LET'S GO:

Switzerland & Austria

"Its yearly revision by a new crop of Harvard students makes it as valuable as ever." —*The New York Times*

"Value-packed, unbeatable, accurate, and comprehensive." —*The Los Angeles Times*

"A world-wise traveling companion—always ready with friendly advice and helpful hints, all sprinkled with a bit of wit." —*The Philadelphia Inquirer*

"Lighthearted and sophisticated, informative and fun to read. [Let's Go] helps the novice traveler navigate like a knowledgeable old hand." —*Atlanta Journal-Constitution*

"All the essential information you need, from making a phone call to exchanging money to contacting your embassy. [Let's Go] provides maps to help you find your way from every train station to a full range of youth hostels and hotels." —*Minneapolis Star Tribune*

"Unbeatable: good sight-seeing advice; up-to-date-info on restaurants, hotels, and inns; a commitment to money-saving travel; and a wry style that brightens nearly every page." —*The Washington Post*

▩ Let's Go researchers have to make it on their own.

"The writers seem to have experienced every rooster-packed bus and lunar-surfaced mattress about which they write." —*The New York Times*

"Retains the spirit of the student-written publication it is: candid, opinionated, resourceful, amusing info for the traveler of limited means but broad curiosity." —*Mademoiselle*

▩ No other guidebook is as comprehensive.

"Whether you're touring the United States, Europe, Southeast Asia, or Central America, a Let's Go guide will clue you in to the cheapest, yet safe, hotels and hostels, food and transportation. Going beyond the call of duty, the guides reveal a country's latest news, cultural hints, and off-beat information that any tourist is likely to miss." —*Tulsa World*

▩ Let's Go is completely revised each year.

"Up-to-date travel tips for touring four continents on skimpy budgets." —*Time*

"Inimitable.... Let's Go's 24 guides are updated yearly (as opposed to the general guidebook standard of every two to three years), and in a marvelously spunky way." —*The New York Times*

Let's Go Publications

Let's Go: Alaska & The Pacific Northwest
Let's Go: Britain & Ireland
Let's Go: California
Let's Go: Central America
Let's Go: Eastern Europe
Let's Go: Ecuador & The Galápagos Islands
Let's Go: Europe
Let's Go: France
Let's Go: Germany
Let's Go: Greece & Turkey
Let's Go: India & Nepal
Let's Go: Ireland
Let's Go: Israel & Egypt
Let's Go: Italy
Let's Go: London
Let's Go: Mexico
Let's Go: New York City
Let's Go: Paris
Let's Go: Rome
Let's Go: Southeast Asia
Let's Go: Spain & Portugal
Let's Go: Switzerland & Austria
Let's Go: USA
Let's Go: Washington, D.C.

Let's Go **Map Guide:** Boston
Let's Go **Map Guide:** London
Let's Go **Map Guide:** New York City
Let's Go **Map Guide:** Paris
Let's Go **Map Guide:** San Francisco
Let's Go **Map Guide:** Washington, D.C.

2 pants   4 sets
2 shirts   underwears/
1 dress   socks
1 sweater   jewelry
2 leggings

1 hiking boots
1 dress shoes
1 concert dress
1 backpack

LET'S GO

The Budget Guide to
Switzerland
& Austria

1997

Jeremy Wyatt Linzee
Editor

Maria Alexandra Ordoñez
Associate Editor

St. Martin's Press ❧ New York

Maps by David Lindroth copyright © 1997, 1996, 1995, 1994, 1993, 1992, 1991, 1990, 1989, 1988 by St. Martin's Press, Inc.

Map revisions pp. xii, xv, 43, 254, 255, 258, 259, 349, 443, 454, 455 by Let's Go, Inc.

Distributed outside the USA and Canada by Macmillan.

About Let's Go

Back in 1960, a few students at Harvard University banded together to produce a 20-page pamphlet offering a collection of tips on budget travel in Europe. This modest, mimeographed packet, offered as an extra to passengers on student charter flights to Europe, met with instant popularity. The following year, students traveling to Europe researched the first, full-fledged edition of *Let's Go: Europe*, a pocket-sized book featuring honest, irreverent writing and a decidedly youthful outlook on the world. Throughout the 60s, our guides reflected the times; the 1969 guide to America led off by inviting travelers to "dig the scene" at San Francisco's Haight-Ashbury. During the 70s and 80s, we gradually added regional guides and expanded coverage into the Middle East and Central America. With the addition of our in-depth city guides, handy map guides, and extensive coverage of Asia, the 90s are also proving to be a time of explosive growth for Let's Go, and there's certainly no end in sight. The first editions of *Let's Go: India & Nepal* and *Let's Go: Ecuador & The Galápagos Islands* hit the shelves this year, and research for next year's series has already begun.

We've seen a lot in 37 years. *Let's Go: Europe* is now the world's bestselling international guide, translated into seven languages. And our new guides bring Let's Go's total number of titles, with their spirit of adventure and their reputation for honesty, accuracy, and editorial integrity, to 30. But some things never change: our guides are still researched, written, and produced entirely by students who know first-hand how to see the world on the cheap.

HOW WE DO IT

Each guide is completely revised and thoroughly updated every year by a well-traveled set of 200 students. Every winter, we recruit over 120 researchers and 60 editors to write the books anew. After several months of training, Researcher-Writers hit the road for seven weeks of exploration, from Anchorage to Ankara, Estonia to El Salvador, Iceland to Indonesia. Hired for their rare combination of budget travel sense, writing ability, stamina, and courage, these adventurous travelers know that train strikes, stolen luggage, food poisoning, and marriage proposals are all part of a day's work. Back at our offices, editors work from spring to fall, massaging copy written on Himalayan bus rides into witty yet informative prose. A student staff of typesetters, cartographers, publicists, and managers keeps our lively team together. In September, the collected efforts of the summer are delivered to our printer, who turns them into books in record time, so that you have the most up-to-date information available for *your* vacation. And even as you read this, work on next year's editions is well underway.

WHY WE DO IT

At Let's Go, our goal is to give you a great vacation. We don't think of budget travel as the last recourse of the destitute; we believe that it's the only way to travel. Living cheaply and simply brings you closer to the people and places you've been saving up to visit. Our books will ease your anxieties and answer your questions about the basics—so you can get off the beaten track and explore. Once you learn the ropes, we encourage you to put Let's Go away now and then to strike out on your own. As any seasoned traveler will tell you, the best discoveries are often those you make yourself. When you find something worth sharing, drop us a line. We're Let's Go Publications, 67 Mt. Auburn St., Cambridge, MA 02138, USA (e-mail: fanmail@letsgo.com).

HAPPY TRAVELS!

WITH OUR RAIL PASSES YOU'LL HAVE UP TO 70% MORE MONEY TO WASTE.

With savings of up to 70% off the price of point to point tickets, you'll be laughing all the way to the souvenir stand. Rail passes are available for travel throughout Europe or the country of your choice and we'll even help you fly there. So all you'll have to do is leave some extra room in your suitcase. To learn more call **1-800-4-EURAIL** (1-800-438-7245).

Rail Europe

Contents

Stuck for cash? Don't panic. With Western Union, money is transferred to you in minutes. It's easy. All you've got to do is ask someone at home to give Western Union a call on US 1 800 3256000. Minutes later you can collect the cash.

WESTERN UNION | MONEY TRANSFER

The fastest way to send money worldwide.

Maps

Acknowledgments

Thanks mucho to our Portuguese brother in arms and the best damn wordslinger this side of any corral. "Fagundes—what's another word for Pirate Treasure?" To those who checked their cards at checkpoint chuck, how will we ever forget you? Thank you Anne for the cure, Gene for the conversation, Kitty for the meow, Brenn-White for the calls, and the Danimal for being all that. Other team thanks go to the Boys, the Bee Gees, the Lindt chocolate factory, the entire cast and crew of the *Sound of Music,* and last but not least, the em-dash. When it's all said and done, though, the biggest thank-you goes to our researchers; you were fantastic—**S&A**

Ali, here's to late nights that just missed dawn. Thank you for the Swiss know-how and the heart of gold. To all those who have made my time so full, I thank you from the bottom of my heart—Dan (free lunch always tastes better), Gaga, Kirsten and Stephanie, Alex, Mike, Amara, Chris, Rock, and all those other late-night dinner types (like Melrose, but much better looking). Thank you Liz for putting up with my dirty dishes, and Murph for all that deep down dirty jazz. To Virginia, a beautiful light, you give meaning to a dusty soul—I couldn't forget about you, even if I was a hundred. And finally to my parents and my sister, to whom this book is dedicated. Words cannot describe the love I have for you—**JWL**

Jeremy, from the interview to the last hours before deadline, it's been a reelin' and rockin' time. Thank you for making me a part of the team, for making me laugh, and for always answering with patience. To the Romance Room thanks for letting me visit and use your computers so often. Rachel D., good luck next year and many thanks for everything this year (e-mail me!). To Cary, Maria, Rachel C., and Kati, in Paris and back home, thanks for being there. Bill, where do I begin? I'll just start by saying thank you for everything. Finally and most especially, to Mom, Dad, Joe, George, Miguel, Julie, Griffin, Gatito, and Winston, my most extra-special love—**AO**

Editor	Jeremy Wyatt Linzee
Associate Editor	Maria Alexandra Ordoñez
Managing Editor	David Fagundes
Publishing Director	Michelle C. Sullivan
Production Manager	Daniel O. Williams
Associate Production Manager	Michael S. Campbell
Cartography Manager	Amanda K. Bean
Editorial Manager	John R. Brooks
Editorial Manager	Allison Crapo
Financial Manager	Stephen P. Janiak
Personnel Manager	Alexander H. Travelli
Publicity Manager	SoRelle B. Braun
Associate Publicity Manager	David Fagundes
Associate Publicity Manager	Elisabeth Mayer
Assistant Cartographer	Jonathan D. Kibera
Assistant Cartographer	Mark C. Staloff
Office Coordinator	Jennifer L. Schuberth
Director of Advertising and Sales	Amit Tiwari
Senior Sales Executives	Andrew T. Rourke
	Nicholas A. Valtz, Charles E. Varner
General Manager	Richard Olken
Assistant General Manager	Anne E. Chisholm

Researcher-Writers

Mary Allison Arwady   *Voralberg, Tirol, Southeast Austria and Liechtenstein*
With her raincoat zipper pulled snugly to her chin, this former swimmer made use of her paddle prowess to become a Noah among RW's, floating in her ark of good cheer and determination above the mist-filled, Paleolithic swamp that the rains made of the Austrian countryside. Allison's cheery telephone calls, assuring us she was fine while a deluge roared in the background, made us fully confident that this stalwart trooper would never jump ship. When not dodging stray storm heads, however, she also persevered through itinerant nocturnal cow parades, brusque yodelers, eerie bone repositories, and shots of Tirolean whisky force-fed by a well meaning octogenarian Alpine *Frau*. Her ford-every-stream, climb-every-mountain determination pulled her through. When her gurgling and grueling itinerary finally dried up we glanced down to see her copy rainbow and found a pot of gold.

Benjamin James Fender   *West and Central Switzerland, Geneva*
With the Queen's English on his lips and the Union Jack wrapped tightly around his pen, our Oxford-schooled Siberian and Icelandic wanderer laced up his boots, hefted his pack and set about to put Sir Edmund Hillary to shame. His consummate passion for all things mountainous shines through his much expanded hiking write-ups; they were so intense that we had to don crampons and polypropylene long underwear just to type them in. When you stand breathless on that devastating Swiss peak, think of Ben, he certainly helped you get there. This Brit also spiced up the fondue pot with his rapid-fire wit, greatly expanding Let's Go's vocabulary with words like "corker" and "gloopy." Perhaps most extraordinary, however, was his penchant for stuffed armadillos—Switzerland seems to be rife with them these days.

Matthew Stamski   *Central and Eastern Switzerland, Zurich*
Leaving his canoe paddles and face paint at home, our anthropology major and erstwhile Samoan chief journeyed to the land of clocks (?) and cheese (!) and managed to acclimate himself quite well. Homesickness never had a chance against Matt's keep on truckin' attitude, though the occasional side trip to a Swiss ethnology museum certainly helped him rekindle old ties. A nature-lover and hiker at heart, Matt gave us earth-conscious restaurant reviews and foot-conscious walks. However, the peaceful life-energies disappeared at night when he traded Alpine Nirvana for Disco Inferno; from the raucous students of Basel, to the Benedictine Monks of Lucerne, to the ibex of the Swiss National Park, Matt's cordiality knew no bounds and resulted in the definitive guide to Swiss nightlife (not an oxymoron).

Christina Svendsen   *Vienna, Salzburg, Northern Austria*
Christina's itinerary was actually a homecoming. A savvy cultural insider, this Viennese near-native waltzed her way back into her beloved city with *dialekt* on her tongue and coffee on her mind, both of which helped her to send back some of the most insightful copy this side of the Danube. Her delightful commentary of Austrian days, filled with medieval wanderings and Baroque lamentations, stocked our sleep with Habsburgs and brooding cafés. With her *Let's Go* radar acutely tuned, she not only found us the best of what's cooking in Vienna with her greatly expanded restaurant section, but was always in the right place at the right time, getting up close and personal with dance-hall gymnasts, Austrian President Thomas Klestil, the Queen of Sweden, and an outlandish pantyhose vendor.

Krzysztof Owerkowicz	*Prague*
Joel Pulliam	*Budapest*
Lisa K. Pinsley	*Munich*

How to Use This Book

I cannot rest from travel; I will drink life to the lees.

—Tennyson

This book is written for those who cannot rest from travel, those who see life as a well of experiences in which to dip one's cup and drink. What you hold in your hands is not an itinerary, but a traveling companion created in the summer of 1996 by a skilled band of four researchers with shoestring budgets and insatiable appetites for uncovering the best, most interesting nooks and crannies. They compiled their information with your interests in mind, answering questions like how to get from place to place, what to savor of the local cuisine, and where to take in the sights, enjoy the evenings, and get some sleep. In the **Essentials** section, we provide over forty pages to guide you through the preparation that an international excursion requires. There you'll find travel organizations, rail passes, customs information, and tipping tips. The book begins with **Switzerland,** starting with a brief section on its history and culture, and then opening with Geneva. **Liechtenstein** comes next, followed by **Austria,** whose first chapter sails from Mozart to Schwarzenegger in a brief look at Austria's history and culture, and whose second chapter starts with Vienna and then works west. As travel to Vienna would not be complete without meeting the rest of its Eastern European Habsburg siblings, Prague and Budapest, and travel to Salzburg is cheaper using the airport of neighboring Munich, we conclude with **Gateway Cities: Prague** and **Budapest** (from *Let's Go: Eastern Europe*), and **Munich** (from *Let's Go: Germany*). The concluding **Appendices** list climate information, public holidays, and include a comprehensive language section for both German and French.

For each entry, **Orientation and Practical Information** maps out the town and compiles the crucial information you'd otherwise forget; read it to learn what each town has, and continue using it as a reference for the length of your stay. You'll find information on public transportation, post offices, budget travel offices, consulates and embassies, American Express, currency exchange, and even laundromats. In large cities, we included all the transport information we could think of, including train schedules, airport shuttle services, even tips for motorists. With your purse in mind, the **Accommodations** and **Food** sections offer ranked evaluations of lodgings, restaurants, cafés, and grocers. The lists start with the best and work their way down in order of preference. Write-ups of each town's **Sights** follow in prose, and are ordered with up-to-date directions and seasoned with wit. This year's guide offers a heavily expanded coverage of **mountain hikes,** and in most locales we also throw in coverage of all the other zany, death-defying mountain activities we could think of, including **skiing, paragliding, canyoning, water sports,** and even **bungee jumping.** In more populous cities, we conclude with **Entertainment** and **Nightlife** opportunities, from wine to Wagner, and then bust through the city limits with **daytrips.**

A NOTE TO OUR READERS

The information for this book is gathered by *Let's Go*'s researchers during the late spring and summer months. Each listing is derived from the assigned researcher's opinion based upon his or her visit at a particular time. The opinions are expressed in a candid and forthright manner. Other travelers might disagree. Those traveling at a different time may have different experiences since prices, dates, hours, and conditions are always subject to change. You are urged to check beforehand to avoid inconvenience and surprises. Travel always involves a certain degree of risk, especially in low-cost areas. When traveling, especially on a budget, always take particular care to ensure your safety.

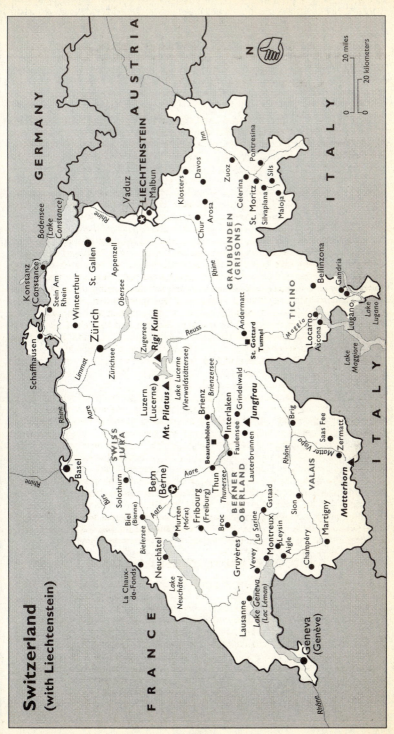

Switzerland
(with Liechtenstein)

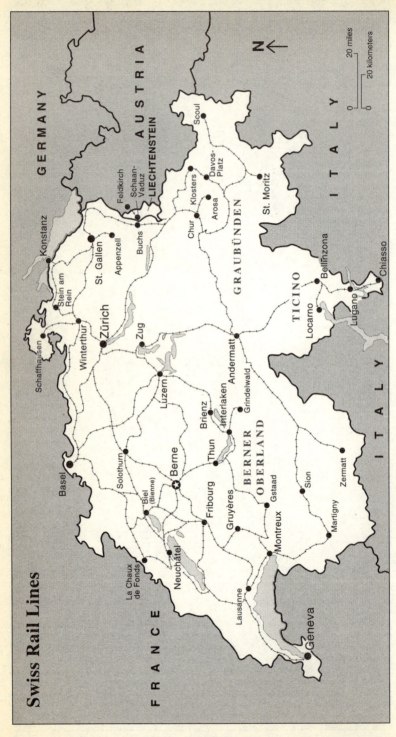

Swiss Rail Lines

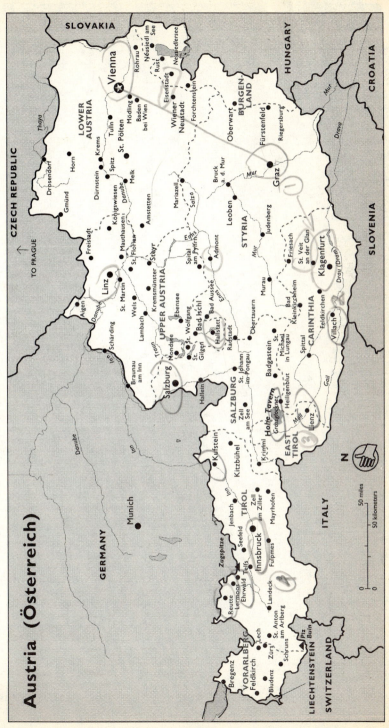

Austria (Österreich)

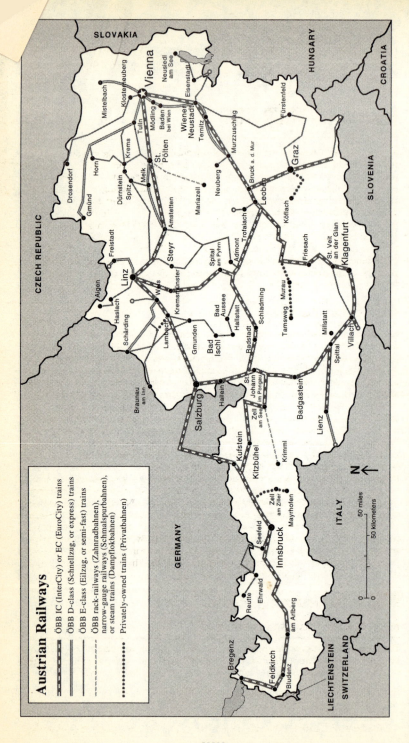

Austrian Railways

ÖBB IC (InterCity) or EC (EuroCity) trains

ÖBB D-class (Schnellzug, or express) trains

ÖBB E-class (Eilzug, or semi-fast) trains

ÖBB rack-railways (Zahnradbahnen), narrow-gauge railways (Schmalspurbahnen), or steam trains (Dampflokbahnen)

Privately-owned trains (Privatbahnen)

ESSENTIALS

PLANNING YOUR TRIP

A vacation is ideally an escape, a spontaneous affair, conceived on a whim and completed without hassle. In today's world, however, escapes are not made without prior planning. Traveling is a complex process, and budget travel is, in many ways, even more difficult—you pay for ease, after all. You will make things a lot easier if you take the time to familiarize yourself with as much as possible before you leave.

You can eliminate a lot of surprises by setting aside the time to plan ahead; read through this chapter before you jump into anything. With a little more research you may find better and cheaper ways of doing things. It is a good idea to have at least a tentative itinerary, and to read through *Let's Go's* listings of those towns. These days, even some hostels require reservations, so you can't always do last-minute planning. Don't be afraid to change your plans, though; just remember: the more knowledge you have, the more prepared you will be for seat-of-the-pants travel.

■ When to Go

Because Switzerland and Austria are a mountain lover's paradise, tourism is a year-round industry. For small towns, especially in West Austria and Eastern Switzerland, prices double and sometimes triple during the winter ski months (generally from Nov.-March). Reservations for most of these towns should be made months in advance. However, much of the flatter, eastern half of the country, including Vienna and Salzburg, see significantly fewer vacationers than normal during this time. The summer provides another heavily touristed period to both countries with locals flocking to tourist spots *en masse* with the onset of school vacations, usually in the last week of June. Be advised that although sites and hotels tend to be cheaper in May and June, rowdy and annoying school groups take their end of the year vacations at this time. They book even the most rural hostels dry years in advance. In July and August, airfares and temperatures rise right along with the population of tourists. The cities tend to be especially busy, as families and college students whiz through on whirlwind summer vacations. Also, almost every city has a gala music festival of some type during these months (see **Festivals** in the **Appendices**, p. 477). April is a particularly colorful month in preparation of Easter celebrations, particularly in Catholic Austria. This could be a good time to go, since many activities abound but tourists are not pouring from every hotel and museum. Finally, small Swiss or Austrian ski playgrounds often become desolate ghost towns when the tourists pack up, some completely closing down during the inter-seasonal periods which usually occurs from mid-April to late-May and mid-Oct. to late-Nov.

■ Useful Information

NATIONAL TOURIST OFFICES

These outposts can provide copious help in planning your trip; have them mail you brochures well before you leave. They will often provide information for travelers with special concerns. Some sell rail passes and can help plan itineraries.

Swiss National Tourist Offices

U.S.: 608 Fifth Ave., **New York,** NY 10020 (tel. (212) 757-5944; fax 262-6116); 150 N. Michigan Ave. #2930, **Chicago,** IL 60601 (tel. (312) 630-5840; fax 630-5848).
Canada: 926 East Mall, Etobicoke, Ont M9B 6K1 (tel. (416) 695-2090; fax 695-2774).

United Kingdom: Swiss Centre, Swiss Court, London W1V 8EE (tel. (0171) 734 19 21; fax 437 45 77).

Austrian National Tourist Offices

U.S.: P.O. Box 1142, **New York,** NY 10108-1142 (tel. (212) 944-6880; fax 730-4568).

Canada: 1010 Ouest rue Sherbourne #1410, **Montreal,** Que. H3A 2R7 (tel. (514) 849-3709; fax 849-9577); Granville Sq. #1380, 200 Granville St., **Vancouver,** BC V6C 1S4 (tel. (604) 683-8695; fax (604) 662-8528).

United Kingdom: 30 St. George St., London W1R 0AL (tel. (0171) 629 04 61; fax 499 60 38).

TRAVEL ORGANIZATIONS

There are a variety of organizations which can help hunt down cheap airfares, railpasses, accommodations, and student discounts.

Council on International Educational Exchange (Council), 205 East 42nd St., New York, NY 10017-5706 (tel. (888) COUNCIL (268-6245); fax (212) 822-2699; e-mail info@ciee.org; http://www.ciee.org). A private, nonprofit organization, Council administers work, volunteer, and academic programs around the world. They also offer identity cards, including the ISIC and the GO25, and a range of publications, including the magazine Student Travels (free).

Federation of International Youth Travel Organizations (FIYTO), Bredgade 25H, DK-1260, Copenhagen K, Denmark (tel. (45) 33 33 96 00, fax 33 93 96 76; email mailbox@fiyto.org). International organization promoting educational, cultural and social travel for young people. FIYTO sponsors the GO25 Card.

TRAVEL PUBLICATIONS

The College Connection, Inc., 1295 Prospect St. Ste. A, La Jolla, CA 92037 (tel. (619) 551-9770; fax 551-9987; email eurailnow@aol.com; http://www.eurailpass.com). Publishes *The Passport,* a booklet listing hints about every aspect of traveling and studying abroad. This booklet is free to *Let's Go* readers; send your request by email or fax only. The College Rail Connection, a division of the College Connection, sells railpasses with student discounts.

The European Festivals Association, 120B rue de Lausanne, CH-1202 Geneva, Switzerland (tel. (022) 732 28 03; fax 738 40 12). Publishes the free booklet *Festivals,* which lists dates and programs of many major European festivals, including music and theater events.

Forsyth Travel Library, P.O. Box 2975, Shawnee Mission, KS 66201 (tel. (800) 367-7984; fax (816) 942-6969; http://www.forsyth.com). A mail-order service that stocks a wide range of city, area, and country maps, as well as guides for rail and ferry travel in Europe; also sells rail tickets and passes. Sells the *Thomas Cook European Timetable* for trains (US$28, or US$39 with full map of European train routes; postage US$4.50 for priority shipping).

John Muir Publications, P.O. Box 613, Sante Fe, NM 87504 (tel. (800) 888-7504; fax (505) 988-1680). Publishes an excellent series of books by veteran traveler Rick Steve. This includes *Europe Through the Back Door,* offering great advice on the dos and don'ts of budget travel (US$19), and *Mona Winks: Self-Guided Tours of Europe's Top Museums* (US$18).

INTERNET RESOURCES

Along with everything else, budget travel is moving rapidly into the information age. With the growing user-friendliness of personal computers and Internet technology, much of this information can be yours with the click of a mouse. There are a number of ways to access the **Internet.** Most popular are commercial internet providers, such as **America On-Line** (tel. (800) 827-6394) and **Compuserve** (tel. (800) 433-0389). The Internet itself can be used in many different forms, but the most useful to budget travelers are the World Wide Web and Usenet newsgroups.

The World Wide Web

Increasingly the Internet forum of choice, the **World Wide Web** provides its users with graphics and sound, as well as textual information. **Search engines** (services that search for web pages under specific subjects) will help you find what you need. **Lycos** (http://a2z.lycos.com), **Infoseek** (http://guide.infoseek.com), and **Yahoo!** (http://www.yahoo.com/Recreation/Travel) are all fine. We at *Let's Go* have come up with some favorite budget travel sites of our own.

Big World Magazine (http://boss.cpcnet.com/personal/bigworld/bigworld.htm), a budget travel 'zine with a great collection of links to travel pages.

City.Net (http://www.city.net) is a very impressive collection of regional- or city-specific web pages. You just select a geographic area, and it provides you with links to web pages related to that area. **USA CityLink** (http://www.usacitylink.com/citylink) has a similar service for the United States

The CIA World Factbook (http://www.odci.gov/cia/publications/95fact) has tons of vital statistics on Switzerland and Austria. Check it out for an overview of the countries' economy, or an explanation of their system of government.

Shoestring Travel (http://www.stratpub.com) is a budget travel 'zine, with feature articles, links, user exchange, and accommodations information.

The Student and Budget Travel Guide (http://asa.ugl.lib.umich.edu/chdocs/travel/travel-guide.html) is just what it sounds like.

Foreign Language for Travelers (http://www.travelang.com) can help you brush up on your German, French, or Italian.

Usenet Newsgroups

Another popular source of information are **newsgroups,** which are forums for discussion of specific topics. One user "posts" a written question or thought, which other users read and respond to in kind. There are thousands of different newsgroups and more crop up every day, so there is information available on almost any topic you can imagine. **Usenet,** the name for the family of newsgroups, can be accessed easily from most Internet gateways.

There are a number of different hierarchies for newsgroups. The "soc" hierarchy deals primarily with issues related to society and culture, such as **soc.culture.austria.** The "rec" (recreation) hierarchy is especially good for travelers, with newsgroups such as **rec.travel.air** or **rec.travel.europe.** The "alt" (alternative) hierarchy houses a number of different types of discussion, such as **alt.politics.france** or **alt.current-events.balkans.** Finally, "Clari-net" posts AP news wires for many different topics, such as **clari.world.europe.austria** or **clari.news.switzerland.**

■ Documents & Formalities

Be sure to file all passport applications several weeks or months in advance of your departure date. Remember, you rely on government agencies to complete these transactions, and a backlog in processing can spoil even the best-laid plans.

When you travel, always carry two or more forms of identification, including at least one photo ID. A passport, along with a driver's license or birth certificate, usually serves as adequate proof of your identity and citizenship. Though most places will simply accept a passport, some establishments, especially banks, require several IDs before cashing traveler's checks. Never carry your passport, travel ticket, identification documents, money, traveler's checks, insurance, and credit cards all together, or you risk being left entirely without ID or funds in case of theft or loss.

If you plan an extended stay in Switzerland or Austria, you might want to register your passport with the nearest embassy, consulate, or consular agent. For general information about documents, formalities, and prudent travel abroad, procure the booklet *Your Trip Abroad.* Send US$1.25 to: Superintendent of Documents, U.S. Government Printing Office, P.O. Box 371954, Pittsburgh, PA 15250-7954 (tel. (202) 512-1800; fax 512-2250).

PASSPORTS

As a precaution in case your passport is lost or stolen, go to an embassy or consulate and ask them to photocopy it and put an official seal on the copy asserting that it is valid. Carry this photocopy in a safe place apart from your passport. Leave another copy at home in case of an emergency. With the sealed copy, a new passport can be issued immediately in the event that yours is stolen. Regardless of whether you get it officially stamped or not, making an unofficial copy is highly recommended. Consulates also recommend that you carry an expired passport or an official copy of your birth certificate (not the original, of course) in a part of your baggage separate from other documents. You can request a duplicate birth certificate from the Bureau of Vital Records and Statistics in your state or province of birth.

Losing your passport can generate a monumental hassle. If you do lose your passport, *immediately* notify the local police and the embassies in Bern or Vienna. You cannot enter another country without your passport. In an emergency, ask for **immediate temporary traveling papers** that permit you to return to your home country. Providing the suggested material can greatly expedite its replacement. Some consulates can issue new passports within two days if you provide adequate proof of citizenship.

Applying for a passport is complicated, so make sure your questions are answered in advance; you don't want to wait six hours in a flickering-fluorescent-lit passport office just to be told you'll have to return tomorrow because your application is insufficient.

United States Citizens may apply for a passport, valid for 10 years (five years if under 18) at any federal or state **courthouse** or **post office** authorized to accept passport applications, or at a **U.S. Passport Agency,** located in Boston, Chicago, Honolulu, Houston, Los Angeles, Miami, New Orleans, New York, Philadelphia, San Francisco, Seattle, Stamford, CT., or Washington D.C. Refer to the "U.S. Government, State Department" section of the telephone directory, or call your local post office for addresses. If your passport is lost or stolen in the U.S., report it in writing to Passport Services, U.S. Department of State, 111 19th St., NW Washington D.C., 20522-1705 or to the nearest passport agency. For more information, contact the U.S. Passport Information's **24-hour recorded message** (tel. (202) 647-0518).

Canada Application forms in English and French are available at all **passport offices, post offices,** and most **travel agencies.** Citizens may apply in person at any one of 28 regional Passport Offices across Canada. Travel agents can direct the applicant to the nearest location. Canadian citizens residing abroad should contact the nearest Canadian embassy or consulate. For additional information, call (800) 567-6868 (24 hrs.; from Canada only) or call the Passport Office at (819) 994-3500. In Metro Toronto, call (416) 973-3251. Montréalers should dial (514) 283-2152. Refer to the booklet *Bon Voyage, But...* for further help and a list of Canadian embassies and consulates abroad. It is available free of charge from any passport office.

Britain British citizens, British Dependent Territories citizens, British Nationals (overseas), and British Overseas citizens may apply for a **full passport.** For a full passport, valid for 10 years (five years if under 16), apply in person or by mail to a passport office, located in London, Liverpool, Newport, Peterborough, Glasgow, or Belfast.

Ireland Citizens can apply for a passport by mail to either the Department of Foreign Affairs, Passport Office, Setanta Centre, Molesworth St., Dublin 2 (tel. (01) 671 16 33), or the Passport Office, 1A South Mall, Cork (tel. (021) 627 25 25). Obtain an application at a local Garda station or request one from a passport office. The new

Passport Express Service offers a two week turn-around and is available through post offices for an extra IR£3.

Australia Citizens must apply for a passport in person at a post office, a passport office, or an Australian diplomatic mission overseas. An appointment may be necessary. Passport offices are located in Adelaide, Brisbane, Canberra City, Darwin, Hobart, Melbourne, Newcastle, Perth, and Sydney. A parent may file an application for a child who is under 18 and unmarried. Application fees are adjusted frequently. For more information, call toll-free (in Australia) 13 12 32.

New Zealand Application forms for passports are available in New Zealand from travel agents and Department of Internal Affairs Link Centres, and overseas from New Zealand embassies, high commissions, and consulates. Completed applications may be lodged at Link Centres and at overseas posts, or forwarded to the Passport Office, PO Box 10-526, Wellington, New Zealand. Processing time is 10 working days from receipt of a correctly completed application.

South Africa Citizens can apply for a passport at any Home Affairs Office. For further information, contact the nearest Department of Home Affairs Office.

EMBASSIES AND CONSULATES

If you are seriously ill or in trouble, your embassy can provide a list of local lawyers or doctors; it can also contact your relatives. If you are arrested, consular officials can visit you in custody, but can do little else to assist you. In extreme cases, they can offer emergency financial assistance, including transferring money.

Swiss Embassies and Consulates

U.S.: Embassy: 2900 Cathedral Ave. NW, Washington, DC 20008 (tel. (202) 745-7900; fax 387-2564). **Consulates:** 665 5th Ave., 8th Fl., New York, NY 10022 (tel. (212) 758-2560; fax 207-8024); other consulates in Atlanta, Chicago, Houston, Los Angeles, and San Francisco.

Canada: Embassy: 5 Marlborough Ave., Ottawa Ont. K1N 8E6 (tel. (613) 235-1837; fax 563-1394). **Consulates:** 1572 Ave. Dr. Penfield, Montreal Que. H3G 1C4 (tel. (514) 932-7181; fax 932-9028); others in Toronto and Vancouver.

United Kingdom: Embassy: 16-18 Montague Pl., London W18 2BQ (tel. (017) 723 07 01; fax 72 70 01; email 100634.3637@compuserve.com; http://www.swissembassy.org.uk). Additional **consulate** in Manchester.

Ireland: Embassy: 6 Alesbury Rd., Bolsbridge, Dublin 4 (tel. (01) 269 25 15 and 269 15 66; fax 283 03 44; email 100634.3625@compuserve.com).

Australia: Embassy: 7 Melbourne Ave., Forrest A.C.T. 2603 Canberra (tel. (06) 273 3977; fax 273 3428). **Consulate:** 420 St. Kilda Rd., 7th Floor, Melbourne VIC 3004; mailing address: Consulate General, P.O. Box 7026, Melbourne VIC 3004 (tel. (03) 98 67 22 66; fax 98 66 49 07).

New Zealand: Embassy: 22 Panama St., Wellington (tel. (04) 472 15 93; fax 499 63 02).

South Africa: Embassy: 818 George Ave. Arcadia 0083, mailing address: P.O. 2289, 0001 Pretoria (tel. (012) 43 67 07; fax 43 67 71).

Austrian Embassies and Consulates

U.S.: Embassy: 3524 International Court NW, Washington, D.C. 20008 (tel. (202) 895-6700; fax 895-6772). **Consulate:** 31 E. 69th St., New York, NY 10021 (tel. (212) 737-6400).

Canada: Embassy: 445 Wilborn St., Ottawa, Ont. K1N 6M7 (tel. (613) 789-144; fax (613) 789-3431).

United Kingdom: Embassy: 18 Belgrave Mews West, London, SW1X 8HU (tel. (0171) 235 37 31; fax 232 80 25).

Ireland: Embassy: 15 Ailesbury Court Apartments, 93 Ailesbury Rd., Dublin 4 (tel. (01) 269 45 77; fax 283 08 60).

Australia: Embassy: 12 Talbot St., Forrest ACT 2603, Canberra (tel. (06) 295 13 76; fax 239 67 51).

New Zealand: Consulate: P.O. Box 31219, Auckland 10 (tel. (09) 489 82 49).

South Africa: Embassy: 1109 Duncan St., Brooklyn, Pretoria 1045 (tel. (012) 46 24 83; fax 46 11 51).

ENTRANCE REQUIREMENTS

Citizens of the U.S., Canada, the U.K., Ireland, Australia, and New Zealand do not need visas for stays of up to three months in Switzerland and Austria (Brits can stay for six months in Austria). South Africans need visas for Austria, but not for Switzerland. All need valid passports to enter Switzerland and Austria and to re-enter their own country. Be advised that you may be denied entrance if your passport expires in fewer than six months. Also, returning to your home country with an expired passport may result in a hefty fine. Australians, New Zealanders, South Africans, and Canadians traveling on to Prague must acquire a visa. Australians and New Zealanders require visas to get to Budapest. Admission as a visitor does not include the right to work, which is authorized only by the Swiss or Austrian governments (see Work, p. 15). Citizens of these countries who wish to stay longer than the allotted time must carry a visa as well as a passport.

CUSTOMS

Unless you plan to import a BMW or a barnyard beast, you will probably pass right over the customs barrier with minimal ado. Most countries prohibit or restrict the importation of firearms, explosives, ammunition, fireworks, controlled drugs, most plants and animals, lottery tickets, and obscene literature and films. To avoid hassles when you transport prescription drugs, ensure that bottles are clearly marked, and carry a copy of the prescription to show to the customs officer. In addition, officials may seize articles manufactured from protected species, such as certain reptiles.

Upon returning home, you must declare all articles that you have acquired abroad and pay a duty on the value of those articles that exceed the allowance established by your country's customs service. Keeping receipts for purchases made abroad will help you ascertain values when you return. Keep in mind that goods and gifts purchased at duty-free shops abroad are *not* exempt from duty or sales tax at your point of return; you must declare these items along with other purchases.

YOUTH, STUDENT, & TEACHER IDENTIFICATION

The **International Student Identity Card (ISIC)** is the most widely accepted form of student identification. Flashing this card can garner you discounts for sights, theaters, museums, accommodations, restaurants (especially student cafeterias), train, ferry, and airplane travel, and other services throughout Switzerland and Austria, as well as most of Europe. Present the card wherever you go, and ask about discounts even when none are advertised. It also provides accident insurance of up to US$3000 with US $100 a day for up to 60 days of hospitalization. In addition, cardholders have access to a toll-free Traveler's Assistance hotline whose multilingual staff can provide help in medical, legal, and financial emergencies overseas.

Many student travel offices issue ISICs, including Council Travel, Let's Go Travel, and STA Travel in the U.S.; Travel CUTS in Canada; and any of the organizations under the auspices of the International Student Travel Confederation (ISTC) around the world (see Travel Organizations, p. 2). When you apply for the card, request a copy of the *International Student Identity Card Handbook,* which lists by country some of the available discounts. You can also write to Council for a copy. The card is valid from September to December of the following year. The fee is US$18. Applicants must be at least 12 years old and must be a degree-seeking student of a secondary or post-secondary school. Because of the proliferation of phony ISICs, many airlines and some other services now require other proof of student identity: have a signed letter from the registrar attesting to your student status and stamped with the school seal, and carry your school ID card. The US$19 **International Teacher Identity Card (ITIC)** offers similar but limited discounts, as well as medical insurance coverage. For replace if lost or stolen. Cheques can be purchased for a fee at American Express Travel Service Offices, banks, and American Automobile Association offices. One can also order them via phone (tel. (800) ORDER TTC (673-3782)), or over America Online. American Express offices cash their cheques commission-free (except where prohibited by law) although they offer slightly worse rates than banks. You can also buy Cheques for Two which can be signed by either of two people traveling together. Request the American Express booklet "Traveler's Companion," listing travel office addresses and stolen check hotlines for Switzerland and Austria, as well as other European countries.

Citicorp: Call (800) 645-6556 in the U.S. and Canada; in the U.K. (0181) 297 4781; from elsewhere call U.S. collect (813) 623-1709. Sells both Citicorp and Citicorp Visa traveler's checks in currencies including Swiss Francs. Commission is 1-2% on check purchases. Citicorp's World Courier Service guarantees hand-delivery of traveler's checks anywhere in the world. Checkholders are automatically enrolled for 45 days in the Travel Assist Program (hotline (800) 250-4377 or collect (202) 296-8728), which provides travelers with English-speaking doctor, lawyer, and interpreter referrals as well as check refund assistance and general travel information. Call 24hr. a day, seven days a week.

Thomas Cook MasterCard: Call (800) 223-9920 in the U.S. and Canada; elsewhere call U.S. collect (609) 987-7300; from the U.K. call (0800) 622 101 free or (01733) 502 995 collect. Offers checks in Swiss francs. Commission 1-2% for purchases. Lower commissions if bought at Thomas Cook. No commission on currency exchanges made at Thomas Cook offices.

Visa: Call (800) 227-6811 in the U.S.; in the U.K. (0800) 895 492; from anywhere else in the world call (01733) 318 949; the call will be a pay call, but you can reverse the charges. If you give them your zip code, they will tell you where the closest office is to purchase their traveler's checks. Call (800) 235-7366 to order traveler's checks by mail. Any kind of Visa traveler's checks can be reported lost at the Visa number.

CREDIT CARDS

Credit cards are invaluable in an emergency—an unexpected hospital bill or ticket home or the loss of traveler's checks. The major credit cards—**MasterCard** and **Visa** are the most welcomed—can also instantly extract cash advances from many banks and teller machines throughout Western Europe in local currency. This can be a great bargain because credit card companies get the wholesale exchange rate, which is generally 5% better than the retail rate used by banks and other currency exchange establishments. You will be charged ruinous interest rates if you don't pay off the bill soon, so be careful when using this service. **American Express** cards also work in some ATMs, as well as at AmEx offices and major airports. All such machines require a **Personal Identification Number (PIN),** which credit cards in the U.S. do not usually carry. You must ask AmEx, MasterCard, or Visa to assign you one before you leave; without this PIN, you will be unable to withdraw cash with your credit card abroad.

American Express (tel. (800) CASH-NOW (528-4800)) has a hefty annual fee (US$55) but offers a number of services. Cardholders can cash personal checks at AmEx offices abroad. Global Assist, a 24-hr. hotline offering information and legal assistance in emergencies, is also available (tel. (800) 554-2639 in U.S. and Canada; from abroad call U.S. collect (301) 214-8228). Cardholders can also take advantage of the American Express Travel Service; benefits include assistance in changing airline, hotel, and car rental reservations, sending mailgrams and international cables, and holding your mail at one of the more than 1700 AmEx offices around the world. MasterCard (tel. (800) 999-0454) and Visa (tel. (800) 336-8472) are issued in cooperation with individual banks and some other organizations.

ELECTRONIC BANKING

Automatic Teller Machines (frequently abbreviated as ATMs; operated by bank cards) offer 24-hr. service in banks, groceries, gas stations, and even in telephone booths across the U.S. ATMs are not quite as prevalent in Britain, Ireland, and continental Europe, but you will find that most banks in the larger cities are connected to an international money network, usually PLUS (800-THE-PLUS (843-7587)) or CIRRUS (800-4-CIRRUS (424-7787)). Depending on the system that your bank at home uses, you will probably be able to access your own personal bank account whenever you're in need of funds. Do this whenever possible, because ATM machines, like credit cards, get the wholesale exchange rate which is generally 5% better than the retail rate most banks use. Using an ATM card offers the traveler great flexibility and is probably the most effective way to carry cash in Europe. It is often easier to avoid the confusion of the ATM machine and walk into the bank itself, withdrawing funds over the counter. Remember to keep an extra card with your passport to avoid the possibility of loss and always keep extra cash or traveler's checks in a secure place as backup.

GETTING MONEY FROM HOME

One of the easiest ways to get money from home is to bring an **American Express** card. AmEx allows card holders to draw cash from their checking accounts at any of its major offices and many of its representatives' offices, up to US$1000 every 21 days (no service charge, no interest). AmEx also offers Express Cash, with over 100,000 ATMs located around the world. Express Cash withdrawals are automatically debited from the Cardmember's specified bank account or line of credit. Green card holders may withdraw up to US$1000 in a seven day period. There is a 2% transaction fee for each cash withdrawal with a US$2.50 minimum. To enroll in Express Cash, Cardmembers may call 1-800-CASH NOW (227 4669). Outside the U.S. call collect (904) 565-7875. Unless using the AmEx service, avoid cashing checks in foreign currencies; they usually take weeks and a US$30 fee to clear.

Money can also be wired abroad through money transfer services operated by **Western Union.** In the U.S., call Western Union any time at (800) 325-6000 to cable money with your Visa or MasterCard. The money is usually available within an hour. Rates are US$29 to send US$250, US$40 for US$500, and US$50 for US$1000.

In emergencies, U.S. citizens can have money sent via the State Department's **Overseas Citizens Service, American Citizens Service,** Consular Affairs, Public Affairs Staff, Room 4831, U.S. Department of State, Washington, DC 20520 (tel. (202) 647-5225; at night and on Sundays and holidays (202) 647-4000; fax (202) 647-3000; http://travel.state.gov). For a fee of US$15, the State Department will forward money within hours to the nearest consular office, which will then disburse it according to instructions. The center serves only Americans in the direst of straits abroad. The quickest way to have the money sent is to cable the State Department through Western Union.

■ Insurance

Beware of buying unnecessary travel coverage—your regular policies may well extend to many travel-related accidents. **Medical insurance** (especially university policies) often cover costs incurred abroad; check with your provider. **Medicare's** foreign travel coverage is valid only in Canada and Mexico. Canadians are protected by their home province's health insurance plan for up to 90 days after leaving the country; check with the provincial Ministry of Health or Health Plan Headquarters for details. The Commonwealth Department of Human Services and Health can provide more information. Your **homeowners' insurance** (or your family's coverage) often covers theft during travel. Homeowners are generally covered up to US$500 against loss of travel documents.

ISIC and **ITIC** provide US$3000 worth of accident and illness insurance and US$100 per day up to 60 days of hospitalization. They also offer up to US$1000 for accidental death or dismemberment, up to US$25,000 if injured due to an airline, and up to US$25,000 for emergency evacuation due to an illness. The cards also give access to a toll-free Traveler's Assistance hotline (in the US and Canada (800) 626-2427; elsewhere call the U.S. collect (713) 267-2525) whose multilingual staff can provide help in emergencies overseas. To supplement ISIC's insurance, **Council** (see Travel Organizations, p. 2) offers the inexpensive Trip-Safe plan with options covering medical treatment and hospitalization, accidents, baggage loss, and charter flights missed due to illness; **Council Travel** and **STA** also offer more comprehensive and expensive policies. **American Express** cardholders receive automatic car-rental and flight insurance on purchases made with the card (tel. (800) 528-4800).

Remember that insurance companies usually require a copy of the police report for thefts, or evidence of having paid medical expenses (doctor's statements, receipts) before they will honor a claim and may have time limits on filing for reimbursement. Always carry policy numbers and proof of insurance. Check with each carrier for specific restrictions and policies.

The Berkely Group/Carefree Travel Insurance, 100 Garden City Plaza, P.O. Box 9366, Garden City, NY 11530-9366 (tel. (800) 323-3149 or (516) 294-0220; fax (516) 294-1096). Offers two comprehensive packages including coverage for trip cancellation/interruption/delay, accident and sickness, medical, baggage loss, bag delay, accidental death and dismemberment, travel supplier insolvency. 24-hr. worldwide emergency assistance hotline.

Globalcare Travel Insurance, 220 Broadway, Lynnfield, MA 01940 (tel. (800) 821-2488; fax (617) 592-7720; email global@nebc.mv.comhttp://www.nebc.mv.com/globalcare). Complete medical, legal, emergency, and travel-related services. On-the-spot payments and special student programs, including benefits for trip cancellation and interruption. GTI waives pre-existing medical conditions with their Globalcare Economy Plan for cruise and travel, and provides coverage for the bankruptcy or default of cruiselines, airlines, or tour operators.

Travel Guard International, 1145 Clark St., Stevens Point, WI 54481 (tel. (800) 826-1300 or (715) 345-0505; fax (715) 345-0525). Comprehensive insurance programs starting at US$44. Programs cover trip cancellation and interruption, bankruptcy and financial default, lost luggage, medical coverage abroad, emergency assistance, accidental death. 24-hr. hotline.

Wallach and Company, Inc., 107 West Federal St., P.O. Box 480, Middleburg, VA 20118-0480 (tel. (800) 237-6615; fax (540) 687–3172; email wallach.r@mediasoft.net). Comprehensive medical insurance including evacuation and repatriation of remains and direct payment of claims to providers of services. Other optional coverages available. 24-hr. toll-free international assistance.

■ Safety and Security

Switzerland and Austria are both relatively free of violent crime, especially when compared to the U.S., but this should not be cause to let your guard down. Tourists are traditionally easy targets, particularly vulnerable to crime for two reasons: they often carry large amounts of cash and they are not as savvy as locals. To avoid such unwanted attention, try to blend in as much as possible. The gawking camera-toter is a more obvious target than the casual local look-alike. Walking into a café or shop to check your map is better than checking it on a street corner. Muggings are more often impromptu than planned. Walking with nervous, over-the-shoulder glances can be a tip that you have something valuable to protect. Act as if you know exactly where you're going. An obviously bewildered bodybuilder is more likely to be harassed than a stern and confident 98-pound weakling.

SAFETY

When exploring a new city, extra vigilance may be wise, but no city should force you to turn precautions into panic. When you get to a place where you'll be spending some time, find out about unsafe areas from tourist information, from the manager of your hotel or hostel, or from a local whom you trust. Especially if you are traveling alone, be sure that someone at home knows your itinerary. Never say that you're traveling alone. Both men and women may want to carry a small **whistles** to scare off attackers or attract attention, and it's not a bad idea to jot down the number of the police if you'll be in town for a couple days.

When walking at night, you should turn day-time precautions into mandates. Stick to busy well-lit streets and avoid dark alleyways. Do not attempt to cross through parks, parking lots or any other large, deserted areas. A blissfully isolated beach can become a treacherous nightmare at dusk. Whenever possible, *Let's Go* warns of unsafe neighborhoods and areas, but only your eyes can tell you for sure if you've wandered into one; buildings in disrepair, vacant lots, and general desertedness are all bad signs. A district can change character drastically in the course of a single block. Simply being aware of the flow of people can tell you a great deal about the relative safety of the area. Many notoriously dangerous districts have safe sections; look for children playing, women walking in the open, and other signs of an active community. If you feel uncomfortable, leave as quickly and directly as you can, but don't allow your fear of the new to close off whole worlds to you. Careful, persistent exploration will build confidence and awareness, making your stay in an area more rewarding.

If you are using a car, learn local driving signals. The leading cause of travel deaths in many parts of the world is injury, with deaths from motor vehicle crashes topping the list. Be sure to park your vehicle in a garage or well-traveled area. Wear your seatbelt at all times; it is law in many areas. Children under 40 lbs. (18kg) should ride only in a specially designed carseat, which can be obtained for a small fee from most car rental agencies. If you plan on spending a lot of time on the road, you may want to bring along some spare parts. Learn your route before you hit the road; some roads have poor (or nonexistent) shoulders, few gas stations, and (depending on where you go) wild animals. In many regions, driving conditions are such that you will need to drive more slowly and more cautiously than you would at home.

Sleeping in your car is one of the most dangerous ways to get your rest. If your car breaks down, wait for the police to assist you. If you must sleep in your car, do so as close to a police station or a 24-hr. service station as possible. Sleeping out in the open can be even more dangerous—camping is recommended only in official, supervised campsites or in wilderness backcountry.

SECURITY

There is no sure-fire set of precautions that will protect you from all of the situations you might encounter when you travel. A good self-defense course will give you more concrete ways to react to different types of aggression, but it might cost you more money than your trip. **Model Mugging**, a national organization with offices in several major cities, teaches a very effective, comprehensive course on self-defense. Contact Lynn S. Auerbach on the East Coast (tel. (617) 232-7900); Alice Tibits in the Midwest (tel. (612) 645-6189); and Cori Couture on the West Coast (tel. (415) 592-7300). Course prices vary from US$400-500. Women's and men's courses offered. Community colleges frequently offer self-defense courses at more affordable prices.

For official **United States Department of State** travel advisories on the U.S. and/or Canada, including crime and security, call their 24-hr. hotline at (202) 647-5225. To order publications, including a pamphlet entitled *A Safe Trip Abroad*, write them at Superintendent of Documents, U.S. Government Printing Office, Washington, DC 20402, or call (202) 783-3238.

Though not prevalent in Switzerland and Austria some may have a few **con artists.** Con artists and hustlers often work in groups, and children, unfortunately, are among the best at the game. These hustlers use tricks which are many and adaptable. Be alert for any suspicious situation. Do not respond or make eye contact, walk quickly away, and keep a grip on your belongings. Contact the police if a hustler is particularly insistent or aggressive.

Don't put money in a wallet in your back pocket. Never count your money in public and carry as little as possible. If you carry a purse, buy a sturdy one with a secure clasp, and carry it crosswise on the side, away from the street with the clasp against you. As far as packs are concerned, buy some small combination padlocks which slip through the two zippers, securing the pack shut. (Even these precautions do not always suffice— moped riders who snatch purses and backpacks sometimes tote knives to cut the straps.) A **money belt** is one of the best ways to carry cash. The best combination of convenience and invulnerability is the nylon, zippered pouch with belt that should sit inside the waist of your pants or skirt. A **neck pouch,** although less accessible, is equally safe. Do avoid keeping anything precious in a fanny-pack (even if it's worn on your stomach); your valuables will be highly visible and easy to steal. In city crowds and especially on public transportation, pick-pockets are amazingly deft at their craft. Hold your bags tightly. Also, be alert in public telephone booths. If you must say your calling-card number, do so very quietly; if you punch it in, make sure no one can look over your shoulder. Making **photocopies** of important documents will allow you to recover them in case they are lost or filched. Carry one copy separate from the documents and leave another copy at home. Keep some money separate from the rest to use in an emergency or in case of theft. Label every piece of luggage both inside and out.

DRUGS AND ALCOHOL

Police officers, members of the *Polizei* or *Gendarmerie,* typically speak little English and tend to be very businesslike. Treat the police with the utmost respect at all times. Imbibing **alcohol** in Switzerland and Austria is generally trouble-free—beer is more common than soda, and a lunch without wine or beer would be unusual. In Switzerland, you must be 16 to drink legally. Each Austrian province sets a legal minimum drinking age; typically anyone over 18 can drink whatever he or she wishes, though beer is easily available at younger ages. **Drugs** could easily ruin a trip. Every year thousands of travelers are arrested for trafficking or possession of drugs, or for simply being in the company of a suspected user. Marijuana, hashish, cocaine, and narcotics are illegal in Switzerland and Austria, and the penalties for illegal possession of drugs range from severe to horrific. It is not uncommon for a dealer to increase profits by first selling drugs to tourists and then turning them in to the authorities for a reward. Even reputedly liberal cities such as Vienna, Salzburg, and Zürich take an officially dim view of strung-out tourists. The worst thing you can possibly do is carry drugs across an international border; not only could you end up in prison, you could be hounded by a "Drug Trafficker" stamp on your passport for the rest of your life. If you are arrested, all your home country's consulate can do is visit you, provide a list of attorneys, and inform family and friends.

Make sure you get a statement and prescription from your doctor if you'll be carrying insulin, syringes, or any narcotic medications. Leave all medicines in their original labeled containers. What is legal at home may not be legal abroad; check with your doctor or the appropriate foreign consulate to avoid nasty surprises.

■ Alternatives to Tourism

PERMITS

To study in Switzerland for longer than three months, you need to fill out a residency permit and receive authorization from the Swiss authorities. To study in Austria, citizens of non-EU countries must have visas. Because of Austria's new EU status, citizens of member countries do not need visas to work or study in Austria. All foreigners, however, must have valid work permits. If you are a student most U.S. university programs will arrange all the permits and cut through all the red tape for you. To work in either country, you must file residency forms. Applying for residency in Switzerland and Austria can only be done from your country of current residence. When you submit your residency application, you must prove that you have been hired and that you have a place to live. It is possible to go as a tourist and look for work, although it is a catch-22. Very few will hire you without a residency permit, but getting one requires a job.

STUDY

Foreign study programs vary tremendously in expense, academic quality, living conditions, degree of contact with local students, and exposure to the local culture and language. Most American undergraduates enroll in programs sponsored by U.S. universities, and many colleges staff offices give advice and information on study abroad. Take advantage of these counselors and put in some hours in their libraries. Ask for the names of recent participants in the programs and get in touch. The Internet has a study abroad website at **www.studyabroad.com/liteimage.html. Council** sponsors over 40 study abroad programs throughout the world. Contact them for more information (see Travel Organizations, p. 2).

American Field Service (AFS), 220 E. 42nd St., 3rd Fl., New York, NY 10017 (tel. (800) AFS-INFO (237-4636), 876-2376; fax (212) 949-9379; http://www.afs.org/usa). Summer, semester, and year-long homestay exchange programs for high school students and graduating high school seniors in Switzerland and Austria. Short-term service projects for adults also offered. Financial aid available.

American Institute for Foreign Study, College Division, 102 Greenwich Ave., Greenwich, CT 06830 (tel. (800) 727-2437; for high school students (800) 888-2247; http://www.aifs.org). Organizes year, semester, quarter, and summer programs for high school and college study in foreign universities. Open to adults. Scholarships available. Programs in Prague and Salzburg.

Austro-American Institute of Education, Operngasse 4, A-1010 Vienna (tel. (1) 512 77 20; fax 513 91 30). An educational exchange program between the U.S. and Austria. Language courses, study-abroad programs.

Council sponsors over 40 study abroad programs throughout the world. Contact them for more information (see Travel Organizations, p. 2).

Central College Abroad, Office of International Education, 812 University, Pella, IA 50219 (tel. (800) 831-3629; fax (515) 628-5316; email admission@central.edu). Offers quarter, semester, and year-long study abroad programs in Austria. US$20 application fee. Scholarships are available. Applicants must be at least 18 years old, have completed their freshman year of college, and have a minimum 2.5 GPA. Programs costs include tuition, housing, and fees.

Eurocentres, 101 N. Union St. #300, Alexandria, VA 22314 (tel. (800) 648-4809; fax (703) 684-1495; http://www.clark.net/pub/eurocent/home.htm) or Eurocentres, Head Office, Seestr. 247, CH-8038 Zürich (tel. (01) 485 50 40; fax 481 61 24). Coordinates language programs and homestays for college students and adults in Lausanne, Neuchâtel, and Lucerne. Programs cost about US$500-5000 and last from 2 weeks to 3 months. Some financial aid is available.

International Schools Services, Educational Staffing Program, 15 Roszel Road, P.O. Box 5910, Princeton, NJ 08543 (tel. (609) 452-0990; fax 452-2690; email edustaffing%ISS@mcimail.com). Recruits teachers and administrators for schools in Africa, Asia, Central and South America, Europe, and the Middle East. All instruction in English. Applicants must have a bachelor's degree and 2 years of relevant experience. Nonrefundable US$75 application processing fee.

Language Immersion Institute, 75 South Manheim Blvd., The College at New Paltz, New Paltz, NY 12561 (tel. (914) 257-3500; fax (914) 257-3569; email lii@newpaltz.edu), provides language instruction at all levels in French, German, Czech, and Hungarian, amongst others. Weekend courses offered at New Paltz and in NYC. They also conduct 2-week summer courses and some overseas courses.

Program fees are about US$275 for a weekend or US$625 per week for the longer courses.

World Learning, Inc., Summer Abroad, P.O. Box 676, Brattleboro, VT 05302 (tel. (800) 345-2929 or (802) 257-7751; http://www.worldlearning.org). Founded in 1932 as The Experiment in International Living, it offers high school programs in Switzerland as well as language-training programs with elective homestays. Programs are 3-5 weeks long. Positions as group leaders are available world-wide if you are over 24, have previous in-country experience, are fluent in the language, and have experience with high school students.

Youth For Understanding (YFU) International Exchange, 3501 Newark St. NW, Washington, DC 20016 (tel. (800) TEENAGE (833-6243) or (202) 966-6800; fax (202) 895-1104; http://www.yfu.org). As one of the oldest and largest exchange organizations in the world, YFU has placed over 175,000 high school students between the ages of 14 and 18 with families worldwide for year, semester, summer, and sport homestays. YFU also offers a Community College program in which international students from 18-22 years of age spend a year or semester with an American family and attend community college.

WORK

There's no better way to submerge yourself in a foreign culture than to become part of its economy. The good news is that it's relatively easy to find a temporary job abroad; the bad news is that unless you have connections, it will rarely be glamorous. You might consider doing the rounds of resort hotels; these places employ many foreigners during the winter and often need English speakers. If you are a full-time student at a U.S. university, one easy way to get a job abroad is through work permit programs run by the **Council on International Educational Exchange (Council)** and its member organizations (see Travel Organizations, p. 2). For a US$225 application fee, Council can procure three- to six-month work permits (and a handbook to help you find work and housing). Austria and Switzerland have offices to help with finding accommodations, openings, and connections.

Transitions Abroad Publishing, Inc., 18 Hulst Rd., P.O. Box 1300, Amherst, MA 01004 (tel. (800) 293-0373; fax (413) 256-0373; email trabroad@aol.com); publishes a bimonthly magazine listing all kinds of opportunities and printed resources for those seeking to study, work, or travel abroad. For subscriptions (USA US$20 for 6 issues, Canada US$26, other countries US$38), contact them at *Transitions Abroad,* Dept. TRA, Box 3000, Denville, NJ 07834.

Surrey Books, 230 E. Ohio St. Chicago, IL 60611 (tel. (800) 326-4430; fax (312) 751-7330) publishes *How to Get a Job in Europe: The Insider's Guide.*

World Trade Academy Press, Suite 509, 50 E. 42nd St., New York, NY 10017-5480 (tel. (212) 752-0329). Publishes *The Directory of American Firms Operating in Foreign Countries* (1996) for US$200, available in bookstores or libraries.

Officially, you can hold a job in European countries (and most others as well) only with a **work permit.** Your prospective employer must obtain this document, usually by demonstrating that you have skills that locals lack. Teaching English abroad is thus a common and practical choice (see also "Volunteering"). In addition, the following *au pair* agencies can help you find work as a nanny in a foreign country.

InterExchange, 161 Sixth Ave., New York, NY 10013 (tel. (212) 924-0446; fax 924-0575). Provides information in pamphlet form on international work programs and *au pair* positions in Switzerland and Austria.

Childcare International, Ltd., Trafalgar House, Grenville Place, London NW7 3SA (tel. (01819) 59 36 11 or 06 3116; fax 06 3461; email offic@childint.demon.co.uk; http://www.ipi.co.uk/childint). Member of the International *Au Pair* Association. Offers *au pair* positions in Switzerland and Austria. UK£60 application fee. The organization prefers a long placement but does arrange summer work.

VOLUNTEER

At the crossroads of work and study lie volunteer jobs. Unlike normal jobs, these opportunities are primarily in the academic or service areas.

Council (see Travel Organizations, p. 2) offers 2- to 4-week environmental or community service projects in over 30 countries around the globe through its Voluntary Services Department (US$250-750 placement fee). Participants must be at least 18 years old.

Service Civil International (SCI-VS), 5474 Walnut Level Rd., Crozet, VA 22932 (tel. (804) 823-1826; fax 823-5027; email scivsusa@igc.apc.org). Arranges placement in workcamps in Europe (ages 18 and over). Registration fees US$50-250, depending on the camp location.

Volunteers for Peace, 43 Tiffany Rd., Belmont, VT 05730 (tel. (802) 259-2759; fax 259-2922; email vfp@vermontel.com; http://www.vfp.org). A non-profit organization that arranges for speedy placement in over 800 countries. 10 to 15 people workcamps in over 60 countries, including Switzerland and Austria. Gives the most complete and up-to-date listings in the annual *International Workcamp Directory* (US$12). Registration fee US$175. Some workcamps are open to 16 and 17 year olds for US$200. Free newsletter.

Willing Workers on Organic Farms (WWOOF) distributes a list of names of organic farmers who offer room and board in exchange for help on the farm. WWOOF-style groups can be found in many countries. Be sure to include an international postal reply coupon with your request. Contact: WWOOF-CH, Postfach, CH-9001 St. Gallen, Switzerland (email fairtours@gn.apc.org).

■ Health

In the event of a **medical emergency,** call the country's **emergency number: 144** in both Switzerland and Austria. Many of the first-aid centers and hospitals in major cities that *Let's Go* lists can provide you with medical care from an English-speaking doctor. Your consulate in major foreign cities should also have a list of English-speaking doctors in town. In most major cities, a rotating pharmacy is open 24hr.—consult the door of the nearest pharmacy to find out which one is open for the night. Hospitals can be found under individual city listings.

If you are concerned about being able to access medical support while traveling, contact one of these two services: **Global Emergency Medical Services (GEMS)** provides its subscribers with 24-hour international medical assistance and support coordinated through registered nurses who have on-line access to your medical information, your primary physician, and a worldwide network of screened, credentialed English-speaking doctors and hospitals. Subscribers also receive a pocket-sized, personal medical record that contains vital information in case of emergencies. For more information, call (800) 860-1111, or write GEMS, 2001 Westside Drive, Ste. 120, Alpharetta, GA 30201. The **International Association for Medical Assistance to Travelers (IAMAT)** offers a membership ID card, a directory of English-speaking doctors around the world who have agreed to treat members for a set fee schedule, and detailed brochures and charts on immunization requirements, various tropical diseases, climate, and sanitation. Membership is free, though donations are appreciated and used for further research. Contact chapters in the **U.S.,** 417 Center St., Lewiston, NY 14092 (tel. (716) 754-4883; fax (519) 836-3412; email iamat@sentex.net; http://www.sentex.net/iamat); in **Canada,** 40 Regal Rd., Guelph, Ontario, N1K 1B5, or 1287 St. Clair Avenue West, Toronto, M6E 1B8 (tel. (416) 652-0137; fax (519) 836-3412), or in **New Zealand,** P.O. Box 5049, Christchurch 5.

BEFORE YOU GO

Always go prepared with any **medication** you may need while away, as well as a copy of the prescription and/or a statement from your doctor—especially if you need to bring insulin, syringes, or any narcotics; this includes birth control pills for women.

Travelers with chronic medical conditions should consult their physicians before leaving. While **Cortisone** is available over the counter in the U.S., a prescription is required in Switzerland. Consult your doctor before you leave for information about this and other drugs in both Switzerland and Austria. Be aware that matching prescriptions with foreign equivalents may be hard; it is best to bring an extra week's supply. Remember that a *Drogerie* only sells toilet articles such as soap and tampons; to purchase any health products (including aspirin, cough drops, contact lens solution, and even condoms) or to get prescriptions filled you must go to an *Apotheke*. Swiss and Austrian **pharmacists** often speak English and can often suggest proper treatment if you describe your symptoms.

If you wear **glasses** or **contact lenses,** take an extra prescription with you and make arrangements with someone at home to send you a replacement pair in an emergency. Glasses-wearers should bring a strap or headband to insure that they don't slip off of your face and plunge into an Alpine gorge while hiking. If you wear contacts, bring glasses, extra solutions, enzyme tablets, eyedrops, etc.—lens supplies abroad, though available, can cost exorbitant sums. If you are accustomed to a heat disinfectant system, check to see if it is safe to switch to a chemical disinfectant system.

Travelers with medical conditions that cannot be easily recognized (diabetes, epilepsy, heart conditions, allergies to antibiotics, etc.) may want to obtain the **Medic Alert Identification Tag** (US$35 the first year and US$15 annually thereafter) from the Medic Alert Foundation, 2323 Colorado Ave., Turlock, CA 95381-1009 (tel. (800) 825-3785). Membership to the foundation provides the tag, an annually updated wallet card, and access to the 24-hr. hotline at (800) 432-5378. The **American Diabetes Association,** 1660 Duke St., Alexandria, VA 22314 (tel. (800) 232-3472) provides copies of *Travel and Diabetes* and ID cards with messages in 18 languages explaining the carriers diabetic status.

ON THE ROAD

Common sense is the simplest prescription for good health while you travel: eat well, drink enough, get enough sleep, and don't overexert yourself. If you're going to be doing a lot of walking, take along some quick-energy foods to keep your strength up. You'll need plenty of protein, carbohydrates, and fluids. The heat, though not Saharan temperatures, can be quite oppressive during the summer, especially in the flatter eastern areas of Austria. Be warned that non-carbonated plastic **water bottles** (like Evian) are impossible to come by in Austria, even in grocery stores. Take a flask, and fill it with **tap water,** which is drinkable.

You may get **diarrhea,** one of the most common symptoms associated with traveling, which may be cured by over-the-counter anti-diarrheals. Carry a canteen or water bottle on your travels, and make sure to drink water frequently to prevent dehydration. Be sure to bring a potent **sunscreen** with you from home, and cover up from the sun with long sleeves and a hat, and, again, drink plenty of fluids. Also, beware of **heat exhaustion.** Symptoms include cessation of sweating, a rise in body temperature, and headache, followed at later stages by mental confusion and possibly death. A heat exhaustion victim should be cooled off immediately with fruit juice or salted water, wet towels, and shade, and then rushed to a hospital.

Extreme cold is no less dangerous than heat—overexposure to cold brings risk of hypothermia and frostbite, and is a serious risk if traveling in the Alps in any season, or at anywhere in the winter. **Hypothermia** is a result of exposure to cold and can occur even in the middle of the summer, especially in rainy or windy conditions or at night. Symptoms include a rapid drop in body temperature, shivering, poor coordination, exhaustion, slurred speech, sleepiness, hallucinations, or amnesia. Seek medical help as soon as possible. To avoid hypothermia, always keep dry and warm and stay out of the wind. In freezing temperatures, **frostbite** may occur. The affected skin will turn white, then waxy and cold. The victim should drink warm beverages, stay or get dry, and gently and slowly warm the frostbitten area in dry fabric or with steady body contact. Never rub frostbite; the skin is easily damaged when frozen. Take serious cases to a doctor or medic as soon as possible.

Travelers to **high altitudes** must allow their bodies a couple of days to adjust to the lower oxygen level in the air before exerting themselves. If you're setting out on long alpine hikes, give yourself an adjustment period before you start. Even marathon runners tire quickly in these parts. Also be careful about **alcohol,** especially if you're used to U.S. standards for beer—many foreign brews and liquors pack more punch, and at high altitudes, where the air has less oxygen, any alcohol will do you in quickly. Drinking games are not an advisable way to spend your time in the Alps.

If you plan to romp in the forest, try to learn any regional hazards. Know that any three-leafed plant might be poison ivy, poison oak, or poison sumac—pernicious plants whose oily surface causes insufferable itchiness if touched. **Ticks** are especially nasty, and can cause tick-borne encephalitis, a viral infection of the central nervous system which is transmitted by tick bites or by eating unpasteurized dairy products and occurs most often in wooded areas. This disease may be referred to as *Gehirn-hautentzündung* (literally, inflammation of the brain; it's similar to meningitis) in Austria. Be extremely careful when walking through the woods; cover as much skin on your lower body with clothing as you can, and consider using a good tick repellent. Do not attempt to get ticks out by burning them or coating them with nail polish remover or petroleum jelly.

Remember to lavish your **feet** with attention. Make sure your shoes are appropriate for extended walking, change your socks often, use talcum powder to combat excess moisture, use lotion when they become too dry, and have some moleskin on hand to pad painful spots before they become excruciating blisters. Do *not* pick at your corns and calluses; the hardened skin offers good protection.

For minor health problems on the road, a compact **first-aid kit** should suffice. Some hardware stores vend ready-made kits, but it's just as easy to assemble your own. Items you might want to include are: antiseptic soap or antibiotic cream, elastic bandage, thermometer in a sturdy case, sunscreen, Swiss Army knife with tweezers and scissors, aspirin, decongestant or antihistamine, moleskin, motion sickness remedy, burn ointment, medicine for diarrhea and stomach ills, bandages and gauze, insect and tick repellent and a large, clean cloth.

AIDS AND STDS

Regardless of travel destination, all travelers should be aware of the facts about **HIV,** the human immunodeficiency virus that causes **AIDS.** People with AIDS have difficulty fighting off even minor illnesses, like the common cold, and frequently catch diseases called opportunistic infections that people with normally functioning immune systems are protected from. It is important to realize that while not everyone who is HIV positive has AIDS, *any person who is HIV positive can transmit this virus* which impairs the immune system and ultimately leads to death.

HIV transmission can occur in several ways. The easiest mode of transmission is through **direct blood to blood contact** with an HIV-positive person; never share intravenous drugs, tattooing, or other needles. The most common mode of transmission is unprotected intercourse. It's important to be aware that there is no assurance that any given person is not infected with HIV or another STD. People who are HIV positive are of all colors, creeds, nationalities, and sexual orientations. Often there are no symptoms for up to 10 years. When having sex, you should always assume the other person is HIV positive. **Safer sex** is sex in which none of your partner's potentially infected blood or sexual fluids come into contact with any of your blood or mucous membranes. Health professionals recommend the use of latex condoms with nonoxynol-9; follow the instructions on the packet. It may not always be easy to buy condoms in small towns. For this reason, it is a good idea to take a supply with you before you depart for your trip.

For more information on AIDS, **Council's** brochure, *Travel Safe: AIDS and International Travel,* is available at all Council Travel offices (see Budget Travel Agencies, p. 25) or call the **U.S. Center for Disease Control's** 24-hr. hotline at (800) 342-2437;

electronic bulletin board at (202) 647-9225) for country-specific restrictions for HIV-positive travelers. Or write to the Bureau of Consular Affairs #6831, Dept. of State, Washington, D.C. 20520. In Switzerland, call (22) 791 46 73, or write to the World Health Organization, Attn.: Global Program on AIDS, 20 Avenue Appia, 1211 Geneva 27, Switzerland.

Sexually transmitted diseases (STDs), such as gonorrhea, chlamydia, genital warts, syphilis, and herpes are a lot easier to catch than AIDS and can be just as deadly. It's a wise idea to actually look at your partner's genitals before you have sex. If anything looks amiss, that should be a warning signal. When having sex, condoms may protect you from certain STDs, but oral or even tactile contact can lead to transmission. Even a high-quality condom still incurs a risk of transmission.

■ Specific Concerns

WOMEN TRAVELERS

Women who explore any area on their own inevitably face additional concerns about safety. In all situations it is best to trust your instincts; if you'd feel better somewhere else, don't hesitate to move on. Consider staying in hostels that offer single rooms that lock from the inside or religious organizations that offer rooms for women only. Stick to centrally located accommodations and avoid late-night treks or metro rides. Hitching is *never* safe for lone women, or even for two women traveling together. Choose train compartments occupied by other women or couples, or ask the conductor to put together a women-only compartment.

When abroad the less you look like a tourist, the better off you'll be. Try to always appear as if you know where you're going (even when you don't), and ask women or couples for directions if you're lost or if you feel uncomfortable. In general, dress conservatively, especially in rural areas. If you spend time in cities, you may be harassed no matter how you are dressed. Don't hesitate to seek out a police officer or a passerby if you are being harassed but remember that the best answer to verbal harassment is often no answer at all. Memorize the emergency numbers, and always carry change for the phone and enough extra money for a bus or taxi. Carry a whistle or an airhorn on your keychain, and don't hesitate to use it. A **Model Mugging** course will not only help prepare you to deal with a mugging, but will also raise your level of awareness of your surroundings as well as your confidence. Offices exist in 14 U.S. states, as well as in Quebec and Zürich (see **Safety and Security,** p. 12). All of these warnings and suggestions should not discourage women from traveling alone—you can still have a perfectly enjoyable time.

Women travelers will likely feel safer and more secure in Switzerland and Austria than in other parts of Europe (like Budapest and Prague)—violent crime is generally rare. Socially defined gender roles are much more clearly demarcated in Switzerland and Austria than in the U.S. or Canada, though women's incomes are catching up with men's. Austria's feminist community thrives in Salzburg and Vienna, where a number of establishments cater to a liberated clientele. Unlike some parts of southern Europe, catcalls and whistling are not acceptable behavior in Switzerland and Austria. Women can rebuke their harassers by loudly saying *"Laß mich in Ruhe!"* (LAHSS MEEKH EEN ROOH-eh: "leave me alone," in German Switzerland and Austria), *"Laissez-moi tranquille!"* (less-AY MWA tran-KEEL, in French Switzerland) or *"Lasciami in pace"* (LAH-shah-mee een PAH-cheh, in Ticino) should suffice to discourage most unwanted attention. Some useful publications include:

A Journey of One's Own, by Thalia Zepatos, (Eighth Mountain Press US$15). The latest thing on the market, interesting and full of good advice, plus a specific and manageable bibliography of books and resources.

Directory of Women's Media is available from the National Council for Research on Women, 530 Broadway, 10th Fl., New York, NY 10012 (tel. (212) 274-0730; fax 274-0821). Lists women's publishers, bookstores, theaters, and newsgroups.

Women Going Places, a women's travel and resource guide emphasizing women-owned enterprises. Geared towards lesbians, but offers advice appropriate for all women. US$14 from Inland Book Company, P.O. Box 12061, East Haven, CT 06512 (tel. (203) 467 42 57), or order from a local bookstore.

Women Travel: Adventures, Advice & Experience, by Miranda Davies and Natania Jansz (Penguin US$13). Information on specific foreign countries plus a decent bibliography and index. The sequel *More Women Travel* is US$15.

OLDER TRAVELERS

Seniors often qualify for hotel and restaurant discounts, as well as discounted admission charges at tourist attractions. In **Switzerland,** women over 62 and men over 65 count as seniors. Seniors qualify for many discounts at hotels with presentation of proof of age upon arrival. Women over 60 and men over 65 make the cut for senior status in **Austria.** A **Seniorenausweiß** (senior identification card) entitles holders to a 50% discount on all Austrian federal trains, Postbuses, and BundesBuses, and works as an ID for discounted museum admissions. The card costs about 350AS, requires a passport photo and proof of age, and is valid for one calendar year. It is available in Austria at railroad stations and major post offices. Both National Tourist Offices offer guides for senior citizens. Senior citizens may also qualify for discounts on tours and transportation and should always inquire as to this possibility. Proof of senior status is required for many of the discounts listed; prepare to be carded.

AARP (American Association of Retired Persons), 601 E St. NW, Washington, DC 20049 (tel. (202) 434-2277). Members 50 and over receive benefits and services including the AARP Motoring Plan from Amoco (tel. (800) 334-3300) as well as discounts on lodging, car rental, and sight-seeing. Annual fee: US$8 per couple; US$75 lifetime membership.

Elderhostel, 75 Federal St., 3rd fl., Boston, MA 02110-1941 (tel. (617) 426-7788; fax (617) 426-8351; http://www.elderhostel.org). You must be 55 or over and may bring a spouse of any age. Programs at colleges and universities in over 50 countries focus on varied subjects and generally last one to four weeks.

Pilot Books, 103 Cooper St., Babylon, NY 11702 (tel. (516) 422-2225). Publishes a large number of helpful guides including *The International Health Guide for Senior Citizens* (US$5, postage US$1) and *The Senior Citizens' Guide to Budget Travel in Europe* (US$6, postage US$1). Call or write for a complete list of titles.

Unbelievably Good Deals and Great Adventures That You Absolutely Can't Get Unless You're Over 50, by Joan Rattner Heilman. After you finish reading the title page, check inside for some great tips on senior discounts and the like. Contemporary Books, US$10.

CHILDREN AND TRAVEL

There are many discounts for families traveling with young children. Children under two generally fly for free with an adult traveler, though they are not guaranteed a seat. International fares are usually discounted 25% for children from two to eleven. Virtually all museums and tourist attractions have a children's rate of admission. Be sure your child carries some form of ID to receive these discounts and in case of an emergency or if he or she gets lost.

Both National Tourist Offices publish books on traveling with children and families; write to them for more information. Not all Swiss and Austrian railways, airplanes, restaurants, hotels, and tours offer children's discounts or rates, but many do. Large cities, and beach-type resorts like Lugano and Neusiedl am See are most amenable to families with small children. Ski villages have numerous guesthouses run by doting grandmother figures, which also bodes well for kids.

Backpacking with Babies and Small Children (US$10). Published by Wilderness Press, 2440 Bancroft Way, Berkeley, CA 94704 (tel. (800) 443-7227 or (510) 843-8080; fax (510) 548-1355).

Take Your Kids to Europe, by Cynthia W. Harriman (US$14), a budget guide geared towards family travel. Published by Mason-Grant Publications, P.O. Box 6547, Portsmouth, NH 03802 (tel. (603) 436-1608; fax (603) 427-0015; email charriman@masongrant.com).

DISABLED TRAVELERS

By and large, Switzerland and Austria are two of the more accessible countries for travelers with disabilities *(Behinderung)*. Tourist offices can usually offer some information about which sights, services, etc. are accessible. In **Switzerland,** most buildings and restrooms have ramps leading up to them. The Swiss Federal Railways have adapted most of their train cars to be wheelchair accessible, and InterCity and long-distance express train have wheelchair compartments. The Swiss National Tourist Office publishes a fact sheet detailing *Travel Tips for the Disabled. Let's Go* attempts to indicate which youth hostels have full or partial wheelchair access. Cities, especially Vienna, Zürich, and Geneva, are very progressive, publishing mounds of information for handicapped visitors. The **Austrian National Tourist Offices** in New York and Vienna offer many pages of listings for wheelchair-accessible sights, museums, and lodgings in Vienna—ask for the booklet *Wien für Gäste mit Handicaps (Vienna for Guests with Handicaps)*. If given three days notice, the Austrian railways will provide a wheelchair that makes it easier to maneuver on a train. The international wheelchair icon or a large letter "B" indicates access.

In **Switzerland,** disabled travelers can contact **Mobility International Schweiz,** Hard 4, CH-8408 Winterthur (tel. (052) 22 26 825; fax 22 26 838). All Hilton, Inter-Continental, and Marriott hotels have wheelchair access, but they aren't cheap. Disabled visitors to **Austria** may want to contact the **Vienna Tourist Board,** Obere Augartenstr. 40, A-1025 Vienna (tel. (1) 211 14; fax 216 84 92), which offers booklets on accessible Vienna hotels and a general guide to the city for the disabled.

American Foundation for the Blind, 11 Penn Plaza, New York, NY 10011 (tel. (212) 502-7600). Open Mon.-Fri. 8:30am-4:30pm. Provides information and services for the visually impaired. For a catalog of products, contact Lighthouse Low-Vision Products at (800) 829-0500.

Mobility International, USA (MIUSA), P.O. Box 10767, Eugene, OR 97440 (tel. (514) 343-1284 (voice and TDD); fax 343-6812). International headquarters in Brussels, rue de Manchester 25, Brussels, Belgium B-1070 (tel. (322) 410 6297; fax 410 6874). Contacts in 30 countries. Information on travel programs, international work camps, accommodations, access guides, and organized tours for those with physical disabilities. Membership with newsletter costs US$25 per year (newsletter only US$15). They also sell the periodically updated and expanded *A World of Options: A Guide to International Educational Exchange, Community Service, and Travel for Persons with Disabilities* (US$14, nonmembers US$16), and offer a series of courses that teach strategies helpful for travelers with disabilities.

Society for the Advancement of Travel for the Handicapped, 347 Fifth Ave., Ste. 610, New York, NY 10016 (tel. (212) 447-7284; fax 725-8253). Publishes quarterly travel newsletter, *SATH News,* and information sheets and booklets (free for members, US$13 each for nonmembers), which contain advice on trip planning for people with disabilities. Annual membership is US$45, students and seniors US$25, agents and corporations US$100.

Twin Peaks Press, PO Box 129, Vancouver, WA 98666-0129 (tel. (360) 694-2462, orders only (MC and Visa) (800) 637-2256; fax (360) 696-3210). Publishers of *Travel for the Disabled,* which provides tips and lists of accessible tourist attractions, in addition to providing advice on other resources for disabled travelers (US$20). Also publishes *Directory for Travel Agencies of the Disabled* (US$20), *Wheelchair Vagabond* (US$15), and *Directory of Accessible Van Rentals* (US$10). Postage US$3 for first book, US$1.50 for each additional book.

The following organizations organize tours or make other travel arrangements for those with disabilities:

Directions Unlimited, 720 N. Bedford Rd., Bedford Hills, NY 10507 (tel. (800) 533-5343, in NY (914) 241-1700; fax (914) 241-0243). Specializes in individual and group vacations, tours, and cruises for those with physical disabilities.

Flying Wheels Travel Service, P.O. Box 382, 143 W. Bridge St., Owatonna, MN 55060 (tel. (800) 535-6790; fax 451-1685). Arranges international trips for groups or individuals in wheelchairs or with other sorts of limited mobility.

The Guided Tour Inc., Elkins Park House, Ste. 114B, 7900 Old York Road, Elkins Park, PA 19027-2339 (tel. (215) 782-1370 or (800) 783-5841; fax (215) 635-2637). This organization, founded in 1972, organizes year-round travel and vacation programs, domestic and international, for persons with developmental and physical challenges as well as those geared to the needs of persons requiring renal dialysis. Call, fax, or write for a free brochure.

BISEXUAL, GAY, AND LESBIAN TRAVELERS

Switzerland and Austria are less tolerant of homosexuals than many other nations; this is especially so in the more conservative western Austria, where open discussion of homosexuality is mostly taboo. Few establishments will turn away homosexual couples, but public displays of affection are a no-no, and in some rural areas could get you arrested. In large cities which tend to be progressive, there is a growing gay and lesbian community. In places like Geneva, Zürich, and Vienna, just about every variety of homosexual organization and establishment exists, from bikers and Christian groups, to bars and barber shops, though they can be difficult to find. Women are accepted in many gay clubs. The German word for gay is *schwule;* for lesbian, *lesben* or *lesbische.* Bisexual is *bisexual,* or simply *bi* (pronounced "bee"). In French, *homosexuelle* can be used to refer to men and women, but the preferred terms are *gai* (pronounced like gay in English) and *lesbienne* (lesbian).

Are You Two...Together? A Gay and Lesbian Travel Guide to Europe. A travel guide with anecdotes and tips for gay and lesbian travelers in Europe. Includes overviews of regional laws relating to gays and lesbians, lists of gay/lesbian organizations, and establishments catering to, friendly to, or indifferent to gays and lesbians. Available in bookstores. Random House US$18.

Ferrari Guides, PO Box 37887, Phoenix, AZ 85069 (tel. (602) 863-2408; fax 439-3952; email ferrari@q-net.com). Gay and lesbian travel guides: *Ferrari Guides' Gay Travel A to Z* (US $16), *Ferrari Guides' Men's Travel in Your Pocket* (US $14), *Ferrari Guides' Women's Travel in Your Pocket* (US $14), *Ferrari Guides' Inn Places* (US $16). Available in bookstores or by mail order. Postage/handling US$4.50 for the first item, US$1 for each additional item mailed within the U.S. Overseas, call or write for shipping cost.

Gay Europe Provides a quick look at gay life in countries throughout Europe. Available in bookstores (Perigee Books, US$14).

International Gay Travel Association, Box 4974, Key West, FL 33041 (tel. (800) 448-8550; fax (305) 296-6633; email IGTA@aol.com; http://www.rainbow-mall.com/igta.) An organization of over 1100 companies serving gay and lesbian travelers worldwide. Call for lists of travel agents, accommodations, and events.

Spartacus International Gay Guides (US$33), Lists bars, restaurants, hotels, and bookstores around the world catering to gays. Also lists hotlines for gays in various countries and homosexuality laws for each country. Available in bookstores. A gay guide to Zurich is also available from this publisher in a German/English edition (22.80SFr). Published by Bruno Gmunder, Postfach 110729, D-10837 Berlin, Germany (tel. (30) 615 00 30; fax 615-9134).

In **Switzerland** there is no official recognition of gay couples though homosexual prostitution has been legal since 1992, and is now on par with heterosexual prostitution. The age of consent in Switzerland is 16. There are several gay working groups in the larger cities. **Homosexuelle Arbeitsgruppe** is a national organization with offices in most cities. **Dialogai,** headquartered in Geneva (av. Wendt 57; mailing address: Case Postale 27, CH-1211, Geneva 7; tel. (022) 340 00 00; fax 340 03 98), formed a partnership with **l'Aide Suisse contre le Sida (ASS),** an organization that works against AIDS. There are several gay publications of note, available in gay centers and bookshops: *Dialogai Info,* provides information on French Switzerland, articles, interviews, etc. For more information on organizations, centers, etc., consult the Practical Information section of the specific city; for information on bars and night-clubs, see the individual Sights and Entertainment sections.

In **Austria,** homosexuality is considered mostly taboo, except in larger cities. The age of consent in Austria is 14. **Homosexuelle Initiative (HOSI)** is a nation-wide orga-nization with offices in most cities, and which provides information on gay and les-bian establishments, resources, and support. HOSI Wien (Vienna) publishes Austria's leading gay and lesbian magazine, the *LAMBDA-Nachrichten* quarterly. There are a number of smaller and alternative organizations throughout the country. Look to HOSI to publish warnings for gay couples about where not to go.

KOSHER AND VEGETARIAN TRAVELERS

National tourist offices often publish lists of kosher and vegetarian restaurants, but the kosher offerings are disappointingly small. The Swiss National Tourist Office dis-tributes the pamphlet *The Jewish City Guide of Switzerland* (published by Spec-trumpress International, Spectrum-House, Tanegg, 8055 Zurich, Switzerland), which lists synagogues, rabbis, butchers, kosher hotels and restaurants, and other useful information and phone numbers for kosher and Jewish travelers. They also publish a fact sheet listing hotels and restaurants that serve vegetarian, organically grown, or whole food. Switzerland and Austria are devoutly carnivorous, although vegetarian restaurants have proliferated along with the blooming alternative scene in larger cit-ies. Dairy products are by and large excellent, fish is common in lakeside resorts, but vegetarians who eat no animal products will have their work cut out for them. Vienna, the center of Austria's minute Jewish population, is the only city in Austria where it is remotely practical to keep kosher.

The European Vegetarian Guide to Restaurants and Hotels (US$14 plus US$1.75) is available from the Vegetarian Times Bookshelf (tel. (800) 435-9610).

The Jewish Travel Guide, lists synagogues, kosher restaurants, and Jewish institu-tions in over 80 countries. Published by Sepher-Hermon Press, 1265 46th St., Brooklyn, NY 11219 (tel. (718) 972-9010; US$14, plus US$2.50 shipping) and in the U.K. by Ballantine-Mitchell Publishers, Newbury House 890-900, Eastern Ave., Newbury Park, Ilford, Essex IG2 7HH (£10; tel. (0181) 599 88 66; fax 599 09 84).

North American Vegetarian Society, P.O. Box 72, Dolgeville, NY 13329 (tel. (518) 568-7970) provides useful publications for vegetarian travelers, including *Transformative Adventures,* a guide to vacations and retreats (US$15).

MINORITY TRAVELERS

It is difficult to generalize and say that either Switzerland or Austria discriminates against any minorities, though minority travelers will undoubtedly encounter odd stares in smaller villages. As always, cities tend to be more tolerant than small towns, but the Swiss and Austrians tend to be much too mild-mannered to hurl crude insults or provoke physical violence anywhere. *Let's Go* asks that its researchers exclude from the guides establishments that discriminate. If in your travels, you encounter dis-criminatory treatment, you should firmly but calmly state your disapproval, but do not push the matter; make it clear to the owners that another hotel or restaurant will be receiving your patronage, and mail a letter to *Let's Go* if the establishment is listed in the guide, so we can investigate the matter next year (see **Helping Let's Go** in the very front of this guide).

TRAVELING ALONE

The freedom to come and go, to backtrack or deviate from a schedule or route is the lone traveler's prerogative. Remember, buddy trips only work out perfectly in Hollywood. If you do travel with friends, consider separating for a few days. You'll get a brief break from each other and the chance to have some adventures of your own. Solo travel in Switzerland and Austria, even for women, is generally safe. Consider indoor accommodations when on your own—lone campers make easy targets for thefts and nocturnal sickos. The biggest disadvantage to traveling alone is the cost. It is much cheaper, especially in exorbitant Switzerland, to rent rooms in pairs, or even triples if possible. For many, however, the absence of partners provides a greater incentive to meet other people—locals and fellow travelers alike.

■ Packing

PACK LIGHTLY...THAT MEANS YOU

If you don't pack lightly, you will pay either with back problems or in postage to mail stuff home. The more things you have, the more things you have to lose. The larger your pack, the more cumbersome it is to store safely. Before you leave, pack your bag, strap it on, and imagine yourself walking uphill for the next three hours. At the slightest sign of heaviness, unpack something. A good general rule is to lay out only what you absolutely need, then take half the clothes and twice the money.

LUGGAGE

Backpack: If you plan to cover most of your itinerary by foot, the unbeatable baggage is a sturdy backpack. Make sure to get a pack with a strong, padded hip belt to transfer weight from your shoulders—pack's weight should rest almost entirely on your hips. Avoid excessively low-end prices—you get what you pay for. Quality packs cost anywhere from US$125 to US$420.

Suitcase/trunk/other large or heavy luggage: Okay if you plan to live in one city and explore from there, but a bad idea if you're going to be moving around a lot.

Daypack: Bringing a smaller bag in addition to your pack or suitcase allows you to leave your big bag in the hotel while you go sight seeing.

Moneybelt or neck pouch: Guard your money, passport, railpass, and other important articles in either one of these, and keep it with you *at all times*. See Safety on p. 12 for more information on protecting you and your valuables.

CLOTHING AND FOOTWEAR

Clothing: No matter what time of year you are visiting Switzerland and Austria, be prepared for cold weather. Mountains, with their shifty climates, dominate much of these countries. In winter, bring warm clothing, such as polypropylene long underwear, pile or wool clothing, hat and mittens, and wind-proof layers. In summer, it is still a good idea to bring a good rain jacket.

Walking shoes: Remember that you will likely be in mountain country, and will definitely be in rain; consider a good water-proofed pair of **hiking boots.** A double pair of socks—light silk or polypropylene inside and thick wool outside—will cushion feet, keep them dry, and help prevent blisters. Bring a pair of flip-flops for protection against the foliage and fungi that inhabit some hostel showers. Talcum powder on your feet can prevent sore and smells, and moleskin is great for blisters.

Rain gear: Essential. A waterproof jacket and a backpack cover will take care of you and your stuff at a moment's notice. Gore-Tex is a miracle fabric that's both waterproof and breathable; it's all but mandatory if you plan on hiking.

MISCELLANEOUS

The following is not an exhaustive list. You'll find the following items valuable: umbrella; resealable plastic bags (for damp clothes, soap, food, pens); alarm clock; waterproof matches; sun hat; moleskin (for blisters); needle and thread; safety pins; sunglasses; a personal stereo (Walkman) with headphones; pocketknife; notebook and pens; plastic water bottle; compass; string (makeshift clothesline and lashing material); towel; padlock; whistle; rubber bands; toilet paper; flashlight; cold-water soap; earplugs; insect repellant; electrical tape (for patching tears); clothespins; maps and phrasebooks; bungee cord; tweezers; garbage bags; sunscreen. Some items not always readily available or affordable on the road: deodorant; razors; condoms; tampons; and contact lens solution. It is also a good idea to bring along a **first-aid kit** (see Health, p. 16).

Sleepsacks: If planning to stay in **youth hostels,** make the requisite sleepsack yourself (instead of paying the linen charge). Fold a full size sheet in half the long way, then sew it closed along the open long side and one of the short sides.

Washing clothes: Sometimes it may be in your best interest to just use a sink. Bring a small bar or tube of detergent soap, a rubber squash ball to stop up the sink, and a travel clothesline.

Electric current: In most European countries, electricity is 220 volts AC, enough to fry any 110V North American appliance. Visit a hardware store for an adapter (which changes the shape of the plug) and a converter (which changes the voltage). You must have both. There is a free pamphlet *Foreign Electricity Is No Deep Dark Secret* by mail from the Franzus Co., Murtha Industrial Park, P.O. Box 142, Beacon Falls, CT 06403 (tel. (203) 723-6664; fax 723-6666).

Film is expensive just about everywhere. Bring lots of film from home, and be aware that, despite disclaimers, airport security X-rays *can* fog film. A lead-lined pouch, sold at camera stores, protects film. Pack it in your carry-on luggage, since higher-intensity X-rays are used on checked luggage.

Packing Light, the Swiss Way

Back in the summer of 1870, when the air was clean and the snow untrammeled, Austrian climbing legend Hermann von Barth took to the hills of the Karwendel Range in the Tirol and climbed no fewer than 88 peaks, 12 of which were first ever ascents. His luggage: a drinking cup, binoculars, smelling salts, a lighter, a paintbrush to paint his name on each peak (!), and a bottle of poison, in case he fell and wasn't able to rescue himself. He never fell.

GETTING THERE

The first challenge in European budget travel is getting there. The airline industry manipulates their computerized reservation systems to maximize profit; finding a cheap airfare in this confusion will be easier if you understand the airlines better than they think you do. There's little institutional incentive for travel agents to do the legwork to find the cheapest fares (for which they receive the lowest commissions); be sure to ask whomever you are calling for special fares and discounts.

In Switzerland, Zürich is the primary travel hub. Paris is a bigger hub, and it could be cheaper to take the TGV to your destination. Vienna is the cheapest destination in Austria, although since Munich has a much bigger airport, it may be more economical to fly into Munich and take a train to your destination. Return-date flexibility is usually not an option for the budget traveler, except on youth fares purchased through the airlines; traveling with an "open return" ticket can be pricier than fixing a return date and paying to change it. Avoid one-way tickets, too—the flight to Europe may be economical, but the return fares can be outrageous. If you show up at the airport before your ticketed date of departure, the airline just might rewrite your ticket, even if it is supposedly precluded by company restrictions.

■ Budget Travel Agencies

Students and people under 26 with proper identification need never pay full price for a ticket. They qualify for startlingly reduced airfares—mostly available from student travel agencies like **Council** and **STA.** These agencies negotiate special reduced-rate

The World At a Discount

Save **20%** to **50%** on Airfare (major carriers)

Save **10%** to **50%** on Museums & Theaters

Save **10%** on AT&T Calls to the U.S.

International Student Identity Card
Carte internationale d'étudiant/Carnet internacional de estudiante

97

ISIC

1997

Family name/Nom de famille/Apellido
YOUNG
First names/Prénoms/Nombres
CHRISTOPHER
Born/Né le/Nacido
5/3/77
Nationality/Nationalité/Nacionalidad
USA
Studies at/Etabl.d'Enseignement/Establ. de Enseñanza
BROWN UNIVERSITY
STUDENT

Save up to **40%** on Train Passes

Save **15%** on Greyhound Travel

Worldwide Discounts in more than **90** countries

Save **10%** to **30%** on Accommodations

The International Student Identity Card
Your Passport to Discounts & Benefits

With the ISIC, you'll receive discounts on airfare, hotels, transportation, computer services, foreign currency exchange, phone calls, major attractions, and more. You'll also receive basic accident and sickness insurance coverage when traveling outside the U.S. and access to a 24-hour, toll-free Help Line. Call now to locate the issuing office nearest you (over 555 across the U.S.) at:

Free 40-page handbook with each card

1-888-COUNCIL (toll-free)

For an application and complete discount list, you can also visit us at **http://www.ciee.org/**

Council

CIEE: Council on International Educational Exchange

bulk purchases with the airlines, then resell them to the youth market. Seniors can also garner mint deals; many airlines offer senior discounts or airline passes and discounts for seniors' companions as well. Sunday newspapers often have travel sections that list bargain fares from the local airport. Outsmart airline reps with the phone-book-sized *Official Airline Guide* (check your local library; at US$397, the tome costs as much as some flights), a monthly guide listing nearly every scheduled flight in the world (with prices) and toll-free phone numbers for all the airlines which allow you to call in reservations directly. *The Airlines Passenger's Guerilla Handbook* (US$15; last published in 1990) is a more renegade resource. On the Web, try the Air Traveler's Handbook (http://www.cis.ohio-state.edu/hypertext/faq/usenet/travel/air/handbook/top.html).

Most airlines maintain a fare structure that peaks between mid-June and early-September. They all practice "yield management," meaning the number of budget-priced seats on any flight is small and constantly subject to change. Midweek (Mon.-Thurs.) flights run about US$30 cheaper each way than weekend flights. Leaving from a travel hub will win you a more competitive fare than departures from smaller cities. Call around. Flying to London is usually the cheapest way across the Atlantic.

Council Travel (http://www.ciee.org/cts/ctshome.htm), the travel division of Council, is a full-service travel agency specializing in youth and budget travel. They offer railpasses, discount airfares, hosteling cards, guidebooks, budget tours, travel gear, and student (ISIC), youth (GO25), and teacher (ITIC) identity cards. U.S. offices include: Emory Village, 1561 N. Decatur Rd., **Atlanta,** GA 30307 (tel. (404) 377-9997); 2000 Guadalupe, **Austin,** TX 78705 (tel. (512) 472-4931); 273 Newbury St., **Boston,** MA 02116 (tel. (617) 266-1926); 1138 13th St., **Boulder,** CO 80302 (tel. (303) 447-8101); 1153 N. Dearborn, **Chicago,** IL 60610 (tel. (312) 951-0585); 10904 Lindbrook Dr., **Los Angeles,** CA 90024 (tel. (310) 208-3551); 1501 University Ave. SE, **Minneapolis,** MN 55414 (tel. (612) 379-2323); 205 E. 42nd St., **New York,** NY 10017 (tel. (212) 822-2700); 953 Garnet Ave., **San Diego,** CA 92109 (tel. (619) 270-6401); 530 Bush St., **San Francisco,** CA 94108 (tel. (415) 421-3473); 4311½ University Way, **Seattle,** WA 98105 (tel. (206) 632-2448); 3300 M St. NW, **Washington, D.C.** 20007 (tel. (202) 337-6464). **For U.S. cities not listed,** call 800-2-COUNCIL (226-8624). Also 28A Poland St. (near Oxford Circus), **London,** W1V 3DB (tel. (0171) 437 7767).
STA Travel, 6560 North Scottsdale Rd. #F100, Scottsdale, AZ 85253 (tel. (800) 777-0112; fax (602) 922-0793). A student and youth travel organization with over 100 offices around the world offering discount airfares (for travelers under 26 and students under 32), railpasses, accommodations, tours, insurance, and ISICs. 16 offices include 297 Newbury Street, **Boston,** MA 02115 (tel. (617) 266-6014); 429 S. Dearborn St., **Chicago,** IL 60605 (tel. (312) 786-9050); 7202 Melrose Ave., **Los Angeles,** CA 90046 (tel. (213) 934-8722); 10 Downing St., Ste. G, **New York,** NY 10003 (tel. (212) 627-3111); In the UK: Priory House, 6 Wrights Lane, **London** W8 6TA (tel. (0171) 938 47 11). In New Zealand: 10 High St., **Auckland** (tel. (09) 309 97 23). In Australia: 224 Faraday St., Carlton, **Melbourne** VIC 3050 (tel. (03) 347 69 11).
Let's Go Travel, Harvard Student Agencies, 67 Mount Auburn St., Cambridge, MA 02138 (tel. (800) 5-LETS GO (553-8746), or (617) 495-9649). Let's Go offers railpasses, HI-AYH memberships, ISICs, ITICs, FIYTO cards, guidebooks, maps, bargain flights, and a complete line of budget travel gear. All items available by mail; call or write for a catalog or see the catalog in center of this publication.
Campus Travel, 52 Grosvenor Gardens, London SW1W OAG (http://www.campus-travel.co.uk). Campus Travel is a large supplier of student travel products in the U.K., with 41 branches throughout the country. Student and youth fares on plane, train, boat, and bus travel. Flexible airline tickets. Discount and ID cards for youths, travel insurance for students and those under 35, and maps and guides. Puts out travel suggestion booklets. Telephone booking service based in the U.K.: in Europe call (0171) 730 3402; in North America (0171) 730 2101; in Manchester (0161) 273 1721; in Scotland (0131) 668 3303; worldwide (0171) 730 8111.

Rail Europe, Inc., 226 Westchester Ave., White Plains, NY 10604 (tel. (800) 438-7245; fax (800) 432-1329; http://www.raileurope.com). Sells all Eurail products and passes, national railpasses, and point-to-point tickets. Up-to-date information on all rail travel in Europe.

Travel CUTS (Canadian University Travel Services, Ltd.), 187 College St., Toronto, Ont. M5T 1P7 (tel. (416) 979-2406; fax 979-8167; email mail@travelcuts). Offices across Canada. Also, in the **U.K.,** 295-A Regent St., London W1R 7YA (tel. (0171) 637 31 61). Discounted flights; ISIC, GO25, and HI cards; and discount travel passes. Offers free *Student Traveller* magazine, and information on Student Work Abroad Program (SWAP).

Usit Youth and Student Travel, 19-21 Aston Quay, O'Connell Bridge, Dublin 2 (tel. (01) 602 1200; fax 671 2408). In the USA: New York Student Center, 895 Amsterdam Ave., New York, NY, 10025 (tel. (212) 663 5435). Additional offices in Cork, Galway, Limerick, Waterford, Maynooth, Coleraine, Derry, Athlone, Jordanstown, Belfast, and Greece. Specializes in youth and student travel. Offers low cost tickets and flexible travel arrangements all over the world. Supplies ISIC and FIYTO-GO25 cards.

■ By Plane

COMMERCIAL AIRLINES

Even if you pay an airline's lowest published fare, you may waste hundreds of dollars. The commercial airlines' lowest regular offer is the **APEX** (Advance Purchase Excursion Fare); specials advertised in newspapers may be cheaper, but have more restrictions and fewer available seats. APEX fares provide you with confirmed reservations and allow "open-jaw" tickets (landing in and returning from different cities). Generally, reservations must be made seven to 21 days in advance, with seven- to 14-day minimum, up to 90-day maximum stay limits, and hefty cancellation and change penalties. For summer travel, book APEX fares early; by May you will have a hard time getting the departure date you want.

Swissair (tel. (800) 221-4750), the national airline of Switzerland, serves most Swiss cities, though their fares tend to be high. They also car rental in conjunction with **Kemwel** and vouchers for over 1500 hotels starting at US$47. They also have **Swisspak,** which is essentially their travel service that puts together customized tours "for all budgets," including a 10% discount for senior citizens over the age of 62 of up to US$100. Further, they have forged a partnership with **Delta, USAir,** and **Singapore Airlines** that allows travelers to accumulate frequent flyer miles and to travel to numerous destinations. Contact the above Swissair number for more information.

Austrian Airlines, 608 Fifth Avenue, New York, NY 10020 (tel. (800) 937-8181 or (212) 265-6350; fax (212) 581 0695), the national airline of Austria, has the most non-stop flights and serves the most cities in Austria, but its fares tend to be high. Austrian Airlines flies daily non-stop from New York to Vienna and has flights from Chicago, London, and Johannesburg to Vienna. Austrian Airlines is associated with **OnePass,** Continental Airlines's frequent flyer program. Members can accrue and redeem their miles on Austrian Airlines flights, with some restrictions. If you are not a member of OnePass (tel. (800) 525-0280), join before you depart on Austrian Airlines. As with any airline's program, you'll earn thousands of miles just on this one round-trip flight. Austrian Airlines also has a partnership with **Delta.** They have moved their operation at JFK International Airport in New York to Delta's Terminal 1A, making domestic-international connections easier. Call Delta for more information (tel. (800) 241-4141 in the U.S and most of Canada.; (800) 361-6770 in Nova Scotia). Dozens of carriers fly to Vienna, albeit often with changes and layovers.

TICKET CONSOLIDATORS

Ticket consolidators resell unsold tickets on commercial and charter airlines at unpublished fares. Consolidators' flights are the best deals if you are traveling: on short notice (you bypass advance purchase requirements, since you aren't tangled in airline bureaucracy); on a high priced trip; to an off beat destination; or in peak season, when published fares are jacked way up. There is rarely a maximum age or stay limit, but unlike tickets bought through an airline, you won't be able to use your tickets on another flight if you miss yours, and you will have to go back to the consolidator to get a refund, rather than the airline. Keep in mind that these tickets are often for coach seats on connecting (not direct) flights on foreign airlines, and that frequent-flyer miles may not be credited.

Consolidators come in three varieties: wholesale only, who sell only to travel agencies; special agencies (both wholesale and retail); and "bucket shops" or discount retail agencies. You, as private consumer, can deal directly with the latter, but you have access to a larger market if you use a travel agent, who can also get tickets from wholesale consolidators. Look for bucket shops' tiny ads in weekend papers (in the U.S., the Sunday *New York Times* is best), and start calling them all. In London, the real "bucket shop" center, the **Air Travel Advisory Bureau** (tel. (0171) 636 50 00) provides a list of consolidators.

Be a smart and careful shopper. Contact the Better Business Bureau to find out how long the company has been in business and its track record. Although not essential, it is preferable to deal with consolidators close to home so you can visit in person if necessary. Ask to receive your tickets as soon as possible so you have time to fix any problems. It may be worth paying with a credit card so you can stop payment if you never receive your tickets. Don't be tempted solely by the low prices; find out everything you can about the agency you're considering, and get a copy of their refund policy in writing. Insist on a **receipt** that gives full details about the tickets, refunds, and restrictions. Consult Kelly Monaghan's *Consolidators: Air Travel's Bargain Basement* (US$5 plus US$3.50 shipping) from the **Intrepid Traveler,** P.O. Box 438, New York, NY 10034; email intreptravel@aol.com), for more information. Also ask about accommodations and car rental discounts.

For destinations worldwide, try **Airfare Busters,** (offices in Washington, DC (tel. (800) 776-0481, Boca Raton, FL (tel. (800) 881-3273), and Houston, TX (tel. (232-8783); **Pennsylvania Travel,** Paoli, PA (tel. (800) 331-0947); **Cheap Tickets,** offices in Los Angeles, CA, San Francisco, CA, Honolulu, HI, Overland Park, KS, and New York, NY, (tel. (800) 377-1000); **Moment's Notice,** New York, NY (tel. (718) 234-6295; fax 234-6450), air tickets, tours, and hotels; US$25 annual fee. For a processing fee, depending on the number of travelers and the itinerary, **Travel Avenue,** Chicago, IL (tel. (800) 333-3335) will search for the lowest international airfare available and even give you a rebate on fares over US$300; **Rebel,** Valencia, CA (tel. (800) 227-3235) or Orlando, FL (tel. (800) 732-3588; or **Discount Travel International,** New York, NY (tel. (212) 362-3636; fax 362-3236) also look for low fares.

Kelly Monaghan's *Consolidators: Air Travel's Bargain Basement* (US$7 plus US$2 shipping) from the Intrepid Traveler, P.O. Box 438, New York, NY 10034 (email intreptrav@aol.com), is an valuable source for more information and lists of consolidators by location and destination. Cyber-resources include **World Wide** (http://www.tmn.com/wwwanderer/WWWa) and Edward Hasbrouck's incredibly informative **Airline ticket consolidators and bucket shops** (http://www.gnn.com/gnn/wic/wics/trav.97.html).

STAND-BY FLIGHTS

Airhitch, 2641 Broadway, 3rd fl., New York, NY 10025 (tel. (800) 326-2009 or (212) 864-2000) and Los Angeles, CA (tel. (310) 726-5000), will add a certain thrill to the prospects of when you will leave and where exactly you will end up. Complete flexibility on both sides of the Atlantic is necessary; flights cost US$169 each way when departing from the Northeast, US$269 from the West Coast or Northwest, and US$229 from the Southeast and Midwest. The snag is that you do not buy a ticket, but the promise that you will get to a destination near where you're intending to go within a window of time (usually 5 days) from a location in a region you've specified. You call in before your date-range to hear all of your flight options for the next seven days and your probability of boarding. You then decide which flights you want to try to make and present a voucher at the airport which grants you the right to board a flight on a space-available basis. This procedure must be followed again for the return trip. Be aware that you may only receive a refund if all available flights which departed within your date and destination range were full. There are several offices in Europe, so you can wait to register for your return; the main one is in Paris (tel. (1) 47 00 16 30). **Air-Tech, Ltd.,** 584 Broadway #1007, New York, NY 10012 (tel. (212) 219-7000, fax 219-0066) offers a very similar service. Their Travel Window is one to four days; rates to and from Europe (continually updated; call and verify) are: Northeast US$169; West Coast US$249; Midwest/Southeast US$199. Upon registration and payment, Air-Tech sends you a FlightPass with a contact date falling soon before your Travel Window, when you are to call them for flight instructions. Note that the service is one-way—you must go through the same procedure to return—and that *no refunds* are granted unless the company fails to get you a seat before your Travel Window expires. It is difficult to receive refunds, and clients' vouchers will not be honored when an airline fails to receive payment.

CHARTER FLIGHTS

The theory behind a **charter** is that a tour operator contracts with an airline (usually one specializing in charters) to fly extra loads of passengers to peak-season destinations. Charter flights fly less frequently than major airlines and have more restrictions, particularly on refunds. They are also almost always fully booked, and schedules and itineraries may change or be cancelled at the last moment (as late as 48 hours before the trip, and without a full refund); you'll be much better off purchasing a ticket on a regularly scheduled airline. As always, pay with a credit card if you can; consider traveler's insurance against trip interruption. Try **Interworld** (tel. (305) 443-4929); **Travac** (tel. (800) 872-8800) or **Rebel**, Valencia, CA (tel. (800) 227-3235) or Orlando, FL (tel. (800) 732-3588).

Eleventh-hour **discount clubs** and **fare brokers** offer members savings on European travel, including charter flights and tour packages. Research your options carefully. **Last Minute Travel Club,** 1249 Boylston St., Boston, MA 02215 (tel. (800) 527-8646 or (617) 267-9800) is among the few travel clubs that don't charge a membership fee. Others include **Moment's Notice** New York, NY (tel. (718) 234-6295; fax 234 6450), air tickets, tours, and hotels; US$25 annual fee and **Travelers Advantage**, Stamford, CT, (tel. (800) 835-8747; US$49 annual fee); and **Travel Avenue** (tel. (800) 333-3335; see Ticket Consolidators, p. 28). Study your contracts closely; you don't want to end up with an unwanted overnight layover.

COURIER COMPANIES AND FREIGHTERS

Those who travel light should consider flying to Europe as a **courier.** The company hiring you will use your checked luggage space for freight; you're only allowed to bring carry-ons. You are responsible for the safe delivery of the baggage claim slips (given to you by a courier company representative) to the representative waiting for you when you arrive—don't screw up or you will be blacklisted as a courier. You will probably never see the cargo you are transporting—the company handles it all—and airport officials know that couriers are not responsible for the baggage checked for them. Restrictions to watch for: you must be over 18, have a valid passport, and procure your own visa (if necessary); most flights are round-trip only with short fixed-length stays (usually one week); only single tickets are issued (but a companion may be able to get a next-day flight); and most flights are from New York. Round-trip fares to Western Europe from the U.S. range from US$250-400 (during the off-season) to US$400-550 (during the summer). **NOW Voyager,** 74 Varick St. #307, New York, NY 10013 (tel. (212) 431-1616), acts as an agent for many courier flights worldwide primarily from New York. They offer special last-minute deals to such cities as London, Paris, Rome, and Frankfurt for as little as US$200 round-trip plus a US$50 registration fee. Other agents to try are **Halbart Express**, 147-05 176th St., Jamaica, NY

11434 (tel. (718) 656-5000); **Courier Travel Service,** 530 Central Avenue, Cedarhurst, NY 11516 (tel. (516) 763-6898); and **Discount Travel International,** 169 W. 81 St., New York, NY 10024 (tel. (212) 362-3636).

You can also go directly through courier companies in New York, or check your bookstore or library for handbooks such as *Air Courier Bargains* (US$15 plus $3.50 shipping from the Intrepid Traveler, P.O. Box 438, New York, NY 10034. *The Courier Air Travel Handbook* (US$10 plus US$3.50 shipping) explains how to travel as an air courier and contains names, phone numbers, and contact points of courier companies. It can be ordered directly from Bookmasters, Inc., P.O. Box 2039, Mansfield, OH 44905 (tel. (800) 507-2665).

A final caveat for the budget conscious: don't get too caught up in the seemingly great deals. Always read the fine print; check for restrictions and hidden fees.

If you really have travel time to spare, **Ford's Travel Guides,** 19448 Londelius St., Northridge, CA 91324 (tel. (818) 701-7414, fax 701-7415) lists **freighter companies** that will take travelers worldwide. Ask for their *Freighter Travel Guide and Waterways of the World* (US$16, plus US$2.50 postage if mailed outside the U.S.).

ONCE THERE

■ Tourist Information and Town Layouts

The **Swiss National Tourist Office** and the **Austrian National Tourist Office** both publish a wealth of information about tours and vacations; every town of any touristic importance whatsoever, and some others, are served by local tourist offices. Even the smallest towns have some sort of bureau. To simplify things, all are marked by a standard green "i" sign. *Let's Go* lists tourist offices in the Practical Information section of each city. The staff may or may not speak English—it is not a requirement in the smaller towns. In Swiss cities, look for the excellent **Union Bank of Switzerland maps,** which have very detailed streets and sites.

One thing to keep in mind is that the Swiss and Austrian creative palate for small-town names is rather dry. Many towns, even within the same state or province, have the same names (Gmünd or Stein, for instance). Before boarding any trains or buses, make sure it is the correct destination. In most small towns, there is generally someone in the train station who can direct you to the local tourist office. For larger cities, there is a branch of the tourist office helping with accommodations in the train station itself. These major stations also have extended hours for currency exchange. Most Swiss and Austrian train stations have luggage storage and bike rentals (at a discount if you have a train ticket for that day, railpasses do count). The **post office** is often next door to the train station, even in larger cities. It is essential to pick up a good **map** of the town or city from the tourist office before embarking on any exploration. Most towns are small enough that all sights are within walking distance. If distances do prove daunting, the buses that go into town generally have several stops within each town. Buy local public transport tickets from *Tabak* stands, which sell them for the cheapest rates around. Most ticket validation is based on the honor system, and many tourists interpret that as a free ride. Though certainly a tempting budget option, Let's Go does not recommend riding for free, or **Schwarzfahren (black riding)** as it is known. Those who get caught pay decidedly unbudget-like fines, and playing "Dumb American" never works.

■ Getting Around

BY TRAIN

European trains retain the charm and romance that their North American counterparts lost generations ago. Second-class travel is pleasant, and compartments, which seat from two to six, are excellent places to meet fellow itinerants of all ages and nationalities. Train trips tend to be short since both Switzerland and Austria are relatively small. Get ready when your stop is near. European trains are very efficient, and generally stop for only two to three minutes before zipping off. For longer trips, make sure that you are on the correct car. On occasion trains are split at crossroads. And when you are in large cities, make sure that you are at the correct train station because there are several (e.g. Vienna, Basel, Zürich, Budapest, Prague). Trains are in no way theft-proof; lock the door of your compartment when you nap, and keep your valuables on your person at all times. And unless you smoke, don't think you'll be able to stand smoking compartments; you won't.

In Switzerland, reservations can only be made on scenic, and not on regular, trains. Yellow signs announce departure times *(Ausfahrt)* and tracks *(Gleis)*. White signs are for arrivals *(Ankunft)*. On major Austrian lines, reservations are advisable; make reservations at least a few hours in advance at the train station (30AS). In Switzerland, children under 16 can travel free when accompanied by an adult with the **Swiss Family Card** (20SFr, no expiration date), which is not connected with the Swiss Family Robinson gift package. Children under six in Austria travel free. Fares are 50% off for children ages six to 14.

The ultimate reference for planning rail trips is the *Thomas Cook European Timetable* (US$28; US$39 includes a map of Europe highlighting all train and ferry routes; US$4 for postage). This timetable, updated regularly, covers all major and most minor train routes in Europe. In the U.S., order it from **Forsyth Travel Library** (see **Travel Publications**) which sells other useful travel books as well. Also look for Lenore Balken's *Camp Europe By Train* (US$15) which covers all aspects of rail travel and includes sections on railpasses, packing, and the specifics of rail travel in each country. Houghton Mifflin recently took over publishing the annual **Eurail Guide:** the *Eurail Guide to Train Travel in the New Europe* (US$15), available in most bookstores. The New Europe guide gives timetables, instructions, and prices for international train trips, day trips, and excursions in Europe. For information write Houghton Mifflin Co., 222 Berkeley St., Boston, MA 02116. Rick Steves' free *Europe Through the Back Door* travel newsletter and catalog, 109 Fourth Ave. N., P.O. Box 2009, Edmonds, WA 98020 (tel. (206) 771-8303; fax 771-0833) provides comprehensive information on railpasses both national and regional.

Switzerland

Getting around Switzerland is extremely easy. Federal **(SBB, CFF)** and private railways connect most towns and villages, with trains running in each direction on an hourly basis. **Schnellzüge** (express trains) speed from metropolis to metropolis while **Regionalzüge** chug into each cowtown on the route. Eurailpasses are valid for the state-run railways that connect major cities and comprise 60% of train service. Each city has small booklets listing train schedules; you can also ask for a free white booklet listing all prices of major fares within the country. The national telephone number for rail information is 157 22 22, with English operators.

Swisspass: Entitles you to unlimited free travel on government-operated trains, ferries, buses in 30 Swiss cities, and private railways, and a 25-50% discount on many mountain railways and cable cars. Second class prices are as follows: a 4-day pass costs US$176; an 8-day pass costs US$220; a 15-day pass US$256; and a 1-month pass US$350 (ages 6-16 half-price, free if traveling with parents and the Swiss Family Card). The pass is sold abroad through Rail Europe or any major U.S. travel agency. Depending on exchange rates, it may be cheaper to buy the pass at train stations in Switzerland. The pass also has a very strict no-replacement policy.

Swiss Flexipass: US$176 (2nd class), valid for any three days of second-class travel within 15 days. Unless you're on a speed tour, the pass may not pay for itself.

Regional Passes: Available in major tourist offices for holders of Eurail Passes (50-175SFr). Available in eight different regions.

Swiss Card: Sold *only* abroad, works as a one-month Half-Fare Card but also gives one free round-trip from an airport or border station (US$96 for one month).

If you are considering driving for any portion of your stay in Switzerland, consider the **Swiss Rail'n Drive Pass,** which works like a Swiss Flexipass combined with three days of car rental with unlimited mileage. Yet, unlike the other passes, the Rail'n Drive pass offers unlimited travel on the some of the private railways, such as the Glacier Express near Zermatt and the Panoramic Express. Furthermore, if you travel with three or four people, only two will have to buy the Rail'n Drive Pass (at a reduced rate for two people) and the others need only buy the Swiss Flexipass. Rail'n Drive passes include car rental with manual transmission only and offer three car categories with differing prices. The second class pass for one adult ranges from US$325-415 (discounts for two people traveling together vary with the season).

Austria

The **Österreichische Bundesbahn (ÖBB),** Austria's federal railroad, operates one of Europe's most thorough and efficient rail networks—a 5760-km system whose trains are frequent, fast, clean, comfortable, and always on or close to schedule. The ÖBB prints the yearly *Fahrpläne Kursbuch Bahn-Inland,* a 5cm-thick compilation of all rail, ferry, and cable-car transportation schedules in Austria. The massive compendium (100AS) is available at any large train station, along with its companion tomes, the *Kursbuch Bahn-Ausland,* for international trains, and the *Internationales Schlafwagenkursbuch,* for sleeping cars.

Austrian Rail Pass: Valid for four days of travel within a 10-day period on all rail lines, including Wolfgangsee ferries and private rail lines. Costs US$111 for 2nd-class, US$165 for 1st class. Also available is the **Austrian Rail Pass Junior,** for travelers under 15. The same discounts as its parent, but for less: 2nd class US$64, 1st class US$95. Children under the age of seven ride free. The card itself has no photo, so you must carry a valid ID in case of inspections. Keep in mind that the Rail Pass Junior is cheaper than many round-trip fares, so it may be an economical option even for short stays. The pass also entitles its holders to a 50% discount on bicycle rental in over 160 railway stations as well as the steamers of Erste Donau Dampfschiffahrts Gesellschaft operating between Passau, Linz and Vienna. Sold in the U.S. by Rail Europe.

Seniorenausweiß: Women over 60 and men over 65 can buy train and bus tickets at half-price after purchasing a Senior Citizen's ID for 350AS. Available at all rail stations and post offices in Austria.

Bundesnetzkarte: Valid for unlimited travel through Austria, including Wolfgangsee ferries and private rail lines. Half-price for Bodensee and Danube ferries. No surcharge on EC and SC first-class trains. One month of 2nd-class travel costs 3800AS (1st-class 5700AS). Picture necessary. Sold only in Austria.

You can **purchase tickets** at every train station, at Bahn-Totalservice stations, and, occasionally, at automats—or from the conductor for a small surcharge. You can pay by check, up to a limit. Over 130 stations accept the major credit cards as well as AmEx Traveler's Cheques and Eurocheques. Many also accept credit cards.

Eurailpasses

Buying a **railpass** is both a popular and sensible option in many circumstances. Ideally conceived, a railpass allows you to go wherever you want whenever you want, and change your plans at will. The handbook that accompanies your railpass tells you everything you need to know and includes a timetable for major routes, a map, and details on ferry discounts. In practice, of course, it's not so simple. You still must stand in line to pay for seat reservations (the only guarantee you have against standing up) and to have your pass validated when you first use it.

More importantly, railpasses don't always pay off. Distance is the fundamental criterion that determines whether or not a pass is a good buy. If you are planning even one long journey, a pass is probably the way to go. To see if a pass suits your itinerary, find a travel agent with a copy of the *Eurailtariff* manual (or call Rail Europe in the U.S. at (800) 438-7245 and ask for the latest edition of the *Rail Europe Traveler's Guide*). Avoid an obsession with squeezing every last kilometer from a pass; you may come home with only blurred memories of train stations.

The Eurail Pass is probably the most popular railpass valid throughout the Continent, including Austria, Switzerland, and Hungary. *Eurail is not valid, however, on many scenic and privately owned mountain railroads in Switzerland, especially in the Berner Oberland.* **Rail Europe,** 226 Westchester Ave., White Plains, NY 10604 (in U.S. tel. (800) 4-EURAIL (438-7145), or (800) 438-7245; fax (800) 432-1329; in Canada tel. (800) 361-RAIL; fax (905) 602-4198; http://www.raileurope.com) is just one of the many organizations that offer a trainload of information and an assortment of railpasses to consider. The various options include: **(1) First-class Eurailpass,** 15 days for US$522, 21 days for US$678, one month for US$838, two months for US$1148, and three months for US$1468; **(2) Eurail Saverpass,** for groups; unlimited first-class travel for 15 days for US$452 per person for two or more people who travel together (3 or more from Apr.-Sept.; also 21-day (US$578 per person) and one-month (US$712 per person) Saverpasses); **(3) Eurail Youthpass,** for travelers under 26; good for 15 days (US$418), one month (US$598), or two months (US$798) of second-class travel; **(4) First-class Eurail Flexipasses,** allow limited travel within a longer period; there are three packages: ten days of travel within a two-month period (US$616); and 15 days of travel in a two-month period (US$812); **(5) Youth Flexipass,** available in flavors of ten days within two months (US$438), and 15 days within two months (US$588).

The **Europass** allows travelers to combine the most popular European countries in one travel plan: France, Germany, Italy, Spain, and Switzerland. Europass offers rail travel through a number of countries determined by the number of travel days selected. For instance, a five- to seven-day trip allows you unlimited travel in three of the participating countries, an eight- to 10-day trip allows you four, and an 11- to 15-day trip allows unlimited travel in all five countries. If you take one of the first two options, the three or four countries you visit must be adjacent to each other. First class prices begin at US$316 (US$237 for two adults traveling together at all times) and the second class youth version (which starts with five to 10 travel days in four countries) at US$210. All passes are valid for two months and come with options for increasing the number of days of travel (for an additional fee). The Europass introduces planning complications that are not present with a simple Eurailpass; you must plan your routes so that they only make use of countries that you've "purchased." They're serious about this: if you've bought Germany and Italy, you can't cut through Switzerland to get to Italy without buying Switzerland, too. You can also add other associate countries (Austria, Belgium, Greece, Luxembourg, the Netherlands, and Portugal) for a nominal fee.

You'll almost certainly find it easiest to buy a Eurailpass *before* you arrive in Europe; contact one of the agencies listed under **Travel Organizations** (p. 2), among many other travel agencies. A few major train stations in Europe sell them too (though American agents usually deny this). If you're stuck in Europe and unable to find someone to sell a Eurailpass, make a trans-Atlantic call to an American railpass agency, which should be able to send a pass to you by express mail. Eurailpasses are not refundable once validated; you will be able to get a replacement if you lose one *only* if you have purchased insurance on the pass from Eurail—something you cannot do through a travel agent. Ask a travel agent for specifics, and be sure you know how the program works before you get to Europe.

Eurail Passes can get you reduced or free passage on some ferry and boat rides, bus routes, and funiculars throughout Switzerland and Austria. It can also get you into certain museums and other attractions. Be sure to ask before you pay full price.

Other Discount Tickets

For those under 26, **BIJ** tickets (Billets International de Jeunesse, sold under the **Wasteels, Eurotrain,** and **Route 26** names) are an excellent alternative to railpasses. Available for international trips within Europe and Morocco and for travel within

France, they save an average of 25-45% off regular second-class fares. Tickets are sold from point to point and allow a number of stopovers along the way. However, you cannot take longer than two months to complete your trip, and you can stop only at points along the specific direct route of your ticket, meaning that you cannot side-track or back-track. You can always buy BIJ tickets at Wasteels or Eurotrain offices (usually in or near train stations). In Switzerland, BIJ tickets are also available from regular ticket counters. Some travel agencies also sell BIJ. In the U.S., contact Wasteels at 7041 Grand National Drive #207, Orlando, FL 32819 (tel. (407) 351-2537; fax 363-1041); in the U.K., call (0171) 834 70 66.

British and Irish citizens **over the age of 60** can buy their national senior pass and receive a 30% discount on first- and second-class travel in Switzerland and Austria. Restrictions on travel time may apply.

BY BUS

Switzerland

PTT **postal buses,** a barrage of banana-colored, three-brake-system coaches delivered to you expressly by the Swiss government, connect rural villages and towns, picking up the slack where trains fail to go. Swisspasses are valid on many buses; Eurailpasses are not. Even with the Swisspass, you might have to pay a bit extra (5-10SFr) if you're riding one of the direct, faster buses. In cities, public buses transport commuters and shoppers alike to outlying areas; tickets must be bought in advance at automatic machines, found at most bus stops. The system works on an honor code and inspections are infrequent, but expect to be hit for 30-50SFr if caught riding without a valid ticket. *Tageskarte,* valid for 24hr. of free travel, run 3-5SFr, but Swiss cities are so small that you might as well travel by foot.

Austria

All public buses in Austria are non-smoking. The efficient Austrian bus system consists mainly of orange **BundesBuses.** Buses are generally local and complement the train system; they serve mountain areas inaccessible by train but do not duplicate long-distance, intercity routes covered by rail. Buses cost about as much as trains, but sadly, no railpasses are valid. Always purchase round-trip tickets if you plan to return to your starting point. Bus stations are usually located adjacent to the train station. Buy tickets at a ticket office at the station, or from the driver; pay based on kilometers traveled. For buses in heavily touristed areas during high season (such as the Groß-glockner Straße in summer), it is advisable to make reservations.

Buy in bulk to save on bus tickets. A **Mehrfahrtenkarten** gives you six tickets for the price of five. A **Seniorenausweiß** for women over 60 and men over 65 entitles senior citizens to half-price fares for a year on both buses and trains (350AS). Anyone can buy discounted tickets, valid for one week, for any particular route. **Children under six** ride free as long as they don't take up a full seat. **Children ages 6-15,** and **large pets** other than seeing-eye dogs, ride for half-price within Austria.

Trips can be interrupted under certain conditions, depending on your ticket. Be sure to ask. Small, regional bus schedules are available for free at most post offices. For more **bus information,** call (0222) 711 01 within Austria (outside Austria dial (1) instead of (0222)).

BY AIRPLANE

Many youths (under 25) are not aware that for long distances (Geneva and Prague, for instance) they can often acquire plane tickets for the same price as the equivalent train destination (though even these can't touch railpass deals). These special fares require ticket purchase either the day before or the day of departure. Look to student travel agencies in Europe (ÖKISTA and SSR, especially) for cheap tickets. The **Air Travel Advisory Bureau** (see Charter Flights, p. 30) can put you in touch with discount flights to worldwide destinations.

In the spirit of the European economic community, Swissair, Austrian Airlines, and Sabena are offering the **Visit Europe** plan. If you fly to any city in Austria, Switzerland, or Belgium from the United States on any carrier, you can fly to any European destination of the following airlines: Austrian Airlines, Swissair, Sabena, Crossair, or Tyrolean for $130 for each flight. You must buy a minimum of three vouchers before you leave the U.S. The vouchers are good for two months. Contact Swissair or Austrian Airlines for tickets.

BY CAR AND VAN

Cars offer great speed, great freedom, access to the countryside, and an escape from the humdrum town-to-town mentality of trains. A single traveler won't save, and will probably lose, by renting a car. Groups of two or three or more can make renting a bargain; groups of four or more definitely make the car cheaper than the train (although gas in Austria costs US$3-4 per gallon). If you can't decide between train and car travel, combine the two; rail and car packages offered by Avis and Hertz are often effective for two or more people who travel together; contact the National Tourist Offices for country-specific plans.

To **rent** a car in **Austria,** you must be over 21 (or older in some cases) and must carry a valid driver's license that you have had for at least one year and an International Driver's Permit or equivalent official validation. Most companies restrict travel into Hungary, the Czech Republic, and Slovakia. In **Switzerland,** the minimum rental age varies by company, but is rarely below 21, and you must possess a valid driver's license that you have had for at least one year. It is probably a good idea to get the IDP as well, though foreign licenses are valid. IDPs can be obtained from the American Automobile Association and the Canadian Automobile Association. Rental taxes are high in Austria (21%). Rates for all cars rented in Switzerland include a 40SFr (about US$27) annual **road toll** called a *vignette*.

You can rent a car from either a U.S.-based firm (Avis, Budget, or Hertz) with its own European offices, from a Europe-based company with local representatives (National and American International represent Europcar and Ansa, respectively), or from a tour operator (Europe by Car, Auto Europe, Foremost, Kemwel, and Wheels International), which will arrange a rental for you from a European company at its own rates. Not surprisingly, the multinationals offer greater flexibility, but the tour operators often strike good deals and may have lower rates. Always check if prices quoted include tax and insurance; some credit card companies will cover this automatically. Ask about student and other discounts and be flexible in your itinerary.

Try **Auto Europe** (well-organized Euro-rent outfit), 39 Commercial St., Portland, ME (tel. (800) 223-5555); **Avis Rent-a-Car** (tel. (800) 331-1084); **Budget Rent-a-Car** (tel. (800) 472-3325); **Europe by Car,** Rockefeller Plaza, New York, NY 10021 (tel. (800) 223-1516); **Europcar,** 145 Avenue Malekoff, 75016 Paris (tel. (1) 45 00 08 06 in France); **Hertz Rent a Car** (tel. (800) 654-3001); **The Kemwel Group** (a British outfit) (tel. (800) 678-0678); or **Payless Car Rental** (tel. (800) 729-5377).

If you're brave or know what you're doing, **buying** a used car or van in Europe and selling it just before you leave can provide the cheapest wheels on the Continent. Check with consulates for different countries' import-export laws concerning used vehicles, registration, and safety and emission standards. *How to Buy and Sell a Used Car in Europe* (US$6, US$1 postage; from Gil Friedman, P.O. Box 1063, Arcata, CA 95518; tel. (707) 822-5001) contains practical information on the process of wrangling for a used car in Europe. *Moto-Europa,* by Eric Bredesen (US$20 plus US$3 shipping to North America, US$7 overseas), available from Seren Publishing, P.O. Box 1212 Dubuque, IA 52001 (tel. (800) 387-6728), is a new comprehensive guide to all these moto-options, as well as useful travel tips. It also includes chapters on leasing and buying vehicles. More general information is available from the **American Automobile Association (AAA),** Travel Agency Services Dept., 1000 AAA Dr., Heathrow, FL 32746-5080 (tel. (800) 222-4357 or (417) 444-7380); the **American Automobile Touring Alliance,** Bayside Plaza, 188 Embarcadero, San Francisco, CA 94105 (tel.

Bikes can also be rented from **Austrian** rail stations. You can return the bike to any other station, and it is half-price with a valid railpass or ticket from that day. Some stations also rent racing, mountain, and tandem bikes (150AS per day with a train ticket). Normal bikes are 90AS, but 50AS with a valid train ticket. Reservations are recommended. Bring photo identification. The eastern part of the country is more level, but the Salzkammergut and Tirol reward effort with more dramatic scenery. One of the most popular bike routes runs along the Danube all the way from Vienna to Passau, Germany. Tourist offices provide regional maps of bike routes.

You can bring your bicycle with you on almost any train in Austria, in the baggage car. You alone are responsible for the bike's safety. The ticket for your bicycle is a **Fahrradmitnahmekarte** (literally, "bicycle take-along ticket"). Look for the *Gepäck-beförderung* symbol (a little bicycle) on departure schedules to see if bikes are permitted, and deliver it to and pick to up from the baggage car.

If you bike **breaks down** on the road, some auto clubs may come to the rescue. Try the **Austrian Automobile, Motorcycle, and Touring Club (ÖAMTC)** (tel. 120 all over Austria) or **ARBÖ** (tel. 123).

BY THUMB

> *Let's Go* strongly urges you to seriously consider the risks before you choose to hitch. We do not recommend hitching as a safe means of transportation and none of the information presented here is intended to do so.

No one should hitch without careful consideration of the risks involved. Not everyone can be an airplane pilot, but almost any bozo can drive a car. Hitching means entrusting your life to a random person who happens to stop beside you on the road and risking theft, assault, sexual harassment, and unsafe driving. If you're a woman traveling alone, don't hitch. It's just too dangerous. A man and a woman are a safer combination, two men will have a harder time finding a ride. Where you stand is also vital. Experienced hitchers pick a spot outside of built-up areas, where drivers can stop, return to the road without causing an accident, and have time to look over potential passengers as they approach. Hitching (or even standing) on super-highways is generally illegal; you may only thumb at rest stops, or at entrance ramps.

Safety issues are always imperative, even when you're traveling with another person. Avoid getting in the back of a two-door car, and never let go of your backpack. Hitchhiking at night can be particularly dangerous; stand in a well-lit place and expect drivers to be leery of nocturnal thumbers. Don't get into a car that you can't get out of again in a hurry. If you ever feel threatened, insist on being let off, regardless of where you are. If the driver refuses to stop, try acting as though you're going to open the car door or vomit on the upholstery.

Often large cities in Switzerland and Austria will have a *Mitfahrzentrale,* where drivers and passengers can request for each other. Consult the Practical Information listings at the beginning of each city, or the local tourist offices for more help.

■ Accommodations

Like most things Swiss and Austrian, accommodations are usually clean, orderly, and expensive. The word *Frühstückspension* indicates that the establishment is a bed-and-breakfast, but virtually all lodging facilities in Switzerland and Austria include breakfast with an overnight stay.

Wherever you stay, be sure to ask for a **guest card.** Normally, the "card" is merely a copy of your receipt for the night's lodging, sometimes only available after staying three nights or more. Guest cards generally grant discounts to local sports facilities, hiking excursions, and town museums, as well as transport within the city or to neighboring hamlets. In Austria, these discounts are funded by the 10AS tax that most accommodations slap on bills. Use the discounts to get your money's worth.

Let's Go is not an exhaustive guide to budget accommodations. Most local tourist offices distribute extensive listings (the *Gastgeberverzeichnis*) and many will reserve a room for a small fee. National tourist offices (see National Tourist Officeson p. 1) and travel agencies (see Travel Organizations, p. 2) will also supply more complete lists of campsites and hotels. Be aware that *Privatzimmer* and *Pensionen* may close their doors without notice; it's always wise to call ahead.

HOSTEL MEMBERSHIP

Prospective hostel-goers should become members of the official youth hostel association in their country. All national organizations are members of **Hostelling International (HI)**. A one-year HI membership permits you to stay at youth hostels all over the world at unbeatable prices. And, despite the name, you need not be a youth; travelers over 26 may only have to pay an occasional slight surcharge for a bed. Save yourself trouble by procuring a membership card at home; some hostels don't sell them on the spot. It is possible to join once you're on the road. Show up at an HI hostel, and ask for a blank membership card with space for six validation stamps. Each night you'll pay a non-member supplement (equal to one-sixth the membership fee) and earn one Guest Stamp; get six stamps and you're a member. Also, most student travel agencies sell HI cards on the spot; otherwise, contact one of the national hostel organizations listed below.

Hostelling International (HI), 9 Guessens Rd., Welwyn Garden City, Hertfordshire AL8 6QW, England (tel. (01707) 33 24 87) is a worldwide federation of national hostelling associations. *Budget Accommodation You Can Trust Vol. 1: Europe and the Mediterranean* (US$11), lists up-to-date information on HI hostels; it's available from any hostel association.

Hostelling International-American Youth Hostels (HI-AYH), 733 15th St. NW, Ste. 840, Washington, D.C., 20005 (tel. (202) 783-6161; fax 783-6171; http://www.taponline.com/tap/travel/hostels/pages/hosthp.html). HI-AYH has 34 offices and over 150 hostels in the U.S. HI-AYH membership cards cost US$25, under 18 US$10, over 54 US$15, family cards US$35. Membership valid for one year from date of issue. Contact HI-AYH for ISIC, student and charter flights, travel equipment, literature on budget travel, and information on summer positions as a group leader for domestic outings.

Hostelling International—Canada (HI-C), 400-205 Catherine St., Ottawa, ONT. K2P 1C3 (tel. (613) 237-7884; fax 237-7868). One-year membership fee CDN$25, under 18 CDN$12, two-year CDN$35; lifetime CDN$175.

An Óige (Irish Youth Hostel Association), 61 Mountjoy St., Dublin 7 (tel. (01) 830 45 55; fax 830 58 08; http://www.touchtel.ie). One-year membership is IR£7.50, under 18 IR£4, family IR£7.50 for each person over 15.

Australian Youth Hostels Association (AYHA), Level 3, 10 Mallett St., Camperdown, NSW 2050 (tel. (02) 565 16 99; fax 565 12 35). AUS$42, renewal AUS$26; under 18 AUS$12.

Youth Hostels Association of New Zealand (YHANZ), P.O. Box 436, 173 Gloucester St., Christchurch 1 (tel. (03) 379 99 70; fax 365 44 76). Annual fee NZ$24.

Hostel Association of South Africa, P.O. Box 4402, Cape Town 8000 (tel. (021) 419 18 53). Annual memberships SAR45; students SAR30; group SAR120; family SAR90; lifetime SAR225.

HOTELS

Hotels are quite expensive in Switzerland and Austria: in Switzerland, rock bottom for singles is US$17-20, for doubles US$22-24; in Austria you should expect to US$30-50 for a single, US$55-75 for a double. Switzerland has set the international standard for hotels; even one-, two- and three-star accommodations may be much nicer than their counterparts in other countries. The cheapest hotel-style accommodations are places with **Gasthof** or **Gästehaus** ("inn") in the name; in Switzerland, **Hotel-Garni** also indicates an inexpensive hotel. Continental breakfast *(Frühstuck)* is almost

always included. Unmarried couples over 21 will generally have no trouble getting a room together.

PRIVATE ROOMS AND PENSIONS

Renting a **private room** *(Privatzimmer)* in a family home is inexpensive and friendly. Such rooms generally include a sink with hot and cold running water and use of a toilet and shower. Many places only rent private rooms for longer stays, or they may levy a surcharge (10-20%) for stays of less than three nights. *Privatzimmer* tend to go for 15-60SFr per person and up in Switzerland. In Austria, rooms range from 150-200AS a night, with rooms in more expensive areas sometimes costing 200AS per night and more. Pensions are somewhat similar to the American and British notion of a bed and breakfast, and to the private rooms described above. You may have a private bathroom, or you may have to share, but almost never with more than four or five people. Pensions are typically a friendly and inexpensive way to see Switzerland or Austria. Rates tend to be slightly higher than those for *Privatzimmer*, though not by much, and the comfort and atmosphere are often worth it.

HOSTELS

Hostels *(Jugendherbergen* in German, *Auberges de Jeunesse* in French, *Albergi della Gioventù* in Italian) are the hubs of the gigantic backpacker subculture that rumbles through Europe every summer, providing innumerable opportunities to meet travelers from all over the world. Most guests are 17-25, but hostels are rapidly becoming a resource for all ages. Many Swiss and Austrian hostels are open to families. Hostel prices are extraordinarily low—US$8-25 per night for shared rooms.

Many hostels are out of the way, conditions are sometimes spartan and cramped, there's little privacy, rooms are usually segregated by sex, and you may run into more screaming pre-teen tour groups than you care to remember. Summer is an especially attractive season for the prepubescent set to invade hostels; try to arrive at a hostel before 5pm to insure that the hordes of children don't deprive you of a room. There is often a lockout from morning to mid-afternoon to let the staff clean in peace. Whenever possible, call the hostel well before you journey over.

Sheet sleeping sacks are required at many of these hostels. Sleeping bags are usually prohibited (for reasons of sanitation), but most hostels provide free blankets. You can make your own sheet sack by folding a sheet and sewing it shut on two sides. The lazier and less domestic can purchase a sleep sack from a department store or by mail (they usually run about US$15).

HI has recently instituted an **International Booking Network (IBN)** which allows you to make confirmed reservations at any of more than 225 hostels throughout the world (US$5 fee and 1 week advance notice). To make prepaid reservations, call or visit hostels on the IBN or IBN booking centers: **U.S.:** (202) 783-6161, **Canada:** (800) 663-5777, **Ireland:** (01) 830 4555, **England:** (0171) 855 215, **Northern Ireland:** (01232) 315 435, **Scotland:** (0178) 45 11 81, **Australia:** (02) 565 1699, and **New Zealand:** (643) 379 9970. If your plans are firm enough to allow it, pre-booking is wise. For US$5, reservations can be made for up to six consecutive nights and for groups of up to nine people, and changes can be made up to three days before the date of the reservation. Credit card (MC or Visa) guarantee required.

The Internet Guide to Hostelling (http://hostel.com), has information on hostel locations, news about hostels and hosteling, lists of budget guides, and budget transportation information.

LONG-TERM STAYS AND HOME EXCHANGE

Home exchange is tourism's symbiosis—thousands of travelers pay a for-profit company to include their house or apartment on a list, and the company in turn unites two parties who plan a mutually thrilling switcheroo. For less than US$80, you can get a list of many thousands of residences owned by people who want to trade their homes. The benefits are manifold: you'll feel like a resident, circumvent hostels, trans-

portation, and restaurant costs, and your own home is taken care of as you cavort in a land far, far away. Discounts are available for customers over 62.

Europa-Let/Tropical Inn-Let, 92 North Main St., Ashland, OR 97520 (tel. (800) 462-4486 or (541) 482-5806; fax 482-0660; email europa-let@wavenet), offers over 100,000 private rental properties (castles, villas, apartments, chalets, etc.) with fully equipped kitchens in 29 countries. Customized computer searches allow clients to choose properties according to specific needs and budget. This service may be especially advantageous for families, business people, large groups, or those planning to stay over one week (less in larger cities).

Fair Tours, CH-9001 St. Gallen, Switzerland (email fairtours@gu.apc.org) is a home exchange program for environmentally conscious travelers, providing them with an opportunity to avoid large-scale commercial tourism. Personal matching service. Send two international reply coupons for further information.

Hometours International, Inc., P.O. Box 11503, Knoxville, TN 37939 (tel. (800) 367-4668; email hometours@aol.com), offers lodging in apartments, houses, and castles in Great Britain, France, Italy, Israel, Portugal, Switzerland, and Spain.

■ Camping and the Outdoors

With over 1200 campgrounds in Switzerland and more than 400 throughout Austria, **camping** is a popular option. In Switzerland, prices average 6-9SFr per person, 4-10SFr per tent—a joy to behold in such an expensive country. In Austria, prices range from 50-70AS per person and 25-60AS per tent (plus 8-9.50AS tax if you're over 15), making camping seldom substantially cheaper than hosteling. You must obtain permission from landowners to camp on private property—don't hold your breath. The traditionally conservative Swiss and Austrians are often very protective of their private property. The Swiss Tourist Office also gives information about sites, though most are open in the summer only. Some campsites are open year-round, and 80 sites are specifically established for winter camping. Camping along roads and in public areas is forbidden. Whether you are camping or just hiking for the day in the Swiss and Austrian mountains, you should keep several things in mind. The first thing to keep in mind: nothing left above the snowline ever decays. In order to keep the mountains beautiful for posterity, do not throw anything away, not even food refuse or paper towels. Save all of your trash and dispose of it when you get back to civilization. Never build fires in the Alps, as grass fires are easily started and the mountains do not recover from the ravages of fire.

WILDERNESS AND SAFETY CONCERNS

The three most important things to remember when hiking or camping: stay warm, stay dry, stay hydrated. The vast majority of life-threatening wilderness problems stem from a failure to follow this advice. If you are going on any hike, overnight or just the day, that will take you more than one mile from civilization, you should pack enough equipment to keep you alive should disaster strike. This includes: raingear, warm layers (not cotton!), especially hat and mittens, first-aid kit, high energy food, and water. *Summer or winter, there are no exceptions to this list.*

All hikers appreciate the beauty of the environment, but many do not recognize its potential dangers. Always check weather forecasts and pay attention to the skies when hiking. Weather patterns in mountainous regions can change instantly. A bright blue sky can turn to rain—or even snow—before you can say "hypothermia." If on a day hike and weather turns nasty, turn back. If on an overnight, start looking immediately for shelter. You should never be forced to rely on cotton for warmth. This "death cloth" will be absolutely useless should it get wet. It retains water, holding it close to your skin and chilling your body. Instead wear synthetic materials designed for the outdoors, or wool. These materials dry faster and pull water away from your body, allowing you to stay warm even when wet.

Without a doubt the most frequent outdoor injury is a twisted ankle. These can be very serious, and could keep you from walking for hours or days. To avoid this, be sure to wear hiking boots appropriate for the terrain you will be hiking. Your boots should be sized so that they fit snugly and comfortably over one or two wool socks and a thin liner sock. Be sure that the boots are broken in. If you feel a "hot-spot" coming on, cover it with moleskin immediately.

If possible you should let someone know that you are going hiking, either a friend, your hostel, a park ranger, or some local hiking organization. If you get into serious trouble, use the Alpine Distress Signal—six audible or visual signals spaced evenly over one minute and followed by a break of one minute before repetition. Listen for a response of signals at 20-second intervals. Whether in a densely populated campground ten minutes from a major city, or alone in the middle of the wilderness, there are several things that you need to remember about camping saftey. A good guide to outdoor survival is *How to Stay Alive in the Woods,* by Bradford Angier (Macmillan, US$8). See **Health** (p. 16) for information about basic medical concerns and first-aid. The most important thing is to protect yourself from the environment. This includes a proper tent with rain-fly, warm sleeping bag, and proper clothing (see **Camping Equipment,** p. 46). Many rivers and lakes are contaminated with *giardia,* a bacteria which causes gas, loss of appetite, and violent diarrhea. Bringing your water to a rolling boil or purifying it with iodine tablets generally affords the best protection.

It is also important to be concerned with the safety of the environment. Because firewood is scarce in popular areas, campers are asked to make small fires using only dead branches or brush; using a campstove is the more cautious (and efficient) way to cook. Don't cut vegetation, and don't clear campsites. Make sure your campsite is at least 150 feet from water supplies or bodies of water. If there are no toilet facilities, bury human waste at least four inches deep and 150 feet or more from any water supplies and campsites. Always pack your trash in a plastic bag and carry it with you until you reach the next trash can.

CAMPING EQUIPMENT

Purchase **equipment** before you leave. Spend time examining catalogs and talking to knowledgeable salespeople. Mail-order firms are for the most part reputable and cheap—order from them if you can't do as well locally. Look for prices on the previous year's line of equipment to decline precipitously (sometimes by as much as 50%) when the new year's line starts to sell, usually sometime in the fall.

Sleeping bags: At the core of your equipment is the **sleeping bag.** Most of the better sleeping bags are rated according to the lowest outdoor temperature at which they will still keep you warm. They are made of either of down (warmer and lighter) or synthetic material (cheaper, heavier, more durable, and warmer when wet). Reasonable prices for good bags: US$65-100 for a summer synthetic, US$136-200 for a three-season synthetic, US$150-225 for a three-season down bag, and upwards of US$250-550 for a winter down bag.

Pads: If you're using a sleeping bag for serious camping, you should also have either a foam pad (US$13 and up for closed-cell foam, US$25 and up for open-cell foam) or an air mattress (US$25-50) to insulate you from the cold ground.

Tents: When you select a tent, major considerations should be shape and size. The best tents are free-standing, with their own frames and suspension systems. Low profile dome tents are the best all-around. Good two-person tents start at about US$135; US$200 for a four-person. Be sure to seal the tent's seams with waterproofer, and *make sure you have a rain fly.*

Backpacks: Buy a backpack with an internal frame if you'll be hiking on difficult trails that require a lot of bending and maneuvering—internal-frame packs mold better to your back, keep a lower center of gravity. In addition, internal frame packs are more manageable on crowded trains, and are less likely to be mangled by rough handling. External-frame packs are more comfortable for long hikes over even terrain since they keep the weight higher and distribute it more evenly. These don't travel as well. Backpacks cost anywhere from US$125-420. Don't economize—cheaper packs may be less comfortable and durable.

Other: Other necessities include: **plastic groundcloth** for beneath your tent, a **waterproof backpack cover,** and a **"stuff sack"** to keep your sleeping bag dry.

Shop around locally before turning to mail-order firms; this allows you to get an idea of what the different items actually look like (and weigh), so that if you later decide to order by mail you'll have a more exact idea of what it is you're getting.

Campmor, P.O. Box 700, Saddle River, NJ 07458-0700 (tel. (800) 526-4784; http://www.campmor.com). Has a monstrous selection of name brand equipment at low prices. One year guarantee for unused or defective merchandise.

Eastern Mountain Sports (EMS), One Vose Farm Rd., Peterborough, NH 03458 (tel. (603) 924-7231). EMS has stores from Colorado to Virginia to Maine. Though slightly higher-priced, they provide excellent service and guaranteed customer satisfaction on most items sold. They don't have a catalog, and they generally don't take mail or phone orders, but if you call the above number, they'll tell you about the EMS branch nearest you.

Recreational Equipment, Inc. (REI), 1700 45th St. E, Sumner, WA 98390 (tel. (800) 426-4840; http://www.rei.com). Stocks a wide range of the latest in camping gear and holds great seasonal sales. Many items guaranteed for life (excluding normal wear and tear).

L.L. Bean, Casco St., Freeport, ME 04033-0001 (U.S. and Canada tel. (800) 221-4221, International tel. (207) 865-3111; U.S. fax (207) 797-8867, Canada and International fax (207) 878-2104). Equipment and preppy outdoor clothing favored by northeastern Americans; high quality and chock-full of information. Call or write for their free catalog. The customer is guaranteed 100% satisfaction or they will replace the item or offer a full refund. Open 24hr., 365 days per year.

Sierra Design, 1255 Powell St., Emeryville, CA 94608 (tel. (510) 450-9555) has a wide array (all seasons and types) of especially small and lightweight tent models. You can often find last year's version for half the price.

HIKING

Free maps for **hikers** are available from even the most rinky-dink of tourist offices. Hiking trails are clearly marked by bright yellow signs indicating the time to nearby destinations, which may or may not bear any relation to your own expertise and endurance. ("Std." is short for *Stunden,* or hours.) Remember that the Alps are not kind to the unprepared. Every summer, dozens die in the Swiss mountains as visitors find that the compelling beauty of the landscape lulls them into attempting hikes or climbs that are beyond their ability. Mountain safety experts often recommend that you can minimize the risks by following five golden rules. First, sudden mists can reduce visibility quickly, so always know where you are, carry appropriate maps and do not rely on the public sign posting. Second, wintry weather can blow into an area in minute. Never be without waterproof clothing, food and extra reserves of stamina. The single biggest cause of hypothermia is wet clothes. Third, only leave marked paths if you are experienced and have reliable advice from locals—there can be hidden dangers like mudslides, loose scree (gravel), ice-cored moraine (glacial refuse), unhikable vegetation or steep snow patches on an innocuous looking fellside. Fourth, under no circumstances whatsoever walk on a snow-covered glacier without ropes, ice-axes, and a practical knowledge of how to use them. Snow may cover crevasses, and there is a hell of a lot more to pulling someone out than waggling a rope in front of them and tugging hard. And finally, watch where you put your feet!

Switzerland and Austria are renowned for their hiking. Mountains dominate much of these countries and millions of people take advantage of them each year. There are hikes available for all levels of talent from simple hikes in the foothills of the Swiss Jura to ice-ax-wielding expeditions through the glaciers of the Berner Oberland. Paths marked *"Für Geübte"* require special mountain climbing equipment and are for experienced climbers only. For lengthy hikes consider taking along a detailed map of the region you will be hiking. The best maps are the **Freytag-Berndt** maps, available in bookstores all over Switzerland and Austria. Purchase them (around US$10), from **Pacific Travellers Supply,** 12 W. Anapamu St., Santa Barbara, CA 93101 (tel. (805) 963-4438), in the U.S. There are several useful publications which you may want to consult before beginning your hiking experience.

100 Hikes in the Alps. Details various trails in Switzerland, France, Italy, Austria, Germany, and Liechtenstein (US$15). Write to The Mountaineers Books, 1001 Klickitat Way, Ste. 201, Seattle, WA 98134 (tel. (800) 553-4453; fax 223-6306).

Walking Austria's Alps, by Jonathan Hurdle. Similar to the above, but Austria-specific. Also order from Mountaineer Books (US$11).

Walking Switzerland the Swiss Way, by Marcia and Philip Lieberman. The "Swiss Way" refers to hiking hut-to-hut. Mountaineer Books also (US$13).

Downhill Walking in Switzerland, (US$12). Old World Travel Books Inc., P.O. Box 700863, Tulsa OK 74170 (tel. (918) 493-2642).

Swiss-Bernese Oberland, by Philip and Loretta Alspach. (US$17 plus US$2.50 handling). Intercon Publishing, P.O. Box 18500-L, Irvine, CA 92623 (tel. (714) 955-2344; fax 833-3156).

Walking Easy in the Austrian Alps, or **Walking Easy in the Swiss Alps.** by Chet and Carolee Lipton. (US$11). Gateway Books, 2023 Clemens Rd., Oakland, CA 94602 (tel. (510) 530-0299; fax 530-0497; orders only (800) 669-0773).

Switzerland

"A pocket knife with a corkscrew, a leathern drinking cup, a spirit-flask, stout gloves, and a piece of green crepe or coloured spectacles to protect the eyes from the glare of the snow, should not be forgotten," wrote Karl Baedeker in his 1907 guide to Switzerland. The Swiss National Tourist Office still suggests ski glasses to avoid **snow blindness,** but somehow the spirit flask has dropped out of the picture.

Hiking offers the most rewarding views of Switzerland. 30,000 miles of **hiking trails** lace the entire country; yellow signs give directions and traveling times (*Std.* or *Stunden:* hours) to nearby destinations. Trails are marked by bands of white-red-white; if there are no markings, you're on an "unofficial" trail, which is not always a problem—most trails are well maintained. Trails that are marked with the blue-white-blue markings indicate that the trail requires special equipment, for either difficult rock climbs or glacier climbing. Lowland **meandering** at its best can be found in the Engadin valley near St. Moritz; for steeper climbs, head to Zermatt or the Interlaken area. **Swiss Alpine Club (SAC) huts** are modest and extremely practical for those interested in trekking in higher, more remote areas of the Alps. Bunk rooms sleep 10 to 20 weary hikers side by side, with blankets (no electricity or running water) provided. SAC huts are open to all, but SAC **members** get discounted rates. The average rate for one night's stay without food is 30SFr for non-members, and 20-25SFr for members. Membership in the SAC costs 126SFr, as a bonus you'll receive the titillating publication *Die Alpen*. Contact the SAC, Sektion Zermatt, Haus Dolomite, 3920 Zermatt, Switzerland (tel. (028) 67 26 10).

Austria

The most scenic way to see Austria is on foot. A membership in the **Österreichischer Alpenverein** provides an in-depth experience with the Tirolean Alps. The group provides a series of **huts** across the Tirol and throughout Austria, all located a day's hike apart from each other. See also the main office listing in Innsbruck (p. 414). This hut-to-hut option is provided to members at half price and a place in any of the huts is always assured, along with use of the kitchen facilities and provisions. Third-party insurance, accident provision, travel discounts, and a wealth of maps and mountain information are also included with membership. For membership information call or stop by the office or write to: Österreich-ischer Alpenverein, Willhelm-Greil-Str. 15, A-6010 Innsbruck (tel. 58 78 28; fax 58 88 42). Membership (US$55, students under 25 US$40, one-time fee US$10) also includes use of some of the huts that the **Deutscher Alpenverein** (German Alpine Club) operate, all of which have beds. Also maintains an office in the **U.K.** at 13 Longcroft House, Fretherne Rd., Welwyn Garden City, Herts. Sleeping in one of Austria's refuges is safer for the environment and generally safer for you—when you leave, you are expected to list your next destination in the hut book, thus alerting search-and-rescue teams if a problem should occur. Prices for an overnight stay without membership in the Alpenverein are 50-150AS, but no reservations are necessary.

The Austrian National Tourist Office publishes the pamphlet *Hiking and Backpacking in Austria*, with a complete list of Freytag-Berndt maps and additional tips. The **Touristenverein "Die Naturfreunde,"** Viktoriagasse 6, A-1150 Vienna (tel. (1) 892 35 34), also operates a network of cottages in rural and mountain areas.

SKIING

Contrary to popular belief, **skiing in Switzerland** is often less expensive than in the U.S. if you avoid the pricey resorts. Ski passes (valid for transportation to, from, and on lifts) run 30-50SFr per day and 100-300SFr per week, depending on the size of the region covered by the pass. A week of lift tickets, equipment rental, lessons, lodging, and *demi-pension* (breakfast plus one other meal, usually dinner) averages 475SFr. Summer skiing is no longer as prevalent as it once was. It is still available in Zermatt, Saas Fee, Les Diablerets, and on the Diavolezza in Pontresina.

Western **Austria** is one of the world's best skiing regions. The areas around Innsbruck and Kitzbühel in the Tirol are saturated with lifts and runs. There's skiing year-round on some glaciers, including the Stubaital near Innsbruck and the Dachstein in the Salzkammergut. High season normally runs from mid-December to mid-January and from February to March. Local tourist offices provide information on regional skiing and can point you to budget travel agencies that offer ski packages.

With peaks between 3000m and 30,000m, the vertical drop is ample—1000 to 2000m at all major resorts. For mountain country, winter **weather** in the Austrian Alps is moderate, thanks to lower elevation and distance from the ocean. Daytime temperatures in the coldest months (Jan. and Feb.) measure around -7°C (20°F), even when the nights are colder. Humidity is low, so snow on the ground stays powdery longer, and ice largely hibernates until spring.

You'll find sundry ways to enjoy the winter wonderland. Some cross-country ski centers charge trail fees to day users, but exempt guests spending their holiday in the area. **Ski schools** throughout Austria will teach anyone to ski. Based on decades of research and racing experience, the **Austrian Ski Method** is a unified teaching concept taught throughout the country. You can **rent skis** at the base of most mountains and at stores in ski villages.

▓ Keeping in Touch

MAIL

Be sure to include the *postal code* if you know it; those of Swiss cities all begin with "CH," Austrian with "A."

Sending Mail from Home

Postcards and letters, when mailed from the U.S. to Europe, cost US40¢ and US60¢, respectively. Between the U.S. and Europe airmail averages a week to 10 days. Generally, letters specifically marked "air mail" travel faster than postcards. U.S. post offices also sell aerograms for US45¢. It is safer, quicker, more reliable, and slightly more expensive to send mail express or registered. Many U.S. post offices offer **International Express Mail** service, which sends packages under 8 ounces to major overseas cities in 48 to 72 hours for US$11.50-14.

Sending mail care of **American Express** is quite reliable. Any office will hold your mail for free if you subscribe to The Card or hold at least one AmEx Traveler's Cheque; otherwise, the office may charge you. AmEx will automatically hold your mail for 30 days; to have it held for longer, write on the envelope, for example, "Hold for 45 days." A complete list of offices is available inside AmEx's free booklet, titled *Traveler's Companion* (tel. (800) 528-4800 in the U.S.).

Other alternatives include a variety of private mail services. **DHL** (tel. (800) 225-5345 in USA and Canada) will send mail to almost all of Western Europe in two to three days for approximately US$30. **Federal Express** (tel. (800) 463-3339 in the U.S. and Canada) will send mail express to Western Europe in two business days for about US$30; other destinations are more variable.

When ordering books and materials from another country, include an appropriate amount of **International Reply Coupons (IRC),** available at the post office (US$1.05), with your request. IRCs provide the recipient of your order with postage to cover delivery. In French **Switzerland,** address mail to Rachel <u>DOBROW</u>, Poste Restante, 1 (city name) Hauptpost, SUISSE. In German Switzerland, send mail to Douglas <u>MILLER</u>, Postlagernde Briefe, 1 (city name) Hauptpost, DIE SCHWEIZ. For Ticino, address letters: Matthew <u>TRIPP</u>, Fermo Posta, 1 (city name) Hauptpost, SVIZZERA. Address **Poste Restante** letters in **Austria** to Postlagernde Briefe. Mark the envelope "BITTE HALTEN" ("please hold"), and address it as follows: Eduoard <u>MÉTRAILLER</u> (name), Postlagernde Briefe, Hauptpostamt, Maximilianstraße 2 (address), A-6020 Innsbruck (postal code and city), AUSTRIA (ÖSTERREICH). Unless you specify a post office by street address or postal code, the letter will be held at the Hauptpostamt (main office).

Mail From Switzerland and Austria

Switzerland and **Austria** both maintain a rapid and efficient postal system. **Letters** take between one and three days for delivery within Switzerland and one to two days within Austria. Airmail to North America takes five to seven days from Switzerland and Austria. Mark all letters and packages *"Mit Flugpost"* or *"Par Avion"* to avoid any bumbling postal official dropping your package in the surface mail box. Allow at least two and a half weeks to Australia and New Zealand.

INTERNATIONAL CALLS

International direct dialing is not complicated. First dial the **international dialing prefix/international access code** from the country you are in (011 in the United States), then the **country code** for the country you are calling. Next punch in the **area code** or **city code** (in the Practical Information listings for large cities). Finally, dial the **local number**. In most countries (excluding the U.S. and Canada) the first digit of the city code is the **domestic long-distance prefix** (usually 0, 1, or 9); omit it when calling from abroad, but use it when dialing another region in the same country. The **country code** for **Austria** is 43; for **Switzerland** 41; for the **U.K.** 44; for **Ireland** 353; for **Australia** 61; for **New Zealand** 64; for **South Africa** 27; for the **U.S.** 1 (For more information see International calls, p. 475)

The quickest (and cheapest) way to **call abroad collect** is to go to a post office—almost all have pay phones—and ask for a *Zurückrufen,* or return call. You will receive a card with a number on it. Call your party and tell them to call you back at that number. At the end of the conversation, you pay for the original call. It's cheaper to use the post office service or find a pay phone, and deposit just enough money to be able to say "Call me" and "I'll give you the number."

Another alternative is the **AT&T Direct** service, which allows you to dial a telephone number from Europe (155 00 11 in Switzerland, 022 903 011 in Austria), to connect instantly to an operator in the U.S. In Austria, the connection to the AT&T operator is a local call—you must keep dropping in change for the length of the call. Rates run about US$1.75-1.85 for the first minute plus about US$1 per additional minute. Calls must be either collect (US$5.75 surcharge) or billed to an AT&T calling card (US$2.50); the people you are calling need not subscribe to AT&T service. For more information, call AT&T (tel. (800) 331-1140, from abroad (412) 553-7458). To connect to the U.S., also try **MCI World Phone** (155 02 22 in Switzerland, 022 903 012 in Austria), or **Sprint Express** (155 97 77 in Switzerland, 022 903 014 in Austria; for more information call (800) 877-4646). For other countries, call: **Canada Direct** (155 83 30 in Switz., 022 903 013 in Aus.; call (800) 565-4708, for information), **B.T. Direct (U.K.)** (155 24 44 in Switz., 022 903 044 in Aus.; call (800) 34 51 44), **Ireland Direct** (155 11 74 in Switz., 022 903 0353 in Aus., call (800) 34 51 44 for more information), **Australia Direct** (155 11 74 in Switz., 022 903 061 in Aus.; call 13 22 00 for more information), **New Zealand Direct** (155 64 11 in Switz., 022 903 064 in Aus., call 123), and **South Africa Direct** (155 85 35 in Switz., 155 85 35 in Aus., call 09 03 for more information). MCI also offers **WorldReach,** a more expensive program through which you can use a calling card to call from one European country to another. For information call MCI at (800) 996-7535.

Internal Calls: Switzerland

> Switzerland is in the process of updating their phone system. Some of the numbers that *Let's Go* lists have not yet been updated and may be incorrect.

Local calls cost 60 centimes. Phones take 10, 20, and 50 centime and 1 and 5SFr coins. Change is not returned; press the red button to make additional calls before the money runs out. City codes are three digits long, numbers themselves six or seven. **Phone cards (Taxcards)** can be bought at any post office, change bureau, or kiosk. In all areas, dial 111 for **information** (including directory assistance, train schedules, and other minutiae), and 191 or 114 for an **English-speaking international operator.** The **police** emergency number is 117, **fire** emergency is 118. The **Anglophone** is at 157 50 14. It provides information ranging from weather reports to English-speaking doctor referrals (1.40SFr per minute).

Internal Calls: Austria

The Austrian telephone and postal system is proof that the term "efficient state monopoly" is not an oxymoron. **Wertkarten (telephone cards)** available in post offices, train stations, and at *Tabak Trafik,* come in 50AS and 100AS denominations, and are purchased for 48AS and 95AS respectively. The rate for local telephone calls is 0.84AS per minute from a pay phone. Card phones are found in even remote villages—they are indicated by blue stickers on the telephone booth. Green stickers mean that a phone accepts incoming calls. All others simply accept coins. When calling from a **post office,** simply take a number, run up a tab while talking, and pay the cashier when you're done. To make **local calls** without a phone card, deposit 2AS to start (less than 3min.) and 1AS for each additional 90 seconds. **Long distance** charges vary—drop in 5AS to start. The display next to the receiver indicates how much money has been deposited by the caller and shows the deductions made during the course of the call. Even when calling collect or using a phone card, you must also pay for the local cost of the call. Between 6pm and 8am on weekdays and from Saturday at 1pm to Monday at 8am, all phone calls within the country are one-third cheaper. This rate does not apply to international calls. For the **police** anywhere in Austria, dial 133; for an **ambulance,** dial 144; for the **fire department,** dial 122.

Let's Go Picks

We have trudged through glacial ice, train stations, and into the farthest reaches of paradises both Alpine and Habsburg. What is the best of the best, you ask? Well, here they are, the Let's Go picks. And the winners are…

SWITZERLAND

Best Hostels
Grindelwald—think the accommodations are nice, wait 'til you see the view (p. 172).
Solothurn—elevator, deck, can you say five-star hotel? (p. 117).
Montreux—drop dead gorgeous (p. 84).
Zurich—rooftop and social scene, dig? (p. 135).
Lugano—villa style, exotic plants, and a pool (p. 184).

Best Museums
Château Chillon, Montreux (p. 87). Kunstmuseum, Bern (p. 158). Art Brut collection, Lausanne (p. 83).
Best places to see stuffed armadillos: Natural History Museum, Sion (p. 102).
Best collection of Samoan and South Pacific artifacts: Villa Heleneum, Lugano

Best Nightlife
Montreux—*pendant le Jazz* (p. 84).
Basel—University town (p. 123).
most tripped out bar: Bikini Test, La Chaux de Fonds (p. 115).

Best Summer Skiing
Zermatt (p. 104). Saas Fee (p. 109). Les Diablerets (p. 109).

Favorite Cities
Grindelwald (p. 172). Locarno (p. 188). St. Gallen (p. 217). Zermatt (p. 104).

AUSTRIA

Best Hostels
Schloßherberge, Admont—huge, renovated castle, towels, hairdryers, ski lifts, sauna, brass fixtures, hanging ivy, private rooms, the list goes on. (p. 328).
Schloßherberge am Wilhelminenberg, Vienna—a view of Vienna that will leave you breathless, plus gorgeous rooms (p. 263).

Best Restaurants
Blue Box, Vienna (p. 268).
Ma Pitom, Vienna (p. 268).

Best Cafés
Hawelka, Vienna (p. 271).
Kleines Café, Vienna (p. 271).

Best Museum
Kunsthistoriches Museum, Vienna (p. 286).

Best Skiing
St. Anton (p. 430)., Lech (p. 432).

Best looking cows: Upper Liechtenstein (p. 227).
Highest per capita Lederhosen rate: Tirol
Favorite Cities: Vienna (p. 249)., Graz (p. 347).

SWITZERLAND

Switzerland
(with Liechtenstein)

GERMANY

AUSTRIA

LIECHTENSTEIN

ITALY

ITALY

FRANCE

N

20 miles
20 kilometers

Bodensee
(Lake Constance)

Konstanz
(Constance)

Vaduz

Malbun

Rhine

Inn

Klosters

Davos

Zuoz

Pontresina

Celerina

St. Moritz

Silvaplana

Sils

Maloja

Arosa

Chur

GRAUBÜNDEN
(GRISONS)

Rhine

Andermatt

St. Gottard
Tunnel

Bellinzona

Gandria

TICINO

Locarno

Ascona

Lake
Lugano

Lugano

Lake
Lugano

Lake
Maggiore

Maggia

Stein Am
Rhein

Winterthur

St. Gallen

Appenzell

Obersee

Zürich

Zürichsee

Zugersee

Rigi Kulm

Reuss

Schaffhausen

Limmat

Aare

Mt. Pilatus

Luzern
(Lucerne)

Lake Lucerne
(Vierwaldstättersee)

Brienzersee

Brienz

Brig

Saas Fee

Zermatt

Matterhorn

Matter Vispa

Rhône

VALAIS

Rhône

Vispa

Basel

Rhine

Birs

SWISS
JURA

Solothurn

Biel
(Bienne)

Bielersee

Neuchâtel

La Chaux-
de-Fonds

Lake
Neuchâtel

Aare

Bern
(Berne)

Murten
(Morat)

Fribourg
(Freiburg)

La Sarine

Broc

Gruyères

Thun

Thunersee

BERNER
OBERLAND

Beautushöhlen

Faulensee

Interlaken

Lauterbrunnen

Grindelwald

Jungfrau

Gstaad

Sion

Martigny

Leysin

Aigle

Champéry

Montreux

Vevey

Lausanne

Lake Geneva
(Lac Léman)

Geneva
(Genève)

Rhône

SWITZERLAND

US$1= 1.20SFr	1SFr =US$0.83
CDN$1= 0.87SFr	1SFr =CDN$1.14
UK£ = 1.86SFr	1SFr =UK£0.53
IR£1= 1.93SFr	1SFr =IR£0.52
AUS$1= 0.93SFr	1SFr =AUS$1.07
NZ$1= 0.82SFr	1SFr =NZ$1.22
SAR1 = 0.27SFr	1SFr =SAR3.75
1AS= 0.12SFr	1SFr =8.63AS
1kč= 0.05SFr	1SFr =21.95kč
1Ft= 0.01SFr	1SFr =126.52Ft

Country code: 41
International Dialing Prefix: 00

Just like the majestic Alps that tower over much of the country, Switzerland *(die Schweiz, la Suisse, la Svizzera, Confederatio Helvetica)* stands staid, placid, and proud. Yet placidity does not necessarily imply simplicity or passivity in Switzerland's case. Comprised of 23 cantons and 3 sub-cantons, Switzerland was first conceived in 1291 and slowly accumulated canton after canton through wars and treaties until the 19th century, united only by treaty and not by language or culture. In fact, internal divisions that transcend cantonal rivalries usually originate from language differences. Some three-quarters of the over 6.75 million population speak a lilting German, as well as their own dialect, *Schwyzerdütsch*. One-fifth speak French, four percent Italian, and the remaining one percent Romansch or Rhaeto-Romanic. In spite of the possible conflicts that could arise in such a delicate union, Swiss politics have an old-fashioned, "small town" feel; approximately 3000 local communes retain a great deal of power, and major policy disputes are routinely settled by national referenda. Two facets of the country's personality are uniform: Switzerland's overwhelming natural beauty and world-class outdoor reputation both of which make it a more than worthwhile travel destination.

While other countries hear the call of imperialism and war, official neutrality since 1815 have spared this postcard-perfect paradise from much of the devastation suffered by the rest of Europe. Neutrality has also nurtured the growth of big money in the staid banking centers of Geneva and Zürich. For many, banking is almost an obsession, as addictive as gambling (dial 166 from anywhere in Switzerland to reach the stock market bulletins hotline). Most residents, however, are more down to earth, and enjoy the pleasures of hiking, skiing, and good food—all Swiss specialties.

One aspect of Switzerland will likely always overshadow whatever internal divisions exist: the majestic Alps with their highest peak, the Dufourspitze, towering at 4,634m. John Keats glorified them in his Romantic poetry, while others have fallen silent against a landscape that defies words. Snow-capped peaks entice hikers, skiers, bikers, and paragliders from around the globe. Fifty-eight percent of the 41,293.2 sq.km Swiss territory is covered by the mountain range that spans five countries. Surprisingly, the Swiss have put 77 percent of country's area to productive use (46 percent meadowland, 25 percent forest, 6 percent arable land). The remaining 23 percent, infertile mountain land, makes up the magnificent and empty area that has helped Switzerland develop one of the most finely tuned tourist industries in the world. Victorian scholar John Ruskin called the Swiss Alps "the great cathedrals of the earth." You're welcome to worship here if you can spare the cash.

■ History and Politics

In Italy for thirty years under the Borgias they had warfare, terror, murder, bloodshed—they produced Michelangelo, Leonardo da Vinci, and the Renaissance. In Switzerland they had brotherly love, 500 years of democracy and peace. What did that produce? The cuckoo clock.
—Orson Welles, *The Third Man*

EARLY YEARS (UP TO 500AD)

Switzerland was too cold for regular habitation until 8000BC, though the mesolithic hunter-gatherers who first inhabited the area were replaced around 6000BC by Indo-European farmers. As civilization progressed, tools and weapons changed from stone to bronze to iron, and by 750BC, Switzerland was an important center of **Celtic** culture. The artistic and warlike **Helvetians** were the most influential Swiss-Celtic tribe. Their attempts to invade Roman Italy in 222BC and again as allies of Carthage between 218 and 203BC (they facilitated Hannibal's famous crossing of the Alps with his elephants) left few long-term gains. Later attempts to advance into Gaul were halted by Julius Caesar in 58BC, who crushed, then colonized the Helvetians. Romanized between 47BC and 15AD, they enjoyed a settled, peaceful, urban civilization for the next two centuries. **Romansch,** a language more closely related to Latin than any other Romance language, is still spoken by denizens of some of the former Roman-occupied territories.

After the first barbarian raids in the 250s (AD), Switzerland became less populous and more militarized, becoming more a frontier in the face of Eastern European invaders and less a peaceful farming province. After the waning of Roman influence in the 5th century, the barbarians began to form permanent settlements. **Burgundians** settled the west, merging peacefully with the Romanized Celts and absorbing their culture and language. The less communicative **Allemanians** populated the center and northeast, eventually pushing the Burgundians west to the Sarine River, which remains the present-day border between German and French Switzerland.

THE MIDDLE AGES (500-1517)

After the Roman influence waned, a period of decline ensued when the only cultivation and activity to be found were on the estates of large landowners. **William Tell** shot an apple off his son's head at about this time (for the whole story, see **Tell-tale** p. 56, or go see the play in Interlaken). The arrival of the Franks in the 530s brought three centuries of foreign influence which aided monastic growth but had little effect elsewhere. After the breakup of the Carolingian empire in the 9th century, the feudal power of the **lords** grew. These lords became vassals of the Frankish king, then the Burgundian dynasty, bringing their own area of influence in the region into allegiance with an external ruler. By 1032 the last Burgundian King died, and his nephew, the King of Germania, incorporated Helvetica into his growing kingdom. Thus, a part of Switzerland enjoyed a stint in the **Holy Roman Empire.** The cities of Zürich and Solothurn prospered, and Bern and Fribourg were established. The **Houses of Savoy, Habsburg,** and **Zähringen** fought over the individual territories after the dissolution of Carolingian rule and the divisions wrought by the 12th-century **Investiture Conflict.** Berthold V of Zähringen died in 1218 without an heir, and the greedy Habsburgs immediately tried to overtake the Zähringenian lands. They were nevertheless thwarted, and in 1231 they signed a letter of franchise guaranteeing freedom to the Zähringenian inhabitants. In 1291, the three forest cantons of **Uri, Schwyz,** and **Unterwald,** in an effort to protect themselves from outside overlords, signed a secret agreement forming the **Ewige Bund (Everlasting League),** in which the cities agreed that an attack on one was taken as an attack on the League After the **Battle of Morgarten** in 1315, in which the Imperial family tried to crush the confederation, Habsburg leaders agreed to a truce and granted the alliance official recognition. Switzerland celebrated its 700th anniversary in 1991.

Tell-tale

First found in a 15th-century ballad, and probably the product of an older oral tradition, the tale of Wilhelm (William) Tell has appeared in wide and varied versions. The culmination of its literary fame came with Friedrich Schiller's drama *Wilhelm Tell* in 1804, and Elmer Fudd's glowing reincarnation of the Swiss national hero in Warner Brothers, Inc. cartoons brought the man of mythic proportion five minutes (literally) of pop-cultural glory. This tale of world renown recounts that sometime in the early 1300s, Tell, together with his young son, visited the town of Altdorf in his native canton of Uri. While in town, the renegade refused to follow the order given by the much-loathed Habsburg governor, and remove his hat in the presence of Gessler's hat (which was sycophantically affixed to a pole in the town square). He was arrested for his disobedience and made to shoot an apple off his son's head as punishment. Legend has it that as Tell prepared to shoot, Gessler found that he had two arrows in his quiver. When he inquired why, Tell told him that if the first arrow missed its mark, he would aim the second at Gessler's heart. Mercifully, Tell scored a bull's-eye, but because of his threat to Gessler was rearrested and sent by boat to a prison on the opposite side of Lake Lucerne. In transit, a violent storm seized the little boat, disturbed its precarious balance, and allowed Tell to overpower his guards. He returned to shore safely, slew Gessler, and lived happily ever after in the history halls of fame. The Swiss herald the myth as a fitting allegory to describe the tenacity of the Swiss people in their struggle for freedom.

Though conflict between the League and the Emperors continued, the three-canton core of Switzerland gradually expanded through merger and conquest over the next several centuries. The confederation's power peaked in the 15th century, but as consolidation increased, social tensions between town and country populations grew. The leadership of **Niklaus von Flüe** (a.k.a. Brüder Klaus), a mystical hermit-farmer, prevented conflict from breaking out over the issue of expansion. The crisis averted, Swiss soldiers became terrifyingly efficient mercenaries for anyone that would hire them, especially the Pope and the northern Italian city-states. In fact, a **Swiss Guard** still defends the Vatican resplendent in their 16th-century clothes and armaments. The **Swabian War** with the Habsburgs of 1499-1500 brought virtual independence from the Holy Roman Empire. Switzerland entered the fray as the French invaded Italy in 1496 to reclaim Naples from the Pope. The confederation was divided, with some cantons favoring the Pope while others supported France, yet after a crushing defeat of Swiss troops by the French, the two countries signed the **Perpetual Peace** agreement in 1516 which made the Swiss mercenaries in French armies, preventing much independent action.

REFORMATION TO REVOLUTION (1517-1815)

The **Protestant Reformation** rocked the confederation to its foundations. Radical theologian **Ulrich Zwingli** of Zürich spearheaded his own brand of reform (see Religion and Philosophy, p. 62). In 1523, the city government of Zürich sanctioned Zwingli's proposed reforms, solidifying his great influence over the local government which would later manifest itself in ugly ways; the differently minded **Anabaptists** were banned and other harsh disciplines were imposed on the city. Another leader of the Swiss reformation was **John Calvin,** a priest and a lawyer born in Northern France whose doctrine urged saintly living in order to "prove" one's chosen status (see Religion and Philosophy, p. 62). He soon took hold of Geneva and instituted puritanical reforms. In 1527, brawls broke out between Roman Catholic and Protestant cantons, culminating in the 1531 defeat of the Protestant cities at Kappel and the death of Zwingli. As a result, Protestants were given the freedom to remain Protestant, but they were prohibited from imposing their faith on others. Religious divisions remained deep, however, and only economic ties held the confederation together.

Despite these religious differences, the confederation remained neutral during the Thirty Years War, escaping the devastation wrought on the rest of Central Europe. The **Peace of Westphalia** in 1648 recognized the independence and neutrality of the 13 cantons. Independence and periodic inter-religious alignments did little to heal the Catholic-Protestant rift, and the next century was characterized by Catholic alliances with France and Spain, as well as Protestant tendencies toward hierarchy, banking, literacy, social control, and witch hunts.

Perhaps upset over former King Louis XVI's loyal Swiss Guards, memorialized at Lucerne, who defended the royal family until their death at the hands of the revolutionaries, French troops invaded Switzerland in 1798 and by Napoleon's order established the **Helvetic Republic.** The relationships between the cantons and the federal government were restructured, and citizens were granted freedom of religion and equality before the law. Napoleon later added six cantons and redesigned the confederation; church and state were separated, free trade was established among the cantons, and the peasantry was emancipated. After Napoleon's defeat, the Congress of Vienna recognized **Swiss neutrality** and created a new conservative constitution, under which the old elites retained some, but not all, of their previous monopoly on wealth and power. It also added two cantons and returned Geneva, annexed to France by Napoleon, to Switzerland, bringing the total to twenty-six.

NEUTRALITY (1815-1945)

A major period of economic growth began after 1815. There was a general improvement in agriculture, while tourism, especially from England, began to develop. However, the industrial sector of the economy made the most significant gains. The exclusion of the British from European markets by the continental blockade during the Napoleonic Wars, while initially detrimental to the textile industry, forced the Swiss to modernize and mechanize.

Unfortunately, this era of material prosperity was not free of political problems. The Mediation Act had disappeared with Napoleon, and established in its place was a new Federal pact that once again established Switzerland as a confederation of sovereign states, united only for common defense and the maintenance of internal order. The formulation and execution of a united foreign policy was still impossible. Because of legal barriers (each canton had its own laws, currency, postal service, weights, measures, and army), the right to reside freely in any canton had also ended, and the inhabitants of one canton regarded the inhabitants of other cantons as foreigners. Furthermore, civil liberties were almost non-existent and religious differences reappeared.

These religious differences led, in 1846, to the formation of a separatist defensive league of Catholic cantons known as the **Sonderbund,** comprising Lucerne, Uri, Schwyz, Unterwalden, Zug, Fribourg, and Valais. In July 1847, the Diet, representing the other cantons, declared the Sonderbund to be incompatible with the Federal Pact, and demanded its dissolution. A civil war broke out that lasted only 25 days and resulted in a victory for the forces of the Confederation.

A **new constitution,** modeled after that of the United States, was established in 1848 (modified in 1874). Finally balancing the age-old conflict between federalism and centrality, it guaranteed republican and democratic cantonal constitutions, and for the first time set up an executive body. The central government established a unified postal, currency, and railway system, and ushered in a free-trade zone among all the cantons. In that same year a crisis arose over Neuchâtel, which had been the property of the King of Prussia since 1707. In the spirit of the Revolutions of 1848, the citizens of Neuchâtel rebelled against the King. Luckily, the King renounced his rights to the territory while at the same time retaining the title of Prince of Neuchâtel, thus allowing Neuchâtel to remain part of Switzerland.

During this time, Switzerland cultivated its reputation as leader in efforts to resolve international conflicts. The **Geneva Convention of 1864** established international laws for the conduct of war and the treatment of prisoners of war. At the same time, the **International Red Cross** set up its headquarters in Geneva. Because it was not embroiled in the tangle of alliances that characterized the turn-of-the-century European balance of power, Switzerland remained neutral throughout the Franco-Prussian war and **World War I** in spite of the country's cultural split. Because forty percent of the total food consumed was imported, the country was dependent on the goodwill of surrounding neighbors for supplies of foreign food. Throughout the century, however, Swiss anxiety grew as Germany and Italian territories united to form nation-states. As a result, in 1874 the constitution was revised to strengthen federal power over the military, as well as over labor laws, due to the rapidly advancing mechanization of industry. Throughout the first half of the 20th century, power increasingly moved to the federal government; in 1912, the cantons yielded their control over civil law, and in 1942 over penal law. In 1920, Geneva welcomed the headquarters of the **League of Nations,** establishing itself as a neutral host state for international diplomacy. **World War II** found Switzerland surrounded by the Axis powers. Trade with both sides and a hard-hitting invasion-contingency plan kept Switzerland neutral. While some Jews and other refugees from Nazi Germany found refuge in Switzerland, the Swiss government, not eager to incur the wrath of the monster that surrounded it on all sides, in general impeded passage through its territory. The Allies were not pleased, and after the war made Swiss diplomacy difficult. Strict neutrality has persisted until the present. But although Switzerland is home to a branch of the **United Nations** and volunteer units of the Swiss army are trained for peace keeping roles with the U.N., it is not a member of the organization.

A heavy cross to bear

After a childhood spent on the shores of Lake Geneva, Henri Dunant, founder of the Red Cross, packed up his bags for Algeria, where he made his fortune as a grain speculator. Bad luck sent him back to Geneva searching for funds. Though he received the needed capital, complications with his business plans ensued, and Dunant became increasingly convinced that French bureaucrats were obstructing his ventures. To rectify the situation, he decided to go straight to the top, to Napoleon III himself.

Procuring an audience with Louis-Napoleon did not prove to be an easy task. Dunant wrote a book "definitively" proving that the French leader was the heir to Emperor Augustus and the crown of the Holy Roman Empire. He had just one copy printed and then undertook to deliver it to the Emperor. By the time Dunant caught up with Louis-Napoleon, the emperor had battled his way into Italy, to the town of Solferino, and had other things on his mind than his ancestry. Dunant was certainly aware why; he had inadvertently landed in the middle of one of history's most brutal battles, in which 33,000 casualties were incurred on the first day alone—the infamous Battle of Solferino. Though clad in a white suit, Dunant rolled up his shirtsleeves in an attempt to save the wounded.

Returning to Geneva, rejected by Napoleon, Dunant recounted the horrors to which he had witnessed. His piece, *A Souvenir of Solferino,* pleaded for the creation of a neutral organization that would offer aid to victims of battle. The idea caught on with the Genevan public administration and Dunant toured Europe in search of further interest and monetary support. The result was the signing of the first Geneva Convention in 1864.

In the meantime, the investors in his failed Algerian venture began wondering what had become of their money. A bankrupt Dunant fled Geneva, only to return to a semi-incognito, hermetic life in Appenzell in 1887. One journalist unearthed the founder of the Red Cross, and exposé followed exposé thereafter. In 1901, Henri Dunant was internationally honored as the joint recipient of the first Nobel Peace Prize. But even fame could not obscure financial debts. The majority of the prize money went to his creditors.

RECENT YEARS (1945-PRESENT)

Switzerland's policy of **armed neutrality** persists to the present; there is no standing army, but every adult male faces compulsory military service. With the threat of an east-west conflict fading, a 1989 referendum proposing to disband the army garnered a surprisingly large number of votes (see p. 60). Switzerland has become increasingly wealthy, liberal, successful, and service-oriented since WWII, yet still fiercely independent and wary of entanglements with the rest of Europe. Apparently Swiss citizens feel strongly about the EU issue; a recent vote which resulted in the rejection of the treaty on a **European Economic Area** (EEA) boasted a voter turnout of almost 80 percent. So while Austria accepted EU membership in early 1995, the "No" vote on the EEA indicates that Switzerland will sit another round out. The division between those who opt to resist change in order to retain *Sonderfall Schweig* (the Swiss Way) and those who envision growth and involvement with the EEC reveals a brutal split along linguistic lines; all six Francophone cantons lean towards integration, while the German-speaking cantons and Italian-speaking Ticino fear being swallowed by their neighbors. Still in the memories of German- and Italian-speaking Swiss are the fascist dictatorships that developed just across the borders only a half-century ago.

GOVERNMENT

Though the existence of twenty-six cantons and four major culturally diverse populations may seem to contradict the stability and harmony that is Switzerland, many Swiss citizens will affirm that this very diversity is what allows this nation to remain truly neutral and democratic (and decentralized). Extensive rights of self-government, active political participation in decision making, and a recognition of basic human rights are the foundations of this democracy.

Over 3000 communes (the smallest administrative unit of government) compose the twenty-six, wholly independent cantons which have existed in Switzerland since the beginning of 1979. Cantons are real states with their own constitutions, legislatures, executives and judiciaries. Legislative power rests with the people or with a parliament elected by them. The cantons themselves are incorporated into the Confederation, which has a two-chamber legislature: the Federal Assembly (consisting of the **National Council,** which represents the people) and the **Council of States,** composed of representatives of the cantons. The 200 seats in the National Council are distributed according to cantonal population, with a minimum of one seat per canton. Decisions of the Federal Assembly take effect only after a majority vote in both chambers has approved the measure.

The executive branch consists of a group a seven members—**the Federal Council**—who are elected for a four-year term by a joint meeting of both legislative chambers. No canton may have more than one representative in the Federal Council at a time. The **President** of Switzerland is then chosen from the ranks of the Federal Council and holds office for only one year, during which he remains responsible for his ministerial department. To maintain a system of checks and balances, the Federal Council provides the legislative branch an annual account of its activities.

Politics play a rather minor role in Swiss daily life, unless there is a **referendum** or **initiative.** An amendment to the constitution can be brought to the fore by an initiative of at least 100,000 votes. 50,000 voters or 8 cantons can demand approval of a federal law passed by both chambers. Any constitutional change must be approved by amajority of the Swiss population by means of referendum before it becomes law.

■ Exiles and Emigrés

Voltaire arrived in Geneva in 1755; since then, the stream of intellectuals, artists, and other soon-to-be-famous personalities to call Switzerland home has reached a steady continuum. The notion of Switzerland as a neutral refuge among more quarrelsome nations has held appeal for many since November 20th, 1815, when the Treaty of Paris recognized Switzerland as the eternally impartial next-door neighbor.

SWITZERLAND

Semper Paratus

We've all got them—Swiss Army knives, Swiss Army watches, etc. But do we ever think about the apparent contradiction held within the ubiquitous brand-name Swiss Army? For a nation that has held to a policy of neutrality since its independence and has been held as the global icon of pacifism in the Cold War era, the concept, let alone the reality, is surprising. Behind the sweet-toothed, storybook façade, however, stands one of the most heavily armed nations per capita in the world and its highly trained army. The mountains bristle with fortifications, its pastures conceal airstrips, its bridges are mined to self-destruct, and in deep caves in the Alpine rock, tanks and fighter jets lurk. Every male stores a gas mask, a repeating rifle and a government-issued (sealed) box of ammunition. Every male citizen must participate in 17 weeks of military training and must return for an annual three-week refresher course until the age of 36 (after that, and until retirement, the course lasts only two weeks). In 1989, the obvious question of what the Swiss are preparing for was raised by a coalition of pacifists, socialists, and religious leaders. They brought the issue to a vote and for the first time in history a European nation was presented with the option of abolishing its army. The referendum drew a passionate response: 37% of the population voted against the army, motivated by the $1000 per capita spent annually on defense and the fragmentation of the work force as men take their weeks of leave. Companies must overhire to compensate, but men also work their way up the business ladder through army contacts (especially if they're selected to join the officer corps) and use refresher courses more as elite alumni meetings than as training. As the Swiss saying goes, "Switzerland does not have an army; it *is* an army." And for the most part, the Swiss like the army, as events like the Zürich Knabenschiessen (marksmanship contests for boys) and national heroes like Wilhelm Tell illustrate. So if a spatter of gunfire breaks the awesome Alpine calm, have no fear—the Swiss men are just keeping fit on a Sunday afternoon.

George Gordon, otherwise known as the opium-smoking Romantic **Lord Byron,** quit England in 1816 and fled to Switzerland where he met **Percy Shelley,** there "on tour." The two composed some of their greatest works while observing the Swiss landscape. Byron wrote his *Sonnet on Chillon* while brooding on Lake Geneva, while Shelley crafted his *Hymn to Beauty* and *Mont Blanc* in the vale of Chamonix. Byron's revelation that "High mountains are a feeling, but the hum of human cities torture" demonstrates an Emersonian encounter with Switzerland's natural beauty. During an especially wet summer in Switzerland, some ghost stories fell into **Mary Wollstonecraft Shelley's** hands; the atmosphere of Swiss mountains rearing through the rain, in addition to the supernatural themes of her nightly conversations, was enough to inspire her to infuse Gothic elements into her latest conception, *Frankenstein.*

The "British Invasion" did not end with the Romantics, however. **Charles Dickens** vacationed in the Lausanne area, and wrote *Dombey and Son* on the shores of Lake Geneva. Along the shores of this same lake in the early 20th-century, **T.S. Eliot** languished as he wrote *The Wasteland.* **James Joyce** fled to Zürich during WWI where he wrote the greater part of his modernist work *Ulysses* between 1915 and 1919; World War II drove him to Zürich once again, where he died in 1941.

From closer neighborhoods, just across the borders in Germany, Austria and Italy, flocked other great minds. **Johann Wolfgang von Goethe** caught his first distant view of Italy from the top of St. Gotthard Pass in the Swiss Alps, the clouded path that would serve as an allegory for the rest of his life. **Friedrich Schiller** wrote his poem about the massive church bell in Schaffhausen and then came forth with the play *Wilhelm Tell,* one of the great Swiss legends. The play was then turned into an opera for which **Rossini** would compose the William Tell Overture (a.k.a. the Lone Ranger theme song). **Friedrich Nietzsche,** while on holiday in the Engadin Valley, conjured up some history and crazy stuff about Superman and Eternal Return in his *Thus Spoke*

Zarathustra. His very complex personal relationship with **Richard Wagner** also began here, while Nietzsche held a professor's chair at Basel University. Most of Wagner's major works were produced during his years in Switzerland.

Zürich and Basel served as a wellspring for intellectual revolution in respect to the sciences; **Albert Einstein** studied there and by 1901 he was a Swiss citizen. His move to Bern to work in a patent office was a pivotal moment in his life, for it was in that city that he conceived the foundation for his theory of relativity and law of equality of matter and energy. This pacifist won the Nobel Prize for physics in 1924. **Karl Jaspers,** the German physician and psychologist of self-fulfillment and self-knowledge, has taught in Basel since 1948, and became a citizen of Basel in 1967.

Switzerland's broad tolerance and neutral status brought it hordes of talented refugees from the World Wars. **Hermann Hesse** moved to the town of Montagnola in southern Switzerland after being branded an enemy of his fatherland during World War I; there he produced his revered works *Steppenwolf* and *Siddhartha.* Such a congregation of artistic personalities, combined with the breakdown of pre-war decadence, culminated to produce the **Dada** explosion in Zürich in 1916, led by **Hans Arp** and **Tristan Tzara. Hugo Ball,** Italian playwright, novelist, actor and dramatist, emigrated as an antiwar activist to Switzerland, and founded the "Cabaret Voltaire" and "Galerie Dada," centers of activities of the Dada movement. His diary, *Die Flucht aus der Zeit,* is a main source of that period. After a war spent in London, to which he had escaped and time spent in Prague, Austrian expressionist painter **Oskar Kokoschka,** also moved to Switzerland in 1953, settling in Villeneuve, a few kilometers beyond the *Château de Chillon.* When Kokoschka died in 1980, his widow, Olda, found herself with an embarrassment of pictures, and subsequently founded the Foundation Oskar Kokoschka in the Musée Jenisch in Vevey. The two German greats, **Thomas Mann** and **Carl Zuckmayer,** also found Switzerland a safe haven. And more recently, writers and scientists from the former Eastern bloc found refuge, notably Russian author **Alexander Solzhenitsyn.**

▓ Art and Architecture

Switzerland's location at the convergence of three cultural spheres—German, French, and Italian—has allowed it to participate intimately in the arts of all its neighbors. This multiplicity of influence has often distracted the Swiss from a unified and independent art of their own; nevertheless, there has been a long line of distinctive, unmistakably Swiss cultural heroes. The Renaissance years brought **Urs Graf** to the fore as a swashbuckling soldier-artist-poet excellently suited to court portraiture. **John Henry Füssli** was the most significant Swiss painter of the 19th century, echoing the advent of Romanticism with his emotionally powerful works, often filled with horrifying images of demons and goblins, doing much to further the popularity of Romanticism in Switzerland. **Ferdinand Hodler,** an early Symbolist painter, worked with powerful images of Swiss landscapes and characters to convey metaphysical messages.

Twentieth-century artist **Paul Klee** was born near Bern, but spent his childhood and early career in Germany, producing highly unique, personal works as a member of *der blaue Reiter* (a school of painters), and also as a member of the Bauhaus faculty. He returned to Switzerland near the start of World War II. The **Zürich School of Concrete Art** between the wars united the Surrealists with the Constructivist ethos that filtered in from Russia and from architectural theory. **Max Bill's** Mondrian-derived canvases, focusing on color relationships and the texture and form of the surface itself, were the essence of Concrete painting. The school also included Paul Klee and **Meret Oppenheim,** a member of the Surrealist movement, famous for her *Fur Cup* and other objects; object art and environment as art were two of the interactions of human and space explored by the group. Sculptor **Alberto Giacometti's** celebrated works in the 1930s were guided by this philosophy of creating a completely new spatial reality within each work. Later, Giacometti rejected the premise of Surrealism in order to concentrate upon representation; his ideas of representation were invariably small, exaggeratedly slender figures, like his *Man Pointing.* **Jean Tinguely** worked in kinetic sculpture, creating mechanized Dada fantasies in celebration of motion as beauty.

The prolific German architect **Gottfried Semper** was born in Switzerland; his works can be seen in most large German cities, particularly Dresden. **Robert Maillart** developed the slab technique for bridge design in 1900, and for the first years of the century produced elegant ferro-concrete bridges that were much more efficient and light in feeling than any that had preceded them. The ferro-concrete building technique was applied to domestic and commercial building by the world-acclaimed architect **Le Corbusier.** Some of the architect's earliest conceptions were formed by his impressions of the Swiss Jura where he grew up; his walks through the Alpine landscape were lessons in seeing. Using rugged materials and geometric shapes, Le Corbusier brought a new and animated spirit to contemporary architecture in Paris, Moscow, Stuttgart, Zürich, and Cambridge, Massachusetts. The house *(la petite maison)* that he built on the edge of the lake at Corseaux-Vevey for his parents in 1924 is now a national monument.

■ Religion and Philosophy

Switzerland contributed largely to the **Protestant Reformation** and adopted its conclusions on a broad scale. Native son **Ulrich Zwingli** (1484-1531) was a contemporary of Luther, and his *Theses,* published at Zürich in 1523, were nearly as influential. These *Theses* expounded a less literal reinterpretation of the symbols and gestures of Catholicism. The two men later quarreled bitterly over fine points of Reform theology. **John Calvin,** Geneva's contribution to Protestantism, took a more philosophical approach, attributing salvation to the knowledge of God's sovereignty through Scripture, and decrying all humanity as corrupt since Adam's fall. For a short time, Geneva was completely under Calvin's control as a theocratic city, and the man's influence spread widely, taking particular hold in England. **Jean Jacques Rousseau,** born in Geneva in 1712 and best known for his *Social Contract* which provided inspiration for the French Revolution, always proudly recognized his Swiss background despite the fact that he spent most of his time outside the country (and that the Swiss burned his books). **Jacob Burckhardt** promoted a new history of culture and art from his Swiss home in the late 19th century. As an expert on the art of the Renaissance period in Italy, his main works include *History of the Italian Renaissance* and *Cicerone: A Guide to the Enjoyment of Italian Art.*

Switzerland became a center of psychological study in the early years of the 20th century when **Carl Gustav Jung's** resided in Basel and Zürich. Jung began his psychological career as an acolyte of Freud, but split with him by 1915 over Jung's publication of *Symbols of Transformation,* a work in direct contradiction of Freud's system. Jung's systems remain interesting to students of spirituality and its role in social structures.

■ Literature

> *"We wanderers are very cunning—the love which actually should belong to a woman, we lightly scatter among small towns and mountains, lakes and valleys, children by the side of the road, beggars on the bridge, cows in the pasture, birds and butterflies."*
> —Hermann Hesse (1877-1962), German-born Swiss novelist,
> *Wandering,* 1920

J.J. Bodmer and **J.J. Breitinger** were among the pioneers of modern literary thought in Switzerland, advocating the supremacy of feeling and imaginative vision that was central to Romanticism. **Madame de Staël** (Germaine Necker, from the prominent Genevan family) was the primary force behind the spread of Romanticism from Germany to France, transmitting the information through her correspondence with

Friedrich Schlegel, a major writer of the early Romantic period, and with her family in France and in the French-Swiss town of Coppet. Mme de Staël, as a result of her political intrigues and alleged rebuff of Napoleon's advances (in a way that Europe could not), was forced into a miserable exile at Coppet.

Hermann Hesse moved to Switzerland in 1899 and became a Swiss citizen in 1924. Earning the Nobel Prize for literature in 1946 for his collected oeuvre, which dealt with contradiction of the body and the spirit, combining Western and Eastern wisdom, Hesse is only one of several well-known and respected Swiss authors. **Benjamin Constant de Rebecque,** a native of Lausanne, one-time lover of Mme de Staël, and author of the novel *Adolphe,* was joined by **Léonard de Sismondi** of Geneva and Mme de Staël in contributing to the French Romantic movement. **Gottfried Keller** was a popular Swiss novelist and poet who was integral to the rising influence of Poetic Realism in late German Romanticism. But it is **Conrad Ferdinand Meyer** who is acknowledged by most authorities as the greatest Swiss poet. His works feature strongly individualistic heroes, and were some of the only German works to effectively unite Romanticism and Realism.

Twentieth-century Switzerland has produced two widely respected modern playwrights and exponents of contemporary literature. **Max Frisch** is lauded for his Brechtian style and thoughtful treatment of Nazi Germany; his most widely known work is the play *Andorra.* **Friedrich Dürrenmatt** has written a number of excellent plays dealing with individual responsibility and morality, most notably *The Visit of the Old Lady* and *The Physicists.* Both Dürrenmatt and Frisch hold critical attitudes towards their home country. **Robert Walser** has been celebrated for his diffuse, existential novels; they were largely ignored until his death in 1956 by an audience expecting clearly defined morals and themes. Posthumously, his novels, poetry, and plays are recognized for their fragile, shady, ironic, and melancholic language.

Switzerland also has a life in the literature of other nations. **Henry James's** Daisy Miller toured here; **Mark Twain** incorporated cuckoo clocks into his revenge fantasies and followed well-touristed paths with his own rough grace, chronicled in his travelogue, *A Tramp Abroad.* The ghosts of geniuses hover in the Alpine countryside surrounding Geneva: Gogol, Dostoyevsky, Victor Hugo, Hemingway, and F. Scott Fitzgerald bicycling through Montreux. It was only when struck by the majesty of the Swiss Alps that David Copperfield, one of Charles Dickens's greatest characters, was able to cry over the death of his wife Dora, "as I had not wept yet.

■ Food and Drink

Little beknownst to those individuals not among the ranks of chefs or culinary experts, Switzerland has one of the finest culinary traditions in all of Europe. The majority of famous French chefs, whose concoctions are so dear to sample, have undergone some schooling in this mountainous land. The reason behind this seemingly odd fact of Swiss life is once again linked to Switzerland's policy of neutrality— the years other culinary giant countries spent in war, the Swiss were able to retain an unbroken dedication to lifestyle. And while most budget travelers may not be able to enjoy the *crème de la crème* of Swiss cuisine, the trickle-down theory operates in full force.

Superseding all regional dishes and possible pretensions to four star cuisine, are Switzerland's culinary masterpieces: **cheese** and **chocolate.** While the words "Swiss cheese" may conjure images of lunchbox sandwiches filled with a hard, oily cheese riddled with holes, the reality is that Switzerland has innumerable kinds of cheese, each of which is made from a particular type of milk and has its own particular flavor and style of production. While the cheese with holes is usually Emmentaler, from the eponymous northwest region, nearly every canton and many towns have their own type of cheese. To name a few of the most well-known types: *Gruyère* is a stronger and tastier version of *Emmentaler; Appenzeller* is a milder hard cheese from the Appenzell region, sometimes using sheep's milk instead of cow's milk; *tome* is a generic term for a soft, uncooked cheese similar to French *chèvre.* In the Italian regions look for more Southern influenced cheeses resembling the *parmeggiani* from Italy more than the cheeses of the north. As far as **chocolate** goes, Switzerland is home to two of the largest producers of chocolate: **Lindt** and **Suchard,** not to mention the local confectioner's concoctions in each town.

Unsurprisingly, the flavor of regional cooking bends with the contours of Switzerland's linguistic topography. The basic geography is simple and logical: Frenchified in the west, Italianish in the south, Swiss-German everywhere else. Each of these regions is represented, however, in the collective pool of "typical" Swiss dishes. A Swiss national menu might include the Zürich speciality, *Geschnetzeltes* (strips of veal stewed in a thick cream sauce, served with *Rösti)*. Other possible contenders are *Luzerner Chugelipastete* (pâté in a pastry shell), *Papet Vaudois* (leeks with sausage from the canton of Vaud), *Churer Fleischtorte* (meat pie originating from Chur), and Bernese salmon.

Three dishes in particular, however, best represent Switzerland. **Rösti,** a patty of hash brown potatoes skilleted and occasionally flavored with bacon or cheese, is as prevalent in the German regions as **fondue** (from the French, *fondre*—to melt) is in the French. Usually made of a blend of Emmentaler and Gruyère cheeses, white wine, *kirsch,* and spices, *fondue* is eaten by dunking small cubes of white bread into a *caquelon* (a one-handled pot) that is kept hot by a flame. White wine is the drink of choice to complement the fondue-tasting palate. **Raclette** is made by cutting a large cheese in half and heating it until it melts. The melted cheese is then scraped onto a baked potato and garnished with any number of other foodstuffs.

The Swiss are particularly good at baking and **confectionery.** To match each type of local cheese, usually there is a bread specific to the region or town. Ask for it by name (e.g. when in St. Gallen, ask for *St. Galler-brot).* Among the most tempting **cakes** are the *Baseler Leckerli* (a kind of gingerbread), *Schaffhauser Zungen, Zuger Kirschtorte* (Kirsch torte of Zug), Engadin nutcakes, the *bagnolet crème* of the Jura (eaten with raspberries and aniseed biscuits), soda rolls, *rissoles* (pear tarts), nougat and pralines of Geneva, and the *zabaglione* of Ticino. *Vermicelli*, not the Italian pasta, but a dessert made of chestnut mousse, is popular all over Switzerland.

Wine was introduced by the Romans, but it was not until the 9th century that beer-drinking laity pried it away from the clergy who used it, of course, for liturgical purposes. By the 19th century production had grown so indiscriminately, and the results so indifferent, that consumers went back to drinking beer. A wine statute in 1953 imposed rigorous quality controls and since then Swiss wine has regained its reputation. Most wine is produced in the west and the Valais, about three-quarters of it white. The wine produced around Lake Zürich and in the Thurgau and Schaffhausen areas is predominantly *Blauburgunder* and a small quantity of a *Riesling-Slyvaner* hybrid. Ticino specializes in reds made from the Merlot grape, and most restaurants offer a house wine as *nostrano* (one of ours). These are usually home-pressed blends, comparatively cheap, and delicious.

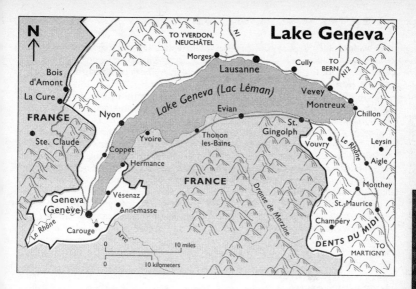

Western Switzerland

LAKE GENEVA (LAC LÉMAN)

> *I should like the window to open onto the Lake of Geneva—and there I'd sit and read all day.*
>
> —John Keats, to Fanny Keats, March 13, 1819

A reliable rule of economic geography says that European incomes rise exponentially as you approach Lac Léman. While this makes Switzerland's most prestigious cities of Geneva, Montreux, and Lausanne slightly intimidating for the budget-bound backpacker, it should not stop one from basking in the lakeside sun for a few luscious moments. The hills that overlook the lake are as near to paradise as you can get, with the view of the blue waters, and on a clear morning, the snowy summits of the Alps floating above the haze. The melding of calm and culture has beckoned intellectuals for centuries, both those like Voltaire and Lenin who appreciated the Swiss guarantee of freedom to think, and those like Stravinsky who just found the Yorkshire a peaceful spot to work. Above all, Switzerland's French-speaking cities are places to *be*, not places to *do*.

▉ Geneva (Genève, Genf)

"I detest Geneva," muttered Napoleon Bonaparte shortly before "liberating" the city in 1798, "they know English too well." They still do—Geneva is very much a cosmopolitan city, with a one-third foreign population. Indeed, it is said that the only things Geneva shares with the rest of Switzerland are its neutral foreign policy and the state religion, banking (Geneva possesses half of Switzerland's banks). The French Emperor had more than linguistic contempt to contend with and knew all to well that the city's citizens have a long and belligerent tradition of doing battle to protect their political and religious independence. In medieval times, the city's strategically desirable site on the outflow to Lac Léman forced it to fend off constant attacks by

65

unfriendly armies. This guard was dropped in 1536, when Geneva openly welcomed a more subtle invader, the Protestant Reformation. The townspeople voted to convert *en masse* and invited the then-unknown twenty-five-year-old John Calvin to their cathedral. His fiery sermons from the pulpit between 1536 and 1564 against the indulgences and superstitions of the 16th century papacy brought in waves of French and Italian refugees fleeing persecution in their Catholic homelands. Geneva was soon known as the "Rome of Protestants."

Geographically vulnerable because it is almost completely surrounded by French territory, Geneva waged a hard-won battle for freedom from the Catholic House of Savoy, whose Duke sought to crush both Protestantism and Genevan democracy. He was driven away from the gates of Geneva by a pot of soup (see **Soup's On** p. 66). Unfortunately, however, religious freedom did not spell tolerance, as Calvin's devout theocracy burned some of the differently-minded at the stake.

The Reformists' ardent zeal continued for at least another century and a half, exemplified by the burning of Rousseau's books in a square just blocks from the house in which he was born. But Geneva's cosmopolitanism eventually won out, and the city became a gathering place for literary elites and free thinkers. Voltaire lived and worked nearby for twenty-three years, just as, later, his compatriot Madame de Staël later held her salons in nearby Coppet. In the early 19th century, mountain-happy romantics such as Shelley and Byron found inspiration in the city's surroundings. Mary Wollstonecraft Shelley created *Frankenstein's* monster here, and George Eliot resided in Geneva, the city of her hero Jean-Jacques Rousseau. One of Geneva's most famous political refugees was Lenin, who bided his time here from 1903-5 and in 1908.

The city's unique atmosphere attracted more than individuals. Under the inspiration of native Henri Dunant, the **International Committee of the Red Cross** established itself in Geneva in 1864, and the First Geneva Convention was signed by nations from around the world in the same year. In 1919, Geneva's selection as the site for the League of Nations confirmed the city's reputation as a center for both international organizations and arbitrations. Geneva still retains the European office of the **United Nations** (responsible for economic and humanitarian programs), and dozens of other international bodies ranging from the Center for European Nuclear Research to the World Council of Churches.

Soup's on

Up until its admittance into the Swiss Confederation, Geneva was under almost constant attack from outsiders. One of the most consistent invaders was the House of Savoy, which Geneva fought on and off for over 200 years. It was during one of their later invasion attempts that they ran full-force into Swiss practicality. On the night of December 11, 1602, the Duke of Savoy's soldiers attempted to scale the city walls. A lone housewife saw the attack and proceeded to dump a pot of boiling soup on their heads, buying enough time for her to sound the alarm. Each year, the **Festival of the Escalade** (climbing) celebrates the event. Citizens in costumes reenact the battle and children eat chocolate *marmites* (pots) filled with marzipan vegetables.

GETTING TO GENEVA

Geneva has two rail stations. **Gare Cornavin,** pl. Cornavin, is the primary station and departure point for all major Swiss and foreign cities. Some major connections are to **Lausanne** (40min., every 20min., 19.40SFr), **Bern** (1hr.45min., every hr., 48SFr), **Zürich** (3hr., every hr., 74SFr), **Basel** (2hr.45min., every hr., 67SFr), **Montreux** (1hr., every hr., 27SFr), **Interlaken** (2hr.50min., every hr., 60SFr), **Paris** (3½hr., 5 daily, 61SFr for ages under 26, plus a reservation fee of 5-20SFr depending upon the time and day of travel, 77SFr for those over age 26, plus same reservation fee), and **Rome** (10hr., 1daily, 109SFr, under 26 84SFr). There is a shuttle leaving Cornavin every 10min. for Cointrin Airport (5:21am-11:15pm, 4.80SFr, railpasses valid; tel. 799 31

11). The reservation and information office is open Mon.-Fri. 8am-6:45pm, Sat. 8am-4:45pm, but expect a long wait. The **Gare des Eaux-Vives,** on the eastern edge of the city on av. de la Gare des Eaux-Vives, serves **Annecy** and **Chamonix** in France. Geneva's **Cointrin Airport** (tel. 799 59 99) is one of **Swissair's** hubs. There is one direct flight daily to **New York,** four to **Paris,** four to **London,** one to **Amsterdam,** and one to **Rome. Air France** has six daily to **Paris** and **British Airways** has seven daily flights to **London.** From the arrivals hall, go up a level and turn left to catch bus #10 to town (2.20SFr). By car, Geneva is more accessible from France than from the rest of Switzerland. To **drive** to Geneva from the west, take A40 or E62 east, which continues on to Lausanne and Montreux; from the south take N201 north; from the north, take E21 from France and E25/62 from Switzerland; from the east, take A40 (E25) west. E62 is also the best way to get to Geneva from Lausanne or Montreux. Don't go crazy looking for the numbers; they are not all that visible. You'll be better off just following the signs for Geneva which are posted on all of the autoroutes. Hugely popular **ferries (CGN)** (tel. 732 39 16) depart from the quai du Mont-Blanc, at the foot of rue des Alpes, for Lausanne (3hr.15min., 29SFr, round-trip 47SFr) and Montreux (4½hr., 34SFr, 55SFr round-trip). Boats leave daily at 9:15am and 2:40pm, and from June to September, at 10:30am and 5:45pm from Jardin-Anglais (tel. 311 25 21). CGN offers many shorter excursions on Lake Geneva; more specific information is available at the tourist office (Eurailpass and Swisspass valid).

ORIENTATION AND PRACTIAL INFORMATION

Geneva has more districts than most cities twice its modest size of 200,000 people. In the *vieille ville,* steep cobbled streets and quiet squares surround the *Cathédrale de St-Pierre* and the university. Heading north, banks, bistros, and boutiques for the beautiful line the Rhône river. The lakeshore tries to assuage the Swiss national yearning for a seaside resort. On a sunny afternoon couples will promenade, ladies of a certain age will walk their poodles, and the ultra-cool will rent a paddle boat (20SFr, by the *Jetée de Pâquis*). Overlooking the city in a northern suburb, the headquarters of the United Nations, Red Cross, World Trade Organization and other international bodies enjoy a panorama of the Alps from their spacious gardens. Be sure to carry your passport with you at all times; the French border is just a few steps from Annemasse (tram #12), and regional buses frequently cross over it. Most buses pass through pl. Bel Air, just by the Pont de l'Ile.

Tourist Office: A small stand sits in Gare Cornavin, but the main office is at 3 rue du Mont-Blanc; exit the right-hand side of the station, and continue down 5min. (tel. 909 70 00, fax 929 70 11). Qualified staff books hotel rooms (5SFr fee), provides information on sights, excursions, and local events, and offers walking tours. Pick up the free city map, the invaluable *Info Jeunes,* which lists inexpensive accommodations, restaurants, and other practical information, the weekly entertainment guide *Genève Agenda;* and the monthly *What's on in Geneva.* Also of note is the excellent and reassuring *Guide to the English-Speaking Community in Geneva.* The key is to ask; the staff can even provide a list of vegetarian or kosher restaurants upon request. Open June 15-Sept. 15 Mon.-Fri. 8am-8pm, Sat.-Sun. 9am-6pm; Sept. 16-June 14 Mon.-Sat. 9am-6pm. There is a new, more colorful **Office du Tourisme,** pl. du Molard 4 (tel. 311 98 27; fax 311 80 52), across the river. They offer all of the same services plus more specific city information, and they make a point of sending no one away unsatisfied. Open Mon. 12:30-6:30pm, Tues.-Fri. 9am-6:30pm, Sat. 10:30am-4:30pm. Budget travelers should head toward the magic bus **Centre d'Accueil et de Renseignements (CAR)** (tel. 731 46 47), at the top of rue du Mont Blanc by Gare Cornavin. Geared toward young people, the office answers all sorts of questions and posts a daily updated list of theatre, music, and other performances. Open June 15-Sept. 15 daily 8am-11pm.

Budget Travel: SSR, rue Vignier 3 (tel. 329 97 34). Very friendly service and special youth and student fares. Open Mon.-Fri. 9am-12:30pm, 1:30-6pm. Visa, MC, AmEx.

Consulates: U.S., rte. de Pré-Bois 29 (tel. 798 16 15). **Canada,** chemin du Pré-de-la-Bichette 1 (tel. 919 92 00). **U.K.,** rue de Vermont 37-39 (tel. 734 12 04). **Australia,**

rue de Moillebeau 56-58 (tel. 918 29 00). **New Zealand,** chemin du Petit-Saconnex 28a (tel. 734 95 30). **South Africa,** rue de Rhône 65 (tel. 849 54 54).

Currency Exchange: In Gare Cornavin. Good rates, no commission on traveler's checks. Will advance cash on credit cards (Visa, MC, AmEx, minimum 200SFr) and arrange Western Union. Open daily 6:45am-9:30pm.

American Express, rue du Mont-Blanc 7 (tel. 731 76 00). Mail held. All banking services; exchange rates similar to those in Gare Cornavin. **ATM** service with AmEx card. Makes hotel (20SFr) and train (10SFr) reservations. Address mail by capitalizing and underlining last name. For example, Bill FERULLO, c/o American Express, Client Mail Service, rue du Mont-Blanc 7, P.O. Box 1032, CH-1211 Geneva 01. Open Mon.-Fri. 8:30am-6pm, Sat. 9am-noon.

Telephones: PTT, Gare Cornavin. Open daily 8am-10pm. Has phone-now-pay-later system that takes Visa and MC.

Public Transportation: Geneva has an efficiently integrated bus and tram network. **Transport Publics Genevois** (tel. 308 34 34), next to the tourist office in Gare Cornavin (open Mon.-Sat. 9am-noon and 2-6pm), provides a free, if somewhat confusing, map of the local bus routes called *Le Réseau.* Or go downstairs and follow the signs marked "i" to find the other branch of the office which holds longer hours (Mon.-Sat. 6:15am-8pm, Sun 6:45am-8pm). 2.20SFr buys an hour of unlimited travel on any bus; 3 stops or less cost 1.50SFr. Your best bet is a full day pass for 5SFr; 6 one-hour trips for 12SFr; or 12 one-hour trips for 22SFR. Buses free with Swisspass, but not Eurail. Buy multi-fare and day tickets at train station, others at automatic vendors at every stop. Stamp multi-use tickets before boarding. Buses run roughly 5:30am-midnight.

Taxis: (tel. 155 17 00), 6.30SFr to start, 2.70SFr per km. Taxi from airport to city around 25SFr.

Car Rental: Hertz, rue de Berne 60 (tel. 731 12 00). **Avis,** rue de Lausanne 44 (tel. 731 90 00). **Budget,** rue de Lausanne 37 (tel. 732 52 52). **Europcar,** rue de Zurich 36 (tel. 731 5150, fax 738 46 50) is probably the cheapest with weekly unlimited-mileage rentals starting at 104SFr per day. All have offices at Cointrin but check for airport-supplements (usually around 11%).

Parking: On street 60c. per hr., 2hr. max. Garage under Cornavin station, entry on pl. Cornavin, is 5SFr per hr. short-stay, 72SFr first day, 24SFr each subsequent day. **Garage Les Alpes,** rue Thalberg has 350 spaces (2SFr per hr. weekdays, 1SFr per hr. nights and weekends),

Hitchhiking: *Let's Go* does not recommend hitchhiking as a safe way to travel. Hitchers say, however, that Switzerland is one of the safer countries in Europe in which to hail a ride. Those headed to Germany or northern Switzerland take bus #4/44 to "Jardin Botanique." Those headed to France take bus #4/44 to "Palettes" and switch to line D to "St. Julien." In summer, **Telstop** has a list of available rides in front of the CAR information booth.

Bike Rental: At the baggage check in Gare Cornavin (tel. 715 22 20; fax 715 22 09). From 21SFr per day, 84SFr per week. Mountain bike 29SFr per day, 116SFr per week. Open Mon.-Fri. 6:50am-6:45pm, Sat.-Sun. 7am-12:30pm and 1:30-5:45pm. Visa, MC, AmEx.

Luggage Storage: Coin-op lockers in Gare Cornavin (5SFr per day for a backpack-sized locker, 3SFr for a smaller one). Open daily 4:30am-12:45am.

Lost Property, rue des Glacis de Rive 7 (tel. 787 60 00). Open Mon.-Thurs. 8am-noon and 1-4:30pm, Fri. 8am-noon and 1-4pm.

Public Markets: Marché des Eaux-Vives, blvd. Helvétique, between cours de Rive and rue du Rhône. Biggest dairy, vegetable, and flower market; stock up on bargain melons and strawberries. Open Wed. and Sat. 8am-1pm. **Plainpalais** has a flea market Wed. and Sat. 8am-6pm.

Laundromat: Salon Lavoir St. Gervais, rue Vallin (tel. 731 26 46), off pl. St. Gervais. Wash 4SFr, dry 1SFr per 12min., detergent 1SFr. Open Mon.-Sat. 7:30am-10pm, Sun. 10am-10pm. **Salon Lavoir de Prieure,** rue du Prieuré 4 (tel. 371 34 26), 2min. from the hostel. Wash 5SFr, dry 1SFr per 10min., 1SFr for detergent. Open daily 7am-11pm.

Library: American Library, rue de Monthoux 3, at Emmanuel Church (tel. 732 80 97). 15,000 titles and a subscription to the *International Herald Tribune.* One-

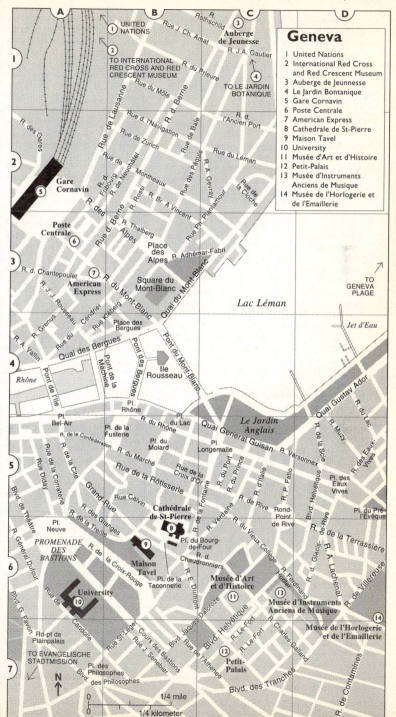

Geneva

1 United Nations
2 International Red Cross and Red Crescent Museum
3 Auberge de Jeunesse
4 Le Jardin Bontanique
5 Gare Cornavin
6 Poste Centrale
7 American Express
8 Cathedrale de St-Pierre
9 Maison Tavel
10 University
11 Musée d'Art et d'Histoire
12 Petit-Palais
13 Musée d'Instruments Anciens de Musique
14 Musée de l'Horlogerie et de l'Emaillerie

month membership (25SFr, less than most books) lets you rent from a small but eclectic collection of books on tape (2SFr per 2 weeks). Open Tues. 12:30-5pm, Wed. 2-8pm, Thurs. 2-5pm, Fri. 12:30-5pm, Sat. 10am-4pm, Sun. 11am-12:30pm.

English Bookstores: ELM (English Language and Media) Video and Books, rue Versonnex 5 (tel. 736 09 45), has a a quality range of new books in English. Bookshop open Mon.-Fri. 9am-6:30pm, Sat. 10am-5pm. the shop next door rents English videos (from 5.50SFr; tel. 736 02 22 open Mon.-Fri. 9am-8pm and Sat. 9am-7pm). **Librairie des Amateurs,** Grand-Rue 15 (tel. 732 80 97), in the *vieille ville*. Classy second-hand dealer among the antique shops on Grand-Rue has a roomful of English books. Open Mon. 2-6:30pm, Tues.-Fri. 10am-6pm and 2-7pm. **Book Worm,** rue Sismondi 5 (tel. 731 87 65), near the train station. An American couple runs this genteel store which buys, sells, and trades used books and classic English language videos (4SFr). Tea room serves pots of tea/coffee (2SFr) two-course lunches (noon-2:30pm, 8.50SFr, including drink) and desserts (3.50SFr). Open Tues.-Sat. 10am-8pm, Sun. 10am-5pm. Visa, MC AmEx. **Payot Libraire,** rue de Chantepoulet 5 (tel. 731 89 50), is the biggest bookstore in Geneva, with an English section that includes *Let's Go*. Open Mon. 1-6:30pm, Tue., Wed., Fri. 9am-6:30pm, Thurs. 9am-8pm, Sat. 9am-5pm. Visa, MC, AmEx.

Gay, Lesbian, and Bisexual Travelers: Dialogai, Case Postale 27, av. Wendt 57 (tel. 340 00 00; fax 340 03 98), Bus #3, 9, or 10 to "Servette-École." Resource group with programs ranging from couples counseling to gay outdoor activities and discussions for young gays. Publishes *Dialogai,* a guide to the gay scene in Switzerland. Unfortunately, phone and center are only open Wed. 8-10pm. Mostly men, though women are welcome. **Centre Femmes Natalie Barney** (women only), av. Peschier 30, CH-1211, Geneva 25 (tel. 789 26 00).

AIDS Group: Groupe SIDA Genève (AIDS Group), rue Pierre-Fatio 17, CH-1204 Geneva (tel. 700 15 00; fax 700 15 47).

Travelers with Disabilities: CCIPH (Centre de Coordination et d'Information pour Personnes Handicapées), rte. de Chêe 54 (tel. 736 38 10). The tourist office also provides a free comprehensive guide to the city for the disabled, called *Guide à l'Usage des Personnes Handicapées,* which lists accessibility of all the main hotels, sights, shops and transport. Huge map included.

Anglo-phone: tel. 157 50 14. A 24-hr. English-speaking hotline answers questions about any aspect of life in Switzerland. Be quick: 2SFr per min.

Late-Night Pharmacy: Every night two pharmacies stay open late. Consult Genève Agenda or call 144 or 111. The pharmacy at the train station has the longest regular hours.

Rape Crisis Hotline: Viol-Secours (tel. 733 63 63). Open Mon. 4-11pm, Tues. 2-6pm, Thurs. 2-9pm, Wed. and Fri. 9am-noon.

Medical Assistance: Hôpital Cantonal, rue Micheli-du-Crest 24 (tel. 372 81 00). Door #3 for outpatient care. Walk-in clinics dot the city; call the **Associaton des Médecins** (tel. 320 25 11).

Emergencies: Police, rue Pecolat 5 (tel. 117), next to post office. **Fire:** tel. 118. **Ambulance:** tel. 144.

Post Office: Poste Centrale, rue de Mont-Blanc 18, 1 block from the Gare Cornavin, in the stately Hôtel des Postes. Mon.-Fri. 6am-6:45pm, Sat. 6-11:30am. Address *Poste Restante* to: 1211 Genève 1 Mont-Blanc. The **Poste de Genève 11,** pl. de la Poste on the Rive Gauche, south of the Rhône, is open Mon.-Fri. 7:30am-6pm, Sat. 8:30-11am. **Postal Code:** CH-1211.

Telephone Code: 022.

ACCOMMODATIONS AND CAMPING

There is no such thing as a budget hotel in Geneva. The best hotels fill quickly even in winter, so reserve well ahead to avoid a hassle. However, you can usually find dorm beds and hostel rooms. If the places listed below are booked, try one of the 25 others listed in *Info-Jeunes,* which you can pick up at the tourist office. Many university dorms rent attractive rooms in the summer for the best prices in town. For longer stays, check the local paper *Tribune de Genève* carries a weekly supplement of classified ads for apartment seekers. For employees of international organizations, the

Centre d'Accueil pour les Internationals de Genève, rue de Varembé 9-11 (tel. 327 17 77, fax 327 17 27) is a centrally located realtor. The tourist office often posts apartment rentals on its noticeboard.

Auberge de Jeunesse (HI), rue Rothschild 28-30 (tel. 732 62 60; fax 738 39 87). Walk 15min. left from the station down rue de Lausanne and then swing a right onto rue Rothschild. Bus #1 (dir. Wilson) terminates right in front of the hostel. Vast, well-tended, modern hostel with a welcoming staff and a sizable lobby, restaurant (dinner 11.50SFr, dessert 1.80SFr), kitchen facilities and TV room with CNN. Flexible 3-night max stay. Reception open in summer 6:30-10am and 4pm-midnight; in winter 6:30-10am, 5pm-midnight.Curfew midnight. Lockout in summer 10am-4pm, in winter 10am-5pm. 23SFr, nonmembers 28SFr. Showers, sheets, and breakfast included. Also has doubles (70SFr, non-members 80SFr) and triples (85SFr, non-members 120SFr), with shower and toilet. Lockers in every dormroom and in the lobby. Laundry 6SFr. Special facilities for disabled guests.

Centre St. Boniface, av. du Mail 14 (tel. 321 88 44). Bus #1 or 4/44 to "Cirque", and continue down av. du Mail; from the station (20min.) heading right on bd. Fazy, across Pont de La Coulouvrenière, and along av. du Mail. This Catholic-run centre has simple spartan rooms which are quiet, exceptionally priced, and just minutes from the *vieille ville.* Reception open Mon.-Fri. 10am-noon and 5-7pm; Sat. 9:30am-noon. Year-round dorms have a lockable wardrobe, but no private lockers (16SFr if you have your own sleepsack, otherwise 24SFr for bed and sheets). From mid-July to late September there are singles of variable quality (39 SFr, students 34SFr) and a few doubles (62SFr, students 54SFr). Try to get one with shower and balcony. Access to kitchen, TV room, and dining room included. No breakfast, but residents get a discount at the restaurant next door, **La Pleine-Lune,** with a card from the center's reception. Reservations preferred.

Hôme St-Pierre, cours St-Pierre 4 (tel. 310 37 07), Bus #5 to "pl. Neuve," or walk 15min. from the train station, crossing the Rhône at Pont du Mont-Blanc, then up the Rampe de la Treille and take the third right. An unforgettable location in a cobbled courtyard opposite the west end of the cathedral in the heart of the *vieille ville.* A residence/hostel for **women only** (ages 17-30), this converted medieval monastery is now run by the Lutheran churches. The well-decorated rooms with soft beds, spectacular rooftop views, kitchen facilities, and warm, homey atmosphere will tempt you to take advantage of the monthly rates (460-590SFr). One dorm is a spacious, state-of-the-art, wooden dream, but the other is up-close-and-personal. No lockout or curfew. Dorms 22SFr. Rarely available singles 35SFr. Doubles 50SFr. Showers and lockers included. Big breakfast (Mon.-Sat.) 7.50SFr. Large kitchens; rich and elegant dining and sitting rooms. Popular and small, so reserve ahead by phone or mail. Reception open Mon.-Sat. 8:30am-1pm and 4-8pm, Sun. 9am-1pm.

Cité Universitaire, av. Miremont 46 (tel. 346 23 55; fax 346 25 10). Ride Bus #3 (dir: Crêts-de-Champel) to the last stop. Find the bus at pl. de 22 Cantons on the far right as you exit the train station. Located far from the station on the other side of the *vieille ville.* Institutional college housing in a modern tower block with heaps of facilities: TV rooms, newspapers, restaurant, disco, ping-pong (paddles at the reception), tennis courts, even internet access. Reception open Mon.-Fri. 8am-noon and 2-10pm, Sat.-Sun. 8am-noon and 6-10pm.Four dorms are available July 1-Sept. 30(15SFr) with very small lockers. 11:30pm curfew; lockout 10am-6pm. Year-round singles 40SFr (students 34SFr), doubles 55SFr (students 50SFr), and studios with kitchenette and bathroom for 61SFr a night. Shower included. No breakfast. Students get 10% off at restaurant downstairs (open 7am-10pm, dinner 9.50SFr, breakfast 4.60SFr, omelettes 4.80-6.40SFr). Thurs. and Sat. the basement becomes *Arcade 46* disco, free for residents.

Hotel Pension Saint-Victor, rue François-le-Fort 1 (tel. 346 17 18; fax 346 10 46; e-mail willacuna@mail.spon.ch; http://geneva.yop.ch/hotels/smp). Bus #1, 3, or 5 to "Place Claparède." Outstanding hotel in the *vieille ville* looks out at the Russian Church across a quiet square. Large, clean, distinguished rooms with great views. Homemade jam and eggs fresh from the owner's farm for breakfast. Friendly anglophone atmosphere. May be more affordable for small groups. Reception open

Mon.-Fri. 7:30-8pm, Sat.-Sun. 8am-8pm.Singles from 60SFr. Doubles from 85SFr. Triples from 110SFr. Breakfast included. Reservations are imperative.

Hôtel de la Cloche, rue de la Cloche 6 (tel. 732 94 81; fax 738 16 12), just off the quai du Mont-Blanc across from the Noga Hilton. Extremely hospitable, family-run hotel on the first floor. Attractively old-fashioned rooms, some with slightly peeling blue wall-paper. Many have a balcony and fantastic view of the *jet d'eau* on Lake Geneva. Reception open 7:45am-11:30pm. Singles (55SFr) and doubles (80SFr) include breakfast. Triples 85SFr, with breakfast 90SFr. Quads 130SFr, with breakfast 140SFr. Only some rooms have showers, otherwise hall showers (2SFr surcharge). Eighteen rooms, so reserve in advance. Visa, MC, AmEx.

Hôtel Beau-Site, pl. du Cirque 3 (tel. 328 10 08; fax 329 23 64). Bus #1 or 4/44 to "Cirque," or walk from the station and turn right on bd. Fazy, crossing the Rhône at Pont de la Coulouvrenière and following blvd. Georges-Favon to pl. du Cirque (20min.). The dark lobby wallpaper and the occasional fireplace smack of elegant, bygone days. Double-paned windows keep out the noise of the busy road. Centrally located. Reception open daily 7am-11pm, but you can call if you'll be arriving later. Singles 59SFr, with shower 64SFr. Doubles 80SFr, with shower 85SFr. Triples 96SFr, with shower 100SFr. Quads 106SFr, with shower 110SFr. Students receive a 10% reduction. Breakfast included. Visa, MC, AmEx.

Hôtel St. Gervais, rue des Corps-Saints 20 (tel./fax 732 45 72). From the train station, cross the street and walk right 3min. down rue de Cornavin. Functional though overpriced rooms in a townhouse near the station. Brand spanking new tartan carpet and modern pictures decorate the hotel, though some of the double beds are small. Reception open 8am-midnight. Singles 62SFr, with shower 98SFr. Doubles 78SFr with shower 105SFr. One triple for 98SFr (without shower). Breakfast included. Visa, MC, AmEx. Advanced phone call preferred.

Hotel Aïda, av. Dunant 6 (tel. 320 12 66; fax 321 28 53). Bus #9, 12, or 15 to Plainpalais, in a busy section of the city. Clean, modern, but fairly simple rooms with above average bathrooms. TV and pictures in every room. Reception open Mon.-Fri. 7am-9:30pm, Sat.-Sun. 7am-noon.Singles 60SFr, with shower 85SFr. Doubles 80SFr, with shower 105SFr. Breakfast included.

Forget-Me-Not, rue Vignier 8 (tel. 320 93 55; fax 781 46 45). Bus #4/44 or tram #12 to "Plainpalais," down av. Dunant and left on rue Vignier. Cement high-rise on a busy street above a pool hall has utilitarian but functional rooms with orange bedcovers, all capped off with a terrace that offers a pleasing view of the Alps. Some have carpeting. Reception open Mon.-Fri. 9:30am-8pm, Sat. 10am-6pm, Sun. 3-6pm, but you can arrive later. Dorms 25SFr. In July and Aug. singles 50SFr, doubles 80SFr; rates decrease after three nights. Breakfast included. Showers. Kitchen Facilities. TV/video room.

Sylvabelle (tel. 347 06 03), Chemin de Conches 10, Bus #8 to "Conches." Nearest camping site to town. Reception open 7-10am and 7-10pm. 6SFr per person, 4SFr per tent, 3SFr per car, shower 2.50SFr. Open Easter to Oct.

Pointe-à-la-Bise (tel. 752 12 96). Bus #9 to "Rive," then bus E (north) to "Bise" (about 7km). 6SFr per person, 9SFr per tent. Open April to mid-Oct. Consult *Info Jeunes* (at the tourist office) for additional locations.

FOOD

Although it's true that you can find anything from sushi to *paella* in Geneva, you may need a banker's salary to foot the bill. For a picnic, shop at the supermarkets on virtually every corner of the city. Many supermarkets also have cafeterias with some of the best deals possible; see the listings below. Or eat at one of the many university cafeterias listed in *Info Jeunes*.

The cheapest way to go, though, is through the *boulangeries* and *pâtisseries*. 6SFr goes a long way when you combine a loaf of bread with an avocado and cheese from **Migros** or **Co-op.** *Patisseries*, pasta, and pizza parlors permeate **Place du Bourg-de-Four**, below Cathédrale de St. Pierre, as do some of the best cafés. By dining in the village of **Carouge** (tram #12 to pl. du Marché), you can combine gastronomy with history. It gained a reputation for fun back in Calvin's day, when those who wished to defy their leader's ban on cafés gathered outside the city limits to chat and drink the night into oblivion.

Restaurant Manora, rue de Cornavin 4 (tel. 909 44 10), 3min. from the station on the right and across from Notre Dame. A lush, green oasis of fruits and vegetables. Huge self-serve restaurant with a selection that's fresh, varied, and of high quality. Wholesome salads (big bowl 4SFr), earthy quiches (6.90SFr including salad), fruit tarts (3SFr), fresh fruit juices (3.90SFr), and main courses starting from 11SFr. Wheelchair accessible. Open Mon.-Sat. 7am-9:30pm, Sun 9am-9pm.

Le Rozzel, Grand-Rue 18 (tel. 311 89 29). Breton-style *crêperie* with outdoor seating on the cobblestones of the most elegant street in the *vieille ville*. Large dinner crêpes (*galettes*, 7-16SFr) or dessert crêpes (4.80-14SFr), and cider (4.50 SFr). Open Mon.-Sat. 8am-8pm, Sun. 11am-7pm. Visa.

La Crise, rue de Chantepoulet 13 (tel. 738 02 64). From the station, go right on rue de Cornavin and make a left on rue de Chantepoulet. Eat among the talkative locals in a tiny grandmother's kitchen. Can't beat the price or the portions: a huge meal (large slice of *quiche* and a plate full of veggies) for a mere 7SFr; a hearty bowl of soup 3SFr, fruit tart 4SFr. Open Mon.-Fri. 6am-8pm, Sat. 6am-3pm.

Auberge de Saviese, rue du Pâquis 20 (tel. 732 83 30). Bus #1: Monthoux. Even Genevois find this a great place to load up on traditional Swiss specialties. Rustic wooden interior with cowbells. Excellent *fondue au cognac* (18.90SFr); a portion of *raclette* with all the trimmings goes for 4.90SFr; pasta dishes (13.30-18SFr) and salads (10-17SFr). Open Mon.-Fri. 8:30am-midnight, Sat. 2:30pm-midnight. Visa, MC, AmEx.

Mañana, rue Chaponnière 3 (tel. 732 21 31). From pl. Cornavin, the first left down rue du Mont-Blanc. Hopping Tex-Mex joint with jolly Mexican guitarist in tow. Enchiladas, burritos, tacos, and quesadillas run 18-20SFr; a boot of beer (we're not kidding) is 5.30SFr. Open Mon.-Fri. noon-2pm and 6-11:30pm, Sat.-Sun. noon-11:30pm. Visa, MC, AmEx. Happy hour at the **Cactus Club** downstairs daily 7-10pm. Live music Wed. and Thurs. nights. DJ other nights.

Navy Club, pl. du Bourg-de-four 31(tel. 310 33 98). The *vieille ville* meets "The Love Boat." Veal sausage with *rösti* and salad is a tasty and traditional way to load on the calories (14.50SFr). Pizzas (12-18SFr); pasta (16-21SFr). Open Mon.-Thurs. 11am-1am, Fri. 11am-2am, Sat. 11am-2:30pm. Visa, MC, AmEx.

Les Armures, rue du Puits-St.-Pierre 1 (tel. 310 34 42). Tell everyone you ate at the five-star hotel where Bill Clinton and Jimmy Carter have eaten. One small step up in price but one giant leap up in atmosphere. The gorgeous cobblestone terrace by the Hôtel de Ville is right around the corner from the Cathédrale de St.-Pierre. Teems with guests from the ritzy Hôtel des Armures. Tasty onion soup 9SFr, good-sized fondue 19SFr, pizzas hover 12-15SFr, and *rösti* 34SFr. Open Mon.-Fri. 8am-3pm and 6pm-midnight, Sat.-Sun. noon-midnight. Visa, MC, AmEx.

Les 5 Saveurs, rue du Prieuré 22 (tel. 731 78 70). Seconds from the hostel. An unlikely combination of dirt-cheap Filipino food (fried chicken, rice and spring rolls 5SFr) and health conscious vegetarian cuisine (400g from the buffet 12SFr; tofu *pulao* 16SFr). Open daily noon-2:30pm, 6-10pm.

Sunset, rue St. Léger (tel. 320 15 13), just off the pl. des Philosophes. Eat out or sit inside with the tropical fish and haphazard bookstall. A vegetarian restaurant with big portions of *pita au champignons* (pita with mushrooms, 15SFr), and gnocchi (15SFr). Open Mon.-Fri. 7:30am-7pm. Visa, MC, AmEx.

Markets

Co-op, Migros, Grand Passage, and **Orient Express** chains can be found throughout the city. On Sundays one of the few places open is Gare Cornavin's **Aperto,** open daily 6am-10pm.

Epa, pl. de Molard. Department store's third floor restaurant serves meals from 8.50SFr to 15.50SFr. Open Mon. 9am-6:45pm, Tues., Wed. and Fri. 8:30am-6:45pm, Thurs. 8:30am-8pm, Sat. 8:30am-5pm.

Co-op, corner of rue du Commerce and rue du Rhône. La Marmite on the first floor has a menu from 9.50SFr and salads (2SFr per 100g). Open Mon. 9am-6:45pm, Tues.-Fri. 8:30am-6:45pm, Sat. 8:30am-5pm.

Migros, av. de Lausanne 18-20, left from Gare Cornavin, beneath the golden arches. Reasonably priced cafeteria with salad bar. Open Mon. 9am-6:45pm, Tue.-Wed. and Fri. 8am-6:45pm, Thurs. 8am-8pm, Sat. 8am-5:45pm.

Kash Express, av. Théodore-Weber 5 (tel. 735 01 00). Kosher grocer. Open Mon.-Thurs. 10am-12:30pm and 3:30-7pm, Fri. 9am-1pm.

Marché des Eaux-Vives, blvd. Helvétique, between cours de Rive and rue du Rhône. Huge dairy, vegetable, and flower market. Open Wed. and Sat. 8am-1pm.

Public Market, rue de Coutance, leading down to the river just above the ponts de l'Ile. Fresh fruits and cheese. Open Mon.-Sat. 8am-6pm. Another produce market is located on the Plaine de Plainpalais (Tues. and Fri. mornings).

SIGHTS

The tourist office provides several **walking tours** during the summer (June 15-Sept. 30; 10SFr). Qualified guides lead different tours each day of the week on Genevan themes: the Reformation, internationalism, the Red Cross, the *vieille ville*. They start at 2:30pm; pick up the tourist office's leaflet for departure points and timetable. If you are here in the winter (or spring or fall), don't fret; the tourist office has a special something for you. Recordings of the tours are obtainable, and a portable cassette player will enable you to walk through 2000 years of Geneva's history *tout(e) seul(e)* (10SFr, 50SFr deposit).

A visit to the *vieille ville* should start at the **Cathédrale de St.-Pierre,** the navel of the Protestant world. The outside shows the signs of clumsy meddling by fashion-conscious bishops. Gothic flying buttresses were added to the already passé romanesque nave, built in 1160 before the cathedral was finished. A Baroque facade was added in the 18th century and a steeple in the 19th. Inside, however, the cathedral is as austerely pure as on the day that Calvin stripped it of its popish baubles. He preached to full houses from 1536 to 1564 and diligent listeners wrote down 2,300 of his sermons. Two blue rose windows shed light on the darkness and cute walnut misericords sit behind the behinds of the choirboys. The brightly painted **Maccabean Chapel,** restored in a flamboyant style, gives the visitor an idea of what the cathedral walls might have looked like before the Reformation. The 157-step **north tower** provides a commanding view of the old town's winding streets and flower-bedecked homes. (Cathedral open daily June-Sept. 9am-7pm; Oct. and March-May 9am-noon and 2-6pm; Nov.-Feb. 9am-noon and 2-5pm. Tower open daily until ½hr. before the church closes. Admission to tower 3SFr. June-Sept: Sat., bell-ringing at 5pm and free organ recital at 6pm.) The ruins of a Roman sanctuary, a 4th-century Basilica, and a 6th-century church are located in a diminutive **archeological site** below the cathedral (open Tues.-Sun. 10am-1pm and 2-6pm. 5SFr, students 3SFr).

Around the cathedral are the oldest buildings in town. One minute from the west end sits the **Maison Tavel,** Geneva's oldest private residence sporting a round tower, mullioned windows, and ten sculptured human and animal heads. The 14th-century structure now houses the **Museum of Old Geneva** (see below). Five cannons stand guard on a nearby street corner opposite the **Hôtel de Ville,** whose older parts date back to1455, though the rest of the structure was constructed in the 16th and 17th centuries. Inside the courtyard, a ramp goes up the square tower, a unique feature which enabled dignitaries to attend meetings on horseback. Rousseau was sentenced to exile for his radical publications here, just a block away from his birthplace. On August 22, 1864, the first **Geneva Convention** (governing conduct during war) was signed here in what is known as the Alabama room, so called because in another international settlement in 1872, the British agreed to compensate America for sinking the Southern ship, the *Alabama*, during the Civil War.

A walk among the **Grand-Rue's** medieval workshops and 18th century mansion displays the hastily added third or fourth floors, the makeshift result of the real estate boom following the influx of French Protestant Huguenots after Louis XIV repealed the Edict of Nantes. Plaques commemorating famous residents abound here, including one at number 40, marking the birthplace of the enlightened philosopher **Jean-Jacques Rousseau.**

The city of Geneva may have overestimated the municipal problem of weary buttocks when it built the **world's longest bench** below the Hôtel de Ville. Stretch out along its 394 feet for a breather before moving onto the rest of the city. Further down, **Le Mur des Réformateurs** stonily faces the Promenade des Bastions. Effigies of Calvin, Cromwell, and company gaze sternly at visitors, probably more than a little peeved that the commemoration of their devout movement has lost out to a clock made of flowers. In front of them is a wooden park and prestigious Geneva University where students sprawl on the lawn by the public library or play with jumbo chessmen. Several museums cluster here, but Calvin would be doing 360s in his grave were he to find out about the existence of the **Russian Orthodox Church,** rue Toepffer, near the Musée d'Art et d'Histoire. Its gilded onion domes and icons will impress even those way past the one-church-too-many stage (1SFr).

A stroll along the lake-front (five minutes from the *vieille ville*) is a rewarding, relaxing, and cost-effective way to enjoy Geneva. One figure gazes perpetually at the water; in 1834, admirers of Jean-Jacques Rousseau finally persuaded the town council to erect a statue in his honor. The council, unwilling to pay too much homage to a radical who had been sent into exile, placed the statue on a tiny island off the Pont des Barques and surrounded it on three sides by walls of poplars, making the free-thinking philospher visible only to those on the lake. The much more visible **jet-d'eau,** down quai Gustave-Ardor, spews a spectacular plume of water 140 meters in the air. At any given time, the world's highest fountain keeps about seven tons of water aloft (operating from March-Oct.). The **floral clock,** in the nearby **Jardin Anglais,** which pays homage to Geneva's watch industry, has the world's largest second hand (2.5m). This is probably Geneva's most over-rated attraction. It was also once the city's most hazardous. Almost a meter had to be cut away from the clock because tourists, intent on taking the perfect photo, continually backed into unfortunate encounters with oncoming traffic. A walk along the rose-lined quais leads to two fun-parks. On the north shore, **Pâquis Plage,** at quai du Mont-Blanc (1SFr), is laid-back and popular with the *Genevois;* further out, on the south shore, **Genève Plage** (6SFr) offers a giant waterslide, an Olympic-sized pool, volleyball and basketball tournaments, and topless sunbathing. However, you should be aware before taking a dip that during a particularly bad outbreak of the bubonic plague the River Rhône, which empties into Lake Geneva, was consecrated by the pope as a "burial" ground for corpses. Be reverent or repulsed, accordingly.

Next to biking, the best way to see Lake Geneva is on one of the **ferry tours** leaving from quai du Mont-Blanc. **CGN** near the pont du Mont-Blanc (tel. 732 39 16) cruises to lakeside towns, including Lausanne, Montreux, and the stupendous Château de Chillon (round trip 47-57SFr, Eurail pass and Swisspass valid). **Swiss Boat** (tel. 732 47 47) and **Mouettes Genevoises** (tel. 732 29 44, fax 738 79 88) provide shorter, narrated winter cruise tours in English, dependent on the weather. Mouettes Genevoises embarks from the quai du Mont-Blanc and offers a two-hour tour (20SFr), a one-hour tour (13SFr), and a 35-minute tour (8SFr). Swiss Boat offers the same deals at the same prices. Call ahead for reservations and departure times.

Further up on the *rive droite,* the lakeside gardens become an attractive series of parks with modern bronzes, fountains, and 19th-century imitation Renaissance villas. The **Museum of the History of Science** (see p. 77), lives in one and the **World Trade Organization** has its headquarters in another, less attractive building further north. Opposite the WTO the basilica-shaped greenhouses of the **Jardin Botanique** (see p. 76) grow a collection of rare plants whose aroma wafts across the rue de Lausanne.

On a hill above these parks sits Geneva's international city, a group of multilateral organizations and embassies, of which the **Red Cross-Red Crescent** headquarters has the most interesting offerings for visitors (see below). Take bus #8. F, Z or walk fifteen minutes from the station. The guided tour of the **United Nations,** on ave de la Paix, is—like Orson Welles's conception of peace—quite dull, despite art treasures donated by all the countries of the world. The constant traffic of international diplomats, brightly clothed in their native garb, provides more excitement than anything the tour guides have to say. A not-so-subtle display of Cold War one-upmanship is the **armillary sphere** depicting the heavens, donated by the U.S. in memory of ex-President Woodrow Wilson. Nearby is the monument dedicated to the **"conquest of space,"** donated by the USSR. Don't miss the lovely view of the lake and Mont Blanc in France. The **Palais de Nations** was originally built for the ill-fated League of Nations and was inaugurated by the flamboyant Aga Khan. It is the second largest building complex in Europe after Versailles. (Open daily July-Aug. 9am-6pm; April-June and Sept.-Oct. daily 10am-noon and 2-4pm; Nov.-March Mon.-Fri. 10am-noon and 2-4pm. 8.50SFr, seniors and students 6SFr, school children under six 4SFr. For information call 907 45 60.) Tours in English go when enough people demand them and at least hourly; they visit the artworks and conference chambers and last about an hour.

MUSEUMS

Petit-Palais, Terrasse Saint-Victor 2 (tel. 346 14 33). Bus #1, 3, or 5 to "Claparède." Just off blvd. Helvétique. This beautiful mansion encompasses the incredibly dynamic period from 1880-1930. The collection exhibits works from the Impressionist, Pointilist, and Cubist, as well as the Expressionist, Fauvist, and Primitivist schools and not simply "name" painters. Open Mon.-Fri. 10am-noon and 2-6pm, Sat.-Sun. 10am-1pm and 2-5pm. 10SFr, students and seniors 5SFr.

Musée d'Art et d'Histoire, rue Charles-Galland 2 (tel. 418 26 00). Bus #1 or 8 to "Tranchées." This museum's eclectic (some would say uneven) collection sprawls over thousands of years, ranging from Egyptian papyrus to post-war avant-garde. The undisputed crown jewel is Konrad Witz's 1444 painting of *Jesus and the Apostles Fishing on Lake Geneva* (not the Sea of Galilee), one of the earliest pictures to use perspective in landscape depiction. Open Tues.-Sun. 10am-5pm. Free.

International Red Cross and Red Crescent Museum, av. de la Paix 17 (tel. 734 52 48). Bus #8, F, V or Z to "Appia." "Each of us is responsible to all others for everything." Dostoyevsky's words serve as the theme for this multi-media museum, which traces the history of the humanitarian organization, from 1864 to the present, through stark exhibits and video footage. 7 million POW records, including de Gaulle's, from World War I are on show and their presentation of current world atrocities pulls no punches. Emotionally involving, and much more interesting than the UN. Open Wed.-Mon. 10am-5pm. 8SFr, students and seniors 4SFr, under 11 free.

Maison Tavel, rue du Puits-St.-Pierre 6 (tel. 310 29 00), next to the Hôtel de Ville (town hall) in the *vieille ville.* This house everything stores everything that the city couldn't bear to throw away: the 1799 guillotine from pl. Neuve, a collection of medieval front doors, and a vast zinc and copper model of the city in 1850 that took 16 years to build. Open Tues.-Sun. 10am-5pm. Free.

Institut et Musée Voltaire, rue des Délices 25 (tel. 344 71 33). Bus #7 to "Délices." The ardent Voltairist might think that the house where he lived from 1755 to 1763 is the best of all possible museums. The enlightened author's letters and manuscripts are candidly displayed along with first editions of his books. Particularly diverting are Huber's cartoons of the philosopher-writer, Frederick of Prussia's sycophantic letters and Voltaire's cantankerous replies to Rousseau. Considerably more effort has gone into cultivating the garden. Exhibits in French. Open Mon.-Fri. 2-5pm. Free.

Musée de l'Horlogerie (Museum of Watches and Enameling), route de Malagnou 15 (tel. 418 64 70). Bus #6 to "Museum." An inexplicably popular array of antique clocks and watches. One clock includes an elephant that wiggles its ears. Open Wed.-Mon. 10am-5pm. Free.

Jean Tua Car and Cycle Museum, rue des Bains 28-30 (tel. 321 36 37). Bus #1, by rue des Grenadiers. Fun collection of 70 cars as well as motorcycles and bicycles, all dating before 1939. Open Wed.-Sun. 2-6pm. 8SFr.

Jardin Botanique, chemin de l'Impératrice 1 (tel. 752 69 69). Bus #4/44 to "Jardin Boutique." Flummoxed flamingos ponder relaxing gardens with a deer park, sweaty greenhouses, and a zone for really smelly plants. Open April-Sept. daily 8am-7:30pm; Oct.-March daily 9:30am-5pm. Free.

Musée Ariana, av. de la Paix 10 (tel. 734 29 50). Bus #8, 18, or F to "Appia." Sparklingly renovated and be-marbled museum of glass and ceramics. Covers seven centuries, but the modern collection is the highlight, starting with *art nouveau*—after that it just gets weirder. Open Wed.-Mon. 10am-5pm. Free.

Musée d' Histoire des Sciences, Villa Bartholoni, 128 rue de Lausanne (tel. 731 69 85), in the park at La Perle de Lac. Bus #4 or 44. This elegant pastel *palazzo* houses esoteric scientific gear in tall glass pods which have apparently beamed down recently from Venus. Downstairs starts sensibly enough with sundials, astrolabes, globes, and an orrery or two, but upstairs gets odder with amputation saws, trepanning kits, a wax model of a syphilis patient, and giant acoustic spoons for measuring the speed of sound in Lac Léman. Exhibits in French. Open Wed.-Mon. 1-5pm. Free.

Museum of Natural History, 1 route de Malagnou (tel. 418 63 00). Massive modern menagerie covering elephants to pterodactyls. On the first three floors the beasts are stuffed; on the fourth floor fossilized. Swiss fauna and minerals get a big show, with a 1:100,000 scale model of the country. Hidden loudspeakers make unnerving wild boar grunts as you pass. Open Tue.-Sun. 9:30am-5pm. Free.

ENTERTAINMENT AND NIGHTLIFE

Genève Agenda and *What's on in Geneva* are available at the tourist office and list events ranging from major festivals to daily movie listings (be warned, a movie runs about 15.50SFr). It would take real effort not to find an enjoyable diversion in Geneva. It is a rare summer day that does not feature a festival or free open air concert. One special option is the hour of **organ music** in the Cathédrale de St.-Pierre. In July and August, don't pass up the unique experience of **Cinelac**—sit near Genève Plage and watch movies on a screen over the lake. Check the listings in *Genève Agenda* for other indoor cinemas, and keep in mind that films marked "v.o." are in their original language with French and sometimes German subtitles; "st.ang." means that the film has English subtitles. *The* party in Geneva is **L'Escalade,** commemorating the dramatic repulse from the city walls of the invading Savoyard troops. The revelry lasts a full weekend and takes place around December 11. Summer festivals include the biggest celebration of **American Independence Day** outside the U.S. on July 4 and the **Fêtes de Genève,** August 15-17, filled with international music and artistic celebration culminating in a famously spectacular fireworks display. **La Bâtie Festival,** a music festival traditionally held in September, draws Swiss music lovers down from the hills for a two-week orgy of cabarets, theater, and concerts by mostly experimental rock and folk acts. Many events are free; students pay half-price for the others (regular prices 10-32SFr). Free jazz concerts take place from July 5 to August 23 on Wednesday and Friday nights at 8:30pm at the *Théâtre de Verdure* in Parc de la Grange. Most parks offer similar free concerts. **Nyan,** a few minutes by train from Geneva on Lac Léman, holds a big name rock festival at the end of July. Tickets run between 30-35SFr per day; details are available from the tourist office.

For budget travelers, shopping in Geneva should be limited to the windows, especially on the upscale Rue Basses and Rue du Rhône; the *vieille ville* contains scads of galleries and antique shops to explore. Those looking for Swiss souvenirs such as Swiss Army knives and watches should head to the department stores. **La Placette** in pl. Cornavin is particularly good for the cheap and chintzy (open Mon.-Wed. and Fri. 8:30am-6:45pm, Thurs. 8:30am-8pm, Sat. 8am-5pm). Exquisite Swiss chocolate can be bought in any supermarket, but the specialty store *par excellence* is **Chocolats Micheli,** rue Micheli-du-Crest 1 (tel. 329 90 06), which makes forty different edible gems; the smell alone in the store inspires lust in the strongest individual (open Tues.-Fri. 7am-6:30pm, Sat. 8am-5pm). Bargain hunters can ogle the goods in a number of markets. Head over to Plainpalais Wednesdays and Saturdays between 8am and 6pm to browse at the **flea market.** A **book market** fills the Esplanade de la Madeleine Monday to Saturday from 8am to 7pm. Or enjoy the more ephemeral wares at the **flower market,** Mon.-Sat. at place du Molard.

Summer nightlife centers around the cafés and the lakeside quais. Cafés abound in Geneva, where the city drinks, converses, and flirts. Two popular areas brimming with cafés are **Place du Bourg-de-Four,** below Cathédrale de St.-Pierre and the village of **Carouge** (tram #12: "pl. du Marché"), which attract young people, especially on those sultry evenings. Those looking for a late night on the town should make friends with a native or bartender and find the location of this week's **squat bar,** a moving party that attracts a trendy and artsy crowd and which serves some of the cheapest drinks in town.

Casting Café, rue de la Servette 6 (tel. 733 73 00). 2 min. walk behind the station or Bus #3, 9, or 10: "Lyon." This theme restaurant/café/bar is *the* place to be. Neon lights, blaring music, and cigarette smoke attract college students to the Wild West, gas station and Hollywood bars. The waitstaff dresses up to play the roles of the characters in the latest American movies showing next door. Drinks are averagely priced, except Saturday and Sunday when the prices are reduced by 85 percent for periods of five minutes which are announced at random times. Open Mon.-Fri. 11am-2am, Sat.-Sun. 2pm-2am. Visa, MC, AmEx.

Post Café, rue de Berne 7 (tel. 732 96 63), just off rue de Mont-Blanc. Tiny bar draws a big crowd. Inexpensive drinks (for Geneva), and friendly atmosphere. Happy hour daily 5-8pm. Mon.-Fri. 6:30am-2am, Sat. 10am-2am, Sun. 5pm-2am.

La Clémence, pl. du Bourg-de-Four 20 (tel. 312 24 92). Generations of students have sat outside and eaten at the famous and traditionally chic bar named after the big bell atop the Cathédrale de St.-Pierre. Come for breakfast (croissant 1.20SFr, coffee 2.70SFr) or beer (3.80-8SFr) or both. Open Mon.-Fri. 7am-1am. Sat.-Sun. 7am-2am.

Flanagan's, rue du Cheval-Blanc 4 (tel. 310 13 14), just off Grand-Rue in the old town. Friendly bartenders pull a good beer in this Irish bar and subdued cellar. Hangout for anglophones of all nationalities. A pint o' Guinness is 7SFr; a lager 6SFr. Happy hours Wed.-Mon. 5-7pm and all day Tuesday; live contemporary music (not Irish though) Thurs.-Sat. Open daily noon-2am.

Lord Nelson, pl. du Molard 9 (tel. 311 11 00). Pseudo-English pub which attracts the young and very young to its outdoor tables. Open Mon.-Thurs. 11:30-1am, Fri. 11:30am-2am, Sat. 2pm-2am, Sun. 2pm-midnight.

Au Chat Noir, rue Vautier 13, Carouge (tel. 343 49 98). Tram #12 to "pl. du Marché," just off the square. Popular venue famous for its jazz acts, but also features rock and sax-moaning blues. Open Sun.-Thurs. 9pm-4am, Fri.-Sat. 9pm-5am.

Arcade 46, av. Miremont 46, in the basement of the Cité Universitaire dorms. Popular with students, this no-frills disco plays music that will take you back to your high school dances, no matter what decade you grew up in. Inexpensive drinks. Open Thurs. and Sat. nights. Entrance free on Thurs. nights (11pm-3am). Sat. nights entrance 10SFr and includes first drink (11pm-4am).

Le Power (tel. 310 15 93), in Passage Malbuisson just off rue du Marché. Currently trendy city center club thumps out house and *"un peu de funk"* nightly from 10pm-5am. Cover of 20SFr includes first drink.

L'Usine, 4 pl. des Volontaires (tel. 781 34 90). Riverside warehouse with submachine gun graffiti is the major center for alternative music and theatre. Entry varies with the gig. See billboards for times.

■ Lausanne

Wedged between some small Alps and Lac Léman, Lausanne is really two cities, one for work and one for play. The *vielle ville* has its bustle and bankers; the lakefront at Ouchy its sunbathers and ice cream. On a warm evening, locals, loners and loungers converge on Ouchy's fountains and restaurants to listen to one of the city's many free concerts, play open-air chess or melt into each other's arms amid the sonorous lull of the waves. Though the flowers and lakeside are less dramatic than at Montreux, the tourist business in Lausanne is a fine-tuned machine, well oiled by the visitors who enjoy its space-aged **Olympic Museum** and the perennial pleasures of ultra-violet radiation. If you don't feel like leaving, don't feel alone; many writers have lazed lakeside.

T.S. Eliot wrote the *Wasteland* here, and nearly a century earlier, Dickens wrote *Dombey and Son* along Lausanne's waterfront, avoiding the company of fellow wordsmiths, Trollope and Thackeray.

ORIENTATION AND PRACTICAL INFORMATION

Lausanne is well-connected by rail to **Montreux** (20min., hourly, 8.40SFr), **Geneva** (40min., every 20min., 19.40SFr), **Basel** (2hr.20min., hourly, 57SFr), and **Zürich** (2hr.20min., hourly, 62SFr). For information call the national train information service (tel. 157 22 22). The superb staff in the station's information office can advise on the complexities of international travel. Direct trains run to **Rome** (11hr., one daily, 73SFr) and **Barcelona** (12hr., one daily, 95SFr); the TGV streaks to **Paris** in under four hours (4 daily, 76SFr, 13SFr reservation required). Lausanne is built on tortuously steep streets and the **train station**, pl. de la Gare (open daily 7am-9pm), is quite an uphill walk. The efficient public transportation system, however, will help you avoid an undignified collapse. The **Métro Ouchy** and bus lines #1, 3 and 5 serve the station. Most buses are routed to pl. St. François, a vital reference point in the center of the city and the location of several banks and one of the main post offices.

Tourist Office: Branch office (tel. 613 73 91) in the station. Open Mon.-Fri. 9am-8pm, Sat.-Sun. 10am-7pm. At the vastly larger **head office**, av. de Rhodanie 2 (tel. 613 73 21; fax 616 86 47), the seats are comfy, the maps are free, and the wait is short. Take the Métro: "Ouchy" or bus #2: "Ouchy." On foot, it's about 1.5km down av. d'Ouchy. Be sure to pick up the staggeringly comprehensive collection of literature they produce. *Useful Information*, and the *Plan Officiel* (map and guide to public transportation) are excellent. As are *Mosaïque*—a guide to the city, which combines a list of hotels and boarding houses with a list of restaurants, night clubs, and upcoming events; and *Pour un Eté 1997*, a guide to free music, theater, and cinema. Staff will make hotel reservations for 4-6SFr. Wheelchair access. Open June.-Sept. Mon.-Fri. 8am-7pm, Sat.-Sun. 9am-6pm; Oct.-May Mon.-Fri. 8am-6pm, Sat.-Sun. 9am-6pm. Also a general tourist information phone line (tel. 617 73 73).

Budget Travel: SSR Voyages, blvd. de Grancy 20 (tel. 617 56 27). Two streets behind the station. Sells and books student tickets and organizes group travel. Open Mon.-Fri. 9:15am-6:00pm.

Currency Exchange: At the station (tel. 312 38 24). Rates comparable to major banks. No commission on traveler's checks. Western Union transfers. Cash advances with Visa, MC, AmEx. Open daily 6:20am-7:30pm.

American Express: av. Mon Répos 14 (tel. 320 74 25). Cashes traveler's checks, sells airline tickets, and holds mail. Open Mon.-Fri. 8:30am-5:30pm. Address mail: Cary HOLLINSHEAD, c/o American Express, Client Mail Service, av. Mon Répos 14, P.O. Box 2072, CH-1002 Lausanne.

Telephones: Public phones await on practically every corner. At the Poste St. François they have call-now-pay-later phones. Open Mon.-Sat. 7:30am-8pm, Sun. 9am-12:30pm and 4-8pm.

Public Transportation: The 5-stop **Métro Ouchy,** with one end in the *vieille ville* and the other at the Ouchy waterfront, is useful for climbing the city's steep streets. The **Métro Ouest** runs from the center of town to the west. The Métro runs Mon.-Sat. 5:30am-12:15am, Sun. 6:15am-12:15am. Buses cross the city and run roughly 6am-midnight (check bus stops for specific lines). Three-Stop tickets are 1.30SFr, 60min. pass is 2.20SFr, 24hr. ticket 6.50SFr. Métro is free with a Swisspass or Museum Passport, but not with a Eurail pass.

Ferries: CGN, av. de Rhodanie 17 (tel. 617 06 66). To **Montreux** (1½hr., 6 per day, last ferry 6:05pm, 17SFr one-way, 30SFr round-trip); **Geneva** (3½hr., 3 per day, last ferry 5:15pm, 29SFr one-way, 47SFr round-trip). Buy tickets at the dock. Eurail pass and Swisspass valid. Open June-Sept. 8am-7:30pm; Oct.-May 8:30am-12:30pm and 1:30-5:15pm.

Taxis: tel. 33 141 33. Usually available at pl. St. François.

Car Rental: Budget, av. Ruchonnet 2 (tel. 323 91 52). **Avis,** av. de la Gare 50 (tel. 320 66 81). **Hertz,** pl. du Tunnel 17 (tel. 312 53 11). **Europcar,** pl. de la riponne 12 (tel. 323 71 42).

Parking: Parking Simplon-Gare, rue du Simplon 34, behind the station, has spots for 2SFr per hr. during the day, 50c. per hr. at night, and 22SFr per day. To park on the city streets, pick up a parking disc from the tourist office. On city streets, white zones indicate unlimited parking, red zones allow parking for 15hr., and blue zones for 90min. Dial up the present time and the maximum stay time, and leave the disc prominently displayed on the dash.

Bike Rental: At the baggage check in the station (tel. (0512) 242 162). Rentals 21SFr per day, 17SFr per ½day. Bikes can be returned at another station for an additional 6SFr. Open daily 6:40am-7:50pm.

Luggage Storage: At the train station. Lockers 3SFr and 5SFr per day. Open 24hr.

Lost Property: pl. Chauderon 7 (tel. 319 60 58). Open Mon.-Fri. 8am-12:15pm and 1:45-6pm; Sat. 8am-noon.

Laundromat: At the youth hostel, even if you're not staying there (5SFr, detergent included). **Quick Wash,** blvd. de Grancy 44, two streets behind the train station, toward the river. Wash and dry around 10SFr. Open Wed.-Mon. 8:30am-8:30pm, Tues. noon-8:30pm.

Library: Cantonal and University Palais de Rumine, pl. de la Riponne 6 (tel. 312 88 31). Open for general borrowing Mon.-Fri. 8am-5:45pm, Sat. 8-11:45am. Reading room open Mon.-Fri. 8am-10pm; Sat. 8am-5pm.

Bookstore: Payot Libraire, pl. Pépinet 3 (tel. 341 31 31). Chain bookstore with English section. Open Mon. 1-6:30pm, Tue.-Fri. 8:30am-6:30pm, Sat. 8:30am-5pm.

24-hr. Pharmacy: Dial 111 to find out which pharmacy is open all night; they rotate daily. **24-hr. medical service:** at the hospital (tel. 314 11 11).

Emergencies: Police: tel. 117. **Fire:** tel. 118. **Ambulance:** tel. 144.

Post Office: Centre Postal, av. de la Gare 43bis (tel. 344 35 14). As you leave the train station, it's on your right. Address *Poste Restante* to: 1000 Lausanne 1 dépot. Open Mon.-Fri. 6:30am-10pm, Sat. 6:30am-8pm, Sun. 9am-noon and 6-10pm. To dispatch your postcard from the site where Edward Gibbon wrote his *Decline and Fall of the Roman Empire* visit **Poste St. Françoise,** 15 pl. St. François (tel. 344 24 16). Open Mon.-Fri. 7:30am-6:30pm, Sat. 8-11am. **Postal Code:** CH-1002

Telephone Code: 021.

ACCOMMODATIONS AND CAMPING

Lausanne's budget accommodations rarely fill completely, but you may need to pick up the tourist office's list of cheap hotels come July and August. They also have a list of private boarding houses and family *pensions.* The owners of these establishments generally prefer stays of at least three days. Those looking for apartments to rent for longer stays should scour the local paper *24 Heures* which carries regular listings, or try the notice boards of big department stores. The tourist office also has a list of (more expensive) furnished apartments to rent.

Auberge de Jeunesse (HI), chemin de Muguet 1 (tel. 616 57 82), corner of ch. du Stade near Ouchy. From the station take bus #1 (dir: Maladière) to "Batelière" and take first left down ch. du Stade.The hostel is at the bottom of the street. From Ouchy or the *vieille ville,* take bus #2 (dir: Bourdonnette) to "Théâtre de Vidy" and continue 100 meters. A short walk to the lake but a long walk to town; be sure to have bus fare. Warm staff makes up for busy road out front and the flimsy outdoor lockers. Attractive balcony and patio. Small enough to get regularly booked-up by German schoolchildren, so reserve ahead in the summer months. Reception daily 7-9am and 5-11pm.Curfew 11:30pm. 25SFr first night, then 22.50SF. Breakfast included. Generous dinner 11SFr. Padlock deposit 5SFr. Laundry 5SF, includes detergent.

Pension Bienvenue, rue du Simplon 2 (tel. 616 29 86), 5min. from the train station, turning right along av. de la Gare, right onto ave. d'Ouchy, and right after the bridge on rue du Simplon. **Women only.** Attractive iron-shaped building with gleaming floors and spotless, palatial bathrooms. Friendly rapport between the long-term guests and the short-term guests. Ask for a south-facing room to minimize train rumbles. Reception open Mon.-Fri. 8-11am and 5-8pm, Sat.-Sun. 8:30-

11am. Call if arriving later. Singles 41.55SFr. Doubles 74.55SFr. Breakfast included. Access to kitchen, laundry facilities, and TV room.

Hotel "Le Chalet," av. d'Ouchy 49 (tel. 616 52 06). Métro Ouchy: "Jordils," or Bus #2 (dir: Bourdonnette) to "Jordils" drops you right in front of the hotel. Gentle and learned older woman proudly maintains this 19th-century Swiss chalet, 3min. from the lake. Composer August Strindberg once stayed here for two years. Old-fashioned dining room is filled with homey clutter. A lush garden partially deters modern noise and pollution. Singles 60SFr. Doubles 85SFr. Breakfast 7SFr. The owner looks you over before letting you in. If you pass the test, it may cost less than 45SFr, and will include showers of grandmotherly love. Don't arrive too late.

Jeunotel, Chemin du Bois-de-vaux 36 (tel. 62 6 02 22; fax 626 02 26). Take bus #2 (dir: Bourdonnette) to "Bois-de-Vaux," cross the street, and follow the signs. A better name would be *Jugend*-hotel, since it is sometimes overrun by raucous German school groups running wild. Barracks-like complex, 2.5km from town. Brutal concrete architecture and thin walls offset by starched white bedspreads and a huge number of beds. A better deal for groups than for singles. Reception open 24hr. Visa, MC, AmEx. Dorms 32SFr. Singles 68SFr. Doubles 80SFr, with shower 98SFr. Triples 102SFr. Quads 136SFr. Buffet breakfast included. Lunch and dinner menus at 10.90SFr and 13.50SFr. Laundry 1.20SFr. Wheelchair facilities.

Camping: Camping de Vidy, chemin du Camping 3 (tel. 624 20 31). Take bus #1,4 to "Maladière" (the last stop) and follow sign onward. Turn left past a church and right on rte. de Vichy, passing the remains of Roman "Lousanna." Year-round campsite with a winning lakeside location. Reception open Sept.-June daily 9am-noon and 5-7pm; July-Aug. 8am-9pm. Free showers. Sites 6.50SFr, students 6SFr, 7-11SFr per tent. Small bungalow (fits 1-2 people) 50SFr. Large bungalow (3-4 people) 86SFr. City tax of 1.20SFr per person and 2.50SFr per car added. Discount tickets for the Bellerive fun-park (2SFr).

FOOD

Lausanne's specialty is fresh perch, caught in Lac Léman. *Perche parfait* is said to swim thrice: once in water, once in butter, and once in wine. *Boulangeries,* where local businessmen on the run buy their sandwiches (3.50-8SFr), appear on every street. Restaurants, cafés, and bars line the pl. Saint-François, while the over-priced eateries lining the Ouchy waterfront welcome with open arms tourists and their open wallets.

Café du Vieil-Ouchy, pl. du Port 3 (tel. 616 21 94), 30sec. from Métro or bus #2 to "Ouchy." Lake frontage, sunset over the mountains, *fondue* bubbling in the pot, cool beer on tap... sounds like you're in for a ghastly evening. Swiss specialties: *rösti* 9.50-20SFr, *fondue* 20SFr, beer 3SFr. Open Thurs.-Tues. 11am-11pm.

Crêperie "La Chandeleur," rue Mercerie 9 (tel. 312 84 19), just below the Cathédrale. Tucked neatly in the hills of the *vieille ville,* this fashionable *crêperie* with its lovely terrace serves over 50 different kinds of dinner and dessert *crêpes* (4-15.50SFr). Salads from 3.80SFr. Normandy cider 4.20SFr, Breton cider 4.50SFr. Open Tues.-Thurs. 11am-10pm, Fri.-Sat. 11am-11:30pm. Visa, MC.

Manora, pl. St-François 17 (tel. 320 92 93). Make your mother proud and fill up at Manora's blooming salad, fruit, and dessert bars. *Menus du jour* run 7-14SFr (one of the best values in town). Open Mon.-Sat. 6:45am-10:30pm, Sun. 8:45am-10:30pm. Hot food served 11am-10pm.

Crêperie d'Ouchy, pl. du Port 7 (tel. 616 26 07). Great for lunch *al fresco* with its many pink and green tables outside. Try a *galette* with *Vaudois* sausage (12SFr) or the chocolate and hazelnut *crêpes* (9.50SFr). Open in summer daily 9am-midnight, in winter 10am-11pm.

Au Couscous, rue Enning 2 (tel. 312 20 17), at the top of rue de Bourg. Serves fashionable Maghreb and Tunisian cuisine plus all things macrobiotic. Its namesake dish is the specialty. Dishes 9SFr-19SFr. Open Mon.-Fri. 11:30am-2:30pm and 6:30pm-midnight, Sat.-Sun. 11:30am-2:30pm and 4:30pm-1:30am.

Il Grottino, rue du Grand-Chêne 4 (tel. 312 76 58), just off pl. St.-François, tucked in its own niche just off the Grand Pont on the St. François side. The overwhelming number of tables for two and the many pairs of heads leaning toward each other in muted conversation tell the tale for this Italian restaurant. Food leans toward fish and seafood. Pizza from 12SFr, pasta 14-22SFr. Open Mon.-Fri. 7am-midnight, Sat. 8am-3pm. The bar **L'Escalier** downstairs has a happy hour Mon.-Fri. 5-7pm. Visa, MC, AmEx.

Markets

Co-op, rue du Petit Chêne. From the train station, head towards the center of town. Open Mon.-Fri. 8am-12:15pm and 1:30-7pm.

Migros, av. d'Ouchy. Down av. de la Gare from the train station and right on av. d'Ouchy. Open Mon. 9am-6:45pm, Tues.-Fri. 8am-6:45pm, Sat. 7:30am-5pm.

Produce markets, from April to mid-Oct. at Ouchy on Sun. 9am-8pm, on rue de Bourg behind the Eglise St.-François Wed. and Sat. mornings, and at rue du Petit-Chêne off pl. St.-François on Fri. mornings. If you are here at the end of Aug. check out the flower and honey market 8-11am, Derrière-Bourg in the vieille ville.

SIGHTS

Lausanne is built on three hills, the highest of which is topped by the Gothic **Cathédrale,** consecrated in 1275 under the auspices of Holy Roman Emperor Rudolph and Pope Gregory X. Medieval architects tried to obscure the building's squatness with an optical illusion: the vaulted roof is skillfully shaped to give the 20-m ceiling a drastic lift. The Protestant Reformation, predicated, in part, by fierce Bernese rule, stripped the cathedral of nearly all its fripperies. The bluish apsidal windows and the rose window in the south transept are happy exceptions. One hundred and five windows (78 of them original) depict the zodiac, the elements, the winds, and other mystical groupings, all arranged into a geometrical scheme. But the windows pale next to the view of city, lake, and mountains rewarding those who struggle up the 200 steps of the tower. (Open July to mid-Sept. daily 7am-7pm; mid-Sept. to June 7am-5pm. Free guided tours (call 323 84 34). Tower open 8:30-11:30am and 1:30-5:30pm. 2SFr, children 1SFr.)

The **Château Saint-Maire,** the former bishop's palace, reigns just past the Cathedral. The structure was built under two bishops who apparently had varying tastes, one wanted something stern and forbidding, while the other fancied brickwork and dinky turrets with little copper spikes on top. The castle is now the seat of government for Canton Vaud. A statue of Major Davel, a Vandois leader beheaded for telling his Bernese overlords to go fry in the ninth circle, stands outside.

Just down the steps by the cathedral entrance stands a symbol of Bern's rule, the 17th-century **Hôtel de Ville,** whose typical Bernese architecture contrasts with the surrounding buildings. At the top of the hour, join Lausannes's *au pairs* and their little charges in front of the ornamental clock here in the **Place de la Palud,** where the history of the canton is depicted on the hour from 9am-7pm.

A large majority of visitors don't go near the *vieille ville,* preferring instead to sun themselves on the Ouchy waterfront or in one of the city's many beautiful parks. In the center of town the **Derrière-Bourg Promenade** depicts in flowers events from the canton's history. Nearby **Mon-Repos** is a green oasis of venerable trees, aviaries, an orangery, and a small circular temple. The **quai de Belgique** in Ouchy is a lakeside promenade flanked by flowers, immaculate gardens, small fountains, and benches. The neo-Gothic **Château d'Ouchy,** a 13th-century castle built on the site of an even older fortress, is still standing and has become a quay-side hotel. The best beach area is in the **Bellerive Complex** (bus #2 to "Bellerive"), a park where scantily-clad locals putt-putt, ping-pong, plunge in, and peel off. (Open mid.-May to Aug. daily 9:30am-until it gets dark, rains, or there is a major earthquake. 4.50SFr, students and seniors 3SFr, 0.50SFr discount after 5pm.)

MUSEUMS

Even die-hard sun worshippers should consider visiting Lausanne's exemplary and eclectic museums. If you are here for three days, a **museum passport** (26SFr, students and seniors 20SFr) will almost surely pay for itself. The passport grants free access to museums and public transportation for three days, and includes a free film at the Swiss Film Archive.

Musée Olympique, quai d'Ouchy 1 (tel. 621 65 11), bus #2 or Métro to "Ouchy" and a short walk along the quay. The terraced lakeside setting with gushing fountains, billowing flags, and statues of firmly-toned torsos gives an appropriately theatrical welcome to the ultra-modern museum of all things Olympic. It's all here: banks of screens endlessly replay great moments to stirring symphonies; interactive audio-visuals narrate the history of the Games; collections of mascots, medals, torches, and curling stones are all stylishly presented. The classiest museum in Switzerland, no question. Fully bilingual English/French. Fully wheelchair accessible, via av. de l'Elysée. Open May-Sept. daily 10am-7pm; Oct.-April Tues.-Sun. 10am-6pm; in addition Thurs. 10am-9:30pm. 14SFr., students and seniors 9SFr, children ages 10-18 6SFr. Visa, MC.

Collection de l'Art Brut, av. Bergières 11 (tel. 647 54 35). An art gallery founded by postwar primitivist painter, Jean Dubuffet, who despised the pretentiousness of the avant-garde art scene so much that he filled his gallery with the works of "non-artists"—the criminally insane, the institutionalized, and children. Watch for gruesome ball-point pen sketches by office-worker Ted Gordon, a cell wall carved with a chamberpot handle, and the toys made by a man who learned carpentry *after* he went blind. Go up the stairs from the west side of pl. de la Riponne, and follow av. Vinet (10min.) or catch bus #2 (dir: Désert) to "Beaulieu." Open Tues.-Sun. 11am-1pm and 2-6pm. 6SFr, students and seniors 4SFr.

Musée de l'Elysée, av. de l'Elysée 18 (tel. 617 48 21), off av. d'Ouchy. Or take bus #8 to "Montchoisi," continue down the hill, and turn right on av. de l'Elysée. An 18th-century mansion that encloses a rarity: a museum devoted entirely to photography. Temporary exhibitions are well presented in a sequence of spacious whitewashed rooms. Open Tues.-Wed. and Fri.-Sun. 10am-6pm, Thurs. 10am-9pm. 5SFr, students 2.50SFr.

Decorative Arts Museum (Musée des Arts Décoratifs), av. Villamont 4 (tel. 323 07 56). Displays high-quality temporary exhibits of modern glasswork, textiles, and graphic art. Open Tues.-Sun. 11am-6pm. 2.50SFr, students 1.50SFr.

Hermitage, rte. du Signal 2 (tel. 320 50 01), on a grassy hill north of the *vieille ville.* Bus #16 to "Hermitage" stops out front, but it is infrequent. Magnificent old house given over to temporary exhibitions of sculptures and paintings which vary in quality from international blockbuster shows on tour to parochial damp squibs. Find out first. Open Tues.-Wed. and Fri.-Sun. 10am-1pm and 2-6pm, Thurs. 10am-10pm. Admission 13SFr, students 5SFr, under 19 2.50SFr, seniors 10SFr. Tours in English Thurs. 8pm, Sun. 3pm.

Museum of Pipes and Tobacco, rue de l'Académie 7 (tel. 323 43 23), behind the cathedral. Bus #16 to "Cathédrale." If you already know the difference between Billiards and Bent Rhodesians, this museum may be hard to match; if not, the walk up to the cathedral may not be worth the puff. Twenty-five hundred pipes, one dizzying atmosphere. Also the meeting place of the ultra-elusive Pipe Club of Lausanne. Open June-Aug. Mon 10am-noon and 3-6pm, Wed. and Fri. 3-6pm; Sept.-May Mon. 10am-noon and 3-6pm. 3.50SFr.

ENTERTAINMENT AND NIGHTLIFE

The **Béjart Ballet, Lausanne Chamber Orchestra, Swiss Film Archives, Municipal Theatre, Theatre of Vidy,** and **Opera House** all enrich Lausanne's cultural life. During the **Festival de la Cité** in the first two weeks of July, the *vieille ville* springs to life with theater and dance events, which are mostly free. If it's Swiss craftwork you're looking for, check out the **Marché des Artisans** in the pl. de la Palud from 10am to 7pm on the first Friday of every month, March-Dec. You can't heave a brick in the pl. St.-François without putting it through the window of a café-bar or hitting the doorman of a night-club. (Warning: *Let's Go* strongly urges you to seriously consider the risks before you choose to heave bricks; Swiss bouncers have a mean streak.) *Lausannois* party-goers inhabit the bars 'til 1am (2am on weekends) and dance at the clubs 'til 4 in the morning. The seriously hardcore then head over to the bar in the train station, which opens at 5am.

Dolce Vita, rue César Roux 30 (tel. 323 09 43). From Pont Bessières up rue Caroline and past the large crossroads. A funky and pungent room with frequent live shows of rap, indie, world music, and blistering acid jazz. Not a pretty place, but one with a lot of substance. Beer 4-5SFr. Open Sun. and Wed. 10pm-3am, Fri.-Sat. 10pm-4am; in summer Thurs. 10pm-3am. Weekend cover 5-25SFr depending on the act. Happy hours Wed.-Thurs. and Sun. 10pm-midnight (beer 2SFr).

Le Lapin Vert, ruelle du Lapin Vert (tel. 312 13 17), off rue de l'Académie, behind the Cathedral. An ancient pub filled with rock music and young students. Look for the green rabbit hanging outside. Open Sun.-Thurs. 8pm-1am, Fri.-Sat. 8pm-2am.

Bellerive's Bar, av. de Cour 99 (tel. 616 96 33). Just a hop, skip, and a stumble away from the hostel, enabling patrons to maximize pre-curfew intake. The comfortable bar stools may make you want to break curfew, but the prices won't. To get there from the hostel, walk up ch. de Stade, hang a right on rue de Cour, and walk about 2 blocks. They offer beer on tap (5.50-7SFr per pint) and a *menu du jour* (14SFr) as well as neighborhood charm and friendly bartenders. Open Mon.-Thurs. 7:45am-1am, Fri.-Sat. 7:45am-2am, Sun. 7:45am-midnight.

Bleu Lézard, rue Enning 10 (tel. 312 71 90), on the corner of rue de Langaliereie and rue Enning. An artsy crowd fills this bistro, gushing over naughty-but-nice desserts (5.50SFr) and beer from nine countries (4.50-6SFr). Window sculptures, re-designed by local artists every two months are *absolutely fabulous*, sweetie darling. Open daily 7am-1am.

Le Barbare, Escaliers du Marché 27 (tel. 312 21 32). Perched on the cobbles by the wooden steps to the cathedral. Sit and sip a devastating hot chocolate that comes in regular, *Viennoise,* and *Liégeoise* (3.50SFr-5.50SFr). Small snacks like *croques monsieur* (toast with cheese and ham, 4.50SFr). Open Mon.-Thurs. 8:30am-11:30pm, Fri.-Sat. 8:30am-midnight.

Ouchy White Horse Pub, av. d'Ouchy 66 (tel. 616 75 75). Perfect for a quiet evening with a terrace just steps up from the waterfront. An authentic pub atmosphere contrasts with the Euro-charm of Lausanne. Beer on tap 5-7SFr for a pint, 0.50SFr cheaper if bought at the bar. *Tapas* 4.50-8SFr; hamburgers, fries and a soda 10SFr. Open Sun.-Thurs. 7am-1am, Fri.-Sat. 7am-2am.

■ Montreux

If you've seen a postcard of Switzerland, it was probably taken in Montreux. The view from the quay in the summertime is a tourist office's dream. With crystal blue water embraced by snow-capped Alps in the distance and marigolds at your feet, Montreux achieves near perfection. Its 10-km lakeside promenade blooms with 250,000 flowers, beckoning ice-cream-licking summer visitors to achieve peaceful karma on the shaded benches among the palm trees and rhododendra. Thirty-one years ago, tourism of the sedate variety was given a dip in its hip and a glide in its stride when **le jazz** arrived. The world-famous **Montreux Jazz Festival,** draws hordes of footloose hipsters to the otherwise peaceful town for two and a half weeks in the beginning of July (see **The Music Festivals,** p. 88, for ticket information). With its fantastic success, the monster-truck of festivals has spawned a matchbox set of lesser ones, featuring jazz, funk, rap, salsa, blues, gospel, and classical music so that the town pulses with concert sounds most evenings.

ORIENTATION AND PRACTICAL INFORMATION

Situated on the eastern edge of the dill-pickle-shaped Lac Léman, Montreux is serviced by trains from many Swiss cities: **Geneva** (1hr., hourly, 27SFr), **Lausanne** (20min., every ½hr, 8.40SFr), **Bern** (1½hr., hourly, 37SFr). Direct trains also go to **Martigny, Aigle, Sion,** and **Brig** and through (literally) the mountains to **Gstaad.** The *Gare de Montreux,* (tel. 963 45 15) on av. des Alpes, is a short stroll away from the city's sites. **CGN** ferries, which go more frequently in the summer, chug passengers between the Swiss Riviera's cities. (**Lausanne,** 1½hr., 17SFr; **Geneva,** 5hr., 34SFr; **Vevey,** 25min., 6SFr. Eurail and Swisspass valid.) To reach the center of town, follow av. des Alpes to the left in front of the train station. To reach the lake, head down the steps opposite the station, then turn left; the lake is on the other side of the buildings directly ahead. The oldest part of the town is set back 800m from the waterfront. Take Grand Rue due west if you want to bike to **Vevey** (see p. 89). Beware that the road undergoes several name changes along the way.

WESTERN SWITZERLAND

Tourist Office: pl. du Débarcadère (tel. 963 12 12; fax 963 81 13), on the lake. Descend the stairs opposite the station and head left on Grand Rue. The office is set back on the right hand side. Fun-loving staff shares an office with desks for festival tickets and excursion information. Free hotel reservation service within Montreux. Festival tickets and local bus and train schedules available. Free photocopied map of Montreux, and the 1SFr map for sale isn't much better. Grab an excellent free map from **Union de Banques Suisses,** av. de Casino 26. The tourist office's *Tourist Info Pass* is a compendium of useful local addresses. Open June-Aug. daily 9am-7pm; Sept.-May 9am-noon and 1:30-6pm. There is a very small **branch office** at the train station.

Budget Travel: SSR Voyages, av. des Alpes 25 (tel. 961 23 00; fax 961 23 06). Open Mon.-Fri. 9am-12:30pm and 1:30-6pm.

Currency Exchange: Good rates at the station. No commission. Also offers Western Union transfers and credit card advances. Open daily 6:40am-9:30pm. Banks in Montreux are generally open Mon.-Fri. 8:30am-12:30pm and 1:30-4:30pm. Rates for travelers checks are better at banks than at the station.

Telephones: Next to the tourist office, in the post office, and at the youth hostel. Phones take both cards and coins.

Buses: Buy tickets at the back of each bus. Look at the map and enter the zone you wish to travel to. Day passes need to be date-stamped on the bus during their first use. 1.70-3.60SFr, juniors (ages 6-20) 1.20-2.40SFr. Swisspass valid. The tourist office will be happy to explain the confusing system if you still have questions. They also offer a 5.50SFr day pass for tourists (April-Oct.). Special late-night buses run during the Jazz Festival.

Ferries: CGN, quai du Débarcadère, next to the tourist office. Mini-cruises to Geneva and Lausanne. Even shorter rides to Villeneuve (near the hostel) and Château de Chillon. Tourist office lists all the excursions offered on Lake Geneva. Buy tickets at the quai, the tourist office, or on board. Eurail and Swisspass valid.

Bike Rental: At the baggage check in the train station. 21SFr per day, 17SFr per ½day; mountain bikes 33SFr per day, 27SFr per ½day. For an additional 6SFr bikes can be returned at other stations (including Martigny, Aigle, and Sion) by prior arrangement. Open daily 5:40am-9:30pm. Visa, MC, AmEx.

Luggage Storage: At the station. Lockers 2SFr, larger backpack-sized lockers 5SFr. Luggage watch 5SFr per bag. Open daily 5:40am-8:45pm.

Laundromat: Salon-Lavoir, rue Industrielle 30. Open Mon.-Fri. 7am-6:45pm.

Bookstore: Payot Libraire, av. du Casino 42 (tel. 963 06 07). Open Mon. 10:30am-12:30pm and 1:30-6:30pm, Tues.-Fri. 8:30am-12:30pm and 1:30-6:30pm, Sat. 8:30am-12:30pm and 1:30-5pm.

Emergencies: Police: tel. 117. **Fire:** tel. 118. **Ambulance:** tel. 144. **Hospital:** tel. 966 66 66. **Emergency Pharmacies:** tel. 962 77 00.

Post Office: Main Office, av. des Alpes 70, near the station. A surfeit of employees to keep things running smoothly. Phones available. Address *Poste Restante* to: CH-1820 Montreux 1. Open Mon.-Fri. 7:30am-6pm, Sat. 8-11am.

Postal Code: CH-1820.

Telephone Code: 021.

ACCOMMODATIONS AND CAMPING

Cheap rooms are scarce in Montreux during the tourist season (late June-Aug.), even in the hostel. Come festival time, revelers often stash their bags in the train station lockers and crash on the lakefront. Be aware that the police will move lake-loungers out at 7am. Bookings for rooms start the previous year, so reserve at least two months in advance to be sure you have a roof over your head during the jazz festival (see **The Music Festivals,** p. 88); don't rely on finding last-minute cancellations. When Montreux is packed, take bus #1 to "Villeneuve," 5km away, where there are a handful of budget hotels, or consider commuting from Lausanne, Martigny or Vevey. Before you leave Montreux, though, ask the tourist office for the list *Pensions et Petits Hôtels,* which has 13 cheapish suggestions.

Auberge de Jeunesse Montreux (HI), passage de l'Auberge 8 (tel. 963 49 34). Completely revamped in 1993, this hostel has kept its purple-trim interior in pristine condition. To get there: if you have a lot of baggage, pick up bus #1 on Grand Rue from the station (dir: Villeneuve) to "Territet." Continue up the street, take the first right (rue du Bocherex), and go down the stairs (passage de l'Auberge). Pleasure-seekers might walk 20min. along the lake: go down the stairs from the station and continue to the quay. Then follow the path along the lake to the left, past the Montreux Tennis Club. The hostel is behind a small underpass and offers a sumptuous lakefront location. Trains rumble all night long just inches from the hostel, but the cheery, rainbow-bright dorms have double-paned windows that keep most residents sleeping soundly. 112 beds in rooms of 4, 6, or 8 beds. Showers, wonderfully clean and private, are across the hall. Friendly, marvelous, and multi-lingual staff (English, French, German, Spanish). Definitely call several weeks in advance during late-June and July when school groups and jazz fans pack it, some making reservations 6 months in advance. Reception open April-Sept. 7-10am and 4pm-midnight; Oct.-March 7:30-10am and 4-11pm. Lockout 10am-4pm. Curfew midnight, but groups and families can request a key. Members 27.40SFr first night, then 24.90SFr. Doubles (5 available) 72.80SFr, then 67.80SFr. Breakfast included. Complete wheelchair access and two special rooms for disabled visitors with bathrooms for regular dorm price. Tasty dinner with salad and dessert 11SFr. Lockers 2SFr deposit. Laundry 8SFr, including detergent. TV room. Free bike- and car-parking are nearby but not affiliated with the hostel. Look for blue and white "P" signs. If full, you might angle for one of the 5 beds at Café Rock (see listing under **Nightlife,** p. 88). Visa, MC, AmEx.

Hôtel du Pont, rue du Pont 12 (tel. 963 22 49), at the top of the *vieille ville,* 800m from the waterfront. Clean but plain rooms overlooking quiet streets, next to woods and a waterfall. All have bathrooms and TVs. The café downstairs is also part of this family-run establishment, and offers evening meals for 13.80SFr. From the station, walk right onto av. des Alpes (3min.), and take a right up rue de la Gare. Follow rue de la Gare up the hill until it becomes rue du Pont. Hôtel du Pont is on the left. Reception open 7am-midnight. Singles 60SFr. Doubles 110-120SFr. Triples 150SFr. Breakfast included. Visa, MC, AmEx.

Hôtel Elite-Garni, av. du Casino 25 (tel. 966 03 03; fax 966 03 10). From the station, go down the stairs onto Grand Rue and turn left, continuing until it becomes av. du Casino. Head on past the shabby neon façade; the Elite-Garni has a city-center location and newly renovated rooms with wood-tiled floors, fluffy comforters, and tutti-frutti shower curtains. All rooms have TV, showers, and telephone. Singles 60-90SF. Doubles 100-160SFr. Closed in Jan. Visa, MC, AmEx.

Hôtel Pension Wilhelm, rue du Marché 13 (tel. 963 14 31; fax 963 32 85). From the station, walk left 3min. up av. des Alpes and turn left onto rue du Marché, up the hill and past the police station. The Wilhelm family has kept this hotel in business since 1870. Convenient location, large bedrooms with matching pastel-colored comforters and bathrooms. Reception open all day, and at night by prior notice. Singles 60SFr, with shower 70SFr. Doubles 90SFr, with shower 100SFr (depending on shower location). 60SFr per person during the jazz festival. Breakfast included. In winter no breakfast, but prices are 5SFr cheaper. Closed in Dec.

Camping: Les Horizons Bleues (tel. 960 15 47), in Villeneuve. Bus #1 to "Villeneuve." From the bus stop, follow the lake to the left (5min.). Supreme lakeside location. Reception open 8am-10pm. 7SFr per person, 4.50-11SFr per tent, 3SFr per car. Free showers. 10% cheaper in winter. Open year-round.

FOOD

Montreux does not offer gastronomic adventure at reasonable rates—prices match the posh country-club atmosphere. If you must dine lakeside, try packing a picnic.

Babette's, Grand Rue 60 (tel. 963 77 96), down the stairs from the train station and to the left. Check out the buns at Bab's, which hovers somewhere between *pâtisserie* and very beige tea-room. Half-baguettes 5SFr; chocolate *crêpes* 6.30SFr— the sinful will add ice cream (2SFr) and suffer the damnation of added poundage; *crêpe vaudoise* 9.60SFr; *pain au chocolate* 1.90SFr.

La Locanda, ruelle du Trait 44 (tel. 963 29 33), a small street off of av. du Casino across from Migros. A hidden, dark-panelled, and romantic restaurant filled with regulars. A pleasant break from the people-watching by the lake. Large pizzas 12-19SFr; healthy portions of pasta from 11SFr; *gnocchi* (14.50-16SFr); and *risotto* (16-17SFr). Open Mon.-Sat. 11am-2pm and 5:30pm-midnight. Visa, MC, AmEx.

Caveau des Vignerons, rue Industrielle 30bis (tel. 963 25 70), at the corner of rue du Marché and rue Industrielle. Swiss dishes are served in this cave amid white-washed walls and candlelight. Cheese *fondue* 20SFr; *raclette* 5.50SFr portion, 25SFr entire meal. They even have the not-really-traditional chocolate *fondue* (11SFr). Open Mon.-Fri. 7am-midnight, Sat. 3:30pm-midnight. Closed the last week in July and the first two weeks in Aug. Visa, MC, AmEx.

The White Horse, 28 Grand Rue, opposite the covered market. Largely Anglophone crowd in this low-key, flag-draped pub. Un-Swiss food at un-Swiss prices. Sandwiches 4.50-6.50SFr; salads 5.50-7.50SFr; spaghetti 11SFr; fish and chips or chicken nuggets 12.50SFr; steak with fries and salad 18SFr. Beer 5.50SFr per pint. Pinball, darts, and füßball to keep you occupied. Open Mon.-Sat. 11am-1am (flexible), Sun. 3pm-midnight.

Restaurant Le Palais "Hoggar," quai du Casino 14 (tel. 963 12 71). Quirky blue-tiled decor and authentic Middle Eastern cuisine are an ideal backdrop for people-watching. *Harira*, a Moroccan soup, is served for 8SFr, and a chicken curry is 20.50SFr. Pick from 20 different dishes of ice cream. Open March-Nov. daily 11am-11pm.

Le Nevada, av. des Alpes 17bis. Central location near the train station. A pleasant restaurant bedecked in pink, serving up filling Italian fare. *Ravioli* or *tortellini* 13.50SFr, or try the more French option of an omelette and salad (10.50SFr). Open Mon.-Sat. 8:15am-7pm.

Markets

Migros, av. du Casino. Restaurant next door. Open Mon. 9am-7pm, Tues.-Wed. 8am-6:30pm, Thurs.-Fri. 8am-8pm, Sat. 7:30am-5pm.

Jelmoli, rue du Théâtre, next to the Migros. Open in summer Mon.-Fri. 8:30am-6:30pm, Thurs. 8:30am-8pm, Sat. 8am-5pm, Sun. 2-6pm. In winter closed Sun.

Co-op, Grand Rue 80. Open Mon.-Fri. 8am-12:15pm and 2-6:30pm, Sat. 8am-5pm.

Marché de Montreux, place du Marché. Outdoor market of fresh fruits, vegetables, meats, cheeses, breads, and pastries along both quai de la Rouvenaz and quai Jaccoud. Every Fri. 7am-3pm. Also look for the **flea market** at this site.

SIGHTS

Montreux's main attraction is the **Château de Chillon** (tel. 936 39 12), a 20-minute walk past the hostel. Built on an island, Chillon is a perfect 13th-century fortress with all the comforts of home: prison cells, torture chamber, weapons room, and latrines that sent the business spinning onto the rocks or unsuspecting marauders below. The *château* inspired narratives by Rousseau, Victor Hugo, and Alexandre Dumas, as well as Lord Byron's *The Prisoner of Chillon*, which tells the tale of a priest manacled to a pillar for four years. See for yourself the proof that Byron was an uncouth cad—his signature is scratched into a pillar in the dungeon where his poem was set. (Open July-Aug. daily 9am-6:15pm; April-June and Sept. daily 9am-5:45pm; Oct. daily 10am-4:45pm; Nov.-Feb. daily 10am-noon and 1:30-4pm; March daily 10am-noon and 1:30-4:45pm. 6.50SFr, students 5.50SFr, ages 6-16 3SFr. Self-guided visit with an explanatory pamphlet available in 13 languages (!) lets you ramble this large site alone.) The Montreux-Vevey **museum passport** covers free entry to nine museums including Chillon (15SFr). A lot less interesting than the castle, the **Musée du Vieux-Montreux,** rue de la Gare 40 (tel. 963 13 53), on the outskirts of the *vieille ville*, describes the history of Montreux through municipal bric-à-brac, with an emphasis on wood working and weights and measures (open Apr.-Oct. 10am-noon and 2-5pm. 6SFr, students and seniors 4SFr).

When the weather isn't too hazy, the best excursion is to climb the **Rochers-de-Nage** (2045m), which sometimes offers views to as far as Mont Blanc and the Matterhorn. An expensive cog railway chugs up Montreux's stately Alps (round-trip 50SFr, one-way 30.80SFr; with Swisspass 31.50SFr and 15.80SFr; with Eurail pass 28.30SFr and 15.40SFr.) You can purchase tickets at the station or the tourist office counter (open April-Oct. Mon.-Fri. 9am-noon and 1:30-5:30pm). To shave a few francs from the price, take the train to Caux (11.80SFr) and walk up from there. The round-trip, following the crest of the ridge, back to Montreux will take about 7 hours. Don't underestimate the power of the mountain.

THE MUSIC FESTIVALS

The Montreux **Jazz Festival,** a world-famous magnet for exceptional musical talent and one of the biggest parties in Europe, pushes everything aside from the first Friday in July through the next 15 days. The 1997 lineup will be made public at Christmas 1996; the 1996 headliners included Quincy Jones, Elvis Costello and Deep Purple, and past guests have included Wynton Marsalis, Etta James, Bobby McFerrin, James Brown, and the B.B. King Blues Band. Jazz legend Miles Davis's last international performance took place here in July 1991, a month before his death. After that, as Quincy Jones pointed out, "everything wants to be here, everyone wants to be at the peak of their creativity." If you can find a room but not tickets, show up anyway for the **Jazz Off,** 500 hours of free open-air concerts given by both young, new bands and celebrated, established musicians. Demand has rocketed festival ticket prices into the stratosphere: individual tickets range from 49 to 129SFr; a festival pass sells for 1300SFr. Standing room tickets range from 29 to 69SFr. Write well in advance for information and tickets from the tourist office. The booking desk (tel. 963 46 90) is open Mon.-Fri. 9am-noon and 1:30-6pm and non-stop during the festival. The **Postal Address** for ticket orders is rue du Théâtres 5. Tickets can also be obtained from Société de Banque Suisse ticket counters in major Swiss cities, from the Swiss National Tourist offices, 608 Fifth Ave., New York, NY 10020 (tel. (212) 757 59 44), or from Swiss Court, London W1V 8EE (tel. (0171) 734 19 21). From mid-March the jazz hotline in Montreux is active (tel. 983 82 82). Most events book out before July, some do so four months ahead.

From late August to early October, the **Montreux-Vevey Classical Music Festival** takes over. Philharmonics from a myriad of metropolises, from Moscow to Memphis, highlight this gathering. Tickets to concerts in Montreux as well as neighboring Vevey, Martigny, St. Maurice, and Chillon, range from 20 to 140SFr. Write to Festival de Musique, rue du Théâtre 5, Case Postale 162, CH-1820 Montreux 2, for information.

NIGHTLIFE

Montreux caters to all tastes, from those who like to high roll or boogie down. Nightlife centers around the polished atmosphere of the bar- and club-lined *quais.*

Casino de Montreux, rue du Théâtre 9 (tel. 962 83 83). From av. du Casino, turn on rue Igor Stravinsky toward the lake. Montreux's fun-focus has no entry fee, but finds other ways to munch your money. 200 slot machines (daily 5pm-3am; must be over 20); *boule,* a roulette variant (8:30pm-1am); **Western Saloon** country music club (Thurs.-Sat. 8pm-3am); **Le Cabaret** nightclub (Mon.-Sat. 10pm-4am); **Platinum,** an underground disco; a piano bar; billiards; and a pool (7SFr; 8:45am-2am). A serenade by the Singing Waiters at the restaurant can not be matched.

The passing of a giant

On July 8, 1991, at the Montreux Jazz Festival, the great jazz trumpeter, Miles Davis, played his last live performance. This was an historic concert, not only because it was the last before Davis's death, but also because it was the first time that Davis had returned to the style of playing with which he began his career. Miles Davis made many contributions to jazz, the last being his "fusion" of jazz and rock. Perhaps his most important contribution, however, was the creation, with Gil Evans, of "cool" jazz. In their pioneering collaboration, Davis and Evans broke away from the frenetic scale structure of be-bop improvization. Davis' smooth, modal improvisations, heard on such albums as *Kind of Blue* and over the rich orchestral settings of the Gil Evans Orchestra on *Sketches of Spain,* influenced a whole generation of artists, including John Coltrane and Bill Evans. Yet, while these and other artists expanded and developed modal jazz, Davis moved on and never looked back. As a result, he did not perform some of his most-loved works for over 20 years. That was until Quincy Jones stepped in. Jones had long wanted to do a concert with Davis and revive Davis' earlier material. Finally, Davis agreed, and the two performed together at Montreux, with the Gil Evans Orchestra (then under the direction of Evans's son, Miles) and the Charles Grundtz Concert Jazz Orchestra, playing songs that hadn't been performed live for a generation. Jones has said that he had never seen Davis as pleased and as connected with the audience in any other concert. Several weeks later, Davis fell ill. He died of pneumonia on September 28, 1991.

Café Rock, rue de l'Auberge 5 (tel. 963 88 88; fax 961 26 27), just up the stairs from the youth hostel. The youth hostel's own little Hard Rock—loud music, young crowd, billiard room, video games, darts and pinball. Beer 6SFr per pint; choose from bottles from 8 countries. They also have five bright white rooms in a quiet annex, which are for rent if the last bed at the hostel is taken. Reception open Mon. 4pm-midnight, Tues.-Thurs. 8:30am-midnight, Fri.-Sat. 8:30am-2am, Sun. 2pm-midnight. Single 50SFr, with shower 70SFr. Double 90SFr, with shower 120SFr. Visa, MC, AmEx.

Opus Café, rue du Marché 23 (tel. 963 28 58). Café combines comfortable atmosphere with a hip crowd defying all age barriers. A drum set, electric and bass guitars, a sax, and synthesizer rest in the corner available to anyone who wants to mix it up a bit. The Café occasionally promotes young Swiss groups. Beer on tap at 5.60SFr per pint; drink list has whiskies at 6-8SFr. Open Mon.-Sat. 5pm-4am.

Duke's, Grand Rue 97 (tel. 963 51 31), 50m away from Auditorium Stravinski. Enter through the class-warfare-inducing Royal Plaza Inter-Continental Hotel. As one of the venues of the Montreux Jazz Festival, this high-class establishment bursts at the seams for 2½ weeks in July. After performing, artists often arrive to hang out with the crowd. Celebrate with the 295SFr champagne, or stick to the impressive 6-7.50SFr range of beers. Sun.-Thurs. open until 1am, Fri.-Sat. until 3am, during Jazz Festival until 6am. Happy hour 6-8pm.

■ Near Montreux

VEVEY

While big sister Montreux has its five-star hotels, boutiques, and golden trumpets, little sister Vevey, just four miles from Montreux along Lac Léman, is famous for its powdered milk. Tour bus operators and grizzled backpackers, apparently uninterested in the lactic residues of the Nestlé corporation, have left this quiet town to its swans. This neglect is a pity, because although Vevey has occasional factories, the views from the rose-lined *quais* are even better than from Montreux. Need some proof? Walking tours will point out the homes of Charlie Chaplin, Jean-Jacques Rousseau, Victor Hugo, Fyodor Dostoyevsky, Le Corbusier, Henry James, and Graham Greene who all would agree. Vevey's charms were immortalized in many a Lost Generation novelist's exegeses on expatriate American decadence.

If Montreux's festivals are mainly audio, Vevey's are mainly video. An **International Comedy Film Festival,** dedicated to Charlie Chaplin, is held in the end of July and features official competition during the day along with more relaxed, open cinema every night at pl. Scanavia (tickets 13SFr). Hordes come out for a cartoon and pasta party that crowns the festival's last evening. Vevey also hosts the **International Festival of Photography and Multimedia** every two years (one month long, during June and July, next in 1998). And the kingpin of them all, the **Fête des Vignerons** (Vevey Wine-Growers Festival) graces Vevey with its presence five times each century. The last celebration, in 1977, lured nearly 200,000 spectators and 4000 participants; the next will be held in all its splendor from late July to mid-August 1999. Make hotel reservations in 1997! Two alternative ways of getting hold of the local grapes are to visit the Folklore Market (in pl. du Marché, mid-July to Aug. Sat. 9am-noon) or to take the **Winetrain,** which winds its way through 13km of villages and vineyards, in the Lavaux wine-growing area (hourly from Vevey station, round-trip up to 9.60SFr, Swisspass and Eurail pass valid). The tourist office has a list of tasting venues and a map with directions to the two wine centers, **Chexbres** and **Puidox.**

A series of small museums complement the town's festivals. The **Swiss Camera Museum,** ruelle des Anciens-Fossés 6 (tel. 921 94 60), just off Grand Place, covers three floors, one blue, one red, one yellow, with cameras from the early days of daguerreotypes through World War I spy cameras, to the present. (Open March-Oct. Tues.-Sun. 10:30am-noon and 2-5:30pm; Nov.-Feb. Tues.-Sun. 2-5:30pm. Admission 5SFr, students 4SFr.) A few minutes along the *quai* towards Montreux brings you to the **Alimentarium/Food Museum** (tel. 924 41 11), on the corner of rue du Léman and quai Perdonnet. The museum tells the story of food from its production in cows to its processing in the human body. Check out the curious blend of educational displays, food processing machinery, and Nestlé commercials. There is also a special exhibit on Chinese food. (Open April-Oct. Tues.-Sun. 10am-5pm, Nov.-March Tues.-Sun. 10:30am-noon and 2-5:30pm. Admission 5SFr, students and seniors 3SFr.) Further along the *quai,* the **Swiss Museum of Games** (tel. 944 40 50), housed in the ivy-clad, 13th-century Château de la Tour-de-Peilz, is much less educational and much more entertaining. Displays detail the history of games, with a particular emphasis on games with wooden bricks. Hands-on exhibits make for good, clean family fun (open Tues.-Sun. 2-6pm; 6SFr, students and seniors 3SFr). A Museum Passport (15SFr) grants free entrance to six museums in the area including those listed above and the **Château de Chillon.**

A budget hostel with 60 dorm beds, the **Auberge pour Jeunes et Familles,** will open at a prime site at Grand Place 5 in mid-1997 (25-35SFr per person; breakfast included). Call the tourist office (tel. 922 20 20) if you want to stay there. You could also look for a bed in one of the Vevey family homes that takes in travelers at around 35SFr per night, such as the **Pension Bürgle,** rue Louis Meyer 16, just off Grand Place (tel. 921 40 23; 36SFr per person including breakfast; dinner 12SFr, and be on time; Visa accepted), or ask for other options at the tourist office. For a little nourishment, check out the **produce and flea market** at the Grand Place (pl. du Marché) on Tuesday and Saturday mornings from 8:30am-noon. The ever-present Migros and Coop glower at one another across av. Paul Cérésole off Grand Place. Food is cheaper away from the lakefront. Next to the station, **Hotel de Famille,** rue des Communaux 20, has a *plat du jour* with dessert for 16SFr. Alternatively, kick it at **Les Temps Modernes,** rue des Deux Gares 6bis (tel. 922 34 39), an industrial factory turned café, record store, and dance studio that (although it still looks and smells like a factory) has become the cultural junction for artists, musicians, and photographers alike. Thursday and Saturday present jazz and contemporary rock concerts (free entry, drinks 1SFr more than usual). Behind the station, head under the underpass at the top of rue de la Clergère, turn left on rue des Deux Gares among the factories. (Salads 5-14SFr. *Plats du jour* 13SFr. Open Mon.-Thurs. 11am-midnight, Fri. 11am-2am, Sat. 5pm-2am.)

Three options are available to reach Vevey from Montreux: train (5min., every ½hr., 2.80SFr), bus #1 to "Vevey" (20min., every 10 min., 2.40SFr), cruise (25min., 5 daily, 6SFr). The full-fledged, ever-so-friendly **tourist office,** Grand Place 29 (tel. 922 20 20; fax 922 20 24) is located under the pillars of the building *La Grenette* at the top of the marketplace. From the station, cross the square (pl. de la Gare) and head down av. Paul Cérésole, where you will have Société de Banque Suisse on the left and a pharmacy on your right. (Tourist office open June 15 - Sept. 15 daily 8:30am-7pm; Sept.16 - June 14 Mon.-Fri. 8:30am-noon and 1:30-6pm, Sat. 8:30am-noon.) **Emergency:** tel. 117. **Postal code:** CH-1800. **Telephone code:** 021.

GSTAAD AND SAANEN

Gstaad is perhaps the most famous little village in the world. Lots of little Swiss villages have stacks of banknotes cozied up in their wooden châlets, but Gstaad became famous because it just couldn't stop. It has a polo field, but not a soccer field. You can buy a Rolex and hire a helicopter on the main street, but you can't do your laundry. Other villages have private schools; Gstaad has the world's most expensive, **Le Rosey** (King Leopold of Belgium made vacationing in Gstaad trendy by dropping in on his kids there). Other villages have fondue parties; Gstaad made the world's biggest fondue and invited 3000 guests. Its creamy-turreted **Gstaad Palace Hotel** set the standard for five-star accommodations when it was built shortly after World War I. The manager once boasted, "Every king is a client, and every client is a king." It was here that Louis Armstrong used to play background music for diners. Alas, the winnowing of world monarchies during the 20th century has forced it to open its doors to less majestic folk to stay in business, but it still manages to keep its full-time bridge tutors and an underwater masseuse well fed.

Apart from goggling at pink princesses on the *piste,* the superlative sports scene is the main reason to come to Gstaad. **White-water rafting** options start from 80SFr at Gstaad (Eurotrek; tel. (01) 462 02 03) and 99SFr at Saanen (Swissraft; tel. 744 50 80). Swissraft also goes **canyoning** (tel. 744 50 80; 80SFr, July-Sept.). Try **ballooning** (Hans Büker; tel. (029) 744 54 85), or **paragliding** (tel. 744 20 05; a day pass at the paragliding school is 31SFr) for a ride into the wide, blue yonder. Those who like something more substantial under their seat can go **horsetreking** (28SFr, tel. 744 24 60). To round out your options, there are 150 kilometers of hardcore **mountain bike trails,** and of course covered tennis courts, saunas, and swimming pools on every corner. For the public pool, hang right on the main road out of the station, and take the first right after the river (tel. 744 44 16; 9SFr, with visitor's card 8SFr; open daily 10am-7pm or later). Armchair sportsmen around in July can waddle to the annual **Swiss Open Tennis Tournament** which attracts all the players who decided to pass up Wimbledon and over 40,000 spectators who each made a similar decision. Call 744 82 82, or fax 744 61 71 for tickets (20-95SFr). In winter, the slopes certainly dominate. A **Gstaad Super Ski Pass** (tel. 882 82; fax 882 60) gives you access to 250km of runs and 69 lifts (day pass 46SFr, 4 day pass 233SFr; includes local transportation). Consult the tourist office for more detailed information.

For a rugged hike with a panorama of Gstaad and the nearby hills, climb up the **Giferspitz horseshoe.** Turn right on the main road from Gstaad station, and head left just before the river on the main road. Take the second big road on the right over the river (with signs to "Bissen;" the turn is 1km from Gstaad). Follow the yellow *Wanderweg* signs for Wasserngrat and power up the steep hill flank to the top cable car station (1936m). For even more heights, the very fit and adventurous (with time on their hands) can continue up to the **Lauenehorn** (2477m) and, after a rocky scramble, further to the **Giferspitz** (2541m), Gstaad's tallest peak. The path circles down to Bissen again, but avoid limping into Gstaad by catching a brief bus ride (1800m of ascent; perfect weather only; allow one whole day; map #5009).

Though hiking offers some grand adventures, Gstaad's sporting reputation really rests on its skiing. In high season there are 250km of runs and 69 lifts. Something is usually open mid-December to the end of April. Truly expert skiers will find little to challenge them but middling ones will be spoiled. The Ski Gstaad pass (tel. 748 82 82; fax 748 82 60) is 50SFr for one day on all sectors, slightly cheaper for fewer sectors. A week of skiing will come to 263SFr. Heliskiing, snowboarding, curling, and skating are also readily available.

There are no hotels in Gstaad with fewer than three stars. Gulp. In the lowest month, May, you *might* squeeze a room from Sporthotel Victoria (tel. 744 14 31) or Sporthotel Rüttie (tel. 744 29 21); 60SFr if you twinkle at them. Try booking a suite at the Gstaad Palace. Just kidding; that will run you a mere 2100SFr. The **Jugendherberge** (tel. (033) 744 13 43), 2mi. away in Saanen, is a godsend. From Gstaad station, take the train (3min., hourly, 2.40SFr), or bus (10min., hourly, 2.40SFr) from Gstaad. One can also walk, turning left on Gstaad's main street. From Saanen station, go ahead past the post office, turn right on the main street, and go straight on at the crossroads following the "Spital" signs (40min.). This slightly chilly rural hostel has an exceptionally warm welcome and is full of family flavor—everyone chips in to wash the dishes. The hostel offers doubles, triples, and quads for couples and families, and rooms with 6 or 8 beds for individuals. (Reception open 7:30am-9am and 5pm-10pm. Curfew 11pm. 25.30SFr first night, 22.80SFr thereafter; add 8SFr per person for doubles. Children ages 2-6 half price; children under 2 stay free. Breakfast and showers included. 3-course dinner 11SFr. Phone ahead in winter.) Sleep under the stars at **Camping Bellerive** (tel. 744 63 30) between Gstaad and Saanen. (Arrive any time; check-in 9-10am and 6-7pm. 8.80SFr, tent 5.30SFr.) Budget diners should take advantage of the **Co-op** supermarket and restaurant, left on the main street from the train station. (Restaurant open Mon.-Fri. 7:30am-6:30pm, Sat. 7:30am-5pm. Supermarket Mon.-Fri. 8am-12:15pm and 1:30-6:30pm, Sat. 8am-4pm.) Slide into the soft leather chairs and have a burger and fries (9.40SFr) at **Richi's Pub** (tel. 744 57 87) on the main street to the right of the station, just after the church (open daily noon-12:30am).

Gstaad's user-friendly **tourist office** (tel. 748 81 81) is on the main road to the right of the train station, just past the railway bridge (open Mon.-Fri. 8:30am-noon and 2-6:30pm, Sat. 9am-noon; July-Aug. 9am-4pm). Saanen's main street also has a tourist office (same hours). The train station in Gstaad has 5SFr and 3SFr **lockers** plus **bike rental, currency exchange,** and a **ski rack.** Try 744 80 80 for **taxis.** By **train,** get to Gstaad from either **Montreux** (1½hr., hourly, 19.40SFr, round-trip 34SFr), or **Interlaken** (2hr., hourly, 21SFr, change trains at Zweisimmen). Catch a **bus** to **Les Diablerets** (50min., 11.40SFr). Gstaad's **post office** is next to the train station (open Mon.-Fri. 7:45am-noon and 1:45-6pm, Sat. 8:30-11am). **Emergency:** tel. 117. **Postal code:** CH-3780. **Telephone code:** 033.

AIGLE AND BEX

Far away from flashbulbs and Hollywood heat, Aigle dozes in the gentle Alpine sun, snuggled up in a green blanket of terraced vines. It's so drowsy that the Chablais wine-growers have even begun to encroach on the town's center, knocking down stone steps to pull the blanket of grapes even tighter to the city's chin. But Aigle (yawn) can't help it. Its south-facing slopes are perfect for grapes, and the narrow strip of the Rhône valley centered on Aigle and stretching from Vevey in the east to Sierre in the west produces nearly all of Switzerland's wine. Four-fifths of the harvest makes full-bodied fruity whites called Fendant and Dorin, but Aigle is also home to most of the domains bottling the less common Swiss reds. The best reason to stop by is the 15th-century grape-garlanded **Château d'Aigle,** which houses the **Musée de la Vigne et du Vin** (tel. 466 21 30). From the station, head down rue de la Gare opposite you, and pass the post office. Just beyond the center of town, there is a large crossroads (pl. du Marché); bear right on av. du Cloître immediately in front of the *imprimerie* (printing shop). With a day's notice groups of 10 or more can taste three Château wines and receive a little souvenir glass as part of their visit (12.50SFr per person. Open April-Oct. Tues.-Sun. 10am-12:30pm and 2-6pm; July and Aug. daily 10am-6pm; 6SFr, students 3SFr.)

If you have a little time before the next train leaves, stroll past the medieval façades of **rue du Bourg** and the **rue de Jérusalem.** If you get hungry, **Restaurant Pizzeria des Alpes,** rue du Bourg 29 (tel. 466 25 18), serves up pizzas (9.50-15.50SFr), but the specializes in *paella,* and horse steaks. The shaded green tables of the restaurant look out on the quiet pedestrian main street and the vine-scored hillsides. (Open Mon.-Fri. 7:30am-11:30pm, Sat.-Sun. 9am-11:30pm; closed Wed. in Sept.-May.) More affordably, there is a **Migros** over the tracks from the station. (Open Mon. 9am-6:30pm, Tues.-Thurs. 8am-6:30pm, Fri. 8am-7:45pm, Sat. 7:30am-5pm.) A vast **Co-op** is visible down the first left as you walk perpendicular to the station along rue de la Gare towards the Château. (Open Mon. 9am-12:15pm and 1:30-6:30pm, Tues.-Fri. 7:45am-12:15pm and 1:30-6:30pm, Sat. 7:45am-5pm.)

Aigle is on the high speed train line from **Montreux** (10min., 2 per hour, 4.80SFr) and **Lausanne** (½hr., 2 per hour, 12.20SFr) that runs along the Rhône valley to **Brig** and **Sion** (35min., 2 per hour, 16.60SFr). It also stops at **Martigny** (15min., 2 per hour, 9SFr). Local trains leave from the square in front of the station for **Leysin** (35min., hourly, 9.60SFr) and **Les Diablerets** (1hr., hourly, 60SFr). The station has **currency exchange** with credit card advances and Western Union transfers, small **lockers** (2SFr) and **bike rental** (21SFr per day). There is an appropriately small and sleepy **tourist office**, 4 rue de la Gare (tel. 466 12 12), on the way to the Château. Ask here about wine tasting at one of the local *caves*. (Open Mon.-Fri. 8am-noon and 1:30-5:30pm). **Emergency:** tel. 117. **Postal code:** CH-1860. **Telephone code:** 024.

One stop and 3.60SFr down the line in **Bex** (pronounced "bay") you can send yourself down the huge **salt mine,** whose mazy tentacles reach 50km under the hillsides. Already 313 yrs. old, the mine still produces 150 tons a year, though the rugged axe-wielding miners of yore have been replaced by little, wimpy squirts of warm water that leach the salt out. The 2½hr. **tour** (tel. (024) 463 24 62; fax 463 24 82) by train and foot through the mineworkings is both spooky and fascinating. From Bex station, follow the brown signs, and be prepared for a 40min. hike. (Open April to mid-Nov. Tours at 10am, 2pm, and 3pm. 15SFr, children 9SFr. Advanced notice is required. Fully wheelchair accessible.)

LEYSIN

Older residents and 19th-century guesthouses still provide the link to Leysin's golden age when it gave intensive "sun therapy" to patients convalescing from tuberculosis. The treatment apparently had some affect—Thomas Malthus's 1798 *Essay on the Principles of Population* has six pages musing on the longevity of Leysin's citizens. The town's sunny terrace, high above Aigle, still watches over the Rhône valley and Dents du Midi as it did in more curative days, though its vacation-inspired, wicker-chaired gentility is occasionally shattered by the lively clutch of American colleges, climbing groups and itinerant rock festivals.

The two sports centers in the village offer their amenities at rather budget un-friendly rates. The pools and Turkish bath, however, in the newer of the two, the **New Sporting Club** (tel. 494 29 21), is only 5SFr and 3SFr with a Leysin holiday card. (Open 9am-9pm but slightly shorter hours for the pools.) There is also **ice skating** at the **Centre des Sports** (tel. 494 13 64) further down the hill near the campsite (open 8am-10pm). The best **mini-golf** in Switzerland provides putt-putt personalities the chance to play. It is on the right as you leave Feyday station. (Open July to mid-Sept. 10am-noon and 2-7pm. 6.50SFr, children 4.50SFr; with visitor's card 3.50SFr, 2.50SFr.) **Mountain bikes** can be rented from Hefti Sports (tel. 494 16 77), 2 minutes from the New Sporting Club on pl. du Marché (35SFr per day). A cable car also bobs up to the nearby summit of Berneuse daily from the New Sporting Club. (June-Oct. and mid-Dec. to mid-April. One-way 13.50SFr, round-trip 18SFr, with visitor's card 9.50SFr, 13SFr. Visa, MC, AmEx.) Another goes to Mayen beneath the highest local top, the craggy **Tour d'Aï** (2331m; same dates and prices). The cable cars can be used for a hike around the two mountain lakes, the **Lac d'Aï** and the **Lac de Mayen,** or a scramble up the two knobbly "towers," the **Tours de Mayen** and the **Tour d'Aï.** The tourist office has maps. To save some money or to make it a full day's outing, you can walk up from Leysin, heading up the steps by the Feydey post office. Go left at the top, and then take, the route d'Aï, the second road on the right (3hr.; 1000m of ascent to the Tour d'Aï). As you go up, the deep misty cleft of the Rhône valley far below makes the jagged Dents du Midi and Mont-Blanc massif beyond seem suspended in space.

Paragliding is offered for those seeking to make their trip slightly more daring. For reservations, call 494 12 02 from 9am-1pm or 494 26 02 in the evening. (100SFr to jump with instructor, 160SFr per day for lessons including flights; all include insurance.) The tourist office arranges 2- and 7-day hiking, paragliding, rock-climbing, and mountain biking packages in the summer (including a 2- to 7-day trek through the Alps on a mule), or 2- and 7-day ski packages in the winter. A 2-day package with Leysin ski passes, half-board at a hotel, and Sporting Club membership starts at 172-187SFr. For all the rookies wanting to try a hand (or foot) at something new, the **Swiss Ski School** (tel. 494 12 02) and **Mountain Climbing School** (tel. 494 18 46) offer lessons. Six half-days of group ski lessons are 130SFr; fees for lessons vary with terrain and ability.

High season in Leysin is unquestionably winter, when you should try to book hotels in advance. Ski pass rates for 1997 will be 38SFr per day for adults, 23SFr for children, and 212SFr for a week (128SFR for children). Prices are 10% lower if you stay in Leysin. In mid-February you can combine your own skiing with gawking at the pros during the **European Snowboarding Championships** held in Leysin every year. The village really spins throughout this week; arrange hotels well in advance.

The friendly **tourist office** (tel. 494 29 21; fax 494 13 64) is in the New Sporting Club just down from pl. du Marché. Get off the train at Leysin-Versmont, and turn right (open Mon.-Fri. 8am-9pm, Sat.-Sun. 9am-9pm). They organize a weekly program of high-energy activities and can advise on accommodations, hikes, and transport. The Leysin Festival at the end of Aug. is a spotty affair—some years they pull stars like Bob Dylan, other years they offer more techno than talent. (Around 45SFr per night. Call 494 29 for details, or surf http://www.hugo.ch.) On a slow night, catch an American flick at the **Cinéma Le Regency,** in the Classic Hotel (open Aug. to mid-June; 13SFr, students 11SFr).

Though Leysin once made a killing on glandular swelling, its old-time health clinics now cater to the wealthy octogenarian set. Those wanting to cough up less have limited options since there is no youth hostel in town. **Club Vagabond,** rte. des Quatre Chalets (tel. 494 13 21; fax 494 13 22), however, more than picks up the slack. Get off the train at Leysin-Feydey, turn left past the post office, and climb the tiny flight of stairs. At the top, turn left, and, when the road forks, take the lower, left hand fork to the Vag. It is slightly past its glory days, but still revered among Leysin's under 30 English speakers for its soap and trash bag parties, live music, Sun. evening barbecues (in summer at 6pm; bring your own meat; 5SFr for bread and salad buffet), and even occasional art exhibitions. Recently renovated, the floors have new carpeting, the walls fresh paint, and the bunk beds firm mattresses. The free-entrance discotheque in the cellar, "The Ice Cave," has, like Gloria Gaynor, survived with its 70s style still intact. Leather armchairs and an English library look out across Leysin's slopes, and the late-night bar serves beer (5SFr; during happy hour 5-7:30pm 4SFr). As "the home of mountain sports," Club Vagabond even offers its own rock climbing and mountain biking packages. (Reception open Tues.-Sun. 8am-5pm; after these hours head to the bar which is open til 3am. 25SFr. Singles 35SFr. Doubles 30SFr. Sheets and towels 6SFr. Breakfast 6SFr.) The cheapest alternative is **Hotel Bel Air,** rue du Commerce, next to the sports center and cable cars (tel. 494 13 39; fax 494 34 21). From Leysin-Feyday turn left, and head in the same direction at the junction down the long hill of rue du Commerce. Many of the rooms have bunks, and its brick terrace overlooks the mountains. (35SFr. Under 12 25SFr. Breakfast included. Evening menu 13SFr. Visa, MC, AmEx.) The **Hotel de la Paix,** av. Rollier (tel./fax 494 13 75), is located opposite the train stop "Versmont" and offers old fashioned rooms with pine walls and fading prints of *belle epoque* Leysin. Red and white striped deck chairs swallow up the older clients. (Reception open daily 8am-9pm. Singles 44-68SFr. Doubles 96-116SFr. Triples with shower 135-150SFr. Breakfast included. Half pension 22SFr, full 36SFr. 10% discount for students.) The **Camping Semiramis** (tel. 494 11 48; fax 494 26 15) is a four-star site beside the Centre des Sports. From Leysin-Village station, walk left on rue de

Village, and turn right onto rte. du Suchet just past the post office (6.50SFr, tent 4.30SFr).

A **Co-op** supermarket is just off the big bend in rue Favez, below pl. Marché and the New Sporting Club (open Mon.-Fri. 8am-12:15pm and 2-6:30pm, Sat. 8am-6pm). Italian pizza and pasta staples receive a good rendition at **La Lorraine** (tel. 494 15 72) and **San Marco** (tel. 494 18 52) around pl. du Marché. Slightly cheaper deals, though, can be found at **Forest Hill** (tel. 494 19 90), above the New Sporting Club, which heaps your plate with spaghetti and salad (10-15SFr) on a rooftop terrace (open daily noon-1pm and 6-10pm). **La Calèche** (tel. 494 24 26), just past the New Sporting Club towards the cable car station, has a long list of main courses (10SFr), plus pork and chicken dishes (12-13SFr).

The only way to reach Leysin by transport is the **cog railway** from Aigle, which leisurely chugs passengers to the top of the steep climb in ½hr. (hourly, 6am-10pm; free with Swisspass but not Eurail). There are four stops, Leysin-Village (7.80SFr), Versmont, Feydey (9SFr), and Grand-Hôtel (9.60SFr). **Ambulance:** tel. 494 27 37. **Police:** tel. 494 25 41. **Emergency:** tel. 117. There are two **post offices**, one next to Feydey station (tel. 494 11 05) and the other down the hill in Leysin-Village on rue du Village (tel. 494 12 05; both open Mon.-Fri. 8am-noon and 2-6pm, Sat. 8-11am). **Postal code:** CH-1854. **Telephone code:** 025.

LES DIABLERETS

It can be pink, latex, and play fanfares at 150 decibels, but if you can't wax it and strap it to your feet it won't even get a surreptitious sideways glance in Les Diablerets. Virtually unknown abroad, the Swiss pile from Geneva and Bern to this unglittery resort every weekend for their nearest summer skiing. Though there may only be five lifts open on Diablerets' glacier in July and August, it's the real thing, and the snow is 100% guaranteed. Come winter, the town is an intimate alternative to the snooty local rivals Gstaad, Crans-Montana, and Verbier. Snowboarders will appreciate the equal status they get here with their two-planked comrades, and hikers can potter peacefully on the surprisingly varied terrain covered by trails.

The summer skiing cable car leaves from the **Col du Pillon** above the village (day pass 49SFr, children 30SFr). A winter day pass includes buses (37SFr, students and children 23SFr). For multiple day excursions you must buy a pass for the whole Diablerets-Villars region (6 days 210SFr, students 178SFr, children 126SFr). There are also special deals for groups, families, and seniors. In the summer you can rent skis, boards, and boot at the top (25SFr). In winter you must rent skis in the village. **Jacky Sports** (tel. 492 32 18; fax 492 31 64), opposite the tourist office, rents equipment in the Swiss Rent-a-Sport system. (Skis 28SFr per day; 6 days 105SFr. Snowboard 38SFr, 130SFr. Ski boots 15SFr, 52SFr. Open daily 8:30am-12:30pm and 2-6:30pm. Visa, MC.) The **ski/snowboard school** (tel. 492 20 02; fax 492 23 48) on the far side of the river offers very competitive prices (6 days of groups lessons 125SFr, children 117SFr). If all this seems confusing, don't panic because you may do better anyway by getting a package. The **Swiss Village Club,** booked through the tourist office, offers half-board in hotels, skipasses, a fondue evening, tobogganing, curling, and skating (3 days and 4 nights 336SFr, 6 days and 7 nights 593SFr).

Other sports are a lot easier to arrange. Jacky Sports rents **mountain bikes** for 35SFr per day. A recommended circuit, also possible on foot, leaves the village from the tourist office. Head around the hairpin turn at the junction with the Col du Pillon road, go straight over, and climb upwards to La Ville where you will have a long view of the Diablerets glacier spilling over the edge high above the village. Turn right along the valley wall to Métraille and La Crua, then begin a long descent to the crag-cradled Lac Retaud and Col du Pillon before free-wheeling back to Les Diablerets. (Full day, with good weather.) If the hike above doesn't tempt, head deeper into the mountains by turning right over the river at the pharmacy, and then right again so that you are facing the **Sommet des Diablerets** (3210m) and the glacier. The valley sides close in as you continue the level riverside walk, depositing you onto the stage of a rugged 200m-high amphitheater at **Creux de Champ** (1320m, 160m ascent., 1hr., very easy).

The path starts to climb steeply up the sides to the refuge at 2280m (1110m, 3hr. above Les Diablerets). The agile can then push on up the scrambly new track (ladders) to **Sex Rouge** (2971m), the cable car terminus on the glacier, which affords an unforgettable 360° Alpine summit panorama (full day hike, high summer and perfect weather only). Once-in-a-lifetime thrills have their outlets too. **Mountain Evasion** (tel./fax 492 32 32) is anything but; they organize **canyoning** (70-120SFr) and **glacier bivouacs** (140SFr). **Paragliding** (60-150SFr) and more canyoning (80SFr) are run by **Centre Paradventure** under Locanda Livia (open daily 9-9:30am and 5:30-6:30pm or call (077) 22 25 82 anytime).

Only two public transport services connect Les Diablerets. The hourly **train** to **Aigle** takes 50min. (9.60SFr). The **post bus** over the mountains to **Gstaad** (11.40SFr) via the Col du Pillon leaves roughly 7 times per day depending on the season. In summer this bus is the only way to reach the Diablerets glacier cable cars at the Col. The first bus goes at 9:30am and the last returns at 4:20pm, so plan accordingly, or prepare yourself for a 45-minute walk.

The helpful but busy **tourist office,** rue de la Gare (tel. 492 33 58; fax 492 23 48), basks in its omniscience 1 min. from the train station. It also co-ordinates an impressive list of weekly activities including, in summer, a free folk music on Fri. in the station square and "sunrise with ibexes" expeditions (35SFr) at the crack of dawn on Fridays. (Open July-August Mon.-Sat. 8am-noon and 2-6pm, Sun. 9am-noon and 3-6pm; mid-Dec. to mid-April Mon.-Sat. 8:30am-12:30pm and 2-6pm, Sun. 9am-noon and 3-6pm; "off season" Mon.-Fri. 8am-noon and 2-6pm, Sat.-Sun. 9am-noon.) The **pharmacy** is just before the bend in the road. (Open Mon.-Sat. 8am-12:30pm and 3-6:30pm, Sun. 10am-noon and 5-6pm, but call 492 32 83 in an emergency.) **Ambulance:** tel. 494 37 27. **Police:** tel. 492 24 88. A right turn out of the station brings you to the **post office** (open Mon.-Fri. 8am-noon and 2:30-6pm, Sat. 7:45-10:45am). **Postal code:** CH-1865. **Telephone code:** 024.

The two cheapest accommodation deals are unfortunately on the outskirts of town. **Les Diablotins,** route du Pillon (tel. 492 36 33; fax 492 23 55) is a big modern block popular with young snowboarding groups. From the station, turn right, bend around the hairpin at the pharmacy, and at the top of the hill, turn right along rte. Pillon. The 20-minute walk can be avoided by calling from the station, they'll send a mini-bus. The 2- to 4-bed rooms are in good shape; all have private sinks and most have balconies. (Reception open 8am-8pm. 31SFr, after 4 days 28SFr; winter 40SFr, 36SFr. Breakfast included. Evening *menu* 15SFr. Snowboards 28SFr per day, 6 days 112SFr. Ski boots 24SFr per day, 6 days 101SFr. Reserve ahead in winter. Visa, MC, AmEx.) **Hotel Mon Séjour** (tel. 492 30 13) is in the nearby hamlet of Vers-l'Eglise. Take the train one stop, wander up the hill past the post office and church, and turn right over the river to get to this family-run chalet with a restaurant near the river. Pack into the intimate dorm (30SFr per night) or the less cramped room (39SFr; reservations preferred). The hotel is immediately above **Camping La Murée** (tel. 492 21 99), an attractive, flat site also next to the river (6.50SFr, tent 9SFr).

Hikers, bikers, and snowboarders usually load up packed lunches from one of the three supermarkets. Near the pharmacy and tourist office, and to the right of the train station, sits the **Grand Bazaar des Alpes** (open Mon.-Sat. 7:30am-6:30pm, Sun. 8am-noon). The **Co-op** awaits on rue de la Gare, left of the station (open Mon.-Fri. 8am-12:15pm and 2:15-6:30pm, Sat. 8am-6pm). The terrace of **Le Muguet** (tel. 492 26 42), opposite the tourist office, puts the glacier center stage. Try a cheese and bacon galette (8SFr) or a dessert crêpe (4.50-9.50SFr) with *cidre* (2.50SFr). Alternatively, cross the channel for their sandwiches (7SFr) and the all-important pot of Darjeeling or Earl Grey tea. Just around the big bend by the pharmacy, **Locanda Livia** (tel. 492 32 80) is an unbuttoned, family Italian restaurant serving pasta (11-18SFr) See if you can navigate your way through the crustacean creation—pasta drowning in mussels, scampi, and prawns. Pizza is served as well (12-18SFr; open Thurs.-Tues. 11:30am-2pm and 6-10pm).

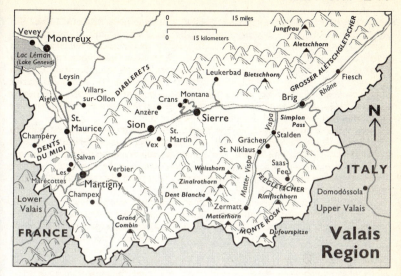

VALAIS (WALLIS)

The territory bounded by Canton Valais sits snugly in the catchment area of the Rhône valley, with most of its settlements lying in the deep wide glacier cleft shaved by the river. In the west, Martigny and Sion are French-speaking; upriver in Brig, Swiss-German dominates. On the right bank rise the southern slopes of the Berner Oberland peaks; on the left bank jut the Valais Alps, with the mighty Matterhorn, along the Italian border. Stereotypically, the Wallisers are supposed to be dour folk with independent minds. Truthfully, they have a vibrant and riotous community life still untouched by the tourism that has engulfed the high mountain villages.

■ Martigny

Martigny is a small town with a big town feel; a busy, concrete, aluminum-processing break from all those creaky wooden chalets. As the gateway for the St. Bernard pass, the town has always had special strategic significance for emperors wishing to control any crawl space between Switzerland and Italy. You can visit unearthed parts of the fort built by the Roman emperor Claudius, the first town in the Valais, and the medieval castle that replaced it. Also of note is a 20th-century addition, the Fondation Gianadda, a leading center for modern art and classical music.

Orientation and Practical Information Frequent trains run both west to **Lausanne** (1hr., every ½hr., 21SFr); **Montreux** (½hr., every ½hr., 13.20SFr); **Aigle** (9SFr); and east to **Sion** (15min., every ½hr., 8.40SFr). Two tiny private lines leave for Orsières, where you can change for **Aosta** in Italy via the Great St. Bernard Pass (30SFr) and for **Châtelard** where you can change for **Chamonix** in France (1hr., 40min., hourly, 28SFr; call 722 20 61 for details). The **train station** provides all of the usual services: **currency exchange, lockers** (3-5SFr), **luggage storage** (5SFr), **bike rental** (21SFr per day), and two **telephones** (services open 5:45am-8:45pm). Martigny's **tourist office**, pl. Centrale 9 (tel. 721 22 20; fax 721 22 24), is straight down av. de la Gare at the far corner of pl. Centrale. (Open July-Aug. Mon.-Fri. 9am-6pm, Sat. 9am-noon and 2-6pm, Sun. 10am-noon and 4-6pm; Sept.-June Mon.-Fri. 9am-noon and 1:30-6pm, Sat. 9am-noon.) The **hospital** (tel. 722 53 01) has a switchboard that can tell you the late night doctor and pharmacy. **Ambulance:** tel. 722 01 76. **Police:** tel. 722 01 76. The large **post office** (tel. 722 26 72), ave de la Gare 32, sits between the station and the tourist office with a phone and a public fax awaiting your next P.R. coup. (Open Mon.-Fri. 7:30am-noon and 1:30-6:30pm, Sat. 7:30-11am.) **Postal code:** CH-1920. **Telephone code:** 026.

Accommodations and Food Travelers stopping over in Martigny are mostly business types, so the budget pickings are meager. Commuting from the recently built **Auberge de Jeunesse** around the corner from the train station in **Sion** is an excellent idea, especially if you have a rail pass (see listing under Sion, p. 99). Otherwise, try the **Hôtel du Stand,** ave du Grand-St-Bernard 41 (tel. 722 15 06; fax 722 95 06), straight past the tourist office, near the **Fondation Gianadda.** This unassuming family hotel comes highly recommended by Swiss regulars. The rooms are spacious and very clean, despite the hotel's unprepossessing cream concrete exterior and the deep-pile puce carpet on the lobby walls. The restaurant downstairs has a *plat du jour* (16SFr) and three course *menus* (22SFr). (Reception open daily 7am-midnight. Singles with shower 65SFr. Doubles with shower 94SFr. Triples with shower 125SFr. Breakfast and parking included. Sauna 5SFr. Visa, MC.) Further out on the same road, the **Auberge de la Poste,** av. du Grand St. Bernard 81 (tel. 722 25 17), has a tree shaded outdoor terrace on a busy crossing and a restaurant serving tasty dishes. (Singles 37SFr. Doubles 60SFr. Visa, MC, AmEx.) **Camping Les Neuvilles,** rue du Levant 68 (tel. 722 45 44), packs its shaded plot with motorhomes. (Reception open Mon.-Sat. 8am-noon and 2-9pm, Sun. 3-9pm. 5.30SFr, high season 6.60SFr, children ages 6-16 half price. Shower included.) From the station head straight on av. de la Gare, take the second left on ave des Neuvilles, and go right onto rue du Levant after the soccer field.

Cafés crowd Martigny's tree-lined Place Centrale, some with *menus* in the 15-20SFr range. For cheaper fare, **Lords' Sandwiches,** ave du Grand St. Bernard 15 (tel. 723 35 98), serves 36 sorts of sandwiches (4-11SFr) including a bacon burger with fries, and the Zeus, an overflowing roast beef sandwich—hey, easy on the ambrosia (open daily 7am-midnight). **Le Rustique,** av. de la Gare 44 (tel. 722 88 33), has crispy savory crêpes (9-13SFr) and sweet crêpes (4.50-9.50SFr), which can be washed down with a mug of cider (3.50SFr; open daily 11:30am-10:30pm). For straightforward Italian food, locals recommend **Le Grotto,** rue du Rhône 3 (tel. 722 02 46), just off pl. Centrale on the left as you walk towards the station (open 8:30am-midnight). The immense **Migros** supermarket at pl. du Manoir 5, just off pl. Centrale, has 18 different boutiques and moving sidewalks to aid your ambulation between them (open Mon.-Thurs. 8:15am-6:30pm, Fri. 8:15am-8pm, Sat. 8am-5pm). Stroll down av. de la Gare on Thursday mornings to buy everything from bread and cheese to t-shirts at the **public market** (7:30am-noon).

Sights and Festivals Martigny's most engaging attraction is the **Fondation Pierre Gianadda** on rue du Forum (tel. 722 39 78; fax 722 52 85). Local engineer Léonard Gianadda discovered the vestiges of a Gallo-Roman temple here in 1976, and, when his brother died in a plane crash two months later, he set up a foundation to show ancient artifacts and modern art together. The "landing-pod" gallery attractively displays classical works like the Octoduran bronzes discovered in Martigny. Around the central courtyard hang blockbuster international traveling exhibitions, with Picasso, Goya, Chagall, and Braque recent features. In 1997, they will warm up with Raoul Dufy (daily 10am-6pm, until June 1) before starting in on a major Joan Miró retrospective (starts June 7, daily 9am-7pm). Descend the stairs to the **Automobile Museum** to scan more than 50 vintage cars—a Rolls Royce Silver Ghost, Bugattis, and gleaming early Peugots—built between 1897 and 1939, most in working condition and all unique. The surrounding garden successfully blends unearthed Roman remains with modern sculptures, including some excellent ones by Brancusi, Moore, Miró, and Rodin. (Fondation open July-Sept. daily 9am-7pm; Oct.-Feb. 10am-noon and

1:30-6pm; March-June 10am-6pm. Both museums 12SFr, students 5SFr, family ticket 25SFr.)

Martigny also has a handful of ruins that are worth a short ramble. Most of the Roman settlement is rather uninformatively uncovered, but the grassy 4th-century **Amphithéâtre Romain** is well worth the short detour over the railway tracks from the Fondation Gianadda gardens (follow the brown signs; free). Re-opened after two decades of excavation work in 1991, it is the spectacular setting for the final contest of the Valais **cow fighting** season at the start of October when it can seat 5000 spectators. Further out from the center the **Semblanet Mill** (tel. 722 51 98) has had its four water wheels, 18th-century threshers, and giant millstones restored to working condition, Follow av. du Grand St. Bernard (open Tues.-Sun. 10am-10pm. 5SFr, children 2SFr).

Le Château de la Bâtiaz, the ruins of a 13th-century castle that once belonged to the bishops of Sion, crouches on a hill overlooking Martigny. Climb the massive stone tower extending over an outcrop of bare rock for a bird's-eye perspective of the flat Rhône floodplain. From the station, head along av. de la Gare, and turn right at pl. Centrale along rue Marc-Morand (open mid-July to mid-Aug. daily 10am-6pm; free). Two other noteworthy buildings are the 17th-century **Grand Maison,** rue Marc Morand 7, near pl. Centrale, which is now an apartment building, but was once a hostel-stop for 18th- and 19th-century literati on their grand tours. Rousseau (1754), Goethe (1779), Stendhal (1800), Byron (1816), and Michelet (1830) all rested their weary heads here. Equally elegant, **Maison Supersaxo,** rue des Alpes 1, behind the tourist office, is the oldest building in Martigny (1440). It was here that Valais bigwig Georges Supersaxo schemed for 6 months about how he would seize the Château Bâtiaz. His siege in 1518 ended in a ruinous fire after which the castle's only residents were an old woman and her three goats. The tourist office runs guided tours of Martigny at 10am and 2pm in July and August. They are the same price as the Fondation Gianadda and include entry to it.

Each year during the first week of October the town hosts the **Foire du Valais,** the regional fair of the Valais canton. Local businesses as well as farmers offer their best, from shoes to marble sculptures. (October 3-12, 10am-9pm. 8SFr, children 4SFr.) The final Sun. always has all-day cow-fighting at the amphitheater and is a must-see if you are in southern Switzerland. The **Foire du Lard** (Bacon Fair) has overtaken the Place Centrale every first Mon. in December since the Middle Ages. Traditionally, Valais mountain folk descended on Martigny to stock up on pork products for the winter, but now the festival has expanded to a large open-air market, though the theme is still "pig." Martigny also sponsors film, theatre, and music festivals throughout the year, notably the **International Folklore Festival** every two years and the annual **Tibor Varga Classical Music Season** which brings big league European orchestras and performers like Alfred Brendel, Vladmir Ashkenazy, and Yehudi Menudia to town every July and Aug. Tickets are available through the Fondation Gianadda (20-80SFr).

For the properly shod, the mountains to the south offer great hiking, but public transportation is awkward. The **Valais Walkers Association** publishes an excellent guide called simply *Randonnées,* available free from the tourist offices. But, unless you have a car, also pick up *Les Sentiers d'Evasion,* a well presented guide to hikes accessible by public transportation published by local train and bus companies. One idea featured is the train and bus to the **Great St. Bernard Pass,** where one can visit the **Hospice Museum** and dog kennels. (Tel. (027) 787 12 36. Open 8am-7pm in high summer while the pass is open. 6SFr, children 4SFr.) You can wind down on the ancient pass path through the "Combe of the Dead" to **Les Toules** reservoir and the village of **Bourg-St.-Pierre** amid grand mountain scenery (2½hr., easy), and then take the bus and train back to Martigny.

■ Sion

"If at first you don't succeed, try, try again" should be Sion's motto. The city lost its bid for the Winter Olympics to Sapporo, Japan way back in 1972, and just recently lost out again in its pursuit of the 2002 Games to Salt Lake City, Utah; but nevertheless it has enthusiastically announced that it plans to re-apply for the 2006 Winter Games. The capital of the Valais region is a city of two halves. A noisy, heavy industrial tangle of towering blocks borders the Rhône, while the quiet, churchy old town cowers beneath two rocky bluffs topped with castle ruins. The moody look of the town inspired writers and poets like Goethe, Rousseau and Rilke who died in neighboring Sierre. Constructed atop Roman ruins, Sion was a political and ecclesiastical capital by the end of the 10th century, when the bishop of Sion was given full temporal power over Canton Valais. The encroachment of the neighboring House of Savoy in the 11th century introduced political instability into the region which lasted for the next five centuries. Much later a large part of the town was destroyed by fire, but in a historical paradox, the flames actually saved Sion. Napoleon had planned to invade it, but saw the ruins and decided to move on. Valais wines slowly ferment here amid vineyards and orchards between the Rhône River and the Alps.

Practical Information From the train station, walk directly up av. de la Gare, and turn right on rue de Lausanne for the **tourist office,** pl. de la Planta (tel. 322 85 86; fax 322 18 82), which offers a free room reservation service. (Open July 15-Aug. 15 Mon.-Fri. 8am-6pm, Sat. 10am-4pm; Aug. 16-July 14 Mon.-Fri. 8:30am-noon and 2-5:30pm, Sat 9am-noon.) **Trains** pass every 30 minutes in each direction along the Rhône valley, going west to **Martigny** (15min., 8.40SFr), **Aigle** (25min., 16.60SFr), **Montreux** (50min., 21SFr), and **Lausanne** (1hr.10min., 27SFr), and east to **Sierre** (10min. 5.40SFr) and **Brig** (½hr., 16.60SFr), where you connect to **Zermatt** (48SFr) and **Saas Fee** (28SFr). The **train station** (tel. 157 22 22) provides **currency exchange** (open daily 6am-8:30pm), **lockers** (small 3SFr, large 5SFr), **luggage storage** (5SFr for 24hr., open 6am-8:45pm), **bike rental** (21SFr), and **telephones. Parking** metered on street sites is 80 centimes per hour, more near the station. The best covered site is under pl. de la Planta near the tourist office. (1-3.20SFr per hour in the day, 20 centimes per hour at night; entry off ave de la Gare.) **Valais Incoming,** av. de Tourbillon 3 (tel. 322 54 35), services **American Express** customers. Address mail, for example George ORDOÑEZ, c/o American Express, Client Mail Service, Valais Incoming-Sion (R), av. Tourbillon 3, P.O. Box 579, CH-1951 Sion (open Mon.-Fri. 8am-noon and 1:30-6pm, Sat. 8am-noon). **Taxis:** 322 33 33. **Emergencies: Police:** tel. 117. **Fire:** tel. 118. **Ambulances:** tel. 23 33 33. The **post office** is at pl. de la Gare, CH-1950 Sion 1, next to the train station and has photocopiers and phones (open Mon.-Fri. 7:30am-noon and 1:30-6:15pm, Sat. 8:15-11am). **Postal code:** CH-1951. **Telephone code:** 027.

Accommodations Built in 1991, the **Auberge de Jeunesse (HI),** av. de l'Industrie 2 (tel. 323 74 70; fax 323 74 38), maintains clean bathrooms, tiny balconies, and lockers in every room. It is also the only hostel in the Rhône valley, so reserve ahead in July and August. The airy dining room leads onto a patio with table tennis, but the showers need a little more oomph. Leaving the train station, walk left and descend the ramp to the rue de la Blancherie; continue left underneath the train tracks. Look for the crazy colorful artwork in front. (Reception open 7:30-9:30am and 5-10pm, but hosts will almost certainly be downstairs in the kitchen. Curfew 10pm, summer 11pm, though keys are often given out. Lockout 9:30am-5pm. Dorms with 4 beds 25.80SFr, subsequent nights 23.30SFr. Doubles 7SFr extra. Breakfast included. Dinner 11SFr if you reserve it. Kitchen facilities 2SFr.) Staying anywhere else will give you a painful sting. The cheapest hotel rooms are at the smartly renovated **Hôtel Elite,** av. du Midi 6 (tel. 322 33 95; fax 322 23 61), located on the edge of the *vieille ville* and surrounded by stores and cafés. From the station, head up av. de la Gare, and turn right. It offers clean-smelling rooms with TVs, phones and private bathrooms. (Reception open 6:30am-midnight. Singles 70SFr. Doubles 120SFr. Breakfast included. Visa, MC, AmEx.) Enterprising (or desperate) travelers seeking a cheap bed can try some of the villages outside Sion. The tourist office's imaginatively titled booklet *Sion* gives details. In Pont-de-la-Morge there are singles for 35-40SFr and doubles for 68-80SFr; in

Saint-Léonard singles 50-70SFr and doubles 70-90SFr. To get to both villages, tackle the local buses at Switzerland's largest post bus station in pl. de la Gare by the train station. **Camping Les Iles** (tel. 346 43 47), rte. d'Aproz, is a lakeside five-star site. Take a very short bus ride past the aerodome to **Aproz.** (Open Jan.-Oct.; 5.80SFr-7.40SFr, tent 6-9SFr.)

Food And Wine The stone streets of the *vieille ville* are flanked by cafés and restaurants, most with white-washed terraces where patrons sip glasses of *Valais Fendant* or *Johannisberg-Tavillon,* the leading labels in town. A solitary vendor hawks fresh produce among a multitude of traders selling clothes on Fridays from 9am to 5pm at the **market,** pl. de la Planta. **Co-op City,** pl. du Midi, right off av. de la Gare along av. du Midi, offers produce galore. (Open Mon. 1-6:30pm, Tues.-Thurs. 8:30am-6:30pm, Fri. 8:30am-8pm, Sat. 8am-5pm.) Not bigger or better or noticeably different the **Migros Centre** has 19 different stores as well as a supermarket and restaurant (7.20-14.90SFr main courses) on av. de France left one block from the station. (Open same hr. as Co-op.) **Manora,** at the corner of av. du Midi and rue de la Dent-Blanche, on the ground floor of the Placette department store and supermarket, is the best of the buffet self-serve restaurants (entrées 4.50-12.90SFr; open daily 8am-8:30pm). Chez Nando, rue Remparts (tel. 322 24 54), sprawls under umbrellas on a pedestrian street near La Placette and has a red and gold chevronned interior. (Spaghetti 11-17SFr, noodles 12.50-18SFr, gnocchi 17SFr, pizzas 10-18SFr. Open daily July-Aug. til late; Sept.-June Tues.-Sun.) **Restaurant la Bergère,** av. de la Gare 30 (tel. 22 14 81), specializes in Italian food (10-17SFr) and sandwiches (5-7SFr; open Mon.-Fri. 6am-1am, Sat. 10:30am-1am, Sun. 5pm-1am). For a classier meal among the wrought-iron balconies and brightly painted houses of the old town, **Brasserie du Grand-Pont,** rue du Grand-Pont 6 (tel. 322 20 09), cooks unusual and experimental food. Try fried calves' brains (14SFr), snails (13SFr) or even alligator (29SFr), or play it safer with spaghetti and pesto (14SFr), shrimp gumbo (8.50SFr), or "Up to Date" salad (15SFr). "Cooking with jazz" they call it. "Blow them horns," we say (open Mon.-Sat. 11am-11pm). Consult the tourist office for organized **wine-tasting excursions,** and a list of local cellars. A long-distance path through the vineyards, *le chemin du vignoble,* passes close to Sion and through tasting territory. Always ring before you arrive at a cave, and try to rustle up a group if you want the proprietor to be more welcoming and forthcoming. One *centre de dégustation* is the Varone vineyard, av. Grand-Champsec 30 (tel. 203 56 83), just across the river. (Open Mon. 2-6:30pm, Tues.-Fri. 10am-noon and 2-6:30pm, Sat. 10am-noon and 2-5pm.)

Sights It's an age-old problem: how to keep the peace between a bossy bishop, a grumpy chapter and a fractious town? Sion's solution was to build the bishop's house, the now-towering **Château de Tourbillon,** on one hill, the chapter's seat, the **Château de Valère** on another, and the municipal powerbase, the **Château de la Majorie** down in the town (a laser is beamed around this power triangle Thurs.-Sat. nightfall-1am). The first two castles stare each other down from across the hilltops and offer panoramas of the entire Valais valley, the Rhône, the Alps, and the city of Sion. From the station, proceed up av. de la Gare opposite you, right on rue de Lausanne, left on rue du Grand-Pont, and then right up the narrow rue des Châteaux just past the bright orange town hall. On the smaller hill, the **Basilique Notre Dame de Valère** boasts the oldest working organ in the world (c. 1390-1430) and presents its annual festival of ancient organ music in July and Aug. every Sat. at 4pm (tickets 20SFr, students 10SFr; call the tourist office or 323 57 67). The Château de Valère also houses recently restored frescoes from the 15th and 16th centuries as well as the **Cantonal Museum of History and Ethnology,** which contains a spotty collection of odds and ends including 7th-century belt buckles, reliquaries, medieval crossbows, the belly armor of 16th-century magnate George Supersaxo, and 18th-century tambourines (tel. 606 46 70; 5SFr, students 2.50SFr). The Château de Valère is open Tues.-Sun. 10am-noon and 2-6pm. The Château de Tourbillon is open Tues.-Sun. 10am-6pm. Both are free; the cost will be on your legs, not your bank account.

On the road to town, the Château de la Majorie is home to the **Musée des Beaux-Arts** (Fine Arts Museum), pl. de la Majorie 15-19 (tel. 606 46 90), which hangs all of the Valais art it can find. The older pictures are unsophisticated, but the photography gallery and modern art exhibition are interesting and experimental (open Tues.-Sun. 10am-noon and 2-6pm; 5SFr, students 2.50SFr). Across the road at the bottom of rue des Château is the incense-filled **Cathédrale Notre Dame du Glaurier** in a peaceful picnic-ready square. A 12th-century belfry has four attractive rows of Romanesque arcades. Inside, below the altar, there is an 11th-century crypt that was discovered in 1985. Two minutes from the south door down passage Supersaxo stands the **Maison Supersaxo** with its ornately carved ceilings and Gothic staircase. The fabulously rich but famously discontented Supersaxo family built the mansion in 1503-5 to show off and irritate their less wealthy rival Cardinal Schiner. (Two public access rooms open Mon.-Fri. 8am-noon and 2-6pm, Sat.-Sun. 9am-noon. Free).

Clearly the most fun of Sion's museums is the **Natural History Museum,** 42 av. de la Gare (tel. 606 47 30), up the road from pl. de la Planta and the tourist office. Knowledgable Swiss museum buffs know by now that Swiss Natural History mean stuffed armadillos, and they will not be disappointed. This collection's sublime attraction, however, is its eccentric hodge-podge of local relics. There is a contorted body of a chamois pulled out of a glacier in 1920 after centuries in the ice; 3- and 5-toed dinosaur footprints from Emossons, the Last Bear in the Valais, helpfully shot by a collector in 1830; a small chalet transferred whole from Zinal (1937); stuffed salamanders, a bison (not local); some live fish and an exhibit on the history of Phylloxera (open Tues.-Sun. 2-6pm. 2SFr, students 1SFr).

The *vielle ville,* with its medieval churches and colorfully painted buildings, hosts yearly music festivals. The open-air **Jazz Festival** takes over the streets at 11pm on Fri. from May through November. (20SFr, festival passes 150SFr; tickets available at tourist office or at the gate.) Throughout Aug. there is an open air theater, and most evenings in summer free concerts of classical music are offered at the Academie de Musique (tel. 322 66 52). Irregularly from July to Sept. there are also major orchestral events during the Valais's Tibor Varga Festival (20-80SFr).

▓ Brig (Brigue)

With its slender-spired churches, narrow houses, and slate-grey squares, Brig is a swatch of northern Switzerland dropped among the chalets and vineyards of the Valais. A junction town at the base of the Simplon, Furka, and Grimsel passes, Brig grew up as a place to change your horses and trade your wares. None of its middlemen fattened themselves so much as the Stockalper family whose pad is Brig's main attraction. Over the course of several generations they scooped together a monopoly on trade to Italy over the Simplon pass. The richest of the lot, Kaspar Jodok van Stozkalper, had exclusive rights to the lucrative salt trade, and between 1658 and 1678 extended his handsome 1533 house in to the largest private residence in Switzerland. The main courtyard has three layers of arcades and square stone towers topped with giant onion domes in three of its four corners. It was never quite finished because peeved townsfolk chased the proto-capitalist bloodsucker into Italy. He later returned, slightly meeker for a quiet retirement.

To get to the **Stockalperschloss** (tel. 923 19 01) from the station, head straight down the tree-lined boulevard Bahnhofstrasse to Stadtplatz, cross to the far side, passing the Sebastionkapelle on your right, and turn left at the end up Alte Simplonstr. (Open June-Sept. Tues.-Sun. with tours on the hour 9-11am and 2-5pm; May and Oct. Tues.-Sun. with tours at 10, 11am and 2,3,4pm. 4SFr, child 1SFr.) During the day the courtyard is always open, as is the lawn below it; both make a good place for a picnic. In July and August. Free German dubbed films are screened in the courtyard on Wed. evenings with a different theme every year.

The ridge above the Rhône valley northeast of Brig has superlative close-up views of the immense **Grosser Aletschgletscher** (glacier) and the snowfields that feed this Amazon of ice. The Jungfrau, Mönch, and other familiar peaks of the Berner Oberland look quite different from this side. Unfortunately a cable car ride is almost essential in this unregulated, unpeopled wilderness, otherwise you will waste all day and your energy slogging up out of the valley to the high mountain pastures. The best viewpoint, tight where the glacier dog-legs, is the **Eggishorn** (2926m), a shapely summit perfectly positioned to see all the highest peaks in Switzerland. The F-O Bahn leaves for **Fiesch** (every ½hr.; 8.40SFr on the F-O Bahn from Brig) from where you can ride a cable car to **Kuhboden** half way up (2212m; one-way 15.60SFr, round-trip 23.80SFr) and **Eggishorn** (2869m; one-way 28SFr, round-trip 38.80SFr). From here it is only a short scramble to the cross on top. You can walk up the clear and simple, but distinctly steep, path from Kuhboden in 2hr. Dozens of tracks criss-cross the Eggishorn ridge and the south bank of the glacier. Allow map #2516, "Aletschgebiet," to sort them out for you; don't rely on free handout maps in this difficult terrain. Also inquire locally about snow and ice, and don't commit yourself to a big hike if there is any. Highly recommended is the trek to the glacier side by the necklace of lakes at **Märjela.** From the Eggishorn cable car station, spiral around the mountain counter-clockwise by dropping down the zigzags, turning left after descending 150m, and crossing the northeast shoulder of the Eggishorn to the highest/rightmost lake. The track then kisses the fractured glacier and follows its flank down to the snout. There are several points at which you can bend left and complete the circle back to Kuhboden, or pass the much-loved Blausee to Bettneralp which has its own cable car to **Betten** near Brig (one-way 12.60SFr). All day hikers may get to **Riederalp** just past the snout, whose cable car goes to **Mörel,** which is even closer to Brig (one-way 11.40SFr). Bettneralp and Riederalp are tiny resorts in their own right with tourist offices (tel. 927 12 91 or 927 13 65) where you should be able to find a dorm bed for the night and guided walks on the glacier.

Brig is admirably connected by public transport, with trains leaving for all the corners of Switzerland. Along the Rhône valley, trains go to **Sierre** (½hr., every ½hr., 12.20SFr); **Sion** (40min., every ½hr., 16.60SFr); **Lausanne** (2hr, hourly, 55SFr); and **Geneva** (2hr.40min., hourly, 55SFr). Through the Lötschberg tunnel, trains head for **Bern** (1hr.40min. hourly, 46SFr) and **Interlaken** (1hr.25min., hourly,38SFr). Through the Simplon tunnel trains lead to **Domodossola** in Italy (½hr., hourly, 12.20SFr) and **Locarno** (2½hrs., hourly, 48SFr, change at Domodossola). From the square outside the station, two tiny lines link Brig to **Zermatt** (1hr.15min., hourly, 37SFr, the "B-V-Z") and to stations towards **Furkpass** for the Aletschgletscher hikes (hourly, **Fiesch** 8.40SFr, **Mörel** 4.20SFr, **Betten** 5.40SFr, the "F-O Bahn"). A mass of bus lines spread their tentacles through the surrounding hillsides, and leave from Bahnhofplatz. The most important leaves hourly for **Saas Fee** (1hr.10min., 17.40SFr) from just left of the station exit.

The station has a **currency exchange** (tel. 922 24 24) that will also do Western Union transfers and credit card advances (open Mon.-Sat. 6:15am-7:30pm, Sun. 8-11:30am and 2-6pm). It also has **lockers** (3SFr and 5SFr), **luggage storage** (open daily 7am-7pm), and a free phone line to all hotels. The **tourist office** (tel. 923 19 01 or 924 31 44) is up the yellow stairs on the first floor. Be warned, they tend to clam up if you ask them about anything outside of Brig, such as the Aletschgletscher cable cars and hikes. (Open Mon.-Fri. 8:30am-noon and 1:30-6pm, Sat. 8:30am-noon; mid-June to mid-Oct. also open Sat. 2-5:30pm.) **Emergency:** tel. 117. **Police:** tel. 922 41 60. **Fire:** tel. 118. The **post office** is directly opposite the train station, Bahnhofstr. 1 (tel. 923 66 56; open Mon.-Fri. 7:30am-noon and 1:30-6:15pm, Sat. 8-11am). **Phones** are next door. **Postal code:** CH-3900. **Telephone code:** 027.

The central **Pension la Poste,** Furkstr. 23 (tel. 924 45 54; fax 924 45 53), is outstandingly clean even by the well-scrubbed, Swiss hotel standards. Cross the square in front of the station, turn right on Viktoriastr., and take the third left onto Furkastr. at the rotary. The rooms have bright paint, showers, and plenty of pine. The restaurant downstairs serves 15 different *rösti* dishes (14-24SFr; reception open 6am-midnight. Dorms 25SFr. Singles 50SFr. Doubles 100SFr. Breakfast included. Visa, MC, AmEx.) **Camping Geschina** (tel. 923 06 88) is 10-15min. from the station by the river. Head straight down Bahnhofstr. to the main square, cross it, take a right past the church, and then go immediately left on Neue Simplonstr. without crossing the river (5.50SFr, tent 10-12SFr, car 5SFr; open May to mid-Oct.).

Noshing options start with the restaurant-cum-supermarket **Migros** on Belalpstr., visible on your left as you leave the station. (Supermarket open Mon.-Fri. 8:15am-6:30pm, Sat. 7:45am-4pm; the restaurant opens a little earlier.) Cheap bars and cafés line the left hand side of the main square, Stadtplatz. **Tea Room Bistro Viva,** Alte Simplonstr. 8, has Altstadt outdoor seating and *älper marcaroni* (8.50SFr), hamburgers (5SFr), and sandwiches (2.90SFr). A long way upmarket and definitely a place for a date, the **Schlasskeller** (tel. 923 33 52; fax 923 69 75) occupies the livable bit of the Stockalper family castle on Alte Simplonstr. Eat under the arcades of the 1533 manor house or in one of the wood-beamed halls inside. Local dishes like "cholera cake" with salad (16SFr) and *fondue* (19SFr) are the specialty, but omelettes (10SFr) and spaghetti (14SFr) can also be found on the menu (open Mon.-Sat. 11am-2pm and 6-10pm. Visa, MC).

■ Zermatt and the Matterhorn

A trick of the valley blocks out the great Alpine summits ringing Zermatt, allowing the Matterhorn (4478m) to rise alone, phoenix-like, above the town. Instantly recognizable and stamped on everything from scarves to pencils by Zermatt's merchants of kitsch, it still causes an intake of breath and a frisson of excitement whenever one looks up. At dawn it blazes bright orange; some days—some weeks—it is completely swathed in clouds, completely hidden from view. Zermatt itself is a missable mix of tourists and rock jocks, but a short hike or cable car ride will lift you away from the crowds to the lonely high Alpine meadows and splintered icefalls that you have been deliciously picturing in your sleep.

PRACTICAL INFORMATION

To preserve the Alpine air from the effects of exhaust fumes, cars and buses are outlawed here; locals in their electrical buggies dodge pedestrians. The only way to Zermatt is by the hourly BVZ (Brig-Visp-Zermatt) rail line. Join at **Brig** (1hr.25min., one-way 37SFr, round-trip 63SFr); **Visp** (if coming from Lausanne or Sion, one-way 34SFr, round-trip 58SFr); **Stalden-Saas** (if coming from Saas Fee; 1hr., one-way 30SFr, round-trip 51SFr); or **Täsch** (every 20min., one-way 7.20SFr, round-trip 14.40SFr). The road head at Täsch has a covered parking lot for 6SFr per day; you can leave your car in an uncovered lot for 3-5SFr per day. The station at Zermatt (tel. 967 22 07) has a free direct phone line to all of Zermatt's hotels.

Tourist Office: Bahnhofpl. (tel. 967 01 81; fax 967 01 85), in the station complex. All the hard facts you could possibly want to know about Zermatt are contained in the chunky free booklet *Prato Borni* and the glossy *Zermatt*. Both appear in summer and winter editions. Panorama plans with suggested hikes are 1.60SFr; to navigate on a hike, however, you will need a real map. Open July–Sept. Mon.-Fri. 8:30am-noon and 2-6pm, Sat. 8:30am-6:30pm, Sun. 9:30am-noon and 4-6:30pm; Oct.-June Mon.-Fri. 8:30am-noon and 1:30-6pm, Sat. 8:30am-noon.

Mountaineering and **Ski School Office** (Bergführerbüro and Skischulbüro), Bahnhofstr. (tel. 966 24 60). From the train station, walk 5min. up the main street on your right, past the post office. Posts a detailed weather forecast every morning covering the next four days. Coordinates private and group climbing expeditions with tours along classic routes and up favorite peaks. In summer, groups go daily to the Breithorn (120SFr), Pollux (230SFr) and Castor (240SFr) tops. The Matterhorn is 670SFr but to attempt this you must have technical experience and spend at least a week in prior training. Prices do not include equipment, hut accommodations, or lifts to the departure points. Whatever you do, get insured (30SFr) or be prepared to risk a 4-figure helicopter rescue bill. Open July-Sept. Mon.-Fri. 8:30am-noon and 4-7pm, Sat. 4-7pm, Sun. 10am-noon and 4-7pm.

Currency Exchange: Banks are mostly open Mon.-Fri. 8:30am-noon and 2:30-6pm.

Telephones: In the train station and the post office.

Bike and Ski Rental: Roc Sport (tel. 967 39 27) and **Slalom Sport** (tel. 966 23 66), both on Kirchstr. (left at the church) rent mountain bikes and skis at reduced rates (10% off) to youth hostelers. Mountain bikes 35SFr per day. Open Mon.-Sat. 8am-noon and 2-7pm, Sun. 8am-noon and 4-6pm. Visa, MC, AmEx.

English Library: In the English Church behind the post office. Small collection of battered novels. Honor system. Bring borrowed books back!

Weather Information: Call 162 or check the window of the Bergführerbüro. **Winter Avalanche Information:** 187

24-hr. Alpine Rescue: tel. 967 20 00.

Emergencies: Police: tel. 117. **Fire:** tel. 118. **Ambulance:** tel. 67 12 12.

Post Office: Bahnhofstr., 5min. walk up the main street, turning right out of the station, in Arcade Mont-Cervin. It has telephones. Address Poste Restante to CH-3920 Zermatt. Open Mon.-Fri. 8am-noon and 1:30-6pm, Sat. 8:30-11am. **Postal Code:** CH-3920.

Telephone Code: 027.

ACCOMMODATIONS

Climbers, hikers, and snowboarders buoy up the demand for budget beds in Zermatt. A healthy supply generally gives them what they want, but finding a dorm bed on the spot can be a squeeze July-Aug., Christmas and New Year's, and Mid-Feb. through mid-March. Many hotels in winter, and all chalets in summer, accept booking only for a week at a time. Every year some campers are tempted to park their bodies illegally in the wide-open spaces above town. This practice is discouraged by the authorities and could incur fines between 50 and 100SFr.

Jugendherberge (HI), Winkelmatten (tel. 967 23 20; fax 967 53 06), is a 15min. walk from the station. Turn right along Bahnhofstr. (the main street), left at the church, cross the river, take the second street to the right after the river (you'll see a yellow Jugendherberge sign), and select the left fork in front of Hotel Rhodania. On the mountain side of town. Slightly overcrowded and sodden shower rooms are amply compensated for by the full frontal view of the Matterhorn. Friendly staff, and a convivial terrace where folks sit around and tell hiking tales. Reception open in summer 7:30-9am and 4pm-midnight; in winter 6:30-9am and 3pm-midnight. No lockout. Curfew 11:30pm. July-Aug., late Dec. to early Jan., and mid-Feb. to mid-April 44SFr, all other times 38SFr. The (only) double room 54SFr and 48SFr. Breakfast, sleepsack, showers, and dinner fit for a king (kosher and vegetarian meals available). Laundry 8SFr small load, 16SFr large load. Closed May and late Oct. to mid-Dec. Visa, MC, AmEx.

Hotel Bahnhof, Bahnhofstr. (tel. 967 24 06; fax 967 72 16). One min. from the station—turn left and its just past the Gornergratbahn. Charming older woman keeps a homely wood-paneled hotel popular with climbers and clean communal types seeking a peaceful break. Dorms 26-28SFr (bring your own sheets). 4-6-bed rooms 32SFrper person. Singles 40-48SFr. Doubles 72-78SFr. No breakfast, but kitchen and large dining room in the basement. Open mid-Dec. to mid-Oct.

Hotel Weisshorn, Bahnhofstr. (tel. 967 11 12; fax 967 38 39). From the train station, turn right along Bahnhofstr. The hotel is 30m past the church, and intrigues with its low ceilings and winding staircases. The beds and bathrooms are clean and cushy. Reception open daily 7am-10pm. Singles 46-50SFr, with shower 63-68SFr. Doubles 84-92SFr, with shower 110-120SFr. Triples 120-132SFr. Reservations necessary in winter high season, but only accepted one week in advance. Visa, MC.

Camping Matterhorn Zermatt, Bahnhofstr. (tel. 967 54 14; fax 967 39 21), is a miniature plot of land 5min. down the main street to the left of the train station. Reception open May-Sept. daily 8:40-9:40am and 5:15-6:15pm. 8SFr, showers included.

Camping Alphubel in Täsch (tel. 967 36 35). Since Zermatt is car-free, caravanners and motorists can park their vehicles and stay here. t5.50SFr, tent 5SFr, car 4SFr, caravan 6SFr. Open May to mid-Oct.

Hutting options: The tourist office has a list of SAC, CAI, and private huts in the Zermatt area. At 23SFr a night they offer a good deal for bona fide climbers; others will find them too high for a proper night's sleep. **Schönbiel** (tel. 967 13 54; 2694m), **Rothorn** (tel. 967 20 43; 3198m), **Gandegg** (tel. 967 21 96; 3029m), **Hörnli** (tel. 967 27 69; 3260m, very crowded), and **Monte Rosa** (tel. 967 21 15; 2795m; crampons and guide advised) are all open July-Sept. and accessible to walker if there is no snow. They require an all day hike from Zermatt.

FOOD AND NIGHTLIFE

Rather than charge Alpine prices for Death Valley food, a surprising number of the cafés along Bahnhofstr. leave both your wallet and your stomach quite content.

Markets

Co-op Center, across from the station. Open Mon.-Fri. 8am-7pm, Sat. 8am-6pm.
Migros, Hofmattstr., down from Bahnhofstr. between the station and the church. Open Mon.-Sat. 8:30am-noon and 2-6:30pm, Sun. 8:30am-noon and 2-6pm.

Restaurants and Bars

Walliser Kanne, Bahnhofstr. (tel./fax 967 22 98), next to the post office. At street level, this establishment offers inventive Swiss food in an ideal people-watching location with dishes such as *käsespätzli* (16.50SFr), *rösti Walliserkanne* (17SFr), deer steaks and dumpling (20SFr), and *apfelstrudel* with vanilla sauce (6SFr), as well as the usual pizza and pasta (13-17.50SFr). Open daily 10am-midnight. Visa, MC, AmEx. Downstairs awaits the **Dance Garage** bar and disco. Beer of the week 4SFr; cider 6SFr. Nachos 5SFr. Open daily 7pm-3am; happy hour until 10:30pm.

The North Wall Bar (tel. 967 28 63). Head over the river on Kirchstr., and take the second right. Also *en route* to the youth hostel. No frills, 100% English speaking climbers' haunt. Skiing and mountaineering videos play every evening. This is also the place to scrounge a job in Zermatt if you're finding it hard to leave. Serves you anything you like as long as its pizza (10SFr, plus 1SFr for fancy topping like mussels) and, at 4.50SFr for 0.5liter, the beer is probably the cheapest in town. Open mid-June to Sept. and mid-Dec.to April daily 6:30pm-midnight.

Café du Pont, Bahnhofstr. (tel. 967 43 43; fax 967 43 42), 7min. from the station at the top of the main street and next to Hotel Weisshorn. Zermatt's oldest restaurant still maintains its romantic atmosphere with subdued lighting and soothing music. It serves stick-to-your-ribs Swiss dishes such as *raclette* (7SFr), *rösti* (14SFr), and *fondue du Pont* (22SFr). Sandwiches 6.50SFr. Open June-Oct. and Dec.-April daily 9am-midnight; food served 11am-3pm and 5-10pm.

Swiss Rock Café, Bahnhofstr. (tel. 967 68 80). Sleek, spanking new restaurant and bar with a bubbling blue waterfall and a line of stuffed parrots. Can you say, "Polly want some World food?" Serves never-ending *bratwurst* with baked potatoes (14SFr), corn on the cob (5SFr), *enchiladas* (18SFr), *dim sum* (18SFr), and Bombay stuffed bread (9SFr). Restaurants open 10am-midnight. Piano bar downstairs has beer at 5.20SFr for 0.5liter. Two drinks for the price of one 6-7pm. Open daily until 2am. Closed May and mid-Oct. to Nov.

Grampi's Pub, Bahnhofstr. (tel. 966 77 88). Central bar flings wide its door during the day and thumps with dance music by night. Beer 3.50SFr for ¼-liter; long list of bottles 4.50-7SFr. Nightly DJ 8:30pm-2am. Open daily 9am-2am.

SKIING, SPORTS, AND ENTERTAINMENT

Seventy-three lifts offering 14,200m of combined elevation and 245km of prepared runs make Zermatt one of the best equipped ski centers in the world. Where it really outshines its rivals, however, is the ski-mountaineering and high-level ski-touring potential. The town also has more **summer ski trails** than any other Alpine ski resort—36 square km of year-round runs between 3900m and 2900m. The **ski school** (tel. 967 54 44) offers group classes for skiing (one day 65SFr, 6 days 215SFr) and snowboarding (a little less). Ski and boot rental should cost the same everywhere—around 43SFr per day, 177SFr per 6 days—but youth hostel residents secure a 10% discount at some stores. Most shops are open daily 8am-noon and 2-7pm. Remember to rent the evening before to maximize your time on the slopes. Zermatt's **ski passes** operate on a regional system. You can buy passes for any combination of the three regions—Matterhorn complex, Gornergrat complex, and Sunnegga complex—and for consecutive days or flexible passes. For example, the Matterhorn region costs 58SFr for one day, 240SFr for 6 days; all three regions together costs 60SFr for one day, and 292SFr for 6 days. In summer only the Klein Matterhorn/Trockener Steg sub-region is open, and you cannot use passes to ascend after 1pm (1 day 58SFr, 6 days 204SFr, 3 days within a 6-day period 150SFr).

Zermatt is at least 3hr. from any worthwhile indoor attraction; when it rains you will quickly wish you had scheduled your trip to North Dakota instead. Zermatt's residents make the most of it by going for a swim or watching a movie. The posher hotels have **swimming pools,** with **Hotel Christionia** (tel. 967 35 66) offering the biggest. Follow the right bank of the river until just past the Rothorn/Sunnegga cable railway station. (10SFr, children 6SFr. Open Mon., Wed., and Fri.-Sat. 8am-8pm, Tues. 2-8pm, Thurs. 8am-10pm.) For movies, your best bet is **Cinema Alpin** on Hofmattstr. (tel. 967 66 36), which has two or three screenings nightly Mon.-Sat. of nearly-new releases, usually in English (15SFr, 13SFr if you stay at the youth hostel; major credit cards accepted). Hofmannstr. heads down to the river from Bahnhofstr. about half-way between the station and the church. The **Alpine Museum** (tel. 967 41 00) has an interesting collection of climbing memorabilia. Cases display oddities picked up after various mountaineering accidents, like the rather dented water bottle of one Dr. W. Moseley, an American who, in the 19th century, "perished on the Matterhorn through sheer imprudence." On show is Whymper's account of the accident on the first ascent of the Matterhorn and, less exciting, a chair in which he was once shaved. (3SFr, children 1SFr. Guide in English 1SFr. Open July-Sept. daily 10am-noon and 4-6pm; Oct. 4-6pm and mid-Dec. to June 4:30-6:30pm.)

Festivities happen mostly in August. The best known is the Alpine Folklore Parade, where locals take a break from their mountain chores mid-month and dust off their alphorns and frilly costumes. There are also irregular classical music concerts in the church (20-25SFr) throughout the month, and at the end of August, the **Matterhorn-lauf,** a fun-run from Zermatt to the Schwarzsee at the foot of the Matterhorn, burns thighs during its 1001m climb.

OUTDOORS AROUND ZERMATT

Outstanding walks into the world of glaciers and high mountains spread from Zermatt in every compass direction. Though these paths are well-made and well-marked, a proper non-panoramic map is essential for safety and adds to your appreciation of the mountains. Lifts and railways to the south and east are also valuable hiking tools; they can save you the collar work of climbing out of the hollow that Zermatt sits in, and allow more time and energy for high altitude exploration. Swisspasses will win you a 25% discount on many of these lifts, but a Eurail pass will win nothing. Prudent walkers will carry rain gear, warm clothes (including a hat and a pair of gloves), food and fluids (not soda), a map, and plenty of cash, even on day hikes and even in the summer months. Zermatt is particularly prone to sudden electrical storms, and you may need to dive to the nearest hut or mechanical lift. The *Bergführerbüro* posts a conservative pictoral weather forecast in its window on Bahnhofstr. To rent hiking boots, try **Skihaus Matterhorn,** Bahnhofstr. (tel. 967 29 56), or **Glacier Sport,** Bahnhofstr. (tel. 967 21 67; one day 14SFr, 7 days 52SFr, and 14 days 80SFr; both stores open daily 8am-noon and 2-7pm).

West and Northwest

West of Zermatt, the mountains are savage, spiky pinnacles. The **Zinalrothorn** (4221m), **Ober Gabelhorn** (4063m), and the **Dent Blanche** (4357m) are regarded today as some of the toughest climbs around the town. However, an easier-paced though long walk to **Zmutt** (1936m, 1hr.) and the **Schönbielhütte** (2694m, 4hr.), leads right along their base and offers the most dramatic encounter with the Matterhorn's north face, its best side. The path is wide, clear, and well-marked, and the views get exponentially better as you rise. From Zermatt, follow Bahnhofstr. past the church and to the river; 100m after hitting the bank, the path shades up right (big sign). A steady gradient pulls you up through Arolla pines to the weathered chalets of the minuscule hamlet, Zmutt. The path then continues through the meadows above a small reservoir giving lengthening views of the Hörnli ridge and the Matterhorn. As you go on, the Matterhorn's north wall, which drops 200m, with an average gradient well over 45°comes breathtakingly into view. This is the hardest regularly attempted Zermatt climb. The path ascends by lakes and waterfalls at the outlet of the rock-strewn Zmuttgletscher and follows the lateral moraine **kame terrace** to the **Schön-bielhütte,** an ideal spot for lunchtime carbo-loading of pasta or rösti while you examine the ice-falls which rise from three sides. On the return journey, the valley frames the **Rimpfischhorn** (4199m) and **Strahlhorn** (4190m; 25km; 1050m of elevation; all day, but nowhere steep and everywhere beautiful).

Southwest

No visit to Zermatt is emotionally complete without struggling up to the **Hörnlihütte,** the base camp for the normal route up the Matterhorn, and a good platform for watching brightly colored dots claw their way upwards along the ridge. Those who have connected with the history and literature of the Matterhorn will appreciate it most, but its 1600m ascent is for the fit and well-booted only. A cable car to the Schwarzsee saves you 900m of elevation (one-way 18.50SFr; round-trip 29.50SFr). Leave Zermatt along the left bank of the Matter Vispa, exactly as for the Zmutt/Schön-bielhütte hike. A mile or so from Zermatt, after a few minutes of climbing, a wide track heads down left across the river marked "Zum See, Schwarzsee and Hörnli-hütte." Take it, and plough up the steep zigzags to the tiny lake, **Schwarzsee** (2552m, 3hr.), admiring the monstrous Gorner gorges on the left. The chapel on the lake was built in an act of piety by a group of climbers caught in a snowstorm whose prayers to Mary were answered when the clouds miraculously lifted. The path becomes rockier and wilder as it joins the true northeast ridge of the Matterhorn, climbing gently at first, but ending in a merciless, exposed arête to the buildings at Hörnli. Rest at the finish and know that there is no way for walkers above the hut. More than 500 people have died in the mile above this point, as a sobering walk around Zermatt's cemeteries will prove. A guide, perfect physical condition, a 4am start and rock climbing experience up to at least PD+ are essential requirements for proceeding past the hut. An alternative route of descent to Zermatt is to bear right at the Schwarzsee to the Furgg cable car terminus, and follow the path down to the beck. It traverses a steep cliff, but is fine underfoot if you don't mind the grade, and has even closer views of the gorges carved by the Gornergletscher.

South

South from Zermatt the Matterhorn changes its clothes again, this time parading the pyramidal west face. This is the way to wilderness—steep icefalls peel off the **Breithorn** (4164m), and below these are the glacier-scoured, sun-bleached boulder fields. The highest **cable car** in Europe alights on the **Klein Matterhorn,** 6km from the Matterhorn. (Operates high season daily 7am-6pm; to **Furi** one-way 8.50SFr, round-trip 11SFr; to **Trockner Steg** one-way 26SFr and round-trip 41.50SFr; **Klein Matterhorn** one-way 44SFr, round-trip 56SFr.) This location makes for great summer skiing and is an easy climbing hub from the top station, though there is no hiking. A track leads out from the tunnel below the viewing platform to **Gobba di Rollin** (3899m) following the T-bar all the way, but needs good weather, caution, and a tortoise pace because of the altitude. From Trockner Steg station (2939m), however, you can walk to Zermatt. Leave the complex on the Monte Rosa side with your back to the Matterhorn, and the path runs left along the gully in front of you (2½hr.).

Southeast and East

Southeast from Zermatt are the **Monte Rosa** (4634m) and the **Liskamm** (4527m), squat blocks that are the highest and the third highest mountains in Switzerland, respectively. Leonardo da Vinci, incidentally, thought the Monte Rosa was the highest mountain on Earth. Among its unlikely conquerors have been Pope Pius XI, who pioneered a new route to the Grenzsattel in 1889, and a youthful Winston Churchill

(1894). Framed by woods and reflected in lakes, it is from this direction that the Matterhorn takes on its best known angle, as manifest by the proliferation of tea towels and cookie tins bearing the same likeness. A rack railway winds up to the best viewpoint, the **Gornergrat** (3090m, one-way 37SFr, round-trip 63SFr), via **Riffelalp** (2211m, one-way 16.60SFr, round-trip 32SFr). Other stops include **Riffelberg** (2582m, one-way 26SFr, round-trip 45SF) and **Rotenboden** (2815m, one-way 32SFr, round-trip 55SFr). The train leaves from opposite Zermatt's main station (daily 7am-7pm). The main path from Zermatt, which begins by following the right bank of the river upstream, calls at all the stations. Since the whole walk to Gornergrat and back demands a lot of stamina, grabbing a lift for part of the ascent will preserve your strength for clambering around the top or taking a more interesting path down. From the top, tracks lead down to the wide, flat Gornergletscher, and along the ridge towards the **Stockhorn** (3532m) to which there is also a cable car (one-way 12SFr, round-trip 24SFr). Each provides a closer encounter with the ice, but loses a fraction of the all-around panorama of summits that makes the Gornergrat so special. A variant of the descent, after the Riffelalp station, is to take the contour around to the Grüensee facing the snout of the Findelngletscher, cross the river, and return to Zermatt by way of the **Moosjesee** and the **Leisee,** two small pools which provide a beautiful foreground to the majestic Matterhorn.

Northeast and Northwest

Compared to the well trodden highways south of Zermatt, the hikes to the north are unsung. Rockier, steeper, and harder, they also lead to proper summits rather than huts or viewpoints. A northeast hike starts from the Zermatt station. Head down to the river beside the Gornergratbahn, cross it, and turn left. Hop on the Sunnegga-Rothorn railway and lift as far as **Blauherd** (2560m, one-way 24SFr, round-trip 32.40SFr). A wide path gently circles the Unterrothorn's right flank to a col at 2981m. Take the blistering series of zigzags on the right (some offering fixed handrails) up to the **Oberrothorn** (3415m) a satisfying rocky fang. A northwest hike begins midway between the church and post office and opposite Hotel de la Poste on Bahnhofstr. The path initially climbs steeply up towards **Alterhaupt** (1961m) and **Trift** (2337m), but then levels off. The little-known glacier cirque beneath the icefalls of the **Ober Gabelhorn** and **Zinalrothorn** makes a turn-around point, but supermen will bear right up the **Metterhorn** (3406m), accessible to agile walkers and often used as an endurance training hike for those about to try the Matterhorn.

■ Saas Fee

Cradled by glaciers, Saas Fee (1809m) occupies one of Switzerland's most glorious sites. Situated in a hanging valley above the Saastal, the city is surrounded by grand 4000m peaks, including the **Dom** (4545m), the second highest mountain in Switzerland. The ice of the Feegletscher comes so low that you can visit the primordial giant on a 20-min. evening stroll.

Skiing, climbing, and hiking dominate the town, just as they do in Zermatt. A cable car to **Felskinn** (2991m) and a discreet underground funicular, the "Metro Alpin," to Mittelallalin (3454m) enable **summer skiers** to enjoy 20km of runs, as well as a stupendous high Alpine view. (Round-trip to Mittelallalin 54SFr; Felskinn 30SFr; 1 day summer skipass 56SFr, 32SFr. No skiing mid to May-June.) In April, a race for truly expert skiers like local resident **Pirmin Zurbriggen** (a zillion times world ski champion) twists down from Mittelallalin to the village amid much festivity. In winter, unquestionably Saas Fee's high season, an immense network of lifts opens up (56SFr per day, children 32SFr; 6 days 260SFr, 150SFr; 13 days 465SFr, 265SFr). The **Ski School** (tel. 957 23 48; fax 957 23 66) offers a week of group skiing lessons (163SFr, snowboarding 150SFr), with lightly reduced rates available in the second half of January. Equipment rental is available at a number of village outlets (skis and boots 65SFr, 6 days 232SFr; snowboard and boots 57SFr, 6 days 207SFr). Torchlit toboggan runs and 20km of prepared winter hiking trails are among the other wintertime treats.

In summer, Saas Fee is among the three or four best places to start Alpinism. The **guide's office** (tel. 957 44 64), by the church, has a selection of climbs to 4000m summits like the **Allalinhorn** for amateurs as well as the experienced (open Mon.-Sat. 9:30am-noon and 3-6pm). Regular hikers have 280km of marked trails to choose from, but the plethora of mountains tends to make for rather steep paths. For a highly recommended half-day walk, take the cable car from the end of main street to **Plattien** (2570m,17SFr). This gives a magnificent picture of the east face of the Dom and Lezspitze. You can walk up by bearing right at the cable car station and left up the zig-zags 5min. further on. From the top, descend for a quarter of an hour, and take the left path heading around the cirque, which spirals slowly down below the Feegletscher. The view opens up to the other high peaks as you drop down to the Gletschersee (1910m) at the glacier snout, and then gently follows the left bank of the outlet stream back to Saas Fee. For a hard, steep, brutal, and blunt walk, hike up to the **Mischabelhütte** (3329m), which has the single best panorama of the Saas Fee cirque accessible to walkers. Coming from the pharmacy along the main street, turn right after the church, and take the right hand fork 100m further on. The track heads straight up the spur of the Lenzspitze, and the views improve monumentally with each step. Check for snow cover before you leave, however. The last part is rocky and becomes very unpleasant with any hint of snow or ice (1550m ascent, a full day hike, June-Sept. only). If you find the thought of steep climbs intimidating, but enjoy feeling gravity's pull, it may be worth getting a **Saas Valley Hiking Pass,** which gives access for a week to all cable cars in the valley, entrance to the ice pavilion at Mittela-llanin, and sports center (149SFr, family rate 299SFr). Do some arithmetic, though, before shelling out so much, and definitely factor in the risk of bad weather. The *wanderpass* is available at the tourist office or any cable car station. Note that most lifts, however, close May to early June and mid-Oct. to mid-Dec.

For rainy day diversion, the Sports Center "Freizeitzentrum Bielen" (tel. 957 24 75), next to the bus station, has an expensive but excellent **swimming pool** and **jacuzzi** complex. (Open high season daily 10am-9pm; low season 1:30-9pm. 12SFr, with guest card 7SFr.)

Drivers can leave their metallic steeds at the lower end of the village with a Saas Fee visitors card from their hotel (1 day 13SFr, 9SFr thereafter). An hourly bus runs to **Brig** (1hr.10min., one-way 17.40SFr, round-trip 33SFr), **Visp** (50min., one-way 13.20SFr, round-trip 26.40SFr; connect here to **Lausanne, Sion,** and the **Valais**), **Stalden Saas** (35min., one-way 10.40SFr, connect here for **Zermatt,** another 30SFr), and **Saas Grund** (10min., 2.80SFr). You need to reserve a place on all buses starting at Saas Fee at least 2hr. before departure. Call 957 19 45 or drop by the bus station. (Ticket office open Mon.-Fri. 7:20am-12:35pm and 1:15-6:35pm, Sat. 7:20am-6:35pm, Sun. 7:20am-12:35pm and 2:15-6:35pm.)

The **tourist office** (tel. 957 14 57; fax 957 18 60), across from the bus station, is small and usually packed. Ask for town maps and information booklets. They may charge up to 5SFr for room reservations, but are full of good advice about hiking and sell a range of maps and guides. (Open Mon. and Wed.-Fri. 8:30am-noon and 2-6:30pm, Tues. 8:30am-noon and 3-6:30pm; July-Sept. and Dec.-April Sat. 8am-7pm, Sun. 9am-noon and 3-6pm; May-June and Oct.-Nov. Sat. 8am-noon and 3-7pm, Sun. 10am-noon and 4-6pm.) The pharmacy, **Alpen Apotheke** (tel. 957 10 30), sits on the main street, down the road to your right as you leave the tourist office (open Mon.-Sat. 8:30am-noon and 2-6:30pm). The bus depot has small **lockers** (2SFr) and is the home of the **post office** (open Mon.-Fri. 8:30am-noon and 2-6pm, Sat. 8:30-11am). **Emergency: 117. Postal code: CH-3906. Telephone code: 027.**

Unlike nearby Zermatt where Neanderthal rock-climber types scrape their knuckles along the ground on every street, Saas Fee attracts mostly clean-living middle managers. Hoteliers have responded accordingly by cutting budget accommodations and initiating town-wide TQM programs, performance targeting, and team-building exercises. All the dorms are over-priced, and hotel rooms cost a small fortune, especially in winter. One of the town's better values is **Pension Garni Mascotte** and its two sister chalets, **Alba** and **Albana** (tel. 957 27 24; fax 957 12 16). With your back to the station, head down the road opposite you just left of the tourist office. At the main street, turn right, and continue up the hill for 200m; Mascotte is on the left. (Alba dorms 27-30SFr. Albana 5-bed rooms 27-32SFr per person, 4-bed rooms 30-35SFr per person, doubles 76-90SFr, all with showers. Smarter rooms in Mascotte 45-55SFr. All prices include breakfast. Half-pension additional 10SFr. Open mid-Dec.-April and July-Sept.) The best budget accommodations, however, are at **Hotel Feehof Garni** (tel. 957 23 08; fax 957 23 09). From the bus station, head down to the main street left of the tourist office, turn left, pass the church and mountain guides' office, and Feehof is on the right opposite Hotel Imseng, which often has a large, **public alphorn** outside. Warm, wooden, and wonderful; nearly all of the creaky pine rooms have balconies, and the beds are deliciously soft. The showers, however, are rather metallic and require an odd little ritual with a vacuum pump. Ah, the quaint idiosyncracies of Alpen charm (in summer 48-52SFr per person; in winter 52-66SFr; showers and breakfast included). Two expensive hotels also have expensive basement dorms. Right behind Feehof, **Hotel Berghof** (tel. 957 24 84; fax 957 46 72) is a three-star hotel with a plush purple-trim lobby. The clean, clinical 48-bed dorm provides fresh insight into Swiss order. Store your bags in the new, unforgettably pink lockers. (35-40SFr. Bring your own sheets. Closed in May.) Continuing past Feehof on the main road to the river brings you to **Hotel Rendez-Vous** (tel. 957 20 40; fax 957 35 34). Though its basement dorms are cramped, its upstairs offers a TV room with leather armchairs and a cheapish restaurant with sheep painted on the wall. (Spaghetti 12-16SFr, *rösti* dishes 13-19SFr, *gemüseteller* 15.50SFr. Reception open 7am-10pm. Dorms 38SFr. Singles 77-99SFr. Doubles 144-188SFr. Breakfast buffet included. Reservation requested 6 months in advance for the winter season.) If you're not burdened by luggage, a spunky, imaginative alternative to staying in Saas Fee is a night in a **mountain hut**. Between July and Sept. the **Mischabelhütte** (3329m; tel. 957 13 17; 26SFr), above Saas Fee, **Hohsaas** (3098m; tel. 957 17 13; 22SFr), and **Weissmieshütte** (2726m; tel. 957 25 54; 25SFr) above Saas Grund, are all accessible. All serve breakfast and dinner to compensate for the tough hike up. The Saas Fee tourist office has a longer list.

There are three largish supermarkets. Nearest the tourist office and Pension Mascotte is the **Supermarkt,** right next to the pharmacy on the main street (open Mon.-Sat. 8:30am-12:15pm and 2:15-6:30pm). The pick of the lot, though, is the super-duper new **Migros,** just down the hill from the church (open Mon.-Sat. 8:30am-12:15pm and 2:15-6:30pm). For cheap filling fast food, try **Charly's Metzg** (tel. 957 29 79), between the tourist office and the main street, which has a menu at 9SFr, *älpermacaroni* for 7.50SFr, and burgers at 5-6SFr. **Spaghetteria da Rasso** (tel. 57 15 26), 2 minutes to the left of the pharmacy under the Hotel Britania, has 14 variations of spaghetti (13-29SFr). Pizzas (15-19SFr), salads (6.50-8.50SFr), and garlic bread (3.50SFr) are also featured on the menu. The shady terrace, grotesque wooden face, and occasional accordionists attract quite a crowd. (Open Dec.-April and July-Oct. daily 11:30am-10:30pm. Visa, MC, AmEx.) A few steps away towards the pharmacy, **Restaurant la Ferme** (tel. 957 14 61) is popular with the locals for serving the best Valais specialties in town. This crusty old chalet with the best mountain view on main street looks as though it should have cows inside. The chefs conjure excellent *käseknöpfli* (15.50SFr), *sennerrösti* (17SFr), *raclette* (8SFr), and *fondue* (24SFr; open daily until 10pm). An alternative for Swiss traditionals is **Restaurant Feeloch** (tel. 957 12 48), under Hotel du Glacier down by Migros (open July-May Mon.-Sat. 6pm-1am).

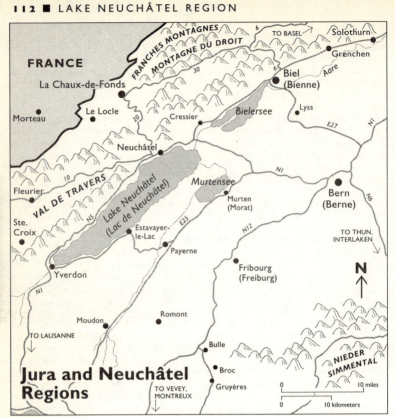

Jura and Neuchâtel Regions

LAKE NEUCHÂTEL REGION

■ Neuchâtel

An 18th-century traveler once called Neuchâtel the "City of Butter." The title probably refers either to the calorie-laden treats in the local *pâtisseries,* or to the unique yellow stone that makes up a large part of the city's architecture. Even after the novelty of the color has worn off, the town possesses a remarkably intact medieval beauty, focused in the graceful **Collegiate Church** and the commanding **château.** Neuchâteloise cuisine boasts quality as distinctive as the city's trademark hue, especially in its *fondue,* sausages, and of course, fresh fish from the lake and nearby rivers. Neuchâtel also produces wines to wash down its culinary offerings; vintnery is a regional obsession. Dozens of tiny vineyards painstakingly produce white wine made from *chasselais* grapes and red *pinot noirs* rivaling those of Burgundy. A regional specialty is the celebrated *l'oeil-de-perdrix* (partridge's eye), a delicate *rosé* of the *pinot noir* variety. Separated from the pulp early on in the production process, the wine has a much more delicate color than its red cousins, and is said to match the color of a partridge's eye, hence the name.

Orientation and Practical Information Neuchâtel regally presides over the longest lake entirely in Swiss territory. The Jura mountains rise from the lake's northeast corner. **Trains** connect Neuchâtel to **Basel** (19 trains per day, 35SFr); **Bern**

(37 trains per day 16.60SFr); **Interlaken** (20 trains per day, 39SFr); **Geneva** (every hour, 41SFr); and **Fribourg** (17 trains per day, 18.20SFr). **Lockers,** 5SFr per day, open until midnight. **Ferries** provide service to **Murten** (15SFr) and **Biel** (22SFr). Facing the lake, the **tourist office** (tel. 889 68 90; fax 889 62 96), in the left corner of the square (open Mon.-Fri. 9am-noon and 1:30-5:30pm, Sat. 9am-noon), dispenses the *Bulletin Touristique,* which contains a helpful city map, and listings (in French) of sights, museums, bars, phone numbers, and *La Route du Vignoble Neuchâteloise,* which lists all the vineyards in the local towns. The **train station** also houses a tourist office geared towards rail travel (open Mon.-Fri. 8:30am-noon, 1:30-6pm; Sat 8:30am-noon). Continue down pl. des Armes to find the **post office** (open Mon.-Fri. 7:30am-6:30pm, Sat. 8-11am) complete with **telephones.** Place Pury is the central **bus stop,** and also the best place to start exploring the town. **Police:** tel. 725 10 17. **Hospital:** tel. 722 91 11. **Postal code:** CH-2001. **Telephone code:** 032.

Accommodations and Food The **Auberge de Jeunesse (HI),** rue de Suchiez 35 (tel. 730 37 09) boasts friendly, multi-lingual management and a fine view of the lake from the immaculate dining room. Spare yourself the three kilometers of uphill hiking and opt for the bus instead. From the station, take bus #6 to "Pl. Plury." Walk in front of the kiosk to the stop for bus #1 (dir: Cormondrèche) and take it to "Vauseyon." At the bus stop, head uphill and take your first right. Follow the pedestrian signs up a flight of stairs and turn right. The hostel is well marked on the left hand side of the street. (Reception open daily 8-9am, 5-9pm. Curfew 10:30pm, but ask for a key. 22SFr first night, then 20SFr. Shower, sheets, and a hearty breakfast included. Closed Oct. 21-April 1.) Closer to town is **Hotel Terminus** (tel. 723 19 19), just across from the train station. (Reception open 7:30am-10pm. Singles 50SFr, 90SFr with shower; doubles 90SFr, 120SFr with shower. Breakfast 7.50SFr.) Ask for the list of *Hôtels et Restaurants de Neuchâtel et Environs* for inexpensive options in nearby towns. The closest **camping** ground is in Columbier: **Paradise Plage** (tel. 841 24 46) is on the lakeside and boasts a 4-star rating. (10SFr per person, 14.50SFr to include single tent, 20SFr to include double; open March-Oct. Prices rise by 2SFr between July 1-Aug. 15).

With its barrage of university students, Neuchâtel offers good, inexpensive meals. A lunchtime *menu* for 15SFr featuring freshly caught fish is not uncommon. Inexpensive cafés and restaurants abound near the university; the #1 bus stops right in front of it (to "Marin"). The student hang-out **Crêperie Bach et Buck,** 22 Ave du Premier-Mars (725 63 53) is especially satisfying if, and only if, you like crêpes (that's all they serve). Though limited, their menu takes one around the world and back, from the Hawaiian crêpe back to the ubiquitous Swiss cheese option. The restaurant offers a serene courtyard and complete meals for under 10SFr. It's located 50 meters from the University toward pl. Pury along av. Premier-Mars (open Mon.-Fri. 11:30am-2pm, also Mon.-Thurs. 5:30-10pm, Fri. 5:30-11:30pm, Sat 11:30am-11:30pm and Sun. 5-10pm). If crêpes aren't your thing, head for **A.R. Knect Boulangerie, Patisserie,** Place des Halles (725 13 21). Lying on the edge of the medievally trendy Maison des Halles, the patisserie serves up meaty sandwiches and flaky pastries for a pittance. West of the Halles des Maison, along Rue Moulins, sits the unassuming bistro **Chauffrage Compris** (tel. 721 43 96). Tucked into the street wall, this bar/restaurant serves up a well endowed *plat du jour* consisting of a meat or fish, vegetable, and a some form of starch. A small, community, everybody-knows-your-name type of place, the Chauffrage Compris exudes character and good feelings. As a bonus, the bar is connected to the **Centre d'Art Neuchâtel (CAN)** (724 01 60), a gallery for starving artists that focuses on the interface of "society and art," and, the hungry artists hope, "food and art" as well (4SFr, students 2SFr; open Wed, Fri, Sat 2pm-7pm; Thurs. 2-9pm; Sun. 2-5pm). With or without a trip to the CAN, the restaurant is a hungry heifer blue light special (open Mon.-Thurs. 6am-1am, Fri.-Sat. 6am-2am, Sun. 2-8pm). **Migros,** 12 rue l'Hôpital, in the center of town, is a good place for groceries and prepared meals (open Mon. 1:15-6:30pm, Tues.-Thurs. 8am-6:30pm, Fri. 7:30am-6:30pm, Sat. 7:30am-

5pm). A branch of the **Co-op** supermarket chain sits down the hill and across the main road from the hostel.

Sights and Entertainment Not surprisingly, the **château** for which the city is named and the neighboring **Eglise Collégiale** dominate the town from their hill-top perches. The 12th-century château served as the seat of the Count of Neuchâtel during the Middle Ages, and still retains essential medieval amenities such as fortified ramparts and murder holes used for dropping hot oil onto unwelcome visitors. The Collegiate Church mixes Romanesque and Gothic architecture, but its true claim to fame is the gaudily painted **Cenotaph**, erected in 1372, an excellent example of medieval art. Its statues of the Counts of Neuchâtel narrowly escaped destruction during the Reformation; the weepers at the base of the monument, mistaken for saints, were not so lucky. (Guided tours in English of the château April-Sept. Mon.-Sat. every hour 10am-4pm, except Sat. at noon and 1pm. Free. Church open daily 8am-6pm.)

The **Tour des Prisons** is but an arrow-shot away on rue de Château, and is worth every centime of the 0.50SFr entry fee. This is the part of your vacation when you can finally rid yourself of that annoying traveling companion. The cells, having seen constant use particularly in turbulent 1848, now have lots of space now in which to store unwanted baggage. The top of the tower provides a magnificent view of the old city and the lake (open April 1-Oct. 1). **La Maison des Halles,** the 16th-century covered market, lends an uncommon style to common activity. The Renaissance architecture of Laurent Perroud houses myriad shops and restaurants; a pleasant location for window shopping and a lunch of *saucisson neuchâteloise* and crusty French bread. The collection of medals, armaments, and paintings found in the **Musée d'Art et d'Histoire,** quai Léopold-Robert, pieces together an eclectic collection of paintings, coins, weapons, and textiles to tell the history of Neuchâtel. The uncanny 18th-century automatons are a special sideshow; performances are on the first Sunday of each month at 2, 3 and 4pm. (Open Tues.-Sun. 10am-5pm. 7SFr, students 4SFr; free on Thurs.)

The local university makes the nightlife predictably lively; the city is famous among regional club-goers for its techno DJs. Across the street from Crêperie Bach et Buck, the **Casino de la Rolande,** 14 faubourg de l'hôpital (724 48 48), has enveloped several smaller bars and turned them into a massive arena of disco worship. During the day, an arm of the Casino, **Arts Café,** serves American style pizzas starting at 12SFr (open Mon.-Fri. 8am-7pm). On weekends, the building transforms itself into a dance complex with occasional live bands and plenty of dancing. Burn baby burn in a disco inferno! (Beers 3-5SFr, admission 10SFr and up depending on the event.) The popular bar **Shakespeare Pub,** rue des Terreaux 7, across from the Musée d'Histoire, turns into a dance cave as the night progresses (or disintegrates), with three levels of leisure suit pleasure for the bachelor or bachelorette. Those so inclined to keep on keepin' on (dig!) should check out **Le Garage**, 4 rue de l'Hôpital, (721 45 45) for after hour grooves. The party goes until 4am, with sporadic specialty nights such as "sex night" (the Swiss were never big on innuendo). For live music, visit **MGM Café** on Rue Moulins just beyond the Chauffrage Compris. Those looking for a sedately fulfilling evening would do well to explore one of the nearby wine-producing villages such as **Cressier** (see below) for dinner and a sampling of the local wine in a café.

■ Near Neuchâtel

CRESSIER

The vines wrapped around the station house make it clear what the little village of Cressier is all about. Wine-making may no longer dominate the economy of this region as it did for centuries, but coaxing the perfect wine from the grapes growing on the sides of the hills remains the regional obsession. Built around a tiny château, the medieval village packs no less than seven **caves** (wine cellars) where one can participate in *la dégustation*, or wine tasting, sampling wines poured by the sunburnt hands that tend the grapes. To enter one of the rich and musty barrel-stacked cellars, ring the doorbell and ask: *"Deguster du vin, s'il vous plaît?"* Choose from *chasselas, pinot noir*, or *l'oeil-de-perdrix*, or leave it to the expert *("Vôtre choix"),* and you'll be poured a glass of Cressier wine, straight out of the vineyard's barrels. Many *caves* line the one and only main street, including the particularly pristine, traditional, and congenial cave of **Jean-Paul Ruedin** (tel. (032) 757 11 51) or the **Lauriers** family (tel. (032) 757 11 62). Though sampling is encouraged, it is considered polite to buy. The cheapest bottles run around 10SFr

Those who speak some French or know something about wine will have a much easier time in the wineries, but anyone can enjoy a charming walk through the vineyards or town streets. To reach the vineyards, and breathtaking views of the valley and **chateau**, follow Rue de Château and the signs for *tourisme pédestre.* This can all be followed by dinner at **La Croix Blanches** (tel. (032) 757 11 66), which serves deliciously fresh trout for 16SFr, and a massive *fondue* for 18.50SFr (open Thurs.-Tues. 11:30am-2pm and 6-10pm). Consider spending a night upstairs in the restaurant's hotel (singles 60SFr, doubles 90SFr with bathroom and breakfast), or try the **Hôtel de la Couronne,** 2088 Cressier (tel. (032) 757 14 58), an inexpensive, and friendly establishment. (Singles 40SFr. Doubles 60SFr. Breakfast 6SFr.) Call the phone number if no one answers the door. For a cheap loaf of bread to go with your wine, there is a **Co-op** next to the church on Rue Gustave Jeanneret (open Mon.-Tues., Thurs.-Fri. 7:45am-12:15pm and 2-6:30pm; Wed. 7:45-12:15pm; Sat 7:45am-noon, 1:30-4pm). Trains run hourly to Cressier from Neuchâtel (3.60SFr).

LA CHAUX-DE-FONDS

Those who are interested in time, or those who simply have a fair amount of it on their hands, may wish to visit La Chaux-de-Fonds. A major center for watchmaking, the town showcases an extravagant **museum** exploring "man and time," which is the focal point of the city's attractions. Another is the city's elevation, which at 1000m makes it the highest in Europe. Downhill and cross country skiing, mountain biking and hiking abound. An hourly train arrives from Neuchâtel (40min., 9.60SFr).

The **Musée International d'Horlogie,** rue des Musées 29 (tel. (032) 967 68 61, fax (032) 967 68 89), is worth the half-hour train ride from Neuchâtel. Not content to display merely examples of the Swiss watch industry, the museum chronicles humanity's quest to measure and use the great continuum, from Stonehenge to the atomic clock. The vast and the minuscule unite in two of the museums's finest pieces. Dardi's astrarium and Ducommun's planetarium illustrate the rigidly timed dance of the planets in the Ptolemian and Copernican systems, respectively. A newer but no less impressive timepiece dominates the area outdoors, above the underground museum. An artistic conglomeration of steel pipes and colored slats, called a **carillon,** measures time to the hundreth of a second, emitting acoustically precise musical ditties in combination with carefully orchestrated panel movements on the quarter of the hour. Those who witness the carillon at work feel strangely like sci-fi extras on the *Forbidden Planet*. The museum can be reached by walking down rue Jacquet-Droz and following the *musées* signs. (Open June-Sept. Tues.-Sun. 10am-5pm; Oct.-May 10am-noon and 2-5pm. 8SFr. students 4SFr.)

Two other museums in La Chaux-de-Fonds deserve mention as well. Fans of 20th-century art will enjoy the **Musée des Beaux-Arts,** rue des Musées 33 (tel. (032) 913 04 44). The collection contains works by a good number of artists, including the town's favorite son Charles-Edouard Jeanneret-Gris (a.k.a. **Le Corbusier**), the architect.The museum also boasts works by such wildly varying artists as Constable, Delacroix, Van Gogh, and Matisse. (Open Tues., Thurs.-Sun. 10am-noon and 2-5pm; Wed. 10am-noon and 2-8pm. 6SFr, students 3SFr, free on Wed.). Housed in an authentic late 16th-century farmhouse, the **Musée Paysan et Artisanal,** 5 Eplatures-Grise, on bus #3 from the train station to "Les Foulets" (tel. (032) 926 71 89), reconstructs the dwelling place, workshop, and general life-style of a rural artisan. (Open May-Oct. Sat.-Thurs. 2-5pm; Nov.-Apr. Wed., Sat., Sun. 2-5pm. 3SFr, students 2SFr.)

Ski enthusiasts will drool at the variety of alpine activity in the area. **Tête de Ran** (1422m), in nearby **Les Hauts-Geneveys** (tel. (032) 853 11 51), offers skiing of the downhill and cross-country varieties (15SFr per day, 13SFr per ½day). Reach Les Hauts-Geneveys by regional rail. A bus runs from the La Chaux-de-Fonds train station to **La-Vue-Des-Alpes** (tel. (032) 853 30 18), which offers both group and private lessons in both forms of skiing (1 day lift ticket 16SFr, half-day 13SFr), and also features night skiing. Buses run three to four times on Wed., Sat., and Sun. Reservations are required (tel. (039) 26 12 75). In summer, bikers and hikers will enjoy miles of well-marked trails that lace the region. (Bikes may be rented at the train station but ask tourist office for trail maps and bike rental information.)

The **tourist office** (tel. (032) 91 96 895; fax 91 96 297) is located at Espacité 1, off av. Léopold-Robert. From the train station, walk one block straight ahead, then turn right onto av. Léopold-Robert and look for the silver tubular tower. *Swiss Family Robinson* meets *Star Trek*. The tourist office is on the first floor. Take the free elevator ride to the 14th floor for a panoramic view of La Chaux-De-Fonds and the surrounding area. (Open May-Oct. Mon.-Fri. 8am-5:30pm, Sat. 10am-2pm; Nov.-Apr. Mon.-Fri. 8am-noon and 1:30-5:30pm, Sat. 9am-noon.) The spotless **Auberge de Jeunesse,** rue du Doubs 34 (tel. (032) 96 84 215, fax 96 82 518), sits at the corner of rue du Doubs and rue du Stand; take the #4 bus, direction: L'Hôpital. Tell the driver you are going to "l'Auberge" and he or she will drop you off right at the door. (Reception open Mon.-Sat. 7-9am, 5-10pm; Sun. 7-9am, 6-10pm. Curfew 10:30pm, but keys available. 23.50SFr first night, 21SFr subsequent nights. Doubles 30SFr and 27.50SFr. Breakfast and sheets included. Handicapped accessible.)

While the **nightlife** may be limited, it does have its hot spots. The **Bikini Test** (tel. (032) 96 82 856) could easily have fit into Wolf's *Electric Kool-Aid Acid Test,* with tripped-out murals on the outside and such oddities as a red, furry, enclosed cab for intimate conversations on the inside. The café, **Le P'tit Paris,** 4 rue du Progrès (tel. (032) 92 86 533), two blocks from the hostel, offers live music on the milder side, including jazz, reggae, and blues acts (Admission around 12SFr. Beers 2.60SFr. Open Mon-Thurs. 8am-midnight, Fri.-Sat. 8am-2am). For food, **La Pinte Neuchâteloise,** rue Léopold-Robert, just past the fountain, offers authentic Swiss cuisine; try the *rösti* for 5SFr. This local watering hole also serves beer for under 3SFr. (Open Sept.-May Wed.-Mon. 8am-midnight; June 1-Aug. 31 open daily 8am-2:30pm and 5pm-midnight.) For portable, do-it-yourself eats look no further than the **Co-op Super Centre** on rue du Modulor off of av. Léopold-Robert (open Mon. noon-6:30pm, Tues.-Wed. and Fri. 8am-6:30pm, Thurs. 8am-8pm, Sat. 8am-5pm).

Man and Machine

Born Charles Edouard Jeanneret-Gris, in 1887, **Le Corbusier,** architect, city planner, and painter has a monumental presence in 20th century art. This son of a La-Chaux-des-Fonds watchmaker accomplished this feat by actually becoming "timeless," revolting against the monumental tendencies of nationalism or historicism found in 19th century art (and probably his father as well). Le Corbusier sought to clean the slate and make way for pure, precise forms, forms that were motivated by their function, rather than their cultural reference. In keeping with this desire, he designed in glass and reinforced concrete, a revolutionary material choice that was to be repeated by countless others throughout the twentieth century. More importantly, he was infatuated with the iconic machines of modernity—the automobile and the airplane among them, and believed that houses and cities should be designed and organized as one would a machine, with regard to the economy of structure and the efficient "use" they offered. As he said in his seminal work, *Toward a New Architecture:* "The house is a machine for living."

■ Solothurn

Snugly sandwiched between the Jura Mountains and the Aare River, Solothurn, boasts one of the best hostels in Switzerland, and eleven of everything else. The eleventh canton to join the Swiss Confederation (in 1481), Solothurn, one of the best-preserved Baroque towns in the country, is home to eleven churches and chapels, eleven historic fountains, and eleven towers. **St. Ursen Kathedrale,** fashioned from pale marble, has eleven bells, and the staircase down from the main door is organized into flights of eleven steps.

Orientation and Practical Information At the edge of the Swiss Jura, Solothurn is easily reached by train from **Basel** (24SFr), **Neuchâtel** (17.40SFr), or **Bern** (13SFr). For tips on hiking in the Swiss Jura, a map of Solothurn, or free room reservations, head to the **tourist office,** Kronenpl. (tel. (032) 62 21 515; fax 62 31 632). From the Solothurn train station, walk through the underpass toward the *Zentrum,* and follow Hauptbahnhofstr. across the bridge and up to the Hauptgasse; the office is to the right, near the cathedral in Kronenplatz (open Mon.-Fri. 8:30am-noon and 1:30-6pm, Sat. 9am-noon). **Rent bikes** (21SFr per day) or **exchange currency** at the **train station** (both counters open daily 5am-8:50pm). **Lockers** and **luggage storage** at the station (5SFr). **Telephone code:** 032.

Accommodations and Food Luxury hostel. An oxymoron, you say? Not in Solothurn. Perched on the river in the *Altstadt,* the **Jugendherberge "Am Land" (HI),** Landhausquai 23 (tel. 23 17 06; fax 23 16 39), is easy to find (a 5-min. walk from the train station, over the Kreuz-acker Bridge, and the first left onto Landhausquai), if you don't mistake it for an art gallery. Opened in September 1994, the place draws you in like a benevolent siren. A central black wrought-iron staircase connects the four white-walled, wood-floored stories, but you can also ride in the great glass elevator. Giant picture windows looking onto the river and modern chrome track lighting keep this *El Dorado* of hostels well-lit day and night. Soothe your aching bones under the hot, high-pressure water of the immaculate showers in the sparkling white bathrooms. Drop your wearied carcass onto a firm bed, rest your head on a soft pillow, and snuggle up under soft sheets (no starchy white sleepsacks here) and a fluffy white comforter, or enjoy the myriad amenities: a pool table, music room, and conference room (for those last-minute press conferences which publicly state your love for Am Land). Sleep in if you wish (there's no lockout), but then you'll miss the unlimited supply of tasty cheeses, crusty bread, fresh juice, yogurt, and other treats that await you in the art deco dining room (served daily 8-10am). All this could be yours for just 24.50SFr (additional nights 22SFr; breakfast included, dinner 11SFr). Sounds too good to be true? There's only one-way to find out... (Reception open 7:30am-10:30pm). The **Hotel Kreuz,** Kreuzgasse 4 (tel. 62 22 020; fax 62 15 232), offers the only other budget alternative. (Singles 42SFr. Doubles 75SFr. Showers included.)

The streets of the *Altstadt* are lined with cafés and restaurants, but the **Taverna Amphora,** Hauptgasse 51 (tel. 62 36 763), outshines almost all others, with its large portions of Greek and Middle Eastern specialties under 20SFr (open Tues. 11am-11:30pm, Wed. 9am-11:30pm, Thurs. 11am-11:30pm, Fri. 11am-12:30am, Sat. 9am-12:30am). **Kreuz,** Kreuzgasse 4 (tel. 62 22 020), offers solid veggie plates in a beatnik atmosphere. Foodstuffs are available at the **Manora grocery store and restaurant,** smack in the middle of the *Altstadt* on Gurzelngasse (open Mon.-Wed. and Fri. 8:30am-6:30pm, Thurs. 8:30am-9pm, Sat. 7:30am-5pm). Stock up at the **farmer's market** on Wed. and Sat. at the Marktplatz (8am-noon).

Sights and Entertainment The city's penchant for quirkiness extends over to its numerous festivals and unusual museums. The beginning of carnival, February 6 in 1997, is marked by **Chesslete,** a procession with bizarre masks and festivities intended to drive away winter. On this day, citizens re-name their town "Honolulu," since the tropical city is directly opposite Solothurn on the other side of the world.

In the heart of the *Altstadt,* the **Museum Altes Zeughaus,** Zeughauspl. 1 (tel. 62 33 528), hoards one of Europe's largest collections of weapons and armor, with over 400 suits standing guard. You can even try a set on to practice your medieval warfare skills. (Open Tues.-Sun. 10am-noon and 2-5pm; Nov.-April Tues.-Fri. 2-5pm, Sat.-Sun. 10am-noon and 2-5pm. 6SFr, students 4SFr.) The **Naturmuseum,** Klosterpl. 2, also within the medieval town's walls, lets kids poke, prod, and touch animals, vegetables, and minerals. (Open Tues.-Wed. and Fri.-Sat. 2-5pm, Thurs. 2-9pm, Sun. 10am-noon and 2-5pm. Free.) Polish history savants can pore over the **Tadeusz Kosciuszko Museum,** Gurzelgasse 12, which details the life of the eponymous revolutionary. The small museum painstakingly maintains the residence as it was when Kosciuszko lived in it. (Open Tues.-Fri. 8am-noon and 1:30-6pm, Sat.-Sun. 2-4pm, if no one is there go to the office directly upstairs and ask for a key. 1SFr.) On the fringes of town, the **Kunstmuseum,** Werkhofstr. 30, houses a small collection of Swiss painters, though a Van Gogh and a few token Impressionists spruce up the walls. (Open Tues.-Wed. and Fri.-Sun. 10am-noon and 2-5pm, Thurs. 10am-noon and 2-9pm. Free.)

A ride on bus #4 yields one of Solothurn's hidden secrets. A 10-minute walk on Riedholzstrasse from the St. Niklaus bus stop (or take the Solothurn-Niederbipp train: "Feldbrunnen") leads to the stately **Schloß Waldegg,** the country estate of the von Besenval family. The castle now preserves the former aristocratic good life and houses the **Ambassadorial Museum,** detailing the history of the French embassy in Solothurn. Stand on the balcony and tell the masses that they can eat cake. (Open Apr. 15-Oct. Tues.-Thurs. and Sat. 2-5pm, Sun. 10am-noon and 2-5pm; Nov.-Dec. 20 and Feb.-Apr. 14 Sat. 2-5pm and Sun. 10am-noon and 2-5pm. Wheelchair accessible and parking available.)

The breathtaking Jura mountains lovingly watch over little Solothurn, and beckon fans of Mother Nature to get up close and personal with their many trails. Stock up on tourist office maps of marked **hiking** and **biking trails** through the Jura. Walking along the river provides gentle terrain and magnificent views of the looming Jura. Walk to nearby Altreu (2hr.) and see the oldest and best-known stork colony in Switzerland (perhaps one of them carried you to your expectant parents). For the more ambitious hiker, the hike to the Weissenstein Alpine center is a rewarding challenge (2hr., trail head at the corner of Wengisteinstr. and Verenawegstr.; follow the yellow signs to Weissenstein). Take the chairlift down from Weissenstein and hop on a train in Oberdorf for the trip back to Solothurn (4.20SFr). In the winter alpine and cross-country skiing dominate the sports scene. Weissenstein (1280m) has seven kilometers of cross country trails and two chairlifts for downhill.

Don't be fooled by the quaint, cobblestone *Altstadt.* When the tiny shops and boutiques close their doors, this village crowds people into its many pubs, cinemas, and other hot spots (ask the friendly hostel receptionist for tips). **Löwen,** Löwengasse 15 (tel. 62 25 055), serves up good beer, cheap Italian food (pasta and pizza for under 15SFr), and a mix of world music (funk, jazz, reggae, and, mercifully, no techno). For funky dance music, spin over to **Kofmel Fabrik. The Cinema Palace** on Hauptgasse shows recently released American films (13-15SFr).

■ Biel (Bienne)

It was in Biel in 1765 that Rousseau spent what he claimed to be the happiest moments of his life. The charms of this town, engulfed by mountains and an alpine lake, evidently were enough to cheer the heart of this generally miserable man. The ancient monastery in which he lived, situated on an island, is now a hotel whose prices give an appropriate lesson on the inequality of man. Culturally, French and German Switzerland have forged a symbiotic relationship in this bilingual town. You get a dose of both as street signs and menus are written in both languages. Though once Biel was considered the Detroit of watch manufacturing, Rolex and Omega factories still call it home. Grapevines (the other regional passion) crawl up the surrounding mountainsides and produce critically acclaimed wines. Perhaps Biel's best features lie outside the town proper; **Lake Biel** provides an excellent starting point for a plethora of moderate **hikes** in the mountains that surround the town.

The two best walks surrounding Biel both pass through magnificent gorges and exemplify the city's dual nature; one features open mountaintop fields ripe for picnics, and the other passes through a rugged canyon with a canopy forest. To get to **Twannbachschlucht,** take the rail car from Biel to Maggligen. (4.20SFr, free with Swisspass or Swiss Card. Leaves twice per hour, 7 days per week.) After tearing yourself away from this magnificent vantage point, follow the signs to **Twannberg** which lead to Twannbachschlucht. The trail follows a ridge perched above Lake Biel and alternately passes through dense forest and open meadows, filled with wild flowers and cushy grass. The journey from Biel to the lakeside town of **Twann** at the bottom of the gorge lasts about three hours. Return to Biel by train or by one of the lake ferries (ferry to Twann 6SFr, Eurail passes not valid), or move on to Neuchâtel. **Taubenloch** is a less ambitious hike, though perhaps a bit more rewarding, and the dense, deciduous canopy of trees is a throwback to Biel's days of fairy tale yore. Enter the canyon at the conjunction of Bozingenstr. and Herman Lienhard-Str. through the Zum Wilden Mann Restaurant's garden (2SFr if anyone is there to take it). The gorge walls shoot upwards over 30m and a mountain stream gurgles and crashes below. Most hikers turn back once they reach the water treatment plant, but those who press on and follow the signs to Frinvillier will find the **Hotel de la Truite** (tel. 35 81 133). The restaurant, in the proprietor's own words, serves "good wandering food." Fresh trout is 14SFr, and a *tulipe* of the local **Schafiser** or **Twanner** wine makes an excellent complement. (Open Mon. 8:30am-1:30pm, Tues. 8:30am-2pm, Thurs. 8:30am-4pm. Fri.-Sat. 8:30am-12:30pm, Sun.9am-1:30pm.) Many vineyards line the lake and can be reached by foot on a self-guided walking tour. (1-4hr., ask the tourist office for map.)

For a more leisurely introduction to the city, consider taking a **boat tour** of the lake. Or soak up some rays by the shore on the Strandboden. To reach the harbor and the beach from the train station, take a left onto Veresiusstr., and then a left onto Quai du Bas. Walk straight and follow the signs. Boat tours range from 12SFr (Biel-Twann) to 33SFr (Biel-Murten) round-trip. The annual **Open-Air Cinema** runs recent releases and classic films on a big screen in the lovely **Schloßpark Nidau**; last year's festival featured the US pop culture hit, *Pulp Fiction.* (Early July. 15SFr. Tickets sold at the tourist office.)

Few budget options bless this shrine of sun-worship. Consider making Biel a daytrip from Solothurn (20min., 8.40SFr), Neuchâtel (20min., 9.60SFr), or Bern (½hr., 10.40SFr). **The Hostel,** Solothurnerstr. 137 (tel. 34 12 965), is reminiscent of Camp Hiawatha and features commune-style management, with no lockout, no curfew, and free luggage storage. Don't think about walking; hop on the #1 trolleybus to "Zollhaus," and then walk away from the town for approximately ten minutes. Call first so they keep the reception open. (22SFr. Breakfast, sheets, and tea included.) For picnic supplies, trust **Migros** Freierstr. 3 (open Mon.9am-6:30pm, Tue-Wed. and Fri. 8am-6:30pm, Thurs. 8am-9pm, Sat. 7:30am-4pm) or the **Co-op** on Rechbergerstr. 1 (open Mon-Fri. 8am-12:30pm and 2-6pm, Sat. 7:30am-4pm).

The Biel **tourist office** is located just outside the **train station,** at Bahnhofpl. (tel. 32 27 575; fax 32 37 757; open May-Nov. Mon.-Fri. 8am-12:30pm and 1:30-6pm, Sat. 9am-noon and 2-5pm; Dec.-April Mon.-Fri. 8am-12:30pm and 1:30-6pm). **Bike rental** at the train station in Biel (21SFr, ½day 17SFr; mountain bike 29SFr, ½day 24SFr). **Lockers** and **luggage storage** at the station (5SFr). **Buch-und Presse Center** on Bahnhofstr. sells English books and magazines (open Mon. 1:30-6:30pm, Tues.-Wed. and Fri. 7am-6:30pm, Thurs. 7am-9pm, Sat. 7am-4pm). **Police:** 32 12 385. **Hospital:** tel. 32 42 424. **Taxi:** 32 21 1111. **Telephone code:** 032.

■ Fribourg (Freiburg)

Fribourg, Bern's sister city to the southwest, lies in a deep wooden gorge, a fact which delights the eyes and disgusts the feet. It straddles the sharp linguistic border between French and German-speaking Switzerland—the river that divides the town is known as the Sarine from the west bank and the Saane from the east. It loops around a lumpy, medieval *vieille ville*. Fortunately tourism takes third place behind the university and Catholicism as a focus of the city's energy; camera-clicking visitors are easily outnumbered by monks and nuns. This plethora of penguins is a manifestation of Fribourg's century-old position as the last redoubt against encroaching Protestantism. Religious foundations sit on every corner, and even the local brew, Cardinal beer, celebrates the career development of a 19th-century bishop.

Orientation and Practical Information Fribourg sits on the main train line between Zürich and Geneva. Frequent connections leave nearly every ½hr. to **Bern** (25min., 10.40SFr) and **Lausanne** (45 min., 21SFr). Other connections include **Neuchâtel** (1hr., hourly, 18.20SFr); **Interlaken** (1hr.20min. hourly, 32SFr); **Murten** (½hr., hourly, 9.60SFr); and **Basel** (1hr.40min., hourly, 43SFr). Fribourg's friendly **tourist office**, av. de la Gare 1 (tel. 321 31 75; fax 322 35 27), is 100m to the right of the station door. (Open May-Sept. Mon.-Fri. 8am-12:30pm and 1:30-6pm, Sat. 9am-12:30pm and 1:30-4pm; Oct.-April Mon.-Fri. 8am-12:30pm, Sat. 9am-noon.) Hotel reservations can be made through the tourist office (3SFr deposit) or at the station. **Currency exchange** is available at the train station (open daily 6am-8:30pm) or at one of the many banks lining rue du Romont. **Lockers** (small 2SFr; large 5SFr) and **luggage watch** (open Mon.-Sat. 6am-8:55pm, Sun. 7am-8:55pm, 5SFr per item), as well as **bike rental** (21SFr per day with ID deposit) are all available at the station. **Buses** for Bulle and the Schwarzsee (each trip 13.20SFr) leave from the station. **Emergencies: Police** 117; **Medical:** tel. 323 12 12. The **post office**, av. de Tivoli, is the unmissable skyscraper left of the train station. It offers money exchange (open Mon.-Fri. 7:30am-noon and 1:30-6:30pm, Sat. 7:30-11am), and phones (open Mon.-Fri. 8am-6:15pm; Visa, MC, AmEx). **Postal code:** CH-1701. **Telephone code:** 026.

Accommodations and Food The **Auberge de Jeunesse** stands at rue de l'Hôpital 2 (tel. 323 19 16). Hang a left out of the train station, and walk past the houses, across av. de Tivoli, past the post office, and onto narrow rue du Criblet. Turn left at the mini-playground, and walk up the path to the hostel. The old Hôpital des Bourgeois has been put to use as a youth hostel, though the long corridors and elevator music reveal the building's past. (Reception open Mon.-Fri. 7:30-9:30am and 5-10pm, Sat-Sun. 7:30-9:30am and 6-10pm. Curfew 10pm, but 50SFr deposit for a key. Dorms 24.35SFr first night, 21.85SFr subsequent nights. Add 7SFr per person for a double. Breakfast, sheets, and locker room-esque showers included. Lockers, laundry (3SFr), and kitchen facilities available. Lunch 11SFr. Open Feb.-Nov. Reservations strongly recommended.) **Hotel du Musée,** rue Pierre Aeby 11 (tel. 322 32 09), above the Chinese restaurant, is tucked in a quiet street, one block away from the Art Museum and the cathedral. Rooms are surprisingly large with deliciously deep-piled carpets. (Singles 40SFr, with shower 50SFr. Doubles 80SFr, with shower 90SFr. Breakfast 5SFr. Visa, AmEx, MC. Reservations preferred.) Campers can catch a GFM bus from the station to "Marly," where **Camping La Follaz** (tel. 436 30 60) offers lakeside plots. (Reception 9am-10pm. 4SFr. Open April-Oct.)

Small cafés selling quasi-Italian or German Swiss food line rue de Romont and especially rue de Lausanne. **Café du Midi,** rue de Romont 25, which buzzes with locals devouring specialty *schöni* fondue (22SFr) and tranche de porc (18SFr) under white umbrellas outside, or surrounded by pine and terracotta inside (tel. 322 31 33; open Mon.-Sat. 7:30am-11:30pm, Sun. 4pm-midnight). **Bindella Ristorante Bar**, rue de Lausanne 38 (tel. 322 49 05), cooks inventive, high quality pasta and pizza dishes, such as spaghetti with mussels and clams (19SFr). Leather sofas line the spacious interior, just the right atmosphere for *jazz e pasta* on the last Thursday of every month at 8:30pm (cover 8SFr; open Mon.-Sat. 9am-11:30pm). Better deals and unusual food lie hidden deeper in the city. Workers and locals pack the bar and restaurant of **Les Tanneurs,** pl. du Petit-St.-Jean (tel. 322 34 17), and its outdoor tables on the pleasant old town square. Plates are piled high with steak and fries (15SFr) and the beer is cheap

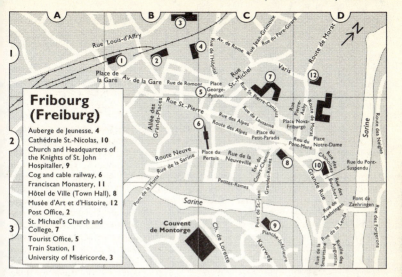

(2.60SFr). Hunt for budget meals at the **market** in pl. Georges-Python (open Wed. 7am-1pm) or in pl. de l'Hôtel-de-Ville (open Sat. 7am-1pm). Neon-orange sign rivals **Co-op** and **Migros** duke it out on rue St. Pierre at #6 and 2. (Both stores open Mon.-Fri. 8am-6:30pm, Sat. 8am-5pm.) While you're there look at the crazy mechanical fountain by Jean Tinguely. Passers-by are usually mesmerized by the cogs and gears for hours.

Sights and Entertainment The picturesque, cobblestoned *vieille ville* warrants a walking tour. From the station or the hostel head down rue de Lausanne to its end at pl. Noca-Friburgo. To the right is the 16th-century **Hôtel de Ville** (town hall) with its pointed clock tower, and in the courtyard in front of it sways the Morat Lime Tree, the last living link with that defining moment of Fribourg's history, the Battle of Morat (1476). Turning right as you face the Town Hall, then left along narrow rue des Epouses, brings you to **St. Nicholas' Cathedral.** For a dizzying panoramic view of Fribourg, climb the 368-step tower. (Cathedral open Mon.-Fri. 6:15am-7pm, Sat. 7:45am-7pm, Sun. 9am-9:30pm. Free. Tower open June-Aug. Mon.-Sat. 10am-12:15pm and 2-5pm, Sun. 2-5:30pm. 3SFr, students 2SFr.) Next door are the **Basilica of Notre Dame** and the **Franciscan Monastery** (open April-Sept. daily 7:30am-7pm, Oct.-March 7:30am-6pm).

At the other end of the cathedral, down rue des Bouchers, is the **Pont de Zähringen,** which gives a good view of the Sarine gorge. If you choose to cross and hike down to rue des Forgerons, it will lead you to the 13th-century **Gottéron Gate; Bern Gate** and **Cat's Tower** stand watch in the other direction. The steep descent down rue de la Samaritaine brings you to a quiet quarter around the Place du Petit-St.-Jean and the 14th-century timber-framed Augustinian Monastery. The two bridges over the Sarine here are the **Pont de Berne,** a wooden covered bridge with boxes of brightly colored flowers peeking out on each side, and the **Pont du Milieu,** an arched stone bridge with an endlessly photographed view of the old town.

There are a series of convents across the river. For a commanding view of the city, head over the Pont de Milieu, right along Karrweg, left up the hill, and right along chemin de Lorette. Here, you can also walk through the ruins of the tower.

The sprawling labyrinthine **Musée d'Art et d'Histoire,** rue de Morat 12 (tel. 322 85 71), maintains one of the largest sculpture and painting collections in Switzerland. There are several rooms of monastic and religious art (14-15th centuries), but the breathtaking exhibits are the macabre metal and bone figures by local artist Jean

Tinguely and the 16th-century statues of apostles from the cathedral, grotesquely shown together in the old town slaughterhouse. A long-promised printing museum is planned to open in 1997. (Open Tues.-Wed. and Fri.-Sun. 10am-5pm, Thurs. 10am-5pm and 8-10pm. Free, except special exhibits 8SFr, students 5SFr.) To pull some strings, head for the **Musée Suisse de la Marionette,** rue Derrière-les-Jardins 2 (tel. 322 85 13), near the pl. du Petit-St.-Jean, which houses hundreds of puppets from around the globe (open Feb.-Dec. Sun. 2-5pm. 4SFr, students 3SFr).

Fribourg will hosts an **International Film Festival,** March 2-9, 1997. It tends to have a Third World theme, as does the **International Folklore Festival** (mid-Aug.; many performances free). Other festivals include the **International Guitar Festival** (end of March), a **Jazz Festival** (July 16-27, 1997), and the **International Curling Festival** (beginning of March). The **Open-Air Cinema** (mid-July to mid-Aug.) is also worth checking out. Ask at the tourist office for tickets (14SFr) or call (041) 240 20 62. For assorted cutlery or that much needed cowbell, you could try the **Flea Market,** on pl. du Petit-St.-Jean on the first Saturday of every month (April-Nov. 7:30am-3pm) or the **Craft Market** on rue de Lausanne (March-Dec. 9am-5pm).

At night, most Fribourgeois sleep, but **Café des Grand Places,** 12 Grand Places (tel. 322 26 58) has an ecumenical selection of live music from funk and blues to salsa and industrial hardcore, plus karaoke on Wed. The restaurant upstairs has *menus* at 13.50SFr and 15.50SFr. (Open Mon.-Thurs. 9am-11:30pm, Fri. 9am-3am, Sat. 5pm-3am, Sun. 5pm-1am. The music starts around 9pm.) Just right from the station, **Café Rock,** bd. de Pérolles 1, has mid-air motorbikes, fenders on the wall, loud music and **Le Sélect** nightclub downstairs (tel. 322 24 14; open til 3am on weekends, *menu* around 14SFr).

■ Near Fribourg

GRUYÈRES

The knobby foothills between Fribourg and Gstaad form La Gruyère, whose 100km of prepared trails await the cardiovascular exploits of the world's cross-country ski-ers. **Gruyères,** a minuscule town and the unofficial capital of the region, also boasts one of the most prestigious **castles** in Switzerland (19 counts of the Gruyère dynasty cavorted about inside from the 11th to the 16th centuries) and its tasty namesake **cheese.** Cow products are churned for visitors daily at 12:30 and 3pm at the **Cheese Dairy.** Enter through the visitor's galley near the train station, and while you enjoy the samples, be sure to check for the alphorn; otherwise scream fraud, it's not real Gruyère cheese (open daily 8am-7pm; free; tours in English).

The two-legged herds amble up the hill to the flower-bedecked main street of the *vielle ville.* The **tourist office** (tel. (026) 921 10 30; fax 921 38 50) lies at the top. (Open mid-June to mid-Sept. Mon.-Fri. 8am-noon and 1:30-5pm, Sat.-Sun. 10:30am-4:30pm; Oct.-May Mon.-Fri. 8am-noon and 1:30-5pm.) **Parking** is available at the base of the hill leading to the "old town." At the top of the road grandly sits the **Château de Gruyères** (tel. (026) 921 21 02; fax 921 38 02), the first Renaissance castle con-structed in the Northern Alps. Built in 1494 for the Counts of Gruyère, it's more of a stately home than a castle, with an eclectic mix of restorations and renovations: 14th-, 18th-, and even 20th-century varieties. (Open June-Sept. daily 9am-6pm, March-May and Oct. daily 9am-noon and 1-5pm; Nov.-Feb. daily 9am-noon and 1-4:30pm; 5SFr, children and students 2SFr, guide 0.50SFr.) To reach the town from Gstaad, change trains at Montboron (15SFr). To get to Gruyères from Fribourg, take the GFM **bus** or **train** to **Bulle** and then hop on a train to Gruyères (15.80SFr). Trains pass through Gruyères hourly in each direction, but be aware that the last train from Gruyères to Bulle leaves at 9:34pm, and the last bus from Bulle to Fribourg departs at 6:28pm.

THE SWISS JURA

The long, narrow sprawl of Lake Neuchâtel divides French Switzerland from the rest of the country. However, the entire Jura region, from Basel all the way south to Fribourg, cannot be divided easily along these same linguistic lines. In Canton Fribourg alone, two-thirds of the people speak French, while the other one-third are native German speakers. At the southern foot of the Jura is Solothurn; curving north brings one to Lac de Neuchâtel (the largest lake lying entirely in Swiss territory), and then northwest to the border lies the town of Basel.

■ Basel (Bâle)

Perched on the Rhine and buffered by France and Germany, Basel (rhymes with nozzle) exemplifies the cultural dimorphism of Northern Switzerland; it is neither French nor German, but takes from both to create a distinct character all its own. An aesthetically beautiful city with a charming cobblestone *Altstadt,* Basel feigns a medieval image, subtly masking the vibrancy of a modern university town. The students at the university, Switzerland's oldest and perhaps most prestigious, inject life (particularly a nightlife) into this ostensibly ancient and sedate town. Majestic and enticing, Basel's sights include café-lined squares, serene churches, world-class museums, and dominating towers, but it is the city's vitality that really draws you in, helping you better enjoy its riches.

The night life of Basel, centered around the gray stoned **Barfüsserplatz,** rages until morning with outdoor cafés, smoky bars, live bands, and dancing. The biggest party of them all, the *Fasnacht,* allegedly rivals Mardi Gras, as residents chase away winter and let it all hang out after Ash Wednesday. The partying hides Basel's industrial side—Switzerland's second largest city is home to the headquarters of pharmaceutical giants Roche, Sandoz, and Ciba-Geigy. The party also gathers steam with the help of the university and its thriving student body, a festive atmosphere that was possibly the drawing point for such noted scholars as Jacob Burkhardt, who coined the term and the notion "Renaissance," and Erasmus, who published both his translation of the New Testament and his satirical masterpiece *In Praise of Folly* here. Basel also boasts a large Jewish community, one of the few in Switzerland.

The **Münster** cathedral presides over the *Altstadt* as a towering conglomeration of red sandstone, stained glass, and sprouting spires. The winding, hilly streets provide homes for 30 carefully orchestrated museums. You can see everything from Picasso to Roman sculpture in one stroll. You can also see the green waters of the Rhine which drift slowly through the city, serpentine and lovely on their way to Germany. It is possible to uncover the dichotomous facets of Basel in a day, but you could perhaps peel the layers off this complex city better in two. Consider Basel a weekend destination.

The goose, the whole goose, and nothing but the goose

In 1529, the residents of Basel enthusiastically joined the Reformation by throwing out the bishop, though they kept his *crozier* (staff) as the town's emblem. The staff is a more appealing symbol than Basel's other emblem, the **basilisk,** a nasty little creature that's part bat, part dragon, and part rooster. In 1474, Basel witnessed what may have been the world's first and only public trial and execution of a chicken. Allegedly, the hen had laid an egg on a dung heap under a full moon, and as everyone knew, such eggs hatch basilisks. The bird was tried, found guilty, and beheaded by the public executioner, and the egg was ceremonially burnt. Modern Basel has several replicas of its namesake monster suspended from buildings, gates, and fountains, but the *crozier,* for aesthetic reasons, is the more prevalent symbol.

GETTING TO BASEL

At the international crossroads amid Switzerland, France, and Germany, Basel is easily accessible from either country. If **driving** from France, take A35, E25, or E60; from Germany, E35 or A5. If traveling within Switzerland, take Rte. 2 north. Basel has an **airport** that serves continental Europe (tel. 325 31 11); all trans-continental flights are routed through Zürich. There are flights several times daily to both Geneva and Zürich. **Shuttle buses** run passengers between the airport and the SBB train station every 20-30 minutes, from 5am until the last plane arrives. By **train**, Basel is connected to **Zürich** (1hr., every 15-30min., 30SFr), **Geneva** (3hr., hourly, 67SFr), **Lausanne** (2½hr., hourly, 57SFr), **St. Moritz** (5hr., 7 daily, 80SFr), **Bern** (1hr., hourly, 34SFr), **Salzburg** (7hr., 2 daily, 124SFr), **Vienna** (10hr., 2 daily, 154SFr), **Paris** (4½hr.-5½hr., 9 daily, 675SFr), and **Rome** (7hr., 2 daily, 1195SFr). The city actually has **three train stations:** the French (SNCF) station (tel. 00 33 36 35 35 36) is next door to the Swiss SBB station (tel. 157 22 22). Trains originating in Germany arrive at the DB station, north of the Rhine down Riehenstr. (tel. 690 11 11). The former two stations are at the end of Centralbahnstr., near the *Altstadt*. International connections are easily made through the French or German stations. **Buses and streetcars** to the city center depart outside the SBB at Centralbahnstr. Buses also leave from the SBB and SNCF to points in **France** and **Germany,** while buses to Germany depart from the DB. Make sure to carry your passport with you for international crossings.

ORIENTATION AND PRACTICAL INFORMATION

Basel sits in the northwest corner of Switzerland, a stone's throw from Germany and a caber toss from France (so close that the *Tour de France* annually bikes through the city). The *Gross-Basel* portion of town, where most sites are located, lies on the left bank of the Rhine on two hills separated by the valley of the Birsig; on the right bank lies *Klein-Basel*. Be sure to pick up a city map (0.50SFr), among other useful publications, at either of the two tourist offices.

Tourist Office: Schifflände 5 (tel. 261 50 50; fax 261 59 44). Take streetcar #1 (from the SBB station) to "Schifflände;" the office is on the river, near the Mittlere Bridge. Also has lists of museums, cultural events, and suggested walking tours for Basel and the surrounding area. Open June-Sept. Mon.-Fri. 8:30am-7pm, Sat. 8:30am-12:30pm and 1:30-6pm, Sun. 10am-2pm; Oct.-April Mon.-Fri. 8:30am-6pm, Sat. 10am-4pm. The **branch office,** located at the SBB station (tel. 271 36 84; fax 272 93 42), also makes hotel reservations (10SFr). Open June-Sept. Mon.-Fri. 8:30am-7pm, Sat. 8:30am-12:30pm and 1:30-6pm, Sun 10am-2pm; Oct.-March Mon.-Fri. 8:30am-6pm, Sat. 8:30am-12:30pm; April-May Mon.-Fri. 8:30am-7pm, Sat. 8:30am-6:30pm.

Currency Exchange: Rates are nearly uniform throughout town. SBB station bureau open daily 6am-9pm.

American Express: Reise Müller, Steinenvorstadt 33, CH-4002 (tel. 281 33 80). Take tram #1 to "Barfüsserplatz;" the office is 1 block from the square. Checks cashed, mail held. Address mail, for example, Alexander SALTONSTALL, American Express Client Mail Service, Steinenvorstadt 33, CH-4002. Open Mon.-Fri. 9am-6:30pm.

Telephones: Outside post office; many elsewhere.

Public Transportation: Trams and buses move Swissly and silently from daily 5:45am-11:45pm. Most sights are within a single zone (#10). One-zone ticket costs 2.60SFr, day ticket 7.40SFr. Tram tickets dispensed from easy-to-use vendors at all stops. Maps are available at the tourist office or at the train station.

Ferries: For those who object to bridges, ferries cross the Rhine whenever someone, generally a commuter, jumps in their boat (1.20SFr; summer daily 9am-7pm, winter daily 11am-5pm). Rhine cruises depart daily, leaving the *Schiffstation* (tel. 639 95 06) by the tourist office. Cruises depart 6 times per day between May 1 and Oct. 13 (round-trip to Rheinfelden 42SFr, round-trip to Waldhaus 18SFr). Tickets can be purchased ½hr. before departure.

Taxis: In front of the train station, or call either 271 11 11 or 271 22 22.
Parking: In many locations, including the SBB station. 2.50SFr per hour.
Bike Rental: Next to the information office in the train station. 21SFr per day. Open: Mon.-Sun. 7am-9pm.
Luggage storage: At all of the stations. 5SFr. Open daily 5:30am-12:15am. Lockers 5-10SFr.
Bookstore: Jäggi Buchhandlung, Freiestr. 32 (tel. 261 52 00), carries English-language paperbacks. Open Mon.-Fri. 9am-6:30pm, Sat. 9am-5pm.
Gay and Lesbian Organizations: Arcados (Gay Center), Rheingasse 69 (tel. 681 31 32; fax 681 66 56), has videos and information. Open June-Aug. Tues.-Fri. noon -3pm and 5pm-9pm, Sat. 11am-5pm; Sept.-May Tues.-Fri. 1-7pm. **Schlez** (Gay and lesbian center), Gartenstr. 55, Case postale 640, CH-4010 (tel. 631 55 88). **Homosexuelle Arbeitsgruppe Basel (HABS),** Lindenberg 23, CH-4058 (tel. 692 66 55). Also has a **Jugendgruppe** (for young gays) and **HUK** (for Christian gays). Ask for the "Schwules Basel" brochure for a listing of groups, bars, discos, saunas, and shops.
Counseling Network: Helping Hand (tel. 143).
Rape Crisis Hotline: tel. 261 89 89. **Hospital:** tel. 265 25 25.
Emergency: Police: tel. 117. **Medical:** tel. 144. All lines have English speakers.
Post Office: Freiestr. 12, at the intersection with Rudengasse. Streetcar #1, 8, or 15 to "Marktplatz"; go 1 block up Gerbergasse to Rudengasse. Open Mon.-Fri. 7:30am-noon and 1:30-6pm, Sat. 8-11am. **Postal Code:** CH-4000 to CH-4060.
Telephone Code: 061

ACCOMMODATIONS AND CAMPING

Basel is a vibrant town with an atmospheric *Altstadt*, eclectically superb museums, and a raucous nightlife, but don't miss it because you didn't *call ahead of time*. There is but one overpacked hostel, and very few hotels even remotely approaching budget status. Just one phone call; you have time right now. Trust us. The truly desperate can try **Stadhof,** Gerbergasse 84 (tel. 261 87 11), which has showerless rooms in extremely limited numbers (Singles 60-70SFr, Doubles 110-120SFr).

Jugendherberge (HI), St. Alban-Kirchrain 10 (tel. 272 05 72; fax 272 08 33). Take Streetcar #1 to "Aeschenplatz," then streetcar #3 to "St. Alban-Tor." Or, a 10- to 15-min. walk from the SBB station down Aeschengraben, then St. Alban Anlage. At the tower, follow the signs for the hostel down the hill. Near a calm, verdant stretch of the river, this efficient, institutional set-up has lockers for every bunk and wheelchair access. Reception open daily 7-10am, 2-11pm. Checkout 10am. Lockout 10am-3pm, though the lounge is open all day. Curfew at midnight, no keys given. 26.80SFr for the first night, 24.30SFr each subsequent night. Showers and breakfast included. Good, solid dinners for 11SFr. Laundry 8SFr.
Hotel-Pension Steinenschanze, Steinengraben 69 (tel. 272 53 53; fax 272 45 73). From SBB station, take a left on Centralbahnstr., and continue walking straight ahead toward Heuwage-Viadukt. More expensive than the hostel, but with added advantages: a private room with TV and CNN; thick mattresses and pillows; private bathroom with a shower spouting hot, high-pressure water; breakfast with unlimited bread, milk, juice, *müesli*, yogurt, and espresso. No curfew. Singles start at 100SFr, but if you are under 25 and hold an ISIC card you get the student rate, 50SFr (3 day max. stay). Doubles with shower start at 140SFr, 100SFr for under-25 with ISIC card. Free daytime luggage storage.
Hecht am Rhein, Rheingasse 8 (tel. 691 2220; fax 681 0788). Cross the Mittlere Rhein Bridge next to the Tourist Office, and make your first right onto Rheingasse. Single without river view 70SFr, with view 80SFr. Doubles 120SFr and 130SFr. In July and August take your chances with lady luck: roll dice for a 10-40% discount off room rates. We're not kidding. Breakfast included.
Camping: Camp Waldhort, Heideweg 16, 4153 Reinach (tel. 711 64 29). Take streetcar #1 to "Aeschenplatz" (one stop), and then streetcar #11 to "Landhof." Backtrack 200m towards Basel, cross main street, and follow signs. Reception open daily 8am-12:15pm, 2:30-10pm. 6.50SFr. Tent 4SFr. Open Mar.-Oct.

FOOD

Basel is a university town, so relatively cheap eateries are fairly numerous, even in the heart of the city. Numerous cafés sprinkle the Marktplatz. Take a walk around the *Alt-stadt* and peruse the myriad menus until one suits your taste and pocket.

Hirscheneck, Lindenberg 23 (tel. 692 73 33). Cross the Wettsteinbrücke and take the first left. An unabashedly left-of-center restaurant/bar where dreadlocks and piercings prevail. Features at least two vegetarian and organically grown dishes daily. Menu 13SFr. Open Mon. 5pm-midnight, Tues.-Thurs. 8am-midnight, Fri. 8am-1am, Sat. 2pm-1am, Sun. 10am-midnight.

Zum Schnabel, Trillengässlein 2 (tel. 261 49 09). Take Streetcar #1 or 8 to "Markt-platz;" walk one block on Hutgasse to Spalenbergasse, and take a left onto Schna-belgasse. A bastion of well-prepared German-style dishes with Italian-speaking servers. A 12.80SFr meal could include *Bratwürst* with caramelized onions, rösti, and a salad. Open Mon.-Sun. 8am-midnight.

Topas Kosher Restaurant, Leimenstrasse 24 (tel. 271 8700). Next to the **Basel Synagogue,** and down the street from the **Marcel Hess** (self-proclaimed "kosher sausage king") **kosher deli.** Entrees 18.50-28SFr. Open Sun. 11:30am-2pm; Mon.-Tues. 11:30am-2pm and 6:30-9pm; Thurs. 11:30am-2pm and 6:30-9pm; Fri. 11:30am-2pm (Fri. dinner and Sat. lunch only if table reserved a day in advance).

Gruner Heinrich Pizzeria, Glockengasse. The hearty Italian food is a plus, but the bistro's location in the heart of the old city is its greatest asset. If it's a nice evening, grab a post-dinner ice cream in nearby Marktplatz, and walk the cobble-stoned streets. Open Tues.-Sat. 9am-midnight, Sun. 5pm-midnight.

Markets

Migros, Steinenvorstadt, Clarapl. or Sternengasse 17. Open Mon.-Wed. 8am-6:30pm, Thurs. 8am-8pm, Fri. 8am-6:30pm, Sat. 7:30am-5pm.

Co-op, opposite train station. Open Mon.-Sat. 6am-10pm, Sun. 9am-10pm.

Public market: On the Marktplatz, fresh fruits, vegetables and baked goods are offered every weekday morning.

SIGHTS AND ENTERTAINMENT

The **Münster,** the crown jewel of Basel's medieval buildings, was built on the site of an ancient Celtic town and Roman Fort, a fact that is catalogued by the archaeological excavation beneath and behind the apse. The church also has other underground activity; amid the wonderful riot of Romanesque and Gothic architecture lies the tomb of Erasmus, a staunch Catholic who remained loyal to his faith even after his beloved Basel joined the Reformation. When he died the city chose to ignore its dogma, however, in lieu of the thinker's great achievements and love for Basel, giving him a Catholic burial in its Protestant Cathedral. Bernoulli, the mathematician who discovered the math of the spiral and several principles concerning flight, also rests here in the cloister. (Blow on the edge of a piece of paper and watch it rise— that's all explained by Bernoulli's principle). The church is lofty and decorated with stained glass and delicate carvings. The red sandstone façade, though, steals the show, featur-ing hundreds of figures in various acts of piety ranging from trumpet-playing to dragon-slaying. The fact that these carvings were carefully designed to morally instruct the peasantry is apparent in the figures of the **Romanesque doorway** on the North wall. One can find the parable of the wise and foolish virgins, as well as the Last Judgment, with naked corpses rising and dressing themselves (after all, it is a major *faux pas* to face Divine Justice in the buff). The Münster **tower** boasts the city's best view of *Klein Basel,* the Rhine, and the Black Forest tower. (25SFr to climb; you must be with at least one another person due to recent suicides.) The picnic tables behind the church, overlooking the Rhine, make an excellent lunch spot. (Open Mon.-Fri. 10am-5pm, Sat. 10am-12pm and 2-5pm, Sun. 1-5pm, Oct.-Easter Mon.-Sun. 11am-4pm.)

Near Barfüsserplatz on Steinenberg, the modern **Jean Tinguely Fountain** juxtaposes the antique *Altstadt.* The fountain features 10 iron sculptures spewing, spraying, and throwing water in a maniacal representation of foolish humans and their foibles. Whether you give it a quick glance or gaze into the depths of watery perception, the fountain is a stand-out in its medieval context.

Walk up Petersgraben to find the University and Petersplatz. The parks forms a *de facto* quadrangle for the university and are ideal for frisbee, picnicking, napping, reading Kant, or any other collegiate endeavor. Bargain-hunters flock here every Saturday morning for the **flea market,** which starts at 9am and goes to the early afternoon. Potential souvenirs such as old coins and beer steins can be found among the flotsam and jetsam, but the friendly students unloading or accruing junk are the best finds. While browsing, strike up a conversation, and you may wind up with a new-found guide to Basel's pleasures both concrete and quixotic.

Nearby, Freiestr., the main shopping avenue, leads to the Marktplatz and the **Rathaus** (City Hall). Erected in the early 1500s to celebrate Basel's entry into the Confederation, the building brightens the entire Marktplatz with its loud red facade adorned with gold and green statues. In 1691, Basel's powerful guilds, in an effort to gain more say in the affairs of state, locked the government inside the Rathaus. While the politicians starved inside, the guilds partied outside, feasting on ale and sweets. The uprising was later dubbed the "Cookie Rebellion." Freiestr. #25 and 34, now restaurant and shop space, are good examples of guild hall architecture. Once the mighty force behind medieval society, the guilds now dabble in various charities.

St. Alban-Tor, by the hostel, is a good place to start a walking tour. It is one of the three remaining towers of the **Old City Wall.** Picnic in the park and play with the passing dogs who walk their owners back and forth, or head down St. Alban-Vorstadt to get to the well-preserved *Altstadt.* A bus tour of the city leaves during the summer from the SBB station (May 1-Oct 31 daily 10am; 20SFr, students 10SFr).

Off Marktplatz, Sattlegasse (Saddler's Street) marks the beginning of the **artisan's district,** with street names such as Schneidergasse (Tailor's Street). Find the **Elf-tausendjungfern-Gässlein** (Lane of 11,000 Virgins) and try to count them all. Legend has it that St. Ursula's pilgrimage of girls to the Holy Land during the Children's Crusade passed through here. While the medieval practice of gaining indulgences by walking this lane is now defunct, people still stagger down here full of the indulgences offered at the nearby clubs. A Gothic fountain, painted in a profusion of colors similar to the scheme of the Rathaus, spices up the nearby **Fischmarket.**

Right next door to the train station is the **Zoologischer Garten** (Basel Zoo) one of the best in Europe, and certainly bigger and cheaper than the one in Zürich. The zoo is most famous for successfully breeding several endangered species and is located on Binningerstr., 10 minutes from the *Altstadt,* down Steinenvorstadt (open daily 8am-6:30pm; 10SFr, students 8SFr).

A university town through and through, Basel's varied nightlife presents an entertaining change of pace from the surrounding bucolic and historical offerings. While parties abound year-round, the carnival, or **Fasnacht,** blows the rest away. At 4am on the Monday after Ash Wednesday (February 14-19 in 1997), the festivities commence with the *Morgenstreich,* the morning parade. The 621-year-old festival features colorful processions, fife and drum music, and traditional lampooning of the year's local and regional scandals. Revelers hide behind brilliant masks in an attempt to scare away winter. Basel attempts to keep Carnival a secret, but those on the anti-winter platform still flock to it in large numbers.

Though *Fasnacht* is *the* party in Basel, the town hardly slumbers the rest of the year. Basel's many cultural offerings include an accomplished ballet and several theaters. Music is especially popular here; one rewarding event is the free weekly **organ recital** at St. Leonard's Church (Wed. 6:15pm). The best sources of information are tourist office pamphlets (in English), which list concerts, plays, gallery exhibits, fairs, and other happenings for a three-month period.

WESTERN SWITZERLAND

MUSEUMS

Basel's 30 museums may seem overwhelming, but deserve more than a casual glance. The **Kunstmuseum** is deservedly the most famous. However, Basel's myriad of smaller art museums emphasize quality over quantity, and some of the most esoteric galleries can be the most fascinating as well. Subjects range from medieval medicine to musical instruments to Monteverdi cars. Pick up the comprehensive museum guide at the tourist office. If you're planning on visiting several museums, it may make sense to buy a **Three-Day Basel Museum Pass,** sold and honored at nearly all the local museums and in nearby **Augst** as well (23SFr, students 16SFr). You don't need to use it right away; the pass is stamped with the date at the first museum. A full-year pass is also available (60SFr, students 40SFr).

Kunstmuseum (Museum of Fine Arts), St. Alban-Graben 16 (tel. 271 08 28). Take Streetcar #2 from the station. In 1661 the culturally minded city bought a private collection and displayed it as the first public gallery not derived from previous royal acquisitions. The collection focuses on the periods between 1400 and 1600, with works from Mathias, Witz, and the Holbeins. The 19th and 20th centuries are also amply represented by Matisse, Braque, Gris, and Van Gogh. The excellent Picasso collection has a heart-warming story behind it: the museum had an opportunity to buy two Picassos but could not raise the money, so Basel granted the money through a resoundingly affirmative referendum. The aged Picasso was so touched that he donated four more paintings. We agree with Picasso—this is a great place and receives a resounding *Let's Go* pick. Open Tues.-Sun. 10am-5pm, Wed. 10am-9pm. 7SFr, students 5SFr. Free on Sunday.

Museum für Gegenwartskunst (Museum of Contemporary Art), St. Alban-Rheinweg 60, by the youth hostel (tel. 272 81 83). Feel the pulsating world beats permeate your body, or explore your innards and orifices on video with the Foreign Body Exhibit. The museum attempts to capture the imagination of the contemporary art scene with its highly energetic exhibits as well as its discerning collection of recent works. Important pieces by Beuys, Stella, and Trockel highlight the collection. Open Tues.-Sun. 11am-5pm. 7SFr, students 5SFr.

Antikenmuseum (Museum of Ancient Art), St. Alban-Graben 5, near the Kunstmuseum (tel. 271 22 02). With many pieces of outstanding quality, the museum exhibits the archaeological discoveries of Greece, Rome, and Byzantium. Basel's own archaeology takes part in the display, with pieces from an ancient Roman settlement found beneath Münster Church. The Medea Sarcophagus, with its writhing bas relief figures, will make you go running for your copy of the *Iliad*. Open Tues. and Thurs.-Sun. 10am-5pm, Wed. 10am-9pm. 5SFr, students 3SFr.

Barfüsserkirche (Historical Museum) Barfüsserplatz. Only here will you see the king of Basel stick his tongue out at you. Originally set on a gate facing the *Klein-Basel* in the 17th century, the *Lälle-Koenig* (king with tongue) is a clock with a protruding tongue that gestures at onlookers every other second. The museum is housed inside an old church which is an exhibit in itself. Open Mon. and Wed.-Sun. 10am-5pm. 5SFr, students 3SFr, first of the month free.

Papiermühle (Paper Mill) St. Alban-Tal 37 (tel. 272 96 52), a quick float down the river from the hostel. Everything you wanted to know about the art of papermaking but were afraid to ask. Feel the wooden water wheel mash trees into modern sheets of paper. Inquire about making your own print. Open Tues.-Sun. 2-5pm. 8SFr, students 5SFr.

Jewish Museum of Switzerland, Kornhausgasse 8 (tel. 261 95 14). Take Tram #37: "Lyss." Small but well-done exhibits with many rare items. The three sections include: the Law, the Jewish year, and Jewish life. Open Mon. and Wed. 2-5pm, Sun. 10am-noon and 2-5pm. Free.

Sammlung Karikaturen and Cartoons (Cartoon and Caricature Collection; *C-D5*), St. Alban-Vorstadt 28 (tel. 271 12 88). Though this collection is more Daumier than Dilbert, the exhibits can still make a fatigued traveler smile. Open Wed. and Sat. 2-5:30pm, Sun. 10am-5:30pm. 6SFr, students 3SFr.

NIGHTLIFE

The bar and club scene of this university town will not disappoint. **Barfüsserplatz** is a good place to start bar-hopping, with lots of students and adults hanging around the outdoor tables or drinking bottles of wine on the steps of the Barfüsserkirche. The two most popular locally produced beers are **Warwick** and **Cardinal.** When the bars close, revelers generally head for the clubs, which may play the hipper-than-thou game. Don't worry, all you need is that thousand watt smile and some clean jeans. Most places have a 21 and older policy, but the crowds get younger on the weekends. Huge parties or "events" thrown in off-beat places (a butcher shop was popular last year) are the in-thing among the movers and shakers of the party scene. Talk to the students at the Petersplatz flea market (see **Sights**) to find the hot spots.

Atlantis, Klosterburg 13. A *Let's Go* pick. Big. Hot. Smoky. Loud. Fun. A large bar that sways to all grooves, including reggae, jazz, rock, and funk, among other world beats. Bands play every night that the Italian soccer team does not. Cover 5-7SFr. Open Sun.-Thurs. 10am-midnight, Fri.-Sat. 10am-1am.

Brauerei Fischerstube, Rheingasse 45. Over the Mittlere Brücke and take the first right. Nary a beer sign in sight, though this bar happens to be Basel's smallest brewery, crafting four of the best beers in town. At this old-school *biergarten,* the delectably sharp *Hell Spezial* goes well with the homemade pretzels on each table. Open Sun.-Thurs. 10-midnight, Fri.-Sat. 10-1am.

Pickwick Pub, Steinenvorstadt (tel. 281 66 87). 100m from Barfüsserpl. This English style pub is a meeting place for students and adults alike. Happy-go-lucky bartenders are prepared to go the distance for you, even if it means going shot for shot. Open Mon.-Thurs. 11am-midnight, Fri.-Sat. 11-3am, Sun. 2pm-midnight.

Caveau Wine Pub, Grünpfahlgasse 6, by the post office. Sedately gentile change from the hops-dominated bar scene. Fine regional wine selection, particularly from Alsace, although the prices may be steep. Glasses 4-6SFr. Open Mon.-Sat. 11am-midnight.

Fifty-fifty, Leonardsburg 1. With its "Happy Days" diner motif, this bar features 50s style Americana on the walls and wine, beer, and "energy drinks" for under 5SFr on the menu. Beers 2.50SFr during happy hour (Mon.-Sat. 5-7pm). Open Mon.-Thurs. 11:30am-2pm and 5pm-2am, Fri. 11:30am-2pm and 5pm-3am, Sat. 5pm-3am, Sun. 6:30am-2am.

Campari Bar, near the Tinguely fountain. On warm summer nights, head over to this elegant outdoor bar surrounded by shady trees. One of the meeting places of the Basel art scene. Open Sun.-Thurs. 5pm-midnight, Fri.-Sat. 5pm-1am.

Babalabar, 74 Gerbelgasse. Dark, modern dance club for the beautiful people. Techno the night away amongst the disco bars and mirrors. Cover about 10SFr depending on night. Open summer Sun.-Thurs. 9pm-1am, Fri.-Sat. 9pm-2:30am; winter Sun.-Thurs. 8pm-midnight, Fri.-Sat. 8pm-whenever.

■ Near Basel: Augusta Raurica

If the medieval remnants in Basel aren't ancient enough for your taste, a day trip to the twin villages of **Augst** and **Kaiseraugst** will take you back another two millennia. Founded in 43 BC, **Augusta Raurica** was the oldest Roman colony on the Rhine, growing into an opulent trading center by the 2nd century AD, with a population of 20,000. After its destruction at the hands of the Alemanni in the late 3rd century, the Romans built a fortress adjacent to the old colony. Excavations, currently underway, continue to uncover temples, baths, theatres, and workshops.

To get to the ruins from Basel, take the hourly regional train three stops to **Kaiseraugst** (4.60SFr). A ferry (tel. 639 95 06) also runs from Schifflände, by the Basel tourist office, to Kaiseraugst (2¼hr., 4 per day, one-way 16SFr, round-trip 29SFr). Ignore the tourist information stand at the train station and follow the easily understandable signs to the **Augusta Raurica.** Also bring a well-stocked picnic to the temples or the amphitheater; the only nearby restaurant with reasonable prices is **Pizzeria Römerhaus** (tel. 811 17 67), just past the museum (open Mon.-Sat. 11am-2:30pm and 6pm-midnight, Sun. 11am-midnight).

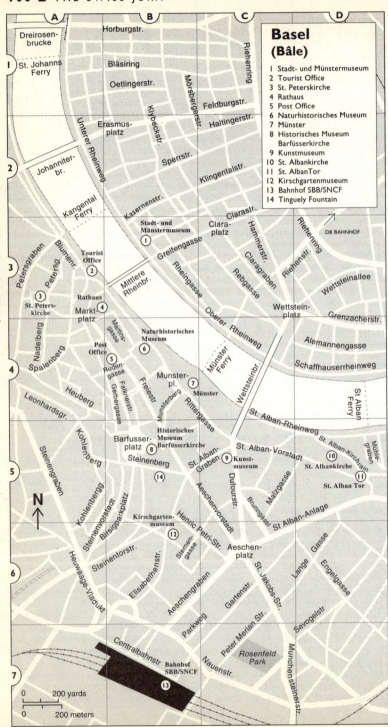

Basel
(Bâle)

1 Stadt- und Münstermuseum
2 Tourist Office
3 St. Peterskirche
4 Rathaus
5 Post Office
6 Naturhistorisches Museum
7 Münster
8 Historisches Museum
   Barfüsserkirche
9 Kunstmuseum
10 St. Albankirche
11 St. AlbanTor
12 Kirschgartenmuseum
13 Bahnhof SBB/SNCF
14 Tinguely Fountain

WESTERN SWITZERLAND

Central Switzerland

▨ Zürich

Switzerland has a bank for every 1200 people, and half of those banks are found in Zürich. The battalions of briefcase-toting, Bally-shoed, Armani-suited executives charging daily through the world's fourth-largest stock exchange and the world's biggest gold exchange help pump enough money into the economy to keep the upper-crust boutiques and expense-account restaurants quite well-fed. However, despite abundance, there is much more to Zürich than money. The city was once the focal point of the Reformation in German Switzerland, led by the 16th-century anti-Catholic firebrand Ulrich Zwingli. This Protestant asceticism was overwhelmed by the avant-garde spirit of 1916, a year in which artistic and philosophical radicalism shook the town's calm institutions. Living at Universitätstr. 38, James Joyce toiled away to produce *Ulysses,* the quintessential modernist novel. Close by at Spiegelgasse 14, Russian exile Vladimir Lenin bided his time, read Marx, and paced up and down this center for capitalism, dreaming of revolution. Next door—and rather troublesome, rumor has it—a group of raucous young artists, calling themselves the Dadaists, were founding the seminal proto-performance art collective known as the Cabaret Voltaire. The *Altstadt* retains some of this youthful irreverent spirit, with lively cafés and bars sprawling onto the narrow, cobblestone streets, and while Zürich's banks and factories may seem to dominate the landscape, a stroll through its manicured parks or along the Zürichsee is exceptionally soothing.

GETTING TO ZÜRICH

Because PTT buses aren't allowed into Zürich proper, it's easier to arrive in the city by plane, train, or car. **Kloten Airport** (tel. 816 25 00) is Swissair's largest hub (tel. 157 10 60), and a layover for many international destinations. Zürich has daily connections to Frankfurt, Paris, London, and New York. Trains leave every 10 to 20 minutes from the airport for the Hauptbahnhof in the city center (train operates 5:37am-12:20am; 5.40SFr; Eurail pass and Swisspass valid). **By car,** N3 east connects to E60, which leads to Zürich from Basel. Take N1 northeast, then connect to E4 or E17 when approaching Zürich from the south (including Geneva). From Austria or southeast Switzerland, get onto N3 west. Zürich is a city of **trains.** The main station is the Hauptbahnhof which faces the legendary Bahnhofstr. on one side and the Limmat River on the other. Connections to all major European and Swiss cities can be made here. To: **Winterthur** (20min., every 15min., 10.60SFr), **Lugano** (3hr., 1-2 hourly, 59SFr), **Lucerne** (1hr., 1-2 hourly, 19.40SFr), **Geneva** (3hr., hourly, 74SFr), **Basel** (1hr., 2-4 hourly, 30SFr), and **Bern** (1hr.10min., 1-2 hourly, 42SFr).

ORIENTATION AND PRACTICAL INFORMATION

Zürich sits smack in the middle of northern Switzerland, not far from the German border, and is surrounded by numerous Swiss playgrounds: the resort lake Bodensee to the north, the ski resorts in the Engadin Valley to the east, and the hiking bases in the Berner Oberland to the south and west. Zürich lies among the lowest land in Switzerland, quite distant from the mountains and skiers that have made the nation famous. The city commands the *Zürichsee* from its northern tip. Fortunately, most of the activity in Zürich is confined to a relatively small, walkable area, even though the suburbs sprawl for miles. The **Limmat River** splits the city down the middle, on its path to the lake. Grand bridges, each offering an elegant view of the stately old buildings which line the river, bind the two sectors together. The university presides over the hillside of the lively far bank, which, like Paris's *rive gauche,* pulses with crowded bars, hip restaurants, and a student's quarter. By contrast, Zürich's real *rive gauche* is rather conservative and very expensive; this stodgy banking community and shopping mecca is in the area surrounding the Bahnhofstr., on the other side of the Limmat. The *Altstadt* straddles the Limmat, and is bounded by the pedestrian zones. Most of Bahnhofstr. lies in this environ. The heartbeat of the city is also confined to this area, and noticeably slows down the farther away you go. **Limmat Quai,** in the *Altstadt,* across the bridge from the Hauptbahnhof, is a favorite strolling destination for many residents and tourists. The **Sihl River** edges the other side of the city, joining the Limmat around the train station. Zürich's industrial district is centered in **Wipinkingen,** a few miles upstream on the river.

Tourist Offices: Main office in the train station at Bahnhofpl. 15 (tel. 211 40 00; fax 211 39 81; hotel reservation service tel. 211 11 31). Exit the station to Bahnhofplatz and walk to the left alongside the building, just behind the taxi stand. Have your questions ready as lines are long and interviews short. You should have little problem signing up for an expensive walking tour of the city (Mon.-Fri. 2:30pm, Sat.-Sun. 10am and 2:30pm; 18SFr; in English). Try not to pay for the maps (1SFr); they are available for free at many hotels and local banks (try the Swiss Bank Corporation at Paradeplatz). Wade through the line for a copy of *Zürich News* and *Zürich Next,* which print restaurant and hotel lists, and information on concerts, movies, and bars (in German and English). Decipher the German *Züri Tip,* a free entertainment newspaper for tips on nightlife and alternative culture. The special reservation desk finds rooms for a 5SFr fee. Staff can answer most questions about Zürich. Open April-Oct. Mon.-Fri. 8:30am-9:30pm, Sat.-Sun. 8:30am-8:30pm; Nov.-March Mon.-Fri. 8:30am-7:30pm, Sat.-Sun. 8:30am-6:30pm. Reservation desk opens 10:30am. Also at **airport terminal B** (tel. 816 40 81), with the same services as the main office, as well as hotel reservations in all of Switzerland for 10SFr; open daily 10am-7pm. The **head tourist office** for the whole country, Bellariastr. 38 (tel. 288 11 11), offers information mainly for convention planners and travel agents; open Mon.-Fri. 9am-6pm.

Budget Travel: SSR, Main office at Bäckerstr. 40 (tel. 297 11 11). Open Mon.-Fri. 9am-6pm. Another office is located at Leonhardstr. 10 (tel. 241 12 08). They arrange package tours for students and can help with most travel questions, from the cheapest way to Greece to what's up in Bali; open Mon.-Fri. 10am-8pm. **Globe-Trotter Travel Service AG,** Rennweg 35 (tel. 211 77 80), specializes in overseas travel and 'round the world fares. Caters to individual travelers and also arranges transport and accommodations in Europe. No package tours; open Mon.-Fri. 9am-12:30pm and 1:30-6pm, Sat. 9am-3pm.

Consulates: U.S., Zollikerstr. 141 (tel. 422 25 66). Open Mon.-Tues. and Thurs.- Fri. 9-11am, Wed. 1:30-4:30pm. **U.K.,** Dufourstr. 56 (tel. 261 15 20). Open Mon.-Fri. 9am-noon and 2-4pm. Visas must be procured at embassy in Geneva. **Canadians, Australians,** and citizens of **Ireland** should contact their embassies in Bern. **New Zealand's** consulate is in Geneva.

Currency Exchange: Train station rates are comparable to most banks. Open daily 6:30am-10:45pm (if desperate, try the currency machine outside the office). Also try **Credit Suisse,** Bahnhofstr. 89. Open Mon.-Wed. and Fri. 8:15am-4:30pm, Thurs. 8:15am-6pm. **Swiss Bank,** Bahnhofstr. 70, is also an option. Open Mon.-Fri. 9am-6:30pm, Sat. 9am-4pm. **ATM machines** are found throughout the city, but most only take MasterCard. **Schweizerischer Bankverein** honors Visa, with branches in Paradeplatz, Bahnhofstr. 70, and Bellevueplatz.

American Express: Bahnhofstr. 20, P.O. Box 5231, CH-8022 (tel. 211 83 70), just after Paradepl. from the train station. Mail held. Travel agency services. Checks cashed and exchanged, but limited banking services. Open May-Sept. Mon.-Fri. 8:30am-6pm, Sat. 9am-noon; Oct.-April Mon.-Fri. 8:30am-5:30pm, Sat. 9am-noon. Traveler's cheque **emergency line** toll-free (tel. 155 01 00).

Telephones: PTT phones at the train station and at Fraumünster post office. Open Mon.-Fri. 7am-10:30pm, Sat. 9am-8pm, Sun. 9am-9pm.

Public Transportation: Swissly efficient trams criss-cross the city, originating at the Hauptbahnhof. Long rides (more than five stops) cost 3.40SFr (press the blue button on automatic ticket machines), and short rides (1hr.) cost 2.20SFr (yellow button). The city is small enough to avoid long rides. Go with the 24-hr. *Tageskarte* if you plan to ride several times; it's a steal at 6.80SFr. Tickets must be purchased

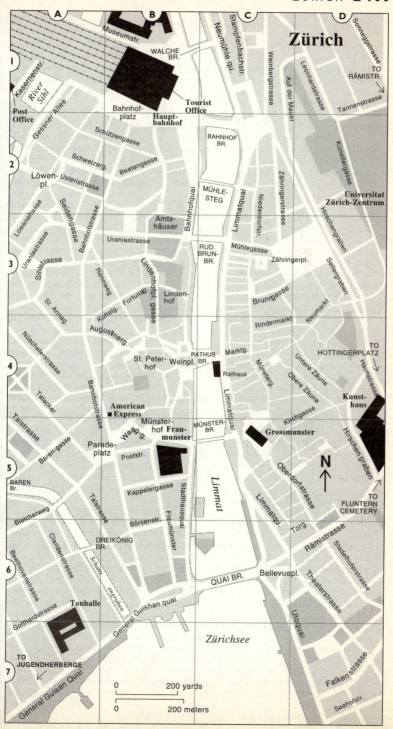

Zürich

CENTRAL SWITZERLAND

Museumstr.

WALCHE BR.

Kasernenstr.

River Sihl

Post Office

Bahnhof-platz

Haupt-bahnhof

Tourist Office

Neumühle qu.

Stampfenbachstr.

Weinbergstrasse

Auf der Mauer

Leonhardstrasse

TO RÄMISTR.

Tannenstrasse

Schmelzstrasse

BAHNHOF BR.

Gessner Allee

Schützengasse

Beatengasse

Zähringerstrasse

Niederdorfstr.

Künstlergasse

Löwen-pl.

Usteristrasse

Schweizerg.

MÜHLE-STEG

Universität Zürich-Zentrum

Lowenstrasse

Seidengasse

Bahnhofstrasse

Uraniastrasse

Amts-häuser

Bahnhofquai

Limmatquai

Hirschengraben

Uraniastrasse

Sihlstrasse

RUD. BRUN-BR.

Mühlegasse

Zähringerpl.

Seilergraben

Rennweg

Lindenhofplgasse

Linden-hof

Brungasse

St. Annag.

Kuttelg.

Fortuna g.

Neumarkt

Nüschelerstrasse

Augustinerg.

Rindermarkt

RATHUS BR.

Marktg.

TO HOTTINGERPLATZ

Talacker

Bahnhofstrasse

St. Peter-hof

Weinpl.

Rathaus

Münsterg.

Untere Zäune

Obere Zäune

Heimatrasse

Talstrasse

American Express

Münster-hof

Frau-munster

MÜNSTER-BR.

Limmatquai

Kirchgasse

Grossmunster

Kunst-haus

Baren-gasse

Parade-platz

Poststr.

Waag-g.

Hirschengraben

BAREN Br.

Talstrasse

Kappelergasse

Stadthausquai

Oberdorfstrasse

TO FLUNTERN CEMETERY

Bleicherweg

Börsenstr.

Fraumünster

Limmatqu.

Rämistrasse

Claridenstrasse

Schanze

DREIKÖNIG BR.

Limmat

Torg.

Stadelhoferstrasse

Beethovenstrasse

engraben

QUAI BR.

Bellevuepl.

Theaterstrasse

Gotthardstrasse

Tonhalle

General Guishan quai

Uloquai

TO JUGENDHERBERGE

General Guisan Quai

Zürichsee

Falken-strasse

Seehofstr.

N

0   200 yards

0   200 meters

before boarding. Validate the ticket by inserting it into the little slot on the ticket machine. Fines start at 50SFr. *Tageskarte* are also valid for ferry rides down the Limmat River within the Zürich Zone (check the maps at each stop, or at the tourist office). They are available at the tourist office, hotels, hostels, the automatic machines, or the **Ticketeria** under the train station in the *Shop-ville* (open Mon.-Sat. 6:30am-7pm, Sun. 7:30am-9pm). Ticketeria also offers 3-day and weekly cards. All public buses, trams, and trolleys run 5:30am-midnight, and on Fri. and Sat. until 2am. Railpasses are valid on all S-Bahnen.

Ferries: Boat trips on the **Zürichsee** leave from Bürgklipl. and range from a 90-min. jaunt between isolated villages (10.80SFr) to a "grand tour" (4-5hr.; 28.40SFr). Ferries also leave from the top of the Bahnhofstr. harbor daily at 11:40am (8SFr). Down at the **Limmat River,** boats run daily from April to Oct. (1hr., 6.80SFr). All ferries are covered on Eurail, and the *Tageskarte* will get reduced rates. Limmat boats leave every half-hour (free with *Tageskarte).* Enjoy a jump-suited night with the "Swiss Elvises," Wed. at 8pm during July on the *Zürichsee* (22AS). For more information, call 482 10 91.

Taxis: Hail a cab or call **Taxi 2000 Zürich** (tel. 444 44 44), **Taxi Zentrale Zürich** (tel. 155 55 15), or **Taxi for the disabled** (tel. 272 42 42). Fare includes tip.

Car Rental: Hertz, Airport (tel. 814 05 11), Morgartenstr. 5 (tel. 242 84 84), Hardturmstr. 319 (tel. 272 50 50). **Avis,** Airport (tel. 241 70 70). The tourist office at the airport and train station also arrange car rental. Others include **Budget Airport** (tel. 813 31 31) and **Europcar,** Josefstr. 53 (tel. 155 40 40; fax 272 05 87).

Parking: Zürich has many public parking garages. Within the city, parking costs 1SFr per hour, half that in the suburbs. Try the garages at the major department stores: **Jelmoli,** at Steinmühlepl. (tel. 220 49 34), **Migros Limmatplatz,** Limmatstr. 152 (tel. 277 21 11), and **Globus,** at Löwenstrasse (tel. 221 33 11). The Zürich police advise parking in the suburbs and taking a tram or train from there. **Universität Irchel** (tel. 257 43 85), near the large park on Winterthurstr. 181 and **Engi-Märt** at Seestr. 25 (tel. 205 71 11), are both suburban lots. Take the tram or train from there. Be sure to pick up the free brochure *Guide for visitors traveling by car* at any tourist office or police station.

Bike Rental: At the baggage counter *(Gepäckexpedition Fly-Gepäck)* in the train station (21SFr per day, mountain bike 29SFr). Open daily 6am-7:40pm. **Free bikes** at Werdmühleplatz and Theaterplatz; open daily 7:30am-9:30pm; passport and 20SFr deposit required.

Hitchhiking: Hitchers to Basel, Geneva, Paris, or Bonn usually take streetcar #4 from the station to "Werdhölzli." Those bound for Lucerne, Italy, and Austria often take streetcar #9 or 14 to "Bahnhof Wiedikon," and walk 1 block down Schimmelstr. to Silhölzli. Hitchers headed to Munich take streetcar #14 or 7 to "Milchbuck," and walk to Schaffhauserstr., in the direction of St. Gallen and St. Margarethen. Hitchhiking is illegal on the freeway. **Mitfahrzentrale** (tel. 261 68 93) matches drivers with riders. Travelers can call and leave a message concerning direction, date, and place where they can be reached. English spoken.

Luggage Storage: Lockers at the train station 4SFr and 8SFr, with 24-hr. access, though you pay extra every time you open the locker. Luggage watch 5SFr at the *Gepäck* counter. Open 6am-10:50pm.

Bookstores: Librairie Payot, Bahnhofstr. 9, has a large selection of English and French literature. Also has travel books, *Let's Go* among them. Open Mon. noon-6:30pm, Tues.-Fri. 9am-6:30pm, Sat. 9am-4pm. **Travel Bookshop** and **Travel Maps,** Rindermarkt 20 (tel. 252 38 83), have travel books and maps. Open Mon. 1-6:30pm, Tues.-Fri. 9am-6:30pm, Sat. 9am-4pm. **Barth Bücher,** in *Shop-ville,* has a smattering of English books. Open Mon.-Fri. 7am-8:30pm, Thurs. 7am-9pm, Sat. 7am-4pm.

Libraries: Zentralbibliothek, Predigerpl. (tel. 261 72 72), is open Mon.-Sat. 8am-5pm, Thurs. and Sun. 8am-7pm. **Pestalozzi Library,** Zähringerstr. 17 (tel. 261 78 11), has foreign language magazines and newspapers. Open Mon.-Fri. 10am-7pm, Sat. 10am-2pm; Oct.-May Mon.-Fri. 10am-7pm, Sat. 10am-4pm. Reading room open Mon.-Fri. 9am-8pm, Sat. 9am-5pm.

Gay, Lesbian, and Bisexual Travelers: Homosexuelle Arbeitsgruppe Zürich, H.A.Z., P.O. Box 7088, CH-8023; meetings at Sihlquai 67 (tel. 271 22 50). **H.A.Z.-**

lesben Schwule! (for lesbians), c/o Urs Bühler, Wildbachstr. 60, CH-8008. **Zart und Heftig** (Gay University Forum Zürich), P.O. Box 7218, CH-8023. **NKCOT** (National Committee for Coming Out Day), Case Postale 7679, CH-8023. **Andershume-Kontiki** (gay publication), Box 7679, CH-8023. **Gay Bikers,** Box 9313, 8036 Zürich. Ask for the **Zürich Gay Guide** at the tourist office which has listings for groups, discos, saunas, bars, and restaurants.

Laundromat: At the **train station,** wash 7.50-9SFr per 6kg. Dry 4.50SFr for 1hr. Soap included. Open daily 6am-midnight. Located under the tracks; ask at the shower desk for laundry services. **Laundry Mühlegasse,** Mühlegasse 11, wash and dry 17SFr per 5kg. Open Mon.-Fri. 7:30am-noon and 1-6:30pm. **Self-Service Wachari,** Weinbergstr. 37, wash and dry 10.20SFr. for 5kg. Open Mon.-Sat. 7am-10pm, Sun. 10:30am-10pm.

Public Showers and Toilets: At the train station. Toilets 1SFr. Showers 8SFr. Open daily 6am-midnight.

All-Night Pharmacy: on Bellevuepl. at Theaterstr. 14.

Emergencies: Police: tel. 117. **Ambulance:** tel. 144. (English speakers). **Medical Emergency:** tel. 261 61 00. **Rape Crisis Line:** tel. 291 46 46.

Post Office: Main office at Kasernenstr. 95/97 (tel. 296 21 11). Take tram #13, 14, or 31 to "Kaserne." Open Mon.-Fri. 7:30am-6:30pm, Sat. 7:30-11am. For *Poste Restante* pick-up open Mon.-Fri. 6:30am-10:30pm, Sat. 6:30am-8pm, Sun. 11am-10:30pm. 1SFr charge for *Poste Restante* after 6:30pm. Address **Poste Restante,** for example, to: Maria <u>MAROULIDOU</u>, Sihlpost, Kasernenstr., Postlagernde Briefe, CH-8021 Zürich. Other **branches** are at the **Hauptbahnhof** next to the tourist office, open Mon.-Fri. 6:30am-10:30pm, Sat. 7:30-11am; **Fraumünster** Kappelergasse, open Mon.-Fri. 7:30am-6pm, Sat. 7:30-11am; and at **Mütlegasse,** open Mon.-Fri. 7:30am-6pm, Sat. 7:30-11am.

Post code: CH-8021.

Telephone code: 01.

ACCOMMODATIONS AND CAMPING

Expensive as Zürich is, there are still a few budget accommodations to be found. Luckily for you, these bargain basement way stations try to emulate the ritzy hotels that made Switzerland famous. They are not five-star hotels, but are generally clean, courteous, and comfortable, and though often somewhat distant from the town center, easily accessible with Zürich's extensive public transportation system. Keep in mind that Zürich is rather sparse in hotel rooms for a city of its renown. Most of its 100 or so hotels are occupied by businesspeople, and its hostels often overflow with school groups. Reserve at least a day in advance, especially during the summer.

Jugendherberge Zürich (HI), Mutschellenstr. 114 (tel. 482 35 44; fax 480 17 27). Trains S-1 or S-8 (Eurail pass, Swisspass valid) to "Bahnhof Wollishofen." Walk straight up the hill from the station, 3 blocks to Mutschellenstr., and turn right. This is a 5-way intersection, so be sure you get on Mutschellenstr. (not Bellarrastr.), which is the farther right-hand street. Pass the Othmar Schoeck fountain on your right. The hostel is 2 blocks down Mutschellenstr. It can also be reached by taking Tram #7 to "Morgantal." Walk 10min. back towards Zürich along Mutschellenstr. Huge, orderly, and impeccably clean, the hostel's pink stucco modern structure looms in a giant corner well outside the city center, concealing diverse travelers within its depths. The kiosk, lounge, and dining room are perhaps the largest, best-stocked, and most comfortable in Switzerland. If you're feeling out of touch, tune in to CNN or watch one of the free nightly laser disc movies. Reception open 24hr. Checkout 6-9am. No lockout. 29SFr, non-members 34SFr. Subsequent nights 26.50SFr, nonmembers 31.50SFr. Doubles 88SFr, nonmembers 98SFr. Dinner 11SFr. Showers, sheets, and breakfast included. Lockers available, but bring your own padlock. Visa, MC accepted.

The City Backpacker-Hotel Biber, Niederdorfstr. 5 (tel. 251 90 15; fax 251 90 24). From the Hauptbahnhof, cross the Bahnhof-Brücke to the left, make a right at the Limmatquai, then walk to Niederdorfstr. Follow Niederdorfstr. until you reach Weingasse with the "Spaghetti Factory" at the corner. The hotel is down the street on the right. In the heart of the *Alstadt,* Biber's rooftop deck provides an ideal picnic or party spot while also providing a perch atop the lively nightlife of Niederdorfstr. Minutes from nearly all points of fascination, it occupies prime real estate. The busy beavers who staff the hotel are incredibly friendly and helpful, a tourist office unto themselves. Pick up a copy of *Swiss Backpacker News* to supplement your itinerary. Reception open daily 8-11am and 3-10pm. 4-6 person dorms 30SFr. Singles 65SFr. Doubles 85SFr, reduced prices in winter. Kitchen facilities and showers included. Lockers available. No breakfast. Sheets 3SFr. Laundry 9SFr.

Martahaus, Zähringerstr. 36 (tel. 251 45 50; fax 251 45 40). Take a left from the station, cross the Balinkof Brücke, and take the second right after Limmat Quai (it will be a sharp right at the Seilgraben sign). Simple but comfortable, with a pleasant dining room and lounge. Many of the rooms have terraces, including some of the dorm rooms. Dorms have partitions and curtains, affording a modicum of privacy. Situated in a prime location on the river, and therefore very busy. Reception open daily 7am-11pm (ring the bell to be let in after that). April 1-Oct. 31 dorms 34SFr, singles 68SFr, doubles 98SFr, triples 120SFr; Nov. 1-March 31 dorms 33SFr, singles 62SFr, doubles 94SFr, triples 111SFr. Showers and breakfast included. Locker deposit 5SFr. Visa, MC.

Justinhaus heim Zürich, Freudenberg 146 (tel. 361 38 06; fax 362 29 82). Take tram #5 or 6 to "Toblerplatz" and walk 10min. along Freudenberg. Perched on a hill overlooking Zürich, the recently renovated hotel features a spectacular view as well as clean and freshly painted rooms. Reception open daily 8am-5pm and 7-8pm. Singles 50-60SFr. Doubles 75-90SFr. Breakfast and kitchen facilities included.

Studenthaus, Rötelstr. 100 (tel. 361 23 13). Take tram #11 to Bucheggpl. and walk downhill 5min. on Rötelstr. Clean student housing during the year turns into a backpacker haven in summer. Youthful feel with a beautiful view of the *Zürichsee* and the city from the rooftop terrace. Phone ahead for reservations. Singles 45SFr. Doubles 60SFr. Kitchen available. Laundry 3SFr. Open July 15-Oct. 15.

Foyer Hottingen, Hottingenstr. 31 (tel. 261 93 15; fax 261 93 19). Take streetcar #3 (dir: "Kluspl."). Staid, quiet, and surrounded by plants and biblical references, the guardian nuns admit **women only** into the dorms. Single men are sometimes allowed to occupy a single room. Reception open 6am-midnight. Curfew midnight (with permission from the nuns). Dorms 25SFr, with partitions 30SFr. Singles 55SFr. Doubles 90SFr. Triples 105SFr. Quads 120SFr. 3min. showers 1.50SFr. Small breakfast included.

Aparthotel, Karlstr. 5 (tel. 422 11 75; fax 383 65 80). Tram #2 or 4 (dir: Tiefenbrunner Bahnhof) to "Fröhlichstr." This family-run hotel is removed from the city center, but lies just one street up from the lake and a 3-min. walk from the beach. A place where everybody knows your name. All rooms have TV and cable. Reception daily 8am-8pm. Singles 68-78SFr. Doubles 98-128SFr. Showers included. Breakfast 12SFr, but **Konditorei Kirch,** across Seefeldstr., has freshly baked goods for less (open Mon.-Fri. 6:30am-6:30pm). No smoking.

Pension St. Josef, Hirschengraben 64/68 (tel. 251 27 57; fax 251 28 08). Hang a left out of the train station, cross Bahnhof-Brücke, up the steps at the Seilgraben sign, and then head right a few hundred meters to the pension (10min.). The exterior is 198 years old, and looks it. The interior, however, is recently renovated and has beautifully polished wood paneling, engravings, and elegant furniture that give it its old-world charm. Despite its location in the center of town, the rooms are gracefully silent. Huge lounge with VCR and cable open to all guests. Possibly the most comfortable place to stay in Zürich. Reception open Mon.-Sat. 7:30am-7pm, Sun. 7:30am-2pm. Singles 70SFr; doubles 105SFr; triples 140SFr; quads 165SFr. Enormous breakfast buffet included.

Oase, Freiestr. 38 (tel. 267 35 35; fax 252 30 15), tram #3 (dir: Kluspl.) to "Hottingerplatz." From the stop, bear left up to Freierstr. and make a left to Oase. Usually a boarding house for students, the Oase is only open March-April and mid-July to Oct. Camp-like atmosphere with murals and hostel-like reception. Call ahead; roving school groups sometimes take over. Reception open Mon.-Fri. 10am-noon. Dorms 40SFr; singles 65-80SFr; doubles 110-130SFr. Breakfast included.

Hotel Seefeld, Seehofstr. 11 (tel. 252 25 70). Take tram #2 or 4 (dir: Tiefenbrunner) to "Opernhaus." This aging, nearly-forgotten hotel is pleasantly uncrowded. It offers somber rooms both near the *Altstadt* and one street up from the lake. Parking available. Singles 64SFr. Doubles 98-128SFr. Triples 135SFr. Showers and breakfast included.

Hotel Splendid, Rosengasse 5 (tel. 252 58 50; fax 261 25 59). Small hotel atop a very popular piano bar. Rooms are small and sparsely furnished. Convenient for Niederdorfstr. bar-hopping, or just for hanging out downstairs and listening to lounge music. Be prepared to stay up late. Singles 58SFr; doubles 96SFr. Showers included. Breakfast 10SFr. Visa, MC, AmEx, Diners Club.

Camping Seebucht, Seestr. 559 (tel. 482 16 12; fax 482 16 60), is somewhat far away, but the scenic lakeside location makes up for it. Take tram #7 to "Wollishofen," and walk the remaining 15min. along the shore to the right; or take bus #161 or 165 (from Bürgkliplatz, at the lake-end of Bahnhofstr.) to "Grenzsteig." Reception open 7:30am-noon and 4-8pm. 6SFr per person, 10SFr per tent. Open early May to late Sept.

FOOD

Zürich boasts more than 1300 restaurants, covering every imaginable ethnic, dietary, and religious preference. Unfortunately, few are affordable for budget travelers. The cheapest meals in Zürich can be found at *Würstli* stands, which sell sausage and bread for 3-4SFr, or at fruit and vegetable stands. For hearty appetites, Zürich prides itself on its *Geschnetzeltes mit Rösti*, slivered veal in cream sauce with country-fried potatoes. Check out the *Swiss Backpacker News* (available at the tourist office and the Hotel Biber) for more on budget meals in Zürich.

Mensa der Universität Zürich, Rämistr. 71. Streetcar #6 (from Bahnhofpl.) to "ETH Zentrum," or walk. Stunningly edible—may we say exquisite—dining hall food. Take a look at the bulletin boards in the university buildings for info on rides, apartments, and rooms for rent, as well as cultural events. Hot dishes 5.50-6.50SFr with ISIC card, salad buffet 6SFr. Open Mon.-Sat. 11am-2:30pm and 5-7:30pm; July 15-Oct. 21 Mon.-Sat. 11am-2pm. Self service cafeteria open Oct. 22-July 14 Mon.-Sat. 8am-4:30pm. **Mensa Polyterrasse** is just down the street at #101 with the same food and prices. Open Mon.-Sat. 11:15am-1:30pm and 5:30-7:15pm. Self service cafeteria 7am-7:30pm, July 15-Oct.21 7am-5:30pm. Both cafeterias close on Sat. from July 15 to Oct. 21. During the semester, the two Mensas open on alternate Saturdays. During vacations Polyterrasse is closed.

Zeughauskeller, Bahnhofstr. 28a (tel. 211 26 90), near Paradepl. Serves up Swiss specialties such as *fondues, rösti,* sausages, and *bratwurst* (everything in the 10-30SFr range) on long wooden tables. This *biergarten* features handsome wood roof beams as well as knights in shining armor on the walls. The outdoor seating provides prime people-watching. Open Mon.-Sat. 11:30am-11pm.

Gleich, Seefeldstr. 9 (tel. 251 32 03), behind the opera house. Herbivore impulses thwarted by industrialization? This completely vegetarian restaurant and bakery may be the oasis of green you need. Salads 6.40-12SFr. Entrées from 10SFr. *Menus* 21-34SFr. Open Mon.-Fri. 6:30am-9pm, Sat. 8am-4pm.

Rheinfelder Bierhalle, Niederdorfstr. 76 (tel. 251 54 64), in the *Altstadt,* and at the other end of the food pyramid. The Rheinfelders liberally wield the meat cleaver and also serve up *rösti* in all its variations. A mainly local crowd enjoys the food as well as the self-proclaimed "cheapest beer in town" (4.10SFr for 0.5liter). Good for people- and party-watching along Niederdorfstr. Entrees 11-30SFr. *Menus* 15-28SFr. Open daily 9am-12:30am.

Hiltl Vegi, Sihlstr. 28 (tel. 221 38 70; fax 221 38 74). Trade carrot sticks with the vegetarian elite at this swanky restaurant *sans* meat, one street towards the Sihl from Bahnhofstr. Salad buffet (9.50SFr) and fresh pastas are among the highlights. Entrées 13.20-18SFr. Open Mon.-Sat. 7am-11pm, Sun. 11am-10pm.

Restaurant Raclette-Stube, Zähringerstr. 16 (tel. 251 41 30), near the Central Library. Swiss *fondues* are at their richest, largest, and cheapest at this small restaurant on the outskirts of the *Altstadt.* The *Rösti* "side-dishes" are a meal in themselves. *Fondues* 18SFr per person but you'll have to share. *Raclette* 7SFr per person. Open Sat.-Thurs. 6-11:30pm, Fri. 11am-2pm and 6-11:30pm. Note: Opening time subject to change in 1997.

Café Chueche, Nagelihof 1 (tel. 262 16 00), tucked just behind Limmatquai. Large salads and eclectic entrées ranges upwards from 9.50SFr. Lasagna with salad (13.80SFr) and freshly-squeezed kiwi-apple juice (4.50SFr) are some of the highlights. Open daily 9am-10:30pm.

Ban Song Thai Restaurant, Kirchgasse 6, near the Grossmünster (tel. 252 33 31). This tiny space bursts with flavor from a narrow street in the *Altstadt*. Specialties include their sticky rice and *pad thai*. Open Mon. 11:30am-3pm, Tues.-Fri. 11:30am-3pm and 6-11:30pm, Sat. 6:30-11:30pm.

Rindermart, Rindermarkt 1, in the *Altstadt*, near Rathausbrücke (tel. 251 64 15). *Crêpes,* desserts, and creamy milkshakes scream to be eaten. Special vegetarian dishes as well as the usual meat and potatoes. Entrées under 17.50SFr. Open Mon.-Thurs. 7:30am-11pm, Fri.-Sat. 7:30am-midnight.

Schalom Café Restaurant, Lavaterstr. 33 (tel. 201 14 76), two blocks behind Mythen Quai. Take tram #5, 6, or 7 to "Bahnhof Enge," on General Willis and a right on Lavaterstr. Leave the *bratwurst* behind—not a pig's knuckle in sight. Kosher delights ranging from falafel (9.50SFr) to salmon (21SFr). Most prices within the 10-30SFr range. Open Mon.-Thurs. 11am-2:30pm and 6-10pm, Fri. 11am-2:30pm; Sat. for groups by reservation only.

Tres Kilos, Dufourstr. 175 (tel. 422 02 35), on the corner of Fröhlichstr. Mexican dishes around 20SFr. Avocado salad (12.50SFr), beers (5.50SFr and up), and free chips with salsa also help to set the mood for your gastronomical rhumba. The *chile con carne* gets rave reviews. Open Mon.-Fri. 11:45am-2pm and 6pm-12:30am, Sat.-Sun. 6pm-12:30am.

Cafés

Sprüngli Confiserie Café, Paradepl. (tel. 252 35 06). A Zürich landmark, founded by one of the original makers of Lindt chocolate, who sold his shares to his brother. The *Confiserie–Konditorei* provides some of the most exquisitely delicious confections in the world, and the café thrives on the *Confiserie's* renown. Lunch menus 16.50-25SFr. *Confiserie* open Mon.-Fri. 7:30am-6:30pm, Sat. 8am-4pm. Café open Mon.-Fri. 6am-midnight, Fri.-Sat. 7:30am-midnight.

Zahringer Café, Zahringerpl. 11 (tel. 252 05 00), across the square from the library. Sip coffee, frappes, and other assorted beverages with the young and hip at this unassuming café. Opens early on weekends so late-night revelers can top off the night with the requisite grease bomb (*rösti* topped with a fried egg 9SFr). Open Tues.-Fri. 6:30am-midnight, Sat.-Sun. 5am-midnight.

Gran-Café, Limmatquai 66 (tel. 252 35 06). Great views abound at this people-watching place *par excellence*. Every plate is meant to be seen, as are the patrons. The ice cream dishes especially are works of art. Entrées start at 9SFr, *menus* at 11.80SFr. Open Mon.-Fri. 6am-midnight, Sat.-Sun. 7:30am-midnight.

Infinito Espresso Bar, Sihlstr. 24 (tel. 212 27 77). Coffee selection broader than Juan Valdez's smile. Espresso starting at 3.30SFr, sandwiches and snacks 3-5SFr. Open Mon.-Wed. and Fri. 7am-6pm, Thurs. 7am-8pm, Sat. 9am-6pm.

Internet Café, Uraniastr. (tel. 210 33 11), is between the observatory and the river. Stave off hunger while surfing the net. Access to the World Wide Web and e-mail for 5SFr per 20min., 9.60SFr for 1hr. Sandwiches and hot pita pockets (12.50SFr) for that biological craving all those machines don't understand. Open Tues.-Sun. 10am-11pm, Mon. 10am-6pm.

Rosika's Rathaus Café, Limmatquai 61 (tel. 262 04 81), across from the Gran-Café. Wave to the passing boats while sipping coffee or a creamy frappe in the shade of an umbrella-shaded table. Coffee and frappes 3.60-7.50SFr, sandwiches 6.50-13SFr. Open daily 7am-midnight.

Markets and Bakeries

Two bakery chains which you can find throughout Zürich, **Kleiner** and **Bachmann,** offer freshly baked bread and *kuchen* for reasonable prices (open Mon.-Wed., Fri. 8:30am-6pm, Thurs. 8:30am-7pm, Sat. 8:30am-4pm).

Farmer's Market, at Burkpl. Fresh fruits and vegetables. Tues. and Fri. 7am-noon.

Co-op Super Center. The Co-op to end all Co-ops straddles the Limmat River next to the train station. You won't go hungry or broke if you watch for free promotional treats. Open Mon.-Fri. 7am-6:30pm, Thurs. 7am-9pm, Sat. 7am-4pm. **Branch** next to the tram stop near the hostel. Open Mon.-Fri. 8am-12:30pm and 1:30-6:30pm, Sat. 7:30-4pm.

Migros, branches near the hostel on Mutschellenstr. (open Mon.-Fri. 7am-6:30pm, Sat. 8am-4pm with adjoining café), under the train station in the *Shop-Ville* passage (open Mon.-Wed. and Fri. 7am-8pm, Thurs. 7am-9pm, Sat. 8am-8pm), and on Falkenstr. off Seefeldstr. (open Mon.-Fri. 7am-6:30pm, Sat. 7:30am-4pm).

SIGHTS

The tourist office leads frequent and expensive **tours** of Zürich. From May to October, tour guides chauffeur visitors around the major sites for two hours. (10am and 2pm year-round. May-October additional tour at noon. 29SFr.) For the same tour plus a cable car and boat ride, tack on an additional 10SFr (May-Oct daily 9:30am; 2½hr.). The cheapest tour is the two-hour **Stroll through the Old Town** (May-Oct. Mon.-Fri. 2:30pm, Sat.-Sun. 10am and 2:30pm; 18SFr.)

Stately and colorful, the **Bahnhofstraße** runs from the station to the *Zürichsee.* Trees lining each side of the street shade shoppers in this causeway of capitalism. One square meter of this will run you 250,000SFr; start saving up for that lemonade stand. Window shop 'til you drop—Cartier, Rolex, Chanel, and Armani flaunt themselves along the boulevard. To avoid the I'll-just-charge-it wallet trap lying in wait for your cash, throw yourself into one of the many, more affordable side streets. Zürich remains the quintessential banker's town. Though banks only give tours to bankers, they don't fault anyone for looking at their lovely interiors. **Bank LEU,** Bahnhofstr. 34, is the fairest of them all with an elegant marble and gold-leafed interior. Halfway down Bahnhofstr. lies **Paradeplatz,** the town center. It is said that Zürich's banks keep their gold reserves in safes directly under the ground here. You won't spot any golden ingots, however, so keep walking. **Bürkliplatz,** at the *Zürichsee* end, hosts a colorful Saturday **market** (May-Oct. 7:30am-3:30pm), with umbrella-hidden vendors hawking everything from vinyl records to giant cowbells.

Two giant cathedrals stare each other down from opposite sides of the river in the *Altstadt.* To the east loom the rather brutal twin towers of the **Grossmünster,** built by Charlemagne on the site of a spirited deer chase. The stark and somber stained-glass windows by **Alberto Giacometti** brighten this otherwise forbidding church. Zwingli spearheaded the Reformation in Switzerland with fiery tirades from the pulpit here. (Open March 14-Oct. 31 daily 9am-6pm; Nov.-March 13 Sun., Tues.-Wed., Fri.-Sat. 10am-6pm, Mon. and Thurs. 10am-5pm.) For a stunning view of Zürich, climb the steps of the **Turm.** (Open May-Sept. Mon.-Sat. 9am-noon and 2-6pm; March-April and Oct. daily 10am-noon and 2-5pm; Nov.-Feb. daily 10am-noon and 2-4pm. 2SFr.) Across the river on the left bank rises the steeple of the dreamier 13th-century **Fraumünster,** founded in the 9th century by the daughters of the local sovereign, with one window by **Augusto Giacometti** and an even more stunning set of stained-glass art by **Marc Chagall.** Catch the stained glass in the morning as it catches the rays of the rising sun. Walk around the Fraumünster to Fraumünsterstr. to admire the ethereal wall paintings in the Gothic archways of the courtyard. The nearby **St. Peter's Church** has the largest clock face in Europe, with the second hand reaching nearly 12 feet long. Noon threatens passersby with auditory nerve damage when the competing bells of the three churches do their stuff. Just down Thermengasse from St. Peter's lie the recently excavated Roman baths of the original, first-century customs post, Turricum. Rub-a-dub-dub, and then head back uphill to **Lindenhof,** the birthplace of Zürich. Now an elevated green with a splendid view of the city, Lindenhof is the original site of Turricum. Play some giant chess under the trees, and then see the Zürich that inspired Nietzsche, Joyce, and Lenin. Get to Lindenhof by climbing the steps at the intersection of Strehlgasse, Rennweg, and Glockengasse.

The university presides over Zürich on the hilltop directly opposite Lindenhof. Walk around the old buildings of the school, the first to admit women in all of Europe, and home, at least temporarily, to Einstein and the discoverers of the electron microscope. To the left of the university's central building is the **Thomas-Mann-Archiv,** Schönberggasse 15 (tel. 632 40 45), which preserves the study and library of its namesake author (open Wed. and Sat. 2-4pm; free). Taking tram #6, 9, or 10 to "ETH" uphill from the university brings one to the grave of fellow author **James Joyce** who lies in the Fluntern Cemetery (Open daily May-Aug. 7am-8pm; March-April and Sept.-Oct. 7am-7pm; Nov.-Feb. 8am-5pm. Free.) Next door is the **Zürich Zoo,** Zürichbergstr. 221 (tel. 252 71 00), featuring over 2000 species of land and water animals. Take tram #5 or 6 to "Zoo." (Open daily March-Oct. 8am-6pm, Nov.-Feb. 8am-5pm. 12SFr, children 6SFr.)

Botanical buffs will want to check out Zürich's many gardens and parks. The University's **Botanical Garden,** Zollikerstr. 107 (tel. 385 44 11), is a well-manicured park of neatly-labeled flora. Even the horticulturally challenged will enjoy lounging on the surrounding grassy hills. Take tram #2 or 4 to "Höschgasse." (Open March-Sept. Mon.-Fri. 7am-7pm, Sat. and Sun. 8am-6pm; Oct.-Feb. Mon.-Fri. 8am-6pm, Sat. and Sun. 8am-5pm.) Escape from the city on tram #3 to "Hubertus," where you can forage through the jungle courtesy of the **Städtgartneri,** Sackzeig 25-27 (tel. 492 14 23). This greenhouse, worthy of Dr. Livingston, shelters several varieties of tropical and sub-tropical plants, including a stunning display of orchids (open daily 9-11:30am and 1:30-4:30pm; free). The lush, tree-filled **Rieterpark,** overlooking the city, creates a romantic backdrop for the **Museum Rietberg,** and is perfect for a peaceful picnic. (Take tram #7 to "Museum Rietburg.")

For a quick and tree-filled jaunt overlooking the city, make the easy hike from Uetliberg to Felsenegg. Uetliberg, also known as the "top of Zürich," is an ideal spot for picnicking with a view of Zürich's urban sprawl on one side and of pristine countryside on the other. The flat walk is a peaceful escape from the city's hustle and bustle. From the Zürich Hauptbahnhof take the train to "Uetliberg" (departs every ½hr.), and follow the yellow signs to Felsenegg (1½hr.). There is a cable car from Felsenegg to Adliswil and another train back to Zürich. (Buy tickets at any train or cable car station or at most hotels. Free with Eurailpass.)

Food and Drink Sampling

Zürich's many food and beverage industries not only offer visitors a behind-the-scenes look but a taste of the action as well. **The Lindt and Sprüngli Chocolate Factory,** Seestr. 204 (tel. 716 22 33), welcomes visitors to its **chocolate museum** (exhibits in German), and invites guests to watch a film on the history of the company and chocolate production. "Physical sensory testing" is not required, but highly recommended (open Wed.-Fri. 10am-noon and 1-4pm). To reach the factory, take the train (S-1 or S-8, 5.40SFr) to "Kilchberg" from the *Hauptbahnhof* or take bus #165 to "Kilchberg." Take a right out of the station, a left down the first street, and an immediate right for a three-minute walk straight to the factory. The **Johann Jacobs Museum: Collection on the Cultural History of Coffee,** Seefeldquai 17 at Feldeggstr. (tel. 388 61 51), unobtrusively housed in a lakeside villa, presents the history of coffee, details its production, and displays elegant coffee services, some pricelessly edged in gold. At the end of the exhibits (all in German, but pamphlet with summaries in English) enjoy a delicious caffeine-filled cup in the drawing room of the villa (open Fri.-Sat. 2-5pm, Sun. 10-5pm; free). Take tram #2 or 4 to "Feldeggstr.," and walk down Feldeggstr. (2min.). The museum is on the right at the end of the street. **Hürlimann Brauerei,** Brandschenkestr. 150, on the outskirts of town, lets its visitors in on the secrets of brewing in the old tradition. Samples are free (mmmm, beer). Tours are by appointment only; call Herr Gyger (tel. 288 26 26) a few weeks in advance. In the same alcoholic vein, **Landolt and Co.,** one of Zürich's prominent wine companies, has a wine warehouse at Bradschenkestr. 60 (tel. 283 26 26) with good prices, a super, mostly anglophone staff, and free wine tastings for the buyers. Offers over 400 wines, 4-5 of which are generally opened daily for the tasting (open Tues.-Fri. 9am-12:30pm and 1:30-6pm, Sat. 9am-1pm).

MUSEUMS

Much of Zürich's banking wealth has been channeled into its universities and museums. Though one would immediately opt to head for the core of the city's art and historical wealth at one of its larger institutions, many of the smaller museums possess unique collections that are not to be missed.

Kunsthaus Zürich, Heimpl. 1 at Rämistr. (tel. 251 67 65). Take tram #3, 5, 8, or 9 to "Kunsthaus." One of the most extensive collections of 15th- and 20th-century art in Switzerland. Grab a map, otherwise you might be confused by your inadvertent jump from Dalí to medieval devotionals. Monet and Picasso hold their own in the sprawling rooms of modern art. Works by Klee, Chagall, and the Dada artists, as well as an entire loft devoted to Alberto Giacometti, round out the stunning assembly, enhanced by temporary exhibits of art from around the world. Open Tues.-Thurs. 10am-9pm, Fri.-Sun. 10am-5pm. 4SFr, students 3SFr. Free on Sundays. Additional admission fee for special exhibits.

Museum Rietberg, Gablerstr. 15 (tel. 202 45 28). Tram #7 to "Museum Rietberg." An exquisite collection of Asian, African, and other non-European art housed in two mansions set in the Rieter Park. **Villa Wesendonck** stores the bulk of the permanent collection, including an ancient golden Buddha from Tibet, a multi-armed Shiva from India, and assorted African tribal costumes. Open Tues.-Sun. 10am-5pm. 5SFr, students 3SFr. Exhibitions and collections 10SFr, 5SFr students. Combinations ticket for Kunsthaus Zürich and Rietberg 20SFr, 10SFr students. **Park-Villa Rieter,** opened in 1994, features an internationally accredited exhibit of Chinese, Japanese, and Indian works. Open Tues.-Sat. 1-5pm, Sun. 10am-5pm.

E.G. Bührle Collection, Zollikerstr. 172 (tel. 422 00 86). Tram #2 or 4 to "Wildbachstr." Walk up Wildbachstr., and turn right onto Zollikerstr. Museum is a few yards down on the right. Prestigious private collection reads like a top ten list of French Impressionists. Monet, Manet, Cézanne, Gaugin, and van Gogh dominate, but Renoir and Degas hold their own. Picasso and Matisse also make guest appearances. Appropriately housed in a stately mansion overlooking the Zürichsee with a view to complement the masterpieces inside. Open Tues. and Fri. 2-5pm, Wed. 5-8pm. 9SFr, students 3SFr.

Schweizerisches Landesmuseum, Museumstr. 2, behind the train station (tel. 218 65 11; fax 211 29 49). Tram #4, 11, 13, or 14 to "Bahnhofquai." This immense museum covers all areas of Swiss life, from its early pre-historic beginnings to the present, with an extensive archaeological collection, and reconstructions of grandiose period rooms. Open Tues.-Sun. 10am-5pm. Free. Special exhibit admission prices vary (about 8SFr).

University of Zürich Museums have a variety of locations. The many specialized schools of the university open the doors of their collections to the public.

Paleontology Museum and the Zoological Museum, Künstlergasse 16 (tel. 257 38 38). Tram #6, 9, or 10 to "ETH." Sharing a building that overlooks Zürich, the museums detail the development of organisms from the first fauna fossils, through prehistoric fish to the humble human head. Both take a hands on approach with interactive computer exhibits and microscope viewing stations. Open Tues.-Fri. 9am-5pm, Sat. and Sun. 10am-4pm. Free.

Museum of Classical Archaeology, Rämistr. 73 (tel. 257 28 20). Tram #6, 9, or 19 to "ETH." This tiny museum on the first floor of the archeological lecture halls has an extensive collection of Greek vases and coins (use the microscope to get up close and personal) and some Mesopotamian and Egyptian artifacts. Temporary exhibits are held in the basement next door to the warehouse of statues. Open Tues.-Fri. 1-6pm, Sat.-Sun. 11am-5pm. Free.

Völkerkundemuseum, Pelikanstr. 40 (tel. 634 90 11). Tram #2 or 9 to "Sihlstr." A collection based on eclecticism—pieces from a myriad of different cultures, ranging from African statues to Tahitian huts. Temporary exhibits highlight the cul-

CENTRAL SWITZERLAND

tures of non-European peoples. Open Tues.-Fri. 10am-1pm and 2-5pm, Sat. 2-5pm, Sun. 11am-5pm. Free.

Museum für Gestaltung (Museum of Design), Ausstellungsstr. 60 (tel. 446 22 11; fax 446 22 33). Tram #4 or 13 to "Museum für Gestaltung." Features outstanding photography, architecture, and design exhibitions, as well as poster and graphics collections. 1997's highlight will be an exhibit on human body forms. Open Tues., Thurs., and Fri. 10am-6pm, Wed. 10am-9pm, Sat. and Sun. 10am-5pm. Special collections by appointment only. 6SFr, students 3SFr. Admission to only the permanent collection 4SFr, 2SFr students.

Mühlerama Museum, Seefeldstr. 231 (tel. 422 76 60). Tram #2 or 4 to "Wildbachstr." Originally built to house a brewery, this fully-operational mill has been processing grain for a different purpose since 1913. Grind wheat on an exercise bike, or watch the flour fly and the wooden parts spin as the miller takes you through the art of making *brot* (bread). You can also eat the fruit of your labors. Open Tues.-Sat. 2-5pm, Sun. 1:30-6pm. 7SFr, students 5SFr.

Beyer Museum of Time Measurement, Bahnhofstr. 31 (tel. 221 10 80; fax 221 33 48). Details the development of the chronograph. Open Tues.-Fri. 10am-1pm and 2-5pm, Sat. 2-5pm, Sun. 11am-5pm. Free.

Zürich Toy Museum, Fortunagasse 15, corner of Renweg 26 (tel. 211 93 05; fax 401 20 36). Zürich's branch of Santa's North Pole has puppets, dolls, and other playthings from the 1700s to the present. Open Mon.-Fri. 2-5pm, Sat. 1-4pm. Free.

ENTERTAINMENT AND NIGHTLIFE

For some time with your feet up, relax at one of the bathing areas that line the shores of the Zürichsee. **Strandbad Mythenquai** is one such locale. Take tram #7 to "Brunaustr." and follow the signs (open Mon.-Fri. 9am-8pm, Sat.-Sun. 9am-7:30pm; 5SFr). Take your time, Zürich's bar and club scene isn't going anywhere. Niederdorfstr. is generally considered the epicenter of Zürich's nightlife; women walking alone, however, may feel uncomfortable in this area at night. Other hot spots include Münstergasse and Limmatquai, both lined with cafés and bars that overflow with people well into the wee hours of the morning. Establishments often charge double drink prices or a hefty cover charge after midnight, so plan your evening accordingly. Many movie theaters offer **English films** with German and French subtitles (marked E/d/f). Check the huge posters which decorate the streets, or try Bellevuepl. or Hirschenpl. Also, have a look at *Zürich News* and *ZüriTip* for film (around 15SFr, Mondays 11SFr) and theater listings, as well as prices.

Casa Bar, Münstergasse 30, a teeny-weeny, crowded pub with first-rate live jazz. No cover, but drink prices are enough to hasten bankruptcy (beers start at 9.50SFr). Open daily 7pm-2am.

Oepfelchammer, Rindermarkt 12 (351 23 36). A popular Swiss wine bar (4-5SFr per glass) with low wooden ceilings and crossbeams, all covered with initials and messages. Free glass of wine for anyone who can climb up and through the rafters—it's harder than it looks. Open Tues.-Sat. 11am-midnight.

Bar Odeon, Limmatquai 2 (tel. 251 16 50), near the Quaibrück. Thornton Wilder and Vladimir Lenin used to get sloshed in this tiny atmospheric joint. Great streetside seating for the artsy crowd that hangs out there. Beers 6SFr and up.

Oliver Twist, Rindermarkt 6 (tel. 252 47 10). Please, sir, could I have some more…Anglophiles? English-speaking crowd enjoys Guinness and British beers in this English pub with an Irish twist. Pint of Guinness 6.50SFr. Open Mon.-Fri. 11:30am-midnight, Sat. 3pm-midnight, Sun. 4pm-midnight.

Emilio's Bagpiper Bar, Zähringerstr. 11 (tel. 252 05 00). Extremely crowded on weekends. A gay bar serving good drinks, snacks, and occasional male stripper shows. (Nice pipes!) Beers 4.30SFr. Open daily 3pm-midnight.

Café Grösenwahn, Theaterstr. 10. A younger crowd grooves to dance and rock music in this dark but playful dance club. Obligatory first drink but no cover. Beers 7SFr and up. Open Sun.-Thurs. 8pm-2am, Fri.-Sat. 8pm-4am.

Cinecittà Bar Club, Stadthausquai 13 (tel. 211 57 52). Attracts all sorts. The bar has a simultaneous scruffy biker and young banker feel, while teens and students bump and grind on the dance floor. Watch for the theme nights (Tues.: 70s night, Fri.-Sat.: Disco, Sun.: Gay night). No cover, but obligatory first drink ranges from 5-15SFr, depending on the night.

■ Winterthur

Once the country home of wealthy industrialists making their fortune in Eastern Switzerland, Winterthur (VIN-ter-tur) now profits from the cultural endowment of its erstwhile philanthropists. Overshadowed in all things commercial by its omnipotent neighbor Zürich, Winterthur fights anonymity with a brave barrage of 15 museums, several private galleries, and two castles in its environs. Though a short march is all that separates the two cities, Winterthur basks in its own cultural grandeur amid rolling hills, green meadows, and sowed fields.

Orientation and Practical Information Winterthur's **tourist office** (tel. 212 00 88; fax 212 00 72) awaits at Bahnhofpl. 12, overflowing with pamphlets on the museums and surrounding area. It also makes hotel reservations for 3SFr (open Mon.-Fri. 8am-noon and 2-6pm, Sat. 9am-noon and 2-4pm). **Currency exchange** (open daily 5:35am-9:45pm), **bicycle rental** (21SFr per day; open Mon.-Sat. 6:40am-7:50pm, Sun. 8:10am-12:30pm), and **luggage storage** (5SFr, same hours as bike rental) are at the **train station.** Trains run to **Zürich** (10.60 SFr. one-way), with connections to **Basel** and **Geneva** twice per hour; trains to **St. Gallen** (18.20SFr) and **Austria** run hourly. **Parking** is available at **Parkhaus Theater am Stadtgarten,** off Museumstr.; **Parkhaus SSB** at the *Hauptbahnhof;* and **Parkhaus Winterthur,** also off Museumstr. The **rape crisis** line is tel. 213 61 61. The **post office** is located conveniently across the street from the train station (open Mon.-Fri.- 7:30am-6:30pm, Sat. 7:30-11am). **Postal code:** CH-8401. **Telephone code:** 052.

Accommodations and Food After exploring the nooks and crannies of the **Schloß Hegi,** drop the backpack and call it a day at the **Jugendherberge Hegi (HI),** Hegifeldstr. 125 (tel. 242 38 40), inside the castle. To reach the castle, take the train or bus # 1 to "Oberwinterthur Bahnhof." After you disembark, backtrack a few steps along Frauenfeldstr., turn left on Hegistr., left again on Hegifeldstr. after going through the underpass, and then walk 10 minutes further. The postal bus from the train station to "Schlossacker" (2.10SFr) is another option. Surrounded by marvelous meadows, hedges, and fruit trees with hens clucking and turkeys gobbling, the hostel offers no-frills, 15th-century living. There are just two dorm rooms and one loft (generally for school groups); however, the people and ambiance are rare treats. The hostel is as convenient to Zürich (Kloten) airport as the Zürich hostel, with an hourly direct train to the airport leaving from Oberwinterthur. The S-12 train from Zürich makes a bee-line to Oberwinterthur five times per day (10.60SFr). (Reception open daily 5-10pm. Lockout Mon. and Fri. 10am-5pm, Tues.-Thurs. and Sat.-Sun. 10am-2pm. 16SFr. No breakfast, but kitchen facilities are available. Open March-Oct.)

Fruit and vegetable **markets** engulf the streets of the *Altstadt* on Tuesdays and Fridays. The **Manor** across from the tourist office also has a café. (Open Mon.-Wed. and Fri. 8am-6:30pm, Thurs. 8am-9pm, Sat. 7:30am-4pm. Restaurant open Mon.-Wed. and Fri. 7am-6:30pm, Thurs. 8am-9pm, Sat. 7:30am-4pm.) **Hegimart** sits across from the Schloß Hegi. (Open Mon.-Wed. and Fri. 8:15am-12:15pm and 2:30-6:30pm, Thurs. 8:15am-12:15pm, Sat. 8am-4pm.) The **Pizzeria Pulcinella,** behind Stadtkirche St. Laurentius, serves up pizzas (13-17SFr) and Italian specialties, none of which top 21SFr (open Mon.-Fri. 11:15am-1:45pm and 5:45-11:30pm, Sat.-Sun. 5:45-10:30pm).

Sights and Entertainment If you've only got time for one museum, make the trip out to the **Oskar Reinhart "Am Römerholz" Collection,** Haldenstr. 95 (tel. 213 41 21), set in the late industrialist's private villa and lush garden at the edge of the forest. (Take bus #10 to Haldengut, on Haldenstr., follow brown "Römerholz" signs uphill to the museum.) The first floor brims to the rim with medieval paintings and

Old Masters, most notably Rembrandt, Rubens, Goya, and Holbein. There is also a healthy collection of Impressionist works, including Manet's *Au Café* and van Gogh's *L'hôpital à Arles*. Sink into the big leather armchairs as you soak in the masterpieces. (Open Tues.-Sun. 10am-5pm. 6SFr, students 4SFr.)

Winterthur's **Kunstmuseum,** Museumstr. 52 (tel. 267 51 62), holds an extensive collection of 16th- to 20th-century Swiss and French works, including Maillol, Bonnard, and Léger, as well as German works from the 19th and 20th centuries. In the summer, temporary exhibits of 20th-century art enhance the collection. Jest with Picasso's bust, the *tête de fou*. To find the museum, walk up the Marktgasse from the station, turn left on Oberer Graben, which will turn into Lindstr.; Museumstr. is the second intersection (open Tues. 10am-8pm, Wed.-Sun. 10am-5pm. 10SFr, students 7SFr). The *Kunstmuseum* building also holds the city **library** (open Mon. 10am-6pm, Tues.-Fri. 8am-6pm, Sat. 8am-4pm). Closer to the town proper, down Stadthausstr. to the right of the train station, the **Oskar Reinhart Foundation,** Stadthausstr. 6 (tel. 267 51 72), balances broad international holdings with exhibitions of 18th- to 20th- century Swiss, Austrian, and German works (open Tues.-Sun. 10am-5pm. 6SFr, students 4SFr). The miniatures of the Dutch "little masters" and timepieces from every corner of the globe await perusal in the early town hall at the **Uhrenmuseum Kellenberger und Museum Jakob Briner,** Marktgasse 20 (tel. 267 51 26; open Tues.-Sat. 2-5pm, Sun. 10am-noon and 2-5pm; free).

Painlessly enter the world of science at the **Technorama der Schweiz,** Technoramastr. 1 (tel. 243 05 05), much farther down Marktgasse, which turns into Obertor, then Römerstr. Or take bus #5 (dir: Technorama) from the train station to the last stop. The center lets its visitors perform hands-on experiments on everything from textile production to sector physics. The museum is a hair-raising experience, complete with giant bubble production, flying bikes, and a Lilliputian train that chugs around the museum's park. Surf the internet exhibit or land a jumbo jet on the flight simulator. (Open Tues.-Sun. 10am-5pm, but also open on the public holidays that fall on Mon. 14SFr, students 10SFr.) For those into bones and stones, the **Naturwissenschaftliche Sammlungen** (Museum of Natural Science), Museumstr. 52 (tel. 267 51 66), displays geological models explaining the creation of the Alps and classifies the flora and fauna of the region (open Tues.-Sun. 10am-5pm; free).

Winterthur's environs also boast two remarkably well-preserved medieval castles. The **Mörsburg** (tel. 337 13 96), former home of the Kyburg family dynasty as early as the 13th century, now holds pieces of 17th- to 19th-century artwork and furniture. Take the bus #1 to "Wallrüti," then follow yellow signs to Mörsburg, a 40-minute hike through the *Schwarzwald*. (Open Mar.-Oct. Tues.-Sun. 10am-noon and 1:30-5pm; Nov.-Feb. Sun. 10am-noon and 1:30-5pm. Free.) The **Schloß Hegi,** Hegifeldstr. 125 (tel. 242 38 40), maintains its 15th-century grandeur overlooking the meadows of Oberwinterthur. Creaky staircases, an 800-year-old tower, working cannons, stained glass, and well-displayed objects detail 15th- to 18th-century life. Still lived in and maintained by original heirs to the castle. Take the train (Eurail pass valid) to Oberwinterthur or bus #1 to "Oberwinterthur" (open March-Oct. Tues.-Thurs. and Sat. 2-5pm, Sun. 10am-noon; free). **Stadtkirche St. Laurentius** (take Unt. Kirchgasse off Marktgasse), built in 1180, and then renovated in the late Gothic style between 1501 and 1515, anchors the town. The Baroque organ dating back to 1766 was acquired from the Salem Cloister in 1809. It includes stained glass windows by **Alberto Giacometti** and a vivid wall painting by Paul Zehnder (church open daily 10am-4pm). The **Stadthaus,** Stadthausstr. 4a, is a monumental sandstone structure built between 1866-1868 by Gottfried Semper, the man behind the legendary Dresden Opera House. Today it holds a concert hall.

■ Lucerne (Luzern)

Though this northern gateway to the Swiss Alps quietly defends its fold with antique towers, turrets, and ramparts, Lucerne's largest fortifications, the majestic peaks of Mount Pilatus and Rigi Kulm, are completely natural. Pilatus rises 2132m in a tumult

Someone back home *really* misses you.
Please call.

With **AT&T Direct**℠ Service it's easy to call back to the States from virtually anywhere your travels take you. Just dial the **AT&T Direct** Access Number for the country *you are in* from the chart below. You'll have English-language voice prompts or an AT&T Operator to guide your call. And our clearest,* fastest connections** will help you reach whoever it is that misses you most back home.

AUSTRIA●◇ 022-903-011	GREECE● 00-800-1311	NETHERLANDS● ...06-022-9111
BELGIUM● 0-800-100-10	INDIA✖ 000-117	RUSSIA●▲♪ (Moscow).755-5042
CZECH REP▲ 00-42-000-101	IRELAND 1-800-550-000	SPAIN◇ 900-99-00-11
DENMARK.................8001-0010	ISRAEL 177-100-2727	SWEDEN 020-795-611
FRANCE................0 800 99 0011	ITALY● 172-1011	SWITZERLAND● ..0-800-550011
GERMANY.................0130-0010	MEXICO▽ 95-800-462-4240	U.K.▲ 0800-89-0011

Can't find the Access Number for the country you're calling from? Just ask any operator for AT&T Direct Service.

Photo: R. Olken

Greetings from LET'S GO

With pen and notebook in hand, a change of clothes in our backpack, and the tightest of budgets, we've spent our summer roaming the globe in search of travel bargains.

We've put the best of our research into the book that you're now holding. Our intrepid researcher-writers went on the road for months of exploration, from Anchorage to Angkor, Estonia to Ecuador, Iceland to India. Editors worked from spring to fall, massaging copy into witty and informative prose. A brand-new edition of each guide hits the shelves every fall, just months after it is researched, so you know you're getting the most reliable, up-to-date, and comprehensive information available.

We try to make this book an indispensable companion, but sometimes the best discoveries are the ones you make on your own. If you've got something to share, please drop us a line. We're Let's Go Publications, 67 Mount Auburn Street, Cambridge, MA 02138 USA (e-mail: fanmail@letsgo.com). Good luck and happy travels!

of craggy rocks, snow, and ice. Separated from Pilatus by the placid Vierwaldstätter-see, or Lake Lucerne, Rigi, as the locals affectionately call it, is a gentler peak (1800m) dotted by meadows, picturesque villages, and grazing cows. The waters of the *see* flow through the city as the Reuss River. The views of the surrounding peaks are breathtaking and have inspired the likes of Twain, Wagner, and Goethe. Turning one's attention back to the city will not disappoint either. The lovely *Alstadt,* a number of museums covering glaciation and Picasso, and scenic bridges help to placate the masses when the sun decides to nap behind low lying clouds.

GETTING TO LUCERNE

Lucerne does **trains** to **Basel** (1hr.10min., 2 every hr., 30SFr), **Bern** (1hr.15min., 1 or 2 every hr., 31SFr), **Geneva** (3hr.15min., every hr., 65SFr), **Interlaken** (2hr., every hr., 23SFr), **Lausanne** (1hr.40min., every hr., 55SFr), **Lugano** (2hr.45min., every hr., 55SFr), **Zürich** (50min., every hr., 19.40SFr), and **Zürich airport** (1hr.15min., every hr., 24SFr). Lucerne does **buses:** local buses depart from the front of the train station and paint every corner of the city (see **Orientation and Practical Information** below for more details). And Lucerne does **cars:** driving from Zürich, take N4 south to N14 south, which enters town on Baselstr. (1hr. from Zürich, traffic permitting).

ORIENTATION AND PRACTICAL INFORMATION

The mammoth train station (complete with book store, grocery store, barbershop, two restaurants, and a maze of lockers) owns the junction of the Reuss River and the Vierwaldstättersee. Most of Lucerne's museums and hotels are located near the quais that line the river and the *see,* but are not confined to any specific area or neighborhood. Numerous bridges connect both sides of the town. The largest one, the See-brücke, is also closest to the center of town activity.

Tourist Office: Frankenstr. 1 (tel. 410 71 71; fax 410 73 34). Follow the "i" signs to the left of the train station, behind the McDonald's. Large selection of maps (free or 1SFr), and hotel reservations made after 11am (5SFr). Also offers **Guided walking tours** that swing past the major monuments. (April 15-Oct. Mon.-Sat. at 9:20am and 2pm; Nov. 4-April 13 Wed. and Sat. 9:30am and 2pm. 15SFr.) Escorted sojourns to the top of Mt. Pilatus are also offered (May 15-Sept. 30 daily at 10:15am, return at 3pm; 85SFr). Ask about the Visitors Card, which, in conjunction with a hotel or hostel stamp, gives discounts at museums, bars, car rental agencies, and more. Open April-Oct. Mon.-Fri. 8:30am-6pm, Sat. 9am-5pm, Sun. 9am-1pm; Nov.-March Mon.-Fri. 8:30am-noon and 2-6pm, Sat. 9am-1pm.

Currency Exchange: At the station. Open Mon.-Fri. 7:30am-8:30pm, Sat.-Sun. 7:30am-7:30pm. The best rates in town, however, are at the **Migros bank,** Seiden-hofstr. 6, off Bahnhofstr.; open Mon.-Wed. and Fri. 9am-5:15pm, Thurs. 9am-6:30pm, Sat. 8:15am-noon, or try the **American Express.**

Budget Travel: SSR Reisen, Grabenstr. 8 (tel. 410 86 56). Student travel and discount flights. Open Mon.-Wed. and Fri. 10am-6pm, Thurs. 10am-9pm.

American Express: Schweizerhofquai 4 (tel. 410 00 77). Offers all services including ATM machines. Address mail, for example: Miguel ORDOÑEZ, c/o American Express, Client Mail Service, Schweizerhofquai 4, P.O. Box 2067, CH-6002. Travel services open Mon.-Fri. 8:30am-6pm, Sat. 8:30am-midnight. Money exchange open Mon.-Fri. 8:30am-5pm, Sat. 8:30am-midnight.

Telephones: PTT services next door to the main post office. Open Mon.-Sat. 7:30am-8pm, Sun. 9am-8pm. Telephones also downstairs in the train station.

Public Transportation: VBL: 1 zone 1.50SFr, 2 zones (to the youth hostel) 2SFr, 3 zones 2.50SFr. *Tageskarte* 10SFr, 2-day pass 15SFr. Swisspass valid.

Taxis: Cab stands are located in front of the train station, at Schwanpl., Pilatusplatz, and in front of the Municipal Theatre, or call 211 11 11.

Car rental: Europcar, Horwerstr. 81 (tel. 310 14 33), advertises special offers for tourists. Compact car 35SFr per day plus 35 centimes per km. **Hertz,** Maihofstr. 101 (tel. 155 12 34).

Parking: Lucerne has 10 parking garages. The most central is **Bahnhof-Parking** under the train station at Bahnhofpl. 2. Also very accessible is **City Parking,** Zürichstr. 35 (tel. 410 11 51). Parking garages run from 25-50SFr per day. Free parking at the Transport Museum.

Bike Rental: At the train station. 22SFr per day. Open daily 7am-7:45pm.

Luggage storage: At the station. Luggage held 5SFr. Open daily 6am-9pm. Small lockers 3SFr, medium 5SF, large 8SFr.

Laundromat: Jet Wasch Bruchstr. 28 (tel. 240 01 51). Full laundry service (wash and dry 16SFr, wash, dry, and fold 19SFr, soap included). English-speaking staff. Open March-Sept. Mon.-Fri. 8:30am-12:30pm and 2:30-6:30pm, Sat. 9am-3pm; Oct.-Feb. Mon.-Fri. 8:30am-12:30pm, Sat. 9am-3pm.

Bookstores: Buchhandlung Josef Stocker, Weinmarkt 8 (tel. 410 49 47). Some English books. Open Mon. 1:30-6:30pm, Tues.-Wed. and Fri. 9am-6:30pm, Thurs. 9am-9pm, Sat. 8am-4pm. **Raeber Bücher,** Kornmarktgasse 7 (tel. 229 60 40). Open Mon.-Fri. 9am-6:30pm, Sat. 8am-4pm.

Gay and Lesbian Organizations: Schwullesbisches Zentrum Uferlos, Geissenteinring 14. **Homosexuelle Arbeitsgruppen Luzern (HALO)** publishes a monthly calendar of events available at the tourist office ranging from Drag Queen parties to Disco nights (mailing address: Postfach 3112, 6002 Luzern, PC-Konto 60-5227-2). For young homosexuals, **Why Not** (mailing address: Postfach 2304, 6002 Luzern) offers Wed. night discussion groups at 8 and 11:30pm at the Zentrum Uferlos.

Emergency: Police: tel. 117. **Fire:** tel. 118. **Ambulance:** tel. 144. **Pharmacy or doctor:** tel. 111.

Post Office: Main branch is near the station on the corner of Bahnhofstr. and Bahnhofpl. **Poste Restante:** Hauptpost, CH-6000 Luzern 1. Open Mon.-Fri. 7:30am-6:30pm, Sat. 8-11am. **Postal code:** CH-6000.

Telephone code: 041.

ACCOMMODATIONS AND CAMPING

Relatively inexpensive beds are available in limited numbers, so call ahead. Also, don't change money at hotels—rates are at least 5% worse than banks.

Jugendherberge (HI), Sedelstr. 12 (tel. 420 88 00; fax 420 56 16). Take bus #18 to "Gopplismoos." After 7:30pm you must take bus #1 to "Schlossberg," and walk 15min. down Friednetalstr. A contemporary building constructed of white concrete block. Some rooms have a beautiful valley view. Reception open daily 7am-9:30am and 4pm-midnight; bring a book or newspaper for the queue. Lockout April-Sept. 10am-2pm, Oct.-March 10am-4pm, but the lounge is always open. Dorms 28.50SFr first night, 26SFr thereafter. Doubles 35.50SFr first night, then 33SFr, with shower 41.50SFr, then 39SFr. Lockers, sheets, shower, breakfast included. Dinner 11SFr. Laundry 10SFr. Visa, MC, AmEx. Crowded in the summer months, so reserve a few days in advance.

Backpackers, Alpenquai 42 (tel. 360 04 20; fax 360 04 42), is a 15min. walk from the station. Walk along the lake on Inseli-Quai, keeping to the left, and over the concrete bridge to Alpenquai. Backpackers is across street from Seepark. Neat 2- and 4-person rooms with balconies facing the lake or Mt. Pilatus, and friendly English-speaking staff. Also across the street from park and beaches. Reception open daily 7-10am and 4pm-midnight. No lockout. Bed in a double 26.50SFr, for a bed in a quad 21.50SFr. Sheets 2SFr. Breakfast 6SFr. Kitchen facilities available. Bike rental 7SFr per day. Tickets sold for Rigi Kulm and Mt. Pilatus.

Touristen Hotel Luzern, St. Karliquai 12 (tel. 410 24 74; fax 410 84 14). From the train station, go underground, exit the complex by the elevator or the steps to the *Altstadt,* walk left along the river to the second wooden bridge, cross it, and make a left onto St. Karliquai. Well located on the river with a view of Mt. Pilatus. Reception open daily 7am-10pm. Bed in a quad 36SFr, students 33SFr; in an 11-bed room 31SFr, students 28SFr. Doubles 98-108SFr. Triples 135SFr. Quads 172SFr. Rooms with shower cost 10SFr more per person. All-you-can-eat buffet breakfast included. Prices in winter are 10-15SFr less per person, but without breakfast—only coffee and tea. All students receive a 10% discount with ID card. Free luggage storage.

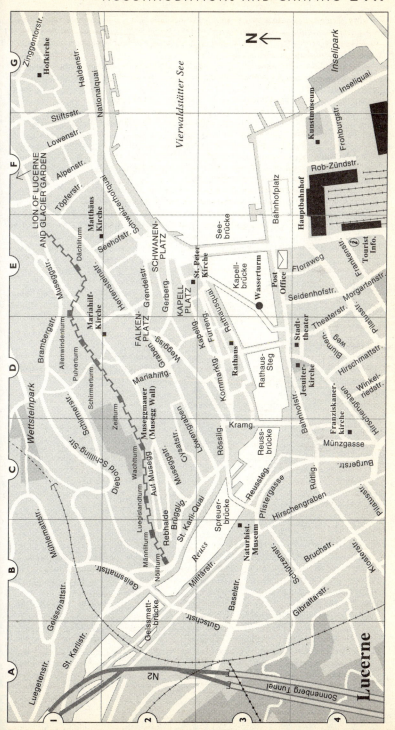

Laundry 10SFr. The Hostel offers free scooter for city travel. Train station pick up for 3 or more people. Visa, MC, AmEx.

Privatpension Panorama, Kapuzinerweg. 9 (tel. 420 67 01; fax 420 67 30), is a hike from the train station. Take bus #4 or 5 (dir: Wesemlin) to "Kapuzinerweg," and walk up the street instead. Clean, quiet, comfortable, and on a hill with absolutely gorgeous views of Pilatus or the *Altstadt*. Homey atmosphere with friendly family patrons. No reception—yodel or ring the bell. Singles 45SFr. Doubles 60-120SFr. Triples 105SFr. Quads 140SFr. Breakfast and parking included.

Pension Pro Filia, at the corner of Pilatusstr. 66 and Zähringerstr. 24 (tel. 240 42 80; fax 240 91 31). From the station, walk 10min. left down Pilatusstr. This sprawling pension is in a residential area, removed from the *Altstadt*. Rooms are so well-maintained and spotlessly clean you might be tempted to move in. It used to be for women only, as the name indicates, but men are now welcome. Reception open daily 7am-9:30pm. Singles 70SFr. Doubles 102SFr, with shower 130SFr. Triples with shower 147SFr. Quad with shower 197SFr. Prices 2-3SFr cheaper in winter. Huge breakfast included. Visa, AmEx.

Hotel Schlüssel, Franziskanerpl. 12 (tel. 210 10 61; fax 210 10 21), near the Franciscan Church. From the station, walk left on Bahnhofstr. along the river, then turn left on Franziskanerpl. One of the cheaper establishments, with a restaurant and outdoor café downstairs. Reception open 8am-midnight. April-Oct. singles 51-62SFr, with shower 74-84SFr; doubles 85-102SFr, with shower 113-158SFr. Nov.-March singles 45-54SFr, with shower 66-77SFr; doubles 81-95SFr, with shower 102-124SFr. Breakfast included. Visa, MC, AmEx.

Camping: Camping Lido, Lidostr. 8 (tel. 370 21 46; fax 370 21 45), is a 30-min. hike from the station on the Lido beach. Cross the Seebrücke, and turn right along the quay, or take bus #2 to "Verkehrshaus." Mini-golf, tennis, and swimming nearby. Reception open daily 8am-6pm. 6SFr. Tent 3SFr. Car 5SFr. Open Mar. 15-Oct.

FOOD

Lucerne's gastronomic taste is overwhelmingly Swiss; ethnic and other specialties are quite expensive. The Saturday morning markets along the river, purveying fresh fruit, vegetables, and meat for an inexpensive picnic, and the restaurants in supermarkets and department stores offer the cheapest meals in town (see **Markets,** below). The restaurant upstairs in the department store **EPA,** at the corner of Rössligasse and Mühlenpl. has 8-14SFr *menus* (open Mon.-Wed. and Fri. 8am-6:30pm, Thurs. 8am-9pm, Sat. 8am-4pm). There is a **Kosher Butcher,** Bruchstr. 26, near Jet Wasch (open Mon.-Tues. and Thurs.-Fri. 9am-noon, Wed. 2:30-5:30pm). **Hotel Drei Könige,** Bruchstr. 35 (tel. 240 88 33; fax 240 88 52), also serves heated kosher food for 45SFr per meal (reception open 7am-1am).

Bistrettino, Theilinggasse 4 (tel. 410 88 08), in the heart of the *Altstadt,* just off Sternenplatz. A speedy Italian joint that serves well-seasoned personal pizzas (11SFr). Feeling Inuit? Try the spaghetti Eskimo with smoked salmon and cream sauce (13.80SFr). Open Mon.-Sat. 9am-11:30pm, Sun. 11am-11:30pm.

Krone, Rössligasse 15 (tel. 419 44 90). Good food with cafeteria-style service. Create your own baguette sandwich, or try the chicken nuggets, kebabs, burgers, or ice cream. All sandwiches under 8SFr. Daily specials feature a *menu* for around 11SFr. Be creative with the colored chalk and blackboard walls. Open daily 10am-11pm. Visa, MC, AmEx.

Restaurant Kapellbrücke, Bahnhofstr. 7 (tel. 210 80 20). A short walk from the train station, the restaurant has outdoor seating on the Reuss river and leather backed cushion seats inside. Mountain murals adorn the walls of this relatively inexpensive Swiss spot. Italian spaghetti with Parmesan cheese and salad for 12.50SFr and full *menus* for under 15SFr.

Markets

Migros, Hertensteinstr. 44, has a wonderful self-serve restaurant in addition to its vast supply of groceries. Open Mon.-Wed. and Fri. 8am-6:30pm, Thurs. 8am-9pm, Sat. 8am-4pm.

Reformhaus Müller, Wienmarkt 1. Sells tofu, lentils, and organic, whole-grain everything else. Open Mon.-Fri. 7:45am-6:30pm, Sat. 7:45am-4pm.

SIGHTS AND ENTERTAINMENT

Much of Lucerne's tourist drawing power comes from the Vierwaldstättersee and the streets of the *Altstadt,* which cobblestone both sides of the Reuss River. The 660-year old **Kapellbrücke,** a wooden-roofed bridge originally built in the early 1300 as part of the city's fortification, is decorated with graphic scenes from Swiss history and has characterized Lucerne's landscape since the Middle Ages. Though the bridge was severely damaged in 1993 by a barge which accidentally set it aflame, efforts were successful in restoring it to its former glory. Down the river, confront your mortality as you cross the covered **Spreuerbrücke,** adorned with Kaspar Meglinger's eerie *Totentanz* (Dance of Death) paintings. The *Altstadt* is famous for its frescoed houses and *oriel* windows, especially the colorful scenes of the Hirschenplatz. The ramparts of the medieval city still tower on the hills above the river; climb them and walk from tower to tower for a magnificent panorama of Lucerne. The clock tower, with its ancient clock mechanism and view of the valleys surrounding Lucerne provides another excellent opportunity for panoptic pleasure. To find it, walk along St. Karli-quai, make a right uphill, and follow the brown signs with the castles on them (open daily 8am-7pm).

The city mascot, the dying **Lion of Lucerne,** carved out of the base of a cliff on Denkmalstr., throws its melancholic and pained eyes over the city. An evocative monument that forces contemplation, world-traveled Mark Twain described the lion as "the saddest and most moving piece of rock in the world." The nine-meter-high monument honors the Swiss Guard who died unsuccessfully defending Marie Antoinette in Revolutionary Paris. Next door is the **Glacier Garden,** with its moon-like landscape of smooth rocks curved and pot-holed into massive other-worldly sculptures. The 7SFr ticket (students 5SFr, with visitors card 5.50SFr) includes admission to the **Glacier Garden Museum,** with its portrayal of prehistoric humans and carefully designed glaciation models. Roam amongst the woolly mammoths and Flintstones, but don't miss the Spiegellabyrinth (mirror maze)—be careful not to lose yourself or your mind. (Open May-Oct. 15 daily 8am-6pm; Oct. 16-Nov. 15 9am-5pm; Nov. 16-Feb. Tues.-Sun. 10:30am-4:30pm; March-April daily 9am-5pm.) Get a combi-ticket (8.50SFr, students 6.50SFr) to view the **Bourbaki Panorama,** down the hill from the Lion Memorial. The largest round panorama mural in the world, it portrays a Franco-Prussian battle and the first active service of the Swiss Red Cross in the process. (Open May-Sept. daily 9am-6pm; March-April and Oct. daily 9am-5pm; Jan.-Feb. Tues.-Sun. 10:30am-4pm. Entry to panorama alone 2SFr, students 1.50SFr.)

Follow Wexstrasse to the **Hofkirche St. Leodegar und Mauritius,** at the end of the Schweizerhofquai. Erected in the 8th century as a Romanesque basilica, it was then refurbished in the 14th century in the Gothic style. Though the church was destroyed by a fire, its towers survived, allowing yet another decorator to get his hands on the confused edifice, which was then finished in the high Baroque. A spectrum of saints greet you as you walk through the oak doors, though the gaudy gilded statues and altars seem almost sinful in their ornamentation. Not to be outdone, the **Franziskanerkirche,** on Franziskanerpl., holds magnificent red and gray marble altars, the central altar flanked by slender stained-glass windows.

A cruise on the **Vierwaldstättersee** (see Near Lucerne, p. 151) deposits visitors in one of the many tiny villages that dot the lakes. It is also a great way to see the countryside. To witness glass blowing or to learn the glass history, alight at **Hergiswil.** For a quick and incredible scenic hike, stop at **Bürgenstock** and climb to ex-U.S. president Jimmy Carter's top choice in Swiss resorts. For easier walking along the lake, pause for a promenade at **Weggis.** To return to Lucerne, simply jump on board again.

CENTRAL SWITZERLAND

Fares are determined by the number of km voyaged (free with Eurail pass, Swisspass, and Swiss Card). Consult the Lucerne tourist office for specifics on each town and the routes of the boats. For a free lakeside dip, walk about 15 minutes along the lake, heading right after you exit the train station, to the **Seepark.**

From August 16 to September 10, 1997, Lucerne will host its **International Festival of Music.** The festival celebrates both classical and contemporary music, sometimes with irreverent tongue-in-cheek interpretations. Outdoor serenades, cruise concerts, and broadcasts at the Lion Monument are all annual highlights. For tickets or further information, contact: Internationale Musikfestwochen Luzern, Postfach/Hirschmattstr. 13, CH-6002 Luzern, Schweiz (tel. 210 35 62; fax 210 77 84).

Every summer, elite crews from all over the world pull their way to Lucerne for the **National and International Rowing Regattas** on the **Rotsee** by the Jugendherberge. Usually held on back-to-back weekends, the 1997 *Internationale Ruderregatta* will take place from July 11-13. For information and entries, contact Regattaverein Luzern, Hans-Peter Roth, c/o Schweizer Bankverein, Postfach 1945, CH-6021 Emmenbrücke (tel. 269 89 89).

MUSEUMS

Lucerne's museums provide more than ample entertainment for rainy or restful days. If you plan to visit several, purchase a museum pass for 25SFr, which is good for one month and available at most museums and the tourist office.

Verkehrshaus der Schweiz (Transport Museum), Lidostr. 5 (tel. 370 44 44; fax 370 61 68), near Camping Lido, is the Disney World of transportation. If you can drive, fly, steer, float, or roll it, it's here. Climb into big rig trucks and jet planes or go for a virtual ride in the virtual reality exhibit. Their are also planetarium shows and 3 daily Imax shows. Open April 4-Oct.31 daily 9am-6pm, Nov. 1-March 31 daily 10am-5pm. 16SFr, students 14SFr. Imax 12SFr. For both 25SFr, students 23SFr. Reduction with Eurail pass or guest card.

Picasso Museum, Am Rhyn Haus, Furrengasse 21 (tel. 410 35 33), presents a slice of Picasso's later life through photographs taken by a close friend, David Douglas Duncan. See Picasso at work, as well as in the bathtub and learning ballet. Also shelters a collection of Picasso's last works, most of them lithographs. Open Apr.-Oct. daily 10am-6pm; Nov.-March daily 11am-1pm and 2-4pm. 6SFr, students 3SFr, with guest card 5SFr.

Natur-Museum, Kasernenpl. 6, has many "hands-on" exhibits, including live animals, and was distinguished in 1987 as "European Museum of the Year." Though it's all done in German with only a small English guide, the language barrier shouldn't be a problem for the Neanderthal club and hand-axe exhibit. It certainly wasn't a problem back then. ("Me Thag. Thag hungry. Mmmm, Thag eat.") Other exhibits include a section on plate teutonics—er, tectonics—and beetles. Open Tues.-Sat. 10am-noon and 2-5pm, Sun. 10am-5pm. 4SFr, students 3SFr. For special exhibits, add 1SFr to the price.

Richard Wagner Museum, Wagnerweg 27. Take bus #6 or 8 to "Wartegg," or walk 25min. along the lake, to the right as you exit the train station. Set in Wagner's secluded former home in the woods overlooking the lake, the museum displays original letters, scores, and instruments of the late composer. Wagner wrote *Siegfried* and *Die Meistersänger* here. The museum also presents a collection of historic instruments from around the globe. The luxurious green lawn extends from the house to the lake and makes for an ideal picnic spot. Open April 15-Oct. Tues.-Sun. 10am-noon and 2-5pm; Feb.-April 14 Tues., Thurs., and Sat.-Sun. 10am-noon and 2-5pm. 5SFr, students and guest card holders 4SFr.

NIGHTLIFE

Lucerne's nightlife is concentrated in the crowded corridors of the *Altstadt*, with its tightly packed pubs and cafés, but also extends to slightly more distant reaches of the town. Directly on the river, **Mr. Pickwick's Pub,** Rathausquai 6 (tel. 410 59 27), has an Anglican feel and friendly bartenders who pump out brews (4.50SFr and up) and music (open Mon.-Sat 11am-12:30am, Sun. 4pm-12:30am). The candle-lit ambiance of the nearby **Hotel des Balances Bar** caters to the older set. Beware of expensive drinks. Up the river, **Hexenkessel** Haldenstr. 21 (tel. 410 92 44), resembles a witch's haunt. Replete with broomsticks, it boils Lucerne's twentysomethings in a two-story cauldron of loud music and DJs (obligatory beer purchase 7SFr, but no cover; open daily 7pm-2:30am). Across the street is the **Kursaal Casino,** Haldenstr. 6. If you win, remember who sent you, if you lose you obviously saw it in Lonely Planet. Feeling like a hot tamale? Try **Cucaracha,** Pilatusstr. 15 (tel. 210 55 77), for a spicy night of Coronas and nachos. (Beers 7.50SFr. Open daily 5pm-midnight.) Wind up the night dancing at **Piranha** (Bundesplatz, above **Zoo**), doors open at 10pm. This is not a place for cold fish. Dance, eat, and thrill to Swiss folklore on the **Night Boat** (tel. 319 01 78) with departures May-Sept. at 8:45pm from piers 5 and 6. (Boat ride 40SFr, with Eurail pass 33SFr; seat reservation, boat ride, entertainment, and one drink 50SFr, with Eurail pass 43SFr.)

■ Near Lucerne

ENGELBERG AND THE VIERWALDSTÄTTERSEE

Lucerne's position in the heart of Switzerland makes it a daytrip departure point *par excellence.* Boat trips from the train station cruise the Vierwaldstättersee; get a list of destinations from the tourist office (day pass for unlimited boat travel 39SFr, free with Eurail or Swisspass). The hour train ride to **Engelberg** is well worth the trip for out-doors people and sight-seers alike (14.20SFr). Ride the world's first revolving cable car to the top of **Mount Titlis** (3020m), the highest outlook in central Switzerland, in just 45 minutes. The gondola gives magnificent views of the crevasses below and peaks above. The black light lit ice grotto at the top, along with the observation deck and restaurants, concludes the trip. (Departs daily from Lucerne at noon. 73SFr, Eurail passes and Engelberg guest card get 20% discount. Guided tours from Lucerne including round-trip rail fare and round-trip Titlis fare only 85SFr, same discounts apply.) One can also visit the glorious glacier lake, **Trübsee**, halfway up Mt. Titlis (round-trip 24SFr, same discounts apply).

Engelberg also attracts hikers to its many trails. There is exceptional hiking from Engelberg to Herrenrüti along the valley floor, next to the cliffs of Titlis (4hrs. round-trip, easy terrain). Ask the tourist office about maps, trail heads, other hikes and guided jaunts. For the faint of heart, try a sedate, yet rewarding trip to the local **Bene-dictine Monastery.** Over 850 years old, the monastery boasts some impressively fine Biblical wood inlay and Switzerland's largest organ. Tours everyday at 4pm are free, but donations are appreciated. Enter through the door marked "Kloster Monastery." As winter rolls around, the skiers roll in. (Ski passes Mon.-Fri. 47SFr, Sat.-Sun. and hol-idays 54SFr. 10% discount with guest card.)

Engelberg's **tourist office,** Klosterstr. 3 (tel. 637 37 37; fax 637 41 56), is a left on Bahnhofstr. after exiting the train station, a right onto Dorfstr., and another right onto Klosterstr. It hosts daily activities (pick up a full itinerary there) like hikes across Gross-Titlis glacier (Tues. 9am, 15SFr, 10SFr with guest card) or on the Brunni trail (Tues. 9am, same prices). Thursday features river rafting for 60SFr (with guest card 45SFr; 9am and 1pm departures). (Office open June 23-Oct. 19 Mon.-Fri. 8am-6:30pm, Sat. 8am-6:30pm, Sun. 4-7pm; Oct.20-Dec.15 Mon.-Fri. 8am-12:15pm and 2-6:30pm, Sat. 8am-6:30pm; Dec.16-April 13 Mon.-Fri. 8am-6:30pm, Sat. 8am-6:30pm, Sun 9am-6pm; April 14-June 21 Mon.-Fri. 8am-12:15pm and 2-6pm, Sat. 8am-6:30pm.)

The quintessential Swiss ski chalet, otherwise known as the **Jugendherberge Berghaus (HI),** Dorfstr. 80 (tel. (041) 637 12 92), is a 10-minute walk out of town. Turn left off Bahnhofstr. onto Dorfstr., and keep walking. (Reception open daily 7:45am-noon and 5-10:30pm. Lockout 9am-5pm, but lounge is always open. 25.50SFr first night, 23SFr thereafter. 5SFr surcharge for non-members. Doubles 31.50SFr, 29SFr subsequent nights. Breakfast and sheets included. Key available on request.)

MOUNT PILATUS AND THE RIGI KULM

> *We could not speak. We could hardly breathe. We could only gaze in drunken ecstasy and drink it in.*
>
> —Mark Twain

Mount Pilatus is the landmark of Lucerne. Soaring 2132 meters into the sky, on a clear day the view from the peak stretches all the way to Italy. Legend has it the devil threw St. Pilatus up here during the Ascension, but *Let's Go* does not recommend the Evil One as a safe mode of transportation—the cable cars are much more reliable. Catch a boat to Alpnachstad and ascend by the **steepest cogwheel train in the world.** Tourist-watch and capitalize on your photo-opportunities. Then return by cable car to Kriens and bus to Lucerne (round-trip 75.40SFr, with Eurail pass 40SFr, half price with Swiss Half-Fare Card). If it's cloudy, don't waste your money—visibility is next to nothing. Though the practice was banned until the 17th century for fear of angry ghosts, it is now legal to climb Pilatus by foot. The hiking trails require sturdy hiking boots and at least 5 hours. The hike can be shortened by meeting the cable car at one of its two stops on the way up the mountain. The hike down takes about 4½ hour. from Pilatus to Kriens. Before starting out on a hike, call 162 for a **weather report** in German, or ask the hotel or hostel owner for a translated forecast.

Across the sea from Pilatus is another majestic, though more subdued peak, the **Rigi Kulm.** Sunrise on the summit of the Rigi Kulm is a Lucerne must. Sunsets get pretty good reviews too. See Mark Twain's 1879 travelogue, *A Tramp Abroad,* for the best account of the ritualistic sunrises on the "Queen of the Mountains." To catch the fantastic sunrise at the peak, as Twain tried to do, stay at **Massenlager Rigi Kulm** (tel. (041) 855 03 03) on the Rigi summit. Part of the Hotel Rigi Kulm, this dormitory has 28 simple bunks (25SFr per night). Trips to Rigi begin with a ferry ride to Vitznau and a cogwheel railroad ride on the mountain railway to the top. Return the same way or hike down to **Rigi Kaltbad** (1hr.) and take a cable car to **Weggis,** returning to Lucerne by boat from there (round-trip 78SFr, same discounts apply).

■ Bern (Berne)

Bern has been Switzerland's capital since 1848, but don't try to imagine it in terms of fast tracks, power politics, or screeching motorcades—the city would rather focus your attention on its Toblerone chocolate and beautiful flowers. Bern was founded by the Duke of Zähringen in 1191, who also named it for his mascot, the bear. Spend a few days here and the tourist industry will brand this fact into your brain. The good Duke's city was burned to the ground in 1405 and was immediately rebuilt in sandstone and mahogany, which has given it an endearing compactness and architectural unity. Situated in a bend of the winding Aare River, its high bridges give wide tree-filled panoramas of the Bernese countryside. To add to the views, the cobblestone streets of the medieval *Altstadt* twist around brightly painted fountains and the 15th-century arcades.

GETTING TO BERN

If **driving** from **Basel** or the north, take N2 south to N1 south. From **Lucerne** (or the east), take 10 west. From **Geneva** or **Lausanne,** take E62 east to E27/N12 north. Finally, from **Thun** or the southeast, take N6 north. The **Bern-Belp Airport** is 20min. from central Bern and is served by Crossair and Air Engadina. Direct flights go daily to Amsterdam, Brussels, London, Lugano, Munich, Paris, Prague, and Vienna. 50min. before each flight an airport bus goes from the station (10min., 14SFr); If you're on it you are guaranteed to make the flight. Bern's **main train station** is a stressful tangle of shops and services. Phones, information, buses, luggage watch, bike rental, and a pharmacy are upstairs; tickets, lockers, police station, and money changers are downstairs. For rail information call 157 22 22 (6am-10pm daily). The **rail information office** is open Mon.-Fri. 8am-7pm, Sat. 8am-5pm. There are direct connections to

Geneva (2hr., every ½hr., 48SFr); **Lucerne** (1hr.20min., 23 daily, 31SFr); **Interlaken** (50min., hourly, 24SFr); **Zürich** (1½hr., hourly, 42SFr); **Lausanne** (1hr.10min., every ½hr., 30SFr); **Basel** (1hr.15min., every ½hr., 34SFr); **Paris** (4½hr., 3 daily, 76SFr); **Prague** (12½hr., 1 daily, 163SFr); **Munich** (5hr.40min., 1 daily, 115SFr); **Rome** (13hr., 1 daily, 74SFr); **Venice** (7hr., 1 daily, 78SFr); and **Berlin** (9hr. 15min., 1 daily, 238SFr).

ORIENTATION AND PRACTICAL INFORMATION

Stately Bern resides in a very diplomatic location, tangential to both the French- and German-speaking areas of the country. Most of medieval Bern is concentrated in front of the train station, and surrounded on three sides by the Aare River.

Tourist Office: Verkehrsbüro, on the street level of the train station (tel. 311 66 11; fax 312 12 33). Distributes maps and copies of *This Week in Bern (Bern Aktuell).* Room reservations are 3SFr. Or try the free 24-hr. board outside the office which has a direct phone line to the hotels, computerized receipts, and directions in German, French, and English. Come here for 2-hr. city tours by bus (mid-May to mid-Oct at 10am and 2pm, mid-Oct. to mid-May 2pm only; 22SFr); foot (May-Oct. at 11am; 12SFr); or raft (May-Sept. at 5:30pm; 35SFr). Open June-Sept. daily 9am-8:30pm; Oct.-May Mon.-Sat. 9am-6:30pm, Sun. 10am-5pm.

Budget Travel: SSR, Rathausgasse 64 (tel. 312 07 24). Take bus #12 to "Rathaus." Sells BIJ tickets. Open Mon.-Wed. and Fri. 9:30am-6pm, Thurs. 9:30am-8pm. **Wasteels,** Spitalgasse 4 (tel. 311 93 93; fax 311 90 10), has BIJ tickets, plane tickets, and currency exchange. Open Mon. 2-6:15pm, Tues.-Wed. and Fri. 9am-12:15pm and 1:45-6:15pm, Thurs. 9am-12:15pm and 1:45-7pm.

Embassies: U.S., Jubiläumsstr. 93 (tel. 357 70 11). Take bus #18 (dir: Tierpark) to "Ka-We-De." Open Mon.-Fri. 8:30am-12:30pm and 1:30-5:30pm. **Canada,** Kirchenfeldstr. 88 (tel. 352 63 81). Open Mon.-Fri. 8am-noon and 1-4:30pm. **U.K.,** Thunstr. 50 (tel. 352 50 21). Open Mon.-Fri. 9am-12:30pm and 2-6pm. **Ireland,** Kirchenfeldstr. 68 (tel. 352 14 42). Open Mon.-Fri. 9:15am-12:30pm and 2-5:30pm. **Australia,** Alpenstr. 29 (tel. 351 01 43). Open Mon.-Thurs. 10am-12:30pm and 1:30-3pm, Fri. 10am-12:30pm. To get to Canadian, U.K., Irish, and Australian embassies, take tram #3 (dir: Saali) to "Thunpl."

Currency Exchange: Downstairs in the train station. No commission on travelers checks. Offers credit card advances, and Western Union transfers. Open daily 6:15am-9:45pm. **ATM machines:** Credit Suisse and Swiss Bank Corp. Visa has advances available at Bank Finalba and Swiss Bank Corp.

American Express: in Kehrli & Oeler, Bubenbergpl. 9 (tel. 311 00 22). From the train station, walk to the bus area across Bahnhofplatz. Mail held 1 month, longer on request. All banking services. 24-hr. toll-free refund service (tel. (046) 05 01 00). Address mail, for example, to Julie ORDOÑEZ, c/o Kehrli & Oeler, American Express Client Mail Service, Bubenbergplatz 9, CH-3001, Bern. Open Mon.-Fri. 8:30am-5:30pm, Sat. 9am-noon.

Telephones: At the train station. Open Mon.-Sat. 6:30am-10pm, Sun. 7am-10:30pm. Major credit cards accepted.

Public Transportation: For all pea-green buses and street cars of the **SVB** (tel. 321 88 88), buy a *Touristen-Karte* from the ticket offices downstairs at the station or at Bubenbergpl. 5. (1-6 stops 1.50SFr; 7 or more stops 2.40SFr; 24-hr. *Tageskarte* 7.50SFr. Swisspass valid.) Maps here as well. Buses run daily 5:45am-11:45pm. **Nightbuses** leave the train station at 12:45am and 2am, covering major bus and tram lines 5SFr (no passes valid). SVB office in the train station. Open Mon.-Wed. and Fri. 6:30am-7:30pm, Thurs. 6:30am-9:30pm, Sat. 6:30am-6:30pm.

Taxis: On Bahnhofpl. and Bollwerk, or call **Bären-Taxi** (tel. 371 11 11).

Parking: Bahnhof (tel. 311 22 52), entrance at Schanzenbrücke or Stadtbachstr. **Bellevue Garage,** Kochergasse (tel. 311 77 76). **City West,** Belpstr. (tel. 381 93 04; 2.80SFr per hr.; 25SFr for 24hr.; 2nd and 3rd day 12SFr).

Car Rental: Avis AG, Wabernstr. 41 (tel. 372 13 13). **Hertz AG,** Kasinoplatz (tel. 318 21 60). **Europcar,** Laupenstr. 22 (tel. 381 75 55).

Bike Rental: Fly-Gepäck counter at the station (tel. 680 34 61). 21SFr per day, mountain bike 31SFr per day. 84SFr and 116SFr per week respectively. Children's bikes available. Reservations recommended. Open daily 6:15am-11:45pm.

Luggage Storage: Downstairs in train station. Small lockers 4SFr, large 5SFr. **Luggage watch** at the Fly-Gepäck counter upstairs 5SFr. Open daily 7am-8:40pm.

Bookstore: Stauffacher, Neuengasse 25. From Bubenbergplatz, turn left on Genfergasse to Neuengasse. Large English language selection. Open Mon. 10am-6:30pm, Tues.-Wed. and Fri. 8am-6:30pm, Thurs. 8am-8:30pm, Sat. 8am-4:30pm. Or **Payot Librairie,** corner of Gurtengasse and Bundesgasse. Open Mon. 2-6:30pm, Tues.-Wed. and Fri. 9am-6:30pm, Thurs. 9am-9pm, Sat. 9am-4pm.

Libraries: Municipal and University Library, Münstergasse 61 (tel. 320 32 11), stacks books for the central library of the University of Bern, and the city's public library as well. Lending library open Mon.-Fri. 10am-6pm, Sat. 10am-noon. Reading room open Mon.-Fri. 8am-9pm, Sat. 8am-noon. **Swiss National Library,** Hallwylstr. 15 (tel. 332 89 11). Lending library and catalog room open Mon.-Tues. and Thurs.-Fri. 9am-6pm, Wed. 9am-8pm, Sat. 9am-2pm. Reading room open Mon.-Tues. and Thurs.-Fri 9am-6pm, Wed. 9am-8pm, Sat. 9am-4pm.

Gay, Lesbian, and Bisexual Organizations: Homosexuelle Arbeitsgruppe die Schweiz-H.A.C.H. (Gay Association of Switzerland), c/o Anderland, Mühlepl. 11, CH-3011. The headquarters of Switzerland's largest gay organizations. **Homosexuelle Arbeitsgruppe Bern (H.A.B.),** Mühlepl. 11, Case Postale 312, CH-3000 Bern 13 (tel. 311 63 53). **Schlub** (Gay Students Organization), c/o Studentinnenschaft, Lercheweg 32, CH-3000 Bern 9 (tel. 381 18 05).

Information: general information tel. 111.

Rape Crisis Hotline: tel. 332 14 14.

Pharmacy: In the train station. Open daily 6:30am-8pm. **Bären Apotheke,** at Bin Zytglogge at the foot of the clock tower. Open Mon.-Fri. 8:30am-6:30pm, Sat. 8:30am-4pm. To find out which is open 24hr. on a given day, call 311 22 11.

Emergencies Police: tel. 117. **Ambulance:** tel. 144. **24-hr. Doctor:** tel. 311 22 11.

Post Office: Schanzenpost 1, next to the train station. Open Mon.-Fri. 6am-11pm, Sat. 6am-6pm, Sun. 10am-noon and 4-10pm. Address **Poste Restante** to Schanzenpost 3000, Bern 1. A tiny town office at the corner of Kramgasse and Krenzgasse is open Mon.-Fri. 7:30am-noon and 1:45-6pm, Sat. 8:30-11am. **Postal codes:** CH-3000-3030.

Telephone Code: 031.

ACCOMMODATIONS AND CAMPING

Bern's shortage of one-star and unstarred hotels can make finding a cheap room difficult. Consider commuting from Fribourg (½hr. by train).

Jugendherberge (HI), Weihergasse 4 (tel. 311 63 16; fax 312 52 40). The hostel is clean, bright, 2min. from the Aare, and on the fringe of the *Altstadt.* From the station, walk straight across the square past the tram lines to Christoffergasse until it ends, then continue around the side of the Parliament on the walkway next to the park. Go through the gate marked "1875," and turn left onto the Bundesstr. Take the *Drahtseilbahn* (funicular) down for 1SFr, or walk the extra 3min. down the path to the left. Once downhill, turn left onto Weihergasse (the path is well marked by white arrows for the hostel). **Warning:** Like many cities, Bern has a nocturnal drug community. Occasionally it settles on an area in front of the Parliament, on a natural path from the town to the hostel. Some residents report being unsettled by this. **You can avoid this area** by coming down Münzrain from Kasinoplatz, and Weihergaasse; the hostel is on the right. The establishment is generally safe and offers a pleasant, tree-shaded terrace. Max. 3-night stay. Reception open June-Sept. daily 7-9:30am and 3pm-midnight; Oct.-May daily 7-9:30am and 5pm-midnight. Lockout June-Sept. 9:30am-3pm, Oct.-May 9:30am-5pm, but the dining room/lounge is always open. 17SFr. 10SFr for a mattress if beds are full. Laundry 6SFr. Breakfast 6SFr. Lunch or dinner 11SFr. Parking available.

Pension Marthahaus, Wyttenbachstr. 22a (tel. 332 41 35; fax 333 33 86). From the station take bus #20 to "Gewerbeschule," then make a right onto Wyttenbachstr. Or from the station, turn left down Bollwerk, then bear right on Lorrainebrücke

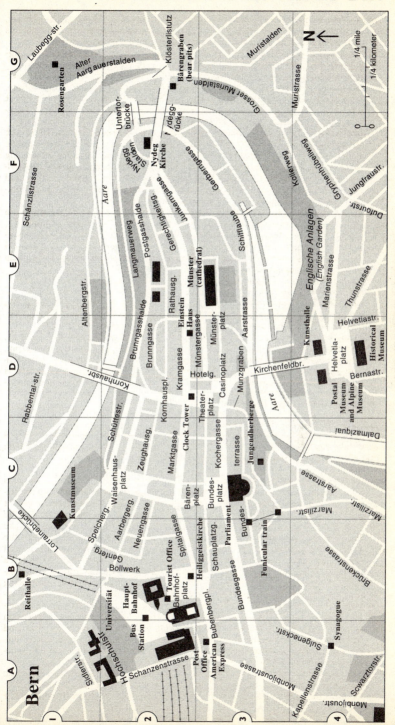

across the river. At the big junction, bear right again on to Victoriarain, and take your first left onto Wyttenbachstr. Matronly hostess maintains a calm, comfortable pension in a very quiet suburb. The bright rooms have been recently decorated. Reception open summer Mon.-Fri. 8am-9pm, Sat. 8am-noon and 1-9pm, Sun. 8am-noon and 3-9pm; winter Sat.-Sun. 8am-noon and 4-9pm. Singles 60SFr, with shower 90SFr. Doubles 95SFr, with shower 120SFr. Triples 130SFR, with shower 155SFr. Prices reduced 5SFr in winter. Breakfast and hall showers included. Laundry 7SFr. Limited parking available. Visa, MC.

Hotel Hospiz zur Heimat, Gerechtigkeitsgasse 50 (tel. 311 04 36; fax 312 33 86). From the train station, take bus #12 (dir: Schosshalde) to "Rathaus." Down the street from the Zytglogge in the *Altstadt,* and just steps from the Bärengraben and the Aare, the hotel has large rooms and a painted fountain outside. The TV room is 18th-century paneled parquet with original tiled stove. Singles 64SFr, with shower 92SFr. Doubles 96SFr. Triples 126SFr, with shower 156SFr. Quads 168SFr. Shower and breakfast included. Restaurant downstairs. Visa, MC, AmEx.

Hotel National, Hirschengraben 24 (tel. 381 19 88; fax 381 68 78). Left off of Bubenbergplatz. Beautiful rooms with Oriental rugs, central location, and a restaurant downstairs with a *menu* (15.50SFr). English-speaking staff. Singles 60-70SFr, with shower 85-100SFr. Doubles 95-100SFr, with shower 125-150SFr. Family room (3-5 people) 140-200SFr. Breakfast included. Reservations recommended in summer. AmEx, Visa, MC, Diner's Club.

Hotel Goldener Schlüssel, Rathausgasse 72 (tel. 311 02 16; fax 311 56 88). Streetcar #9 or 12 to "Zytglogge." A newly renovated hotel, with a popular restaurant-café downstairs, right in the center of town. Reception open daily until 11pm. Singles 75SFr, with shower 95SFr. Doubles 110SFr, with shower 135SFr. Breakfast included. Reservations preferred May-Oct. Visa, MC.

Camping: Camping Eichholz, Strandweg 49 (tel. 961 26 02). Take streetcar #9 to "Wabern" (last stop), backtrack 50m and take first right. 5.50SFr, students 4.30SFr, children 2.90SFr. Tent 4.30SFr or 8.60SFr depending on size. Also sports a few rooms with 2 beds for 13SFr plus 5.50SFr per person. Showers 15SFr; electricity 3SFr; laundry 5SFr. Reserve ahead. Open May-Sept.

FOOD

The **Bärenplatz** is a lively square with myriad cafés and restaurants, most of them with *menus* and lighter fare in the 9-17SFr range. Don't miss Bern's specialties: **Gschnätzltes** (fried veal, beef, or pork) and **sur chabis** (a sauerkraut). Sweet teeth will enjoy an airy **meringue** or the world-renowned **Toblerone chocolate.**

Manora, Bubenbergplatz 5A (tel. 311 37 55), over the tramlines from the station. The closest of the self-serves to the youth hostel, Manora serves big platefuls that are indisputably nutritious. The regulars hover over the fruit tarts and freshly squeezed orange juice. Salad bar (4.20SFr). Pasta main courses (8SFr-10SFr). Open Mon.-Sat. 7am-10:45pm, Sun. 9am-10:45pm.

Zähringer und Schopbar, Hallerstr. 19 (tel. 301 08 60), at the crossing with Gesellschaftstr. This neighborhood joint cooks up great Swiss dishes, with six menus (16.50-18.50SFr). Shaded outdoor tables. Open daily 9am-midnight.

Restaurant Ratskeller, Gerechtigkeitsgasse 81 (tel. 311 17 71). The Ratskeller offers a modern version of traditional Bernese fare like poached brains (14.50SFr); the less daring can opt for a *menu du jour* at 16.50SFr. Outside seating under the arcades provides a view of the *Altstadt.* Open daily 10am-11:30pm.

Schoog-Dee, Bollwerk 4, behind the train station (tel. 311 37 08). Take bus #20 to "Bollwerk." The Thai and Chinese specialties are one of Bern's best deals. Dim sum (13.50SFr), Thai shrimp chow mein (10.20SFr). Open Mon.-Fri. 11am-2pm and 5-11:30pm, Sat. 5-11:30pm, Sun. 4-11pm. Visa, MC, AmEx.

Café des Pyrenées, Kornhausplatz (tel. 311 60 44). A buzzing bistro-café complete with a small terrace surrounded by plants and bushes. A shortish menu has inventive sandwiches (calamari 6.50SFr) but conservative spaghettis (10-11SFr). Next to the menu, the spirits list looks extravagant, with six types of Spanish brandy. Open Mon.-Thurs. 9am-11pm, Fri. 9am-midnight, Sat. 8am-5pm.

CENTRAL SWITZERLAND

Pizza Camargue, Kramgasse 42 (tel. 311 82 77). Humming with local life, it's a good spot for *Altstadt* people-watching under the arcades. Choose from pasta (14SFr), gnocchi (17SFr), or pizzas (13.80-19SFr). Beer (0.3 liter 3.40SFr).

Markets

Migros, on Kramgasse. Open Mon.-Wed. and Fri. 8:30am-7:30pm, Thurs. 8:30am-9:30pm, Sat. 8am-4pm.

Reformhaus M. Siegrist, Marktgasse-Passage, is a popular health food market. Open Mon. 2-6:30pm, Tues.-Fri. 8am-12:15pm and 1:30-6:30pm, Sat. 7:45am-4pm.

Fruit and vegetable market, sprawls its fresh produce daily over Bärenplatz (open May-Oct. 8am-6pm); Tuesdays and Saturdays it spreads into Bundeplatz as well (year round). The onion market on the fourth Mon. of Nov. is probably Bern's single best known festival.

SIGHTS

The massive **Bundeshaus** dominates the Aare river and reminds passing rafters that Bern is boss. You can receive an introduction to Swiss politics here at the **Parlamentsgebäude** (free 45min. tour every hr. 9am-noon and 2-4pm; watch from the galleries when Parlament is in session). A stroll down Kockergasse and Herrengasse brings you to the other source of law in this town, the 15th-century Protestant **Münster.** The imagination of the late-Gothic period runs riot in the portal sculpture of the Last Judgment. The white-robed goody-goodies stand smugly on the left, while the naked damned trot off unhappily to the fiery furnaces rightward. Climb the highest spire in Switzerland for a fantastic view. (Open Easter-Oct. Tues.-Sat. 10am-5pm, Sun. 11am-5pm; Nov.-Easter Tues.-Fri. 10am-noon and 2-4pm, Sat. 10am-noon and 2-5pm, Sun. 11am-2pm. Tower closes ½hr., before church. 3SFr.)

Heading down Münstergasse, take a right, and then the first left to come to the **Zytglogge** (clock tower). Built in the 13th century, it is now famous for its astronomical time piece with moving figures. Crane your neck and join the crowd 4min. before each hour to watch bears dance, jesters beat drums, and a squeaky, golden rooster announce the hour (tours of the interior May-Oct. daily at 4:30pm; 6SFr). The city's bright red, blue, and gold fountains were the flight of fancy of Hans Gieng who loyally carved them on Bernese themes between 1539 and 1546.

Down Kramgasse and Gerechtigkeitsgasse one finds the slender copper spire of the **Nydegg Kirche,** built on the remains of the Nydegg imperial fortress which was destroyed in the mid-13th century. The **Bärengraben** (bear pits) is across the bridge. It dates back to the 15th century and features the mascots of Bern who lumber back and forth munching on carrots. (Open April-Sept. daily 8am-6pm; Oct.-March 9am-4pm. Feed the bears 3SFr.) On Easter, newborn cubs emerge for their first public display. The path snaking up the hill to the left leads to the **Rosengarten;** sit among the blooms and admire one of the best views of Bern's *Altstadt.*

Elsewhere, the **Botanical Gardens** of the University of Bern, Altergrain 21 (tel. 631 49 11), thrive on the banks of the Aare, with exotic plants from Asia, Africa, and the Americas photosynthesizing cheek to leaf with native Alpine green. (Park open March-Sept. Mon.-Fri. 7am-6pm, Sat.-Sun. 8am-5pm. Greenhouse open 8-11:30am and 2-5pm. Free.) To get to the gardens, take bus #20 to "Gewerbeschule" and backtrack to the entrance either downhill from the bus stop or the bridge. A walk southwards along the Aare (or bus#19 to "Tierpark") leads to the **Dählhölzli Städtischer Tierpark** (Zoo), which houses a comprehensive menagerie of European animals plus moose and musk oxen. Some animals roam in semi-natural setting, while others have roofs over their heads. (Tel. 3512 06 16. "Vivarium" open in summer daily 8am-6:30pm, in winter 9am-5pm. Entrance closes ½hr. earlier. 6SFr, students 4SFr, children 3SFr. Parking available.)

MUSEUMS

Several of Bern's many outstanding museums cluster together at **Helvetiaplatz,** across the **Kirchenfeldbrücke** (streetcar #3 or 5). Consider purchasing a **day ticket**

(Tageskarte) for the museums at Helvetiapl. For 7SFr (students 5SFr), the ticket grants admission to the Alpine Museum, Historical Museum, Kunsthalle, Natural History Museum, PTT Museum, and the Rifle Museum.

Kunstmuseum, Hodlerstr. 8-12 (tel. 311 09 44), near the Lorrainebrücke. The ground floor tells the story of modern art using the world's largest Paul Klee collection—2500 works, from his school exercise books to his largest canvases, and some pictures by his chums Kandinsky and Feininger. Upstairs has a briefer collection of the century's big names: lots of Braque, plus Picasso, Matisse, Dali, and Miro. The basement is mainly Swiss, but there is an unexpected room of the Italian *trecento* including Duccio and Fra Angelico. Open Tues. 10am-9pm, Wed.-Sun. 10am-5pm. 6SFr, students 4SFr.

Albert Einstein's House, Kramgasse 49 (tel. 312 00 91). This small apartment where the theory of general relativity was born in 1905 is now filled with photographs, a few of Einstein's letters, and resonating brain waves, but not much else. Open Feb.-Nov. Tues.-Fri. 10am-5pm, Sat. 10am-4pm. 2SFr.

Museum of Natural History, Bernastr. 15 (tel. 350 71 11), off Helvetiapl. Most people come to see "Barry," the now-stuffed St. Bernard who saved over 40 people in his lifetime. The other stuffed beasties, however, are much better. See the anteater, the sea elephant, and a whole floor of beetles, and believe in the wonder of creation again. Some labels are only in German, but a Riesengürteltier is an armadillo in anybody's language. Open Mon. 2-5pm, Tues.-Sat. 9am-5pm, Sun. 10am-5pm. 3SFr, students 1.50SFr, free on Sun.

Bernisches Historische Museum, right off Helvetiapl. 5 (tel. 350 77 11). Exhibits Flemish tapestries, replicas of rural Swiss rooms, and booty from the Burgundian wars of 1476. Open Tues.-Sun. 10am-5pm. 5SFr, students 3SFr. Additional charge for special exhibitions, free on Sat.

Swiss Alpine Museum, Helvetiaplatz 4 (tel. 351 04 34). Vast, spell-bindingly intricate models of Switzerland's most popular mountains, and the story of Switzerland's beautiful maps. A mountain or map lover's must-see. Open mid-May to mid-Oct. Mon. 2-5pm, Tues.-Sun. 10am-5pm; mid.-Oct. to mid-May Mon.2-5pm, Tues.-Sun. 10am-noon and 2-5pm. 5SFr, students and seniors 2.50SFr

Kunsthalle, Helvetiapl. 1 (tel. 351 00 31). No permanent collection. It shows very contemporary art, often by unknowns, so it's potluck. Even the official pamphlet says it is "ready to take risks." Open Tues. 10am-9pm, Wed.-Sun. 10am-5pm. 6SFr, students 3SFr.

ENTERTAINMENT AND NIGHTLIFE

Artsy Bern has symphonies, concerts, and theater performances galore. The many theaters offer light to heavy fare in the city's squares during the summer. In winter shows go up at the Stadttheater (in Kornhausplatz) and other smaller venues. Productions at the **Stadttheater** (tel. 311 07 77) range from operas to ballets during the Sept. to June season. Tickets are 6-115SFr; students receive a 50% discount. For more information, write to: Theaterkasse, Kornhauspl. 18, CH-3000 Bern 7. (Open Mon.-Fri. 10am-6:30pm, Sat. 10am-6pm, Sun. 10am-12:30pm.) The theater season ends in June, but the **Berner Altstadtsommer** picks up the slack in July and Aug. with dance and music concerts, ranging from tango, jazz, and funk to choral concerts. All are in the squares of the *Altstadt* and are free.

The **Gurten Festival** has attracted such luminaries as Bob Dylan, Elvis Costello, INXS, and Björk to its July stage. For ticket information, contact the Bern Tourist Office (tel. 311 66 11), or write to "Gurten Festival, Billett-Versand, Postfach, 3000 Bern B." Ticket prices are around 55SFr per day. Jazz lovers should plan to arrive in early May for the **International Jazz Festival,** whose headliners have included Count Basie and other jazz legends. For tickets, go to the Bankverein Swiss Bank ticket counter in any branch. Bern's **Symphony Orchestra** plays in the fall and winter at the Konservatorium für Musik at Kramgasse 36. For tickets, call 311 62 21.

A Bern tradition that should not be missed is a drink at the **Klötzlikeller Weine Stube,** Gerechtigkeitsgasse 62 (tel. 311 74 56). Bern's oldest wine cellar resides in a

The Berner Oberland

TO BERN
Steffisburg
Thun
N
Oberhofen
Spiez
Faulensee
Krattigen
Reichenbach
TO AIGLE
Frutigen
Adelboden
Balmhorn
Kandersteg
Lötschbergtunnel

Brienzer Rothorn
Brienz
Tannenhorn
Hohgant
Oberried
Brienzersee
Giessbach
Beatenberg
Iseltwald
Beatushöhlen
Thunersee
Interlaken
Faulhorn
Därligen
Leissigen
Wetterhorn
Dreispitz
Wengen
Grindelwald
Lauterbrunnen
Eiger
Schilthorn
Mürren
Mönch
Gimmelwald
Stechelberg
Jungfrau
Blümlisalp
Wannenhorn
Breithorn
Aletschhorn
Eggishorn

0   5 miles
0   5 kilometers

brick-roofed cavern under the *Altstadt's* arcades. You may hear the singing from out-side (open Tues.-Sat. 4pm-12:30am). Bars and late-night cafés line the Bärenplatz. **Art Café,** Gurtengasse 3, is a café by day and a bar for an artsy, cigarette-smoking, hand-waving set at night. The black and white decor and 18 vast Donald Ducks *après* War-hol give a *Der Stijl* meets Disney feel. Spirits list (6-7SFr; open Mon.-Thurs. 7am-12:30pm, Fri.-Sat. 7am-7pm and 8pm-2:30am, Sun. 6pm-12:30am). **Reithalle,** in a graf-fiti-covered warehouse, provides an industrial setting in which one can explore Bern's underground music scene. From the corner of Bollwerk and Hodlerstr. (near the Lorrainebrücke), walk through the parking lot, under the train tracks, and into the building in front on the left. (Shows Fri. and Sat., and occasionally other nights. Cover 15SFr.)

THE BERNER OBERLAND

Pristine and savage, comfortable and remote, the hulking peaks and isolated lodges of the Berner Oberland are at the heart of Switzerland, geographically and emotionally. When World War II threatened to engulf the country, it was this area, *le réduit,* that the Swiss army resolved to defend to the last. A young, international, and somewhat rowdy crowd migrates here every summer to get its fill of crisp Alpine air and clear, starry nights. Bring your camera and take lots of pictures. Don't be stingy. Film is cheap; the views are priceless. Opportunities for paragliding, mountaineering and whitewater rafting are virtually unparalleled here and bewitch not only rubber-boned physical types but also romantics searching for a memory to last a lifetime.

You have to be iron-willed to stick to a budget in the Oberland. Though the heartiest adventures can cost three-figure sums, what really hurts is the cost of transportation. You can keep this to a minimum by using a town or village as a hub. The Thun-Interlaken-Brienz rail link is a standard priced Swiss railway, but the Berner Oberland Bahn, the string of mountain trains that link Interlaken to the valleys, and the various cable cars that lift visitors to the breathtaking peaks, charge high altitude fares, and do not accept railpasses. Eurail pass sometimes ekes out only a 25% discount, and even the magic Swiss Pass, valid on trains to Grindelwald, Wengen, Lauterbrunnen, and Mürren loses its power here. It barely scrapes together a 25% reduction in rates to the higher peaks, including the First, Schilthorn, Jungfraujoch, Männlichen, and the Rothorn. Drivers be forewarned that certain towns, notably Mürren and Wengen, are closed to cars. Of uncertain value is the 15-day **Berner Oberland Regional Pass** (190SFr, 155SFr with Swisspass or Half-Fare Card; *Eurail pass not valid)*, which gives free travel for five days on many railways and cable cars (e.g. Rothorn, Schynige Platte, First, Niesen) and half-price travel on the remaining ten days. The biggest money-suckers, the Schilthorn and Kleine Scheidegg-Jungfraujoch, are only a feeble 25% cheaper with this pass. A seven-day variation is also available with three free days and four half-priced days (150SFr, 120SFr with Swisspass or Swiss Half-Card). Both can be bought at train stations or any tourist office. The only good news for Eurail pass holders is that the useful **Thunersee** or **Brienzersee** ferries are free (Swisspass valid also). These yield hidden surprises like the **Giessbach Falls** (Brienzersee) or the **Beatushöhlen Caves** (Thunersee) which would be inaccessible without them. The only drawback is that the boat service ends around 7pm in summer and 5pm in the spring and fall (winter hours are extremely limited), while the last trains leave at midnight.

■ The Thunersee

Two jade-green lakes framed by steep wooded mountainsides and the distant snowy summits of the Jungfrau sandwich the town of Interlaken. The westerly **Thunersee** is more settled and the mountains are less stark than around its twin, the **Brienzersee**, but its northwestern shores are dappled with castles.

Its three significant towns, **Thun, Spiez,** and **Interlaken** all lie on the main railway line that goes from Bern to Interlaken and then Lucerne. To get to the smaller villages nearly everyone opts for the boats that putter between the Thun and Interlaken West railway stations, calling at a dozen tiny landing stages on the way. There are thirteen daily from June to September, nine daily in October, April, May, and one daily November through March. The whole trip from Thun to Interlaken takes two hours. Boats are free with Eurail, Swisspass, and Berner Oberland pass. A day pass on the Thunersee and Brienzersee costs 42SFr.

THUN

Thun straddles the Aare river as it leaves the Thunersee on its way to Bern. The station is on the south bank, while the main street, the tree-lined boulevard Bälliz, runs along an island in the river. The oldest squares and the castle lie on the north bank.

To get to the **Schloß Thun** from the station, bear left down Bahnhofstr., go over two bridges, right on Obere Hauptgasse, and then left up some stone steps called Risgässli, turning left again at the top. The castle, now guarded by **goats,** was built in 1429. It surrounds the **Turm Zähringer,** which currently houses a historical museum (tel. 223 20 01), whose inexplicable upper floors juxtapose a vicious collection of weaponry with a selection of antiquated musical instruments. The lower floors of the castle display a collection of pottery and regimental tunics. The Turm, built in 1186, was the site of a gruesome fratricide in 1322, when Eberhard of Kyburg unsportingly threw his brother Hartmann out of a window. The Romanesque square tower with four corner turrets looks especially imposing with the Alps as a backdrop. The courtyard below the tower has a 96-foot-deep well. (Open June-Sept. daily 9am-6pm; April-May and Oct. daily 10am-5pm. 5SFr, student 2SFr.) The Schloß also hosts summer classical music concerts (call 223 35 30 or contact the tourist office). Returning back down the Risgässli steps and left at the bottom brings you to Thun's **Kunstmuseum,** Hofstetterstr. 14 (tel. 225 84 20; fax 225 82 63; bus #6 to "Thunerhof"), which stages exhibitions of contemporary art. Call ahead to find out if all the rooms will be open. (Open Tues. and Thurs.-Sun. 10am-5pm, Wed. 10am-9pm. 4SFr, students 3SFr.) Further on, the **Brahms promenade** celebrates the composer's three years sojourn in Thun. Past the Casino, go up left to **Jakobstübeli,** a small hill with a great view of the lake and the Jungfrau mountains.

On the south shore, 15 minutes walk to the right of the station, is the pink **Schloß Schadau,** Seestr. 45 (tel. 223 14 32), in the Walter Hansen Schadaupark. This Victorian folly in a tree-lined garden on the waterfront houses more than 4000 cookbooks and an important collection of historical menus owned by the **Swiss Gastronomy Museum.** (Open June-Aug. Tues.-Sun. 10am-5pm; March-May and Sept.-Oct. 1-5pm. 4.50SFr, students 3.50SFr.)

The best of Thun's castle quartet is **Schloß Oberhofen** (tel. 243 12 35), an early 13th-century fortress bought in 1926 by an enterprising American lawyer. Leaving the exterior intact, he completely renovated the castle, decorating each room in a different historical style. The Turkish smoking room on the top floor of the tower invites debauchery. There is a also a 17th-century prison, a frescoed chapel, and a lot more to see. The castle and the park are right next to the **Oberhofen** boat landing. (Open May to mid-Oct. daily 10am-noon and 2-5pm. Garden open 9:30am-6pm. 5SFr, students 3SFr.) **Schloß Hünegg** (tel. 243 19 82) clings to a cliff above the boat landing at **Hilterfingen.** The most elaborate of the Thunersee castles, its rooms exemplify Victorian excess, some decorated beyond beautiful. (Open mid-May to mid-Oct. Mon.-Sat. 2-5pm, Sun. 10am-noon and 2-5pm. 3SFr, student 1.50SFr.)

Trains leave every hour for **Interlaken** (14SFr) and every half hour for **Spiez** (6SFr) and **Bern** (11.40SFr). The station has **lockers** (5SFr), **currency exchange** (open daily 5:50am-8:40pm), and **bike rental** (21SFr per day; open Mon.-Sat. 7am-7:50pm, Sun. 8:20am-noon and 2-7:50pm). The rail **information desk** can provide any information you might need to get out of the tiny town (open Mon.-Fri. 8am-6:30pm, Sat. 8am-5pm). The **boat landing** (tel. 223 53 80) is just to the right of the train station. Boats depart for **Interlaken West** (15.60SFr), **Spiez** (7.80SFr), **Faulensee** (8.60SFr), **Hilterfingen** (4.40SFr), and **Oberhofen** (5SFr). Thun's **tourist office,** Seestr. 2 (tel. 222 23 40), is outside and to the left of the station. Ask about housing, and pick up a free map. (Open July-Aug. Mon-Fri. 9am-7pm, Sat. 9am-noon and 1-4pm; Sept.-June Mon.-Fri. 9am-noon and 1-6pm, Sat. 9am-noon.) **Parking** is available at the Parkhaus Aarestr., on Aarestr. (1.30SFr per hour, 15SFr per day). The **post office** is at Bälliz 60, opposite the Mühlebrücke (open Mon.-Fri. 7:30am-noon and 1:30-6pm, Sat. 7:30am-11am). **Postal code:** CH-3600. **Telephones** await next door. **Telephone code:** 033.

A 2SFr bus ride to nearby Gwatt brings you to the lakeside **Younotent** (tel. 222 23 40), where you can get a semi-outdoor bed (17SFr) from mid-June to mid-September. The only budget hotel in Thun itself is **Hotel bio-pic,** Bälliz 54 (tel. 222 99 52; fax 223 34 97). Bear left out of the station along Bahnhofstr., cross one branch of the river and take the first left. Reservations made either by phone or at the tourist office are recommended. (Singles 36-52SFr, with shower 62SFr. Doubles 64-86SFr, with shower 102SFr. Breakfast included.) **Hotel Metzgern** (tel. 222 21 41; fax 222 21 82) sits in the heart of town on Rathauspl. (Singles 50-55SFr. Doubles 100-110SFr. Breakfast included. Visa, MC accepted. Closed Monday.) Camp at **Bettlereiche** (tel. 336 40 67) in Gwatt. It's 45 minutes to the right of the station on the lake, or take bus #1 to "Bettlerreniche." (8.80SFr. Tent 6.30-16SFr. Cars free. Open April-Sept.)

Food in Thun is surprisingly cheap. Both **Migros** and **Coop** have markets and restaurants, and are located on Allmendstr. on the island (open Mon.-Fri. 8am-6:30pm, Thurs. 8am-9pm, Sat. 7am-4pm). At the open air market in the *Altstadt*, across the river from the train station, vendors hawk souvenirs, clothes, and food (open Sat. 8am-9pm). A food market takes over Bälliz on the island all day on Wednesdays.

Thun's sole vegetarian joint, **bio-pic,** downstairs in the Hotel bio-pic, offers hearty meals for under 14SFr (open Mon.-Fri. 7am-6:30pm, Sat. 7am-4pm). Restaurants on Bahnhofstr. are cheap as well. Also, south of the river on Aarestr. in the *Aare-Zentrum* is **Le Pavillon,** a self-service restaurant featuring spicy, Asian specialties as well as Swiss staples (open Mon.-Fri. 7:45am-6:30pm, Sat. 7:45am-4pm). For delectable pastries and sandwiches try **Konditorei Steinmann,** Bälliz 37 (tel. 222 20 47; open Mon.-Fri. 7:15am-6:30pm, Sat. 7am-4pm).

A popular local walk with a distant view of the Jungfrau mountains is the climb up **Heilingenschwendi,** the hillside above Thun on the lake's north shore. From town, pass by the *Kunstmuseum* and the casino to the village of Seematten where the lake proper starts. Turn left, cross the river, and head up through the wooded ridge to Heilingenschwendi (1152m). From the village of Schwendi near the top, you can head back to Oberhofen on the right, keeping the castle on the right (600m ascent, half day). Either the bus or the ferry can take you back to Thun.

SPIEZ AND FAULENSEE

Spiez is happy to forgo the proud bombast of prim chalets or grand monuments. Quiet and understated, it fills its tiny harbor with bobbing boats and surveys the **Thunersee** from its gentle hills. Half-hourly **trains** connect the town with **Bern** (15.80SFr), **Thun** (4.60SFr), and **Interlaken** (8.40SFr), and the **boat service** has an hour-long trip to Thun and Interlaken. **Schloß Spiez** (tel. 654 15 06) was a medieval fortress that became a residential castle for Oberlander bigwigs like the Bubenbergs and Erlachs. The castle is next to the dock; from the station, go down the ramp to Hotel Krone, and cross over onto Seestr., following it around to the right before heading left on Schlossstr. A stone tower with unconventional spiral shutters leads to a quiet grassy courtyard, a tenth-century churchyard, and a rose garden. Inside the fortress is the historical museum with a mesmerizing tower view. (Museum open July-Aug. Mon. 2-6pm, Tues.-Sun. 10am-6pm; April-June and Sept.-Oct. Mon. 2-5pm, Tues.-Sun. 10am-5pm. 4SFr, student 1SFr.) Around the corner, the **Wine-Making Museum,** Spiezbergstr. 48, has rustically decorated rooms, a caste-maker's workshop, and a pressing shed (open May-Oct. Wed. and Sat.-Sun. 2-5pm; free).

Spiez's **tourist office,** Bahnhofstr. 12A (tel. (033) 654 21 38; fax 654 21 92), right around the corner from the train station, sells maps of hiking trails and helps find inexpensive private rooms. (Open July-Aug. Mon.-Fri. 8am-noon and 1:30-6:30pm, Sat. 9am-noon and 2-4pm; June and Sept. Mon.-Fri. 8am-noon and 2-6pm, Sat. 9am-noon; Oct.-May Mon.-Fri. 8am-noon and 2-6pm.) If you continue down to Oberlandstr., there are banks, a **Migros** and a **Co-op Center.** (Both open Mon.-Thurs. 7:30am-12:15pm and 1:30-6:30pm, Fri. 7:30am-12:15pm and 1:30-9pm, Sat. 7:30am-4pm.) There is a **post office** to the left of the station (open Mon.-Fri. 7:30am-noon and 1:45-6pm, Sat. 8:30-11am). The **Postal code** is CH-3700. **Telephone code:** 033.

Budget accommodations are almost non-existent in Spiez. Plain but clean rooms, some affording great views, abound at **Hotel Krone,** Oberlandstr. (tel. 654 41 31; fax 654 94 31. Singles 45-52SFr; doubles 80-95SFr. Open May-March.) Better options exist in surrounding villages. Nearby, **Faulensee** has its own minuscule **Jugendherberge (HI)** at Quellenhofweg 66 (tel. 654 19 88; fax 654 17 10) on the lakeshore. Hike from Spiez's train station by following directions to the castle. However, instead of hanging left onto Schlossstr., turn right, and follow the shoreline past the harbor and the tree-covered knolls (40min.). Or, wait for a bus at the station to "Faulensee-Oberdorf," and turn left along Quellenhofweg. Easiest is the journey by boat—most steamers stop at the hostel. Check the itinerary at the landing to make sure. After the boat landing follow the Wanderweg signs to the right. (Reception open 7-9am and 5-9pm. Lockout 9am-5pm. 21SFr, 18.50SFr subsequent nights. Breakfast included. Lunch or dinner 11SFr. Reservations encouraged. Open March-Oct.) In Spiezwiler (take a bus from the station), **Hotel Rössli** on Frutigenstr. offers dorms (9.50SFr) and breakfast (11.50SFr), or, **camp** at **Panorama Rossern,** Aeschi (tel. 654 43 77). To find the campsite, catch the bus to Mustermattli (2SFr), then follow the signs (6.40SFr; tent 6-7SFr; open May-Sept.).

The mountain piercing the sky is the **Niesenberg** (2363m). Hikes on it, while not for beginners, are not remotely as spine-tingling as they look from a distance, and the view from the top is a corker. Pick up hiking maps at tourist offices in Interlaken, Thun, or Spiez. A funicular chugs to the top. Its builders pushed out the frontiers of human achievement by building steps alongside the track, which thereby became the **longest flight of steps in the world.** Thunder-thighed locals pound all 11,674 of them in the annual **Niesen Steps Race.** The hourly Lötschberg train from Spiez (7.20SFr round-trip) connects with the funicular at Mülenen (May-Oct.; 23SFr one-way, 38SFr round-trip, 12SFr one-way to Schwandegg). Hiking routes head down from the summit to **Mülenen** (3hr.) and **Wimmis** (3½hr.).

Another possibility is the 3-stop funicular ticket (31SFr), which is valid on the train to the top. For more scenic bliss, hike down to Schwandegg (1hr.15min.), and take the train again through the woods to Mülenen. To spend a night in an unspoiled, friendly *Berggasthaus,* visit the **mountain guest-house** on the summit (rooms 38SFr per person, breakfast 14SFr). The hotel has a roomy dining area, as well as a large terrace and wine cellar hewn into the rock-face. For reservations, call 676 11 13, or take advantage of the bargain **"Sunset-Sunrise"** package at the hotel, offering dinner, breakfast, and round-trip transportation; sunrise and sunset included (110SFr).

BEATENBERG AND THE CAVES

Not much more than a sprinkle of *châlets,* Beatenberg is known as the sun-terrace of the Berner Oberland. Perched 600m above the Thunersee the town offers hiking and leisurely mountain walking for all levels. Bus #21 from Interlaken to Thun stops in the village, where there is a **tourist office** (tel. (033) 841 12 86; fax 841 18 08; open Mon.-Fri. 8am-noon and 2-6pm, Sat. 9am-noon and July-Aug. also Sat. 3-5pm).

The superb Güggisgrat ridge above the châlets rewards a short climb with long views. Yellow signs from the village center point the route up the Niederhorn (1950m). The hike is essentially straight up (830m ascent, 2½hrs.). Four miles of airy ridgeway then lead northwest to the Gemmenalphorn (2061m) at an easy gradient. Dozens of paths loop back to civilization; Map #5004 will untangle them. A gondola can save you the climb up the Niederhorn (20SFr one-way, 30SFr round-trip; closed two weeks in Nov. and two weeks in April). It starts at the eastern (Interlaken) end of the village. The restaurant (tel. (033) 841 11 97) at the top has dorm beds (30SFr; breakfast included), as well as singles (45SFr), and doubles (90SFr).

Down from Beatenberg village, **Beatushöhlen,** or St. Beatus' Caves, riddle the hillside for over 8km. You can explore the first 100m of glistening stalactites, waterfalls, and clear pools, and also visit the cell of the sixth-century Irish hermit, Beatus. Legend has it that the Augustinian monk had to fight off a dragon in the caves before he could preach the gospels in peace. They were probably both after the natural air-conditioning—even on a hot summer day the interior of the caves stays a cool 8-10° Celsius. Half-hour tours leave every ½hr. from the entrance to the caves. To get there walk 15min. up the hill from the Beatushöhlen dock, 30 minutes by boat from Interlaken, or take bus #21 which runs between Thun and Interlaken (8.20SFr round-trip from Interlaken). One can also walk from Interlaken (2hr.). The admission fee includes entry to the **Caving Museum** (tel. (033) 841 16 43.), 5 minutes down the hill. This tiny room chronicles the discovery and mapping of Switzerland's grottos. (Caves open April-Oct. daily 9:30am-5pm. Museum open April-Oct. daily 10:30am-5pm. 12SFr, students 10SFr.)

■ The Brienzersee

The more rugged of the sister lakes, the Brienzersee lies still and clear beneath sharply jutting cliffs, sharp peaks, and dense forests. Cruises on the lake depart from Interlaken's Ostbahnhof. (June-Sept. every hour 9am-5pm; April-May and Oct. five daily; Nov.-March no service; free with Swisspass and Eurailpass.) Brienz, at the eastern end of the lake, is the only town. The south shoreline, having escaped human attention save for the hamlet of Iseltwald, makes a great hike.

BRIENZ AND THE ROTHORN

Brienz straggles for several kilometers the thin strip of level land between the lake and the steep, wooded fell-side. The station, dock, and Rothorn rack railway terminus occupy the center of town, flanked on the Hauptstr. by the post office, banks, and a supermarket. At the west end of town is Brienz-Dorf wharf; at the eastern end of town lie the hostel and the two campsites.

The campy **Ballenberg Swiss Open-Air Museum,** on the outskirts of town along Lauenenstr. (tel. 951 11 23; fax 951 18 21), is a 50-hectare country park, displaying examples of traditional, rural dwellings from every region of Switzerland, with anachronistically dressed Swiss artisans busily working away. Though the freshly laundered clothes and showered faces sterilize peasant life of its nastiness, brutishness, and shortness, the park is certainly a colorful excursion. The park is about an hour's walk from the Brienz train station, but an hourly bus (round-trip 5.60SFr) connects the two. Alternately, the local train to Meiringen and Lucerne halts in Brienzwiler opposite the museum (open mid-April to Oct. daily 10am-5pm. 12SFr, with visitor's card 10.80SFr). At the other end of town you can visit the **Wood-Carving Museum** on Schleegasse (tel. 951 17 51; open Mon.-Fri. 8-11am and 2-5pm; free) or the **Violin-Making School** on Oberdorfstr. (tel. 951 18 61; open Wed. 2-4pm, closed in July-Aug.; free). Many local wood-carvers let you watch them work; contact the tourist office for a map locating the workshops.

For the more authentic Switzerland, you can ascend the **Rothorn** (2350m) with its outstanding view of the Brienzersee and the Berner Oberland mountain chain, well beyond the familiar Eiger, Mönch, and Jungfrau. From June to October, the **Brienz Rothorn Bahn** (tel. 951 12 320) huffs and puffs its way up hourly. Over 100 years old, this small open train is the only steam rail line left in Switzerland (the others axed in the never ending Swiss quest for precision). The one-hour trip is pricey (40SFr, round-trip 62SFr, free or 50% off with regional pass, Swisspass 25% off; Eurail pass not valid), but as you rise the 1800m of ascent, your feet will bless every red centime. A ticket to **Planalp** in a hanging valley at 1341m leaves you 2½hr. from the top (26SFr). While descending, the view is breathtaking and the pace easy. Either follow the railway down, turning left below Planalp through Baalen and Schwanden (3½hr.), or leave the summit in an eastwards direction towards the lake, and turn right at the Eiseesaltel, continuing down to Hofstetten, Schwanden, and Brienz (4hr.). The tourist office publishes a leaflet, *Wanderberg*, with these options clearly marked. For a romantic encounter with rosy-fingered dawn over the Oberland glaciers, or, alternately, a dark, cloudy, 7am start on top of a mountain, you can stay on the peak of the Rothorn at the *Berggastehaus* there (tel. 951 12 32; fax 951 37 95; dorms 32SFr; singles 70SFr; doubles 130SFr; breakfast included; no showers).

Twenty minutes by the hourly train or 1hr.15min. by boat (10.60SFr), Brienz makes a peaceful daytrip from Interlaken. Guests of the hotels at Brienz get free **visitor's cards,** good for lots of discounts and some freebies, including free water skiing on Mondays (notify the tourist office by 4pm). *Gäste-Information* (Visitor Information) is a free booklet from the tourist office listing all the deals and dozens of free events. Brienz's **tourist office,** Hauptstr. 143 (tel. 952 80 80; fax 952 80 88), across and left from the train station, suggests trails for hikers of all levels. Ask here about *Privatzimmer* or find out about the events for the week, such as guided hikes, tours of the wood-carving school, "carve your own cow" fests, and other stimulating happenings. (Open July-Aug. Mon.-Fri. 8am-6:30pm, Sat. 9am-noon and 4-6pm; Sept.-June Mon.-Fri. 8am-noon and 2-6pm, Sat. 8am-noon.) The **train station** rents **bicycles** for 21SFr per day, **exchanges currency,** and offers **small lockers** (2SFr). The **post office** (tel. 951 25 05) is also nearby (open Mon.-Fri. 7:45am-noon and 1:45-6pm, Sat. 8:30-11am). **Postal code:** CH-3855. **Telephone code:** 033.

From the station turn right and walk towards the end of the lake for 15 minutes to find the **Brienz Jugendherberge** (HI), Strandweg 10 (tel. 951 11 52; fax 951 22 60).

The lake-side hostel rents hiking boots (5SFr) and bicycles (10SFr for 1 day, 15SFr for 2) to its mountain-hungry guests. (Reception open daily 8-9am, 5-6pm, and 7-9pm. Dorms 23SFr, after first night 20.50SFr. Doubles 28SFr, then 25.50SFr. Dinner 11SFr. Kitchen facilities. Open March-Nov.) The cheapest hotel in town is **Hotel Sternen am See,** Hauptstr. 92 (tel. 951 35 45), left from the station, with a winning lakeside terrace. (Reception open 8am-8pm. Singles 50-60SFr. Doubles 80SFr, with shower 120SFr. Triples 110SFr, with shower 150SFr. Quads with shower 180SFr. Breakfast included. Visa, MC.) Continue past the hostel to hit two waterfront campgrounds: **Camping Seegärtli** (tel. 951 13 51; 7SFr, tent 4-7SFr, car 3SFr; open April-Oct.) and **Camping Aaregg** (tel. 951 18 43; fax 951 43 24; reception open 7am-noon and 2-8pm; 7SFr, tent 13SFr; open April-Oct.). A **Co-op** nests on Hauptgasse across from the station (open Mon.-Thurs. 7:45am-6:30pm, Fri. 7:45am-8:30pm, Sat. 7:45am-4pm). **Restaurant Adler,** Hauptstr. 131 (tel. 951 41 00), has a terrace with a spectacular view of the bright green Brienzersee and the Axalphorn. (Main dishes 14.80-18.80SFr. Open June-Oct. daily 7:30am-11:30pm, Nov.-May Tues.-Sun. 7:30am-11:30pm.) **Steinbock Restaurant,** further along Hauptstr. (tel. 951 40 55), has outside tables and a low-ceilinged, wooden interior with subdued lighting. Main courses start at 11SFr (open daily 11am-11pm).

There is a swimming pool complex near the hostel (open June-Sept. daily from 9am; 4SFr adults, 2SFr children; one free admission with the visitor's card). Brienz's cinema, just left of the station on the quay side, dubs many of its films into German, but English language originals sometimes slip through the net (Thurs.-Sun. 8:30pm). Take note of the local by-law which forbids mushroom picking until the 8th of each month. Even then, it's probably better to keep your fungal forays furtive.

THE SOUTH SHORE

Boat service gives easy access to the wild, romantic south shore of the Brienzersee. Float 10 minutes from Brienz or one hour from Interlaken to **Giessbach Falls,** and climb for hours along its 14 frothy cascades. A funicular runs up the hill, but you can walk up in 15 minutes by turning left at the tiny dock. (Funicular open May to mid-Oct. 3SFr one-way, 5.50SFr round-trip; 2.50SFr and 3SFr respectively for students and Regional Pass holders.) The classic view is from the hotel, but the path that criss-crosses the falls, passing behind the falls, provide a deafening, dampening experience. Trails stretch around the lake from the falls to **Iseltwald,** a small village whose only tourist attraction is professional fishing. The hike is 1½hr.; the village is gloriously sleepy and served by postal bus and steamer. Iseltwald's campground, **Camping du Lac** (tel. (033) 845 11 48), has many conveniences, from water sport facilities to a seafood restaurant (7.90SFr, tent 5-10SFr; open May-Sept.).

To reach a satisfying little peak, the **Axalphorn** (2321m), you can take a bus from Brienz station to Axalp (8.40SFr one-way, 16.80SFr round-trip) and head up either the east or west ridge (800m ascent, half-day). You will need Map #5004 and navigational aptitude as both paths are indistinct in places.

MEIRINGEN AND REICHENBACH FALLS

Though **Meiringen** is seven miles from the Brienzersee, its water-related attraction still makes for a great day trip from Brienz or Interlaken. Travel to the town is given added convenience by its strategic rail position; the hourly train from Interlaken and Brienz to Lucerne both stop in Meiringen. The spooky **Gorge of the Aare,** a 200-meter-deep cleft cut by the river Aare, sports vertical sides scraped clean by erosion. With only a meter separating the two sides at their narrowest point, direct sunlight hardly ever reaches the bottom. To reach the gorge, follow signs from Meiringen's main street (2km). On Wednesday and Friday in July and August the gorge shines under floodlights after 9pm (open April-Oct.; 5SFr, students 3.50SFr).

More famous, but less spectacular, the **Reichenbach Falls** hurl their glacier water into the Aare at Meiringen. Sherlock Holmes and Professor Moriarty tumbled together into the falls on May 4, 1891, apparently ending the greatest struggle between good and evil in the history of the detective novel. The public outrage incited by the calamitous end of its favorite hero helped revive the flagging series. Walk down Meiringen's main street and turn right over the river to Reichenbach. A **funicular** leads to the falls (open mid-May-Sept., 4.40SFr one-way, 6.50SFr round-trip), or you can walk. Continuing onwards and you will soon get into the deserted high alpine pastures of the Rosenlaui valley ending in the ice-fall of the Rosenlaui glacier and the shapely Wellhorn peak (600m ascent, half-day). There is a **Sherlock Holmes Museum** (tel. 971 42 21) in the old Anglican church in Meiringen which has a "replica" of 221B Baker Street (open May-Sept. daily 10am-6pm; Oct.-April Wed.-Sun. 3-6pm; 3.80SFr). In grateful response to the interest in their small hamlet piqued by the popular author, the inhabitants of Meiringen have installed a statue of Sir Arthur Conan Doyle, the author of the Sherlock Holmes mysteries, in town. For details on local accommodations and other excursions see the **tourist office** (tel. 971 43 22) near the station.

■ Interlaken

Interlaken was so named in 1130 by two ruthlessly literal-minded Augustinian monks because it fills the gap between the Thunersee and the Brienzersee. Most of its visitors, however, have come not for the lakes but for the arc of giant mountains to the south, the Eiger, Mönch, and Jungfrau. Although the sight of the Jungfrau rising 4158 meters above the flower gardens lining Höheweg is entrancingly beautiful, realize that Interlaken is a way-station for the villages to the south and not much of a destination in itself.

One of the eeriest and most fascinating sights in the Berner Oberland is the face in the **Harder Mountain.** No human hand sculpted it, but there it is, looking out over Interlaken with its brooding gaze. Locals call it the **Harder Mann.** On a clear day he is easy to see, a pale triangular face resting against a pillow of trees on one side and a wedge of naked rock on the other. His black moustache has a certain despondent droop, and his deep-socketed eyes have a melancholic, hunted look. There are many legends about the Harder Mann, some of them dark: a man, guilty of murder or rape, fled to the mountains and was turned to stone, his face left behind for all eternity. But for the children of Interlaken, there is a brighter side. Every year, they're told, the Harder Mann comes down from the mountains to fight off winter. On January 2, they celebrate this fight, donning wooden masks of the Harder Mann face and throwing a carnival. Hikers may hike this landmark but should not leave the marked paths. Deaths are reported every summer when people attempt to master parts which have been roped off.

ORIENTATION AND PRACTICAL INFORMATION

Interlaken lies south on N6, west on N8, and north on Route 11, and has two train stations. The **Westbahnhof** (tel. 826 47 50) stands in the center of town bordering the Thunersee, near most shops and hotels; trains from Bern, Basel and other western towns stop here first. The **Ostbahnhof** (tel. 822 27 92), on the Brienzersee, is 10 minutes away from the town center by foot or bus (2.20SFr) but is near the youth hostel. Mainline trains arrive from **Bern** (24SFr), **Basel** (54SFr), **Zürich** (59SFr), **Geneva** (60SFr), **Lucerne** (23SFr), and **Lugano** (67SFr) among others. Trains to the **mountains** leave every ½hr. from Interlaken Ost, the front half of the train going to **Lauterbrunnen** (6SFr), **Wengen** (11.40SFr), **Kleine Scheidegg** (33.60SFr) and the **Jungfraujoch** (153.20SFr round-trip, but see The Jungfraujoch, p. 175); and the rear end rumbling along to **Grindelwald** (9SFr). Swisspass is valid up to Grindelwald, Wengen and Mürren (14.40SFr, change at Lauterbrunnen) and gets you a 25% discount above these stops. Eurail gets you a 25% discount on mountain trains but no free rides. Polyglot computers on the platform at either station spew tourist information in English, German, and French. Both also have direct free phones to all the hotels with price details posted.

Tourist Office: Höheweg 37 (tel. 822 21 21), in the Hotel Metropole. From West-bahnhof, take a left on Bahnhofpl. and a right on Bahnhofstr., which turns into Höheweg; from the Ostbahnhof, turn left, and keep going. Provides maps and schedules for free. Sells tickets to the Jungfraujoch, and maintains a TV link to all the cable cars and railway stations. Open July-Aug. Mon.-Fri. 8am-6:30pm, Sat. 8am-5pm, Sun. 5-7pm; Sept.-June Mon.-Fri. 8am-noon and 2-6pm, Sat. 8am-noon.

Currency Exchange: Good rates at the **train station,** but you might do 1% better in town. No commission on traveler's checks. Credit card advances and Western Union transfers. Open daily 8am-noon and 2-6pm.

Taxis: City Taxi: tel. 155 23 60, **ABC Taxi:** tel. 155 27 10.

Parking: Lots at each train station, at the back of the Casino, and on Centralstr.

Bike Rental: At either **train station,** 21SFr per day, 29SFr for mountain bikes. Open daily 5am-10pm. **Zumbrunn Velo,** Postgasse 4 (tel. 822 22 35); 8SFr per day, 18SFr for mountain bikes.

Bookstore: Buchhandlweg Haupt, Höheweg 11 (tel. 822 35 16). Selection of English-language books (and German-French dictionaries). Restock *Let's Go* here. Open Mon.-Fri. 10am-6:30pm, Sat. 8:30am-4pm.

Library: Marktpl. 4 (tel. 822 02 12). German, French, and English books. Open Mon.-Tues. and Thurs.-Fri. 4-6pm, Wed. 9-11am and 3-7pm, Sat. 10am-noon.

Laundry: Postgasse 10. Open Tues.-Fri. 8am-noon and 1:30-6pm, Sat. 8am-4pm.

Snow and Weather Info: tel. 855 10 22.

Pharmacy: call 111 to find out which pharmacy is open late. **Grosse Apotheke,** Bahnhofstr. 5A is open Mon.-Fri. 7:30am-12:15pm and 1:15-6:30pm, Sat. 7;30am-5pm. Visa, MC, AmEx.

Emergency: Police: tel. 117. **Doctor:** tel. 823 23 23. **Hospital:** tel. 826 26 26.

Post Office: Marktgasse 1 (tel. 824 89 50). From the Westbahnhof go left on Bahnhofpl., right on Bahnhofstr., and left on Marktgasse. Open May-Sept. Mon.-Fri. 7:45am-6:15pm, Sat. 8:30-11am; Oct.-April Mon.-Sat. 7:45am-noon and 1:30-6:15pm, Sat. 8:30-11am. **Postal Code:** CH-3800.

Telephone Code: 036.

ACCOMMODATIONS AND CAMPING

Hotels in the mountains are going through a lean patch and Interlaken is seriously over-bedded, so finding a place to sleep is easy. Self-catering *châlets* can be rented by the week, but get a list from the tourist office first, because there may not be any available in high season.

Balmer's Herberge, in the nearby village of Matten on Hauptstr. 23-25 (tel. 822 19 61; fax 823 32 61). Take bus #5 to "Hotel Sonne" (2.20SFr) and backtrack one minute, or walk 15min. from either station. From Westbahnhof, take a left on Bahnhofpl., and a right on Bahnhofstr., a right on Centralstr. After the post office, Centralstr. will become Jungfraustr.; at the end, dodge right off Gasthof Hirschen and Balmer's is on the left. Sign in and return at 5pm when beds are assigned (no reservations). When you see Americans in Interlaken, it's not hard to guess where they're staying. A back-to-the-mother-tongue break for monolingual English-speakers, Balmer's is the country's oldest private hostel, and a legend on the international hostelers' circuit. During U.S. college vacations, it takes on a distinctive frat-party, summer-camp atmosphere, replete with fast-flowing beer and numerous lounges, about which veterans hold strong opinions for and against. "Uncle Erich" provides tons of services for his guests: currency exchange, mountain bike rental (20SFr per day), discount excursions, nightly movies, four TVs with CNN and MTV, book exchange, kitchen facilities (1SFr per 20min.), laundry (8SFr per load), a mini-department store (open daily until 10pm), safety deposit boxes (1SFr for the entire stay), and oodles of information. A newly-built **club-room** with a doo-wop-ditty **jukebox,** live music by staff members, a **game-recreation room,** with pool table and darts, and summer **bonfires** in the nearby forest (shuttle bus free) all entertain Balmer's guests into the wee hours of morning. Partake of the entertainment with caution—wake-up calls are at 7:30am. The staff makes a real effort to get guests out on the trails and slopes, and from May-Oct. sells expeditions of **river rafting** (75SFr), **canyoning** (80SFr), **rock-climbing** (75SFr), **bungee-jumping** (the longest in the world at 180m; also a 100m jump for the beginner) off a cable car near Lucerne (148SFr); or combinations of these in an **Adventure-Package.** Some prefer the frigid but fantastic **ice-climbing** (110SFr) or the beautiful tandem **paragliding** off local mountains (year-round, 100-170SFr). In the winter there are free sleds and a 20% discount on ski and snowboard rental. Many of those in the dorms or Balmer's tent value comradeship above comfort. Reception open daily 9:30am-noon and 4:30-11pm; winter 6:30am-9am and 4:30-11pm. Dorms and tent 17-19SFr. Singles 40SFr. Doubles 56SFr. Triples 66SFr. Quads 84SFr. If beds are full, crash on a mattress, 11SFr. Showers 1SFr per 5min. of hot water. Breakfast included. Don't worry, no one gets turned away, but it's best to show up early. Balmer's takes credit cards with a 50SFr minimum and a 5% surcharge (Visa, MC, AmEx).

Jugendherberge Bönigen (HI), Aareweg 21 (tel. 822 43 53; fax 823 20 58). Take bus #1 (dir: Bönigen) to "Lütschinenbrücke" (2 stops), and follow the signs for 2min. to the left, or walk from *Ostbahnhof* for 20min. Turn left and left again on the main road. The *jugi* is the ying to Balmer's yang. The turquoise lake laps fifteen seconds from the door, the birds sing, and there are gnomes in the garden (3 large, 6 small and a gnomehouse). The six-bed dorms are equally peaceful, but the 25-bed behemoths on the top floor are less loved. Reception open daily 6-10am and 4-11pm. No lockout. Dorms 18.30SFr first night, then 15.80SFr. Add 4SFr per person for a 4-bed family room. Doubles 62.60SFr. Showers, sheets, and lockers included. Breakfast 7SFr, good dinner 10.50SFr. Kitchen facilities 50 centimes. Laundry around 8SFr. Bike rental 10SFr. Open Feb.-Oct.

Heidi's Garni-Hotel Beyeler, Bernastr. 37 (tel. and fax 822 90 30). From the Westbahnhof, turn right, then bear left on Bernastr. (right behind the Migros market), and walk straight for about 3min. A friendly, family-run hotel in a rambling old house on a quiet but convenient street. Wood-beamed TV room with CNN. Lots of info on things to do, and a very bouncy dog called Pedro. Cheap, livable rooms all have showers and bathrooms. Open year-round. Doubles 60-70SFr. Triples 90SFr. 4-bed rooms 100SFr. Visa, MC.

Alp Lodge, Marktgasse 59 (tel. 822 47 48; fax 822 92 50). Take a left from Westbahnhof, bear right on Bahnhofstr. and left down Marktgasse at the post office. The hotel is down an alley by the pink Hotel Bellevue, just opposite Mr. Hong's. Jazzy, primary colors in the halls and funky, home-painted safari animals in the rooms. The staff are a gas and the rooms sparkle, though the stairwell carpet may get a bit frayed. Reception open 7am-9pm. 27-29SFr per person, with shower 37-39SFr. Breakfast included. Open mid.-Dec. to Oct.

Happy Inn Lodge, Rosenstr. 17 (tel. 822 32 25; fax 822 32 68). From the Westbahnhof, walk left as you exit the station, make a right on Bahnhofstr., walking to the post office, and then make a right onto Rosengasse. Look for the bright yellow happy face. This small hotel provides some hostel-type dorms, and also quads and doubles with a less institutional feel. Thin walls do little to block out the occasional bands playing downstairs at the restaurant/bar, **Brasserie 17,** however. 6-bed dorms 26SFr, without breakfast 19SFr. Doubles 82SFr, without breakfast 70SFr. Quads 136SFr, without breakfast 108SFr. MC, AmEx.

Camping

Interlaken has seven campsites and Böningen three more. Amenities vary enormously so pick up a checklist from the tourist office.

Camping Sackgut (tel. 822 44 34), is closest to town, just across the river from the Ostbahnhof. Head as if you are going to town, taking a right across the first bridge and right on the other side. 7.60SFr. Tent 6.50-14SFr. Open May-Sept.

Camping Jungfraublick (tel. 822 44 14; fax 822 16 19). 5min. past Balmer's on Gsteigstr.; take bus #5 from Westbahnhof. The views here are splendid, and the location is quiet and peaceful. 7.80SFr; off-season 7SFr. Open May.-Sept.

Camping Seeblick (tel. 822 02 36). Near the youth hostel on the Brienzersee. Take bus #6 to "Lütschinenbrücke" and turn left. 7.70SFr. Tent 6.30-17SFr. Open April to mid-Oct.

Five other sites are clustered together near the Lombach River and the Thunersee in Unterseen; from the Westbahnhof, cross the Aare River on Bahnhofstr. and follow the signs down Seestr. 7.40-10.50SFr.

FOOD

Interlaken's restaurants, unlike its accommodations, are as expensive as the rest of Switzerland. Generally, the Balmer's crowd eats at Balmer's *(fondue, Bratwurst,* and burgers all under 10SFr), and the youth hostel crowd eats at the hostel (11SFr).

Châlet Oberland, Postgasse (tel. 821 62 21). A romantic, rustic wooden chalet interior for upmarket traditional Swiss food. Live but discreet music. Turkey *schnitzel* with mushroom sauce 16SFr, Berner *bratwurst* and *rösti* 15SFr. Open Sun.-Thurs. 11am-11:30pm; Fri.-Sat. 11am-1am. Visa, MC, AmEx.

Vegetaris, in the Hotel Weisseskreuz, am Höheweg (tel. 822 59 51). Uses soy in more ways than you thought possible. A creative break from *Gemüseteller.* Salad buffet (7SFr and 12SFr), good soups (6SFr), and specials 14.50-24.50SFr. Open in summer daily 8am-12:30am; in winter Thurs.-Tues. 8am-11:30pm.

Pizpaz, Bahnhofstr. 1 (tel. 822 25 33) is a buzzing, central Italian restaurant with pinkish outdoor tables. "Farinaceous dishes" (presumably pasta) 9.50-16.50SFr, pizzas 10.50-17SFr, shrimp and gorganzola *risotto* 17.50SFr. Open July-Aug. daily 11am-midnight; Sept.-June Tues.-Sun. 11am-midnight. Visa, MC, AmEx.

Confiserie Rieder, Marktgasse 14 (tel. 822 36 73). Neat pyramids of homemade truffles, sweet-smelling strudel in the bakery, meringues heaped with ice cream, and sorbets in the tea room...anyone? Open Tues.-Fri. 8:30am-6:30pm, Sat. 8:30am-6pm, Sun. 1-6pm.

Markets

Migros, across from the Westbahnhof, also houses a restaurant with giant prancing cows on the ceiling. Market and restaurant open Mon-Thurs. 7:30am-6:30pm, Fri. 7:30am-9pm, Sat. 7:30am-4pm; restaurant also open Sun. 9am-5pm.

Co-op, on Bahnhofstr. on the right as you cross the river into Unterseen. Restaurant open Mon.-Thurs. 8am-6:30pm, Fri. 8am-9:30pm, Sat. 8am-5:30pm, Sun. 9am-5:30pm. Supermarket open Mon.-Thurs. 7:30am-6:30pm, Fri. 7:30am-9pm, Sat. 7:30am-4pm.

SIGHTS

OK, it's raining in Interlaken, and time for some "sights." Passionate about model railways or wet marmots? Well, you're in luck. The **model railway exhibition,** Rugenparkstr., right out of the Westbahnhof, has 40 models and is the leading rainy-day activity. (Open May-mid.-Oct. daily 10am-noon and 1:30-6pm; 7SFr, children 3SFr.) The marmots scuttle around at the **Alpine Wildlife Park** on Brienzstr., on your first right over the river as you head from the Ostbahnhof to town (free). The **Chäs-Dörfli,** behind Centralstr. 3, sneaks a peak at the (un?)wholesome art of cheese-making. (Open summer Mon. 1:30-6:30pm, Thurs.-Fri. 8am-noon and 1:30-6:30pm, Sat. 8am-noon and 1:30-4pm; winter Tues.-Fri. 2-4pm.)

There is a market every Tuesday from June to mid-September on Jungfraustr. The **Bödeli** complex behind the Casino has an **indoor public swimming pool** (tel. 822 24 16; open Mon. 1:30-9:30pm, Tues.-Fri. 9am-9:30pm, Sat.-Sun. 9am-6pm; 8SFr, children 4.50SFr) and an **indoor skating rink.**

OUTDOORS NEAR INTERLAKEN

Because of its central location, Interlaken is the base for many outdoor excursions, boasting a plethora of nausea-inducing, pants-wetting, heart-attack-producing activities such as bungee jumping, parachuting, glacier climbing, canyoning, kayaking, and paragliding. Guests at Balmer's can sign up near the Herberge's reception desk for those run by **Adventure World** (see Balmer's on p. 167 for outdoor activity offerings). **Alpin Zentrum,** Interlaken's main "adventure coordinator," will help you try out a myriad of these daredevil pursuits. On the water, there's **river rafting** (half-day 61-81SFr) and **canyoning** (half-day 80-120SFr). On land, struggle up and rappel down the alps on your **climbing** adventure (half-day 75SFr). In the air, enjoy the graceful, peaceful beauty of **tandem paragliding** (half-day 120SFr or 230SFr, depending on altitude of flight), or experience the free-fall rush of **bungee jumping** from the Schilthorn (100m, 129SFr; 180m, 259SFr, prerequisite of one previous jump). Alpin Zentrum also offers combined packages of all their activities (300-350SFr). For information and reservations, contact Alpin Zentrum, P.O. Box 3800, Interlaken (tel. 823 43 63; fax 822 73 07).

Interlaken's *Flugschule,* **Ikarus,** offers intensive and expensive classes in parachuting and paragliding, as well as a one-day program of tandem paragliding (starting at 100SFr). Contact Claudia or Hanspeter Michel, Brunngasse 68, CH-3800 Matten b, Interlaken (tel. 822 04 28). **Alpin Raft,** another Interlaken-based group, also offers rafting (50-108SFr), canyoning (75-120SFr), and kayaking (50-70SFr). Contact Heinz Looshi, Postfach CH-3852, Riggenberg (tel. 823 41 00; fax 823 41 01).

On the Brienzersee, minutes from Interlaken, sea-kayaking provides a strenuous day in the sun, and on the water (contact Alpin Raft; 54-70SFr). **Euro-trek** leads guided boat trips on the Vierwaldstättersee near Lucerne, and on the Brienzersee (71SFr and up). Contact Euro-trek Abenteuerreisen, Malzstr. 17-221, CH-8026 Zürich (tel. (01) 462 02 03). For those who enjoy getting really cold and wet, Alpin Zentrum and **Alpine Guides** (Hano Tschabold, Bergführer, CH-3852 Ringgenberg; tel. 22 05 69) offer **glacier climbing** (June-Oct., 117SFr), one day **rock-climbing courses** (95SFr), and one-day **glacier walks** (98SFr) every day in summer. Interlaken's winter activities range from tame skiing to snowboarding, ice canyoning, snow rafting, and glacier skiing. Contact either the **Verkehrsverein Interlaken,** Höheweg 37 (tel. 822 21 21; fax 822 52 21) or Alpin Zentrum.

With all these activities, the situation is very fluid; companies tend to come and go as individual guides and instructors move into and out of Interlaken. Shop around, and watch for insurance and who pays for travel to the start point in the fine print.

HIKES FROM INTERLAKEN

Interlaken is in a deep valley, so to get picture-perfect views you have to sweat. For a scenic stroll, a gentle lakeside path rings the Brienzersee, with the south shore generally preferred. Start at Böningen or the youth hostel garden. The best half-day hike is the climb up the **Harderkulm** (1322m). The white wall of the Jungfrau, Eiger, and Mönch peaks looks touchably close, towering 3700 meters above Interlaken's rooftops. On a clear day, the view from the top is hard to leave, but unfortunately you don't get much of it on the climb up, a steep, dull, zigzag through dense woods. From Interlaken Ost, head as if into town, and take the first road bridge across the river on your right. On the other side, the path has yellow signs (destination: "Harderkulm") which later give way to white-red-white *bergweg* flashes on the rocks. When you reach the house in a clearing you are halfway from Interlaken West, turn left and left again across the river on Bahnhofstr., later called Scheidgasse. After 7 minutes, you intersect with Beatenburgstr. at the edge of town; the path rises at the junction on the other side of the road. Neither path is very difficult, but mud can make both gloopy after rain (750m ascent, 2hrs. up, 1hr. down). A restaurant at the top serves spaghetti for 11.50SFr and *rösti* with fried eggs for 11.80SFr, but try to bring liquids with you to protect your bank balance. To facilitate your ascent, a funicular climbs up from the start of the Interlaken Ost path (roughly May-Oct. 12.40SFr one-way, 20SFr round-trip; 25% discount with Eurail pass and Swisspass). For the fit, the walk extends wonderfully. Head up the path that clings to the crest of the ridge—the views improve, the gradient lessens, and you start to lose the accursed trees. Paths dive down rightward to Ringgenberg and Niederried from where you can catch a bus back to Interlaken.

A gruesome hike for a hot, clear day is the climb up **Schynige Platte** (2070m). Though very long and very steep, the panoramic view is one of the best in the Jungfrau region. Take bus #5 south of Interlaken (or any of the mountain trains from Interlaken Ost) to the village of Wilderswil, across the river; the path heads up (and up and up) from the back of the churchyard (1500m of ascent, full day, steep in places). In May and early June check first for snow by watching the TV at the tourist office or big hotels. From roughly June to mid-October, a railway leaves from Wilderswil (30.80SFr one-way, 50.60SFr round-trip; 25% discount with Eurail pass and Swisspass), but if you are thinking of taking the railway up and walking down, bear in mind that you will be out of sight of the Jungfrau massif, and that walking off Schynige Platte northwards to Zweilütschinen, while possible, is extremely steep and only for the experienced.

NIGHTLIFE

Interlaken's nightlife heats up during high season, but never gets exactly red hot. The fun starts at **Buddy's,** Höheweg 33, a small, crowded English pub in the Hotel Splendid. An Interlaken tradition, it has cheap beer and popular snacks (beers 3.20-5.30SFr; open daily 10am-12:30am). The drunken herds then migrate to Interlaken's oldest disco, **Johnny's Dancing Club,** Höheweg 92, downstairs in the Hotel Carlton. (Drinks from 5.50SFr. Sat. cover 7SFr. Open Dec.-Oct. Tues.-Sun. 9:30pm-2:30am.)

Interlaken is a good place to cleanse yourself of that nagging desire to see leather-clad Swiss men slap their thighs, toot their alpen horns, dong their cowbells and yodel a bit. The **Swiss Folklore Show** at the Casino will expunge some of these lacks in your life for only 16SFr at 9pm, daily in July and August and sporadically from May to October (tel. 827 61 00). You can dine with your fellow *lederhosen* lovers at 7:30pm on *fondue* and ice cream for another 23.50SFr. The other apex of Interlaken's cultural life is the summer production of Friedrich Schiller's play *Wilhelm Tell* (yup, in German). 250 local men with bushy beards and local lasses with flowing locks ham the tale of Swiss escape from the thumbscrew of Austrian rule. The showmanship is superb; 20 horses gallop by in every scene, and a magnificent mock-village amphitheater around the corner from Balmer's allows the cast to make real bonfires. A cunning distraction leaves you pondering whether they actually shoot the apple off the wee lad's head, however. The audience stamps their feet with delight, or possibly just to keep them warm. (Shows late June to early July Thurs. 8pm; mid-July to early Sept. Thurs. and Sat. 8pm.) Tickets (12-32SFr) are available at the *Tellbüro,* Bahnhofstr. 5A (tel. (036) 822 37 23; open May-Sept. Mon.-Fri. 8:30-11:30am and 2-5pm; Oct.-April Tues. 8-11am and 2-5pm, or at the theater on the night of the show; an English synopsis of the show is also available for 2SFr).

■ The Jungfrau Region

A few miles south of Interlaken, the hitherto middling-sized mountains rear upwards, immediately transformed into hulking white monsters. Welcome to the Jungfrau, home to Europe's largest glacier, as well as many of its steepest crags and highest waterfalls. The Jungfrau area's list of firsts reflects its irresistible appeal to sportsmen: the first part of Switzerland opened up to tourists, the first Alpine mountaineering, the first skiing. Impressive, yes, but also approachable, since settlements survive in improbable hollows and discreet cable cars whip you up to the grandest summits. In summer the Jungfrau region's hundreds of kilometers of hiking blast the senses with spectacular mountain views, meadows of wildflowers, roaring waterfalls, and pristine forests. In winter, the skiing is divine—almost literally, in fact, since Emperor Hirohito came here to learn the rudiments (bringing thousands of Japanese in his wake).

The three most famous peaks in the Oberland are the **Jungfrau,** the **Eiger,** and the **Mönch.** In English, that's the Maiden, the Ogre, and Monk. Natives say that the monk is protecting the maiden by standing between her and the ogre. Actually the Jungfrau is 4158m high, so she'd probably kick the Eiger's puny little 3970m butt.

Commitment to tourism is total: some villages have even gone car free, with most locals scooting around in electric buggies instead, sneaking up silently behind visitors and scaring the hell out of them. The quietest periods are Nov. and April-May. Both valleys become busier and considerably more expensive during ski season; on the bright side, jobs teem for dishwashers, bartenders, and chalet staff.

Keeping to a strict budget in these villages is even trickier than elsewhere in the Oberland. Fortunately, every village has dorm beds and most have supermarkets. More importantly, the best things in life, and especially in the Jungfrau area, are free. The budget killers in this region are the punishingly expensive buses, trains, and cable cars. If you do shell out the cash for a ticket for the Jungfraujoch or Schilthorn, make sure that the weather is cloudless in order to justify the expense. To maximize time in the mountains and minimize transportation costs, *Let's Go* strongly recommends that you use a village as a base for day hikes: there is no virtue in touring the villages which are really only service stations to springboard visitors into the hills.

GRINDELWALD

The town of Grindelwald, beneath the north face of the **Eiger,** is a skier's and climber's dream. The lush green valley ringed with blue glaciers glinting in the sun is Switzerland distilled to its purest and most stunning. Though it only has two important streets, Grindelwald is the most developed part of the Oberland's two major valleys, and isolated *châlets* dot the slopes for several miles. To get there, take the Berner-Oberlander-Bahn from the Interlaken Ostbahnhof (one-way 9SFr), remembering to sit in the rear half of the train. To go to other villages by train you will need to change trains at Zweilütschinen. This is true for Mürren (18.60SFr), Wengen (15.60SFr), and Lauterbrunnen (10.20SFr). Trains to Kleine Scheidegg and the Jungfraujoch start from the station but also call at Grund station near the river. Kleine Scheidegg is 26SFr one-way and 45SFr round-trip; the Jungfraujoch is 137SFr, or 99SFr on the first train of the day (the "Good Morning Ticket"). Swisspass and Eurail pass get a 25% discount to these two destinations. There is also a bus from Balmer's (round-trip 13.60SFr).

The popular **Sport-Zentrum** in the town's center has modern facilities which become cheap with a visitor's card from the cheap hostel or hotel (tel. 854 12 30; open in summer Mon., Wed., and Fri. 10am-10pm, Tues., Thurs., and Sun. 10am-6:45pm, Sat. 1:45-6:45pm; in winter Mon. and Wed. 2-10pm, Sat. and Sun. 2-6:45pm). The **swimming pool** is 10SFr and 7.50SFr for children (2.50SFr and 2SFr with visitor's card). From July to Easter the **skating rink** is 7.50SFr, 5.50SFr for children (2SFr and 1.50SFr with visitor's card). The **climbing room** is 5.50SFr year-round; they also have **table tennis,** and a **sauna,** and a **weight room.**

Grindelwald's hotel prices push most budget travelers into dorms; fortunately these are thick on the ground to cater to the hiking/skiing crowd. Two superb hostels, however, are far more comfortable than most of the hotels. The **Jugendherberge (HI)** (tel. 853 10 09; fax 853 50 29) is a ranking contender for the title of World's Best Youth Hostel. To get there, head left from the station for 5-7minutes, then cut up the hill to the right for 8 minutes; there is a small brown sign at the turn. Warm, wood living rooms and dorms still smell of freshly cut pine. The surprisingly private dorms have state-of-the-art bar code locks and balconies facing the Eiger. It's expensive but a tremendous deal. (Reception open Mon.-Sat. 6:30-9:30am and 3pm-midnight, Sun. 6:30-9:30am and 5-11pm. No lockout. 29.50SFr first night, 27SFr thereafter. Quad or double with sink 34.50SFr, then 32SFr. Double with shower 45SFr then 42.50SFr. Giant dinner 11SFr. Laundry 1.60SFr. Huge lockers and proper bed linen, not sleeping sacks, included.) Its rival is the bright blue **Mountain Hostel** (tel. 853 39 00; fax 853 47 30) at the Grund station next to the river. Turn right out of the station, then right down the hill just after the bus station. At Hotel Glacier, turn right, and head just past the station. Renovated in 1996, it has gleaming 4-6 bed dorms and a plush reception area with ping-pong and pool tables. (Dorms 29-34SFr. Double 34-39SFr per person. Buffet breakfast included. Outside cooking facilities 0.50SFr.) To see two glaciers from your bedroom windows, you need to stay at the friendly **Monty's/Alpenpub** (tel. 853 11 05; fax 853 44 84) above a kicking bar. It's 20 minutes from the center of town following the main street right from the station, and 2 minutes past the church on the right. (Reception open until 12:30am. Dorms 30SFr. Singles 55SFr. Doubles

90SFr in high season (July-Sept., Dec. and Feb.-March) and 5-10SFr per person less in low season. Breakfast 10SFr. Visa, MC, AmEx. Reserve in winter high season.) **Hotel Glacier** (tel. 853 10 04; fax 853 50 04) is closer to town. Turn right from the station and right past the bus station. Its dorm is large and spartan. (No lockout. Dorms 28SFr. Sheets 2SFr. Breakfast included. Visa, MC, AmEx.) The restaurant of the three-star hotel upstairs has entrées starting at 11.50SFr. One hour from town (see Hiking, p. 173) but a step from the upper Glacier, **Hotel Wetterhorn** (tel. 853 12 18) has dorms for 42.50SFr, including breakfast. The Grosse Scheidegg bus (5.40SFr) stops at the door. *Zimmer frei* (room for rent) notices are also posted on the information board at the bus station, though most rooms require a one-week minimum. **Gletscherdorf** (tel. 853 14 29; fax 853 31 29) is the nearest of all Grindelwald's **campgrounds.** From the station, turn right, take the first right after the tourist office, and then the third left. Small, with clean facilities and a phenomenal view of the mountains (9SFr, tent 4-9SFr). **Camping Eigernordwand** (tel. 853 42 27) is across the river and to the left of the Grund station (9.50SFr, tent 5-7SFr).

Frugal gourmets shop at the **Co-op** across from the tourist office (open Mon.-Thurs. 8am-6:30pm, Fri. 8am-9pm, Sat. 8am-5pm). A **Migros** is further along the main street away from the station. (Open Mon.-Thurs. 8am-noon and 1:30-6:30pm, Fri. 8am-noon and 1:30-9pm, Sat. 8am-5pm.) For huge plates of *rösti*, omelettes, salads, and fresh-baked desserts, hit the **Tea Room Riggenburg** (tel. 853 10 59) on the main street past the tourist office away from the station. Main courses run 12-16SFr, or try their more extravagant frozen desserts (8.50-20SFr).

The **tourist office** (Verkehrsbüro; tel. 854 12 12; fax 854 12 10) is located in the Sportzentrum; turn right from the train station, ignoring the "i" sign which points down the hill. It provides travelers with hiking maps, chairlift information, and a list of free guided excursions in the area; they also find rooms in private homes (25-50SFr) though these often require a three-night minimum stay. (Open July-Aug. Mon.-Fri. 8am-7pm, Sat. 8am-5pm, Sun. 9-11am and 4-6pm; Sept.-June Mon.-Fri. 8am-noon and 2-6pm, Sat. 8am-noon and 2-5pm.) For outdoor activities, walk from the station past the tourist office to the joint **Bergführerbüro** (Mountain Guides Office; tel. 853 52 00; fax 853 12 22) and **Ski School** (tel. 853 20 21). The office sells maps for hiking and coordinates rugged activities such as glacier walks, ice climbing training, and mountaineering. (Open June-Oct. Mon.-Fri. 9am-noon and 3-6pm, Sat. 9am-noon and 3-6pm, Sun. 4-6pm. Reserve a few days ahead for the multi-day expeditions.) There is a **post office** opposite the station with **phones** (open Mon.-Fri. 8am-noon and 1:45-6pm, Sat. 8-11am). **Postal code:** CH-3818. **Telephone Code:** 036

Hiking and Outdoor Activities near Grindelwald

Only Zermatt could possibly challenge Grindelwald's claim as the superlative hiking center in Switzerland. The town has nearly everything: easy valley walks, hiker's peaks, high altitude level walks, visitable glaciers, and mountains that stretch even top climbers. The terrain varies in every direction; moreover, a competent network of railways, cable cars and buses makes the most exciting areas accessible without hours of uphill toil. Ride **Europe's longest chairlift** to the top of the **First Mountain** for awesome scenery (27SFr, round-trip 43SFr) and good access to the Faulhorn and Schwarzhorn peaks. Other transport links north and east are the bus to **Bussalp** (1807m, 8 daily, 14SFr one-way, 28SFr round-trip, half price with Swisspass and Eurail pass), and the bus to **Grosse Scheidegg** (1926m, 11 daily, 7.80SFr and way, 15.60SFr round-trip, half price with passes). Intelligent combinations are possible for non-circular hikes. Examples are First one-way plus Bussalp one-way (41SFr); First and Grosse Scheidegg (42SFr); First and Schynige Platte (62.80SFr).

In the southerly and westerly directions, the **Männlichen mountain** (2230m) separates the Grindelwald and Lauterbrunnen valleys; its summit affords a glorious vista of the Eiger, the Mönch, and the Jungfrau. The **Grindelwald-Männlichen gondola** transports passengers there from the Grindelwald-Grund station (27SFr, round-trip 43SFr, 50% off with Eurail, 25% off with Swisspass). Take the railway up to Kleine Scheidegg, enjoy the short walk to Männlichen and come down the cable car for

50SFr. The **Kleine Scheidegg** railway costs 26SFr one-way and 43SFr round-trip. Finally, the tiny **Pfingstegg cable car** that gives you a lift on the path to the Lower Glacier costs 9.20SFr one-way and 14SFr round-trip. Show your railpass at all trains and lifts. If you plan to use one lift and return a different way, you should inquire about discounts. (Firstbahn and buses tel. 853 36 36; Männlichen tel. 853 38 29; Kleine Scheidegg tel. 828 71 11.)

Many tops have places to spend the night and nothing is more beautiful than waking up to a still dawn over the mountains. At Kleine Scheidegg (2061m), there are dorm beds at **Grindelwaldblick** (tel. 855 13 74; 32-35SFr) and **Bahnhofbuffet** (tel. 855 11 51; 28-50SFr). At Männlichen, a bunk is 35SFr (tel. 853 10 68; 2227m), and on the Faulhorn, dorms are 33SFr (tel. 853 27 13, 2681m). Finally **Berggasthaus First** at the cable car terminus has a **touristenlager** for 38-40SFr including breakfast and 20SFr for an evening meal (tel. 853 12 84). Don't miss out on these soul-stirring opportunities to commune with the hills.

Grindelwald has many too many **hikes** to list. The following are suggestions only and can be endlessly modified. A classic, level mountain-top walk is from Männlichen to Kleine Scheidegg or vice-versa (1hr.) and gives wide airy panoramas and a close up view of the Eiger. Every September, a marathon, beginning in Interlaken, finishes on this ridge, 2061 meters above the start line. Descending from either end to Grindelwald Grund station takes 3-4hr. at a gentle pace through trees and forests. Another classic level walk is from **First** to **Schynige Platte** or in reverse, taking you past hidden high-level alpine valleys, the lovely *Bachsee* (2265m), and up to the Faulhorn peak (2680m). The path is as wide as a road, and the walk is a full day. A variant on the latter is to take the cable car to First, hike up the Faulhorn, and descend to Bussalp, and catch the bus back to Grindelwald. This captures the long views and marmot-filled glens of the longer walk, but is cheaper on the transport bill, and makes for a more manageable day.

You can visit either of the Grindelwald glaciers easily. Take Grindelwald's main street right from the station past the church, and turn right just after Monty's (yellow sign: "Hotel Wetterhorn"); then follow the signs from the Hotel Wetterhorn (1½hr. up, at an easy gradient). The cliffs of the Wetterhorn are frightening; watch out for **Engi**, the house perched half way up. Alas, it is hard to get a better view of the **Upper Glacier**—paths go up both sides via Restaurant Milchbach or the Schreckhornhütte. However, both are tricky, exposed, and the former has terrifying ladders. The **Lower Glacier** is much more approachable. Turn right just after the church, cross the river, and go up the zigzags to Pfingstegg; you can take a detour to the Glacier Gorge (which charges admission) on the way. At Pfingstegg (1392m) turn right to the glacier and follow the edge as far up as you please (1½-3hr. up, 45min.-2hr. down).

Some people aren't happy unless they get to the *top* of something. If the Faulhorn strikes you as a tame little hill, the Schwarzhorn (2928m), offers a simple but challenging alternative. From Grosse Scheidegg or First, go up through the high valley of Chrinnenboden; the finish is steepish, but the panorama from the top covers a dozen 4000-m peaks and excels in every compass direction. Allow three to four hours for the ascent; time for the descent will depend on whether you choose to go down by bus and cable car or foot.

Mountaineers should contact the Mountain Guide Office (see above) for climb details, but should note that even the first train to Jungfraujoch is too late for the high peaks, and that an overnight at the Mönchsjochhütte will be required. The guides lead big climbs most summer days. For two people the Eiger is 890SFr, Mönch 560SFr, and Jungfrau 900SFr. Contact the Bergführerbüro at least three days in advance. They will also give you skills training for a day, weekend, or week, but, again, give them notice so that they can get a group together.

Adventure World coordinates high adrenaline activities as at Interlaken (tel. 826 77 11; write to Adventure World, 3800 Interlaken), **paragliding** (120-200SFr), **rock climbing** (75SFr), **canyoning** (85SFr), and **rafting** (85SFr) among them. In **winter** the skiing is phenomenal. Ski passes are 100SFr for two days, 254SFr for a week, and 400SFr for two weeks (80SFr, 204SFr, and 320SFr respectively for those aged 16-29;

50SFr, 127SFr, and 200SFr respectively for those under 16). Beady-eyed rental companies are vigilant concerning one another's prices, so there isn't much to choose from.
The activity isn't jut limited to skiing and snowboarding, however. For 5-10SFr you
can rent a sled from a ski rental store and sled down 2000 meters of mountainside;
some mountain paths also get cleared so you can even hike in winter—the path up
Faulhorn is one example.

THE JUNGFRAUJOCH

The most arresting ascent in this area is up the **Jungfraujoch** (Yoong-frow-yock), a
head spinning, breath-shortening, 3454m above sea-level adventure on the highest
railway in Europe. The track is chiseled out of solid mountain and tunnels right
through the Eiger and Mönch mountains. The **Jungfrau** itself, higher than the "joch,"
is almost always inaccessible. The construction of the railway was one of the greatest
engineering feats of all time, taking 16 years and a work force of 300 men. The line
was to have gone even higher to the Jungfrau summit itself (4158m) but by 1912
when the Jungfraujoch was reached the project was so over budget that the final
700m were left to the gods and to serious mountaineers. The top now shelters
Europe's highest manned meteorology station and the **Sphinx laboratory** for the
study of cosmic radiation, ideally situated because of the lack of pollution in the rar-
efied air (open daily 8am-5:30pm). The half-million visitors a year can also make a trip
to the **Ice Palace,** a weirdly smooth maze cut into the ice with cutesy ice sculptures,
go for a **sled ride** driven by Siberian huskies (10SFr), or ski (30SFr; the slope is very
short), as well as gaze down the 24-km **Aletschgletscher,** Europe's longest, and, at
900m, also thickest glacier. If the weather is perfect, the best venture is the ½hr. paddle across the snow to the **Mönchsjoch** climbing hut. You will feel like you are floating on top of the world.

   Trains start at Interlaken's *Ostbahnhof* and travel to either Grindelwald or Lauterbrunnen, continuing to **Kleine Scheidegg** and finally to the peak itself, "the top of
Europe." The entire trip costs a scary 153SFr, but if you take the 6:34am train from
Interlaken Ost, the 7:05am from Lauterbrunnen or the 7:18am from Grindelwald, the
fare is reduced to 115SFr (called the "Good Morning" ticket). From November-April,
this train departs 1hr. later. In all seasons you must leave the top by **noon** on this
ticket (with Eurail 116SFr, morning ticket 101SFr; with the Swisspass 105SFr, 90SFr).
All tickets are round-trip—there is no way down from the top except by train. If you
are staying in Grindelwald the prices are slightly lower (137SFr, morning ticket
99SFr). Before spending so much, try to avoid going on a cloudy day when you will
miss the mind-blowing view. An extra day's hostel bill waiting for clear skies is money
well-spent. Call 855 10 22 for a **weather forecast** and use the cable TV channel that
broadcasts live pictures from the Jungfraujoch and other high altitude spots like the
First and Männlichen (in all tourist offices, station and big hotels). Also bring winter
clothing and food— it can be 10°C (14°F) on an ordinary looking July day, and in winter alcohol thermometers crack and car antifreeze tends to freeze solid.

WENGEN

Tiny Wengen occupies the only ledge along the cliff-curtained *Lauterbrunnental.*
From its scoop out of the Männlichen, the mountain that separates the Grindelwald
and Lauterbrunnen valleys, it offers the best of two worlds: sight of the raw grandeur
of the crags and waterfalls, but local slopes just gentle enough to make for some really
fine hiking and skiing. Though car-free, Wengen is easily accessible because it is a
stop for the half-hourly trains headed from **Interlaken** (11.40SFr) and **Lauterbrunnen**
(5.40SFr) to **Kleine Scheidegg** (19.60SFr) and the **Jungfraujoch** (126SFr, morning
ticket 88SFr). Leave cars in the Lauterbrunnen multi-story parking garage (9SFr per
day).

   The village is most famous for hosting the World Cup's (skiing, not soccer) longest
and most dangerous downhill race every January, the **Laubehorn.** In 1997 the races
will take place between January 17-19 (tickets 20SFr per day, training runs free).

Wengen will be bursting, but hotels generally won't allow you to book rooms until about two weeks beforehand so that they can guarantee all the racers and support crews a place to sleep. The downhill course starts at 2315m above Kleine Scheidegg, curls around Wegenalp, and ends at Ziel (1287m) at the eastern end of the village, a drop of nearly 3500 feet in around 2½ minutes. **Ski passes** for the Wengen-Kleine-Scheidegg-Männlichen area start at 52SFr for one day, and 95SFr for two days; for longer periods, you must purchase a Jungfrau regional pass. Passes are 50% cheaper for children aged 6-16 and around 20% cheaper for those aged 16-20. Many shops rent skis with nearly identical prices. Look for 28SFr per day, 115SFr per week plus 19SFr per day and 85SFr per week for ski boots. There are two ski schools; the **Swiss Ski School** (tel./fax 855 20 22), by the Co-op, 1 minute right of the station, is the cheaper of the two. (Open late-Dec. to early April Sun.-Fri. 8:30am-noon, 1-2:30pm, and 3:30-6pm, Sat. 9-11am and 4:30-6:30pm. 198SFr for 6 half-days of groups lessons.) The other is **Private Ski School** (tel./fax 855 29 39), 3 minutes to the left of the station (220SFr for 4 half-days of group lessons). **Snow information:** tel. 855 35 10. **Weather:** tel. 157 45 06.

To reach the **tourist office** (tel. 855 14 14; fax 850 30 60), turn right from the station, then take an immediate left. They issue competent hiking details and will find you a tennis partner. (Open mid-June to mid-Oct. and mid-Dec. to March Mon.-Fri. 8am-noon and 2-6pm, Sat. 8:30-11:30am and 4-6pm, Sun. 4-6pm; mid-Oct. to mid-Dec. and April to mid-June Mon.-Fri. 8am-noon and 2-6pm, Sat. 8:30-11:30am.) At the **station** you can **exchange currency,** book hotel rooms through an information board, and watch the cable-car TV channel. The **pharmacy** (tel. 855 12 46), left out of the station, is 2min. past the tourist office (open Mon.-Fri. 8am-noon and 2-6:30pm, Sat. 8am-noon and 2-5pm). A public **laundry** hides under the Hotel Silberhorn between the station and the tourist office (open daily 7am-9:30pm). For a **doctor** call 855 15 03; for the **hospital,** 826 26 26. The **post office** next to the tourist office has **telephones** (open Mon.-Fri. 8am-noon and 1:45-6pm, Sat. 8-11am). **Postal code:** CH-3823. **Telephone code:** 033.

The funkiest place to eat, sleep, drink, and groove is **Hot Chili Peppers** (tel. 855 50 20), opened in May 1996 and smack dab in the center of town. The decor of this Tex-Mex eatery turned hostel, is decidedly freaky-styley. Turn left from the station, head past the tourist office; it will be on your left hand side. The newly renovated dorm is 24-26SFr; a backpacker's breakfast is 6SFr. Smart, clean, freshly painted singles are 38-48SFr and doubles 76-96SFr including breakfast depending on the season. (Tacos and burritos 5-9SFr. Chips and salsa 5SFr. Sangria 5SFr. Beer 5-6SFr.) Much closer to what you expect budget accommodations in Wengen to look like, **Eddy's Hostel** (tel. 855 16 34; fax 855 39 50) has large yet intimate dorms annexed to Hotel Eden (in summer 26SFr; in winter 30SFr). Eddy's Corner also has beer at 4.50SFr per pint and main courses like *bratwurst* and spaghetti (7.50SFr and up). Whip out your traveler sized bassoon to play at the informal and free folklore evenings on Fridays. Simple, livable rooms with back-to-the-70s orange hall showers are available at **Hotel Bären** (tel. 855 14 19; fax 855 15 25). From the station turn right under the railway and the hotel is 2 minutes on the right. (Singles 50SFr. Doubles 100SFr. 6-bed dorms 35SFr per person including breakfast. Open Dec.-Oct. Visa, MC, AmEx.)

Unless you eat at the Hot Chili Peppers or Eddy's, Wengen is expensive. Opposite the station, the **Co-op** is co-operatively central (open Mon.-Fri. 8am-12:15pm and 1:30-6:30pm, Sat. 8am-6pm), while fancier fodder can be found at the **Victoria Lauberhorn** immediately past the tourist office. Try their chocolate and vanilla ice cream *crêpes* (10.50SFr). Pasta ranges from 9.80SFr to 19.50SFr; *raclette* is 9.80SFr and vegetarian options 9-15.50SF (open daily 9:30am-11:30am).

The **swimming pool,** first left past Eddy's, is open-air but heated. (Open Mid-June to August 10am-6:30pm; 6SFr, children 3SFr, with guest card 4SFr, 2SFr.) In July and August the ice rink keeps the ice nice and cold. (Open Mon.-Fri. 1:45-6pm. 8SFr, children 5SFr, cheaper with guest card.) The big party in town gets down during the Lauberhorn Race. Also join in the summer jollity on **Dorfsonntag** in mid-July.

Hikes from Wengen

Wengen snoozes beneath the steep flanks of the **Lauberhorn** (2472m) and **Männlichen** (2343m) mountains. The ultimate view of the Eiger Norwand and a superb all around panorama make the climb worthwhile. Since hiking down the sharp gradients is more comfortable than hiking up, make use of the **Männlichen cable car** (one-way 19.60SFr, round-trip 32SFr; closed briefly Nov. and May) and the railway to Kleine Scheidegg (one-way 19.60SFr, round-trip 32SFr). For the best route up, turn right just after Eddy's Hotel, and follow the yellow signs and train tracks which snake around the Lauberhorn to Wengeneralp and Kleine Scheidegg. From here, the view unfolds eastwards to the Eiger and Wetterhorn north faces. Turn left up the Lauberhorn across the level track to Männlichen, and slither abruptly back to Wengen from the col between Männlichen and the Lauberhorn. (1350m ascent, all day if you take a leisurely pace.) You can buy a combination ticket lifting you up to Kleine Scheidegg and down from Männlichen which turns the excursion into a half-day outing (39.60SFr). For mountaintop sleeping, see Grindelwald, (p. 172).

For a perfect view of the Lauterbrunnen valley, turn right out of the station under the tracks to the Ziel chair lift. Just past the lift there are some benches at Staubachbänkli facing the staggering vertical crags and free-falling spume of the cascades above Lauterbrunnen and Stechelberg (1hr. round-trip, an evening stroll). The walk extends by skirting the valley wall, and dropping into the secluded cove above the Trümmelbach Falls. Descend steeply to the valley base, and ½hr. more brings you to Lauterbrunnen from where a 5.40SFr train ride can save you the hike back to Wengen. (A half day through spectacular landscapes.) In winter there are cleared hiking trails all around Wengen (e.g. Kleine Scheidegg to Männlichen) and guided walks.

LAUTERBRUNNEN VALLEY

The "pure springs" that give Lauterbrunnen its name are the waterfalls that plummet down the sheer walls of the narrow, glacier-cut valley. Stark but beautiful, untamed yet serene, the valley is reminiscent of a time when valleys were valleys. Back to Eden. Or Elysia. Or something like that.

Lauterbrunnen feels small, dwarfed by vertical rock cliffs. An easy 40-minute hike or a quick postal bus ride from the main street (hourly, 2.80SFr), are the fabulous **Trümmelbach Falls,** 10 consecutive glacier-bed chutes that gush up to 20,000 liters of water per second and generate mighty winds and a roaring din in the process. Explore tunnels, footbridges, and an underground funicular. (Open July-Aug. 8am-6pm; April-June and Sept.-Nov. 9am-5pm. 10SFr, with visitor's card 9SFr.) Continue along the river to **Stechelberg,** a scattered, three-horse town with a **Co-op** (open Mon. and Wed.-Fri. 8am-noon and 2:30-6pm, Tues. 8am-noon, Sat. 8am-noon and 2-4pm); the **Breithorn campground** (tel. 855 12 25; 5.90-6.50SFr per person; open year-round); and the **Schilthorn Bahn cable car** leading to **Gimmelwald** (one-way 7.20SFr), **Mürren** (14SFr), **Birg** (32.20SFr), and the **Schilthorn** (46SFr). To reach all, follow the signs; the **Co-op** and **campground** are near the post office. Since Gimmelwald and Mürren are carless, you may want to leave your car at the uncovered parking near the cable car (day 5SFr, week 21SFr, month 30SFr).

Lauterbrunnen village is further down the valley and has a wider range of shops and service plus an array of cheap, basic beds. The **station** connects half-hourly with **Interlaken Ost** (6SFr), **Wengen** (5.40SFr), **Kleine Scheidegg** (25SFr), the **Jungfraujoch** (round-trip 136.80SFr), and **Mürren** (every 15min., 8.40SFr). The station has **lockers** (2SFr) and **currency exchange.** The small **Lauterbrunnen tourist office** (tel. 855 19 55; fax 855 36 04) is 200m to the left of the station on the main street. (Open Mon.-Fri. 8am-noon and 2-6pm, in July and Aug. also Sat.-Sun. 10am-noon and 3-6pm.) The **post office** is between the train station and the tourist office (open Mon.-Fri. 7:45-11:45am and 1:45-6pm, Sat. 7:45-11am). **Telephone code:** 033.

Next to the post office lies a small but satisfactory **Co-op** (open Mon.-Fri. 8am-noon and 2-6:30pm, Sat. 8am-noon and 1:30-5pm). **Matratzenlager Stocki** (tel. 855 17 54), a farmhouse/hostel, offers a full kitchen stacked with spices and a mellow atmosphere. Leave the train station from the back, descend the steps, cross the river, turn right, and walk 200m. The sign on the house on your right will read *Massenlager*. (Check in before 6pm without fail. 10SFr. Open Jan.-Oct. Reservations strongly advised.) Even more central, **Chalet im Rohr** (tel. 855 21 82), on the main street opposite the church, has 40 beds and a lived-in feel (24-26SFr. No breakfast. Kitchen facilities 1SFr. Parking available). Lauterbrunnen also has two souped-up campsites with dormitory accommodations and cheap restaurants. **Camping Jungfrau** (tel. 856 20 10; fax 855 20 20), up the main street from the station toward the large waterfall, provides cheap beds, kitchens, showers, lounges, and a grocery store. (Open 8am-noon and 2:30-8pm. 8.20-9.60SFr. Tent 6-15SFr. Dorms 14-20SFr. Laundry 7SFr. Restaurant *menus* 10-11SFr. Visa, MC, AmEx.) **Camping Schützenbach** (tel. 855 12 68; fax 855 12 75) can be reached by following the signs toward Trümmelbach from the station (15min.). Take a left on the main road and a left over the river by the church. The communal bathrooms will definitely bring you back to summer camp days. (Reception open 6:30am-noon and 2-7pm. 8SFr. Tent 4SFr. Dorms 14-16SFr. 4-bed "tourist rooms" in barrack-like huts 18-20SFr per person. Doubles with sinks 44-52SFr. Shower 0.50SFr. Kitchen facilities 1SFr. Laundry 5SFr.)

Being at the bottom of a trough, Lauterbrunnen's **hikes** are either very steep or very flat. The best flat walk is a tour of the waterfalls. Starting on the western side, continue along the main road past the church. In succession the Staubbachfall, Spissbachfall, Agertenbachfall, Mümenbachfall crash from overhead, leaving dark cones on the rock where the wind has blown the spray. Crossing over the river by the Stechelberg power station (5-7km) brings you face to face with the Staldenbachfall and Mattenbachfall. The return leg passes the Trümmelbachfälle, the cascade which funnels the waters of the Jungfrau glaciers, and the Hasenbachfall, providing in the process a glorious view of the slopes of the Laubehorn. (3hr. with virtually no climbing; the best walk in the area during a prolonged wet spell.)

Imboden Bike Adventures (tel. 855 21 14), on the main street, rents out mountain bikes at 30SFr per day and bursts with suggestions about where to go with them. A favorite is the **Mürren Loop**, where you take your bike for free on the funicular to Grütschalp (6.60SFr), pedal along to Mürren and Gimmelwald, then free-wheel it down to Stechelberg and Lauterbrunnen. Imboden lets you leave the bike at Central Sport in Wengen opposite the tourist office or the sports center in Mürren for no charge (open Tues.-Sun. 9am-noon and 2-6:30pm).

If it's raining you could try the open air **pool** (tel. 855 32 74) between the station and the tourist office (open daily 9:30am-6pm; 5SFr, children 3SFr, with guest card 4SFr and 3SFr). If the rain gets truly torrential there is the **Museum of the Lauterbrunnen Valley** (tel. 855 35 86) across the river from the church, which has exhibits on lead sulphide mining, early alpine mountaineering and skis. (Open mid-June to Sept. Tues., Thurs., and Sat.-Sun. 2-5:30pm. 3SFr, with visitor's card 2SFr.)

MÜRREN AND THE SCHILTHORN

Either take the cogwheel train from Lauterbrunnen (8.40SFr), ride the cable car from Stechelberg (14SFr) or Gimmelwald (7.20SFr), or hike from Gimmelwald up to **Mürren**, a car-free skiing and sport resort. Just as the Japanese swarm around Grindelwald, Brits muddle around Mürren as they have done since George Bernard Shaw came for Fabian fresh air and Field Marshal Montgomery for mushrooms. The 2970-m **Schilthorn**, made famous by the Alpine exploits of James Bond in *On Her Majesty's Secret Service*, is a short (albeit expensive) cable car trip from Mürren (one-way 32SFr, round-trip 55SFr). The hike up the Schilthorn takes about 4hr. Perfect hiking shoes are a must; the ascent is one of the rockiest and snowiest around. At its apex spins the immoderately priced **Piz Gloria Restaurant.** Daily menus run 16-17SFr. Warm up (summer or winter) with *Glühwein* (7SFr), or take in the astounding 360° Alpine panorama from the Schilthorn station's deck, or the restaurant which fully rotates every hour. The staff at the Mürren stop courteously remind you that there is very little to do at the top when it's cloudy. At each of the stops of the cable car up to the Schilthorn (Birg, Mürren, Gimmelwald), beautiful and often rocky hiking paths lace the mountains, and eventually lead back to the valley; these make the best walks in the area. It's often snowy at the top in early summer, so if you want to hike down consider the one-way trip to **Birg** (18.20SFr), from where the view is nearly as good. Check with the tourist office for maps before embarking on any of these, however, and get a weather forecast—the TV link at the cable car station broadcasts the local conditions at the summit. From the train station take either road to the other end of the village (10min.).

The **tourist office** (tel. 856 86 86; fax 856 86 96), in the sports center, is 10 minutes from the Schilthorn cable car station and 5min. from train station, taking the right fork. It is all knowing; ask here for hiking trails and skiing prices (open Mon.-Wed. and Fri.-Sat. 9am-noon and 1-6:30pm, Thurs. 9am-noon and 1-8:30pm, Sun. 2-6pm). Ask at the tourist office for *Privatzimmer*, check the chalkboard for dorm room announcements (30-35SFr), or get the list of cheap sleeps in Mürren. The **pharmacy** is on the upper street near the tourist office (open Mon.-Sat. 9am-noon and 4-6pm). **Medical assistance:** tel. 855 17 10. **Police:** tel. 855 28 17. **Alpine rescue service:** tel. 855 45 55. The **post office** is on the station side of the main street (open Mon.-Fri. 8am-noon and 2-5pm, Sat. 8-10:15am). **Postal code:** CH-3825. **Telephone code:** 033.

To rest your weary body after a long day of hiking, seek shelter at the **Chalet Fontana** (tel. 855 26 86). It's run by a bubbly Englishwoman and has lovely, distinctive rooms in the center of town. (Mid-May to mid-Sept. 35-45SFr per person, breakfast included; mid-Sept.-mid-Dec. 30SFr per person, no breakfast.) **Hotel Belmont** (tel. 855 35 35; fax 855 35 31) is right next to the train station and has bunk beds in bright, clean newly decorated rooms. (27SFr or 35SFr. Doubles 90SFr, with shower 130SFr. Breakfast included. Open mid-Dec. to mid-Nov. Visa, MC, AmEx.)

There is a **Co-op** on the town's main walkway (open Mon.-Fri. 8am-noon and 1:45-6:30pm, Sat. 8am-4pm), but eating out in Mürren is unexpectedly cheap. The **Snack Bar** on the main road, near the station end of the town, has Swiss treats like *bratwurst* and french fries (7.50SFr) and Italian rib-stickers like "big pasta" (6SFr) available for take out (open daily 10am-8pm, but closes earlier if the weather is bad). Next door to the Co-op is **Restaurant Stägerstübli** (tel. 855 13 16), a family joint with a tiny wooden interior. The creamy rich *raclette* (12.50SFr) melts in your mouth (entrées 11-20SFr; open daily 8:30am-11:30pm).

Mürren pioneered two graceful ways of enjoying the mountains. In 1910 the first balloon crossing of the Alps was made from the village, a fact now celebrated annually in September, when the town hosts an **international ballooning week** that fills the skies with big colorful bulbs. The other sport, **skiing,** took off with even more panache. Mürren was the stage for the first major ski race (1922), the first ski school (1930), and the first World Championship (1931). **Ski passes** for the Mürren-Schilthorn area are 50SFr for one day and 254SFr for a Jungfrau regional week pass; children aged 6-16 gain a 50% reduction, teenagers 16-20 a 20% discount. The **ski school** (tel. 855 12 47) has a comprehensive spread of classes for downhill, slalom, and snowboarding, and a palette of special events such as torchlit ski expeditions. Six half-days of group lessons cost 123SFr. The calf-killing **Inferno Run** seeks volunteers every year to race from Lauterbrunnen to the top of the Schilthorn, a 2150m climb that only sinewy superstars finish. Finally the **indoor swimming pool,** in the sports center by the tourist office, is open Mon.-Wed. and Fri.-Sat. 1-6:45pm, Thurs. 1-8:45pm and Sun. 1-5:45pm (when raining open at 10am; 7SFr, children 3.50SFr).

GIMMELWALD

A tiny speck on the massive valley wall, Gimmelwald is accessible only by foot or the Schilthorn cable car (6.80SFr) from Stechelberg or Mürren. The town was once a remarkably secluded, peaceful, romantic village undisturbed by tourists, and remained so until travel writers started advertising it as such, with predictable results. Sorry. A steep but scenic trail leads from Stechelberg, taking the left fork at the point where the road ends. The normal approach is to walk 20 minutes down from Mürren, taking the left fork just after the post office as you walk from the station; follow the yellow signs. Gimmelwald has a **post office** (open Mon.-Fri. 8:30am-10:15am and

4-5pm, Sat. 8:30-10:15am) and its **postal code** is CH-3825. There is a **telephone** near the cable car station. **Telephone code:** 033.

Accommodations in Gimmelwald are definitely back to basics, but do not feature straw pillows or necessitate sharing your bed with farm animals. Next door to the cable car station awaits the hiker's mecca, the **Mountain Hostel** (tel. 55 17 04), not to be confused with the Grindelwald hostel of the same name. Loosely run by a relaxed couple of villagers, Petra and Walter, the hostel exudes friendliness and communalism, and hostel groupies happily do limited chores. Though there are no meals, a kitchen is offered, and life's essentials— bread (2.50SFr), milk (2SFr), and chocolate (2SFr)—can be purchased. Be warned that there is no market in Gimmelwald—bring other food from the **Co-op** in Lauterbrunnen, Mürren (½hr. uphill), or Stechelberg. You can reserve, but only one day in advance. Arrive early as beds fill fast. (Dorms 15SFr, showers 1SFr. Sheets and sleds included.) Though the **Pension Gimmelwald** is located temptingly close to the Mountain Hostel, *Let's Go* believes that the Mountain Hostel is a much better choice than its neighbor. At **Hotel Mittaghorn** (tel. 55 16 58), up the hill toward Mürren, sample some *Glühwein* (mulled wine) made by the owner, Walter. (Doubles 60SFr. Triples 85SFr. Quads 105SFr. Dorms 25SFr. Meals 15SFr if ordered in advance. Open May-Nov.)

The descent to Stechelberg—down the hill by the Mountain Hostel, over the river, and down through the woods—is still civilized and gives a great long shot of the sheer rock slabs lining the Lauterbrunnen valley. It's a grand approach to the **Trümmelbach Falls** (1½hr.), with a return facilitated by the cable car. The hikes from Gimmelwald, wild, lonely, and remote, radiate in other directions. Five minutes after the river crossing on the Stechelberg path, you can fork right, and climb along the flank of the unsettled Lauterbrunnen valley head. At the top lies the tiny Oberhornsee (2065m), a midget lake fringed by a gargantuan cirque of glaciers. If you head off early you are likely to meet wild chamois. (1100m of climbing. Full day. Map #5004.) The **Sefinental**, left from the crossroads by the mountain hostel, offers a level riverside path into a corridor below the crags of the Gsaltenhorn (3436m), but you need to come back on the same path that you went in. It's a good walk for tired legs with only 250m of ascent. (3hrs. to the end and back at a leisurely pace.) However, the climb up the Schilthorn (2970m), zigzagging straight up the hill, is for *übermenschen* only; there is often snow at the top (1600m ascent).

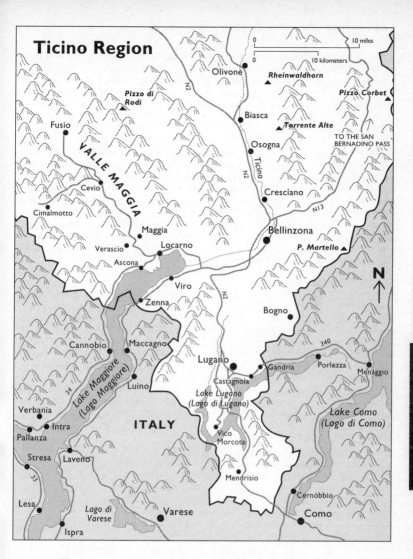

Ticino Region

Olivone · Rheinwaldhorn · Pizzo Corbet

Pizzo di Rodi · Biasca

Fusio · Osogna · TO THE SAN BERNADINO PASS

Torrente Alte

VALLE MAGGIA · Cevio · Cresciano

Cimalmotto · N13

Maggia · Bellinzona

Verascio · Locarno · P. Martello

Ascona

Viro

Zenna · Bogno

Cannobio · Maccagno

Luino · Lugano · Gandria · Porlezza · Menággio

Verbania · Castagnola · *Lake Lugano (Lago di Lugano)* · Lake Como (Lago di Como)

Intra

Pallanza · ITALY · Vico Morcote

Stresa · Laveno

Mendrisio · Cernóbbio

Lesa · *Lago di Varese* · Varese · Como

Ispra

Eastern Switzerland

ITALIAN SWITZERLAND (TICINO)

The Swiss took Ticino from Italy in 1512 and never gave it back. Ever since, the Italian-speaking canton of Ticino (Tessin, in German and French) has been renowned for its refreshing juxtaposition of Swiss efficiency and Italian *dolce vita*. The ring of the Italian accent is not all that sets the region apart from the rest of Switzerland; the southern climate turns it into a lush Mediterranean garden. Emerald lakes, luxurious vegetation, castles overlooking vineyards, and defiant stone houses scattered along winding lanes render Ticino's hilly countryside as romantic as Lugano and Locarno, its famed resorts. Industrialization has only touched this region insofar as it has emptied its smaller towns. A **Ticino Card** is available for use on cable cars, museums, castles, and other attractions (valid for 3 consecutive or non-consecutive days, 70SFr, children 6-16 years old and students under 21 45SFr).

■ Lugano

Arcaded passageways explode with blood-red geraniums, and orange tiles dribble up and down the hills that make up this hybrid Swiss town. Lugano, Switzerland's third-largest banking center, hides from German Switzerland in the dramatic crevassed bay between San Salvatore and Monte Brè. With Italian language, food, and architecture, Lugano holds onto its Swiss identity by a fingernail. Never fear, though, trains, buses, and services are all extraordinarily efficient. A striking contrast from the rugged, frost-bitten Alpine areas that surround it, this sun-drenched oasis is the retirement fantasy of Switzerland's northern residents and draws many elderly tourists to the relaxing shores of Lago di Lugano. Once the most polluted lake in Europe, it has been made swimmable by means of an extensive purification program.

GETTING TO LUGANO

Lugano's **train station** has service north to **Locarno** (1hr., every ½hr., 15.80SFr); **Basel** (4½hr., hourly, 77SFr); **Bern** (4½hr., hourly, 74SFr); **Lucerne** (3hr., hourly, 55SFr); **Zürich** (3hr., hourly, 59SFr); and south to **Milan, Italy** (1½hr., hourly, 14SFr). From **Geneva** in the west, change trains in **Domodossola, Italy** (50SFr. from Domodossola to Lugano, Swisspass valid). From **Chur** and **St. Moritz** in the east, take a postal bus to **Bellinzona,** where you can catch a train to Lugano (3½hr., 3 daily, 60SFr plus 5SFr reservation fee; Swisspass valid). For more info on trains, call 157 22 22. **Buses:** Chur to Bellinzona (63SFr and 5SFr reservation fee); St. Moritz to Bellinzona (54SFr and 5SFr reservation fee). For info call 807 85 20. To reach Lugano **by car,** take route N2/E35 (or just follow the signs). The small **Lugano-Agno Airport** services Crossair flights from **Basel, Bern, Geneva, London, Nice, Rome,** and **Zürich.** Trains go to Lugano train station from Agno Airport (every 20min., 4.20SFr).

ORIENTATION AND PRACTICAL INFORMATION

Lugano has a large pedestrian zone dotted with cobblestone *piazze.* It is triangularly bounded by the ridge on which the train station sits, Corso Pestalozzi, and the Fiume Cassorate. At the center of all the *piazze* sits the arcaded and café-inundated **Piazza della Riforma.** Northwest of this lies the **Piazza Cioccaro,** which is home the **funicular** (ascending cable car) that carries passengers from Lugano's center on the waterfront to the train station on one of the hills overlooking the bay (0.80SFr, free with Swisspass). With easy connections to Bellinzona, Zürich, Basel, and Milan, Lugano's location makes it an ideal vacation spot. The town itself boasts an extensive public transportation system. Buses run from the neighboring towns into the center, and also criss-cross the city (0.90-1.70SFr per ride, 24hr. "Carta Giorno" 4.40SFr, Swisspass valid). If you can find your way around the winding roads, the uphill journey from town to the station takes only 15 minutes.

> **Tourist Office:** in the Palazzo Civico, Riva Albertolli, at the corner of Piazza Rezzonico (tel. 921 46 64; fax 922 76 53). From the station, cross the footbridge labeled "Centro," and proceed down via Cattedrale straight through Piazza Cioccaro as it turns into via Pessina. Then take a left on via del Pesci, and another left on Riva via Vela, which becomes Riva Giocondo Albertolli; the office is just past the fountain on the left, across the street from the ferry launch. Or take bus #5 to "Centro," head down via della Posta until the water, turn right on riva Albertolli and the office is 100m to your right. Pick up maps, or make hotel reservations (4SFr). The tourist office also offers a free guided city walk from April-Oct. on Tuesdays at 9:30am, starting at Chiesa degli Angioli. It also offers a wide range of inexpensive

Lugano

Autosilo (Parking), 13
Bagno Publico, 17
Basilica del Sacro Cuore, 15
Cathedral San Lorenzo, 5
Chiesa Loreto, 2
Chiesa San Rocco, 8
Chiesa Santa Maria degli Angioli, 3
Museo Cantonale d'Arte, 7
Palazzo dei Congressi, 11
Parco Civico, 12
Parco Tassino, 16
PTT Centro (Post Office), 6
Stazione F.F.S. (Train Station), 4
Tourist Office, 9
Villa Ciani, 10
Villa Malpensata, Museo d'Arte Moderna, 1
Villa Saroli, 14

guided excursions beginning at 15SFr per person, such as a walk up Monte San Salvatore. Open April-Oct. Mon.-Fri. 9am-6:30pm, Sat. 9am-12:30pm and 1:30-5pm, Sun. 10am-2pm; Nov.-March Mon.-Fri. 9am-12:30pm and 1:30-5pm, Sat. 9am-12:30pm and 1:30-5pm.

Consulates: U.K., 19 via Motta/32 via Nassa (tel. 923 86 06).

Currency Exchange: Good rates in the train station. Open Mon.-Sat. 7:10am-7:45pm, Sun. 8am-7:45pm.

American Express: in **VIP Travels,** 10 via al Forte, P.O. Box 3530, CH-6901 (tel. 923 85 45; fax 922 02 66). Standard services, mail held, but traveler's checks cannot be cashed. Open Mon.-Fri. 8:30am-noon and 2-6pm, Sat. 9am-noon.

Telephones: At the train station, the post office, and the youth hostel.

Public Transportation: Buses run from the neighboring town to the center of Lugano and also traverse the city. Schedules and automatic ticket machines at each stop (0.90-1.70SFr per ride, 24-hr. "Carta Giorno" 4.40SFr; Swisspass valid).

Taxis: Associazone Concessionari Taxi (tel. 922 88 33 or 922 02 22).

Car Rental: Avis, 8 via C. Maraini (tel. 922 62 56). **Budget,** 14 via C. Maraini (tel. 964 17 19). **Hertz,** 13 via San Gottardo (tel. 923 46 75).

Parking: Several parking garages, but few provide long-term parking (*Autosilo* in Italian). **Comunale Balestra,** on via Pioda, offers hourly rate (1SFr), daily ticket (10hr. 15SFr), and a half-day ticket (5hrs. 10SFr). Open 7am-7pm. **Autosilo Central Park** has hourly rates (1SFr) and allows a maximum of 12hr. (21SFr). Open 7am-7pm. For info regarding parking, call 800 71 76. City parking meters scattered about are 1SFr per hour.

Bike Rental: At the baggage check in the train station (21SFr per day, 6SFr to return bike to another station). Open daily 5:20am-8:45pm.

Luggage Storage: Lockers at the train station (5SFr). Open daily 5:20am-8:45pm.
Lost Property: Polizia Communale, piazza della Riforma (tel. 800 71 10).
English Bookstore: Melisa, 4 via Vegezzi (tel. 923 83 41), stocks such intriguing titles as *The Self Shiatsu Handbook, Zen and the Art of Motorcycle Maintenance,* and V.S. Naipaul's *A Way in the World.* Open Mon.-Fri. 8am-noon and 1:30-6:30pm, Sat. 8am-noon and 1:30-5pm.
Library: Biblioteca Cantonale, 6 viale Cattaner (tel. 923 25 61). Open Mon.-Fri. 9am-7pm, Sat. 9am-noon and 2-5pm; July-Aug. closed on Sat.
Medical Services: Doctor or dentist (tel. 111).
Emergencies: Police: tel. 117. **Ambulance:** tel. 144. **Fire:** tel. 118.
Post Office (PTT): via della Posta, 2 blocks up from the lake near via al Forte. Open Mon.-Fri. 7:30am-noon and 1:15-6:30pm, Sat. 8-11am. Telephones, telegraphs and fax services available at the Via Magatti entrance to the PTT building. Open Mon.-Fri. 7:30am-8pm, Sat. 9am-7pm, Sun. 9:30am-12:30pm and 2:30-7pm.
Postal code: CH-6900.
Telephone code: 091.

ACCOMMODATIONS

Though Lugano's lakesides are lined with five-star hotels and restaurants, surprising bargains can be found even in the center of town.

Ostello della Gioventù (HI), Lugano-Savosa, 13 via Cantonale (tel. 966 27 28; fax 928 23 63). Take us #5 (from the left of the station, go down the second ramp, cross the street, and uphill 100m) to "Crocifisso" (6th stop), then backtrack a few steps and turn left up Via Cantonale. Friendly and helpful English-speaking staff. Call ahead as it is a deservedly popular spot. Jasmine and wisteria flowers climbing the walls, a full-sized pool out back, and a peaceful neighborhood. This place feels like home, if your home is a lush villa with stunning gardens and various tropical flora. Reception open 7am-noon and 3-10pm. No lockout. Strict curfew at 10pm. Dorms 17SFr. Singles 31.50SFr, after 3 nights 28SFr, with kitchenette 41.50SFr and 38SFr respectively. Doubles 43.50SFr, over 3 nights 40SFr, with kitchenette 53.50SFr and 50SFr respectively. Sheets 2SFr. Breakfast 6SFr. Key available. 1SFr for kitchen use after 7:30pm only. Apartments available for families (7-day min. stay; 70-100SFr per day). Open mid-March to Oct.
Casa della Giovane, 34 corso Elvezia (tel. 922 95 53), 3 blocks from the hospital and across the street from Basilica Sacro Cuore. A 20-min. walk from the station, left on Piazzale della Stazione, right on via San Gottardo, and a sharp right on via Cantonale. Follow via Cantonale as it becomes corso Pestalozzi, and make a left on corso Elvezia; look for a beautiful peach brick building about four blocks on your right. Or take bus #9 (leaves opposite train station) to "Corso Elvezia." For **women only.** Wooden floors and modern furniture garnish big, bright rooms that are exceptionally clean. Colorful cafeteria nostalgic of nursery school, and service even more friendly than those halcyon days of milk and cookies. Beautiful rooftop terrace with views of lake and mountains allows you to get a serious tan. Reception open 7am-10pm. Under age 18, curfew 9:30pm; ages 18 and up 11:15pm weekdays, 2am weekends. Dorms 20SFr. Breakfast 4.50SFr. Lunch or dinner 12SFr. Doubles with bathrooms available during summer, with breakfast and one meal 35SFr, with all three meals 40SFr. Lockable armoires in dorms and rooms. Laundry 3SFr. During the school year, make reservations.
Hotel Montarina, 1 via Montarina (tel. 966 72 72; fax 966 12 13), just behind the train station. Walk 200m to the right from the station, cross the tracks, and hike up the hill. The lush grounds are reminiscent of Fantasy Island, but the rooms are sized for Tattoo. Reception daily 9am-9pm. Cramped dorms 20SFr, sheets 6SFr. Singles 50SFr. Doubles 80SFr. Buffet breakfast 15SFr. Open April-Oct.
Hotel Pestalozzi, 9 Piazza Indipendenza (tel. 921 46 46; fax 923 20 45). Live it up for a night by staying in this upscale version of a budget hotel. A smattering of affordable singles and doubles with huge, fluffy white pillows and floral wallpaper. Turkish rugs on the floors. Reception open 24hrs. Singles 54-92SFr. Doubles 96-148SFr. Triples 125-200SFr. Breakfast included. Reserve ahead. Visa accepted.

Villa Serva, 36 via Tesserete (tel. 923 60 17; fax 943 47 81), is a 15-min. walk from the station, exit station, and go left until second ramp, walk down ramp and then along via Gottardo for 250m, right on via Tesserete. Or take bus #9 to "Sassa." Clean rooms spruced up by the occasional painting. Outdoor pool and grapevine draped lattice greets you as you enter. Singles 46-72SFr. Doubles 108-130SFr.

Hotel Zurigo, 13 corso Pestalozzi (tel. 923 43 43; fax 923 92 68). Just down the street from the Pestlozzi, and across the street from the AmEx office. Clean and spacious. All rooms have telephones and yellow walls. Rooms with showers also have TV. Reception open daily 6am-midnight. Singles 55SFr, with shower 80SFr. Doubles with shower 90SFr, with shower and toilet 120SFr. Triples with shower 160SFr. Breakfast and parking included. Hotel closed in Dec.

Camping: There are 5 campsites nearby, all in **Agno.** Take the Ferrovia-Lugano-Ponte-Tresa (FLP) train to Agno (4.20SFr). From the train, turn left, and turn left again on Via Molinazzo for **La Palma** (tel. 605 25 21) and **Eurocampo** (tel. 605 21 14; fax 605 31 87). 7.50SFr, tent 4-15SFr. All sites are open April-Oct.

FOOD

As the central city in the Ticino, Lugano knows the way to its visitors' hearts. Serving up plates of *penne* and *gnocchi* and freshly twirled pizzas, Lugano's many outdoor restaurants and cafés pay homage to the canton's Italian heritage. It doesn't take a genius to realize that Lugano's specialty is sausage. *Spätzle* steps aside here in deference to spaghetti. For a simple meal, your might try **Ristorante Inova,** on the third flood of the department store Inovazione in piazza Dante. They have the same old self-serve goodies: salad bar (4.20SFr-9.90SFr), grand pasta bar (6.90-9.60SFr per plate), and other warm entrées-of-the-day (8-13SFr; open Mon.-Sat. 7:30am-10pm, Sun. 10am-10pm.) For some quick *al fresco* shopping and eating, **Via Pessina** livens up at midday with outdoor sandwich and fruit shops. Try the Salumeria at 12 via Pessina for quick sandwiches to go (2.50-6SFr).

La Tinèra, 2 via dei Gorini (tel. 923 52 19). Tucked away in a tiny alley off a quiet cobblestone road, this low-lit, romantic, underground restaurant is full of Ticinese ambience and not to be missed. You can't go wrong with the daily specials (10-15SFr). The *pollo alla compagnola* (13.50SFr) looks particularly scrumptious. Open Mon.-Sat. 11am-2:30pm and 6-10pm. Visa, MC, AmEx.

Pestalozzi, 9 piazza Indipendenza (tel. 921 46 46), in the hotel. This non-alcoholic restaurant offers ten vegetarian dishes (10.50SFr and up), including tofu burgers (check the daily menu). Lasagne Bolognese 8.50SFr. Open daily 11am-10pm.

Ristorante Sayanara, 10 via Soave (tel. 922 01 70), in the piazza Cloccaro. You can't miss the fluorescent orange chairs that clash with the peachy tablecloths. A huge lunchtime crowd comes for the homemade pasta (12-16.50SFr) and pizza (11.50SFr and up). Open daily 8am-midnight. Visa, MC, AmEx.

Ristorante Cantinone, piazza Cioccaro (tel. 923 10 68), across from Sayanara. It competes with its cross-piazza rival for lunchtime clients, offering more of the same—pizza (10.50-17SFr) and pasta (12.50-16.50SFr). Large salads 16SFr and up. Open daily 9am-midnight. Visa, MC, AmEx.

Bistro Tango, piazza della Riforma (tel. 922 27 01). Take a break from pizza and head for the border. Central and South American food in a lively tango atmosphere. Tacos and burritos 15SFr. Open daily 11:30am-1am. Visa, MC, AmEx.

Markets

Migros, 15 via Pretoria, in the center of town, offers freshly made pasta and delicious Italian *ciabatta,* as well as the usual fare. Also a **branch** located around the corner from the hostel. Open Mon.-Fri. 8am-6:30pm, Sat. 7:30am-5pm.

Public Market, piazza della Riforma. Displays the seafood and produce of the region. Tues. and Fri. 7am-noon.

Reformhaus Müller in the Quartiere Maghetti (next to Chiesa San Rocco) for health food. Open Mon.-Fri. 8am-6:30pm, Sat. 8am-5pm.

EASTERN SWITZERLAND

SIGHTS AND ENTERTAINMENT

The vaults and arches of the 16th-century **Cathedral San Lorenzo,** just below the train station, are chock-full of brilliant frescoes. The statues and stained glass inside are masterpieces in themselves. To soak in the spectacular view of the Lago di Lugano with the striking contrast between the blue lake and the sienna Ticinese rooftops, cross the street and follow the curved path down the hill. The **Chiesa San Rocco,** on via Canova, dating from 1349, houses an ornate Madonna altarpiece and Passion frescoes by Discopoli. **Basilica Sacro Cuore,** on corso Elevezia, about four blocks from piazza Indipendenza, and across from the Casa della Giovane, is a national monument featuring Swiss hikers walking alongside the disciples in the altarpiece fresco. A tribute to the combination of church and state, the Swiss flag is tucked into nouveau Biblical scenes. The most spectacular frescoes are Bernardino Luini's *Crucifixion* and *Last Supper* in the **Chiesa Santa Maria degli Angioli,** on piazza B. Luini. They pulse with loud, crowded color, denying their centuries of age. These precursors to neon could keep even the most sinful dozer awake (open daily 8-11:45am and 3-5:45pm).

Lugano lost one of its largest assets in a rush of art-world intrigue. The **Thyssen-Bornemisza Gallery,** in Villa Favorita, Castagnola (tel. 962 17 41), has a fascinating international history (see **Art for Art's Sake** p. 187; open April 4-Nov. 3 Fri.-Sun. 10am-5pm. 10SFr, students 6SFr). The **Museo d'Arte Moderna,** Villa Malpensata, 5 riva Caccia (tel. 944 43 70), still has paintings on the wall, holding yet another impressive collection of 20th-century art, European and American, as well as yearly retrospectives and special exhibitions. (Open Tues.-Fri. 10am-noon and 2-6pm, Sat.-Sun. 10am-6pm; 8SFr, students 5SFr.) The **Museo Cantonale d'Arte,** 10 via Canova (tel. 910 47 80), features 19th- and 20th-century works, including Swiss artists such as Klee, Vela, Ciseri, and Franzoni, and foreign artists such as Nicholson, Morandi, Degas, and Renoir. Temporary exhibits focus on modern art. Much of the permanent collection may be removed for temporary exhibits (open Tues. 2-6pm, Wed.-Sun. 10am-6pm; admission to special exhibits 10SFr, students 5SFr, to permanent collection 7SFr, students 5SFr). The Brignoni family heirlooms at the **Museo delle Culture Extraeuropee,** 324 via Cortiuo (tel. 971 73 53), on the footpath to Gandria in the Villa Heleneum, does not include cuckoo clocks or Swiss army knives; the family chose instead to collect masks, shields, carvings, and weapons from everywhere—from Samoa to Africa. Check out the real, dead shrunken heads from Papua New Guinea (open March 5-Oct. 31 Tues.-Sun. 10-5pm; 5SFr, students 3SFr).

Lugano's waterfront parks are an ideal place to spend a few hours. The **Belvedere,** quai riva Caccia, a sculpture garden stretches along the lakeside promenade in the direction of Paradiso. Lugano is chock full o' summer **festivals.** At the end of June, the **Tour de Suisse** comes to a dramatic finish in Lugano, and from the end of June to early August, **Cinema al Lago** shows films on the lakeside beach. A huge screen is installed at the water level on the lake, where 1000 seats are available for viewers. The films are international, and draw stars from Italy, France, Britain, and the U.S. In early July, Lugano's **Jazz Festival** heats up at no charge. Previous performers include Miles Davis and Bobby McFerrin. The **Blues to Bop Festival** celebrates the tradition of R&B, blues, and gospel at the end of August. The town wraps up its festive season with the **Wine Harvest Festival** in late September/early October, drinking in the Indian summer and its fermented fruits.

The surrounding mountains are as clean and pure as they day they were created, untouched by the pollution that once plagued the lake. The tourist office and hostel both have topographic maps and trail guides (the tourist office sells them, while the hostel lends them). The bay's guard towers, **Monte Bré** (933m) and **Monté San Salvatore** (912m), are both easily scaled by a day hike. San Salvatore is the more striking of the two, with craggy cliffs extending to the water. There is a church dating back to the 13th century on the top. The trail head is just past the funicular station at Paradiso (about a 15-minute walk from the tourist office, to the right along the shore). The trail is marked but a map is still useful; the climb to the top takes about 1hr.15min. After studying the lake, Lugano, and the Alps, follow the signs to Carona, a small village halfway up the mountain that has an Olympic size pool with high dive (1SFr). Continue walking to Morcote, on the shore, where you can catch a ferry back to Lugano (14SFr, Swisspass valid). The walk from the summit takes about 3½hrs. Both mountains are serviced by funiculars (11SFr one-way, 17SFr round-trip, students aged 16-18 6SFr one-way, 9SFr round-trip). For more information contact the San Salvatore Funicular office at 994 13 52, or the Monte Bré office at 971 31 71.

The arcades of the *città vecchia* come alive at night as people meander through the piazzas and along the lake. The outdoor cafés of the piazza della Riforma are especially lively. The slot machines spin at **Casinò Kursaal di Lugano** (tel. 923 32 81), near the tourist office. (Casino open daily 9pm-2am for game tables, noon-midnight for slots; pants and shirt collars required after 8pm.) The **Pave Pub,** riva Albertolli 1 (tel. 922 07 70), offers 50 different beers and an English pub atmosphere with a great lakeside view of the lit fountains. (Beers start at 45SFr; open daily 11am-1am). **B-52,** 4 via al Forte (tel. 923 96 58) draws a young crowd that loves to mix and mingle (open Tues.-Sun. 10pm-3am). The Latin American **Mango Club**, 8 piazza Dante (tel. 922 94 38), gets nice and spicy (opens at 11pm, goes until last person leaves).

Bathers can enjoy Lugano's only sand beach at **Lido Beach** (tel. 971 40 41), just across the Fiume Cassarate on Viale Castagnola. (Open May and Sept. daily 9am-6pm; June and Aug. 15-Sept.1 9am-7pm; July-Aug. 14 9am-7:30pm. 6SFr.)

Art for art's sake? Whatever.

The **Thyssen-Bornemisza Gallery,** in Villa Favorita, once housed one of the most outstanding private collections in Europe, until the owner, a fantastically rich, old Baron, and his young Spanish wife (a former beauty queen) started looking around for a permanent home for all of those Rembrandts, Dürers, Van Goghs, and Kandinskys. In the international bidding war that ensued, the collection first moved into the hands of the Spanish government for a while to up the ante. When Spain became attached to the paintings, he talked them into building a museum and paying him a cool US$350 million for the stash. Spain wins, Switzerland loses, end of story. The Villa is still maintained by the very piqued Swiss and open to the public with some leftovers and pleasure-dome architecture. Learn a lesson in Swiss tact by asking the guides—with the best look of open innocence you can muster—where all of the paintings have gone.

■ Near Lugano: Gandria

A picturesque walk along the lake shores, through overgrown vegetation just above the lapping waters (1hr.), leads to the precariously perched village of Gandria, lazing away the days in a placid corner of the Lago di Lugano. It can also be reached by boat from Lugano (½hr., every ½hr.; 10SFr, round-trip 16SFr, Swisspass valid; first boat at 8:30am, last boat at 10:15pm). A small fishing village and once a smuggling port for pirates, Gandria's winding streets are preserved from the ravages of modern design and technology—city ordinances forbid construction, and prohibit cars—but not the ravages of modern tourists. One foot off the boat, and the proliferation of restaurant advertisements and souvenir shops betrays a tourist trap. **Hotel Locanda Gandriese** (tel. (091) 971 41 81; fax 976 06 57) offers clean rooms overlooking the lake (singles 50SFr, doubles 86SFr, triples 110SFr; breakfast included). The **Hotel Miralgo** (tel. (091) 971 43 61) offers clean rooms, with a unique scheme incorporating pink sheets, green rugs, and floral patterned chairs (38SFr per person; breakfast included).

There may not be much to do in this town, but an afternoon having ice cream while hanging above the lake is always pleasant. The **Chiesa Parrochiale San Vigilio** offers a cool spot to beat the heat and view some well-carved sculpture and internal architecture. A short boat ride from Gandria's town center to **Gandria-Cantine** (boat stop "Museo delle Dogane") leads to the **Swiss Customs Museum.** The museum glorifies those brave men and women who keep gold pure and smugglers on the lookout. Several hands-on exhibits show the intricacies of detecting fake I.D.'s and searching cars, while others show slices of the life of a turn-of-the-century border policeman. (Open daily 1:30-5:30pm. Free. Exhibits in Italian and German, with some introductory notes in English and French.)

■ Locarno

On the shores of Lago Maggiore, which straddles Italy and Switzerland, Locarno basks in warm near-Mediterranean breezes and bright Italian sun. Luxuriant palm trees replace the ruggedness of the Alps and provide a dramatic contrast to the rest of Switzerland. More serene than even its Italian cousin to the south, Locarno offers balmy evenings and *al fresco* living to its visitors. For much of the inter-war era, hopes for peace were symbolized by "the Spirit of Locarno"—a futile attempt in 1925 by England, France, and Italy to appease Germany after World War I. History records that Locarno was chosen over other Swiss cities because the mistress of one of the representatives insisted that the conference be held on the Maggiore. Perhaps the *bella donna* needed some work on her tan. Sun-worshippers flock in droves to pay homage to the UV deities in this relatively unspoiled resort town that receives over 2200 hours of sunlight per year—the most in all of Switzerland. Nestled in the Ticinese foothills, Locarno is also an excellent starting point for mountain hikes along the pristine Verzasca and Maggia valleys, or for regional skiing. If you're not up for the mountains, the lake and the city provide ideal lounging spots for weary travelers. James Joyce loitered around Maggiore's waters in 1917, waiting for Ezra Pound to send back a critique of *Ulysses*. Locarno's arcades brim with live music, kinetic cafés, and feisty *flaneurs*. The town blends an ideal mixture of Swiss orderliness and efficiency with Italian energy, food, spirit, and exuberance. People talk loudly with Italian hands, yet stay on time with Swiss watches.

GETTING TO LOCARNO

Trains run most frequently to **Bellinzona** (20min., every ½hr., 6.60SFr), connecting every hour north to **Lucerne** (2hrs.40min., 54SFr) and **Zürich** (3hrs., 57SFr) and south to **Lugano** (15.80SFr) and **Milan** (2hrs.20min., 23SFr). If you are heading west to **Zermatt** (82SFr), **Montreux** (69SFr), or **Geneva** (5hrs.20min., 84SFr), change trains in **Domodossola**, Italy. Call 157 22 22 for more information on trains. **Buses** depart from the train station or from the lake side of Piazza Grande to Locarno and to nearby towns such as Ascona (#31) and Minusio. Buses also run regularly through the **San Bernadino Pass** to Eastern Switzerland. **By car,** Locarno is accessible from motorway N2, which extends from Basel to Chiasso (exit: Bellinzona-süd).

ORIENTATION AND PRACTICAL INFORMATION

Piazza Grande, home of the International Film Festival, anchors Locarno, with all of the town's cultural and commercial life gravitating around its century-old Lombardian arcades. **Città Vecchia,** in the old town and worth visiting for its 16th-and 17th-century architecture, not to mention its extravagantly economical accommodations, lies just above Piazza Grande. **Via Ramogna** connects the Piazza to the train station and ferries groups of gawking tourists to the Madonna del Sasso via the funicular which ascends from the street. **Via Rusca,** extending from the other side of the Piazza, winds up at the Castello Visconti. South of the Piazza lies the residential district, laid out in a traditional grid plan. The vacation homes of many Swiss are here.

> **Tourist office:** Largo Zorzi, on Piazza Grande (tel. 751 03 33). From the main exit of the train station, walk diagonally to the right, and cross via della Stazione; follow this street through the pedestrian walkway (via alla Ramogna). When you come out, cross Largo Zorzi to your left; the tourist office is in the same building as the *Kursaal* (casino). Hotel reservations are a 5SFr deposit, deducted from the price of the hotel room. The office also organizes **bus excursions** around Lago Maggiore and beyond. City tours in English leave the tourist office March 25-Nov. 1 Mon. at 9:45am. Pick up a map of Locarno and choose from among the many brochures

that highlight local points of interest. Open March-Oct. Mon.-Fri. 8am-7pm, Sat.-Sun. 9am-noon and 1-5pm; Nov.-Feb. Mon.-Fri. 8am-noon and 2-6pm.

Currency exchange: Try any one of the banks lining Piazza Grande. Good rates are also at the train station. Open daily 5:45am-9pm.

Telephones are located at the train station, post office, and along Piazza Grande.

Ferries: Navigazione Lago Maggiore, 1 Largo Zorzi (tel. 751 18 65; fax 751 30 24), presents tours of the entire lake, all the way into Italy. A full day on the Swiss side of the lake costs 10SFr. Trips to Ascona (10min., 7 daily, round-trip 10SFr) and especially the Island of Brissago (20min., 6 daily, round-trip 19SFr), an island famous for its gardens and cigars, are well worth the visit.

Car rental: Europcar, 5a Viaggi Verbano (tel. 791 43 24).

Taxi: tel. 743 11 33.

Parking: Metered public parking found on via della Posta and major streets (1SFr per hr.). Also, the 24-hr. parking garage, **Autosilo Largo SA** (tel. 751 96 13), awaits beneath the *Kursaal,* and is accessible by via Cattori.

Bike rental: At the train station. 21SFr per day, 84SF per week; mountain bike 29SFr per day. To return a bike to another station 6SFr (open daily 5:45am-9pm).

Luggage storage: At the train station. 5SFr. Open daily 5:45am-9pm. **Lockers** 2SFr.

English bookstore: Fantasia Cartoleria Libreria, 32 Piazza Grande. English books, travel books, and maps (open Mon.-Fri. 8am-6:30pm, Sat. 8am-5pm).

Emergencies: Police: 117. Fire: 118. Road rescue: 163. **Weather:** 162. **Medical Assistance:** 111. **Ambulance:** 144.

Post office: Across the street from the train station. Open Mon.-Fri. 7:30-11:30am and 2-6pm, Sat. 8:15-11am.

Postal code: CH-6600.

Telephone code: 091.

ACCOMMODATIONS

Pensione Città Vecchia, 13 via Toretta (tel./fax 751 45 54). From the Piazza Grande, turn right on via Toretta (look for a brown sign with the *pensione*'s on it) and continue to the top. The pink stucco façade blends well with the Mediterranean theme. With a great price and a location to match, it's no small wonder that it's always full. Reserve weeks in advance. Reception open daily 8am-9pm. Check-in 1-6pm; you must have a reservation if you come between 6-9pm (or at least call from the station). No curfew. 22SFr per person, sheets 4.50SFr. Breakfast 4.50SFr. Open March-Oct.

Reginetta, 8 via della Motta (tel./fax 752 35 53). Run by the world-traveled Miss Bertolutti (the currency-postered walls are proof), this traveler's haven provides bright, spacious and impeccably clean rooms. Walk along the arcades to the end of Piazza Grande, and make a right onto via della Motta. Look for the huge, framed jigsaw puzzles on the walls. The friendly owner offers good advice on local sights; check the chalkboard for local events of interest. Reception open daily 8am-9pm. 39SFr per person, 45SFr with breakfast. Showers included. Open March-Oct. only. Visa, MC, AmEx.

Ostello Giaciglio, 7 via Rusca (tel. 751 30 64; fax 752 38 37). Walk to the end of the Piazza Grande, make a right onto via della Motta, and take the left fork in the road onto via Rusca. Brightly colored, sunshiny dorms for 4, 6, or 8 people. Kitchen facilities available, along with a sauna (20SFr) and tanning salon (10SFr) in case an inadvertent cloud invades Locarno's air space. 30SFr per person, no breakfast. If the hostel is full, walk across the street to **Hotel Garni Sempione** to find the hostel's supervisor. Visa, MC, AmEx.

Hotel Garni Stazione/Albergo Garni Montaldi, 7 Piazza Stazione (tel. 743 02 22; fax 743 54 06). Two jointly run hotels, both just behind the station. The former is part of an antique apartment building with clean sparkling white rooms (some with a good view). Reception for both places open 24hr. 40SFr per person, breakfast included. The newly renovated Albergo is quite a bit more expensive. 70-95SFr per person, breakfast included. Visa, MC, AmEx.

Delta Camping, 7 via Respini (tel. 751 60 81; fax 751 22 43). A 20-min. walk along the lakeside from the tourist office brings you to this campstyles of the rich and famous; a reservation fee of 75SFr, which is not deducted from the bill, is recommended for July and August. Offers a rock beach nearby and an enticing view of the lake. No dogs allowed. Reception open daily 8am-noon and 2-9pm. 13SFr, kids ages 2-14 5SFr. Site 20-30SFr, lake site 30-40SFr. Open March 1-Oct. 31.

Rivabella (tel. (091) 745 22 13; fax 745 66 38). in nearby **Tenero,** is much more affordable and is accessible by boat or a 45min. walk along the water in the opposite direction of Delta Camping. 9SFr. Tent 18SFr.

FOOD

Panini and pasta reign supreme in Locarno, as gruyère cheese gives way to Gorgonzola. While the majority of restaurants lean toward the expensive side, most offer pasta and pizza in the 10-20SFr range.

Inova, 1 via della Stazione (tel. 743 76 76), left as you exit the station. Huge self-serve restaurant. Wooden food bars bring otherwise financially inaccessible luxuries such as fruits and vegetable to your fingertips: fruit bar (4-6.80SFr), salad bar (4.20-10.50SFr), grand pasta buffet (9.60SFr). Also a tantalizing host of desserts. Open Mon.-Fri. 8:30am-6:30pm, Sat. 8am-5pm.

Casa de Popolo, Piazza del Corporazioni (tel. 751 12 08). Specializes in pizza (10-16SFr) and fresh pasta (12-18SFr), with courteous Italian waiters and a gurgling fountain in front of the outdoor seating. Open Mon.-Sat. 7am-midnight, Sun. 5pm-midnight. Visa, MC, AmEx.

Contrada, 26 Piazza Grande (tel. 751 48 15), offers outdoor dining ideal for people-watching. Pizzas and pasta (10.50-15SFr). Ask for the list of daily specials (14SFr). Open Mon.-Sat. 8am-6:30pm. Visa, MC.

Lungolago Bar, corner of Lungolago G. Motta and via Bernadino Luini (tel. 751 52 46), features a beautiful lakeside terrace and lively nightlife. *Panini* from 5SFr, pizzas 10.50-14SFr, beer 3.30SFr. Open daily 7am-1am.

Gelatina Primavera, 4 via all'Ospedale (tel. 31 77 36), across the street from the Chiesa San Francesco. Feel like those 2200 hours of sun are hitting you all at once? Grab one of their delicious store-made ice cream cones and cool off. Sandwiches from 5.50SFr and brick oven pizza from 11SFr. Open Wed.-Mon. 8am-midnight, Sat.-Sun. 10am-midnight.

Al Böcc, 14 Piazza Grande (tel. 751 49 39), opposite the lake side of Piazza Grande. Busy little sandwich shop on the piazza. Sandwiches 3-6SFr. Serves warm *focaccia* bread (4.50-6.50 SFr). Open daily 6:30am-midnight. Visa, MC.

SIGHTS AND ENTERTAINMENT

A 15-minute walk up shaded via al Sasso, by a mountain stream, leads to the shocking yellow and orange church of **Madonna del Sasso** (Madonna of the Rock). A popular pilgrimage destination, the church was under construction longer than it has been a site. It took three centuries to complete, but only celebrated its 200th birthday in 1992. The interior overwhelms with its breathtaking frescoes, ornate carvings, and brilliant painting, while the outdoor terrace pacifies with its tranquil view of Locarno and the lake. Painstakingly carved scenes of the *Pietà, The Last Supper,* and *Lamentation* stand proudly on the porticoes of the church grounds. The lady of the house herself, the **Madonna,** is tucked away in the museum next door, as are masterpieces by Ciseri and Raphael. (Grounds open daily 7am-10pm, Nov.-Feb. 7am-9pm. Museum open April-Oct. Mon.-Fri. 2-5pm, Sun. 10am-noon and 2-5pm. Admission to museum 2.50SFr, students 1.50SFr.)

Closer to sea level the cavernous **Chiesa Sant' Antonio** presides over the outskirts of the *città vecchia.* Built between 1668 and 1674 it features vaulted ceilings and an immense and colorful fresco depicting Christ being taken off the cross. Founded by the brethren of St. Francis of Assisi shortly after his death, the **Chiesa San Francesco** unassumingly sits on the Piazza San Francesco. The church's current architecture, mellowed by old cobblestones and fading frescoes, is a melange of styles starting from the 13th century. Downhill from Chiesa San Francesco along via Ripacanova, the **Castello Visconteo,** an archaeological exhibit in itself, gazes on Locarno. The medieval castle, constructed between the 13th and 15th centuries, now houses the **Museo Civico e Archeologico,** which exhibits Roman glassware, pottery, and coins. Be sure to check the wall placards indicating each room's function in medieval times; also keep an eye out for the 17th-century frescoes painted for the viscounts who inhabited the castle. (Open April-Oct. Tues.-Sun. 10am-noon and 2-5pm. 5SFr, students 3SFr.)

A mildly interesting collection of modern art, donated to the city of Locarno by Jean and Marguerite Arp, is displayed in **La Pinacoteca Casa Rusca,** Piazza di Sant' Antonio 1 (tel. 756 34 58), a recently restored 18th-century villa. Both the Arps have work in the collection as does Max Bill, and other talents of the 20th century (open Tues.-Sun. 10am-noon and 2-5pm; 5SFr, 3SFr students). The **Casorella,** via F. Rusca 5, highlights the works of regional artists, and displays an impressive array of Roman coins found in the Locarno area. (Open April-Oct. Tues.-Fri. 2-5pm, Sat.-Sun. 10am-noon and 2-5pm. Free.)

As the sun sets and the temperature drops, gamble at the **Kursaal** (casino) next to the tourist office, which resembles a video arcade more than a casino (open Sun.-Thurs. noon-2am, Fri.-Sat. noon-4am; must be over 19; proper attire required). Catch a movie at the **Cinema Rex** on via Bossi, or nurse a long drink at one of the numerous cafés along the Piazza Grande. The **Record Rock Café,** Via Trevani 3 (tel. 751 4433), a Hard Rock look-a-like, pumps out American and English rock along with contemporary hits. Posters range from Queen to the Beatles; they adorn the walls amid various guitars and records. Live bands play from September to June. (Open July-Aug. Tues.-Sun. 5pm-1am; Sept.-June Tues.-Sun. 4pm-1am. Cover 10SFr.)

Locarno is the ideal starting/stopping/break point for outdoor enthusiasts. For the faint of heart or short of breath, ride to up to **Cimetta,** which hangs over Locarno at a lofty 1671m by taking the Madonna Funicular to the Cardada Cable Car, which, in turn, takes you to the Cimetta chair lift. (Round-trip 33SFr; funicular only round-trip 6SFr, with Swisspass 4.50SFr; Locarno-Cardada 28SFr round-trip. Cable cars depart twice per hour, funicular every 15 min.) To escape the city, head out on Postal Bus 630-55 to **Sonogo** (1hr., 15.80SFr, Swisspass valid) and bask amid the extraordinarily rugged peaks at the end of **Val Verzasca** (Verzasca valley). From the bus stop, make your first left and follow the yellow signs to Lavertezzo. Pass through cool, shady glens and rocky riverbeds as you follow the Verzasca river through the pristine valley. Peaks rise on either side as you walk (primarily downhill) by deserted villages and cascading waterfall. Close to **Lavertezzo,** the river eases its rapid, crashing pace and offers the soul-cleansing cold of its refreshing pools to hikers, thermally overloaded or otherwise. Pick your swimming hole carefully, however, as current can be fast and colder than you think. Climb the **Ponte dei Salti,** a vaulted stone bridge built at the end of the Middle Ages, and gaze into the clear green ponds. The walk from Sonogroto Lavertezzo take about 3½hr., but you can lengthen or shorten your walk as you like by meeting the postal bus at a number of other stops along the valley. The trail is marked by yellow signs with direction and town names and also by painted red stripes sandwiched by two white stripes.

The Locarno Film Festival

Each year in the first weeks of August, Locarno hosts an **International Film Festival** which has perhaps the most widely-attended world premieres of movies anywhere. In 1997 the festival hits Locarno August 7-17. Unlike Cannes, no snooty invitations are required. Thousands of big-screen enthusiasts squeeze themselves like sardines into the Piazza Grande and watch whatever happens to be playing that night on the 800ft. movie screen—Europe's largest. More than 100,000 spectators participate in the event annually, making it definitively Switzerland's biggest party. In past years Woody Allen, Milos Forman, Stanley Kubrick, Spike Lee, and Bernardo Bertolucci have all screened films here. Officially, Locarno's festival focuses on the promotion of young filmmakers and new film movements.

During the festival, accommodations are gone with the wind. Make reservations at least six months in advance if you don't want to be left without shelter. For festival information, as well as information about student discounts, contact International Film Festival, Via della Posta 6, CH-6600 Locarno (tel. 751 02 32; fax 751 74 65). Available tickets are: one screening 15SFr, 2 screenings 25SFr, whole day (3 screenings) 30SFr. Information in the U.S.: East Coast: Norman Wang and Sophie Gluck, New York (tel. (212) 226-3269; fax 941-1425); West Coast: Bill Krohn, Los Angeles (tel./fax (213) 883-0078).

■ Near Locarno: Ascona

Queen of the Lago Maggiore, Ascona rules with a languorous hand. Ascona has welcomed many diverse groups to her shores. In the Renaissance, a small bunch of sculptors and artists established their studios in Ascona. Their legacy is emblazoned in the façades that grace the **Casa Serodine.** More recently, a group of hippies "colonized" **Monte Verità,** Ascona's beautiful mountain, seeking a return to truth through natural living. Their efforts are immortalized in the **Museo Casa Anatta** (tel. 791 01 81), at the summit of Monte Verità, a 20-minute walk up a stairway from the town center. (Open April-June and Sept.-Oct. Tues.-Sun. 2:30-6pm, July-Aug. Tues.-Sun. 3-7pm. 5SFr, students 3SFr.) Take bus #33 from the post office, as it winds its way to the top. With the utopian, heavily sedated ascetics taking the high road, the burghers colonized the lower *città vecchia* as a bastion of good taste and expensive delicacies. Jewellers, *haute couture* boutiques, and exclusive art galleries line the narrow winding streets. Ascona tries to go incognito as the quaint fishing town of yore. Don't believe the hype, in reality it is an *Über-*resort, with many plentifully starred hotels as yet untouched by the *hoi polloi.*

Down the road from the bus stop to the right is the **Collegio Pontificio Papio,** otherwise known as Ascona 90210. Founded in the 16th century, the private school brilliantly displays the coat of arms of the Papio family of Ascona. The **Chiesa Santa Maria della Misericordia,** built in 1399, smells of incense and looks its age with fading yet communicative frescoes from the 16th century. The church now presides over the school, reminding students to be pious, a task which is not hard for the students who labor away in paradise. **The Chiesa S.S. Pietro e Paolo,** in the heart of the pedestrian sector of Ascona, was constructed in the 16th century, but Baroque restoration coated the church's interior walls with colorful frescoes. Ascona's **Museo Comunale d'Arte Moderna,** 34 via Borgo (tel. 791 67 57), displays an extensive permanent collection including such artists as Klee, Utrillo, Amiet, and Jawlensky, as well as a collection of caricatures done both in color and black and white. (Open March-Dec. Tues.-Sat. 10am-noon and 3-6pm, Sun. 10am-noon. 3SFr, students and seniors 2SFr.) Private galleries line the winding streets, promoting such artists as Niki de St. Phalle, Chagall, and Braque. A testimony to Ascona's incorporation of history and capitalism is the **Castello dei Ghiriglioni** at the far end of Piazza Motta. Touted as a site of historical interest, the lone remaining tower of the 13th-century castle is now a hotel and restaurant. The **Museo Epper,** 14 via Albarelle (tel. 791 19 42), beyond the Castello, presents temporary exhibits and retrospectives of 20th-century artists. (Open March-June, Sept.-Oct. Tues.-Fri. 10am-noon and 4-6pm, Sun. 4-6pm; July-Aug. Tues.-Fri. 10am-noon and 8-10pm, Sat.-Sun. 8-10pm. Free.)

In late June and early July, Ascona sets up the bandstands and claps its hands to the beat of the **Festa New Orleans Music.** Local cafés and the waterfront host musicians who bring the night to life with jazz, gospel, soul, blues, and even zydeco. This ain't your mama's sippin' jazz—it's the real thing with acts from jazz hotspots the world over. The 1997 festival will be held from June 27-July 5; entrance is 5SFr per night, 30SFr for the whole festival. If you're planning a trip, other events include an international horse jumping competition at the end of July, an international music festival (late Aug.-mid-Oct.), and an international puppet festival (Sept. 5-15). Locarno's younger crowd flocks to Ascona's subterranean dance club, **Cincilla,** via Moscia 6 (open Wed.-Thurs. and Sun. 11pm-3am, Fri.-Sat. 11pm-4am). The club is a little heavy on the zebra motif, but heavy on the groove also.

EASTERN SWITZERLAND

A village of only 4500 inhabitants, Ascona together with its neighboring twin, Losone boasts over 3000 hotel beds. Unfortunately, close to none fall into a budget price range. Try the rooms above the **Ristorante Verbano** (tel. 791 12 74) on via Borgo near the museum (44SFr per person, breakfast included), or ask the tourist office for a list of **camere private** (private rooms), which run 24-65SFr per person. Grab a bite to eat at **Otello** on via Papio 8 (tel. 791 33 07), just down the street to the right from the bus stop. Their specialty is *crêpes* (8.50SFr and up), but they also have an expensive Chinese and Italian kitchen. During the jazz festival and on other random occasions, you can hear New Orleans original jazz in the bandstand on the terrace in back (open Sun.-Thurs. 7am-midnight; Fri.-Sat. 7am-1am; Visa, MC). Of the pricey lakefront cafés, try the orange-umbrellaed **Osteria Nostrana,** Piazza Motta 53 (tel. 791 51 58), which serves pizza and spaghetti (11.50-18.90SFr; open daily 9:15am-midnight; Visa, MC, AmEx). And then there is always the **Co-op.** You can't miss the orange sign from the bus stop (open Mon.-Fri. 8am-6:30pm, Sat. 8am-5pm).

Ascona's **tourist office** (tel. 791 00 90; fax 792 10 08) is in the Casa Serodine, just behind the Chiesa S.S. Pietro e Paolo with its sumptuous Baroque façade (open March 20-Oct. 20 Mon.-Fri. 9am-6:30pm, Sat. 9am-6pm, Sun. 9am-2pm; Oct. 21-March 19 Mon.-Fri. 9am-12:30pm and 2-6pm). **Guided tours** of Ascona leave the tourist office from March-Nov. on Tues. and Fri. at 10am (5SFr, approx. 1½hr.).The tourist office **exchanges currency,** but the train station in Locarno offers better rates and hours. **Telephones** are at the post office. **Buses** run from Ascona to Locarno (2.40SFr) every 15 minutes. (line #31, leaving Piazza Grande and the train station in Locarno, and via Papio in Ascona). **Parking** in Ascona shouldn't be too difficult, though they do not allow cars in the center of town. Try your luck at the **Autosilo** at the corner of via Papio and via Buonamno. The **post office** is at the corner to the left of the bus stop, on via della Posta (open Mon.-Fri. 7:30am-noon and 1:45-6pm, Sat. 8-11am). **Postal code:** CH-6612. **Telephone code:** 091.

■ Bellinzona

The capital of Ticino, the "beautiful zone," *"citta dei castelli"* (city of castles), "gateway to the Alps," Bellinzona has many monikers. However, this southern gateway is primarily viewed as a crossroads, linking the sojourner to the Ticinese pearls, Lugano and Locarno. In the process, however, Bellinzona has evolved into a pearl itself, with dramatic (though no longer strategic) castles and old Italian façades and arcades. Relieved of its martial duties, Bellinzona presently serves as a cultural link between the German and Italian regions of Switzerland. As its name testifies, Bellinzona's body lies in Switzerland, but its heart is with *Italia* to the south.

Getting to Bellinzona The easiest way to arrive in Bellinzona is via **train.** There are direct connections to **Basel** (4hr., hourly, 70SFr), **Lugano** (½hr., 3 every hr., 10.40SFr), **Locarno** (20min., 2 every hr., 6.60SFr), **Lucerne** (2hr.15min., 50SFr), **Zürich** (2½hr., every hr., 54SFr), **Milan** (2hr., hourly, 23SFr), **Rome** (7hr., 3 daily, 61SFr), and **Venice** (5hr., daily, 39SFr). Further connections can be made in Zürich. If you are heading west toward **Geneva** (5½hr., 10 daily, 87SFr), change trains in Domodossola. Call 157 22 22 for more information on trains. **Post buses** leave from the stations for **Chur** (2½hr., 5 daily, 53.20SFr) and other destinations in Eastern Switzerland. **By car,** Bellinzona can be reached from the north via routes N2/E35 or N13/E43; from Lugano or the south, take N2/E35 north; from Locarno or the west, take route 13 east.

Orientation and Practical Information Bellinzona's **tourist office,** 2 via Camminata (tel. 825 21 31; fax 825 38 17), is adjacent to the City hall and makes hotel reservations for free. From the train station, walk left 10 minutes in a straight line along viale Stazione, past piazza Collegiata, along via Nosetto, and you'll spot the big blue "i" sign directly in front of you at piazza Nosetto. (Open May-Sept. Mon.-Fri. 8am-6:30pm, Sat. 9am-5pm; Oct.-April Mon.-Fri. 8am-noon and 1:30-6:30pm, Sat. 8-11am.)

The train station provides **currency exchange, luggage storage** (5SFr at the baggage check), **lockers** (3SFr), and **bike rental** (21SFr per day, also at the baggage check; open daily 6am-9pm). **Telephones** line the viale Stazione near the post office and the larger piazzas. **Public parking** is available on an hourly basis at the train station or in the Colletivo at piazza del Sole (open daily 8am-7pm; 1SFr per hr.). The ultra-new **post office** on viale Stazione is a block left from the train station (open Mon.-Fri. 8am-noon and 2-5pm). **Postal code:** CH-6500. **Telephone code:** 091.

Accommodations and Food

Bellinzona, in all its efforts to attract tourists, has yet to build a youth hostel. **Hotel Moderno Garni,** 17b viale Stazione (tel. 825 13 76), gives you a two-star hotel at one-star prices. From the train station, head left on viale Stazione. For the reception, turn right on via Claudio Pelladini and take another immediate right on via Cancelliere Molo. Pleasant rooms with flowery sheets and some with balconies. (Reception in the hotel's café. Open daily 6:30am-midnight. Singles 55SFr. Doubles 90SFr. Triples 120SFr. Quads 160SFr. Shower and breakfast included. Visa, MC.) **Hotel San Giovanni,** 7 via San Giovanni (tel. 825 19 19), provides clean, smallish rooms, with large windows useful for catching warm summer breezes and showers and bathrooms on each floor. From the station, take a left on viale Stazione, and turn right down Scalinata Dionigi Resinelli; continue straight for 100m. (Reception open daily 6:30am-midnight. Singles 50SFr. Doubles 90SFr. Breakfast included, parking available.) If you are willing to put up with a hotel that's slightly run-down for the sake of convenience, try **Hotel Metropoli,** 5 via Ludorizo il Maro (tel. 825 11 79), just across the street and to the right of the train station. Spotless white sheets and high ceilings. (Reception open 8:30am-midnight. Singles 50SFr. Doubles 90SFr. Breakfast included. Visa, MC, AmEx.) Take postal bus #2 to "Arbedo Posta Vecchia" for **Camping Bosco de Molinazzo** (tel. 829 11 18; fax 829 23 55; 4.80-6.20SFr, children half-price; tent 5.20SFr, car 16SFr; open April 3-Oct. 6)

When you get the munchies, lunch at **Ristorante Inova,** viale Stazione 5 in the Inovazione. The mass-produced meals offer surprises like sautéed salmon. (Entrées 10-13SFr, salads 4.20-9.90SFr. Open Mon.-Fri. 8:30am-6:30pm, Sat. 8am-5pm.) For sunbathing and checking out the local fanfare, grab a prime seat, a cappuccino (3SFr), and a *panino* (5SFr) at **Peverelli Panetteria Tea Room Pasticceria** in piazza Collegiata, off viale Stazione (open Mon.-Fri. 7am-7pm, Sat. 7am-6pm). To rustle up your own grub, garner supplies at **Migros** on piazza del Sole, across from the Castelgrande entrance (open Mon.-Fri. 7am-6:30pm, Sat. 7am-5pm). To stock up on organically grown fruits and veggies, tofu burgers, and vitamins, head to **Bio Casa,** near the tourist office (open Mon.-Fri. 8:30am-6:30pm, Sat. 8am-5pm). Also check out the huge **outdoor market** along the via Stazione, purveying everything from typical fruits and breads to incense and rugs (Sat. 8am-noon).

Sights and Entertainment

The **Castelgrande** stands tall and proud over Bellinzona, on the site of earlier Roman defenses. Above it soar the *bianca* (white) and *nera* (black) towers, both 28m high, marking the Bellinzona landscape. The castle sprawls over the city center making it look as if a colony of rolling green hills had suddenly become armed and dangerous. Mr. T says, "I pity the fool who mess wit' them hills." The Duke of Milan constructed the most significant additions to the castle in 1487. Subsequent centuries saw the destruction and dilapidation of the castle. Restoration began in 1980 and was completed in 1992, giving the castle an entirely new interior. It now displays the 15th-century frescoes that adorned its walls and other archaeological finds from the hills of Bellinzona. The Castelgrande can be reached via an elevator near Piazza del Sole, or by walking up the paths that wind up the hill from Piazza Collegieta and Piazza Nosetto. (Open in summer Tues.-Sun. 10am-12:30pm and 1:30-5:30pm, in winter Tues.-Sun. 9am-noon and 2-5pm. Museum 4SFr, students 2SFr.)

The **Castello di Montebello** beckons visitors from its hillside niche across the river valley. For the intermediate castle conqueror, Montebello features assailable towers and its own working moat and drawbridge. It's a quick climb up the steps of the old city wall, behind the post office. (Open in summer Tues.-Sun. 9am-noon and 2-6pm; in winter Tues.-Sun. 9am-noon and 2-5pm. Admission to the archaeological and civic museum 2SFr, students 1SFr.) Two hundred and thirty meters above the city level, the **Castello di Sasso Corbaro,** smallest of the three castles, surveys the Ticinese mountains. The castle was built during a 6-month Herculean effort in 1470, by the strict order of the Duke of Milan after the battle of Giornico. It can be reached from the Castello di Montebello by walking for 15 minutes up Strata di Castello, through woods and vineyards, or by via Ospedale with the best view of valley from its tall peak. (Open April-Oct. Tues.-Sun. 10am-12:30pm and 1:30-5:30pm, Nov.-March Tues.-Sun. 9am-noon and 2-5pm.) The **museum** in the Castello di Sasso Corbaro presents an exposition of Ticinese life and manners, with typical dress, tools, weapons, and even exhibits on how to mill wheat and corn (same hours as the Castello; 4SFr, students 2SFr). A **"3 Castelli" ticket,** granting entry to the museums at all three castles, can be purchased for 8SFr (students 4SFr) at any of the castles or the tourist office. On the outskirts of Bellinzona, cloistered in the late 15th century **Chiesa Santa Maria della Grazie,** blazes a brilliant fresco of the Crucifixion, surrounded by fifteen panels of the Life of Christ. From the train station, walk 15 minutes to the left, or take bus #4 to "Cimiterio" (open daily 6:15-11:45am and 2-6:45pm).

The annual **Blues Festival** in Bellinzona draws crowds from throughout Switzerland in late June. Concerts are held in the piazzas and are free to the public. Previous performers include Luther Allison and Joe Louis Walker. Contact the tourist office for more information. Near Bellinzona is **Alcatraz** (tel. 859 31 34), the biggest dance club in Ticino, drawing disco tykes and tycoons from Locarno to Bellinzona. To get there take the train to nearby **Riazzino**, but hurry, Cinderella—the club closes at 3am, but the last train back is at midnight.

The Ticino river provides an ideal spot for idle strollers to enjoy the mountain air and scenery. Follow it all the way down to the Maggiore if you like. For a slightly more strenuous hike with grand views of Sasso Corbaro and the valley, make the 45-min. walk to Prada. From Bellinzona, take a short postal bus ride to Monti di Ravecchia. The trail begins at the hospital parking lot and follows an ancient mule path, leading to the now deserted town of Prada, an ancient trading post possibly dating to pre-Roman times. A concerned group of nuns has managed to preserve the town's church.

■ Near Bellinzona: San Bernardino Pass

A short bus ride from Bellinzona, the San Bernardino Pass leads into the heart of the Alps and from there into literature and the imagination. The harsh, weather-beaten, snow-capped peaks immediately conjure up the age old struggle between man and the elements—one pictures long rope-trains of hikers with their wool hats and leather straps, or one grabs for an old copy of Hemingway or a Baedeker and a swig of whisky. The hiking and biking through this romantic playland reveal vistas and natural wonders that will put a swing in anyone's stride and a good, clean whistle on your lips. The San Bernardino **tourist office** (tel. (091) 832 12 14; 1626m) has information on hiking and skiing, including maps (open Mon.-Fri. 8:30am-noon and 2-5pm; Sat.-Sun. 8:30am-noon). From the bus stop walk straight 10 meters and make your first left, walk straight on this road for 200m (there are no street names), and the tourist office is on the left. Grab a pizza (12SFr) at **Ristorante Pizzeria Postiglione** (tel. 832 12 14), at the bus stop (open Tues.-Sun. 9:30am-10pm) or stock up on trail mix at the **Satellite Denner.** Go right from the bus stop—opposite direction from the tourist office—and the supermarket is 100m away on your left (open Mon.-Fri. 8:30am-noon and 3-6:30pm; Sat. 8:30am-noon and 2-5:30pm). Bushed after a long climb from Bellinzona? Stay at the alpine hut, **Capanna Genziana** (tel. (091) 832 12 04). To reach the hut, continue past Denner, over a small stream, and bear left. Then bear right at the next intersection, and follow the signs to the San Bernardino Pass; the hut is on your right. Sparse rooms with bunk beds provide all you need (25SFr; breakfast included).

There are several hikes that lead up to the village of **Ospizio** and the **San Bernardino Pass** (2065m). The easiest way is to follow the road past the Capanna Genziana for 1½hr. There are trails through the taiga and alpine trees, but these are only sporadically marked by white and red paint marks or posts. Make sure you have a map and a friend when using the trail system. The shores of the pure alpine lake, Lago Moesola, await, as do commanding views of the valley. This is a congregation point for cyclists and hikers among the stately and solitary Alps. A small restaurant marks the village of Ospizio, where you can refuel and exchange stories with other pass breakers. A postal bus travels on to **Thusis** (22SFr); from there, catch a train to **Chur** (12.20SFr), or keep on truckin'; the valley seems to go on forever.

GRAUBÜNDEN (GRISONS)

The largest, least populous, and most Alpine of the Swiss cantons, Graubünden's remote valleys and snow-clad peaks are bound to bring out the wild-hearted, lusting-for-life yodeler in everyone. Deep, rugged gorges, forests of larch and fir, and eddying rivers imbue the region with a wildness seldom found in ultra-civilized Switzerland. The area is also a microcosm of Swiss cultural heterogeneity—from valley to valley the language changes from German to Romansch to Italian, with a wide range of dialects in between. Though only 1-2% of the country converses in the ancient Romansch tongue, it is a fiercely preserved subject in schools and books, especially hymnals, and is recognized as an official language, whereas Swiss-German is not.

Once a summer visiting spot, the region was changed forever by the St. Moritz hotel pioneer Johannes Badrutt in 1864. The innkeeper made a bet with four British summer visitors: if they came back in the winter and didn't like it, he would pay their travel costs from London and back. If they did like it, he'd let them stay as long as they wanted, *for free*. Alas, that was the last of cheap housing in Graubünden. It made the area a popular ski resort but now even the youth hostels have lamentably high prices. This may be the Switzerland of Heidi, but it is also now a point of mountain pilgrimage for Hollywood celebrities and existing royal families. Diamonds, gold, and furs, oh my! Yet the environs retain their original untamed nature once you step off the beaten (gilded?) track.

Travel around the Graubünden is made easier with the **Graubünden Regional Pass,** which allows 5 days of unlimited travel in a 15-day period, and a 50% discount on the other days (133SFr, children 16 and under 66.50SFr), or 3 days of unlimited travel in a 7-day period, also with a 50% discount on the other days (100SFr, children 50SFr). The Regional Pass is issued in Switzerland only from May through October. The ubiquitous **Swisspass** is valid as well. Visitors should plan excursions carefully in this part of the country; high season, when reservations are absolutely indispensable, runs December to mid-April and peaks again in July and August. In May and early June virtually everything shuts down as locals take their own vacations.

▓ Chur

The capital of Graubünden, Chur may be Switzerland's oldest settlement; it was a thriving religious and commercial center as early as 400AD when the Romans established the town as a key checkpoint on the north-south passageway. Chur fails to measure up to any standard as a cultural mecca, but it is an important transport nexus between the Engadin Valley and the rest of Switzerland. Should masked bandits commandeer your train and throw you off at Chur, don't be afraid to leave the train station and explore this transportation hub, however. The sights are all within walking distance of the town's center, making Chur an easily manageable city. The 12th-century Romanesque **cathedral,** at the top of the old town, boasts eight altarpieces in addition to the **Hochaltar,** a stunning flamboyant masterpiece of gold and wood. The crypts, where the Capuchin martyr St. Fidelis is buried, also house the **Dom-museum**

(tel. 252 92 50), replete with many dated religious relics (open Mon.-Sat. 10am-noon and 2-4pm; request key at Hofstr. 2). The **Martinskirche,** down some stairs, counters the Cathedral's grandiose flair with understated simplicity; the church's sole decorations are three stained-glass windows designed by Augusto Giacometti. Chur's **Bündner Kunstmuseum** (tel. 257 28 68), at the corner of Bahnhofstr. and Grabenstr., gathers the canton's treasures, including an impressive collection of the works of three Giacomettis: Giovanni, Alberto, and Augusto. (Open Tues.-Wed. and Fri.-Sun. 10am-noon and 2-5pm, Thurs. 10am-noon and 2-8pm. 8SFr, students 5SFr.)

Budget accommodations are few and far between. Alas, the *Jugendherberge* has departed in hopes of a better life in youth hostel heaven, and finding a private room is perhaps more difficult than teaching a fish to ride a bicycle. On the outskirts of the old town, **Hotel Rosenhügel,** Malixerstr. 32 (tel./fax 252 23 88), possesses a friendly English-/French-/Italian-/German-speaking receptionist and a panoramic view of the city. From the train station (15min.), head right, and take Engadinstr.; follow it straight (even as it becomes Grabenstr.) to the intersection. At the intersection, continue on Malizerstr. (the road with an incline), and the hotel is 5min. away on your right. (Reception open 8am-midnight. Singles 45SFr, with view 50SFr. Doubles 90SFr, with shower 100SFr, and toilet 120SFr. Breakfast and parking included. Visa, MC, AmEx.) Try the hotel's restaurant (open Sun.-Thurs. 7:30am-10:30pm, Fri.-Sat. 7:30am-midnight) and its pizza (10.50SFr and up). If you've got a tent buried somewhere in your backpack, try **Camp Au Chur,** Felsenaustr. (tel. 284 22 83). Au dear. The site features a très large sports complex featuring tennis, swimming, and an excellent Rhine-side location. Take bus #2 direct to "Obere Au." Walk past the sports complex cash registers, and hang a left on the gravel path; the campsite is a 5-minute walk from there (one person 12.40SFr, two people 15.70SFr; must have your own tent). The **Co-op Center,** at the corner of Alexanderstr. and Quaderstr., off Bahnhofstr., mimics fine dining with a café of its own. (Market open Mon.-Thurs. 8am-6:30pm, Fri. 8am-9pm, Sat. 8am-5pm.) Cross-town rival **Migros,** at the corner of Gäuggelistr. and Gürtelstr., off Engadinstr., offers much of the same. (Market and restaurant open Mon.-Thurs. 8am-6:30pm, Fri. 8am-9pm, Sat. 8am-5pm.) Or step up to the classy atmosphere of **Restaurant Welschdörfli** in the Hotel Chur, Welschdörfli (tel. 252 52 44), where you have a choice of pizza (10.20-16.80SFr), pasta (11.50-19.90SFr), or a specialty from the Greek kitchen (4.80-20.50SFr; open Mon.-Fri. 7am-midnight, Sat. 6pm-midnight, Sun. 7pm-11pm). Hit the alternative scene at **Shoarma-Grill,** Untergasse 5 (tel. 252 73 22), packed with twentysomethings, world music, and alternative beats. (Kababs 7.50SFr, falafel 6.80SFr, beers start at 3.50SFr. Open Mon.-Fri. 11:45am-2pm and 5pm-midnight, Sat. 11:45am-midnight.) For all its lack of flavor, a surprisingly lively young crowd takes Chur by night.

From the Ticino, **postal buses** run between Chur and **Bellinzona** (2hr.15min., 5 daily, 50SFr plus 5SFr reservation fee). Chur is accessible to the rest of Switzerland by rail via **Zürich** (1½hr., every ½hr., 37SFr). Direct trains also connect Chur to **Basel** (2½hr., hourly, 59SFr), **Disentis** for the **Furka-Oberalp line** (2½hr., hourly, 25SFr), **Arosa** (1hr., hourly, 11.40SFr), **St. Gallen** (1½hr., hourly, 32SFr), and **St. Moritz** (2hr., hourly, 39SFr). The **train station** provides **currency exchange** (open daily 5:40am-9:15pm), **luggage storage** (5SFr), and **bike rental** (21SFr) at the baggage check (daily 5:40am-9:15pm), and **lockers** (2SFr) and **telephones** all day long. Chur's **tourist office,** Grabenstr. 5 (tel. 252 18 18; fax 252 90 76), will help you find a room for a 2SFr fee. From the train station, walk to the left and up Bahnhofstr.; at the second intersection (Postplatz), make a left on Grabenstr. (open Mon.-Tues. 1:30-6pm, Wed.-Fri. 8:30am-noon and 1:30-6pm, Sat. 9am-noon). The tourist office offers walking tours of the city in English on Mondays at 2:30pm, meeting at the Rathaus (6SFr, children under 16 3SFr). Graubünden's **regional tourist office,** Alexanderstr. 24 (tel. 254 24 24; fax 254 24 00), also located in Chur, brims with brochures covering every city in the canton. From the station, head down Bahnhofstr. and take an immediate left on Alexanderstr. (open Mon.-Fri. 8am-noon and 1:30-5:30pm). English books are available at **F. Schuler,** Gäuggelistr. (open Mon. 1-6:30pm, Tues.-Thurs. 8:30am-6:30pm, Fri. 8:30am-9pm, Sat. 8:30am-4pm). **Emergency:** tel. 117. **Postal code:** CH-7000. **Telephone code:** 081.

■ Arosa

Once a simple farming village, Arosa's fate was transformed by a certain Dr. Herwig's "discovery" of Arosa's salutary climate in 1888. Since then, Arosa has metamorphosed twice, first into a spa for the treatment of tuberculosis, and then into a skiing and hiking mecca. Sitting just below craggy peaks that seem to ooze granite, the town possesses outstanding views, as well as clean air, and hides at the end of an alpine valley. Hiking in the above tree-lined landscape, skiing the slopes, lolling in the sun next to a mountain stream, or sipping cappuccino on an outdoor terrace are all acceptable activities in this mile-high village. Arosa's biggest asset is that it is slightly less glitzy and glamorous than its sister resorts in the Engadin Valley.

In winter, 14 **ski lifts and cableways** hoist skiers to the 70-km network of slopes in the Arosa-Tschuggen ski area. The ticket offices in Arosa seem to love making **passes** (day passes, morning passes, afternoon passes, 1½-day passes, "choose-your-day" passes, etc., etc.); don't exhaust your entire vacation pondering all of your options. Passes issued for the use of all 14 lifts and cableways run 49SFr per day, 239SFr for one week, and 362SFr for two weeks; for those with small children in need of a little practice, the smaller Tschuggen sector day pass is 30SFr. Children under 15 ski for half-price; young people 16-19 get a 15% discount. Arosa's mountain peaks barely dip under 2000m, and the tallest, the **Weisshorn,** towers 2653m above sea level. For those affected by vertigo, Arosa's 25km of cross-country ski trails, ice rinks, indoor tennis courts, and swimming pools are perfect winter treats.

When the snow melts, Arosa's snow-covered hillsides transform into golf courses and flower-covered **hiking** paths, with over 200km for rambling and prancing. Every Tuesday, Wednesday, and Thursday from mid-June to mid-October, an alpine guide leads 7- and 9-hr. hikes at beginner, intermediate, and advanced levels for only 10SFr (contact the tourist office). The comprehensive system of cable cars provide scenic (and physically non-taxing) trips into the valley's upper reaches. The **Weisshornbahn** leaves from just behind the train station and whisks travelers to the top of the Weis-serhorn in a 100 person cable car. (Departs every 15min.; one-way 9SFr, round-trip 30SFr; 30% discount with SwissPass.)

From the summit (2496m), one can see all of the Engadin and back to San Bernardino. For more snow-capped peaks than you can shake a walking stick at, hike off the stoically gallant peak, and follow the yellow signs down along the ridge to the Hörnli-Express. (Return to Arosa on the Hörnli-Express is valid with your ticket up the Weis-shornbahn. 1½hr.; Hörnli tickets one-way 24SFr, round-trip 30SFr. 30% reduction with Swisspass.) There are also myriad splendid hikes back down to Arosa from the Weisserhorn peak, most take about 2-2½hrs. For a mellow hike below treeline, cruise along the ridge overlooking the Obersee to the small town of Maran, where you can catch a bus back to Arosa (1hr., start at the hill to the right of the Co-op, as you face the Co-op). For the more sedentary, the fish of the Obersee and local rivers bite frisk-ily. (Permits sold at the tourist office; day 25SFr, week 65SFr, 2 weeks 100SFr, month 125SFr.) The Untersee's free beach welcomes swimmers and sunbathers.

Orientation and Practical Information Arosa's pastel pink **tourist office,** Poststr. (tel. 377 51 51; fax 377 31 35), can help arrange ski lessons and hiking trips, and makes free hotel reservations. Head right from the station, and then take the first right onto Poststr. Or take the free **bus** that leaves from the newsstand two stops to "Kursaal." (Open Dec. 7-April 13 Mon.-Fri. 9am-6pm, Sat. 9am-5:30pm, Sun. 10am-noon and 4-5:30pm; April 14-Dec. 6 Mon.-Fri. 8am-noon and 2-6pm, Sat. 8am-1pm; June 29-Aug. 17 Sat. also open 2-4pm.) The **train station** provides **currency exchange** (Mon.-Sat. 5:30am-8:05pm, Sun. 6:30am-8:05pm), **lockers** (2SFr), **bike rental** (21SFr), and **telephones.** Secluded Arosa is accessible by **train** only via a scenic route from **Chur** (1hr., every hr., 11.40SFr). **Parking** is free in the summer at the **Parking Garage Obersee,** but the rates are steep during the ski season. Beware—a traffic ban has been imposed from midnight to 6am every night, and if broken could impart large fines. Climb on board the **free public bus,** which stops at the Hörnli and Prätschli ski lifts, the Untersee, the train station, and everywhere in between. **Emergency:** tel. 117. The **post office** is in Arosa's main square, just right of the train station (open Mon.-Fri. 7:45am-noon and 1:45-6:30pm, Sat. 8-11am). **Postal code:** CH-7050. **Telephone code:** 081.

Accommodations and Food Arosa's hotels tend to demand high prices for "Bliss at 1800 Meters," but there are a number of budget options. Arriving in town without making reservations first is a no-no. Most places set arbitrary opening dates, including the accommodations listed below, so it is impossible to foretell what will be open at any given time. The **Jugendherberge (HI),** Seewaldstr. (tel./fax 377 13 97), is equipped with a friendly, multilingual staff. The pale yellow building was recently renovated, and offers inexpensive rooms in a prime location. Walk right from the station, and turn on the first street to your right (Poststr.); then go past the tourist office, and bear left down the hill (you'll see a sign). Or take the free bus from the newsstand, get off two stops later at "Kursaal," continue past the tourist office, and bear left down the hill. (Reception open daily 7-9:30am and 5-10pm. No lockout. Curfew 10pm, but you can get a key. Dorms 24SFr; doubles, triples, quads 29SFr per person. In high season (Dec. 26-Jan. 10, Feb.-mid-March, and Easter week) dorms 36SFr, doubles, triples, quads 46SFr. Sheets and hearty breakfast included. Show-ers.50SFr. Lunch pack 7.50SFr. Dinner 12SFr. Open mid-June to mid-Oct. and mid-Dec. to mid-April.) Hidden up in the woods, **Pension Suveran** (tel. 377 19 69; fax 377 19 75) is the quiet, homey, wood-paneled châlet that you came to Switzerland in search of. It also offers the least expensive housing in Arosa aside from the youth hostel. To the right of the Co-op, head up to the left on the small walkway; at the top, turn right, walk, and follow the sign up the gravel path. (In summer, 42SFr per person with 5SFr added for stays less than 3 nights. In winter 53SFr per person with a 10SFr supplement. Breakfast included. For a single room, add 5SFr in both seasons.) **Hotel Garni Haus Am Wald,** behind the train station and 150m to the left of the Weisshornbahn (tel./fax 377 31 38), offers clean, bright rooms with a small café downstairs. Call ahead to make sure they are accepting guests. (In summer, singles 45-55SFr, doubles 90-104SFr. In winter singles 70-80SFr, doubles 120-140SFr.) **Camping Arosa** (tel. 377 17 45; fax 377 30 05) is open year-round in a quiet riverside location and offers showers and cooking facilities (7.30-8.30SFr per person, plus tax, children 4-4.50SFr, tents 4.50SFr). For a tasty and scenic meal, head to **Orelli's Restaurant,** Poststr. (tel. 377 12 08), after the post office and before the tourist office. Make sure to eat on the south-facing deck. A family-oriented restaurant with special kids' meals and senior citizen discounts, Orelli's also has a special vegetarian menu (14-16.50SFr), salad buffet (6.20-14SFr), and warm entrées (10-16SFr). (Open 7:30am-9pm. Closed in May and Nov. Visa, MC.) **Café/Restaurant Oasis** (tel. 377 22 20), diagonally across the street from Orelli's, has an outdoor deck just over Poststr, good for people watching and mountain gazing. Cheap entrées include spaghetti *bolognese* with parmesan cheese (11SFr), spaghetti and tomato sauce with parmesan cheese (11SFr), or chicken cordon bleu with fries for 15SFr (open daily 8:30am-11pm; during May, June, Sept., Oct., and Nov. closed Sun.). Bag your groceries at the **Co-op,** just before the tourist office on Poststr. (open Mon.-Fri. 8am-12:30pm and 2-6:30pm, Sat. 8am-4pm), or at **Denner Superdiscount** in the main square. (Open Mon.-Wed. and Fri. 8:30am-12:15pm and 2:30-6:30pm, Sat. 8:30am-12:15pm, and 1:15-4pm.) The 1997 International Jazz Festival will be held July 17-20 with free admission to various local venues. The festival features New Orleans style jazz played by American, Swiss, Australian, and English bands. Previous performers include Tuba Fats and Jambalaya.

■ Davos

A famed international vacation venue, Davos is the strongest challenger to St. Moritz's hegemony as the ski and spa capital of Graubünden. Settled in 1289 by the Walsers, Davos emerged as a health resort in the 19th century, and quickly developed into a finely-tuned skiing center of international renown. Part of Davos's appeal is its mixture of town and country; while most ski resorts feel as remote as the mountains on which they rest, Davos maintains a cosmopolitan atmosphere while perched high in the Swiss Alps.

Orientation and Practical Information Davos is easily accessible from the rest of Switzerland by **train** through **Chur** (1½hr., hourly, 26SFr, change in Landquart) or **Klosters** (8.40SFr) on the Rhätische Bahn lines. The town is divided into two areas, **Davos-Dorf** and **Davos-Platz** (each with its own train station), which are linked by the long **Promenade.** Davos maintains an intra-city **bus** line which travels between the two train stations, with stops near the major hotels and the youth hostel on the Davosersee (2SFr). Davos-Dorf is closer to most hotels and the Bergbahn, while Davos-Platz is the center of administration, with the tourist office and the main post office. Drivers to Davos will find many **parking lots** along the Promenade and Talstr., but should be aware that the Promenade has one-way traffic heading west (parking is generally 1SFr per hr.; free parking at Kongresszentrum). The high-tech **main tourist office,** 67 Promenade in Davos-Platz (tel. 415 21 21; fax 415 21 00), plans skiing and hiking packages, helps find rooms, and generally knows all. Walk up the hill to the right of the Davos-Platz train station, and then right along Promenade for 5min. The tourist office is on the left. A smaller **branch** office, across from the Davos-Dorf train station, also offers information and kindly calls hotels. (Both offices open June 22-Sept. 28 and Dec. 1-April 15 Mon.-Fri. 8:30am-6pm, Sat. 8:30am-4pm; April 16-June 21 Mon.-Fri. 8:30am-12:30pm and 1:45-6pm, Sat. 8:30am-12:30pm;

Sept. 30-Dec. 1 also open Sat. 1:45-4pm. Telephone hours: June 22-Sept. 28 and Dec. 1-April 15 Mon.-Fri. 8am-7pm, Sat. 8am-4pm; April 16-June 21 8am-12:30pm; Sept. 30-Dec. 1 8am-12:30pm and 1:45-4pm.) Both train stations **exchange currency** (open daily 7am-8pm), **store luggage** (Platz luggage open Mon.-Sat. 4:30am-8pm, Sun. 5:30am-8pm; Dorf luggage open daily 6:50am-9pm; 5SFr at both stations), and provide **lockers** (2SFr) and **telephones**. Rent bikes at the Davos-Dorf station (21SFr per day). Davos's main **post office** is in Davos-Platz, at 43 Promenade (open Mon.-Fri. 7:45am-6pm, Sat. 8:30am-11pm). **Postal code:** CH-7270. **Telephone code:** 081.

Accommodations and Food The **Jugendherberge Höhwald (HI)**, in Davos-Wolfgang (tel. 416 14 84; fax 416 50 55), has seen its share of ski seasons. The old house sits directly on the Davosersee, and is complete with a large front porch and swimming dock. Take the bus in the direction of Davos-Wolfgang to "Hochgebirgsklinik," backtrack 100m and turn left; or head right from the Davos-Dorf train station, and walk ½hr. along the Davosersee. (Reception open 8-11am and 5-9pm. No lockout. No curfew, but quiet time from 10:30pm. Dorms in summer 22.70SFr first night, 20.20SFr thereafter; in winter 23.10SFr, 20.60SFr. Doubles in summer 28.20SFr per person first night, 25.70SFr thereafter; in winter 28.60SFr, 26.10SFr. Family rooms available. Sheets, showers, and breakfast included. Kitchen facilities 2SFr. Lunch pack or dinner 11SFr. Closed April 22-June 7 and Oct. 24-Dec. 13.) The **Gasthaus Seehorn** (tel. 416 31 61; fax 416 62 51) is also on the Davoser See, halfway to the other end, on the left side from Davos-Dorf. It has a friendly international staff and a lovely outdoor deck overlooking the mountains and water. (Singles 50SFr; doubles 100-122SFr. Add 6SFr for stays of only one night and for using a double room as a single. Breakfast included. Open Dec.-April 15, June-Nov. 1.) **Hotel Edelweiss**, Rosswiedstr. 9 (tel. 416 10 33; fax 416 11 30), in Davos-Dorf provides bright, clean rooms that are a welcome break from the chic hotels just up the hill. (Reception open 7am-10pm. In summer, singles 38-105SFr; doubles 80-170SFr. In winter, singles 47-105SFr; doubles 96-170SF. Breakfast included. Visa, MC, AmEx. Closed April-June 15.) Wherever you stay, ask for the Davos **visitor's card,** which entitles you to free unlimited travel on the city bus, as well as reductions for theater performances, concerts, ice rinks, swimming pools, and golf. **Camping Färich**, in Davos-Dorf (tel. 416 10 43), is a four-star facility that lies relatively close to the ski lifts and attractions of the town. Take bus #1 (dir: Pischa) to "Stilli" (4.80-5.80SFr, children half-price; tent 5.20SFr; open May 18-Sept. 29). The newly re-modeled, bright, and flowery **Café-Konditorei Weber,** 148 Promenade (tel. 416 24 13) in Davos-Dorf, offers colorful and friendly service to match. Choose from the daily *menu*, which includes at least one vegetarian dish (10-18SFr), or order a la carte (from 11SFr; open daily 6:30am-7pm). Grab a Bud and a bar stool—American style—at **Café Carlo's**, 58 Promenade (tel. 413 17 22), in Davos-Platz across from the tourist office offers a daily *menu* (12.50-15.50SFr), salad (6-10SFr), sandwiches (10-14SFr), and pasta (12.50-18SFr; open daily 8am-midnight; Visa, MC, AmEx). Haven't had your *rösti* fix for the day yet? Shame on you. Head for the **Röstizzeria** at 128 Promenade, where you can satisfy your craving for 14.50SFr and up, or choose pizza (11SFr and up; open Mon.-Sat. 5pm-midnight, Sun. 11am-2pm and 5pm-midnight). For a local hole in the wall, try **Restaurant Helvetia**, Talstrasse 12 (tel. 413 56 44), a 10-minute walk out of the train station and to the right. Decorated with sports memorabilia and other oddities (look for the New Hampshire "Davos" vanity plate), the restaurant serves up spaghetti (9.50SFr) and *kalbswurst* with *rösti* (14SFr; open Mon.-Sat. 10am-2pm and 5pm-midnight). For hiking snacks, stop by **Migros** on the Promenade in both Davos-Dorf (open Mon.-Fri. 8:30am-12:30pm and 1:30-6:30pm, Sat. 8am-4pm) and Davos-Platz (open Mon.-Fri. 8:30am-6:30pm, Sat. 8am-4pm).

Sights and Entertainment Davos provides direct access to three mountains: the **Parsenn, Schatzalp,** and **Jakobshorn,** and five **skiing areas,** covering every degree of difficulty. **Day passes** start at 25SFr for the Schatzalp and go all the way to 46SFr for the Jakobshorn. **Regional ski passes** are offered for the Davos-Klosters area, including unlimited travel on most transport facilities (2 days 113SFr, week 288SFr). Comprehensive information and maps are available at the tourist office. In summer the lifts service hikers. (Jakobshorn 23SFr up, 20SFr down, 27SFr round-trip. Schatzalp 10SFr up, 8SFr down, 12SFr round-trip.) Apart from winter downhill skiing, Davos boasts 75km of **cross-country trails** throughout the valley, including one trail flood-lit at night and a trail on which dogs are allowed. **The Swiss Ski School of Davos,** 157 Promenade, offers lessons, starting at 30SFr for a half-day downhill lesson, 50SFr for a half-day snowboard lesson (tel. 416 24 54; fax 416 59 51 for information and booking). Europe's largest natural **ice rink** (22,000 square meters) reserves space for figure skating, ice dancing, hockey, speed skating, and curling (tel. 415 21 15; 5SFr; skates can be rented at the rink). Davos does not wilt when the snow melts. Instead, the town refocuses itself and offers indoor/outdoor **swimming pools** with sauna and solarium (6.50SFr, students 4.50SFr), and of course, the **Davosersee,** in which you can swim and fish, and on which you can sail and windsurf. Fishing permits available at the tourist office (day 72SFr, week 209SFr, month 443SFr). A highlight in the end of July is the **Swiss Alpine Marathon,** a grueling 67km mountain race (always the last Sat. in July; July 26 in 1997). Davos' snowless slopes uncover a web of over 450 km of **hiking** trails. The exquisite mountains engulfing the Metro-Davos area provide views deep into the Dolomites and all along the valley. One possible day hike begins at the top of Jakobshorn (2590m) and traverses a ridge over Jatzhorn (2682m) to Tällifurgga (2568m). See the areas where only the boldest hike and ski. meander down the velvety green ski slopes to the village of Sertig Dörfli. The hike from the summit to Sertig Dörfli takes 3hr., Davos Platz is another 2½hr. from Sertig Dörfli, walking down the Sertigtal valley.

A hike (or funicular ride) up to the Schatzalp reveals the **Alpine Garden** with 800 different species of plants. (Open mid-May to Sept. daily 9am-5pm. 3SFr. Guided tours in German every Mon. at 2pm—other languages by arrangement.) Once you've finished exercising your muscles, exercise your eyes at the **Davos Kirchner Museum** (tel. 413 22 02), the frosted glass structure across from the grand Hotel Belvedere on the Promenade, which houses one of the most extensive collections of Ernst Ludwig Kirchner's artwork. His creations are best known as archetypes of the German Expressionism movement of the early 20th century. Kirchner lived in Davos for nearly 20 years before his death, and is buried in the Davos cemetery. (Museum open mornings from July 15-Sept. 30, exhibitions Tues.-Sun. 10am-noon. 7SFr, students 4SFr; during exhibitions 9SFr, students 6SFr.) Davos's **Heimatmuseum** (tel. 416 17 82), on Museumstr. behind the train station in Davos-Dorf, displays a collection of centuries-old furniture and crafts of the Graubünden region. (Open June to mid-Oct. and Jan. to mid-April Wed., Fri., and Sun. 4-6pm, or by appointment.) Before catching the train out of Davos, stop by the **Evangelische Kirche St. Johann** in Davos-Platz, across from the post office, up the hill from the train station. The church, built in 1335, has gone through several renovations, including the installation of a stained glass window by Augusto Giacometti in 1928.

De luge

Before the advent of spandex uni-suits and titanium, flying down mountains was a very simple affair. As early as 1883, the natives of Arosa increasingly found their rustic sleds missing, and the hills outside the town sprinkled with very bored and very insane recovering English invalids. These dashing chaps officially brought the sport of Tobogganing to Switzerland in 1883 when they started the Davos Tobogganing club and inaugurated the famed Cresta Run. Among the many innovations tested on the Arosa hills were iron runners and the implementation of the head-first plunge. A quote from *The Bystander* in 1905 perhaps summed it up best: "Tobogganing itself is absurd. It glories in being absurd."

■ Klosters

Across the Gotschna and Parsenn mountains lies Davos' sister ski resort, Klosters. A smaller, more subdued town, you'd think Klosters would suffer in Davos' shadow. Yet Klosters' charm and surprisingly mellow atmosphere draws just as many skiers. A favorite spot of winter repose for Charles, Fergie, and your other favorite royal soap stars (when they aren't divorcing, cavorting, or carousing), Klosters is a four-star resort that embraces its glitzy visitors as well as its lovely countryside. Its hotels and ski runs blend tactfully into the Swiss countryside. And while Davos makes an extra effort to be a city, Klosters succeeds in keeping a low profile; even its upper-crust hotels look like unassuming Swiss châlets.

If you're looking for entertainment in Klosters, one word sums up your best options: **skiing.** Klosters, combined with the mountains in the Davos area, has some of the best skiing in Switzerland, with 315km of trails. **Ski passes** for the Klosters-Davos region run 113SFr for two days and 288SFr for one week (includes public transportation). For just the Klosters area, a Grotschna, Parsenn, Strela/Schatzalp, Madrisa one-day ticket goes for 52SFr, one week 246SFr. The **ski school** in Klosters, located conveniently in the tourist office, offers private, group, and snowboard lessons for children and adults; class instruction starts at 40SFr per day (call 422 13 80 the day before to book private lessons). All of these packages combine with 40km of cross-country trails, an ice rink, and sled runs to make Klosters a winter *Wunderland*. In summer, the tourist office makes available an extensive list of **hiking** suggestions, including exact directions, elevation levels, anticipated times, and a map of the 250km of trails. From early July to early October, the mountain cable car to the **Madrisa** provides a fantastic opportunity to explore the peaks all the way into Austria (15SFr up, 10SFr down, 18SFr round-trip). Guided tours (typically a 4-5hr. hike each day) include accommodations, breakfast, and dinner, and start at 80SFr for the two-day hike and 155SFr for the three-day hike (tel. 422 23 23; advance booking recommended; don't forget your passport).

Klosters offers plenty of bang for your shoe leather, even for the less ambitious. The **Gotschna-bahn** cable car whisks you up to Gotschnagrat (2285m) for incredible views of the Silvrettagletscher, Klosters, and the quintessentially Swiss valley embracing the village. Take a leisurely 3-hr. walk down to Klosters, crossing the ski runs just below the striking, jagged peak known as Casanna Alp. Drop below treeline and follow the signs to Serneuser Schwendi and Klosters. Got vertigo? Stay closer to the luscious green valley floor and make a large loop, going from the Klosters Protestant church up-valley on Monbielstr. to Monbiel. Loop around toward the left and follow the signs to Pt. 487 and Monbieler Wald. The trail comes to fruition at the Alpenrösli restaurant, from where you can grab Talstr. back to the hostel. The **Klosters Adventure Program** offers guided hikes and mountain tours, canyonning, and river rafting, as well as mountain bike tours, paragliding, and the **Rock Adventure Garden** every Monday through Friday from mid-June to mid-October. These events are generally free for people staying at Adventure hotels, including the Jugendherberge Soldanella. Big discounts with only a guest card. (Guided hikes: adventure hotel guests free, with guest card 15SFr. Mountain bike tours: guests free, with guest card 15SFr. River rafting: guests 130SFr, with guest card 135SFr. Canoeing: guests 140SFr, with guest card 145SFr.)

Like everything else in Klosters, the **Jugendherberge Soldanella (HI),** Talstr. 73 (tel. 422 13 16; fax 422 52 09), is quietly elegant, laid back, and unassuming. Head right from the Klosters-Platz train station, bear left at the rotary, turn right on Talstr., and hike 10 minutes uphill. This massive renovated Swiss châlet with wood paneling and a stunning view down the valley allows its guests to relax in the garden and enjoy a view of the Madrisa as well as distant glaciers from the flagstone terrace staffed by a friendly and knowledgeable family. (Reception open daily 7-9:30am and 5-10pm. No lockout, no curfew. Quiet time from 10pm. Dorms 25.50SFr first night, 23SFr thereafter. Doubles 36.50SFr, then 34SFr. Add 1.90SFr tax in summer and 2.20SFr tax in winter to each day. Sheets, shower, and savory breakfast included. Family rooms

EASTERN SWITZERLAND

available. Dinner 11SFr. Closed May to mid-June and Nov. to mid-Dec. Visa, MC, AmEx.) **Gasthaus Casanna,** 171 Landstr. (tel. 422 12 29; fax 422 62 78), offers pink-flowered comforters that clash with the brown carpeting, and a restaurant that serves diverse *fondues.* (In summer singles 50SFr; doubles 100SFr. In winter singles 60SFr; doubles 120SFr. Breakfast included.) Better yet, choose from the impressive list of **private rooms** starting at 15SFr (available at the tourist office). **Chesa Grischuna,** Bahnhofstr. 12 (tel. 422 22 22), to the right of the Klosters-Platz train station, cooks up some rather expensive meat dishes, but if you stick to the cheeses and salads, you can still enjoy a filling dinner (cheese plate 8SFr, salads 8.50-16SFr, soups and sandwiches 9-12SFr, vegetarian plate 18.50SFr). Make reservations during winter—even the celebrities who come here do. (Open daily 7am-11pm, or until the last person leaves; kitchen open for hot food daily 11:30am-9:30pm. Visa, MC, AmEx. Closed May and Nov.) **À Porta,** Bahnhofstr. 22, on the corner with Landstr. (tel. 422 14 96), is a nearly 70-year-old, family-run restaurant and bakery that serves fresh pizzas starting at 12SFr and German-Swiss dishes, such as *rösti* with ham and onions (14.50SFr; open daily 7:30am-10:30pm; closed Mon. and Tues. during Nov., May, and June). **Tasty bakery** serves sugary treats and fresh bread (open daily 10:30am-6:30pm), or stop by the **Co-op,** halfway to the train station, for sustenance (open Mon.-Fri. 8am-12:30pm and 2-6:30pm, Sat. 8am-4pm).

Klosters, like Davos, is divided into **Klosters-Platz** and **Klosters-Dorf;** the two are connected by a 20-minute walk, a 5-minute bus ride, or a 3-minute train ride. There are **tourist offices** in both Platz and Dorf, but the **main tourist office** is in Klosters-Platz (tel. 410 20 20; fax 410 20 10). From the train station, walk to the right, make a right at the Co-op, and cross the street to the building with the "i." The friendly and cheerful staff can help locate lodgings, suggest hikes, and even exchange currency. They also work closely with the ski school in planning ski packages. (Open in summer Mon.-Fri. 8am-noon and 2-6pm, Sat. 8am-noon and 2-6pm; in winter (Dec.-April) Mon.-Fri. 8am-noon and 2-6pm, Sat. 8am-noon and 2-6pm, Sun. 4-6pm; during low season, Sat. 8am-noon.) **Trains** arrive in Klosters-Platz and Klosters-Dorf, from **Chur** (1hr., hourly, 18.20SFr, change in Landquart) and **St. Moritz** (2hr., hourly, 32SFr). The Klosters-Platz **train station** provides **currency exchange** (open daily 6am-8:30pm), **lockers** (2SFr), **luggage storage** (open daily 6am-7pm; 3SFr), and **telephones.** The local **bus** in Klosters runs between Dorf and Platz and the major ski lifts (1-6 stops 1SFr, 7-10 2SFr, more than 10 3SFr). The bus is free with the **Klosters guest card,** which is also valid for bargain tickets to events and a number of reductions for local facilities; it is available in your hotel or at the tourist office. **Parking** is free in summer; in winter, parking cards for public parking run 20SFr for eight days, 40SFr for 16 days, and 80SFr for one month. They're available at the tourist office or from the local **police** (tel. 422 17 13). **Postal code:** CH-7250. **Telephone code:** 081.

■ Engadin Valley

Swiss skiing connoisseurs often rate the Engadin Valley behind the Jungfrau and Matterhorn regions. That's quite a glowing compliment considering that the skiing in Switzerland outranks almost everything anywhere else. But not so fast. Hiking here will make you swoon, too. The trails lead you away from the resort façade that encrusts the valley and into the Swiss wilderness, and whether you're out for a stroll along a babbling brook or scaling ancient glaciers, the Engadin delivers beauty and adventure. Most local tourist offices can recommend excellent hikes and set you up with maps. Perched proudly at the center of Upper Engadin, glitzy and glamorous St. Moritz is the hub of the Valley; most of the other villages make nice day trips.

SKIING

Spas propelled the Engadin Valley into the limelight, but ski slopes have kept it there. Three hundred and fifty kilometers of **ski trails** and 60 **ski lifts** lace the lower Graubünden, and thousands of ski bunnies gather here each year. Ski rental is standard throughout the region (downhill 35-45SFr per day, cross-country 25SFr). Novices should head for **Zuoz** or **Corviglia,** experts for **Diavolezza, Corvatsch, Piz Nair,** or **Piz Lagalb** (tel. (081) 833 88 88 or fax 833 76 68 for more information). Anyone hoping to catch a glimpse of Hollywood should head for **St. Moritz.** Passes covering transport and T-bars for the entire area run 48SFr per day (available in St. Moritz only), 286SFr per week, 442SFr for two weeks, and 900SFr for the season (all lifts; they also include access to indoor swimming pools). Cross-country fanatics can plant their poles at the world-famous **Engadin Ski Marathon,** stretching from Maloja to Zuoz. The race takes place every year on the second Sunday in March (call (081) 842 65 73 or fax 842 65 25 for an application/registration form; entry fee 70SFr). **Ski schools** in just about every village offer private lessons.

ST. MORITZ

In St. Moritz are the hangers-on of the rich…the jewel thieves, the professional backgammon players and general layabouts, as well as the high-class ladies of doubtful virtue (if such a thing still exists)…

—Peter Viertel

St. Moritz (1856m) is one of the most famous ski resorts in the world. Chic, elegant, and exclusive, it caters to all of Robin Leach's favorites. This "Resort at the Top of the World" will convert almost anyone into a window-shopper, as you are tamed by the like of Armani, Versace, and Gaultier. Surveying the lake below, St. Moritz glitters in the sunny heights of the Engadin hillsides. This focal point of the Engadin also provides you with a great place to test out your mud-caked boots, but clean them off before you do any star gazing—in St. Moritz, the streets of the town, which are tread by many of your favorite Hollywood friends, are posh and polished. The Alpine wilderness is kept neatly at bay from this town. The glamor of the town is nothing new. St. Moritz played host to the Olympic Games in 1928 and again in 1948. It's no wonder that the town offers every winter sport imaginable from world-class skiing (call 833 88 88 for ski packages) and bobsledding to golf, polo, and cricket tournaments on the frozen lake, to *skikjöring*—a sport similar to water skiing in which the water is replaced by ice and the motorboat is replaced by a galloping horse. Surprisingly, a larger number of guests travel to St. Moritz in the summer than in the winter. **Wind surfing** is one draw (tel. 833 44 49; sailboard: 2hr. 30-40SFr, private lessons 50SFr per hr.; 10 lessons 240SFr). **River rafting** is certainly another. (With Eurotrek (tel. (01) 462 02 03), ½day 80SFr, day 140SFr; with Swissraft (tel. (081) 911 52 50), ½day 60SFr, day 143SFr.) **Horseback riding** (tel. 833 57 33; 45SFr per hr., 80SFr for 2hrs.), and **clay pigeon shooting** (tel. 828 81 88; 15SFr) also add to the annual tourist flow.

The **Engadiner Museum,** 39 via dal Bagn (tel. 833 43 44), down Via dal Bagn from the tourist office, opens a window on daily life in the Engadin Valley. The house, built in 1905, was constructed as a typical example of Engadin architecture and is filled with antique furniture and curiosities. Explore the tiny doorways and intricate wood carvings and inlays of this mountain den. (Open June-Oct. Mon.-Fri. 9:30am-noon and 2-5pm, Sun. 10am-noon; Dec.-April Mon.-Fri. 10am-noon and 2-5pm, Sun. 10am-noon. 5SFr, students 4SFr, children 2.50SFr. Buy a pass here for both museums for 10SFr, students 8SFr.) One street up from the Engadiner Museum sits the domed tower of the **Segatini Museum,** 30 via Somplaz (tel. 833 44 54), dedicated to the Italian Expressionist painter. The museum is housed in a stone basilica and features some of Segantini's well known, wall-sized Alpine landscapes and portraits. (Open June-Oct. Tues.-Sat. 9am-12:30pm and 2:30-5pm, Sun. 10:30am-12:30pm and 2:30-6:30pm; Dec.-April Tues.-Sat. 10am-12:30pm and 3-5pm, Sun. 3-5pm. 7SFr, students 5SFr, children 2SFr.) The leaning tower at the top of the village does not bear any resemblance to the one of Italian fame; rather, it is all that is left of the 13th-century **St. Mauritius Church,** which was pulled down in 1890.

A pleasant **day hike** from St. Moritz to Pontresina takes you past the Olympic Ski Jump, towering glaciers and through narrow alpine valleys. From St. Moritz-Bad, at the junction of Via Mezdi and Via Teglatscha, walk to the **Hahnensee,** an Alpine lake. From there, follow the signs to Fuorcla-Surlej. The trail then snakes along to the Ova da Roseg and the Roseg valley downstream to Pontresina. (Walking time approx. 6hr.) To scout out the slopes on foot, before the ski season begins, ride up to **Corviglia** (one-way 14SFr, round-trip 21SFr) from St. Moritz and pick your line down (approx. 2hr.). From the top of Corviglia you can also take another lift up to **Piz Nair** (3075m; one-way from Corviglia 14SFr, round-trip 21SFr) and hike down to Survetta Lake (2580m) after enjoying the rooftop view of the Engadin. Picnics at **Survetta lake,** underneath the majestic **Piz Julier** (3380m) are a must. Rested and ready, follow the Ova da Survetta back down to the Signalbahn or St. Moritz. (Total time approx. 3hr.)

To find the **Jugenherberge Still (HI),** 60 Via Sur Punt (tel. 833 39 69; fax 833 80 46), follow the signs around the lake to the left of the station (30min.), or hop on the postal bus that leaves from the train station (dir: "Maloja") to "Hotel Sonne" (2.40SFr.), and from the bus stop go left on Via Sur Punt for 10min. The hostel is run more like a Republican convention than a youth hostel—huge, carpeted lobby, impersonal staff, spotlessly clean, and terse announcements over the intercom system reminding everyone that there are only 30 minutes remaining for breakfast. Finding the reception is an adventure in this enormous modern building; follow the red signs. (Reception open daily 7-9am, 4-5:30pm, 6-8pm, and 9-10pm. No lockout. Curfew midnight, but quiet hour starts at 10pm and keys available for late night expeditions. Dorms 41.50SFr first night, 39SFr thereafter. Doubles 108SFr, then 103SFr. Doubles with shower 130SFr, 125SFr thereafter. 5SFr surcharge for non-members. Sheets, showers, lockers, breakfast, and dinner included—show up before 7:15pm to get dinner. Laundry 4SFr. Visa, MC, AmEx.) You might opt instead to take the "See" exit at the train station and drop all your belongings at **Hotel Bellaval,** 55 via Gravass (tel. 833 32 45; fax 833 04 06). With its prime location on the lake and right behind the train station this hotel is the diamond in the rough of St. Moritz. (Reception open daily 7:30am-10pm. Singles 55SFr. Doubles 106-146SFr. Prices 5SFr per person more July-Aug.; 7SFr more Feb.-Easter. Huge delicious breakfast included. Closed Oct.-Dec. and Easter-May. Visa, MC, AmEx.) **Camping Olympiaschanze** (tel. 833 40 90) offers an agreeable location on its own little pond. Follow via Grevas from the station to via San Gian, then watch for signs (total 40min.). Or catch the postal bus to **St. Moritz-Bad Signal,** and walk along the foot path across the street to the right (away from the lake) for 10min. (tel. 833 40 90; 4.20-6SFr, children half-price, tent 5-6SFr; open May 18-Sept. 29).

Living the four-star lifestyle of St. Moritz is expensive. Unfortunately, *looking* as though you're living it is almost as pricey. An outdoor lunch at the **Giardino Café,** 54 via dal Bagn (tel. 832 21 71), on the flower-ridden terrace of the Hotel Schweizerhof, is a prime spot for mountain gazing. Try the verdant salad buffet (7-9SFr), daily special (16-18.50SFr), or choose something from the grill (12-21SFr; open 10am-6pm, contingent upon the weather). Or grab a floral cushioned lawn chair and relax on the deck of **Au Réduit,** 10 via Maistra, Réduit Passage (tel. 833 66 57), just around the corner from the tourist office. Specializes in homemade pasta (15-20SFr) and pizza (14-17.50SFr). Occasional live music played on the deck during the summer and year-round laid back atmosphere prevails (open 11am-1am, pizza after 6pm; Visa, MC, AmEx) The **Restaurant Engadinia** Piazza da Scoula (tel. 833 32 65), serves up your classic Swiss favorites including bratwurst with fries (16SFr) or the more Italian spaghetti Bolognese (16.50SFr; open Mon.-Sat. 8:30am-11pm). It never hurts to forage for groceries at the **Co-op Center,** one square up from the tourist office or on 20 via dal Bagn, *en route* to the youth hostel (open Mon.-Fri. 8am-12:15pm and 2-6:30pm, Sat. 8am-12:15pm and 2-5pm). And if you're here Jan. 23-Feb 1, 1997, try the culinary delights of the week-long annual **St. Moritz Gourmet Festival.**

The resort's give-as-much-information-as-possible **tourist office** *(Kurverein),* 12 via Maistra (tel. 837 33 33; fax 837 33 77), is located in the heart of town. From the train station, cross the street, climb Truoch Serlas, and take via Serla to the left past the post office. As you pass the Badrutt Palace Hotel on your left, make a right up the

Réduit Passage. Emerge from the shopping arcade onto via Maistra, and the tourist office is on the right. Stop by for free hotel reservations, skiing information, and advice on hiking in the smaller towns of the Engadin Valley. (Open July-mid-Sept. and mid-Dec. to mid-April Mon.-Sat. 9am-6pm; May and Nov. Mon-Fri. 8am-noon and 2-6pm.) The **train station** provides **currency exchange** (open daily 6:50am-8:10pm), **luggage storage** (5SFr; open daily 7:30am-6:15pm), **bike rental** (21SFr per day; open daily 7:30am-6:15pm), **lockers** (2SFr), and **telephones.** From the Matterhorn to the Engadin Valley, the legendary **Glacier Express** covers the 270km to **Zermatt** in a leisurely 8-hr. chug (1 daily, 140SFr, Swisspass valid), affording ample time to take in the magnificent Alpine landscapes while crossing 291 bridges and 91 tunnels. If you can't sit still for that long, the **Bernina Express** makes the excursion to **Tirano, Italy** (2½hr., hourly, 27SFr, Swisspass valid); it is the only Swiss train which crosses the Alps without a single tunnel. Trains also run every hour to **Chur** (2hr., 39SFr), **Celerina** (5min., 2.40SFr), **Pontresina** (15min., 4.20SFr), **Zuoz** (30min., 8.40SFr), and **Zernez** (1hr., 15.80SFr). Yellow **postal buses** (*not* the local blue buses) cover almost all the same routes as the trains, and are also your only access from the southwest tip of the Upper Engadin Valley since St. Moritz is the railway terminus. Buses run twice every hour to **Silvaplana** (15min., 3.60SFr), **Sils** (20min., 6SFr), and **Maloja** (40min., 9SFr), and depart from the left of the train station. **Emergency:** tel. 111. The **post office** is located on via Serla (open Mon.-Fri. 7:45am-noon and 1:45-6:15pm, Sat. 8-11am). **Postal code:** CH-7500. **Telephone code:** 081.

SILVAPLANA

At the foot of the Julier mountain pass, Silvaplana (1815m) is situated amidst the magnificent Upper Engadin lake country. Not unexpectedly, the town's main attraction is its **See** (lake). Silvaplana's beaches beckon sun-worshipers, campers, sailors, windsurfers, and hikers eager to soak their aching feet. The "Gorge" of Switzerland, the water's edge is host to a bevy of neoprene clad itinerant windsurfers. Rent sailboards next to the campground (tel. 828 92 29; 1hr. 20-25SFr, with wetsuit 25-30SFr; 2hrs. 30-40SFr, with wetsuit 40-50SFr; 1 day 50-60SFr, with wetsuit 60-80SFr; group lesson start at 50SFr per hour, but longer lessons of 9hrs. (240SFr) or 18hrs. (380SFr) are recommended for beginners; open June 15-Sept. 15 daily 9am-7pm). While the lake is free for all to enjoy, wind-surfing, sailing, and fishing fees reflect the lake's prime location and southern winds. Fishing *Tageskarten* (day tickets) start at 28SFr and weekend tickets will run you 66SFr. Monthly permits cost 132SFr. All permits are available at the tourist office. In August, Silvaplana hosts the **Nitro-Cup** (International Slalom Windsurfing Competition) and in July the **Swiss National Sailing and Windsurfing Championships.** Unfortunately, due to rising temperatures, the Corvatsch glacier is no longer large enough for summer skiing. Not to worry, snow is guaranteed in the winter. A cable car (tel. 828 82 42) ascends from **Surlej** (on the other side of the lake) high up into the **Piz Corvatsch** peak region (21SFr, round-trip 30SFr). The intermediate station of **Murtèl** (17SFr, round-trip 24SFr) is the center of an extended and varied ski region with links to Sils' **Furtschellas** runs and the downhill run past the Hahnensee Lake to St. Moritz (daily ski ticket 47SFr, children 34SFr; half-day 39SFr, children 29SFr; Graubünden pass and Swiss Card receive a 50% discount, Swisspass gets 25% reduction). From the Corvatsch cable car station, yodel your way up the rest of the glacier to **Piz Corvatsch** (3451m), from where you can see the entire glacier and the striking surrounding peaks. Resist the urge to jump into this seemingly large bowl of Ben and Jerry's glacial vanilla, it's a long way out and an even longer fall. The trip up takes 1-1½hr.; the trip down is approximately 20 minutes of hiking and 10 minutes of world class glissading. The **Wanderbillet** takes you from Surlej up to Corvatsch and then halfway down to Murtèl (25SFr, children 16 and under 13SFr), also a prime area for invigorating treks that traverse the valley. For a hike below the glaciers, walk from the mid-station to Fuorcla Surlej (2755m), and down to Pontresina crossing the mountain range along the Roseg valley (total trip takes approx. 4hrs). For flat-landlubbers, Silvaplana's **Sportszentrum Mulets** (tel. 828 93 62) offers tennis (18SFr per hr.), volleyball (20SFr for 2hrs.), and a soccer field (60SFr for 2hrs.) in summer,

EASTERN SWITZERLAND

which freezes over in winter for ice-skating, hockey, and the esoteric and bizarre European pastime, curling. Silvaplana offers ideal conditions for kiting, and in early September 1997, the town will host its third annual **kite festival.**

Silvaplana and its lake are a mere 1-hour hike or 10-minute bus ride from St. Moritz (every ½hr., 7am-8pm, 3.60SFr). The **tourist office,** at the corner of via Maistra and via dal Darrer (tel. 838 60 00; fax 838 60 09), can help plan a hike, arrange a wind-surfing lesson, or make free hotel reservations. Walk 2 blocks left from the post office (open Mon.-Fri. 8:30am-noon and 2-6pm, Sat. 9am-noon and 4-6pm). While this village of 870 residents has its share of hotels, most only offer rooms starting at 70SFr. Instead, stay at the youth hostel in St. Moritz or Maloja, or sleep on the beach at **Camping Silvaplana** (tel. 828 84 92; 7.60SFr, tent 6-8SFr; open mid-May to mid-Oct.). Grab some grub at **Volg,** to the left of the tourist office. (Open Mon.-Fri. 8am-noon and 2-6:30pm; Sat, 8am-noon and 2-4pm.) **Postal code:** CH-7513. **Telephone code:** 081.

SILS (SEGL)

More than a century ago, **Friedrich Nietzsche** praised Sils as "the loveliest corner of the Earth." This contributed greatly to the town's present fame, if you want to call it that. Though Sils thrives mainly on its tourist industry, its quiet winding streets and placid, bovine-filled meadows mask any sign of a vacation resort, and, except for allowing the occasional post card sporting kiosk to blossom in its town center, this is a feel that Sils plans to keeps. A **traffic ban** has been imposed on all automobiles in town, except for residents entering or exiting (Sils has generously built a parking garage to make up for the inconvenience). A short bus ride from St. Moritz (a **postal bus** leaves every ½hr. from 7am-8:30pm; 6SFr), Sils is the perfect antidote to the kitsch of many Swiss ski resorts. The town is divided into two areas: **Sils Baselgia,** a small cluster of homes near the **Silsersee,** and **Sils Maria,** the town center. After a morning hike, stop by the **Nietzsche House** (halfway between the post office and the tourist office along Sils' main road), where the philosopher lived during summers from 1887-88, and drifted into syphilitic madness. The house details many key events in his life. All exhibits are in German, though Nietzsche's works are available for sale in four languages (open Tues.-Sun. 3-6pm; 4SFr, students 2SFr).

Sils' side valleys, untamed and teeming with flora and fauna, are accessible only by foot; a 2-hour jaunt through **Val Fex** to **Curtins** is the hike of choice. The path begins just in front of the tourist office and winds its way beneath glaciers and 3000m peaks. If the hiker in you is dormant, **horse-driven omnibuses** make the round trip in 2 hours (20SFr). Grab your team in front of Hotel Maria, just to the right of the post office. Those who wish to commune with nature on a higher level may ascend the **Furtschellas** cable car (tel. 826 54 46; 12SFr up, 10SFr down, 18SFr round-trip), for a fascinating view of the entire Upper Engadin Valley. From here, hike north to **Murtèl,** where you can catch the cable car back to **Surlej** (12SFr). The walk to Murtèl features rocky traverse and wide open green fields. The Furtschellas cable car is a 10-minute walk to the right of the post office (the opposite direction from the tourist office). For a mellow afternoon beneath the snowy peaks and along the breezy shores, walk along the Silsersee to Maloja (2hrs.), taking the boat back at the end of your journey (tel. 826 53 43; 4 daily in both directions; one-way 12SFr, round-trip 18SFr). From Dec. to April, Furtschellas and its 14 downhill runs offer skiing the way it is meant to be—without waiting (daily ticket 47SFr, children 34SFr; half-day 39SFr, children 29SFr). If you wish to take private or group lessons at the downhill or cross-country ski school, contact the tourist office.

The town's studied tranquility doesn't come cheaply. Sils' housing choices are limited, with few hotels in the budget range. **Pension Schulze** (tel. 826 52 13), up the street behind the tourist office, houses you in large rooms with delicious scents wafting from the downstairs bakery/café up to your room. (Reception open daily 7:30am-noon and 2-6:30pm. Singles 60SFr, with shower 70SFr. Doubles 120SFr, with shower 140SFr. Breakfast included.) To carbo-load for the hikes ahead, dash to **Volg,** just left of the post office (open Mon.-Fri. 8am-noon and 2-6:30pm, Sat. 8am-noon and 2-

4pm). **Restaurant Survial** (tel. 826 55 50), across the street from Pension Schulze, offers homemade pastries, Italian cuisine, and Swiss specialties. Menus range from 16-26SFr. (Open daily. Full menu served 11:30am-2pm and 6-9pm. Shorter menu served 2-6pm. Closed Oct. 15-Dec. 15.) The **tourist office** (tel. 838 50 50; fax 838 50 59), down the street to the left from the post office, provides maps for hiking and skiing and can call hotels for vacancies. (Open Mon.-Fri. 8:30am-noon and 2-6pm, Sat. 9am-noon and 4-6pm; April-June and Oct.-Dec. closed on Sat.) All references to and directions from the post office refer to the Sils Maria **post office** (at the bus stop "Sils/Segl Maria"). **Postal code:** CH-7514. **Telephone code:** 081.

CELERINA

Celerina possesses all the merits of the more famous Engadin towns, skiing, hiking, biking, and *fondue*-ing, yet resides just outside the resort veneer created by the likes of St. Moritz. The proudest moments in Celerina's history came when St. Moritz hosted the Winter Olympics in 1928 and 1948. Remnants of the games can be seen in the **Bob-run** and **Cresta-run,** both of which came to a dramatic, revelry-filled finish in Celerina. Each run is re-built every year around the end of November by 14 specialized laborers from the village of **Naturns, Italy.** They use 5000 cubic meters of snow and 4000 cubic meter liters of water to make a mush that is used like cement to form each canal. The exclusive band of crazed thrill seekers, better known as the **St. Moritz Tobogganing Club,** presides over the runs, yet offers nonmembers a chance to ride on most mornings for a stiff fee. Bob runs will run you 190SFr, includes one run, one photo, one drink, and one certificate (tel. 833 41 10). The **Cresta Run** (Tobogganius Stupidus) is a modified, head first toboggan ride down the icy course (first 5 rides with lessons costs 450SFr, subsequent rides cost 44SFr; tel. 833 31 17). Aside from the runs, Celerina offers…well…hmmm…hiking and skiing away from the large crowds. The **Celerina gondola** and **Marguns chairlift** brings you to the midst of 80km of hiking trails in the summer. (Celerina-Marguns 12SFr one-way, 18SFr round-trip; Marguns-Corviglia 8SFr one-way, 12SFr round-trip.) In the winter its all snow, baby (tel. 833 43 70; daily ticket 50SFr, half-day 42SFr, children 35SFr). A moderate hike from Marguns (the top of the Gondola), the Chna Saluvan sits just below the mighty peak of the same name. Traverse the valley and head down to Alp Clavadatsch, and finally back to Celerina. The hike will take you from the rocky alpine backside of the ski area down through the green, open fields rising above Celerina (total time approx. 4hr.). Of course there is more hiking to be had, just ask the friendly **tourist office** in the middle of town (tel. 833 39 66; fax 833 86 66). From the train station, walk right; from the bus stop, walk right. The staff is a solid resource for hiking and skiing information, but hotel bookings are not their forte. (Open Mon.-Fri. 8:40am-noon and 2-6pm, Sat. 9-11am and 3-5pm; May-June and mid-Oct. to mid-Dec. closed on Sat.) Unfortunately, super-cheap housing has been run out of town by valley competition. However, the friendly family at the **Hotel Trais Fluors-Garni** (tel. 833 88 85; fax 832 10 01) can put you up in spacious, clean rooms with old-fashioned floral wallpaper and wood cabinets. Feels like home, but smells like a bakery—sweets and breads abound in the in-house bakery downstairs. (Singles June-Oct. 42-55SFr, Dec.-April 51-58SFr. Doubles June-Oct. 46-49SFr per person, with shower 55-70SFr. Dec.-April 49-53SFr, with shower 58-72SFr. Breakfast included. Closed May and Nov.) Across from the tourist office is a **Volg** supermarket (open Mon-Fri. 8am-noon and 2-6:30pm, Sat. 8am-noon and 2-4pm). Down the street from the tourist office, in the direction of the 14th-century Romanesque **Church of San Gian** (with frescoes and painted wood ceiling), lurks a **Co-op** (open Mon.-Fri. 8am-12:15pm and 2-6:30pm, Sat. 8am-12:15pm and 2-5pm). The Church of San Gian proudly stands on a knoll just outside of town. In the center of the valley, the crumbling spire and ancient graveyard add a sense of history to the modern ski lifts and hotels. If the Co-op or Volg aren't going to cut it, head for the pueblo-style interior of **Restaurant La Court** (tel. 837 01 01), directly in front of Hotel Trais Fluors and right on the river. Eat under the restaurant's huge skylight or outside on the river. (Salad buffet 7.70SFr, homemade lasagna 13.50SFr. Open daily noon-10pm.) The closest town north of **St.**

Moritz, Celerina is easily accessible by foot (45min.), **train** (2.40SFr), or **postal bus** (2.80SFr). **Postal code:** CH-7505. **Telephone code:** 081.

PONTRESINA

Pontresina lies in one of the highest wind-sheltered valleys of the Upper Engadin, along a mountainside terrace facing southwest. Surrounded by alpine meadows and fragrant cembra-pine and larch woods, it is a popular starting and stopping point for outdoors people. Rather than the credit cards and love-you-dahlings of St. Moritz, Ice axes and crampons abound, making for a much more rugged feel. Rather than Holly-wood shimmer, this *Burg* is internationally acclaimed thanks to the skiers' paradise of **Diavolezza,** the only glacier in the entire Engadin Valley that still offers summer ski-ing on its perpetual snow (all the other glaciers have melted due to rising tempera-tures and are no longer large enough for summer skiing). The summer ski lift operates in June and July daily from 8:30am to noon, and in August depending on snow conditions (tel. 842 64 19; daily ticket 35SFr, children 16 and under 25SFr; win-ter tickets 44SFr, ½day 36SFr; children 31SFr, 26SFr).

When summer closes the ski lift, trade your ski boots for hiking boots and explore the nearby valleys and vales. The tourist office has extensive hiking maps and sugges-tions. One nearby hike takes you along a green ridge, just below the mighty 3157m **Piz Muragl.** From Pontresina, walk or take the postal bus one stop to "Punt Muragl." From there a funicular will take you to **Mouttas Muragl** (2456m; from 8am-11pm, every ½hr.; 16SFr, round-trip 25SFr). Follow the yellow signs to **Alp Languard** (2330m; approx. 2½hrs), hike down to Pontresina (1hr.), or take the chairlift down (one-way 13SFr, round-trip 19SFr; open 8:30am-5:30pm).

To see global warming in action, hike to the receding **Morteratsch Glacier.** From the train station, walk towards town on via de la Stazium, and hang a right at the trail sign just before the second bridge. Walk for 2 hours along the valley floor through pine groves and tall grassy meadows. Or you can take the train (1 per hr., one-way 3.60SFr) to "Morteratsch." From the train station, bear right and follow the signs to the glacier (approx. 45min.). Follow the signs marking the glacier's recession since the turn of the century along the gushing river created by the melting waters. Though disappearing, the glacier is still a massive wall of ice and snow, seemingly arrested in motion as it crawls through the rugged valley. If you still have the energy, walk up along the glacier's edge to Chna. da Boval for scenic respite. (2hrs. from "Morter-atsch" train stop.)

The **Mountaineering School Pontresina** offers daily guided hikes over the Dia-volezza glacier, the Pers glacier, and down through the Morteratsch glacier and val-ley. No technical equipment or experience is necessary, but a raincoat, warm clothes and rubber-soled hiking boots are a must (20SFr, children 7-16 10SFr; lasts approx. 4hrs.). School also leads more mellow hikes daily through regional valleys (Val Fex on Mon., 4½hrs.; or Val Roseg on Fri., 5½hrs.; each 30SFr). As guests of Pontresina, you will be ecstatic to learn that you are entitled to a number of **free sports, tours,** and **excursions,** such as free trout-fishing in **Lej Nair** and **Lej Pitschen,** free botanical excursions, free mushroom picking outing under the guidance of a local expert, free guided hiking tours into the **National Park** (see also p. 211), and free excursions to experience an unforgettable sunrise on **Piz Lagalb.** Horse-drawn carriage excursions and winter sleigh rides leave from the railway station (tel. 842 60 57 for booking). The town's historical monument is located at the highest part of the village. From the outside, the **Church of Santa Maria** resembles many of the numerous Romanesque churches in Graubünden. The interior is blessed with magnificent ancient wall paint-ings. (Open June and Sept. Mon.-Fri. 3:30-5:30pm; July-Aug. Mon. and Wed.-Fri. 3:30-5:30pm, Tues. 10-11:30am; first half of Oct. Mon.-Fri. 3-5pm). The **Museum Alpin,** chesa Delnon (tel. 842 72 73), up the street from the tourist office on your left, pre-sents life in the Engadin as it used to be (void of tourists) by tracing the changes done to a simple wooden farmhouse from the middle ages onwards. Don't miss the impres-sive blend of music and picture in the slide show thriller *Mountain Experience* from 4:30-5:15pm (open mid-June to mid-Oct. Mon.-Sat. 4-6pm; 5SFr, children 2SFr).

EASTERN SWITZERLAND

The **Jugendherberge Tolais (HI),** in the modern, rust-colored building directly across from the train station, is quite convenient for early-morning ski ventures (tel. 842 72 23; fax 842 70 31). The hostel boasts its own full-fledged restaurant, and friendly service that blows St. Moritz away. Inside the hostel, yellow *Wanderweg* signs tell you the hostel's elevation and where everything is, from the toilets to dining facilities. Call early for quads and doubles. (Reception open in summer daily 6:45-9am, 4-6:30pm, and 7:30-9pm; in winter daily 7:30-9am, 4-6:30pm, and 7:30-9pm. No lockout. Quiet hour 10pm. Curfew 11pm, but anyone can ask for the house key. Dorms 30.25SFr first night, 27.75SFr thereafter. Doubles 110.50SFr, then 105.50SFr. Quads 161SFr, then 151SFr. Lockers, sheets, and breakfast included. Lunch 11SFr. Dinner 11SFr, mandatory July-Aug and Feb.-March 15. Laundry 5SFr. Open June 16-Oct. 18 and Dec. 15-April 7. Visa, MC, AmEx.) **Hotel-Pension Hauser,** 165 Cruscheda (tel. 842 63 26; fax 842 65 41), is another option. Head left from the tourist office uphill along Cruscheda. Tucked in a residential neighborhood, you will feel right at home, and once you've slept in the inviting beds, you might never want to get up and hit the slopes. (Reception open in summer 7:30am-midnight. Singles 55-65SFr, with shower 65-75SFr. Doubles 110-130SFr, with shower and toilet 150-180SFr. Parking and buffet breakfast included. Open mid-Dec. to mid-April and mid-June to mid-Oct.) Right in the heart of town, **Pension Valtellina** (tel. 842 63 63) features old-style rooms with wood cabinets and flowing drapes. A bastion of Italy in a Swiss German neighborhood. (Singles 46-54SFr. Doubles 92-104SFr. Breakfast included. Closed June.) The tourist office also has an extensive list of **private rooms** in Pontresina starting at 25SFr per person. **Camping Plauns** (tel. 842 62 85) offers all the amenities a tent-dweller could hope for, and is in a beautiful location. From the train station, walk 3km towards the Bernina Pass to Morteratsch; the trail is well marked (7.50SFr per person, tent 9SFr; open June to mid-Oct). Pontresina's dining choices are more limited. If the soft scent of chlorine triggers your appetite, then try **Bistro im Hallenbad** (tel. 842 73 41), in the swimming complex across from the tourist office and 50m up the hill, offers a hearty daily menu (16SFr), with soup or salad (16SFr), and a daily vegetarian dish (9.50-12SFr) that should suit you fine. They also have a chlorine-free outdoor patio. Feel free to take a dip in the indoor pool either before or after your meal (7SFr, students 3.50SFr; open Mon.-Fri. 9am-8:30pm, Sat.-Sun. 10am-6:30pm). The **Co-op** resides at the corner of via Maistra and via da Mulin (open Mon.-Fri. 8am-12:15pm and 2:30-6:30pm, Sat. 8am-5pm).

Pontresina's **tourist office,** in the center of town (tel. 842 64 88; fax 842 79 96), plans those free excursions, has a long list of hikes, and will call hotels for vacancies. From the train station, head right and follow via de la Stazium to town. At the fork in the road, bear left; when the road ends, turn right on via Maistra. The tourist office will be on your left. (Open Mon.-Fri. 8:30am-noon and 2-6pm, Sat. 8:30am-noon and 3-6pm, Sun. 4-6pm; mid-Oct. to mid-Dec. and mid-April to mid-June Mon.-Fri. 8:30am-noon and 2-6pm, Sat. 8:30am-noon; mid-Dec. to mid-April Mon.-Fri. 8:30am-noon and 4-6pm; July-Aug. Sundays 4-6pm.) **Postal buses** connect Pontresina to the villages of the Upper Engadin Valley all the way to **Maloja.** Trains run to Pontresina from **St. Moritz** (10min., every ½hr., 4.20SFr) and **Chur** (2hr., hourly, 39SFr; change at Samdan). The train station provides **currency exchange** (daily 6:40am-7pm), **luggage storage** (5SFr), **lockers** (2SFr), **telephones** (24hr.), and **bike rental** (21SFr) at the baggage check (daily 6:40am-7pm). **Postal code:** CH-7504. **Telephone code:** 081.

THE SWISS NATIONAL PARK

Switzerland's only national park is flanked by the towns of **Zernez** and **S-chanf.** Elsewhere-extinct wildflowers decorate and **ibex** and **deer** roam free in this naturalistic nirvana. The park spearheads many re-introduction programs for nearly extinct animals, such as the much underrated bearded vulture, and, as a result, forbids fires, dogs, hikes off of the well-groomed and marked trails, or picking mushrooms (even of the Funkadelic variety). The official park town, Zernez, is accessible by rail from **St. Moritz** (1hr., hourly, 15.80SFr) or **Chur** (2hr.45min., hourly, change at Samedan, 46SFr). The **National Park House** in Zernez displays the highlights of the park, as well as relevant scientific information. Its location at the park's extremity is a good starting point for hikes through the park itself. The Park House also organizes lectures on various topics, such as dinosaurs and the pre-historic humans of the area. (Open June-Oct. Wed.-Mon. 8:30am-6pm, Tues. 8:30am-10pm. 4SFr, students 3SFr. Lectures and film shows 4SFr, students 3SFr. Admission to the park itself is free.) Call the Park House at (081) 856 13 78 for more information or contact **Zernez's tourist office** (tel. (081) 856 13 00; fax 856 11 55). To reach the Park House, walk past the bus stop directly in front of the train station, and make a left. Then walk past the **Co-op** (snagging picnic supplies along the way; open Mon.-Fri. 8am-noon and 2-6:30pm, Sat. 8am-noon and 2-4pm), and turn right at the intersection; Park House will be 200m on the right.

Only one road penetrates the park with **PTT buses**. Departing from the train station, the bus takes hikers and strollers to the nine stops within the park. Needless to say, the limited hiking potential is made extremely accessible by this venue, the flora, fauna, and footpaths all within easy reach. To see the quest to save the endangered bearded vulture, take the bus to stop #7 and climb through the **Val dal Botsch** to **Margunet** (2328m), where the birds are being re-introduced. If the vultures don't grab you, the views certainly will. Hike back down over the Stabelchod pass (1958m) back to stop #8 or to the closer stop #9 (total time approx. 3hr.).

If you feel a bus ride would spoil the naturalistic theme of the park, hike directly from the Park House to **Chamana Cluozza**. From the Park House, head to the right, and cross the covered bridge 200m to the right. Follow the signs to Cluozza. The trail starts out as a switchbacked fire access road, but soon turns into a soft pine-needle-cushioned trail leading up the foothills facing Zernez. The trail quickly climbs to 2329m. Be sure to make the 15-min. detour to **Bellavista,** when you near the summit, for spectacular views of the mountain, the valley, and Zernez. From Bellavista, continue to follow the signs to Cluozza through the Alpine forest, and then move out onto the rocky ridge traversing the Val Cluozza. Descend to the river and then back up the other side of the valley (only 100m up) to the **Chamana Cluozza.** This alpine hut (tel. (081) 856 12 35) is one of the few places to sleep in the park. Re-carbo-load with spaghetti dishes starting at 11SFr. Water and bathroom facilities are also available. (Accessible by foot only, 3hr. from Zernez, 2½hr. back. 25SFr. Breakfast included. Open June-mid-Oct.) Rest up and spend the night before scaling **Spi Murter** (2545m), a majestic peak presiding over the valley. From the summit, hike down the **Plan dals Poms** to bus stop #3, and take the bus back out of the park (Cluozza to bus stop #3, 3½hr.).

Across the park from Zernez, **S-chanf** lies another possible base camp for hikers heading into the park, or for those seeking to enjoy Engadin Valley skiing. For more information contact **S-chanf's tourist office** in the Banca Raiffeisen (tel. (081) 854 13 48; open Mon.-Tues.and Fri. 8:30am-11am and 4-5:30pm, Wed. 8:30am-11am and Thurs. 8:30am-11am and 4-6:30pm). Walk left from the station downhill, and turn left at the church (2min.) to reach **Gasthaus Sternen,** via Maistra (tel. (081) 854 12 63). Though dwarfed by the vibrant Parc-Hotel Aurora next door, the *Gasthaus* is sufficient for a good night's sleep before the next day's hike (summer 45SFr per person, with shower 55SFr; winter 55SFr; breakfast included).

ZUOZ

Burnt to the ground by residents in 1499 to keep the Austrians from getting at it, Zuoz was rebuilt in the early 16th century, and today is considered the best preserved medieval village in the Upper Engadin. Dominated by patrician houses, fountains, and carved troughs, it has retained its original character. Come to experience the sounds of Switzerland's leftover Latin dialect, Romansch. Zuoz is not for the thrill-seeker, but the town has a few ancient customs that may baffle the accidental tourist. On March 1, the **Chalandamarz** engulfs all of Engadin as young boys wander from house to house, ring huge bells, and sing songs to drive off evil spirits and welcome the spring. The more peculiar **San Gian's Day** commemorates John the Baptist (though it originated in pagan fertility rites) on June 24, when village boys spritz girls with water from Zuoz's many fountains. Good Swiss fun.

The small **Church San Luzius,** on via Maistra, has sweet-smelling pine pews and hymnals in Romansch. Next door is the **prison tower,** filled with menacing implements of torture (ask the tourist office for the key). The *graffito* carvings in Zuoz are eye-catching in their detail—look up at **Crusch Alva** in the main square. The town woos bikers with 37km of marked trails, and hikers can use the Inn River as a starting point for many delightful hikes. The path to **Punt Muragl** (4hr.) follows the En/Inn River along the Engadin's green valley floor. A relaxing walk follows the twisting swirling rapids past smaller villages and towns. To put a bit of altitude into your walk, the trail from Zuoz to Madulain takes approximately 2hr. and follows the above-treeline ridge overlooking the valley floor. The trail crosses others leading to alpine huts, such as the Chamana d'Es-cha (a full day hike away), or the terraced farms and vineyards of the other valley villages. To find the trail start just uphill from Zuoz's main square, and head 300m up Somvih street.

For a more rugged afternoon, follow the Ova d'Arpiglia to a crashing 20m waterfall. Start on the other side of the train tracks and the highway at the Resgia Parking lot past the Restaurant Dorta, and follow the signs to Sagl d'Arpiglia along a magnificent rock strewn gorge. After admiring the falls from below, climb the "Stairway to Heaven," a steep, green meadow to the right of the falls that seems to reach the sky, replete with purple wildflowers and Jurassic looking leaves and fronds. Once you reach the top of the stairway, chase butterflies to you heart's content in the tiny valley's swath of grassy meadow. Follow the signs from this perfect picnic haven back to Zuoz (whole trip only about 1½hrs., including butterflies).

For a hearty day hike, starting again at the Resgia parking lot, follow the up-and-down trail to Munt Seja and the Alpine Lej da Prastinaum (lake Prastinaum). The trail winds through high valleys hidden behind the auspices of the Engadin valley, and the entire route from Zuoz and back is marked by signs to Munt Seja, Lej da Prastinaum, Alp Arpiglia, and finally Zuoz (approx. 3-4hr. to the lake, 2hr. down).

The 400-year-old **Chesa Walther** (tel. 854 13 64), just before the tourist office, offers indescribably lovely rooms with ivy walls and antique furniture. (35-38SFr. Breakfast not included. Kitchen facilities 5SFr.) **Restaurant Murütsch,** downstairs in the hotel, serves pizza starting at 12.50SFr. **Restaurant Dorta** (tel. 854 20 40) is around the corner from the train station. From the station, head left, and walk under the tracks; the restaurant will be on your left. This elegantly ancient establishment serves numerous regional specialities such as *rösti* (9SFr), *raclette* (9.50SFr), and *fondue* (23SFr; open Tues.-Sun. 6pm-1am; Visa, MC, AmEx). Load up at the bright, new **Co-op** across from the station (open Mon.-Fri. 8am-12:15pm and 2-6:30pm, Sat. 8am-12:15pm and 2-5pm), or at the **Volg** supermarket next door to the tourist office (open Mon.-Fri. 8am-noon and 2-6:30pm, Sat. 8am-noon and 2-4pm).

The **tourist office** (tel. 854 15 10; fax 854 33 34), on via Maistra, provides keys for the church and tower and suggests hikes in the area. From the station walk up La Passarella, directly across from and perpendicular to the station. At the top of the pedestrian walkway, turn right on the main street, and the tourist office will be past the main square on your right. (Open July-Aug. and Dec-April Mon.-Fri. 9am-noon and 2-6pm, Sat. 9-11am; May-June and Oct.-Nov. Mon.-Fri. 9am-noon and 3-5pm). Zuoz is a short **train** ride from **St. Moritz** (½hr., hourly, 8.40SFr) on the way to the **Swiss National Park.** The **train station** provides **luggage storage** (5SFr), **bike rental** (21SFr), **currency exchange** (Mon.-Sat. 7am-6:30pm, Sun. 8:35-11:50am and 1:40-6:25pm), and **telephones. Postal code:** CH-7524. **City code:** 081.

MALOJA

Crown of the Upper Engadin, the village of Maloja (1815m) with its 230 inhabitants precariously rests on the 360m precipice that separates the Engadin Valley from the **Bregaglia Valley**. This peaceful, family oriented playground also lies on the source of the **Inn River.** Just 32km from the Italian border, the town's official language is Italian and both Catholic and Protestant churches have a following here. On most mornings and late afternoons, the **Malojaschlange,** a stream of confused clouds occasionally taking the form of an enormous twisted snake, creeps over the pass as they are pushed by gusty winds and cannot adjust to the altitude change quickly enough. During most of the day, though, artist **Giovanni Giacometti** found he could not remember "a sun so bright and clear as shines upon the plateau of Maloja." The brightness enticed not only Giacometti, but also ensnared Italian expressionist painter **Giovanni Segantini**, who spent the last 15 years of his life in Maloja and was buried in the village's idyllic mountain cemetery in 1899. Private pictures, sketches, documents, and personal memorabilia are on display in the artist's refurbished studio, **Atelier Segantini** (open July 7-Oct.12 Tues.-Sun. 3-5pm; 2SFr). The **Belvedere Tower**, a 15-minute walk from the post office, was begun in 112 (no, that's not a typo), and after serving numerous functions throughout the centuries, was given to the town in 1988. Today it houses various exhibits on the Engadin and Bregaglia Valleys. The observation tower provides a phenomenal panoramic view which extends across the border into Italy. Hold on to your hat; they're not kidding when they talk about the strength of the Maloja winds. Feel the Malojaschlange ruffle your hair as it blows over the valley floor (open daily 9am-5pm; free). Fauna, flora, and **Gletschermühlen** (massive glaciated pot holes, some 15ft wide and 30ft deep) in the protected nature reserve surround the tower.

Hiking in this region is glorious. Spend a rigorous afternoon climbing the **Septimer Pass** to **Juf**, the highest village in Europe. Guided tours of this climb take place every other Tues. (June 25-Oct. 1, 50SFr); meet the group at the PTT station at 6:45am (rise and shine!). To spend the day steeped in the history of this Alpine region, join the guided historical tour departing from outside the Maloja tourist office for the heart of the Bregaglia Valley (June 20-Oct. 3 Thurs. 8am; 12SFr). For more information regarding these and other guided mountain tours, contact Maloja's tourist office. In the opposite direction, a 6-hour trek over the hills to the northeast will take you through **Grevasalvas**, the village where *Heidi* was filmed, all the way to **Signal**, where you will find Heidi's hut. From there, a cable car departs for St. Moritz. The hike to Grevalvas begins to the left of **Aparthotel Interhomeutoring**, follow the signs to Signal Cable Car. To cut this hike down to Heidi size, take the postal bus from Maloja (dir. St. Moritz) to "Plaun da Lej," and begin there. Don't forget your blonde braids. The Giant-60ft.-Godzilla-Heidi-destroys-Manhattan tour, if you choose to begin in Maloja, takes approximately 7-8hr.

On the Italian frontier, 22km farther down the valley from Maloja, lies **Soglio**, a matchbox Swiss-Italian village with narrow, crooked streets and ancient homes. Soglio's reputation results from its position on the legendary **Panorama Highway**, a footpath that commences at **Casaccia**, just south of Maloja. The route follows the Bregaglia valley downstream, making for a net downhill trip. The path meanders up and down ridges, past waterfalls, bright Alpine blossoms, and deserted Roman ruins. Views of the needlepoint peaks still towering overhead, alternate with tree enshrouded patches on the **wanderweg**. The hike lasts about 4-5hr. and does have some uphill sections before you reach the grassy hills and gnarly streets of Soglio. The natives call the trail "the beauty of the Graubünden" with good reason. To hike the Panorama Highway, you can get to Casaccia by foot (the path starts 200m to the right of the post office, just before the Sporthotel and across from the youth hostel), or catch the **postal bus** which runs every ½hr. (3.60SFr). The bus will also take you all the way to **Soglio** in 1hr. if you please (11.40SFr; change in Promontogno). There is no tourist office in Soglio; for lodging you need look no further than **La Soglina**, a pair of hotels run by the same enterprising *famiglia*. **Stüa Granda** (tel. (081) 824 19 88) is the less expensive of the two and has beautiful wood-beamed rooms for 60-70SFr per person. Rooms can be had for 48SFr per person in the **Casa Giovanni** next door, with breakfast included for both. Casa Giovanni rooms are only available from June-Oct, and Stüa Granda is closed between January 7 and February 7. Try the hotel's restaurant for carbo-loading on spaghetti plates starting at 14SFr or sample something from the vegetarian menu (plates 12-24SFr; open daily 6am-midnight, kitchen open daily 11:45am-10pm).

Maloja is also blessed with its own **Jugendherberge (HI)** (tel. 824 32 58; fax 824 35 71). Walk 200m to the right from the post office. Once a Swiss-Italian farmhouse, the hostel's dark wood walls and quiet yard work to camouflage it among the other build-ings in Maloja; a disguise that the big blue Hostelling International sign works decid-edly against. The hostel is divided between two houses—one, like Charlie Watts, is old but with character, the other, like Lars Ulrich, is newer, but not as fun to inter-view. (Reception open daily 8-9am, 5-6pm, and 8-9pm. No lockout, no curfew, but quiet time start at 10pm. Dorms 23.70SFr first night, then 21.20SFr. Nonmembers add 5SFr. Sheets, showers, and breakfast included. Kitchen facilities 2.50SFr. Laundry 10SFr. Open July-Oct. and Dec.-May.) **Camping TCS** (tel. 824 31 81), surprisingly close to the town center (15min.), also doubles as a windsurfing landing and beach. Cross the street from the bus stop, walk to the right, and take a left on the small street after Hotel Schweizerhaus that leads to the lake (4.60-5.40SFr, children half-price; tent 4.20-5.30SFr; tax 2SFr; open June-Sept.). Fill your grocery bag at the **Alimentari** across the street from the post office. Maloja's **tourist office** (tel. 824 31 88; fax 824 36 37), sits just beyond the youth hostel, 300m to the right of the post office. (Open Mon.-Fri. 8:30-noon and 2-6pm, Sat. 9-11am and 3-5pm; closed on Sat. during the low season.) **Postal buses** run between Maloja and **St. Moritz** 7am-7pm (40min., every ½hr., 9SFr). **Postal code:** CH-7516. **Telephone code:** 081.

THE BODENSEE

The third largest lake in Europe, the Bodensee forms a graceful three-cornered border at the conjunction of Austria, Switzerland, and Germany. Ancient castles, manicured islands, and endless opportunities to achieve a melanomic crisp draw residents of all three countries (and then some) to the lake throughout the summer.

▓ Constance (Konstanz)

Spanning the Rhine's exit from the Bodensee is the elegant university city of Con-stance. Although technically lying in Germany, it extends into Switzerland, a fact which saved it from the bombing that leveled many Germany cities of similar size. Its German/Swiss mix, and the fact that Constance belonged to Austria until 1805, give it an open, international feel. The narrow streets wind around beautiful painted Baroque and Renaissance façades in the central part of town, while along the river promenades, gabled and turreted 19th-century houses gleam with undeniable gentil-ity. Local students and visitors crowd the old resort beaches on the edge of town. Be aware that, because most of the city is in Germany, currency is in Deutschmarks and most phones lie in Germany.

Orientation and Practical Information The **tourist office** in the arcade to the right of the train station (tel. 13 30 30; fax 13 30 60), provides an excellent walk-ing map and lots of information about the area. They find rooms for a three-night min-imum stay in private homes (DM5). Ask for the free self-guided walking tour brochure, which includes a map, suggested route, and a brief explanation of the many sites. (Open May-Sept. Mon.-Fri. 9am-6:30pm, Sat. 9am-1pm; Oct.-April Mon.-Fri. 9am-noon and 2-6pm, also April and Oct. only Sat. 9am-1pm.) Hourly trains con-nect Constance to **Kreuzlingen** (2min., 2.40SFr), **Stein am Rhein** (½hr., 9SFr), and **Schaffhausen** (1hr., 15SFr). Constance's **Mitfahrzentrale,** Münzgasse 22 (tel. 214 44), can help you find a ride (open Mon.-Fri. 9:30am-1pm and 2-6pm, Sat. 9:30am-2pm), or check the university **rideboard** and hope to find someone you can trust. **Buses** in Constance cost DM2.20. You can buy a 6-ride ticket (DM10) for the Meersburg-Con-stance **ferry** from any machine. The tourist office offers a 2-day pass (31SFr) including transportation on buses, the ferry, the **Weiße Flotte** shipline to Meersburg and Mainau, as well as a city tour and admission to Mainau (see p. 440). Ships depart about once per hr. from behind the Constance train station to all ports on the Bod-ensee, including one that stops at various points in Germany (June-late Sept. daily).

For more information and schedules independent of the tourist office, you can contact the **Weiße Bodenseeflotte** counter directly (tel. 28 13 89), in the harbor behind the train station. (Open Sun.-Fri. 7:40am-6:10pm, Sat. 7:40-8:15pm. Trips on the lake are ½-price with Eurail pass, trips west of Konstanz are free with Eurail pass.) **Private boats** run hourly from behind the train station to the **Freizeitbad** and the **Freibad Horn** (June-Aug. daily 10:30am-5:30pm; May and Sept. Sun. only; one-way 2.50-3SFr). **Paddleboats and rowboats** can be rented at Am Gondelhafen (tel. 218 81) for about DM14 per hour from 9am-dusk. **Police:** 110. **Postal code:** D-78462. **German telephone code:** 0049. **Telephone code:** 07531.

Accommodations and Food Far and away the top choice of Constance's two youth hostels is the clean, comfortable **Jugendherberge Kreuzlingen (HI)**, Promenadenstr. 7 (tel. (071) 688 2663; fax (071) 688 47 61; use the Swiss access code, 0041), resting in an old manor house on the water in Kreuzlingen, Switzerland (but actually the closer hostel to downtown Constance). Take the train or walk to **Kreuligen Hafen** from the Hauptbahnhof, exit the station, go left on Bahnhofpl., make your first left, and cross the tracks. After the tracks, turn right, and follow the road next to the tracks to the Kreuzlingen Hafen train station (two stops away from the Konstanz station). From the station, turn left onto the main road, and walk 5min. until you reach the traffic light. Cross the train tracks on your left, and walk up the gravel path marked with a sign for the hostel. (Reception open daily 5-9pm. First night 21.20SFr, subsequent nights 18.70SFr. March-April and Oct.-Nov. 18.70SFr, 16.20SFr. Breakfast and sheets included. Dinner 11SFr. Closed Dec.-Feb.) **Jugendherberge Otto-Moericke-Turm (HI),** Zur Allmannshöhe 18 (tel. 322 60; fax 311 63), is probably the world's only hostel housed in a former water tower. Take bus #4 to "Jugendherberge." (Reception open daily 4:30-5:30pm. Curfew 10pm. DM18.50, non-members DM24.50. Breakfast included. Sheets DM5.50. Open March-Oct. Call ahead.) **Jugendwohnheim Don Bosco,** Salesianerweg 5 (tel. 622 52; fax 606 88), is an excellent alternative to the hostels. From the station, take bus #1 to "Salzberg." Go back 25m, and take the path on the left that becomes Brandesstr. At the intersection, take Händelstr. until it reaches the alley; turn left, walk 150m, and look for the big yellow building on your left. Choose from 39 channels (MTV, of course) in the comfortable dayroom. (Curfew 12:30am, but get a key. 4- to 8-bed rooms DM25. Doubles DM30 per person. Extremely rare singles DM35. Sheets DM5. Call ahead.) **Campingplatz Konstanz-Bruderhofer,** Fohrenbühlweg 50 (tel. 33 057), offers a cheaper alternative; take bus #1 to "Staad." The campground is along the water. Call ahead; it fills up fast. (DM6, tent DM5-8. Open April 15-Sept.)

The **University Mensa** dishes out Constance's cheapest food. Lunches, including dessert and a view of the lake, cost DM3-4 (DM1 discount with student ID). Take bus #9, 9a, or 9b from the station. (Open Oct. 9-July 14 Mon.-Thurs. 11:15am-1:30pm and 5-6:15pm, Fri. 11:15am-1:30pm, cafeteria open Mon.-Thurs. 8am-6:30pm; July 15-Oct. 8 open Mon.-Fri. 11:15am-1:30pm, cafeteria open Mon.-Thurs. 8am-5pm, Fri. 8am-3pm.) Stroll through the area around Rheingasse, the oldest part of Constance and now the center of its vibrant alternative scene, complete with health-food stores, left-wing graffiti, and student cafés. **Sedir,** Hofhaldestr. 11, serves big bowls of vegetarian noodles for DM10 (open Mon.-Fri. 11am-2pm and 6pm-midnight, Sat.-Sun. 6pm-2am). For a good *Biergarten* atmosphere and cheap pizzas (from DM10), try **Seekuh,** Kouzilstr. 1 (tel. 272 32). You can dine outside under a hanging garden or inside in the all-wood barroom (open Sun.-Thurs. 6pm-1am, Fri.-Sat. 7pm-2am). For more traditional Italian food, try **Mamma Mia,** St. Johanngasse 9 (tel. 270 07), with incredibly fast and polite service. (Pizza DM9-14, pasta dishes starting at DM11. Open daily 11:30am-2pm and 5pm-midnight.)

Sights and Entertainment Constance's **Münster,** built over the course of 600 years, has a soaring Gothic spire and 17th-century vaulting. The cathedral, dominating from a distance, really jumps out at you as you happen upon it in the *Altstadt.* (Open mid-April to mid-Oct. Mon.-Sat. 8am-5:30pm. Admission to tower DM1, students DM.50.) The elaborate frescoes on the 14th-century **Rathaus** depict Constance's history, and the delightful inner courtyard deserves a glance. Wander down **Seestraße,** near the yacht harbor on the lake, or **Rheinsteig** along the Rhine, both picturesque waterside promenades. The tree-filled **Stadtgarten,** next to Constance's main harbor, provides peace and an unbroken view down the length of the Bodensee. A voluptuous revolving statue guards the Gondelhafen harbor.

Constance boasts a number of **public beaches;** all are free and open from May to Sept. **Strandbad Horn,** the largest and often the most crowded, sports a section for nude sunbathing. In inclement weather, head next door to **Freizeitbad Jakob,** Wilhelm-von-Scholz-Weg 2 (tel. 661 63), an ultra-modern indoor-outdoor pool complex with thermal baths and *faux*-summer sun lamps. For both, walk ½hour along the waterfront from the train station, or take bus #5 (open daily 9am-9pm; DM8, students DM5). **Strandbad Konstanz-Litzelstetten** and **Strandbad Konstanz-Wallhausen** can both be reached via bus #4. The twentysomething set frolics on the beach at the university (bus #4 to "Egg;" walk past the *Sporthalle* and playing fields, or take a 10min. walk down through the fields if coming from the youth hostel). The university beach can also be reached by walking out the lakeside of the mensa, to the footbridge, and then following the signs.

The **Bodensee-Festival,** featuring concerts by the Bodensee Symphony Orchestra, occurs in nearby Meersburg on May 14-21. Constance holds fireworks shows over the Bodensee every August 2—find a good spot and enjoy. The **Stadt Theater,** Konzilstr. 11 (tel. 13 00 50; fax 13 00 55), offers a wide assortment of dramatic productions by international playwrights. (Box office open Mon.-Fri. 10am-12:30pm and 5-6:30pm, Sat. 10am-1pm.)

■ St. Gallen

In the 7th century, St. Gall, an Irish missionary, attempted a whirlwind tour of the pagan regions near the Alps. When he reached a small town near the Bodensee he decided that he had enough with proselytizing, and became a hermit in the Alpstein. In 719, while on a pilgrimage, St. Otmar founded a monastery to honor the solitary St. Gall. Piously named, St. Gallen flourished as a religious and cultural center, even through the city's eventual industrialization. In 1983, the city library was named a world heritage treasure by UNESCO. Today St. Gallen fuses the likes of the monastery's stupendous Baroque library and the city's magnificent cathedral with a modern university and lively cafés, boutiques, and bars. The youthful crowd that fills the streets makes this medieval city of learning and piety come alive, and though a compelling city in itself, St. Gallen's' proximity to the Bodensee, Zürich, Germany, Austria, and smaller mountain villages make it even more of a regional hotspot.

ORIENTATION AND PRACTICAL INFORMATION

While much of St. Gallen is centered around the *Altstadt* near the *Kloster,* the city's tendrils spread far into the surrounding hills. St. Gallen has excellent hourly rail connections to **Zürich** (1hr., 26SFr), **Geneva** (4hr.20min., 87SFr), **Bern** (2½hr., 59SFr), **Lugano** (4hrs., 74SFr), **Münich** (3hr., 60SFr, under 26 49SFr), and **Bregenz** (16SFr, under 26 11SFr).

Tourist Office: Bahnhofpl. 1a (tel. 227 37 37; fax 227 37 67). From the train station, cross straight through the bus stop, and pass the fountain on the left; the tourist office is on the right. The English-speaking staff makes free hotel reservations within St. Gallen. Maps, brochures, and a city tour are also available. (Tour June 12-Sept. Mon., Wed., Fri. 2:30pm. 15SFr, including museum admissions.) Office open Mon.-Fri. 9am-noon and 1-6pm, Sat. 9am-noon.

Telephones: At the train station and along most streets.

Currency Exchange: Union Bank of Switzerland, Bahnhofpl. is convenient. Open Mon.-Wed. and Fri. 8:30am-4:30pm, Thurs. 8:30am-6:30pm.

City Buses: Convenient buses cross the hills and valleys of the St. Gallen region. Single fare 1.80SFr, *Tageskarte* (day card) 7SFr, 12 rides 18SFr. Buy tickets at each stop; multi-fares and *Tageskarten* available at large kiosks or the VBSG Transit Authority across the street from the train station in Bahnhofpl.

Taxis: Sprenger AG, Rohrschacherstr. 281 (tel. 222 23 33).

Car Rental: Budget Rent-A-Car, City Garage AG, St. Leonhardstr. 35 (tel. 222 11 14; fax 222 01 57). 118SFr per day, weekend package Fri.-Mon. 201SFr. **Herold Autovermietung AG,** Molkenstr. 7 (tel. 220 20 30; fax 223 88 31). 72SFr per day, 3 days 151SFr.

Parking: Neumarkt Parking Garage, Lily Garage AG (tel. 222 11 14). Open Mon.-Sat. 5am-12:40am. From 5am-9pm 2SFr per hr., from 9pm-5am, 1SFr per hr. **Rathaus Parking Garage** (tel. 223 11 25). Open 24hr. From 7am-10pm 1.80SFr per hr., from 10pm-7am 0.50SFr per hr. Park outside in one of the **blue zones** that cover most of the city for 5.50SFr per day.

Luggage storage: At the train station. Lockers 2SFr. Luggage watch 5SFr (open Mon.-Fri. 7:30am-7:45pm, Sat.-Sun. 7:30am-noon and 2-6pm).

Laundromat: Quick Wash, Rohrschacherstr. 59 (tel. 245 31 73). Soap 1.50-5SFr, wash 4-7SFr, dry 1.80-3.80SFr. Open Mon.-Sat. 8am-10pm.

Post Office: St. Leonhardstr. 7, across the street and to the right of the train station exit. Open Mon.-Fri. 7:30am-6:30pm, Sat. 7:30-11am.

Postal code: CH-9000.**Telephone code:** 071.

ACCOMMODATIONS

Jugendherberge St. Gallen (HI), Jüchstr. 25 (tel. 245 47 77; fax 245 49 83). From the train station, take the Trogenerbahn (Orange Train) from the smaller Appenzeller/Trogener station to the right, or from the Marktpl. take the train (dir: Speicher-Trogen) to "Schülerhaus." Walk up the hill on the right, make a left across the train tracks at the sign, and walk downhill 2min. Perched on a hill overlooking St. Gallen, the hostel is filled with bright murals and posters. Clean, quiet, with a panoramic breakfast room, outdoor terrace dining, barbecue pit, and chess, checkers, and backgammon. Reception open Mon.-Sat. 5-10:30pm, Sun. 6-10:30pm. Checkout 9am. Dorms 23SFr, 20.50SFr subsequent nights; doubles 64SFr, 59SFr subsequent nights. Rare single 57SFr, 54.50SFr subsequent nights. Lockout 10am-5pm, but lounge is open. Staff speaks English. Parking available. Closed Dec. 15-March 7.

Hotel Weisses Kreuz, Engelgasse 9 (tel. 223 28 43; fax 223 28 77). Sits atop a lively, neon blue alternative bar. Good spot for delving into the *Altstadt's* nightlife. 5% student discount on room. Reception open 5am-midnight. Singles 40-60SFr, doubles 70-100SFr. Breakfast and hall showers included.

Hotel Elite, Metzgergasse 9-11 (tel. 222 12 36; fax 222 21 77), one block over from the Weisses Kreuz. Clean, plain rooms, all with telephone and wall-embedded radio. Singles 54-100SFr; doubles 108-150SFr. Breakfast included.

FOOD

Restaurant Spitalkeller, Spitalgasse 10 (tel. 222 50 91). From Marktplatz, head down Marktgasse, and make your first left on Spitalgasse. Hearty alpine food for mountain men and women taking a break from the wilderness. Local sausage specialties can stay the appetite of any flannel-clad lumberjack. Appenzeller macaroni with sausage or Ticino *rösti* (with tomatoes and cheese) 11.50SFr. Daily *menus* 13SFr and up. Open Tues.-Sat. 8am-midnight.

Pizzeria Boccalino, Burggraben 20 (tel. 222 96 66). From Marktgasse, turn onto Spisergasse and left onto Burggraben. Italian-speaking waiters (who understand English and German as well) serve filling pasta and pizza dishes (13-18SFr) upstairs and downstairs in this upscale restaurant. Pizza Margherita 11SFr. Open Mon.-Sat. 10:30am-11pm.

Christina's, Webergasse 9 (tel. 23 88 08). A sleek, new-age, indigo-tinted bar/café/restaurant. Vegetarian specialties, fresh salads, and bread, as well as more hearty fare. Veggie dishes 16SFr and up. Fish and meat dishes 19SFr and up. Open Tues.-Thurs. 9:30am-11:30pm, Fri.-Sat. 9:30am-12:30am, Sun.-Mon. 3-11:30pm.

Markets

Migros, St. Leonhardstr., two blocks up from the train station. Open Mon.-Wed. and Fri. 8am-6:30pm, Thurs. 8am-9pm, Sat. 7:30am-5pm. Restaurant open Mon.-Wed. and Fri. 6:30am-6:30pm, Thurs. 6:30am-9pm, Sat. 6:30am-5pm.

Reformhaus Müller, Spisergasse 13, sells organically grown goodies and health foods. Open Mon.-Fri. 8am-6:30pm, Sat. 8am-5pm.

Birreria, Brühlgasse 45, over 700 types of beer let you take a barley trip around the globe without moving your lazy gut. Open Mon. 11:30am-7pm, Tues.-Wed. 10:30am-7pm, Thurs.-Fri. 10:30am-12:30am, Sat. 9am-12:30am.

Public market, on the Marktpl. Fresh produce, bread and meat available daily from 9am-7pm.

SIGHTS AND ENTERTAINMENT

St. Gallen's main attraction is the **Stiftsbibliotek** (Abbey library; tel. 227 34 15) and the Abbey which houses it. The library itself maintains a collection of 140,000 volumes and 2000 manuscripts, 500 of which date back to the 13th century. The Stiftsbibliotek is a living, lending library serving scholars the globe over; Umberto Eco was seen sniffing around the library to get inspiration for *The Name of the Rose.* A mummified Egyptian (who evidently spent too much time studying) presides over the collection from the far side of the room. However, the ancient manuscripts on display and the books which line the main reading room are over-shadowed by the breathtaking **Baroque reading room.** The room was built between 1758 and 1767, and has never required restoration. The parquet floors and the ceiling paintings are among the most exquisite examples of the period in Switzerland. (Open June-Aug. Mon.-Sat. 9am-noon and 1:30-5pm, Sun. 10:30am-noon and 1:30-4pm; May and Sept.-Oct. Mon.-Sat. 9am-noon and 1:30-5pm, Sun. 10:30am-noon; Dec.-March Tues.-Sat. 9am-noon and 1:30-4pm; April Mon.-Sat. 9am-noon and 1:30-5pm. 5SFr, students and children 3SFr.) The **Kathedrale St. Gallen** (tel. 227 33 88), part of the Abbey, was founded in the 8th century, but took its present form in the mid-18th century, remaining one of the most beautiful cathedrals in Europe. Dark frescoes cover the ceiling, faintly reminiscent of the Sistine, while incredibly detailed wood carvings and gold moldings adorn everything from confessionals to grates. (Open daily 9am-6pm except for mass on Sat. and Sun.) The Abbey courtyard is a great place for a picnic or a sunbath. Near the Catholic Abbey, the **Evangelical Church of St. Lawrence,** founded in the 9th century, sits unassumingly next to its ornate sister (open Mon.-Fri.9:30-11:30am and 2-4pm). Across the train tracks to the left and uphill (something of a walk from the center of town), the **Peter and Paul Wildpark** (tel. 222 67 92), on Rosenberg in Romontum, is where the ibex was saved from near extinction. The animals now roam the grounds freely (open 24hrs.; free). Explore the campus of the **St. Gallen University** by taking bus #5 from the station (dir: Rotmonten) to "Hochschule" beyond the university. There is also a huge park donated to the city of St. Gallen in 1963, which provides a magnificent view of the city and the Bodensee.

To conclude the month of June, St. Gallen's celebration of music and general debauchery takes over the fields surrounding the town, June 27-29 in 1997. The **Open Air St. Gallen Music Festival** features over 20 live bands which appeal to everyone from the young to the very old. Past headliners included Red Hot Chili Peppers, Cypress Hill, the legendary B.B. King, and the Godfather of Soul, James Brown. You must buy a ticket for the all three days; though they run a steep 135SFr, housing is included if you bring a tent and camp out (showers and toilets available). Or stay in St. Gallen and take the free shuttle bus from the train station to the concert grounds. For information about tickets and bands, call 223 41 01 or write to: Open Air St. Gallen, Bahnhofstr. 6, CH-9000, St. Gallen, Switzerland. The **Stadttheater,** Museumstr. 24 (tel. 242 06 66) hosts over 200 concerts and dramatic works annually (Sept.-June). There are several **movie theaters** at Marktplatz (movie info tel. 122).

MUSEUMS

St. Gallen's aptly named Museumstraße holds four museums; all of which can be visited with the same ticket.

Historical Museum, Museumstr. 50 (tel. 244 78 32). The local half presents models, recreations, and interpretations of St. Gallen's history. The ethnological half displays an impressive collection of artifacts hailing from a cornucopia of world cultures. Inuit kayaks mingle with Hindu musical instruments, along with masks, weapons, and pan pipes from Asia, Africa, and the Pacific Islands. Open Tues.-Sat. 10am-noon and 2-5pm, Sun. 10am-5pm. 6SFr, students 2SFr.

Natural History Museum, Museumstr. 32 (tel. 245 22 44). Almost everything Mother Nature has birthed in the last four billion years can be found here: geological exhibitions, dinosaurs, some taxonomy and more. Open Tues.-Sat. 10am-noon and 2-5pm, Sun. 10am-5pm. 6SFr, students 2SFr. **Kunstmuseum,** in the same building as the Natural History Museum, juxtaposes modern art on the top floor with works by more traditional, older 19th- and 20th- century artists.

Kirchofer House Museum, Museumstr. 27 (tel. 244 75 21). Modest art collection, but impressive array of coins, all displayed in the house of one of St. Gallen's first families. Stare down the bones of a local cave bear and enjoy local farmhouse paintings. Open Tues.-Sat. 10am-noon and 2-5pm. 6SFr, students 2SFr.

NIGHTLIFE

Filou, Schwertgasse (tel. 244 74 54). Smoky bar pumps 80s rock for a twentysomething crowd. Good luck finding space to dance on the weekend. Open Mon.-Sat. 5pm-midnight. No cover.

Goliath, Goliathstr. 27, is a dark, local joint with red velvet walls, low ceilings, and a crooked wooden bar. A diverse crowd populates the bar adding to the unique atmosphere. Open Sun.-Fri. 8:30pm-midnight, Sat. 8:30pm-12:30am.

Ozon, Goliathgasse 28 (tel. 244 81 24). Non-stop chrome and mirrors lend the illusion of size to this compact club. If the flashing lights and smoke don't blind you, the drink prices will (beer starts at 8SFr). Cover charge usually 10SFr. DJ spins a different theme every night (techno on Thurs.). Open Sun., Tues.-Thurs. 10pm-2am, Fri. and Sat. 10pm-3am.

Trischli, Brühlgasse 18 (tel. 226 09 00). Dance floor action is projected onto a big screen and surrounding little screens. Local bands, karaoke, and other theme nights (foxtrot, anyone?). Open July-Aug. daily 10pm-5:30am; Sept.-June 9pm-whenever people leave. Sun.-Wed. no cover. Thurs.-Sat. 7-17SFr.

■ Near St. Gallen: Appenzell

The jewel of Appenzellerland, Appenzell can't help but flaunt its beautiful location in the foothills as well as its well preserved *Altstadt.* A stroll along Appenzell's streets reveals a remarkable number of centuries-old buildings, all of which—the tourist office will remind you—support the town's claim to being one of the most "authentic" Swiss villages. The Rathaus, which houses the museum, town hall, cantonal library, and the tourist office, is itself remarkable, especially the **Grossratssaal,** with intricately carved, wood-paneled walls and frescoes dating from the 16th century. The Rathaus building was built in 1563 and managed to escape any Baroque intrusion on its heavy wooden beams and parquet floors.

The town's location in the heart of the *Alpstein,* or foothills of the Alps, makes it ideal for moderate to difficult **hikes,** without the temperature extremes of Zermatt or the Ticino region. Appenzell also has one of the most extensively marked networks of trails in Switzerland, creating a web that connects the small towns of the canton to the larger urban areas such as St. Gallen and Winterthur. Many trails, anticipating hikers, have *Gasthöfe* (guest houses) and restaurants along the way for the road-weary. Ask for the *Wandervorschläge: Appenzellerland* at the tourist office for a detailed map, complete with timed distances.

For an easy walk through the green pastures whose product eventually become the renowned Appenzeller cheese, walk along the Sitter River to Weissbad by exiting the tourist office, turning left on Hauptgasse, and following the signs to Weissbad at the river (approx. 1hr., 32m elevation change). You can then take the Appenzeller-bahn back (free with Eurailpass). Climb to Hirschberg (1167m) for a more difficult hike and for panoramic views and breathtaking scenery. Afterward, backtrack for 25 minutes, and turn right for Mendli. From here, you can also take the train back to Appenzell (hiking time approx. 3hrs.20min.). For some experience above the treeline, take the train to Jakobsbad and then a cable car to the top of Mt. Kronberg (1663m; 21SFr round-trip for cable car; 14SFr with Eurailpass). Follow the trail through remote villages all the way back to Appenzell (approx. 3hrs.). If you can't make it the last 15 minutes to Appenzell, crash at **Gasthof Freidenberg** (tel. (071) 87 12 40), which provides the best panoramic view in Appenzell of the Alpstein from its hilltop locale. From the rear exit of the train station walk about 12 minute, mostly uphill, and follow the signs, eventually taking the gravel footpath up the hill to the Gasthof. (Reception and restaurant closed on Wed. Singles 58SFr. Doubles 98-116SFr. Breakfast included.) The restaurant downstairs offers huge portions, and all prices are under 27SFr (even the steak). Particularly picturesque and helpful is the **Haus Lydia,** Eggerstandenstr. 53 (tel. (071) 787 42 33). A family member will pick you up at the train station if you call ahead. Otherwise walk 20min. from the station, right on Grin-gelstr., left on Weissbadstr., right on Gaiserstr., and right onto Eggerstrandenstr. Run by a friendly, English-speaking family, the house offers large rooms with great views of the mountains and a kitchen for guest use. (37.50SFr per person. Breakfast included. Reservations required.) The **Gasthaus Hof** (tel. (071) 787 22 10; fax (071) 787 58 83), near the center of the *Altstadt,* is a bustling family-run restaurant, with rooms upstairs. (Dorms 25SFr per person. Doubles 65SFr. Breakfast included. Restau-rant open daily 8am-midnight.) For more Swiss specialties, with a cheesy twist, try some of the Appenzeller specialties at **Restaurant Traube,** Marktgasse 7 (tel. (071) 787 14 07; open 9am-midnight; closed in February). For hiking sustenance, try the **Co-op,** Marktgasse 14. Walk along Rathauspl. to the Marktgasse on the left, and look for the orange sign behind the Marktpl. (Open Mon. 1-6:30pm, Tues.-Fri. 8am-12:15pm and 2-6:30pm, Sat. 8am-4pm.)

The Appenzell **tourist office** (tel. (071) 788 96 41; fax (071) 788 96 49) is in the **Rathaus** building. From the train station, walk down Bahnhofstr., bearing right as the road curves and intersects the Hauptgasse; the tourist office is to the left of the church. They provide detailed hiking maps and specific dates for all of Appenzell's intriguing festivals—don't miss the early October *Viehschau* (cattle show), or the diz-zyingly more captivating goat show the following day. They also make hotel reserva-tions for free by phone, but a 20SFr deposit on the room is required if made in person. Cable car excursions can also be booked here (round-trip 21-27SFr). (Open June.-Oct. Mon.-Fri. 9am-noon and 2-6pm, Sat. 9am-noon and 2-4pm; Nov.-May Mon.-Fri. 9am-noon and 2-5pm, Sat. 9am-noon.) The tourist office offers different tours and activities every day, ranging from a tour of the Appenzeller Alpenbitter factory (Wed. 10am, free, meet at main factory entrance, Weissbadstr. 27) to a course in woodcarv-ing (Thurs. 2pm, make your own butter dish 20SFr; register before 5pm the previous day). **Buses** connect Appenzell to the smaller towns of the canton, and the **Appen-zellerbahn** chugs to St. Gallen every hour (1hr., one-way 10.20SFr). There is a huge parking lot across from the Co-op, as well as along the Sitter river, across the bridge from the St. Mauritius Church.

Tucked inside the **Rathaus** and the adjoining Haus Buherre Hanisefs, the **Museum Appenzell,** Hauptgasse 4 (tel. (071) 787 9631) holds a six-floor collection of Swiss crafts, costumes, and culture. (Open April-Oct. daily 10am-noon and 2pm-5pm; Nov.-March Tues.-Sun. 2pm-4pm. 5SFr, students 3SFr.)

■ Schaffhausen

The only Swiss city north of the Rhine and surrounded by Germany on three sides, Schaffhausen understandably retains a rather Teutonic language and look. While the town's outlying areas have thrived off the hydroelectric power generated by the Rhine's roar, the well-preserved medieval *Altstadt* remains an anachronistic complement to such modern-day advancements. *Oriel* (bay) windows, gilded shopkeepers' signs, fountains, and cobblestones fill the pedestrian Marktplatz and *Altstadt*. Schaffhausen is proud of its history and architecture as manifested in the fact that citizens painstakingly rebuilt the buildings accidentally bombed by the U.S. in World War II in the same fashion as the originals. Tourists from the tri-country area who are cruising the Rhine, the Bodensee, and the Rhinefalls (in nearby Neuhausen, 5min. by bus, ½hr. by foot) flock to the city to catch a glimpse of Schaffhausen's colorful exterior decor. The **Munot Fortress,** dating back nearly 500 years, stands tall and proud above the city, a testimony to the Schaffhausen community. Half a millennium ago, the people volunteered to build the medieval fortress in their spare time so that the city would be protected. Though well-intentioned, the huge fortress was never used, as it was too small to house the entire town. It is large enough, however, to host today's sporadic concerts and annual festivals.

Orientation and Practical Information Schaffhausen is accessible by bus, train, and boat. Numerous ferries traverse the Bodensee and arrive in Schaffhausen with departures to Stein Am Rhein (3 daily, 13.80SFr) and Constance, Germany (3 daily, 26SFr). Purchase a **Tageskarte** (26SFr) and get one day of unlimited travel on Bodensee area railways, waterways, and roadways, including those belonging to Schaffhausen, Stein am Rein, Konstanz, and St. Gallen. **Trains** arrive every hour from Zürich (15.80SFr) and St. Gallen (26SFr), and Winterthur (9.60SFr). PTT **buses** connect Schaffhausen to the smaller towns of St. Gallerland (2SFr). The local **tourist office** (tel. 625 51 41; fax 625 51 43) looks out onto the lively Fronwagpl. (Open April-Sept. Mon.-Fri. 10am-noon and 2-5pm, Sat.-Sun. 10am-12pm; Oct.-May Mon.-Fri. 2-5pm.) From the train station, head down Schwertstr., the narrow street to the right as you leave, and walk until you reach the main square and fountain; the tourist office is on the right at the back of the square. Pick up maps, hotel listings, and hiking route information, or take the city tour in German, French, or English. (Tour April-Oct. Mon., Wed., and Fri. at 2:15pm. 1½hr. 10SFr, children 5SFr.) The train station is a good place for **currency exchange** (open daily 5:30am-8:10pm), **bike rental,** and **luggage storage** (both open Mon.-Fri. 6am-8pm, Sat.-Sun. 8am-8pm; bikes 21SFr per day, storage 5SFr). At the station you can also pick up groceries at **Migros.** (Open Mon.-Wed. and Fri. 8:15am-6:30pm, Thurs. 8:15am-9pm, Sat. 7:30am-4pm.) **Parking** is available in the parking garage off of Rheinstr., in the lots near the Münster, off of Moeratz, and behind the train station. **Postal code:** CH-8200. **Telephone code:** 053.

Accommodations and Food Schaffhausen's **Jugendherberge (HI),** Randenstr. 65 (tel. 625 88 00; fax 624 59 54), is in the newer section of town (newer meaning early 19th century). Once a villa, the building now houses the mammoth youth hostel, with high garden walls and ample outdoor lounging areas. (Reception open 5:30-10pm. Checkout 9am. Curfew 10pm, but keys available. Dorms 21.50SFr first night, 19SFr thereafter. Doubles and singles 27SFr per person, 24.50SFr. Members only. Breakfast, sleepsack, and showers included. Kitchen facilities 2SFr per meal.) **Hotel Steinbock,** Webergasse 47 (tel. 625 42 60), hidden in the bowels of the *Altstadt*, has a lively bar downstairs. Walk from the tourist office along the Vorstadt, and then left on Webergasse. (Reception open 2pm-midnight. Singles 46SFr; doubles 75SFr; triples 95SFr. Showers included. No breakfast. Closed Sundays.) **Camp** at the edge of the Rhine at **Camping Rheinwiesen** (tel. 659 33 00; 4.20SFr per person, tent 5.30SFr; July-Aug; 6.20SFr per person; tent 6.30SFr), 3km from Schaffhausen. Take the bus to "Langswiesen" or the train to Stein am Rhein.

The Fronwagpl. comes alive during the day with outdoor cafés, restaurants, and live entertainment, ranging from mimes to fire-breathers. Schaffhausen's modern **Migros** puts up a good medieval front, blending harmoniously with the rest of the Vorstadt. (Open Mon.-Wed. and Fri. 8:15am-6:30pm, Thurs. 8:15am-9pm, Sat. 7:30am-4pm.) Stock up on farm fresh produce at the **farmer's market** every Tuesday and Saturday from 7am-noon at Johannkirche. **Biona-fehr,** hidden on Löwengässchen, vends vitamins, minerals, and natural food (open Tues.-Fri. 8:15am-12:15pm and 1:15-6:30pm, Sat. 8am-4pm). **Restaurant Fallun,** Vorstadt 5 (tel. 625 32 21), has been a Schaffhausen landmark for years. The former Falken brewery is still home to many beer drinking traditions and clubs, and sports an inexpensive but hearty Swiss menu. Create your own *rösti* for 7.90SFr and up. Free beer with lunch if you show them your *Let's Go*. **La Rondine,** Webergasse 27 near the Hotel Steinbock, specializes in pasta and pizza. (Open Mon., Wed.-Thurs., Sun. 10am-2pm and 5-11:30pm, Fri.-Sat. 10am-2pm and 5pm-2:30am. Entrées 10-16SFr.) The owner of **Restaurant Tiergarten,** across from the Allerheiligen Monastery, adds atmospheric spice by serving a different national cuisine each year. Past influences include the Caribbean and Greece. Find out where he's off to next, or dig into one of the seasonal specialties, such as longhorn sheep in winter. *Bratwurst* and *rösti* for 14.50SFr are among the permanent Swiss classics. (Open daily 9am-11pm.)

Sights and Entertainment   At the corner of the Vorstadt and Löwengässchen in the *Altstadt,* watch for the gilded *oriel* (bay) windows on the **Goldener Ochsen,** dating back to the Middle Ages. The entire *Altstadt* is dotted with colorful fountains and frescoes; the intricate clocks and carvings also hark back to the days of yore. Of particular note is the **Knight's House,** Vordenstr. 65, which is covered by brilliantly colored frescoes portraying scenes from Greek and Roman mythology in high Renaissance style. The 16th-century **Munot Fortress** brings one back to the days when hot oil was used a weapon and not a hair-care product. Cavernous ground floors, narrow, winding staircases, and dimly lit interiors spook even the most brazen. Get to the other side of town and climb the steps, starting at the overpass (open May-Sept. daily 8am-8pm; Oct.-April daily 9am-5pm). On the outskirts of the *Altstadt,* the **Münsterkirche** and the **Kloster Allerheiligen** maintain a peaceful oasis in the midst of the hustle and bustle of the power plants nearby. The church was built in the 11th century, but was stripped of ornamentation during the Reformation, leaving the holy confines stark and majestic. The adjoining monastery is a labyrinth of porticoes and courtyards, housing a music school, museum, and the enormous **Schiller Bell,** which inspired the famous poem by Schiller, though he never actually saw the bell—his chum Goethe described it to him. The monastery also shelters well-tended herb gardens still used for medicinal purposes. The **Museum Zu Allerheiligen** holds the **Natural History Museum** (tel. 625 43 77; fax 625 43 70) and the **Kunstverein Schaffhausen** both reside there. The history museum showcases the eras of Schaffhausen's history, from a reconstruction of the Paleolithic Cave through exquisite 18th-century antiques. The basement presents the progression of the textile industry in Schaffhausen, once the town's life-blood (open Tues.-Sun. 10am-noon and 2-5pm; free). The **Hallen Für Neue Kunst,** Baumgartenstr. 23 (tel. 625 25 15), in a former textile factory, has a vast collection of avant-garde art from the 60s and 70s, including Andre, Nauman, and Weiner. (Open May-Oct. Thurs. 5-7pm, Sat.-Sun. 11am-5pm, other days by appointment, Nov.-April by appointment only.) The **Stadttheater,** Herrenacker 23 (tel. 625 05 55), offers a diverse selection of concerts and plays (open Mon.-Fri. 2-6pm, Sat. 9:30-11am).

A short bus ride from the train station to **Neuhausen** (bus #1 or 9) leads to the **Rheinfalls,** which are supposedly the largest falls in Europe. Follow the brown arrows from the "Rheinfalls" stop to the falls. Once at the falls, walk along the river's edge, or cross the bridge to get nearer to the massive column of water (1SFr). There was so much water that Goethe thought it was the source of the ocean. Contact **Rhein Travel,** Schlauchbootfahrten, 8455 Rüdlingen (tel. (01) 867 06 38), for information about river rafting. Float into the falls from downstream with **Rhyfall Mändli** (tel. 672

EASTERN SWITZERLAND

48 11). Boats depart approximately every 45 minutes from Schloß Laufen (June-Aug. 11am-6pm, May-Sept. 11am-5pm; 5.50SFr, children 3SFr). Let the rushing river lull you to sleep at the **Jugendherberge Dachsen (HI)** (tel. 659 61 52; fax 659 60 39). Best reached by train ("Schloß Laufen am Rheinfall," two stops from Schaffhausen stop). Walk up the stairs to the castle and follow the signs for the hostel. The hostel fills up quickly; make reservations in advance. (Reception open 7-10am and 5-10pm. 22SFr, 19.50SFr for subsequent nights. One triple and one quad available 24SFr per person, 21.50SFr subsequent nights (suites do not include breakfast). Members only. Breakfast included. Kitchen facilities 2SFr.)

The **Bannerstube** (tel. 659 67 67) in the castle serves a few reasonably priced dishes and has a fantastic view of the falls. (Soups 5.50-7.50SFr. Pasta dishes start at 12.50SFr. Children's menu (under 9SFr) also available. Open daily March-Dec. 11:30am-2pm and 6:30-9:30pm.)

■ Stein am Rhein

Stein am Rhein (not to be confused with Stein) is roughly the Swiss equivalent of America's Plymouth or Williamsburg—the entire hamlet a proud showcase of Switzerland's modest origins, with museums, reconstructions, and reenactments. A port-of-call of sorts for the tourist-packed ferries that cruise around the lake, it has also seen fit to merge its medieval architecture and docile streets with the rather profitable Bodensee tourist trade. However, though its petite *Altstadt* is lined with souvenir shops and cafés, the beautiful and carefully maintained medieval buildings are among the loveliest to be found anywhere. Residents like their small village and intend to protect if from the ravages of modernity and expansion.

Orientation and Practical Information Stein am Rhein's **tourist office** (tel. 741 28 35; fax 741 51 46) lies on the Oberstadt, to the left of the Rathaus. Stop by for hotel tips, maps, and cruise information (open Mon.-Fri. 9-11am and 2-5pm). From the train station, walk down Bahnhofstr., bear right going downhill, walk across the bridge, and arrive in the *Altstadt*. Before you do, **exchange currency** and **rent bikes** at the **train station** (open Mon.-Fri. 5am-11pm, Sat.-Sun. 5:55am-11pm). Trains connect Stein am Rhein to Schaffhausen (6.60SFr), St. Gallen (23SFr), Winterthur (11.40SFr), and Konstanz (9SFr). **Buses** connect the string of small towns in the area to Stein Am Rhein, as well as to Germany. **Boats** depart three times daily (once on Sun.) for Schaffhausen (1hr.15min.; 13.80SFr), Constance (2hr.15min.; 16.60SFr), and other Bodensee towns. **Parking** is available along the Hemihoferstr., off of the Untertor (lot open 10am-6pm). The **post office** is carefully hidden from the main street on Brodlaubegasse. From the Rathaus, walk down Rathauspl., and take a right onto Brodlaubegasse. The post office is straight ahead on the right. (Open Mon.-Fri. 7:30am-noon and 1:45-6pm, Sat. 8-11am.) **Postal code:** CH-8260. **Telephone code:** 054.

Accommodations and Food A 10-minute walk along Hemihoferstr. leads to the suburban **Jugendherberge (HI),** Hemihoferstr. 711 (tel. 741 12 55; fax 741 51 40). From the train station, take the bus to "Strandbad," cross the street, and walk the gravel path to the end. You'll see the flags in front of the hostel across the street. The hostel is clean, and the English-speaking staff is very friendly. Some rooms have a great view of the Rhine. (Reception open 7:30-9am and 5:30-10pm. Curfew 10:30pm but keys available. 21.50SFr, 19SFr subsequent nights; doubles 27SFr, 24.50SFr subsequent nights. 5SFr surcharge for non-members. Breakfast, sheets, and showers included. Open March-Oct.) Head to the gilded **Co-op** at the corner of Rathauspl. and Schwarzhorngasse for picnic supplies. (Open Mon.-Fri. 8:15am-12:15pm and 2pm-6:30pm, Sat. 7:30am-4:50pm). People-watch along the Rathausplatz in one of the many restaurants and cafés with outdoor seating. **The Spaghetteria,** Schifflände (tel. 741 22 36), sits directly on the Rhine and serves up cheap but tasty Italian fare, with pasta dishes starting at 11SFr, and beers at 4.20SFr for ½liter. It's also home of the world's longest piece of spaghetti at 188.8m. (Open March 15-Oct. 31 daily 9am-midnight. Free beer with lunch if you show your *Let's Go.*) The **Restaurant Roten Ochsen,** Rathausplatz 9 (tel. 741 23 28) cooks up Swiss dishes (9-28.50SFr) and tosses a mean salad (11-16.50SFr). (Open Tues.-Thurs. and Sun. 9:30am-11:30pm, Fri.-Sat. 9:30am-12:30am.)

Sights and Entertainment Stein am Rhein first came to prominence in the 12th century with the establishment of the **Kloster St. George** (tel. 741 21 24), a Benedictine monastery, perhaps the best preserved in the German-speaking world. The monks' rooms haven't changed since the 16th century. The intricate frescoes, wood carvings on the paneled walls, and the parquet floors are of particular note (open March-Nov. 10am-noon and 1:30-5pm; 3SFr, students 1.50SFr).

To the right of the Kloster, the stately **Rathaus** surveys Stein am Rhein's main thoroughfare. The outside is spectacularly decorated with colorful frescoes (as are the rest of the square's buildings) depicting everything from wine-making to mythology. The third floor holds a to-die-for collection of his and her armor (for the lady may we suggest a nice hauberk, and for the gentleman, why look at these chain-mail stockings). For a viewing, call 741 54 25. On the Untertor, the **Wohnmuseum Lindwurm,** Understadt 33 (tel. 741 25 12; fax 741 45 82), reconstructs domestic life in the 19th century. The building's delicate façade is a masterwork of 19th-century architecture (open March-Oct. Wed.-Mon. 10am-5pm; 5SFr, students 3SFr). Down the street, Mike D, Adrock, and MCA could learn a lesson or two at the **Phonograph Museum,** Rathauspl. 17 (tel. 741 31 97), where your great-grandfather's wax mixes it up in the halls of vinyl (open March-Oct. daily 10am-5pm). Near the Rhine, on the quiet Schwarzhorngasse (a left off of the main street from the Monastery), the **Puppenmuseum,** Schwarzhorngasse 136 (tel. 741 39 66), displays every kind of doll you can imagine, from ancient, balding babies to recent facsimiles of Swiss girls at play (open mid-April to mid-Oct. Tues.-Sun. 11am-5pm; 5SFr, students 4SFr).

A vigorous 20-minute hike from the town center through vineyards and forest leads to the **Burg Hohenklingen.** From the main square, walk to the parking lot outside the *Fußgängerzone,* and follow the yellow *Wanderweg* signs up the hill to the castle. Built in the 13th century, the castle now serves as a popular but expensive restaurant (tel. 741 21 37; open Tues.-Sun. 11am-2pm and 5:30-9:30pm). Walk through the restaurant and climb the ladder-steps to the top of the **Turm** for a breathtaking view of the town and the Rhine.

EASTERN SWITZERLAND

LIECHTENSTEIN

Famous chiefly for its wines, royal family, and, yes, postage stamps, Liechtenstein's minute size (at 160 sq. km, about the same as Manhattan) and population (30,629 people) render it a favorite among sadistic geography teachers. The principality itself is more of a tourist attraction than any individual sight it contains. Though brochures entreat visitors to "go *to* Liechtenstein, not through it," most travelers breeze right through, only pausing long enough to buy the official "*Hurra! Ich bin da*" (hurray, I'm here!) postage stamp or hastily record the visit in a passport.

The only German-speaking monarchy in the world, Liechtenstein remains one of the last vestiges of the former Holy Roman Empire. Recognized as a country since 1719, it's been without an army since 1868—the last active unit was an 80-man force that patrolled the Italian border and saw no action other than the occasional blizzard on the Stelvio Pass. The principality has used the Swiss franc as its currency since 1924 and has adopted the Swiss postal and telephone systems. Liechtenstein's official language is German, though many among the predominantly Roman Catholic population also speak English and French. Although **biking** is a dream in the flatter areas of this green kingdom, there's an efficient and cheap **postal bus** system linking all 11 villages (most trips 2.40SFr; Swisspass valid). A one month bus ticket (20SFr) covers all of Liechtenstein and includes buses to Swiss and Austrian border towns such as Feldkirch and Buchs. If you plan to stay more than three days (a sojourn which may tax the imagination), it's a great buy. To enter the principality, catch a postal bus from Sargans or Buchs in Switzerland, or Feldkirch just across the Austrian border. Each of the three trips costs 3.60SFr. There is only one **telephone code** for all of Liechtenstein: 075. For **police,** call 117; for **fire,** call 118.

■ Vaduz

More a hamlet than a national capital, Vaduz is Liechtenstein's tourist center—and not a budget-friendly place. Tour buses deposit their loads directly in front of the dozens of souvenir shops and postcard stands on the main streets, while restauranteurs inflate menu prices knowing that hungry tourists have to eat. Above the town sits the 12th-century **Schloß Vaduz,** regal home to Hans Adam II, Prince of Liechtenstein. Along with *Seine Durchlaucht* (His Highness), the castle houses an excellent collection of Dutch and Flemish art, gathered by the royal family over the last 400 years. Unfortunately, the ruler's residence is off limits to the bourgeois masses. Much of the art, however, makes its way to the **Staatliche Kunstsammlung,** Städtle 37, next to the tourist office (open daily 10am-noon and 1:30-5pm; Apr.-Oct. 10am-noon and 1:30-5:30pm; 5SFr, students 3SFr). In addition, much of the Prince's art eventually ends up on postage stamps, and therefore in the one-room **Briefmarkenmuseum** (Stamp Museum) on the other side of the tourist office. The museum features rare postage from around the globe as well as one of the staples of the country's GDP—nearly one-fourth of Liechtenstein's income comes from its postage stamps (open Sept.-Mar. daily 10am-noon and 1:30-5pm; Apr.-Oct. daily 10am-noon and 1:30-5:30pm; free). If the idea of seeing 300 types of skis and 180 pairs of boots thrills you, check out the **Ski Museum,** Bangarten 10 (tel. 232 15 02), up the road to Schaan and on the left (open Mon. and Fri. 2–6pm or by appointment; 5SFr).

Groups of ten or more people can arrange to visit the **Hofkellerei des Regierenden Fürsten von Liechtenstein** (Wine Cellars of the Ruling Prince of Liechtenstein), and taste wines from the private vineyards of the Prince. Reservations are required. Write to: Feldstr. 4, FL-9490 Vaduz, or call for the wine tasting (tel. 232 10 18; fax 233 11 45).

Liechtenstein's **national tourist office,** Städtle 37 (tel. 392 11 11 or 232 14 43; fax 392 16 18), one block up the hill from the Vaduz-Post bus stop, stamps passports

(2SFr), distributes free maps and advice on hiking, cycling, and skiing in the area, locates rooms free of charge, and makes hotel reservations at any of the country's 46 hotels and guest houses (2SFr). (Open June-Oct. Mon.-Fri. 8am-noon and 1:30-5:30pm, Sat.-Sun. 9am-noon and 1-4pm; Nov.-March Mon.-Fri. 8am-noon and 1:30-5:30pm; April-May Mon-Fri 8am-noon and 1:30-5:30pm. English spoken.) If the tourist office is closed and you are in desperate need of a passport stamp, head to the postage museum. For **currency exchange** at acceptable rates, go to Switzerland. No kidding. Liechtenstein's banks charge exorbitant rates. (If you must, change money in the train stations in **Buchs** and **Sargans** and use a credit card whenever you can.) The main **post office** is near the tourist office (open Mon.-Fri. 8am-6pm, Sat. 8-11am; **postal code:** FI-9490). **Cycling** enthusiasts can rent trusty steeds (20SFr per day) at the train station in Buchs or Sargans leaving an ID as deposit. **Swimmers** bathe at the swimming pool, Muhlehölz, Schaanerstr. 60, just down the street from the youth hostel (see below). The complex boasts two high dives and a child wading pool. Walk out of the hostel's driveway and toward the main road, but instead of turning left, continue straight. (Open June-Aug. Mon. 10am-8pm, Tues.-Sun. 9am-8pm. May and Sept. Mon 10am-7pm, Tues.-Sun. 9am-7pm. 4.50SFr, children 2SFr, with a 10SFr lock deposit.)

Liechtenstein's lone **Jugendherberge (HI),** Untere Rütigasse 6 (tel. 232 50 22, fax 232 58 56), is in **Schaan,** one town over from Vaduz. Take the bus (from the Vaduz bus stand, dir: Schaan) to "Mühleholz." Walk toward the intersection with the traffic lights and turn down Marianumstr. Walk 4-5 minutes and follow the signs to this newly renovated and spotless pink hostel, set on the edge of a farm. The hostel is an arcade junky's paradise, with füßball, pinball, air hockey, and video games in the basement and ping pong tables outside. (Reception open Mon.-Sat. 7-9:30am and 5-10pm, Sun. 6-10pm. Curfew 10pm. Members only. 26.30SFr. Doubles 32.30SFr per person, family quads 28.30 per person. Laundry facilities. Showers and breakfast included. Dinner 12SFr. Open March-Nov. 15.) If the hostel is full, walk about 10 minutes back up the road toward Vaduz or take the bus (dir: Schaan) to "Falknis" for **Hotel Falknis** (tel. 232 63 77) right near the stop. (Singles and doubles 50SFr per person. Breakfast and showers included. Closed Dec. 24-Jan. 15). Eating out cheaply in expensive Liechtenstein is extremely hard; shop at **Denner Superdiscount,** Aulestr. 20, next to the Old Castle Inn for an inexpensive picnic (open Mon.-Fri. 8:30am-1pm and 1:30-6:30pm, Sat. 8am-4pm). In the same shopping complex try **Azzuro Pizza** (tel. 232 48 18). Take out or stand at the white tables to eat (open Mon.-Sat. 8am-8pm, Sun. 10am-5pm). For an unusually mechanized treat, pop in 2SFr in the ice cream machine just opposite the post office. Pull out the cone and watch the ice cream automatically swirl in, no hands necessary.

■ Upper Liechtenstein

It seems impossible that a country so small could have regions, but the clusters of villages in the upper country do have a character of their own. They are all accessible by short bus rides (under 40min.). The old Valaisian-style houses and the chapels of **Masescha, Steg,** and **Malbien** stand out. The "upper" in Upper Liechtenstein does not refer to a northern position but to the elevation; high on top of the mountains one is surrounded by clouds, cows, and a gorgeous view of the **Rhine Valley.**

Triesenberg, the principal town, was founded in the 13th century by a group of Swiss immigrants known as the Walsers. Overpopulation, oppression, and natural disaster drove them from Valais to present-day Liechtenstein, where they chose the highest arable mountain as the site for their village. The **Walser Heimatmuseum** chronicles the Walsers' religious customs, the construction of their huts, their cattle trades, and craft work in the villages. The ground floor houses wood sculptures by folk artist Rudolf Schädles. (Open June-Aug. Tues.-Fri. 1:30-5:30pm, Sat. 1:30-5pm, Sun. 2-5pm; Sept.-May Tues.-Fri. 1:30-5:30pm, Sat. 1:30-5pm. 2SFr, students 1SFr.) The **tourist office** (tel. 262 19 26), is in the same building as the museum and has the same hours. For a night's repose, the **Pension Schönblick,** Winkel 617 (tel. 262 19 05 or 262 30 94), offers warm beds fifteen minutes from the tourist office. Turn left onto the main street, away from the church, and walk almost all the way to Rotenboden, in Winkel. The tourist office also has a detailed map. The hotel offers rustic rooms with spectacular views of the valley below. (Singles 40SFr. Doubles 70SFr. Breakfast and showers included. Open year-round.) Liechtenstein's two **campgrounds**, peaceful almost to a fault, are easily accessible by postal bus. **Bendern** (tel. 373 12 11) is on the Schellenberg line (3SFr per person, 2-4SFr per tent). **Camping Mittagspitze** (tel. 392 36 77 or 392 26 86) lies between Triesen and Balzers on the road to Sargans. (Reception open 7am-noon and 2-10pm. 8SF per person. Tent 5SFr.)

Malbun, on the other side of the mountain from Triesenberg, dubbed "the undiscovered St. Moritz," offers secluded and affordable ski slopes and has served as a training ground for many an Olympian. Highlights are two chairlifts, four T-bars, two ski schools, and a dearth of other skiers. (Daypass 32SFr. Weekly pass 139SFr, off-season 129SFr.) Ski school **Malbun A.G.** (tel. 263 97 70 or 262 19 15) offers one-day classes (45SFr), five-day classes (140SFr), and even private snowboard lessons (1 day 190SFr). **Franz Beck** (tel. 262 29 34) rents skis (1 day 43SFr, including boots and poles) and snowboards. The Valüna valley, 2km from Malbun, offers 4-track, lighted cross-country ski trails. For those who want to say "been there, done that" with grand panache, try **bungee jumping** in Liechtenstein. Call 263 46 27 and speak to Günter (140SFr), or try **paragliding** (tel. 232 72 88, 150SFr including photos). Malbun's **tourist office** (tel. 263 65 77) is open June-Oct. and mid-Dec. to mid-April Mon.-Wed. and Fri. 9am-noon and 1:30-5pm, Sat. 9am-noon and 1:30-4pm. The superb duo of chalet-cum-hotels **Hotel Alpen** and **Hotel Galina** (tel. 263 11 81 and fax 263 96 46) are the hotels of choice in Malbun. Family-run, with wood paneling and a heated swimming pool, these hotels are perfect for après-ski unwinding. (Singles and doubles 40-65SFr per person, with shower 65-100SFr. Breakfast and pool included. Reception in Hotel Alpen for both. Open June-Sept. and Dec. 15-April 15.)

As two-thirds of the country is undeveloped mountains, **hiking** in Upper Liechtenstein offers breathtaking views and forest trails. The upper country has 150 km of trails, clearly marked with the yellow *Wanderweg* signs. Tourist offices in Vaduz, Triesenberg, and Malbun offer a free booklet of short hike suggestions; detailed maps cost 14.50SFr at any bookstore or the tourist offices. The top pick of the suggested **hikes** is the round-trip from **Gnalp to Masescha** and back (roughly 3hr.). Other popular power-hikes to prominent peaks include the **Pfälzer-Hütte** (2108m, through Augustenberg to Bettlerjocht; 4-5hr.), **Schönberg** (2104m; 4-5hr.), and **Galinakopf** (2198m; 6-7hr., depending on the route). **Alpine guides** offer group and private climbing courses in the region (in Liechtenstein as well as in neighboring Austria and Switzerland, contact Bargetze Michael, pat. Bergführer, Lavidina 755, FL-9497 Triesenberg; tel. 268 10 05). However, a guided tour isn't necessary; less challenging do-it-yourself hikes start from the Triesenberg church ("Philosophenweg") and run from **Masecha** and back (2-3hr.), or from the parking lot at Malbun near the postal bus stop ("Sass") to Kirchli and down (1-2hr.). The **Liechtenstein Alpine Association** offers guided full- and half- day hikes every Thursday in summer. Routes are published in the previous Saturday's newspaper, with a contact number, or consult the tourist office.

AUSTRIA

US$1= 10.36 Schillings (AS)
CDN$1= 7.55AS
UK£1= 16.09AS
IR£1= 16.72AS
AUS$1= 8.02AS
NZ$1= 7.09AS
SAR1= 2.30AS
1SFr= 8.63AS
1kč= 0.39AS
1Ft= 0.07AS

10AS = US$0.96
10AS = CDN$1.33
10AS = UK£0.62
10AS = IR£0.60
10AS = AUS$1.25
10AS = NZ$1.41
10AS = SAR4.34
10AS = 1.16SFr
10AS = 25.44kč
10AS = 140.66Ft

Country Code: 43
International Dialing Prefix: 900 from Vienna, 00 from elsewhere

Three horizontal bars of red, white, and red adorn the flag of the Federal Republic of Austria (Österreich). Legend has it that the flag was a tribute to the great warrior **Friederich Barbarossa**, who had a penchant for getting covered with blood (not his own) during battles. The only part of his body not slathered with gore was the cloth underneath his waistbelt. At 32,276 square miles, the country is almost exactly the size of Maine, and lies at the same latitude as Maine's northern tip. Austria comprises nine semi-autonomous provinces, or Bundesländer. Counterclockwise from the northeast they are: Vienna (Wien), Lower Austria (Niederösterreich), Upper Austria (Oberösterreich), Salzburg, Tyrol (Tirol), Vorarlberg, Carinthia (Kärnten), Styria (Steiermark), and Burgenland. The concern for these political divisions varies according to region, but it is important to remember that Austria is relatively young as a nation while many of its regions have been constructing identities for centuries. The Tirolers get really emotional about their "Tirolness;" they nearly seceded from Austria after WWI to stay united with Südtirol. The Styrians are also extremely micro-patriotic (possibly because no one else can understand their dialect). International borders are also important. Though Austria has maintained a core despite being surrounded by seven countries—Hungary, the Czech Republic, Germany, Switzerland, Italy, Slovakia, and diminutive Liechtenstein—many of its inhabitants were once on the other side of what in many cases is now an arbitrary line. The Burgenlanders, for example, are very distinct because of their Hungarian heritage.

Austria's population of 7.8 million is 99 percent German-speaking, but that statistic belies the presence of significant ethnic minorities. The Slovenes of southern Carinthia and the Croats in Burgenland are guaranteed rights by the terms of Article Seven of the Austrian State Treaty of Vienna of 1955. A Hungarian minority inhabits a number of Burgenland towns and villages, and there is a small Slovak community in Vienna. Eighty percent of the Austrian population is Roman Catholic; a further 4.9 percent is Protestant, most ascribing to the Augsburg Confession.

Despite all its political transformations Austria maintains an overpowering physical beauty. With onion-domed churches set against snow-capped Alpine peaks, lush meadows blanketed with edelweiss, pristine mountain lakes, dark cool forests, and mighty castles towering over the majestic Danube, Austria truly is as dreamy as the photos you've seen. Situated in the eastern portion of the European Alps, more than half of the country is covered by mountains. Western Austria, in particular, is dominated almost entirely by them, rising to the Großglockner, the highest peak in Austria at 3,797m (12,457 feet). Humans clearly play a lesser role in these areas; the two largest cities contain barely 300,000 people between them. The mountains generate year-round tourism: alpine sports dominate the winter scene, while lakeside frolicking draws visitors in the warmer months. The exception to this alpine environment is generally found in the eastern part of the country, where agricultural plains and lush vineyards abound. Rivers also play an important role. The Danube, Europe's longest river, has been central to Austrian industry and aristocracy since the beginning, with both the Babenburgs and the Habsburgs setting up residences on its shores. Vienna, once the imperial residence and now the country's capital, is also built around it. To cap off all this scenery, forests and meadows cover two thirds of the total area of Austria, making it the most densely forested nation in Europe.

■ History and Politics

Perhaps the most remarkable aspect of Austrian history is the absence of a consistently Austrian identity. For centuries the locus of an empire that stretched throughout Europe, Austria, though consistently ruled by ethnic Germans, included a myriad ethnic mix—Magyars, Slovenes, Flemings, Slavs, and Italians were all part of the empire. It was not until the 19th century that anything resembling a transcendent nationalism could be detected. This movement ran simultaneous to the German exaltation of the *Volk* and shared the same goal— to create a nation out of a multi-ethnic empire. However, this empire was soon dismantled following World War I, when Austria was stripped of its imperial possessions, and the Austrian Republic was born. The existence of a national state, even then, did not a nation make: Austria attempted to join the Greater German Republic in fear that the arbitrary rump Austria wouldn't be economically viable.

The separation of the two, forced by foreign armies and international treaty, was finally ended by Hitler's seduction, which plunged the nation into barbarism, war, and defeat. A unique and lasting Austrian identity has been formed, in part, as a reaction to the horrors of Nazism. The Second Austrian Republic, founded in 1945 separated Austria from Germany, creating a meaningful Austrian homeland and national identity in the process. Since World War II, Austria has made a distinct effort to develop this selfhood, though the bonds of nationalism are still not as strong here as elsewhere. This is by no means a liability—internationally neutral, democratic, Western-oriented, and a newly admitted member of the European Union, the Second Republic has fashioned a progressive social democratic welfare state that seems to work as well as any in the hemisphere.

EARLY HISTORY

Though humans have inhabited Austria since Paleolithic times (80,000-10,000 BC), little evidence of this lengthy period remains. Around 5000 BC, hunter-gatherers began to settle the highlands, where they farmed, raised stock animals, mined **salt,** and periodically froze in the Alpine passes. One of the latter was discovered in 1991, his body mummified in the glacial ice of the Ötztal Alps.

Around 400 BC, the **Celts** took control of the salt mines and established the kingdom of **Noricum,** which developed a successful culture and economy based on a far-ranging salt and iron trade. The **Romans** to the south appreciated the trade-link, but ended up conquering their Austrian neighbors (30-15 BC) in order to secure the Danube frontier against the marauding Germans. During the centuries of the *Pax Romana,* Noricum thrived, and an urban economy developed, spurring the creation of cities such as **Vindobona** (Vienna), **Juvavum** (Salzburg), **Aguntum** (Lienz), and **Brigantium** (Bregenz). **Marcus Aurelius** wrote his famous *Meditations* and then died in Vindobona, starting a long tradition of Viennese artistic emigrés. Roman roads along the Danube and through the Alps allowed legions, traders, and missionaries (both Pagan and Christian) free access until the end of the second century, when the frontier began to weaken. An increase in Germanic raids finally resulted in the Roman abandonment of the province in the 5th century.

Over the next three centuries, Huns, Ostrogoths, Lombards, and others occasionally rampaged through the territories but failed to establish any more than a transitory presence. The region was primarily occupied by three different groups: **Alemanni** in the south, **Slavs** in the southwest, and **Bavarians** in the north. Modern placenames ending in *-itz* indicate Slavic origins, while endings *-heim* and *-ing(en)* reveal Germanic settlement. The few Celts left in the highlands retained both Celtic place names and **Christianity,** though the new lowland settlers were not converted until the arrival of Irish missionaries in the early 7th century. Further Christianization was carried out by the dukes of Bavaria, who did so in an attempt to bring a semblance of law and order to the area and create a power base free of Frankish influence. With the missionaries' successes, **Salzburg** became an archbishopric in 798; it remained Austria's ecclesiastical capital well into the modern era.

Try as they might, the Bavarian dukes, most notably **Duke Tassilo III** (740-788), were unable to secure Austria as their own personal power base. **Charlemagne,** crowned Holy Roman Emperor, claimed eastern Austria as a border province of the Carolingian empire, and began to develop a distinct concept of Austria as an entity in order to prevent war with the Bavarians, who, having retained control of western Austria, sought to expand their influence eastward. The name *Österreich* means "Eastern Empire," referring to the easternmost lands that Charlemagne conquered. Eager to keep the area out of Bavarian hands, the Carolingian emperors had placed the *Mark* (borderland) of *Österreich* in the charge of a non-Bavarian *Markgraf,* or **margrave.**

THE HOUSE OF BABENBERG

The invasion of the Asian **Magyars** ended with their defeat at Lechfeld at the hand of **Otto I,** the first magnate elected in Germany to continue the Holy Roman Empire. He restored the *Mark* and installed **Leopold of Babenberg** as margrave in 976.

The house of Babenberg ruled *Ostarrîchi,* as eastern Austria was now known, from 976 to 1246. The Babenbergs stabilized the frontiers, extending their protectorate north of the Danube and farther east and south into Magyar (later Hungarian) lands. Monasteries and abbeys founded by the Babenbergs played an important role in the re-colonization of the depopulated country with **German settlers,** who cleared the country for farming and increased the Germanic hold over the developing Austrian consciousness. Though they took the side of the Pope during the **Investiture Conflict,** disagreeing with Henry IV who took upon himself the authority to appoint clergy, the Babenbergs, including **Leopold III** (1095-1136), later Austria's patron saint, were generally very loyal to the Holy Roman Emperors. This eventually earned them, in 1156, the elevation of their margraviate into a duchy.

The Babenberg territories benefited economically from traffic with the east during the Crusades. The family also secured a large part of the ransom that England paid to rescue **Richard the Lionheart,** who had been detained in Austria by **Leopold V** on his way home from the Third Crusade. Leopold used the ransom to fortify the towns of Wiener Neustadt and Vienna. In that same year, 1192, Leopold V obtained the Duchy of **Styria** (today southeast Austria) through a contract of inheritance. In the first half of the 13th century, cultural life at the court of the Babenbergs was in full bloom. **Minnesängers** (minstrels) wrote epic ballads (including the **Nibelungenlied**) and **Romanesque architecture** came to a late fruition.

THE RISE OF THE HABSBURGS

The last Babenburg, **Friedrich II** "the Quarrelsome," was faced by an angry emperor to the west, rebellious nobles to the north, and nervous Hungarians (they were under threat of Mongol invasion) to the east. He died childless at the hands of the latter in 1246, leaving Austria fragmented and unruly. Order was restored by the Bohemian King **Ottokar II,** who married Friedrich's sister, reconquered Styria, and attached the Duchy of **Carinthia** (now south-central Austria) to his holdings.

Meanwhile, after the 19-year *Interregnum,* a new Emperor had emerged in the Holy Roman Empire—the Swiss **Rudolf of Habsburg,** who demanded the Slavic Ottokar's allegiance. When Ottokar refused, Rudolf attacked with support from the Austrian nobility, defeating Ottokar at Marchfeld in 1278. In 1282, Rudolf granted his two sons the Duchies of *Ostarrîchi* and Styria, thus laying the foundations for Habsburg dynastic rule in the region. The Habsburgs would retain power in Austria almost continuously until 1918, through 19 Habsburg emperors and one empress.

At the inception of Habsburg rule, the family's dominance was far from secure. It was primarily weakened by the lack of primogeniture, or full inheritance by the first son; instead, the lands were divided among all the sons. Even though the territories tended to agglomerate themselves again, this made for at least temporary instability. There were incessant revolts, even by the Swiss, who had earlier belonged to one of the most loyal Habsburg territories. During the late Middle Ages, the Habsburgs focused on expanding their holdings and defending their inflating borders. Rudolf the Founder's short rule (1358-1365) was marked by the acquisition of the Earldom of **Tirol** (now southwest Austria). He founded the **University of Vienna** and commissioned improvements to St. Stephen's in Vienna as well. When Rudolf felt his family had been passed over by the Luxembourg Emperor Karl IV, he forged several documents, later called the **Privilegium maius,** to demonstrate his dynasty's higher rank. Rudolf's descendant, Emperor **Friedrich III,** affirmed the claims made in these documents and strategically arranged the marriage of his son, **Maximilian I,** to the heiress of the powerful Burgundian kingdom, which gave Austria control of the Low Countries. In response to incursions by the imperial Turkish forces along the Danube and Drau Rivers, Maximilian consolidated his regime through various **centralizing reforms.** During his rule, Vienna became a center of humanistic culture. In 1493, Maximilian became the first Habsburg to claim the title of Holy Roman Emperor without papal coronation, which gave the family hereditary rights to the imperial throne. Through his prudent marital alliances, he ensured the hereditary succession of lands far and wide and laid the foundations for the vast territory to come under Habsburg rule during the pinnacle of the empire. Maximilian not only married well—his wife was heiress to the duchies of Burgundy as well as territories in western France—but deftly arranged the marriage of his son Philip as well. He was married to the daughter of Spain's royal duo, Ferdinand and Isabella, heirs to the combined **Kingdom of Spain.** The child produced by this union was **Karl V** (known as Charles I in Spain). He not only combined the inheritance of his four grandparents: Austria, the Netherlands, Aragon and its Italian and Mediterranean possessions, Castile, and the Spanish Americas, but also was elected Holy Roman Emperor in 1519 as well, adding Germany to the list. Dwarfing any other political entity in Europe the Habsburg empire became the first on which the sun never set.

Under Karl V, the Habsburgs came the closest to their prophetic motto **"A.E.I.O.U.,"** meaning *"Alles Erdreich ist Österreich untertan"* (Austria is destined to rule the world). A less boastful and probably more accurate motto might have been the popular couplet written by the shrewd organizer of this whole affair, Maximilian, which stated: *"Bella gerant alii, tu felix Austria nube"* (Other nations go to war while you, lucky Austria, marry). It seems that the 1960s owe a creative debt to Maximilian, for penning the original "Make love, not war."

THE HABSBURG EMPIRE

The massive territory and majestic imperial sheen concealed anxieties among the Habsburgs. The **Ottoman Empire,** which had been encroaching on Europe since the 14th century, began to threaten the continent more and more in the 1500s and 1600s. After the conquest of Constantinople, the Turks consistently undertook expeditions farther west, becoming a permanent threat to the Habsburg patrimonial lands. In 1529, their armies reached the gates of Vienna only to be beaten back.

This was not sufficient to quell the disturbances, however. The Ottoman threat placed a huge strain on the stagnant Austrian economy; the emperors required a monstrous army to defend the territories and also spent lavishly on construction and art to divert cultural attention from their French counterparts. Social unrest, fomented by the **Reformation,** further threatened to undermine stability. Burghers and nobles were drawn to Protestantism because it affirmed rationality. Peasants found the doctrine attractive because it freed them from onerous tithes to the

Church. Social hierarchies, though, kept the two groups from forming a united front against the emperor and Church. Along with the reformation came an increase in literacy. Now able to read the Bible themselves, the peasants realized that there was no biblical sanction for serfdom. Predictably upset, they rebelled. The Austrian rulers hired mercenaries who mercilessly crushed the rebels in the **Peasants' Wars** of 1525-6. Several leaders tolerant of Protestantism followed, allowing it to flourish peacefully. However, the protestant Bohemians felt that their religious liberties were being infringed upon by the Habsburg emperor **Matthias** (1612-1619), especially when he sent two emissaries to sort things out. The taking of matters into their own hands resulted in the **defenstration of Prague** (1618), in which the emissaries were thrown out of a window. This act of defiance was then followed by the overthrow of Matthias. His successor Archduke **Ferdinand II** (1619-1637) was not so easily handled. His victory during the early stages of the resultant and largely religiously fueled **Thirty Years' War** (1618-1648) over the Protestant forces commanded by **Frederick V,** won the Habsburgs hereditary control of Bohemia, and led to the forcible return of most of the peasants to Catholicism and the consolidation of the Catholic church. The culmination of the war was not so beneficial for the Habsburg dynasty, however; the **Peace of Westphalia** (1648) brought about the independence of the German States that the Habsburgs had been trying to consolidate under their dominion.

In 1683, the Ottoman Turks sat on Vienna's doorstep once again. Austria's brilliant military response was largely the handiwork of **Prince Eugene of Savoy.** The Prince's triumph had a drastic impact on Western Europe which as a result was never colonized by the Ottoman empire and converted to Islam. Not content to rest at home, Prince Eugene pressed his forces into Turkish lands, capturing Hungary, Transylvania and Croatia. His martial exploits culminated in the **Peace of Belgrade** (1739) in which the two empires negotiated a common boundary that was for the most part respected until the twentieth century. Victory over the Turks generated an era of celebration; to honor Austrian prowess, magnificent buildings were constructed and wounded castles, churches, and monasteries were finally repaired. Opera flourished under the auspices of Johann Josef Fux. This patriotic exuberance, tempered by a deep religious conviction, was the prevailing trademark of the Austrian **Baroque.** After Eugene of Savoy rescued Vienna from this second Turkish siege, **Leopold I** gave him control of the army. Eugene also successfully led the Habsburg troops against the French during the **War of Spanish Succession,** which raged in Europe from 1701 to 1714, with **Louis XIV** attempting to defend his newly inherited Spanish empire, passed to him by **Charles II,** ruler of Spain. When the war ended with the signing of the **Treaty of Utrecht** in 1713, France kept Spain, but the Habsburgs gained Belgium, Sardinia, and parts of Italy. By 1718, the Habsburg emperors had direct control of Bohemia, Moravia, Silesia, Hungary, Croatia, Transylvania, Belgium, Lombardy, Naples, Sicily, and, of course, Austria.

By the 1730s, however, the empire was extremely decentralized and poorly run. The nobles maintained great power, though the majority of the population were still serfs. The minuscule middle class and guild artisans were held in check by Austria's inconvenient location, out of the way of most major trading routes. A benevolent and loyal man, Emperor **Karl VI** did not know how to run his empire. His diplomatic and military failures in life were matched by his failure at his death to leave a male heir. After constant political deal-making he was able to win the acceptance of the **Pragmatic Sanction** of 1713, in which most of the powers in Europe had agreed to recognize succession of the Habsburgs through the female line if the male line fell extinct, allowing Charles' daughter **Maria Theresa** to become empress in 1740. Maria Theresa married Franz Stephan of Lorraine in 1736, who, though elected Emperor of the Holy Roman Empire in 1745, was overshadowed throughout his life by his wife's personality and intelligence.

Meanwhile, Prussian King **Friedrich the Great** was beginning the military expansions that would one day lead to a powerful German state. One of his many successful campaigns snatched away Silesia (now southwest Poland), one of the empire's most prosperous provinces; Maria Theresa spent the rest of her life unsuccessfully maneuvering to reclaim it. The empress was, however, able to maintain her rule during the **Wars of Austrian Succession** from 1740 to 1748 with help from the Hungarians, but she lost the Italian lands of Lombardy. Diplomatic warfare ensued, waged by her wily foreign minister **Count Kaunitz,** who reconsidered the age-old rift between France and Austria and proposed an alliance between the two. The marriage of Maria Theresa's daughter to the future Louis XVI was one such outcome of what came to be known as the **Diplomatic Revolution** of 1756. Kaunitz's new alliance was not as successful as he planned and the stalemate that resulted from the **Seven Years War** (1756-1763) underscored the waning influence of the Austrian empire and the rise of Prussia as a great power. Maria Theresa and her son **Josef II** undertook a series of enlightened reforms to stimulate the economy, such as improving tax collection, increasing settlements, encouraging religious freedom, aiding industry, and decreasing feudal burdens. A new state system transformed the agglomeration of lands that had hitherto been only loosely connected into a tightly administered central state. Under Maria Theresa and the enlightened Joseph, the empire, and Vienna in particular, became a center of culture and commerce. **Christoph Willibald Gluck, Josef Haydn,** and **Wolfgang Amadeus Mozart** composed their main works in the Theresian court of imperial Vienna. When Josef took over after the death of Maria Theresa in 1780, the process toward a centralized and "rationally" governed Austria was greatly accelerated. In 1781 Josef issued the **Toleration Patent,** giving numerous Protestant sects religious freedom, and liberated the serfs everywhere except Hungary (their emancipation soon followed). Though Josef initially encouraged public political consciousness and expression, his development of one of the first centralized bureaucratic governments came towards the end of his reign to rely on the influence of the Ministry of Police, which he systematically employed to censor the media and repress political dissidents.

THE END OF THE HOLY ROMAN EMPIRE

The doctrines behind the **French Revolution** gained ground in 18th-century Austria and represented a serious threat to Austrian absolutism. **Emperor Franz II,** grandson of Maria Theresa and nephew of the newly headless French Queen **Marie Antoinette,** joined the coalition against revolutionary France. The French Revolutionary **National Assembly** declared war on Austria in 1792, a war that would continue through France's Second Revolution and showcase the military genius of a young commander General **Napoleon Bonaparte.** The defeat of the Austrians in Northern Italy, and the ensuing **Treaty of Campo Formio** in 1797, in which Austria recognized French possession of Belgium and parts of Italy, became the first in a long series of his victories. The reorganization of Germany performed by the treaty heralded the final demise of the Holy Roman Empire. Facing the inevitable, Franz II renounced his claim to the now-defunct Holy Roman crown in 1804 and proclaimed himself Franz I, Emperor of Austria—only at this point was an Austrian empire as such founded. At the **Congress of Vienna** in 1815, which redrew the map of Europe after Napoleon's defeat, Austrian Chancellor of State **Clemens Wenzel Lothar Metternich,** "the Coachman of Europe," restored the old order in Europe while masterfully orchestrating the re-consolidation of Austrian power. Metternich preached the gospel of "legitimacy" and stability—in other words, the perpetuation of conservative government—to achieve a balance of power in European politics. His machinations ushered in a long period of peace in Europe, during which commerce and industry flourished.

1848 AND THE REIGN OF FRANZ JOSEF

The first half of the 19th century was marked by immense technological progress **Industrialization** took over, accompanied by rapid population growth and urbanization, and the working and middle classes were born. The French philosophy of a **middle-class revolution** reached Austria in the spring of 1848. Students and workers joined together in an insurrection, building barricades, taking control of the Imperial palace, and demanding a constitution and freedom of the press. Metternich's government was so taken by surprise that Metternich himself resigned and fled to England. A constituent assembly, the *Konstitutierende Reichstag,* abolished feudalism in all non-Hungarian lands. Ethnic rivalries and political differences divided the revolutionary forces, however, and the Habsburgs were able to suppress the revolution in October of 1848. The year 1848 also marked the brutal suppression of a rebellion in Hungary (with help from Russia), the forced abdication of the weakened emperor **Ferdinand I,** and the coronation of **Kaiser Franz-Josef I,** whose reign (1848-1916) stands as one of the longest of any monarch in history. The new leader created a highly centralized state based on an alliance of the army, police, and the bureaucracy of both the government and the Catholic Church.

Losses to France and Italy were overshadowed by **Bismarck's** victory over the Austrian armies in 1866, which dislodged Austria from its position of leadership in Germany and established Prussia in its place. Franz-Josef was forced to assent to what passed as a constitutional monarchy, but he remained firmly in control, and the Austrian state actually became more centralized and autocratic than it was before. Under the terms of the **Ausgleich** (compromise) of 1867, a dual monarchy was established, giving **Hungary** the co-equal status of kingdom alongside Austria, with foreign policy, finance, and defense in the hands of the emperor, who remained Austrian. In reality, German speakers still dominated the so-called **Austro-Hungarian Empire,** with the Magyars next in the pecking order and all the subject peoples at the bottom. This construction was fundamentally flawed in its lack of concern for the countless other nationalities represented in the dual empire; Czechs, Poles, Slovenes, and Croats, to name just a few. To its credit, the Austrian Kingdom had by 1907 ceded basic civil rights to the population and accepted universal male suffrage, with the first general elections to the Imperial Council *(Reichsrat)* taking place that year.

Along with liberalism and socialism, a new movement began to take hold in Austria during this period. **Pan-Germanism,** the desire to abandon the eastern empire and unite with the German Reich, flourished under the leadership of **Georg von Schönerer,** whose doctrines were to have a profound influence on Adolf Hitler. By the turn of the century, Vienna was in political turmoil; the anti-Semitic **Christian Socialists,** under **Karl Lueger,** were on the rise. *Ruhe und Ordnung* (peace and order) was the Kaiser's motto, but his policies amounted in practice to trying to stop the irreversible tide of modernity. (He was known, for instance, to eschew indoor plumbing.) Austria continued to be treated as a Great Power in Europe, if only because it suited the purposes of the Prussian-dominated German Reich.

The long period of peace that lasted until the First World War was safeguarded by a complicated system of European **alliances** in which minor disputes could easily escalate into a conflict involving dozens of nations. In 1879 Austria-Hungary joined the German Empire, which, with the addition of Italy in 1882, formed the **Triple Alliance,** balancing the **Triple Entente** of France, Britain, and Russia (and later, the U.S.). Meanwhile, burgeoning nationalist sentiments, especially among the Serbia-inspired South Slavs, led to severe divisions within the multinational Austro-Hungarian Empire. The demands of the working class for better pay and more humane working conditions were another vexing problem for the government.

WORLD WAR I AND THE FIRST REPUBLIC

Brimming with ethnic tension and locked into the rigid system of alliances, the Austro-Hungarian Empire was a disaster waiting to happen. The spark that set off the explosion was the assassination of **Franz Ferdinand,** the heir to the imperial throne, by a Serbian nationalist named **Gavrillo Prinzip** on June 28, 1914. Austria's declaration of war against Serbia set off a chain reaction that pulled most of Europe into the conflict: Russia ran to support Serbia, Germany to support Austria and France to support its Entente partner, Russia. The technologically and organizationally backward Austrian army performed with spectacular ineptitude on the battlefield and was defeated every time it faced serious competition. Only the subordination of the Austrian forces to the German command saved the empire from immediate collapse. Austria's wartime fortunes rose and finally fell with Germany's.

Franz Josef died in 1916, leaving the throne to his grandnephew **Karl I,** who tried to extricate Austria from the war with its empire intact. The Entente powers, recognizing that the Habsburg goose was already cooked, rebuffed Karl's advances and proclaimed a goal of self-determination for the Habsburg nationalities. On November 11, 1918, a week after signing an armistice with the Entente, Karl abdicated, bringing the 640-year-old dynasty to a close.

Worry over economic viability due to the fact that industry was mostly located in what were now Slavic lands following World War I caused revolution in the streets of Vienna, and brought about the proclamation of the **Republic of Deutsch-Österreich** (German Austria), a constituent component of the Greater German Republic. The Entente was, however, leery of a powerful pan-German nation, and ruled out a merger of the two nations, forbidding Austria from calling itself German Austria. The new **Austrian republic** or the **First Republic,** as it is known, consisted of the German-speaking lands of the former Habsburg empire minus those granted to Italy, Czechoslovakia, and Hungary—or, in the famous words of French Premier Georges Clemençeau, "what's left over." The old empire had sprawled over 676,615 square kilometers and encompassed some 51.4 million people. After World War I, the new republic covered only 83,850 square kilometers and 6.4 million inhabitants.

The new Austria experienced an unhappy **inter-war period.** The break-up of the empire undermined economic life as former markets became independent sovereign states and closed their borders to Austrian goods. Vienna's population was on the verge of famine. By the middle of the 1920s, however, the Austrian government had succeeded in stabilizing the currency and establishing economic relations with neighboring states. As in Germany, **Communists** attempted to revolt, but the Social Democrats suppressed the rebellion without relying on the right. Political divisions were sharp, especially between "Red Vienna" and the staunchly Catholic provinces; Social Democrats (Reds) and Christian Socialists (Blacks) each regarded the other not just as opposing parties, but as opposing *Lager* (camps). The parties set up paramilitary organizations, and political violence became a fact of life. On this shaky democratic foundation, the authoritarian **Engelbert Dollfuss** created a government in 1932 with a majority of one vote in the National Assembly.

THE ANSCHLUß

The minority **Austrian Nazis** had been agitating for unification with Germany since Hitler took power, but their demands became more menacing after his stunning success facing down the Western powers. Four months after the establishment of the authoritarian Federal State of Austria, Nazi sympathizers attempted a coup in which they murdered Dollfuss. Dollfuss's successor, **Kurt Schuschnigg,** put down the insurgents but faced a stepped-up campaign of agitation by Hitler's agents. Schuschnigg sought to maintain Austria's sovereignty by allying with Italy and Hungary. In 1938, however, Hitler met with Schuschnigg in Berchtesgaden and threatened to invade Austria if **Arthur Seyss-Inquart,** a Nazi, was not named Interior Minister. With the Austrian police thus under their control, the Nazis brought Austria to near chaos. On March 9, 1938, hoping to stave off a Nazi invasion, Schuschnigg called a referendum four days hence on unity with Germany. One day before the plebiscite was to take place, Nazi troops crossed the frontier. Although Josef Goebbels' propaganda wildly exaggerated the enthusiasm of Austrians for Hitler (as did a phony referendum in April, in which 99 percent of Austrians approved of the Anschluß), the myth that Austria was merely a prostrate victim is equally fallacious. When German troops marched into Vienna on March 14, thousands of Austrians turned out to cheer them on. The German Nazi **Racial Purity Laws** were subsequently extended to Austria, a disaster for Austrian Jews, who were deprived of their basic civil and human rights. Many managed to emigrate, but few were allowed to flee after March, 1938. Those left in Austria perished later in Nazi extermination camps. Today, less than .05% of Austria's population is Jewish.

THE SECOND REPUBLIC

After the German defeat in World War II, a coalition of Christian Socialists and Social Democrats declared a Republic with **Karl Renner** as president. The Allies did not impose reparations payments on Austria as they did on Germany, but they did occupy the country and withhold recognition of sovereignty for the decade following the war. The country was divided into four parts; Britain, France, and U.S. held the west, while the eastern portions, including Vienna, came under **Soviet** control. When Stalin assented to free elections, the Soviet-occupied zone voted overwhelmingly to rejoin their western compatriots in a united, democratic Austrian nation. The Austrian **Declaration of Independence** of 1945 proclaimed the existence of an Austrian nation which, unlike the First Republic, claimed no fraternity with Greater Germany. Under the **Constitution Act** and the **State Treaty** of 1955, signed in Vienna's Belvedere Palace, Austria declared its absolute neutrality and earned national sovereignty. **Austrian nationalism,** which under the First Republic had been almost a contradiction in terms, has blossomed in the post-war period.

GOVERNMENT AND POLITICS

The foundation for the Second Republic of Austria is built upon the federal constitution of 1920 and its 1929 amendment. The constitution provides for a bicameral parliament, consisting of a popularly elected lower house, or **Nationalrat,** headed by a **Chancellor,** and an upper house, or **Bundesrat,** whose delegates are appointed by the provincial parliaments. The constitution also created the office of **Federal President,** a largely ceremonial and theoretically non-partisan post. Since the President lacks executive power in peace time, his role is mostly confined to signing treaties and laws, and other similarly formal roles.

Politics in the Second Republic have since been dominated by the **Socialist Party of Austria** (*Sozialistische Partei Österreichs*—**SPÖ**), which was renamed the **Social Democratic Party of Austria** (*Österreichische Sozialdemokratische Partei,* same abbreviation) in 1991. Despite being the majority, though, they have often been compelled to govern in coalition with the second-largest party, the **People's Party of Austria** (*Österreichische Volkspartei*—**ÖVP**), the descendant of the Christian Socialists. In 1949, in the first elections in which fascist and extreme nationalist parties were allowed to compete, the fascist League of Independents tallied a surprising 10 percent of the vote. The League later renamed itself the **Freedom Party** (*Freiheitliche Partei Österreichs*—**FPÖ**) and took on yet another face-lift this past year, renaming itself the **Freedom Movement** (*Die Freiheitlichen*—**F**). It continues to perform strongly, and controls the legislature in the federal state of Carinthia.

As much as politics in the First Republic were characterized by bitter struggle and confrontation, postwar politics have been defined by cooperation, accommodation, and consensus building. In 1966, just as the German Social Democrats were entering the government for the first time in the postwar era, the SPÖ went into opposition for the first time. Four years later, the SPÖ came roaring back under the leadership of the charismatic **Bruno Kreisky,** and in 1973 it gained an absolute majority, which it held until 1983. Under the SPÖ's stewardship, Austria built up one of the world's most successful **industrial economies**—Austria's unemployment and inflation rates are enviably low, even as Austrians enjoy the security of a generous, comprehensive **welfare state.** In the elections of 1983, the SPÖ lost ground and had to form the **Small Coalition** with the FPÖ (which was then under the control of its liberal wing). **Fred Sinowatz** replaced the venerable Kreisky as chancellor. When the FPÖ fell back under the sway of the far Right, the SPÖ abandoned the Small Coalition and returned to the **Grand Coalition** with the ÖVP, which, though shaken by internal disputes, has persisted until today for lack of any alternative. Sinowatz resigned in the wake of a scandal in 1986; he was replaced by the current federal Chancellor, **Franz Vranitzky.** The Coalition remained strong in the recent 1995 elections, with the Social Democrats on top and the Freedom Movement losing some of its seats.

Disturbingly, the Freedom Movement, under the leadership **Jörg Haider,** often labeled a neo-Nazi, continues to do well among younger voters, especially as anxiety about immigration from Eastern Europe grows. Even worse, Austrians elected **Kurt Waldheim** to the largely symbolic and ceremonial Austrian presidency in 1986 despite evidence strongly suggesting that he helped arrange the deportation of Jews to extermination camps when he was an officer in the German army. As an international pariah (he was barred from making state visits to most places, forbidden even to enter the U.S.), Waldheim was a serious embarrassment for Austria. The current President, **Thomas Klestil,** is more widely accepted, despite his confession of a long-term love affair with one of his aides.

THIS YEAR'S NEWS

December's 1995 elections were a continuation of the status quo with little change witnessed in the government. The Grand Coalition of the SPÖ and ÖVP held on to its majority, and Franz Vranitzky remains the Chancellor. Austria's application to the **European Union** was accepted in early 1995, and the Austrian Schilling joined the European **Exchange Rate Mechanism** shortly thereafter. Though long restricted from entering the forthcoming **European Monetary Union** due to the fact that their budget deficit has been above 3 percent of Gross Domestic Product, Finance Minister **Viktor Klima** has recently announced that Austria will reach the quota and take part in the Monetary Union by 1998. The government hopes to achieve this by streamlining subsidies, cutting welfare benefits and public expenditures, and beginning a more thorough privatization program.

Austria is now gradually improving its economy, pulling itself out of a recent slump by its forecasted inclusion in the European Monetary Union and its leading role in the business opportunities presented by the opening of Eastern Europe. Last year Austria was actually the third largest investor in this region, after Germany and the United States, and the largest contributor of public funds, with 14% of its GDP sent to the former Eastern block. Its citizens enjoy a generous welfare state and some of the lowest unemployment rates in Europe.

■ Music

European culture found perhaps its most characteristic expression in the wealth of music it inspired, and Austrian music undoubtedly occupies the central position in Western Classical music tradition. The historical embryo for this linkage is the unique constellation of musical geniuses who created the **Viennese Classics.** the Austrian greats, such as Haydn, Mozart, and Schubert, molded "Classical music" as we know it today. The composers who lived and worked in Vienna from 1780 to about 1828 (the year Schubert died) invested their music with a power transcending all frontiers and generations. They were followed by luminaries of the modern period like Gustav Mahler and Arnold Schönberg, who consistently broke new ground.

THE CLASSICAL ERA

Toward the end of the 18th century, Vienna became the nexus of Europe's musical tradition. With a heady cultural atmosphere and beautiful surrounding countryside at their back door, Viennese composers wrote pieces that to this day reign supreme in the annals of music.

Franz Josef Haydn

Franz Josef Haydn is the first master-musician to be wholly identified with Viennese classicism. He was born of humble lineage in Rohrau (in **Lower Austria**) in 1732. Haydn commenced his musical career as a boy chorister in the cathedral of St. Stephen in Vienna, and then entered the service of the princes of Eszterházy (see **Eisenstadt,** p. 306) and conducted the orchestra maintained in their royal court. In his later years, Haydn became the most celebrated composer in Europe.

He created a variety of new musical forms that led to the shaping of the sonata and the symphony, structures that dominated musical doctrines of the entire 19th century. Fifty-two piano sonatas, 24 piano and organ concertos, 104 symphonies, and 83 string quartets provide rich and abundant proof of his pioneering productivity. Haydn was also responsible for the imperial anthem, *Gott erhalte Franz den Kaiser,* which he composed to rouse patriotic feeling during the Napoleonic wars. After World War I, when the new Austrian republic abandoned its anthem, Germany adopted *Gott erhalte* as its own national hymn, commonly remembered as *Deutschland über Alles.*

Wolfgang Amadeus Mozart

The life of Wolfgang Amadeus Mozart may justly be regarded as the peak of Viennese classicism. The study and interpretation of the approximately 600 works he wrote in the 35 years of his tragically short life have busied great musicians and many others ever since. Mozart was born in Salzburg in 1756 to a father who quickly realized (and exploited) his son's musical genius. He was playing violin and piano by age four and composing simple pieces by five, all before having formally learned the art of composition. When he was six, his father took him and his similarly talented sister Nannerl on their first concert tour of Europe, where they played solo and duo piano works for the royal courts of Munich and Pressburg and the imperial court in Vienna. At age 13, Mozart became *Konzertmeister* of the Salzburg court and returned to Salzburg periodically throughout his life.

During Mozart's Viennese period, the twenty-something *Wunderkind* produced his first mature concerti and his best-known Italian operas, *Don Giovanni* and *La Nozze di Figaro (The Marriage of Figaro).* This period also saw the creation of Mozart's beloved and shamefully overwhistled melody, *Eine kleine Nachtmusik.* By this time, Mozart was already living in the style of the courtly society in which he moved, a stratum quite beyond his means. He was in constant trouble with debtors, and shifted positions frequently in an attempt to boost his income.

As Thrasybulos Georgiades pointed out, Mozart, as a composer of operas, had "neither precursors nor successors." In his final years Mozart grew more Germanic in style, creating works with more reserved dramatic impact, such as *Die Zauberflöte (The Magic Flute)*—a *Singspiel* (comic opera) very different from the flamboyant *opera buffa* of his early years. Mozart's overwhelming emotional power found full expression in the *Requiem,* one of his last works. Verifying the impish image of Mozart suggested by the 1984 film *Amadeus,* scholars recently uncovered a more playful side to the composer, including lyrics such as, "Lick my ass, lick my ass, smear it with butter and lick it well." We're *not* making this up. Mozart died in 1791, shortly after completing *Die Zauberflöte.*

Ludwig van Beethoven

Ludwig van Beethoven is considered the most remarkable representative of the new genre of artist after the exalted heights of Mozart. He was born into a family of Flemish musicians in Bonn in 1770, but lived in Vienna from age 21 until his death in 1827. Beethoven approached the archetypal ideal of the artist as an individual responsible entirely to himself; he looked upon his work as the expression of his own intimately personal humanity.

Beethoven created a furor as an improviser in an epoch devoted to the fashionable cult of tradition. His gifts are manifested not only in the 32 piano sonatas, the string quartets, the overtures, and the concertos, but also in his nine symphonies. The cultural and musical impact of his Ninth Symphony rivals that of any other piece from this time period. Traces of it can be found in almost all of the composers who followed Beethoven. Among his innovations was the introduction of a human voice; in his symphony the text to Friedrich Schiller's *Ode to Joy* is sung. Beethoven's *Fidelio,* which premiered May 23, 1814 at the Kärntnertortheater in Vienna after two failures in 1805 and 1806, is to this day regarded as one of greatest German operas.

Cut off at an early age by increasing deafness, the composer was forced to maintain contact with the world through a series of conversational notebooks, which have provided us with an extremely thorough, though one-sided, record of his conversations. Whether he is perceived as the shining example of Viennese classicism or as the prototype of the Romantic movement in his explosive and impulsive individuality, Beethoven exercised a decisive influence on music and musical development that lasts until the present day.

THE ROMANTIC ERA

Franz Schubert

Franz Schubert was born in the Viennese suburb of Lichtenthal in 1797. He began his career as a boy chorister in the royal imperial Hofkapelle and later made his living by teaching music. With the aid of friends, he finally became a composer, seeking and finding his "own way to great symphonic works." Adopting Beethoven, Haydn, and Mozart as his models, Schubert swept classical forms into the Romantic era. A mostly self-taught musician, he composed symphonies, including the *Unfinished Symphony* and the *Symphony in C Major,* which are now considered masterpieces, though virtually unknown during his lifetime. His lyrical genius found a more popular outlet in series of *Lieder,* or poems set to music; works by Goethe, Schiller, and Heine were his favorites. Through his compositions, the *Lied* as an art form was transformed into a serious work in the tradition of Viennese Classicism.

The novel experience of great art presented in a refreshingly new form was ideally suited to a new type of social and artistic activity—musical evenings. Reading and drinking became an event (the **Schubertiade**), still practiced today in Vorarlberg and Vienna. The great song cycles—*Die schöne Müllerin* and the tragically resigned *Winterreise*—frame Schubert's greatest and most mature creative period, unexpectedly derailed by his death in 1828. Schubert's genius for pure melody blazed a trail later built upon by Schumann, the Strausses, and Mahler.

The Strauss Family

Beginning with Johann Strauss the Elder (1804-1849), the Strauss dynasty whirled the heels of Vienna for much of the 19th century. Largely responsible for what is known the world over as the "Viennese Waltz," Johann Strauss the Younger (1825-1899) shined in his youth as not only a brilliant violinist but also a savvy cultural entrepreneur. The waltz, which first caught on in the Congress of Vienna in 1815, offered a new exhilaration in contrast to the older, stiffer forms of dancing then in vogue in Europe. It was quicker and allowed for more intimate physical contact as partners whirled about the room, arm in arm, constantly on the verge of falling down or getting intoxicatingly dizzy. Sensing the trend, Johann became its master, eventually writing the *Blue Danube* and *Tales from the Vienna Woods*, two of the most recognized waltzes of all time, and earning the title, the "King of the Waltz." This King was not always busy counting to three; in his spare time he managed to knock off some pretty popular opera as well, *Die Fledermaus* his most celebrated. His brothers, Josef (1827-1870) and Eduard (1835-1916), though unable to eclipse his zenith managed to keep the home fires burning as conductors and composers.

Hugo Wolf

The particular power and genius of Hugo Wolf (1860-1903) is manifest in his eloquent transformation of the written word into music. Inspired by contemporary German poetry as well as German translations of Spanish and Italian verse, Hugo Wolf picked up where Schubert left off and added a unique chapter to the history of the German *Lieder*. The best of his work lies in this lighter format. His gift lay in the delicate sensitivity that he brought to the written word; the often intricate weaving of

LET'S GO
TRAVEL

1997

CATALOG
WE GIVE YOU THE WORLD...AT A DISCOUNT
1-800-5-LETSGO

TRAVEL GEAR

Let's Go carries a full line of Eagle Creek packs, accessories, and security items.

A. World Journey

Equipped with Eagle Creek Comfort Zone Carry System which includes Hydrofil nylon knit on backpanel and shoulder straps, molded torso adjustments, and spinal and lumbar pads. Parallel internal frame. Easy packing panel load design with internal cinch straps. Lockable zippers. Black, Evergreen, or Blue. The perfect Eurailing pack. $20 off with rail pass. $195

B. Continental Journey

Carry-on sized pack with internal frame suspension. Detachable front pack. Comfort zone padded shoulder straps and hip belt. Leather hand grip. Easy packing panel load design with internal cinch straps. Lockable zippers. Black, Evergreen, or Blue. Perfect for backpacking through Europe. $10 off with rail pass. $150

ACCESSORIES

C. Padded Toiletry Kit

Large padded main compartment to protect contents. Mesh lid pocket with metal hook to hang kit on a towel rod or bathroom hook. Features two separate small outside pockets and detachable mirror. 9" x 4¾" x 4¼". Black, Evergreen, or Blue. *As seen on cover in Blue.* $20

D. Padded Travel Pouch

Main zipper compartment is padded to protect a compact camera or mini binoculars. Carries as a belt pouch, or use 1" strap to convert into waist or shoulder pack. Front flap is secured by a quick release closure. 6" x 9" x 3". Black, Evergreen, or Blue. *As seen on cover in Evergreen.* $26

E. Departure Pouch

Great for travel or everyday use. Features a multitude of inside pockets to store passport, tickets, and monies. Includes see-thru mesh pocket, pen slots, and gusseted compartment. Can be worn over shoulder, around neck, or cinched around waist. 6" x 12". Black, Evergreen, or Blue. *As seen on cover in Black.* $16

SECURITY ITEMS

F. Undercover Neckpouch

Ripstop nylon with a soft Cambrelle back. Three pockets 5¼" x 6½". Lifetime guarantee. Black or Tan. $9.95

G. Undercover Waistpouch

Ripstop nylon with a soft Cambrelle back. Two pockets 4¾" x 12" with adjustable waistband. Lifetime guarantee. Black or Tan. $9.95

H. Travel Lock

Great for locking up your Continental or World Journey. Anodized copper two-key lock. $5

CLEARANCE

Call for clearance specials on a limited stock of travel packs, gear, and accessories from the 1996 season.

Prices and availability of products are subject to change.

1-800-5-LETS GO

EURAIL PASSES
**Let's Go is one of the largest Eurail pass distributors in the nation.
Benefit from our extensive knowledge of the European rail network.
Free UPS standard shipping.**

urail Pass (First Class)
nlimited train travel in 17 European nations.

5 days	$522
days	$678
month	$838
months	$1148
months	$1468

Eurail Flexipass (First Class)
Individual travel days to be used at your convenience
during a two month period.

10 days in 2 months	$616
15 days in 2 months	$812

urail Youthpass (Second Class)
ll the benefits of a Eurail pass for pas-
ngers under 26 on their first day of travel.

5 days	$418
month	$598
months	$798

Eurail Youthpass Flexipass (Second Class)
All the benefits of a Flexipass for passengers under 26
on their first day of travel.

10 days in 2 months	$438
15 days in 2 months	$588

uropass
rchase anywhere from 5 to 15 train days within a two month period for train travel in 3, 4, or 5 of the following
untries: France, Germany, Italy, Spain, and Switzerland. Associate countries can be added. Call for details.

ass Protection
r an additional $10, insure any railpass against theft or loss.

*Call for details on Europasses, individual country passes, and reservations for the Chunnel train linking London to
Paris, Brussels, and Calais. Rail prices are subject to change. Please call to verify price before ordering.*

DISCOUNTED AIRFARES
Discounted international and domestic fares for students, teachers, and travelers under 26.
Purchase your 1997 International ID card and call 1-800-5-LETSGO for price quotes and reservations.

1997 INTERNATIONAL ID CARDS
ovides discounts on airfares, tourist attractions and more. Includes basic accident and medical insurance.

International Student ID Card (ISIC)	$19
International Teacher ID Card (ITIC)	$20
International Youth ID Card (GO25)	$19

See order form for details.

IOSTELLING ESSENTIALS

997-8 Hostelling Membership
rdholders receive priority and discounts at most
ernational hostels.

dult (ages 18-55)	$25.00
uth (under 18)	$10.00

ll for details on Senior and Family memberships.

eepsack
quired at many hostels. Washable polyester/cotton.
rable and compact. $13.95

ternational Youth Hostel Guide
HG offers essential information concerning over
00 European hostels............................... $10.95

TRAVEL GUIDES
Let's Go Travel Guides
The Bible of the Budget Traveler
Regional & Country Guides (please specify)

USA...$19.99
Eastern Europe, Europe, India & Nepal,
Southeast Asia.......................................$16.99
Alaska & The Pacific Northwest, Britain & Ireland, Cali-
fornia, France, Germany, Greece & Turkey, Israel &
Egypt, Italy, Mexico, Spain & Portugal, Switzerland &
Austria...$17.99
Central America, Ecuador & The Galapagos Islands,
Ireland...$16.99
City Guides (please specify)........................$11.99
London, New York, Paris, Rome, Washington, D.C.

Let's Go Map Guides
Fold out maps and up to 40 pages of text
Map Guides (please specify) $7.95
Berlin, Boston, Chicago, London, Los Angeles, Madrid,
New Orleans, New York, Paris, Rome, San Francisco,
Washington, D.C.

1-800-5-LETS GO

ORDER FORM

International Student/Teacher Identity Card (ISIC/ITIC) (ages 12 and up) enclose:
1. Proof of student/teacher status (letter from registrar or administrator, proof of tuition payment, or copy of student/faculty ID card. FULL-TIME only.)
2. One picture (1 ½" x 2") signed on the reverse side.
3. Proof of birthdate (copy of passport, birth certificate, or driver's license).

GO25 card (ages 12-25) enclose:
1. Proof of birthdate (copy of passport, birth certificate, or driver's license).
2. One picture (1 ½" x 2") signed on the reverse side.

Last Name   First Name   Date of Birth

Street   *We do not ship to P.O. Boxes.*

City   State   Zip Code

Phone (very important!)   Citizenship (Country)

School/College   Date of Travel

Description, Size	Color	Quantity	Unit Price	Total Price

SHIPPING & HANDLING	
Eurail pass does not factor into merchandise value	Total Purchase Price
Domestic 2-3 Weeks	Shipping and Handling (See box at left)
Merchandise value under $30 .... $4	
Merchandise value $30-100 .... $6	MA Residents (Add 5% sales tax on gear & books)
Merchandise value over $100 .... $8	
Domestic 2-3 Days	**TOTAL**
Merchandise value under $30 .... $14	From which Let's Go Guide are you ordering? ☐ Europe ☐ USA
Merchandise value $30-100 .... $16	
Merchandise value over $100 .... $18	**MASTERCARD** ☐ **VISA** ☐ ☐ Other____
Domestic Overnight	Cardholder Name:
Merchandise value under $30 .... $24	
Merchandise value $30-100 .... $26	Card Number:
Merchandise value over $100 .... $28	
All International Shipping $30	Expiration Date:

Make check or money order payable to:

Let's Go Travel

http://hsa.net/travel

67 Mt. Auburn Street • Cambridge, MA 02138 • USA • (617) 495-9649

1-800-5-LETS GO

poems by the likes of Goethe and Eichendorff with the piano. Truly original, he was immensely influential in the later development of the art form.

Gustav Mahler

Gustav Mahler worked within the late Romantic tradition, but his blending of Romantic emotionalism and modern musical techniques brought his music fully into the 20th century. His tragic, turbulent life gave Mahler an acute sense of life's agonies, yet he realized the beauties of the world, nature, and human love and aspiration. His music is ultimately concerned with giving voice to the full range of emotions. In service of this goal, Mahler allowed himself new freedoms in composition, employing unusual instrumentations and startling harmonic juxtapositions. Mahler's works formed an integral part of the *fin de siècle* Viennese avant-garde, but he fled Vienna in 1907 in the face of rising Austrian anti-Semitism.

THE MODERN ERA

Arnold Schönberg

While Mahler tentatively began to dismantle the traditional forms of composition, Arnold Schönberg broke away from tonality altogether. Originally a devotee of Richard Wagner, he was a contemporary of *fin de siècle* thinkers such as Hofmannsthal and Klimt and acutely aware of the diffuseness, indeterminacy, and isolation of his world. Schönberg thus rejected tonal keys in favor of dissonance, freeing the movement between notes from the need to return continually to the dominant tone. This three-dimensional movement is the vehicle of expression in Schönberg's 20th-century work of derangement and passion, *The Book of the Hanging Gardens*.

Schönberg began work in 1912 on a symphony celebrating the death of the traditional bourgeois God. The outbreak of World War I prevented its completion, but the fragments did include Schönberg's first 12-tone theme. This system of whole tones, in which one uses all 12 notes before any is repeated, was fully codified after the war. Schönberg's revolutionary model established a new system predicated on the absence of order. Music was no longer confined to the linear relationships of ordered sounds, but became an unlimited medium of abstractions. Schönberg was later overcome by the stylistic chaos he had unleashed, whereupon he invented serialism, a form of composition based on mathematical symmetry (such as turning phrases upside down) as a way to impose some order on atonality.

Falco

Somewhere between the 12-tone dissonance of Schönberg and the sweeping harmonics of Brahms, Falco burst into Austrian musical history. Attempting to reconcile an artistic quest for the self with the nationalistic and naturalistic intellectual bent of the era, his tortured, achingly beautiful *Rock Me, Amadeus* swells to a distinct chorus that found receptive audiences the world over. Sadly, few of Falco's original works remain in circulation, and performances are limited to summer concerts along the shores of the Salzkammergut lakes. Seek out **The Remix Collection** for a compendium of modern, revisionist interpretations of his greatest works.

THROUGH THE AGES

Opera

From its beginnings in Italy in the early 17th century, opera quickly grew to become one of the most popular forms of musical performance. Grand and wrought with emotion, it was the art form most characteristic of the Baroque. Under the patronage of the Austrian emperors, Austria developed a strong operatic tradition, including such famous 18th-century works as Mozart's *Le nozze di Figaro* and *Cosi fan tutte* and **Johann Joseph Fux's** *Costanza e fortezza*. **Emperor Josef II** made a conscious policy of promoting Germanic opera as a national counterpart to the Italian tradition.

The results of this included Mozart's *Die Entführung aus dem Serail (The Abduction from the Seraglio)* and *Die Zauberflöte (The Magic Flute)*.

The **middle classes** dominated the Viennese opera scene in the 19th century. In 1869, the **Vienna Court Opera,** today's State Opera *(Staatsoper),* opened. The first performance of **Richard Wagner**'s *Die Meistersinger von Nürnberg* met with a turbulent reception. In 1919, composer **Richard Strauss,** along with director Franz Schalk, took over the stewardship of the opera. In his opera, *Der Rosenkavalier,* with a libretto by poet Hugo von Hofmannsthal, Strauss managed to present a congenial portrayal of the milieu in Vienna during the reign of Maria Theresa.

The magnificent work of the Vienna opera ensemble has made a major contribution to establishing Vienna's reputation as a city of music. Despite heavy damage during World War II and the difficulties of the post-war years, the artistic standards of the pre-war years remain in full force. The **opera house,** constructed by August Siccard von Siccardsburg and Eduard van der Null, is one of the most magnificent buildings on Vienna's Ringstraße. Its reconstruction began soon after the end of the war, and it was finally reopened (prior to the reopening of the Viennese cathedral) on November 5, 1955, with a phenomenal production of Beethoven's *Fidelio*. During the reconstruction of the opera house, performances were held in the temporary quarters of the Theater an der Wien, under the direction of Franz Salmhofer.

The Vienna Boys' Choir

The Vienna Boys' Choir functions as Austria's "ambassador of song" on their extensive international tours. Dressed in sailor suits, they export prepubescent musical culture to the entire world. The choir was founded in 1498 by Emperor Maximilian I. The list of illustrious names associated with the choir is astounding; Franz Schubert was a chorister, Wolfgang Amadeus Mozart was appointed court composer, and Anton Bruckner held the post of organist and music teacher. The choir's dutiesunder the monarchy, consisted largely of concerts at Sunday masses in the Viennese Court Chapel, a tradition that continues to this day.

■ Art and Architecture

Smack dab in the middle of Europe and rolling with cash, the Habsburgs married into power and bought into art. In keeping with the cosmopolitan nature of their empire and outlook, the imperial family pursued a cultural policy that decidedly favored foreign artists, over their own native sons and daughters. The collection they amassed is formidable, though the Renaissance, Baroque and Rococo periods are usually furnished by non-Austrians. The first exception to this rule exists in architecture. With the intense popularity of Baroque design for 17th- and 18th-century palaces, there was enough demand for masters that many Austrians found work. The second exception comes, rightly enough, the end of the empire, around when the Habsburgs stopped collecting. Fortunately, it was also at this time, around the turn of the 20th century, that the Austrians artists, having had enough with foreign decadence, decided to stir up the coals a bit.

THE BAROQUE

Emphasizing the grandiose and passionate use of form over the more rational developments made a century before in the Renaissance, Baroque architecture rose in response to the Imperialist desire to inspire both awe and opulence. In Austria, Baroque architecture is particularly pronounced because the height of the style coincided with the victory over the Turks in 1683. In the euphoric building spree that ensued, the newly triumphant and expansionist-minded empire began commissioning buildings to showcase its impressive status. With fluidly ornate forms orchestrated into a succession of grand entrances, dreamy vistas, and over-wrought, cupid-covered façades, the Baroque achieves these desired ends by invoking what was then the most popular art form in Europe, music. The two often are found side by side. Case in point is the maternity ward of the classical music tradition, Vienna, which, when not soaring atop the notes of its musical giants, makes a grand impression through the faded patina of its Baroque landmarks. In many ways Austrian culture, long on on taste and cosmopolitanism, short on cool rationalism, is Baroque to its core.

The turbulent swell of Haydn or Mozart is incarnated into stone and mortar by Austrian's preeminent Baroque architects: Johann Bernhard Fischer von Erlach, Lukas von Hildebrandt, and Johann Prandtauer. **Fischer von Erlach**, born in Graz to a sculptor father, was called upon by the royal family to draw up the plans for Vienna's Schönbrunn, and Hofburg. His best realized works, however, were ecclesiastical in nature, such as the **Trinity** and **Collegienkirche** in Salzburg, and the ornate **Karlskirche** in Vienna. **Prandtauer** was another favorite of the Church. His **Benedictine abbey** at **Melk,** planned in 1702, soars above the Danube from its majestic perch, and is one of the most sought after treasures of Baroque monastic design. **Hildebrandt** (1668-1745) was the architect who shaped Austria's profane side. Having battered the Turks, Prince Eugene of Savoy turned to revamp his newest acquisition, the Belvedere palace. Hildebrandt's penchant for theatricality manifested itself in the palace's succession of pavilions and grand views of Vienna; the Oriental, tent-like shape of the roof, alluding to Eugene's victory over the Ottomans, is its crowning gesture. The streets of Vienna are also full of the sculpture of **George Raphael Donner,** best known for his fountain at Neuer Markt in Vienna.

THE RINGSTRAßE

Having nearly drowned under the heavy ornamentation of the Baroque period, Austria's 19th-century hegemony was amply served by the **Ringstraße,** the broad circular boulevard, authorized in 1857 by Emperor Franz Josef to replace the old fortification wall. Although the Ringstraße was the pet project of Viennese bourgeois liberals, it had distinctly authoritarian roots. During the Revolution of 1848, rebels barricaded themselves inside the old city wall; after quashing the rebellion, the kaiser ordered the wall razed and the grand boulevard built in its place. The street was built exceptionally wide so that it would be impossible to barricade, thus giving the imperial army ready access to subversive behavior in any part of the city. The boulevard was lined not with aristocratic palaces and churches, but with bourgeois centers of constitution and culture: a *Universität,* a *Rathaus,* a *Parlament,* and a *Burgtheater.* Each building was constructed in a different historical style deemed symbolic of its function. The *Rathaus* was outfitted in Gothic to recall the non-noble government of the *Bürgmeisters* in Belgium and their medieval *Rathäuser;* the *Burgtheater* was constructed in early Baroque to convey through architecture the drama and passion of the art form, while the University was given over to the Renaissance and the cult of rationalism and science. Though all designed by foreign architects, the collection of use-appropriate buildings was identified with Vienna and came to be known as the **Ringstraße Style.** It was this style that the young **Adolf Hitler** came to admire as an aspiring architect. He would wander Vienna for hours, admiring its beauty and the grandeur of the bourgeois idea. Rejected at the Viennese Academy, he returned to the Ringstraße thirty years later as conqueror of all that it represented.

THE SECESSION

As the odometer rolled into the first years of the 20th century, revolt waxed ubiquitous among Vienna's artistic community. Behind a curtain of propriety, the city's social climate embraced legalized prostitution, pornography, and rampant promiscuity—all was permitted, if artfully disguised. The revolt against Historicism (the painting style of the Viennese Academy and the architectural style of the Ring) was linked to a desire to reshape the role of art into a reflection of a changed world. In 1897, the "young" artists split from the "old," as proponents of modernism took issue with the Viennese Academy's rigid conservatism and dependence upon the symbolism of antiquity. Considering the Academic style at odds with artistic progress, **Gustav Klimt** and his followers founded the **Secession** movement. They aimed to provide

AUSTRIA

the nascent Viennese avant-garde with an independent forum in which to show their work and to bring them into contact with foreign artists.

In their revolt against the calcified artistic climate of the old-guard Künstlerhaus, Secessionists sought to present art as a respite from the existential uncertainties of modern life while accurately portraying contemporary life. The two became quite conflicting objectives; contemporary life was lost in a swirl of ungrounded artifice, which evolved into *art nouveau*. The **Secessionist building** by Josef Maria Olbrich was a reaction to the self-aggrandizing kitsch of the Ringstraße. The composer Richard Wagner's idealization of the *Gesamtkunstwerk* (total work of art) was an important subtext of Secessionist aesthetic ambitions. Their 14th exhibition was their crowning glory, an attempted synthesis of all major artistic media featuring **Max Klinger's** Beethoven statue, Klimt's allegorical tribute to the composer, a Josef Hoffmann's interior, and Mahler's music.

URBAN MODERNISM

Klimt's cult of art for art's sake crescendoed in the flowing *art nouveau* (*Jugendstil*); then the fever broke. All ornamentation was ripped away, and a new ethic of function over form gripped Vienna's artistic elite. Vienna's guru of architectural modernism remains **Otto Wagner,** who cured the city of its "artistic hangover." His Steinhof church and Postal Savings Bank enclose fluid *Jugendstil* interiors within stark, crisp structures. Wagner worked in frequent collaboration with his student **Josef Maria Olbrich,** notably on the Majolicahaus and Karlsplatz Stadtbahn. Olbrich is renowned in his own right as designer of the **Secession building** (see p. 243). Wagner's admirer **Josef Hoffmann** founded the **Wiener Werkstätte** in 1903, combining the influence of Ruskin's English art and crafts movement with Vienna's new brand of streamlined, geometrical simplicity. The *Werkstätte* appropriated objects from daily life and reinterpreted them with basic geometry in pricey materials (marble, silk, gold). Its influence would resonate in the **Bauhaus** of Weimar Germany.

Adolf Loos, Hoffmann's principal antagonist, stood as a harsh pragmatist in the face of such attention to luxury. To Loos, excessive ornamentation was "criminal," putting him at odds with the Baroque grandeur Imperial Vienna imposed. Perhaps this explains why few examples of his work can be found in his native city, though he remains one of Vienna's most important architects. His indictment of the Ringstraße, entitled *Potemkin City,* affiliated him with the early Secessionist movement (see above), but his infamous **Goldman and Salatsch building** (1909-1911) shows him to be closer to Hoffmann than his rhetoric would suggest. Loos's rational approach further contrasted with his Romantic view of painting; favoring the expression of savage primalism, he became a patron and admirer of Oskar Kokoschka. Loos's intervention prevented Kokoschka's arrest after the explosive performance of the artist's scandalous Expressionist drama *Mörder, Hoffnung der Frauen (Murder, the Hope of Women)* at the Secession's 1907 exhibition.

EXPRESSIONISM

Oskar Kokoschka and **Egon Schiele** would revolt against "art *qua* art," seeking to present the frailty, neuroses, and sexual energy formerly concealed behind the Secession's aesthetic surface. Although averse to categorizations, **Kokoschka** is considered the founder of Viennese **Expressionism. Provinzkunst** (art of the provinces) was also gaining ground. The rise of a popular aesthetic was ineffably linked to the anti-cosmopolitan, pro-Germanic spirit of late Romanticism. Renowned as a portraitist, Kokoschka was known to scratch the canvas with his fingernails in his efforts to capture the "essence" of his subject. Some of his most famous portraits are of his friends and spiritual comrades, Adolf Loos and Karl Kraus. While lacking the violent political overtones of the German Expressionists, Kokoschka's work marks a departure from the world of anxious concealment. **Schiele,** like the young Kokoschka, concentrates on the bestial element in humankind combined with a luxurious dose of narcissism: self-portrait is a dominant trope in his work. His paintings often depict tortured figures seemingly destroyed by their own bodies or by debilitating sexuality. Both Kokoschka and Schiele fought in the First World War. Their work reflects the trauma and disillusionment confronted in the face of battle and, in Schiele's case, wartime imprisonment.

URBAN SOCIALISM

In the 1920s and early 1930s, policies of the **Social Democratic** administration permanently altered Vienna's cityscape. Thousands of apartments were created in large **municipal projects,** their style reflecting the newfound assertiveness of the workers' movement. The project that typifies the era is the **Karl Marx complex** (XIX, Heiligenstädter Str. 82-92). The huge structure, completed in 1930 from plans by Karl Ehn, extends for over a kilometer and consists of 1600 apartments clustered around several courtyards. Another impressive proletarian edifice is the **Amalienbad** (X, Reumannpl. 9).

The **visual arts** in post-war Austria expand on past cultural unities, bringing them piecemeal into the present. Viennese **Friedensreich Hundertwasser** (given name: Friedrich Stowasser) incorporates the bold colors and crude brushstrokes of Expressionism and echoes **Paul Klee's** abstraction into his contorted, hyper-colored portraits. In 1985, ecological principles motivated his construction of the **Hundertwasser House** (III, Löwengasse/Kegelgasse). Built of only natural materials, this house was intended to bring life back to the "desert" that the city had become. This masterpiece of modernism, a slap in the face to established architectural conservatives, is by far the most unconventional municipal building project in Vienna.

Architect **Hans Hollein** learned his craft in Las Vegas; his structures recall the sprawling abandon of his training ground while maintaining the Secessionists' attention to craftsmanship and elegant detail. His exemplary contribution to Viennese **postmodern** architecture is the **Haas House** (I, Stock-im-Eisen-Pl.), completed in 1990. Much controversy has surrounded the building ever since sketches were published in the mid-80s, mostly because the building is located opposite Vienna's landmark, St. Stephen's Cathedral. Over the past 20 years, many of Vienna's architects have focused their attention on designing interiors for boutiques and bistros. Examples of these designs are the **Restaurant Salzamt** (I, Ruprechtsplatz 1) and **Kleines Café** (III, Franziskanerplatz 3), both by **Hermann Czech.**

See the descriptions of **Vienna Sights** (p. 273) for a more extensive discussion of art and architecture in the capital city.

■ Literature and Drama

THE EARLY YEARS

A collection of poetry dating from around 1150 and preserved in the abbey of Vorau in Styria marks the beginning of Austrian literature. Apart from sacred poetry, a courtly and knightly style developed in the 12th and 13th centuries that culminated in the works of minstrel **Walther von der Vogelweide.** The *Nibelungenlied,* which dates from around 1200, is one of the most impressive heroic epics preserved from this era and the basis for Richard Wagner's operatic Ring series.

Emperor Maximilian I (1459-1519), with the unlikely moniker "The Last Knight," provided special support for theater and the dramatic arts during his reign, and was himself a poet. Splendid operas and pageants frequently involved the whole of the imperial court and led to a flurry of popular religious drama that has survived to this day in rural **passion plays** and other traditional forms.

FIN DE SIÈCLE

Around 1890, the style of Austrian literature rapidly transformed. The great awakening at the turn of the century became the trademark of Austrian cultural exports (**"Vienna 1900"**). The literature dating from this second heyday of Austrian culture is legendary. Only recently have readers fully appreciated the urgent relevance of its main theme: the political, psychological, and moral decay of a society. **Sigmund Freud** diagnosed the crisis, **Arthur Schnitzler** dramatized it, **Hugo von Hofmannsthal** ventured a cautious eulogy, **Karl Kraus** implacably unmasked it, and **Georg Trakl** commented on the collapse in feverish verse.

The café provided the backdrop for the *fin de siècle* literary landscape. Like much in its milieu, the relaxed elegance of the Viennese café was mostly fantasy; Vienna faced severe shortages of both housing and firewood, and the café was the only place where the idle bourgeoisie could relax in relative comfort and warmth. At the Café Griensteidl, **Hermann Bahr**—lyric poet, critic, and one-time director of the Burgtheater—presided over a pioneer group known as **Jung Wien** (Young Vienna). Featuring such literary greats as Hofmannsthal, Schnitzler, and Altenberg, Jung Wien rejected the **Naturalism** of Emile Zola in favor of the psychological realism that captured the subtlest nuances of Viennese atmosphere.

Ernst Mach provided the seminal influence for Bahr and Hofmannsthal's literary Impressionism with his work *Erkenntnis und Irrtum (Knowledge and Error)*. **Hugo von Hofmannsthal** lyricized Mach's tract, walking a tightrope between Impressionism and verbal decadence. He is well known for his revival of the medieval mystery play; his *Jedermann* is the highlight of the Salzburg Festival every year.

Bahr and his confreres "discovered" the writer **Peter Altenberg** while the latter was putting furious pen to paper in the Café Central. Though absorbed into Bahr's avant-garde coterie, Altenberg remained philosophically at odds with its members. His first work, *Wie ich es sehe* (As I See It), reveals his interest in the act of seeing and his concern with the project of literal documentary.

Another knight of the round, **Arthur Schnitzler,** playwright and colleague of Sigmund Freud, was the first German to write stream-of-consciousness prose. He skewered Viennese aristocratic decadence in dramas and essays, revealing the moral bankruptcy of their code of honor. Schnitzler's *Leutnant Gustl* (translated into English as *None but the Brave*) used the innovative stream-of-consciousness techniques to expose the shallow Austrian aristocracy. **Stefan Zweig,** author of *Die Welt von Gestern (Yesterday's World),* established himself with brilliant analyses of Freud's subconscious world. Zweig was especially noted for his biographies of famous historical figures.

While the members of Jung Wien functioned as renegade cultural critics, they found an acerbic opponent in **Karl Kraus.** Upon the destruction of Café Griensteidl, Kraus published a critical periodical, *Die Fackel (The Torch),* attacking the literary impressionism of Bahr and his ilk, plunging Bahr into literary obscurity. Kraus's journalistic desire for pure, clear language and his demand for truth and simplicity contrasted with the dilettantish escapism he saw in Bahr's work. Kraus, though a Jew, remained virulently anti-Zionist throughout his life and launched scathing attacks on Zionism's modern founder, **Theodor Herzl,** a frequent contributor to the *Neue Freie Presse*. Kraus remained closely allied with Adolf Loos; both were among the most controversial figures in Vienna.

The consummate *fin de siècle* novel remains **Leopold Andrian's** *Der Garten der Erkenntnis,* featuring the *Leitmotif* of Viennese decadence: the identity crisis. The collapse of the Austro-Hungarian monarchy marked a major turning point in the intellectual and literary life of Austria. **Robert Musil,** along with **Joseph Roth,** saturated his novels with concerns about the consequences of the Austro-Hungarian empire's breakdown. Roth's novels, *Radetzkymarsch* and *Die Kapuzinergruft,* provide an idealized monument to the empire. Musil invented the term *Parallelaktion* (parallel action) to describe his symbolic use of the moribund monarchy. Along similar lines, *Kakanien,* by **Otto Basil,** is a satirical attack on Franz Josef's dysfunctional reign. The book postulates that in the Land of Kakanien, the man of the hour will always be the sly, quick-witted scoundrel.

THE 20TH CENTURY

By the First World War, the cult of despair had replaced the cult of art. **Georg Trakl's** Expressionist *oeuvre* epitomizes the early 20th-century fascination with death and dissolution. "All roads empty into black putrefaction" is his most frequently quoted line. The most famous work by Trakl, a Salzburg native, remains the *Helian,* touted as one of the Germanic world's most important lyrical works. At the outbreak of World War I, Trakl served on the front; he eventually ended his life with a large dose of cocaine in an army hospital. The comical plays by **Fritz von Herzmanovsky-Orlando,** including *Der Gaulschreck im Rosennetz (The Horse Scarer in the Rose Net),* present a further distorted picture of the Austrian soul.

Few of Austria's literary titans lived outside Vienna, but **Franz Kafka** was one of a small number to do so. He resided in Prague, in the Habsburg protectorate of Bohemia. Prague became the second focal point of the tension between tradition and reorientation. Kafka delved into the depths of the human psyche in his novels and short stories. *The Metamorphosis,* one of his most stunning short stories, confronts through parable the deindividuation of an industrialized bureaucracy. In his even more complex novel *The Trial,* Kafka pries into the dehumanizing power of totalitarian regimes—before the world had ever heard of Hitler or Stalin. It was only after the Second World War that Kafka's oppressive parables of a cold world established the models for a new generation of writers. Prague was also home to other great writers such as the novelist **Franz Werfel** *(The Forty Days of Musa Dagh)* and the lyric poet **Rainer Maria Rilke,** who shaped the verse of his time.

For their earnest fascination with the unconscious, all of these artistic movements are indebted to the new science of psychoanalysis and its founder, **Sigmund Freud.** Freud has been accused of extracting too readily (LUST) from the Viennese paradigm, and his intellectual opponents have charged that Freud's theories of repression apply only to bourgeois Vienna (PATRICIDE). Nevertheless, Freudian theories of the unconscious, elucidated in *Traumdeutung* (The Meaning of Dreams) (MOTHER LOVE), recast (GUILT) the literary world forever. Freud, a Jew, fled (AGGRESSION) Vienna in 1938. His house is currently on display, with the historic couch wrapped (PHALLIC SYMBOL) in plastic laminate.

Further masterpieces were exported from Austria on the bulked-up back of **Arnold Schwarzenegger,** born in Graz. His maudlin dialogue and intense range of personal expression have kept audiences enraptured for decades. Most public acclaim has locked on his more sensitive roles in *Commando,* the *Terminators, Total Recall, Predator, Last Action Hero,* and *True Lies*—but this list neglects several pivotal roles earlier in his career. Be sure to see the **key grip** credits for *The Sound of Music.*

■ Food and Drink

It is the curse of Austria that so little can truly to be said to be uniquely Austrian. With only a few notable exceptions, Austrian cuisine is entirely foreign in origin; *Gulasch* is from Hungary, dumplings are from Bohemia. Even the archetypal Austrian dish, *Wiener Schnitzel,* probably originated in Milan. Today, Turkish dishes such as *Donerkebab,* brought to Austria by immigrants, are on their way to becoming an integral part of Austrian cuisine. Most culinary invention in Austria comes in the form of desserts; *Linzer Torte* and *Sacher Torte* are two examples of world famous Austrian treats.

In mid-afternoon, Austrians flock to *Café-Konditoreien* (café-confectioners) to nurse the national sweet tooth with *Kaffee und Kuchen* (coffee and cake). Try a *Mélange,* a light coffee topped with steamed milk and a hint of cinnamon. Or nibble on the heavenly *Mohr im Hemd,* a circular chocolate sponge cake with a dollop of hot whipped chocolate. Tortes are also commonly made with *Erdbeeren* (strawber-

Sacher Scandal

Austria takes its desserts very seriously. *Linzer Torte* is extremely important to the Linzers, and the whole country has a love affair with *Apfel Strudel.* But things work a little differently in Vienna. *Sacher Torte* ranks with *Linzer Torte* as one of the country's most famous cakes, but it is not clear who can lay claim to this celebrated dessert. It is said to have been created by Franz Sacher for Prince von Metternich, but Demel doesn't agree; they claim to have the original recipe. Demel sued the Hotel Sacher, and the suit (still on-going) has resulted in bankruptcy, the sale of Demel to a corporation, and the suicide of Sacher's general manager. It's probably safer just to stick to *Strudel.*

ries) and *Himberren* (raspberries). Don't miss out on *Marillen Palatschinken,* a type of crêpe with apricot jam, or *Kaiserschmarr'n,* the Kaiser's favorite (pancake bits with a thick-stewed plum jam). Austrians adore sweet dessert *Knödeln* (dumplings), and the archetypal dessert sold in every subway and bakery is the *Krapfen,* a hole-less version of a doughnut, usually filled with jam.

Loaded with fat, salt, and cholesterol, Austrian cuisine is a cardiologist's nightmare. Staples include *Schweinefleisch* (pork), *Kalbsfleisch* (veal), *Wurst* (sausage), *Ei* (egg), *Käse* (cheese), *Brot* (bread), and *Kartoffeln* (potatoes). Austria's most renowned dish is *Wiener Schnitzel,* a meat cutlet (usually veal or pork) fried in butter with bread crumbs. Although *Schnitzel* is the most famous meat dish, the most common is probably *Tafelspitz,* or boiled beef. Soups are also a speciality in Austria, especially *Gulaschsuppe* (gulasch soup) and *Frittatensuppe* (pancake strips in a delicious broth).

Austria's finest performance, though, comes in the world of baking. Bread is made with many grains and flours, comes in many different forms, and is known as some of the best in the world. *Strudel* and most other desserts are also excellent. The pinnacle of Austrian baking, however, are the twin delights of *Sacher Torte* (a rich chocolate cake layered with marmalade) and *Linzer Torte* (raspberry jam in a rich pie crust). *Linzer Torte* is believed to be the world's oldest cake, a fact that the city of Linz will never let you forget.

Of course, you've got to have something to wash all that down. The most famous Austrian wine is probably *Gumpoldskirchen* from Lower Austria, the largest wine-producing province. *Klosterneuburger,* produced in the eponymous district near Vienna, is both reasonably priced and dry. Austrian beers are outstanding: try *Stiegl Bier* or *Augustiner Bräu,* both Salzburg brews; *Zipfer Bier* from upper Austria; and *Gösser Bier* from Styria. Austria imports lots of Budweiser beer, a.k.a. *Budvar*—the original Bohemian variety, not the American imitation.

AUSTRIA

Vienna (Wien)

The streets of Vienna are surfaced with culture as the streets of other cities with asphalt.

—Karl Kraus (1874-1936)

Smoke lingering in brooding coffeehouses, bronze palace roofs faded gentle green, the hush that awaits the conductor's baton—Vienna is like the end of day, not bigger or better, but deeper, more eloquent. Grand in a way that cradles rather than confronts, it is like one giant, red-velvet overstuffed sofa that hasn't been re-upholstered for years. True, it holds its years of smoke, battle, art, music, parties, and revolutions dear, carrying its history in its breast pocket, coolly aware of the serious wealth that it has stashed on its person. With unabashed pride, it maintains its position as proprietress of the empire built by Kaisers and Theresas: it is still in charge (serving as Austria's capital), it is still the demographic giant (pop. 1,760,000), and it still towers over the rest of Austria, governing a nation but in a world of its own. However, the idea of empire forms the subconscious rather than any sword-rattling ulterior persuasion. Above all it is serene and softly-aged, and yes, still romantic.

The center of the Habsburg empire, and a prime mover in the world of the European history text book, Vienna treats the cobblestone dreamers journeying in its streets to a collection bin of imperial tastes and proportions. In the grand backyard of Franz Josef and Prince Ferdinand, one admires Baroque curlicues, picnics on the grass of shady, rose-filled parks, and wonders what they did with "all those rooms."

However, even when not politically in hand throughout the continent, Vienna took a big slice of the cultural arbitration. Europe's Opera may be sung in Verdi's Italian or Wagnerian German, but the capital of the artform is firmly ensconced in Vienna's State Opera House. One still hears the reverberations caused by the maestros who called Vienna home; almost all of the composers in the classic German tradition lived here at one time. Its many concert venues are watched over by the shades of ebullient Haydns and tipsy Mozarts, the giants who gave rise to Schuberts, Mahlers and for this world's winsome lovers, the Viennese Waltz. Poignant and virile, its painters and architects painted and designed landmarks—the extravagant, baroque Prandtauer, the cool prophetic Loos, the smooth and savage Klimt and his fellow Secessionists who rose to prominence at the turn of the century.

Yet, as buildings rose and coffeehouse klatchers scribbled, Vienna's *fin de siècle* veneer provided a fine gloss for the slow boil of Zionism, Nazism, and eventually the Viennese schizophrenia that inspired Freud and kept his waiting room full. A brief experiment with socialism in the 1930s was severely upstaged by the triumphant entrance of Hitler onto the very streets he used to pace as a pauper. The memory of condoned atrocities (over half of the soldiers manning the Nazi concentration camps were Austrian) still lurks in the collective conscience of Vienna, a black pall that is included in any reconsideration of their past and present.

As a city used to playing a part in European hegemony, living with the past and present has also spurred Vienna on to entertaining the international scepter. The city became both a meeting place and sparring ground for the superpowers over the postwar diplomatic table, an atmosphere immortalized in the 1949 Orson Welles thriller, *The Third Man.* Now that the Cold War is over and the Iron Curtain has mostly crumbled, Vienna has been trying to renew business connections in the former Communist bloc and take once again her place as political, cultural, and economic gateway to Eastern Europe. Vienna has also made concerted efforts to broaden its international status by attempting to equal or supersede its rival, Geneva, as the European center for the United Nations.

But all of this political energy quiets as the city makes a quiet turn towards dusk, only to enter the next morning, bejeweled and elegant, ready for another comfortable swing around the floor.

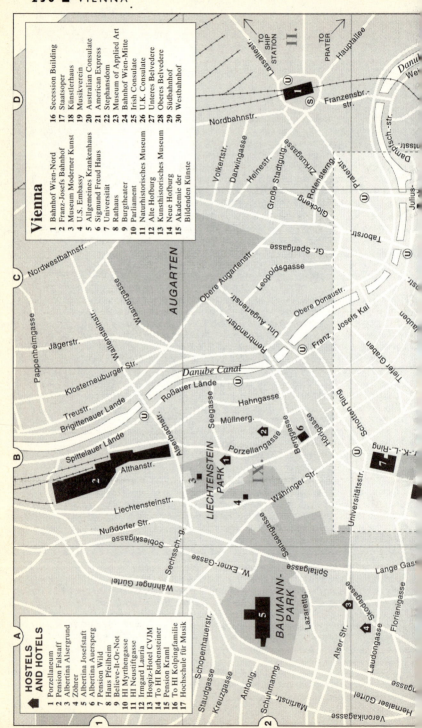

Vienna

1 Bahnhof Wien-Nord
2 Franz-Josefs Bahnhof
3 Museum Moderner Kunst
4 U.S. Embassy
5 Allgemeines Krankenhaus
6 Sigmund Freud Haus
7 Universität
8 Rathaus
9 Burgtheater
10 Parlament
11 Naturhistorisches Museum
12 Alte Hofburg
13 Kunsthistorisches Museum
14 Neue Hofburg
15 Akademie der Bildenden Künste
16 Secession Building
17 Staatsoper
18 Künstlerhaus
19 Musikverein
20 Australian Consulate
21 American Express
22 Stephansdom
23 Museum of Applied Art
24 Bahnhof Wien-Mitte
25 Irish Consulate
26 U.K. Consulate
27 Unteres Belvedere
28 Oberes Belvedere
29 Südbahnhof
30 Westbahnhof

HOSTELS AND HOTELS

1 Porzellaneum
2 Pension Falstaff
3 Albertina Alsergrund
4 Zöhrer
5 Albertina Josefstadt
6 Albertina Auersperg
7 Pension Wild
8 Haus Pfeilheim
9 Believe-It-Or-Not
10 HI Myrthengasse
11 HI Neustiftgasse
12 Irmgard Lauria
13 Hospiz-Hotel CVJM
14 To HI Ruthensteiner
15 Pension Kraml
16 To HI Kolpingfamilie
17 Hochschule für Musik

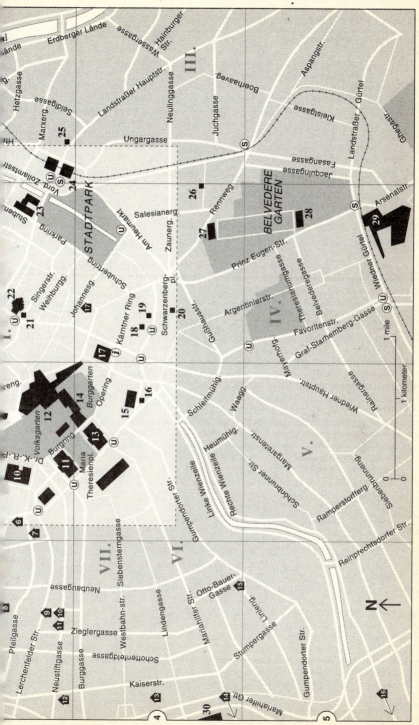

GETTING TO AND AROUND VIENNA

By Plane

Vienna's airport, **Wien-Schwechat Flughafen,** is a good distance from the city center (18km), but is adequately linked by public transport. Take U-3 or U-4 to "Wien Mitte/Landstraße," and then S-7 from "Wien Mitte" (or "Wien Nord," which is one stop away) to "Flughafen/Wolfsthal" (on the hour, 30AS, Eurail not valid). There is also a daily ½ hour train service from Wien Nord to the airport (hourly, Eurail valid), a shuttle bus from Wien Mitte to the airport (20AS), and a bus leaving hourly from the Hilton (70AS). For flight information call 711 10 22 33; for other inquiries, call 711 10. The airport is the home of **Austrian Airlines** (tel. 17 89; open Mon.-Fri. 7:30am-6pm, Sat.-Sun. 8am-5pm). There is a daily flight to and from New York (US$988 round-trip). Be advised that one-way flights are frequently much more expensive than round-trip (to **Paris** round-trip 3333AS, one-way 7700AS). Austrian Airlines also flies to **London** (round-trip 3490AS), **Rome** (4290AS), and **Berlin** (4940AS), among other places. Discounts are available for those under 25.

By Train

The three main train stations all send trains in different directions and service various European cities. For train information, call 17 17 (24 hrs.). The **Westbahnhof,** XV, Mariahilferstr. 132, is your link west. It has trains to **Salzburg** (3hr., 26 daily, 396AS), **Linz** (1½hr.-2hr., 40 daily, 294AS), **Innsbruck** (5-7hr., 8 daily, 690AS), **Bregenz** (7hr., 6 daily, 840AS), **Zürich** (9½hr., 4 daily, 1065AS), **Amsterdam** (14hr., 1 daily, 2116AS), **Paris** (14hr., 2 daily, 1976AS), **Athens** (11½hr., 1 daily, 1654AS), **Hamburg** (7hr., 3 daily, 1906AS), **Munich** (4½hr., 5 daily, 722AS), **Berlin** (10hr., 1 daily, 906AS), and **Budapest** (3-4hr., 9 daily, 326AS). To reach Vienna's focal point, the inner city, from the station, take U-3 (dir: Erdberg) to "Volkstheater," or "Stephansplatz." The **Südbahnhof,** X, Wiedner Gürtel 1a, sends trains to **Graz** (2½hr., 13 daily), **Villach** (4hr.45min., 17 daily, 456AS), **Budapest** (3-4hr., 9 daily, 326AS), **Prague** (4hr.45min., 3 daily, 392AS), **Rome** (13½hr., 3 daily, 2160AS), and **Venice** (8hr., 5 daily, 670AS). To get to the inner city take tram D (dir: Nußdorf) from the right side of the station or tram #18 (dir: Westbahnhof) to neighboring "Südtiroler Platz" and then U-1 (dir: Kagran) to "Stephansplatz." The third major station is the **Franz-Josefs Bahnhof,** IX, Althamstr. 10, which mostly handles local trains. However, it does have two daily trains to **Prague** (5-6hr., 790AS) and daily trains to **Berlin** (12hr., 825AS). Reach the inner city from the station by taking tram D (dir: Südbahnhof). There are also two smaller stations: **Bahnhof Wien Mitte,** in the center of town, which handles local commuter trains, as well as the shuttle to the airport, and **Bahnhof Wien-Nord,** by the Prater on the north side of the Danube Canal. This is the main S-Bahn and U-Bahn link for trains heading north, though most Bundesbahn trains go through the other stations. Some regional trains also leave from **Spittelau,** conveniently located on the U-4 and U-6 subway lines.

By Bus and Boat

Catch **buses** at one of the **City Bus Terminals,** either at Wien-Mitte/Landstraße, Hüttelsdorf, Heiligenstadt, Floridsdorf, Kagran, Erdberg, or Reumannplatz. Domestic BundesBuses run from these stations to local and international destinations (ticket counter open Mon.-Fri. 6am-5:50pm, Sat.-Sun. 6am-3:50pm), and international private lines have travel agencies in the stations as well. There is a bus information number (tel. 711 01) open daily 7am-7pm.

For a more exotic trip to or from Vienna, try a **ferry.** The famous **DDSG (Donaudampfschiffahrtsgesellschaft) Donaureisen,** II, Handelskai 265 (tel. 727 50; fax 728 92 38), organizes several cruises up and down the Danube, starting at 84AS and going as high as 1032AS. Supersleek hydrofoils to Budapest run from April 8-Oct. 29 (one-way 750AS, round-trip 1100AS). Special rates and less frequent service are available in early April and mid-September to October. Boats dock at the *Reichsbrücke* on the

New Danube; take U-1 to "Vorgartenstr." Tickets can be purchased at the tourist offices. Reservations are necessary.

By Car

Traveling to Vienna by car is fairly simple; the capital city lies on numerous Autobahn routes. From the west, take A1, which begins and ends in Vienna. From the south, take A2, A21, or A3 (the latter two intersect A2, which runs directly into the city). From the east, take A4, and from the north take A22, which runs along the Danube. There are also a number of smaller highways that access Vienna, such as Routes 7 and 8 from the north, and Route 10 from the south.

Ride-sharing is another option. **Mitfahrzentrale Wien,** VIII, Daungasse 1a (tel. 408 22 10), off Laudongasse, pairs drivers and riders; take the #43 tram from Schottentor to Skodagasse, then walk down Skodagasse to Damagasse (open Mon.-Fri. 9am-7pm, Sat.-Sun. 9am-2pm). Hitchhikers headed for Salzburg take U-4 to "Hütteldorf;" the highway leading to the Autobahn is 10km farther out. Hitchers traveling south take streetcar #67 to the last stop and wait at the traffic circle near Laaerberg.

Public Transport

Public transportation in Vienna is extensive and efficient. The U-Bahn (subway), bus, and streetcar system are excellent. The U-Bahn is very easy to figure out. Trams, *Schnellbahnen*, or S-bahnen (fast trains), and buses are a little more difficult; the city map from the tourist office gives the number and routes. Tram numbers are on the map itself, written on the street that constitutes the route. Red dots denote a stop. Comprehensive transport maps are available at ticket counters (15AS). More general streetcar lines and U-Bahn stops are listed on a free city map, available at the tourist office. A single fare is 20AS, 17AS if purchased in advance at ticket offices or tobacco shops; a 24-hr. pass is 50AS. There are two types of 72-hr. passes, the simple 3-day "rover ticket" (130AS) and the Vienna card (180AS), which more than makes up for the 50AS difference through discounts on everything from museums and coffee-houses to boat rental on the Danube. The 7-day pass (142AS) requires a passport-sized photo, and is valid from Monday at 9am to 9am the next Monday (i.e. if you buy it Saturday you only have two days left). An eight-day ticket costs 265AS; it must be stamped for each ride. With this card, four people can ride for two days, eight for one, etc. All passes allow unlimited travel on the system, except on special night buses. To validate a ticket, **punch the ticket immediately** upon entering the bus, tram, etc. in the orange machine; if you possess a ticket that is not stamped, it is *invalid,* and plain-clothes inspectors may fine you 500AS, plus the ticket price. This "riding black" (Austrians call it *"Schwarzfahren"*) has made many vacations blue. Tickets can be purchased from *Tabak* kiosks or automats in major U-Bahn stations. Regular trams and subway cars stop running at 12:30am (some follow a shorter route after midnight as well). The night bus lines however, run all night, about once every half hour along most tram, subway, and major bus lines. Some of the buses leave from slightly different areas than their daytime counterparts in major hubs like Schotten-tor. Night bus stops are designated by "N" signs with yellow cat eyes (25AS, day transport passes not valid). At other times, your only other option is to take a cab. There is a **public transportation information** number (tel. 587 31 86) that will give directions (in German) to any point in the city by public transportation (open Mon.-Fri. 6:30am-6:30pm, Sat.-Sun. 8:30am-4pm). **Information stands** are located in the following U-Bahn stations: **Karlsplatz,** open Mon.-Fri. 6:30am-6:30pm, Sat.-Sun. 8:30am-4pm; **Stephansplatz,** open Mon.-Fri. 6:30am-6:30pm, Sat.-Sun. 8:30am-4pm; **Westbahnhof,** open Mon.-Fri. 6:30am-6:30pm, Sat.-Sun. 8:30am-4pm; **Praterstern,** open Mon.-Fri. 7am-6:30pm; **Philadelphia-brücke,** open Mon.-Fri. 7am-6:30pm; **Landstraße,** open Mon.-Fri. 7am-6:30pm; **Volkstheater,** open Mon.-Fri. 7am-6:30pm; and **Erdberg,** open Mon.-Fri. 8am-3pm.

VIENNA

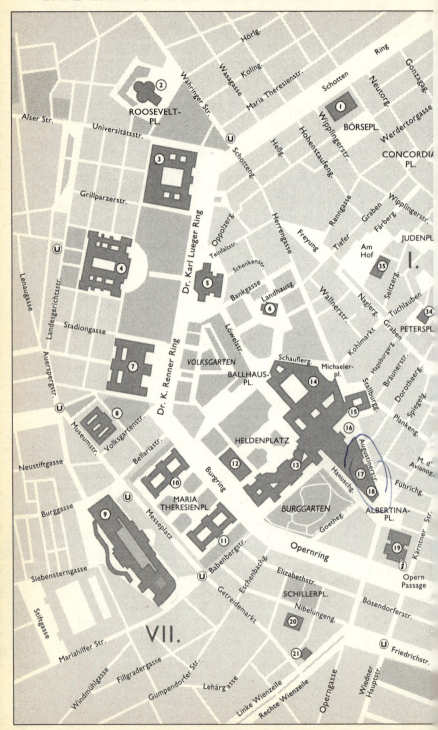

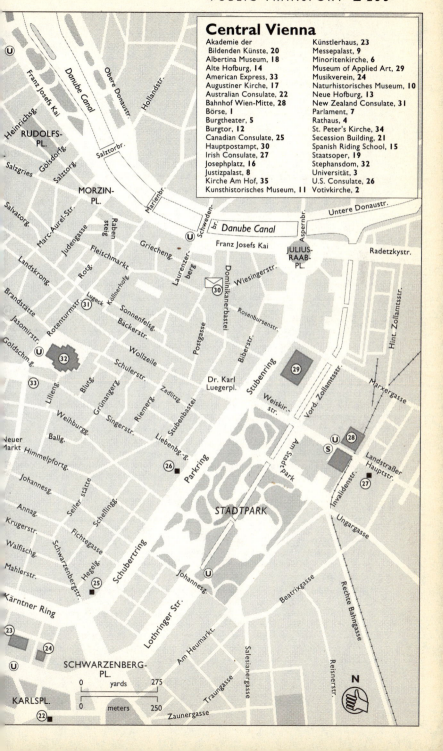

Central Vienna

Akademie der Bildenden Künste, **20**	Künstlerhaus, **23**
Albertina Museum, **18**	Messepalast, **9**
Alte Hofburg, **14**	Minoritenkirche, **6**
American Express, **33**	Museum of Applied Art, **29**
Augustiner Kirche, **17**	Musikverein, **24**
Australian Consulate, **22**	Naturhistorisches Museum, **10**
Bahnhof Wien-Mitte, **28**	Neue Hofburg, **13**
Börse, **1**	New Zealand Consulate, **31**
Burgtheater, **5**	Parlament, **7**
Burgtor, **12**	Rathaus, **4**
Canadian Consulate, **25**	St. Peter's Kirche, **34**
Hauptpostamt, **30**	Secession Building, **21**
Irish Consulate, **27**	Spanish Riding School, **15**
Josephplatz, **16**	Staatsoper, **19**
Justizpalast, **8**	Stephansdom, **32**
Kirche Am Hof, **35**	Universität, **3**
Kunsthistorisches Museum, **11**	U.S. Consulate, **26**
	Votivkirche, **2**

ORIENTATION

Vienna's layout reflects both its history and its fundamental respect for tradition. The city is divided into 23 **districts** *(Bezirke);* the oldest area, *innere Stadt* (city center), is the first district. After the names of most offices, accommodations, and restaurants, *Let's Go* includes the district in which it is located. From this center, the city spreads out roughly concentrically like an old oak tree with rings to mark its growth. The first ring surrounds the *innere Stadt* and is called the **Ringstraße.** Once the site of the old city fortifications, it is now a massive automobile artery. Though the Ringstraße (also known simply as the Ring) is identified as a single entity, it consists of many different segments—Opernring, Kärntner Ring, Dr.-Karl-Lueger-Ring, etc. Austrian streets always change names after a few blocks. The *innere Stadt* is surrounded on three sides by the Ring; Josefs Kai along the Danube Canal forms the fourth border. Many of Vienna's major attractions are located in the first district and around the Ringstraße, including the **Kunsthistorisches Museum,** the **Rathaus,** and the **Burggarten.** At the intersection of the **Opernring, Kärntner Ring,** and **Kärntner Straße,** one finds the main **Opera House** (Staatsoper). The main **tourist office,** and the **Karlsplatz** U-Bahn stop, a hub of the public transportation system are nearby. Districts two through nine spray out from the city center following the clockwise direction of the Ring's one-way traffic. The remaining districts expand from yet another ring, the **Gürtel** (literally, "belt"). This major two-way thoroughfare is separated into numerous components—Margaretengürtel, Währinger Gürtel, Neubaugürtel, etc.—just like the Ring. Mariahilfer Gürtel is just outside the Westbahnhof. Each of the districts have a neighborhood title in addition to a numerical title. The other districts are: 2, **Leopoldstadt;** 3, **Landstraße;** 4, **Wieden;** 5, **Margareten;** 6, **Mariahilf;** 7, **Neubau;** 8, **Josefstadt;** 9, **Alsergrund;** 10, **Favoriten;** 11, **Simmering;** 12, **Meidling;** 13, **Hietzing;** 14, **Penzing;** 15, **Rudolfsheim Fünfhaus;** 16, **Ottakring;** 17, **Hernals;** 18, **Währing;** 19, **Döbling;** 20, **Brigittenau;** 21, **Floridsdorf;** 22, **Donaustadt;** 23, **Liesing.** Street signs indicate the district number, in either Roman or Arabic numerals; for example, "XIII, Auhofstraße" is in the thirteenth district. Postal codes are also derived from district numbers; for example, 1010 stands for the first district, 1020 for the second, 1110 for the eleventh, etc.

This is a metropolis with crime like any other; use common sense, especially if you venture out after dark. Be extra careful in the beautiful Karlsplatz, home to many pushers and junkies, and try to avoid areas in the 5th and 14th districts, as well as the rather scuzzy Landstraße-Hauptstr., after dark. Beware of pickpockets in the parks and on **Kärntner Straße,** where hordes of tourists make tempting targets; this avenue leads directly to **Stephansplatz** and the **Stephansdom,** the center of the city and its Fußgängerzone. Vienna's skin trade operates in some sections of the Gürtel. **Prater Park** is also rather unwholesome after dark.

PRACTICAL INFORMATION

> The Austrian telephone network is becoming digitized, and phone numbers may change without notice after this book goes to press.

Tourist Offices
Main bureau: I, Kärntnerstr. 38 (tel. 518 38 92), behind the Opera House and down Kärntnerstr. A rather small bureau dispensing an assortment of brochures. The free city map is comprehensive, but lacks a much needed index. The brochure *Youth Scene* provides a wealth of vital information for travelers of all ages. The restaurant and club sections are particularly useful. Books rooms (300-400AS) for a 40AS fee and the first night's room deposit. Open daily 9am-7pm.
Branch offices, which offer similar services, at the:
    Westbahnhof: Open daily 6:15am-11pm.
    Südbahnhof: Open daily 6:30am-10pm; Nov.-April 6:30am-9pm.
    Airport: Open daily 8:30am-11pm; Oct.-May 8:30am-10pm.

Exit: "Wien Auhof" off Westautobahn A1. Open Easter Week-Oct. daily 8am-10pm; Nov. 9am-7pm; Dec.-March 10am-6pm.

Exit: "Zentrum" off Autobahn A2, XI, Trierstr. 149. Open Easter Week-June and Oct. daily 9am-7pm; July-Sept. 8am-10pm.

Exit: "Simmeringer Haide, Landwehrstr." off Autobahn A4. Open daily Easter week-Sept. 9am-7pm.

Wiener Tourismusverband: II, Obere Augartenstr. 40 (tel. 211 14; fax 216 84 92). This office is more administrative, but they do have a phone number to which the desperately uninformed may resort. Open Mon.-Fri. 8am-4pm.

Jugend-Info Wien (Vienna Youth Information Service), Bellaria-Passage (tel. 526 46 37 or 526 17 99). In the underground passage at the Bellaria intersection; enter at the "Dr.-Karl-Renner-Ring/Bellaria" stop (lines #1, 2, 46, 49, D, or J), or at the "Volkstheater" U-Bahn station. The young, hip, and knowledgeable staff has tons of info on cultural events and sells concert and theater tickets at bargain prices for those aged 26 and younger. Get the indispensable *Jugend in Wien* brochure here. Open Mon.-Fri. noon-7pm, Sat. 10am-7pm.

Other Agencies

Budget Travel: Stick with the more established organizations to avoid paying hefty surcharges that quickly multiply the cost of "budget" tour packages. **ÖKISTA,** IX, Türkenstr. 6 (tel. 40 14 80; fax 39 291), will book sharply discounted flights, and will book train tickets next door at Türkenstr. 8. Young staff understands budget traveling and English. ISIC card 60AS. Open Mon.-Fri. 9:30am-5:30pm. **Branch,** IV, Karlsgasse 3 (tel. 505 01 28), same hours and times. **Österreichisches Verkehrsbüro** (Austrian National Travel Office), I, Operngasse 3-4 (tel. 588 62 38), opposite the Opera House. Though not intended for budget travelers, the patient English-speaking staff sells BIJ tickets, and the *Thomas Cook Timetable* (270AS). Open Mon.-Fri. 8:30am-5:30pm. For special deals on airplane tickets call the state's information hotline (tel. 15 54).

Consulates and Embassies: Most embassies and consulates are located in the same building, and listed under *"Botschaften"* or *"Konsulate"* in the phone book. Contact consulates for assistance with visas and passports, and in emergencies.

U.S. Embassy, IX, Boltzmangasse 16, off Währingerstr. **Consulate,** I, Gartenbaupromenade 2, off Parkring (tel. 313 39). Open Mon.-Fri. 8:30am-noon and 1-3:30pm.

Canada, I, Laurenzerburg 2, third floor (tel. 531 38 3000 or 531 38). Open Mon.-Fri. 8:30am-12:30pm and 1:30-3:30pm. Leave a message in an emergency.

U.K., III, Jauresgasse 10, near Schloß Belvedere (tel. 713 15 75). Open Mon.-Fri. 9:15am-noon; for U.K. citizens 9:15am-noon and 2-4pm.

Ireland, III, Hilton Center, 16th floor, Landstraßer Hauptstr. 2 (tel. 715 42 47; fax 713 60 04).

Australia, IV, Mattiellistr. 2-4 behind the Karlskirche (tel. 512 85 80). Open Mon.-Fri. 9am-12:30pm; for Australian citizens 9am-12:30pm and 2-5pm.

New Zealand, XIX, Springsiedlegasse 28 (tel. 318 85 05; fax 37 76 60). Open Mon.-Fri. 9am-5pm.

South Africa, XIX, Sandgasse 33 (tel. 32 46 93).

Currency Exchange:

Banks are usually open Mon.-Wed. and Fri. 8am-3pm, Thurs. 8am-5:30pm. Most close mid-day from 12:30-1:30pm. Bank and airport exchanges use the same official rates (minimum commission 65AS for traveler's checks, 10AS for cash). Many offer cash advances with Visa or MasterCard (look for the signs).

ATMs are marked by green and blue signs, and are located everywhere. Nearly all accept MasterCard, Eurocard, Visa, and Cirrus cards. Signs on the ATM indicate which cards work. If the ATM seems broken, call the **Bankomat-Service Sperrtelefon,** (tel. (0660) 53 72). If you have problems withdrawing from your Visa or MasterCard, consult their offices in Vienna: **MasterCard/EuroCard,** III, Hintere Zollamtsstr. 17 (tel. 717 01). **Visa,** I, Wipplingerstr. 4 (tel. 534 87; fax 534 87 47). There are also **bill exchange** machines dotting the *innere Stadt*, including

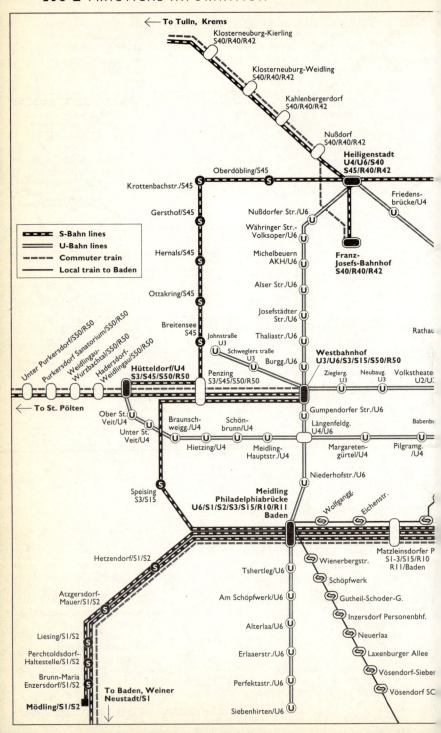

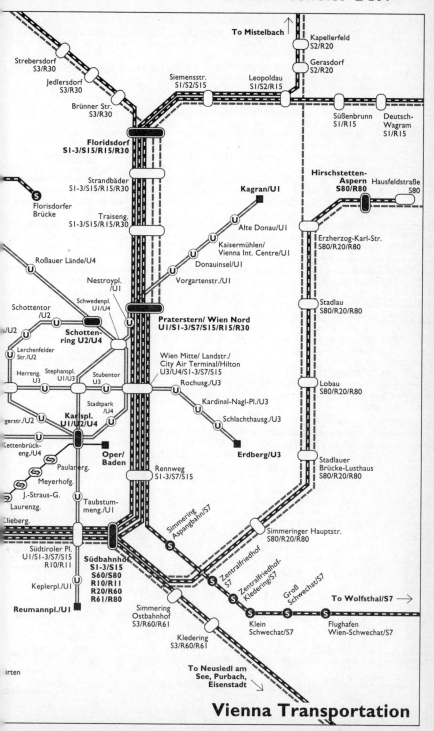

Vienna Transportation

one at the intersection of Graben and Kohlmarkt down the street from Stephanspl., and one outside the casino, a few steps away from the main information office at Kärntnerstr. These machines have very expensive rates—only change here in a weekend emergency. The **casino** is also a possible place to procure emergency cash (open late weekend nights). They have better rates than at the bill exchange machines, though not as good as banks.

Main Post Office exchanges currency daily 24hr. (60AS per traveler's check, no surcharge for cash). It offers some of the best rates in town.

Train station exchanges offer longer hours and lighter commission (50AS charge for changing up to US$700 of traveler's checks). **Westbahnhof,** (open daily 4am-10pm); **Südbahnhof** (May-Oct. open daily 6:30am-10pm; Nov.-April 6:30am-9pm); **City Air Terminal** (open daily Mon.-Fri. 9am-1pm and 1:30-3pm); and the **airport** (arrivals hall open daily 6:30am-11:30pm, departures hall 6am-9pm). **American Express** (see below). 15AS charge for cash.

American Express: I, Kärntnerstr. 21-23 (tel. 515 40), down the street from Stephanspl. (For 24-hr. refund service or lost traveler's cheques call toll-free (066) 68 40 or 935 121 152.) Holds mail for 4 weeks for AmEx customers only. Address mail, for example, as follows: "Daniel <u>FEINBERG</u>, c/o American Express, Client Mail Service, Kärntnerstr. 21-23, P.O. Box 28, A-1015 Vienna, Austria." Theater, concert, and other tickets sold for a 22% commission. Open Mon.-Fri. 9am-5:30pm, Sat. 9am-noon.

Telephones: I, Börsepl. 1, near the Schottenring. Open daily 6am-midnight. Also at the 4 main post offices: the **Hauptpostamt, Südbahnhof, Franz-Josefs Bahnhof,** and **Westbahnhof.** Phone booths are sprinkled throughout the city (for the Superman in us all). Deposit 1AS and up for local calls, 9AS for long-distance calls. Although coin-operated phones are still widely used, *Wertkarten* (phone card) telephones are generally more convenient; **phone cards** are available at post offices and train stations for 48AS (worth 50AS of phone calls) and 95AS (worth 100AS of phone calls).

Bisexual, Gay, and Lesbian Organizations

While the gay and lesbian community in Vienna is not large, the city poses little threat to visitors. Occasional acts of hate are directed at property, not persons, and are few and far between. Bisexual, gay, and lesbian life in Vienna is more integrated than in other cities; homosexuals are not necessarily segregated to certain "gay clubs." The German word for "gay" is *schwul,* "lesbian" is *lesbisch* or *lesben,* and "bisexual" is *bi* (pronounced BEE). Pick up a copy of *Connect,* a Viennese gay magazine available at most newsstands, for up-to-date information and articles. (See Bisexual, Gay, and Lesbian Cafés and Clubs under Nightlife, p. 293).

Rosa Lila Villa, VI, Linke Wienzeile 102 (tel. 586 81 50). A favored resource and social center for Viennese homosexuals and visiting tourists. Friendly staff provides counseling, information, nightclub listings, and other services. Situated on a main thoroughfare, the large pink and purple building with the inscription "Lesbian and Gay House" makes a rather striking impression on the more conservative passers-by. This, according to the staff, is the whole point. Lending library available. Open Mon.-Fri. 5-8pm. See Nightlife, p. 293.

Homosexuelle Initiative Wien (HOSI), II, Novaragasse 40 (tel. 26 66 04). Call the Rosa Lila telephone Tues. and Fri. 6-8pm. Open Tues. at 8pm. Lesbian group and telephone network Wed. at 7pm. Youth group and telephone network Thurs. at 7pm. Also prints a rather political newspaper, *Lambda Nachrichten.*

Internationale Homosexuelle Studentinnen, IX, Rooseveltspl. 5a (tel. 43 93 54). This student and faculty group is able to provide counseling or will steer you elsewhere for help. Meets Sat. at 5:30pm in the GEWI area in Rooseveltspl.

Schwulengruppe der Technische Universität (tel. 588 01-5890). A gay student counseling group. Open Thurs.-Fri. 2-4pm. Meets only during the term.

Other Practical Information

Taxis: (tel. 313 00, 401 00, 601 60, 814 00, or 910 11). Taxi stands at Westbahnhof, Südbahnhof, and Karlspl. in the city center. Accredited taxis have yellow and black signs on the roof. Basic charge 24AS, plus per mile charge. 12AS surcharge for taxis called by radiophone; 10AS surcharge for late nights (11pm-6am), Sun., and holidays. 12AS surcharge for luggage weighing more than 20kg, 24AS for more than 50kg.

Car Rental: Avis, I, Opernring 3-5 (tel. 587 62 41). Open Mon.-Fri. 7am-6pm, Sat. 8am-2pm, Sun. 8am-1pm. **Hertz,** Schwechat Airport (tel. 700 70), open Mon.-Fri. and Sun. 8am-11pm, Sat. 8am-8pm; I, Kärnter Ring 17 (tel. 512 86 77), open Mon.-Fri. 7:30am-6:30pm, Sat. and Sun. 8am-4pm; and XI, Simmeringer Hauptstr. 2 (tel. 79 54 26 71), open daily 8am-6pm. **Budget Rent-a-Car,** III, Landstraßer Hauptstr. 2 (tel. 714 65 65), open Mon.-Fri. 8am-6pm, Sat. 8am-2pm, Sun. 9am-1pm.

Auto Repairs: If your car needs fixing call **ÖAMTC** (tel. 120) or **ARBÖ** (tel. 123).

Parking: In the first district, parking is allowed for 1½hr., Mon.-Fri. 9am-7pm. One must first buy a voucher (6AS per ½hr.) at a *Tabak* and display it, with the time, on the dashboard. It's better to park cars outside the Ring and walk into the city center. Garages line the Ringstraße, including two by the State Opera, one at the Franz-Josef Kai, and one at the Marek-Garage at Messepalast. Good luck.

Bike Rental: The best bargain is at Wien-Nord and the Westbahnhof stations. 100AS per day; 45AS with train ticket from the day of arrival. Elsewhere in the city, such as on the Donauinsel, rentals average 30AS per hr. Pick up the *Vienna By Bike* brochure at the tourist office for more details.

Luggage Storage: Lockers at all train stations (40AS per 24hr.). Adequate for sizeable backpacks. Checked luggage 30AS. Open daily 4am-1:15am.

Lost Property: Fundbüro, IX, Wasagasse 22 (tel. 313 44 92 11). Call 790 94 35 00 within 3 days for items lost on public transport. Open Mon.-Fri. 8am-noon.

Bookstores: Shakespeare & Company, I, Sterngassse 2 (tel. 535 50 53; fax 535 50 53 16; e-mail bookseller@shakespeare.co.at). Eclectic and intelligent. Great English magazine selection, occasional readings or book signings. Open Mon.-Fri. 9am-7pm, Sat. 9am-1pm. **British Bookshop,** I, Weihberggasse 24-26 (tel. 572 19 45). Lists language seminars and other English-language events. Open Mon.-Fri. 9am-6pm, Sat. 10am-1:30pm. **Frauenzimmer,** Lange Gasse 11 (tel. 406 86 78; fax 407 16 20). Women's bookstore with some English language books and women's travel literature. Open Mon.-Fri. 9am-6pm, Sat. 9am-1pm.

Laundromat: Münzwäscherei Karlberger & Co., III, Schlachthausgasse 19 (tel. 78 81 91). Wash 90AS per 6kg, dry 10AS. Soap 10AS. Open Mon.-Fri. 7:30am-6:30pm, Sat. 7:30am-1pm. **Münzwäscherei Margaretenstraße,** IV, Margaretenstr. 52 (tel. 587 04 73). Take bus #59A from the U-Bahn U-4 "Margaretengürtel" station to "Kloster-Neugasse." Wash 95AS per 6kg load, dry 25AS; soap included. Open Mon.-Fri. 7am-6pm. Closed July 15-Aug. 6. Many hostels also offer access to a washer, dryer, and soap for about 50-70AS.

Public Showers and Bathrooms: At Westbahnhof, in Friseursalon Navratil. ½hr. shower 48AS, ½hr. bath 60AS. Extra 10AS for either on Sundays. Toilets in all underground stations (1-5AS). Art nouveau decor around toilets in I, Graben.

Snow reports: Vienna, Lower Austria, and Styria (tel. 15 83); Salzburg, Upper Austria, and Carinthia (tel. 15 84); Tirol and the Voralberg (tel. 1585).

Crisis Hotlines: All can find English speakers.

House for Threatened and Battered Women: 24-hr. emergency hotline (tel. 545 48 00 or 408 38 80).

Rape Crisis Hotline (tel. 523 22 22). Open Mon. 11am-6pm, Tues. 2pm-6pm, Wed. 10am-2pm, Thurs. 5pm-11pm. For **immediate help** in a rape situation call 717 19 24hr.

Frauentelefon: (tel. 408 70 66). Discussion arena for women's issues.

Advice Center for Sexually Abused Girls and Young Women: (tel. 526 49 94). Mon.-Fri. 9am-1pm.

Psychological Hotline: (tel. 310 87 80). Open Mon.-Fri. 8pm-8am, Sat.-Sun. 24hr.

English-language "Befrienders" Suicide Hotline: (tel. 713 33 74). Open Mon.-Fri. 9:30am-1pm and 6:30-10pm, Sat. and Sun. 6:30-10pm.

Poison Control: (tel. 406 43 43). Open 24hr.

VIENNA

Medical Assistance: Allgemeines Krankenhaus, IX, Währinger Gürtel 18-20 (tel. 404 00). A consulate can provide a list of English-speaking physicians.

AIDS Groups: AIDS-Informationszentrale Austria, VIII, Lenaugasse (tel. 40 22 353; fax 40 22 35 36). **AIDS-Hilfe Wien,** VIII, Wickenburggasse 14 (tel. 408 61 86; fax 408 64 11). Mon.-Tues. and Fri. 9am-2pm, Wed. 8am-1pm, Thurs. 4-8pm.

Emergencies: Police: (tel. 133); **Fremdenpolizei** (foreign police) headquarters at IX, Wasagasse 22 (tel. 313 44 0). Though they don't handle emergencies, they are responsible for student and worker visas. **Ambulance:** tel. 144. **Fire:** tel. 122. Alert your consulate of any emergencies or legal problems.

Post Offices: Hauptpostamt, I, Fleischmarkt 19. Vast structure containing exchange windows, telephones, faxes, and *natürlich,* mail services. Open 24hr. **Branches** at the train stations: **Südbahnhof,** open 6am-midnight; **Franz-Josefs Bahnhof,** open 24hr.; and **Westbahnhof,** open 24hr. Address **Poste Restante** to "Postlagernde Briefe, Hauptpostamt, Fleischmarkt 19, A-1010 Wien." Post office branches are distributed throughout the city; just look for the yellow sign with the trumpet logo. **Postal Codes:** Within the 1st district A-1010, in the 2nd A-1020, in the 3rd A-1030…in the 23rd A-1230.

Telephone Code: 0222 from within Austria, 1 from outside the country.

ACCOMMODATIONS AND CAMPING

One of the few unpleasant aspects of Vienna is the hunt for cheap rooms during peak season (June-Sept.). Don't leave your shelter to the vagaries of chance; write ahead or call for reservations at least five days in advance. Otherwise, plan on calling from the train station between 6 and 9am during the summer to put your name down for a reservation. If your choice is full, ask to be put on a waiting list, or ask for suggestions—don't waste time tramping around. Places fill quickly. The list of budget accommodations in Vienna is available at almost every tourist office. Those unable to find a hostel bed should consider a *Pension.* One-star establishments are generally adequate and are most common in the seventh, eighth, and ninth districts. Singles start around 350AS, doubles 500AS. The summer crunch for budget rooms is slightly alleviated in July, when university dorms are converted into makeshift hostels. Bear in mind that these "dorms" are not dormitories, but single and double bedrooms, and are priced accordingly.

If you're looking for a place to stay for a longer period of time, try **Odyssee Reisen and Mitwohnzentrale,** VIII, Laudongasse 7 (tel. 402 60 61). They find apartments for 225-350AS per person per night. A week runs about 1200AS and a month starts at 2000AS. They charge 20% commission on whatever you pay for the first month (20% for the following months; up to 120% total). Bring your passport (open Mon.-Fri. 10am-2pm and 3-6pm). Otherwise, visit either *Österreichische Hochschülerschaft* at Rooseveltplatz 5 or the first floor of the NIG building on Universitätstr. near the *Votivkirche,* where university students advertise for flatmates.

Hostels and Dormitories

The Myrthengasse Cluster

Myrthengasse (HI), VII, Myrtengasse 7 (tel. 523 63 16 or 523 94 29; fax 523 58 49). From the Westbahnhof take U-6 (dir: Heiligenstadt) to "Burggasse-Stadthalle," then bus #48A (dir: Ring) to "Neubaugasse." Walk back on Burggasse one block, and take the first right on Myrthengasse (15min.). From the Südbahn-hof, take bus #13A (dir: Skodagasse/Alerstr.) to "Neustiftgasse." Walk two blocks to your left on Neustiftgasse, and make a left onto Myrthengasse. A peaceful, leafy courtyard for your bread and cheese feast, as well as comfortable, modern rooms with light pine furniture. Is often overrun by adolescent schoolchildren. 2-, 4-, and 6-bed rooms with sink, shower and lockers. No lockout. 160AS, nonmembers 200AS. Laundry 50AS. Lunch, dinner 60AS. Wheelchair access.

Believe It Or Not, VIII, Myrthengasse 10, apt. #14 (tel. 526 46 58). Ring the bell; if no one answers in the afternoon or evening (until 11pm) try the caretaker's home phone (tel. 526 10 88). Funky and extremely social, Believe It Or Not gives hosteling an even more bohemian twist. Across the street from the Myrthengasse (see p. 262), apartment #14 offers two bedrooms, with bunks rising to the spacious ceilings, and a fully operational kitchen. All this space to groove comes complete with a gonzo caretaker who kicks you out from 10:30am-noon to clean and then leaves you alone for the rest of the day. Her personal crash-course on Vienna is a must. Reception open 8am until early afternoon—call if in doubt. 160AS. From Nov.-Easter the rate drops to 110AS. Reservations recommended.

Neustiftgasse (HI), VII, Neustiftgasse 85 (tel. 523 74 62; fax 523 58 49). Follow the directions to Myrthengasse—Neustiftgasse is around the corner. Managed by the same friendly people who manage Myrthengasse, with access to all Myrthengasse facilities encouraged. 2-, 4-, and 6-bed rooms, all with showers, and some co-ed rooming. Reception open 7:30-11am and 4pm-midnight. Lockout 9am-4pm. Curfew 1am. 155AS, nonmembers 195AS. Breakfast (7-8:30am) and sheets included. Lunch or dinner 60AS. Laundry 50AS, soap included. Reservations recommended. Wheelchair accessible.

Other Hostels

Gästehaus Ruthensteiner (HI), XV, Robert-Hamerlinggasse 24 (tel. 893 42 02; fax 893 27 96), is 3min. from the Westbahnhof. Exit on the Äußere Mariahilferstr. (beyond the Gürtel); turn right as you leave the station, then make your first left on Palmgasse, and go onto Robert-Hammerlinggasse, to the middle of the second block. About 15min. from the city center. All rooms are bright and very clean. Really friendly here, with a beautiful oasis of ivy and sun for a courtyard—complete with barbecue and oversized chess set. Reception open 24hr. No curfew, no lockout, and a flexible 4-night max. stay. 10-bed rooms 139AS per person. 3-5-bed rooms 159AS. Doubles 225AS. Singles 239AS. Sheets (except for the 10-bed rooms) and showers included. Breakfast 25AS. Lockers and kitchen facilities available. Bicycle rental July-Sept. 89AS per day. Reservations recommended.

Jugendgästehaus Wien Brigittenau (HI), XX, Friedrich-Engels-Pl. 24 (tel. 332 82 94-0 or 330 05 98; fax 330 83 79). Take U-1 or U-4 to "Schwedenplatz" and then tram N to the end station at "Floridsdorfer Brücke/Friedrich-Engels-Pl.," and follow the signs. It is the large green building behind the tram stop to the left of the tracks and across the street. 25min. from city center. The building has a lot of room and exceptional facilities for the disabled. Reception open 24hr. Lockout 9am-3pm. Dorms 140AS. Doubles with shower 280AS. Free lockers. Breakfast included. Laundry 50AS. Sizable lunch and dinner 60AS. 6-night max. stay.

Turmherberge Don Bosco, III, Lechnerstr. 12 (tel. 713 14 94). Take the U-3 to "Kardinal Naglpl.," then exit into Drorygasse, turn right on Erdbergstr., and continue until you hit Lechnerstr. (10min.). Stark rooms in the bell tower of a former monastery. This place bakes when the weather turn warm. Rather brusque reception. Austerity does have its rewards, however—beds are 70AS.

Kolpingfamilie Wien-Meidling (HI), XIII, Bendlgasse 10-12 (tel. 83 54 87; fax 812 21 30). Take U-4 or U-6 to "Niederhofstr." Head right on Niederhofstr. and take the fourth right onto Bendlgasse. This well-lit, modern hostel has 190 beds and stores valuables at the reception. Kind of boring, but then you didn't come to sit in the youth hostel, did you? Flexible reception times, but always open 6am-midnight. Check-out 9am. Lockout midnight-4am. Curfew midnight. 4, 6, and 10-bed rooms 145AS, 130AS, and 100AS per person respectively. Doubles 500AS. Nonmembers 20AS surcharge. Showers included. Linen 65AS. Breakfast 45AS.

Schloßherberge am Wilhelminenberg (HI), XVI, Savoyenstr. 2 (tel. 485 85 03-700; fax 48 58 50 37 02). From U-6 stop "Thaliastr," take tram #46 (dir: Joachimsthalerplatz) to "Maroltingergasse," or from Schottentor take tram #44 to "Wilhelminenstr.," and take bus 146B from this stop to "Schloß Wilhelminenberg" (on the way to Vienna this bus becomes #46). The bus will pull up to the palatial castle and you will think *Let's Go* is pulling your leg. Your accommodations are actually on the left of the palace, and, though not as opulent, are still beautiful. Situated in the Viennese countryside, bordering the Vienna woods, the hostel has a fantastic—repeat, fantastic—view of the city. Impeccably clean with 164 beds all arranged in quads with bathrooms attached. Curfew 11:45pm. 287AS per person (or 210AS in large groups). Reserve by fax, letter, or call at least 2 days in advance.

Hostel Zöhrer, VIII, Skodagasse 26 (tel. 46 07 30; fax 408 04 09). From the West-bahnhof, take U-6 (dir: Heiligenstadt) to "Alserstr.," then take streetcar #43 (dir: Schottentor) two stops to "Skodagasse." From the Südbahnhof, take bus #13A to "Alserstr./Skodagasse." About 10min. from the city center. Crowded but comfort-able and in a good location. Rose garden adjacent to a courtyard and furnished kitchen. Reception open 7:30am-10pm. No curfew. No lockout. Checkout 9am. 36 beds. 5, 6, or 7-bed rooms, with showers, 170AS per person. Breakfast (7:30-9:30am), sheets, and kitchen facilities included. Laundry 60AS. Front door/locker key deposit 50AS with ID, 100AS without.

Jugendgästehaus Hütteldorf-Hacking (HI), XIII, Schloßberggasse 8 (tel. 877 15 01 or 877 02 63; fax 87 70 26 32). From Karlsplatz, take U-4 to the end station "Hüt-teldorf," walk over the footbridge, and follow the signs to the hostel (10min.). Weary backpackers take bus #53B from the side of the footbridge opposite the sta-tion to its stop at the hostel. From the Westbahnhof, take S-50 to "Hütteldorf." About 35min. from the city center, this secluded hostel sits in one of Vienna's most affluent districts with great views of northwest Vienna. Often packed with high school groups. 271 dorm beds in 2, 4, 6, and 8-bed rooms. Some of the doubles have showers. Reception open 7am-11:45pm. Lockout 9am-4pm. Curfew 11:45pm, but ask for a digital card that will open the doors after curfew. 153AS per person, 183AS with shower. Breakfast included. Two-course menu 62AS, 3-course 71AS. Lunch package 71AS. Laundry 50AS per load.

University Dormitories

From July through September, the following university dorms are converted into hotels, generally consisting of singles and doubles, with a few triples and quads thrown in. These rooms don't have much in the way of character, but their cleanli-ness and relatively low cost are sufficient for most budget travelers.

Porzellaneum der Wiener Universität, IX, Porzellangasse 30 (tel. 31 77 28 20). From the Südbahnhof, take streetcar D (dir: Nußdorf) to "Fürstengasse." From the Westbahnhof, take streetcar #5 to the Franz-Josefs Bahnhof, then streetcar D (dir: Südbahnhof) to "Fürstengasse" (20min.). Nice plaster entryway, marked by a flag display worthy of the U.N. Good location 10min. north of the Ring. Reception open 24hr. Singles 175AS; doubles 350AS. Sheets and showers included. Reserva-tions recommended.

Ruddfinum, IV, Mayerhofgasse 3 (tel. 505 53 84). Just a few yards down Mayerhofg. from U-1 stop "Taubstummeng." Rock on, dude! Buy a beer at the reception and veg in front of MTV. Why should your vacation be different from your college days? The more intense guests watch CNN. Large rooms in a well-managed facility. Great location. Reception open 24hr. Singles 260AS; doubles 440AS; triples 570AS. Sheets, showers, and breakfast included.

Katholisches Studentenhaus, XIX, Peter-Jordanstr. 29 (tel. 34 92 64). From the Westbahnhof, take U-6 (dir: Heiligenstadt) to "Nußdorferstr.," then streetcar #38 to "Hardtgasse," and turn left onto Peter-Jordan-Str. From the Südbahnhof, take street-car D to "Schottentor," then streetcar #38 to "Hardtgasse." A laid-back atmosphere in the one of the leafier parts of the 19th district. Unexciting, but the price is right. Singles 230AS; doubles 332AS. Showers and sheets included. Call ahead.

Haus Döbling, IXX, Gymnasiumstr. 85 (tel. 34 76 31; fax 34 76 31 25). From U-6 stop "Nußdorfstr.," take S-bahn 38 (dir: Grinzig) to "Hardtgasse." Large, boxy grey institution. Pokes fun at its own architectural style with a Fisher-Price-esque sculp-ture of huge tumbling cubes in primary colors scattered in the leafy courtyard. Reception open Mon.-Fri. 8-10am and 2-4pm, Sat. 8-10am. Just follow the signs reading Verwaltung. Singles 270AS; doubles 340AS. Breakfast and showers included. Large parking area.

Gästehaus Pfeilgasse, VIII, Pfeilgasse 6 (tel. 401 74). Take U-2 to "Lerchenfelder-str." Head right on Lerchenfelderstr., right on Lange Gasse, and then left on Pfeil-gasse. The homesick will not be reminded of home, but of their freshman dorms (except these rooms have clean sheets and no U2 posters). Reception open 24hr. Singles 260AS; doubles 440AS; triples 570AS. Showers and breakfast included.

VIENNA

Studentenwohnheim der Hochschule für Musik, I, Johannesgasse 8 (tel. 514 84 48; fax 514 84 49). Walk three blocks down Kärnterstr. away from the Stephansdom, and turn left onto Johannesgasse. Fantastic location. Dinner and lunch are scrumptious and inexpensive. Reception open 24hr. Singles 380AS, with bath and toilet 450AS; doubles 660AS; triples 720AS; quads 880AS; quints 1100AS per person. Breakfast and showers included. Open July-Sept.

Albertina Hotels Austria, I, Fürichgasse 10 (tel. 512 74 93; fax 572 19 68), also commandeers dorms during the summer months. Call them to find out which of the three dorm locations they are opening up, or to reserve a room.

Albertina Auersperg, VIII, Auerspergstr. 9 (tel. 406 25 40). Nicest of the three. Modern rooms. Practically on the Ring and a hop, skip, and jump from U-2 stop "Lerchenfelderstr." up Alserstr. Singles with sink 355AS, with shower 500AS; doubles with sink 580AS, with shower 820AS; triples with shower 1200AS. Breakfast and sheets included. Call central number first.

Albertina Josefstadt, VIII, Buchfeldgasse 16 (tel. 406 52 11), behind the Rathaus. Take U-2 to "Rathaus" and walk one block up Schmidgasse to Buchfeldgasse. Also has a fantastic location and is a little cheaper than Auersperg. Call central number first to see if it is open for guests.

Albertina Alserstraße, VIII, Alsterstr. 44 (tel. 406 32 31). Take U-6 to "Alsterstr.," then take tram #43 (dir: Schottentor) to "Langegasse." Turn back and the hotel is on the left. Cheapest of the three. Call central number first.

Hotels and Pensions

Check the hostels section for good singles deals as well. The prices are higher here, but you pay for convenient reception hours, no curfews, and no lockouts.

Pension Kraml, VI, Brauergasse 5 (tel. 587 85 88; fax 586 75 73), is off of Gumpendorferstr. From the Westbahnhof, walk across the Gürtel and up Mariahilferstr., and take the fourth right onto Otto-Bauer-Gasse; make the first left on Königseggasse, then the first right (15min.). From the Südbahnhof, take bus #13A (dir: Alserstr./Skodagasse) to "Esterházygasse" (15min.). About 10min. from the city center. Tidy, comfortable, new, and run by a cordial family. Lots of space in the well-lit larger rooms, with wooden floors and high ceilings. Reception open 24hr. year-round. Singles 280AS; doubles 570-590AS, with shower 680AS, with shower and private toilet 780AS; triples 750AS, with shower 875AS; quad with shower and toilet 1160AS. Buffet breakfast—bread, yogurt, cheese, eggs—in the pension's privately owned pub. Call ahead.

Lauria, VII, Kaiserstr. 77, apt. #8 (tel. 522 25 55). From the Westbahnhof, take tram #5 four stops to "Burggasse," #77 Kaiserstr. is right there on the intersection. From Sudbahnhof, take tram#18 to the Westbahnhof, change there to the #5 and follow direction above. Fun and eclectic—a Hawaiian, ethno-Elvis feel inside an old-fashioned, semi-*Jugenstil*, Austrian apartment building. One pleasant mattress-packed dorm room with huge ceilings and lots of triples and doubles. No curfew. Co-ed rooming. Dorm beds 160AS; double 530AS, with bunk 480AS, with shower 700AS; triple 700AS, with shower 800AS; quad 850AS, with shower 940AS. Kitchen facilities. TV. Reservations strongly recommended but require a 2-day min. stay. Bring lock for lockers. Visa and MC accepted.

Hospiz-Hotel CVJM, VII, Kenyongasse 15 (tel. 523 13 04; fax 523 13 04 13). From the Westbahnhof, cross the Gürtel, walk 1 block down Stallgasse and turn left on Kenyongasse (3min.). This large, old building, now part of the Austrian YMCA, provides a quiet location close to the station. Big, institutional feel. Reception open daily 8am-10pm. Singles 350AS, with shower 380AS; doubles 640AS, with shower 680AS; triples 900AS, with shower 990AS; quads 1160AS, with shower 1280AS. Floor space (on mats, bring a sleeping bag) is available for groups only (150AS). Ample parking. Key to entrance and room provided. Visa, MC.

Pension Hargita, VII, Andreasgasse (tel. 526 19 28 or 932 85 64). Take U-3 to "Zieglergasse," and head down Mariahilferstr. (directly across the street) to Andreasgasse. The sun shines brightly through the windows on the rustically carved wood and ethnic rugs of this newly renovated *Pension*. Comfortable aesthetics and a good location. Singles 400AS, with shower 450AS; doubles 550AS, with shower 650AS, with shower and private toilette 800AS. Breakfast 40AS.

Pension Wild, VIII, Lange Gasse 10 (tel. 43 51 74). Take U-3 to "Volkstheater," then U-2 to "Lerchenfelderstr." Lange Gasse is the first street to the right. From the Süd-bahnhof, take bus #13A (dir: Alserstr./Skodagasse) to "Piaristengasse." Take a left onto Lerchenfelderstr., and take the second left onto Lange Gasse. 30 beds, with kitchen access. Reception open daily 7am-10pm. No curfew, but take a key if you plan to stay out late. Singles 460-550AS; doubles 590-690AS; triples 860-960AS. Breakfast and shower included. Reservations recommended.

Pension Falstaff, IX, Müllnergasse 5 (tel. 317 91 27; fax 31 79 18 64). Take U-4 to "Roßauer Lände," cross Roßauer Lände, and head down Grünentorgasse, taking the third left onto Müllnergasse. This small pension is much quieter than its boisterous namesake. A dusty stillness reigns in this world of linoleum. It has a campy flavor all its own. Singles 360AS, with shower 470AS; doubles 600AS, with shower 720AS, with private toilet 820AS. Extra bed 200AS. Breakfast included.

Hotel Quisisana, VI, Windmühlgasse 6 (tel. 587 71 55; fax 587 71 56). Take U-2 to "Babenbergerstr.," turn right down Mariahilferstr. for three blocks, and bear left on Windmühlgasse. An old-fashioned hotel run by a charming older couple—it's diffi-cult to feel uncomfortable here. Singles 320AS, with shower 370AS; doubles 500AS, with shower 600AS; triples 750AS; quads 1000AS. Breakfast 40AS.

Camping

Wien-West I (tel. 914 14 49) and **II** (tel. 914 23 14), at Hüttelbergstr. 40 and 80, respectively, are the most convenient campgrounds; both lie in the 14th *Bezirk* about 8km from the city center. For either, take U-4 to the end station at "Hüttel-dorf," then switch to bus #14B or 152 (dir: Campingpl. Wien West). 65AS, children 35AS. Tent or car 61AS. Both offer laundry machines, grocery stores, and cooking facilities. I is open July 15-Aug. 28. II is open March-Jan., and also rents 4-person bungalows (April-Oct. 450AS).

Aktiv Camping Neue Donau, XXII, Am Kaisermühlen 119 (tel. 220 93 10). Near the U-1 stop "Kaisermühlen." Tents 40AS per person, electricity 48AS. Large tents or trailers 64AS per person, electricity 68AS. Open May-mid-September.

FOOD

"Here the people think only of sensual gratifications."
—Washington Irving, 1822

In a capricious world full of uncertainty, the Viennese take it as a given that the least you can do is face it with a full stomach. Food is not mere fuel for the body; it is an aesthetic and even philosophical experience that begins when you wish someone *"Mahlzeit"* (enjoy). Food and drink are inseparably linked here, and both are con-sumed in great quantities. Cafés, *Beisln* (pubs), and *Heurigen* (wine gardens) each possesses their own peculiar balance between consumption and entertainment. One would do well to search the **Entertainment** and **Nightlife** sections for a splendid night out or the **Food** listings for good culinary suggestions.

Viennese culinary offerings reflect the crazy patchwork empire of the Habsburgs. Boiled beef is one of the few dishes actually originating in Austria, a hearty national treasure. Otherwise, many of the specialties betray an association with former prov-inces. *Serbische Bohnensuppe* (Serbian bean soup) and *Ungarische Gulaschsuppe* (Hungarian spicy beef stew) are two examples of Eastern European influence. *Knödel*, bread dumplings found in most side dishes, originated in the former Czecho-slovakia. Even the famed *Wiener Schnitzel* (fried and breaded veal cutlets) was first cooked in Milan. Of course this works both ways. As any Austrian schoolchild can tell you, crescent-shaped bread and pastries, *kipferln,* were first made by Viennese bak-ers to celebrate the end of the Turkish sieges. It was only later that the French co-opted the design to make croissants. The *Gästehäuser* and the *Beisln* serve inexpen-sive rib-sticking meals that are best washed down with much beer. The *Würstel-*

stände, found on almost every corner, provide a quick, cheap lunch. A sausage runs in the neighborhood of 25AS. Vienna is most renowned for its sublime desserts and chocolates—unbelievably rich, and priced for patrons who are likewise blessed. Most residents, however, adamantly maintain that the sumptuous treats are worth every *Groschen.* Unless you buy your sin wholesale at a local bakery, *Sacher Torte, Imperial Torte,* and even *Apfel Strudel* cost up to 40AS.

The restaurants near **Kärntnerstraße** are generally expensive. A better bet is the neighborhood north of the university and near the Votivkirche (U-2 to "Schotten-tor"), where **Universitätsstraße** and **Währingerstraße** meet; reasonably priced *Gast-stätten, Beisln,* and restaurants are easy to find. The area radiating from the **Rechte** and **Linke Wienzeile** near the **Naschmarkt** (U-4 to "Kettenbrückegasse") is home to a range of cheap, often ethnic restaurants, and most of the nearby 7th district **(Neu-ban)** is funky and pleasant. The **Rathausplatz** hosts inexpensive food stands most of the year themed around whatever the current festival happens to be. At Christmas-time, the **Christkindlmarkt** offers hot food and spiked punch amidst vendors of Christmas charms, ornaments, and candles. From the end of June through July, the **Festwochen** (weeks of celebration) bring foodstuffs of many nations to the stands behind the seats of the various art and music films (stands open daily 11am-11pm). Another outdoor option is the open-air Naschmarkt, where you can nibble on aro-matic delicacies (vegetables, bread, and ethnic food) while shopping at Vienna's pre-mier flea market (U-4 to "Kettenbrückengasse"). The Naschmarkt is an especially filling option for vegetarians in this carnivorous city. Come before 11am, and walk to the far end of the Naschmarkt to find the cheapest prices from local farmers (open Mon.-Fri. 7am-6pm, Sat. 7am-1pm). The open-air **Brunnenmarkt** (U-6 to Josefstädter-str., walk up Veronikagasse, after a block turn right) is extremely colorful and tends to have lower prices because it's located in a traditional workers' district. The reliable **Weinerwald** chain for chicken-lovers has many branches in the first district (Anna-gasse 3, Freyung 6, Bellariastr. 12, Schottengasse with a particularly nice garden; open daily 7am-midnight).

As always, supermarkets provide the building blocks of cheap, solid meals, but prices vary tremendously. The lowest prices can be found at **Billa, Konsum, Hofer,** and **Sparmarkt**—slightly less common are **Ledi, Mondo, Renner,** and **Zielpunkt.** Kosher groceries can be bought at the **Kosher Supermarket,** Hollandstr. 10 (tel. 216 96 75). Be warned that most places, including restaurants, close Saturday afternoons and all of Sunday (on the first Sat. of every month, most shops close at 5 or 6pm.) In winter visit the excellent and inventive **Bäckerei Schwarz,** XIII, Anhofstr. 138 (tel. 877 24 75; take the U-4 to "Hütteldorf"). In general, restaurants stop serving after 11pm. To conquer summer heat, seek out the **Italeis** or **Tichy** ice cream vendors, or visit the delicious **Gelateria Hoher Markt,** I, Hoher Markt just off Rotenturmstr. Expatriate Italians flock here to sample all 23 mouth-watering flavors of ice cream (open daily March-Oct. 9am-11pm).

Restaurants

The Innere Stadt

Trzesniewski, I, Dorotheergasse 1 (tel. 512 32 91), is 3 blocks down the Graben from the Stephansdom. A famous stand-up restaurant, this unpronounceable estab-lishment has been serving petite open-faced sandwiches for over 80 years. Favorite toppings include salmon, onion paprika, and egg. The design is dark and spare: classic early 20th century. This was the preferred locale of Franz Kafka, among oth-ers. 19 varieties of spreads on bread, 8AS per *Brötchen* (baguette). Ideal for a snack while touring the city center. Lots of vegetarian options. Open Mon.-Fri. 8:30am-7:30pm, Sat. 9am-1pm; first Sat. of the month 9am-6pm. Another **branch** at VII, Mariahilferstr. 26-30 in the Hermansky department store. Same hours.

Levante, I, Wallnerstr. 2 (tel. 533 23 26). Walk down the Graben away from the Stephansdom, bear left on Kohlmarkt, and then right on Wallnerstr. (3min.). A hot spot among students, this Greek-Turkish restaurant features a stunning street-side dining area and a myriad of affordable dishes, including plenty of vegetarian delights. Entrées 78-130AS. **Branches** at I, Wollzeile 19 (off Rotenturm, U–3 or U-1 to "Stephanspl."); Mariahilferstr. 88a; and VIII, Josefstädterstr. 14 (by the "Rathaus" U-2 stop). All open daily 11:30am-11:30pm.

Ma Pitom, I, Seitenstettengasse 5 (tel. 535 43 13). In the "Triangle" area—walk down Potenturmstr., take a left on Fleischmarkt, a quick right onto Rabensteig, and another quick right onto Seitenstettengasse. Low vaulted white ceilings and candles set on closely packed round black tables. Sophisticated, relaxed and cultured atmosphere—the black and white photos on the wall are by Mapplethorpe. If you sit outside, try to find a table between the tree-lined wall and the lit stained glass windows of Ruprechtskirche. The melted cheese on the brick-oven pizza (61-80AS) is absolutely beautiful—they must melt it with wine. Also a night-spot and gallery, with occasional live music or readings. Open Mon.-Thurs. 11:30am-3pm and 5:30pm-1am, Fri.-Sat. 11:30am-3pm and 5:30pm-2am, Sun. 5:30pm-1am.

Brezelgwölb, I, Lederhof 9 (tel./fax 533 88 11). Excellent hearty cuisine even the Viennese call *"Altwiener"* (old Viennese). The atmosphere of this old-fashioned *Backstube* is enhanced by cobblestones and classical music. Don't leave without seeing one of the rare standing pieces of the medieval city wall in the courtyard—the rest was torn down to build the Ringstraße. You might need a reservation in the evening. Open daily 11:30am-1am, heated food until midnight.

Zu den Drei Hacken, I, Singerstr. 28 (tel. 512 58 95), is a 5-min. walk down Singerstr. from the Stephansdom. A unique experience with its ancient wooden floors, fading black and white photographs, and dusty walls. This 200-year-old establishment was the preferred dining spot of Schubert and has fantastic tables outside. The Drei Hacken serves only traditional Austrian food (including boiled beef). The food is remarkable but, be warned, the prices follow suit. English menu. Entrées 86-200AS. Open Mon.-Fri. 9am-midnight, Sat. 9am-2pm.

Bizi Pizza, I, Rotenturmstr. 4 (tel. 513 37 05), on the corner of Stephanspl. Good food and a great deal in the heart of the city. This self-service restaurant, now an institution among the young and cashless, boasts a deliciously fresh salad bar (small plate 30AS, large plate 50AS) and huge individual pizzas (60-75AS, slices 27AS). Try the spinach pizza. Open daily 11am-11pm. **Branch** with the same hours at Franz-Josefs-Kai (tel. 535 79 13).

La Crêperie, I, Grünangergasse 10 (tel. 512 56 87), off Singerstr. in the Stephansplatz area. A very enthusiastic decorator gave this interior a sweetly kitschy patchwork of Versailles and Louis XIV; Baroque wallpaper with gilded *fleur-de-lys* and metallic tassles and fringes alternate with indoor sculpted bushes and a bar disguised as a rustic, paint-peeling outdoor gazebo. Scrumptious *crêpes*, both sweet and savory (30-200AS). Open daily 11:30am-midnight.

Café Ball, I, Ballgasse 5 (tel. 513 17 54), near Stephanspl., off Weihburggasse. On a narrow cobblestone lane, the black and white stone floor tiles, dark wood, and brass bar create an elegant, bohemian feeling. Falafel 45AS. Open Mon.-Thurs. 10:30am-midnight, Fri.-Sat. 10am-2pm, Sun. 6pm-midnight.

Margaritaville, I, Bartensteingasse 3 (tel. 405 47 86). Serves interesting Mexican food, most notably the *Fasita Lupita*. This place gets very hip and very hopping at night. Entrées 85-200AS. Tiny outdoor garden. Open Mon.-Sat. 6pm-2am (heated food until 1am), Sun. 6pm-midnight.

Outside the Ring

Tunnel, VIII, Florianigasse 39 (tel. 42 34 65). Take U-2 to "Rathaus," and with your back to the Rathaus, head right on Landesgerichtstr., then left on Florianigasse. Pronounced "Too-nehl" by the locals. Dark and smoky, with funky paintings, thick, heavy tables to gather around, and the occasional divan instead of chairs. The Tunnel is an extremely popular place, prized for its dilapidated hipness, its live music downstairs every night, and its really affordable food. Italian, Austrian, and Middle Eastern dishes, with vegetarian options as well (40-120AS). Some of the cheapest beer in Vienna (½L *Gösser* 24AS), the best pizza (50-80AS), and a breakfast menu (29AS) until 11:30am. Open daily 9am-2am.

Blue Box, VII, Richtergasse 8 (tel. 523 26 82). Take U-3 to "Neubaugasse," turn off of Mariahilferstr. into Neubaugasse, then take your first right onto Richtergasse. You absolutely can't come to Vienna and miss this place. Although the interior looks more like a nightclub than a restaurant—jaundiced orange chandelier, blue leather couches, and lots of posters advertising alternative rock concerts—the emphasis is on the food. Dishes are fresh, flamboyant, and above all, original. They often center around themes, whether regional (Russia, Louisiana, Tuscany) or general (sailors' fare, "color lessons," picnics, garlic). DJs pick the music to make an interesting juxtaposition with the meals. As the night wears on, Blue Box becomes more of a club. And it's even a great place to come for breakfast (until 5pm). Choose from Viennese, French, English, vegetarian, you name it. Open Tues.-Thurs. 10am-2am, Fri.-Sat. 10am-4am, Sun. 10am-2am, Mon. 6pm-2am.

Amerlingbeisl, VII, Stiftgasse 8 (tel. 526 16 60) Turn off Mariahilferstr., about half-way between the U-2 "Babenberger" and the U-3 "Neubangasse" stops, into Stift-gasse. After a couple of blocks you'll hit a cluster of outdoor restaurants. Walk past the first to Amerlingbeisl, a gem with live music, an idyllic tree-roofed courtyard, and excellent Viennese pub food. It's actually affordable. Entrées 74-105AS, breakfast 48-85AS. Open daily 9am-2am, heated food served until 1am.

Restaurant am Radetzkyplatz, III, Radetzkypl. 1 (tel. 712 57 50). An old, mellowed, grand Austrian pub. At least 150 years of beer (0.50L 28AS) and food (58-160AS) give the place worn bar railings and faded green walls. Sit outside under the striped awning and enjoy some of the cheapest prices in Vienna. Robust servings and veggie options. Open daily 8am-11pm.

Schweizerhaus, II, Straße des l. Mai 116 (tel. 218 01 52). Take U-1 (dir: Kagran) to "Praterstern," exit the station, and take a left under the bridge. Walk into the park, and follow the main thoroughfare (*des Ersten Mai*). Operated by the Kolarik family since 1920, "Swiss House" is one of Austria's most loved *Biergarten*. Think beer, oceans of it. The tray-toting waiters have perfected the technique of serving mass quantities of brew. *Budvar*, the Czech *Budweiser* (far superior to its American brother), on tap. The garden is enormous, packed, and fun. To complete the experience, try the *Schweinstelze*, the largest piece of meat served anywhere (enough grilled pork for three big bad wolves) only 89AS. Spicy potato pancakes, two for 24AS. Food from 35-128AS. Open 10am-11pm.

Fischerbräu, XIX, Billrothstr. 17 (tel. 319 62 64). Take U-6 to "Nußdorfer Straße," walk up Währinger Gürtel, take a left on Döblinger Hauptstr., and another left onto Billrothstr. Popular spot for young locals. The leafy courtyard and jazz music make this an ideal spot to consume the home-brewed beer (large 36AS) and delicious food. The veal sausage (56AS) and the chicken salad (82AS) are excellent. Open Mon.-Sat. 4pm-1am, Sun. 11am-1am. Jazz brunch Sun. noon-3pm.

Thai Kitchen, V, Schönbrunnerstr. 23 (tel. 586 78 85). Take the U-4 to "Ketten-brückestr.," make a 180-degree turn as you exit, and walk up the Rechte Wienzeile to Wehrgasse; keep going until you hit Schönbrunnerstr. This tasteful restaurant with Thai sculptures and bamboo serves fresh authentic *nouveau* Thai cuisine. Entrées 100-200AS, lots of vegetarian options. Open Tues.-Sun. 6-11:30pm, Sat.-Sun. also noon-2pm. In good weather, they open ½hr. later.

Elsäßer Bistro, IX, Währingerstr. 30 (tel. 319 76 89). Take tram #40 or 41 from Schottentor to "Spitalgasse." Within the palace now housing the French Cultural Institute—just walk in the fenced garden and follow your nose. Really wonderful food which even French expatriates acknowledge as authentic. Most dishes hover at or below 100AS. Open Mon.-Thurs. 9:30am-7:30pm, Fri. 9:30am-4:30pm.

Nells, XVII, Alseggerstr. 26 (tel. 479 13 77). Take tram #40 from Schottentor to "Alseggerstr." The garden tables, warm wooden interior, and original interpretations of traditional Viennese food draw a hip twentysomething crowd. Lots of different beers and *heuriger* wines. Open Mon.-Sat. 4pm-2am, Sun. 11am-1am.

Hatam, IX, Währingerstr. 64 (tel. 310 94 50). Take trams #40, 41, or 38 to "Spital-gasse." Persian food at decent prices. Try their unbeatable *gorme sabse,* or grab a *Döner* to go (35-55AS, entrées 70-160AS). Open daily 11:30am-11:30pm.

Schnitzelwirt Schmidt, VII, Neubaugasse 52 (tel. 523 37 71). From U-2 or U-3 stop "Volkstheater," take bus #49 to "Neubaugasse" (5min.). Offers every kind of *Schnitzel* (58-108AS) imaginable. Huge portions and low prices for the most carnivorous of desires and frugal of budgets. Open Mon.-Sat. 11am-11pm.

Stomach, IX, Seegasse 26 (tel. 310 20 99). Take tram D (dir: Nußdorf) from the Ring to "Fürstengasse," then walk down Porzellangasse to Seegasse, and turn right. First-class Austrian cooking with a Styrian kick; lots and lots of vegetarian food (90-190AS). Drop-dead gorgeous inner courtyard. Come early to get a table. Open Wed.-Sat. 4pm-midnight, Sun. 10am-10pm.

Quick Sandwiches, VII, Mariahilferstr. 64 (tel. 523 74 26). Near the U-3 stop "Eigler-str." Come here to fill up without emptying out your wallet. At first the decor will make you think you're in McDonald's, until you look up to see the crêpe butter-flies. Permanently stocked with little old ladies drinking mugs of beer, even around breakfast-time. Sandwiches hover at the 15AS mark. Open Mon.-Sat. 7am-8pm.

Café C.I. (Club International), XVI, Payergasse 14 (tel. 408 72 61). At the Brunnen-markt in Yppenplatz; take the U-6 to "Josefstädterstr.," walk up Veronikagasse, and turn right on Payergasse (or take tram #44 here from Schottentor). Pleasant Aus-trian, Greek, and Italian dishes at very pleasant prices (40-80AS). Lots of vegetarian and macrobiotic options, plus breakfast served all day. Every Thursday has some sort of cultural program, usually readings or art exhibitions. A bit of a nightspot as well. Open Mon.-Sat. 8am-2am, Sun. 10am-2am.

University Mensa, IX, Universitätsstr. 7, on the 7th floor of the university building, midway between U-2 stops "Rathaus" and "Schottentor." Open to all. Visitors can ride the old-fashioned elevator (no doors and it never stops; you have to jump in and out) to the sixth floor and take the stairs to the seventh floor. Typical univer-sity meals in the dining hall 20-50AS. Open Mon.-Fri. 8am-3pm. Other inexpensive student cafeterias serve their constituencies at:

Music Academy, I, Johannesgasse 8 (tel. 512 94 70). Open Mon.-Fri. 7:30am-2pm. Food served 11am-2pm.

Academy of Applied Art, I, Oskar-Kokoschka-Pl. 2 (tel. 718 66 95). Open Mon.-Thurs. 9am-6pm, Fri. 9am-3pm.

Academy of Fine Arts, I, Schillerpl. 3 (tel. 58 81 61 38). Open Mon.-Fri. 9am-5:30pm. Closed June to early Sept.

Vienna Technical University, IV, Wiedner Hauptstr. 8-10 (tel. 586 65 02). Open Mon.-Fri. 11am-2:30pm.

Catholic University Student's Community, I, Ebendorferstr. 8 (tel. 408 35 87 39). *Menu* 33-40AS. Open Mon.-Fri. 11:30am-2pm.

Economics University, IX, Augasse 2-6 (tel. 310 57 18). Open Mon-Fri. 7:30am-7pm, holidays only until 3pm.

Coffeehouses and Konditoreien

> *"Who's going to start a revolution? Herr Trotsky from Café Central?"*
> —anonymously quoted on the eve of the Russian Revolution

There is a steadfast rule for the Vienna coffeehouse—the drink matters, but the atmo-sphere where it is consumed *really* matters. The 19th- and 20th-century coffeehouse was a haven for artists, writers, and thinkers who flocked to its soft, brooding interior because their apartments were often unheated and lacked telephones. There they wrapped themselves in the dark wood and dusty velvets, ordered a cup of coffee and stayed into the night, composing operettas, writing books, and cutting into each other's work. The bourgeoisie followed suit, and the coffeehouse became the living room of the city and an important piece of its history. At its tables gathered the intel-lectual world of Vienna and, in many cases, Europe. A grand culture grew up around them. Peter Altenberg, "the café writer," scribbled lines, Kokoschka sallied forth, and Leon Trotsky played chess. **Adolf Loos,** prophet of 20th-century minimalist architec-ture, designed the interior of the **Museum Café** in smooth, spacious lines. No longer the tumult of bristling writers and modern artists that they once were, they are packed with their illustrious pasts. The best places resist massive decorative over-hauls, allowing a noble, comfortable decrepitude.

Viennese coffee is distinct, not quite as strong as an espresso, but with more kick than your average Coffeemate Dripmaster. One orders a *Kleiner* (small) or *Grosser* (large) and signifies one's potency—*Brauner* (brown, with a little milk) or *Schwarzer* (black, enough said). There is also a *Melange* (coffee with steamed milk), which is not unlike a cappuccino, and *Mazagron,* which is iced and laced with rum.

Another Viennese quintessential is *Mokka mit Sclagrahm,* a mocha coffee with whipped cream. Be traditional and order an *Einspänner* (coffee and a glass filled with whipped cream beside it), or wow the whole café by drinking a *Kaisermélange*—a regular *mélange* with the yolk of an egg mixed in. Opulent pastries complete the picture. *Apfel Strudel,* cheesecakes, tortes, *Buchteln* (warm cake with jam in the middle—diabolical), *Palatschinken, Krapfen,* and *Mohr im Hemd* have all been an important factor in Vienna's placement on the culinary map. Occasionally, one must go to the counter to select and pay for a pastry, giving the receipt to the waiter, who will serve you accordingly.

In these living rooms of Vienna, time effectively stops. The waiter (often outfitted with black bow tie) will serve you as soon as you sit down, but will leave you alone for the rest of the stay. If your water glass, however, keeps on being filled hours after you've finished your coffee, then you should probably take the hint and order something else. Coffeehouse etiquette also dictates lingering in the dim hush. Signal to the waiter that you are ready to leave by asking to pay: *"Zahlen bitte!"* A waiter will never approach without a summons—it is considered rude to rush patrons. Before you settle up, however, do as the Viennese and starving artists do and did—relax with a **newspaper** for free. Daily newspapers and magazines are neatly racked and provided free of charge for patrons. Both can be found in English. The *Konditoreien* are no less traditional, but with the focus shifted onto their delectable creations rather than their coffee. These pastries are somewhat of a national institution, and while Switzerland may have its gold reserves, the currency in Austria could be backed by its world-renowned *Sacher Torte.*

The Innere Stadt

Café Hawelka, I, Dorotheergasse 6 (tel. 512 82 30). Three blocks down Graben from the Stephansdom. Dusty wallpaper, dark wood, and red-striped velvet lounges that haven't been upholstered in years—the Hawelka is shabby and glorious. Josephine and Leopold Hawelka put this place on the map when they opened it in 1937, and it is now revered (Leopold received an award from the Austrian government and Josephine a visit from Falco—see the picture). *Buchteln* (served only at 10pm) 30AS. Coffee 25-40AS. Open Mon., Wed.-Sat. 8am-2am, Sun. 4pm-2am.

Café Museum, I, Friedrichstr. 6 (tel. 56 52 01). Near the Opera; head away from the *innere Stadt* to the corner of Operngasse and Friedrichstr. Built in 1899 by Adolf Loos, with striking, curved, red leather and lots of space. Simple and elegant, this spacious and comfortable meeting place attracts a mixed bag of artists, lawyers, and students. There are chess tables in back. Open daily 7am-11pm.

Kleines Café, I, Franziskanerplatz 3. Turn off Kärtnerstr. into Weihburgasse and follow it to the Franziskanerkirche. Whimsical mix of the traditional and the funky. Brown leather and wood, the low gently vaulted ceiling, floor tiles, art exhibits, and nightclub posters coexist harmoniously. The salads here are minor works of art. Yes, it's *klein* (small). Open Mon.-Sat. 10am-2am, Sun. 1pm-2am.

Café Alt Wien, I, Bäckergasse 9 (tel. 512 52 22). Dimly lit place and on a street behind the Stephansdom with ancient restaurants and cobblestone passages. Smoky red sofas and layers of *avant-gardiste* posters on the wall. At night it's very happening. Open Mon.-Thurs. 10am-2am, Fri.-Sun. 10am-4am.

Café Haag, I, Schottengasse 2. From U-2 stop "Schottenring," head left down Schottengasse. Gracefully classic, old-Vienna atmosphere without the formaldehyde museum feeling of stasis or preservation. Cool garden (the former Scottish cloister) for hot feet. Great pastries. Open Mon.-Fri. 7:30am-8pm, Sat. 10am-6pm.

Café Central, I, at the corner of Herrengasse and Strauchgasse, inside Palais Ferstel. This opulent café is steeped in history. Theodor Herzl and Sigmund Freud just begin a guest list that reads like the later chapters of your high school European history text. It was also the reknowned hangout of satirist Karl Kraus, obsolete hero Vladimir Ilych Ulianov (better known by his pen name Lenin), and Leon Trotsky, who played chess at Central, fingering imperialist miniatures with cool anticipation. Alfred Polgar used the name of the café to skewer the intellectual pretensions of the Viennese bourgeoisie in his essay *Theorie de Café Central.* Oh, they serve coffee, too, which comes with a little chocolate. Open Mon.-Sat. 9am-8pm. Live piano music 4-7pm.

Demel, I, Kohlmarkt 14. Walk 5min. from the Stephansdom down Graben. *The* Viennese *Konditorei*. The atmosphere is near-worshipful in this legendary cathedral of sweets. A fantasy of mirrored rooms and cream walls, topped by the display case of magical desserts. Waitresses in convent-black serve the divine confections (35-48AS). Don't miss the *crème-du-jour*. Open daily 10am-6pm.

Hotel Sacher, I, Philharmonikerstr. 4 (tel. 512 14 87), around the corner from the main tourist information office. This historic sight has been serving the world-famous **Sacher Torte** (45AS) in red velvet opulence for years. During the reign of Franz Josef, elites invited to the Hofburg would make late reservations at the Sacher. The emperor ate quickly and Elisabeth was always dieting—nobody dared eat after the imperial family had finished—so all the guests left hungry and had a real dinner later at Hotel Sacher. Exceedingly elegant; most everyone is refined and bejeweled. Open daily 6:30am-11:30pm.

Café-Restaurant Burggarten, I, Burggarten (tel. 533 10 33). Walk away from the Ring toward the backside of the Hofburg. Unobtrusive little place next to the old green glass of the vaulted, palm-filled, otherworldly greenhouse. Look out into the liveliest part of the Burggarten, where students come in droves to tan and chat and choose from vegetarian, Italian, or even seafood entrées (60-90AS). Open daily 10am-11pm.

Cafe MAK, I, Stubenring 3-5 (tel. 714 01 21). Located in the MAK museum. Take tram #1 or 2 to Stubenring. The place is light, bright, white, and it gets very tight at night. Starkness as an aesthetic statement. Can get very lively with a student crowd after 10pm. Open Tues.-Sun. 10am-2am, warm food until midnight.

Outside the Ring

Café Sperl, VI, Gumpendorferstr. 11 (tel. 586 41 58), is 15min. from the Westbahnhof. Built in 1880, Sperl is one of Vienna's oldest and most beautiful cafés. Although some of the original trappings were removed during renovations, the *fin de siècle* atmosphere remains. Franz Lehár was a regular here; he composed operettas at a table by the entrance. Also the former home for Vienna's Hagenbund, an *art nouveau* coterie excluded from the Secession. Coffee 25-40AS; cake 28AS. Billiards daily 9:30am-9:30pm. Open Mon.-Sat. 7am-11pm, Sun. 5-11pm; July-Aug. closed Sun.

Café Drechsler, VI, Linke Wienzeile 22 (tel. 587 85 80). By Karlspl., head down Operngasse and continue on Linke Wienzeile. *The* place to be the morning after the night before. Early birds and night owls roost here over pungent cups of *Mokka*. Great lunch menu—try *Spinatz*. Open Mon.-Fri. 4am-8pm. Sat. 4am-6pm.

Café Wortner, IV, Wiedner Hauptstr. 55 (tel. 505 32 91). Walk down the thoroughfare from Karlsplatz. Sit in the elaborate garden around the water-spitting angel fountain, or come inside for the warm dozing-off quietness. This 100-year-old café also offers chess and billiards (60AS per hour). Ask a waiter when the next jazz-matinee, discussion group or gallery exhibit is being held. Open Mon.-Fri. 7am-11pm, Sat. 8am-8pm.

Café Stein, IX, Währingerstr. 6 (tel. 319 72 41). Walk down Währingerstr. from Schottentor. Chrome seats outside to see and be seen, or clustered tables indoors in the smoky red-brown and metallic interior. Anyone hitting a positive number on the hipness scale puts an appearance in here. Intimate and lively, it slides into night as "Stein's Diner," with live DJs. Also offer billiards and Internet access (55AS per ½hr., 10am-11pm, reserve your slot in advance). Open Mon.-Sat. 7am-1am, Sun. 9am-1am. Stein's Diner in the basement open Mon.-Sat. 7pm-2am.

Café Bauernfeld, IX, Liechtensteinstr. 42 (tel. 317 83 65). Take tram D to "Fürstgasse." Silly, good-humored place with a Christmas-light-wreathed fish tank alongside bizarre fresco pieces that look as if they date from the 1940s. Be careful, the patched brown leather couches are so big you might lose your date. Billiards, popcorn, and lots of students from the Porzellaneum. Open Mon.-Fri. 9am-2am, Sat. 2pm-2am, Sun. 2pm-midnight.

Café Prückel, I, Stubenring 24 (tel. 512 61 15). Spacious, with high ceilings. A 50s renovation has given it faded lime green tablecloths, and time has conferred a noble slouch. Patronized by art students from the MAK (Museum of Applied Arts), which is down the street. Open daily 9am-10pm.

> ### Taster's choice
>
> Legend dates Vienna's love affair with coffee back to the second Turkish invasion of 1683. Two months into the siege, Vienna was on the verge of falling to the Turks, until a Polish-born citizen named **Kolschitzky** volunteered his services. A dashing adventurer who had spent time within the Sultan's territories, Kolschitzky used his knowledge of Turkish language and customs to slip through the enemy camp and deliver a vital message to the relief forces under the Duke of Lorraine. The Duke then engaged the Turks in a bitter battle which sent them fleeing, leaving most of their camp behind. Kolschitzky claimed as his only compensation the many sacks of greenish beans left by the routed armies of the Sultan. The grateful city readily granted this reward, and Kolschitzky opened the first Viennese coffeehouse, **Zur Blauen Flasche,** became a huge success, and died a wealthy and revered man.

SIGHTS

Viennese streets are laden with memories of glorious people and times past. You can get the best feel for the city by simply wandering the paths once trodden by the likes of Klimt, Freud, and Mozart. *Vienna from A to Z* (30AS from tourist office, higher prices in bookstores) provides all you need for a self-guided tour. The array of cultural offerings in Vienna can be mind-boggling; the free *Museums* brochure from the tourist office lists all opening hours and admission prices. Individual museum tickets usually cost 20-80AS, but the **Vienna Card** transportation pass will bring you big discounts. Whatever you do, don't miss the **Hofburg,** the **Schloß Schönbrunn,** the **Kunsthistorisches Museum,** and the **Schloß Belvedere.** The range of available **tours** is equally overwhelming—walking tours, ship tours, bike and tram tours, bus tours, tours in a cup, tours over easy. Call the tourist office in advance to make sure that the tours are operating on schedule. The DDSG company (tel. 727 50 451) runs three-hour **riverboat tours** from April to October (220AS). Boats depart from the Schwedenplatz, near the Kunsthaus Wien. Information on 90-minute **walking tours** is available from the tourist office (120AS, under 18 60AS, with Vienna card 95AS). All of these tours are very worthwhile, but "Vienna in the Footsteps of the Third Man" tour, which takes you into the sewers and the graffiti-covered catacomb world of the Wien River's underground canals, is simply not to be missed (bring your own flashlight). **Tours** on turn-of-the-century "old-timer" trams run from May to October. (Tel. 587 31 86. 1½hr. 200AS. Departs from the Karlsplatz near the Otto Wagner Pavilion on Sat. 11:30am, 1:30pm; and Sun. 9:30, 11:30am, and 1:30pm.) The legendary drivers of *Fiakers,* or horse-drawn carriages, are happy to taxi you wherever your heart desires; be sure to agree on the price before you set out. **Cycling tours** take place daily all year round. Call **Vienna-Bike,** IX, Wasagasse (tel. 319 12 58) for bike rental (60AS) or a 2-3hr. tour (200AS). Early booking is advised. **Bus tours** operate through various companies: **Vienna Sight-seeing Tours,** III, Stelzhamergasse 4/11 (tel. 712 46 83); **Cityrama,** I, Börgegasse 1, (tel. 534 13); and **Vienna Line,** I, Johannesgasse 14 (tel. 51 24 93 50). Tours start at 200AS.

The Innere Stadt

The **First District** *(die Innere Stadt)*, Vienna's social and geographical epicenter, is enclosed on three sides by the massive **Ringstraße** and on the northern end by the **Danube Canal.** Though *"die Innere Stadt"* literally translates to "the inner city," it thankfully carries no connotation of American inner-city ills. Vienna's perfectly preserved *Altstadt* (old town) was the gallery that the artists of Austria, and in some cases Europe, rushed to fill. Due to the generous hand of wealthy monarchs and 20th-century nation builders, it has been maintained and preserved, yet allowed to fade to its noble patina. With the mark of master architects on everything from palaces and theaters to tenement housing and toilet bowls, the *Innere Stadt* is a testament to the genius which flowed through Vienna's veins. The historic transformations of the Austrian aesthetic are also apparent as smooth *Jugendstil* designs peep out amid Rococo ornament—strange, yet, harmonious bedfellows.

From Staatsoper to Stephansplatz

Apart from St. Stephan's Cathedral, no other building is as close to the hearts of the Viennese as the **State Opera House** or *Staatsoper*. Its construction was given first priority in the massive Ringstraße project (see p. 278), and the grand building was completed in 1869. Due to a construction mistake, however, the foundation was dug too deep and a full story of the building's grandeur was axed. Franz Josef agreed with the general consensus when he remarked that the building was "a little low." The two architects so badly wanted to create a worthy edifice that the lukewarm reactions at its opening drove one to suicide and caused the other to die two months later "of a broken heart." The emperor was so shocked that for the rest of his life, he only answered in two phrases whenever he was presented with something: *"es ist sehr schön, es hat mich sehr erfreut"* (It's very beautiful, I enjoyed it very much). Opinions about the Opera House changed as the years progressed, and Vienna's collective heart broke when the Opera was destroyed by Allied bombing in 1945. The exterior of the opera house was meticulously restored and re-opened in 1955. The list of former directors is formidable, including Gustav Mahler, Richard Strauss, and Lorin Maazel. If you miss the operas, at least tour the gold, crystal, and red velvet interior. (Tours July-Aug. daily 11am-3pm on the hour; Sept.-June upon request. 40AS, students 25AS.) Actually seeing an Opera is cheaper, though—*par terre* standing room tickets with an excellent view are only 20AS and standing room anywhere else costs 15AS. Every February, the crystal and champagne **Opernball** waltzes its way, white-tied and well-heeled, into the Viennese social calendar.

Just across from the Opera lies another reminder of turn-of-the-century top hats and white gloves—the flag-bedecked **Hotel Sacher.** Even today a hotel and restaurant of prestige, this legendary institution, once run by the formidable, cigar-smoking Anna Sacher, served magnificent dinners over which the imperial elite discussed affairs of state. Equally important, the hotel's *separées* provided discreet locations where the elite also conducted affairs of another sort.

Behind the Sacher in Albertinaplatz lies a memorial to a more disturbing time in Viennese history: Alfred Hrdlicka's painful 1988 sculpture **Monument Gegen Krieg und Faschismus** (Memorial Against War and Fascism. This work memorializes the suffering of Austria's people—especially its Jews—during World War II. The twisted figures, especially the man on hands and knees, are a reminder of the horror of the Nazi period, in particular, the shameful events after the German *Anschluß,* when Viennese Jews of all ages were forced to scrub the streets clean of the anti-Nazi posters which had been posted by the Social Democrats.

From Albertinaplatz, Tegetthoffstr. leads to the spectacular **Neuer Markt.** In the middle stands the **Donnerbrunnen,** a fountain by Georg Raphael Donner, wherein the graceful Danube is surrounded by four gods representing her tributaries. The 17th-century **Kapuzinerkirche** springs from the southwest corner of the square. Inside is the **Imperial Vault** *(Gruft),* securing the remains (minus heart and entrails) of all the Habsburg rulers since 1633. Empress Maria Theresa, buried next to her beloved husband Franz Stephan of Lorraine, rests in an ornate Rococo sepulcher surrounded by delicate cherubs and a dome of wedding cake proportions. Maria Theresa was crushed by the death of her husband, and visited his tomb frequently. Having grown old and unable to overcome gravity, the Empress had an elevator built to make her visits easier. On her last trip, the elevator stalled three times, prompting the old dame to exclaim that the dead did not want her to leave. She was buried there a week later (open daily 9:30am-3:30pm; 30AS, children 20AS).

Just a quick step down Donnergasse lies **Kärntner Straße,** a grand boulevard lined with chic-but-*cher* cafés and boutiques, as well as street musicians playing everything from Peruvian folk to Neil Diamond ballads. Heading left brings the visitor back to Vienna's heart. Look at the **Stephansdom** as reflected in the glass and aluminum of the **Haas Haus.** The view is even better inside the Haus, which has a café on the top floor. The Haus, considered something of an eyesore by most Viennese (much to the dismay of architect Hans Hollein), was opened in 1990.

Stephansplatz to Michaelerplatz

From the Stephansplatz, walk down Rotenturmstr., cross Fleischmarkt to Rabensteig, and then turn left onto Seitenstettnegasse to reach Ruprechtsplatz, adorned with a slew of street cafés and the Romanesque **Ruprechtskirche,** the oldest church in Vienna. The north side of the square looks out onto the **Danube Canal,** the waterway that defines the northern boundary of the *Innere Stadt.* Once you've taken in the quay, walk back down Ruprechtsstiege, onto Seitenstettengasse, and find the **Synagogue,** Seitenstettengasse 2-4. This building, one of over 94 temples maintained by Vienna's 180,000 Jews until 1938, was saved from Nazi destruction only because it stood on a residential block. Most of the other synagogues were destroyed by the Nazis on November 9-10, 1938, during the **Kristallnacht** (Crystal Night) pogrom. The night received that name because the glass shards that were found on the streets the next day glittered like crystal. Over 50 years later, fewer than 7000 Jews reside in Vienna, and the synagogue is patrolled by an armed guard.

Back at the top of Seitenstettengasse runs **Judengasse** (literally "Lane of the Jew"), a reminder of Vienna's segregationist ghetto policy toward its Jews. **Hoher Markt** lies down the street; this square stands on the site of the Roman encampment **Vindobona,** and served as the town's center during the Middle Ages. The most memorable piece of architecture in the square is much more recent—glance up at the **Ankeruhr clock** at noon to see this *Jugendstil* diversion in its full glory. Built in 1911, the mechanical timepiece has twelve historical figures that rotate past the old Viennese coat of arms accompanied by music of their period. The figures depict the city's history from the era of Roman encampment up to Joseph Haydn's stint in the Boys' Choir. (One figure per hour, except at noon, when all appear in succession.)

Wipplingerstraße heads west (right) from Hoher Markt past the impressive baroque façade of the **Bohemian Court Chancellery,** now the seat of Austria's Constitutional Court. The **Altes Rathaus,** Friedrich-Schmidt-Pl. (tel. 53 43 67 79), stands directly across from here. Occupied from 1316 until 1885, when the government moved to the Ringstraße, the building's courtyard contains a fountain by George Raphael Donner displaying a scene from the legend of Andromeda and Perseus (open Mon.-Thurs. 9am-5pm.; tours Mon.-Fri. 1pm). **Judenplatz,** on the opposite side of the Chancellery, presents a statue of Jewish playwright Ephraim Lessing. Originally erected in 1935, the statue was torn down by Nazis and only returned to Judenplatz in 1982.

A quick right off of Wipplingstr., down Stoss im Himmel, will reward the visitor with **Maria am Gestade,** a gem of a Gothic church with an extraordinarily graceful spire of delicately carved stone. The stained glass above the altar is one of the few remarkable examples of the art in Vienna. Head back past Judenpl. and down Drahtgasse, which opens into the grand courtyard **Am Hof.** The Babenbergs used this square as the ducal seat when they moved the palace in 1155 from atop **Leopoldsberg** (in the Wienerwald) to the present site of Am Hof 2. The square where medieval jousters once collided now houses the **Church of the Nine Chairs of Angels** (built 1386-1662). At the request of Baron von Hirsch, Pope Pius VI gave the papal blessing here on Easter in 1782. Emperor Franz II proclaimed his abdication as Holy Roman Emperor in 1806 from the terrace. Am Hof was in use long before the Babenbergs, as evidenced by the **Roman ruins** (open Sat.-Sun. 11am-1pm). In the middle of the square stands the **Mariensäule,** erected to fulfill a vow sworn by Emperor Ferdinand III when the Swedes threatened Vienna during the Thirty Years War. A rather intimidating Mary crowns the pillar, while four ferocious cherubs cutely dispatch the evils of hunger, plague, and war.

A jaunt down Steindlgasse from Am Hof onto Milchgasse leads to Petersplatz, home of the **Peterskirche.** Charlemagne, legend says, founded the first version of St. Peter's on this site in the 8th century, but town architects just couldn't resist tinkering with it throughout the ages. The present Baroque ornamentation was completed in 1733, with Rottmayer on fresco duty. Head out Jungferngasse to the **Graben,** one of Vienna's main shopping drags; this pedestrian zone offers *Glühwein* (spiked hot punch) during the Christmas season. The Graben is a good example of Viennese architectural evolution. Historicist and Secessionist façades stare warily at each other. One of the most interesting sights is the underground *Jugendstil* public toilets, which were designed by Adolf Loos. The **Pestsaüle** (Plague Column), in the square's center, was built in 1693 in thanks to God for the passing of the Black Death. According to the inscription, the monument is "a reminder of the divine chastisement of plagues richly deserved by this city," proving that the Viennese had ways of dealing with guilt complexes long before Freud.

At the western end of the Graben, away from the Stephansdom, Kohlmarkt leads off to the left, past **Demel Café**—though few sweet teeth can pass Demel without a purchase, and the **Looshaus** (1910). The latter architectural wonder was branded "the house without eyebrows" by contemptuous contemporaries. Admirers of both Classical and *Jugendstil* styles were scandalized by the elegant simplicity of this building; the bottom two floors are decorated with green marble, and the top four floors are of pale green stucco with (gasp!) no façade decoration. Franz Josef was reportedly so disgusted with the atrocity built outside his bedroom window that he refused to use the Hofburg gate that faced it. The Looshaus sits on **Michaelerplatz,** named for the **Michaelerkirche** on its eastern flank. The church was purportedly founded by Leopold "the Glorious" of Babenberg, as an expression of gratitude to God for his safe return from the Crusades. The church's Romanesque foundation dates back to the early 13th century, but construction continued until 1792 (note the Baroque embellishment over the doorway). In the middle of the Michaelerplatz, lie the **excavated foundations** of Old Vienna.

Ecclesiastical Vienna: The Stephansdom

Vienna's most treasured symbol, the **Stephansdom,** known affectionately as "Der Steffl" to locals, fascinates viewers with its Gothic intensity and smoothly tapered **South Tower** (found on most city postcards). The **North Tower** was originally intended to be equally high and graceful, but construction ceased after a disturbing tragedy. It seems that a young builder named Hans Puchsbaum wished to marry his master's daughter Maria. The master, rather jealous of Hans' skill, agreed, on one condition: Hans had to finish the entire North Tower on his own within a year. Faced with this impossible task, Hans despaired, until a stranger offered to help him as long as Hans abstained from saying the name of God or any other holy name. Hans agreed, and the tower grew by leaps and bounds. The young mason spotted his love in the midst of his labor, and wishing to call attention to his progress, called out her name: "Maria." With this invocation of the Blessed Virgin, the scaffolding collapsed, and Hans plummeted 500 feet to his death. Rumors of a devilish pact spread, and work on the tower ceased, leaving it in its present condition. Less supernatural forces almost leveled the entire church; Nazi artillery at the end of WWII did massive damage. The painstaking reconstruction is chronicled by a series of photos inside. The exterior of Stephansdom boasts some remarkable sculptures and monuments, and deserves a lap around before you enter the building. The oldest sections, the Romanesque **Riesentor** (Giant Gate) and **Heidentürme** (Towers of the Heathens), were built during the reign of King Ottokar II, when Vienna was a Bohemian protectorate. Habsburg Duke Rudolf IV later ordered a complete Gothic retooling, earning the sobriquet "the Founder." (Tours of the cathedral in English Mon.-Sat. at 10:30am and 3pm, Sun. and holidays 3pm; admission 30AS. Spectacular evening tour July-Sept., Sat. 7pm; admission 100AS). Inside, some of the important pieces include the Albertine Choir built in the beginning of the 14th century, and the pulpit and organ loft by **Anton Pilgram.** Both works by this master are exquisite examples of late-Gothic sculpture, so delicate that Pilgram's contemporaries warned him that the fragile organ pedestal would never bear the organ's weight. Pilgram replied that he would hold it up himself and carved a self-portrait at the bottom, bearing the entire burden of the structure on its back. The high altar piece of the **Stoning of St. Stephen** is another must-see. You can view the Viennese sprawl from the **Nordturm** (North Tower; open daily 9am-6pm, Oct.-Mar. 8am-5pm; elevator ride 40AS). The ambitious can climb the 343 steps of the South Tower for a better 360-degree view not to mention a (fenced) walk along the outer side of the tower (open 9am-5:30pm; 20AS). Walk downstairs to the entrance of the **Catacombs,** where thousands of plague-victim skeletons line the walls. Look for the lovely **Gruft** (vault), which stores all of the Habsburg innards. Everyone wanted a piece of the rulers; the Stephansdom got the entrails, the Augustinerkirche got the hearts, and the Kapuzinergruft, apparently drawing the short straw, got the leftovers. Morbid thrill-seekers can see the urns containing the royal digestive systems as a skeleton-filled room or two. (Tours every ½hr. Mon.-Sat. 10am-noon and 2-5pm, Sun. and holidays 2-5pm. 50AS.)

Imperial Vienna: The Hofburg

The sprawling **Hofburg** (Imperial Palace) can be read like an architectural history book of the Habsburg family. Its construction began in 1279, and additions and renovations continued virtually until the end of the family's reign in 1918 as it became a mini-city. On the whole, the palace is not particularly unified nor exceptionally beautiful, but it does provide an appropriate testimony to the peculiar splendor of the Habsburg Empire. Today, the complex houses the Austrian President's offices and the performance halls of the Lipizzaner stallions and the Vienna Boys' Choir. The hours will fly as one loses one's self amidst the pomp and circumstance. (Tel. 58 75 55 45 15. Enter at Michaelerpl. 1; Imperial apartments open daily 9am-5pm.)

A stroll along the perimeter is the best way to start a tour. From the Michaelerplatz and facing the palace, start your journey to the left to find the **Stallburg** (Palace Stables) right inside the passage, home to the Royal Lipizzaner stallions of the **Spanische Reitschule** (Spanish Riding School; tel. 533 90 32; fax 53 50 10 96). This renowned example of equine breeding is a relic of the Habsburg marriage to Spanish royalty. The Reitschule performances (April-June and Sept. Sun. 10:45am, Wed. 7pm; March and Nov. to mid-Dec. Sun. 10:45am) are always sold out; you must reserve tickets six months in advance. (Write to "Spanische Reitschule, Hofburg, A-1010 Wien." If you reserve through a travel agency, you pay at least a 22% surcharge. Write only for reservations; no money will be accepted. Tickets 240-800AS, standing room 190AS.) Watching the horses train is much cheaper. (March-June and Nov. to mid-Dec. Tues.-Sat. 10am-noon; Feb. Mon.-Sat. 10am-noon, except when the horses tour. Tickets sold at the door at Josefspl., Gate 2, from about 8:30am. 100AS, children 20AS. No reservations.)

Keep walking around the Hofburg, away from the Michaelerkirche, to wander through the Baroque **Josefsplatz,** with an equestrian monument to Emperor Josef II. The modest emperor would no doubt be appalled at his statue's Roman garb, but the sculptor probably couldn't bring himself to depict the decrepit hat and patched-up frock coat favored by Josef. The stunning **Augustinerkirche** sits on this square also. The church was built in the 14th century; its Gothic insides restored in the 18th century. The church is the proud possessor of the hearts of the Habsburgs, which are enshrined in the crypt below. Augustinerstr. leads right past the **Albertina,** the palatial wing once inhabited by Maria Christina (Maria Theresa's favorite daughter) and her hubby Albert. The Albertina now contains a film museum and the celebrated **Collection of Graphic Arts** with pieces by Dürer (tel. 534 83; open Mon.-Thurs. 10am-4pm, Fri. 10am-1pm).

Upon rounding the tip of the Albertina, cut around the monument to Erzherzog Albrecht and stroll through the exquisite **Burggarten** (Gardens of the Imperial Palace). The gorgeous, gently sloping grass makes a perfect picnic spot. The opposite end of the garden opens onto the Ring and the main entrance to the interior of the Hofburg, just a few meters to the right. Enter through the enormous stone gate into the sweeping **Heldenplatz** (Heroes' Square). The equestrian statues (both done by **Anton Fernkorn**) depict two of Austria's greatest military commanders. The one of Archduke Karl portrays him on a charger triumphantly reared on its hind legs with no other support, a feat of sculpting never again duplicated, even by Fernkorn. The poor man went insane, supposedly due to his inability to achieve the same effect in his portrayal of the second statue, Prince Eugene of Savoy. To the right is the grandest part of the Hofburg, the **Neue Hofburg** (New Palace), built between 1881 and 1913. The double-headed golden eagle crowning the roof symbolizes the double empire of Austria-Hungary. The building, however, even in all its splendid majesty is only a part of what the Habsburgs intended. Planned in 1869, the Neue Hofburg's design called for a twin across the Heldenplatz. Both buildings were also to be connected to the Kunsthistorisches and Naturhistorisches Museums by arches spanning the Ringstraße. WWI put an end to the Empire and its grand designs. In 1938, Hitler spoke from the Neue Hofburg balcony to a huge, applauding crowd in the Heldenplatz following the *Anschluß*. By 1945, the length of the entire Heldenplatz was covered with potato plants to feed the starving surviving citizens of the city. In the present day, the Neue Hofburg palace houses branches of the Kuntshistorisches Museum, including an extensive weapons collection, as well as an assortment of antique instruments; among the harps and violins are Beethoven's harpsichord and Mozart's piano, which has a double keyboard—the top for the right hand, the bottom for the left. The **Ephesus Museum** contains the massive findings of an Austrian excavation of Roman ruins in Turkey (see Art Museums, p. 286). Also within the Neue Hofburg is the exquisite **Nationalbibliothek** (National Library), which boasts an outstanding collection of papyrus scriptures and musical manuscripts. The library's **Prunksaal** (Gala Hall) is an awesome display of High Baroque. (Tel. 53 41 03 97. Open Jan.-May and Nov.-Dec. Mon.-Sat. 10am-noon, June-Oct. Mon.-Sat. 10am-4pm.) The Hofburg continues to have some connection with the Austrian government; the building attached to the Neue Hofburg is the **Reichskanzleitrakt** (State Chancellery Wing), most notable for the labors of Hercules, a group of buff statues said to have inspired the eleven-year-old and 98-pound weakling, Arnold Schwarzenegger, then on his first visit to Vienna, to begin his journey towards universal pumptitude.

The arched stone passageway at the rear of the Heldenplatz leads you to the courtyard called **In der Burg,** surrounded by the wings of the **Alte Hofburg** (Old Palace). In the center is a monument to Emperor Franz II. Turn left under the arch of red and black stones, crowned by a black eagle on a gilded shield, to arrive at the **Schweizerhof** (Swiss Courtyard), named for the Swiss mercenaries who formed the Emperor's personal guard. This is the oldest part of the Hofburg. Although the building is now mostly Renaissance architecture, there are some remnants of the medieval fortress so necessary for the upwardly-mobile aristocratic dynasty. The Habsburg stronghold was frequently under attack, twice by the Viennese themselves. On the right side of the courtyard stands the **Schatzkammer** (treasury), which contains such famous wonders as the crowns of the Holy Roman and Austrian Empires. The **Holy Lance** is, legend states, the one that pierced Christ's side during the Crucifixion. It was in front of this lance that the young Hitler was purportedly inspired to return to Germany and found the Nazi party. Just ahead is the Gothic **Burgkapelle** where the **Wiener Sängerknabenchor** (Vienna Boys' Choir) performs (see Music, p. 288).

Back at In der Burg, turn right to find yourself under the intricately carved ceiling of the **Michaeler Küppel.** The solid wooden door on the right leads to the **Schauräume,** the former private rooms of Emperor Franz Josef and Empress Elisabeth. (Open Mon.-Sat. 8:30am-noon and 12:30-4pm, Sun. 8:30am-12:30pm. Tours 40AS, students 20AS.) Amid all the Baroque trappings, the two most personal items seem painfully out of place; Emperor Franz Josef's military field bed and Empress Elisabeth's personal wooden gym bear mute testimony to two lonely lives. The door on the left opens to reveal the **Hofsilber und Tafelkammer,** a display of outrageously ornate cutlery, trays, and pitchers that once adorned the imperial dinner table (open Tues.-Fri. and Sun. 9am-1pm; admission 30AS, students 5AS).

Monumental Vienna: The Ringstraße

The Hofburg's Heldenplatz gate presides over the northeastern side of the Burgring segment of the **Ringstraße.** In 1857, Emperor Franz Josef commissioned this 57-m-wide and 4-km-long boulevard to replace the city walls that separated Vienna's center from the suburban districts. The military, still uneasy in the wake of the revolution attempted nine years earlier, demanded that the first district be surrounded by fortifications; the erupting bureaucratic bourgeoisie, however, protested for the removal of all formal barriers, and the opening of space in the city. Imperial designers struck a unique compromise; the walls would be razed to make way for the Ringstraße, a sweeping circle of traffic efficient for the large-scale transport of forces yet visually unobtrusive and thereby non-threatening. The mass traffic of the Ringstraße, a pathway around the inner city with no specific destination, creates a psychological "edge" or border, isolating life inside from that without. This massive architectural commitment attracted participants from all over Europe. Urban planners put together a grand scheme of monuments dedicated to some staples of Western culture: scholarship, theatre, politics, and art. The collected Historicist result became known as the **Ringstraße Style.**

The **Hofburg,** the nexus of Vienna's imperial glory, extends from the right side of the Burgring. On the left is **Maria-Theresien-Platz,** flanked by two of the monumental foci of culture: the **Kunsthistorisches Museum** (Museum of Art History) and, on the opposite side of the square, the **Naturhistorisches Museum** (Museum of Natural History). When construction was completed on the museums, the builders stepped back and gasped in horror; they had put Apollo, patron deity of art, atop the Naturhistorisches Museum, and Athena, goddess of science, at the crown of the Kunsthistorisches Museum. The horror subsided when they realized all could be mended— tour guides claim that each muse is intentionally situated to *look upon* the appropriate museum (see Art Museums, p. 286). The throned Empress Maria Theresa, surrounded by her key statesmen and advisers, is immortalized in a large statue in the center of the square. The statue purportedly faces the Ring so that the Empress may extend her hand to the people.

As you continue clockwise around the Ring, the stunning rose display of the **Volksgarten** is on your right (see Gardens and Parks, p. 283), across the Ring from the **Parlament** building. This gilded lily of Neoclassical architecture, built from 1873-83, is the first of the four principal structures designed to fulfill the program of bourgeois cultural symbolism. Now the seat of the Austrian National and Federal Councils, it was once the meeting place for elected representatives to the Austro-Hungarian Empire. Before the *fin de siècle* artistic revolution, mid-19th-century architects consistently turned to historical reference when designing buildings of important political and social position. Here, all of the architectural forms in this edifice were supposed to evoke the great democracies of ancient Greece. (Tours Sept.-June Mon.-Fri. at 11am and 3pm; July-Aug. Mon.-Fri. 9, 10, 11am, 1, 2, and 3pm; Easter holidays 11am and 3pm.)

Just up the Dr.-Karl-Renner-Ring is the **Rathaus,** another masterpiece of historical symbolism. The building is an intriguing remnant of the late 19th-century neo-Gothic style, with Victorian mansard roofs and red geraniums in the windows. The Gothic reference is meant to recall the favored style of the *Freistädte* (free cities) of old; the first grants of trade-based municipal autonomy appeared at the height of the Gothic period in the early 12th-century. The Viennese, emerging from imperial constraints through the strength of the growing bureaucratic middle class, saw fit to imbue their city hall with the same sense of budding freedom. There are numerous art exhibits inside, and the city plans outdoor festivals in the square outside.

The **Burgtheater,** across the Rathauspark and the Ring, responds well to the long, articulated front of the Rathaus, the building's Baroque and Rococo flourishes capturing the soaring spirit of the art form. Inside, frescoes by Gustav Klimt, his brother, and his partner Matsch depict the interaction between drama and history through the ages. Apparently, Klimt used contemporary faces as models for the audience members; notables of the day used to send Klimt gifts in hopes that they would be immortalized in one of the murals. (Tours Sept.-Oct. and April-June Tues. and Thurs. 4pm, Sun. 3pm; July-Aug. Mon.-Sat. 1, 2, and 3pm; Nov. and March upon request.)

Immediately to the north, on Karl-Lueger-Ring, is the **Universität.** This secular cradle of rationalism is rendered unequivocally in the Renaissance style. The university was the source of the failed 1848 bourgeois uprising, and thereby received the most careful attention; above all, the architectural symbolism had to be *safe*. It was necessary to dispel all of the ghosts of dissatisfaction and revolt in the building's design. Therefore, the planners took as their model the cradle of state-sponsored liberal learning—Renaissance Italy. In that culture, there existed the quintessential safe blend of discovery *sans* subversion; the Renaissance generated intellectual pursuits in the name of, not in confrontation with, the state. Inside the university (also known as the **Schottentor**) is a tranquil courtyard with busts of famous departed professors filling the archways.

The surrounding side streets gush the typical assortment of university-bred cafés, bookstores, and bars. To the north, across Universitätsstr., the twin spires of the **Votivkirche** come into view. This neo-Gothic wonder and home of a number of expatriate religious communities with services in English is surrounded by rose gardens where students study and sunbathe in warm weather. Frequent classical music concerts afford opportunities to see the chapel's interior; look for posters announcing the dates throughout the year. The Votivkirche was commissioned by Franz Josef's brother Maximilian as a gesture of gratitude after the Kaiser survived an assassination attempt in 1853. The Habsburgs habitually strolled around town with a full retinue of bodyguards—supposedly incognito, though everyone knew who they were. The emperor *demanded* that his subjects pretend to not recognize the imperial family. On one of these constitutionals, a Hungarian insurrectionist leapt from nearby bushes and attempted to stab the emperor; Franz Josef's collar was so heavily starched, however, that the knife drew no blue blood, and the crew of bodyguards dispatched the would-be assailant before he could strike again.

Outside the Ring

Operngasse cuts through Opernring, leading to the Ringstraße nemesis, the **Secession Building,** perhaps the greatest monument of turn-of-the-century Vienna. The cream walls, restrained decoration, and gilded dome clash strongly with the Historicist style of the Ringstraße. This is exactly the point (open Tues.-Fri. 10am-6pm and Sat.-Sun. 10am-4pm). Otto Wagner's pupil Josef Olbrich built this *fin de siècle* Viennese monument to accommodate artists who scorned historical style and broke with the rigid, state-sponsored **Künstlerhaus.** Note the inscription above the door: *"Der Zeit, ihre Kunst; der Kunst, ihre Freiheit"* (To the age, its art; to art, its freedom). The Secession exhibitions of 1898-1903, which attracted cutting-edge European artists, were led by Gustav Klimt. His painting, *Nuda Veritas* (Naked Truth) became the icon of a new aesthetic ideal. Wilde's *Salomé* and paintings by Gauguin, Vuillard, van Gogh, and others created an island of modernity amidst an ocean of Habsburgs and Historicism. The exhibition hall remains firmly dedicated to the display of cutting-edge art (see Art Museums, p. 286). Those ensnared by the flowing tendrils of *Jugendstil* can find plenty of other *fin de siècle* works in Vienna—ask the tourist office for the *art nouveau in Vienna* pamphlet, with photos and a discussion of the style's top addresses in town.

The **Künstlerhaus,** Karlspl. 5, from which the Secession seceded, is just to the east, down Friedrichstr. This exhibition hall, attacked for its stodgy taste by Klimt and company, continues to display collections that can be quite worthwhile. Next door the acoustically miraculous **Musikverein** houses the **Vienna Philharmonic Orchestra** (see Music, p. 288). The **Karlskirche** lies on the other side of Friedrichstr., across the gardens of the Karlsplatz. Completed in 1793, this stunning church was built to fulfill a vow Emperor Karl VI made during a plague epidemic in 1713. Byzantine wings flank minaret-like Roman columns, and a Baroque dome towers atop a classical portico in a curious amalgam of architectural styles. This unique blend is continued by the reflecting pool and modern sculpture in front of the church designed by 20th-century sculptor **Henry Moore.**

Modern Architecture: Wagner and his Disciples

Moore's additions to the Karlsplatz area and the Resselpark complemented the genius of Otto Wagner, the architect responsible for the massive **Karlsplatz Stadtbahn Pavilion.** This is just one of the many enclosures that he produced for the city's rail system when the structure was redesigned at the turn of the century. All of the U-6 stations between Längenfeldgasse and Heiligenstadt are other examples of Wagner's work. His attention to the most minute details on station buildings, bridges, and even lampposts gave the city's public transportation an elegant coherence. Wagner's two arcades in Karlsplatz are still in use: one functions as an entrance to the U-Bahn station, the other as a café. Wagner diehards should also visit the acclaimed **Majolicahaus,** at Wienzeile 40, a collaborative effort by Wagner and Olbrich. Olbrich's *Jugendstil* ornamentation complements Wagner's penchant for geometric simplicity. The wrought-iron spiral staircase is by Josef Hoffmann, founder of the *Wiener Werkstätte*, an arts-and-crafts workshop that was as vital a part of *Jugendstil* as was *art nouveau.* The Majolicahaus' golden neighbor, the palm-leafy **Goldammer** building, is also a Wagnerian mecca. In order to see the finest examples of Wagner's work and *Jugendstil* architecture, however, one must journey outside the city center.

Otto Wagner's **Kirche am Steinhof,** XIV, Baumgartner Höhe 1 (tel. 910 60 23 91), stares down from high on a hill in northwest Vienna. The church combines streamlined symmetry and Wagner's signature functionalism with a decidedly Byzantine influence. The church has, at 27 seconds, the longest reverberation in the world. Koloman Moser, vanguard member of the Secession, designed the stained-glass windows, while *Jugendstil* sculptor Luksch fashioned the statues of Leopold and Severin poised upon each of the building's twin towers. The floor is sloped to facilitate cleaning, and holy water runs through pipes to keep it pure. Even the pews are functionally designed; they give nurses easy access to the worshipers, a relic of the days when Steinhof served as the provincial lunatic asylum. (Take bus #48A from U-2 or 3 stop "Volkstheater" to the end of the line. Open Sat. 3-4pm. Free. Guided tours in German only.)

Postsparkasse (Post Office Savings Bank) is technically inside the Ring at George-Coch-Pl. 2. A bulwark of modernist architecture, the building raises formerly concealed elements of the building, like the thousands of symmetrically placed metallic bolts on the rear wall, to positions of exaggerated significance. This was Wagner's greatest triumph of function over form; don't miss—you can't miss—the heating ducts. The distinctly *art nouveau* interior is open during banking hours free of charge (open Mon.-Wed. and Fri. 8am-3pm, Thurs. 8am-5:30pm).

Modern Architecture: Hundertwasser and Public Housing

Having built massively opulent palaces and public edifices before the war, post-WWI Vienna turned its architectural enthusiasm to the mundane but desperately necessary task of building public housing. The Austrian Social Democratic Republic set about building "palaces for the people." While they are lovely in the eyes of certain theorists, these buildings stand as testaments to a largely discredited system in both politics and art. Whatever a person's political opinions, one cannot help but be impressed by the sheer scale of these apartment complexes. The most famous and massive is the appropriately christened **Karl-Marx-Hof,** XIX, Heiligenstadterstr. 82-92 (U-4 or 6 to "Heiligenstadt"). This single building stretches out for a full kilometer, and encompasses over 1600 apartments, with common space and interior courtyards to garnish the urban-commune atmosphere. The Social Democrats used this Hof as their stronghold during the civil war of 1934, until army artillery shelled the place and broke down the resistance.

Breaking with the ideology of *"Rot Wien"* (Red Vienna, the socialist republic from 1918 until the Anschluß) which had resulted in sterile housing complexes like Karl-Marx Hof, Fantastic Realist and environmental activist Friedenstreich Hundertwasser designed **Hundertwasser Haus,** III, a fifty-apartment building at the corner of Löwengasse and Kegelgasse. Completed in 1985, the building makes both an artistic and a political statement. Trees and grass were built into the undulating balconies to bring life back to the "desert" that the city had become. Irregular windows, oblique tile columns, and free-form color patterns all contribute to the eccentricity of this blunt rejection of architectural orthodoxy. Take streetcar N from "Schwedenplatz" (dir: "Prater"). Architectural politics aside, this place is fun, bordering on the ridiculous; Hundertwasser's design team must have included droves of finger-painting toddlers.

Kunst-Haus Wien, another Hundertwasser project, is just three blocks away at Untere Weißgerberstr. 13. The house is a museum devoted to the architect's graphic art (see Art Museums, p. 286); it's worth a visit just for a walk on the uneven floors (straight lines were "too mechanical, inhuman") and a drink of *Melange* in the café (open 10am-midnight; enter on Weißgerberlände after museum hours). Hundertwasser fanatics may want to check out the **Müllbrennerei** (garbage incinerator) visible from the U-4 and U-6 lines to "Heiligenstadt." This huge jack-in-the-box of a trash dump has a high smokestack topped by a golden disco ball.

Palatial Vienna: Schwarzenberg, Belvedere, and Schönbrunn

The elongated **Schwarzenbergplatz** is a quick jaunt from Karlsplatz along Friedrichstr., which becomes Lothringerstr. During the Nazi era, the square was called "Hitlerplatz." At the far end, a patch of landscaped greenery surrounds a fountain and a statue left to the city as a "gift" from Russia. The Viennese have attempted to destroy the monstrosity three times, but this product of sturdy Soviet engineering refuses to be demolished. Vienna's disgust with their Soviet occupiers is evident in their nickname for an anonymous Soviet soldier's grave: "Tomb of the Unknown Plunderer." Behind the fountain is the **Schwarzenberg Palace.** Originally designed by Hildebrandt in 1697, it is now a swank hotel. Rumor has it that daughters of the super-rich travel here annually to meet young Austrian noblemen at the grand debutante ball that makes its luxurious entrance each year.

While grand in its own right, the Schwarzenberg Palace is but a warm-up for the striking **Schloß Belvedere,** IV, whose landscaped gardens begin just behind the Schwarzenberg. The Belvedere was once the summer residence of Prince Eugene of Savoy, Austria's greatest military hero. His distinguished career began with his routing of the Ottomans in the late 17th century. Though publicly lionized, his appearance was most unpopular at Court; Eugene was a short, ugly, impetuous man. The Belvedere summer palace (originally only the **Untere** (Lower) **Belvedere**) was ostensibly a gift from the emperor in recognition of Eugene's military prowess. More likely, the building was intended to get Eugene out of the imperial hair. However, having conquered the Turks, Eugene was possessed with a larger bank account than his Habsburg neighbors (a fact that certainly didn't improve their relationship) and, as an accomplished collector and patron of the arts, he decided to make some improvements on his newest acquisition. The result is the **Obere** (Upper) **Belvedere,** a masterpiece of the great Baroque architect Hildebrandt. The palace was not designed as a residence but as a place to throw parties to an opulent and bacchanalian excess. The building certainly impresses with its Baroque dress, and the effect is enhanced by one of the best views of Vienna, higher than the Hofburg. This bit of architectural bombast did not settle well with the Habsburgs; the symbolism of Eugene looking down on the Emperor and the rest of the city was a bit unsettling to the royal family. To top it off, the roof of the Obere Belvedere supports a facsimile of an Ottoman tent, which called undue attention to Eugene's martial glory. After Eugene's death, the Habsburgs snatched up the building (he never married or had children), and Archduke Franz Ferdinand lived there until he was assassinated in 1914. The grounds of the Belvedere, stretching from the Schwarzenberg Palace to the Südbahnhof, now contain three spectacular gardens (see Gardens and Parks, p. 283) and an equal number of well-endowed museums (see Art Museums, p. 286). The nearest U-Bahn stops to both palaces are "Stadtpark" or "Karlsplatz."

In truth, the Habsburgs need not have fretted over being shown up by Prince Eugene; **Schloß Schönbrunn,** XIII, the imperial summer residence, makes Belvedere appear waifish in comparison. The original plans were designed to make Versailles look like a gilded outhouse. The cost, however, was so prohibitive that the main building of the original plan wasn't even started. Nevertheless, Schönbrunn remains one of the greatest European palaces. Building finally began in 1695, but it was Maria Theresa's 1743 expansion that is most apparent (U-4 to "Schönbrunn").

The view of the palace's Baroque symmetry from the main gate impresses, but it's only a faint preparation for the spectacle that stretches out behind the palace. The view is a rigid orchestration of various elements including a **palm house,** a **zoo,** a massive **sculptured fountain of Neptune,** and bogus **Roman ruins,** all set amongst geometric flower beds and handsomely coiffed shrubbery. Walk past the **flower sculptures** to reach Schönbrunn's most frivolous pleasure, the *Schmetterlinghaus* (Butterfly House), where soft-winged beauties fly free in the tropical environment. The compendium is crowned by the **Gloriette,** an ornamental temple serenely perched upon a hill with a beautiful view of the park and much of Vienna. Drink a somewhat pricey *Mélange* in the new café here and survey your prospects (palace Park open daily 6am-dusk; free).

Tours of some of the palace's 1500 rooms reveal the elaborate taste of Maria Theresa's era. The **Great Gallery's** frescoes are a highlight. This room was a popular spot for the giddy Congress of Vienna, which loved a good party after a long day of divying up the continent. The six-year-old Mozart played in the **Hall of Mirrors** at the whim of the Empress, and to the profit of the boy's father. However, the **Million Gulden Room** wins the prize for excessiveness; Indian miniatures cover the chamber's walls. In summer, concerts and festivals abound in the Hof. (Palace apartments open daily April-Oct. 8:30am-5pm; Nov.-March 8:30am-4:30pm. 80AS. Guided tours available in English.)

The **Schönbrunn Zoo** (Tiergarten) attracts many visitors. Built for Maria Theresa's husband in 1752, it is the world's oldest menagerie. The style is allegedly Baroque, but the conditions border on the Gothic; some of the cages are minuscule. The zookeepers, to be fair, are aware of this fact, and are trying to remedy the animals' environments. (Zoo open Nov.-Jan. daily 9am-4:30pm; Feb. and Oct. 9am-5pm; March 9am-5:30pm; April 9am-6pm; May-Sept. 9am-6:30pm. 70AS.)

Former Vienna: The Zentralfriedhof

The Viennese like to describe the **Zentralfriedhof** (Central Cemetery), XI, Simmeringer Hauptstr. 234, as half the size of Geneva, but twice as lively. The phrase is not only meant to poke fun at Vienna's rival but also to illustrate Vienna's healthy attitude towards death. In the capital city, the phrase "a beautiful corpse" is a proud compliment, and the event of one's death is treated accordingly. And death doesn't get any better than at the Zentralfriedhof. The tombs in this massive park (2 sq. km with its own bus service) memorialize the truly great as well as those who wished to be so considered after their demise. This is the place to pay respects to that favorite Viennese decomposer. The second gate (**Tor II**) leads to the graves of Beethoven, Wolf, Strauss, Schönberg, Moser, and an honorary monument to Mozart. Amadeus' true resting place is an unmarked mass paupers' grave in the **Cemetery of St. Mark,** III, Leberstr. 6-8. **Tor I** of the Zentralfriedhof leads to the **Jewish Cemetery** and Arthur Schnitzler's burial plot. Various structures throughout this portion of the burial grounds memorialize the millions slaughtered in Nazi death camps. The state of this section mirrors the fate of Vienna's Jewish population. Many of the headstones are cracked, broken, lying prone, or neglected, because the families of most of the dead are no longer in Austria to tend the graves. To reach the cemetery, take streetcar #71 from "Schwarzenbergplatz" (35min.). (Open April and Oct. 7am-5pm; May and Sept. 7am-6pm; June-Aug. 7am-7pm; Nov.-March 7am-dusk.)

Gardens and Parks

Gardens, parks, and forests are common Viennese attractions, brightening the urban landscape with scattered patches of greenery. Plots of land in sections of the 14th, 16th, and 19th districts were distributed to citizens short of food after WWII, to let them grow their own vegetables. Although the shortage is now long gone, these community *Gärten* still exist, full of roses and garden gnomes and marked by the huts of the original caretakers. The city's primary public gardens were opened and maintained by the Habsburgs throughout the last four centuries, recently becoming public property. Especially noteworthy are the gardens of **Schloß Schönbrunn, Palais Belvedere,** and the **Augarten.** These meticulously groomed Baroque wonders have admirably preserved the intentions of their 18th-century landscapers.

The **Augarten,** Obere Augartenstr., is the oldest extant Baroque garden in Austria; it was commissioned by Kaiser Josef II in the 17th century as a gift to the citizens of Vienna. Children play soccer on the lawns between flowers and various athletic facilities (including a swimming pool and tennis courts) which were opened in 1940. Of interest in the Augarten is the **Vienna China Factory,** founded in 1718, and the **Augarten Palace,** residence of the Vienna Boys' Choir. You can't miss the **Flakturm,** a daunting concrete tower constructed as an anti-aircraft defense tower by the Nazis during World War II. This structure and other similar creations in parks around the city were so sturdily constructed that an attempted explosive demolition failed (the walls of reinforced concrete were up to 5m thick). They stand as sad memorials to the country's intimate relationship with the Third Reich. To reach the park, take streetcar N (dir: "Friederich-Engels-Pl.") from "Schwedenpl." to "Obere Augartenstraße," and walk to the left down Taborstr.

By the Danube

The **Danube** provides a number of recreational possibilities northeast of the city. The recurrent floods became problematic once settlers moved outside the city walls, so the Viennese stretch of the Danube was restructured from 1870 to 1875, and again from 1972 to 1987. This generated recreational areas, such as new tributaries (including the **Alte Donau** and the **Donaukanal**) and the **Donauinsel,** a thin slab of island stretching for kilometers. The Donauinsel is devoted to bicycle paths, swimming, barbecue areas, boat rental, and summer restaurants. Several bathing areas line the northern shore of the island, along the Alte Donau. (Open May-Sept. Mon.-Fri. 9am-8pm, Sat.-Sun. 8am-8pm. Admission starts at 50AS.) Take U-1 (dir: Kagran) to "Donauinsel" or "Alte Donau." One of the most **spectacular views** of Vienna can be had from the Donaupark. Take the elevator up to the revolving restaurant in the **Donauturm** (Danube Tower), located near the United Nations complex (U-1 to "Kaisermühlen/Vienna International Center"). Also of note is the **Donau Insel Fest,** which brings various stages for jazz or stadium rock in late June (past guests include Joe Cocker and Sheryl Crow).

The **Prater,** extending southeast from the Wien-Nord Bahnhof, is a notoriously touristed amusement park that functioned as a private game reserve for the Imperial Family until 1766 and as the site of the World Expo in 1873. The park is squeezed into a riparian woodland between the Donaukanal and the river proper; it boasts ponds, meadows, and stretches of lovely virgin woods. The area near the U1 stop "Praterstern" is the actual amusement park offering various rides, arcades, restaurants, and casinos (entry to the complex is free, but each attraction charges admission, generally 20AS). Rides range from garish thrill machines and wonderfully campy spook-house rides to the stately 65-meter high **Riesenrad** (Giant Ferris Wheel). The wheel, which has one of the prettiest views of Vienna, is best known for its cameo role in Orson Welles' postwar thriller, *The Third Man.* This wheel of fortune *extraordinaire* is cherished by locals as one of the city's more obscure symbols. (Open Feb.-Nov. 10am-10pm, sometimes 11pm. 50AS. Ride lasts 20min.) Beloved by children during the day, the Prater becomes less wholesome after sundown; peepshows and prostitution abound.

The Danube Canal branches into the tiny river **Wien** near the Ring; this sliver of a waterway extends to the southwest, past the *innere Stadt* and Schloß Schönbrunn. First, however, the Wien, replete with ducks and lilies at its narrowest point, bisects the **Stadtpark** (City Park), off the Park Ring. Built in 1862, this was the first municipal park outside the former city walls. The sculpted vegetation provides a soothing counterpoint to the central bus station and Bahnhof Wien-Mitte, just yards away. One of

Hot to trot

White, royal, dancing, and one of the biggest tourist attractions in Vienna? No, it is not the Royal Ballet's performance of *Swan Lake*. In Vienna, these three traits classify horses—more specifically, the Lipizzaner stallions of the *Spanische Reitschule* (Spanish Riding School). The Royal Stables, on an architectural level one of the most important Renaissance buildings in Vienna, were built as a residence for the Archduke Maximilian in the mid-16th century, and later (when he became Emperor), were converted to the stables of the royal stud. The choice of Lipizzaner horses, known for the their snowy-white coat and their immense physical strength and grace, was a circumstantial one for the royal (now federal) breed. Originally a mixture of Arab and Berber stallions, the Spanish Lipizzaner breed was founded by order of the Austrian Emperor in Lipizza, near Trieste, upon the Habsburg's annexation of the Spanish realms in the late 16th century. Once the stud line had been established, the Lipizzaners were imported to Austria proper, to dance in the spotlight of the Renaissance heyday of *haute école* horsemanship. And while audiences to their performance may marvel at how these beautiful beasts can stand making all of those little prancing steps, they should also marvel at the Lipizzaners survival over the centuries. Aficionados of horsemanship will recount the several times the stud almost became extinct. They ran from the French in the Napoleonic wars and barely survived the poverty that ensued after World War I and the breakup of the Empire. During WWII they were moved to a safe haven in Czechoslovakia. In 1945, U.S. General Patton flagrantly violated his own orders to stay put by leading a madcap Eastern push to prevent the plundering Russians, who confiscated just about everything in their path, from reaching the four-legged treasures first. In the early 1980s, an epidemic of virus in the stud killed upwards of thirty of the brood mares, and today, stud farmers worry that the decreasing number of Lipizzaners may lead to health problems resultant from inbreeding

Vienna's most photogenic monuments, the **Johann-Strauss-Denkmal** resides there. (Take U-4 to "Stadtpark," or walk down Parkring.)

Along the Ring

Stroll clockwise around the Ring to reach the **Burggarten** (Gardens of the Imperial Palace), a wonderfully kept park with monuments to such Austrian notables as Emperor Franz Josef and Emperor Franz I. The **Babenberger Passage** leads from the Ring to the bubble-gum-sweet **Mozart Memorial** (1896), which features Amadeus on a pedestal, surrounded by instrument-toting cherubs. In front of the statue is a lawn with a treble clef crafted of red flowers. Reserved for the Imperial family and members of the court until 1918, the Burggarten is now a favorite for young lovers and lamentably hyperactive dogs. Walk behind the Hofburg to the area near the vaulted greenhouse/café to find students sun bathing in this prime hangout for the twenty-something set.

The Heldenplatz, farther up the Ring, abuts the **Volksgarten,** once the site of the Bastion Palace destroyed by Napoleon's order. Be sure to seek out the **"Temple of Theseus,"** the monument to Austrian playwright Franz Grillparzer, and the **Dolphin Fountain,** a masterful bit of sculpting by Fenkhorn. The Volksgarten's monument to Empress Elisabeth who was assassinated in 1898 by an Italian anarchist, was designed by Hans Bitterlich. The throned empress casts a marmoraceous glance on Friedrich Ohmann's goldfish pond. The most striking feature of this space, though, is the **Rose Garden,** populated by thousands of different rose species.

West of the 13th *Bezirk* is the **Lainzer Tiergarten** (Lainz Game Preserve). Once an exclusive hunting preserve for the Habsburgs, this space is enclosed by a 24-km wall and has been a protected nature park since 1941. Wild animals roam the grounds freely. Aside from hiking paths, restaurants, and spectacular vistas, the park encloses the **Hermes Villa.** This erstwhile retreat for Empress Elisabeth now houses exhibitions by the Historical Museum of the City of Vienna. Take U-4 (dir: "Hütteldorf") to "Hietzing," change to streetcar #60 to "Hermesstr.," and then take bus #60B to "Lainzer Tor" (open April-Nov. Wed.-Sun. and holidays 9am-4:30pm).

The **Türkenschanz Park,** in the 18th *Bezirk,* attracts a plethora of leashed dachshunds bristling at the peacocks. The long-haired garden is a wonderful pit stop on the way up to the *Heurigen* of the 19th district. In the summer, you can feed the duckies or gaze in Monet-like rapture at the water lilies. In the winter, come for sledding or ice-skating. Whenever you visit don't miss the well-beloved Turkish fountain with its graceful arabesques. You can enter anywhere along Gregor-Mendel-Str., Hasenauerstr., or Max-Emmanuelstr.

The **Pötzleindorfer Park,** at the end of tram line #41 (dir: Pötzleinsdorfer Höhe) from Schottentor, feeds into the lower end of the Vienna Woods. Come here to see wild deer roaming through the overgrown Alpine meadows and woodland. Far to the north and west of Vienna sprawls the illustrious **Wienerwald,** made famous by Strauss' celebrated waltz, "Tales of a Vienna Woods." The woods, jealously conserved by the Viennese, extend up to the slopes of the first foothills of the Alps. Take U-4 or U-6 to "Heiligenstadt" and bus #38A to "Kahlenberg." No visit to Vienna is complete without a trek up here. The area around Kahlenberg, Cobenzl, and Leopoldstadt is criss-crossed with hiking paths (*Wanderwege*) marked by bars of colors painted on the tree trunks. This is where the Turks camped in 1683 when they besieged Vienna. Now the area is overflowing with the elderly hobbling through the woods (the #38A isn't nicknamed "the Granny-mover" for nothing). Stride by them and through the incredible natural beauty of the hills as the countless German Romantics did before you. Or, follow in the Pope's footsteps, and visit the **Leopoldskirche,** a kickin' pilgrimage site.

MUSEUMS

Vienna owes its vast selection of masterpieces to two distinct factors: the acquisitive Habsburgs, and Vienna's own crop of unique art schools and world-class artists. See p. 242 for the complete story of Vienna's artistic heritage. All of the distinctly Viennese movements, and many other styles culled from myriad nations and epochs, await in Vienna's world-class assortment of exceptional museums. Though painting and architecture may dominate, Vienna's treasures are as diverse as the Habsburg possessions. The Ephesus Museum and the Museum für Völkerkunde with its collection of Benin bronzes are two examples of the Habsburg collecting prowess. Other subjects range from "Horseshoeing, Harnessing, and Saddling" to "Heating Technology." An exhaustive list is impossible to include here; be sure to pick up the *Museums* brochure at the tourist office.

Art Museums

Kunsthistorisches Museum (Museum of Fine Arts; tel. 521 77), across from the Burgring and the Heldenplatz on Maria Theresa's right. The world's fourth-largest art collection. The works by Bruegel are unrivaled, and the museum possesses entire rooms of Rembrandt, Rubens, Titian, and Velazquez. Ancient and classical art are also well-represented here, including an Egyptian burial chamber. The lobby is pre-Secession Klimt, a mural depicting artistic progress from the classical era to the 19th century, painted in the Historicist style he would later attack. Open Tues.-Wed. and Fri.-Sun. 10am-6pm. Picture gallery also open Thurs. until 9pm. Another **branch** of the museum resides in the Neue Burg (Hofburg) and contains the Arms and Armor Collection (the second largest collection in the world), and Ancient Musical Instruments Collections. Same hours as picture gallery. 100AS, students and seniors 50AS.

Austrian Gallery (in the Belvedere Palace) III, Prinz-Eugenstr. 27, behind Schwarzenbergplatz. The collection is split into two parts. The **Upper Belvedere** (built in 1721-22 by Hildebrandt) houses Austrian Art of the 19th and 20th centuries. Most of the famous Secessionist works can be found here; especially well-represented are Waldmüller, Makart, Schiele, Kokoschka, and Klimt (whose gilded masterpiece, *The Kiss,* has enthralled visitors for nearly a century). Also check out the breathtaking views of the city from the upper floors. Use the same ticket to enter the **Lower Belvedere,** where the **Baroque Museum** has an extensive collection of sculptures by Donner, Maulbertsch, Messerschmidt, and David's famous portrayal of Napoleon, gallantly reared on his horse as he rides into battle. The **Museum of Medieval Austrian Art** is also here. Romanesque and Gothic sculptures and altarpieces by *Süddentisch* masters abound. Both Belvederes open Tues.-Sun. 10am-5pm. 60AS, students 30AS.

Akademie der Bildende Kunst (Academy of Fine Arts) I, Schillerplatz 3, near Karlsplatz (tel. 58 81 62 25). Designed in 1876 by Hansen, famed for the Parlament, Musikverein, and Börse. The building has a collection that contains Hieronymus Bosch's *Last Judgment* and works by a score of Dutch painters, including Rubens. Open Tues. and Thurs.-Fri. 10am-2pm, Wed. 10am-1pm.

Secession Building, I, Friedrichstr. 12 (tel. 587 53 07), on the western side of Karlspl. Originally built to house artwork that didn't conform to the Kunsthaus' standards, giving the break-out prophets of modern art space to hang their work—Klimt, Kokoschka, and the "barbarian" Gauguin were featured early on. Rather than canonize these early pioneers, the museum continually seeks to exhibit what is new and fresh. Substantial contemporary works are exhibited here, while the Belvedere remains the best collection of Secessionist work. Klimt's Beethoven Frieze is the major exception—this 30m-long work is Klimt's visual interpretation of Beethoven's Ninth Symphony. A series of serpentine scenes depict humanity's weaknesses and desires. Open Tues.-Fri. 10am-6pm, Sat.-Sun. 10am-4pm. 30AS and 15AS. Special exhibition 60AS, students 30AS.

Museum Moderner Kunst (Museum of Modern Art; tel. 817 69 00). Two locations. The first is in the Liechtenstein Palace, IX, Fürstengasse 1. Take streetcar D from the Ring (dir: Nußdorf) to "Fürstengasse." These are the same Liechtensteiners who own that tiny country between Switzerland and Austria. They still hold the deed to this palace and another inside the First *Bezirk,* as well as others throughout the country. The *Schloß,* surrounded by a manicured garden, boasts a collection of 20th-century masters, from Magritte to Motherwell. The second location is at the **20er Haus** (tel. 799 69 00), III, Schweizer Garten, down Arsenalstr., and opposite the Südbahnhof. Its large, open Bauhaus interior provides the perfect stage for the substantial collection of ground-breaking 60s and 70s work—Keith Arnnat and Larry Poons among them, along with contemporary artists. Open Tues.-Sun. 10am-6pm. Admission to one of the two 45AS, students 25AS; for both 60AS; children 30AS. Disabled facilities.

Österreichisches Museum für Angewandte Kunst (MAK) (Austrian Museum of Applied Art), I, Stubenring 5 (tel. 711 36). Take U-3 to "Stubentor." The oldest museum of applied arts in Europe. Otto Wagner furniture and Klimt sketches sit amidst crystal, china, furniture, and rugs dating from the Middle Ages to the present. Don't miss Philips Starck's coolly svelte armchair. Open Tues.-Wed., Fri.-Sun. 10am-6pm, Thurs. 10am-9pm. 90AS, students 45AS.

Kunst Haus Wien, III, Untere Weißgerberstr. 13 (tel. 712 04 91). Take U-1 or U-4 to "Schwedenpl.," then bus N to "Radetzkypl." This museum, built for the works of Hundertwasser, is also one of his greatest achievements. The crazily-pastiched building hosts international contemporary exhibits. Ya gotta love what he does with the floor. Open daily 10am-7pm. 60AS, students 44AS.

Kunsthalle Wien, IV, Treitlstr. 2 (tel. 586 97 76), in Karlspl. across from the Secessionist building. Holds some stellar international exhibits. Open Wed.-Mon. 10am-6pm, Thurs. 10am-8pm.

Museum für Völkerkunde, I, Neue Burg 1, Heldenplatz (tel. 534 30-0). The Habsburg agents brought back a surprisingly good collection of African and South American art. Visit Benin bronzes and West African Dan heads, or Montezuma's feathered headdress. Open Wed.-Mon. 10am-4pm, tours available Sun. 11am.

Other Collections

Historisches Museum der Stadt Wien (Historical Museum of the City of Vienna), IV, Karlspl. 5, to the left of the Karlskirche (tel. 505 87 47). This museum has a collection of historical artifacts and paintings that document the city's evolution from the Roman encampment and booty from the Turkish sieges through 640 years of Habsburg rule. Memorial rooms to Loos and Grillparzer, plus temporary exhibitions on Viennese themes. Open Tues.-Sun. 9am-4:30pm. 30AS.

Sigmund Freud Haus, IX, Berggasse 19, near the Votivkirche. U-2 to "Schottentor," up Wahringerstr. to Berggasse. This meager museum, where a cigar is just a cigar, was Freud's home from 1891 until the *Anschluß.* Almost all of Freud's original belongings moved with him out of the country, including the leather divan. Lots of photos and documents, though, including the young Freud's report cards. Open daily July-Sept. 9am-6pm; Oct.-June 9am-4pm. 60AS, students 40AS.

Naturhistorisches Museum (Natural History Museum), across from the Kunsthistorisches Museum. Displays the usual animalia and decidedly unusual giant South American beetles and dinosaur skeletons. Two of its star attractions are man-made: a spectacular floral bouquet comprised of gemstones, and the Stone-Age beauty *Venus of Willendorf.* Open Mon. and Wed.-Sun. 9am-6pm; in winter, first floor only 9am-3pm. 30AS, students 15AS.

Bestattungsmuseum (Undertaker's Museum), IV, Goldegasse 19 (tel. 50 19 52 27). The Viennese take their funerals very seriously, giving rise to a morbidly fascinating exhibit that, in its own way, is as typically Viennese as *Heurigen* and waltzes. Contains items such as coffins with alarms (should the body decide to rejoin the living) and Josef II's proposed reusable coffin. Open Mon.-Fri. noon-3pm, by prior arrangement only.

Jewish Museum, I, Dorotheergasse 11 (tel. 535 04 31). This new museum explores Judaism as well as the history and contributions of Austria's Jewish community. Exhibits on Freud and psychoanalysis, as well as works by Arnold Schoenberg and Bronica Killer-Pinell. Open Sun.-Fri. 10am-6pm, Thurs. 10am-9pm.

Künstlerhaus, Karlsplatz 5 (tel. 587 96 63). Temporary exhibits, usually contemporary and non-European art. Open Mon.-Wed. and Fri.-Sun. 10am-6pm, Thurs. 10am-9pm. 90AS, students 40AS.

ENTERTAINMENT

Music

> The State Opera and the Philharmonic Orchestra are closed in July and August. The Vienna Boys' Choir is on tour in August. The Lippizaner Stallions do not dance in July and August. Many an unsuspecting tourist has carefully planned a trip, only to be disappointed by these most inconvenient facts of Viennese life.

Like its architecture and art, Vienna's music always teeters on the cutting edge. Mozart, Beethoven, and Haydn created their most stunning masterpieces in Vienna, comprising the "First Viennese School." A century later, *fin de siècle* Expressionist composers Schönberg, Webern, and Berg teamed up to form the Second Viennese School. Every Austrian child must learn to play an instrument during his or her schooling, and the **Konservatorium** and **Hochschule** are world-renowned for the high quality of their musical instruction. Even pampered Habsburg heirs became instrumentally deft enough to star in private performances. Throughout the year, Vienna presents performances ranging from the above-average to the sublime, and much of it is surprisingly accessible to the budget traveler.

"Too many notes, dear Mozart" was Josef II's observation after the premiere of *Abduction from the Seraglio.* "Only as many as are necessary, Your Majesty," was the genius's reply. The Habsburgs may be forgiven this critical slip; their support of opera is one of their principal contributions to Vienna and to the globe. The **Staatsoper** remains one of the top five companies in the world and performs about 300 times per year from September through June. **Standing-room tickets** provide the opportunity to see world class opera for a pittance. Those with the love, the stamina, or the desire to say "been there" should start lining up on the western side of the Opera (by Operngasse) half an hour before curtains open (2-3hr. in tourist season) in order to get tickets for the center—the side views are rather limited. Buy a ticket (balcony 20AS, orchestra 30AS, formal dress *not* necessary) and find a space on the rail. Tying a scarf around the rail will reserve your spot if you wish to grab a coffee or *Wurst* before the performance. Those feeling lucky should try the box office a half-hour before curtain; students can buy any unclaimed tickets for 50AS (ISIC *not* valid; bring a university ID). Advance tickets range from 100-850AS and go on sale a week before the performance at the **Bundestheaterkasse,** I, Hanuschgasse 3 (tel. 514 44 22 60), next to the opera along the Burggarten. Get there at 6-7am of the first day for a good seat; Viennese will camp overnight here for the major performances. They also sell tickets for the three other public theaters: the **Volksoper, Burgtheater,** and **Akademietheater** (open Mon.-Fri. 8am-6pm, Sun. 9am-noon; ISIC *not* valid; university ID required). The Volksoper shows operas and operettas in German, translated if need be; the other two feature classic dramas in German. Discount tickets go on sale a half-hour before performance, at the individual theater box offices (50-400AS). Nearby **fiakers** (horse and carriage rides) journey home from performances in style; agree on a price with the driver beforehand—a 40-minute ride can cost as much as 800AS.

The **Wiener Philharmoniker** (Vienna Philharmonic Orchestra) is known worldwide for its excellence. The top-notch orchestra includes Gustav Mahler among its directors; a bust in his honor stands in the concert hall. Regular performances take place in the **Musikverein,** I, Dumbastr. 3 (tel. 505 81 90), on the northeast side of Karlspl. The Philharmoniker also play at every Staatsoper production. Tickets to Philharmoniker concerts are mostly available on a subscription basis, so the box office of the Musikverein normally has few tickets for sale; check on ticket availability at the Musikverein (ticket office open Sept.-June Mon.-Fri. 9am-6pm, Sat. 9am-noon). Write to the "Gesellschaft der Musikfreunde, Dumbastr. 20, A-1010 Wien" for more information. The **New Year's concert** by the Vienna Philharmonic Orchestra, a tradition since the 18th century, is broadcast the following morning by the ÖRF (Austrian Broadcasting Corporation). Vienna's second fiddle, the **Vienna Symphony Orchestra,** is frequently on tour but plays some concerts at the Konzerthaus, III, Lothingerstr. 20 (tel. 72 12 11).

The 500-year old **Wiener Sängerknabenchor (Vienna Boys' Choir)** is another famous and beloved musical attraction in town. The pre-pubescent prodigies perform Sundays at 9:15am (mid-September-June) in the **Burgkapelle** (Royal Chapel) the oldest section of the Hofburg. Reserve tickets (60-280AS) at least two months in advance; write to the "Hofmusikkapelle, Hofburg, A-1010 Wien." Do not enclose money. Pick up tickets at the Burgkapelle on the Friday before mass from 11am to noon, or on the Sunday of the mass by 9am. Unreserved seats go on sale from 5pm on the preceding Friday, with a maximum of two tickets per person. Standing room is free. They also perform every Friday at 3:30pm at the Konzerthaus in the months of May, June, September, and October. For tickets (370-420AS) write to: "Reisebüro Mondial, Faulmanngasse 4, A-1040, Wien" (tel. 58 80 41 41; fax 587 12 68).

Awe-inspiring and free musical experiences can be had at the **Sunday High Masses** celebrated at 10am in the major churches (Augustinerkirche, Michaelerkirche, Stephansdom). The music is extremely powerful in its proper context and atmosphere. Although the big guns take a summer siesta every year, Vienna has held a summer festival, *"Klangbogen,"* every year since 1952, highlighted by the **Wiener Kammeroper** (Chamber Opera), which performs Mozart's operas in an open-air theater set among the ruins of Schönbrunner Schloßpark. Pick up a Klangbogen brochure at the tourist office. One free treat not to be missed is the **nightly film festival** in July and August, found in the Rathauspl. at dusk. Taped operas, ballets, operettas, and concerts enrapture the young and old audience.

Vienna hosts an array of important festivals annually, with the vast majority centered around music. 1997 will be the 200th anniversary of Franz Schubert's birth. Look for tourist office's monthly calendar for dozens of concerts and performances, many hosted by the *Musikverein* and the *Konzerthaus,* that are currently in the planning stages. The **Vienna Festival** (mid-May to mid-June) has a diverse program of exhibitions, plays, and concerts. Of particular interest are the celebrated orchestras and conductors joining the party. Avant-garde theater has a remarkable representation here as well. The Staatsoper and Volkstheater will host the annual **Jazzfest Wien**

VIENNA

during the first weeks of July, featuring many famous acts. For information, write to "Jazzfest Wien, Estepl. 3/13, A-1030, Wien" (tel. 712 34 34). From the end of July to the beginning of August the **Im-Puls Dance Festival** attracts some of the world's great dance troupes and offers seminars to enthusiasts (for information, call 93 55 58). Some of Vienna's parties are thrown by the parties (political, that is); the Social Democrats host a late-June **Danube Island Festival,** and the Communist Party holds a **Volkstimme Festival** in mid-August. Both cater to a young crowd with rock, jazz, and folk music.

Theater and Cinema

In the past few years, Vienna has made a name for itself as a city of musicals, with productions of West End and Broadway favorites such as *Phantom of the Opera* and *Les Misérables,* and the long-running home-grown favorite *Elisabeth,* a very creative interpretation of the late empress' life. The **Theater an der Wien,** VI, Linke Wienzeile 6 (tel. 588 30), once produced musicals of a different sort; this 18th-century edifice hosted the premieres of Beethoven's *Fidelio* and Mozart's *Die Zauberflöte (The Magic Flute).* The nobility found that Mozart had crossed the line of good taste by composing an opera in German (such an *ugly* language), so they blocked the scheduled premiere. The masterpiece was finally performed in the Theater an der Wien, thrilling the peasants, because they could finally understand the plot. In remembrance of this past, the Staatsoper still occasionally sends productions of Mozart opera to be performed here.

English-language drama is offered at **Vienna's English Theatre,** VIII, Josefsgasse 12 (tel. 402 12 60; box office open Mon.-Fri. 10am-6pm, Sat. and Sun. 10am-4pm, shows usually at 7:30pm; tickets 150-420AS, students 100AS on night of performance). The **International Theater,** IX, Porzellangasse 8 (tel. 319 62 72; tickets 220AS, under 26 120AS) is another English venue. Look for the posters around the city. **Films** in English usually play at **Burg Kino,** I, Opernring 19 (tel. 587 84 06; last show usually around 8:30pm, Sat. around 11pm), **Top Kino,** VI, Rahlgassel 1, at the intersection with Gumpendorferstr. (tel. 587 55 57; open daily 3pm-10:30pm), and **Hadynkino,** on Mariahilferstr. near the U-3 stop "Neubangasse" (last show usually around 9:30pm). As English becomes extremely fashionable, more theaters show movies in English or with subtitles—look in the newspaper for film with the letters OF, OV, EOV, or OmU after the title. **Votivkino,** on Währingerstr. near Berggasse and Schottentor, is an art-house popular with the university crowd; it shows everything with German subtitles. **Artis Kino, Filmcasino,** and **Stöberkino** also show subtitled art and foreign films. Be warned—in Vienna, you pay for the row you sit in, and seats are assigned. Ushers check if you buy a first row ticket, then sit in back. On Monday, however, all seats are discounted to 60AS. In summer, there is an **open air theater** in the Augarten park; all seats are 70AS and the show begins at 9:30pm (bring mosquito repellent). Take tram #31 from Schottenring; dismount at "Gaußplatz." Every fall, there is a city-wide **film festival,** the *Viennale.* During the rest of the year, the Austrian **Filmmuseum** (Augustinerstr. 1; tel. 53 37 05 40) has festivals of classic and avant-garde films

Heurigen (Wine Gardens)

Created by imperial edict in the early 18th century, *Heurigen* are one of Vienna's most beloved institutions. Citizens have collectively met, discussed, and celebrated life in these pastoral settings for generations, with no signs of letting up. To this day, the *Heurigen,* marked by a hanging evergreen at the door, continue to sell their new wine, mineral water, and rustic snacks. Beer, coffee, and soda are not allowed, and the *Heuriger* owners would not have it any other way.

The wine called *Heuriger* is young wine from the most recent harvest and has typically been grown and pressed by the *Heuriger* owner himself. Good *Heuriger* is generally white (*Grüner Veltliner* or *Riesling* are best), fruity, and full of body. *Heuriger* is ordered by the *Achtel* or *Viertal* (eighth or quarter liter respectively). In local parlance, one doesn't drink the wine, one "bites" it, a term meant to convey its youth and freshness. *G'spritzer* (wine and mineral water) is a popular combination, and patrons frequently order a bottle of wine and water to mix themselves.

Half of the pleasure of visiting a *Heuriger,* however, comes not from the wine but from the atmosphere. The worn picnic benches and old shade trees provide an ideal spot to contemplate, converse, or listen to *Schrammelmusik,* sentimental, wine-lubricated folk songs played by aged musicians who inhabit the *Heuriger.* Often, though, drunken patrons take the matter into their own hands and begin to belt out verses praising the *Bäckchen* (cheeks) of girls in the Wachau. Once upon a time, patrons would bring picnics with them, but sadly those days seem to be gone. However, a *Heuriger* generally serves simple buffets (grilled chicken, salads, pretzels, etc.) that make for enjoyable and inexpensive meals. Those looking for some down home fare should order a portion of *Brattfett* or *Liptauer,* a spicy paprika and cream cheese concoction, to spread on your bread.

At the end of the summer, *Sturm* (cloudy, unpasteurized wine) is available at the *Heurigen;* the drink is very sweet but not quite as potent. At the end of August or the beginning of September in **Neustift am Wald,** now part of Vienna's 19th district, the *Neustifter Kirtag mit Winzerumzug* rampages through the wine gardens; local vintners march in a mile-long procession through town, carrying a large crown adorned with gilt nuts. After the **Feast of the Martins** on November 11, the wine remaining from last year's crop becomes "old wine," no longer proper to serve in the *Heurigen.* The Viennese do their best to spare it this fate by consuming the beverage in Herculean quantities before the time's up. Grab a *Martinigänsl* (goose) and a liter of wine to help the locals in their monumental task. *Heurigen* generally cluster around each other in the northern, western, and southern Viennese suburbs, where the grapes grow. **Grinzing** is the most famous region, which explains the large number of coach tours. The wine is rather strong here, perhaps in an effort to distract patrons from the high prices. Better atmosphere and prices are to be found in **Sievering, Neustift am Wald, Stammersdorf,** and **Neuwaldegg.** The least expensive and least touristed *Heurigen* can be found in Stammersdorf and **Strebersdorf** (from Schottentor, bus #31 and 32, respectively). True *Heuriger* devotés should make the trip to **Gumpoldskirchen,** a celebrated little vineyard village with decent bus and train connections to Vienna and Mödling. Most vineyard taverns are open 4pm-midnight. *Heuriger* costs about 25AS per *Viertel.* Casual dress is fine.

Buschenschank Heinrich Niersche, XIX, Strehlgasse 21 (tel. 440 21 46). Take bus #41A from the U-6 stop "Währingerstraße/Volksoper" to "Pötzleindorfer Höhe;" walk uphill one block and make a right on Strehlgasse. Hidden from tourists and therefore beloved by locals. The beautiful garden overlooks the fields of Grinzing; an oasis of green grass, cheerful voices and relaxation. *Weiße G'spritzer* (white wine with tonic water) 18AS. Open Thurs.-Mon. 3pm-midnight.

Heuriger Josef Lier, XIX, Wildgrubengasse 44 (tel. 32 23 19). Take tram #38 from Schottentor to the end of the line, walk up the Grinzigersteig to the Heiligenstädter Friedhof (cemetery), then leave the asphalt for Stadtwanderweg 1 along Schreiberbach onto Mukental and then finally Wildgrub (10min. after you leave the cemetery). This *Ur-Heuriger* looks the way places in Grinzing must have been before the advent of the tour bus. Set right in to the vineyards, it boasts a panoramic view of Vienna from the natural beauty of the Vienna Woods. Only one white and one red wine here—Josef Lier's own, from the vineyards you're sitting in. The food is equally *Alt-Wiener* and equally excellent—boiled eggs, pickles, *Liptauer,* and *Wurst,* to name just a bit.

Zum Krottenbach'l, XIX, Krottenbachstr. 148 (tel. 440 12 40). Take bus #35A (dir: Salmannsdorf) from U-6 stop "Nußdorferstraße" to "Kleingartenverein/Hackenberg." With a terraced, multi-level garden built onto the fertile slopes of Untersievering, the *Heuriger* offers a lush perch from which to savor the fruit of the vine. An underground spring flows in a careful aqueduct through the terraces, gurgling into fountains and running past tables. Rustic tavern with thick wooden beams. Hot and cold buffet. Open daily 3pm-midnight.

VIENNA

Thicker than blood

The Viennese connection to wine is a strong one, so strong that the fruit of the vine played a vital role in the Habsburg's rise to power. In 1273 Ottokar II of Bohemia, Rudolf of Habsburg's one rival to the throne of the Holy Roman Empire, holed himself up in Vienna, where he enjoyed strong support. Rudolf marched to the town walls and told the Viennese in no uncertain terms that if Ottokar did not go, the surrounding vineyards would. The Viennese got their priorities straight; vine cultivation has not only outlasted poor Ottokar but the Habsburg dynasty as well. The *Heurigen*, or wine gardens, owe their existence to another Habsburg. In 1784, Josef II, the man who gave Vienna the Edict of Tolerance and the reusable coffin, promulgated another enlightened edict allowing wine growers to sell their most recent vintage, as well as food and fruit juices. Farmers soon started to sell their crops and their pork and poultry out of the rooms where potential customers used to sample their wines. Those rooms have evolved into the buffets that now serve the patrons.

Buschenschank Helm, XXI, Stammersdorferstr. 121 (tel. 292 12 44). Take Tram #31 to the last stop, make a right by the *Würstelstand,* then a left. The family who owns and staffs this establishment generate a friendly atmosphere. The garden itself is quite attractive with great old trees. Open Tues.-Sat. 2:30pm-midnight.

Franz Mayer am Pfarrplatz Beethovenhaus, XIX, Pfarrpl. 2 (tel. 37 12 87). From U-4 or U-6 "Heiligenstadt," take bus #38A to "Fernspechamt/Heiligenstadt" (the first stop after you turn the corner onto Grinzigerstr). Walk up the hill, and head right onto Nestelbachgasse. Beethoven used to stay in the *Heuriger* when it offered guest quarters. Patios are festive and cool. Open Mon.-Fri. 4pm-midnight, Sun. and holidays 11am-midnight. Live music 7pm-midnight.

Weingut Heuriger Reinprecht, XIX, Cobenzlgasse 22 (tel. 32 14 71). Take U-4 or U-6 to "Heiligenstadt," then bus #38A to "Grinzing." This *Heuriger* is a fairy-tale stereotype—picnic tables as far as the eye can see under an ivy-laden trellis, with *Schrammel* musicians strolling from table to table. Although this is one of the more touristed establishments, don't be surprised to hear whole tables of nostalgic Austrians break into verse with the accordion. Note the incredible bottleopener collection as you walk in. *Viertel* of red wine costs 30AS. Open Mar.-Nov. daily 3:30pm-midnight.

WINTER IN VIENNA

The Viennese don't let those long winter nights go to waste. Christmas festivities begin in November with *Krampus* (Black Peter) parties. Krampus is a hairy devil that accompanies St. Nicholas on his rounds and gives bad children coal and sticks. On November 5th, people in Krampus suits can be found everywhere from nightclubs to supermarkets, rattling their chains and chasing passersby.

As the weather gets sharper, all the summertime *würstel* huts turn their coats and begin roasting *Maroni* (roasted chestnuts) and *Bratkartoffeln* (potato pancakes) on charcoal grills. Cider, punch, and *Glühwein,* a hot, spiced wine that warms you to the tips of your toes with the first sip are also featured at street-side stands. **Christmas markets** (*Christkindlmärkte*) also open around the city. The somewhat tacky **Rathausplatz** *Christkindlmärkte* (open daily 9am-8pm) is probably the most well-known of the yule marketplaces. You can usually manage to find excellent *Lebkuchen* (similar to gingerbread—try the *Heidelberger* variety) and beeswax candles. **Schloß Schönbrunn's** *Weihnachtsmarkt* (Mon.-Fri. noon-7pm, Sat.-Sun. and holidays 10am-7pm) also offers exquisite traditional wares, although you definitely pay for your prizes. For a funkier off-beat angle to Christmas shopping, head to the Spittelberg market (Mon.-Fri. 2-8pm, Sat.-Sun. and holidays 10am-8pm), where artists and university students put their creations up for bidding. Most of the theaters, opera houses, and concert halls perform Christmas pieces in December. (See Music, p. 288 or Theater and Cinema, p. 290.)

As soon as the Christ child has visited every Christmas tree (no, Santa Claus does not come to Austria), the Viennese immediately begin gearing up for New Year's Day. The twin high points of the New Year's season are the **Silvester concert** (New Year's concert) by the Viennese Philharmonic, broadcast worldwide and the flashy **Imperial Ball,** in the Hofburg (for tickets, write to "Kongresszentrum Hofburg, A-1014 Wien;" tel. 587 36 66-23; fax 535 64 26). For those not endowed with seven-digit incomes, however, the City of Vienna organizes a huge chain of parties in the Inner City within walking distance of each other. Just follow the **Silvesterpfad,** marked by lights hung over the street, to run into everything from outdoor karaoke and jazz bands to waltzing in the streets. Rumor has it every year that the great bell of St. Stephen's squatter tower will be rung on New Year's. The bell hasn't been rung for over 100 years because it is too powerful and experts fear the foundations of the church might crack.

New Year's is barely over before Lent arrives in February, and the **Fasching** (carnival season) spins the city into a bubbly daze of bedlam. These are the weeks of the Viennese waltzing balls. The most famous is the **Weiner Opernball** (Viennese Opera Ball), which draws the Princess Stephanies and Donald Trumps the world over. Tickets must be reserved years in advance (international celebrities, write to the Opernball-Büro, A-1010 Wien, Goethegasse 1; tel. 514 44 26 06 for tickets). However, you don't have to sit out if you can't make the Opernball—*Fasching* is a democratic season and there are balls for all tastes, the well-padded and the out-at-the-elbows. Even the kindergartners in public pre-schools have *Fasching Krapfen* parties, and McDonald's puts up carnival crêpe banners. For an absolutely cost-free *Fasching* celebration, come to the **carnival parade** that winds its way around the Ring, merrily stopping traffic the day before Lent begins. For the more temperately minded, the city sets up an enormous outdoor skating rink in the Rathausplatz in January and February. Come for a spin or just enjoy the madcap atmosphere.

NIGHTLIFE

In its dark, soothing bars and on its groovy, kinetic dance floors, Vienna parties until dawn. From the dilapidated and crawling college pub to the swank and stylish watering hole, the right place for every kind of thirst and wallet can be found. Certain areas contain a high bar to cobblestone ratio, making a night of bacchanalian wandering deliriously easy. One such area, recommended to the loud, crowded, and smoky type, is the **Bermuda Dreieck (Triangle),** named after its frequenters who, listing to port like over-stuffed Spanish treasure galleons, lose their wind and their way and slowly sink. This is an area of about ten bars down Rotenturmstr., away from the Stephansdom. Follow Rotenturm to Fleischmarkt, where Rabensteig connects and follow Rabensteig to Seitenstettengasse on your left. If your vision isn't foggy and your compass is still oriented at this point, continue on to Ruprechtsplatz, where pub tables line up against the walls of Ruprecht's church, which sternly overlooks the revelry. Here is some of the best summer outdoor seating in Vienna, with cobblestones, stained glass, and the neighboring Danube. Revelry moves inside from 11pm until 2 or even 4am. For more relaxed, less seasick action, head to the smooth **Bäcker-straße**—cool, ancient grottos where the lights are dim and the beer is perfect. Though not as packed with bars, the **Eighth District,** behind the University, and the area around **U-3: "Stubentor Station"** have been known to down many. Bars are known by the moniker *Beisl* or *Lokal.* Use these words when asking the inebriated local where he has come from and where you should go.

The Club scene whirls and rages every night of the week, later than bars. DJs spin wax until at least 4am or even 6am. A fact of Viennese dance life: it starts late. If you arrive at some place at 11pm, it will a scene from your junior high school dance. As usual, the best nights are Friday and Saturday. The cover charges are reasonable and the theme nights frenetic and varied enough to please everyone. While techno still rears its digitalized head, house and soul enjoy a strong following as well.

A couple of other hints about nightlife: First, pick up a copy of the indispensible *Falter* (280AS) at a newsstand. This is a complete guide to nocturnal events, from

Opera schedules to club listings. Second, regular public transportation ceases operating at around midnight; find a night bus schedule and plan accordingly.

Bars

The term "bar" is loosely defined in Vienna. Many restaurants (see Restaurants, p. 267) live a Dr. Jekyll-Mr. Hyde dual existence as a place to both eat and party.

The Innere Stadt

Benjamin, I, Salzgries 11-13 (tel. 533 33 49). Just outside of the Triangle area. Go down the steps from Ruprecht's church, left onto Josefs Kai, and another slight left on Salzgries. Dark and quintessentially groovy. Persian rugs hang on the walls, candles shine from wine bottles covered with wax. Filled with old, eclectic furniture. Can get rowdy on weekends, but the place designates a separate area for the cool and mellow. Student crowd and great beer—*Budvar* and *Kapsreiter* (37AS and 43AS respectively). Open Sun.-Thurs. 7pm-2am, Fri.-Sat. 7pm-4am.

Krah Krah, I, Rabensteig 8 (tel. 533 81 93). From Stephanspl., head down Rotenturmstr., and continue straight and slightly to your left on Rabensteig. Quintessential "Triangle" spot. Long bar serves 50 kinds of beer on tap. Popular outdoor seating until 10pm. Open Sun.-Wed. 11am-2am, Thurs.-Sat. 11am-3am.

Zwölf Apostellenkeller, I, Sonnenfelsgasse 3, behind the Stephansdom (tel. 52 62 77). To reach this underground tavern, walk into the archway, take a right, go down the long staircase, and discover grottoes that date back to 1561. One of the best *Weinkeller* (wine bars) in Vienna, and a definite must for catacomb fans. Beer 37AS. *Viertel* of wine starts at 25AS. Open Aug.-June daily 4:30pm-midnight.

Esterházykeller, I, Haarhof 1, off Naglergasse (tel. 533 34 82). Perhaps the least expensive *Weinkeller* in Vienna; try the *Grüner Veltliner* wine from Burgenland (26AS). Open Mon.-Fri. 11am-11pm, in winter also Sat.-Sun. 4-11pm.

Kaktus, I, Seitenstettengasse 5 (tel. 533 19 38). In the heart of the triangle. Packed with the bombed and the beautiful late at night. Candles and atmospheric slouch. Open Sun.-Thurs. 6pm-2am, Fri.-Sat. 6pm-4am.

Roter Engel, I, Rabensteig 5 (tel. 535 41 05), just across from the Krah Krah. Artsily-decorated bar with live music nightly ranging from bubble-gum pop to electrifying blues. Some of us would like to know where they manage to dig up so many good Austrian and German bands. Cover 50-100AS. Open Mon.-Wed. 3pm-2am, Thurs.-Sat. 3pm-4am, Sun. 5pm-2am, in summer 3pm-2am.

Bierleutgeb, I, Bäckerstr. 12 (tel. 512 26 37). One of the Bäckerstraße's cool subterranean grottos. Excellent beer-bar, mainly Ottakring on tap. Also a restaurant with lots of Styrian specialties. Open Mon.-Thurs. 5pm-1am, Fri. 5pm-2am.

Jazzland, I, Franz-Josefs-Kai 29 (tel. 533 25 75). U-1, U-4 to "Schwedenplatz." Jazz music of all styles and regions—check the schedule first. Excellent live music filters through the soothing brick environs. Hefty cover 120-250AS. Open Tues.-Sat. 7pm-2am. Music 9pm-1am.

Santo Spirito, I, Kampfgasse 7 (tel. 512 99 98). From Stephanspl., walk down Singerstr., and make a left onto Kumpfgasse (5min.). This bar will change your idea of classical music forever. The stereo here pumps out Rachmaninoff's second piano concerto while excited patrons co-conduct. Little busts on the wall pay homage to famous composers. Owner takes a vacation in July, otherwise open daily from 6pm until people leave.

MAK Café, I, Stubenring 5 (tel. 714 01 21). U-4 to "Stubentor," then left on Stubenring. This café, located in the Museum of Applied Arts, has a historic feel. Its 9-m Baroque ceiling, set in white, is tastefully contrasted by touches of pine, glass, and aluminum. The outdoor seating is equally impressive. Artists, students, and visitors to the MAK museum partake of the space. Open daily 8:30am-2am.

Thelonius Monk, I, Sonnenfelsgasse 13 (tel. 512 16 31). Live jazz, cocktails, mellowness. Open daily 9pm-4am, closed July-September.

Aera, I, Gonzagagasse 11 (tel. 533 53 14) warms up slowly as an Italian, Viennese, and vegetarian restaurant and phases into its true self around midnight—a twenty-something, chrome energetic nightspot.

Outside the Ring

Alsergrunder Kulturpark, IX, Alserstr. 4 (tel. 407 82 14). Located on the old grounds of a turn-of-the-18th-century hospital, Kulturpark is not one bar but many of them. A favorite outdoor hangout for the Viennese who flock here to the beer garden, *Heurige,* champagne bar…the list goes on. All sorts of people decorate the park, and all sorts of night life—just about anything you might want for a happening night out. Open every night from April.-Oct. 4pm-2am. Also, call about the frequent concerts held here.

Chelsea, VIII, Lerchenfelder Gürtel 29-31 (U6). The best place in Vienna for live "alternative" music. Period. Open daily 4pm-4am.

Miles Smiles, VIII, Langegasse 51 (tel. 405 95 17), as in Miles Davis. U-2 to "Lerchenfelderstr." Head down Lerchenfelderstr., and take the first right. Cool as "Sketches of Spain." The music is post-1955 jazz. Open Sun.-Thurs. 8pm-2am, Fri.-Sat. 8pm-4am.

Europa, VII, Zollergasse 8 (tel. 526 33 83). Buy a drink, scope the scene, and just vogue, Katya. Adorned with concert posters and funky light fixtures, the hip twentysomething crowd of Vienna hangs out here late at night on the way to further intoxication. Open daily 9am-4am.

Känguruh, VI, Bürgerspitalgasse 20 (tel. 597 38 24). Decent little bar; offers over 70 brands of beer. Snacks also available. Open daily 6pm-2am.

Discos and Dance Clubs

U-4, XII, Schönbrunnerstr. 222 (tel. 85 83 18). Around the corner from the U-4 "Meidling Hauptstr." stop. In earlier days, this was *the* disco in Vienna, and it still gets very crowded. A behemoth with all the trappings including two separate dance areas, dancer's cage, and random slide shows. Five floors and rotating theme nights please a varied clientele. Cover 50-100AS. Open daily 11pm-5am.

Mekka, VII, Mariahilferstr. 19-21. Take U-2 to "Babenbergerstr.," and walk up Mariahilferstr. It's on your left (3min.). This is the newest place in town, and it just got renovated. Candlelight, arabesque curves, chrome, and an oriental fringe along the bar. Three DJs mix house and techno. Some Sat. (or rather Sun. mornings), Mekka holds "After Hours," where the bar and the dance floor stay open until noon the next day. Cover 50-100AS. Open Tues.-Sat. 4pm-6am.

Titanic, VI, Theobaldgasse 11 (tel. 587 47 58). From the U-2 "Babenbergerstr." station, walk up Mariahilferstr. past Mekka and take the third left. No pretensions, just deep, sweaty grooves in the cavern-like interconnected rooms. Two dance floors, concrete and crowded, with lots of soul. Occasionally they do slip in some older music. No cover. Open Sun.-Thurs. 7pm-2am, Fri.-Sat. 7pm-4am.

B.A.C.H., Bachgasse 21 (tel. 450 18 58). Lots of live funky concerts and theater acts as well as straight-up dancing in this subterranean nightclub. Definitely left of center. Open Sun.-Thurs. 8pm-2am, Fri. and Sat. until 4am.

Volksgarten, I, Burgring/Heldenpl. (tel. 63 05 18). Nestled on the edge of the Volksgarten Park, near the Hofburg. Zip up the leisure suit and strap on the platform soles. Definite 70s vibe. Comfy red couches provide the perfect spot for wallflowers to mellow. In good weather, the club rolls back the roof so clubbers can pulse under the stars. Mon. "Vibrazone" kicks out the funk and groove while the Sun. morning breakfast club, which starts at 6am and runs until 2pm, is the place to prolong Saturday's buzz. Cover 70-100AS. Open daily 10pm-5am.

Bisexual, Gay, and Lesbian Cafés and Clubs

For recommendations, support, seasonal parties, or just to make contacts, call or stop by the **Rosa Lila Villa** (see Practical Information, p. 256). The helpful staff can give you lists of events, clubs, cafés, and discos (available in English). They also sponsor **Frauenfeste** (women's festivals) four times per year.

Café Willendorf, VI, Linke Wienzeile 102, in the Rosa Lila Villa (tel. 587 17 89). A café, bar, and restaurant with an outdoor terrace and excellent, creative vegetarian fare. Open daily 7pm-2am, meals until midnight.

Berg das Café, IX, Berggasse 8 (tel. 319 57 20). A mixed café/bar at night. Casual hang-out by day. Open daily 10am-1am.

Why Not, I, Tiefer Graben 22 (tel. 535 11 58). A relaxed bar/disco for men and women. Fri.-Sat. 11pm-6am, Sun. 9pm-2am. Women only one Thurs. per month, 11pm-3am.
Eagle Bar, VI, Blümelgasse 1 (tel. 587 26 61). A bar for men. Diverse clientele derived from the leather and/or denim set. Open daily 9pm-4am.
Nightshift, VI, Corneliusgasse 8 (tel. 586 23 37). A bar for men, preferably in black leather. Sun.-Thurs. daily 10pm-4am, Fri.-Sat. 10pm-5am.
U-4, see Discos and Dance Clubs, p. 295. Thurs. nights are "Gay Heavens Night," 11pm-5am.
Café Savoy, VI, Linke Wienzeile 36. A café-bar for gay men and women of mixed ages. Open Tues.-Fri. 5pm-2am, Sat. 9am-6pm and 9pm-2am.

■ Daytrips from Vienna

For other possible daytrips, see **Eisenstadt** (p. 306) and **Baden bei Wien** (p. 304).

MÖDLING

"You must take a good look around Mödling; it's a very nice place."
—Ludwig van Beethoven to the painter August von Kloeber

"Poor I am, and miserable," Beethoven wrote upon his arrival in Mödling. Seeking physical and psychological rehabilitation, he schlepped all this way for that *je ne sais quoi* only a mineral spring could offer. He wrote his *Missa Solemnis* within Mödling's embrace, and his spirits thoroughly improved. Take his happy-camper transformation as a good omen; whatever the baths' medicinal effects, they certainly offer a soothing respite from travel stress.

About 20min. from Vienna by S-Bahn (Eurail Pass valid), thanks to its surroundings Mödling maintains the charm that has drawn nobility and artists to it since the Babenberg reign. Minstrel Walther von der Vogelweide performed his epics in town. Later, other musical geniuses, including Schubert, Wagner, and Strauss, made their way here to glean inspiration from the stunning scenery. Most of the artists of the *fin de siècle*, such as musician Hugo Wolf, poet Peter Altenberg, and painters Egon Schiele and Gustav Klimt, planted at least temporary roots at the spa. In his house on Bernhardgasse, Arnold Schönberg developed his 12-tone chromatic music and posed for the renowned Oskar Kokoschka portrait.

This elegant and serene town of 20,000 permanent inhabitants is hidden among the trees of the Wienerwald. There are 85km of marked hiking trails in and around Mödling, leading to the ruins of the **Babenbergs' Castle,** the Neoclassical **Liechtenstein Palace,** and the Romanesque **Liechtenstein Castle** (both in Maria Enzersdorf, a neighboring town). The well-preserved *Altstadt* proudly presents two Romanesque churches (check out the amazing stained-glass in the **Pfarrkirche St. Othman** and the majestic **Karner** tower topped by a huge black onion dome) and a charming Renaissance **Rathaus.** Mödling's **City Museum,** Josef Deutsch Pl., displays archaeological finds that trace the town's history back to 6000 BC (open April-Dec. Sat.-Sun. 10am-noon and 2-4pm).

To this day, Mödling remains a favorite recreational destination; the **Stadtbad** (city bath) down Badstr. has huge outdoor and indoor swimming pools, a sauna, sunbathing, massage therapy, and zillions of screaming children climbing on a funky orange octopus thing—go in the morning when everything is much more sane. There are also facilities for golf, tennis, horseback-riding, and fishing. In the evening, summer clientele naturally flock to the *Heurigen,* enjoying the cool night breeze and the healthy grapes.

For information, brochures, and *Privatzimmer* lists, head to the **tourist office** (*Gästedienst*), Elisabethstr. 2 (tel. (02236) 267 27), next to the Rathaus. From the train station, walk up the hill and left down Hauptstr. all the way to the end at the Rathaus (10 min.). (Office open Mon.-Fri. 8am-noon and 1-4pm.) Mödling's proximity to Vienna makes for an excellent day trip. Trains leaving from the Südbahnhof pass

VIENNA

through Mödling all day (30AS), and a bus leaves every hour from Südtiroler Platz in Vienna. The bus from the Vienna Kennedybrücke also runs into Mödling.

Buses from Mödling (dir: Hinterbrühl) run through **Heiligenkreuz,** a beautifully pink Baroque Cistercian monastery on a hillside. Founded by Leopold V, the man who imprisoned Richard the Lionheart for ransom, it was originally intended as a "school of love" and a reform of the pre-existing Benedictine order. Life at Heiligenkreuz was never particularly austere. You can visit the Weinkeller where the monks pressed their own grapes, or walk through the chapel which still has ornamentation and beautiful stained glass windows despite several medieval missives from church elders who threatened that if the decoration was not taken down within 2 years, the abbot, prior, and cellarer would have to fast on bread and water every sixth day until it was removed. Visiting the abbey itself is only possible by tour (open 9am-6pm; 45AS, children 25AS). The same bus that goes to Heiligenkreuz halts one stop later at **Mayerling,** the hunting lodge where heir to the throne Archduke Rudolf shot his bourgeois lover, Marie Vetsera, whom court protocol forbid him to marry, and then killed himself.

KLOSTERNEUBURG

Easily accessible via the buses from Heiligenstadt (every ½hr., 27AS), Klosterneuburg is an 8-century-old monastery founded by Leopold III in 1114. The church contains the renowned high Gothic masterpiece, the Verduner Altar. (Stiftsmuseum open May 1-Sept. 15 Sat.-Sun. and holidays 10am-5pm.) In 1730, Karl IV moved into Klosterneuburg and began the building of a palace that was to echo the monastery in size and thus symbolize the equivalent importance of *Gottesreich* and the *Kaiserreich*— God's kingdom and the Emperor's kingdom. The wildly extravagant Baroque style will keep the crowds from the tour bus oohing and aahing. Note especially the crown of the Holy Roman Emperor at the crest of the palace. Klosterneuburg library is also stupendous, with over 200,000 ancient tomes. Call the Stiftsmuseum (tel. (02243) 62 10) early to arrange a tour.

Klosterneuburg also has a **Jugendherberge** at Hüttersteig 8 (tel. (02243) 83 501) to which the forlorn traveler unable to find a bed in Vienna could easily commute. It's a bit of a steep climb but it offers 65 beds at 120AS a piece. It occasionally fills up with groups of screaming kids. (Open Jan. 5-Sept. 15.)

Lower Austria

Lower Austria

Though it bears little resemblance to the foreign stereotype of Austria, the Danube province of **Niederösterreich** (Lower Austria) is the historic cradle of the Austrian nation. Forget *The Sound of Music*. Rolling, forested hills replace jagged Alpine peaks, and lavender wildflowers stand in for hillside edelweiss. The region gets its name not because it is at the bottom of the state, but rather because it is situated at the lower end of the Danube's flow. Niederösterreich is also billed as "the province on Vienna's doorstep," a name which refers not to doormat status but to geographic fact: Lower Austria encircles the pearl of Vienna. Anyone who enters or departs Vienna over land must pass through the province. This also explains the rugged castle ruins, which were once defensive bastions against invading imperial Turkish forces, and now look wistfully across the Hungarian border. The province also accounts for one-quarter of the nation's land mass and 60% of its wine. Try the local *Wienerwald* cream strudel while sipping some *Schnapps;* the pastry is a sinful mixture of flaky crust, curds, raisins, and lemon peel. It tastes *far* better than it sounds.

The **Wachau** region of Lower Austria, located between the northwestern foothills of the Bohemian Forest and the southeast Dunkelsteiner Wald, is a magnificent river valley. The celebrated Wachau wines can today be savored at the wine cellars of any local vintner. Off the beaten tourist route, the **Waldviertel** region is a vast tract of mountains and trees stretching between the Danube and the Czech Republic. Though the regional villages and hamlets are treasure troves of history, the chief attractions are the densely forested woodlands, interspersed with lakes and pools, where hiking paths meander hundreds of miles over hill and dale. Enjoy the forest, but beware—dangerous ticks have been known to fall from the trees onto anything or anyone walking beneath. These ticks carry a virus that results in *Gehirnentzündung* (literally, inflammation of the brain), a disease similar to meningitis; see **Essentials: Health,** p. 16, for more preventative advice.

■ St. Pölten

If cities are like women, then St. Pölten (pop. over 50,000) is an aging opera star currently undergoing the latest of a series of make-overs to cover up the scars from World War II and the pockmarks of her industrial heritage. It does, however, still play a convincing *ingénue*. Granted a city charter in 1159 by Bishop von Passau, it is legally the oldest city in Austria and, because of its train link, offers a convenient exit from Vienna for a day of baroque wandering. Serving not only as the capital of Niederösterreich, but as a transportation hub for all those traveling east of Vienna, the pretty, pastel town with its baroque face offers a bustling shopping district and a number of museums and theater festivals. Because of St. Pölten's easy train access, many guests visit every year, though a good number are just passing through.

Orientation and Practical Information The city is divided by the Kremsergasse. Leaving the train station and crossing the Bahnhofplatz, Kremsergasse is at ten o'clock. Follow it until you hit the Rathausgasse and then turn right to reach St. Pölten's heart, the **Rathausplatz,** or town hall square. The **tourist office** (tel. 533 54; fax 525 31 or 28 19), is here in the Rathauspassage, the tunnel under the cotton-candy colored Rathaus. Tourist officials will provide oodles of information about St. Pölten, regional events, and the wonders of the surrounding Lower Austrian lands (in English upon request). The eager staff will also give you a room list, suggest a madcap night on the town (ask for the *IN Szene* brochure), lead tours of the city (call for times), or distribute a **cassette tour** (20AS; Office open Mon.-Fri. 8am-6pm, Sat. 9:30am-6:30pm). What the staff will not do is make room reservations; look next door on the wall of the Reisebüro for a free telephone from which you can make reservations. The best place to exchange money is the **Postsparkasse Österreichischer Bank (PSK),** Rathausgasse 2 (tel. 35 45 71; fax 35 45 75), across the street from the post office. **Trains** are located at Bahnhofpl. abutting the pedestrian zone. The station has every service you could hope for, including direct trains to Hütteldorf and the Westbahnhof in Vienna two or three times every hour. **Lockers** are available 24hr. (small 30AS, large 40AS). You can **rent bikes** (tel. 528 60;100AS, 50AS with train ticket; open daily 5:45am-10pm). Right in front of the train station, the **bus** depot has buses running to **Melk** and to **Krems.** A complete schedule is available for free at the bus stop, or call 35 34 66. The main **post office,** Bahnhofpl. 1a, is right next to the train station. (Open Mon.-Fri. 7am-8pm, Sat. 7am-4pm, Sun. 8am-10am.) **Postal code:** A-3100. **Telephone code:** 02742.

Accommodations and Food Unfortunately, St. Pölten lost its only youth hostel two years ago. *Privatzimmer* (private rooms) are another budget option, but most of these lie outside the city limits. Travelers bent on visiting may consider staying in the hostels in **Krems** (tel. (02732) 834 52, p. 314), **Melk** (tel. (02752) 26 81, p. 317), or **Vienna.** Another option is **Gasthof Graf,** Bahnhofpl. 7, across the street from the train station and beyond the McDonalds; it's home to 50 clean, sunny rooms with TVs and comfortable beds, many with shower and toilet. (Singles 290-355AS. Doubles 560-740AS. Parking available. Breakfast included.) The Stüberl downstairs offers regional cuisine at reasonable prices (entrées 55-88AS; open Mon.-Fri. 7am-10pm, Sat. 7am-2pm). It has garden seating open in summer and live music on Thurs. 8pm.

St. Pölten's local specialties include oysters, fried black pudding, and wonderfully savory Wachau wine. Many shops and cafés can be found in the *Fußgängerzone* surrounding the Dom and the Rathaus. **B&B (Bier & Brötchen),** Schreingasse 7 (tel. 520

72), has soup and sandwiches, good beer, and outside seating (open Mon.-Fri. 10:30am-11pm, Sat. 9:30-2pm; live music the first Sun. of the month from 10am-2pm). **Café Melange,** Kremsergasse 11, on the second floor, is a comfortable Viennese café with newspapers and lingering guests. It tends to draw a younger crowd. **Don Paolo Ristorant,** Linzerstr. 16, serves inexpensive pizza. (Open Mon.-Fri. 11am-2pm and 4pm-midnight, Sat. 11am-2pm, 5pm-midnight, Sun. 4pm-midnight.) **Domstüberl,** Domplatz 7, is a real unvarnished country stüberl. The *dirndl* crowd lets loose on the benches in the square, while the woozier patrons pass the afternoon inside the smoky atmosphere of dark wood, and soccer decals. One can pick up the makings of a cheap and healthy lunch at the St. Pölten branch of **Julius Meinl,** Kremsergasse 21 (open Mon.-Fri. 7:30am-6pm, Sat. 7:30am-12:30pm).

Sights and Entertainment Like many Austrian towns, about 40% of St. Pölten was destroyed or damaged during World War II. Thankfully, many 17th-century structures, designed by the prolific architects Jakob Prandtauer and Joseph Munggenast, were restored to their original grandeur. The overriding Baroque presence makes the city an architectural bonanza. Prandtauer's florid, baroque *Schlag* is put into relief by the masterful turn-of-the-century *Jugendstil* (art nouveau) buildings of Joseph Maria Olbrich that somehow escaped most of the explosives. St. Pölten has borrowed much of its contemporary culinary and artistic offerings from its surroundings: the vineyards of the Wachau and the forested Waldviertel.

The Rathausplatz at St. Pölten's core was erected in the 13th century, though recent archeological excavations reveal that a Roman settlement had sprouted there in the first millennium. The building to the left of the city hall, at Rathausplatz 2, is called the **"Schubert Haus,"** after Franz Schubert's frequent visits to the owners, Baron von Münk and his family. A neo-Grecian Schubert (bare chested, no less) conducts and composes above the window at the portal's axis. The expansive front of the **Institute of Mary Ward** *(Institut der Englischer Fräulein)* founded in 1706 at Linzer Str. 9-11 for the instruction of girls from noble families, sports a magnificent white on pink façade with Corinthian columns and vaguely religious, life-size reliefs.

St. Pölten's **Wiener Straße** has been a thoroughfare since the Romans rolled through. After 1100, it became the central axis of the bourgeois-trader settlement established by the Bishop of Passau. At the corner of Wienerstr. and Kremsergasse stands the oldest pharmacy in St. Pölten, the **Hassack-Apotheke,** happily curing headaches and hemorrhoids since 1595. Note their beautifully painted shutters. **Herrenplatz** has seen the haggling of St. Pölten's daily market for centuries. A narrow alley just after Wiener Str. 31 leads to the **Domplatz,** which still has charm despite its current parking lot status. The remains of the Roman settlement of Aelium were discovered here when some clumsy sewer installers tripped over Roman hypocausts, an ancient floor heating system. Be sure to stop by the actual **Dom** (cathedral) with its pleasant salmon tones and gilded baroque encrustations.

St. Pölten maintains a few good museums. The encyclopedic **Stadt Museum,** Prandtauerstr. 2, near the Rathaus, often has special exhibits on cultural and historical themes in addition to its very thorough permanent collection on the history of St. Pölten from pre-Roman times to the present. (Everything from transplanted church pews, to Roman coins, to 18th-century cloth samples. Open daily 9am-5pm. 50AS, students 20AS.) Part of the exhibit is located in **Schloß Pottenbrunn** outside of St. Pölten. Buses run from the Bahnhof to the Schloß every hour. St. Pölten also has two **theaters.** The open-air theater called **"Die Bühne im Hof,"** (the stage in the courtyard) at Linzerstr. 18 (tel. 352 291; fax 522 94), has mostly modern theater and dance pieces. The tourist office offers a program detailing the productions. Prices range from 70-350AS, depending on what's showing, with students and seniors receiving 50% off the subscription price. More traditional operas and ballets take place at the **Landeshauptstadt Theater,** Rathauspl. 11 (tel. 35 20 26 19). Tickets run 160-290AS, but standing room tickets can be obtained from the box office on the evenings of performance. Seasonal festivities include the **St. Pöltner Festwoche,** which brings all kinds of cultural events to the local theaters and museums at the end of May. In the summer the Landeshauptstadt Fest comes to St. Pölten for one Friday in July; the town is filled with stages and stands for a day of open-air concerts and dancing. Finally, during Sept., there is a Baroque Festival, and from the end of Sept. to the beginning of Oct. the **Sacred Music Festival** displays organ and sacred music concerts in the churches of St. Pölten for free.

For some more earthly pleasures, check out the **flea market** that comes to the Einkaufszentrum Traisenpark from 8am-3pm every Sunday and lays out crafts, toys, art, antiques, books, furniture, everything you could dream of and more to haggle over. The **Naturfreunde Reisebüro,** Heßstr. 4 (tel. 572 11), organizes bike tours in the surrounding area as well as further afield in places like India and East Africa.

■ Mariazell

The local Benedictine superior's motto for Mariazell is *"Gnadenzentrum Europas,"*—Europe's Center of Mercy. While this may be something of an exaggeration, time spent in Mariazell does feel blessed. The attractions of this little town tilting precariously on the side of the Alps seem rather schizophrenic at times; Mariazell is at once an unabashed resort town and the most important pilgrimage site in Central Europe. The faithful come here to pay homage to a miraculous Madonna of linden wood, a hand-carved statue which was once the possession of the traveling monk Magnus, who in 1157 established a chapel in Mariazell (see below). Those of a different faith come to ski or bronze their bodies near the waters of the Erlausee.

Orientation and Practical Information The **tourist office,** Hauptpl. 13 (tel. 23 66; fax 39 45), has copious pamphlets describing seasonal activities (skiing, boating, fishing, praying), as well as bus and train information and accommodations listings. The multi-lingual staff also makes free reservations. The office and Mariazell itself is a 20-minute jaunt from the **train station;** turn right on St. Sebastian, as you exit the station, and walk until you see a fork in the road. Follow the left fork up the hill to Wienerstr., turn right, and intersect the **Hauptplatz.** The office is straight ahead. (Open June-Sept. Mon.-Sat. 9am-12:30pm and 1:30-5:30pm, Sun. 9am-noon; Oct.-May Mon.-Fri. 9am-1pm and 2-4:30pm, Sat. 9am-noon and 2-4pm, Sun. 9:30am-noon.) To **exchange money,** stop by the **Sparkasse** just behind the post office on Grazerstr. 6 (tel. 23 03; open Mon.-Fri. 8am-noon and 2-4pm, Sat. 8-11am). There is also a 24-hr. **ATM** there. **Telephones** are found at the post office, bus and train stations, and the Hauptpl.

Mariazell is difficult to access by train. The **train station,** Erlaufseestr. 19 (tel. 22 30), is most useful for **renting bikes** (50AS per day) and **luggage storage** (30AS per day; open daily 5am-6:40pm). Besides the touristy old steam train that runs around the Erlausee, the **Mariazellerbahn** is the only train entering and exiting the town, and it does so via **St. Pölten** (2½hr., every 2-3hr. 156AS, Eurail pass valid). Driving to Mariazell is shorter (1hr.), but you'll miss the scenic train ride, which steams through parts of the Alps practically inaccessible by car or by foot and is a tourist attraction in its own right. Take this train in the winter if possible, the views are even more spectacular. To reach Mariazell **by car** from **Vienna,** take Autobahn A1 west to St. Pölten, and exit onto route 20 south to Mariazell. From **Leoben** or **Bruck an der Mur,** take route S6 to Kapfenberg and then route 20 north to Mariazell. From **Graz,** take route S35 north to Bruck an der Mur, then route S6 to route 20 north.

The **bus station** is directly behind the post office near the Hauptplatz (open Mon.-Fri. 8am-noon and 2-4pm, Sat. 8-11am). Bus routes are only a fraction less exasperating than train connections. Buses to **Bruck an der Mur** leave five times per day (5:45, 6:25, 7:50am, 3:30, and 6:10pm; 94AS), twice for **Graz** (5:45am and 3:30pm), and twice for **Vienna** (3hr., 170AS). For more bus information, stop by the **Postautodienst** desk at the bus station (open Mon.-Fri. 9:30-11:30am and 2:30-4:30pm, Sat. and Sun. 9:40-10:10am and 3:15-3:55pm). For the latest **snow conditions** in the region, call 42 20. For medical **emergencies,** call the St. Sebastian Hospital, Spitalgasse 4 (tel. 22 22). The local **pharmacy** is **"Zur Gaudenmutter,"** Grazer-Str. 2 (tel. 21 02; open

Mon.-Fri. 8am-noon and 2-4pm, Sat. 8am-noon, Sun. 9am-noon). Upstairs at the **post office** there are telephone centers and fax machines. (No traveler's checks exchanged. Open Mon.-Fri. 8am-noon and 2-6pm, Sat. 8-10am.) **Postal code:** A-8630. **Telephone code:** 03882.

Accommodations and Food Mariazell's **Jugendherberge (HI),** Fischer-von-Erlach-Weg 2 (tel. 26 69; fax 26 69 88), is immaculate. Designed for large groups, the hostel is equipped with a huge breakfast room, activity rooms, a basketball court, and a huge, green, grassy hill, complete with cows out back. The rooms are a bit snug, with lockers and showers on the hall. From the station, walk straight on Wiener-Str., through Hauptpl. and P.-Abel-Pl., straight onto Wiener Neustädterstr., and then turn left on Fischer-von-Erlach-Weg (½hr.). (Reception open 5-10pm year round. Curfew 10pm, but sign out a key. No lockout, members only, and reservations recommended. In summer 165-185AS; in winter 175-195AS. 20AS surcharge for one night stays. Breakfast included. Owners may close for vacation around Oct. or Nov.) One alternative is a room at **Haus Maria Molnar,** Brünnerweg 5 (tel. 46 86), near the train station. Frau Molnar, a lively, helpful soul, offers wonderful singles and doubles, all with sinks and most with a great view of the mountains. (180AS per person, more than 3 nights 160AS. In summer, showers or baths 20AS. Breakfast included. Add 10AS to all prices in winter.) Enjoy the comforts of home at **Haus Wechselberger,** Bilderiweg 8 (tel. 23 15). The Wechselberger family rents out a few rooms in their house, complete with antique beds with high, ornately decorated head and foot-boards. Several rooms have balconies with views of the surrounding hills. (170-180AS, add on 10AS in winter. Toilet and showers on the hall. Breakfast included.) Though crowded, **Camping Erlaufsee,** behind the Hotel Herrenhaus near the west dock (tel. 21 48 or 21 16), is in a lovely spot just by the lake on Erlaufseestr., equipped with hot showers, toilets, refrigerator, and activity room. (35AS per person, children under 15 15AS, 20-40AS per tent space.)

Try **Café Oberfeichtner,** Ludwig-Leber-Str. 2, for a good meal and lively patrons. (Pizza and other entrées about 65-95AS. Open Mon.-Fri. and Sun. 10am-10pm, Sat. 10am-midnight.) Cheap food and occasional live music can also be found at **Stüberl Goldener Stiefel,** corner of Wiender Neustädtstr. and Dr.-Karl-Lueger-Str. (tel. 27 31. Pizza 45-80AS. Open Mon.-Sun. 8:30am-midnight.) There is a **Julius Meinl** supermarket on Wiener-Str. (open Mon.-Fri. 5am-6pm, Sat. 8am-noon), and of course many wonderful *lebkuchen* stands outside the church.

Sights and Entertainment Mariazell literally means "Mary's chapel." This pilgrimage town has received hundreds of thousands of pious wanderers over the centuries, all journeying to visit the **Madonna** within the **Basilica** (tel. 25 95). The Basilica, in the middle of the Hauptplatz, is capped by black baroque spires visible from any spot in town. Mass quantities of gold and silver adorn the **High Altar,** which depicts a huge silver globe with a snake wound around it. The **Gnadenaltar,** in the middle of the church, is where the miraculous Madonna rests. Empress Maria Theresa donated the silver and gold grille that encloses the Gnadenaltar. (Free guided tours with appointment through the Superiorat, Kardinal-Tisserant-Pl. 1; Basilica open for visits, without the tour, daily 6am-7pm.) The church's amazing **Schatzkammer** (treasure chamber) contains gifts from scores of pious Europeans. (Open Mon.-Fri. 10am-noon and 2-3pm, Sat.-Sun. 10am-3pm. 10AS.)

With **skiing, tobogganing, hiking, windsurfing, tennis, biking,** and **whitewater kayaking,** Mariazell caters to throngs of bronzed-skinned, ultra-healthy (rhymes with wealthy…) outdoor types. Located just under the **Bürgeralpe** and a short jaunt away from the **Gemeindealpe,** Mariazell is an ideal ski region—one of the closest, in fact, to Vienna. There is a **cable car** (tel. 25 55) up to the top of the Bürgeralpe a six-minute walk away from the Hauptpl. at Wienerstr. 28. (Cars leave every 20min. Open July-Aug. 8:30am-5:30pm; April-June and Oct.-Nov. 9am-5pm; Sept. 8:30am-5pm. Round-trip 85AS. One-way uphill 60AS. One-way downhill 40AS. With guestcard or student ID 75AS, 55AS, and 40AS respectively.) Ski lifts and trails line the top (2-day

Mary, Mary, quite contrary

In 1157, Magnus the Good Monk set out on a mission in the mountains. Ever prepared, he took along a servant, a horse, and his precious hand-carved statue of the Holy Mary. One night, however, Magnus and his companion had the bad fortune to encounter a robber who, upon seeing how fiercely the monk defended the statue, drew his dagger and demanded that Magnus hand over the treasure. Fearlessly, Magnus rose and held the statue at arms length in front of him. The mesmerized robber dropped his dagger and muttered "Maria," giving the monk and his companion time to flee. When they were at a safe distance away, they set up camp and went to bed. Shortly after midnight, Magnus heard a woman's voice pleading with him to wake up and flee. The monk opened his eyes to a shimmering vision of Mary, insisting that he take the statue and run. The monk woke his companion, and they took off into the night with a pack of robbers in hot pursuit. *Grace à* Mary, the two had something of a head start, but were brought to a sudden standstill when they encountered a huge stony cliff. Without hesitation, Magnus held the statue aloft and said a heartfelt prayer. With a great rumble and creak, a narrow passage opened in the stone, just wide enough for the two travelers. They walked into a lush green valley where they were met by bewildered lumberjacks who made them feel quite at home. At his request the locals built a little wooded "chapel," or "Zell," for the miraculous Mary statue. This valley became known as "Maria in der Zell" or "Mariazell."

pass 430AS, single day pass 235AS). Five kilometers away from Mariazell in Mitterbach (you can get here by bus or by the steam engine train) are the Gemeindealpe, offering more lifts and trails. Reach the top (1623m) via the **Gemeindealp chairlift** (tel. 42 11 or 32 92), which is open June-Sept. daily 8am-noon and 1-4:30pm (roundtrip 120AS). For ski information on the Bürgeralpe, Gemeindealpe, Gußwerk, Tribein, and Köcken-Sattel Mountains (no lifts here) contact the Mariazell tourist office. In the summer, hiking prevails in these areas.

All of Mariazell's water sports revolve around the **Erlaufsee**, a wondrous Alpine oasis six kilometers outside the city limits. Five kilometers of lakeside beaches allow for some of the best sunbathing in central Austria. **Buses** (tel. 21 66) run from Mariazell to the Erlaufsee at 9:10am, 1:10pm, 3pm, and 3:15pm (20AS). **Steam train engines** (tel. 30 14), proclaimed by the tourist office as "the oldest in the world," also whizz around the Erlaufsee. (Runs July-Sept. on weekends and holidays. 30AS, roundtrip 50AS.) Once at the water's edge, try renting an **electric boat** (100AS for ½hr.), or a **paddle/row boat** (70AS for ½hr.) from **Restaurant Herrenhaus** (tel. 22 50). Those interested in **scuba diving** in the Erlaufsee can contact **Harry's Tauchschule,** Traismauer 5 (tel. (02783) 77 47), for information about lessons and equipment rental. However, you first need a doctor's certificate that verifies that you are fit enough to dive; call 27 71 for more information. Rent **mountain bikes** from Sport Zefferer on Wiener Neustädterstr., up the street from the tourist office. (Open Mon.-Sat. 8am-noon and 2-6pm. 100AS per day.)

APPROACHING BURGENLAND

South and southeast of Vienna, from the easternmost portion of the Wienerwald to northwest Burgenland, lies a region of rolling hills and dense woodlands. Oddly enough, the Burgenland doesn't get its name because the region has a plethora of castles (*Burg* means castle), but because there are so many towns that end in "-burg" (e.g. Piesburg, Wieselburg, Eisenburg). Burgenland was once the scene of a vicious Trojan-type war between the Huns and the Burgens, complete with an *Iliad*-type epic studied in local schools. The villages that extend south from Vienna along Autobahn A2 are primarily grape towns, with vineyards producing world famous wines and friendly taverns serving them. Textiles and foodstuff factories, plus major chemical and iron plants abound in this industrial center, driving the tourist-independent economy. The River Leitha runs along the Burgenland border north of Wiesen to Wiener Neustadt and to nations east, while the peaks of the Rosaliengebirge glower over the southern part of the region near the Hungarian border.

■ Baden bei Wien

Baden is the favorite weekend spot for Viennese trying to get away from it all. Since the age of Roman rule, bathers have cherished the spa for the therapeutic effects of its sulphur springs. All day, every day, a supply of water with a natural temperature of 36°C (96°F), springs from the ground. The Holy Roman Emperors used Baden as a summer retreat; the honor became official in 1803 when Emperor Franz I decided to move the court here during the summer months. The Emperor gave Baden an imperial reputation, and over the years some big names came here to catch a little R&R: Grillparzer, Mozart, Schubert, Strauss, Beethoven and, of course, Falco.

Under imperial patronage in the 19th century, Biedermeier culture flourished; city notables generated magnificent specimens of architecture and art and encouraged the burgeoning science of horticulture. As a tribute to the Emperor's presence, Baden created a rosarium covering 90,000 square meters of park; the enormous garden contains over 20,000 roses. The park extends from the center of town to the Wiener-wald. In one step, you can depart the carefully tended roses and enter the enormous, trail-laced tract of woodland.

Orientation and Practical Information There's only one problem in paradise: Baden is built for an imperial budget. Nevertheless, because it is so lovely and so well connected to Vienna by public transportation (a mere 27km away), Baden makes an excellent day trip. **By car** from the west, take the West Autobahn to "Alland-Baden-Mödling (Bundesstr. 20)." From Vienna, take the Süd Autobahn, and exit at "Baden." The Vienna local railway runs a direct **train** from Vienna to Josefplatz, just outside the Baden *Fußgängerzone*. (Leaves the Vienna Westbahnhof at 10am and 4:15pm. ½hr. Return trips leave Josefpl. at 8:40am and 3:05pm.) Better yet, take the **Badner Bahn,** a tram that runs every 15 minutes between Josefplatz and the Opera House in Vienna. Still another option is the Wiener-Lokal Bahn, which runs from the main station in Baden, located on Waltersdorferstr., to the Wien Meidling in Vienna. These trains run every 30min.-1hr. Regular trains stop in Baden on their way to and from Vienna every 15 minutes (34AS to Vienna). The main Baden **bus** stops are at the Wiener-Lokal Bahn and Josefpl. Approximately 50 buses run per day between Baden and Vienna (stops at Heinrichshof/Opera in Vienna; last bus from Vienna 3:10am, last bus from Josefpl. 2:21am; 58AS).

Baden's **tourist office** *(Kurdirektion)* is located at Brusattipl. 3 (tel. 868 00 310; fax 441 47). Get there by going to Josefplatz (where you will be if you took the bus or tram) and walk towards the hot springs fountain to the Erzherzog-Rainer-Ring. Follow this to your second left, which will be Güner Markt. In the left corner will be the tourist office. They offer free *Altstadt* tours every Monday at 2pm and Thurs. at 10am (1hr.30min.), as well as free guided **hiking** or **biking** tours, or a wine region tour (Wed. at 3pm; 2hr.). **Wine-tastings,** for a fee, are held Thursdays 4-7pm or upon arrangement. The patient, English-speaking staff will give you all the brochures and information necessary to make a thorough visit. (Open May-Oct. Mon.-Sat. 9am-12:30pm and 2-6pm, Sun. 9am-12:30pm.) **Bike rental** can be found at the **train station** (50AS) or **Windrad** on Vöslauerstr. 38 (tel. 492 22). (Open Mon.-Fri. 8am-6pm, Sat. 8:30am-12:30pm; 60AS per day, mountain bikes 200AS.) There is **luggage storage** (30AS per bag) at the train station. **Public toilets** are at Grüner Markt and in the *Bahnhof*. **Postal code:** A-2500. **Telephone code:** 02252.

Accommodations and Food If you would like to spend the night in Baden, despite admonishments from the budget fairy, the tourist office will introduce you to the owner of a *Privatzimmer.* The inexpensive options are limited. **Haus Taschler,**

Schlossergasse 11 (tel. 484 41), is a beautiful house set on a tiny, ivy-laden alley off of Gutenbrunner Park, halfway between Josefpl. and the Strandbad. Clean, well-furnished rooms, and kitchen facilities are available for 180AS, including private shower. Call in advance; the place fills easily and prefers long-term guests. **Pension Steinkellner,** Am Hang 1 (tel. 862 26), is another possibility. It offers decent rooms at, for Baden, reasonable prices. (Singles 290AS, with shower 300AS.)

There are many (though not necessarily inexpensive) food options to choose from. **Café Damals,** Rathausgasse 3 (tel. 426 86), in a cool, ivy-hung courtyard on the right facing the Hauptpl., is a relaxing place to lunch and linger, despite the rather un-nostalgic Austrian Top 40 music. Try one of their delicate salads (40AS; open Mon.-Fri. 9:30am-11pm, Sat. 9:30am-5pm, Sun. 11am-5pm). **Zum Vogelhändler,** Vöslauerstr. 48 (tel. 852 25) is a full *Beisl*-type hangout where the Baden youth flock to imbibe the local wine and snack on small, hot dishes. Try their specialty, *nockerl* (60-87AS). The **Happy Chinese Restaurant,** Völauerstr. 19 (tel. 873 76), around the bend from Josefpl., has a refreshing garden overlooking a babbling brook, and a cheap lunch *menu* (50AS): soup, spring roll, and main course (open daily 11:30am-2:30pm and 5:30-11:30pm). **Bier-Pub Einhorn,** Josefpl. 3, is where the nightlife is to be found, if "nightlife" is really the word for it. Go for snacks (38-120AS), drinks, and the saloon-like decor (open Mon.-Thurs. 10:30am-2am, Fri. 10:30am-4am, Sat. 9:30am-4am, Sun. 4pm-2am). Cheap food is also to be found at all of the *"Buschenschanken."* For a bite to eat on the run, **Billa** is at Wassergasse 14 on the way from the train station to the pedestrian zone (open Mon.-Thurs. 7:30am-6:30pm, Fri. 7:30am-8pm, Sat. 7am-1pm). A fresh **farmer's market** rests at Grüner Markt (Mon.-Fri. 8am-7pm, Sat. 8am-1pm).

Sights and Entertainment The baths were the biggest attraction back in the days of Mozart and Beethoven (and even the days of the Romans), and remain the bait that draws guests today. The sulfur springs burst forth at a natural temperature of 36°C. Though they smell like sulfur (bad), they're warm and relaxing and good for you. The visitors who keep to a budget can take advantage of two outdoor thermal pools; the largest one, the **Strandbad,** is at Helenenstr. 19-21 where the common visitor can splash around in the hot sulfur thermal pool, and then cool down in the normal chlorine pools. It's very Roman. (Entrance: whole day Mon.-Fri. 79AS, Sat.-Sun. 92AS. After 1pm, 66AS and 79AS, respectively. Swimming pool only, 25AS.) For a smaller outdoor thermal experience, visit the pool at Marchetstr. 13 (49AS), behind the Kurdirection. The **Kurdirektion** itself, at Brusattipl. 4 (tel. 445 31) is the center of all curative spa treatments. It houses an indoor thermal pool mostly used for patients, but is also open to common visitors (72AS). Underwater massage therapy (295AS), sulfur mud baths (305AS), regular or "sport" massages (310AS) are all offered. Some resort hotels also have private thermal pools; ask at the tourist office for the list of exorbitant prices.

Baden has a lovely pedestrian area, centered around the Hauptpl., containing the **Dreifaltigkeitsäule** (trinity column), a *Pestsäule* (plague column) erected in 1718 as a sign of thanks to God that the plague spared Baden. The Hauptplatz also contains the **Rathaus** and Franz Josef I's summer residence at #17. Around the corner at Rathausgasse 10 is the **Beethovenhaus,** the house in which the composer spent his summers from 1804-1825, and one of the few lodgings he wasn't thrown out of for continuously making music (pesky kid). Beethoven composed part of the *Missa Solemnis* and much of his *Ninth Symphony* here. Come visit the museum and view tasteful relics such as the composer's death mask and locks of his hair (open Tues.-Fri. 4-6pm, Sat.-Sun. and holidays 9-11am and 4-6pm.)

North of the Hauptplatz via Maria-Theresa-Gasse, lies the glory of Baden, the **Kurpark.** Set into the southeast edge of the Wienerwald, this meticulously landscaped garden is a shady delight for leisurely strollers. It houses a monument to Mozart and to Beethoven. The park is also a gambler's joy: the **Casino** lies within its grounds. Entrance is free, and a variety of betting tables have different stakes (must be 19 or over, semi-formal dress required). Underneath the casino are the **Römer Quelle** (Roman Springs) where water gushes forth from the rock. The delightful **Theresien-**

garten was laid out in 1792, when the Kurpark was still called "Theresienbad." The **flower clock** in the middle of the Kurpark grass began ticking in 1929. The park became an important frolic zone in Europe when the Congress of Vienna met in the early 19th century; the highest-ranking European political figures were granted permission to escort the Imperial Court here. After Sunday Mass, throngs of townsfolk would gather to watch the dignitaries strut through the park. The **Emperor Franz-Josef Museum,** Hochstr. 51 (tel. 411 00), perches atop the Badener Berg at the end of the park (follow signs through the "Sommerarena" via Zöllner and Suckfüllweg), and holds exhibitions of folk art, such as weapons, sacred art, and a history of photography (open Apr.-Oct. Tues.-Sun. 1-7pm; Nov.-Mar. Tues.-Sun. 11am-5pm). A **Doll and Toy Museum,** Erzherzog-Rainer-Str. 23 (tel. 410 20), displays over 300 dolls from different countries, including a 12mm doll made in the South Tirol in the early 1800s. Also in the collection are teddy bears, Japanese ceremonial dolls, and marionettes from Prague (open Tues.-Fri. 4-6pm, Sat.-Sun. and holidays 9-11am and 4-6pm).

Baden's **Beethoven Festival** takes place from mid-Sept. to early Oct., with performances by famous Austrian artists. Not to be outdone, the Town Theater features Beethoven films during the festival. (For ticket reservations, contact: Kulturamt der Stadtgemeinde Baden, Hauptpl. 1, A-2500 Baden; tel. 86 80 02 31; fax 86 80 02 10.) From late June to mid-Sept., the **Summer Arena,** inside the Kurpark grounds, offers a magnificent, open-air setting for performances of classic Viennese operettas, including works by Fall and Lehár. (Tickets 90-420AS, standing room 30AS.) For tickets, call 485 47, stop by the box office in the Stadttheater on Kaiser-Franz-Ring-Str., or write to: Stadttheater Baden Kartenbüro, Theaterpl. 7, A-2500 Baden (open Tues.-Sat. 10am-noon and 5-6pm, Sun. and holidays 10am-noon). Or get last minute tickets 30 minutes before the concert at the door. On summer days, Baden's **orchestra** performs four or five concerts a week, weather permitting.

In the blooming days of June, Baden holds the **Badener Rosentage,** a multi-week celebration of local roses at the height of the season. The wide range of activities are in most cases free. World class horse racing also occurs near the Casino from May to Sept. Call 887 73 or 886 97 for more specifics.

In Sept., Baden hosts **Grape Cure Week,** a Bacchanalian gathering of stands from local wineries in the Hauptplatz, all selling fresh grapes and grape juice (open daily 8am-6pm; first 500 guests get free grape juice). The idea is that one needs to periodically irrigate one's system, and the best way to do this is by eating a lot of grapes (1kg of grapes per day; this increases to 2kg within three weeks!). It is thought that this fights off disease and provides the body with essential nutrients. Some take the cure to heart, but for most, it's an excuse to party.

For more details, stop by one of the *"Buschenschanken."* Baden rules state that the individual *Lokalen* can only stay open for two weeks at a time, which they do on a rotating schedule, available at the tourist office. Look for the gathered branches outside the doors indicating that the store is open. The nearby town of **Sooß** is filled to the brim with *Heurigen,* all along the Haupstr. Reach Sooß by walking or biking across the Radweg (Schimmergasse) off Josefpl (20min. by bike, 1hr. on foot).

■ Eisenstadt

> *Where I wish to live and die.*
>
> —Josef Haydn

Haydn, *Heurigen,* and Huns are three H's that pushed Eisenstadt into cultural significance. It was here that **Josef Haydn** composed the melodies that inspired Mozart. His wish to live and die in Eisenstadt was happily met by the **Esterházy** family for whom he worked. The Esterházys were powerful Hungarian landholders who to this day are one of the wealthiest families in Europe. The family was instrumental in helping the Habsburgs maintain their power. They first lived in Eisenstadt when it was part of Hungary, and decided to keep their palace even when borders changed. Today they own many of the vineyards that made the region famous. The grapes that grow in this area make divine **heurige** (new wine), which many compare to the wine produced in Bordeaux.

Orientation and Practical Information Situated only 50 kilometers from Vienna, Eisenstadt is centered around the Hauptstraße, which is the major component of the city's pedestrian zone. To get there from the train station, leave the front door of the Bahnhof and follow Bahnstr. (which becomes St. Martinstr. and Fanny Eißlergasse) to its middle (10-15min. walk). When you enter Hauptstr., the **Schloß Esterházy** will be on your left at the end of the street. Find the **tourist office,** Franz Schubertpl. 2 (tel. 673 90; fax 673 91), by going right onto Hauptstr., crossing Lisztgasse, walking through the rather uninteresting Colmarplatz, and then going left past the Hotel Burgenland. The office will be on your left, inconspicuously sheltered under the burgundy aura of the hotel. The people here are extremely friendly and speak English. If you are in a bind, they will help you make a reservation. They have prepared lots of information including lists of accommodations, musical events, tours upon reservation (500 AS) and *Heurigen* calendar. (Open May-Oct. Mon.-Sat. 9am-5pm, Sun. 9am-1pm.)

To get to Eisenstadt **by car,** take Bundesstr. 16 from Vienna south. From Wiener Neustadt, take Bundesstr. 153 east. There is an underground **parking garage** conveniently located just outside the Esterházy Palace in the Zentrum (25AS per hour). The **train station** is a bit of a walk away from the city center at the end of Bahnstr. A direct train leaves from **Wien Meidling** in Vienna roughly 2-3 times per hour (1hr.; 69AS). Another option is to take a train from the Vienna Südbahnhof (1½hr., hourly, 68AS) and switch trains in Neusiedl am See. Connections to **Vienna Süd** (1½hr., hourly, 68AS) can be made in Neusiedl am See (17AS). The train station **rents bikes** (100AS per day, 50AS with train ticket, or 150-200AS for a mountain bike), **stores luggage** (30AS per bag per day), and happily dispenses train information (open Mon.-Fri.7:30am-8:15pm, Sat.-Sun. 8:40am-8:15pm, or call 626 37). The **bus station** (tel. 23 50) is located on the Dompl. next to the *Dom,* down Pfarrgasse from Esterházypl. A bus information office is there to answer questions about bus schedules and prices (open Mon.-Fri. 9am-noon and 2-4:30pm; tel. 623 50). Buses run to **Rust, Mörbisch, Wiener Neustadt, Vienna,** and other destinations (consult information office for prices and times). **Telephones** are located at the post office, Hauptpl., the Bahnhof, and just outside the Esterházy Palace. The best exchange rates are available at **Creditanstalt Bankverein** on the corner of St. Martin and Dompl. (open Mon.-Thurs. 8am-1pm and 2-4pm, Fri. 8am-3pm). Public **bathrooms** are at Dompl., the Esterházy Palace, and the parking lot behind Colmanpl. near the tourist office. The **post office** (tel. 651 71), is located near the other end of Hauptstr., on the corner of Pfarrgasse and Semmelweise. It has telephones, and package services and the best rates for traveler's checks. (Open Mon.-Fri. 7am-7pm, Sat. 7am-1pm.) **Postal code:** A-7000. **Telephone code:** 02682.

Accommodations and Food With no youth hostel in the vicinity, the next cheapest thing is to rent a *Privatzimmer,* but there are very few of these. Most are on the outer city limits, and they are limited to renting space only during July and Aug. The youth hostels in **Neusiedl am See** (tel. 22 52) and **Wiener Neustadt** (tel. 296 95) are cheaper and only one hour away. Definitely consider Eisenstadt as a day trip.

During July and Aug., booking in advance is recommended to avoid getting shut out by itinerant throngs. A friendly manager tends bar at **Hotel Franz Mayr,** Kalvarienbergpl. 1 (tel. 627 51), directly across from the Bergkirche. All rooms have shower and toilet. (Singles 400AS. Doubles 700AS. Triples 850AS. Quads 900AS. Breakfast included. Reservations recommended.) At **Wirtshaus zum Eder,** Hauptstr. 25 (tel. 626 45), centrally located in the Hauptpl., one can engage in deep conversation over wine in the airy courtyard, with its oil paintings and clean, white awnings. (Singles 440-590AS. Doubles 590AS. Triples 790AS. Breakfast included.)

Gasthaus Kiss, Neusiedlerstr. 34 (tel. 61 182), cooks up huge servings of hearty Austrian food in a snug inn. **Café Central**, Hauptstr. 40 (tel. 645 08), despite its rip-off of the Viennese coffee klatch location extraordinaire of the same name, is a pleasant, unassuming little café in a shady, walled courtyard off of the main street. It draws a mainly student crowd with offerings such as hot milk and rum (31AS) and a filling tuna salad (42AS). The **Schloß-café,** is at the corner of Museumgasse and Unterbergstr., just down the street from the Landesmuseum. The run-down decadence of its dark brown, ersatz marble, cloth topped tables, and chairs the color of green watered silk, is simply from another era. Linger and wait for Altenberg or Trotsky to walk in the door. Prices are old-fashionedly low, too. Eisenstadt also has a few grocery stores: **Spar Markt,** at Esterházystr. 38 and on Bahnstr. 16-18 (open Mon.-Fri. 7am-12:30pm and 2-6pm, Sat. 7am-noon), and **Julius Meinl,** at Hauptstr. 13 (open Mon.-Fri. 8am-6pm, Sat. 7:30-noon). Along with a cool, crisp glass of wine, one can get a modest and decently priced bite to eat at one of the many **Heurigen.**

Sights and Entertainment Schloß Esterházy is still owned by the Esterházys, an aristocratic family claiming descent from Atilla the Hun. In a fit of largesse they leased the family home to the provincial government, giving the public access to some of its magnificent rooms. The government occupies 40% of the castle. Some rooms are used for office space, the others are opened to the public. The remaining 60% is still the private living space of the Esterhàzy family. The government thought they were getting a good deal when they completed the bargain at a cool 125,000AS, but the wily Esterhàzys had inserted a clause in the lease that made the government responsible for the cost of renovating and keeping up their part of the house. Rumor has it the government has spent more than 40 million shillings on the upkeep of just the silk tapestry in the Red Salon.

Built on the footings of the Kanizsai family's 14th-century fortress, the castle-turned-palace was only painted the cheerful hue it is today when the Esterhàzy family showed allegiance to the great Austrian Empress in the 18th century by painting it *Maria Theresien gelb,* or Maria Theresian yellow. Probably the most famous and most magnificent room of the palace is the **Haydnsaal** (Haydn Hall), where the hard-working composer conducted the court orchestra almost every night from 1761 to 1790. The Haydnsaal is considered *the* acoustic mecca for classical musicians. When the government took over the room, the marble floor was removed and replaced with a wooden one. Now the room is so acoustically perfect that seats for concerts in the room are not numbered—supposedly every seat provides the same magnificent sound. Guests are invited to sing, or, failing that (they usually do), a piece of Haydn's is played, so that they may wander and revel in acoustic perfection. Even when the music stops, the room is still a Baroque symphony of red velvet, gold, monumental oil paintings, and careful woodwork. (Tours of the *Schloß* daily every hr. 9am-4:30pm; 40AS, students and seniors 30AS. Tour lasts 40 min. and includes a number of splendid reception rooms designed to showcase the Esterhàzy wealth.)

Though the *Kapellmeister* was employed in the palace's concert hall, he actually lived around the corner. His modest residence has been converted into the **Haydn-Haus,** Haydngasse 21 (tel. 626 52), exhibiting some of his manuscripts and other memorabilia. Though the occupants who came after Haydn added on to the house, most of the articles are originals. (Open Easter-Oct. daily 9am-noon and 1-5pm. 30AS, students 15AS. A combi-ticket for the Haydnmuseum and the Landesmuseum is 40AS, students 20AS.) Having composed in Eisenstadt, Haydn now decomposes there. The *maestro* lies buried in the **Bergkirche** (tel. 626 38), placed there in 1932 after scientists had removed his head searching for manifestations of musical genius on the skull's surface. For years, it was on display at the Vienna Music Museum (look Mommy, it's Haydn's brain!)—fortunately, body and head were reunited in 1954. (Church open Easter-Oct. daily 9am-noon and 1-5pm. 20AS, students 10AS.) Entrance fee to the Bergkirche also allows admission to the **Kalvarienberg,** an annex to the Bergkirche where one finds the 12 Stations of the Cross. The fixed yet passionate expressions on the hand-carved biblical figures' faces gives this extended shrine a peculiarly disturbing impact. Stand in the central nave to see if you can tell which of the Doric columns are real and which are painted on the wall.

The **Jüdisches Museum,** Unterbergstr. 6 (tel. 651 45), celebrates the Austrian Jewish heritage, with an emphasis on religious holidays. A small synagogue and a disturbing black room, with a Nazi banner proclaiming Jewish undesirability, complete the collection. (Open May-Sept. Tues.-Sun. 10am-5pm. 50AS, students 40AS.) Around the corner on Wertheimer-Str., near the hospital, is a small **Jewish cemetery** with headstones dating back several decades. The old Esterházy family in Eisenstadt was known for its hospitality toward Jews, a hospitality that played a major part in their rise to power.

For a more frivolous way to spend the afternoon, stop by the **Burgenländische Feuerwehrmuseum** at Leithabergstr. 41 (tel. 62 105). Austria's first fire-fighting museum displays cute little fire-buggies— cross-bred offspring of a steam engine and a circus wagon. Also on hand are spectacular fire helmets; certainly these were worn by Greek gods, not mere mortals. (Open Mon.-Fri. 10am-noon and 1-4pm.)

Eisenstadt certainly celebrates Haydn's life. From May to Oct., there are **Haydnmatinees** (tel. 633 84 15; fax 633 84 20) in which four fine fellows, bewigged and bejeweled in baroque costumes of imperial splendor, bring you half an hour of impeccable Haydn. And you thought KISS had great stage gear. (Tues. and Fri. 11am in Schloß Esterházy. 80AS.) There are also **Haydnkonzerte** at the Schloß (May, June, Sept. and Oct. Sat. at 7:30pm; July and Aug. Thurs. at 8pm. 80-250AS. No shows in the winter; the place is impossible to heat.) True Haydn enthusiasts should visit from when the delicate tapestry of sound from Eisenstadt's favorite can be savored during the **International Haydntage 1997.** Schedule also available at the tourist office; tickets run 160-1000AS.

Of course, leaving Eisenstadt without wine is like leaving Linz without the *torte*. Plan to visit Eisenstadt in late June during **Bergler Kirtag,** a big bash when every local winery floods the Hauptplatz with stands of kegs, flasks and bottles to sell their goods. If you miss this, try again in mid-Aug. during the **Festival of 1000 Wines,** when wineries from all over Burgenland crowd the Orangerie of the Schloß with their Dionysian delicacies. At any other time of the year, fresh wine is available straight from the source in the local wineries themselves. Most are small and aren't allowed to open for more than three weeks per year to sell their wine. Fear not, however—the wineries stagger their opening times so that wine is always available. To find out which *Buschenschank,* or *Schenkhaus,* is open, ask the tourist office for the schedule, or look in the local newspaper. Most of the *Buschenschanken* are clustered in Kleinhöfler Hauptstraße. If you like music with your wine, visit during the month of June when the **Eisen Stadt Fest** provides all kinds of sounds from *schrammelmusik* to rock.

NEUSIEDLER SEE

Covering 320 square km, the Neusiedler See is a vestige of the body of water that once blanketed the entire Pannenian Plain. With no outlets or inlets save underground springs, this steppe lake is only two meters at its deepest; it periodically recedes to expose thousands of square meters of dry land—indeed, in the mid-19th century, the lake desiccated entirely. Warm and salty, the lake is a haven for birds and humans alike. More than 250 species of waterfowl dwell in the thickets formed by its reeds, and every summer thousands of sun-hungry vacationers flock to various resorts for swimming, sailing, fishing, and cycling.

■ Neusiedl am See

Less than an hour from Vienna by express train, Neusiedl am See is the gateway to the Neusiedler region. The principle attraction here is the lake itself, not the town, so consider Neusiedl a day at the beach. There are two train stations in Neusiedl. The first, the **Hauptbahnhof,** is located 15 minutes by foot from the center of town. (Service to and from Eisenstadt 17AS; to Vienna 68AS round-trip 98AS.) **Luggage storage** is available at 30AS per day (information and ticket window open daily 5am-9pm). To get to town, take a right onto Bahnstr., follow the slope of the road right onto Eisen-städterstr. which will become Obere Hauptstr. and then the Hauptplatz.

The **tourist office,** in the Rathaus on the Hauptplatz (tel. 22 29; fax 26 37), distrib-utes pamphlets about the resort town, provides assistance with accommodations and offers advice on boat and bike rental. (Open July-Aug. Mon.-Fri. 8am-7pm, Sat. 10am-noon, 2-6pm and Sun. 4-7pm; May-June and Sept. Mon.-Fri. 8am-4:30pm; Oct.-April Mon.-Thurs. 8am-noon and 1-4:30pm, Fri. 8am-1pm.) **Raffeisbank,** Untere Hauptstr. 3 (tel. 25 64), has the best rates for your ducats. The other **train station** and the adja-cent **bus station** are located by making a right at the end of Untere Hauptstr. onto Seestr. As this is more central to the town, you might want to see if your train stops at **Neusiedl Bad.** The bus station, Seestr. 15a (tel. 24 06), also offers a **Fahrradbus** which carries bikers and their metallic steed on bus #1173 to and from Mörbisch and Neusiedl. Also service to Vienna (85AS) and Bruck an der Leitha hourly (34AS). As the town is spread out, it may make your day easier to rent a bike at **Radverleih Imbiß,** to the right of the train station (160AS per day). Dial 133 in case of **emergency.** The **post office,** on the corner of Untere Hauptstr. and Lisztgasse, has a small **telephone center.** (Open Mon.-Fri. 8am-noon and 2-6pm, Sat. 8-10am.) **Postal code:** A-7100. **Telephone code:** 02167.

You're here, you've got your bathing suit and towel, now where's the **beach?** Head down Seestr., all the way to the end (1km), or catch the bus from the Hauptbahnhof and the Hauptplatz that runs hourly until 6pm. The beach is a bit rocky, but still pleas-ant (admission 12AS, children 4AS). The **Segelschule Neusiedl am See** (tel. 87 60) located at the docks farthest to the right will get you out on the water in a laser, Hobie Cat, or sailboard. (1hr. 140-340AS, half or full day 345-1730AS; open daily 8:30am-6pm.) Close by, there are also **motorboats** (130-150AS per hr.), **paddleboats** (80AS per hr.), and **rowboats** (40AS per hr.) at **Bootsvermietung Leban,** down by the end of Seestr.

Heavy tourist activity, partly assured by Neusiedl's proximity to Vienna, makes find-ing accommodations trying. To reach the newly renovated **Jugendherberge Neusiedl am See (HI),** Herberggasse 1 (tel./fax 22 52), find Wienerstr., and then take a left onto Goldberggasse. The hostel is on the corner of Goldberggasse and Herberggasse. It's an uphill walk, but don't get discouraged—the renovations have equipped the hostel with a sauna and winter greenhouse, both adequate spots to unlace your smoking boots and stretch out tired toes. The hostel sports 86 beds in 20 quads and three doubles. There are showers in every room, but the bathrooms are on the hall. (Reception open daily 8am-2pm and 5-10pm. 161AS. Under 19 145AS. Breakfast included. Sheets 15AS. Key deposit 100AS. Reservations recommended. Open March-Oct.) **Gasthof zur Traube,** Hauptpl. 9 (tel. 24 23), has a cordial staff and nice, pink rooms, each replete with a shower and toilet. 315AS. (Prices drop after four nights; add 10AS in high season. Breakfast included.) **Rathausstüberl** (tel. 28 83; fax 28 83 07), around the corner from the Rathaus on Kirchengasse, has a lovely shaded court-yard and great wine and food, including plenty of fresh fish and vegetarian dishes. Dig the plastic lobster and rainbow fish display out front. (Entrées 70-150AS. Open March-Dec. daily 10am-midnight.) Rathausstüberl doubles as a sunny *Pension* as well. 315-355AS per person with breakfast buffet (reservations recommended). On your way to the beach pick up a picnic at **Billa** grocery store on Seestr. (Open Mon.-Thurs. 7:30am- 6:30pm, Fri. 7:30am-8pm, Sat. 7am-1pm.)

■ Rust

During the summer, tourists inundate this tiny, self-appointed wine capital of Austria to partake of the fruit of the vine. Ever since 1524, when the Emperor granted the wine-growers of Rust the exclusive right to display the letter "R" on their wine bar-rels, Rust has been synonymous with good wine— make that really good wine. The town is particularly known for its production of sweet dessert wines, styled *"Aus-*

bruch" (literally "break out"). These wines are very high in quality because the grapes are allowed to dry up and sweeten a bit more than regular wine-grapes (on their way to raisin-hood). Then the center is "broken-out" and its juice is pressed. The quantity of dessicated grapes needed for a bottle is astounding, resulting in the high cost of the area's wine. The income from the wine (or maybe its inebriating qualities) enabled the town to purchase its independence from Kaiser Leopold I in 1861. The price: 60,000 gold guilders and 30,000 liters of the priceless "Ausbruch" wine. (Leopold: "Quick, my corkscrew!")

Wine isn't Rust's only attraction, however. The town's beautifully unspoiled and relatively untouristed town center, with its medieval houses and nesting storks, not to mention Rust's location smack on the top source of the prime bathing areas in the *Neusiedlersee,* make this one of the most addictively beautiful places of the Austrian countryside.

Orientation and Practical Information Rust is 10 kilometers east of Eisenstadt on the Neusiedler See. **By car** from Eisenstadt, take Bundesstr. 52 straight into Rust. From Vienna, take Autobahn A4 to Neusiedl am See, Bundesstr. 50 south until Seehof, and then follow signs. **Buses** run between Eisenstadt and Rust several times per day (34AS), between Rust and Vienna (Wien Mitte/Landstraße) four times a day (120AS), and once per day to and from Neusiedl am See (52AS). Rust does not have a train station. The **bus station** is located just behind the post office at Franz-Josef-Pl. 14. (The trip between Rust and Neusiedl am See takes roughly 30 min.) To reach the award-winning *Fußgängerzone,* leave the post office and turn left. You will almost immediately come to an intersection of Oggauerstr. and Conradplatz. Take a left onto Conradpl. until you come to a triangular platz. In front of you will be the **Rathaus.** The **tourist office** *(Gästeinformation),* inside the *Rathaus* (tel. 65 74; fax 502), hands out maps, plans bicycle tours, and gives out information on wine tastings, the beach, and *Privatzimmer* lists (open Mon.-Fri. 9am-noon and 2-6pm, Sat. 9am-1pm, Sun. 10am-noon; Oct.-April Mon.-Fri. 8am-noon and 1-4pm). The hyperbionic display board outside the tourist office displays all the best accomodations; green lights indicate vacancies. The best place to **exchange money** is at the **Raiffeisenkasse Rust,** Rathauspl. 5 (tel. 285), open Mon.-Fri. 8am-noon and 1:30-4pm. The Raiffeisenkasse also has a 24hr. **ATM. Reisbüro Blaguss** in the Rathaus and the **Ruster Freizeitcenter** office by the beach (tel. 595; open 8am-10pm) are open late, providing cash exchange in an emergency. The **post office** has a **telephone** center and will exchange money but not traveler's checks. (Open Mon.-Fri. 8am-noon and 2-6pm.) **Postal code: A-7071. Telephone code: 02685.**

Accommodations and Food Tourists pack Rust in July and Aug., but a spot in one of Rust's 1200 beds is usually available. If not, try the **Jugendherberge** in **Neusiedl am See** (tel. (02167) 2252; 145AS per night). Rust's hostel recently closed, so a reservation at one of the many *Privatzimmer* is strongly recommended. Be warned: prices in the high season are bound to rise. **Haus Rennhofer,** Am Hafen 9 (tel. 316), has small rooms conveniently located on the street closest to the shore. Rooms are clean and airy, most with balconies; there's also a sunbathing yard. (Singles, doubles, and triples 160AS per person, breakfast and showers included.) Down the street, **Haus Schuh,** Am Hafen 13 (tel. 61 93), has two double bedrooms with private baths, toilets, and balconies. (160AS. Breakfast included.) There's always room for tent-dwellers at **Ruster Freizeitcenter** (tel. 595), which offers warm showers, washing machines, a game room, a playground, and a grocery store. (Reception open 7:30am-10pm. 44-55AS. Children 16-27AS. Tent 38-44AS. Showers included.) The campgrounds are conveniently located about 5 minutes away from the beach. Camping guests receive free entrance into the beach area.

For the truly hungry, **Zum Alten Haus,** corner of Raiffenstr. and Franz Josefpl. (tel. 230), serves up gargantuan portions (we're not kidding!) of *Schnitzel* and salad for only 80AS. (Open Tues.-Sun. 9am-10pm.) Since they're not selling wine to Kaiser Leopold anymore, the local vineyards opt to open a restaurant instead called a *Bus-*

chenschenk (tavern) where one can grab a small inexpensive snack along with superb wine. To avoid being taxed as full-fledged restaurants *Buschenschenken* are allowed to stay open, or *"ausg'steckt,"* for six months per year in Rust. The calendar detailing openings is available at the tourist office. For the ultimate in elegance, allow yourself to be seated at **Peter Schandl,** Hauptstr. 20 (tel. 265). Fresh, white, outdoor seating. Beautiful salads. Heavenly wine. A bit on the more expensive end, but a wonderful experience (wine from 16AS; 70AS for the classic Ausbruch). Or come to the corn-cob hung **Alte Schmiede,** (tel. 467) at Seestr. 24. Both the courtyard roofed with live grape vines and the stone-and-wood interior are funky. Listen to the daily (often live) gypsy music while feasting on traditional Austrian food with a Hungarian twist (also a variety of vegetarian dishes). **A & O Markt Dreyseitel,** on Weinberggasse between Mittergasse and Schubertgasse (tel. 238), sells the raw materials for a meal (open Mon.-Fri. 7am-noon and 3-6pm).

Sights and Entertainment By day, Rust's visitors enjoy any one of a number of outdoor activities. Sun bunnies enjoy lounging and splashing on the south shore of the **Neusiedler See.** There is a **public beach** (tel. 591; fax 59 14) complete with showers, lockers, WC, telephones, water slide, and snackbar (30AS per person, after 4pm 70AS). Though the murky waters of the lake daunt some swimmers, the water is actually of drinking quality. The muddy color comes from the shallow, clay bottom that is easily disturbed (the deepest section is 2m). For those still not convinced, the beach also has a chlorine pool. Be sure to keep track of the entrance card with its metallic strip—you'll need it to exit the park again. To reach the beach, walk down the Hauptstraße, take a left onto Am Seekanal and a right onto Seepromenade. Seepromenade is the street that cuts through all of the marsh lands (about 7km) surrounding the perimeter of the lake. These marsh reeds (which sometimes are almost 2m high) make it a bug-infested place, inconvenient for bathing anywhere other than at the designated areas.

The **storks,** some of Rust's most favored guests, however, thrive from this vegetation. These large, white, majestic birds have been nesting atop the chimneys for years; signs on the corner of Seezeile and Hauptstr. indicate their rooftop hangouts. Locals began to voice their concern over the dwindling number of these endangered birds; so in 1987, Rust and the **World Wildlife Federation** initiated a special joint program to protect the storks and eventually increase their number. The program involved fudging with nature's delicately balanced ecological system. The storks eat mainly frogs, fish, snakes, and beetles—critters found mostly amongst Neusiedler See's reedy marshes. When the reeds grew too tall, the storks had difficulty finding food. So, the city of Rust borrowed cattle from another part of Austria and plunked them down in the marshes to act as natural lawnmowers. They are proud to announce that their tampering is working; nine pairs of storks came to roost in 1996, hatching 20 little storklings (question: who brings the storks *their* babies?) The storks, aside from their storklings, have hatched a second post office, the "**Storks' Post Office,** A-7073 Rust," at the Rathaus. You can support the birds by having your mail delivered with the stork postmark.

If lounging at the beach strikes you as too inactive, try **renting a boat** from **Family Gmeiner** next to the beach on the water's edge (tel. 493 or (62683) 55 38). **Sailboats** are 90AS per hour or 270AS for five hours. **Paddleboats** are 70AS per hour and 270AS for five hours. **Electric boats** are 110AS per hour and 330AS for five hours. The same company also runs **Schiffsrundfahrten** (boat tours) which will tour the lake or transport you to Illmitz on the opposite shore. Boats leave Rust every Tues., Fri.-Sun. and Holidays at 10am and 4pm. Return from Illmitz at 11am and 5pm. (Boats run April 30-Sept. 25.) Besides swimming, boating, and bird-watching, tourists flock to the Neusiedler See area to go **biking.** The lake area is criss-crossed with bicycle routes, many along the lake shore or winding their way in and out of the little towns of both Austria and Hungary. The route is about 170km in its entirety, but families and those out for less intense biking can do a part of the stretch and then take the bus back, or take the Illwitz boat to the opposite shore and then bicycle back. Buses to Neusiedl am See (one in the morning and one in the afternoon, approximately 9am and 4pm) have bike racks set up inside and a big sign saying *"FAHRRADBUS"* (bikebus) on the windshield. For more bus information, call the information number (tel. (02167) 24 18) or the Neusiedl office (tel. 24 06 540).

Rust's name is derived from the word for "elm tree," as is its Hungarian moniker, "Szil." Early morning strolls down the 16th-century elm-lined streets of the *Altstadt* are accompanied by chiming church bells and crowing roosters. The *Altstadt* is one of the three in Austria to have won the title of *"Modelstadt"* from the Europa-Rat committee in Strasbourg (the other two cities are Salzburg and Krems). The award praises the preservation of traditional Austrian buildings. To learn more, participate in one of the hour-long **tours,** featuring discussions of Rust's history, culture, wine, and storks (May-Sept. Wed. and Sat. 10am at the tourist office; 25AS, with guest card 20AS). Tours are ordinarily only offered in German, but English tours can be arranged for groups of 10 or more. Wine garden tours are offered Thurs. at 6pm at **Familie Just** and Friday at 5pm at **Familie Beilschmidt's.**

Rust's **Fischerkirche,** around the corner from the tourist office, was built between the 12th and 16th centuries; it's the oldest church in Burgenland. Because Rust is such a small town, the Romanesque and Gothic sections have survived untouched by the ravages of Baroque remodeling. Check out the beautiful medieval frescoes and the brick floor. (100AS, students 50AS; tour 5AS; open May-Sept. Mon.-Sat. 10am-noon and 2:30-6pm, Sun. 11am-noon and 2:30-6pm; Oct.-April Mon.-Fri. 11am-noon and 2-3pm, Sun. 11am-noon and 2-4pm.) The tours are by pre-arrangement only. Call Frau Kummer (tel. 550).

Rust also houses the only **Weinakademie** in Austria. This institution offers different courses to teach people about wine, including everything from how to cultivate it to basic bartending and legal points. They also hold wine tours and tastings in the region. The offices are at Hauptstr. 31 (tel. 64 51 or 453; fax 64 31. Open July to mid-Sept. daily 2-4pm, Oct.-June Sat.-Sun. and holidays 2-4pm; 60-80AS for 5-10 tastes.) Many town vintners *(Weinbauer)* offer wine tastings and tours of their cellars and vineyards. **Rudolf Beilschmidt,** Weinberggasse 1 (tel. 326), is one such proprietor (tours May-Sept. every Fri. at 5pm). **Familie Just,** Weinberggasse 16 (tel. 251), also offers vineyard tours and tastings (April-Sept. every Tues. at 6pm; 60AS).

■ Near Rust: Mörbisch

The tiny village of Mörbisch lies five kilometers along the Neusiedler See to the south, easily within cycling distance of Rust. Buses from Eisenstadt to Mörbisch leave every two hours (18AS). From Neusiedl am See to Mörbisch buses leave twice per day (22AS), and many buses go through the Rust-Mörbisch stretch (17AS) on their way to other places. However, a walk from Rust along the five-kilometer country lane to Mörbisch can easily be done (about 1½hr.) and provides a fantastic foray into the countryside. The road, usually used by small vineyard tractors and the worn-out country bikes of the vineyard wives, runs through the fertile vines that have brought such fame to the region. Take a look at the *Hütterhütte* (stone huts) where young men would spend weeks of their lives in solitude, guarding the wine grapes from man and bird. Whitewashed houses, brightly painted doors, and dried corn hanging from the walls mark the village, the last settlement on the western shore of the lake before the Hungarian border. The village is centered around Hauptstraße. On this street one finds the **tourist office,** at #23 (tel. (02685) 88 56; fax 84 039). It has very helpful brochures on Mörbisch and the surrounding Burgenland region, as well as a list of accommodations. (Open July-Aug. daily 9am-6pm; May-June and Sept. Mon.-Fri. 9am-5pm, Sat. 9am-1pm; April and Oct. Mon.-Fri. 9am-5pm.) The town also has its own beach, whose biggest draw is its floating theater. Each summer, it hosts an operetta festival—the **Mörbisch Seefestspiele.** The operetta slated for 1997 is *Pariser Leben* by Jacques Offenbach. Performances float atop the See every Friday, Saturday, and Sunday from July 11 to Aug. 24, 1997. Tickets run from 200-700AS, and can be ordered by calling the tourist office or from the Burgenland information center at

Schloß Esterházy in Eisenstadt (see Eisenstadt, p. 306). **Blaguss Reisen** in Vienna (tel. (02682) 662 10; fax 662 10-14) arranges a shuttle bus to Mörbisch at 6pm from Wiedner Hauptstr. 15 in Vienna. It returns after the fat lady has sung (180AS round trip). Reserve a seat when ordering tickets.

THE DANUBE (DONAU)

The "Blue Danube" is largely the invention of Johann Strauss's imagination, but this mighty, muddy-green river still merits a cruise. The legendary **Erste Donau Dampfschiffahrts-Gesellschaft (DDSG)** runs ships daily from May to late Oct. The firm operates an office in **Vienna,** II, Handelskai 265, by the Reichsbrücke (tel. (0222) 727 50; fax 218 92 38). Cruises run from Vienna, passing Krems and Melk en route. East of Vienna, hydrofoils run to Bratislava, Slovakia and Budapest, Hungary. All of the cruises are expensive (at least double the train fare); fortunately, Eurail passes are valid on river jaunts. Families may travel for half-price (minimum one parent and one child ages 6-15; children under 6 accompanied by a parent travel free). **Bicycle rental** is possible at the Melk, Spitz, and Krems docks (combined with cruise 35AS per day, each additional day 70AS; without a cruise 150AS; bring a private bike on board for 35AS). Pets pay half fare, though Rufus will have to wear a muzzle, available on board, at all times during the cruise.

The **ferries** run from Vienna to Krems (5hr. upstream, 4hr. downstream; round-trip 318AS) and from Krems to Melk (3hr. upstream, 2hr. downstream; round-trip 230AS). Express boats will take you to Bratislava (1hr.45min., 330AS) or Budapest (6hr. upstream, 5hr. downstream, one-way 750AS, round-trip 1100AS). Children and seniors are eligible for a further 50% off. See the DDSG and tourist offices for prices on other special ship/bus and ship/train ticket combinations. Specialty tours include the Nibelungen tour, which goes through the areas described in the saga, a summer solstice cruise (Sonnendfahrt), which steams by the solstice bonfires in the Wachau valley during the shortest night of the year, and a Henrigen Ride with a live *Liederabend* trio. To really bury yourself in Austrian culture, however, strap on your blue suede shoes for "The King Lives" tour with a crew of Elvis imitators. Find out how "Hunk a' hunk a' burnin' love" sounds with a German accent on this Blue Hawaii meets the Blue Danube extravaganza.

Cyclists should take advantage of the **Lower Danube Cycle Track,** a velocipede's Valhalla. This riverside bike trail between Vienna and Naarn links several Danube villages, including Melk and Dürnstein. The ride offers captivating views of crumbling castles, latticed vineyards, and medieval towns, but your attention is inevitably drawn back to the majestic current of the river. Ask at any area tourist office for a route map and bike rental information. Many of the train and ferry stations grant DDSG ticket holders a discount on bicycle rentals.

Between Krems and Melk along the Vienna-Grein route numerous ruined castles testify to the magnitude of Austria's glorious past. One of the most dramatic fortresses is the 13th-century **Burg Aggstein-Gastein,** which commands the Danube from its pinnacle. The castle was formerly inhabited by Scheck von Wald, a robber baron known by fearful sailors as **Schreckenwalder** (terrible forest man). The lord was wont to impede the passage of ships with ropes stretched across the Danube, and then demand tribute from his ensnared victims. According to legend, he forced many of his prisoners to jump from the castle ramparts into the river valley more than 300m below.

■ Krems and Stein

Krems is made up of two towns: the modern yet quietly baroque **Krems** and the medieval gem, **Stein.** Located in the Danube valley at the head of the Wachau region, a region known particularly for its rich wine heritage, the double city is surrounded by the lush, green, terraced hills; these are the vineyards, thick with grapes. Wines and a central trade location were factors in the early rise of the settlement; Krems is first mentioned in 995 AD. In Stein, the medieval half of this urban binarism, one is taken back to, if not 995 itself, then somewhere thereabouts. The crooked, narrow, cobblestone passages wind and twist back on themselves, bordered by stuccoed walls that lean with age. The double-whammy of the dual city deal is completed by Krems, whose modern *Fußgängerzone* (when you're dealing with 995, Baroque is modern) is a good place for some serious shopping (don't get too serious) for everything from Reeboks to fancy underwear.

Ah, but don't forget the wine. Not only are there 120 different wines produced by the vineyards, but Krems-Stein was the stomping ground for French wine legend **Hans Moser,** who developed the **"raised vine" technique** which raised the vines off the ground where they had lain, technologically impaired, for centuries. This technique is now standard procedure for all those who ferment grapes. Head for the hills to see Hans' technique in action, or, better yet, head for **Kellergasse,** the high street in Stein that lies next to those hills of plenty, where one can sample the fruit of the vine in the many *Heurigen* that dot the street and take in a great view of the **Stift Göttweig,** which lies across the Danube.

Orientation and Practical Information Though Krems is accessible by **train** and **ferry** most visitors arrive on bicycles; the **train station** is a five-minute walk from the pedestrian zone. Exit out the front door of the Bahnhof, cross Ringstr. and continue straight onto Dinstlstr. which leads to the *Fußgängerzone.* The station has **lockers** for 30AS, **luggage storage,** and **bike rental** (open daily 5:30am-6:45pm; tel. 825 36 44). Most of the trains leaving Krems are regional trains. The *Regionalzug* connects Krems through Tulln to Vienna at the new Spittelau station (136AS); connections to other big cities can be made through St. Pölten. Directly in front of the station is a **bus depot,** with routes to Melk and St Pölten.

Krems lies along the popular Donau route from Passau through Linz to Vienna. People arrive daily by **ferry** (headquarters of the DDSG in Vienna). The ferry station is on the riverbank close to Stein, near the intersection of Donaulande with Dr.-Karl-Dorrek-Str. To reach Krems from the ship landing station, walk on Donaulände until it becomes Ringstr., and then take a left onto Utzstr. To reach Stein from the landing, first follow Dr.-Karl-Dorreck-Str. and then take a left onto Steiner Landstr.

Krems' **tourist office** is housed in the Kloster Und on Undstr. 6 (tel. 826 76; fax 700 11). To get there from the train station, take a left on the Ringstr. and follow it (about 10-12min.) until you get to Martin-Schmidt-Str., on your right. Follow this to the end; the office is across the street and to the right. They have amassed tons of information on accommodations, sports, and entertainment, as well as the indispensable *Heurigen Kalendar* (which lists the opening times of regional wine taverns). The tourist office offers a tour of the surrounding wine area with wine-tasting, snack, and a wine cellar tour (Thurs. at 2pm; 410AS). The office also has a tour of Stein which includes admission to the Steiner Kunsthalle (Wed. 2pm; 180AS). All tours leave from the tourist office and require at least 15 people and a reservation. It is, however, possible to rent Walkman tours (60AS) on the spur of the moment. (Office open Mon.-Fri. 9am-6pm, Sat.-Sun. 10am-noon and 1-6pm; mid-Nov. to Mar. Mon.-Fri. 8am-5pm.) Though **ATM** machines dot the shopping streets, the **post office** is the best place for **currency exchange** (tel. 826 06), and is right off Ringstr. on Brandströmstr. (Open Mon.-Fri. 8am-noon and 2-6pm, Sat. 8-11am.) You can rent **bikes** at the Donau Campground (40AS per half day, 60AS per day), at the ferry landing (90AS per day, 40AS per day with a valid ship ticket), or at the train station (same prices as at the ferry landing). **Postal code:** A-3500. **Telephone code:** 02732.

Accommodations and Food No matter where you stay, ask your hosts for a **guest card** that makes you eligible for a cornucopia of discounts. The **Jugendherberge Radfahrer (HI),** Ringstr. 77 (tel. 834 52; for advance bookings call the central office in Vienna tel. 586 41 45; fax 586 41 453), is a spotlessly clean hostel accommodating 52 in comfortable quads and six-bed rooms. Located on the Passau-Vienna bike path, the hostel has a garage for bikes, as well as a private toilet and shower in each room. (Members only. Reception open 7-9:30am and 5-8pm. 150-160AS, with a surcharge of 20AS if you stay less than three nights. Tax, breakfast and sheets included. 135AS without breakfast. Lockers 10AS. Open April-Oct.) **Haus Puchmayer,** Steiner Landstr. 79 (tel. 787 49), in the middle of Stein, has a few beds available in airy rooms with sinks when everything else is full. (Doubles only, with toilet and shower on the hall. 440AS, after 2 nights 400AS. Breakfast included.) If all else is full, try walking down the Steiner Landstrasse and checking out one of the many *Privatzimmer* advertised by little red and white flags with the words, *"Zimmer frei."* Or, stay at **ÖAMTC Donau Camping,** Wiedengasse 7 (tel. 844 55), which rests on the Danube, right by the marina. (Reception open 7:30am-10am and 4:30pm-7:30pm. 50AS per person plus 10.50AS tax, children 35AS; 30-60AS per tent depending on size (no tents provided), 40AS per car. Showers included. Energy connection 25AS. Facilities for disabled guests. English spoken. Open Easter to mid-Oct.)

The area around the pedestrian zone overflows with restaurants and streetside cafés. The **Schwarze Kuchl,** Unterer Landstr. 8 (tel. 831 28), offers a small salad buffet for 28AS (large 48AS), soup for 20-30AS, and bread for 5AS (open Mon.-Fri. 8am-7pm, Sat. 8am-1pm, first Sat. of the month until 5pm). Right next door is the famous **Konditorei Hagmann** (tel. 83 167), known throughout Krems for its outstanding pastries and chocolates. Try the **Kremser Kugel,** a Mozart Kugel-esque goody filled with apricot and nougat. (Open Mon.-Fri. 7am-7pm, Sat. 7am-1pm, first Sat. of the month until 6pm.) **Haus Hamböck,** Kellergasse 31 (tel. 845 68) in Stein, has a charming leaf terrace with a view of the town's spires and a restaurant bedecked with old *Faß* (kegs), presses, and other vineyard tools. The jolly proprietor will gladly take you on a free tour of the cellar and give a free tasting. (Glass of wine about 22AS, snacks 30-50AS; open daily 3pm-til people leave.) The cheapest eats in town are available at **Julius Meinl,** corner of Gaheisstr. and Obere Landstr. (Open Mon.-Fri. 8am-6pm, Sat. 7:30am-noon, first Sat. of the month until 6pm.)

Sights and Entertainment Krems and Stein lie snuggled between the Donau and the steep wine hills behind them. These lovely terraced hills, with the vines photosynthesizing in neat little rows, immediately command attention. A visit to Krems wouldn't be complete without visiting one of the **Heurigen** (wine cellars), which are allowed to open every other month for three weeks. The exact calendar can be obtained from the tourist office; the *Heurigen* are arranged so that they're open only from April to Oct. every year. A walk along Kellergasse in Stein provides one with a number of them to choose from, one of which will probably be open. If you don't have time to sit at a *Heurigen,* at least stop by the **Weingut Stadt Krems,** Stadtgraben 11 (tel. 826 62 21 or 826 62 23; fax 801 269), on the edge of the pedestrian zone. This winery does not have a restaurant attached, but they do offer free tours of the cellar and bottling center. Afterward, free tastings often lead to the purchase of a bottle or two (40-100AS). This winery belongs to the city, and is one of the oldest in all of Austria (founded in 1210; open for tours Mon.-Fri. 8am-noon and 1-4pm, Sat. 8am-noon).

The *Fußgängerzone,* the center of mercantile activity, runs down Obere and Untere Landstr. The entrance to the pedestrian area is marked by the **Steiner Tor,** one of four medieval city gates flanked by two Gothic towers. Various market places line Obere Landstr. The first is the Dominikanerpl., housing the **Dominikaner Kirche,** which now contains the **Krems History Museum,** a portion of which is the **Vintner's Museum** (tel. 80 13 38 or 80 13 39), where guests learn about wine cultivation, and then taste wines from all over the area. Call the museum or the tourist office for exact opening times and prices. Further down the pedestrian zone is the **Pfarrkirche Platz,** home of the Renaissance **Rathaus** and the **Pfarrkirche,** with its piecemeal Romanesque, Gothic, and Baroque architecture. While there, walk up the hill to the **Piaristen-Kirche,** with its newly renovated, life-size statues depicting Jesus' crucifixion in stations outside the church. Finally, at the end of the pedestrian zone is the **Simandlbrunnen,** a fountain depicting a husband kneeling in front of his domineering wife in fright, begging for the house keys so he can stay out late with "the boys."

The word "Simandl" means "push-over." In Stein almost every building on the **Steiner Landstr**. is a stunningly preserved vestige of the Middle Ages. Don't stop here, however. Climb the hill to the ancient and now profaned **Frauenbergkirche** and the wonderful **Heurigen** that dot the area.

Culturally, the city enjoys a number of theater and music events and other rotating exhibits. The **Kunsthalle Krems** (tel. 836 69) has recently opened a new building (close to the entry to Stein) on the corner of Steiner Landstr. and Dr.-Karl-Dorreck-Str. The Kunsthalle is a large exhibition hall that always has a large cultural or historical exhibit, usually focusing on post-modern and non-European art. Be sure not to miss its annex in Stein's Minoritenkirche, which has its own tiny modern sculpture garden (40-90AS, discounts for students, seniors and groups of eight or more; open daily 10am-4pm). Each year the Austrian **Donaufestival,** one day of open-air music and dancing at the end of June, kicks off a summer of cultural activities, including theatre, circus, symposiums, *Lieder,* folk music, and even flamenco. From mid-July to the beginning of Aug., Krems hosts a **Musikfest,** featuring a number of organ, piano, and quartet concerts that take place in the Kunsthalle, and in the various *Kirchen.* Tickets are available at the Kunsthalle, Minoritenpl. 4, A-3504 Krems (tel. 826 69). For the month of Aug., Krems is a technicolor dreamcoat, as artists plaster the streets with colorful banners and flags for the **Steiner Flag Festival.** The **Motorrad-Museum Krems-Egelsee,** idling at Ziegelofengasse 1 (tel. 41 30 13), will keep the moto-maniac in you entranced for an afternoon. The museum features an extraordinary collection of exhibits on the history of motorcycles and motor technology. (Open daily 9am-5pm; Sept.-June Sat.-Sun. 9am-5pm. 40AS, students 20AS.) Finally, throughout the year, myriad **churches** often have sacred music and organ concerts, which are overwhelmingly beautiful and usually free. Stop by the tourist office for a schedule.

■ Melk

On March 24, 1089, the Austrian Margrave Leopold II turned over the church and castle atop the Melk cliff to Benedictine Abbot Sigibod. This act begat the **Benedictine Monastery** and, subsequently, the village Melk. Floating majestically over the town, the enormous white and yellow monastery is a treasure trove for Baroque enthusiasts and an important site of the history of the Catholic Church in Austria. Indeed, Austria invested heavily to restore this wedding cake of a building and the restoration project, begun in 1978, was completed in 1996, just in time to celebrate Austria's 1000th birthday, whose motto was "Ostarrichi-Österreich 996-1996." Melk is still a living monastery, home to 25 active monks who toil away inside, praying, brewing drinks, and teaching the youth of Austria at the monastery school.

Each year over 400,000 guests visit Melk, many making a daytrip from Vienna or Krems. A large number of the visitors are cyclists touring the Danube from Passau to Vienna, and many others are religious buffs. Maria Theresa visited Melk on her way back to Vienna after being crowned empress in Prague in 1743. She was presented with a meal, a private tour of the monastery, and the keys to the city. She politely refused the keys, saying that they would be better off in the hands of the abbot, though in queen-like diplomacy she hastily added, "If I had never come here, I would have regretted it." Down below the abbey are Renaissance houses in narrow pedestrian zones, romantic cobblestone streets, old towers, and remnants of the old city wall from the Middle Ages.

Orientation and Practical Information Melk's **tourist office,** on the corner of Babenbergerstr. and Abbe-Stadler-Gasse, next to the Rathausplatz (tel. 23 07 32 or 23 07 33; fax 23 07 37), is equipped with plenty of pamphlets and maps to edify travelers about town history and athletic activities in the Wachau region. The office has large **lockers** (10AS) and bike racks for those looking to make Melk a day-trip. They make reservations for free. The office is located eight minutes by foot from the train station; walk down Bahnhofstr. and then straight on Bahngasse, which spills into Rathausplatz. Turn right at the Rathausplatz and cross it, staying to the right side.

This will take you to Abbe-Stadler-Gasse, which leads right to the front door of the tourist office. (Open July-Aug. daily 9am-7pm; Sept.-Oct. Mon.-Fri. 9am-noon and 2-6pm, Sat. 10am-2pm; Apr.-June Mon.-Fri. 9am-noon and 2-6pm, Sat. 10am-2pm.) Public **telephones** are located outside the train station, post office, at the end of the Hauptplatz, and at the monastery. **Trains** link Melk to Amstetten and St. Pölten. **Bike rental** (100AS, 50AS with rail ticket), **currency exchange,** and **luggage storage** (30AS) are all available at the station. Just outside the station's main entrance is the **bus depot;** take bus #1451 from Melk to Krems (64AS), and #1538 from Melk to St. Pölten (46AS). Buses run less frequently than trains. Melk is also on the DDSG-Donaureisen **ferry** route from Passau to Vienna (tel. 727 50; from Vienna 530AS; from Krems 238AS). The **post office** is at Bahnhofstr. 3. (Open Mon.-Fri. 8am-noon and 2-6pm, Sat. 8-10am.) **Postal code:** A-3390. **Telephone code:** 02752.

Accommodations and Food Head back to Krems if everything is full in Melk. The recently renovated **Jugendherberge,** Abt-Karl-Str. 42 (tel. 26 81; fax 42 57), is about a 10-minute walk from the Bahnhof; turn right as you exit and follow the green signs. The hostel offers 104 beds, all in quads with private showers, and toilets on the hall. Rooms are clean with plenty of storage space. In summer, guests can eat at benches outside in an ivy-hung yard or make use of the ping-pong tables, volleyball net, and soccer area. (Reception open daily 8-10am and 5-9pm. 147AS, after 2 nights 123AS, under 19 120AS and 107AS respectively. Tax 10.50AS. Breakfast included. Open April-Oct.) Another option is renting a *Privatzimmer* (complete list from the tourist office). **Camping Kolomaniau** (tel. 32 91), overlooks the Danube next to the ferry landing. (Reception open 8am-midnight. 35AS. Children 20AS. Tent 35AS. Car 25AS. Tax 10.50AS. Showers 15AS.) **Gasthof Goldener Stern,** Sterngasse 17 (tel. 22 14), has respectable rooms and hearty Austrian fare at the restaurant downstairs. Try their specialty—*Linsen mit Speck, Würstel, und Semmelknödel* (lentils with bacon, sausage, and dumplings; 75AS). (Reception for *Gasthof* open daily 7am-midnight. Singles 260-290AS. Doubles 400-500AS. Shower and toilet on hall. Prices drop the longer you stay. Breakfast included.)

Restaurants abound on the Rathausplatz, but look elsewhere for the less tourist-oriented joints. A five-minute walk west through the Hauptpl. brings you to **Restaurant zum "Alten Brauhof,"** Linzerstr. 25 (tel. 22 96), with a charming outdoor seating area that almost looks out on the Danube. Try the *Grillhendl* (roasted chicken; 75AS) or buttery *Schnitzel* (85AS). Admire the synthetic palm trees and oh-so-chic decor at **Il Palio,** Wiener-Str. 3 (tel. 47 32) which serves beer and some of the cheapest ice cream in Austria. (Open daily 9am-midnight.) Or visit the **Melkerstübel,** Wienerstr. 5 (tel. 28 27), near the Klostersteig. It serves both traditional Austrian fare and original vegetarian-friendly creations, made from fresh vegetables, *volkorn* grains, and occasionally even tofu. Don't miss the dippy, color-pencil drawings on the menu or the plaques of poems in the side garden where several tables are set. The *menu,* at 65-80AS for three courses, is a very decent bargain. **SPAR Markt,** Rathauspl. 9, has bread to spread, pears to share, apples to grapple, oranges to...well, nothing actually rhymes with "oranges." (Open Mon. and Wed.-Fri. 7am-6pm, Sat. 7am-noon.)

Sights and Entertainment To visit Melk is to visit the **Benediktinerstift,** which perches resplendent atop the town and commands marvelous views of the city and the surrounding Danube countryside. The "profane" wing, for those less holy, is open to the public and includes the imperial chambers where notables such as Emperor Karl VI, Pope Pius VI, and Napoleon took shelter. No signs saying "Napoleon wuz here," but a great and informative exhibit nonetheless.

Stroll through the cool, marble halls and take a look at the Habsburg portraits which line the wall. In an act of political deference, Franz I points to his wife, the ever dominant Maria Theresa. ("Franz, you will obey!") The stunning **abbey library** is brimming with sacred and secular texts that were painstakingly hand-copied by monks. The two highest shelves in the gallery are fake; in typical Baroque fashion, the monks sketched book spines onto the wood to make the collection appear more for-

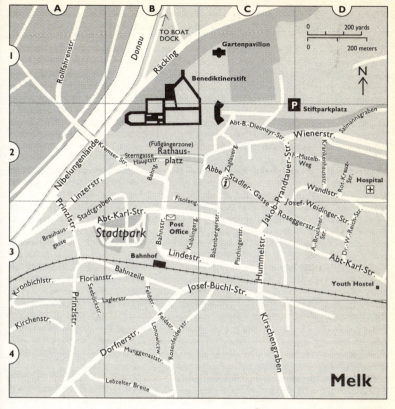

Melk

midable. The church itself, maintained by 25 monks, is a Baroque masterpiece. Maria Theresa donated the two skeletons that adorn the side altars. They are unknown holy men from the catacombs of Rome, special presents from the powerful empress ("well, let's see…for Krems a church, for Mariazell some gold, for Melk—oh yeah, how about those two dead guys?"). By far the centerpiece of the monastery, however, is the **Melker Kreuz** (Melk Cross)—gold, jewels, the works, circa 1363. Stolen twice, the Cross always exposed its thief and returned to its home in Melk through supernatural movement. Perhaps this is why the Melkers chose the aggressive slogan *"Non coronabitur nisi legitime certaverit"* (without a legitimate battle there is no victory) as the philosophy of their monastery. The monks of Melk do not live in the dusty shadow of nine centuries past, however. To show that they are with it, they not only allow temporary exhibits of contemporary art, but also commissioned modernist artist Peter Bischof to create new, harmonious paintings over the irreparable frescoes in the interior of the main courtyard. (Open Apr.-Oct. daily 9am-5pm; May-Sept. daily 9am-6pm. Last entry an hour before closing. Nov.-March, "must-have" guided tours at 11am and 2pm, or by arrangement. 50AS, students 25AS, tour (highly recommended) 10AS. Tour in English leaves at 3pm. Call 231 22 32 for more info.) Sunday services are at 7am, 9am and from May-Oct. another mass is added at 11am.

Five kilometers out of town is **Schloß Schallaburg** (tel. (02754) 63 17), one of the most magnificent Renaissance castles in central Europe. The Schloß is a 10-minute bus ride away; by foot, take Kirschengraben, off Lindestr. and Bahnhofstr., out of town and turn right under the Autobahn. The castle's architecture is reason enough to visit; Romanesque, Gothic, Renaissance, and Mannerist influences converge in the terra-cotta arcades of the main courtyard. The floor consists of a 1600-piece **mosaic** (remember, there was no puzzle box top to help the designer). This castle is known as the International Exhibition Center of Lower Austria (tel. 63 17); the staff pulls out all the stops in bringing foreign cultures to life. (Open May-Sept. Mon.-Fri. 9am-5pm, Sat.-Sun. 9am-6pm. 60AS, students 20AS.) Buses leave from Melk's Bahnhof daily at 10:30am and 3:10pm; each departs from the castle 15 minutes later (one-way 30AS, students 15AS). The castle houses special temporary exhibits each year that are usually worthwhile. Check with the tourist office for specific information.

Hikers can enjoy the network of trails surrounding Melk that wind through tiny villages, farmland, and wooded groves. Ask at the tourist office for the highly recommended map, which lists area sights and hiking paths, and for the handouts on the 10-kilometer Leo Böck trail, six-kilometer Seniorenweg, and 15-kilometer Schallaburggrundweg. **Cyclists** might enjoy a tour along the Danube on the former canal-towing path, in the direction of Willendorf; ask for the Danube *cycle track* map. The **Venus von Willendorf,** an 11cm, beautifully over-proportioned stone figure, and one of the world's most famous fertility symbols, was discovered there in 1908. Thought to be 30,000 years old, she is now on display in Vienna. Then, perhaps, take a ferry to the other side of the Danube to **Arnsdorf,** where the local *jause,* or Austrian version of British high tea, here called the *Hauerganse* (vintner's special) will load enough carbos to send you through the vineyards and apricot orchards back towards Melk. On the return trip, you will pass an unusual forest called the **Heiratswald,** or Marriage Woods. The romantic city awards newlyweds who marry in Melk a young sapling tree, which the happy couple plants and tends for the rest of their lives. For those planning on eloping, sorry, the woods are full.

Another cycling route will take you by the mystical basin stones scattered in the Dunkelstein woods and in small streams. According to legend, these stones are pieces of a footstep left behind by the devil. Strange stones also figure in the cow and calf. Looking down towards the Danube from the **Schobühel** monastery when the water is relatively low, you can see two rocks in the middle of the river. People in the region have named the two rocks the cow and the calf; brave swimmers periodically swim out and "ride" them, a practice the "beasts" don't seem to mind.

Finally, the **Sommerspiele Melk** (Melk Summer Festival) comes to town in early July. In 1996, the festival kicked off with a bonfire, a fireworks and water display set to music, and an open-air play by Grillparzer. There was also live music. Big crowd, hefty party, look for a repeat of this in 1997.

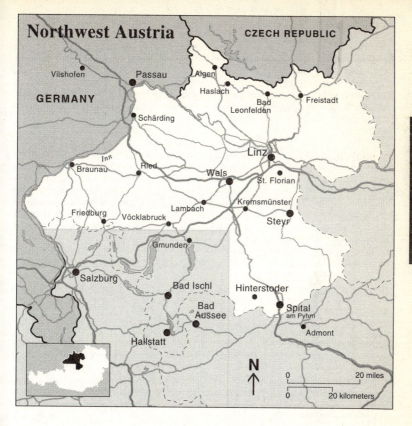

Northwest Austria

Oberösterreich (Upper Austria) is the country's Rust Belt of sorts. Austria's primary source of industrial wealth, it certainly hasn't tried to take of its blue-collar image and woo the tourists. The provincial capital is **Linz,** a major center of iron, steel, and chemical production and home to many modern Danube port installations. The area is Austria's second most productive source of oil and natural gas since World War II, and several large-scale hydroelectric power stations have been built along the *Donau* (Danube) and its tributary, the Enns.

This is not Austria's favorite showcase; the mountains are less rugged and tourism is not the largest employer. However, the relatively flat terrain of the area makes for wonderful **bicycling tours,** heavily touted by the region's tourist offices and popular with vacationing locals. Well-paved bike paths wind their way through the entire province, easy enough for cyclers of any age. A popular "cultural tour" of Upper Austria makes a circuit from Linz, through **Steyr,** and on to **Wels,** and several hotels in these towns offer special discounts for travelers on wheels. Four tours start from Wels and lead to the surrounding *Möst* country, where the local apple cider, unique for its pungent, vinegar-like flavor, is brewed. Get information on Upper Austrian biking through the tourist offices in Linz, Wels, or Steyr.

Bike paths also follow the Danube as it winds its way from Germany southeast towards Vienna, bisecting the province along its path. Oberösterreich gets its name not by virtue of being in the north, but by where the flow of the Austrian Danube starts. The sister province Niederösterreich (Lower Austria), therefore, is where the river flows into Hungary. The province encompasses everything north of Salzburg, but not quite north of Vienna (that becomes Niederösterreich). Oberösterreich is composed of three distinct regions: the **Mühlviertel** in the north; the **Innviertel** to the west of Linz in the Danube valley; and the **Pyhrn-Eisenwurz** in the south, smothered by Alpine foothills and limestone crags.

■ Linz

The provincial capital of Upper Austria and one-time home to Kepler, Mozart, Beethoven, Bruckner and Hitler, Linz proudly sits on the banks of the blue(ish) Danube and magisterially rules over the industrial sector of Austria. Although the city of 208,000 inhabitants is the third largest in the country (after Vienna and Graz), and occupies a prime location in the heart of Austria, the city's stigma of being an industry-oriented town sadly and unfairly keeps tourism at arm's length. Bookended by Vienna to the east and Salzburg to the west, Linz suffers from a middle-child syndrome of the Jan Brady strain: it's not as cosmopolitan as Vienna, yet it's not as quaintly provincial as Salzburg, either. But just as Jan would don a zany black wig in order to be different, Linz, too, invests that extra effort to make itself stand out, partly through the natural friendliness of its citizens (they haven't reached the tourist saturation point of Vienna and Salzburg) and partly through their annual festivals—the orgiastic summer music festival, the **Brucknerfest,** with its opening laser and water show, and the vibrant, pulsing **Pflasterspektakel** (street performer's fair), which draws artists (and crowds) from all over the world.

GETTING TO LINZ

Transport to Linz is simple. Frequent **trains** connect Linz to major Austrian and European cities. To **Vienna** (2hr., every ½hr., 264AS); **Salzburg** (1hr.20min., every ½hr., 192AS); **Innsbruck** (3hr.20min., hourly, 476AS); **Munich** (3hr., hourly, 472AS); **Prague** (4hr., 4 daily, 296AS). All **buses** arrive and depart from the Hauptbahnhof where schedules are also available. It is easier to purchase tickets from the bus driver rather than to make plans based on a sporadically open ticket window. Motorists to Linz can arrive on the main West Autobahn (A1 or E16).

Linz is not Lienz, a small Italo-Austrian city in East Tirol. Many a naive tourist has inadvertently ended up in the wrong town. When asking for information, be sure to state the city's complete name, Linz an der Donau.

ORIENTATION AND PRACTICAL INFORMATION

Linz, capital of Upper Austria, lies on both sides of the **Danube,** which curves west to east through the city; most of the *Altstadt* sights crowd along the southern bank, near the **Nibelungenbrücke** (Nibelung Bridge). This pedestrian area includes the huge **Hauptplatz,** just south of the bridge, and extends from there down **Landstraße,** which ends near the train station. Linz is mid-way between Salzburg and Vienna and also between Prague and Graz, making Linz a transportation hub that conveniently services further travel through Austria and Eastern Europe.

Tourist Office: Hauptpl. 5 (tel. 23 93 17 77). The helpful, friendly, and multilingual staff will help find accommodations at no charge. Pick up the walking tour brochure *A Walk Through the Old Quarter* for a quick summary of the *Altstadt's* main attractions. Open May-Sept. Mon.-Fri. 7am-7pm, Sat. 9am-7pm, Sun. 10am-7pm; Oct.-April Mon.-Fri. 8am-6pm, Sat. 9am-6pm, Sun. 10am-6pm.
Telephones: In the post office. Open 24hr. Phone booths on the street, and clustered at Schillerpl., Taubenmarkt, and Hauptpl.

Currency Exchange: Banks vary with rates and commissions. Bank hours are Mon.-Wed. 8am-4:30pm, Thurs. 8am-5:30pm, Fri. 8am-2pm. Change larger amounts of cash at the post office, which offers better rates (60AS commission).

American Express: Bürgerstr. 14 (tel. 66 90 13). The best place to cash traveler's checks (all types) but they don't change cash. Address mail, for example, to Joe ORDOÑEZ, c/o American Express Client Mail Service, Bürgerstr. 14, A-4021 Linz, Austria. Open Mon.-Fri. 9am-5:30pm, Sat. 9am-noon.

Local Public Transportation: All corners of the city are easily accessible through Linz's public transport system. Two streetcars (#1 and #3) start near the Hauptbahnhof and run north through the city, along Landstr., Hauptpl., and across the Nibelungenbrücke. Several buses criss-cross Linz as well. Nearly all vehicles pass through **Blumauerplatz**, down the block and to the right from the train station. The public transport hub closer to the city center is **Taubenmarkt**, just south of Hauptpl. on Landstr. A ticket for 4 stops or less ("MINI") costs 10AS; more than 4 ("MIDI") 18AS; and a 24-hr. ticket ("MAXI") 35AS. Buy tickets from any machine at all bus or streetcar stops (be aware that the machine gives no change), and stamp them before boarding; those caught *Schwarzfahren* (riding *sans* ticket) fork over 400AS. Multiple journey tickets can be purchased at tobacconists and the tourist office.

Ferries: The German company **Wurm & Köck** has begun ferrying between Passau (tel. (0851) 92 92 92, fax (0851) 355 18) and Linz (tel. (0732) 78 36 07 or 77 10 90; fax 783 60 79). The Passau-Linz journey takes 5-7hr., depending on the current (one-way 228AS). Boats arrive and leave Linz at the Donau Schiffstation, on the south side of the river, stopping at a number of small Austrian and Bavarian towns along the way. Combinations with ferry, train, and bus are possible. Discounts are available for seniors and children under 14.

Taxis: Taxi stands located at the Hauptbahnhof, Blumauerpl., and Hauptpl., or call the **Green Taxi Co.** (tel. 69 69).

Parking: Free parking at Urfahrmarkt.

Bike Rental: At the train station (24hr.; 100AS per day, 50AS with valid ticket), or at the Neues Amtsgebäude, Urfahrmarkt 1 (open daily 10am-6pm; 60AS per day). Linz's flat terrain is covered with bike paths; pick up a map at the tourist office.

Luggage storage: At the train station. (Large lockers 30AS, small 20AS; 2-day limit.) Luggage watch is 20AS per bag per calendar day.

Gay-Lesbian Information Centers: Homosexuelle Initiative Linz (HOSI), Postfach 43 (tel. 60 98 98). Discussion tables Thurs. 8pm at Gasthaus Agathon, Kapuzinerstr. 46.

Auton. Frauenzentrum (Women's Center), Altstadt 11/1 (tel. 21 29). Open for information Tues.-Thurs. 10am-noon and 1-4pm. Also offers rape crisis advice.

AIDS Hotline: AIDS-Hilfe Oberösterreich, Langgasse 12 (tel. 21 70). Gay information telephone line open Mon. and Wed. 5-6pm.

Pharmacies: *Apotheken* rotate late-night hours (any *Apotheke* has a schedule of who's open). **Central Apotheke,** Mozartstr. 1 (tel. 77 17 83). Open Mon.-Fri. 8am-noon and 2-6pm, Sat. 8am-noon.

Emergencies: Police: tel. 133. **Ambulance:** tel. 144. **Fire:** tel. 122.

Post Office: Bahnhofpl. 11, by the train and bus stations. Exchange open daily 7am-5pm. Mail services open Mon.-Fri. 7am-8pm, Sat. 8am-4pm. Information open Mon.-Fri. 7am-5pm, Sat. 8am-4pm. Wheelchair accessible. **Postal code:** A-4020.

Telephone Code: 0732.

ACCOMMODATIONS AND CAMPING

Linz suffers from a lack of cheap rooms, so it's usually best to stick to the youth hostels. While *Privatzimmer* can provide alternatives in most other cities, Linz is just urban enough that locals aren't allowed to rent rooms privately. Wherever you stay, call ahead to ensure a room; vacancies never remain so for long.

If affordable accommodations are fully booked in Linz, consider taking the train to the nearby town of **Steyr** (45min., hourly, change trains in St. Valentin). See the Steyr section (p. 329) for complete accommodation information.

NORTHWEST AUSTRIA

Jugendherberge Linz (HI), Kapuzinerstr. 14 (tel. 78 27 20), near the Hauptplatz, offers the cheapest bed in town at an excellent location. From the train station, take streetcar #3 to "Taubenmarkt," cross Landstr., walk down Promenade, continue on Klammstr., and turn left on Kapuzinerstr. The hostel is on the right (20min.). Airy rooms in a quiet area, including a courtyard laden with picnic tables and roaming cats. Accommodates 36 in 2- to 6-bed rooms. Reception open daily roughly 8-10am and 5-8pm. No curfew; ask for a key. Rooms have private showers. 115AS, under 19 95AS, nonmembers 30AS surcharge for first night. Lockers included, sheets 20AS. Laundry and kitchen facilities available. Call ahead.

Jugendgästehaus (HI), Stanglhofweg 3 (tel. 66 44 34). From Blumauerpl. (near the train station), catch bus #27 (dir: Schiffs-wert) to "Froschberg." Walk straight on Ziegeleistr., right on Roseggerstr., and on to Stanglhofweg. The bland exterior conceals a liveable interior. Clean and spacious with lots of closet space. Showers in every room, and toilets off the hall. Reception open daily 8am-4pm and 6-11pm. Singles 303AS. Doubles 203AS. Quads 153AS per person. 8AS tourist surcharge. Breakfast included. Often overrun with school groups. Call ahead.

Goldenes Dachl, Hafnerstr. 27 (tel. 67 54 80). From the Hauptbahnhof, take bus #21 to "Auerspergplatz." Walk in the same direction as the bus along Herrenstr. for half a block, then take a left onto Wurmstr.; Hafnerstr. is your first right. On foot, take a right on Bahnhofstr., and bear left onto Volksgartenstr. before Blumauerpl. Follow it until it hits Herrenstr; Wurmstr. is your first left. Narrow corridors and staircases allow for large rooms. Run by a motherly, elderly woman with an eye for comfort. Singles 260AS. Doubles 460AS, with shower 480AS. This little *Pension* only has 15 beds—call ahead.

Gasthof Wilder Mann, Goethestr. 14 (tel. 65 60 78). From the train station, walk down Bahnhofstr., turn left on Landestr. at Blumauerpl., then right on Goethestr. (7min.). Large, bright rooms, often with sofa, table, and chairs. Restaurant with garden seating downstairs. Reception open daily 8am-9pm. Singles 300AS, with shower 370AS. Doubles 520AS, with shower 620AS. Breakfast 50AS.

Camping Pleschinger See (tel. 24 78 70). Located directly on the Linz-Vienna biking path on Pleschinger lake. Tents only. 20AS per person. Open May- late Sept.

FOOD

Avoid paying through the nose by ducking into the alleys along the Hauptplatz and Landstraße to find a restaurant. Generally, the further you move away from the Hauptplatz, the cheaper restaurants get. Of course, anyone who leaves Linz without indulging in its namesake dessert, the **Linzer Torte,** will have defeated part of the purpose of visiting. The *Torte* is unique for its deceptively dry ingredients—very little flour is used, and absolutely no cream at all. The secret is in the red currant jam filling, which slowly seeps through and moisturizes the dry, crumbly crust. Not all *Linzer Tortes* are the same; the best should be allowed to sit for at least two days after baking to allow for maximum jelly saturation.

Weinstube Etagen Beisl, Domgasse 8, 2nd fl. (tel. 77 13 46), off the Hauptplatz. Mingle with the locals and wash down the *Oma's Pfandl* (granny's frying pan) special with beer until the wee hours of the morning. Dirt-cheap prices. Hot entrées 65-80AS. Open Tues.-Sat. 6pm-2am.

Mangolds, Hauptpl. 3. Ovo-lacto Vegetarian Valhalla. This cafeteria-style restaurant in screaming primary colors offers only the fresh stuff. Nearly all the vegetables are organically grown; all the eggs are organically laid. Extravagant salad bar. 39-60AS for entrées. Open Mon.-Fri. 11am-9pm, Sat. 10am-4pm.

Levante, Hauptplatz 13 (tel. 79 34 30; fax 79 34 30 17). Finally, real Turkish and Greek food at real prices. A branch of the well-known Vienna restaurant. Open daily 11:30am-11:30pm.

Gasthaus Goldenes Schiff, Ottensheimerstr. 74 (tel. 23 98 79). On the scenic banks of the Danube. From the Hauptplatz, cross the bridge, turn left, go around the Babylonian gardens (actually the Neues Rathaus), and walk upstream along the river for 7min. Removed from the *Altstadt,* but well worth it. Locals pile in the *Gastgarten* for the under-100AS full course diners. Open Wed.-Sun. 9am-10pm.

Jindrak Konditorei, Herrenstr. 22, though other branches dot Linz. Rumored to serve the best *Linzer Torte* (22AS) in Linz. Mouth-watering sweets lined up behind the counters. Buy penny candy or pastries, or sit and enjoy a piece of what they're famous for. Open Mon.-Fri. 8am-6:30pm, Sat. 8am-6pm.

Café Traxlmeyer, Promenadestr. 16. Big, gentle orange café with garden tables and a Viennese flavor. Foamy *mélanges, Tortes* (24AS), newspapers—contemplate wrapping up your afternoon sometime next week. Open Mon.-Sat. 8am-10pm.

Markets

Billa Supermarket, at the intersesction of Landstr. and Mozartstr. Open Mon.-Thurs. 7:30am-6:30pm, Fri. 7:30am-8pm, Sat. 7am-1pm.

Julius Meinl, Landstr. 50, along tram route #3. Open Mon.-Fri. 8am-noon.

SIGHTS AND ENTERTAINMENT

Start your exploration of Linz at the **Hauptplatz,** which hugs the Danube's south bank. The enormous plaza was constructed in the 14th and 15th centuries when the inhabitants of Linz prospered by taxing the large quantities of salt and iron passing through the town. The focus of the square is the marble **trinity column,** offered as a sign of gratitude for the city's being spared from war, famine, and the plague in the 18th century. The Baroque **Altes Rathaus**—under renovation until 1998—is crowned by an octagonal tower and an astronomical clock. To this date only two people have ever addressed the public from the Rathaus balcony, Adolf Hitler and Pope John Paul II. Free-spirited star-gazer Johannes Kepler (the fellow who corrected his predecessors and said that planets travel in ellipses not circles) wrote his major work, *Harmonices Mundi,* while living around the corner at Rathausgasse 5. On nearby Domgasse stands Linz's glorious twin-towered **Alter Dom** (Old Cathedral); the 19th-century symphonic composer and organist extraordinaire, Anton Bruckner, played here during his stint as church organist. To the south, the neo-Gothic **Neuer Dom** (New Cathedral) may seem even more impressive; erected in the 19th century, this Godzilla-esque edifice is the largest church in all of Austria. For an inexpensive outing and sheer olfactory ecstasy, visit the **Botansicher Garten** (southwest of the Neuer Dom), which shelters a world-famous cactus and orchid collection. (Open May-Aug. daily 7:30am-7:30pm; Oct. and March 8am-6pm, Sept. and April 8am-7pm; Nov.-Feb. 8am-5pm. 10AS, under 18 free.)

Cross the **Nibelungenbrücke** to reach the left bank of the Danube. This area of Linz, known as **Urfahr,** was once another city altogether, until it was swallowed up by Linz in the early decades of this century. Local Linzers keep this old neighborhood a secret from tourists, but it boasts some of the oldest buildings in the city. While you are on this side of the Danube, catch a captivating view of Linz from the apex of the **Pöstlingberg** (537m). To reach the summit, take streetcar #3 to the end of the line "Bergbahnhof Urfahr," which is at the base of the mountain (Landgutstr. 19). From there, either hike up .5km by following Hagenstr. (off Rudolphstr., which is off Hauptstr. near the bridge), or hop aboard the **Pöstlingbergbahn** (tel. 78 01 75 45), which provides a scenic 20-min. ascent in a San Francisco-style trolley car. (Runs daily 5:20am-8pm, every 20min. One-way 25AS, round-trip 40AS, children half-price.) The twin-towered **Pöstlingbergkirche** (Parish Church), the city symbol, stands guard over the city from the hill's crest. To indulge your nascent romanticism, take the Grotten-bahn into the fairy-tale caves of Pöstlingberg, complete with dwarves, dragons, and Prince Charming models. (Open Easter-Nov. Mon.-Fri. 9am-6pm, Sat.-Sun. and Advent 10am-5pm. 45AS, under 15 20AS.)

Linz is also equipped with many intriguing museums. The **Neue Galerie,** Blütenstr. 15 (tel. 23 93 36 00), boasts one of Austria's best modern art collections, with works by Klimt, Kokoschka, and Lieberman. (Open June-Sept. Mon.-Fri. 10am-6pm, Sat. 10am-1pm; Oct.-May Mon.-Wed. and Fri.-Sun. 10am-6pm, Thurs. 10am-10pm. 40AS, students 20AS). The city's history is presented by the **Linzer Schloßmuseum,** Tummelpl. 10 (tel. 77 44 19; open Tues.-Fri. 9am-5pm, Sat.-Sun. 10am-6pm; 50AS, students 30AS); and the **Stadtmuseum Nordico,** Bethlehemstr. 7 (tel. 23 93 19 12; open Tues.-Fri. 9am-6pm, Sat.-Sun. 2-5pm; 30AS, students 20AS). The brand new **Ars Electronica,** Hauptstr. 2, bills itself as the "museum of the future." What Buck Rogers could only dream about—computer animation, engineered simulation, high-tech visualization, and maybe even a little virtual stimulation.

Linz also offers a variety of cultural events. In September, the city hosts the month-long **Brucknerfest,** when the works of Linz's native son, Anton Bruckner, are performed at the Brucknerhaus concert hall, known for its acoustic perfection. (Tickets 220-900AS, standing room 40-50AS; buy tickets at the Brucknerhaus-kasse, Untere Donaulände 7 (tel. 77 52 30; fax 761 22 01) on the Hauptplatz side bank of the Danube; open daily 10am-6pm, or write to "Brucknerhaus-kasse, Untere Donaulände 7, A-4010 Linz.") You don't always have to buy tickets—the opening concert (the end of the first week in Sept.), billed as *Klangwolke* (Cloud of Sound), includes a spectacular open-air laser show accompanied by Bruckner's 7th Symphony, broadcast live into the surrounding Donaupark, to the thrill of 50,000 Bruckner fans (and you thought The Who whipped the audience into a frenzy). During the third weekend of July, the city hosts a **Pflasterspektakel,** a free, international street performers' festival. Every few steps down the Landstraße and Hauptplatz, different performers from as far away as Australia perform everything from Houdini acts and fire-eating to outdoor theater and bongo drum concerts. Young, funky, crowd converges on Linz for these 2-3 days—it's a very fun social scene.

Afraid things may die down at night? Don't worry, the nightlife is sleepy but still has a pulse. Prod it awake at the **Bermuda Dreieck** (Bermuda Triangle), behind the west side of the Hauptplatz (just past the Chinese restaurant). Frequented by Linzers as well as tourists, this area has the highest bars and nightclubs to square meter ratio. In the Hauptplatz itself, try the **Alte Welt Weinkeller,** Hauptpl. 4, a popular hangout for Linz's youth. Soak up wine and spirits in this arcaded Renaissance-era edifice (open Mon.-Sat. 5pm-2am, food served 6-11pm). The **17er Keller,** on Hauptpl. 17, will serve you an apple-juice and cinnamon flavored tequila while you listen to their mix of jazz, funk, blues, and acid jazz (open Mon.-Sat. 7pm-2am, Sun. 7pm-1am). For reggae and a bit of dancing in an unconventional, mellow, mixed-ages crowd, drop by the **Afro-Musik Café,** Klammstr. 1 (tel. 277 233), off of Promenadegasse and around the corner from the youth hostel. Very obliging DJ. (Open 4pm until whenever people leave—officially 4am, sometimes earlier.) Gays and lesbians patronize the subdued **C+C Café,** Bethlehemstr. 30 (tel. 770 862), managed by a charming, grandmotherly hostess who arguably may be the nicest *Linzerin* in all the city. (Open Mon.-Fri. from 6pm, Sat. from 7pm; in winter, open Fri.-Sun. from 3pm. Closes whenever people go home.) *Linzers* also flock to the other side of the Danube for after-hours entertainment. Grab a bench at **Fischerhäusl,** Flußgasse 3, which owns the two beer gardens on your left as you cross the bridge (open daily 11:30am-midnight; shorter hours in winter).

■ Near Linz

MAUTHAUSEN

About half an hour down the Danube from Linz in Mauthausen stand the remains of a Nazi concentration camp (*Konzentrationslager,* abbreviated KZ). Unlike other camps in south Germany and Austria, Mauthausen remains very much intact. The barracks in which 200,000 mostly Russian and Polish prisoners toiled, suffered, and died are clearly visible, rise bleakly from the landscape, powerfully making the memorials which enjoin the world to "Never Forget" almost superfluous. The terrible **Todessteige** (Staircase of Death) leads to the stone quarry where inmates were forced to work until exhaustion. The steep but even steps in place now have been added for tourists' safety—when the inmates worked here there was nothing but a twisted, stony path dotted with boulders and jagged rocks. As prisoners descended, the last in line was frequently violently pushed so that the entire group tumbled down the path. As they carried the 50kg stones out of the quarry on their shoulders, they were often beaten. Occasionally the SS simply pushed prisoners off the heights on to the rocks and into the deep murky pond below—the surrounding cliff was cruelly known as **Parachuter's Wall.** The inner part of the camp is now a museum. You can visit the barracks (inmates polished the floors and walls every single day and were only allowed to enter barefoot in the Nazi's cleanliness mania), roll call grounds, ovens, and torture rooms. The central part contains an explanatory display with documents and photographs (20AS, students 10AS). To reach the camp from **Linz,** take a train to Mauthausen, with a transfer in St. Valentin (round-trip 114AS). Beware, the Mauthausen train station is 6km away from the camp. The **BundesBus** (one-way 44AS) will drop you off at the base of the hill in residential Mauthausen, where the camp resides, and is only a 2-km walk. Buses are few and far between, however, and almost never run on weekends. A better and more popular option is to rent a **bicycle** from the Mauthausen train station (100AS, 50AS with that day's train ticket or Eurail Pass; open daily 5am-6pm). If traveling **by car,** exit Autobahn A1 (Vienna-Linz) at Enns. (Mauthausen open Feb. to mid-Dec. daily 8am-6pm. Trains run hourly.)

ST. FLORIAN ABBEY

Seventeen kilometers from Linz lies the Abbey of St. Florian, Austria's oldest Augustinian monastery. According to legend, the martyr Florian was bound to a millstone and thrown in the Enns river. Although he perished, the stone miraculously floated and is today the abbey's cornerstone. The complex owes much of its fame to composer Anton Bruckner, who began his career here first as choirboy, then teacher, and finally organist; his body is interred beneath the organ, allowing him to feel the vibrations of his well-loved pipes for eternity. The abbey (tel. (07224) 89 02 10; fax 89 02 60) contains the **Altdorfer Gallery,** dedicated to 15th-century artist Albrecht Altdorfer of Regensburg; the altarpieces on display show his commitment to the Danube School's revolutionary painting style. The fourteen **Kaiserzimmer** (Imperial rooms), built for the possibility of a visit by the Emperor, will astound you with their Baroque splendor. The spectacular, recently renovated church (the only portion of the abbey accessible without a tour) houses the enormous **Bruckner Organ.** You can hear a 20-min. concert on the monster instrument every day; the abbey is open at 2:30pm (30AS, students 20AS). An obligatory tour of the abbey excluding the *Kaiserzimmer* is offered daily every hr. 10-11am and 2-4pm (45AS, students 40AS; Abbey open April-Oct.). To reach the abbey, take bus #2040 or 2042 from **Linz** to "St. Florian Stift," but pick up the bus again at "St. Florian Markt" downhill in downtown St. Florian or "Lagerhaus." Both are a 15-min. walk from the abbey (round-trip 68AS; ½hr.).

KREMSMÜNSTER

The fabulous **Kremsmünster Abbey,** lying 32km south of Linz, is Austria's oldest order, dating from 777 AD (an auspicious year for an abbey). Some 75 monks still call it home today, and it administers parish churches as far-flung as Brazil. The abbey still owns most of the land in the area, including wine-producing vineyards and 3800 hectares of woods. The **library,** which has two rows of books on every shelf and hidden doors in the bookcases, is Austria's third largest and boasts many medieval tomes. Although visitors aren't allowed to touch the books, ask your guide to take out any volume and page through it for you. The **Kaisersaal,** built by the monks for the worst case scenario of a shatteringly expensive visit by the Austrian monarch, is a rich Baroque gallery complete with marble columns and somewhat cartoonish ceiling frescoes which make the rooms seem much higher than they actually are. The library, Kaisersaal, rooms of paintings, and the **Schatzkammer** (treasure room), sheltering a beautifully engraved golden chalice dating from the time of Charlemagne, are all part of the abbey's **Kunstsammlung** (art collection) tour. The monks' collection of minerals and semi-exotic animal specimens is on display in the seven-story **Sternwarte.** Also on display is the **Fischkalter,** five fantastic fish fens for feeding the fasting friars' friends fresh flounder. Actually the Fischkalter is a series of arcaded pools set with pastoral statues spouting water. The entire chamber is studded with stag antlers mounted on wooden heads—see if you can find the one with a radish in its mouth. (Tours of Kunstsammlung April-Oct. 10-11am and 2-4pm; 1hr.; 45AS, students 20AS. Sternwarte tour May-Oct. 10am, 2, and 4pm; 1½hr.; 50AS, students 20AS. Both tours include the Fischkalter. Without joining a tour, you can visit the central chapel for free, or see the Fischkalter alone for 10AS.)

The town of Kremsmünster itself boasts twisty medieval streets and precariously steep stairway paths overgrown with moss and wildflowers. Come eat fresh fruit at the open air market in the Marktplatz (Fri. 1-6pm), or stop by **Café Schlair** (tel. (07583) 77 72), for pastries and fresh fruit or berry drinks (25-40AS; open daily 8am-6:30pm, but closed Wed. afternoon). If you stay the night, try the **Bauernhof Gossen-hub,** Schürzendorf 1 (tel. (07583) 77 52), a lovely farmhouse with clean, simple rooms for 160AS (40AS surcharge for stays of less than three days).

To get to Kremsmünster and the abbey, take a **train** from **Linz** to Kremsmünster (45min., every hr., one-way 64AS). Bundesbus routes also head to town, but infrequently. Head straight out of the train station, follow Bahnhofstr. as it curves left, then right, and then left again, and continue onto Marktpl. The path up to the abbey starts at the **tourist office,** Rathauspl. 1 (tel. (07583) 72 12; open Tues.-Fri. 9am-noon, Tues. and Fri. also 3-6pm).

■ Admont

The tiny town of Admont, "the gateway to the Gesäuse" Alpine region, is situated just over the Styrian border on the River Enns. Benedictine monks first built an abbey here in the 11th century and although fire has repeatedly ravaged the complex, the stubborn friars have refused to let the church go up in smoke. The current **Benedik-tinerstift** (Benedictine abbey) was completed in 1776. The highlight is the frescoed **library,** the largest monastery collection in the world, with over 150,000 volumes, including displayed illuminated manuscripts dating back to the 9th century. Joseph Stemmel's four statues dominates the central gallery. *Death* portrays a human skeleton (look closely—the wings are actually hanging folds of skin). In *The Last Judgment,* the devil, complete with beard, glasses, and grin, was given the facial features of a disliked abbey treasurer. *Hell,* Stemmel's most famous work, combines seven figures for seven sins, including wrath (the crazed main figure) and intemperance (with bottle and sausages). *Heaven* is positively tame compared to the first three. Sixty-eight gilded **busts** of philosophers, poets, and historians glare disdainfully from the walls at the intellectually inferior. Try to find the hidden stairways that lead to the upper balconies, or ask a guide for assistance. The same building holds the **Schatzka-mmermuseum** (tel. (03613) 23 12), which contains Admont artifacts, and a **natural history museum,** full of bottled snakes, insects, and other assorted animalia. (Library and museums open May-Sept. daily 10am-1pm and 2-5pm; April and Oct. daily 10am-noon and 2-4pm; Nov.-March by appointment. Combined admission to all 3, 60AS, students 30AS. English info sheets 5AS.) Also in the complex is the **Heimatmuseum,** which displays local historical paraphernalia. (Open May-Oct. daily 9:30am-noon and 1-4:30pm. 20AS, children 10AS.) The abbey isn't entirely secular, however; take a moment to stroll by the huge neo-Gothic **church** in the middle of the grounds (free).

The Admont **tourist office** *(Fremdenverkehrsbüro;* tel. (03613) 21 64; fax 36 48) will track down a room for free. To reach the tourist office from the train station, turn left down Bahnhofstr. and take the second right at the conspicuous post office; the office is five minutes away, on the left. (Open Mon.-Fri. 8am-noon and 2-6pm, Sat. 9am-noon; Sept.-May Mon. 8am-noon, Tues.-Fri. 8am-5pm.) The other reason to come to Admont is honestly the youth hostel, **Schloß Röthelstein**—reputedly the most beautiful hostel in Europe. The hostel is in a restored 330-year-old castle, high above the town and boasts two winter ski lifts, winter ice skating, a sauna (costs extra), a private tennis court, a soccer field, and even a small track. Indoors, a huge stone hall with draped ivy, chandeliers and two floors of arches serves as the main eating area, and an exquisite *Rittersaal* (knights' hall) serves as a concert venue. The dorm-style rooms are usually reserved for groups; individual travelers stay in doubles or quads and are often given a double to themselves if there's space. You'll forget you're in a hostel when you see the large rooms and windows, brass fixtures, wood furniture, private telephones, and elegant lamps. The private bathrooms clinch it: gleaming white with blue accents, towels, drinking glasses and even hair dryers. All this elegance comes with a higher-than-usual price (255AS), but its definitely worth it. The only challenge is getting there; yes, it is that lone castle sitting high on the hill, and yes, you have to walk all the way up there. Consider storing heavy bags at the train station (20AS overnight) and prepare for a 45-50min. walk. From the train station, turn left down Bahnhofstr. and left again at the post office. Cross the tracks, and continue straight down that road for 20-25min. Don't turn right at the Fußweg path sign to the castle, unless you want an extremely steep and slippery footpath directly up the mountain; instead continue down the main road past the lumberyard. Turn right at the large sign for "Schloßherberge Röthelstein" and follow the paved road as it curves up and up and up, ending at the castle. Those with cars can park directly at the hostel. An infrequent morning bus will take travelers from the station to the base of the uphill path, but the hard part is still ahead. (Open Jan.-Oct. Hearty meals available for 50AS.)

If the trek is too intimidating, try **Frühstückspension Mafalda**, on Bachpromenade 75 (tel. (03613) 21 88), which grants two pillows per bed, and showers and toilets in each of its three doubles and three singles. (Singles 240AS; doubles 420AS. 40AS surcharge for one-night stays.) At the post office, turn left and cross over the rail tracks, then make the next two rights and cross over the same ones; Mafalda is right under the tracks—a fact all too apparent when you try to doze off at night. Other rooms closer to the town center run 180-250AS; ask at the tourist office for assistance. The **ADEG supermarket** is on the way to the tourist office (open Mon.-Thurs. and Sat. 7:30am-noon, Fri. 7:30am-noon and 3-6pm). **Buses** depart from the front of the office; **trains** run to **Selzthal,** the regional hub (every 1-2hr., 34AS). Get to Selzthal from Linz (2hr., 168AS. See **Linz**, p. 322.) **Postal code:** A-8911.

■ Steyr

Steyr is famous for its iron trade and notorious as a jewel of ancient city planning. Two mountain rivers, the **Enns** and the **Steyr,** dice the city into three parts, each with a different ambience. The city's appearance, depicted on an etching handed down from 1554, has been preserved until this day. No single structure dominates the city landscape. The various buildings politely stand side-by-side, untouched by the ravages of industrialization. This comely surface hides Steyr's unique position in the annals of modern technology. In 1884, Steyr was the first town in Europe to use electric street lighting. Who would have guessed?

Orientation and Practical Information The **tourist office** in the Rathaus, Stadtplatz 27 (tel. 532 29; fax 532 29 15), provides maps and other information, and exchanges money when the banks are closed. From the train station, walk right on Bahnhofstr. across the bridge, and make a left on Enge Gasse, which leads straight to the Stadtplatz. (Open June-Sept. Mon.-Fri. 8:30am-6pm, Sat. 9am-noon; Oct.-May Mon.-Fri. 8am-6pm, Sat. 9am-noon.) The main **post office** is next to the train station (open Mon.-Fri. 7am-8pm, Sat. 8-11am). There's also a **branch office** off the Stadtplatz, Grünmarkt 1 (open Mon.-Fri. 7:30am-6:30pm). Steyr is most easily reached by **train** from **Linz** (45min., one-way 78AS, round-trip 140AS). The station rents **bicycles** for further travel (open daily 6am-7pm). Small (20AS) and large (30AS) **lockers** are also available at the train station. Pick up a brochure from the tourist office detailing the **biking trails** in the area. Cyclists are offered discounts in some of Steyr's (more expensive) hotels. To get around within the city, several city **buses** connect the *Altstadt,* the train station, and the surrounding communities. There is a local women's center with a lesbian emphasis: **Frauennotruf Steyr,** Wehrgrabengasse 85 (tel. 657 49). **Postal Code:** A-4400. **Telephone Code:** 07252.

Accommodations and Food The most likely place to find inexpensive accommodations is at the **Jugendherberge (HI),** Hafnerstr. 14 (tel. 455 80). Turn right on Bahnhofstr. as you exit the train station, and then turn right on Damberggasse. Walk under the bridge, keep to the right, and begin your slow ascent up the windy hill. Take the second right, then bear right on Bikto-Odlergassestr., past the **Spar Markt** on the left (open Mon.-Fri. 8am-6pm, Sat. 8am-noon). The hostel lies just beyond (15min.). Situated in a residential apartment community, the hostel glows with the bizarre, aged, green and orange tones of its 70s retro styling, and its brown, plastic-furry bed coverings—don't worry, the Village People will be back. It is usually filled to the brim, primarily with schoolchildren, in the months of April through June. (Reception open daily 6-10pm, but you can drop your luggage off by 3pm on weekdays and 5pm on weekends if needed. Curfew 10pm. 76AS; nonmembers 83AS, under 19 69AS, 76AS. Sheets, shower, and breakfast included.) If the hostel fails, try **Albrecht Julius,** Alois-Huemer-Str. 1 (tel. 540 78), on city bus route #1 about 2km outside the city's center. Get off on Fleischmannstr., and continue down the main road; Alois-Huemerstr. is the second and last street on the left. Single and double rooms with sinks, hall showers, and a sauna (!) for common use. The hostess will pick you up from the train station (160AS per person, breakfast included; call ahead). For natural air-conditioning, try **Campingplatz Forelle Steyr,** Kematmüllerstr. 1a (tel. 680 08; fax 614 68; 25AS; open April 4-Oct. 31).

Cheap meals can be found on Pfarrgasse between the Stadtplatz and the parish church, where **Pizza-Kebab Ömer** heats up pre-made pizzas (80AS for a 2-person pie, 40AS for ½pie) as well as kababs (40AS; open daily 10am-10pm; take out only). The best place to soak in the Stadtplatz atmosphere is at **Café Arabia,** Stadtpl. 11 (tel. 422 80). Enjoy an *Apfel Strudel* (24AS) or a medium-sized entrée (48-68AS) on their sidewalk patio (open Mon.-Sat. 7am-midnight, Sun. 7am-10pm).

Sights Discover the city with the tourist offices' complimentary map and sightseeing guide. The focal point of the *Altstadt* is the **Stadtplatz,** which is packed with 15th-century buildings. Other action can be found at the 16th-century **Leopoldibrunnen** (Leopold fountain), which, with its ornamental, wrought-iron spigots and bright flowers, vies with the Rococo **Rathaus** across the square for the title of ornamental heavyweight champion. The town hall was designed by Gotthard Hayberger, Steyr's famous mayor, architect, and Renaissance man-about-town. The former **Dominican Church** *(Marienkirche),* also crammed into the Stadtplatz, was born a Gothic building but put on a Baroque face in the early 17th century. Be sure to follow the Berggasse, one of the numerous narrow lanes typical of Steyr, up to the pink **Lamberg Schloß,** where the **Schloß Galerie** showcases temporary art exhibits (open Tues.-Sun. 10am-noon and 2-5pm; free). If you're not in the museum mood, then wander in the cool green courtyards of the palace.

A pair of famous composers lived in Steyr's *Altstadt* as well, producing some of their best-known works in town. Franz Schubert once occupied the lavender house on the west side of the Stadtplatz, now a **Drogerie Market (dm);** he composed the *Trout Quintet* here. Up the street is the **Stadtpfarrkirche** (City Parish Church), where Steyr's Stevie Wonder, Anton Bruckner, banged away the chords to his final two symphonies on the church organ.

Be sure to sidestep into the narrow, capillarial alleys that branch out from the Stadtplatz and the adjacent Eugegasse, famous for their low-hanging arches (Bang! Damn those short medieval guys). The rambling streets across the Steyr river from the Stadtplatz give off an Italianate feel. Also on the left bank of the Steyr is **St. Michael's Church,** a towering presence that stands at the confluence of the two rivers. It boasts a remarkable gable-fresco painting on its Baroque façade.

Unfortunately, most of Steyr's beautiful residences have been transformed into banks or shops, with modern interiors hidden behind the ornate façades; the major exception is the **Innerberger Stadel,** Grünmarkt 26. Now a museum, it contains a plethora of puppets, a vast utensil collection, an extensive stuffed bird collection, and a gallery with mannequins in military uniforms from around the world. Look kids, a museum for us! (Open Tues.-Thurs. 10am-4pm. Jan.-Nov. free, Dec. 25AS.) A series of idyllic, ivy-laden footbridges built into the cliff lead across the river to the **Museum Industrielle Arbeitswelt,** Wehrengrabengasse 7 (tel. 673 51), with hands-on technological exhibitions celebrating the advance of manufacturing and industry (open Tues.-Sun. 10am-5pm; 55AS, students 35AS).

THE MÜHLVIERTEL

Regional tourist offices consistently extol the wondrous quality of the Mühlviertel atmosphere. Here, they announce, is "some of the cleanest air on earth." There is some truth to what they say. Traveling north from the smoggy environs of Linz, your lungs will quickly corroborate their claim; the only pollutants here are the cows. The Mühlviertel was once the stomping grounds of pagan Celts until the Christians stormed in during the Middle Ages and decided to civilize, decorating the terrain with churches constructed out of the local granite. The granite, Celt-proof, is also home to the famed mineral rich waters of the region, considered curative in homeopathic circles. The woodland walks and quiet agricultural fields are also equally soothing and highly recommended.

Although the Mühlviertel is still considered part of industrial Austria, the region's industry is really of the arts-and-crafts variety. Along the popular vacation route **Mühlviertel Weberstraße** (Fabric Trail), analogous on a bumpkin scale to the Middle Eastern Silk Road, various towns of textile interest display their unique method of linen preparation. The Mühlviertel has been producing this stuff for centuries. You can also follow the **Gotische Straße,** where you'll encounter multitudes of High Gothic architectural wonders. Or try the **Museum Straße,** which boasts more **Freilichtmuseums** (open-air museums) than you can shake a loom at. These museum villages typically recreate the 15th- and 16th-century peasant lifestyle in a functional hamlet. Iron, from Steiermark (Styria), flows through the Mühlviertel on its way to Bohemia along the **Pferdeisenbahn,** an ancient trade route once traversed by horsedrawn caravans of the past, now a favorite hiking route. All through this pastoral countryside, *Bauernhöfe* (farm houses) open their doors to world-weary vacationers in search of a little rural R&R. Nifty tourist brochures document all these trails. For more info about *Bauernhöfe*, area hiking, and the Mühlviertel in general, contact the **Mühlviertel Tourist Office,** Blütenstr. 8, A-4040 Linz, Postfach 57 (tel. (0732) 23 50 20 or 23 81 55).

▓ Freistadt

Owing to its strategic location on the **Pferdeeisenbahn, Freistadt** was a stronghold of the medieval salt and iron trade. Well preserved from its former days, one can journey around its outer and inner wall fortifications, view the span the horizon from its watch tower, feast inside its castle, and swim in the surrounding moat. It is often likened to Germany's Rothenburg, another town that seems untouched by time for the past, oh, five or six centuries.

In 1985, Freistadt received the International Europa Nostra Prize for the finest restoration of a medieval *Altstadt*. While it is also the main city in industrial Mühlviertel, Freistadt still basks in fresh air and lush, verdant crop fields; coming up from Linz, you'll be surprised by the sudden shift from brick walls to rolling pastures. Come sit in one of the many **Gastgärten** perched on the city's inner wall overlooking the moat and enjoy the locally brewed **Freistädter Bier.**

NORTHWEST AUSTRIA

Orientation and Practical Information Freistadt, at the juncture of the **Jaunitz** and **Feldiast** Rivers, is easily reached from Linz. **Trains** run every two hours from **Linz** (round-trip 155AS) and arrive at the Hauptbahnhof, 3km outside of town. You can **rent bikes** (50AS with valid ticket or Eurail Pass) and **store luggage** (20AS) here. To hoof it to the city center, turn right, and walk down the street (it will merge with Leonfeldner Str.); then turn left onto Bahnhofstr. (which becomes Brauhausstr.), and follow it until the end, at Promenade/Linzer Str. At this intersection, the main gate to the town, the **Linzertor**, will be visible; the **Hauptplatz** lies within. Alternatively, catch the city shuttle bus from the back of the station to the Hauptplatz (10AS). However, the shuttle only runs weekdays, leaving the train station twice daily at 8:25am and 11:25am. **Taxis** to the old town cost roughly 70-100AS. Taking a **bus** from **Linz** might be a more viable alternative. Buses #2232 and 2084 leave from Linz at the main train station every hour (round-trip 122AS) and drop you off at Böhmertor in Freistadt, which lies just outside the city walls, a 2-minute walk to the Hauptplatz. The tiny town **tourist office**, Hauptpl. 12 (tel. 29 74), finds accommodations for free and provides information about the surrounding Mühlviertel villages (open Mon.-Fri. 9am-noon and 2-5pm, Sat. 9am-noon). The **post office** is at Promenade 11, at the intersection with St. Peterstr. They only exchange hard cash (no traveler's checks; open Mon.-Fri. 8am-noon and 2-5:30pm, Sat. 8-10:30am). **Postal code: A-4240. Telephone code: 07942.**

Accommodations and Food Freistadt has a few reasonably priced accommodations. The *Schloß* looms ominously behind Freistadt's **Jugendherberge (HI)**, Schloßhof 3 (tel. 43 65). From the tourist office, walk around the corner to the red building right off the Hauptplatz, next to Café Lubinger. The hostel is busy with students from April to July and during the early fall, but it's so empty during the rest of the year that the owner is rarely in. Fun pine-and-brick place with hand-painted stripes, silly cartoons, trees, and homemade paintings on the walls. Very comfortable and clean. Call ahead and leave a message; the accommodating proprietor will wait from 6-8pm to give you a key; if no one is there or you don't arrive in time, try her at home. (Katherine Pichles; tel. 24 73. 70AS, 20AS surcharge for nonmembers. Sheets 40AS. Showers and toilets off the hall. Kitchen facilities available below in the youth center.) For a perfectly positioned place, pick **Pension Pirklbauer**, Höllgasse 2/4 (tel. 24 40). Located in the *Altstadt* right next to the Linzertor. All rooms with shower, toilet, telephone, and TV. Ask in advance, and you can have breakfast in the *Gastgarten* overlooking the old moat. (Singles 220AS; doubles 380AS. Breakfast included.) **Camping Freistadt**, Buchtastr. 10 (tel. 26 24), is only a 7-minute walk out the Böhmertor (follow the signs). In the propietor's big backyard with a nice view of the *Altstadt*. (Reception open daily 8-10am and 5-10pm. 40AS; children 20AS; tent, car, or caravan 5AS; showers 15AS.)

There are a variety of cheap eats at cozy *Gasthäuser;* prowl around for different offerings. Enjoy a *tête-à-tête* at **Café Vis à Vis**, Salzgasse 13 (tel. 42 93). It offers local fare, such as *Mühlviertel Bauernsalat mit Suppe* (farmer's soup and salad, 60AS) and *Freistädter* beer in a garden crowded with young people (open Mon.-Fri. 9:30am-midnight, Sat. 5pm-1am). **Foxi's Schloßtaverne**, Hauptpl. 11 (tel. 39 30), right next to the tourist information center, is patronized by an older but no less raucous crowd. Weekday *menus* offer a soup, main course, and side order (70-88AS). Their Greek salad (75AS) is humongous. Last but not least, **Café Lubiner**, at Hauptpl. 10 is known to have the best ice cream in all of Mühlviertel (12AS for soft-serve, 7AS per scoop of the hard stuff). Pastries and ice cream inside available for take-out or sit in. (Open Sun.-Fri. 8am-7pm, Sat. 8am-6pm.) The most convenient grocery store is **Uni Markt**, Pragerstr. 2, at the intersection of Pragerstr. (an extension of Promenade) and Froschau (behind the Böhmertor side of the *innere Stadt;* open Mon.-Thurs. 8am-12:30pm and 2:30-6pm, Fri. 8am-6pm, Sat. 7:30am-noon).

Sights and Entertainment Start your tour of Freistadt by clambering around the remarkably well preserved 14th-century castle. Its tower, the **Bergfried,** houses the **Mühlviertler Heimathaus** (tel. 22 74). This regional museum displays traditional tools, clothing, and other period pieces, including clocks and playing cards. (Obligatory tours May-Oct. Tues.-Sat. 10am and 2pm, Sun. 10am; Nov.-April Tues.-Fri. 2pm. 10AS.) Descend through an archway down the Ölberggasse with its cobbled shoulder-width twistings and its lovely, hidden garden, or walk around the old moat that circumscribes the old city, now a stretch of gardens and mossy duck ponds. Numerous **hiking trails** branch out from Freistadt to amazing Mühlviertel destinations; consider hiking out of town and catching a **bus** back to Freistadt. The **Pferdeeisenbahnwanderweg** is a 237km hiking trail along the former medieval route. There are no organized tours of the area; instead, pick up a map from the tourist office (10AS) or stop by **Wolfsgruber Bookstore,** Pfarrgasse 16, for help in planning your excursion (open Mon.-Fri. 7:30am-noon and 2:30-6pm, Sat. 7:30am-noon). You could also take a mildly strenuous 1-hour hike up the zig-zagging Kreuzweg to **St. Peter's Church.** The walk is peppered by several beautiful monuments. A large map on the Promenade illustrates other local hiking paths, and the tourist office provides free bus schedules and inexpensive hiking maps.

Freistadt's pride and joy is the **Freistädter Brauerei,** a community-owned brewery in operation since 1777; don't be surprised to see "I only drink Freistadt beer" stickers posted around the steering wheels of most of the buses in the area. In 13th-century Freistadt, every male citizen was granted the right to brew and sell his own beer. In 1363, realizing that there was a profit to be made via the popular froth, Herzog Rudolph IV forbade anyone within a mile of the city to make or sell beer. The issue was finally resolved in 1737 when all small breweries were dissolved and a commonly held community brewery established. The brewery is still there, located just outside the town walls at Promenade 7. The brewery conducts free tours and concludes with equally **free beer.** Tours every Wednesday at 2pm between September and May. To join a tour, ask at a local *Gasthaus* that serves *Freistädter* beer (they almost all do) or call the brewery for more info (tel. 57 77).

Southeast Austria

Austria's harshest peaks guard the Italian and Slovenian borders from the southern regions of **Carinthia** (Kärnten) and **East Tirol** (Osttirol). Italian architecture, a sunny climate, and a distinctly laid-back atmosphere give Carinthia a somewhat Mediterranean feel, not unlike Switzerland's Ticino region. The palpable warmth of the local population, however, can be deceiving. Four percent of the state's inhabitants are ethnic Slovenes (Austria's only significant national minority), and the xenophobic Carinthian Homeland Movement makes no secret of its desire to send them packing. In the "Town-Sign War" of the 1970s, for example, the Slovenes lobbied for bilingual street signs (in both German and Slovene); the measure was soundly defeated by the Austrian majority. The current unrest in the former Yugoslavian republics has also exacerbated the situation; tensions remain heated in discussions of minority affairs. The former president of the provincial government was Jörg Haider, present leader of the arch-conservative Freedom Movement which still controls the Carinthian legislature (see Government and Politics, p. 237).

Also encompassing the provinces of **Styria** (Steiermark) and **Burgenland,** southeastern Austria's rolling Alpine foothills and gentle valleys are topographically unexciting by Austrian standards—which explains the relative dearth of tourists. Styria's rich deposits of iron ore made it very exciting to some, however, and Styria became one of Europe's first centers of primitive industry. The region also cashes in on the gold and precious stones of Graz, its burgeoning provincial capital. The countryside in Burgenland is drenched with endless fields of sunflowers, rows of yellow faces all oriented like solar panels. The vineyard-covered land belonged to Hungary until 1918, and Magyar influence is still ubiquitous in food, architecture, and dress.

■ Klagenfurt

At the crossroads of north-south and east-west trade routes, the initial settlement of Klagenfurt has burgeoned into a major summertime destination. Billed as "the Rose of the **Wörthersee,** the easy-going, southernmost provincial capital of Austria attracts thousands of work-weary Austrians who unwind in its beachfront suburbs. Many have playfully dubbed Klagenfurt the Austrian Riveria. This obvious refusal to ignore Austria's landlocked status does carry a certain bit of accuracy, however. Situated only 60km north of Italy, locals of this Carinthian capital lead a lifestyle similar to their southern counterparts, enjoying a culture of European pleasures: casual strolls around a palette of outdoor cafés, Italian Renaissance courtyards, wrought iron tracery, and tree-lined avenues framed by Alpine peaks.

GETTING TO KLAGENFURT

Planes arrive at the **Klagenfurt-Wörthersee Airport** (tel. 41 50 00). Flights from **Vienna** are prohibitively costly for anyone on a budget, but arrive approximately every two hours (round-trip 3400AS). To get to the airport from the train station, take bus #40, 41, or 42 to "Heiligenplatz" and switch to bus #45, taking it all the way to "Flughafen." **By car,** Klagenfurt can be reached by Autobahn A2 from the west, Route 91 from the south, Route 70 from the east, and Route 83 from the north. From **Vienna** or **Graz,** take Autobahn A2 south to Route 70 west. **Trains** chug to the **Hauptbahnhof** (tel. 17 17) at the intersection of Südbahngürtel and Bahnhofstr. (open 24hr.). To reach the town center from the train station follow Bahnhofstr. to Paradieserstr, turn left, and Neuerpl. is two blocks down on the right. Trains travel to **Lienz** (1hr.40min., 2 daily, 216AS); **Salzburg** (3hr., 9 daily, 316AS); the **Vienna Sudbahnhof** (4hr.15min., 12 daily, 416AS.); and **Villach** (½hr., several daily, 64AS). Other connections can be made in Salzburg or Vienna. The **Ostbahnhof,** at the intersection of Meißtalerstr. and Rudolfsbahngürtel, is for shipping only. **Buses** depart across the street from the train station. There are **BundesBus routes** to most destinations in Car-

Southeast Austria

inthia (**Villach** 68AS, **Pörtschach** 34AS, **St. Veit** 48AS, **Friesach** 82AS, and **Graz** 176AS). The ticket window (tel. 581 10) is open Mon.-Fri. 6am-6pm, Sat.-Sun. 7am-6pm.

ORIENTATION AND PRACTICAL INFORMATION

Alterplatz, Neuerplatz, and **Heiligengeistplatz,** the town's bus centers, comprise the three-ring circus of the city's center. They are encompassed by the **Ring,** the inner district of Klagenfurt, which bustles with social and commercial activity and is bounded by St. Veiter Ring, Völkermarkter Ring, Viktringer Ring, and Villacher Ring. Streets within the Ring generally run north to south and east to west, creating a grid-like pattern. The **Lendkanal,** a narrow waterway, and **Villacherstr.** lead from the city's center to the Wörthersee about 3km away.

> **Tourist Office: Gäste Information** (tel. 53 72 23; fax 53 72 95; email Klagenfurt-Info@w-see.or.at; http://www.w-see.or.at/Klagenfurt/) is on the first floor of the Rathaus in the Neuerplatz. The well-staffed, English-speaking office supplies visitors with colorful English brochures and helps find rooms for no fee. From the station, walk down Bahnhofstr., and turn left onto Paradiesergasse, which opens into Neuerpl. Open May-Sept. Mon.-Fri. 8am-8pm, Sat.-Sun. 10am-5pm; Oct.-April Mon.-Fri. 8am-5pm. **Branch office** (tel. 236 51) outside Minimundus. Open mid-May to mid-Sept. daily 9am-8pm.
> **Currency Exchange:** Best rates at the main post office and its train station branch.
> **Telephones:** Phone centers at both post offices.
> **Public Transportation:** Klagenfurt boasts a punctual and comprehensive bus system. The central bus station is located at Heiligengeistpl. Single-fare rides 20AS. Buy individual tickets or a 24-hr. pass (40AS) from the driver. *Tabak* kiosks sell blocks of tickets at reduced rates. Pick up a *Fahrplan* (bus schedule) at the tourist office. *Schwarzfahrer,* or illegal riders, are heavily looked down upon; violators face a hefty 400AS fine.
> **Car Rental: Hertz,** Villacherstr. 4 (tel. 561 47). **Avis,** Villacherstr. 1c (tel. 559 38).
> **Bike Rental:** At the Hauptbahnhof (90AS, 50AS with train ticket for that day) or at the main tourist office (70AS for 24hr.). The tourist office distributes a pamphlet entitled *Radwandern,* detailing local bike paths and sights easily reached by bike.
> **Luggage storage:** At the train station. 20AS per piece. Lockers 20AS. Open 24hr.

Gay, Lesbian, and Bisexual Information: Gay Hot-Line Klagenfurt, Postfach 193 (tel. 50 46 90). Hotline open Wed. 6-8pm. **Bella Donna Frauenzentrum** (Women's Center), Villacherring 21/2 (tel. 51 42 01). Open Mon.-Fri. 9am-1pm.

AIDS Hotline: AIDS-Hilfe Kärnten, 8 Maistr. 19/4 (tel. 551 28). Open Mon-Tues. and Thurs. 5-7pm.

Pharmacy: Pharmacies abound, **Landschafts-Apotheke,** Alterpl. 32, and **Obir-Apotheke,** Baumbachpl. 21, provide 2 distinguished options.

Medical Assistance: Klagenfurt Krankenhaus, St.-Veiter-Str. 47 (tel. 538).

Emergency: tel. 133. **Ambulance:** tel. 144. **Medical Assistance:** tel. 141. **Police:** tel. 53 33, in an emergency 133.

Post Office: Main post office, Pernhartgasse 7 (tel. 556 55). Open Mon.-Fri. 7:30am-8pm and Sat. 7:30am-1pm. **Currency exchange** open Mon.-Fri. 7:30am-5pm. **Train station branch,** Bahnhofpl. 5. (tel. 58 10). Open 24hr.

Postal Code: A-9020.

Telephone Code: 0463.

ACCOMMODATIONS AND CAMPING

Though the summer heat dries up the pool of available rooms, there is *some* compensation for the sudden dearth; two student dormitories convert to youth hostels during July and August. The tourist office will help sniff out accommodations for no fee; it also distributes helpful pamphlets: *Hotel Information*, with a city map; *You are Welcome*, both in English; and *Ferienwohnunger, Ferienhäuser, Privatequartiere*, listing private rooms in German. If you're staying in a hotel or *Pension*, ask for the **Gästepaß** (guest card), which entitles you to a free city guide and discounts at specified cafés, museums, and other area attractions.

Jugendherberge Klagenfurt, Neckheimgasse 6 (tel. 23 00 20; fax 23 00 20 20), at the corner of Universitätstr. and Neckheimgasse, is close to the university and a 20-min. walk from the Wörthersee. From the Hauptbahnhof, take bus #40, 41, or 42 to "Heiligengeistpl.," switch to bus #12, and disembark at "Jugendgästehaus," or, since bus #12 runs infrequently, catch bus #10 or 11 to "Neckhcimgasse." (Catch all at stand 2 at Heiligerplatz.) This spic-and-span hostel, designed for the Jetson family, features a bubblegum-pink and baby-blue color scheme and assorted foliage. All rooms are quads with bunk beds, private showers, and toilets. Reception open daily 7-9am and 5-10pm. 175AS. Nonmembers 215AS. Curfew 10pm. Breakfast (7-8am) and sheets included. Dinner 80AS. Key deposit 200AS, or leave a passport, or student ID. Reservations recommended.

Jugendgästehaus Kolping, Enzenbergstr. 26 (tel. 569 65; fax 569 65 32). From the station, head down Bahnhofstr., turn right at Viktringer Ring, left at Völkermarkter Ring, right at Feldmarschall-Conrad-pl., which becomes Völkermarkterstr., and, finally (whew!), right on Enzenbergstr. (20min.). Run by the friendly family Kolping, this dormitory provides simple rooms decorated by a single cross. Reception open 24hr. 150AS, with private shower 190AS, under 18 170AS, surcharge for one-night stay 20AS, surcharge for singles 40AS. Breakfast included. Open only when school is out—early July to early Sept.

Pension Klepp, Platzgasse 4 (tel. 322 78). The closest accommodation to the train station in town, Klepp is a 10-min. walk from both the station and the city center. From the station, follow Bahnhofstr., take the third right onto Viktringer Ring, and then the second right onto Platzgasse. Comfortable rooms with large windows as well as hall toilets and showers. Singles 250AS; doubles 450AS.

Jugendheim Mladinski Dom, Mikschallee 4 (tel. 356 51, fax 356 51 11). Follow the directions to Jugendgästehaus Kolping, but instead of turning down Enzenbergstr., continue down Völkermarkterstr., and turn right on Mikschallee (25min.). Another option is to take bus #40, 41, or 42 to Heiligergeistpl. and then bus #70 or 71 (dir: Ebental) to "Windischkaserne" from stand #13, and keep walking the direction the bus goes (bus runs Mon.-Sat. until 6:50pm). Mladinski Dom serves as a student dorm during the school year, converting to a pleasant bed-and-breakfast early July to early Sept. It has a gym and parking, as well as private toilets and showers. Reception open Mon.-Fri. 6am-midnight, Sat.-Sun. 24hr. Curfew 10pm, but key available. Singles 255AS; doubles 410AS; triples 435AS. Children under 12 110AS, under 6 70AS. Breakfast 25AS. Discount after 3 nights 20AS.

Hotel Liebetegger, Völkermarkterstr. 8 (tel. 569 35; fax 56 93 56). From the train station, walk up Bahnhofstr., and make a right on Burggasse, which becomes Salmstr. When Salmstr. ends, curve to the left around Feldmarshall-Conradplatz, and bear right onto Völkermarkterstr. (10min.). Small but adequate rooms. Reception on the 2nd floor. Singles 220AS, with shower 250AS, with shower and toilet 350AS; doubles 350AS, with shower and toilet 600AS; triples 550AS, with shower and toilet 750AS. Breakfast 50AS.

Klagenfurt-Wörthersee Camping-Strandbad (tel. 211 69; fax 211 69 93) is at the Metnitzstrand right off Universitätsstr. From the Hauptbahnhof, take bus #40, 41, or 42 to the end station at "Heiligengeistpl.," then bus #12 to the end station "Strandbad Klagenfurter See." Turn left immediately upon disembarking, and walk for 2min.; the campsite will be to the left, on the edge of the Wörthersee. Grocery store, miniature golf, and beach on the grounds. May to mid-June and late Aug. to Sept. 50AS, ages 3-14 25AS. Site 100AS. Small site 20AS. Mid-June to late-Aug. 80AS per person, ages 3-14 40AS. Year-round tax for persons over 18 12AS. Showers and beach entry included. Open May-Sept.

FOOD

Like its Italian counterparts, Klagenfurt finds gastronomical and cultural sustenance in the myriad cafés that freckle the old city's squares and streets. You don't have to walk far or look hard to find an inexpensive place to eat. Neuerplatz, Kardinalplatz, and Burggasse overflow with small eateries. Though a bit expensive, **Café Musil** is the city's most famous place to stop for delectable cookies, cakes, and coffee. Café Musil operates a small stand at Neuerpl. (open Mon.-Sat. 8:15am-7:30pm, Sun. 9am-7:30pm), along with a fairly dressy, larger bistro at 10 Oktoberstr. 14 (open until 10pm). The tourist office prints a helpful brochure called *Sonntagsbraten,* listing the addresses and opening hours of Klagenfurt's cafés, restaurants, clubs, and bars.

Rote Lasche (Red Tongue), Villacherstr. 21, on the corner of Villachstr. and Villacher Ring. This ultracool, vegetarian-specialty restaurant is best categorized under "Eatery of the Absurd." Inspired and decorated by Klagenfurter absurdist artist Victor Rogy, the diner-like restaurant is upholstered wall-to-wall with his artwork, from the 4-meter red rubber tongue that greets you at the door and lends its name to the restaurant to the racks of postcards displaying some of his tamer works. The impeccably tuxedoed waiters help complete the sensory overload by delivering, arguably, the most delicious vegetarian dishes in Austria. Banana curry rice (69AS). Peppers stuffed with potato purée (88AS). Open Mon.-Fri. 11am-midnight, Sat. 11am-3pm.

Zuckerbäckerei-Café-Konditorei-Imbisse D. Todor, Feldmarschall-Conrad-Pl. 6 (tel. 51 18 35). Now *that's* a mouthful. This everything-in-one café is a quick and inexpensive haven for any meal. Chow down on *Salatschüssel* (salad dish; 35-50AS) and *Schinken-Käse Toast* (ham and cheese on toast; 30AS) in the sun-drenched, ivy-enclosed *Gastgarten* out back. Also serves ice cream (7AS), candy, and freshly baked goods (12-28AS). Open Mon.-Fri. 7am-9pm, Sat. 7am-2pm.

Café Pumpe, Lidmanskygasse 2 (tel. 571 96), down the block from Café Musil. Here, at their favorite hangout, the locals may at first deal you lengthy stares. Don't worry, the beer they serve helps smooth the road for even the greenest of foreigners. A salt-of-the-earth crowd helps season Pumpe's famous *goulash* (small 40AS, medium 58AS, groß-me-out 76AS). Midday *menu* 59, 69 and 79AS. Open Mon.-Fri. 9am-10pm, Sat. 9am-1:30pm.

Rathausstüberl, Pfarrplatz 35 (tel. 579 47), is on a hidden cobblestone street right by the Pfarrkirche. Freshly prepared Carinthian specialties at attractively low prices. *Käsnudel mit grünem Salat* (cheese and potato dumplings with green salad) and other daily specials 75AS. Italian entrées 65-78AS. People-watch on the outdoor terrace on balmy summer evenings. English menus available. Open Mon.-Fri. 8:30am-midnight, Sat. 8:30am-2pm and 7pm-2am.

Markets

Every Thursday and Saturday from 8am-noon, the compact **Benediktinerplatz** on the lower westside of the *Altstadt* welcomes a barrage of rickety, wooden stands showcasing fresh fruits and vegetables.

SPAR Markt, just off Heiligengeistpl. on Hermangasse. Open Mon.-Fri. 8am-6:30pm, Sat. 8am-1pm. Another on Bahnhofstr. with a small, cheap restaurant inside. After 3pm, breads and sweets in the *Konditorei* are half-price. Open Mon.-Fri. 7:30am-6:30pm, Sat. 7:30am-1pm.

Konsum, next to the main bus terminal at Bahnhofpl. 1. Open Mon.-Fri. 8am-6pm, Sat. 8am-noon. There's another branch directly behind the hostel, on Universitätsstr. Open Mon.-Fri. 8am-12:30pm and 2:30-6pm, Sat. 8am-noon.

Biokost, Wiesbadener Str. 3, is a health-food market right off of Neuer Platz. Open Mon.-Fri. 7:30am-6:30pm, Sat. 7am-12:30pm.

SIGHTS AND ENTERTAINMENT

A tour of Klagenfurt should begin with a walk through the city's *Altstadt.* If you're not interested in having the tourist office's pamphlet, *A Walk Round Klagenfurt's Old Town,* navigate your journey, seek out one of the free guided tours leaving from the front of the Rathaus (July-Aug. Mon.-Sat. 10am; usually in German). Buildings in this part of town display a strange amalgam of architectural styles: Biedermeier, Italian Renaissance, Mannerist, Baroque, and *Jugendstil* façades all attempt to upstage each other. At the edge of the **Alter Platz** stands the 16th-century **Landhaus,** originally an arsenal and later the seat of the provincial diet. Its symmetrical towers, staircases, and flanking projections gracefully create a courtyard sprinkled with the banana-yellow umbrellas of numerous outdoor cafés. The flourishes of the interior are what truly deserve accolades—665 brilliant coats of arms blanket the walls (it took artist Johann Ferdinand Fromiller nearly 20 years to complete them all). Don't let the ceiling's "rounded" edges fool you. The room is perfectly rectangular (open April-Sept. Mon.-Fri. 9am-noon and 12:30-5pm. 10AS, students 5AS).

A brisk stroll through Kramergasse, one of the oldest streets in Klagenfurt, leads directly to the **Neuer Platz.** Here, merry-go-rounds for the kids, cafés for adults, and soapboxes for cantankerous university ideologues are all readily available amid the torrent of motion and activity. Standing proudly over the eastern end, a (rather large) statue of (rather large) Maria Theresa glares regally at the skateboarders launching themselves off her pedestal. And that's not her only indignity; the 60-ton half-lizard, half-serpent, braces-needing, copper creature spitting water in her direction is the **Lindwurm,** Klagenfurt's heraldic beast. Legend has it that this virgin-consuming monster once terrorized the Wörthersee area and prevented the settlers from draining the marshes. Enter Hercules, monster-slayer and all-around *übermensch.* He quickly dispatched the beast in Schwarzeneggerian fashion and saved the village; the women of Klagenfurt would swoon when they recounted how the hero craftily lodged a barbed hook in the throat of a sacrificial cow to put an end to the monster. Today, the Lindwurm still terrorizes Klagenfurt, albeit more subtly—Puff the Magic Dragon-esque stuffed animals turn up *everywhere.*

Two blocks south of Neuer Platz, off Karfreitstr., is Klagenfurt's **Domplatz** and **Kathedrale.** Rebuilt after being destroyed by Allied bombing in 1944, the nondescript modern exterior of the building and surrounding square make the church easy to miss. This would be a shame—the cathedral's interior is gloriously decorated with high arches, crystal chandeliers, pink and white floral stucco, and a brilliant gold altar. Other ecclesiastical paraphenalia is on display in the tiny **Diözesanmuseum** (tel. 502 498) next door, Lidmanskygasse 10, including the oldest extant stained-glass window in all of Austria, a humble, 800-year-old sliver portraying Mary Magdalene. (Open mid-June to mid-Sept. daily 10am-noon and 3pm-5pm; mid-Sept. to mid-Oct. and May to early June 10am-noon. 30AS, students 10AS, children 5AS.)

Klagenfurt and its suburbs are home to no fewer than 23 castles and mansions; the tourist office's English brochure *From Castle to Castle* suggests a path to view them all, and gives details on architecture and visiting possibilities. One can also pick up the German *Museumswandern* brochure, giving addresses and opening hours for the city's 15 museums and 22 art galleries.

One of the largest museum was also 19th-century enlightened despot Franz Josef's favorite museum, the **Landesmuseum,** Museumgasse 2 (tel. 53 63 05 52). The former Habsburg emperor's most cherished exhibit was **Prohaska,** a stuffed dog that, prior to stuffing, served as the regimental mascot and faithful friend of Field Marshall Radetsky. Other guests also admire the Celtic and Roman artifacts, 18th-century musical instruments, or giant Großglockner relief map. Also on display is the **Lindwurmschädel,** a fossilized rhinoceros skull, discovered in 1335, that served three centuries later as the inspiration for the heinous Lindwurm statue in the Neuerplatz. (Museum open Tues.-Sat. 9am-4pm, Sun. 10am-1pm, Mon. during inclement weather. 30AS, children 15AS.) The **Kärntner Landesgalerie** (tel. 53 63 05 42), at Burggasse 8, two blocks east of Neuerplatz, is home to an eccentric collection of 19th- and 20th-century artwork, with a focus on Carinthian Expressionism. Slog through the first couple of rooms of newer art to get to the good stuff; Werner Berg's *Pigs' Heads,* is a grotesque still-life parody that could turn even the staunchest of carnivores into a vegetarian. (Open Mon-Fri. 9am-6pm, Sat. and Sun. 10am-noon. 20AS, students and children 5AS.) The **Robert Musil Museum,** Bahnhofstr. 50 (tel. 50 14 29), honors the work of its namesake, Austria's most famous modern bard, with an archive of his writings. (Open Mon.-Fri. 10am-noon and 2-4pm, Sat. 10am-noon. Ring bell to be let in. Free.)

Klagenfurt's most shameless concession to tourist kitsch is the **Minimundus** park, Villacherstr. 241 (tel. 21 94), minutes from the Wörther See. The park remains entertaining despite the masses of camera-clicking, finger-pointing tourists. Artists have created intricately detailed models of over 160 world-famous buildings and sights— all on a 1:25 scale. You'll be on eye level with the Parthenon, Big Ben, and the Taj Mahal, along with plenty of more obscure buildings. For a taste of home, depending on where home is, check out the Sydney Opera House, a Maori Communal House, Groot Constantia, Westminster Palace, the White House, or the Statue of Liberty. At night, an outstanding lighting system illuminates the models. From the main train station, take bus #40, 41, 42 to "Heiligengeistpl.," then switch to bus #10, 11, 20, 21, or 22 (dir: Strandbad), and disembark at "Minimundus." (Open April and Oct. daily 9am-5pm; May-June and Sept. 9am-6pm; July-Aug. Sun.-Tues. and Thurs.-Fri. 8am-7pm, Wed. and Sat. 8am-9pm. 85AS, children 6-15 25AS, seniors 65AS, groups with 10 people 60AS per person. Extensive and fairly necessary English guidebooks 30AS.) All profits go to the Austrian "Save the Child" society, so you can feel slightly better as your *Schillings* are sucked up.

Next door to Minimundus is **Happ's Reptilien Zoo,** its cages enclosing a host of the Lindenwurm's descendants. Evidently Mr. Happ defines the term "Reptilien" rather loosely—along with the puff adders, tortoises, and iguanas, the zoo also features spiders, scorpions, rabbits, guinea pigs, and local Wörther See fish. Every Saturday, there's a piranha and crocodile show; every Sunday, the snakes shimmy freely around the garden. (Open May-Sept. daily 8am-6pm; Oct.-April daily 8am-5pm. Admission 70AS, students 60AS, children 30AS.) The **planetarium** (tel. 217 00), behind the zoo, has a show daily (75AS, under 18 45AS) and stargazing at 9pm on clear Wednesday nights (50AS, children 30AS).

To maximize your entertainment *Schilling,* read the tourist office's *Veranstaltung-Kalender* (Calendar of Events) available in English. The tourist office also distributes brochures listing concerts, gallery shows, museum exhibits, and plays, including the cabaret performances in the **Theater im Landhauskeller** throughout July and August. Tickets are available through **Reisebüro Springer** (tel. 387 05 55; 120AS, students 80AS; performances in German). The **Stadttheater,** built in 1910, is Klagenfurt's main venue for major operas, plays, and traveling dance troupes. To enjoy a cultivated night on the town, call the Stadttheater box office. (Tel. 540 64. Tickets 40-520AS; 50% discount for students and seniors. Open mid-Sept. to mid-June Tues.-Sat. 9am-noon and 4-6pm. At all other times, contact the tourist office.) The best of

Klagenfurt's limited nightlife can be found in the pubs of the **Pfarrplatz.** Keep your eyes open for the **Disco Bus** (tel. 50 53 11) which often runs from 9:30pm to 3:15am, picking up and dropping off party-goers at various area discos and bars (only in July and August; bus leaves from Heiligengeistpl.; round-trip 20AS).

On a humid spring or summer day, you may choose to skip the *Altstadt* altogether to join the crowd basking in the sun and lolling in the clear water of the nearby **Wörther See.** This water-sport haven is Carinthia's warmest, largest, and most popular lake. The two closest beaches to Klagenfurt are the **Strandbad Klagenfurt See** and the **Strandbad Maiernigg.** (Both open 8am-8pm. 35AS, children 15AS; after 3pm 20AS, children 7AS. Family card with one adult and up to five children 50AS, with two adults, 80AS. 50AS key deposit for a locker.) The former is crowded but easily accessible by public transportation, and only a 20-min. walk from the hostel. From the Hauptbahnhof, take bus #40, 41, or 42 to the end station, "Heiligengeistpl.," then bus #10, 11, or 12 to "Strandbad Klagenfurter See." To enjoy the water without getting wet, rent a **rowboat** (½hr. 24AS), **pedal boat** (42AS), or **electric boat** (66AS); beach admission not required. Strandbad Maiernigg is far from the noise and fuss of its busier counterpart, but you'll need a car or a bicycle to get there. From downtown, ride along Villacherstr. until it intersects Wörther See Süduferstr., and then follow signs to "Wörther See Süd." **Stadtwerke Klagenfurt Wörthersee-und-Lendkanal-Schiffahrt** (tel. 211 55; fax 211 55 15) offers scenic cruises on the lake and short rides down the canal. The 2-hour cruise (round-trip 170AS) takes you as far as **Velden,** on the opposite shore, and allows stops at designated docks along the way. You can purchase tickets in advance at the Stadtwerke Klagenfurt information center in Heiligengeistpl. For bike trips, pick up a *Radwandern* brochure, free at the tourist office, suggesting seven one-and-a-half-hour tours, 20 two-hour tours, and 12 four-and-a-half-hour tours.

THE DRAUTAL

Bordered by Italy to the south and Slovenia to the southeast, the **Drautal** (Drau Valley) in central Carinthia, with its moderate climate, well-endowed watering holes, and proximity to southern Europe, evokes locales decidedly un-Teutonic. The region gingerly combines skiing and water sports in high- and low-lands carved by the river **Drau,** between the Höhe Tauern and the Villacher Alps. The region's largest peaks soar a mere 2000m, a baby-step above the timberline. The mountains are favored not just with lumber and plenty of snow but with valuable minerals: iron ore, lead, tungsten, zinc, and manganese. Nestled among these lazy peaks is the partially navigable Drau and its tributaries, plus numerous popular lakes, streams, and warm-water springs, where curative spas tempt visitors even in the coldest months. One especially scintillating pastime involves lounging in the shallow end of a toasty bath while commenting on the probable body temperature of the various skiers spread-eagled on the slopes of the surrounding mountains.

Though the Drautal has the transportation hub of **Villach** and the important electronic components industry at its core, it still manages to unwind at a variety of lakeside resorts. These include the Millstätter See, the serpent-shaped Ossiacher See near Villach, and the baths of its many smaller towns and villages, such as the Broßer-Mühldorger See near Gmünd, the Afritzer See near Afritz, and the Faaker See near Villach, with an enchanting island in its center. Fitness buffs can enjoy trails, marked through meadows and mountains, as well as manifold water sports and mountain biking, an increasingly popular activity in Carinthia. When the frost arrives, you can return to ice-skate on the lakes where you backstroked months ago.

■ Villach

Awe-inspiring mountain backdrops and an intriguing, multicultural atmosphere make Villach (pop. 55,000) an unforgettable and occasionally unfathomable city. Situated just north of the border between Austria, Italy, and Slovenia, Villach is distinctly schizophrenic; even the street musicians betray the influence of cultural neighbors in the inflections of their traditional Carinthian, German, Italian, and occasionally American folk songs (listen for John Denver's *Take Me Home, Country Roads*). The august **Villach Kirchtag** manages to celebrate the former three all at once with food, song, and dance. Nevertheless, Villach still shifts uneasily under its burden of problems. Although Carinthia declared its allegiance to Austria in the famous referendum of October 19, 1920, the present war-torn situation of former Yugoslavia has subtly, but painfully refocused attention on ethnic differences here.

Orientation and Practical Information Villach sprawls on two sides of the River Drau. Bahnhofstr. leads from the train station, over a 9th-century bridge, to the economic and social heart of Villach, the **Hauptplatz.** Narrow cobblestone paths are woven throughout this area in the center of town, revealing hidden restaurants and cafés with every new corner. The square is flanked by two sweeping arcs of stores, and is closed off at one end by a towering church, with the Drau river forming the other boundary.

Villach's **tourist office,** Europapl. 2 (tel. 04 22 41), cheerfully gives advice on the town's attractions and area skiing, and also helps find accommodations for free. From the train station walk out to Bahnhofstr., take a left onto Nikolaigasse right after the church, and walk 50m (5min.). The ivy-covered office is on your right. (Open July 21-Aug. and late Dec.-March Mon.-Fri. 8am-6pm, Sat. 9am-noon; April-July 20 and Sept.-Nov. Mon.-Fri. 8am-12:07pm and 1:30-6, Sat. 9am-noon.) An **ATM** is conveniently located on Hauptpl., under the **Bank fur Kärnten und Steiermark. Telephones** are available at the post office.

Villach has **Trains** to **Vienna Südbahnhof** (456AS), **Innsbruck** (396AS), **Klagenfurt** (64AS), **Salzburg** (264AS), and **Graz** (356AS). A free city **bus** service travels a circuit every 20 minutes (Mon.-Fri. 8:40am-6:20pm, Sat. 8:40am-12:20pm). A **taxi** stand is located at the Bahnhof, or call 288 88, 310 10 or 322 22. **Car rental** services are available at **Hertz,** inside the **Springer Reisebüro** at Hans Gasser-Pl. 1 (tel. 269 70; open Mon.-Fri. 8am-noon and 2-5pm). You can **rent bikes** at the **train station,** (100AS per day, 50AS with train ticket or Eurail Pass), or at **Das Radl** Italienstr. 22b (tel. 269 54). **Luggage storage** is also found at the train station (30AS per day; open daily 6:30am-8:30pm). The local **hospital** is at Nikolaigasse 43 (tel. 208). Dial 20 30 for **police** headquarters. The mailman cometh to the main **post office** (tel. 26 77 10), at the right of the train station. **Currency** is **exchanged** here also (open Mon.-Fri. 7am-5pm). **Postal code: A-9500. Telephone code:** 04242.

Accommodations and Food Few budget accommodations are accessible by foot in Villach. If you have a car, pick up a *pension* list at the tourist office to find outlying bargains. The most reasonably priced option is **Jugendgästehaus Villach (HI),** Dinzlweg 34 (tel. 563 68). From the train station walk up Bahnhofstr., go over the bridge, and through Hauptpl. Then turn right on Postgasse, walk through Hans-Gasser-Pl., which merges into Tirolerstr., and bear right at St. Martinstr.; Dinzlweg is the first street on the left (20-30min.). The hostel is tucked away past all of the tennis courts. This pleasant facility, plastered with neon yellow and orange à la 1976, houses 150 in spacious 5-bed dorm rooms, each with its own shower. Make reservations—the hostel is often full with school groups. (Reception open daily 7-10am and 5-10pm. Curfew 10pm. 155AS. Breakfast (7:30-8:30am) and sheets included. Lunch or dinner 75AS each. Bike rental 15AS per hour, 80AS per day. Keys available with a deposit of a passport or ID.) **Pension Eppinger Grete,** Klagenfurterstr. 6 (tel. 243 89), has 16 beds in the center of town. From the station, walk up Bahnhofstr. and turn left onto Klagenfurterstr. (5min.). The tiny *Pension* is in a small alleyway on the right.

(Singles 200-300AS; doubles 300-400AS; triples 450-480AS. Showers and toilet off the hall. No breakfast, but there's a bakery across the street.)

Eating in Villach delights both palate and pocketbook. **Lederergasse** overflows with small, cheap restaurants, while sprawling **Kaiser-Josef-Platz** and the **Hauptplatz** seat swankier sunglass-sporting patrons. **Ristorante Flaschl,** on Seilergasse, behind the **Bank für Kärnten und Steiermark,** offers genuine Italian fare in a plaster grotto with dark red lights (pizzas and pastas 65-105AS; open Mon.-Fri. 5pm-2am, Sat. 6pm-2am). **Pizzeria Trieste,** Weißbriachgasse 14 (tel. 25 00 58), bakes up its popular pies for 65-100AS (open daily 10am-11pm). Overlooking the Drau at Nikolaipl. 2 is **Konditerei Bernhold** (tel. 254 42), Villach's answer to Vienna's Demel, the legendary cathedral of sweets. Snack on sundry colorful pastries (12-29AS), devilish ice cream concoctions, and refreshing mixed drinks—sip nonchalantly on a cappuccino (28AS) as you watch the ships cruising up and down the Drau (open Mon.-Fri. 7:30am-7pm, Sat. 8am-7pm, Sun. 9:30am-7pm). Pick up a picnic lunch at the **Julius Meinl supermarket,** Hauptpl. 14 (open Mon.-Fri. 8am-6:30pm, Sat. 7:30am-noon), or the less expensive **SPAR Markt** in the Hans-Grasser-Platz or at 10 Octoberstr. 6 (open Mon.-Fri. 7:30am-6:15pm, Sat. 7:30am-noon).

Sights and Entertainment Any tour of Villach must traverse the bustling **Hauptplatz,** the commercial heart of the city for 800 years. The southern end of the square lives in the mighty Gothic shadow of the **St. Jakob-Kirche,** only one of Villach's 12 lovely churches. Slightly raised on a stone terrace, this 12th-century church was converted during the Reformation in 1526, and thereby became Austria's first Protestant chapel. In the Counter-Reformation, however, it switched back to Catholicism, and today is still a gorgeous Catholic church with all the trimmings. Inside, the high altar's gilt Baroque canopy dazzles the most jaded eyes; don't let the glitter obscure the staid Gothic crucifix suspended just in front. An ascent up the tallest steeple in Carinthia (94m), the church's **Stadtpfarrturm** (tel. 20 54 75), affords an equally dazzling sight of Villach and its environs. (Open June-Sept. Mon.-Sat. 10am-6pm; July-Aug. also Fri. until 9pm; Oct. Mon.-Sat. 10am-4pm; May Mon.-Sat. 10am-4pm. 20AS, students and children 10AS.)

Learn more about Villach's history at the **Stadtmuseum,** Widmanngasse 38 (tel. 20 53 49). Along with archaeological and mineral displays from 6 millennia, the museum features clocks, hats, lots of paintings of men in those uncomfortable-looking 18th-century collars, and the original gold-on-black Villach coat of arms from 1240—an eagle talon clutching a mountain top. Through the stone-paved courtyard, containing remnants of the old city wall, one finds life-sized dioramas of miners, and gems displayed on black velvet. (Museum open May-Oct. daily 10am-4:30pm; Nov.-April Mon.-Fri. 10am-6pm, Sat. 10am-noon and 2-5pm. 30AS, students 20AS, children under 15 free.)

A quick five-minute walk lifts you from the congested streets of the Hauptplatz to the small **Schillerpark,** home of the **Relief von Kärnten,** an enormous topographic model of Carinthia. Walk up Hauptplatz until it turns into 10 Oktoberstr., then turn left on Peraustr.; the park is one block in on your right. (Open May-Oct. Mon.-Sat. 10am-4:30pm. 20AS, students 10AS, under 15 free.) Two more blocks down Peraustr. looms the Baroque **Heilig-Kreuz-Kirche,** the dual-towered, pink edifice visible from the city bridge. If you meander inside the church, gaze up into the colorful mural inside the high, newly renovated dome. On the other side of the Drau, the **Villacher Fahrzeugmuseum** (tel. 255 30 or 224 40) is parked at Draupromenade 12. Hundreds of antique automobiles present a rubber-burning ride into the history of transportation. (Open Mon.-Sat. 9am-6pm, Sun. 10am-5pm; Oct.-May daily 10am-noon and 2-4pm. 50AS, ages 6-14 25AS, family pass 100AS.) A **Puppenmuseum** (doll museum) is at Vassacherstr. 65 (tel. 228 55; open May-Oct. daily 10am-6pm).

The **Villach Kirchtag** (church day), held since 1225 on the first Saturday of August, is, despite its moniker, far from holy. The town celebrates its "birthday" with raucous revelry (entrance into the *Altstadt* 60AS, in the evening 70AS). Kirchtag is also the culmination of Villach's annual fair, the **Villacher Brauchtumswoche,** in which folklore presentations of several nationalities are given. January or February marks the annual **Carnival** with parades and festivities in the snow.

Ferries cruise the waters of the **Drau,** departing from the dock beneath the north end of the main bridge. (Two-hour cruises run mid-June to mid-Sept. 9:30, 11:40am, 2, and 4pm; May to early-June and late Sept. 2pm. 105AS, ages 6-15 half-price.) This is assuming the river cooperates; note the high-water marks on the first corner house on Lederergasse from the flood of September, 1882, or the marks on house #25 from the 1965 and 1966 deluges.

Less crowded than the Wörther See, the **Faaker See** is a small but no less beautiful lake at the foot of one of the mountains between Villach and its suburb **Maria Gail.** The sleek peaks around Villach also make for excellent **skiing,** with a plethora of resorts to woo the winter traveler. A one-day regional lift ticket valid for four areas costs about 300AS (children 180AS); other combinations are available as well.

If you'll be in Carinthia for an extended period, consider investing in a **Kärnten Card,** good for up to three weeks of unlimited use of trains and buses and free admission to most area sights and museums. The card is great deal at 265AS, children ages 6-14 130AS, and is available at area tourist offices.

THE MURTAL

Eons ago, before the mining of iron ore and manganese became the *de rigeur* south Austrian vocation, the **River Mur** in central and southern Styria carved a valley among the Gleinalpe to the west, Seetaler Alpen to the south, and Seckauer and Niedere Tauern to the north. Long, upland, pastured ridges flank the valley. Half of the region is covered by forests, and another quarter by grasslands and vineyards.

The Mur has its source in the Salzburger Land, and it eventually joins the Drau in erstwhile Yugoslavia. Low hills (at most 2000m high) make the region a cyclist's and walker's nirvana. With the possible exception of cultured Graz, there's certainly no urbanism to get in your way—maybe a mountain beast or terrible forest man (see **Danube** in Lower Austria).

With its two main towns—Leoben and Graz— the Murtal represents yesterday's Austria. The mostly rural countryside helps retain the charm of an earlier age; industry here remains dependent upon the mineral resources ensconced within the womb of the rounded mountains. Almost every house in the valley proudly displays an *Alte Bauernkalender* (Old Farmer's Calendar), a tradition for some 250 years. The calendar is a small, colorfully illustrated booklet, the equivalent of an American *Farmer's Almanac;* many visitors consider it the superlative Styrian souvenir. Its main purpose—other than mass retail—is forecasting weather; many are convinced that meteorologists are less reliable than the book's conjectures.

The **Steirische Eisenstraße** (Styrian Iron Road) winds through valleys and waterfalls from Leoben to Styria's pride and joy, the Erzberg (Iron Mountain), and on through the Enns Valley.

■ Leoben

Cloistered in the heartland of Austria's "Iron Belt," Leoben (pop. 35,000) lies cradled between a ring of mountains and the Mur river, which borders all but its southern edge. Although 1000-year-old Leoben is the second-largest city in Styria (only Graz is larger), it still maintains a pastoral, even rustic, atmosphere. Leoben's claim to fame is its southernmost position on the **Steirische Eisenstraße** (Styrian Iron Road), the former commercial iron trade route; Leoben is the proud home of a rather competitive **Mining University,** as well as seven other research institutions. Iron-ically, the world of heavy labor and industry doesn't mar the natural beauty of Leoben. Three-quarters of the town's area is woodland, crowned by the idyllic city park "Am Glacis," visited by, among other notables, Emperor **Napoleon Bonaparte.** Nine times

Leoben's floral splendors have garnered it the title of "most beautiful town in Styria" in the **Provincial Flower Competition,** and nearly all residents boast kaleidoscopic backyard gardens brimming with tiger lilies and marigolds that would make even Martha Stewart jealous. Leoben makes a nice change of pace from the more hectic, bustling, tourist-oriented sites in Austria. And while in town, take the opportunity to enjoy the local specialties, such as mushroom goulash, "Shepherd's Spit," and the excellent (and cheap) local *Gösser* beer.

Orientation and Practical Information Leoben is just minutes from Autobahn A9, which runs south to Graz and northwest toward Steyr and Linz. The town's **train station** funnels several major routes to the transit hub at **Bruck an der Mur** (15min., every 20min., 34AS); **buses** also run from Leoben to the rest of Styria. Direct trains run to **Graz** (every 2hr., 110AS) and to **Vienna** (every 90min., 252AS). Trains to **Salzburg** (316AS) and **Klagenfurt** (every 2hr., 228AS), but nearly every train passes through Bruck an der Mur before continuing on its journey. The Mur acts like a moat around the town; from the train station, you must cross the river to reach the heart of Leoben. Franz-Josef-str. and Peter-Tunner-str. run parallel for the length of the town, leading to Hauptplatz and beyond.

The **train information counter** (tel. 425 45) at the station can help decipher the snarl of rail lines (open Mon.-Fri. 9am-noon and 2-4pm). The train station also has small- and medium-sized **lockers** for 20AS, and **luggage storage** (open Mon.-Sat. 5am-10pm, Sun. 6am-10pm; 30AS). The main **bus station,** located on the way to the tourist office, is a 10-minutes walk from the train station, at the corner of the Franz-Josef-Str. (the main town artery) and Parkstr. Pick up bus schedules from the train station.

Leoben's **tourist office,** Hauptpl. 12 (tel. 440 18; fax 482 18), will help you plan your visit to the Murtal. Although they won't make reservations, they're more than happy to dispense a hotel list and a complimentary map (open Mon.-Thurs. 7am-noon and 1:30-5pm, Fri. 7am-1pm). To reach the Hauptplatz, walk straight out of the train station, cross the river, and take your second right onto Franz-Josef-str. Follow Franz-Josef-Str. past the bus terminal to the main square. The tourist office is on the right. **Telephones** are available at either location. A new underground **parking garage** is right under the Hauptplatz, in addition to the one located on Kärtnerstr. (5AS per ½hr.). **Taxi stands** are at the Hauptpl. and at the Hauptbahnhof. Drop a postcard at the Otto Wagner-esque **post office** at Erzherzog-Johann-str. 17 (open Mon.-Fri. 8am-7pm, Sat. 8-10am). **Postal code:** A-8700. **Telephone code:** 03842.

Accommodations and Food Leoben has few—make that no—budget accommodations and only nine establishments total. The closest thing to a good deal is **Hotel Altman,** Südbahnstr. 32 (tel. 422 16), with 22 beds and a small bowling alley in a convenient, albeit busy, location. The three-lane bowling alley tends to fill with local folks joyfully and copiously partaking in the beverage that has been linked to the sport since the time of Adam—beer. To reach the hotel, walk out of the train station and immediately turn left on Südbahnhofstr. Walk alongside the rail tracks for 10min.; the hotel is on the right. Private TV sets, showers, and hard-wood floors help make Altman more luxurious than most hotels in this price range. (Singles 290AS; doubles 480AS. Breakfast included. Other meals 55-155AS. Bowling alley open Tues.-Sun. 10am-midnight; 10AS per 10min. English spoken. Free parking. Visa, MC.) If the price seems too steep, hostels await in neighboring towns from May to September; try the **Jugendherberge (HI)** in Bruck an der Mur Theodor-Körner-str. 37 (tel. (03862) 534 65; fax 560 89), 16km to the east, with 50-beds divided up into quads and larger dorms. The owner will even pick you up from the station if you let him know when you're arriving.

Fans of Italian or typical Austrian cooking will have no trouble in Leoben. For starters, try **Gasthof Familie Hölzl,** Kärtnerstr. 218 (tel. 421 07), across from the Stadttheater, which seems caught between two worlds with an Italian flag motif and *Wiener Schnitzel.* Spaghetti and pasta (60-76AS), olive oil drenched salads (42-54AS), and fish entrées (95-98AS) are also featured on the menu (open Mon.-Fri. 8am-8pm, Sat. 8am-

2pm). Or explore the **Kirchgasse,** where there are a number of cheap restaurants and pubs. Another alternative is **La Pizza,** on Langgasse 1 (tel. 453 47), which has large pizzas for two 59-94AS. Stand-up counters only; take out a pie and enjoy it by the river (open Mon.-Fri. 11am-2pm and 5-10pm, Sat.-Sun. 11am-10pm). Potential picnickers can pack perishables at the **private markets** along Franz-Josef-str. or at **Billa,** Langgasse 5 (open Mon.-Thurs. 7:30am-6:30pm, Fri. 7:30am-8pm, Sat. 7am-1pm). A **farmer's market** sets up in the Kirchplatz (Tues. and Fri. 7am-1pm).

Sights and Entertainment The majority of Leoben's limited attractions lie cluttered around the **Hauptplatz,** a 10-minute walk from the train station; cross over the bridge, and bear right onto Franz-Josef-str. Sights are designated by a square block with a bizarre imprint of an ostrich eating iron horseshoes with one held daintily between its toes and the other protruding from its beak. This city symbol alludes to Leoben's dependence on the iron trade—in the Middle Ages, ostriches were thought capable of eating and digesting iron. That's a goose you say? When it was made, no one was sure what exactly an ostrich looked like.

Most of the buildings in the Hauptplatz are former homes of the **Hammerherren** (Hammer men), another reminder of the iron trade. The most ornate of the bunch is the 1680 **Hacklhaus,** bearing a dozen statues on its pink façade. The top six figures represent six of the 12 Christian virtues. Justice holds a sword and a balance, Hope brandishes an anchor, and Wisdom views the world through the mirror in his hand. The bottom figures depict the four seasons including Old Man Winter on the bottom row, warming his icy fingers over a roaring fire. Standing guard at the entrance to the Hauptplatz are the **Denkmäler und Monumente** (statues and monuments), beautifully crafted works erected to ward off the fires and plague that devastated much of Styria in the early 18th century. Look for Florian, the fire-proof saint, and the reclining Rosalia, the saint responsible for fending off plagues.

Just outside the Hauptplatz is the **Pfarrkirche Franz Xaver,** a rust-colored church with twin towers built in 1660-1665 by the Jesuits. The simple façade belies an elaborate interior and a high altar bedecked with remarkable Solomonic columns. Next door is the **Museum der Stadt Leoben,** Kirchgasse 6, a rich collection of portraits and documents that traces the city's historical development (open Mon.-Thurs. 10am-noon and 2-5pm, Fri. 10am-1pm; 20AS, students 5AS). An ever-vigilant fungus, the **Schwammerlturm** (Mushroom Tower) stands guard over the bridge that crosses the Mur.

You'd be hard-pressed, however, to find any mushrooms sprouting in Leoben's meticulously manicured gardens. For more flora, stroll through the **Stadtpark "Am Glacis"** one block past the Hauptplatz. There, you can visit the **Friedensgedenk-stätte** (Peace Memorial), which commemorates the peace treaty with Napoleon, signed here in 1797. The small museum showcases an exhibit detailing the political and military events surrounding the treaty, including the very feather pen that Napoleon used to inscribe his signature (open May-Sept. daily 9am-1pm and 2-5pm; free).

A scenic 30-minute walk along the Mur rewards you with the chance to inspect the **Gösser brewery.** Examine antique brewing machinery, wander around inside the **Göss Abbey** (the oldest abbey in Styria), and then guzzle down a free *Stein* of fresh brew. Regardless of whether you make a tour (though the free beer is worth it), try visiting the **beer museum,** with exhibits on the brewery's history and revolutionary changes in brewing techniques. (Tours by arrangement; call 226 21. Museum open Mon.-Fri. 8am-noon and 2-4pm. Tours last 90min.) The **Stadttheater,** at Kärntnerstr. 224 (tel. 406 23 02), is the oldest functioning theater in all of Austria (box office open Mon.-Sat. 9:30am-12:30pm and Thurs.-Fri. 4pm-6:30pm). The theater is, however, on vacation from June-September. The city fills the summer void with the **Leobener Kultursommer,** a program of theater, classical and pop concerts, literary readings, and treasure hunts for children. Pick up a free program from the tourist office detailing dates, locations, and prices—tickets range from 0-200AS.

▒ Riegersburg

Dramatically perched atop an extinct volcano, the majestic Riegersburg castle stands watch over the diminutive valley town that bears its name. Riegersburg—the town—has known little peace since its founding in the 9th century BC. Roman domination and Hungarian invasions periodically forced the citizens to ascend the remarkably steep hill and seek solace and safety on its rocky summit. During the 17th century, with the mighty forces of the Ottoman empire only 32km away, Riegersburg was once again compelled to entrust its fragile existence to the stalwart bulwarks of the castle. Baroness Katharina Elisabeth Freifrau von Galler completed the castle in a flurry of construction and transformed it into one of the largest and most impregnable fortresses in all Austria. 108 rooms were surrounded by two miles of walls with five gates and two trenches. The fearsome and imposing castle withstood the Ottoman onslaught—in 1664 Riegersburg and the surrounding villages drove the Ottomans back in the great battle of Mogersdorf. Despite the cheerful vineyards that now grow at the foot of the castle, Riegersburg's daunting appearance and the **Witch Museum** that it houses still evoke spooky trepidation of fairy-tale proportions.

Orientation and Practical Information Riegersburg serves as an excellent stopover on the route from Graz into Hungary. A one-way ticket from nearby Feldbach (10km) to the border town Szentgottard costs 60AS (½hr., 6 per day). Getting to Riegersburg, however, can be quite tricky; poor train-bus connections necessitate careful planning, especially if you only want to make the small town a day-trip. Take the **bus** all the way (departing Graz from Andreas-Hofer-Platz Mon.-Sat. 12:35pm, Mon.-Fri. 5:30pm, and Sun. 10:45am; 100AS) or take the train from Graz to Feldbach (1hr., hourly, 100AS) and switch to the bus from the Feldbach train station into Riegersburg (½hr., 5 daily on weekdays, 0-2 on weekends, 20AS). Buses leave Riegersburg for Graz at the ungodly hours of Monday-Saturday 5:40am and 6:05am and on Sunday at a more pious 5:35pm. Buses to Feldbach are more frequent, but none run on Sundays. If you do get stuck in Riegersburg, call a **taxi** (tel. (03152) 25 35) to take you back to Feldbach (170-210AS). Otherwise, the small **tourist office** (tel. 8670), actually a corner of a craft shop across from Saurugg on the way up to the castle, can help you find a room. (Open April to mid-Oct. daily 10am-6pm, mid-Oct.-March 10am-noon and 2-6pm.) The **post office** stands at Riegersburgstr. 26 (open Mon.-Fri. 8am-noon and 2-6pm). You can **change money** there, or stroll to **Raiffeisen Bank,** down the street at Riegersburg Str. 30 (open Mon.-Fri. 8am-noon and 2-4:30pm). **Postal code:** A-8333. **Telephone code:** 03153.

Accommodations and Food The **Jugendherberge "Im Cillitor" (HI)** (tel. 8217), is directly on the path up to the castle, and actually incorporated into the fortress walls. Walk up Riegersburg Str. toward the castle, take a right at the tourist office, and struggle up the last, extremely steep 100m. Large keys, noisy locks, and spears in the reception area all evoke a distinctly medieval atmosphere. Iron bars traverse the few geranium-filled windows (now we've got you, my pretty...) of the large dorm rooms. (Curfew 10pm. 135AS, under 19 115AS; nonmembers 30AS surcharge. Breakfast included, other meals 50-60AS; sheets 30AS. Showers, toilets off the hall. Generally open May-Sept., but call ahead since the hostel sometimes randomly closes if there are no groups there). At the bottom of Riegersburg's hill is **Lasslhof** on Riegersburgstr. 20 (tel. 201 or 202), a yellow hotel with a popular bar/restaurant. The proprietor collects "art," loosely defined, and the common areas overflow with an eclectic mix of framed works. (Reception open 8am-10pm. 170-240AS; July 15-Sept.15 surcharge for singles 30AS. Breakfast with fresh bread included. English spoken.) At the restaurant downstairs, gorge yourself on *Wiener Schnitzel* with potatoes and salad (75AS), or snack on the *Frankfurter mit Gulaschsaft* (38AS). Otherwise, stock up on groceries at **Saurugg,** right across the street from the tourist office (open Mon.-Fri. 7am-noon and 2:45-6:15pm, Sat. 7:15am-12:15pm).

Sights and Entertainment Riegersburg relies heavily on the revenue from tourists who gawk at the well-preserved remains of the huge medieval fortress, the town's only real attraction. But like the foreign invaders of the past, sightseers must also tackle the treacherously steep, stone-paved path leading up to the castle. Bring sturdy shoes and bottled water, lest you share the fate of many a young 17th-century Turk. The path itself is arguably the best part of the castle: sweeping views of the surrounding farms and rolling hills reward visitors at every turn, and benches, vineyards, stone arches, and monuments provide good excuses to catch your breath. The ruts in the stone path near the top were carved by the thousands of horse-drawn carts in the centuries before Goodyear. At the top, the castle houses several well-displayed exhibits and museums. The **Burgmuseum** showcases 16 of the castle's 108 rooms, chock-full of art and historical notes on the Liechtenstein ruling family (yes, like the country), who own this and other Austrian castles. The **Weiße Saal** (White Hall), in particular, with its wedding-cake ceiling flourishes, and crystal chandeliers, looks as though it should be filled with elegantly dressed couples waltzing around the floor. The **Witches' Room** contains an eerie collection of portraits of alleged witches (among them, Katharina "Green Thumb" Pardauff, who was executed in 1675 for causing flowers to bloom in the middle of winter) and a real iron maiden. The **Hexenmuseum** (Witch Museum) is spread out over 12 more rooms; it presents the most expansive witch trial in Styrian history (1673-1675). Filled with torture devices, funeral pyres, and other ghastly exhibits, the museum testifies to the horrific ramifications of prejudicial hysteria. (Open April-Oct. daily 9am-5pm. Hour-long tours (in German) on the hour, or you can walk through yourself with a short English sheet; 95AS, students 50AS). You can best appreciate the castle's ageless beauty from among the web of gravel paths and stone staircases. Carefully study the elaborate iron pattern covering the well in the castle's second courtyard; it is said that any woman who can spot the horseshoe amidst the complex design will find her knight in shining armor within a year. In the shadow of the castle whimpers a rather meager zoo, the **Greifvogelwarte Riegersburg,** which showcases caged birds of prey. (Open Easter-Oct.; shows with trainers dressed in castle finery Mon.-Sat. 11am and 3pm, Sun. 11am, 2pm, and 4pm. Admission 50AS, students and children 30AS; show 60AS, students 40AS.)

■ Graz

As Austria's second-largest city, with 100,000 more people than Salzburg, and a thriving arts community thanks to its 45,000 university students, Graz just can't understand why it doesn't attract more tourists. For centuries this capital of Styria (pop. 250,000) has been a center of arts and sciences that can rival any other in the Teutonic world. Graz's prosperity and international renown brought Emperor Friedrich III here in the mid-15th century. Astronomer Johannes Kepler was similarly lured to the city's Karl-Franzens-Universität, founded in 1585 as a Jesuit College. As further testament to this cultural citadel, it's telling that the actor **Arnold Schwarzenegger** was reared in Graz before he bade Hasta La Vista, Baby! to his family and trainer (who still live here) and marched off to become Conan, the Terminator, and, in the biggest leap of Hollywood imagination, Danny DeVito's twin brother. The small pond where he proposed to his wife, Maria Shriver, is now a site of pilgrimage for die-hard fans, despite the bemused protestations of tourist officials who say it's "nothing special."

Ever since Charlemagne claimed this strategic crossroads for the Carolingian empire, Graz, today 60km from the Slovenian and Hungarian borders, has witnessed over a thousand years of European-Asian hostility. The ruins of the fortress perched upon the **Schloßberg** commemorate the turmoil; the stronghold has withstood battering at the hands of the Ottoman Turks, Napoleon's armies (three times), and most recently the Soviet Union during World War II. The celebrated castles are the few remaining testaments to Graz's long history of military and political upheaval.

The city itself, full of classic red-tiled roofs, refreshing parks, museums, and monuments, provides a welcome respite from the throngs of tourists in Austria's Big Three—Vienna, Salzburg, and Innsbruck. Innumerable theaters, the **Forum Stadt-**

park, the renowned **Steirischer Herbst** (an avant-garde festival founded in 1968 and held every October), and the summer music festival **Styriarte,** have contributed to the culture you'd expect of a university town. In several ways Graz culturally challenges its elite big sister Vienna. Graz's *fin de siècle* period is occurring now, and judging by its artistic offerings—Stravinsky instead of Strauss, Mamrt instead of Mahler—Graz is fast becoming a cultural epicenter for Austria.

GETTING TO GRAZ

Flights arrive at the **Flughafen Graz,** Flughafenstr. 51, 9km from the central city. For flight information call 29 02. All trans-continental flights are routed through Vienna. **Currency exchange** is available here daily 6am-12:45pm and 2:30-7pm. The **information office** at the airport is open daily 6am-8pm. Airport shuttle bus #631 departs from Hotel Daniel Europlatz 1 (adjacent to the Hauptbahnhof) six times daily, at 5:15, 7:10, and 9:45am, and 12:25, 2:15, and 5:10pm. The shuttles also stop at Hotel Weitzer and Griesplatz before arriving at the airport 30 minutes later. The same service also comes from the airport to Graz six times daily, with the last bus leaving the airport at 6:45pm (one-way 20AS). **Trains** depart from the **Hauptbahnhof** Europapl. (tel. 98 48; for train info call 17 17; information line open 7am-9pm), or pick up a free *Bahneurbindungen* (train timetable). The **Ostbahnhof** on Conrad-von-Hötzendorf-str. is a freight station; don't get off here unless you came in a crate. There are direct connections to **Salzburg** (4¼hr., 6 daily, 396AS), **Linz** (3½hr., 4 daily, 336AS), **Innsbruck** (6hr., 4 daily, 540AS), **Vienna** (2½hr., 9 daily, 296AS), **Zürich** (10hr., 1 daily, 996AS), **Paris** (14½hr., 1 daily, 1976AS, 1740AS if under 26), and **Münich** (6hr., 1 daily, 746AS) among others. Further connections can be made through Vienna. The **Graz-Köflach Bus (GKB)** departs from Griespl. for West Styria. Its **office,** Köflnehergasse 35-41 (tel. 59 87), is open Mon.-Fri. 8am-5pm. For the remainder of Austria, the **BundesBus** departs from Europapl. 6 (next to the Hauptbahnhof) or, more often, from Andreas-Hofer-Platz. Its main office at Andreas-Hofer-Pl. 17 (tel. (0660) 80 20) is open Mon.-Fri. 6am-6:30pm. The Branch office at the Hauptbahnhof is open Mon.-Fri. 9am-noon.

ORIENTATION AND PRACTICAL INFORMATION

Graz straddles the River Mur in the southeast corner of Austria, on the northern edge of the Graz plain, serving as a gateway to Slovenia (50km south) and Hungary (70km east). Fully two-thirds of Graz's five square km consist of beautiful parklands, earning it the nicknames "Garden City" and "Green City." The **Hauptplatz** main square, on the corner of Murgasse and Sackstr., forms the social and commercial center of the city. The *Platz* is directly in front of the Rathaus and lies in the shadow of the **Schloßberg** fortress ruins. **Herrengasse,** which runs from the Hauptplatz to Jakominiplatz, forms the heart of the pedestrian zone and is lined with cafés, clothing boutiques, and ice cream shops. **Jakominiplatz** (Yah-to-MEE-nee-platz) near the Eisernes Tor and five minutes from the Hauptplatz by foot, is the hub of the city's bus and streetcar system. The Graz **Universität** is tucked away in the northeast part of Graz, near the posh residential district of St. Leonhard. The **main train station** lies on the other side of the river, a short ride away by streetcars #1, 3, or 6 from Hauptplatz. To get to the city center by foot from the train station, follow Annenstr. up and over the Hauptbrücke (15min.). If you're staying in Graz for at least three days, take advantage of the tourist office's **Graz Card** (180AS) which entitles you to three days of free bus and tram travel, 10-60% reductions on most museums and tours, and 5-10% discounts at some shops and restaurants. Arnold says: "Get it. The Graz Card is great."

> **Tourist Office: Main office,** Herrengasse 16 (tel. 807 50; fax 807 50 15; e-mail heinzkaltschmidt@computerhaus.at). Cordial staff gives away one city map and sells a more detailed version (25AS), books rooms (30AS fee), and supplies information on all of Styria, including the location of Arnold Schwarzenegger's former home in the nearby village of Thal. The office is littered with posters and pamphlets of cul-

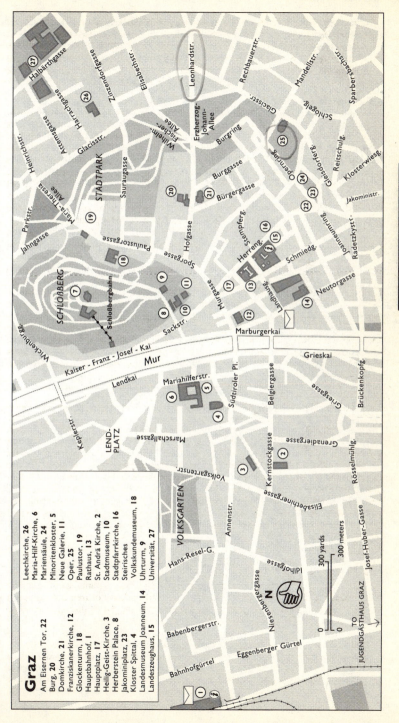

Graz

Am Eisernen Tor, 22
Burg, 20
Domkirche, 21
Franziskanerkirche, 12
Glockenturm, 18
Hauptbahnhof, 1
Hauptplatz, 17
Heilig-Geist-Kirche, 3
Herberstein Palace, 8
Jakominiplatz, 4
Kloster Spittal, 4
Landesmuseum Joanneum, 14
Landeszeughaus, 15

Leechkirche, 26
Maria-Hilf-Kirche, 6
Mariensäule, 24
Minoritenkloster, 5
Neue Galerie, 11
Oper, 25
Paulustor, 19
Rathaus, 13
St. Andrä Kirche, 2
Stadtmuseum, 10
Stadtpfarrkirche, 16
Steirisches
Volkskundemuseum, 18
Uhrturm, 9
Universität, 27

tural goings-on. Procure a brochure of area hotels and a separate listing of private rooms. Open in summer Mon.-Fri. 9am-7pm, Sat. 9am-6pm, Sun. and holidays 10am-3pm; other months open Mon.-Sat. 9am-6pm, Sun. and holidays 10am-3pm. **Branch office** (tel. 91 68 37) at the main train station. Open Mon.-Fri. 9am-6pm, Sat. 9am-6pm, Sun. and holidays 10am-3pm.

Consulates: U.K., Schmiedgasse 10 (tel. 82 61 05). **South Africa,** Villefortgasse 13 (tel. 32 25 48).

Currency Exchange: Best rates at the American Express office; second-best at the main post office. Most banks open Mon.-Fri. 8am-noon and 2-4pm. On Sunday, exchange offices at both post office branches are open. Also at the train station; open Mon.-Fri. 7:30am-1:30pm and 2-6pm, Sat. 7:30am-1:30pm.

American Express: Hamerlingasse 6 (tel. 81 70 10; fax 81 70 08). Holds mail and exchanges currency (40AS for the latter service). Address mail, for example, as follows: Virginia BRAME, c/o American Express, Client Mail Service, Hamerlingasse 6, A-8010 Graz. Open Mon.-Fri. 9am-5:30pm.

Telephones: In the main post office.

Public Transportation: Grazer Verkehrsbetriebe, Hauptpl. 14 (tel. 88 74 08). Open Mon.-Fri. 8am-5pm. Purchase single tickets (20AS) and 24-hr. tickets (40AS) from the driver, and booklets of 10 tickets (150AS) or week-tickets (92AS) from any one of the *Tabak* stores sprinkled through Graz. Tickets are valid for all trams and buses, and also for the cable car that ascends to the Schloßberg. Children half-price for all tickets. Be sure to stamp your ticket, or face the wrath of a 500AS fine. Most tram lines run until 11pm, and most bus lines run until 9pm; check the schedules posted at every *Haltestelle* (marked with a green "H") for details. To decipher the confusing mesh of bus and tram routes, ask for a *Netzplan* at the small green GV booth in Jakominiplatz, in front of the McDonald's.

Taxi: Funktaxi, Griespl. 28 (tel. 983). **City-Funk,** Glockenspielpl. 6 (tel. 878). We want the funk!

Car Rental: Avis, airport and Schlögelgasse 10 (tel. 81 29 20; fax 84 11 78). **Budget,** Bahnhofgürtel 73 (tel. 91 69 66; fax 916 68 34), and airport (tel. 291 54 13 42). **Hertz,** Andreas-Hofer-Pl. (tel. 82 50 07; fax 81 02 88). **Europcar,** airport (tel. 29 67 57; fax 24 25 47).

Automobile Clubs: ÖAMTC, Giradigasse (tel. 50 42 61) and **ARBÖ,** Kappellenstr. 45 (tel. 271 60 00). Car trouble? Call 120 or 123.

Bike Rental: At the train station. 90AS per day, 50AS with Eurail Pass or valid ticket.

Luggage Storage: At the train station. 30AS per day, 4am-10pm. **Lockers** are also available (small 20AS, large 30AS).

Bookstores: Englische Buchhandlung, Tummelpl. 7 (tel. 82 62 66). Sells virtually every book you might ever want, in English. Hardcovers are sometimes cheaper than paperbacks, but then you have to carry them. Open Mon.-Fri. 9am-6pm and Sat 9am-noon. Experience reverse culture shock at **American Discount**, on Jakoministr. 12 (tel. 83 23 24), a warehouse of every imaginable American magazine, comic book, and basketball jersey. Open Mon.-Fri. 9am-12:30pm and 2:30pm-6pm, Sat. 9am-12:30pm.

Student Resources: The **student administration office** of the university has billboards papered with concert notices, student activity flyers, and carpool advertisements for all of Austria. To find the hall, walk through the emergency exit *(Notausgang)* of the bathroom in the upper restaurant of the *Mensa* (see below).

Gay, Lesbian, and Bisexual Organizations: Rosarote Panther/Schwul-lesbische Arbeitsgemeinschaft Steiermark, Postfach 34 (tel. 47 11 19). **Frauenberatungstelle** (Women's Information Center), Marienpl. 5/2 (tel. 91 60 22).

Laundromat: Putzeri Rupp, Jakominstr. 34 (tel. 82 11 83), has do-it-yourself (5kg. load 65AS) as well as professional handling. Both open Mon.-Fri. 8am-4pm, Sat. 7am-noon.

AIDS Hotline: Steirische AIDS-Hilfe, Schmiedgasse 38 (tel. 81 50 50). Drop-in hours Mon. and Wed. 11am-1pm, Tues., Thurs., Fri. 5pm-7pm.

Pharmacy: Bärenapotheker, Herrengasse 11 (tel. 83 02 67), across the street from the tourist office, is one of the oldest in Graz. Open Mon.-Fri. 8am-12:30pm and 2:30-6pm, Sat. 8am-noon.

Hospital: Krankenhaus der Elisabethinen, Elisabethinergasse 14 (tel. 90 63), near the hostel.

Emergencies: Police: tel. 133. **Ambulance:** tel. 144.

Police: At the main train station (tel. 888 27 75). Open 24hr. Outside doors open 8am-5pm; ring the doorbell at other times.

Post Office: Main office, Neutorgasse 46. Open Mon.-Fri. 7am-11pm, Sat. 7am-2pm, and Sun. 8am-noon. A **branch office,** Europapl. 10, is next to the main train station. Open 24hr. **Postal code:** A-8010; branch office A-8020

Telephone code: 0316

ACCOMMODATIONS

Sniffing out a cheap bed in Graz may require a bit of detective work; most budget hotels, guest houses, and pensions run from 300-450AS per person, and several are located in the boondocks. Luckily, the web of local transport provides a reliable and easy commute to and from the city center. Also, be sure to ask the main tourist office about the list of *Privatzimmer* (most 150-300AS per night), especially in the tourist-bloated summer months of July and August.

Jugendgästehaus Graz (HI), Idlhofgasse 74 (tel. 91 48 76; fax 91 48 76 88), is a 15-min. walk from the train station. Exit the station and cross the street, head right on Eggenberger Gürtel, take a left at Josef-Huber-Gasse (after the Nissan dealership), then take the first right at Idlhofgasse; the hostel is hidden behind the parking lot on your right. Or, from Jakominipl., take bus #31 (dir: Webling), #32 (dir: Seiersburg), or #33 (dir: Gemeindeamte) to "Lissagasse" (last bus around midnight) and walk 2min. back to the hostel. Plain, clean, spacious rooms with large lockers and private toilet and shower in quads and doubles. Omnipresent insomniac school groups, but the management goes out of its way to fit in backpackers if there's no room in town. Reception open Mon.-Sat. 7am-11pm, Sun. 7-9am and 5-10pm. No lockout. No real curfew—the door locks at 11pm, but the security system lets late-comers in every half-hour until 2:30am, and if that's still too early, just pick up a key at the desk. Curfew hours should clue you in to the management style here: congenial and laid-back. 6- or 8-bed dorms 135AS per person. Doubles 440AS; quads 680AS. Surcharge for first night 20AS. Nonmembers 40AS extra per night. Breakfast and yellow-and-white checked sheets included. Laundry 45AS.

Hotel Strasser, Eggenberger Gürtel 11 (tel. 91 39 77; fax 91 68 56), a 5-min. walk from the train station. Exit the station, cross the street, and head right on Bahnhof-gürtel; the hotel is on the left, across from a huge sign for *Kaiser Bier*. Though located off a busy street, thick glass windows keep the large, wood-paneled rooms relatively quiet. Singles 340AS, with shower 440AS; doubles 560AS, with shower 660AS; triples 840AS; quads 1000AS. Breakfast included. English spoken. Restaurant downstairs. Free parking.

Hotel Zur Stadt Feldbach, Conrad-von-Hötzendorfstr. 58 (tel. 82 94 68; fax 84 73 71), is a 20min. walk south of Jakominipl., or, from Hauptpl. or Jakominipl., take either tram #4 (dir: Liebnau) or #5 (dir: Puntigam) to "Jakominigürtel." The hotel is on the street corner to the right. This modest, 30-bed hotel with simple, no-non-sense furnishings earns points for their colorful comforter covers. 24-hr. reception on the second floor. Singles 350AS; doubles 500AS, with shower 650AS; triples with shower 750AS. Breakfast 50AS.

Gasthof Schmid Greiner, Grabenstr. 64 (tel. 68 14 82). From the bus station take bus #58 (dir: Mariagrün) to "Grabenstr." Get off the bus, turn right, walk 30m, and head right on Grabenstr. for 10min. A peaceful establishment imbued with old-world charm. Snow-white comforters, antique wood furnishings, and delicate lace curtains grace the tidy rooms. Ring the bell to get let in; if at first you don't succeed, however, try, try, again on the other side of the building. Singles 340AS; doubles 460AS, with toilet 480AS.

FOOD

Graz's 45,000 students sustain a bonanza of cheap eateries. Inexpensive meals can be found at the Hauptplatz and at the **Lendplatz,** off Keplerstr. and Lendkai, where concession stands sell *Wurst,* ice cream, beer, and other fast food until about 8pm. Numerous markets are located on Rösselmühlgasse, an extension of Josef-Huber-Gasse, and on Jakoministr. directly off Jakominipl. Low-priced student hangouts also line Zinzendorfgasse near the university. If you order a salad in Graz, it will likely be dressed with the local dark pumpkin seed oil.

University Mensa, Sonnenfelspl. 1 (tel. 32 33 62), just east of the Stadtpark at the intersection of Zinzendorfgasse and Leechgasse. Walk, or take bus #39 to "Uni./ Mensa." The best deal in town; just walk down the stairs into the basement and grab a tray. Simple and satisfying set *menus,* with meat or vegetarian *(Vollwert)* for 30-55AS. Be on the alert for blue tickets, distributed only to university students, that shave 8AS off the price of a meal. Open Mon.-Fri. 11am-3pm. For slightly more expensive à la carte meals (soup or salad 49AS), explore the restaurant upstairs. Open Mon.-Fri. 9:30am-3pm.

Gastwirtschaft Wartburgasse, Halbärthgasse 4. Trendy posters and loud music make this indoor/outdoor restaurant Graz's premier student hangout. Tasty food compensates for the wait. Lunch specials 50-60AS. Pasta, vegetarian, and meat dishes 42-120AS. Open Mon.-Thurs. 9am-1am, Fri. 9am-4am, Sat. 6pm-1am.

Mangolds Vollwert Restaurant, Griesgasse 11, by the river off Grieskai. This vegetarian nirvana is a healthy alternative to cholesterol-laden Austrian cuisine. Geometric pastel hangings and dangling lights set off colorful salads, fresh squeezed juices (orange-lemon-pineapple-banana 29AS), and unidentifiable, but tasty, healthy entrées 45-60AS. Cafeteria-like dining hall with real tablecloths and café next door. Daily lunch specials (39-50AS) include soup, salad, and dessert. Open Mon.-Fri. 11am-8pm, Sat. 11am-4pm. Café opens at 10am.

Calafati, Lissagasse 2 (tel. 91 68 89), a 3-min. walk from the hostel. Lunch combinations (main course, soup or spring roll, and dessert, 42-55AS) make this slightly out-of-the-way Chinese restaurant quite a bargain. Several vegetarian and take-out options 65-78AS. Lunch bargain daily 11:30am-3pm; dinner daily 5:30-11:30pm.

Pfeffermühle, Idlhofgasse 68 (tel. 91 82 73), is just to the left when you walk out of the hostel and features cheap Austrian classics. Enjoy a huge plate of *Wiener Schnitzel* 49AS in the small restaurant or guest garden behind. Open Mon.-Fri. 11am-2:30pm and 5-11pm.

Café-Pizzeria Catherina, Sporgasse 32 (tel. 82 72 63). Ramble up Sporgasse to reach this popular pizzeria, which also serves breakfast. Ham and two eggs, American style 32AS. Take-out pizza slices 21AS are the perfect size to combat late-night munchies. Whole pies 55-82AS. Salads 28AS. Open Mon.-Sat. 7:30am-midnight, Sun. 9:30am-midnight.

Markets

Graz is blessed with a seemingly countless number of small grocery stores that sell all the necessary ingredients for a picnic lunch; pick up a few bites and sup under a tree in the relaxing, quiet **Volksgarten** located right off Lendplatz. There are also **outdoor markets** at Kaiser-Josef-Platz and Lendplatz, where vendors hawk their fruits and vegetables amidst a dazzling splash of reds, greens, and yellows (open Mon.-Sat. 7am-12:30pm). Other markets are run Mon.-Fri. 7am-6pm and Sat. 7am-12:30pm in the Hauptplatz and Jakominiplatz.

Feinkost, Bahnhofgürtel 89, 2min. from the train station. A small fruit, vegetable and essential food shop, with three conveniently located stores (open Mon.-Fri. 8am-6pm, Sat. 8am-12:30pm). **Feinkost Exler** is a quick jaunt to the left from the youth hostel, open Mon.-Fri. 7am-1pm and 3-6pm, Sat. 7am-noon. **Feinkost Muhrer** borders closely on Hauptpl. in Franziskanerpl, open Mon.-Fri. 6:30am-7:30pm, Sat. 6:30am-noon.

Interspar is a huge market at the intersection of Lazarettgasse and Lazarett-gürtel in the enormous City Park shopping mall. Open Mon.-Wed. 9am-7:30pm, Thurs. 9am-8pm, Fri. 9am-7:30pm, Sat. 8am-1pm. A **branch** is next door to the *Mensa.* Open Mon.-Fri. 8am-1pm and 4-6:30pm, Sat. 7:30am-12:30pm.

SOUTHEAST AUSTRIA

SIGHTS

"Tastes, architecture, and slaps in the face are all different" is an old Styrian saying, and the buildings of Graz prove at least the first two. The central *Altstadt* (old city) packs dozens of classical arches, domes, and red-tiled roofs into a twisting maze of cobblestone streets, while the stark modern buildings of Technical University, a few blocks away, are just one example of the influence of Graz's well-known modern School of Architecture. A fun and easy way to systematically explore diverse Graz is through the tourist office's guide in English, *A Walk through the Old City* (10AS). From April through October, the office also leads tours of the old city every day starting at 2:30pm in front of the office (75AS; in English and German). November through March they're only offered on Saturdays. The tourist office itself is a sight; situated in the **Landhaus**, which is still the seat of the provincial government, the building was remodeled by architect Domenico dell'Allio in 1557 in masterful Lombard style. Walking through the arch to the right leads one to an arcaded stone courtyard, flowing with geraniums in summer, a glorious reminder of the Italian Renaissance. On the other side of the tourist office, you'll find the most bizarre yet fascinating attraction in Graz, the **Landeszeughaus** (Provincial Arsenal), Herrengasse 16 (tel. 87 73 6 39 or 87 72 7 78), built from 1642 to 1645 by Anton Solar. Back in the 17th century, when Ottoman invasions from the east were as regular as the seasons, Graz's rulers assessed the need for an on-premises weapons stash. The result of their efforts, after some political haranguing, is this armory—the world's largest, with 30,000 harnesses and weapons dating from the Late Middle Ages to the early 19th century. In the early 18th century, the Turkish menace dissipated, and the court war council in Vienna sought to replace the temporary enlisted mercenaries with a standing army. Thus, the task of protecting the frontiers, previously carried out by local forces in the countryside, would be undertaken by the state. The government foolishly resolved to permanently dispose of all antiquated weapons, an idea that incensed the locals. They wanted the arsenal to stand forever as a monument to the soldiers' bravery and faithfulness in the fight against the "sworn enemy of Christendom." Empress Maria Theresa consented to maintain this unique historical monument in its original condition. Today, the former armory of the Styrian estates contains an eerie four-story collection of scintillating spears, muskets, and armor—enough to outfit 28,000 burly mercenaries (and you thought Ah-nold got all the hardware). It is the only antiquated arsenal in the world still preserved in its entirety. (Open April-Oct. Mon.-Fri. 9am-5pm, Sat.-Sun. 9am-1pm. 25AS, seniors 10AS, students free. Free English info sheet.)

The **Zeughaus** is just a tiny part of the collection of the **Landesmuseum Joanneum,** the oldest public museum in Austria. The assembled holdings are so vast and eclectic that officials have been forced to categorize the legacy and house portions in separate museums scattered throughout the city. Admission to each museum is 25AS, seniors 10AS, students free. The **Neue Galerie,** Sackstr. 16 (tel. 82 91 55), off the Hauptpl., showcases off-beat, avant-garde contemporary works, as well as a collection of 19th- and 20th-century paintings in the gorgeous **Palais Herberstein.** Be sure to catch a glimpse of the mountains from the palace's weatherbeaten courtyard (open Tues.-Fri. 10am-6pm, Sat.-Sun. 10am-1pm; free). For an even more impressive collection of works from the Middle Ages and the Baroque period, check out the **Alte Galerie,** Neutorgasse 45 (tel. 80 17 47 70). Especially awe-inspiring are the larger-than-life statues that comprise Veit Königer's "Group of Annunciation" and Bruegel's graphic and grotesque "Triumph of Death," in which archduke and peasant alike are slaughtered by an army of skeletons (open Tues.-Fri. 10am-5pm, Sat.-Sun. 10am-1pm). The **Natural History Museum,** encompassing geology, paleontology, mineralogy, zoology, and other -ologies, is at Raubergasse 10 (open Mon.-Fri. 9am-4pm, Sat.-Sun. 9am-noon).

One of the more prominent additional museums is the **Stadtmuseum,** Sackstr. 18 (tel. 82 25 80), with exhibits on area history (open June-Oct. Tues. 10am-9pm, Wed.-Sat. 10am-6pm, Sun. 10am-1pm). For religious icons and art, visit the Mariahilferplatz 3. (Tel. 91 39 94. Open Tues.-Wed. and Fri.-Sat. 10am-5pm, Thurs. 10am-7pm, Sun.

10am-1pm.) The **Hans-Mauracher-Museum,** Hans-Mauracher-Str. 29 (tel. 39 23 94), is dedicated to the eminent Graz sculptor (open Tues.-Thurs. and Sun. 10am-5pm). The **Abteilung für Volkskunde,** Paulustorgasse 13 (tel. 83 04 16), showcases ethnic and social history (open April-Oct. Mon.-Fri. 9am-4pm, Sat.-Sun. 9am-noon). The **Robert Stolz Museum,** Mehlpl. 1 (tel. 81 59 51), offers exhibits and concerts honoring the native conductor. (Open April-Sept. Tues.-Fri. 2-5pm, Sat.-Sun 10am-1pm; Oct.-March Tues.-Thurs. 2-5pm, Sun. 10am-1pm.)

Across Herrengasse from the Landzeughaus is the lemon yellow **city parish church,** originally the Abbey Church of the Dominicans in the 16th century. Done up in late Gothic style, the church suffered severe damage from World War II air raids, and subsequently, several of the window paintings were obliterated. When Salzburger artist Albert Birkle designed new stained-glass windows for the church in 1953, one of his windows made worldwide news: the left panel behind the high altar portrays the scourging of Christ, who is silently watched over by two figures bearing uncanny resemblance to Hitler and Mussolini. Organ concerts are held here early July to early September on Thursdays at 8pm (70AS, students 40AS).

Dominating the inner city of Graz is the towering **Schloßberg** (Castle hill) the one-time site of a fortress built in the Middle Ages. Rising 473m, the steep Dolomite peak has had a long, colorful history. Its strategic location helped Styria successfully defend against marauding Turkish forces in the 16th and 17th centuries, and the French troops 100 years later. The 16th-century **Glockenturm** (bell tower) and the 13th-century **Uhrturm** (clock tower) perched atop the peak can be seen from almost any spot in Graz. The Uhrturm acquired its present appearance—the circular wooden gallery with oriels, and the four huge clockfaces 5.4m in diameter—when the Schloßberg castle was reconstructed in 1556. But remember, if you set your watch by the Uhrturm's faces, the clocks' hands are reversed, so that the big hand indicates the hour, not the minute. Originally, the clock only had one big hand, visible from town, and set to show the hour. The huge bell in the Glockerturm, galled the "Lisl," has sounded since 1578.

Napoleon never did manage to defeat the Schloßberg fortress until *after* he conquered the rest of Austria. Then he razed the fortress in an infantile, jealous rage. The town, however, managed to rescue the bell and clock towers by paying the little Emperor a sizeable ransom. You can see the fortress-turned-park by ascending the **Felsenstieg,** a beautiful, dramatic stone staircase snaking up the mountain from Schloßbergpl., or by taking the **Schloßbergbahn cable car,** which has its ground station on Kaiser-Franz-Josef-Kai 38. (Tel. 88 74 13. Cable car runs daily every 15min. April 9am-10pm; May-June 8am-11pm; July-Aug. 8am-midnight; Oct.-March 10am-10pm. One-way 20AS, round-trip 40AS; children half-price; public transport passes valid.) Almost obscured by the great views, a small **Garnisons museum** showcases cannons and military equipment (open daily 10am-5pm; 20AS, students and children 10AS).

Descend the hill on the eastern side near the Uhrturm via Dr.-Karl-Böhm-Allee, pass through the Paulustor arch, and you'll arrive at the lovely floral **Stadtpark** (city park), which separates the old city from the lively university quarter. The carefully tended gardens attract walkers, sun-bathers, and frisbee players and provide a large island of calm right in the heart of the city. Graz acquired the ornate central fountain, depicting eight figures holding huge spitting fish, at the 1873 Vienna World's Fair. Paris snatched up the two complementary side pieces, now in the *place de la Concorde.* The **Künstlerhaus,** also nestled in the Stadtpark, is a museum that showcases eclectically themed exhibitions ranging from Tibetan artifacts to Secessionist paintings (open Mon.-Fri. 10am-5pm, Sat.-Sun. 10am-1pm; 40AS, students 20AS). The 13th-century Gothic **Leechkirche,** Zinzendorfgasse 5, between the Stadtpark and the university, is the oldest structure in Graz. Inside the relatively small chapel, a wooden altar with white, three-dimensional figures presents a sharp contrast to the glittery gold of most Austrian churches.

South of the fountain, the Stadtpark blends into the **Burggarten,** a bit of carefully pruned greenery complementing what remains of Emperor Friedrich III's 15th-century **Burg.** Freddie had the initials "A.E.I.O.U." inscribed on his namesake wing of the palace. This cryptic inscription is varyingly interpreted as "*Austria Est Imperare Orbi Universo*," "*Austria Erit In Orbe Ultima*," or "*Alles Edreich Ist Österreich Untertan*"—all three roughly translate to "Austria will rule the world." Friedrich's son, Maximilian I, enlarged the building and, in 1499, commissioned the unique Gothic double spiral staircase, thus predating Watson and Crick by almost 500 years. He also inserted the **Burgtor** (Castle Gate) into the city walls. Stroll through the courtyard and out through the giant gate to find Hofgasse and the **Dom** (cathedral); its simple Gothic exterior belies the exquisite Baroque embellishments inside. In 1174, Friedrich III had the existing Romanesque chapel retooled to make the three-bayed cathedral late-Gothic style. In 1485, a picture of the "Scourges of God" was mounted on the south side of the church to remind Christians of the most palpable Trinity of the time: the Black Death, attacks by Ottoman Turks, and the invasion of the locusts, the combination of which wiped out 80% of the population in 1480.

Inside the cathedral, a beautiful silver and gold organ and thick marble pillars await visitors. The huge fresco over the lintel, ostensibly Christ, actually bears the features of Emperor Friedrich III—worshippers believed that if they caught a glimpse of his eyes, they would pass without harm. Originally, the front of the church was covered by a thick wooden gate, since the commoners were only supposed to hear the priests and never see them. The Emperor got a choice seat high above the left side, and was able to watch mass as well. The priest controlled the hands of the clock under the organ from the pulpit and could stop them if he felt the need to pray longer.

Next door, the solemn 17th-century Habsburg **Mausoleum,** regarded as the best example of Austrian Mannerism, stands atop a grey stone staircase. Look to the right for the golden eagle, the world's largest weather vane. The domed tomb was intended for the Emperor Ferdinand II but actually holds the remains of his mother, Archduchess Maria. Master architect Johann Bernard Fischer von Erlach designed the frescoes inside (open Mon.-Thurs. and Sat. 11am-noon and 2-3pm; free). The **Opernhaus** (opera house), at Opernring and Burggasse, was built in under two years by Viennese theater architects Fellner and Helmer. The two drank their cup of inspiration from the masterful fonde of Fischer von Erlach. The Graz **Glockenspiel** (bell tower), located just off Enge Gasse in the Glockenspielpl., opens its high wooden doors every day at 11am, 3pm, and 6pm to reveal life-size wooden figures spinning to a slightly out-of-tune Austrian folk song. The black and gold ball underneath turns to show the phases of the moon.

To the west of Graz proper, **Schloß Eggenberg,** Eggenberger Allee (tel. 58 32 64), stands as an artifact of past grandeur. Built under the auspices of the Imperial Prince Ulrich of Eggenberg, this grandiose palace holds the regional hunting museum, coin museum, and an exhibition of Roman artifacts. The city wasted no modesty on the elegant **Prunkräume** (literally, resplendent rooms), designed around the theme of cosmology and astronomy. Count the palace windows—all 365 of them—each representing…well, you know. To see the apartments of state, known for their 17th-century frescoes and ornate chandeliers, you must join one of the free tours (in German; hourly 10am-noon and 2-4pm). The enchanting **game preserve** that envelops the palace proves that nature's handicraft is every bit as magnificent as the work of bishops or princes. Royal blue peacocks wander and squawk freely. Take tram #1 (dir: Eggenberg) all the way to "Schloß Eggenberg." (*Prunkräume* open April-Oct. daily 10am-1pm and 2-5pm. Hunting museum open March-Nov. daily 9am-noon and 1-5pm. Coin museum open Feb.-Nov. daily 9am-noon and 1-5pm. Artifacts open daily Feb.-Nov 9am-1pm and 2-5pm. Game preserve open May-Aug. daily 8am-7pm; March-April and Sept.-Oct. daily 8am-6pm; Jan.-Feb. and Nov.-Dec. daily 8am-5pm. Admission to the entire complex 80AS, students 40AS, entrance to only the gardens 2AS.) Classical concerts are given in the *Planetensaal* (Planet Hall; tel. 82 50 00) in the palace in August and September Mondays at 8pm. Tickets start at 130AS.

ENTERTAINMENT

The vibrant, dynamic population of Graz prides itself on being able to cultivate high art while simultaneously being able to let it all hang out. Entertainment in Graz has something to suit even the most curmudgeonly vacationer. For progressive, envelope-pushing drama, Graz's remarkable neo-Baroque **Opernhaus** (opera house), at Opernring and Burggasse (tel. 80 08), sells standing-room tickets (25-35AS) at the door an hour before curtain call. The yearly program includes operas and ballets of worldwide repute; for many young hopefuls, Graz is considered a stepping stone to an international career. One big show comes to the Opera House each July, while the regular companies are on vacation; 1995 brought the musical "Cats," 1996 the Bolshoi Ballet. The **Schauspielhaus,** a theater at Freiheitspl. off Hofgasse (tel. 80 05), also sells bargain seats just before showtime. Regular and student tickets and performance schedules are available at the **Theaterkasse,** Kaiser-Josef-Pl. 10 (tel. 80 00; fax 800 85 65; open Mon.-Fri. 8am-6:30pm, Sat. 8am-1pm). Tickets and information are available at the Zentralkartenbüro, Herrengasse 7 (tel. 83 02 55).

In late September and October, the **Steierischer Herbst** (Styrian Autumn) festival celebrates avant-garde art with one month of modern abstractions. Contact the director of the festival, Sackstr. 17 (tel. 82 30 07; fax 83 57 88; email stherbst@ping.at; http://www.ping.at/members/stherbst) for more details. Since 1985, Graz has hosted its own summer festival, **Styriarte,** as well. Mostly classical concerts are held daily from late June to early July in the gardens of the Eggenberg Palace, the large halls of Graz Convention Center, and the squares of the old city. The renowned Graz conductor, Nikolaus Harnoncourt, sets the tone. (Tickets for most events start at 200AS.) The award-winning movie theater **Rechbauerkino,** Rechbauerstr. 6 (tel. 83 05 08), occasionally screens undubbed American flicks (tickets 80AS, 60AS on Mon.), and Tuesday is English Film Night at the **Royal Kino,** on Conrad-von-Hötzendorfstr., a few blocks south of Jakominiplatz (tickets prices same). Of course, the best things in life are free—stroll down **Sporgasse,** a narrow cobblestone path squeezed between two rows of brightly lit shops, or meander down **Herrengasse** to hear the trumpets and violins echoing against the façades of the *Altstadt.* Also be sure to consult the cultural magazine, *Graz Derzeit,* available free at the tourist office, for a daily, mind-boggling list of events and details on prices and locations (also at http://www.iic.wifi.at/graz/veranstaltungen/derzeit).

NIGHTLIFE

Each day when the sun sets on Graz, the quarter of a million inhabitants change into their party threads and collectively paint the town red. The hub of after-hours activity can be found in the **"Bermuda Triangle,"** an area of the old city behind the Hauptplatz and bordered by Mehlplatz, Färbergasse, and Prokopiagasse. Like the one in Vienna, the Triangle's dozens of beer gardens and bars are packed with people all night, every night; sitting in an outdoor café is *de rigeur,* at least until 11pm, when local ordinance requires that festivities be continued indoors. The area is as patronized by Graz students as by Armani-clad business-mongers, but more scholars can be found in the pubs lining Zinzendorfgasse and Halbärthgasse, near the university.

Kulturhauskeller, Elisabethstr. 30, underneath the Kulturhaus. Young crowd and cool locale dictate the loud, sometimes overwhelming music in this bar. The partying doesn't really get started until 11pm on weekends. Tall glass of *Weißbier* 34AS. No shorts or military duds. IDs checked (19+). Obligatory coat check and security fee 20AS. Open Mon.-Sat. 8pm-3:30am.

Café Harrach, Harrachgasse 26 (tel. 32 26 71). Quaff a beverage at this local student haunt, which serves an more sophisticated clientele in its quiet, outdoor seating. A half-liter of *Gösser* goes for 29AS, but most everybody's throwing back white wine spritzers (26AS). Open Mon.-Fri. 9am-midnight, Sat.-Sun. 7pm-midnight.

Tom's Bierklinik, Färbergasse 1 (tel. 84 51 74) has the largest stock of international beers in Austria. Go ahead and try prescriptions from Hawaii, Trinidad, or India (all 75AS), or just get a local fix with a glass of *Murauer Pils* (32AS). Walk-in hours daily 8pm-4am. No appointment necessary.

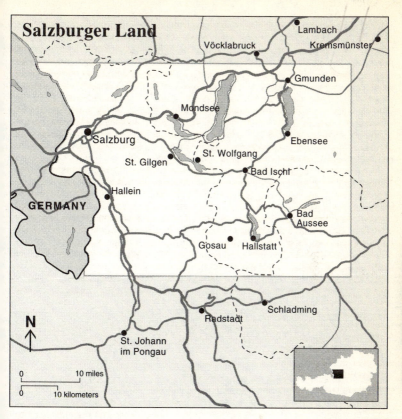

Salzburger Land

N

| 0 | 10 miles |
| 0 | 10 kilometers |

Salzburger Land

Once one of Europe's most powerful archbishoprics, the province of Salzburg remained an autonomous entity until 1815, when the Congress of Vienna awarded it to Austria. The region built up its tremendous wealth with "white gold"—the salt industry that flourished from the Iron Age onward. The name "Salzburg" comes from *Salz,* the German word for salt, and several localities in the region also have some derivative of *Hall* (an archaic Celtic term for salt) in their name. Although tourism displaced the salt trade long ago, figures of St. Barbara, the patron saint of miners, are still found everywhere. The major attraction of Salzburger Land is the Baroque magnificence of its capital city, Salzburg. The dramatic natural scenery and placid lakes of the Salzkammergut, which straddles the provincial boundaries of Salzburg, Styria, and Upper Austria, are also among Austria's favorite vacation spots.

Though all this mineral mining may seem soporific, when the Salzburger Land lets down its hair, it does so in style. Every three years, on the last Sunday in July, a historic **Pirates' Battle** is held on the River Salzach at **Oberndorf.** The pirates' camp is situated below the State Bridge. According to the ritual plot, the brigands attack and rob a saltboat and then fire on the town of **Laufen,** on the opposite (Bavarian) side of the river. Eventually, the defeated pirates try to escape. They are arrested and condemned to death, but their sentence is quickly modified to "death by drowning in beer," which signifies the beginning of a lavish feast.

■ Salzburg

For the city of Salzburg (pop. 150,000), the three most important factors about real estate are Mozart, Mozart, and Mozart. *The Sound of Music* is a close fourth. Though wedged between three foliage-covered peaks and dotted with church spires, medieval turrets, and resplendent palaces, Salzburg nevertheless considers its forte to be not its spectacular sights, but its historical and current performance relationship with the music of its favorite son Wolfgang Amadeus Mozart, whose presence is felt throughout the city, from its narrow alleys to its grand music halls. The city's adulation for the composer reaches a deafening roar every summer during the **Salzburger Festspiele** (summer music festival), when financially endowed admirers from the world 'round come to pay their respects. The *Festspiele* is a five-week event featuring hundreds of operas, concerts, plays, and open-air performances. Of course, Salzburg is also the best place to pay homage to the saccharinely trilling von Trapp family of *The Sound of Music* fame. Tour guides will never let you forget that the movie was filmed here.

The one-two combination of "Wolfie" and his later fellow Salzburger musicians make the otherwise peaceful town a beacon for tourists, rich and poor. Never mind that both Mozart and the von Trapps eventually left, finding Salzburg a bit too stifling (the former fled from the oppressive bourgeois atmosphere and his over-managerial father, the latter from the tone-deaf Nazis). This Little City That Could couldn't keep away the onslaught of visitors even if it wanted to.

GETTING TO SALZBURG

Flughafen Salzburg (airport; tel. 85 20 91) serves continental Europe and is located 4km west of the city center in the Maxglan section. Bus #77 (dir: Bahnhof from the airport, Walserfeld from the train station) connects the train station with the airport and makes runs every 15 to 30min. (daily 5:55am-11:26pm.; ride lasts 15min.) A taxi from the train station to the airport costs 90-120AS (ride lasts 10-15min.). For flight information, call **Austrian Airlines** (tel. 87 55 44; fax 85 92 22). Daily flights jet between major European and Austrian cities including **Paris, Amsterdam, Vienna,** and **Innsbruck.** The following airlines have connections in Salzburg: Aeroflot, Air Link, Air Salzburg, Austrian Airlines, Lufthansa, Sabena, Lauda Air. The cheapest way to get to Salzburg is to fly into the larger hub, Munich, and take the train from there (2hr., every ½hr., 280AS).

Salzburg has two main train stations. The **Hauptbahnhof** on Südtiroler Platz is the first depot when coming from Vienna; the **Rangier Bahnhof** is the first stop when coming from Innsbruck. The Rangier is used to load cargo and is much farther from the center of town; don't get off here. Though the following is by no means an exhaustive list, Salzburg connects directly to many major international and domestic cities. The reservation office at the station is open daily 7am-8:15pm. Trains go to **Innsbruck** (2hr., hourly, 336AS); **Graz** (4½hr., hourly, 396AS); **Vienna** (3½hr., every ½hr., 396AS); **Budapest** (7½hr., 9 daily, 670AS); **Munich** (2hr., every ½hr., 280AS); **Zürich** (6hr., 6 daily, last connection at 4pm, 806AS); **Prague** (connect in Linz, 4 daily, 462AS); **Venice** (7½hr., 7 daily, last connection at 10:15pm, 434AS). Call 17 17 for train schedule information.

The **regional bus depot** is right outside the main train station. The BundesBus makes outstanding connections to the Salzkammergut region. **Mondsee** (50min., hourly, 54AS); **St. Wolfgang** (1½hr., hourly, 81AS); and **Bad Ischl** (1½hr., every 2hr., 95AS) are among the destinations. For schedule information call 167.

Motorists coming from Vienna can exit at any of the numerous Salzburg-West exits on Autobahn A1. Among these, the Flughafen exit is near the airport; the Salzburg Nord exit is near Itzling and Kasern; and the Salzburg Süd exit lies south of the city near Schloß Hellbrunn and Untersberg. Routes A8 and E52 lead from the west into Rosenheim, and then branch off in different directions to Munich and Innsbruck. Autoroute A10 heads north from Hallein to Salzburg. To reach the Salzkammergut area and the scenic road to the top of Gaisberg, take the "Grazer Bundesstraße," (route #158) from Gnigl behind Kapuzinerberg. Since public transportation is efficient within the city limits, consider the "Park and Ride" **parking lots.** Park for free when you get off the highway and take the bus into town. The best is **Alpensiedlung Süd** on Alpenstr. (exit: Salzburg Süd). A bigger lot is open in July and August at the Salzburger Ausstellungszentrum (exit: Salzburg-Mitte).

ORIENTATION AND PRACTICAL INFORMATION

Salzburg, capital of the province of the same name, lies at the midpoint of Austria's length, 470m above sea level. Three wooded hills surround the town, which hugs the banks of the **Salzach River** a few kilometers from the German border. The Hauptbahnhof is located at the northern side of downtown, and is a short bus ride to downtown proper on buses #1 (dir: Maxglan), 5 (dir: Birkensiedlung), 6 (dir: Parsch), 51 (dir: Salzburg-Süd), or 55 (dir: Rif). Downtown is divided by the river. On the west bank is the *Altstadt,* with the **Mönchsberg** (Monk's Mountain) towering above it; on the east side is the *Neustadt,* which has **Mirabellplatz** at its heart. From the bus, disembark at "Mirabellplatz" or "Mozartsteg" to access the city sights. By foot, the inner city is a 10- to 15-minute walk from the train station. Exit the building, turn left, and follow Rainerstr. until it becomes Mirabellpl. Most hostels are on the east side of the river, while a quick jaunt over the Salzach to its west bank leads to the heavily touristed pedestrian district.

Agencies

Tourist Office, Mozartpl. 5 (tel. 84 75 68 or 88 98 73 30; fax 88 98 73 42), in the *Altstadt.* From the train station, take bus #5, 6, 51, or 55 to "Mozartsteg," and curve around the building into Mozartpl. On foot, make a left on Rainerstr., go to the end, and cross the Staatsbrücke over the Salzach, then continue following the river's west bank upstream to Mozartsteg (20min.). Free hotel maps at all branches. Reservations 30AS, 60AS for three or more people, plus a deposit of 7.2% deductible from the first night's stay. The understaffed, overworked offices will let you know which hostels still have rooms available. The office also peddles a "Salzburg Card," offering free entrances and other price reductions for attractions, museums, and restaurants, as well as free use of the bus system (24-hr. card 180AS, 48-hr. 260AS, 72-hr. 350AS). Unless you plan to cram four or five major attractions into each day, the cards are probably not worth it. The free hotel map is exactly the same as the 10AS city map. Open June-Aug. daily 9am-7pm; Sept.-May 9am–6pm. Hours may vary by 15min.-1hr. each month. Other **branches** are located at the **train station platform #2a** (tel. 87 17 12 or 87 36 38), open Mon.-Sat. 8:45am-8pm; at the **airport** (tel. 85 24 51 or 85 24 52), open daily 9am-9pm; and at the Salzburg-West **exit** off the Autobahn.

Budget Travel: ÖKISTA, Wolf-Dietrich-Str. 31, A-5020 Salzburg (tel. 88 32 52; fax 88 18 19), near the International Youth Hotel. Open Mon.-Fri. 9:30am-5:30pm. **Young Austria,** Alpenstr. 108a (tel. 625 75 80; fax 62 57 58 21), part of the *Österreichisches Jugendferienwerk.* Open Mon.-Fri. 9am-5pm, Sat. 9am-noon. Both have discounts, especially for travelers under 26.

Consulates: U.S. Consulate Agency, Herbert-von-Karajan-Pl. 1 (tel. 84 87 76), in the *Altstadt.* Open Mon., Wed., and Fri. 9am-noon. **U.K.,** Alter Markt 4 (tel. 84 81 33). Open Mon.-Fri. 9am-noon.

Currency Exchange: Banking hours are Mon.-Fri. 8am-12:30pm and 2-4:30pm. Currency exchange at the train station open daily 7am-9pm. **Rieger Bank** *(C4),* Alter Markt 14, is also open May-Oct. on Sat. afternoons and Sun. 10am-5pm. Banks offer better rates for cash than AmEx, but commissions are often higher. **Panorama Tours** offers cash currency exchange at bank rates with no commission to guests taking their tour.

American Express: Mozartpl. 5 (tel. 84 25 01; fax 842 50 19). All banking services; expect excruciatingly long lines in summer. For cashing and exchanging traveler's checks, AmEx charges up to 40AS per transaction, but it's less than what the banks charge. Cardholder mail held, sightseeing tours booked, music festival tickets reserved. Address mail, for example: Melissa WATT, c/o American Express, Client

Mail Service, Mozartplatz 5, A-5020 Salzburg. Open Mon.-Fri. 9am-5:30pm, Sat. 9am-noon.

Thomas Cook: Reisen & Freizeit, Rainerstr. 24 (tel. 87 94 96; fax 87 91 66). No exchange, but refunds on lost traveler's checks.

Telephones: Metered phones at the train station post office. Open 24hr. Also at Residenzplatz post office. Open Mon.-Fri. 7am-7pm, Sat. 8-10am.

Transportation

Public Transportation: Information at Griesgasse 21 (tel. 62 05 51, ext. 553). Punch your ticket when you get on board to validate it. An extensive network of 18 buses cuts through the city, with central hubs at "Hanusch-Platz" by Makartsteg, "Äußerer Stein" by the Mozartsteg, the Mirabellplatz, and at the Bahnhof. Tickets can be purchased at any *Tabak* 14AS per ride, on the bus 21AS, or at the automatic vending machines 17AS. Ages 6-15 7AS. 24-hr. passes available from Tabaks (30AS). Maps available from the tourist office. Buses usually make their last run from downtown to outer destinations at 10:30-11:30pm, and earlier for less frequented routes. Check the schedule posted at bus stops.

Parking: If you can, consider the "Park and Ride" options (see Getting to Salzburg, p. 358). If you must drive into the city, the **Altstadt-Garage** inside the Mönchsberg is open 24hr. **Mirabell-Garage** in Mirabellplatz is open 7am-midnight. **Parkgarage Linzergasse** at Glockengasse, off Linzergasse, is open Mon.-Fri. 7am-11pm, Sat. 7am-2pm. Blue lines on the sidewalk indicate that parking is available with a ticket from a nearby automated machine. Other parking lots at the airport, Hellbrunn, and Akademiestr. (15AS per hr.).

Taxis: Taxi stands in the *Altstadt* are at Alter Markt and Anton-Newmayr-Platz (tel. 81 11). The city transportation also runs a **BusTaxi** at night daily 11:30pm-1:30am when the public buses stop. Pick it up at the bus stops at Hanuschplatz and Theatergasse (every ½hr.), and tell the driver where you need to go. 30AS per person for any distance within the city limits.

Car Rental: It is much cheaper to rent by prior arrangements with travel agents abroad. **Avis,** Ferdinand-Porsche-Str. 7 (tel. 87 72 78; fax 88 02 35), and **Budget,** Rainerstr. 17 (tel. 873 45; fax 88 23 87), are located at the airport. The cheapest car rental place is **Kalal,** Alpenstr. 2 (tel./fax 62 00 06). All offer unlimited mileage and full insurance.

Bike Rental: At the train station counter #3 (tel. 88 87 54 27). Climb every mountain and ford every stream with a bicycle. 100AS per day, 50AS with a train ticket from that day. Five-day rental packages 200AS. Bike paths wind all through the city, especially in the *Altstadt.*

Hitchhiking: Hitchers who are headed to Innsbruck, Munich, or Italy (except Venice) take bus #77 to the German border. Thumbers bound for Vienna or Venice take bus #29 (dir: Forellenwegsiedlung) until the Autobahn entrance at "Schmiedlingerstr." They also take bus #15 (dir: Bergheim) to the Autobahn entrance at "Grüner Wald."

Other Practical Information

Luggage Storage: At the train station. Large lockers 30AS for two calendar days. Small lockers 20AS. Luggage check costs 20AS per piece per calendar day for a maximum of 30 days. Open 24hr.

Bookstore: Bücher Schneid, Rainerstr. 24 (tel. 87 17 85). Restock *Let's Go* or pick up other English-language books. Open Mon.-Fri. 8:30am-6pm, Sat. 8am-noon. **American Discount,** hidden in a passage in Alter Markt 1 (tel. 75 75 41), sells American magazines, boxing gloves and paperbacks.

Gay, Lesbian and Bisexual Organizations: Homosexuelle Initiative (HOSI), Müllner Hauptstr. 11 (tel. 43 59 27). Sponsors discussion groups. Club open Wed. and Sat. 10pm-midnight, Fri. 9pm-midnight. **HUK-Salzburg** (Gay Christian Organization), Philharmonikergasse 2 (tel. 84 13 27). **Frauenkulturzentrum** (Women's Center), Markus-Sittikusstr. 17 (tel./fax 87 16 39). Center open Mon. noon-4pm, Tues.-Thurs. 10am-4pm. Women's café Wed.-Sat. 8pm-midnight.

Laundromat: Laundromat Wgescheid, Paris-Londronstr. 14 (tel. 87 63 81), between Linzergasse and the ÖKISTA. Industrial sized machines can handle up to

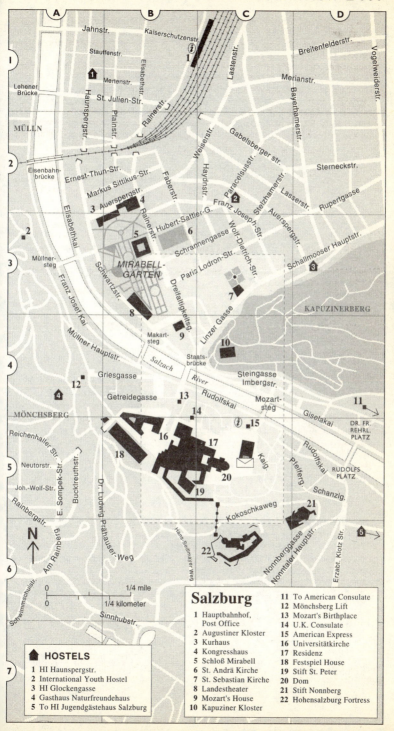

Salzburg

1 Hauptbahnhof, Post Office
2 Augustiner Kloster
3 Kurhaus
4 Kongresshaus
5 Schloß Mirabell
6 St. Andrä Kirche
7 St. Sebastian Kirche
8 Landestheater
9 Mozart's House
10 Kapuziner Kloster
11 To American Consulate
12 Mönchsberg Lift
13 Mozart's Birthplace
14 U.K. Consulate
15 American Express
16 Universitätkirche
17 Residenz
18 Festspiel House
19 Stift St. Peter
20 Dom
21 Stift Nonnberg
22 Hohensalzburg Fortress

HOSTELS

1 HI Haunspergstr.
2 International Youth Hostel
3 HI Glockengasse
4 Gasthaus Naturfreundehaus
5 To HI Jugendgästehaus Salzburg

7kg. Self-service laundry. 100AS for wash, soap, and dry; 150AS for someone else to do your dirty laundry. Open Mon.-Fri. 7:30am-6pm and Sat. 8am-noon. **Constructa**, Kaiserschützenstr 10 (tel. 87 62 53), across from the train station. Self service and drop-off services available.

Public Toilets: In the *Altstadt*. Under the archway between Kapitel and Domplatz (7AS). Cheaper ones in the Festungsbahn lobby (3AS).

Pharmacies: To get rid of the sniffles, visit **Elisabeth-Apotheke,** Elisabethstr. 1 (tel. 87 14 84), a few blocks left of the train station. **Alte f.e. Hofapotheke,** Alter Markt 6 (tel. 84 36 23), is the oldest pharmacy in Salzburg. Pharmacies open Mon.-Fri. 8am-12:30pm and 2:30-6pm, Sat. 8am-noon. There are always three pharmacies available for emergencies. Check the door of any closed pharmacy to find an open one.

Rape Hotline: tel. 88 11 00.

AIDS Hotline: AIDS-Hilfe Salzburg, Saint-Julienstr. 31 (tel. 88 14 88).

Medical Assistance: When the dog bites, when the bee stings, when you're feeling sad, call the **Hospital,** Müllner Hauptstr. 48 (tel. 44 82).

Emergencies: Police: tel. 133. Headquarters at Alpenstr. 90 (tel. 63 83). **Ambulance:** tel. 144. **Fire:** tel. 122.

Post Office: Hauptbahnhof (tel. 889 70). Mail your brown paper packages tied up with strings at the main office next to the train station. Address **Poste Restante** to "Postlagernde Briefe, Bahnhofspostamt, A-5020 Salzburg." Office open 24hr., but Poste Restante must be picked up Mon.-Fri. 7am-6:30pm. **Postal code:** A-5020. **Branch Office** at Residenzpl. 9 (tel. 84 41 21). Open Mon.-Fri. 7am-7pm, Sat. 8-10am. **Postal Code:** A-5010

Telephone Code: 0662

ACCOMMODATIONS AND CAMPING

Salzburg has no shortage of hostels—but, then again, it has no shortage of tourists either. Real estate in Salzburg is even more expensive than in Vienna; most of the affordable accommodations are located on the outskirts of town, easily accessible by local transportation. To hunt down rooms in *pensionen* and private homes, go to the tourist office—it's a very good place to start. Ask for their list of private rooms (separate from the hotel map). The tourist office charges 7.2% of your room fee to make reservations. From mid-May through mid-September hostels fill by mid-afternoon; call ahead. During the festival, never show up without prior arrangements, and certainly not later than noon. Hotels are booked months in advance, and most youth hostels and *Gasthäuser* are full days before. Hostels have long abandoned the old practice of letting late stragglers crash on the floor. Most places will accept reservations, but space is so tight that they certainly won't hold them indefinitely. Cancel your reservations if you change plans so as not to cause fellow travelers trouble. The *Hotel Plan* (available at the tourist office) provides information on hostels. An underutilized resource is the **HI booking network** (see Hostel Membership, p. 41).

Hostels and Dormitories

Gasthaus Naturfreundehaus/Bürgerwehr, Mönchsberg 19c (tel. 84 17 29), towers over the old town from the top of the Mönchsberg. The easy way (by elevator): take bus #1 or 2 (dir: Maxglan) to "Mönchsbergaufzug," disembark, and stroll from the main tourist office down Getreidegasse until the end when you reach the elevator (it's just through the stone archway). The elevator takes you to the top of the mountain (round-trip 25AS, last elevator at 11pm). At its summit, turn right, climb the steps, and go down the paved path to the left following signs for "Bürgerwehr" or "Panoramaterrasse." Go through the stone arch of the old fortress, and take the small dirt path to the immediate left. The *Gasthaus* lies about 50m ahead on the right. Look for the red umbrellas; it may look like a restaurant, but it's not, it's a hostel. The not-so-easy way: hike up the 332 stairs at Toscaninihof (next to the Festspielhaus), bearing right the whole time on the paths at the top until you come to the red-umbrella-bedecked *Gasthaus*. Great view. Great price. Great hostel. The vista comes to you direct from five-star hotel territory. Genial, folksy proprietors have their hands full with running the terrific restaurant downstairs as well. Only

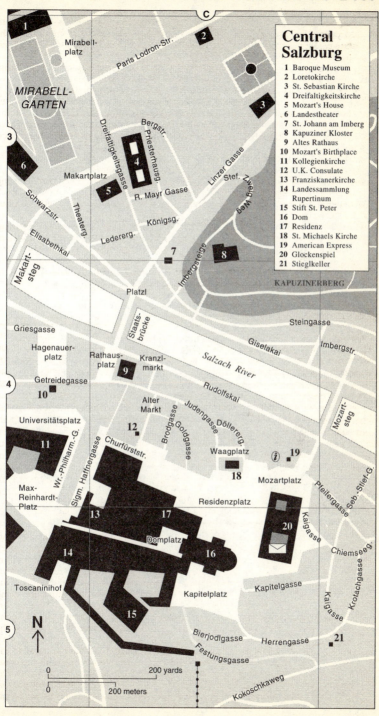

Central Salzburg

1 Baroque Museum
2 Loretokirche
3 St. Sebastian Kirche
4 Dreifaltigkeitskirche
5 Mozart's House
6 Landestheater
7 St. Johann am Imberg
8 Kapuziner Kloster
9 Altes Rathaus
10 Mozart's Birthplace
11 Kollegienkirche
12 U.K. Consulate
13 Franziskanerkirche
14 Landessammlung Rupertinum
15 Stift St. Peter
16 Dom
17 Residenz
18 St. Michaels Kirche
19 American Express
20 Glockenspiel
21 Stieglkeller

SALZBURGER LAND

Mirabell-platz

Paris Lodron-Str.

MIRABELL-GARTEN

Bergstr.

Priesterhausg.

Dreifaltigkeitsgasse

Makartplatz

R. Mayr Gasse

Linzer Gasse

Stef.

Zwieg Weg

Königsg.

Schwarzstr.

Theaterg.

Ledererg.

Elisabethkai

Imbergstege

KAPUZINERBERG

Makart-steg

Platzl

Staats-brücke

Griesgasse

Steingasse

Hagenauer-platz

Giselakai

Imbergstr.

Rathaus-platz

Kranzl-markt

Salzach River

Getreidegasse

Rudolfskai

Universitätsplatz

Alter Markt

Judengasse

Döllererg.

Brodgasse

Goldgasse

Mozart-steg

Churfürststr.

Waagplatz

ⓘ

Wr.-Philharm.-G.

Sigm. Haffnergasse

Mozartplatz

Max-Reinhardt-Platz

Residenzplatz

Pfeifergasse

Seb.-Stief-G.

Kaigasse

Domplatz

Toscaninihof

Kapitelgasse

Chiemseeg.

Kapitelplatz

Kaigasse

Krotachgasse

N

Bierjodlgasse

Herrengasse

Festungsgasse

0   200 yards

0   200 meters

Kokoschkaweg

accommodates 28 in doubles, triples, quads and 6-bed rooms, so call ahead and let the proprietors know in advance how many nights you're staying. Reception open daily 8am-10pm. Curfew 1am, so start hustling up those stairs at quarter 'til. 120AS per person. Showers 10AS per 4min. Breakfast 30AS. Sheets 10AS. Open May to mid-Oct.

International Youth Hotel, YoHo, Paracelsusstr. 9 (tel. 87 96 49), off Franz-Josef-Str. From town, take bus #15 (dir: Bergheim) to "Paracelsusstr." Or more easily, exit the train station to the left, make another left onto Gabelsbergerstr. through the tunnel. Then make the second right onto Paracelsusstr (7min.). A loud, boisterous pit stop for homesick Americans who come for the camaraderie, and to play a couple rounds of "You Go to [insert college], Do You Know [insert peripheral high school buddy]." The hostel restaurant's perpetual happy hour makes it more popular than most local bars. Clean and orderly, most of the time. *The Sound of Music* screened daily. Reception open daily 8am-10pm. "Curfew" 1am (not very strict); theoretical quiet time starts at 10pm, but don't expect it to quiet down until 2-3am. Dorms 130-140AS per person. Doubles 340-360AS. Quads 600-640AS. Showers 10AS per 6min. Breakfast 15-40AS. Dinner entrées 60-75AS. Lockers 10AS. Stylish sleepsacks 20AS.

Institut St. Sebastian, Linzergasse 41 (tel. 87 13 86 or 88 26 06; fax 87 13 86 85). From the station, turn left on Rainerstr., go past Mirabellpl., make a left onto Bergstr., and a left at the end onto Linzergasse. The hostel is through the arch on the right, near the fire station. This privately owned hostel-like accommodation, built right on the St. Sebastian church grounds, received a much-needed facelift recently, and the entire complex is clean and modern. Located smack-dab in the middle of the historic *Neustadt,* the institute is a female-only university student dorm, but travelers of either gender are welcome. The cemetery of the St. Sebastian church abutting the dormitory makes for a very quiet neighborhood. Reception open daily 9am-10pm; Sat.-Sun. closed noon-3pm. No curfew. Only 90 beds, so reservations are strongly recommended. Dorms 160AS. Singles 300AS, with shower and toilet 350AS. Doubles 540AS, with shower and toilet 600AS. Triples 690AS, with shower and toilet 810AS. Sheets 30AS, but sheets and breakfast included with singles, doubles, and triples. Kitchen facilities available, including refrigerators with little lockable cupboards inside—ask for a key at the reception. Pots and bowls can be rented. During Oct.-June only the dorms are open.

Jugendgästehaus Salzburg (HI), Josef-Preis-Allee 18 (tel. 84 26 70 or 84 68 57; fax 84 11 01), just southeast of the *Altstadt.* Take bus #5, 51, or 55 to "Justizgebäude," or walk right from the tourist office southeast (upstream, or with traffic) along the river, bear right onto Hellbrunnerstr., right again onto Nonntaler Hauptstr., and then take the first left. Sunny, spacious rooms off brightly colored corridors. Omnipresent school groups make frequent use of the on-site video game room, café, and disco. Ridiculous reception hours. Here it goes: open Mon.-Fri. 7-9am, 11-11:30am, noon-1pm, 3:30-5:30pm, 6-9:30pm, and 10pm-midnight; Sat.-Sun. 7-9am, 11-11:30am, noon-1pm, 4:30-7:30pm, and 10pm-midnight. No lockout. Curfew midnight. Dorms 160AS. Double with shower 520AS. Quads with shower 840AS. Nonmembers pay 40AS extra first night. Shower, breakfast, and sheets included. Lunches, bag lunches, and dinners 68AS. Kitchen, laundry facilities, and lockers available. Bike rental 90AS per day. Reservations recommended. Very nice disabled facilities.

Haunspergstraße (HI), Haunspergstr. 27 (tel. 87 50 30; fax 88 34 77), just minutes from the train station. Walk straight out Kaiserschützenstr. (past the Forum department store), which becomes Jahnstr. Take the third left onto Haunspergstr., and turn left onto Haunspergstr. A student dormitory, but transforms into a hostel for July and Aug. It won't accept groups; die-hard backpackers, rejoice! Clean, spacious rooms, ideal for hanging out. Houses 125 in 2- to 4-bed rooms. Staff occasionally disappears from the office; just wait. Reception open daily 7am-2pm and 5pm-midnight, but hostel fills by late afternoon. Curfew midnight. 135AS per person in doubles, triples, and quads. Nonmembers 40AS one time surcharge. Sheets, showers and breakfast included. Laundry 70AS. Open July-Aug.

Glockengasse (HI), Glockengasse 8 (tel. 87 62 41; fax 876 24 13). Walk out the east exit of the station onto Gabelsbergerstr., turn right on Bayerhamerstr., and cross Schallmooser Hauptstr. to the foot of the Kapuzinerberg (mountain). The wooden benches in the mess hall and the rickety bunk beds in the crowded downstairs afford a "Little House on the Prairie" schoolhouse atmosphere—so does the endless parade of school groups. Reception open daily 7-9am and 3:30pm-midnight. Lockout 9am-3:30pm. Curfew midnight. 130AS, subsequent nights 125AS. Breakfast and sheets included. Lockers 100AS deposit. Open April-Sept.

Eduard-Heinrich-Haus (HI), Eduard-Heinrich-Str. 2 (tel. 62 59 76; fax 62 79 80). It's a bit *fa* (a long, long way to run), *so* (a needle pulling thread) take bus #51 (dir: Salzburg Süd) to "Polizeidirektion." Cross the street, continue down Billrothstr., and turn left on the Robert-Stolz-Promenade footpath. Walk 200m, and the hostel is behind the thick of trees on the right. Young people swarm to this woodsy area near university housing. All rooms have 6 beds and are large enough not to be cramped. Some of the rooms are occupied by permanent students during the year, so significantly more space is available in July and Aug. Reception open daily 7-9am, 5pm-midnight. Lockout 9am-5pm. Curfew 11pm. Dorms 135AS. Showers and lockers included. Breakfast served 7-8am.

Aigen (HI), Aignerstr. 34 (tel. 62 32 48; fax 232 48 13). Lots of jungle-like potted plants in the reception and hallways. The rooms themselves are huge, bare 6-bedders with wooden floors. TV and fitness room available. Take bus #5 from the station to "Mozartsteg," then bus #49 (dir: Josef-Käut-Str.) to "Finanzamt" and walk 5min. along the road; it's the yellow, estate-like building on your right. If you've missed the bus, walk from the tourist office over the river on Mozartsteg, turn right on Imbergstr., and follow the street around the rotary as it becomes Bürglsteinstr., and then bear right onto Aignerstr. (½hr.). Reception open daily 7-9am and 5-11pm. Curfew midnight. 140AS, nonmembers 180AS. Breakfast, showers, and sheets included. No lockers.

Hotels and Pensions

Pensionen within the city are scarce and expensive, and service is at times a crapshoot. Better quality at lower prices can be found in farther environs, and public transportation puts these places within minutes of downtown Salzburg. Rooms on Kasern Berg are officially out of Salzburg, so the tourist office doesn't recommend them, but the sugar-sweet hosts and bargain prices make them little-known steals. They can be reached by taking any northbound regional train (4-min. ride, generally every ½hr. daily from 6:17am-11:17pm, 17AS, Eurail Pass valid) to the first stop "Salzburg-Maria Plain," and walking the lone road up the hill. All the pensions are along this road, and if you call in advance, they will even pick you up at the Kasern station. Or, take bus #15 (dir: Bergheim) from "Mirabellplatz" to "Kasern" and then hike up the mountain (15min.). By car, exit Autobahn A1 on "Salzburg Nord." Yet another option in an emergency is to go camping, a possibility even for domestic souls who have never spent a night under the stars. Some of the campsites have beds in pre-assembled tents. Whatever you decide, eschew proprietors who accost you at the train station—they often charge outlandish prices for sparse rooms in La-La Land. This goes for the train station at Kasern Berg as well as the Hauptbahnhof in the Salzburg. Don't trust people who come up to you as you get off the train, and no matter what never pay in advance.

Haus Lindner, Panoramaweg 5, formerly Kasern Berg 64 (tel. 45 66 81 or 45 67 73). Frau Lindner's house is on a little gravel road set about 15m back from the main Kasern Berg street. She and her sisters rent 30 private beds in three separate houses, which all share a breakfast room in Haus Lindner. Rooms are spacious with hardwood floors. Throw rugs give the place a "Mom-I'm-home" feel. Families with children are welcome, and the playground is located in the rear. 160-200AS per person in doubles, triples, and quads. Shower and breakfast included.

Haus Rosemarie Seigmann, Kasern Berg 66 (tel. 45 00 01). Rosemarie is a welcoming, English-speaking hostess offering hand-painted cupboards, flowered curtains, and stuffed animals to keep you warm at night. Listen to birds singing from the stone terrace overlooking the Alps. Bright rooms with fluffy comforters. 170-180AS per person in doubles and triples. Breakfast and showers included. If no rooms are available, she'll call around for you.

Germana Kapeller, Kasern Berg 64 (tel. 45 66 71), just below Haus Lindner and hence closer to the train station, but with smaller rooms. *Dirndl*-clad English-speaking hostess oversees enchantingly traditional rooms and screens *The Sound of Music* upon group demand (guests only). 160-180AS per person. Showers and complete breakfast included. Call ahead.

Haus Moser, Turnebuhel 1 (tel. 45 66 76), above Haus Rosemarie Seigmann; climb up the hidden stairs on the right side of Kasern Berg road. A mountainside, dark-timbered home with spacious rooms filled with fur rugs and deer heads. 170AS per person for singles, doubles, triples, and quads. "Welcome drink," all-you-can-eat breakfast, and shower included.

Haus Ballwein, Moostr. 69 (tel. 82 40 29). Take the south-bound bus #60 to "Gsengerweg," which stops right in front of the pension (8min. to city center). Spotless rooms decorated in pastels and beautiful new furniture. The country farmhouse has wonderful farmland for hiking and offers a relaxing rural reprieve from the bustle of city tourism. Amazing breakfast includes eggs from the pension's own chickens. 200AS per person, in room with shower 240AS. Breakfast included.

Haus Kernstock, Karolingerstr. 29 (tel. 82 74 69; fax 82 74 69). Take bus #77 (dir: Flughafen) to "Karolingerstr.," and then follow signs for the street number, as the road twists strangely (15min. from rail station). Gigantic rooms with balconies, private baths, and handpainted cupboards. Amiable hostess has 4 bikes which she lends to guests, and also offers *Sound of Music* screenings. 220-250AS per person for doubles, triples, and quads. Cable TV. Breakfast included. Visa, MC.

Pension Sandwirt, Lastenstr. 6a (tel. 87 43 51). Close proximity to the Hauptbahnhof makes Sandwirt stand out from the other average *Pensionen*. From the station, exit from the platform #13 staircase, make a right on the footbridge, and at the bottom, turn right onto Lastenstr. The *Pension* is behind the building with the large post sign (3min.). Singles 280AS. Doubles 440AS, with shower and toilet 500AS. Triples 570AS, with shower and toilet 630AS.

Haus Elisabeth, Rauchenbichlerstr. 18 (tel. 507 03). Take bus #51 to the end "Itzling-Pflanzmann," walk up Rauchenbichlerstr. over the footbridge, and continue right along the gravel path. Amazing rooms with balconies and sweeping views of the city. Hostess believes in stuffing her guests with a plentiful breakfast of corn flakes, yogurt, bread, jam. Singles with shower 300AS. Doubles 500AS. Single night surcharge of 10%. Breakfast included.

Gasthof Wastlwirt, Rochusgasse 15 (tel. 82 01 00). Near the hip residential community of Maxglan on the other side of the Mönchsberg. Take bus #1 or #2 to "Schwendenstraße," and walk down Rachusgasse following the sign to the Stiegl brewery. Gasthof Wastlwirt also feeds guests in the traditional *Gastgarten* downstairs (open Mon.-Fri. 10am-midnight). Singles 360AS. Doubles 550AS. Triples, quads and quints 250AS per person. Breakfast included. Ample parking available.

Camping

Camping Stadtblick, Rauchenbichlerstr. 21 (tel. 45 06 52; fax 45 80 18), next to Haus Elisabeth. By car, take exit "Salzburg-Nord" off A1. Situated behind a copse of trees, with a sweeping view of the city. 65AS, 60AS for *Let's Go*-toting students. Tent 15AS. Car 25AS. Bed in a tent 80AS. Mobile home for four, TV and showers included, 125AS per person. Laundry 70AS. Comprehensive store and homemade food on the grounds. Open March 20th to Halloween.

Camping Nord-Sam, Samstr. 22-A (tel. 66 04 94). Take bus #33 (dir: Obergnigl) to "Langmoosweg." Shady, flower-bedecked campsites with a small swimming pool to boot. Mid-June to Aug. 50AS per person, campsite 95AS. Apr. to mid-June and Sept.-Oct. 40AS per person, campsite 76AS. Laundry 75AS. Open April-Oct.

FOOD

Blessed with fantastic beer gardens and countless pastry shop patios, Salzburg begs its guests to eat outdoors. The *Salzburger Nockerl* is the local specialty. A large soufflé of eggs, sugar, and raspberry filling is baked into three mounds which represent the three hills of Salzburg. Another specialty is *Knoblauchsuppe* (garlic soup), a rich cream soup loaded with croutons and pungent garlic—a potent weapon, use it only as a last resort against irritating bunkmates. During the first two weeks of September, local cafés dispense *Stürm,* a delicious, cloudy cider (appropriately, reminiscent of a storm) that hasn't quite finished fermenting.

There are more of the world-famous **Mozartkugeln** (Mozart's balls, er, chocolate, actually) lining café windows than notes in all of Mozart's works combined. They were invented by a Salzburg confectioner in 1890, but the production of the candy has since moved into modern industrial methods. Although the mass-produced *Kugeln* wrapped in gold and red are technically *echt* (authentic), try to sniff out the rarer, handmade ones wrapped in blue and silver, impossible to find outside of Salzburg. Reasonably priced samples are sold individually at the **Holzmayr** confectioners in the Alter Markt (5AS each, 7AS for the real, handmade McCoy). *Kugeln* are made by covering a hazelnut-marzipan with nougat, and then dipping it in chocolate; the blue and silver variety have more marzipan than the mass-produced ones.

Bars, restaurants, and cafés are difficult to classify because, more often than not, they become each of those things at different times during the day. *Beisl,* for example, serve coffee in the morning, tea in the afternoon, and beer in the evenings.

Restaurant Zur Bürgerwehr-Einkehr, Mönchsberg 19c (tel. 84 17 29). Follow the directions to the Naturfreundenhaus/Bürgerwehr. The mom-and-pop owners of the Naturfreundehaus (see Hostels and Dormitories, p. 362) operate this restaurant at the top of the Mönchsberg with the best view in town of the *Altstadt,* the Festung, Kapuzinerberg, the Salzach. On sunny days, escape the tourist throng below and repose on the red patio. One of the most reasonably priced menus around. Schwarzenegger-size full meals from 68-108AS. Mmmm, these are a few of our favorite things. Kitchen open May-Oct. daily 10am-9pm.

Humboldt-Stuben, Gstättengasse 6 (tel. 84 31 71). Hamburgers and cheeseburgers for 39AS. Affordable traditional Salzburger specialities: *Pinzgauer Kasnock'n* (88AS), *Salzburger Nockerl* for two (96AS). Over 20 vegetarian salad offerings on the salad bar. Located right under the Mönchberg Elevator. Super-crowded at night. Open daily 10am-1:30am.

Der Wilde Mann, Getreidegasse 20 (tel. 84 17 87) in the passage. Huge portions of *Wiener Schnitzel,* potatoes, and *Stiegl Bier* for the wild man (or woman) in all of us. Lovely carved wooden furniture and an incredible tiled oven, all in the most traditional Austrian style. Entrées 70-120AS and worth every *Groschen.* Pleasantly less touristed than nearby bistros. Open Mon.-Sat. 9am-9pm.

Zum Fidelen Affen, Priesterhausgasse 8, off Linzergasse (tel. 87 73 61). Join the young and local clientele sitting on picnic benches in the street. Drinks 30AS. Full meal of salad and main course 78-90AS. Try the spinach *Spätzle* (potato-based noodles) or the garlic noodles. Open 5:30-11pm.

Trześniewski, Getreidegasse 9 (Mozart's Birthplace; tel. 84 07 69). Behind the chocolate counter and butcher shop. Kafka's favorite hangout in Vienna now has a new franchise on the ground floor of Mozart's *Geburtshaus;* you can ponder over who would roll over in his grave first while indulging in their wonderful open-faced sandwiches (9AS; be advised that you will probably need about four to make a good lunch). Open daily 8:30am-6pm.

Shakespeare, Hubert Sattlergasse 3, off Mirabellplatz (tel. 87 91 06). To eat, or not to eat—that's no question: to eat, by Jove! Won ton soup, Greek salad, *Wiener schnitzel,* or just about anything else for 23-90AS. Speaketh thy mind, we shall hear. Doubles as bar(d)—great music. Open daily 10am-1am, but the Chinese cook takes Sundays off. Visa, MC.

University Mensa, Sigmund Haffnergasse 6 (tel. 241 39), is located in the *Altstadt,* to the right inside the courtyard of the law school behind the iron fence. A good deal for penny-pinchers. Three hot dishes available everyday. *Menu I* (28AS) is forgettable. Go for *Menu II* (39AS) or *Menu III* (55AS). Vegetarian meal daily 39AS. Read menus carefully so you don't choose extras. Desserts and drinks aren't included. Open Mon.-Thurs. 9am-4pm, Fri. 9am-3pm. Be sure to bring valid student ID. ISICs accepted.

Fischmarkt, at Hanuschplatz on the *Altstadt* side of the river. Two mammoth trees reach through the roof. Hang out with locals and partake in the pleasures of imported Danish seafood. Very casual and very crowded—you may have to eat outside. *Fischbrötchen* 16-25AS, beer 20AS. Sells fresh seafood by the kilogram. Open Mon.-Fri. 9am-6pm, Sat. 9am-noon.

Vegy, Schwarzstr. 21 (tel. 87 57 46). A health food restaurant and shop with only vegetarian selections. Vegy will seat you at a table or sell you a quick meal or groceries to go. Very filling food, if somewhat small portions for your buck. Open Mon.-Fri. 10:30am-6pm. Another branch at Wolf-Dietrich Str. 17 closes at 4:30pm.

Pizza Casanova, Linzergasse 23 (tel. 87 50 31). Don't be put off by the burlesque joint with the same name next to it—Pizza Casanova knows that the way to a man's heart is through his stomach. Large pies 66-105AS, with a healthy selection of veggie and whole-grain pizzas. Open daily 11am-3pm and 6-11pm.

Nudelboutique, Eugen-Mullestr. 85 (tel 42 29 99). Take bus #29 to the end of the line. Far from the bustle of the tourist pits, Nudelboutique offers a wide array of affordable noodle dishes, including vegetarian plates, to satisfy the Wiener Schnitzeled-out. Open Mon.-Sat. 11am-2pm and 6-10pm.

Cafés

Café Tomaselli, Alter Markt 9 (tel. 84 44 88). A favorite haunt for wealthier Salzburger clientele since 1705. In 1820, Mozart's widow and her second husband came here to write the dead man's bio. Today, it's one of the most famous cafés in Austria. Have some tea (a drink) with jam and bread. Pay the drink server and dessert server separately. Open daily 7am-9pm.

Café Fürst, Brodgasse 13 (tel. 84 37 59), near Alter Markt. Faces off with the equally haughty Café Tomaselli, across the Alter Markt. Specializes in the original *Mozartkugeln,* although at 10AS a pop it's best to savor slowly. Vast selection of candies, chocolates, pastries, tortes, *Strudels,* and cakes. Catch one of the splendiferous tables outside if you can. Branch also in Mirabellplatz. Open Mon.-Fri. 8am-9pm, Sun. 9am-9pm, in winter open until 8pm.

Kaffeehäferl, Getreidegasse 25 (tel. 84 43 49), in the passage across from McDonald's. An unpretentious little courtyard café, Kaffeehäferl provides a needed respite from the rush of tourists steaming down G-street. The neighboring flower shop adds to the olfactory pleasure. *Quiche Lorraine* 45AS, banana milkshake 35AS. Open Mon.-Sat. 9am-7pm, Sun. noon-7pm.

Café Bazar, Schwarzstr. 3 (tel 87 42 78). Actually affordable drinks and small meals in a tree-lined garden along the banks of the Salzach. Yogurt with raspberry juice 34AS. The place to go for Turkish coffee. Open Mon-Sat. 9:30am-11pm.

Café im Kunstlerhaus, Hellbrunnerstr. 3 (tel 84 56 01). Low-key café popular with students, artists, and those who enjoy the student-art atmosphere. Have a *mélange* and sink into your seat. Open Mon.-Fri. 11am-11pm.

Markets

In most cases, markets are open Mon.-Fri. 8am-6pm, Sat. 8am-noon.

Hofer, Schallmooser Hauptstr. (an extension of Linzergasse) and Franz-Josef-Str.

SPAR is widespread and can be found in the Getreidegasse and Mirabellplatz.

KMG, across the street from the Hauptbahnhof.

Open-air markets, Universitätpl. in the *Altstadt.* Fresh *Semmeln* (rolls) stuffed with tomatoes, cheese, *Wurst,* and leafy greens are particularly filling. Open Mon.-Fri. 6am-7pm, Sat. 6am-1pm. A larger, cheaper market for locals takes place Thurs. mornings (6am-2pm) in the Mirabellplatz extending down into Hubert-Sattlergasse. If you're in town on Sat. (6am-1pm), you can pick up your organic tomatoes and sausage lard at the Max Rheinhardtplatz in the *Altstadt.*

BEER GARDENS AND BARS

Munich may be the beer capital of the world, but a good deal of it flows south to the beer gardens (*Biergärten*) of Austria. Beyond Mozart and *The Sound of Music,* beer gardens are an essential part of Salzburg's charm, an absolute must for visitors. Many of the gardens also serve moderately priced meals, but like everything else in Salzburg, they tend to close early. Many of these oases of lager are clustered in the center of the city, especially around the Salzach River. Nightclubs in the *Altstadt* generally attract younger folk and tourists. For a less juvenile atmosphere, hit the other side of the river—especially along Giselakai and Steingasse.

Augustiner Bräu, Augustinergasse 4 (tel. 43 12 46). From the *Altstadt,* pick up the footpath at Hanuschplatz and follow it alongside the river walking with the current (pick up the footpath at Hanuschplatz). Go left up the flight of stairs just past the Riverside Café, cross Müllner Hauptstr., and continue walking up the hill. Augustinergasse is the first left. The brewery is inside the *Kloster* building with the big tower, and is a Salzburg legend. The great beer brewed by the Müllner Kloster is poured into massive *Steins* from even more massive wooden kegs. Garden seats 1300, indoor salons seat an additional 1200. Numerous sausage and bread concession stands inside placate grumbling stomachs. Liters 48AS (be nice, and tip the tap-*meister* 2AS), half-liter 24AS (but they're only for light-weights). Open daily 3-11pm.

Sternbräu, Getreidegasse 34 (tel. 84 21 40). Formerly a place where beer was brewed, now just a place to drink and eat in mass quantities. Located in the *Altstadt,* this place has two beer gardens, a restaurant, and a self-service snack bar with sausages and smaller meals. Get there by ducking into any number of passages at the end of Getreidegasse. Open daily 9am-11pm.

K&K Stieglkeller, Festungsgasse 10 (tel. 84 26 81), off Kapitelplatz near the Festungsbahn. Perched halfway up the mountainside on the way to the *Festung,* this garden has a fantastic view of all the roofs and spires of the *Altstadt.* Stiegl beer on tap. They also serve reasonably priced food. Be careful not to wander in accidentally around 7:30pm, when the *Keller* hosts a Sound of Music Live dinner show. Open May-Sept. daily 10am-10pm.

Pub Passage, Rudolfskai 22-26, right under the Radisson Hotel by the Mozartsteg bridge. A shopping promenade for youthful clubbing. All these bars are located in the corridors of the "mall" and are open until 2-4am. They include: **Speedy Bar,** with swift service; **Tom's Bierklinik,** which brags beers from all over the world; **The Black Lemon,** which offers Latino night every Wed.; **Bräu zum frommen Hell,** an inferno of 80s music; and **Dips & Co.,** a new Tex-Mex dive furnished with *Beetlejuice* set designs.

2 Stein, Giselakai 9 (tel. 88 02 01). Or not to Stein. Possibly the coolest bar in town. Previously a gay bar, now a favorite spot for a mixed clientele of both genders. Open daily 5pm-4am.

Felsenkeller, in a small cave in the cliff near the Festspielhaus. Live music every Wed. and Sat. after 7:30pm. Open Sun.-Fri. 3:30pm-midnight, Sat. 10pm-1am and 4pm-midnight.

Schnaitl Pub, Bergstr. 5-7 (tel. 87 86 78), near the Staatsbrücke, attracts a student crowd with cheap drinks and progressive rock. Squint through the clouds of smoke and you may catch a glimpse of a live concert. Open daily 6:30pm-2am.

CLOUD, Ledergasse 10, near Anton-Neumayr-Pl. (tel. 87 67 28). Disco with a small-ish dancefloor. Hipper-than-thou attitude keeps most tourists out, and even some locals. Sneakers, hiking boots, and other "day clothes" prohibited. Maria's hand-made curtain-wear notwithstanding, the von Trapp kids wouldn't stand a chance. Open 10pm-4am. 18 and over.

Bovine Befuddlement

Salzburg's pride, the **Hohensalzburg** fortress, was once saved from imminent destruction by its clever archbishop. During the **Peasant Wars** (see The Habsburg Empire, p. 232), the peasants surrounded the fortress with the intention of starving the archbishop out. Though the archbishop only had one cow left, he wanted to discourage the peasants by tricking them to believe that he had more. He painted the one remaining beast with different spots on both sides and paraded him back and forth along the castle wall in distinct view of the peasants below. Since the peasants were simple-minded folk, the ploy worked and they promptly cancelled their embargo attempts. Talk about a tanning.

Frauen Café, Sittikusstr. 17 (tel. 87 16 39). A relaxed lesbian hangout where women convene to drink and chat. Café open Wed.-Sat. 8pm-midnight.

Schwarze Katze, Fruhdiele, Auerspergstr. 45 (tel 87 54 05). For all those who miraculously found a late night scene in Salzburg and/or got locked out of their respective hostels, the Black Cat magnanimously opens its doors from 4am to noon, Tues.-Sun. Dark, low-key atmosphere guaranteed not to grate on early morning nerves.

SIGHTS

The Altstadt

Salzburg sprang up under the protective watch of the fortress **Hohensalzburg** (tel. 80 42 21 23), which towers atop the imposing Mönchsberg. Built between 1077 and 1681 by the ruling archbishops, the *Festung* is now the largest totally preserved castle in Europe. The only way to actually see the splendid rooms inside, however, is to participate in a guided tour. These first-rate tours wind through torture chambers, formidable Gothic state rooms, the fortress organ, and the impregnable watchtower that affords an unmatched view of the city. The tour also includes the archbishop's medieval indoor toilet—a technological marvel in its day—with an advanced 2m drop below. This was only to be used by the archbshop's family and close personal friends. (Fortress open daily 8am-7pm; Oct.-May 8am-6pm; 50-min. tours daily July-Aug. 9am-5pm; April-June and Sept.-Oct. 9:30am-5pm; Nov.-March 10am-4:30pm. 30AS, students with ISIC and children 20AS. Tour in German and English 30AS, seniors 25AS, students 25AS, children 25AS.)

The **Rainer Museum,** inside the fortress, displays even more instruments of torture: the chastity belt, the rack, the standardized test form… (open May-Oct., free with tour; otherwise 30AS, students and children 15AS). To reach the fortress, take the overpriced **Festungsbahn** (cable car) from the tiny Festungsgasse, a winding lane behind Kapitelplatz, or walk up the steep Festungsgasse to the top. Cars run every 10 minutes (Open Oct.-April 9am-5pm; May-Sept. 8am-9pm. Since the cable car terminates in the fortress keep, descent by foot is only possible with admission to the fortress. 57AS, children 31AS; round-trip 67AS, 36AS.) The myriad footpaths atop the Mönchsberg give an eagle's eye view of the city; hikers meander down the leafy trails to the *Altstadt* below, or descend by the **elevator** built into the mount at Gstättengasse 13, near Café Winkler (open daily 7am 11pm; 15AS, round-trip 25AS).

At the bottom of the Festungsbahn is **Kapitelplatz,** home of a giant chess grid, a horse-bath fountain depicting Poseidon wielding his scepter over the mass expanse of water, and tradesmen bartering their wares. Standing at the chess grid, the entrance to **St. Peter's Monastery,** through the cemetery, is at the back right corner. The lovely cemetery, **Petersfriedhof** (St. Peter's cemetery), is one of the most peaceful places in Salzburg—maybe because guided tours are forbidden to enter. The various headstones are works of art, some dating back to the 1600s. Though a popular subject for romantic painters, this secluded spot is best known as the place where Liesl's Nazi boyfriend Rolf blew the whistle on the von Trapp family in *The Sound of Music* (open June-Aug. daily 9am-8pm; Sept.-May 10am-7pm). On the left side of the *Friedhof* is the entrance to the **Katakomben** (catacombs) where Christians allegedly worshiped in secret as early as 250AD. (Hourly tours in English and German May-Sept. 10am-5pm; Oct.-April 11am-noon and 1:30-3:30pm. 12AS, students 8AS.) Exit the cemetery down the little path in the corner opposite the entrance off Kapitelplatz to find **St. Peter's Church.** The once stoic collegiate church received a Rococo facelift in the 18th century, and now green and pink moldings curl delicately across the graceful ceiling, and gilded cherubim blow golden trumpets to herald the stunningly decorated organ. The steeple tower with its clock and depiction of St. Peter are also newer additions (open daily 9am-12:15pm and 2:30-6:30pm).

The courtyard on the other side of the gate facing St. Peter's entrance leads to the monastery **Toscaninihof.** Here lies an entrance to the Mönchberg Parking Garage, as well as stairs leading up the cliff to Mönchsberg. Part of the **Felsenreitenschule** makes up one wall of this enclosure. Many of the events of the Music Festival take place here. Because the opera house is not open to the public, a poster-sized photo has been fixed to the wall depicting the stone arches which comprise the rear wall of the house's stage. These arches, hewn out of stone for the spectators, were formerly the Rock Riding School for the archbishops' horses, but are better-known for their appearance in *The Sound of Music* in the dramatic penultimate scene. Above the poster on the wall is a huge outdoor organ which once performed, but now only serves as ornamentation.

The distinctive dome of the **Universitätskirche** (University Church), stands watch over the Universitätsplatz, near the daily farmer's market. Generally considered Fischer von Erlach's masterpiece, this massive chapel is quite celebrated in European Baroque circles (see The Baroque, p. 242); it is one of the largest on the continent. The pale interior and enormous dome create a vast open space pierced only by the natural light radiating from the apse and accented by the Baroque sunbursts-and-cherubim sculpting at the focal point of the nave.

From the Universitätsplatz, there are several passages which lead through tiny courtyards filled with geraniums and creeping ivy. They eventually give way to the stampede of **Getreidegasse.** Be sure to forge a mini-exploration through this labyrinth of winding pathways and façades dating to the 17th and 18th centuries. One of the most well-preserved (and well-touristed) streets in Salzburg, Getreidegasse's shops have wrought iron signs, dating (they claim) to the Middle Ages when the illiterate needed pictorial aids to understand which store sold what. Some of us suspect a few of these are modern tourist revivals...golden arches, for example, don't objectively suggest hamburgers... Maybe Pavlov could explain.

Wolfgang Amadeus Mozart was unleashed upon the world from what is now called **Mozart's Geburtshaus** (birthplace) Getreidegasse 9 (tel. 84 43 13; fax 84 06 93), one of Salzburg's most touristed attractions. The long red and white flag suspended from the roof serves as a beacon for music pilgrims worldwide. Though he eventually settled in Vienna, his birthplace holds the most impressive collection of the child genius's belongings: his first viola, violin, a pair of keyboard instruments, and even a lock of hair purportedly from his egg-shaped noggin. Do not overlook the incredible set of dioramas from previous *Festspiele* productions of Mozart's operas. (Open Sept. to mid-June daily 9am-6pm; mid-June to Sept. daily 9am-1pm, but in summer come before 11am to beat the crowds. 62AS, students and seniors 47AS, children 17AS.)

At 17, Salzburg's favorite son moved across the river; **Mozarts Wohnhaus**, Marktpl. 8 (tel. 84 43 13; fax 84 06 93), was the composer's residence from 1773 to 1780. The house suffered major damage in World War II air raids, but has since periodically undergone renovations, and reopened on his 240th birthday, January 27, 1996. A statue in honor of Salzburg's hero rests in Mozartplatz. For those with true Mozart mania, the **Mozarteum**, Schwartzstr. 26-28, holds the enormous **Mozart Archives.** Inside the grounds stands a tiny wooden shack, transplanted from Vienna; this is the **Zauberflötenhäuschen,** where Wolfgang Amadeus supposedly composed *The Magic Flute* in just five months. The Mozarteum was originally constructed for the Salzburg Academy of Music and the Performing Arts; regular performances are now held in the concert hall (see Entertainment, p. 375).

The **Neugebäude** (tel. 80 42 22 76; fax 80 42 21 60), opposite the AmEx office, supports both the city government's bureaucracy and a 35-bell **Glockenspiel.** Bells ring daily at 7am, 11am, and 6pm. Be sure to attend one of the daily performances; the delightful, slightly off-key carillon rings out a Mozart tune (specified on a notice on the corner of the Residenz), and the tremendous pipe organ atop the Hohensalzburg fortress bellows a response.

Long before the Mozart era, Archbishop Wolf Dietrich dominated the town's cultural patronage. Composer and clergyman are still intertwined yearly, when the Salzburger Festspiele brings opera to the courtyard of the archbishop's magnificent **Residenz** facing the Glockenspiel (tel. 80 42 26 90; fax 80 42 29 78). The ecclesiastic elite of the Salzburger Land have resided here, in the heart of the *Altstadt,* for the last 700 years. Tours of the pad feature the imposing Baroque staterooms *(Prunkräume),* with an astonishing three-dimensional ceiling fresco by Rottmayr. The Residenz also houses a **gallery** (see Museums, p. 374; tours are held daily in July-Aug. (min. 3 people) every ½hr. from 10am-4:30pm; Sept.-June Mon.-Fri. hourly from 10am-3pm; 40min.; 45AS, students and seniors 35AS).

Dead-center in the Residenzplatz is the in-your-face 15m horse fountain—incidentally, the largest Baroque fountain in the world, complete with amphibious horses charging through the water (observe the webbed hooves). Appropriately, **fiakers** (horse-drawn carriages) congregate around the fountain, which explains the barnyard odor and heaps of horse manure. (Carriage rides 350AS for 20-25min., 680AS for 50min. Be sure to ask if the driver speaks English.) The Baroque **Dom,** forms the third wall of the Residenzplatz. Wolf Dietrich's successor, Markus Sittikus, commissioned the cathedral from Italian architect Santino Solari in 1628. The three dates above the archways list the years that the cathedral underwent renovations. The statue in front of the Domplatz depicts the Virgin Mary. Around her swarm four lead figures representing Wisdom, the Church, Faith, and the Devil. Mozart was christened here in 1756 and later worked at the *Dom* as *Konzertmeister* and court organist.

The New City

Cross the river on the Staatsbrücke to the *Neustadt* (new city). The Staatsbrücke is the only bridge from the *Altstadt* over the Salzach open to motorized traffic in the new city; the bridge opens into **Linzergasse,** a medieval-esque shopping street much in the style of the Getreidegasse. From under the stone arch on the right side of Linzergasse 14, you can ascend a staircase of tiny stone steps up the side of the Kapuzinerberg. At its crest stands the simple **Kapuzinerkloster** (Capuchin Monastery) that Wolf Dietrich ordered built in the late 16th century. The monastery itself is a sight to behold, but the real draw is the view of the city below. Farther along Linzergasse, but much less crowded at #41, is the 18th-century **Sebastianskirche;** its graveyard contains the gaudy tiled mausoleum of Wolf Dietrich and the tombs of Mozart's wife Constanze and father Leopold (open daily 7am-7pm).

From Linzergasse you can cut across Dreifaltigkeitsgasse to the **Mirabellplatz** to discover the marvelous **Schloß Mirabell.** The supposedly vowed-to-celibacy Archbishop Wolf Dietrich built this rosy-hued wonder in 1606 for his mistress Salome Alt and their ten children, christening it "Altenau" in her honor. When successor Markus Sittikus imprisoned Wolf Dietrich for arson, he seized the palace for himself and changed its name. Although the castle is now the seat of the city government, many of the mayor's gorgeous offices are usually open for public viewing (open Mon.-Fri. 7am-4pm). The *Schloß* also hosts classical concerts in the evening; some swear that the **Marmorsaal** (Marble Hall) rivals all other European concert halls. Next to the palace sits the delicately manicured **Mirabellgarten.** which includes extravagant rose beds, labyrinths of groomed shrubs, and 15 grotesque marble likenesses of Wolf Dietrich's court jesters. Students from the nearby Mozarteum often perform here. Maria also made this one of her stops in *The Sound of Music* as the children danced around and sang "do-re-mi." Slightly more adorable than the children are the vertically challenged statues in the **Dwarf Garden,** a favorite Mirabellgarten play area for Salzburg toddlers.

What about Joe?

Legend has it that the resident monks of the Kapuzinerkloster, clad in their coffee-colored robes with white hoods, inspired the world's first cup of *cappuccino.* A café proprietor with an overactive imagination observed the pious gents on a noonday stroll and *voilà.* The country's resident food buffs and cultural authorities, Austrian schoolchildren, will tell you that the Italian cappuccino is no more than a rip-off of the much older *Kapuziner,* still ordered in Viennese cafe today.

The Sound of Music

In 1964, Julie Andrews, Christopher Plummer, and a gaggle of 20th-Century Fox crew members arrived in Salzburg to film *The Sound of Music,* based on the true story of the von Trapp family. Ever since then, Salzburg hasn't hesitated to cash in on its celluloid notoriety. Consequently, many people come to Salzburg to see just this. There are three official companies which run Sound of Music Tours. They are all very similar and often the best choice is the one that stops closest to your accommodation; many hostels and pensions work exclusively with one of the firms, and offer discounts. **Salzburg Sightseeing Tours** (tel. 88 16 16; fax 87 87 76) and **Panorama Tours** (tel. 87 40 29; fax 87 16 18) operate rival kiosks on opposite sides of Mirabellplatz, but their tours are pretty much comparable (330AS, students 300AS; Salzburg Sightseeing offers a discount for *Let's Go*-toting non-students as well; tours leave from Mirabellplatz daily at 9:30am and 2pm). Panorama will also do currency exchange at competitive bank rates without commission. The renegade **Bob's Special Tours,** Kaigasse 19 (tel. 84 95 110; fax 84 95 23) has no high-profile kiosk, but they offer a special touch by driving around in a minibus. This enables them to show a bit more of the *Altstadt,* a location that the big tour buses can't reach (330AS; tours run every day in summer at 9am and 2pm; in winter 10am). All three companies offer free pick-up from your accommodation and last 3½-4 hours. Generally, they're worth the money if you've only got a short time in Salzburg. The tours take you outside of Salzburg into the Salzkammergut lake region as well.

If you have time, however, you may consider renting a bike and doing the tour on your own. 20th-Century Fox certainly took a lot of artistic license with the film— much of the story is made up for Tinseltown purposes. For example, Maria was a nun-apprentice in the film, whereas in reality she merely taught at the abbey. **Nonnberg Abbey** lies high above the city near the Festung. They filmed the scene where the nuns sing "How do you solve a problem like Maria?" and parts of the wedding scene here. You can reach the abbey by walking out of the Kapitelplatz along Kapitelgasse, and turning right onto Kaigasse where there are stairs up to the nunnery. The darling little gazebo where Liesl and Rolf unleashed their youthful passion is on the grounds of **Schloß Hellbrunn** (see Near Salzburg, p. 377). The gazebo is disappointingly small, but makes a pretty picture. On a nice afternoon, the walk back from Hellbrunn to the *Altstadt* is glorious and passes the castle used for the front of the von Trapp home. Head straight all the way down Hellbrunner Allee from the Hellbrunn parking lot until it turns into Freisaalweg. At the end of Freisaalweg, turn right on Akadmiestr., which will end at Alpenstr. and the river. You can take the river footpath all the way back to Mozartsteg and the Staatsbrücke (1hr.).

The yellow castle with the long yellow wall (Maria sang "I Have Confidence" here) serves as the front of the house and is on Hellbrunner Allee. The house is now a student dorm for music students at the Mozarteum. The back of the von Trapp house (where Maria and the children fell into the water after romping around the city all day) was filmed at the **Schloß Leopoldskron** behind the Mönchsberg, now a center for academic studies. It is easily reached by bike, or by walking. Take bus #55 to "Pensionistenheim Nonntal," walk left up Sunnhubstr., and then left again up Leopoldskroner Allee to the castle. There is also a public **pool** at Leopoldskron (35AS) which might be a nice way to relax after a long morning of sightseeing.

Within the *Altstadt* itself, there are several film locations. The **Petersfriedhof** is the cemetery where the family hid behind headstones at the end, and where Rolf blew the whistle. The **Felsenreitenschule** (Rock Riding School) is where the family sang their final performance, while all the Nazis swayed so touchingly to the melodious song "Edelweiss." The opera house is closed to the public now, but there is a picture of the inside affixed to the wall at Toscaninihof. There is also a set of stairs there; if you walk up them to the right, sometimes you can lean over the wall and get a glimpse of the stage from above. It depends on whether the top to the house has been left open or not. The **Mirabellgarten** by Mirabellplatz was a favorite haunt of Maria and the children while they made their forbidden daytrips. Several statues and fountains should look familiar.

The von Trapps were actually married in the church at Nonnberg Abbey, but Hollywood decided to use the church in **Mondsee** instead. The sightseeing tours allow its guests to waddle around Mondsee for 45min., but it's really worth a whole daytrip. Mondsee boasts a beautiful lake with sailing and paddleboating facilities and coffee and pastry shops. Buses leave the Salzburg train station from the main bus depot (45min., hourly, one-way 52AS). The hills that are alive with the sound of music (where Maria rapturously twirls around in the opening scene) are partway along the Salzburg-St. Gilgen route, near Fuschl, but any of the hills in the Salzkammergut region could have fit the bill; for your own re-creation and recreation purposes, try the Untersberg, just south of Salzburg (see Near Salzburg, p. 377).

As if this wasn't enough saturation, the Stieglkeller hosts an overpriced **Sound of Music Live Dinner Show** (tel. 84 00 82; fax 84 50 21). Performers sing your favorite film songs, while they serve soup, *Schnitzel* with noodles, and crisp apple strudel, (Show daily at 8:15pm, tickets 360AS, ages 6-15yrs. 220AS. Dinner and 7:30pm show 520AS, ages 6-15yrs. 320AS. Open daily May-Sept.)

MUSEUMS

Unfortunately, Salzburg's wide variety of small, specialized museums gets lost behind the shadow of the *Festung, The Sound of Music,* and the *Festspiele.* Should you desire to indulge in your own personal museum-fest, combi-tickets are available (60AS, students 20AS) for the Carolino Augusteum, the Bürgerspital, the Domgrabung, and the Folklore Museums. Also try browsing around in the small private galleries on Sigmund-Haffner-Gasse.

Rainer Museum, inside the fortress. Can be visited separately. Medieval relic displays, including torture devices. Open June-Oct. 10 8am-7pm, Oct. 11-May 8am-6pm. 30AS, students 15AS.

Dom Museum (tel. 84 41 89; fax 84 04 42). Inside the *Dom* by the main entrance. Houses an unusual collection called the **Kunst- und Wunderkammer** (Art and Miracles chamber), which includes conch shells, mineral formations, and a two-foot whale's tooth. All of these curiosities were accumulated by the archbishop to impress distinguished visitors. The bottom floor always houses a temporary exhibit which attempts to do the same. Open mid-May to mid-Oct. Mon.-Sat. 10am-5pm, Sun. 11am-5pm. 40AS, ages 16-18 10AS, ages 6-15 5AS.

Domgrabungsmuseum, entrance on Residenzplatz (tel. 84 52 95), displays excavations of the Roman ruins under the cathedral. Open May-Oct. Wed.-Sun. 9am-5pm. 20AS, under 19 10AS.

Museum Carolino Augusteum, Museumplatz 1 (tel. 84 31 45; fax 84 11 34). Named after Emperor Franz I's widow, Caroline Augusta. Roman and Celtic artifacts including excellent, mosaics and burial remains preserved compliments of the region's salt on the lower floors. Gothic and Baroque art on the upper floors. Open Wed.-Sun 9am-5pm, Tues. 9am-8pm. 40AS, students 15AS.

Trachtenmuseum (National Costume Museum), Griesgasse 23 (tel. 84 31 19), near Anton- Newmayr-Pl. Displayed within is the traditional garb of Austrian folk past and present. *Lederbosen, Dirndls,* 8-in. dragon headed boots (just kidding). Open Mon.-Fri. 10am-noon, 2-5pm, Sat. 10am-noon. 30AS, students 20AS.

Folklore and Local History Museum, Hellbrunn Monatsschlößchen (the little month-castle; tel. 82 03 72 21). The castle got its name when someone bet Archbishop Markus Sittikus that he couldn't build a castle in a month. As one of the archbishop's many weakness was gambling, he accepted the challenge and began spending the church's money on architects, engineers, and laborers who toiled round-the-clock. He won. Open Easter-Oct. daily 9am-5pm. 20AS, students 10AS.

Rupertinum Gallery, at Wiener Philharmonikergasse 9 (tel. 80 42 23 36; fax 80 42 25 42). The works of Kokoschka, Klimt, and lesser known living artists are housed in an older, gracefully arched building touched up by Hundertwasser. Very interesting temporary exhibits and small sculpture garden. Open Tues.-Sun. 10am-5pm, Wed. 10am-9pm; July-Sept. Thurs.-Tues. 10am-6pm, Wed. 10am-9pm. 50AS, students 35AS, under 15 free.

Residenz Gallery, Residenzpl. 1 (tel. 84 04 51). Not really known for its permanent collection, the gallery is better known for its rotating exhibits with occasional works by Titian, Rubens, and Bruegel. Open April-Sept. daily 10am-5pm; Oct.-March Thurs.-Tues. 10am-5pm. 45AS, students 34AS, combination ticket with the Residenz Prunkräume 70AS.

Baroque Museum (tel. 87 74 32), resides in the Orangerie of the Mirabellgarten, with wall after wall of tribute to the ornate aesthetic of 17th- and 18th-century Europe. In the 19th century, parts of the city walls were destroyed by Napoleon; the rubble was buried under the current site of the Mirabellgarten, and the hill it forms now serves as the favorite sledding place for the children of Salzburg. Remember: reduce, reuse, recycle! Open Tues.-Sat. 9am-noon and 2-5pm, Sun. 9am-noon. 40AS, students and seniors 20AS, ages 6-14 free.

Haus der Natur (Museum of Natural History), Museumpl. 5 (tel. 84 26 53; fax 84 79 05), across from the Carolino Augusteum. One of Austria's best natural history museums displays everything from gems to live alligators. 36-tank aquarium. Open daily 9am-5pm. 50AS, students 30AS.

Bürgerspital Museum, Bürgerspitalgasse 2 (tel. 84 75 60), near the Festspielhaus. Sundry musical instruments and other local arts and crafts. Open Tues.-Sun. 9am-5pm. 30AS, students 10AS.

Zoo at Hellbrunn (tel. 82 01 76; fax 82 01 766). Lions and tigers and bears, oops, that's Oz. All behind less than intimidating fencing. Plan about 2hr. Open Oct.-March 8:30am-4pm; April-Sept. 8:30am-6pm. 60AS, students 35AS.

ENTERTAINMENT

The Music Festivals

The renowned **Salzburger Festspiele** (Festivals) were founded by Max Reinhardt, Richard Strauss, and Hugo von Hofmannsthal in 1920; every year since, Salzburg has become a musical mecca from late July to the beginning of September. A few weeks before the festival, it's not unusual to bump into world-class stars in Getreidegasse, taking a break from rehearsal. On the eve of the opening of the Festival, more than 100 dancers don regional costumes, accessorized with torches, and perform a *Fackeltanz* (torch-dance) on the Residenzplatz.

In the month of festivities, almost every public space is overrun with operas, dramas, films, concerts, and tourists. The complete program of events is printed a year in advance (10AS) and is available from any tourist office. Inside, all crucial concert locations and dates are listed. For the best seats, requests must be made in person or by mail months in advance. Remaining tickets are then distributed to ticketing agencies, who sell them at 30-40% mark-ups. To place orders, write to **Kartenbüro der Salzburger Festspiele,** Postfach 140, A-5010 Salzburg (fax 84 66 82), no later than the beginning of January. A pamphlet is then printed listing remaining seats. While there are cheap tickets to the operas (around 300AS), concerts (around 100AS), and plays (around 100AS), as well as some standing room places (50-100AS), these are gobbled up quickly by subscribers or local student groups. Usually what's left are very expensive tickets (upwards of 1000AS) and modern music concerts featuring avant-garde composers—you may be able to purchase these for as little as 200AS. Middle-man ticket distributors also sell marked-up cheap tickets, a legal form of scalping—try American Express or Panorama Tours. If you are 26 or younger, you may have a chance at getting cheap subscription tickets (2-5 tickets at 200AS apiece)—all you have to do is write about eight months in advance to: Direktion der Salzburger Festspiele, attn: Alexander von Donat, Hofstallgasse 1, A-5020 Salzburg.

The powers that be have discontinued hawking last-minute tickets for dress rehearsals to the general public; nowadays, you've got to know somebody to get your hands on one of these cheap tickets ("Oh, sure, Placido and I go *way* back!"). Those without the foresight to be hit by an international opera star while walking across the street should take advantage of the **Fest zur Eröffungsfest** (Opening Day Festival), when concerts, shows, and films are either very cheap or very free. Tickets for these events are available on a first-come, first-serve basis the week of the opening; they and a Fest zur Eröffungsfest schedule are available at the *Tageskasse* in the Großes Festspielhaus on Hofstallgasse. Also on this day, the traditional folksingers begin performing at 8 and 10pm. The traditional **Fackeltanz** (torchdance) is performed around the horse fountain with hundreds of torch-carrying dancers aerobically lighting up the area and kicking off the festivities. The only other event available without prior planning is **Jedermann**. This modern morality play by Hugo von Hofmannsthal is performed every year on a stage set up in front of the *Dom*. At the end, people placed in strategic locations throughout the city cry out the eerie word "Jedermann" which can be heard echoing all over town. Locals actually have shouting contests to be awarded the opportunity to be one of the ghostly criers. Standing room places are available and are sold the same day. Check with the Festspielhaus or a ticketing agency (60AS).

Even when the *Festspiele* are not in full force, there are a lot of other concerts and events. The **Mozarteum** (Music School) performs a number of concerts on a rotating schedule, available at the tourist office. Though many of the performances sell out early, some tickets are usually left over and can be obtained through Kartenbüro Mozarteum, Postfach 345, Schwarzstr. 36, 1st Stock, A-5024 Salzburg (tel. 87 31 54; fax 87 29 96; open Mon.-Thurs. 9am-2pm, Fri. 9am-4pm). They are also certain to have one cycle of concerts dedicated to students (80AS). In the summer, cruise through the well-postered Aicher Passage next to Mirabellplatz to see what concerts are being advertised.

For a bit more money but a lot more fun, check out the **Mozart Serenaden** (Mozart's Serenades) at Hellbrunn. These are evening concerts in Hellbrunn (more often in July-Aug.) where Mozart favorites (e.g. *Eine kleine Nachtmusik, Requiem*) are performed with the musicians dressed in traditional Mozart garb (knickers, white hair, etc.); an intermission buffet is also included. Afterwards guests have the option of getting a bit wet in the tour of the **Wasserspiele** (Water Games). In winter, these concerts are at Mirabellplatz instead. For information and tickets, write Konzertdirektion Nerat, A-5071 Salzburg Siezenheim 342. (Tel.43 68 70; fax 85 30 73. Tickets 300AS, with the *Wasserspiele* 350AS, available at the Schloß Hellbrunn ticket window. Open on concert days only 10:30am-12:30pm and after 3pm.)

For a particularly enchanting (and expensive) evening, attend one of the **Festungskonzerte** (Fortress Concerts) up in the ornate *Fürstenzimmer* (Prince's chamber) and *Goldener Saal* (Golden Hall) in the Fortress. There is a concert nightly (program of pieces available at tourist office) and tickets are available for 270AS one hour before the concert begins from the box office. For more information contact Festungskonzerte Anton-Adlgasserweg 22, A-5020 Salzburg (tel. 82 58 58; fax 82 58 59; open daily 9am-9pm).

A less tourist-oriented concert activity is the year-round **Salzburger Schloßkonzerte,** held in Schloß Mirabell or the Residenz. Mozart's music is still number one on the play rotation, but at least it's not a monopoly. Tickets for the classy concerts are 350-380AS, students 250AS, and are available at the *Tageskasse* in Schloß Mirabell daily from 7am to 4pm. In July and August, an **outdoor opera** is occasionally performed in the historical hedge theater of Mirabellgarten. (Tickets 300AS, students 150AS, standing room 120AS from the Schloß Mirabell *Tageskasse,* or from Konzertbüro Steinschaden & Hiller; tel. (06246) 76 11 73.)

Throughout the summer months (May-Aug.) there are various outdoor performances in the Mirabellgarten, including concerts, folk-singing, and dancing. The tourist office has a few leaflets on what's planned, but strolling through in the evening might prove just as effective. Other good concert information is sometimes posted on the church doors, particularly around Easter and Christmas. Great music is also performed during most services. Mozartplatz and Kapitelplatz are also popular stops for street musicians and touring school bands.

The **Dom** also has an extensive concert program. The organ concerts are on Thurs. and Fri. afternoons beginning at 11:15am. Tickets are available at the door (100AS, students 70AS). The organ has four separate pipe sections, so the sound produced has a dramatic "surround sound" effect. They also have periodic evening concerts—check the door to see the upcoming program.

At the **Salzburger Marionettentheater** (tel. 87 24 06; fax 88 21 41), recorded *Festspiele* opera performances are played back with hand-made marionettes playing the roles. The theater is small in order to accommodate the diminutive size of the actors. (Info: Marionettentheater Schwarzstr. 24, A-5020 Salzburg. Open on performance days Mon.-Sat. 9am-1pm, and two hours before the start of performance. Tickets 250-400AS, students 200AS.) For English **movies,** the program of films in **Das Kino** are reliable. Cinemas rotate a few films during the month, with offerings often in English with German subtitles.

■ Near Salzburg: Lustschloß Hellbrunn and Untersberg

Just south of Salzburg lies the unforgettable **Lustschloß Hellbrunn** (tel. 82 03 72; fax 82 03 72 31), a one-time pleasure palace for Wolf Dietrich's nephew, the Archbishop Markus Sittikus. The sprawling estate includes fish ponds, trimmed hedge gardens, the "I am sixteen, going on seventeen" gazebo, and tree-lined footpaths through open grassy fields, perfect for picnicking or a round of ultimate frisbee. The neighboring **Wasserspiele** (Water Gardens) are perennial favorites; Markus cracked himself up with elaborate water-powered figurines and a booby-trapped table, which could spout water on his drunken guests. Prepare yourself for an afternoon of wet surprises. (Open July-Aug. daily 9am-10pm; May-June and Sept. daily 9am-5pm; April and Oct. daily 9am-4:30pm. 48AS, students 24AS. Castle tours 20AS, students 10AS.) The **Steintheater,** on the palace grounds, is the oldest natural theater north of the Alps. In the adjoining park, the tiny hunting lodge **Monats-schlößchen** received its moniker from a speed of legendary proportions; local artisans supposedly finished construction of the mini-palace within a month. The lodge is now the **Folklore and Local History Museum** (see p. 374). To reach the palatial grounds, take bus #55 (dir: Anif) from the train station, Mirabellplatz, or Mozartsteg to "Hellbrunn," or bike 40min. down Hellbrunner Allee, a beautiful tree-lined path. An adjacent **zoo** (see p. 375) sports vultures along with other local fauna. Yodel a quick hello to the lonely goat herds.

A little farther south of Hellbrunn is the **Untersberg peak,** where Charlemagne supposedly rests, preparing to return and rule over Europe once again. Don't call it a comeback. You can ride a **cable car** (tel. (06246) 87 12 17 or 724 77) to the top and experience a spectacular view of Salzburg and the Alps. Take bus #55 to "Untersberg." (Cable car runs July-Sept. daily 8:30am-5:30pm; March-June and Oct. 9am-5pm; Dec.-Feb. 10am-4pm. Up the mountain 115AS, down 100AS, round-trip 190AS; children 60AS, 45AS, and 90AS respectively.)

THE SALZKAMMERGUT

East of Salzburg, the landscape swells into towering mountains interspersed with unfathomably deep lakes. Corny as it sounds, this is Austria's primary honeymoon destination—really. The Salzkammergut takes its name from the long-abandoned salt mines which, in their glory days, underwrote Salzburg's architectural treasures. The region is remarkably accessible, with 2000 kilometers of footpaths, 12 cable cars and chairlifts, and dozens of hostels. Though towns near the Autobahn bustle with tourists and merrymakers, some distant villages host the hardy few who make their way across a lake by ferry. Winter brings mounds of snow to the valleys and downhill skiing to the slopes.

Hostels abound, though you can often find far superior rooms in private homes and *Pensionen* at just-above-hostel prices. *"Zimmer Frei"* signs peek out from virtually every house. **Campgrounds** dot the region, but many are trailer-oriented. Away from large towns, many travelers camp discreetly almost anywhere without trouble. Hikers can capitalize on dozens of **cable cars** in the area to gain altitude before setting out on their own, and almost every community has a local trail map publicly posted or available at the tourist office. At higher elevations there are **alpine huts**—check carefully at the tourist office for their opening hours. These huts are leased through the **Österreichischer Alpenverein** (Austrian Alpine Club), which supplies mountains of information of all sorts; the central office of the ÖAV is in Innsbruck (tel. (0512) 594 47) with a branch in Linz (tel. (0732) 77 32 95). The regional branches are staffed by volunteers who have experience in their particular area.

Within the region there is a dense network of **buses.** Most routes run 4 to 12 times per day, and since the mountainous area is barren of rail tracks, buses are the most efficient and reliable method of travel into and through the lake region. Check at the Bad Ischl kiosk (tel. (06132) 231 13) or any other Salzkammergut town bus station for special leaflets detailing bus-and-hike routes; look out especially for the *Postbus: Salzkammergut* brochure, a map of the area with all the bus route.

Hitchers from Salzburg allegedly take bus #29 to Gnigl, and come into the Salzkammergut at Bad Ischl. The lake district itself is one of the rare, refreshing Austrian regions in which hitchhikers have been known to make good time. Two-wheeled transportation is much more entertaining, but only if you get a good **bike**—some mountain passes top 1000 meters. Pedaling the narrow, winding roads that line the lake banks is far less strenuous and equally scenic. Most of the train stations in the region rent bikes. Reasonably priced ferries serve each of the larger lakes. The **Wolfgangsee** line is operated by the Austrian railroad, so railpasses get you free passage; on the private **Attersee** and **Traunsee** lines, Eurailpass holders receive a discount.

On January 5, the **running of the figures with special caps** (*Glöcklerlaufen*) takes place after dark in the Salzkammergut. These *Glöckler* derive their name from the custom of knocking at the door (the verb *glocken* means "to knock"), not from the bells attached to their belts (although the noun *Glocke* coincidentally means "bell"). These caps, reminiscent of stained glass windows, have an electric light inside. In return for their Happy New Year wish, the runners are rewarded with a special doughnut, the *Glöcklerkrapfen.* The masked figures are usually given money and refreshments by the citizenry, which indicates something about their origin—a long, long time ago, seasonal workers needed such handouts to survive.

While much of the Salzkammergut is technically in the province of Upper Austria, the region culturally associates itself more with Salzburgerland and Tirol. Every February brings **Carnival,** called *Fasnacht* in Western Austria and elsewhere known as *Fasching.* Carnival commences with the January ball season. In the countrified areas, traditional processions of masked figures are the most important events of the season. Also part of the processions are *Schiache* (ugly masks with connotations of evil). The large Tirolean Carnival celebrations require months of preparation, and only men may perform. At the **Ausseer Fasching,** the carnival at Bad Aussee, *Trommelweiber* (women with drums, who are really men in white nightdresses and night-caps) march through the town. The Carnival near Ebensee culminates in the **Fetzenfasching** (carnival of rags). The people sing in falsetto, pretending to imitate spooky voices, and wave old umbrellas.

On the Sunday after November 25, about 30 bird-catcher clubs in the Salzkammergut region organize a **bird exhibition.** The birds are kept in living rooms during the winter and then released. A **Christmas passion play** is performed every fourth year (next in 1998) at Bad Ischl.

■ Bad Ischl

For centuries, Bad Ischl (population 15,000) was a mere salt mining town, and would have remained so had it not been for a certain Dr. Franz Wirer, a Viennese physician who came to Bad Ischl in 1821 to study the potentially curative properties of the heated brine baths. Pleased with his findings, he began to prescribe his patients brine bath vacations in Bad Ischl as early as 1822. Real fame descended on the resort only when the brine's healing powers kept the Habsburgs from sputtering into extinction. The infertile couple Archduke Francis Charles and Archduchess Sophia journeyed to

Bad Ischl seeking a cure for their state of childlessness. The magical, mystical, almost Hans Christian Andersen-esque results were three sons, the so-called **Salt Princes.** When the first Salt Prince, Franz Joseph I, ascended the throne in 1848, he proceeded to make Bad Ischl his annual summer residence, vacationing here for 40 years. It was the ideal base for practicing his favorite hobby—hunting—while still entertaining guests and performing other kaiserly functions. Bad Ischl quickly became an imperial city, attracting noblemen, aristocrats, and artists. Stressed-out composers Brahms, Bruckner, and Lehár came here to find a little R&R. Bad Ischl is one of the few towns in the region not on a lake, which eliminates half the fun of visiting the Salzkammergut, but German vacationers (including German Chancellor Helmut Kohl) flock to the town anyway.

Orientation and Practical Information Bad Ischl lies at the junction of the **Traun** and **Ischl** rivers, which form a horseshoe around the town center. The Ischl is a small river which runs from the Wolfgangsee to the Traun on the way to the Danube. Bad Ischl is also within splashing distance of seven Salzkammergut oases: the Hallstättersee, Gosausee, Wolfgangsee, Mondsee, Attersee, Traunsee, Grundlsee, and the Altausee.

If traveling **by car,** Bad Ischl lies at the junction of Rtes. 158 and 145. From **Vienna,** take the A1 West Autobahn to Rte. 145 at the town of Regau. From **Innsbruck** or **Munich,** take the A1 East past Salzburg, and exit onto Rte. 158 near Thalgau. From **Salzburg** proper, the best way is to take Rte. 158 straight (on ramp near Gaisberg), which wanders through the beautiful towns of St. Gilgen and Fuschl. **Buses** leave from Salzburg to Bad Ischl every 2 hours (#3000; 100AS), making stops in Fuschl and St. Gilgen (St. Gilgen-Bad Ischl 48AS). Bus #2560 travels to St. Wolfgang through Strobl, where you can catch a ferry on the Wolfgangsee connecting St. Gilgen, Strobl, and St. Wolfgang (48AS). There is only one **train** that comes through the station, running from Attnang-Puchheim in the north, through Gmunden (64AS), Bad Ischl, Hallstatt (50AS), Bad Aussee (64AS) to Attnang-Puchheim and back. Longer trips with connections go to **Vienna** (376AS), **Linz** (168AS), and **Zell am See** (276AS).

The **train station** has **bike rental** (100AS per day, 50AS with train ticket; open daily 7am-8pm). There are no lockers, but **baggage check** is available (30AS per piece per day, open daily 7am-7:30pm). Bad Ischl's **bus station** is to the right when facing the train station on Bahnhofstr. The **tourist office** is straight out of the train station and two minutes down the road, across from the huge yellow Kaiser Therme building at Bahnhofstr. 6 (tel. 277 570 or 235 200, fax 277 577-7). The office has extensive lists of *Pensionen* and *Privatzimmer,* and will help look for a room, although you must make reservations yourself. A free basic English brochure is available for the asking. (Open June-Sept. Mon.-Fri. 8am-6pm, Sat. 9am-4pm, Sun. 9-11:30am; Oct.-May Mon.-Fri. 8am-noon and 2-5pm, Sat. 8am-noon.) The **post office** is a 2-minute walk from the train station, on the corner of Bahnhofstr. and Auböckpl. (Open June-Sept. Mon.-Fri. 8am-8pm, Sat. 8-11am; Oct.-May Mon.-Fri. 8am-7pm, Sat. 8-10am.) There are metered **telephones** inside, and coin- and card- operated phones near the train station. **Postal code**: A-4820. **Telephone code:** 06132.

Accommodations and Food Every guest who stays the night must register with his or her individual hotel or pension and pay a *Kurtax,* which is a tax levied by the local government (June-mid-Sept. 14-19AS per person per night depending how close to the city center the lodging is; Oct.-May 12-13AS). But in return, the local **guest card** gives discounts on museums, mountain cable cars, and other treats. Bad Ischl's **Jugendherberge (HI),** Am Rechenstag 5 (tel. 265 77; fax 265 77 57), is minutes away from the Kaiser's summer residence. From the tourist office, walk left on Bahnhofstr., turn right on Kaiser-Franz-Josef-Str., bear right at the fork, and watch for the *Jugendherberge* sign to the left, near the bus parking lot. The hostel offers many comfortable one- to five-bed rooms off long corridors, but it often fills with groups.

It's prudent to call in advance. (Reception open daily 8-9am and 5-7pm. Quiet hour in the hostel 10pm, but keys are available to come and go later than that. 130AS, plus the *Kurtax*. Sheets, showers, and breakfast included. Lunch and dinner available.) Some hotels are within budget limits. Try **Haus Stadt Prag,** Eglmoosgasse 9 (tel. 236 16), with large and airy rooms awaiting your tired bones. From the train station, walk left on Bahnhofstr., turn right on Kaiser-Franz-Josef-Str., and bear left at the fork. Continue down Salzburgerstr., and bear left again on Stiegengasse, at the *Goldschmied* sign. Follow Stiegengasse down and go up the steps—Haus Stadt Prag is the pink, balconied building on your right. (Singles 250AS, with shower and toilet 320AS. Doubles 500AS, with shower and toilet 600AS. Triples with shower and toilet 850AS. Breakfast included.)

Restaurants are tucked into every possible spot along Schulgasse and the other streets of the pedestrian zone. Almost as famous as the Kaiser himself is the **Konditorei Zauner,** Pfarrgasse 7 (tel. 235 22). Established in 1832, this place has a reputation for heavenly sweets and tortes, and even makes the tourist office's short list of sights. Zauner also operates a riverside restaurant-café on the Esplanade; it's probably out of the question to actually eat at either, but it's worth it to sit at one of the riverside tables along the Esplanade and have a cup of coffee (22AS and up) or grab an ice cream (7AS) to go. When Bad Ischlers make a run for the border, they head to **Amigos Tex-Mex Restaurant,** Auböckpl. 9 (tel. 213 17), across from the Konsum. This restaurant's tongue-in-cheek slogan, "Warm beer, lousy food, shitty service," obviously goes ignored by the thick crowd of devotees who would endure the amenities of a Gulag cafeteria if only for morsel of its stand-up-and-shout chili (65AS). Burgers with fries run 60-76AS; cheese enchiladas 65AS. Nearly all entrées are under 100AS. (Open Mon.-Fri. 11:30am-2pm and 5:30-11:30pm, Sat.-Sun. 5-11:30pm.) The **Happy Dragon China Restaurant,** Pfarrgasse 2 (tel. 234 32), boasts a riverside garden and has a lunch *menu* with soup, spring roll, and main course for 64AS. Most dinners run 83-99AS. Vegetarian options available (open daily 11:30am-2:30pm and 6-11pm). The **Konsum grocery store** is conveniently located at Auböckpl. (open Mon.-Fri. 7:30am-6pm, Sat. 8am-12:30pm). There is an **open air market** every Friday (7am-noon) in the Salinenplatz.

Sights and Entertainment Other than the baths, Bad Ischl's main attraction is what the Habsburgs left behind. The tourist office gives walking tours on Tues. mornings in summer, meeting at 8:30am at the office. (Free with guest card, otherwise 30AS, register by the day before, and in case of bad weather they'll try again Thursday). Austria's last Emperor, Kaiser Franz Josef, received a house at the edge of town as a wedding gift, which quickly became known as the **Kaiservilla** (tel. 232 41). The emperor made it his summer getaway palace and crammed it with expensive hunter kitsch—the interior motif is strictly dead-animal-Ma-where-should-I-put-it, most evident in the villa's foyer which displays a pantheon of horns and antlers of various sizes, each with the date and place of the animal's untimely demise at the hands of Franzl himself, printed on it. Although entrance to the Kaiservilla is only possible through a guided tour in German (95AS, with guest card 90AS, students 65AS (you must ask), children 40AS) the tour is definitely worth it. Among other things, it includes Franz Josef's Lederhosen and hunting paraphernalia, the old red armchair where he napped every afternoon (you can see his favorite position from the area where the chair is worn and indented), and the desk where he signed the declaration of war against Serbia in 1914 that led to World War I. You can also wander through the surrounding 14-hectare **Villapark,** a verdant pasture where the regal couple spent several cool summer afternoons. (35AS, children 25AS; to the park and obligatory tour of the Kaiservilla (in German) 95AS, with guest card 90AS, children 40AS. Tours given May-Sept. daily 9-11:45am and 1:10-4:45pm. Open weekends in April.) At the rear of the grounds lies the empress's **Marmorschlößl** (tel. 244 22), which houses a **Photo Museum.** The emperor commissioned this decidedly marble palace so that she could sleep solo. To reach the Kaiserpark and both castles, head left from the tourist office onto Bahnhofstr, and right on Franz-Josef-Str. to the villa's entrance.

(Open April-Oct. daily 9:30am-5:30pm. 12AS with guest card, children 10AS, plus entrance to the Kaiserpark.) The **Museum of the City of Bad Ischl,** Esplanade 10 (tel. 254 76), houses some exhibits on the history of the salt-mining town and its baths. It is housed in the former "Hotel Austria," where the young Emperor Franz Josef announced his engagement to the 16-year-old Bavarian princess Elisabeth von Wittelsbach in 1853, known affectionately as "Sisi." (Open Dec.-Feb. and Easter-Dec. Tues., Thurs.-Sun. 10am-5pm, Wed. 2-7pm; July-Aug. also Mon. 10am-5pm. 45AS, with guestcard 40AS, students 25AS.) An unfairly overlooked city monument in Bad Ischl is the **Stadtpfarrkirche** (city parish church), on Kaiser-Franz-Josef-str., dedicated to St. Nikolaus (*not* Santa Claus). The capacious church differs from other parish churches in its open airy architecture, provided by the absence of pillars in the church's interior. The Stadtpfarrkirche is most renowned, however, for its magnificent **Kaiserjubiläumsorgel** (Emperor's Jubilee Organ); organ virtuoso and composer Anton Bruckner played in 1890 for the royal wedding service of Duchess Marive Valerie and Duke Franz Salvator. To this day, the organ is regarded as one of the best in the world, attracting famous talent to its double-keyboard.

A tour through Bad Ischl's **Salzbergwerke** salt mines (tel. 239 48) imparts a didactic but amusing glimpse of the trade that brought wealth and fame to the Salzkammergut. (Open July-Aug. daily 10am-4:45pm, May 6-June and Sept. 1-22 9am-3:45pm. 135AS, with guest card 120AS, children 65AS.) The mines are outside of the city in Perneck, and are best reached by car via Grazerstr. to Pernechstr. City bus #8096 also travels to Perneck and leaves from the Bahnhof two to five times daily, the last bus returning from Perneck at 4:15pm.

Whether or not the **salt baths** themselves really contain curative powers, something must be said for the relaxed atmosphere of the town. For those interested in partaking in the mud or salt baths, saunas, massages, or acupuncture, the bath facilities are concentrated in one resort complex called **Kaiser Therme,** across from the tourist office on Bahnhofstr. 1 (tel. 233 24; fax 233 24 44). Try the underwater massage therapy, water gymnastics programs, or the "mind gymnastics," which are quasi-yoga sessions, not a series of math problems. The rates are steep for such lofty experiences, but for a one-time splurge, they won't break the bank. An underwater massage runs 393AS for 20min. A full-body mud bath (including the shower afterward) is 294AS. 50min. of acupuncture therapy costs 396AS, or splash around in the salt baths on your own (135AS for 3hr.). Do remember, however, that most things more complicated than swimming in the pools requires a doctor's prescription.

For the low-down around town, pick up the brochure *"Bad Ischl Events"* from the tourist office. Free outdoor **Kurkonzerte** occur two to three times per day at the Kurpark, the voluptuously green garden outside the Kurhaus along Wirerstr. The exact program of pieces performed by the 20-piece Kurorchestra is posted weekly on kiosks, in the hotels, and at the Kurhaus itself. Every year in mid-August, the **Bad Ischler Stadtfest** comes to town for a weekend of music—classical, pop, jazz, boogie-woogie, oom-pah-pah bands, etc. Just before the Stadtfest on August 15th, the Bad Ischlers celebrate the Kaiser Franz Josef's birthday with live music late into the night on the Esplanade, explaining that the Kaiserfest is only a small remembrance of the elaborate partying that used to take place while the Kaiser was alive and summering in Bad Ischl. Around Easter the town holds a more outward-looking "Country Music Festival" with bands from Austria and the U.S. who will play everything from bluegrass and Cajun to something mysteriously "Texmec" in the stadium where horse dressage displays are usually held (space for camping tents available). In late summer the **Bad Ischl Operetten Festspiele** celebrates the musical talent of the composer Franz Lehár, the Lawrence Welk of opera, who lived in Bad Ischl for 30 years. The concerts are every Wednesday through Friday, from mid-July to the beginning of September. Each year's Festspiele features two operas, one of which is by Lehár. Tickets range 140-500AS, and are available from Büro der Operettengemeinde, Wiesengerstr. 7, A-4820 Bad Ischl (tel. 238 39; fax 233 84; open Mon.-Fri. 8am-noon). If your desire runs rampant to get to know the genius who created *Gypsy Love, The Merry Widow,* and *The Land of Smiles,* visit the **Lehár villa** (tel. 269 92), former home of the composer. (Open Easter and May-Sept. daily 9am-noon and 2-5pm. 50AS, with guest card 45AS, students 25AS).

A network of **hiking paths** webs around the town and is mapped out in detail on a 98AS map available at the tourist office. Bikers can invest in a 95AS trail map, as well. In winter, the town valiantly battles against the shift in tourist attention to neighboring ski resorts. Besides, an excellent network of **cross-country skiing** trails from easy to difficult, shown on the free maps at the tourist office, Bad Ischl offers all sorts of Yule festivities from a **Christkindlmarkt** (Christmas market), advent caroling, in the Kurhaus, and tours of elaborate **weihnachtskrippen** (nativity scenes) in the area, or horse-drawn sleigh rides (Pferdeschliffen) through the snow. In both summer and wintry weather, the **Katrin Seilbahn** (cable car) runs to the summit of nearby Mt. Katrin (1544m), a peak also laced with fine hiking trails. Get to the cable car by taking city bus #8095 from the train station or Schröpferpl., leaving every two hours. The last bus back leaves the Seilbahn at 4:55pm. The Seilbahn (tel. 237 88) is open mid-May to Oct. and Dec.7-Easter. (Open daily 9am-4pm. Up 139AS; down 109AS; round-trip 159AS, with guest card 139AS.) A **flea market** comes to Bad Ischl every first Sat. of the month from Apr.-Oct. at the Esplanade.

▓ Mondsee

The Salzkammergut's warmest lake, the **Mondsee** (Moon Lake), derives its romantic name from its crescent shape. The entire lake is actually privately owned, but available for general use. The town of Mondsee (pop. 2000) lies at the northern tip of the crescent, close to Autobahn A1. For a more scenic drive, take route 158 from Salzburg to St. Gilgen, and then route 154 along the edges of the lake to downtown Mondsee. The town has no train station, but is accessible by bus #3010 from **Salzburg** (50min., hourly, last one at 8:20pm, 57AS). Although it is the closest lake resort to Salzburg, Mondsee is also one of the least touristed; perhaps it has something to do with the fact that the town is not directly on the beach itself, but 200m away—light-years by Salzkammergut standards. Still, air-conditioned tour buses rumble through the town several times daily to see the local **Pfarrkirche,** a Gothic church re-designed with a bright yellow Baroque exterior; its towers dominate the town skyline. Once a Benedictine monastery, the parish church is best known for its use in *The Sound of Music's* wedding scene. The organ was played in the movie as well. Next door is the **Museum Mondsee,** which houses a mildly interesting collection of regional archaeological finds and religious artifacts, including some beautifully illuminated manuscripts. (Open May-Oct. daily 9am-6pm; from mid-Oct. to the month's end, Sat.-Sun. and holidays 9am-6pm. 25AS, students 12AS.) The **Freilichtmuseum,** on Hilfbergstr. up the street behind the church, is an open-air museum with a 500-year-old traditional smokehouse, common in this area and in parts of Bavaria. Smokehouses have no chimneys; in days past the smoke wafted through the roof of its own accord. This served the practical purpose of drying the *Getreide* (cereal or grain) that hung from the ceiling, and asphyxiating all humans who dared enter pre-maturely. (Open May-Sept. daily 9am-6pm; April and mid-Oct. to the month's end Sat.-Sun. and holidays 9am-5pm. 25AS, students 12AS.)

The **tourist office** *(Tourismusverband),* Dr. Franz Müllerstr. 3 (tel. 22 70; fax 44 70), is a 5-minutes walk from the bus station, halfway between the church and the lake. From the bus stop, head up the road past the post office, turn right, and continue to the end. Turn right again, and the office is on the left. The English-speaking staff will gladly give out every brochure they have and find accommodations for free. To get a good feel for the region, pick up the sightseeing pamphlet (free) of the Mondsee area, which suggests three different routes to follow. The shortest takes one to two hours, and covers just the town highlights; the longest takes six to seven hours and requires a car. (Open July-Aug. Mon.-Fri. 8am-7pm, Sat. 9am-7pm, Sun. 9am-1pm; Sept.-June Mon.-Fri. 8am-noon and 2-6pm.) Up the street toward the church from the tourist office, the **Tabak** store sells no fewer than 9 daily **English newspapers,** and 11

English **magazines**. The **post office,** on Franz Kreuzbergerstr. across from the bus station, is the most convenient place for **currency exchange** (open Mon.-Fri. 8am-noon and 2-6pm, Sat. 8-10am). **Postal code:** A-5310. **Telephone code:** 06232.

Mondsee is brimming with *Pensionen* and *Privatzimmer,* as well as hotels; ask at the tourist office or watch for signs to find the most convenient location with vacancies. The **Jugendgästehaus (HI),** Krankenhausstr. 9 (tel. 24 18, fax 241 875), offers doubles, quads, and dorms. From the bus station, walk up Kreuzbergerstr. toward the post office, turn right on Rainerstr., walk up the hill, and then go left on Pflegerstr., which splits into Krankenhausstr. to the left. The hostel is hidden away on the left. Bunkbeds are tucked into every possible nook, making the rooms a little snug. It's normally filled with groups; call first. Tread on brown carpets reminiscent of your grandmother's hide-the-stain approach. (Reception open daily 5-10pm. Curfew 10pm. Members only. Dorm and 4 bed-rooms 140AS per person. Doubles 340AS. Private showers in the doubles and quads. Breakfast included.)

For tasty inexpensive eats, **Pizzeria Nudelini** (tel. 41 93), upstairs from Café Mexico in the blue building just down from the church, features cheap individual pizzas (65-100AS) and noodle dishes (85AS). (Open daily 11am-2pm and 5:30-11pm. On "swimming weather" days, the staff takes the day off and then opens 5:30pm-midnight.) For delicious coffee and cake at a better price than at the flamboyant cafés in front of the church, head to **Café Übleis,** next to the tourist office at Badgasse 6 (tel. 24 33). They specialize in home-made *Mozartkugeln* (8AS) and soft-serve ice cream (20AS; open daily 10am-10pm). Hot 59-73AS lunches are served at the **China Restaurant** (tel. 4468) on Rainerstr. near the bus stop. One of the few Austrian-Chinese restaurants to feature seafood—squid dishes (115-145AS) and prawn dishes (160-190AS)—they also have a lunch menu that includes soup (59-73AS; open daily 11:30am-2:30pm and 6-11pm; Visa, MC). The most convenient supermarkets are the **SPAR Markts** on Herzog-Odilostr., just past the main square on the way up to the hostel, and on Rainerstr. (all open Mon.-Fri. 7:30am-6:30pm, Sat. 7:30am-noon).

Mondsee's true attraction is the **lake.** During the summer months the waters buzz with activity; in winter, though, everyone seems to hibernate. The **public beach** (tel. 22 91) is generally a safe place to swim. Jumping in at other random places along the shore is not permitted, as the lake is protected by wildlife conservation laws; use the designated beach areas. (30AS, children 12AS, prices go down after 1:30pm. Open May-Sept. daily 9am-7:30pm.) Sailboats, paddle boats, and motor-boat rentals are available by the hour from **Peter Hemetsberger,** Seebadstr. 1, next to the public beach (tel. 24 60). The beach also has water skiing; one round costs 100AS, two attempts at the slalom course 80AS. Contact **Sportland Mondsee,** Prielhofstr. 4 (tel. 40 77).

For entertainments other than the lake itself, partake of Mondsee's numerous cultural offerings, including the **Musiktage,** an annual classical music festival, which swings by in early September. (Tickets 200-450AS; write to "Postfach 3, A-5310 Mondsee" by July 31 for ticket information; or call 22 70; fax 3544.) Also, every year Hugo von Hofmannsthal's 1922 morality play, **Jedermann,** is performed in the open-air theater, the **Freilichtbühne.** Performances of this Salzburger favorite occur every Saturday from mid-July to mid-October, and tickets cost from 80-120AS; they are sold at the tourist office.

■ St. Wolfgang

More than a thousand years ago, the world-weary bishop of Regensburg (named Wolfgang) left the big city and set out for greener pastures in the Salzkammergut, finally ending his journey on the pacific shores of the Wolfgangsee (it was called Abersee at the time). After performing several miracles, Wolfgang was eventually canonized, and soon thereafter up to 70,000 disciples made pilgrimages to visit St. Wolfgang each year. The influx of visitors hasn't decreased since; in a wry twist of events, the formerly hermetic village, St. Wolfgang (pop. 3000) is arguably today the most touristed lake resort in the Salzkammergut region. Most are drawn to St. Wolfgang by the legendary **Pilgrimage Church** overlooking the Wolfgangsee and home of the famous Michael Pacher altar; others come for the **Schafberg,** a mountain peak offering the best vista of the lake region. They stay, however, for the idyllic landscape, the swimming, the hiking, and just plain good living. In the winter season, St. Wolfgang all but shuts down, getting some much needed rest before the next onslaught of tourists arrive with the first bloom.

Orientation and Practical Information St. Wolfgang rests lazily on the shore of Wolfgangsee, across the water from St. Gilgen. Access to St. Wolfgang is easiest **by car;** from **Vienna,** take the Autobahn A1 west until you hit Mondsee, at which point head south through St. Lorenz, Scharfling, and on to St. Wolfgang. From **Salzburg,** take Rte. 158 east through Hof, Fuschl, and St. Gilgen. **Buses** run often between **Bad Ischl** and St. Wolfgang (hourly, 40AS) and **Salzburg** and St. Wolfgang (hourly, 81AS, change at Strobl). **Train** connections can be made at either Bad Ischl or Salzburg. The ÖBB also operates the Wolfgangsee **ferry,** which connects the lakeside villages of St. Wolfgang, St. Gilgen (48AS), and Strobl. Boats depart from St. Wolfgang Markt and St. Wolfgang Schafbergbahnhof hourly.

St. Wolfgang's main drag is its only drag—the streets Pilgerstraße and Michael-Pacher-Straße run into each other and form a quasi-**pedestrian zone.** Automobiles are strictly prohibited from traveling down this thoroughfare at most times of the day—either park in one of the lots at either end, or, if you want to simply bypass the town, take the tunnel that circumnavigates downtown St. Wolfgang, coming out the other end. The **bus** stop is at the end of the west tunnel entrance, outside the post office. To get to the **tourist office,** Pilgerstr. 28 (tel. 22 39; fax 22 39 81), make a left and walk down Pilgerstr. for one minute. Watch for the poorly marked green building on the left, labeled **Marktgemeindeamt.** The helpful, English-speaking office hands out oodles of information, including a thick booklet of accommodations; they'll also reserve a room for free. Another **branch office** is located further down the block, next to Hotel "Peter." A 24-hr. **electronic accommodations board** can be found within the kiosk (Main office open May-Oct. Mon.-Fri. 8am-6pm, Sat. 8am-noon; Nov.-April Mon.-Fri. 8am-noon and 2-5pm, Sat. 9am-noon. Branch office open daily 10am-7pm.) The **Rieger Bank,** Marktpl. 87 (tel. 28 07), and at the Info Kiosk (tel. 30 92) **exchanges money** daily from 9am to 7pm, at hefty rates. The **post office** at the bus station (tel. 22 01) will also change money. (Open Mon.-Fri. 8am-noon, 2-6pm, Sat. 8-11am; exchange open Mon.-Fri. 8am-5pm.) In case of emergency, call the **police** (tel. 133). Telephones are behind the post office. **Postal code:** A-5360. **Telephone code:** 06138.

Accommodations and Food Almost 2000 tourists troop through St. Wolfgang every sunny summer day. The tourist office's brochure features a list of hotels, pensions, and private rooms that just keeps going and going. There is no youth hostel in St. Wolfgang, but the gentleman who runs **Haus am See** on Michael-Pacher-Str. 98 (tel. 22 24) also manages a youth hostel in Vienna during the winter. Richard, the enthusiastic proprietor, pampers his guests with a 40-bed *pension* right on the lake, and its own swimmable shore. To get to Haus am See from the tourist office, simply continue down the main road away from the post office for 7min., until you get to the east entrance of the tunnel; the Haus is just beyond, on the right. Look for a *Zimmer frei* banner. (Singles from 200AS. Doubles 360-550AS. Two-room quads 800-1000AS. All showers and toilets in the hall. Prices depend on balcony and view. Breakfast included. Parking available. Open May-Oct.) Haus Am See also has a renovated boathouse down on the shore, where beds start at 150AS. Also check out **Gästehaus Raudaschl,** Deschbühel 41 (tel. 25 61), is on the way to the major hiking paths. From the tourist office, continue down the main road, and make a left at the Hotel Peter. Climb up the small hill, and the pension is on the left (5min). This smaller pension offers a private shower and private balcony in each of its seven well-furnished rooms. Keep an eye out for the taxidermic animals that silently decorate the staircases. (Singles 210AS, 250AS for single nights. Doubles start at 380-420AS. Breakfast included. Open May-Oct.)

Most of St. Wolfgang's restaurants and *Imbiße* price their wares very competitively. Stand at any of the snack shacks lining the main road, where almost nothing is above 45AS. *Konditoreien* also serve up a local speciality—the *Schafbergkugel* (23AS), named after the mountain. A variant of the *Mozartkugel*, the *Schafbergkugel* is a supersweet treat about the size of your fist. It probably tastes better, too, unless *your* hands are made from nuts and marzipan and dipped in creamy milk chocolate. Pick one up at **Bäckerei Gandl,** Markt 44 (tel. 33 17; open Mon.-Sat. 7am-6pm, Sun. 8am-6pm). Cheap pizzas are easy to come by at **Pizzeria Julio,** Au 36 (tel. 31 57). Pies range from 69AS for a cheese to 110AS for a seafood pizza. Smaller pies are 60AS, pastas 68-95AS. The pizzeria also hosts a traditional Hungarian goulash party every Friday evening. Julio's is located on the hill above the east tunnel entrance (open daily 11am-midnight). **Hauer's Imbißstube,** a **self-service restaurant,** stands at the corner of Michael-Pacher.-Str. and Deschbühelstr., across from the Hotel "Peter" and serves up Austrian standards for under 90AS in its guest garden or indoor seating (open daily 9am-5:30pm).

Sights and Entertainment For St. Wolfgang's top attraction, follow the throngs to the **Wallfahrtskirche** (Pilgrimage Church), in the center of town. While the tiny chapel built on this site by St. Wolfgang went up in smoke in the Great Fire of 1429, the present church still honors Wolfgang's sense of humility, with its single tower and arched arcades looking out onto the tranquil lake. Inside the church, however, the meek are swiftly disinherited; look no further than **Michael Pacher's altarpiece** to get a taste of the extreme limits of ecclesiastical grandeur and luxury. Completed by Pacher in 1480, the altarpiece actually has two pairs of altar wings—originally, these were opened depending on the holiness of the day. In more pious times, the inner shrine was only revealed on Easter and Christmas. Fully closed, Pacher's altar displays scenes of a humble pilgrim's life. When the outer wings are opened, eight scenes in the life of Christ are revealed. The final pair of wings displays the Coronation of Mary, with Christ blessing his mother.

Pacher's altar is almost outdone (but not quite) by the **Schwanthaler Altar,** which stands in the middle of the church behind wrought-iron gates. Installed in 1676, the frenetic, high Baroque altar was originally made to replace Pacher's "obsolete" one, but the sculptor Thomas Schwanthaler himself self-sacrificially persuaded the abbot to leave Pacher's masterpiece alone. Together the two altars crowd and almost overwhelm the rather small church; try not to miss its other little treasures, such as Schwanthaler's **Rosenkranzaltar** (Rose Garland Altar), in the Maria Chapel.

St. Wolfgang's second largest attraction is the **Schafbergbahn** (Schafberg Railway), a romantic steam engine that laboriously ascends to the 1732-meter summit of Schafberg mountain. The railway was built in 1892, and in 1964 Hollywood found it *so* precious that it was given a cameo in *The Sound of Music,* with the children waving out of its windows. At the top, dozens of trails unravel down the mountain, leading to several nearby towns, including St. Gilgen, Ried, and Falkenstein. Train tickets run as steep as the mountain (up 140AS, halfway-up 110AS, round-trip 250AS), but because the Schafbergbahn is operated by the ÖBB, Eurail Pass is valid. (Train runs early May to mid-Oct., once per hour daily 7:15am-6:40pm. Tickets for the 7:15 and 8:30am trains to the top sell for the halfway up price.) If you are paying full price to go up and down, you might as well take up the special deal offered by the **Berghotel Schafbergspitze**—a mountain inn peeking over the Schafberg's steepest face. For 500AS per person, you get a round-trip ticket on the railway, plus a night's lodging at the beautiful hotel, with breakfast (tel. 22 32 18; reserve in advance).

Nature-lovers can enjoy themselves here too—the **lake** provides plenty of watersport activities. If you like swimming, you can dive off the deep end at **Strandbad Ried** (tel. 25 87; 40AS, children 20AS). Water skiing is available through **Stadler,** on the Seepromenade (tel. (0663) 917 97 43). One round costs 120AS; daredevils can try the water-ski jump. Rent **boats** at the beach on Robert-Stolz-Str., across from the tennis courts. Both motor boats (½hr. 90AS, 1hr. 150AS) and pedal boats (½hr. 50AS, 1hr. 90AS) can be hired (open in the summer daily 8am-7pm).

SALZBURGER LAND

With the mountains at the edge of the lake, **hiking** is another possibility. All trails are marked clearly and are described in detail in the free, English *Info* brochure obtainable from the tourist office. The tourist office also sponsors guides for Thursday morning hikes July to mid-September. (Free, except for the 52AS boat ride. Meet at the office at 9:30am, no registration necessary.) Every third Sunday in October, St. Wolfgang holds a **race around the lake,** a distance of 27 kilometers. The start and finish line is the St. Wolfgang Markt; the record stands at 1½ hours.

Lazier folk can take advantage of the Wolfgangsee **ferry,** also operated by the ÖBB. The boat stops in St. Gilgen, Strobl, Fürberg, and other lesser landings (every 1hr., 52AS to St. Gilgen, Eurail valid). Hop aboard from either the St. Wolfgang Markt landing or the pier at the St. Wolfgang Schafbergbahnhof. (Ferries run early May-mid-Oct. daily approximately once per hour 8:15am-6:15pm).

■ Hallstatt

Perched on the banks of the **Hallstätter See,** in a valley surrounded on all sides by the sheer rocky cliffs of the Dachstein mountains, Hallstatt is quite simply, in the words of Alex von Humboldt, "the most beautiful lakeside village in the world." The tiny village of 1100 inhabitants seems to defy gravity, with medieval buildings clinging to the face of a stony slope. 4500 years ago, a highly advanced Celtic culture thrived in Hallstatt, but its settlers did not come for the view. Hallstatt was a world-famous settlement back when Rome was still a village, thanks to its salt. The surrounding mountains were slavishly mined for salt—the famed "white gold" of the Salzkammergut. The well-preserved archaeological remains of Hallstatt were so extensive that the whole pre-historical period in Celtic studies (800-400BC) is dubbed the "Hallstatt period." The present tourist pit-stop seduces visitors with both scenery and its history. To enjoy both simultaneously, hike up above the town to the 700-year old **Rudolfsturm** (Rudolph's tower). Perched on a mountain 855m above the village, the lonely tower guards the entrance to the Salzburg Valley, site of a famous prehistorical burial ground and of a modern salt mine installation.

Orientation and Practical Information Hallstatt stands poised on the **Hallstätter See,** a pristine emerald oasis at the southern tip of the Salzkammergut. Its charm lies in its isolation, and the fact that it hangs (though not precariously) off a cliff—two things that make it a royal pain in the rear to access. If **driving** from **Salzburg** or the Salzkammergut towns, take Rte. 158 to Bad Ischl, and then Rte. 145 in the direction of Bad Aussee. After passing the small town of Bad Goisern, it's approximately 5km to the narrow road leading along the Hallstätter See into Hallstatt (watch for the signs). Once in town, there is a strict limit on the number of cars. If just staying for a day, ample **parking** lots are available by the tunnels leading into town. If intent on driving all the way through Hallstatt on the road, narrow and deluged with pedestrians, beware that two electronic gates pose further obstacles daily 10am-6pm. A gate pass is required to open the gates, and is available to those staying in Hallstatt from their hotel or *Pension*. The first time in, park your car at the lot outside of the gate, and walk into town to the tourist office or hotel; obtain a pass, and fetch your car later. Traveling **by train** is only slightly easier. Hallstatt's **train station** lies on the opposite bank of the lake from downtown, in the middle of proverbial nowhere. After every train arrives, there is a **ferry** across to town; don't worry about missing it, as it waits for all the passengers from the train (20AS). It comes to a stop at Landungspl. The tourist office and the main square are a 2-minute walk to the left, at the second plaza—then again, everything is within 15-minute of everything else anyway. To escape the town by rail, ferries depart roughly ½ hour before the train. Ferry schedules can be picked up at the train station, Landungspl., or the tourist office. The only train route traveled is from Stainach-Irnding to Attnang-Puchheim and back; further connections can be made at Attnang-Puchheim (hourly 6am-6pm; 110AS). The last ferry from the Hallstatt Bahnhof back to town leaves at roughly 6:30pm. If you do happen to arrive later, stay on the train to the next stop (Obertraun), and take a taxi

(150AS), or walk (5km) to downtown Hallstatt. From **Salzburg,** the **bus** is the best option; transfer in Bad Ischl. This bus stops in the tunnel above the Hallstatt town center (144AS). Depending on the route, another connection may be necessary at Gosamühle. The main bus stop in Hallstatt is "Hallstatt-Lahrs" at the edge of downtown on Seestr. and near the **Salzbergwerke.** The route goes from Bad Ischl through Hallstatt to Obertraun.

Hallstatt's main byway, **Seestraße,** hugs the lakeshore all through town. The **tourist office** *(Tourismusbüro),* in the Kultur- und Kongresshaus at Seestr. 169 (tel. 82 08; fax 83 52), finds vacancies among the plentiful, cheap rooms for no fee. While the office also sells a map for 10AS, you can pick up a free one at many souvenir kiosks. (Open July-Aug. Mon.-Fri. 8:30am-6pm, Sat. 10am-6pm, Sun. 10am-2pm; Sept.-June Mon.-Fri. 9am-noon and 1-5pm.) **Public toilets** are available behind the Prehistoric Museum. The **post office,** down Seestr. from the tourist office, offers the best **exchange** rates. (Open June 15-Sept. 15 Mon.-Fri. 8am-noon and 2-6pm, Sat. 8-10am; Sept. 16-June 14 Mon.-Fri. 8am-noon and 2-6pm.) **Exchange office** open Mon.-Fri. 8am-5pm. **Postal code:** A-4830. **Telephone code:** 06134.

Accommodations and Food *Privatzimmer* at just-above-hostel prices speckle the town. Wherever you tuck yourself in, don't forget to ask your host or hostess for Hallstatt's free **guest card,** which offers discounts on mountain lifts and sporting facilities in Hallstatt, Gosau, Obertraun, and Bad Goisern. Establishments may not always automatically give guests the guest card, but all provide it on request. While the largest **Jugendherberge,** Salzbergstr. 50, is limited to groups, **Gasthaus Zur Mühle,** Kirchenweg 36 (tel. 8318), is a quasi-hostel with 3- to 18-bed rooms and lots of English-speaking backpackers. It's also close to the city center. From the tourist office, walk a few steps up the hill as if heading toward the Heimatmuseum, swing right at the end of Platz, and the hotel is through the little tunnel on the left, right next to the cascading waterfall. (Reception open daily 8am-2pm and 4-10pm. 100AS. Showers and lockers included. Sheets 35AS. Breakfast 35AS. Lunch and dinner available at the restaurant downstairs.) **Frühstückspension Sarstein,** Gosaumühlstr. 13 (tel. 82 17), offers the prettiest accommodations in town, luring visitors with homey rooms, wonderful vistas of the lake and village, and a beachside lawn for sunning and swimming. From the tourist office, head toward the ferry dock and continue along the road nearest the lake for 7-8 minutes, past the Pfarrkircher steps. (190-210AS, with private bathroom and shower 280AS. Hall showers 10AS. Breakfast included.) Frau Sarstein's sister **Franziska Zimmerman** lives up the block toward town at #69 (tel. 83 09) and offers similar (but fewer) accommodations (190AS; showers 10AS; breakfast included). **Frühstückspension Seethaler,** Dr.-F.-Mortonweg 6 (tel. 84 21), sits on the hill near the tourist office. Head uphill, bear left, and follow the signs. Basic rooms with hall toilets and showers and a breakfast included (185-205AS). **Camping Klausner-Höll,** Lahnstr. 201 (tel. 83 22), lies three blocks past the bus stop on Seestr., one street up from the public beach. (Check-out noon, gate closed daily noon-2:30pm and 10pm-7am. 45AS. Tax 10AS. Children under 14 25AS plus a 5AS tax. Tent 40AS. Car 30AS. Breakfast 60-95AS. Showers included. Laundry facilities available.)

Hallstatt has so many attractive restaurants that it can be difficult to decide among them. Many of them, however, will bore a hole through your wallet—avoid lake-side establishments where you pay double for the view. **Gasthaus zur Mühle,** below the hostel, offers one of the best deals in town. Pizza (68-94 AS) and pasta (68-88AS) are the specialties, although there is also a wide range of salads (54AS and up). Three kinds of canneloni (one vegetarian) are sold for 88AS each. (Open daily 11:30am-2pm and 5-10pm.) Another local favorite is the **Gasthaus zum Weißen Lamm,** across from the Heimatmuseum (tel. 83 11). This restaurant has a "mountain man's cellar" with a mining motif. They offer two daily *menus* for lunch and dinner, all with appetizer, main course, and dessert *(menus* 85-110AS; open daily 11am-3pm and 5-10pm).

Sights and Entertainment Hallstatt packs some heavy punches for tourists despite its lean frame. The tourist office sells a 30AS English cultural guide, but you don't really need it. Simply exploring the narrow, crooked streets is entertainment in itself. Depending on one's point of view, a visit to St. Michael's Chapel at the **Pfarrkirche** is macabre, poignant, or intrusive. Next to the chapel is the parish "charnel house"—a bizarre repository for sundry skeletons. Walking into the creepy crypt is like stumbling onto an Indiana Jones set. Bones from the surrounding cemeteries are transferred here after 10 to 20 years, because the graveyard is too small to accommodate all those who wish to rest there. (They're buried vertically as it is.) Each neatly placed skull is decorated with a flower (for females) or ivy (for males), and inscribed with the name of the deceased and the date of death. (Open May-Sept. daily 10am-6pm. In winter, call the Catholic church at 82 79 for an appointment. 10AS.)

In the mid-19th century, Hallstatt was the site of such a large Iron Age archaeological find. Among the finds were a plethora of artifacts, a pauper's grave, and the well-maintained crypts of the ruling class, all circa 1000-500BC. The **Prähistorisches Museum** (Prehistoric Museum), across from the tourist office, exhibits some of the relics unearthed in the region. Finds from the famous excavation site on Hallstatt's *Salzberg* (salt mountain) are displayed here; they give scientific proof of prehistoric salt-mining activity. Extensive salt-trading brought bronze ornaments from Northern Italy and amber from the east coast to this remote valley. (40AS, with guest card 35AS, students 20AS). The price of admission also covers entrance to the **Heimatmuseum,** around the corner, with exhibits on the artifacts of daily living, such as clothes, kitchen utilities, and mining tools. It also maps the work of Dr. Franz Morton, who studied the development of local fauna (both museums open May-Sept. daily 10am-6pm; Oct.-April 10am-4pm).

The 2500-year-old **Salzbergwerke** is the oldest saltworks in the world, although it's more of a tourist attraction these days. The guided tours (1½hr.) lead you down a mining slide and to a mysterious, eerie lake. The tour guide's ghost stories sound even scarier in German. (Open June to mid-Sept. 9:30am-4:30pm; April-May and mid-Sept. to Oct. 9:30am-3pm. 135AS, with guest card 120AS, students 60AS, children under 6 35AS.) To reach the salt mines, wander up the steep path near the Pfarrkirche to the top (1hr.). Or take the **Salzbergbahn,** at the southern edge of town, following the black signs with the yellow eyes to the bottom of the train station. If walking from the tourist office, head away from the ferry dock along the lake, and turn right at the large bus circle. (June to mid-Sept. 9am-6pm; April-May and mid-Sept.-Oct. 9am-4:30pm. One-way 55AS, with guest card 45AS. Round-trip 97AS and 80AS, respectively, children 65AS.) The last train up runs ½ hour before the last tour starts (June-Sept. at 4pm, for example).

Hallstatt offers some of the best scenic day hikes in the Salzkammergut. The tourist office offers a 70AS English Dachstein hiking guide, detailing 38 hikes in the area, as well as a 35AS mountain bike trail map. Beyond the Salzbergwerk is the **Echental,** a valley carved out millennia ago by glaciers, and now blazed with trails leading deep into the valley. Hardy (or foolhardy) hikers can attempt the **Gangsteig,** a slippery, nefarious, primitive stairway carved onto the side of the cliff that comprises the valley's right wall. It's marked for experienced hikers only. Those without the gumption or experience to delve so deep into the forest can visit the Waldbachstub waterfall or the **Glacier Gardens** in the valley. These beautiful hills, nooks, and crannies are the scars left in the glacier's wake. The melting glacier water ("glacier-milk") was filled with so much sand and silt, and rushed past at such a high velocity, that it had the same effect as a sand-blaster, permanently scouring the rocks. To reach the Echental, head toward the Salzbergwerk, and continue on either "Malerweg" or "Echenweg;" about 20 minutes later, a sign will post the area's layout. Gangstieg is about 1hr. from there on the right, and the gardens are about 40min. on the left side, right before the mountain tunnel. In winter, a free ski bus (tel. 231 13; with guest card only) runs to Obertraun and Krippenstein, leaving Hallstatt at 9:30am, 10:55am, and 12:55pm, with the last bus returning to Hallstatt at 4:05pm.

■ Near Hallstatt: Obertraun

At the end of the lake in Obertraun, the prodigious **Dachstein Ice Caves** give eloquent testimony to the geological hyperactivity that forged the region's natural beauty. (Open May to mid-Oct. daily 9am-5pm. Admission to either Giant Ice Cave or Mammoth Cave 79AS, children 38AS, combined "Gargantuan Experience" 106AS, children 55AS.) To reach the caves from Hallstatt, catch the bus at the stop near the lake, 6-7 minutes from the tourist office in the direction away from the ferry dock (25AS one-way). Obertraun is also accessible by boat or train, but the bus runs most frequently and drops you right at the **Dachstein Cable Car** station. Ride the cable car up 1350m to "Schönbergalm." (Open daily 9am-5pm. Round-trip 155AS, with guest card 140AS, children 100AS.) For info on the caves, call (06131) 362. The **tourist office** stands in the Gemeindeamt, Obertraun 180 (tel. (06131) 351; open Mon.-Fri. 8am-noon and 2-6pm, in summer also Sat. 9am-noon). Obertraun's sparkling **Jugendherberge (HI),** Winkl 26 (tel. (06131) 360), is a refuge for summer hikers and winter skiers alike. (Reception open daily 8-9am, noon-1pm and 5-7:30pm. Lockout 2-5pm. Flexible 10pm curfew. 130AS, under 19 110AS. Breakfast 50AS.)

Central Tirol

The Central Tirol region is a curious amalgam—parts of Tirol, Salzburg, Carinthia, and East Tirol, wedged between Italy and Germany, have established a unique flavor defined by Alpine terrain, not provincial boundaries. Central Tirol enthralls visitors with breathtaking vistas of rugged mountains and sweeping valleys. The Zillertal Alpen overwhelm with their enormity and grandeur; the sight of mountaintop rock and *névé* (partially compacted granular snow) is, simply stated, unforgettable. Jagged contours in the Kaisergebirge above St. Johann and Kufstein, in the northwest, fade slightly to the rounded shapes of the Kitzbühel Alpen to the south, but the peaks rise again just past Zell am See. Mountainous crags create two of the most spectacular natural wonders in all of Europe; if you're within hours of Central Tirol, take a detour to the **Krimmler Waterfall** or the **Großglockner Straße**—words don't do them justice. Bring lots and lots and lots of film; we guarantee you'll use it.

East Tirol is the geopolitical oddity of the region. It's technically a semi-autonomous, wholly-owned subsidiary of the province of Tirol, though the two share no common border. In the chaos following World War I, Italy stealthily snatched South Tirol, the connecting portion, away, leaving the province awkwardly divided by an Italian sliver. Although East Tirol resembles its mother province culturally and topographically, Easterners retain a powerful independent streak.

■ Kitzbühel

Posh Kitzbühel (or "Kitz," the nickname witty tourist officials have tried to popularize) is a cross between glitzy St. Moritz and gaudy Atlantic City—wealthy visitors pump enough cash into the local casinos to keep the cobblestone streets in good repair and the sidewalk cafés flourishing. At night, affluent international playchildren gather in Kitzbühel's tiny pubs and discotheques to squander inherited money on drink and debauchery in this land of Visa and Eurocard. To add to the created glamor, the annual Miss Austria beauty pageant waltzes its wares every March before these voracious pleasure seekers. Most visitors here are older (read: financially secure) Germans and Brits.

Since 1928, when the city's first downhill run was built on the towering **Hahnenkamm** (1960m), Kitzbühel has been a mecca for skiing pilgrimages. Its "Ski Circus" consists of six different peaks, making it Austria's largest and most popular ski area. The annual international Hahnenkamm race (see **Sights and Entertainment**) boasts what is generally acknowledged as the toughest course in the world and thus manages to attract amateurs, professionals, and spectators alike. Despite its popularity, Kitzbühel hasn't expanded much geographically—the town still makes do with only two traffic lights.

GETTING TO KITZBÜHEL

Kitzbühel lies on Route 161 north/south and at the east terminus of Route 170. **By car** from Salzburg, take Route 21 south to 312 west; at St. Johann in Tirol, switch to 161 south, which leads straight to Kitzbühel. From Innsbruck, take Autobahn A12 east; at Kramsach, switch to Route 171 north, and then take Route 170 east to Kitzbühel. Several major rail lines converge on the town. The routes from München and Innsbruck funnel through Wörgl and into Kitzbühel before running onto Zell am See. Kitzbühel has two **train stations,** one at each side of the "U" formed by the rail tracks. From Salzburg, you arrive first at the **Hauptbahnhof;** from Innsbruck or Wörgl, at the **Hahnenkamm Bahnhof.** There are direct connections to **Innsbruck** (1hr., 10 daily, 156AS), **Salzburg** (3hr., hourly, 228AS), **Vienna** (6hr., 7 daily, 560AS), and **Zell am See** (1hr., every ½hr., 94AS); other connections can be made in Innsbruck, Salzburg, or Munich (256AS). For **train information,** call 40 55. **Bus stops** are adjacent to both train stations, with schedules at the tourist office.

N

GERMANY

Hallein

Kufstein

St. Johann in Tirol

Wörgl

Kitzbühel

Jenbach

Zell am See

Lend

Zell am Ziller

Krimml

Kaprun

Innsbruck

Mayrhofen

Badgastein

Großglockner

Heiligenblut

0   15 miles
0   15 kilometers

Lienz

Brixen (Bressanone)

ITALY

Central Tirol

CENTRAL TIROL

ORIENTATION AND PRACTICAL INFORMATION

Kitzbühel sits prettily on the banks of the Kitzbüheler Ache river. Nearby, the warm, mud-bearing Schwarzsee proffers its luscious and mythically curative waters. The town cowers under a number of impressive peaks, including the Kitzbüheler Horn (1996m) and the Steinbergkogel (1971m). Kitzbühel's *Fußgängerzone,* at the center of town, hosts multitudes of cafés and benches, where the paparazzi lie in wait for innocently strolling celebrities. The city center is a maze of twisting streets; if you get confused look for the *Zentrum* (center) signs to point you back.

Tourist Office: Hinterstadt 18 (tel. 21 55 or 22 72; fax 23 07). Head straight out the main door of the *Hauptbahnhof,* down the street, and turn left at the main road; at the traffic light, turn right, and walk toward the shops. As the road winds left, continue until you reach the pedestrian zone and turn right (across from Louis Vuitton). The tourist office is near the Rathaus at the end of the street. From the Hahnenkamm Bahnhof, walk down Joseph-Heroldstr., take the first major left onto Klostergasse and follow it as it curves right. Then turn right onto Reischstr., and walk through the arch at the end; the tourist office will be on your left. Though the friendly staff doesn't make reservations, the free telephone at the **electronic accommodations board** outside is helpful (in operation daily 6am-10pm). Maps and basic English brochures are also outside after hours. A small bank branch in the office exchanges money during the high season. Free hour-long **tours** of Kitzbühel (in English) start at the tourist office during the summer every Thursday at 8:45am. From July 16-Aug. 13 the office also offers a cultural tour which leave from its doors daily at 9:15am. Office open July-Sept. and mid-Dec. to late April Mon.-Fri.

8:30am-6:30pm, Sat. 8:30am-noon and 4-6pm, Sun. 10am-noon and 4-6pm; Oct. to mid-Dec. and late-April to June Mon.-Fri. 8:30am-noon and 2:30-6pm.

Budget Travel: Reisebüro Eurotours, across the street from the tourist office (tel. 31 31; fax 30 12). Provides discounts on package tours and makes local room reservations for a fee. Exchanges currency, but may not have the best rates. Open Mon.-Fri. 8:30am-noon and 3-6:30pm, Sat. 8:30am-noon and 4:30-6:30pm, Sun. and holidays 10am-noon and 4:30-6:30pm.

Currency Exchange: The most widely accepted forms of currency are Visa and MasterCard. Exchange, however, is available at all banks, travel agencies, and the post office. The post office and most banks have **ATMs** located outside. Also try **Reisebüro Eurotours** (tel. 31 31), across from the tourist office.

Telephones: At the rail stations, post office, and behind the tourist office.

Taxis: If not on the street or at the stand in front of Hauptbahnhof, call 28 11, 22 83, or 17 18. Taxis run until 2am.

Car Rental: Hertz, (tel. 48 00; fax 721 44), on Josef-Pirchlstr., at the traffic lights on the way into town from the main station. Open Mon.-Fri. 8am-noon and 2-6pm, Sat. 9am-noon. Travelers with a valid guest card get a 20 percent discount.

Bike Rental: At the main train station (tel. 505 53 85). Road bikes 90AS per day, 50AS with train ticket for that day. Mountain bikes 200AS and 150AS respectively.

Parking: There are four lots in Kitzbühel: **Griesgasse, Pfarrau, Hahnenkamm,** and **Kitzbühlerhorn.** The latter two are next to the two major ski lifts. In the winter, a free park and ride service operates between the four. Free parking is available at the Fleckalmbahn for those using the cable car (open 8am-6pm), and winter parking at Hahnekamm costs 50AS per day.

Luggage Storage: Both stations. Open daily 6:30am-10:30pm. 30AS per piece.

English Newspapers: Vendors at both train stations sell English newspapers. Tabaks and bookstores in the town center stock USA Today, The International Herald Tribune, Time, and Newsweek.

Laundromat: Dry cleaning at **Phönix Reinigung,** Graggaugasse 6 (tel. 30 55). Open Mon.-Fri. 8am-6pm.

Ski Conditions: tel. 181 or 182, in German

Hospital: Städtisches Krankenhaus, Hornweg 28 (tel. 60 10).

Emergencies: Red Cross Ambulance Service, Wagnerstr. 18 (tel. 40 11). **Police:** tel. 133. **Fire:** tel. 122. **Medical:** tel. 144.

Police: Rathaus (tel. 26 26).

Post Office: Josef-Pirchlstr. 11 (tel. 27 12). From the tourist office, walk left down Hinterstadt along the *Fußgängerzone,* and turn left at the end; then walk past the church and follow the street as it curves around at a right angle. Office is on the left side of the street. It lists bus schedules, and has telephones, a fax, and an expensive, self-serve copier inside. Open Mon.-Fri. 8am-noon and 2-6pm, Sat. 8-11am. **Currency exchange** Mon.-Fri. 8am-noon and 4-5pm.

Postal code: A-6370.

Telephone code: 05356.

ACCOMMODATIONS AND CAMPING

Kitzbühel has almost as many guest beds (7445) as inhabitants (8000), but the only **youth hostel** is far from town and restricted to groups. The town center is dominated by pricey hotels with fancy pastel façades. They offer enticing views, but not an affordable stay. Austrians claim that in Kitzbühel, you pay German prices for German comfort (read: twice the price, half the comfort). Rooms during the summer generally run 200 to 300AS per person; expect to shell out an extra 100AS during the winter. The Hahnenkamm Ski Competition in January creates a bed shortage so great that most residents are willing to vacate their homes and rent them to visitors. Wherever you stay, be sure to ask for your **guest card** upon registration—it entitles you to discounts on all sorts of town facilities and local attractions.

Hotel Kaiser, Bahnhofstr. 2 (tel. 47 08 or 47 09), located right down the street from the main train station. The native English-speaking owner and staff, all former backpackers, are happy to greet road-weary travelers. The hotel has a sun terrace, an inexpensive bar, and an Austrian restaurant (dinner only, sign up in the morning).

Expect a ripping game of soccer to be on in the TV room. Singles 170AS, with private bathroom 210AS. Doubles 280AS, with private bathroom 360AS. Breakfast included. Laundry facilities 50AS (wash and dry). Major credit cards accepted. Ample parking available.

Pension Hörl, Josef-Pirchlstr. 60 (tel. 31 44). Coming from the main train station, take a left after Hotel Kaiser; Pension Hörl will be on the left. Quiet and unassuming, with simple rooms and reasonable rates. If they can't find you a bed here, they'll try to put you up at their nearby **Gästehaus Hörl** (Bahnhofstr. 8). Summer 160-220AS per person, with private shower 190-260AS. Winter prices start at 40AS more. Breakfast included. English spoken.

Pension Neuhaus "Motorbike," Franz-Reichstr. 23 (tel. 22 00). Facing the tourist office, walk through the archway to the left and follow Franz-Reichstr. on the right (look for Wienerwald). The pension is on the left, enticingly close to the chairlift. Its name is not capriciously chosen; the English-speaking proprietors here *really* like motorcycles, as the interior of the relaxed bar attests. Still, sporting chic Kawasakis, the chopper crowd is more hubris than Harley. Rooms house up to 6 people. Summer rates start at 200-300AS per person, winter rates at 300-400AS. Breakfast included.

Camping Schwarzsee, Reitherstr. 24 (tel. 28 06; fax 44 79 30). Take the train to the "Schwarzsee" stop (one stop past the "Hahnenkamm" stop coming from the main train station) and walk toward the lake. If you're up for the half-hour walk, turn right at the tourist office and pass under the archway. Bear right at the Wienerwald up Franz-Reischstr., which becomes Schwarzseestr. and leads to the lake. 76AS per person, ages 2-12 65AS, under 2 free. Guest tax 6AS per day. Tent 92AS, caravan 90-100AS. Dogs 40AS. TV hook-up 20AS per day. In high season (July 1-Aug. 15) 85AS per person, all other prices the same.

FOOD

There are few reasonably priced restaurants in Kitzbühel; most establishments prepare food for the more cultured palates and price their dishes accordingly. To find less expensive meals, escape the *Fußgängerzone,* and turn the corner, looking for simple havens to avoid astronomic gastronomic adventures.

Huberbräu-Stüberl, Vorderstadt 18 (tel. 56 77). Located smack in the center of town, Huberbräu offers high-quality traditional cuisine at comparably low prices, making it a hangout for local Kitzbühelers. Besides their *Wiener Schnitzel* (98AS) or pizza "margherita" (65AS), check out the incredibly filling *prix fixe* menu—soup, entreé, potato, and dessert (90AS). Open daily 8am-midnight.

Café-Restaurant Prima Angebot, Bichlstr. 22 (tel. 38 85), on the second floor. Inexpensive meals on a sunny patio with an eye-boggling vista of the mountains. This self-serve eatery chain has a wide selection of food, including spaghetti (55AS), *Wiener Schnitzel* (78AS), and a salad bar. Open daily 9am-10pm.

La Fonda, Hinterstadt 13 (tel. 73 673). A Tex-Mex joint deep in the heart of Kitzbühel, down the road from the tourist office. Serves cheap, snack-style meals such as hamburgers, nachos, Texas spare ribs, potato skins, Australian meat pies, and tacos. Nothing over 80AS; no Ted Turner either. Open daily 11am-1am.

Pik-As, Josef-Heroldstr. 17 (tel. 742 19), on the way out to the Hahenkamm lift. Why this place? Bik-As it serves a variety of international dishes, as well as a healthy selection of salads. Interesting Tirolean-Italian combinations, something like Mozart writing *The Marriage of Figaro.* The Hendel salad (110AS) is the house specialty. Pasta dishes 75AS; steak 200AS; tacos 110AS; vegetarian dishes 80-88AS. Open Mon.-Sat. 10am-midnight.

Markets

SPAR Markt, Bichlstr. 22 (tel. 50 91), on the corner of Ehrengasse and Bichlstr. Open Mon.-Fri. 8am-6pm, Sat. 7:30am-1pm.

Billa Markt, Hammerschmiedstr. 3 (tel. 42 54), next to the Hotel Hummer. Open Mon.-Thurs. 7:30am-6:30pm, Fri. 7:30am-8pm, Sat. 7am-1pm.

Farmer's market, in front of the tourist office. On Wed., Fri., and Sat. mornings, several small stands sell meat, cheese, and produce.

SIGHTS AND ENTERTAINMENT

Set against the snow-capped mountains, the stark and somber church steeples of Kitzbühel dominate the diminutive skyline. The **Pfarrkirche** (parish church) and the **Liebfrauenkirche** (Church of Our Lady) lie in an ivy-enclosed courtyard on the holy hill, both surrounded by a beautiful cemetery. Between the churches stands the **Ölberg Chapel**, dating from 1450, with frescoes from the late 16th century. The town **fountain** in the Hinterstadt was built to mark the 700th anniversary of the town in 1971. The local **Heimatmuseum**, Hinterstadt 34, stocks its wares in Kitz's oldest house, which dates from the 12th century. Its three floors contain a rich collection of instruments both rustic and rusty, including prehistoric, European mining equipment and the first metal bobsled. (Open Mon.-Sat. 9am-noon. 30AS, with guest card 25AS, children 5AS.)

Few visitors remain at ground level for long; the Kitzbühel **ski area,** jovially dubbed "Ski Circus," is simply one of the best in the world. Site of the first ski championships in 1894, the range challenges skiers and hikers with an ever-ascending network of lifts, runs, and trails. These very mountains honed the childhood skills of Olympic great Toni Sailer; bow before you ascend. If you spot a skiing retinue, chances are good that they're chasing European royalty down the slopes—Princess Stephanie of Monaco is one of many regal vacationers. In January, Kitzbühel hosts the true *crème de la crème* during the **Hahnenkamm Ski Competition.** Held since 1931, the race is part of the annual World Cup. This is the best time to make it to Kitzbühel—the atmosphere is an electric 24-hour party for seven days straight. Entry tickets are available at the gate.

Amateurs, however, can also partake of Kitzbühel's skiing. A one-day ski pass (350-390AS, under 15 half-price) grants you free passage on 64 lifts and the shuttle buses that connect them. Lift ticket prices drop after the first day. All of the passes may be purchased at any of the following lifts: Hahnenkamm, Fleckalm, Hornbahn, Bichlahn, Gaisberg, Resterhöhe, and at the Kurhaus Aquarena (pool, sauna, solarium). You can **rent skis** from virtually any sports shop in the area. Try **Kitzsport Schlechter,** Josef-Heroldstr. 19 (tel. 43 73), or **Sport Pepi,** next door (also tel. 43 73). Downhill equipment rental runs 180-350AS per day; lessons cost 500AS per day. Ask at the tourist office about prefabricated **ski packages:** one week of lodging, ski passes, and instruction (available right before Christmas and after Easter). Rock-bottom for a week-long package without instruction is 3900AS.

An extensive network of 70 **hiking trails** snakes up the mountains surrounding Kitzbühel. Some of the best views are from the Kampenweg and Hochetzkogel trails. Most are accessible by Bichalm bus (26AS, with guest card 20AS), which leaves once per hour, 8am-5:10pm, from the Hahnenkamm parking lot. Get an English map *(Panoramakarte)* from the main tourist office. After ski season, ride the **Hahnenkammbahn** to reach some of the loftier paths (open daily 8am-5:30pm; 160AS, with guest card 140AS, children 80AS, dogs 25AS). You might also consider climbing up yourself (approx. 2hr. of varying terrain)—the descent is free on this and most other area cable cars. At the top are two cafeteria-style restaurants, as well as the small **Bergbahn Museum Hahnenkamm.** One floor is packed with historical information on the cable car and its founding. The best exhibits, however, are videoclips of past Hahnenkamm races, and a **larger-than-life skier** into which you insert 10AS and climb inside. Assume the tuck position, look through the viewer, and, for three minutes experience a breath-taking, virtual run down the Hahnenkamm (museum free). The **Kitzbüheler Hornbahn** lift ascends to the **Alpenblumengarten,** where more than 120 different types of Alpine flowers blossom each spring. If you're feeling healthy, the hike up takes about four hours. (Open late-May to mid-Oct; cable car ride 80AS per section; gondola 160AS, with guest card 140AS, children 80AS.) The smaller **Gaisberg, Resterhöhe,** and **Streiteck** lifts also run in the summer. A 3-day **summer holiday pass** is valid for unlimited use of all cable cars, free Bichalm bus service, and Aquarena pool entrance (340AS, children 170AS). Guest card holders can take advantage of the tourist office's *wunderbar* **mountain-hiking program.** The guided hikes

(2½-6hr.) cover more than 100 routes, with two offered daily: one easy and one more difficult. The guides (Pepi, Klaus and Madeleine) are friendly and knowledgable. On Thursday the hike is given in English. (June to mid–Oct. daily at 8:45am from the tourist office. Free, although you pay for any cable car rides). Free three-hour cycling tours are also available June through October on Mondays, Wednesdays, and Saturdays, leaving at 9:30am from the tourist office. Register one day in advance; a minimum of five people is necessary. Former Olympic and world ski champion, Ernst Hinterseer, leads hikes every Friday down the famous Streif downhill course (July 15-Sept. 15; 240AS, children 75AS). Trails for mountain biking also abound; rent a mountain bike from **Stanger Radsport,** Josef-Pirchlstr. 42 (tel. 25 49), for 250AS per day. A booklet detailing bike paths through the Kitzbüheler and other Alps is available at the tourist office (54AS).

The **Schwarzee** (black lake), 2.5km northwest of Kitzbühel, is famous for its healing mud packs. Remember when you made mud pies? This is better. The lake sits in the shadow of sharp cliffs and is a popular swimming spot. (Open daily 7am-8pm. Entrance 45AS, with guest card 40AS, children 12AS; half price after 1pm. Electric boats 80AS per ½hr., 150AS per 1hr., and rowboats 40AS per ½hr., 70AS per 1hr.) To get to the Schwarzee, follow directions to Camping Schwarzee.

Eclecticism reigns at the *gratis* music concerts during July and August; the repertoire runs the gamut from local, folk harpists to brass Sousa bands. Check for signs posted around town, or call the tourist office for the identity of the day's performers. (Every Tues. and Fri., weather permitting, in the center of town at 8:30pm. Also, Wed. at the Chamber of Commerce at 8pm. Tickets required.) **Casino Kitzbühel,** near the tourist office, opens July 8 to September 30 daily at 7pm. Go on, raise the stakes—you've got to finance that lift ticket for tomorrow (no cover; must be 18 or older; semi-formal dress). At the end of July, the **Austrian Open** Men's Tennis Championships come to town, frequently drawing athletes such as Michael Stich and Goran Ivanesivic to the Kitzbühel Tennis Club. Call 33 25 (fax 33 11) for information about tickets.

■ Kufstein

Dubbed the "pearl of Tirol" by its 15,000 inhabitants, beautiful Kufstein rests at the foot of the **Kaisergebirge** mountains just a few kilometers south of the German border. Like other towns in the Tirol, Kufstein offers the requisite spectacular view of snow-capped mountains, sweeping valleys, etc. But the town also sports its own nifty castle, which perches high atop a bluff in the center of Kufstein and lords over her subjects. Its extreme proximity to Bavaria makes Kufstein a prime target for German vacationers.

Practical Information Kufstein is a popular stopping point for vacationers traveling between Innsbruck or Salzburg and Munich. All routes have connections in **Wörgl;** from Wörgl to **Kufstein** (½hr., hourly, 34AS); from **Innsbruck** (112AS); from **Salzburg** (264AS).

Kufstein is neatly bisected by the Inn river, with nearly all of its tourist sites located on the picturesque eastern side. Before you cross that bridge, however, head for the town's **tourist office,** Münchnerstr. 2 (tel. 622 07; fax 614 55). From the train station, head straight out and walk toward the river; the office is on the left, right before the bridge. Staff can help track down accommodations and will provide information about city tours and hiking groups, but they do not make reservations. (Open mid-June to Sept. Mon.-Fri. 8:30am-12:30pm and 1:30-5:30pm, Sat. 9am-noon; Oct. to mid-June Mon.-Fri. 8:30am-12:30pm and 2-5pm, Sat. 9am-noon.) **Telephones** are at the train station, outside the tourist office, or to the right of the post office. The **Sparkasse,** Oberer Stadtplatz 1, across the street from the post office, cashes American Express traveler's cheques and changes money. (Open Mon.-Wed. 8am-noon and 2-4pm, Thurs. 8am-noon and 2-6pm, Fri. 8am-noon and 1-4pm.) A 24-hr. **ATM** is also located on Oberer Stadtplatz, across the street from the *Fußgängerzone.* The **train** station (tel. 69 21) has **luggage storage** (30AS per day) and rents **bikes** (90AS, with a train ticket for that day 50AS). They can also **exchange currency** until 8:30pm. For a **taxi,** either go to the train station, or call 696 90. **Emergencies: Medical:** tel. 122. **Fire:** tel. 144. **Police:** tel. 133. The main **post office** is located down the street to the left as you walk out of the train station (open Mon.-Fri. 8am-noon and 2-6pm). A branch with longer hours is at Oberer Stadtplatz. Go over the bridge and continue up the hill through the pedestrian zone, which empties into Oberer Stadtplatz; the post office is across the street, on the right (open Mon.-Fri. 7am-7pm, Sat. 7-11am). **Postal code:** A-6330. **Telephone code:** 05372.

Accommodations and Food

If you're traveling alone, make every effort to call ahead; cheap accommodations, especially singles, are hard to come by. The multitude of hotels in and around the city center cater to those who have other people carry their luggage; go and gawk at them, sigh regretfully, turn around, and walk back across the river. Most of the inexpensive pensions can be found across the railroad tracks. Check out the large rooms of **Haus Hauber,** Zellerstr. 33 (tel. 635 39). To find Haus Hauber use the overpass; head over the rail tracks and then turn right. At the first intersection turn right again; Haus Hauber is the yellow house on the left, just down the hill (150AS per person, 165AS with breakfast; showers included). Another inexpensive option, on the castle side of the river, is **Landhaus Zech,** Hochwachtstr. 29 (tel. 621 75). Cross the river, continue up the hill through the pedestrian zone, and take the first major right onto Kinkstr. Then take the fifth left onto the wide Mitterndorferstr. (at the sign for Hotel Alpen Rose). Continue bearing left along the quadrail, and take every left fork. Hochwachtstr. connects with Mitterndorferstr. after three or four blocks; turn right and Landhaus Zech is on your right. Spacious rooms with showers off the hall (50AS per night; breakfast included). Another option is **Gasthof Zellerhof,** Schluiferstr. 20 (tel. 624 15), on the train station side of the river. After the overpass, turn left immediately and continue until you reach the end of the small road. Make a right on Schluiferstr.; Gasthof Zellerhof is just across the two-lane road (270AS per person; breakfast included). **Camping Kufstein,** Salunerstr. 36 (tel. 636 89) lies right on the Inn river, with the castle in (distant) view. From the tourist office, cross the river and turn right immediately. Walk 15-20 minutes along the river, past where Schubertstr. crosses it. The campsite is visible from the river promenade, near Hotel Zum Bären (48AS, children 35AS, tents 33AS, cars 33AS, campers 58AS, showers 10AS).

Fortunately, most restaurants in Kufstein are reasonably priced and competitive with each other. Loiter around the pedestrian zone to survey the more popular eating establishments. At night, **Singer-Imbiß** opens up on Oberer Stadtplatz. They'll fry up a large *Schnitzel*-burger for 45AS, or a hamburger for 30AS (open daily 6pm-midnight). Specializing in Greek cuisine, **Kink-Café,** Kinkstr. 28 (tel. 616 57), on the castle side, has takeout and sit-down service. (Greek salad 70AS, Kebab with bread 45AS. Open Wed.-Mon. 10am-midnight.) Finally, the **Inntal Center,** an American-style shopping mall located at the intersection of Hans-Reichstr. and Feldgasse., houses the mother of all supermarkets, **Eurospar,** with twenty aisles of sundry goods (open Mon.-Fri. 8:30am-6:30pm, Sat. 8am-12:30pm).

Sights and Entertainment

You can't miss Kufstein's main attraction—the imposing **Festung** (castle), built in 1393. This behemoth structure, which rests on a gigantic rock foundation in the middle of the pedestrian zone, is the epicenter of activity in Kufstein, often serving as a concert arena for up-and-coming European rock groups or long-established classical ensembles. (Entrance to the castle is free; check posters for upcoming concerts.) It is also the home of the **Heldenorgel** (Hero's Organ), the largest open-air organ in the world. Built in 1931 to commemorate the fallen soldiers of World War I, the organ can be heard for miles around on a quiet day. You can listen as the 4607 heavy, metal pipes toot their stuff every day at noon; from June to mid-September there is an additional concert at 6pm. For a concert-like experience, pay the 10AS ticket price for a seat in the listening area, at the bottom of the

Festung where the acoustics are best. If you don't want to pay for a seat, but still want to hear some pipes, stay down in town—the overhanging eaves make the pipes almost inaudible from atop the castle. The pipes are also on display a few minutes before each concert. Climb the stairs that lead to the Festung and follow the signs to "Heldenorgel," or ride the *Festungslift* (elevator) up (20AS, round-trip 25AS). The castle is also the site of two other attractions, the **local museum** and the **planetarium** (tel. 650 50). The museum documents the illustrious 1200-year history of Kufstein, displaying objects ranging from prehistoric artifacts discovered in the Kaisergebirge to the imperial artifacts of Maximilian I (open 9am-5pm; 34AS). To see the museum you need to go on an hour-long tour of the castle (April-June and Aug.-Oct. 26, Tues.-Sun. at 9:30am, 11:30am, 1:30pm, 3pm and 4:30pm; July-Aug., daily every ½hr. 34AS, children 20AS). The planetarium features light shows and movies in the summer. (Open April 8-Oct. 29 Tues.-Sun. every 2hr.; 42AS.) A **guided tour** of the Festung is offered in German during the summer (April 1-Oct. 26 Tues.-Sun., every 1½hr.; 17.50AS).

During the summer, Kufstein is a popular point of origin for **hiking** expeditions in the Kaisergebirge. The tourist office heads three-hour tours into the wilderness each Thursday and Friday at 10am in the summer (free with guest card; you must call in advance). A chairlift, the "Wilder Kaiser," expedites hiking journeys by whisking you halfway up the mountainside (one-way100AS, children 40AS, round-trip 130AS; tickets available at the lifts). Though the lifts provide merely bunny-slope-style skiing in the winter, Kufstein is in close proximity to "Ski World," another Tirolean multi-mountain alpine ski resort extravaganza. A ski bus travels from Kufstein's tourist office to the slopes (free with guest card). Finally, don't miss the free open air concerts at Unterer Stadtplatz (June-Sept. Mon. at 7:45pm).

THE ZILLERTAL ALPS

The Zillertal Alps are a popular destination for Austrians who seek a weekend escape from camera-clicking foreign hordes. Keeping international tourism to a minimum; the Zillertal's residents have defiantly crafted a mountainside paradise for locals to relish. Transportation in the region is simple and convenient, thanks to the **Zillertalbahn** (better known by its nifty nickname, the **Z-bahn**), an efficient network of private buses and trains connecting all the villages (railpasses not valid; tel. (052) 244 24 58). This line would make the Swiss proud; it arrives late *at most* twice per year. The starting point is **Jenbach,** and the route's southern terminus is at **Mayrhofen** (round-trip 114AS); you can also reach Jenbach by train from Innsbruck (½hr.; 60AS; Eurail valid). The Z-bahn has two types of trains, the **Dampfzug** and the **Triebwagen.** The Dampfzug is an old, red steam train, targeted at tourists; it costs twice as much and moves half as fast. Less romantic is the Z-bahn's bus line, which runs through the towns. The Triebwagen and the Z-bahn Autobus each leave daily every hour 6am-8pm. (Zell am Ziller to Jenbach 47-106AS.)

In the Zillertal, skiing reigns supreme. If you plan to stay in the area for more than three days, the most economical alternative is the **Zillertal Super Skipass** (tel. 716 50), valid on all of the area's 151 lifts (4 days 1170AS, 7 days 1800AS, 10 days 2350AS). This includes the **Gletscherbahn,** which provides access to year-round skiing on the **Hintertux Gletscher** (glacier) (4 days 1410AS, 7 days 2225AS, 10 days 2960AS; children discounted 40%, under 18 discounted 20%). Passes are also available to ski four of six days, five of seven days, six of seven days, and 10 of 14 days. The cost of the lift ticket includes unlimited use of the Zillertalbahn transportation network. Passes can be purchased at any valley lift station.

The Zillertal Alps also have some of the most glorious **hiking** in western Austria— the region claims more footpaths than roads and more Alpine guides than policemen. The popular four out of six days **Z-Hiking Ticket** is valid on all lift stations in the Zillertal (including Zell am Ziller, Fügen, Mayrhofen, Gerlos, and Hintertux) and runs

(310AS, children ride free with the purchase of two regular tickets). Procure passes at any lift or at the railway stations in Zell am Ziller and Mayrhofen. When strolling around the mountain paths, be especially careful where you place your feet; whatever you do, don't dislodge any stones into the **Wetter See** (Weather Lake), under the shadow of Mount Gerlos. According to local lore, anyone who throws a rock into its waters will be pummeled by torrential thunderstorms, hail, and winds. Imagine what would happen if you threw garbage in!

■ Zell am Ziller

Twenty kilometers south of Jenbach and deep in the Ziller valley rests the quiet resort town of **Zell am Ziller.** Having billed itself as the "second smallest community in Tirol," it features neither gilt palaces nor Golden Arches, and is in many ways just another of the Zillertal's many ski villages—a few restaurants, some quaint cottages, and a cable car or two. However, thanks to the *Gauderfest*, and the Paragliding World Championships, it packs a bit more heat than your average alpine village. A monk laid the foundation stone for Zell am Ziller in the second half of the 8th century, but materialism soon took over the construction plans, as locals discovered that they could grow rich from the vast natural resources of the central Zillertal. However, gold mining and the other forms of exploitation that flourished from the 17th to the 19th centuries did little to tarnish the breathtaking, natural beauty of Ziller.

Orientation and Practical Information Zell is located at the south end of the Zillertal, between Jenbach and Mayrhofen (60AS by train to or from Jenbach). Private bus and train lines operate, so most railpasses are not valid in this region. The town **tourist office** is at Dorfplatz 3a (tel. 22 81; fax 22 81 80). From the rail station, head right along Bahnhofstr.; at the end, turn right on Dorfplatz. The office is on your left, just before the rail tracks (4min.). Pick up a town map, skiing information, and a *Frühstückspension* list if you want to track down a room on your own, although the staff will make reservations for free. Inquire here about weekly organized **hikes,** free with guest card. (Open July-Sept. Mon.-Fri. 8am-6pm, Sat. 9am-noon and 4-6pm; Oct.-Nov. and May-June Mon.-Fri. 8am-noon and 2-6pm; Dec.-April Mon.-Fri. 8am-noon and 2-6pm, Sat. 9am-noon and 4-6pm.) **Christophorus Reisen,** Bahnhofstr. (tel. 25 20), handles all **budget travel** concerns. **Exchange currency** at all banks and travel agencies; **banks** offer the best rates (open Mon.-Fri. 8am-noon and 2-5pm). **Raiffeisenbank** (tel. 22 15) stands across the street from the tourist office, with a 24-hr. electronic **ATM** outside; a **Sparkasse** and a **Volksbank** sit farther down the street. The **train depot** for the Zillertalbahn is at Bahnhofstr. 8 (tel. 22 11). Z-bahn trains leave hourly for Jenbach or Mayrhofen until 6pm. **Telephones** are available here; **buses** (Z-bahn buses and yellow Bundesbuses) leave from the front of the station. For a **taxi,** call 26 25, 23 45, or 22 55. In an **emergency,** call the **fire** department (tel. 22 12 or 122), **ambulance** (tel. 144), or the **police** (tel. 22 12 or 133). The **post office,** Unterdorf 2 (tel. 23 33), has **telephones** outside and **faxes** inside. When Bahnhofstr. intersects Dorfplatz, turn left. (Open Mon.-Fri. 8am-noon and 2-6pm, mid-Dec.-mid-March and July-Sept. Mon.-Fri. 8am-noon and 2-6pm, Sat. 9-11am.) **Postal code: A-6280. Telephone code: 05282.**

Accommodations and Food With two guest beds available for every resident, there's certainly no shortage of lodgings in Zell. The owner of **Haus Huditz,** Karl-Platzer-Weg 1 (tel. 22 28), provides beverages, conversation *(auf Deutsch),* and luscious down comforters. Spread yourself out in the huge rooms with terraces. From the tourist office, cross the rail tracks and continue onto Gerlosstr.; bear left onto Gaudergasse (at the *Mode Journal* building) and look for Karl-Platzer Weg on the left (10min.). Reception open daily 8am-noon and 1-10pm. In summer 190AS per person, 170AS additional nights; in winter 200AS per person. 7-min. shower tokens 15AS. Breakfast included. **Camping Hofer,** Gerlosstr. 33 (tel. 22 48), sports hot water showers, laundry machines, and free weekly hikes for campers, including a 3am sunrise hike. In summer, 50-55AS per person; in winter, 55-60AS. Guest tax 12AS.

When you stop for a bite to eat, savor some of the local specialties. *Zillertaler Kasrahmspätzln,* comprised of doughy noodles cooked with onions and garnished with cheese, is a plain but nevertheless enticing dish (80AS), served up deliciously by the **Gasthof Kirchenwirt** at Dorfplatz 18 (tel. 22 80; open daily 8am-2pm and 6pm-9pm). A traditional summer dish is the *Scheiterhaufen,* a monstrous mixture of rolls, apples, eggs, milk, lemon, cinnamon, sugar, butter, and raisins drizzled with rum. *Zillertaler Krapfen* are sweet, heavy doughnuts in every bakery. Not to be eaten before a long hike, however.

Dorfplatz is flanked by all sorts of red meat outlets. Check out the **Zeller Stuben,** Unterdorf 11 (tel. 22 71). Cheap food, including self-service half-chickens (80AS) and *gulaschsuppe* (35AS). The sit-down restaurant upstairs features 5 daily menus including soup, entrée, and dessert for 120-140AS. Childrens' and vegetarian menus are available (open daily 11am-9pm). Enjoy a pizza (80-150AS) at **Zellerhof,** Bahnhofstr. 3 (tel. 26 12; open daily noon-2pm and 5-10pm). Cap off dinner with a decadent visit to **Café-Konditorei Gredler,** Unterdorf 10 (tel. 24 89), where 1995 Confectioner of the Year, Tobias Gredler, whips up gorgeous desserts for you to enjoy on the café's riverside patio (strawberry torte, 30AS). From the tourist office, follow the railroad tracks in front of the brewery to find the **SPAR Markt** (open Mon.-Fri. 7:30am-noon and 2-6:30pm, Sat. 7:30am-1pm).

Skiing and Entertainment Zeller skiing comes in two packages: either the **Super Skipass** (for more than 3 days; see The Zillertal Alps, p. 397) or **day passes,** valid on the Kreuzjoch-Rosenalm and Gerlosstein-Sonnalm slopes. (1 day 340AS, children 205AS, 2 days 610AS, 3 days 860AS.) Single tickets are also available for non-skiers who tag along to watch. Obtain passes at the bottom of the **Kreuzjoch** (tel. 716 50), **Gerlosstein** (tel. 22 75), or **Ramsberg** (tel. 27 20) cable cars. The lifts run every 15 minutes and are all open daily 8:30am-4:30pm. **Summer skiing** is also possible at the **Hintertux Glacier,** 15 kilometers south of Zell am Ziller, accessible by Z-bahn and Bundesbus (one-day lift tickets 340AS, youth 280AS, children 205AS). **Ski rentals** are available at any of Zell's sporting goods stores; try **Sport Peudl,** Gerlosstr. 6 (tel. 22 87) or **Ski School Lechner,** Gerlosstr. 7 (tel. 31 64; open daily 8am-noon and 3-6pm). At both, skis cost 140-180AS per day and 600-690AS per week. For more information on area skiing, see The Zillertal Alps, p. 397.

Register in any town hotel or *Pension* to get a **guest card;** among other benefits, the card offers is a free **hike** led by the tourist office (June-Sept.; you must register one day in advance at the tourist office). The cheapest **bike rentals** can be found at **Sb-Markt Hofer** (tel. 22 20). 1 day 50AS, 3 days 120AS, 1 week 250AS; mountain bike 1 day 170AS, 3 days 410AS). Two of the three ski lifts in Zell's vicinity also offer **Alpine hiking:** the **Kreuzjochbahn** (open daily 8:30am-12:15pm and 1-4:45pm; round-trip 150AS, 100AS to the mid-station) and the **Gerlossteinbahn** (open daily 8:30am-12:20pm and 1-5:10pm; round-trip 100AS). Also try the **Grindlalmbahn** nearby (open 8am-8pm; round-trip 55AS). The **Paragliding World Championships** glide into Zell during the last week of June, when dozens of Icarus' modern day counterparts fill the skies. You can try too; tandem flights cost 700-900AS. The term "take-out" will take on a whole new meaning when you trust your life to the gliding guides at **Pizza-Air,** Zelbergeben 4 (tel. 22 89; fax 228 94).

The first Sunday in May brings the **Gauderfest** to Zell am Ziller, when the whole town gets sauced in a three-day celebration of cold, frothy beverages. The name is not derived from the German word "*Gaudi,*" meaning fun, but from the farmer's estate that owns the local private brewery. The *Bräumeister's* vats, Tirol's oldest, concoct the beloved and rather potent Gauderbock especially for the occasion. There is also a little rhyme for the festival: "*Gauderwürst und G'selchts mit Kraut, / hei, wia taut dös munden, / und 10 Halbe Bockbier drauf, / mehr braucht's nit zum G'sundsein!*" ("Gauder sausage and smoked pork with sauerkraut, / Hey, how good it tastes, / and 10 pints of beer to go with it, / what more could you need for your health!") It's in near-incomprehensible Austrian dialect, but fear not—pronunciation deteriorates throughout the evening of festivities, so by midnight you'll blend in just fine. The most important element of the festival is the **Ranggeln** (traditional wrestling) for the title of Hogmoar. There are also animal fights (attended by a veterinary surgeon) and customs such as the **Grasausläuten** (ringing the grass in order to wake it up and make it grow). Revelry continues into the night with Tirolean folk singing and dancing. By June, at least half of the residents are sober enough to court the tourist trade.

THE HOHE TAUERN NATIONAL PARK

The enormous **Hohe Tauern range** is part of the Austrian Central Alps, comprising parts of Carinthia, Salzburg, and Tirol. This range, spanning about 10 towns across the south of Austria, boasts 304 mountains over 3000 meters and 246 glaciers. The valleys were molded during the ice age, and are now partitioned by expanses of ice, snow, and massive alluvial cones, mountain pasture land, with alpine heaths of grass, and forested bulwarks helping to fend off erosion and avalanches. The region of rock and ice at the very heart of this alpine landscape remains largely unspoiled. Early this century the magnificence of the region prompted conservationists to lobby for the creation of a **national park.** In Salzburg and Carinthia, between 1958 and 1964, large tracts of mountain land were declared preserves. Finally, on October 21, 1971, the provincial government leaders of Carinthia, Salzburg, and Tirol signed an agreement at Heiligenblut to "conserve for present and future generations the Hohe Tauern as a particularly impressive and varied region of the Austrian Alps." Thus designated, the **Hohe Tauern National Park** became the largest national park in all of Europe. Officially enclosing 29 pre-existing towns with a total of 60,000 residents.The Glocknergruppe, forming the heart of the park, boasts the highest of the Hohe Tauern peaks, as well as glaciers with dazzling ice slopes. A number of lakes crowd together amidst the Glocknergruppe, including the Weißsee, the Tauernmoos See, the Grünsee, and the Stausee. The spectacular **Gloßglockner Straße** (Großglockner Road) runs north to south through this region, and the **Krimml Waterfall** is in the far west.

The Hohe Tauern are accessible by **car, bus,** and, in certain parts, **train.** Schnellstraße 167 runs north to south, intersecting Schnellstraße 168, which runs west to Krimml. If you drive, make sure your brakes work, as there are multiple blind spots. Any imperfection could cause you to plunge forever into a ravine. Shift your car to low gear, drive slowly, brake sporadically, and *never* pass anyone, even a turtle-paced coal truck. The federally-owned **BundesBus** travels down the main arteries flowing through the Hohe Tauern. Bus #3230 runs from Böckstein to Badgastein twice per hour, and bus #4094 runs from Zell am Ziller to Krimml five times per day. A rail line from Zell am See terminates at Krimml; trains run nine times per day in each direction. Another line runs south from Salzburg through Badgastein to Spittal an der Drau, with trains approximately every two hours. For general information about the park, contact Evidenzstelle des Nationalpark-Rates, Rauterplatz 1, 9971 Matrei i.O., (tel. (04875) 51 61 71; fax (04875) 51 61 20), or an area tourist office.

■ Großglockner Straße

The stunningly beautiful **Großglockner Straße** is deservedly one of Austria's most popular attractions. More than a million visitors annually brave the nausea-inducing trek to gaze and gawk at this veritable wonder. Skirting the country's loftiest mountains, Bundesstraße 107 winds for 50 kilometers amid silent Alpine valleys, meadows of *edelweiss,* tumbling waterfalls, and a staggering glacier. Conjure up all the superlatives you know—they won't begin to do the road justice. Many of the high-mountain-sweeping-panorama-hairpin-turn-sports-car commercials (and you thought German words were long) are filmed here. Switzerland and France used the Großglockner example when engineering their own mountain highways. Consider the Austrian work ethic that made it possible—in only five years (1930-35), during a global economic crisis, over 3000 workers constructed the Großglockner Straße, reducing in part the massive unemployment of the time.

The trip up to Edelweißspitze (the highest point of the Großglockner Straße) and then to Kaiser-Franz-Josephs-Höhe, takes you from the flora and fauna of Austria into the habitat of the Arctic. Although tours generally run between **Zell am See** or **Lienz** and the park at **Kaiser-Franz-Josefs-Höhe** (the midway point), the highway is officially only the 6.4km beginning at **Bruck an der Großglockner** and ending at **Heiligenblut.** Coming from Zell am See, you'll pass the **Alpine Nature Exhibit** (2300m elevation) on the way up to Kaiser-Franz-Josephs-Höhe. If you are on the earlier bus in prime season, you can get off here and take the next bus to the top, one hour later. Well designed nature exhibits, a 25-minute movie (in German), and less expensive souvenirs are some of the attractions (open daily; free; English headphones 20AS). At Franz-Josefs-Höhe, you can gaze on Austria's highest peak, the **Großglockner** (3797m), and ride the **Gletscherbahn** funicular (tel. 25 02 or 22 88) to Austria's longest glacier, **Pasterze Glacier** (mid-May to Oct. daily hourly from 9:30am-5pm; roundtrip 95AS, children 50AS). The **Gamsgrube Nature Trail** is a spectacular path along the glacier, culminating in the **Wasserfallwinkel** (2548m). The duration of the trip is 1½hr.—beware of patches of quicksand, unique to this part of the Alps.

The Großglockner Straße snakes through the **Hohe Tauern National Park.** Remember, the park was created to safeguard indigenous flora and fauna such as the stone pine, ibex, grouse, griffon vulture, and the ubiquitous marmot. Before starting out on a hike, check with park officials; all hikes in the area pose dangers, and some regions are strictly off-limits. Contact the **Regional Großglockner Association** (tel. (04824) 20 01 21) in Heiligenblut or the **Carinthian Park Center** (tel. (04825) 61 61), in a small town called Dollach, 10km from Heiligenblut (offices open Mon.-Fri. 9am-5pm). Another option is to hire a guide for hikes, rock and ice climbing, or ski touring. Pick up the brochures **Bergführer und Bergsteigerschulen** at any of the areas tourist offices. For information on sleeping in regional Alpine huts (open only mid-June to Sept.), contact **Edelweißhütte** (tel. (06545) 425); they also operate a road-side information kiosk by the Edelweißspitze.

TRANSPORT ON THE GROßGLOCKNER

Lienz and Zell am See are the two main gateways into the Großglockner. You can travel between the cities, switching buses at the road's midway point and main attraction, Kaiser-Franz-Josefs-Höhe, or, as most people choose, ride from one city to Kaiser-Franz-Josefs-Höhe and back. Either way total transport time (with scenic rest stops in between) will be at least five hours of intense self-discipline as you attempt to resist the urge to snap blurry photos through moving bus windows. Many visitors come here for weeks and feel much more refreshed dividing the five hours over several days. If you are only giving one day to the road, resist the urge to disembark at any of the cutesy villages along the way; buses come so infrequently that you'll be stuck in Nowhere for several lonely and boring hours. Furthermore, you'll take away from precious time that could better be spent at Kaiser-Franz-Josefs-Höhe. Try to choose a clear day—there's no need to pay the park entrance fee on a day when viewing conditions are utterly horrid. For drivers, the road is most easily traversed from June to September. Parking areas are strategically situated at various look-out points along the road, and traffic is banned from 10pm to 5am. Further, the road is closed entirely from November to April, when it is common for single snowfalls to accumulate 18m of snow. For information on the road's condition (in German) call the information office (tel. (04824) 2606), or try the Heiligenblut toll booth (tel. (04824) 2212) or Ferleiten toll booth (tel. (06546) 517).

Many visitors traverse the Großglockner Straße in a tour bus or rental car, neither of which are recommended for those with light pocketbooks or weak stomachs. The hairpin curves winding on narrow roads are simply dizzying, and driving through the mountains incurs a hefty 350AS toll. If you buy a day pass (400AS), you have access to the entire Hohe Tauern for the day and need not pay a return fare, so daytrippers should hang on to their receipts.

Wise budget travelers travel by **BundesBus.** Recognizing the incredible demand for a cheap method of traveling the Großglockner Straße, the federally-owned postal bus offers daily return trips from Zell am See or Lienz to Kaiser-Franz-Josefs-Höhe, sometimes accompanied by a pleasant narration, compliments of the bus driver. Watch in disbelief (and horror) as he (or she) dispenses educational facts about the Hohe Tauern (in German), and delivers and picks up mail along the road, all the while nonchalantly navigating the harrowing loops of the road.

Starting from the north, bus #3064 leaves Zell am See for Kaiser-Franz-Josefs-Höhe (226AS) from the main bus station behind the post office, swinging by the stop directly across from the train station. In 1996, one bus ran daily between June 16 and October 13, leaving Zell am See at 9:50am and leaving Franz-Josefs-Höhe at 2:45pm. In addition, another bus ran between July 6 and September 8, leaving Zell at 8:50am and Franz-Josefs-Höhe at 3:45pm. If you're traveling from the south, the odyssey begins with a bus from Lienz to Kaiser-Franz-Josefs-Höhe (round-trip 185AS; 2hr.15min. each way). In 1996, one bus ran up between June 16 and September 28, leaving Lienz at 7:45am, and two ran down, leaving Franz-Josefs-Höhe at 10:28am and 2:45pm. In addition, between July 6 and September 8, buses left Lienz at 10am and 11:25am, and Franz-Josefs-Höhe at 4:05pm.

Travel to and from Lienz may even be cheaper with the new 24-hour **Verkehrs Verbund Kärnten** card (80AS), which provides for unlimited train travel in one region of Carinthia. It is also valid on buses and will save you a bundle on the Großglockner, although you still have to pay the road entrance fee. Buy the red and yellow card at the Lienz train station; the driver can only give you the regular rate. Travel to the valley village of Heiligenblut is also advisable for stays in the Hohe Tauern. (Zell am See to Heiligenblut round-trip 135AS; Lienz to Heiligenblut round-trip 116AS, one-way 64AS, Heiligenblut to Franz-Josefs-Höhe round-trip 74AS.)

For anyone planning a lengthy stay in the area, BundesBus offers a **National Park Ticket** good for 10 days of unlimited travel between Lienz, Heiligenblut, Hochtor, and other stops in the region and reduced fares on cable cars and other sights. The bus to the Krimmler Wasserfälle (see p. 406), the Gletscherbahn in Kaprun, and the Schmittenhöhebahnen in Zell am See (see p. 405) are all fare game. (mid-June to mid-Oct.; 590AS, children 295AS.) For more details, the brochure *Der BundesBus ist WanderFreundlich* (available at the bus stations in Lienz and Zell am See and the tourist offices in Lienz and Heiligenblut) contains a schedule of bus departure times, destinations, maps, hiking paths, and general information.

▓ Zell am See

Surrounded by a ring of snow-capped mountains that collapse into a pale turquoise lake, Zell am See (pronounced "Tsell am Zay") is one of Europe's prettiest small towns and a fine base for exploring the Hohe Tauern National Park. There's really not much to *see* here, but you'll never get locals to admit that. They insist that the mountains are sights enough. Indeed, Zell am See's horizon is dominated by 30 "three-thousanders," that is, 30 peaks over 3000m tall. For *wanderlust*-filled tourists, the surrounding alpine terrain offers hiking and skiing challenges a-plenty, while the cool blue of the lake calls to those who desire summer rest and relaxation. With a reported two million guests coming every year, the town has seen a large increase in tourism since the year 748, when Zell was founded as a small monastery, or monks' "cell." While making merry in the water, raise your eyes and inhale the splendor of the Schmittenhöhe mountain just above or the 3203m Kitzsteinhorn to its southwest.

GETTING TO ZELL AM SEE

Zell am See lies at the intersection of Route 311 from the north and Route 168 from the west. It's also accessible by Route 107 from the south, which runs into Route 311 north. From Salzburg, take Route 21 south to 312 south; at Lofer, switch to 311 south to Zell. The **train station** (tel. 321 43 57) is at the intersection of Bahnhofstr. and Salzmannstr., on the waterfront. There are direct connections to **Innsbruck** (1½-2hr., 8 daily), **Vienna** (4hr.15min., 6 daily), and **Kitzbühel** (50min., 15 daily); further connections to international destinations can be made in Innsbruck or Salzburg. The **BundesBus station** is on the Postplatz, behind the post office and facing Gartenstr. Buses leave daily to Salzburg (118AS) and travel along the Großglockner Straße (buy tickets from the driver).

ORIENTATION AND PRACTICAL INFORMATION

Zell am See's relative proximity to the German border makes it a prime destination for international tourists. The town's accessibility to Salzburg and Innsbruck and its magnificent mountain slopes make it popular among Austrians, too. Zell am See's *Fußgängerzone* lies to the north of the train station, though most abandon it for the slopes during winter days.

Tourist office: Brucker Bundesstr. 1 (tel. 726 00; fax 20 32), within easy walking distance of the train station. From the station, take a right, bear left before the brick street onto Dr. Franz-Rehrl-Str., and then right onto Brucker Bundesstr. Look for the large green "i" immediately before the intersection with Mozartstr. A nifty computer displays and prints information on accommodations, events, and services in German or English, even when the office is closed (machine operates daily 8am-midnight). Though the extremely pleasant staff can't make reservations, they are more than happy to ferret out vacancies or overwhelm you with brochures. Open July to mid-Sept. and Christmas-Easter Mon.-Fri. 8am-6pm, Sat. 8am-noon and 4-6pm, Sun. 10am-noon; Easter-June and Sept.-Christmas Mon.-Fri. 8am-noon and 2-6pm, Sat. 8am-noon and 4-6pm, Sun. 10am-noon.

Telephones: Available at the post office or at Track 1 at the train station.

Taxis: Available at the train station, or by calling 27 22, 735 73, or 575 51.

Car Rental: Hertz, Postpl. 3 (tel. 41 16), through the Eurotours Travel Agency.

Automobile Clubs: ÖAMTC (Austrian Automobile and Touring Club), Loferer Bundesstr. (tel. 41 32). In case of a breakdown, dial 120.

Parking: Large public parking garage at the Kurcenter sport center, past the post office on the left.

Bike Rental: At the train station. 90AS per day, 50AS with Eurail Pass.

Luggage Storage: At the train station. 30AS for 24hr. in high-tech, electronic lockers; accommodations for both bags and skis.

Dry Cleaning: Phönix Reinigung, Schmittenstr. 6 (tel. 27 02), does expensive dry cleaning. Open Mon.-Fri. 8am-noon and 2-6pm, Sat. 8am-noon.

Hospital: Hospital Zell am See, on the northern end of the lake (tel. 36 31).

AIDS Hotline: AIDS-Hilfe Außenberatungsstelle Zell am See, Saalfenderstr. 14 (tel. 20 10). Hotline open Thurs. 5-7pm.

Emergencies: Mountain Rescue: Bergrettung Zell am See (tel. 84 97) or the police, Bruckner Bundesstr. (tel. 37 01).

Post Office: Postplatz 4 (tel. 37 91). **Exchanges currency** and traveler's checks at prime rates. Open early July to mid-Sept. Mon.-Fri. 7:30am-6:30pm, Sat. 7:30-11am; mid-Sept. to early July Mon.-Fri. 7:30am-6:30pm, Sat. 7:30-10am.

Postal Code: A-5700

Telephone Code: 06542

ACCOMMODATIONS AND CAMPING

Although Zell am See has more than its share of four-star hotels (and prices), the town has not forgotten the budget traveler. Many affordable accommodations roll out the red carpet for backpackers and other cost-conscious travelers. Wherever you stay, ask for a guest card to take advantage of town discounts.

Haus der Jugend (HI), Seespitzstr. 13 (tel. 551 71 or 571 85; fax 571 854), is an amazing, 4-yr.-old hostel on prime lakefront property. Exit the rear of the train station, turn right, and walk along the well-lit footpath beside the lake; at the end of the footpath, take a left onto Seespitzstr. (15min.). Large, immaculate rooms, each with shower, toilet, and a lakeside terrace. Other goodies include a TV room with VCR, a pinball machine, and a small snack shop in the reception area. Sometimes filled with screaming school groups, so reserve ahead. 106 beds divided into doubles, quads and 6-bed rooms. Throw down some plush carpet, hang a picture or two, and you'd be paying triple the price. Reception open daily 7-9am and 4-10pm. Check-out 9am. Lockout noon-4pm. Curfew 10pm. 170AS, each additional night 145AS. Over 25, 9.50AS tax per night in summer, 10.50AS in winter. Breakfast and sheets included. Lunch and dinner 60AS each. Lockers available for a 10AS refundable deposit. Key deposit 200AS. Open Dec.-Oct.

Pensione Sinilill (Andi's Inn), Thumersbacherstr. 65 (tel. 735 23), on the north shore of the lake, but you'll think you died and went to heaven. Call ahead and Andi will pick you up; or take the BundesBus (dir. Thumersbach Ort) to "Krankenhaus" (14AS, last bus 7:14pm). Turn left upon exiting, walk about 200m, and look for a *Zimmer Frei* sign on the left side of the street. Paradise for backpackers and road-weary travelers. Andi's swimming trophies, and stories, Joy's culinary and karaoke prowess, and the friendliest hound this side of the Großglockner provide an eminently homey atmosphere. 160-200AS per person. Camping in the front yard 50AS. Hallway shower. Lumberjackian breakfast and late-night conversation over beer or hot rum tea included.

Frühstückspension Annemarie, Gartenstr. 5 (tel. 28 51), a 5-min. walk from the lake. Follow the directions to the tourist office, continue along Brucker Bundesstr., and turn left onto Gartenstr. at the large parking sign. Spacious rooms, sweeping lawn, and an ideal location for skiers at the foot of the Zellerbahn lift. In summer 200AS; in winter 230-250AS. Showers and breakfast included.

Camping Seecamp, Thumersbacherstr. 34 (tel. 21 15, fax 21 15 15), in Zell am See/Prielau, just down the road from Pension Sinilill. This campground is the Ritz-Carlton of sites. Situated on the lakefront, they offer phones, a restaurant, a café with terrace, and even a small shopping market. Reception open 7am-noon and 2-10pm. 92AS per person, ages 2-15 45AS; tents 50AS, trailers 100-120AS. Showers included.

Camping Südufer, Seeuferstr. 196 (tel. 562 28, fax 56 22 84), accessible only by car, caravan, or motorcycle. A bit removed from the lake and almost opposite the town center. 61AS per person, ages 10-15 30AS, under 10 25AS, dogs 20AS; tents 40-65AS, cars 25AS, motorcycles 15AS, caravans 60-70AS. Electricity 8AS per kilowatt hour. Cable TV hook-up 20AS. Laundry facilities, small convenience store.

FOOD

Here in the Pinzgau region, food is prepared to sustain the farmers during their strenuous labors. Try the *Brezensuppe* (a clear soup with cheese cubes) as an appetizer, and then *Pinzgauer Kasnocken* (homemade noodles and cheese, topped with fried onions and chives). Top it all off with yummy *Lebkuchen Parfait* (spice cake parfait). *Blattlkrapfen* (deep-fried stuffed pancakes) and *Germnudeln* (noodles served with poppy seeds, butter, and sugar) have also survived generations of finicky eaters. The fat-saturated beer and deep-fried red meats that are the specialties here will keep you prostrate hours longer than you wish.

Ristorante Pizzeria Giuseppe, Kirchgasse (tel. 23 73), next to the *Bier Stad'l* in the *Fußgängerzone;* from the station walk past the church and continue straight. Plenty of options for the vegetarian. English menu. Pasta dishes 78-115AS; pizza: small 50-88AS, large 72-125AS; salads 55-89AS. Open daily 11:30am-2:30pm and 5-11pm. Major credit cards accepted.

Pizza Mann, Bruckner Bundesstr. 9 (tel. 473 57). "They serve Pizza, man!" (79-102AS). In May and June Thurs. and Fri. are a bargain travelers dream: all-you-can-eat pizza for 85AS (starting at 7pm). Also pasta 69-74AS and salads 30-60AS. Open daily 11am-midnight.

Crazy Restaurant, Bruckner Bundesstr. 10-12 (tel. 25 16-58; fax 25 16-55) serves Mexican and American foods. Very popular with young, English-speaking tourists. Buffalo wings 75AS; ribs 130AS; burritos 120AS; salads: small 55AS, large 85AS; and the must share with your date classic: "Breath-killer garlic bread" 30AS. Children's portions available. Open daily 6pm-midnight.

Fischrestaurant "Moby Dick," Kreuzgasse 16 (tel. 33 20), near the lakefront. Don't let the big one get away. Moby Dick offers a staggering double fishburger with potatoes and salad for only 75AS. Single fishburger 25AS. Even has a few entrées that feature fish straight from the lake (most entreés 85-105AS). Open Mon.-Fri. 8am-6pm, Sat. 8am-1pm.

Markets

SPAR Markt, Brucker Bundesstr. 4. Open Mon.-Fri. 8am-6:30pm, Sat. 7:30am-1pm.
Billa Markt, on Schulstr., near the Mozartstr. intersection. Open Mon.-Thurs. 7:30am-6:30pm, Fri. 7:30am-8pm, Sat. 7am-1pm.

SIGHTS

Zell is clustered in the valley of the clear blue **Zeller See.** Dip your toes in the lake at one of three beaches: **Strandbad Zell am See,** near the center of town (walk toward the lake down Franz-Josef-Str.), **Strandbad Seespitz,** by the Haus der Jugend, and **Thumersbacher Strandbad** on the eastern shore. (Open late May to early Sept.; 62AS, children 36AS.) **Boat tours** around the lake depart from and return to the Zell Esplanade, off Salzmannstr., along the river. Eight round trips leave on the hour or half-hour and last 40 minutes (daily 10am-5:30pm; admission 75AS, ages 6-14 40AS). One-way trips across leave every ½ hour. (June-Aug. 9am-7:45pm, Sept.-May 9am-6:10pm; 37AS, children 21AS). Purchase tickets on the boat. From the lake, the land rises swiftly into verdant peaks, crowned with a dusting of snow above the treeline. You can conquer these local mountains by riding one of the town's five **cable-cars.** Take the BundesBus (dir. Schmittenhöhebahn/Sonnenalmbahn Talstation; 19AS) to find the **Schmittenhöhebahn,** about two kilometers north of town on Schmittenstr. (Mid-May to late-Oct. daily 8:30am-5pm. One-way up 175AS, children 90AS; round-trip 220AS, with guest card 200AS, children 110AS.) The **Sonnenalmbahn,** which travels half the height, is adjacent to the Schmittenhöhebahn. It connects to the **Sonnkogelbahn,** which rises to 1834 meters. (Early June to early Oct. daily 9am-5pm. One-way up 95AS, with guest card 85AS, children 50AS; round-trip on either lift 120AS, with guest card 110AS, children 60AS. A combination ticket for both lifts sells for Schmittenhöhebahn fares.) The **Zeller Bergbahn** (780-1335m) is right in the center of town, at the intersection of Schmittenstr. and Gartenstr. (Early June to late Sept. daily 9am-5pm. Round-trip 135AS, with guest card 125AS, children 70AS; one-way up 105AS, with guest card 95AS, children 50AS.) Journey to the **Schüttdorf** suburb to find the **Areitbahn** (736-1370m; early June to late Sept. daily 9:15am-5pm; fares are the same as for the Zeller Bergbahn). In Kaprun, one town over and accessible by bus, the **Kitzsteinhorn** mountain (3203m) and its glacier offer year-round skiing. Between June 10 and October 18, a day pass costs 330AS, children 210AS. Skis, boots, and poles run 195AS per day, and are available at **Intersport Brundl** in the Alpine Center (tel. (06547) 862 13 60)

Skiing, of course, is not only limited to the summer. Every winter Zell am See inevitably transmogrifies into an Alpine ski resort. In the high season, lift tickets for the Schmittenhöhe area, as well as for the Kitzsteinhorn-Kaprun area, start at 400AS per day, 240AS for children. A bus connects the two areas (free with valid pass). For a report in German of the ski conditions in the Schmittenhöhe area call 36 94; for the Kitzsteinhorn-Kaprun area call (06547) 84 44.

The Zell area provides lots of opportunities to put those expensive hiking boots to work. The Schmittenhöhe lift alone provides five brochures (with English translations) detailing hikes ranging from the leisurely stroll to the self-torture variety. In the former, the Erlebnisweg Höhenpromenade can't be beat. It's a one-hour hike with a 115m elevation change, connecting the top stations of the Schmittenhöhe and Sonnkogel lifts. Seventeen displays on history, nature and ecology along the way exercise your mind. The brochure *Three Panorama Round Trips of the Schmittenhöhe,* available at any cable-car station, gives more light hiking options. Free guided hikes leave from the lower stations (July-Oct. Mon.-Fri.). Also, contact the **Schmittenhöhebahn Aktiengesellschaft** (tel. 36 91), or the lower station for more details. For longer hikes, pick up a *Wanderplan* or consider the *Pinzgauer Spaziergang,* a leisurely but very long 10 hour hike. The trail head is located at the upper terminal of the Schmittenhöhebahn; the trail is marked as *"Alpenvereinsweg"* number 19 or 719, and a brochure is available. There are free daily guided hikes and more challenging possibilities at the Kitzsteinhorn, as well as extended-stay hiking passes. For **rafting** (480AS), **canyoning** (520AS), **paragliding** (800AS), **climbing** (420AS), or **mountain bike** information, contact **Adventure Service,** Steinergasse 9 (tel. 35 25; fax 42 80). Back in town, a large **sports center,** the Kurcenter, has an indoor swimming pool, sauna, and solarium for cold, ugly days.

Finally, no visit to Zell would be complete without a glimpse of the toilet Franz Joseph used when he visited the Schmittenhöhe. This, and four floors of equally eclectic exhibits (the largest pike ever caught in the lake, old gingerbread-making utensils and hundreds of minerals) join the erstwhile royal throne in the entertaining **Heimatmuseum** (tel. 470 34) located in the Vogtturm (tower), Kreuzgasse 2. The tower itself is more than 1000 years old, and has cracks in the walls (now secured by steel retaining bars) due to the vibrations caused by cannon fire through the roof hatches. Zell's enemies of old, however, were probably unphased: the cannons were fired at oncoming thunderstorms, a practice that was believed to disperse the clouds. This continued until the science of meteorology reached Zell sometime in the mid-19th century (open Mon.-Fri. 1-5pm, rainy days 11am-5pm; 20AS, ages 6-18 10AS).

NIGHTLIFE

If all the exercise from skiing and hiking isn't enough, cut some serious rug at one of the local clubs. To really get hammered check out the local bar game, **Nageln,** in which drinkers compete to see who can drive a nail into a tree stump first, with the *sharp* end of a hammer.

Bierstad'l, Kirchengasse 1 (tel. 470 90). Thirty-three different brews in stock; you'll be on the floor by number nine. Dark beer enthusiasts must try the EKU 28, billed as the strongest beer in the world (.3L 83AS). Open daily 8pm-3am.

Crazy Daisy's, near the tourist office at Brucker Bundesstr. 10-12 (tel. 25 16 58; fax 25 16 55). A predominantly English-speaking crowd floods into Daisy's every day during happy hour for their 2-for-1 deal—order 1 beer, get another free. Open in summer daily 8pm-1am; in winter 4pm-1am; happy hour in summer 9-10pm; in winter 4-6pm.

Pinzgauer Diele, Kirchengasse 3 (tel. 21 64). Two bars and a small dance area, guaranteed to get you moving. A mostly under-25 crowd. Mixed drinks 50-95AS, beer 60-75AS. Cover 80AS. Open Wed.-Mon. 10am-3am.

■ Near Zell am See: Krimml

Amidst the splendor of Alpine crags and glades, Mother Nature cuts a truly extraordinary **waterfall** near Krimml, in southwest Austria. This superlative cascade doesn't unleash the monstrous energy of Niagara (though tourist officials say Krimml is becoming an increasingly popular honeymoon destination) or match the sheer height of Angel Falls—nevertheless, with three cascades, each falling up to 140m, it is the highest falls in Europe. Set in a beautiful, unspoiled forest, the surrounding wilderness and the stoic presence of the mountains make the **Krimmler Wasserfälle** a recommended stop on any tourist's route. The waterfall is part of the **Höhe Tauern National Park**.

You can reach Krimml, the waterfall's base town, by **train** or **bus;** trains come only from the east, through Zell am See (1½hr., 9 daily, round-trip 190AS), but many buses run from Zell am Ziller (round-trip 179AS). From Zell am Ziller, get off at the first bus stop in Krimml and follow the signs pointing to the falls. From Zell am See, take the train to "Krimml Bahnhof," cross the street to catch the bus (19AS) to "Mautstelle Ort," two stops away, and follow the signs to the falls. Another option is to **hike** the

3km from the train station to the falls; follow the signs on the footpath (admission 15AS) and stay on the left side of the brook; beware of stray cattle. Don't forget a raincoat and camera bag; the mist is very wet. The lowest major cascade is visible a few meters past the entrance booth and to the left, but the well maintained path will take you up into the forest along the falls with plenty of lookouts. The highest point is 1½ hours up.

The only significant attraction in Krimml is the waterfall, rendering the tourist office largely unnecessary. But if you insist, Krimml's main **tourist office** (tel. (06564) 239) is a short walk from the "Mautstelle Ort" bus stop. Head toward the church spire; the office is directly behind the church, adjacent to the **post office** (tourist office open Mon.-Fri. 9am-noon and 2:30-5pm). For English brochures and pamphlets about the falls, try the Österreichischer Alpenverein's **tourist information booth** located along the path to the falls (open daily 9am-noon and 2-6pm). This organization first built the path in 1900-1901 and, today, provides mounds of hiking information and maintains the benches sporadically situated along the route up to the falls. Munchies are available at the myriad **food stands** on the path, but prices are inflated. Stock up at the **Nah und Frisch** market between the bus stop and falls instead.

▓ Lienz

> **NOTE:** Lienz is distinct from Linz, which is in northeast Austria. Lienz is pronounced "LEE-ints"; Linz is known as Linz an der Donau. Make the distinction before boarding any trains.

Sandwiched between the bald, angry peaks of the Dolomites and the gentle, snowcapped summits of the Hohe Tauern mountains, Lienz is surprisingly captivating in its duality. Although the Alpine vista and the Austrian low-slung houses decked in pastel reds and yellows betray its Austrian heritage, there is something pungently Italian in its dusty cobblestone roads, hazy summer heat, and authentic pizzerias. Even the weather cooperates; the valley around Lienz registers about 2000 sunshine hours per year, making it one of Austria's sunniest regions. Perhaps Lienz has been so doubly blessed because of its pervading religious ethos—residents leave flowers and burn candles in front of the crucifixes at traffic intersections, and niches in building façades hold statues of the Virgin Mary.

GETTING TO LIENZ

Lienz lies at the conjunction of several highways: Route 108 from the northwest, 106 and 107 from the northeast, 100 from the west, and E66 from the east. **By car** from Salzburg, take Autobahn A10 south to 311, and just before Zell am See switch to 107 south to Lienz. From Innsbruck, take Autobahn A12 east to 169 south. At Zell am Ziller, switch to 165 east, and at Mittersill take 108 south to Lienz. However, it is somewhat more direct from Innsbruck to go through Italy. **Trains** arrive at the **Hauptbahnhof,** Bahnhofpl. (tel. 660 60). There are direct connections to points all over Austria, including **Klagenfurt** (1hr.40min., 3 daily, 216AS), **Innsbruck** (3-3½hr., 4 daily, 332AS), the **Vienna Südbahnhof** (6hr., 2 daily, 560AS), and **Villach** (1hr.15min., 1 daily, 168AS). There are indirect connections (most through Innsbruck or Vienna) to **Graz** (456AS), **Salzburg** (296AS), and **Zell am See** (186AS). The station is open daily 5am-11pm. **Buses** leave from the station in front of the *Hauptbahnhof* for destinations all over the region and throughout Austria. (Ticket window (tel. 670 67) open Mon.-Fri. 7:45-10am and 4-6:30pm, Sat. 7:45-10am.)

ORIENTATION AND PRACTICAL INFORMATION

Bordered in the south by the jagged Dolomites (the mountain range Austria shares with Italy and Slovenia), Lienz is the unofficial capital of **East Tirol** (Osttirol), a discontinuous portion of the Austrian province of Tirol. Lienz is approximately three

CENTRAL TIROL

hours by train from Innsbruck or Salzburg, but just 40 kilometers from the Italian border. The town is split by the **Isel River,** which feeds into the Drau.

Tourist Office: Tourismusverband, Europapl. (tel. 652 65; fax 65 26 52). From the train station, turn left onto Tirolerstr. and right onto Europapl. at the SPAR Markt (3min.). The courteous staff showers you with brochures, most with English translations, including a complete listing of private accommodations and prices, entitled *Lienzer Dolomiten Preisliste.* The booklet *Information für unsere Gäste* lists area restaurants, hotels, emergency and service numbers, and schedules and opening hours for local cultural events and museums. An electronic accommodations board, basic, brochures, and a room price list are outside after hours. Open July-Aug. and mid-Dec. to March Mon.-Fri. 8am-7pm, Sat. 9am-noon and 5-7pm, Sun. 10am-noon and 5-7pm; April–June and Sept. to mid-Dec. Mon.-Fri. 8am-noon and 2-6pm, Sat. 9am-noon.

Currency Exchange: Best rates are in the post office. Exchange desk open Mon.-Fri. 8am-noon and 2-5pm. Also at the train station.

Telephones: In the post office. There are also a number of phone booths across the street from the station.

Taxi: Call 654 50, 638 63, or 640 64.

Bike Rental: At the train station. 90AS per day, 50 AS with train ticket or Eurail. Mountain bikes 200AS.

Parking: Free parking at the Europaplatz, as well as lots across from the train station, on Tinderstr.

Automobile Association: OAMTC, Tirolerstr. (tel. 633 32).

Luggage Storage: At the train station. 30AS per piece per day. Lockers 30AS.

Hospital: Emanuel-von-Hibler-Str. (tel. 606). **Ambulance:** tel. 144 (also for water rescue).

Emergencies: Police: Hauptpl. 5 (tel. 63 15 50, 626 00 or 133). **Fire:** tel. 122. **Mountain Rescue:** tel. 140.

Post Office: Boznerpl. 1 (tel. 66 88), on the corner of Hauptpl. across from the train station. Open Mon.-Fri. 8am-8pm, Sat. 8-11am. **Postal Code:** A-9900 **Telephone Code:** 04852

ACCOMMODATIONS AND CAMPING

Although the Lienz Youth Hostel closed in 1993, the town still offers affordable accommodations, most just beyond the Hauptplatz and town center. Most *Pensionen* and *Privatzimmer* have rooms that cost between 250-300AS per person.

Gasthof Goldener Stern, Schweizergasse 40 (tel. 621 92). A renovated 13th-century mansion with low-vaulted ceilings, rope bannisters, old-fashioned lamps, and a smattering of antique furniture. From the train station, cross Tirolerstr., and bear left into Hauptpl. Walk through the square, veer right onto Muchargasse, through Neuerpl. when Muchargasse becomes Schweizergasse. The Gasthof will be on your right (10min.). July to mid-Sept. singles 240AS, with toilet and shower 350AS; doubles and triples 230AS per person, with toilet and shower 330AS per person. Mid-Sept. to June 10AS less per person. Showers 20AS. Breakfast included. Discounts for stays of 3 nights or more.

Frühstückpension Gretl, Schweizergasse 32 (tel. 621 06, fax 619 79). Right down the street from Goldener Stern in the large unmarked glass doors. Reception to the right. Offers similar facilities to Goldener Stern in slightly smaller rooms and without the historic setting, but all rooms have private toilet and shower. Lovely geraniums in summer. Reception open from 8am-8pm; after that, better luck down the street. 250AS per person for fewer than 4 nights. Ample breakfast included.

Egger, Alleestr. 33 (tel. 720 98). From the station, walk through the Hauptplatz, bear left on Rosengasse and then bear right when you reach the Il Gelato ice cream shop onto tree-lined residential Alleestr. Walk about 10 minutes down Alleestr. and it's the white house on your left. Large, well-lit rooms, and the owner, a warm, elderly woman, greets guests with open arms. 20min. from the station. 160-170AS per person. 10AS surcharge for stays of less than 3 nights. Generous breakfast and showers included.

Camping Falken, Eichholz 7 (tel. 640 22; fax 64 02 26). Located just across the Drau River near the foot of the Dolomites. From the station, make a left onto Tirolerstr. and a left at the Sport Hotel, pass through the tunnel, then over the Drau, and continue straight when the road splits. Follow the road as it curves left, and after passing the soccer and track facilities, head left down the small paved footpath, through the field. The campsite is just beyond the **Gasthof** of the same name. (15-20min. from station) July-Aug. and mid-Dec. to Mar., 60AS per person, under 15 45AS, 105AS per campsite. In the off-season 45-50AS, 30-35AS, and 90-95AS, respectively. People over 15 must pay 7AS tax per night. Showers, laundry facilities, and a small store. Reservations strongly recommended in July-Aug. Gate closed daily 10pm-7am.

FOOD

Calorie-laden delis, bakeries, butcher stores, and cafés lie in wait in the **Hauptplatz** and **Schweizergasse.**

Imbiße Köstl, Kreuzgasse 4 (tel. 620 12). Dynamo mother-daughter duo prepares the cheapest eats in town (19-49AS) in this diner-style restaurant. Chow down on the *Wienerschnitzel* (49AS), curry *Würstl* (27AS), or sully your fingers with the pastries on display (8-17AS). Eat in or take out. Open Mon.-Thurs. 7:30am-8pm, Fri. 7:30am-10pm., Sat. 7:30am-noon.

Pizzeria-Spaghetteria "Da Franco," Agydius Peggerstr. (tel. 699 69). To get to Franco's, head through Hauptpl. to Johannespl., turn left at Zwergerstr., and continue down the small alley. This relatively new enterprise is captained by Franco, a native Italian who decided to try to make it up north. Watch him through the window as he conjures up the best *gnocchi* you've ever tasted. Pizzas 65-110AS, smaller pizza or pasta portions 15AS less. Eight salads 40-105AS. Open in summer daily 11:30am-2:30pm and 6pm-midnight; in winter open Mon.-Sat. 11:30am-2pm and 5:30pm-midnight. Visa, MC, AmEx.

China Restaurant Sechuan, Beda-Webergasse 13 (tel. 651 22). Tasty entrées (most 75-85AS) and a 55AS lunch special with soup or spring roll (11 entrée choices) reward those willing to cross the River Isel. Beautiful porcelain soupspoons. Cross the bridge adjoining the Neuerpl., bear right in the gardens, and turn left onto Marcherstr. (3-5min.). The restaurant is on the left. Open daily 11:30am-2:30pm and 5:30-11:30pm.

Café Wha, Schweizergasse 3. Wha? Wha not? Younger, body-pierced, alternative crowd rocks and rolls way past the midnight hour. Strain your eyes through the smoke and check out the bizarre modern art hanging on the walls or venture into the back room for a game of pool. Beer 24-35AS, wine 21-25AS. Open daily 6pm-1am.

Markets

SPAR Markt, across Europapl. from the tourist office. Open Mon.-Fri. 7:30am-6:30pm, Sat. 7:30am-1pm.

ADEG Aktiv Markt, Südtirolerpl. Next to the tall pink Hotel Traube, and in Hauptpl. Open Mon.-Fri. 8am-6pm, Sat. 8am-noon.

Bauernmarkt (farmer's market), Marktpl. Farmers sell local produce. Sat. 8am-noon.

SIGHTS AND ENTERTAINMENT

Above Lienz, the **Schloß Bruck,** home of the **East Tirolean Regional Museum,** houses everything the town didn't have the heart to throw away, from Roman remains to carved Christmas *crèches*. This lonely castle was once the mighty fortress of the fearless counts of Gorz (circa 16th century) before it fell to the even more fearless Habsburgs. Inside the fortress, the **Kapelle zur Alterheiligsten Dreifaltigkeit** boasts surprisingly well-preserved (and less anatomically correct) frescoes dating from the 15th century. The **Rittersaal** (Knights' Hall) houses an incredible 34-square-meter tapestry comprised of 42 different squares tracking the life and death of Christ. The work of local *fin de siècle* painter **Albin Egger-Lienz** is accumulated in a gallery inside the Regional Museum. From the Hauptplatz walk 15 minutes down Muchargasse, Schweizergasse, and Schloßgasse, turn right onto Iseltalerstr., then take your first left and climb up the path to the castle. Alternatively, take the BundesBus from the train station (dir: "Matreier Tauernhaus" or "Lucknerhaus") to "Lienz Schloß Bruck Heimatmuseum" (19AS) or the free city bus to "schloßgasse." (Castle open mid-June to mid-Sept. daily 10am-6pm; mid-Sept. to Oct. and April to mid-June Tues.-Sun. 10am-5pm. 50AS, students, children and seniors 25AS.)

Across the river from the main part of town is the exquisite parish church of **St. Andrä,** which dominates Lienz from its lofty situation above the River Isel. The church was built around 1450 on Romanesque foundations; a porch and crypt from 1204 are still partly intact, as are the remains of an early Episcopal church. Look closely at the door handles—they're actually figures of saints. The church contains 14th-century murals and the elaborate marble tombs of the 16th-century counts of Gorz. A chapel memorializes citizens who died during the World Wars—Albin Egger-Lienz is also buried here. To visit St. Andrä, turn onto Beda-Weber-Gasse from Linker Iselweg, and make a left onto Patriasdorferstr.

For an easy-going introduction to the area's Alpine wonders, take the **Hochstein-bahnen** chairlift, from the base station near the castle at the intersection of Iseltaler-Str. and Schloßgasse, 1500 meters up to the **Sternalm.** (Lift runs late June to mid-Sept. Wed.-Sun. 8:45am-11:45pm and 1-5:15pm. Round-trip 100AS, children 50AS; family pass 200AS.) From the summit you can absorb the spectacular confrontation of the unforgiving Dolomites to the south and the gently rounded Hohe Tauern to the north. Also at the summit of the chairlift is the **Moosalm Children's Zoo,** with a complete menagerie of rabbits, goats, and ducks available for your petting pleasure (open daily 10am-5:30pm; free). The **Zettersfeld** chairlift provides access to hiking on the 1930-meter Zettersfeld peak. Take the free blue and white Stadtbus (July to mid-Sept.) from the train station to the last stop, "Zettersfeld Talstation." (Lift open late June to early Oct. Fri.-Tues. 9-11:45am and 1-4:45pm. Round-trip 120AS, children 60AS; family pass 250AS. A three-day cable car pass is available.) The **Dolomiten-Wanderbus** delivers nature lovers to another challenging hiking base, the **Lienzer Dolomitenhütte** (1620m). More than 40 trails of varying difficulty spiral off from this Alpine hut. (Buses leave from the right side of the train station (when facing the station) mid-June to late Sept. 8am, 1:10pm, and 4:30pm; one-way 75AS; round-trip 120AS.) For additional mountain hiking information, contact Lienz's chapter of the **Österreichischer Alpenverein,** Franz von Defreggerstr. 11 (tel. 489 32; open Mon., Wed., and Fri. 9am-noon). Eighteen huts are in the region.

Aquaphiles can also venture on the five-kilometer hike to the **Tristacher See,** a sparkling blue lake hugging the base of the Rauchkofel mountain. Ask at the tourist office for the brochures *Wandertips* and *Radtouren in der Ferienregion Lienzer Dolomiten* (Bike Tours in the Linzer Dolomites). Couch potatoes can enjoy the lake's facilities (25AS), by hopping on the free **Bäder- und Freizeitbus** (Bath- and Freetime-Bus) in front of the train station; disembark at the end station, "Parkhotel Tristacher-see" (bus runs daily July to early Sept).

Lienz also serves as an excellent base to attack the ski trails comprising the **Lienzer Dolomiten Complex.** During the high season (mid-Dec. to April), a one-day ski pass costs 290AS, seniors and youths 230AS, under 15 145AS. (Off-season 275AS, seniors and youths 220AS, under 15 145AS. Half-day tickets 230AS, seniors 185AS, under 15 115AS; off-season 220AS, seniors 175AS, under 15 115AS.) The **Skischule Lienzer Dolomiten** (tel. 656 90, fax 710 80) at the Zettersfeld lift offers hour-long private lessons at 410AS per person (190AS for each additional person). The four-hour daily skischool costs 440AS, and private snowboard lessons are also available. **Hans Moser und Sohn,** at the apex of the Zettersfeld lift (tel. 691 80 or 681 66), supplies **ski or snowboard rental;** a complete set of downhill equipment, here or elsewhere, will run 210AS per day, children half-price. For a **ski report** in German, dial 652 00.

During the second weekend of Aug., the sounds of alcohol-induced merriment reverberate off the daintily painted façades of Lienz's town buildings in celebration of the **Stadtfest** (admission to town center 50AS). The summer months also welcome the reaffirmation of Tirolean culture and heritage in a series of **Platzkonzerte.** Watch grandfathers dust off their old *Lederhosen* (leather pants) and perform the acclaimed shoe-slapping dance. (Free; consult the booklet *Informationen für unsere Gäste.*) On the third Sunday of January, the world's greatest male cross-country skiers gather in Lienz to compete in the 60 kilometers **Dolomitenlauf.**

Winter-phobic athletes have their turn on the second Saturday of Sept., when the competition to become the **Dolomitenmann** drives hundreds to engage in the bizarre tetrathalon consisting of *Berglauf* (mountain hiking), paragliding, kayaking, and mountain biking. Lienz also hosts mountain bike races in June, and snowboard competitions in winter (including the past World Championships in 1996). Free city tours (in German) leave the tourist office Mondays and Fridays at 10am. National park tours are offered in summer on Wed. and Thurs.

West Austria

West Austria

The western provinces of Tirol and Vorarlberg are to Austria as Bavaria is to Germany: a haven of tradition, a postcard icon, a tourist's fantasy of what Austria must be like. As you kick back in a mountain chalet with yodeling old folks in *Lederhosen,* it's hard to imagine Austria as an autocratic, aggressive empire or an unindicted co-conspirator in the Third Reich. Patriotic and particularist almost to a fault, **Tirol** (12,648 sq. km., pop. 630,358) is the most traditional and most beautiful of Austria's federal states. Catholicism is ubiquitous here; Madonnas, saintly icons, and Christ-figures appear on every roadside. Only 13% of the territory is inhabited, with most of the people gathered in the Inn valley. Tirol counts almost 600 peaks over 3000m as well as 169 ski schools to coax skiers down them. Five glacier regions offer year-round skiing as well.

Perched on the intersection of three nations, the residents of the **Vorarlberg** (1004 sq. mi., pop. 322,551), Austria's westernmost province, speak like the Swiss, eat like the Germans, and deem their land a world unto itself. From the tranquil Bodensee in the west, the country juts increasingly upward with each easterly move; at the boundary with Tirol, the Arlberg Alps form an obstacle only passable by the 10km Arlberg Tunnel. The unforgiving terrain that characterizes West Austria isn't hospitable to agriculture or manufacturing (except chocolate), so tourism is by far the leading industry. In fact, Tirol earns more foreign currency from tourism than any other province. The skiing in the region is perhaps the best in the world—we only say "perhaps" because we don't want to offend the Swiss.

■ Innsbruck

Although Innsbruck, rich with the cultural artifacts of emperors and queens past, harbors a lot of beautiful history in its roofs and historic gates, it is the mountains that will cause one's jaw to drop. They are everywhere, these white-haired, primordial giants. They rise above the town's Baroque façades and quiet cobblestones, conveniently shield it from northerly winds, and contribute to its mild climate. They also help, along with the more than one hundred and fifty cable cars and chairlifts and an extensive network of mountain paths, to garner Innsbruck, the capital of Tirol, enthusiastic thumbs up from passers-through, even the ones who just cleaned up Vienna and Salzburg. Many see it as the third member of the triumvirate, the provincial counterpart to Vienna's cultural and political dominance and Salzburg's musical notoriety. The city was officially founded in 1180, when a local count fancied that the River Inn would make a convenient plumbing system for his castle. Realizing a one-sided moat wasn't enough, he added on protective towers and bulwarks as appendages. Many people were drawn by this protection and the population soon sky rocketed. Innsbruck takes much pride in preserving its Baroque buildings, architectural reminders of a cultural past that was once graced by the Habsburgs. Of all the cities in his empire, Maximilian I thought Innsbruck the fairest of them all. Perhaps the Olympic search committees for the winter games in 1964 and 1976 thought so too, choosing Innsbruck as their location and thrusting the city into the international limelight. Though the gold, silver, and bronze hubbub has subsided, the mountain vistas rising from every angle are still enough to inspire awe.

GETTING TO INNSBRUCK

By car, Innsbruck can be reached from the east or west via Autobahn A12. From Vienna, take A1 west to Salzburg, and then A8 west to A12. From the south, take A13 north to A12 west. If coming from Germany or a smaller city to the north, take A95 (from Germany) to Route 2 east. **Flights** arrive and depart from **Flughafen Innsbruck,** Fürstenweg 180 (tel. 22 22). The airport is 4km from the town center. Bus F shuttles to and from the main train station every 20 minutes (21AS). **Austrian Airlines** and **Swissair,** Adamgasse 7a (tel. 58 29 85) have offices in Innsbruck. Austrian Airlines has daily flights from New York or Boston to Innsbruck, via Vienna (from US$800 roundtrip), and Swissair has daily flights from New York or Boston to Innsbruck via Zürich. (Also see **Essentials: Getting There,** p. 25.)

Trains leave from the **Hauptbahnhof** on Südtirolerpl. (tel. 17 17; open 7am-9pm). Buses A, D, E, F, J, K, R, S, and #3 all take you there. There are daily trains to **Ehrwald** (2hr., 2 daily), **Bregenz** (2hr.40min., 6 daily), **Salzburg** (3hr., 14 daily), **Vienna** (5hr.20min., 14 daily), **Graz** (6hr., 3 daily), **Basel** (5hr., 1 daily), **Zürich** (3hr.45min., 3 daily), **Munich** (1hr.50min., 18 daily), **Berlin** (12½hr., 2 daily, night trains), **Hamburg** (11hr., 4 daily), **Brussels** (12hr., 2 daily, night trains), **Paris** (11hr., 2 daily, night trains), and **Rome** (9hr., 2 daily). The station has **lockers** (48hr. 30AS) that fill quickly in summer, **luggage storage** (open July-Aug. 6:30am-midnight; Sept.-June 6:30am-10:30am; 30AS), **bike rental,** and **showers** (20AS). Two quick photo machines are also available. The **Westbahnhof** and **Bahnhof Hötting** are cargo stops. For connections to the rest of the Tirol, take a **post bus** from the station on Sterzingerstr., adjacent to the Hauptbahnhof (tel. 58 51 55; open Mon.-Sat. 7am-7pm, Sun. 8am-6pm for calls). For information, contact the **Postautodienst,** Eggerlienzstr. 130 (tel. 57 66 00).

ORIENTATION AND PRACTICAL INFORMATION

Most of Innsbruck lies on the eastern bank of the **River Inn.** Because of Innsbruck's compact size, nearly any two points lie within easy walking distance of each other, making public transportation largely unnecessary. **Maria-Theresien-Str.** is the main thoroughfare; constantly crowded with tourists and open-air cafés, this well-trafficked road runs north to south and offers perhaps the best view in the city of the surrounding mountains. Be advised, however, that only taxis, buses, and trams are actually allowed to drive on this street. To reach the **Altstadt** from the main train station, turn right and walk until you reach Museumstr., then turn left and walk for about 10 minutes. Or take trams #3 or 6, or city bus A, F or K from the train station to "Maria-Theresien-Str." Small starter maps of the city are available at the train station information booth, the *Jugendwarteraum,* or any tourist office. Continue down Museumstr. and toward the River Inn (following a straight course onto Burggraben, across Maria-Theresien-Str. and onto Marktgraben) to reach the **University district,** near Innrain. The university itself is a walk to the left down Innrain.

Tourist Offices

Innsbruck's myriad tourist offices seem to suffer from terminal confusion over who does what. In the end, they all accomplish pretty much the same services with equal competence and friendliness. If you don't have long to explore Innsbruck, a 2hr. city bus tour, including a walk through the *Altstadt* and visit to the ski jump, leaves from the train station (in summer noon and 2pm, in winter noon only; 160AS).

Jugendwarteraum, in the Hauptbahnhof near the lockers (tel. 58 63 62). Helps young travelers get directions, suggests hostels, and hands out free maps and skiing information. English spoken. Open Mon.-Fri. 11am-7pm, Sat. 10am-1pm. Closed July-Aug.

Innsbruck-Information, central office at Burggraben 3, on the edge of the *Altstadt* just off the end of Museumstr. (tel. 53 56; fax 53 56 14). **Branches** are located at the train station (tel. 58 37 66; open April-Oct. 8am-10pm, Nov.-March 9am-9pm) and major motor exits (on the Brennerautobahn, Inntalautobahn, and the road leading to Feldkirch and Zürich). The central office is huge and high-tech, with hundreds of brochures. These tourist offices are overseen by a private, profit-maximizing consortium of local hotels and are the place to arrange tours and concert tickets, but not the place to reserve budget accommodations. Staff is also happy to help bewildered tourists with questions on almost anything. Main branch open Mon.-Sat. 8am-7pm, Sun. and holidays 9am-6pm.

Österreichischer Alpenverein, Wilhelm-Greil-Str. 15 (tel. 595 47; fax 57 55 28). The Austrian Alpine Club's main office. Provides mountains of alpine hiking information, as well as discounts for alpine huts and hiking insurance. Membership in the club costs 460AS, ages 18-25 and over 60 300AS, under 18, 120AS. Club's services available to members only. Open Mon.-Fri. 9am-1pm and 2-5pm.

Tirol Information Office, Maria-Theresienstr. 55 (tel. 512 72 72; fax 512 72 72 7; e-mail tirol@tis.co.at; http://www.tis.co.at/tirol), dispenses excellent information on all of the Tirol, but is mostly for people planning trips in advance. Open Mon.-Fri. 8:30am-6pm.

Other Agencies

Budget Travel: Tiroler Landesreisebüro, on Wilhelm-Greil-Str. at Bozner Platz (tel. 598 85). Discounts on plane and bus tickets. Open Mon.-Fri. 9am-noon and 2-6pm. Visa, MC, AmEx.

Currency Exchange: Main post office and its main train station branch. Open daily 7:30am-8pm. Tourist office exchange (office on Burggraben) open daily 8am-7pm. Better rates at Innsbruck's banks open Mon.-Fri. 8am-noon and 2:30-4pm.

American Express: Brixnerstr. 3 (tel. 58 24 91). Take a right from the train station, and then your first left. Mail held. Address mail as follows: Mike PATTERSON, c/o American Express, Client Mail Service, Brixnerstr. 3, A-6020 Innsbruck, Austria. All banking services. Charges no commission to exchange its checks; small fee for cash. Open Mon.-Fri. 9am-5:30pm, Sat. 9am-noon.

Consulate: U.K. Matthias-Schmidtstr. 12 (tel. 58 83 20). Open Mon.-Fri. 9am-noon.

Telephones: At either post office, in the train station near the information office, and at the restaurant end of the large hall.

Transportation

Local Public Transportation: Buses run in circuits that split the city and surrounding areas into 3 zones. Single rides within 1 zone cost 21AS, 1-day tickets 30AS; both tickets are available from the driver, or from Innsbruck-Information. Week-long bus passes that are good from Monday to Monday (105AS) as well as 4-ride tickets (54AS) can be purchased at the Postautodienst, Eggerlienzstr. 130 (tel. 57 66 00) or from any *Tabak* store. The 4-ride ticket can be used by more than 1 person (e.g., 4 people for 1 ride or 4 rides for 1 person). An excellent city map detailing all the bus and tram routes along with a booklet with all departure times is available at Innsbruck-Information. Punch your ticket when you board the bus, and push the white button to tell the driver to stop at the next stop. Push it again to open the doors. From outside the bus, push the flashing green button on either

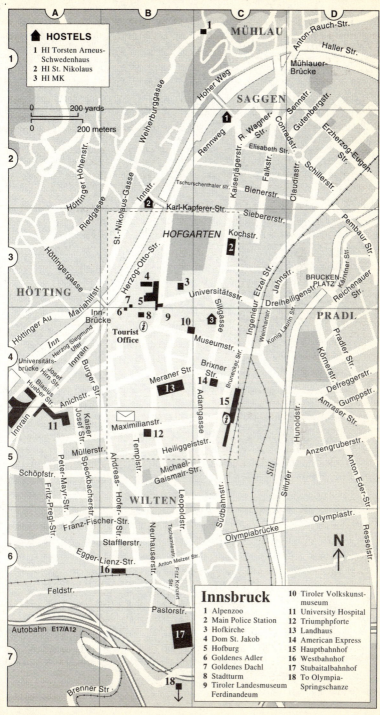

HOSTELS

1 HI Torsten Arneus-
   Schwedenhaus
2 HI St. Nikolaus
3 HI MK

0   200 yards

0   200 meters

MÜHLAU

SAGGEN

HOFGARTEN

HÖTTING

PRADL

BRUCKEN-
PLATZ

WILTEN

Tourist
Office

N

Innsbruck

1 Alpenzoo
2 Main Police Station
3 Hofkirche
4 Dom St. Jakob
5 Hofburg
6 Goldenes Adler
7 Goldenes Dachl
8 Stadtturm
9 Tiroler Landesmuseum
   Ferdinandeum
10 Tiroler Volkskunst-
   museum
11 University Hospital
12 Triumphpforte
13 Landhaus
14 American Express
15 Hauptbahnhof
16 Westbahnhof
17 Stubaitalbahnhof
18 To Olympia-
   Springschanze

WEST AUSTRIA

side of the doors. Most buses stop running between 10:30 and 11:30pm, but check each line for specifics.

Taxis: Innsbruck Funktaxi (tel. 53 11, 17 18 or 455 00). About 100AS from the airport to the *Altstadt,* dig?

Car Rental: ARAC, Amraserstr. 84 (tel. 34 31 61 or 34 31 62). **Avis,** Salurner Str. 15 (tel. 57 17 54). **Budget,** Leopoldstr. 54 (tel. 58 84 68; fax 58 45 80) or at the airport (tel. 28 71 81). **Europcar/Interrent,** Salurnerstr. 8 (tel. 58 20 60; fax 582 06 09). **Hertz,** Südtiroler Pl. 1 (tel. 58 09 01; fax 58 09 01 17).

Automobile Organizations: ARBÖ, (tel. 123). **ÖAMTC,** (tel. 120).

Hitchhiking: Hitchers reportedly go to the Shell gas station by the DEZ store off Geyrstr. near Amras, taking bus K to "Geyrstr."

Bike Rental: Main train station (tel. 503 53 85). Open April to early Nov. 90AS per day, 50AS per day with Eurail pass or train ticket from that day. For mountain bikes near the station (220AS per day), walk straight out onto Salurnerstr. and visit **Sport Neuner** at #5 (tel. 56 15 01). Or try **City Mountain bike rental,** Innstr. 95 (tel. 28 65 15).

Ski Rental: Skischule Innsbruck, Leopoldstr. 4 (tel. 58 23 10). Skis, boots, and poles with insurance (250AS). The same can be had in the nearby Stubai Valley at **Stubaier Gletscherbahn** (tel. (0522) 681 41) for 270AS.

Other Practical Information

Luggage storage: Baggage watch at the train station (July-Aug. open daily 6:30am-midnight., Nov.-June daily 6:30am-10:30pm; 30AS). **Lockers** are also available (30AS).

English Bookstores: Restock *Let's Go* at **Buchhandlung Tirolia,** Maria-Theresien-Str. 15 (tel. 596 11; fax 58 20 50). Open Mon.-Fri. 9am-6pm, Sat. 9am-12:30pm. Lots of hiking maps and travel literature at **Freytag-Berndt Buchhandlung und Landkartensortiment,** Wilhelm-Greil-Str. 15 (tel. 58 51 30 or 57 24 30). Open Mon.-Fri. 8:30am-12:30pm and 2-6pm, Sat. 9am-noon.

Library: Innsbruck Universität Bibliothek, Innrain 50, near the intersection with Blasius-Heuber-Str. Take bus O, R or F to "Klinik." Open Mon.-Fri. 9am-8pm, Sat. 9am-6pm.

Gay, Lesbian, and Bisexual Organizations: Homosexuelle Initiative Tirol, Innrain 100, A-6020 Innsbruck (tel. 56 24 03); **Frauenzentrum Innsbruck** (Women's Center), Liebeneggstr. 15, A-6020 Innsbruck (tel. 58 08 39).

Laundromat: Waltraud Hell, Amraserstr. 15 (tel. 34 13 67). Take a right out of the train station, a right after the post office, and head under the train tracks onto Amraserstr. Turn right, go over the river and continue for another two blocks. Hell is just past Gumppstr., on the left. Wash, dry, and contemplate Dante (small load 95AS, large load 106AS, soap included). If all the machines are full, the attendant will hold your stuff and heave it into the first available inferno for no charge. Open Mon.-Fri. 8am-6pm.

Public showers: At the train station, near the rest rooms (20AS).

Mountain guide information office: tel. 532 01 78. Open Mon.-Fri. 9am-noon.

Weather report: tel. 28 17 38.

Snow Report: Call **Tirol Information Office** (see above) at 532 01 70.

AIDS Hotline: AIDS-Hilfe Tirol, Bruneckerstr. 8, 6020 Innsbruck (tel. 56 36 21; fax 563 62 19). Information, counseling, support, and HIV testing. English spoken, anonymity assured.

Medical Assistance: University Hospital, Anichstr. 35 (tel. 50 40). **Ambulance Service,** Monte-Pianostr. 18 (tel. 26 77 55).

Emergencies: Police: tel. 133. Headquarters at Kaiserjägerstr. 8 (tel. 590 00). **Ambulance:** tel. 144 or 334 44. **Fire:** tel. 122. **Mountain rescue**: 140.

Post Office: Maximilianstr. 2 (tel. 500), down from the Triumph Arch. From the train station, walk straight onto Salurner Str.; after 2½ blocks, the street becomes Maximilianstr.; the post office is located close to the transition, on the corner of Fallmerayerstr. Open 24hr. Address **Poste Restante** to *Postlagernde Briefe,* Hauptpostamt, Maximilianstr. 2, A-6020 A-6010 Innsbruck. Branch next to the train station (tel. 59 93 40). Open Mon.-Sat. 7am-9pm, Sun. 9am-noon.

Telephone Code: 0512.

Central Innsbruck

1 Main Police Station
2 Kapuzinerkirche
3 Dom St. Jakob
4 Hofburg
5 Landestheater
6 Alte Universität
7 Tiroler Volkskunst-
   museum
8 Hofkirche
9 Goldenes Dachl
10 Goldenes Adler
11 Stadtturm
12 Tiroler Landesmuseum
   Ferdinandeum
13 Spitalkirche
14 Rathaus
15 Landhaus
16 Servitenkirche
17 American Express
18 Hauptbahnhof
19 Triumphpforte

0   100 yards
0   100 meters

N

HOFGARTEN

Inn

Herzog-Otto-Str.

Herrengasse

Rennweg

Kaiserjägerstr.

Badg.

Pfarrg.

Universitätsstr.

Hofg.

Herzog-Friedrich-Str.

Riesengasse

Kiebachgasse

Stiftgasse

Burggraben

Angerzellg.

Prof.-Franz-Mair-G.

Stillgasse

Schlosserg.

Klara-Pölt-Weg

Marktgraben

Museumstr.

Stainerstr.

Maria Theresien Str.

Sparkasse
Platz

Erlerstr.

Gilmstr.

Meinhardstr.

Anichstr.

Bozner
Platz

Brixner Str.

Fallmerayer Str.

Meraner Str.

Wilhelm Greil-Str.

Adamgasse

Südtiroler Platz

Landhaus
Platz

Salurner Str.

Welserg.

Sterzinger Str.

Maximilianstr.

Lieberstr.

Leopoldstr.

Heiliggeiststr.

Müllerstr.

WEST AUSTRIA

ACCOMMODATIONS AND CAMPING

Though there are 9000 beds available in Innsbruck and suburban Igls, inexpensive accommodations are scarce in June when only two hostels are open; book in advance if possible. Join **Club Innsbruck** by registering at any central Innsbruck accommodation for one or more nights. Membership provides you with discounts on museums, free bike tours, and ski bus service, and the option to participate in the club's fine hiking program (June-Sept.). Ask at the tourist office if your accommodation is included.

Hostels and Dormitories

Hostel Torsten Arneus-Schwedenhaus (HI), Rennweg 17b (tel. 58 58 14; fax 585 81 44), along the river. Take bus C from the station to the "Handelsakademie" stop, continuing in the direction of the bus, to the end and straight across Rennweg to the river, or walk right from the station, and make a left onto Museumstr. Take a right at the end of the street onto Burggraben and follow it under the arch and onto Rennweg (20min.). This 95-bed hostel offers convenient location and a front-yard view of the Inn River. The rooms hold 3-4 people with showers and bathrooms inside. Reception open daily 7:30-9am and 5-10pm, but during the summer weekdays the front desk is open all day to leave luggage. Lockout 9am-5pm. Curfew 11pm, but one can ask for a key. 120AS per person per night, shower included. Breakfast 7-8:30am (45AS). Dinner 60AS. Sheets 20AS. Reservations recommended, but only by postcard, not by phone. Open July-Aug.

Jugendherberge Innsbruck (HI), Reichenauer Str. 147 (tel. 34 61 79 or 34 61 80; fax 346 179 12). Take bus R for 6 stops and then bus O to "Jugendherberge," or follow the same directions as Jugendheim St. Paulus to get to Reichenauerstr. Tinted octagonal windows make the 178-bed hostel resemble an office building, and the English-speaking staff are as efficient and knowledgeable as any corporate secretaries. Three large lounges with hot plates, TV, and a small (German) library. Large turquoise lockers in the room to offset the green flowered quilts and orange and brown sheets the Partridge family left behind. **Innsbruck Studentenheim (HI),** at the same address, is an extension intended for groups. Reception open 7-10am and 5-10pm. Lockout 10am-5pm. Curfew 11pm, but quiet time begins at 10pm. Six-bed rooms 135AS. Four-bed rooms 165AS. Price drops considerably if you stay for more than one night: six-bed room 105AS and four-bed room 135AS. Nonmembers pay 40AS more. Singles 340AS. Doubles with shower 240AS per person. Breakfast (7-8am) and sheets included. Dinner available 6-8pm. Laundry facilities (45AS), but you must notify the desk by 5pm if you intend to do laundry (bring your own soap). Often crowded with Americans, but they'll honor phone reservations as long as you show up by 5pm. Extension open July 15-Aug. 31; main hostel open year-round.

Jugendheim St. Paulus (HI), Reichenauer Str. 72 (tel. 34 42 91). Take bus R or O to "Pauluskirche" or walk right from the main train station, turn right on Museumstr., and take the first left fork after the train tracks on König-Laurin-Str. When the street ends, make a right onto Dreiheiligenstr., which merges into Reichenauer Str. The hostel is just past St. Paul's Church on your right under the rainbow (25min.). Negatives: 54-bed facility divided into 5 rooms, nearby church bells, trough-like bathroom sinks. Positives: roses, a comfortable TV lounge, kitchen facilities, helpful staff, and the cheapest beds in town. You make the call. 3-night max. stay. Reception open 7-11am and 5-9pm. Lockout 11am-5pm. Curfew 11pm, but you can leave your passport for a key. 100AS per person. Showers included. Breakfast 30AS. Sheets 20AS. Open mid-June to mid-Aug.

Jugendherberge MK (HI), Sillgasse 8a (tel. 57 13 11; fax 53 46 99), near the main train station. From the station, walk right until you reach Museumstr. Turn left and then take your first right onto Sillgasse. This 105 bed hostel features a hip, friendly staff and a very social breakfast café. Drink coffee and bask in rolls, butter and jam while listening to U2 or Acid Jazz. Also beautiful basketball court, pingpong, and *Fußball*. Reception open 7-9am and 5pm-9pm. Lockout 9am-5pm. Curfew midnight. 150AS, nonmembers 160AS. Sheets 20AS. Showers and breakfast included. Open July-Sept. 15.

Technikerhaus, Fischnalerstr. 26 (tel. 28 21 10; fax 28 21 10 17). Though a bit far from the train station, this recently renovated student housing complex converts into a pleasant hostel during the summer months, conveniently located near the university district and the *Altstadt.* From the train station walk straight out Salurnerstr. to your first right, Maria-Theresien-Str.; then take your first left onto Anichstr. Walk over the bridge on Blasius-Hueber-Str., turn left on Fürstenweg, and finally another left onto Fischnalerstr. Or take bus R and disembark at "Unterbergerstraße/Technikerhaus." Restaurant and TV room. Breakfast room looks as if it came out of a Disney animator's sketchbook. Reception open 24hr. Singles, doubles and triples 235AS per person. Showers included. Breakfast 40AS. Reservations recommended. Open mid-July to Aug.

Internationales Studentenhaus, Rechengasse 7 (tel. 50 15 92 or 59 47 70; fax 501 15). From the station, walk straight out Salurnerstr. and right on Maria-Theresien-Str. Take the first left off Maria-Theresien-Str. onto Anichstr. Go down Anichstr. and then take a left onto Innrain. Pass the main university complex and take a right onto Rechengasse. Or take bus O, R or F to "Klinik" on Innrain and walk right on Rechengasse. Bus C to "Studentenheim" will also do the trick. A modern 560-bed dormitory with English-speaking staff. Parking available at several parking garages located a short distance away on Innrain. Reception open 7am-2am, but call in advance. Singles 260AS, with private shower 350AS. Doubles 440AS, with private shower 600AS. All-you-can-eat American buffet breakfast 70AS. Laundry facilities. Open July-Aug. Due to renovations prices in 1997 may be significantly higher. Call for more information.

Hotels and Pensionen

Haus Wolf, Dorfstr. 48 (tel. 58 40 88), in the suburb of Mutters. Take the Stubaitalbahn (STB) to "Birchfeld," and walk down Dorfstr. in the direction the tram continues. (The STB stop is on the third traffic island in front of the train station, 25AS, week-long ticket 85AS. Last STB at 10:30pm. Tickets available from the driver.) Unload your pack, take in the amazing view, bask in the maternal comfort, and eat, eat, eat at breakfast; there's no place like home, but this fabulous place comes close. Let the proprietress Titti Wolf spoil you in her Alpen paradise. The tram ride up is 30min. of scenic bliss; the beds are at least 8 hours of heaven. Singles, doubles, and triples 190AS per person. Breakfast and shower included.

Haus Kaltenberger, Schulgasse 15 (tel. 57 55 47), just down the road from Haus Wolf in Mutters. Take the STB to "Mutters," walk toward the church, turn right on Dorfstr. and take the first left onto Schulgasse. Gorgeous mountains out the front door, homemade strawberry jam, and a guest register full of satisfied comments. 180AS per person. Breakfast and showers included.

Haus Rimml, Harterhofweg 82 (tel. 28 47 26), a 20min. bus ride from the train station. Follow directions to Camping Innsbruck Kranebitten below, but walk downhill and turn left. Consummately comfortable—private showers, knickknacks galore, and large singles. Jolly owners have breakfast waiting. 250AS per person, with private shower 300AS. Breakfast included. Call ahead. Open Dec.-Oct.

Pension Paula, Weiherburggasse 15 (tel. 29 22 62). Satisfied guests frequently return to this inn-like home down the hill from the Alpenzoo. Take bus K from the Hauptbahnhof to "St. Nikolaus," and then walk uphill. Fantastic views of the river and city center. Singles 320AS, with private shower 420AS. Doubles 520AS, with private shower 600AS, with private shower and bathroom 640AS. Breakfast included. Reservations recommended—it is almost always full.

Camping

Camping Innsbruck Kranebitten, Kranebitter Allee 214 (tel. 28 41 80). From the main train station, take bus LK at Bozner Pl. to the stop "Klammstr." If bus LK eludes you, take bus F, R or O to "Klinik," and switch to the LK there. Reception open July-Aug. 7am-9pm; April-June and Sept.-Oct. 7am-noon. If reception is closed, find a site and check in the next morning. 60AS, children under 15 45AS. Tent 40AS. Car 45AS. Tax 6AS. Shower included. Washing machines available.

WEST AUSTRIA

FOOD

Most tourists first glimpse cosmopolitan Innsbruck from the glamour of **Maria-Ther-esien-Str.** Rather than gawk at the overpriced delis and *Konditoreien,* escape the *Alt-stadt* and its accompanying local profiteers. Cross the river to Innstr., in the university district, and uncover a myriad of ethnic restaurants, low-priced *Schnitzel Stuben,* and Turkish grocers.

Al Dente, Meranestr. 7 (tel. 58 49 47). Snug place with smooth, stylish wood, can-dlelight, salad bar, and delicious pasta. After finishing your entrée (82-138AS), pol-ish your meal off with yummy *tiramisú* (46AS). Plenty of vegetarian options. English menus. Open Mon.-Sat. 7am-11pm, Sun. and holidays 11am-11pm. Visa, MC, AmEx, Diners Club.

Philippine Vegetarische Küche, Müllerstr. 9 (tel. 58 91 57), at Lieberstr., one block from the post office. A vegetarian rest stop on a highway of meat, this whimsically decorated two-floor restaurant serves up some of the best food in carnivorous Inns-bruck. Zucchini cream soup or carrot-lemon juice, as well as typical tofu and tor-tellini (82-138AS). Daily special 45-98AS. Mid-day meals including soup and entrée 75AS. Open Mon.-Sat. 10am-11pm. Visa, MC.

Churrasco la Mamma, Innrain 2 (tel. 58 63 98). Outdoor seating next to the river—watch the moon rise, fall in love, but before you do, remember to eat. Pasta 84-116AS. Brick oven pizza 68-118AS. Open daily 9am-midnight.

Crocodiles, Maria-Theresien-Str. 49 (tel. 58 88 56). This tiny restaurant, located off of Maria-Theresien-Str. on the right side of Intersport Okay, serves up 33 different types of pizza, including 7 vegetarian options, from its old-fashioned brick oven. English menus and a "croco-crew" of waiters available to help you decide. Large pizzas 55-85AS. Open Mon.-Fri. 10am-10pm, Sat. 10am-2pm.

Baguette, Maria-Theresien-Str. 57, conveniently located in front of the *Triumphpforte* just down the road from the post office. This air-conditioned cor-ner café, serves up fresh bread, pizza, and cheese-covered baguettes. Exotic drinks for 17-21AS. Small salads 13AS, sandwiches 25-35AS. Open Mon.-Fri. 7am-6:30pm, Sat. 9am-12:30pm. The branch at Innrain 31 opens at 7:30am on Sat.

Gasthof Weißes Lamm, Mariahilfstr. 12 (tel. 28 31 56). Home-style, Tirolian restau-rant, popular with local crowd. 100AS can go a long way with their heaping por-tions and special menus (soup, entrée, and salad 80-115AS). Other entrées 100-200AS. Open Mon.-Wed. and Fri.-Sun. 11:30am-2pm and 6-10pm.

Salute Pizzeria, Innrain 35 (tel. 58 58 18). Popular student hangout located down the street from the university. Small pizzas (35-80AS), large (50-100AS), Pasta (55-75AS), and salads (35-55AS). Open daily 11am-midnight.

University Mensa, Herzog-Siegmund-Ufer 15 (tel. 58 43 75), on the 2nd floor of the new university at Blasius-Hueber-Str. near the bridge. Student cafeteria open to the public. No student ID necessary. Meals 47-60AS. Open in summer Mon.-Fri. 11am-1:30pm; in winter, 11am-2pm.

Markets

Innsbruck has many small supermarkets, generally open Monday through Friday and Saturday morning.

M-Preis Supermarket, with the lowest prices around. Branch on the corner of Reichenauer Str. and Andechstr. Another branch on the corner of Salurner Str., near the rail station, and at Innrain 15. Open Mon.-Fri. 8am-6:30pm, Sat. 7:30am-1pm.

Indoor Farmer's Market, in the *Markthalle* on the corner of Innrain and Marktgra-ben, right behind the *Altstadt* (look for the spinning apple). Stands selling the four food groups, gorgeous flowers, and much, much more. Open Mon.-Sat. 7am-1pm.

SIGHTS

The **Goldenes Dachl** (Little Golden Roof), on Herzog Friedrichstr., smack in the mid-dle of the Altstadt, serves as the city's center and is its most potent symbol. It's not much of a roof really; it's more of an ostentatious balcony cover, built to commemorate the marriage of the Habsburg couple Maximilian I and Bianca, the great-great-great-great-great-great grandparents of Maria Theresa. Beneath the 2657 shimmery gold shingles, Max and his precious wife would cheer their minion of jousters and dancers of yore in the square below. Today, representations of the roof grace post-cards, parking signs, and even lingerie displays. Inside the building, the new **Maximilianeum,** serves as a memorial to Innsbruck's favorite ruler. (Open daily 10am-6pm; 60AS, students 30AS, seniors 50AS, family pass 120AS.) The structure behind the Goldenes Dachl used to be a royal palace, but was reconstructed in the 19th century to house the city government.

The Goldenes Dachl sits amid a number of splendid 15th- and 16th-century buildings. To the left, the façade of the **Helblinghaus,** a 15th-century Gothic town residence, is flushed salmon pink and blanketed with 18th-century baroque floral stucco. Climb the 168 narrow stairs of the 15th-century **Stadtturm** (city tower), across from the Helblinghaus, to soak in the panoramic view. Look up before you climb—on a clear, sunny day, space in the tower can be tighter than a pair of Jordache jeans and even harder to walk around in. (Open daily 10am-5pm; July-Aug. 10am-6pm. 22AS, children 11AS.) The 15th-century **Goldener Adler Inn** (Golden Eagle Inn) is a few buildings to the left of the Goldenes Dachl. The plaque on the wall reads like your high school textbook: Goethe, Heine, Sartre, Mozart, Wagner, Camus, and even Maximilian I ate, drank, and made merry here. A block behind the Goldenes Dachl, look for the twin towers of the baroque **Dom St. Jakob** (built between 1717-1724) with its superb *trompe l'oeil* ceiling by C. D. Asam depicting the life of St. James, and an altar decorated with Lukas Cranach's *Intercession of the Virgin.* Much of the church was destroyed in a 1944 air raid, but renovations through 1993 restored the finely molded stucco to its original lovely light pink. (Open 8am-6:30pm; April-Sept. 8am-7:30pm. Free.)

The influence of the Habsburgs is obvious at the intersection of Rennweg and Hofgasse where the grand **Hofburg** (Imperial Palace), **Hofkirche** (Imperial Church) and **Hofgarten** (Imperial Garden) converge. Built between the 16th and 18th centuries, the Hofburg brims with the trappings of the old dynasty. Empress Maria Theresa plumply rules over nearly every room, and a portrait of Maria's youngest daughter, Marie Antoinette (with head) shines over the palace's main banquet hall. Enjoy the delicate furniture and grand rooms on your rococo wanderings. A leisurely wander takes about half an hour. (Open Tues.-Sun. 9am-noon and 1-5pm; Nov.-April Tues.-Sat. 10am-noon and 1-5pm. Last entrance 4:30pm. 55AS, students 35AS, children 10AS. English guidebook 25AS.) The Hofkirche holds an intricate sarcophagus, decorated with scenes from Maximilian I's life as well as the **Kaisergrab,** twenty-eight larger-than-life bronze statues standing guard lest anyone try to "grab" the Kaiser. The statues of King Arthur, Theodoric the Ostrogoth, and Count Albrecht of Habsburg were designed by Dürer. Max isn't here, however, though that is hardly the emphasis of the guidebooks. The monument was never completed to his specifications, and he was buried outside of Vienna. The Silver Chapel, off the main church, is, however, the final resting place of Emperor Ferdinand II. (Open daily 9am-5pm; July-Aug. 9am-5:30pm. 20AS, students 14AS, children 10AS.)

A combi-ticket (50AS, students 39AS, children 25AS) will also admit you to the collection of the **Tiroler Volkskunstmuseum** (Tirolean Handicrafts Museum) in the same building. Built between 1553 and 1563 as the "New Abbey," the building was converted into a school in 1785 and has served as a museum since 1929. Dusty implements, peasant costumes, and furnished period rooms provide a brief introduction to Tirolean culture. See how the Tiroleans worked, dressed, fell asleep, moved dirt, and carried things. (Open Mon.-Sat. 9am-5pm, Sun. 9am-noon; July-Aug. Mon.-Sat. 9am-5:30pm. Museum alone 40AS, students 25AS, children 15AS.) The nearby **Hofgarten** is a beautifully groomed, shaded picnic spot by day, complete with ponds, gorgeous flowers, and a concert pavilion. The knee-high chess set in the middle of the park adds a physical dimension to the cerebral game. ("Whew, that's heavy—check!") A butterfly house is open in the park June to September.

The collection of the **Tiroler Landesmuseum Ferdinandeum,** Museumstr. 15, several blocks from the *Hauptbahnhof,* includes exquisitely colored, delicately etched stained-glass windows, several outstanding medieval altars and paintings, plus works by several eminent Tiroleans and a small selection of others (Schiele, Klimt, and a tiny Rembrandt). (Open May-Sept. daily 10am-5pm and Thurs. 7-9pm; Oct.-April Tues.-Sat. 10am-noon and 2-5pm, Sun. 10am-1pm. 50AS, students 30AS.)

A block or two up Rennweg from the Schwedenhaus youth hostel, the Battle of Bergisel is brilliantly portrayed in over 1000 square meters of 360° carnage in the **Rundgemälde** (panoramic painting; open April-Oct. daily 9am-4:45pm; 26AS). Backtrack a bit, cross the covered bridge over the Inn, and follow the signs up to the **Alpenzoo** (tel. 29 23 23), the loftiest zoo in Europe, with every vertebrate species indigenous to the Alps. When you've had your fill of high-altitude baby boars, descend on the network of scenic trails that weave across the hillside. If you'd rather ride to the zoo, catch tram #1 or 4 or bus C, D or E to "Hungerburg Funicular Railway" and take the cable car up the mountain. (Zoo open in summer daily 9am-6pm; in winter 9am-5pm. 60AS, students 30AS.)

Back in town, a stroll along **Maria-Theresien-Straße** with the baroque grandeur of its pink and yellow houses gives a clear view of the snow-capped mountains of the *Nordkette* (Northern range). The beginning of the street is marked by the **Triumphpforte** (Triumphal Arch) built in 1765 to commemorate the betrothal of Emperor Leopold II. The rectilinear, colonnaded façade of #43 marks the Neoclassical **Altes Landhaus,** built between 1725 and 1728 by G.A. Gumpp. Farther down, the **Annasäule** (Anna Column), erected between 1704 and 1706 by the provincial legislature, commemorates the Tiroleans' victory after an unsuccessful Bavarian invasion during the War of Spanish Succession. Don't miss the view of the Alps from this point. The 17th-century **Palais Troyer-Spaur** and the **Palais Trapp-Wolkenstein** opposite it are also on this street. Under the balcony of the latter, you can spot the coat of arms of the von Trapp family, of *Sound of Music* fame.

Grassmayr Bell-Foundry (tel. 594 16) is run by the Grassmayr family who has been crafting bells for 14 generations. Church bells take two months, but they'll make small ones for tourists. Watch ore being smelted. ("Holy Hot Metal, Batman!" Open Mon.-Fri. 9am-6pm, Sat. 9am-noon.) **Basilika Wilten** and **Stiftskirche Wilten,** across from the Railway Museum, are beautiful Rococo and Baroque churches, respectively. Other museums in the area, including the **Kaiserschützen** and the **Bergisel,** exhibit enough old military equipment to fend off legions of tourists. (Why do they call it tourist season if we can't shoot 'em?) The **University of Innsbruck** lies behind the *Altstadt,* down the river on Innrain.

Outside the city proper, Archduke Ferdinand of Tirol left a stash of 16th-century armor and artwork (including pieces by such masters as Velazquez and Titian) at **Schloß Ambras.** The medieval castle was a royal hunting lodge between the 11th and 15th centuries but was rebuilt by Ferdinand into one of the most beautiful Renaissance castles and gardens in Austria. A portrait gallery with detailed historical accounts depicts European dynasties from the 14th to the 19th centuries. To reach the palace, take streetcar #6 (dir: "Igls") to "Schloß Ambras," and follow the signs (open April-Oct. Mon. and Wed.-Sun. 10am-5pm; Dec. 27-March 31 guided tours from 2-3:30pm. 60AS, children and students 30AS). Feel queasy thinking of all the daredevils who have propelled themselves over the **Olympische Skischanze** (Olympic Ski Jump) in Bergisel. Take streetcar #1, 6, or the STB to "Bergisel." From their vantage point, the brave Olympians stared out over Innsbruck and, in particular, at a graveyard located right under the hill from the stadium. It was clear where a bad landing would lead. Further down the *Brennerautobahn* (motorway) spanning the Sil River is the tallest bridge on the continent, the 2330ft high **Europabrücke.**

OUTDOORS INNSBRUCK

A **Club Innsbruck** membership (see Accommodations, p. 418) lets you in on one of the best deals in all Austria. The club's excellent mountain **hiking** program provides guides, transportation, and equipment (including boots) absolutely free to hikers of all ages and experience levels. Participants assemble in front of the Congress Center (June-Sept. daily at 8:30am), board a 9am bus, and return from the mountain ranges by 5pm. Not a strenuous hike, but the views and mountains are phenomenal and the guides are qualified and friendly. This is a perfect, free way to get up into the mountains and see an Alpine hut for yourself. Free lantern hikes also leave every Tuesday at 7:45pm for Gasthof Heiligwasser, just above Igls; enjoy an Alpine hut party once there. If you wish to attack the Alps alone, pick up a free mountain guide booklet at any of the tourist offices.

The Club Innsbruck membership also significantly simplifies winter ski excursions; just hop on the complimentary club ski shuttle (schedules at the tourist office) to any suburban cable car (Dec. 21-April 5). Membership has other privileges as well; the Club card entitles you to discounts on ski passes. **Innsbruck Gletscher Ski Pass** (available at all cable cars and at Innsbruck-Information offices) is a comprehensive ticket valid for all 52 lifts in the region. (3 days 1180AS, 6 days 2140AS; with Club Innsbruck membership, 980AS and 1780AS, respectively.) Passes available for skiing on 3 out of 4 days and 3 of 6 days. The tourist office also rents equipment, available on the mountain. (**Ski rentals:** alpine (boots, poles, skis) approximately 270AS per day; cross-country 160AS per day. **Bobsled:** 300AS per person per ride.)

The summer bus to **Stubaier Gletscherbahn** (for glacier skiing) leaves at 7:20am and 8:30am. Take the earlier bus—summer snow is often slushy by noon. There are also buses at 9:45am, 11am, and 5pm in the winter (1hr.20min., round-trip 150AS). The last bus back leaves at 4:30pm, when the lifts close. One day of winter glacier skiing costs 420AS; summer passes cost 330AS after 8am, 275AS after 11am, and 170AS after 1pm. Ski rental (approximately 270AS) is available at the glacier. Innsbruck-Information and its train station branch offer the most reliable daily glacier ski packages: 660AS in summer, including bus, lift, and rental, and 540AS in winter (cheaper because the bus is free).

For a one-minute thrill, summer and winter bobsled rides are available at the Olympics bobsled run in Igls (tel. 37 75 25; fax 33 83 89), 5km from Innsbruck (although the summer rides are akin to spruced-up *Cool Runnings* carts with wheels). Professionals drive the 4-man bobs, and reservations are necessary. (In winter Tuesdays at 10am, and Thursdays from 7pm on. In summer Thurs., Fri. and Sat. from 4:30-6pm. 360AS per person.) For a calmer ride try the **Hafelekar Cable Car** (daily; 264AS with Club Innsbruck card).

When you descend from Alpine peaks, peruse the monthly cultural brochures available at the tourist office for comprehensive listings of exhibitions, films, and concerts. Posters plastered on the kiosks at Innsbruck University reveal even more cultural options. During August, Innsbruck hosts the **Festival of Early Music,** featuring concerts by some of the world's leading soloists on period instruments at the Schloß Ambras and Congress Center. Organ recitals are also given on the Hofkirche's 16th-century Ebert organ. (For festival tickets, call 53 56 21; fax 53 56 43.) Several of the festival's performances are held at the **Tiroler Landestheater** across from the Hofburg on Rennweg (tel. 52 07 44; tickets available Mon.-Sat. 8:30am-8:30pm, Sun. 6:30-8:30pm or 7-8pm at the door before the performance; 40-540AS). Top-notch plays, operas, and dance performances are presented most nights throughout the year here as well (same box office times; tickets 65-440AS, but **student rush tickets,** available to anyone under 21 and students under 27, sell for 80AS in any price category half an hour before the show).

The **Tiroler Symphony Orchestra** of Innsbruck (tel. 58 00 23) plays in the Congress Center, across from the Landestheater between October and May (tickets 280-440AS; children and students receive a 30% discount). Chamber music concerts cost 160-260AS and the same discounts apply. Many Tuesday nights in summer, **classical music concerts** are held in the Spanish mall at Schloß Ambras (tickets 140-380AS). Late June to mid-July brings the **International Dance Summer.** Chestnuts in the *Altstadt,* cribs in the folklore museum, and caroling at the congress center are all components of the annual **Christmas market,** held Nov. 22-Dec. 23.

Bottom Taler

American currency has its foundations in the small town of Hall, a few miles downriver from Innsbruck. Here, in the 16th century, Duke Sigmund (a Habsburg) coined the *Joachimsthaler,* a silver coin. Over the next century, this coinage, shortened to Taler, gained acceptance through Europe. When a bunch of upstarts in the American colonies didn't feel like paying taxes anymore and declared independence, they adopted this name for their new currency, the dollar. Hall has yet to see any royalties.

NIGHTLIFE

Though most visitors collapse into bed after a full day of Alpine adventure, there is still enough action to keep a few party-goers from their pillows. Much of the lively nightlife revolves around the students, making the **university quarter** a mecca for late-night revelry. The **Viaduktbogen,** a cluster of bars and music joints along Ingenieur Etzel Str., presents another intriguing option.

Hofgarten (tel. 58 88 71), hidden inside the Hofgarten park. Follow Burggrabenstr. around under the archway and past Universitätstr.; enter the park after passing the Landestheater through the small gateway. Follow the path and you'll hear the crowd gathering. The elegantly lit garden and white tent splendor resemble a party Jay Gatsby would be proud to host. The crowd starts gathering around 8pm, and by 10pm hundreds of students and professionals fill the outdoor tents and tables. Snack food 50-100AS, beer 28-48AS, wine spritzers 31AS. Open in summer daily 10am-1am, in winter Mon.-Sat. 5pm-1am, Sun. 10am-6pm.

Treibhaus, Angerzellgasse 8 (tel. 58 68 74). Hidden in an alley to the right of China Restaurant, this is Innsbruck's favorite student hangout. Colorful plastic squiggles on the ceiling and a brightly lit tent outside. Extensive Volksgarten series includes free concerts on Saturday evening, while jazz reigns supreme on Sundays. Jazz and blues festivals throughout the summer. Food 50-95AS. Mon.-Fri. 9am-1am, Sat.-Sun. 10am-1am.

Jimmy's, Wilhelm-Greilstr. 17 (tel. 57 04 73), on the Landhaus Platz end, tucked inside an office building. The front end of an old-fashioned bright yellow Opel sticks out of the bar. Happy Days meets Hard Rock; they elope and head for the Tirol. Packed with students who revere Jimmy's Italian, Mexican, and American food, especially the "Go to Hell" (actually a heavenly pasta; 50-105AS). Open Mon.-Fri. 11am-1am, Sat.-Sun. 7pm-1am. Visa, MC, AmEx.

Krah Vogel, Anichstr. 12, off Maria-Theresienstr. (tel. 58 01 49). Mellowed, amber wall and sleek black railings line this modern, hip bar, packed with people. Check out the "black box room," a sensory walk through the jungle—in the dark. Big screen TV and outdoor tables. Häagen-Däzs ice cream (48AS), beer (27-39AS), and food (38-178AS). Open Mon.-Sat. 9:30am-1am, Sun. 4pm-1am.

Utopia, Tschamlerstr. 3 (tel. 58 85 87; http://www.utopia.or.at). More of an alternative music concert venue than a club, but most Fridays are gay disco nights. Rave and techno otherwise.

■ Seefeld in Tirol

With the '64 and '76 Olympiads padding its resumé, ritzy Seefeld in Tirol lays a serious and confident claim to winter sports mecca status. Innsbruck twice used Seefeld's terrain for nordic skiing events (though a disappointing snowfall in '64 forced the use of an appalling 20,000 metric tons of imported snow). Although skiing is the cash cow, lush meadows and breathtaking Alpine scenery invite travelers in all seasons. Seefeld is the picture-perfect Austrian village; feast your senses on towering peaks and bubbling fountains, and hear the clip-clop of Haflinger mountain horses pulling Tirolean wagons around the narrow cobblestone streets (1hr. tour 400AS). Winter quickens the stream of tourists headed to Seefeld. Be sure to make reservations at least a month in advance.

Orientation and Practical Information On the northwest perimeter of suburban Innsbruck, Seefeld in Tirol perches on a broad plateau 1180m above sea level, surrounded by the **Hohe Munde, Wetterstein,** and **Karwendel** mountain ranges. The town is only 26km from Innsbruck and is thereby easily reached by road and rail (17 trains from Innsbruck daily, 40min., 48AS, round-trip 90AS). Sit on the right (approaching Seefeld) for the best view of the valleys down below. If you can dislodge your transfixed eyeballs from the window once the train comes to a stop, head straight down the street in front of the train station to the center of town, where restaurants and horse-drawn carriages await.

Seefeld's **tourist office,** Klosterstr. 43 (tel. 23 13; fax 33 55; http://www.tis.co.at/tirol), is well equipped to handle the town's celebrity status. The helpful and knowledgeable staff gives away plenty of information in English, Italian, French, Spanish, *und natürlich,* German. From the train station, walk straight out the main door, cross the street, and head up Bahnhofstr. (which becomes Klosterstr. after the Münchner Str. intersection). The tourist office, housed in the Rathaus, is on the right. (Open June-Sept. Mon.-Sat. 8:30am-6:30pm; Oct. to mid-Dec. and end of March to June Mon.-Sat. 8:30am-noon and 3-6pm; mid-Dec. to end of March Mon.-Sat. 8:30am-6:30pm, Sun. 10am-12:30pm and 4-6pm.) You can **exchange money** at local banks (open Mon.-Fri. 8am-12:30pm and 2-4pm) and at the post office until 5pm. Walk straight out of the train station to find an **ATM.** The **post office** (tel. 23 47; fax 38 73) is right down the road from the tourist office (open Mon.-Fri. 8am-noon and 2-6pm; Dec. 16-April 15 and July-Sept. also open Sat. 9am-noon). The **telephones** inside take *Wertkarten* (open Mon.-Fri. 8am-noon and 2-6pm, Sat. 8am-noon). **Luggage storage** (30AS) and **bike rental** (50-90AS per day) are available at the train station. **Trains** run frequently between **Salzburg** (792AS round-trip), **Munich** (470AS round-trip), and **Innsbruck** (90AS round-trip). If the station bikes are all rented, try **Sport Sailer** (tel. 25 30) in Dorfplatz. A mountain bike there costs 220AS for a full day (open July-mid Sept. 9am-12:30pm and 2-6pm; mid-Sept.-Dec. 9am-noon and 3-6pm). For a **taxi,** call 26 30, 22 21, or 22 67. Wash clothes at **Tip-Top Laundromat,** Andreas-Hofer-Str. 292 (tel. 20 44), located behind the train station and to the right (open Mon.-Fri. 8am-12:30pm and 2:30-6pm, Sat. 9am-noon). **Snow report:** tel. 37 90. **Postal code:** A-6100. **Telephone code:** 05212.

Accommodations and Food Seefeld boasts seven five-star hotels (that's *thirty-five* stars!), but no hostel—this proliferation of constellations means that the price of a bed rises 400-2400AS, depending on the season. It is probably best to consider Seefeld as a **day trip** from Innsbruck. However, *Privatzimmer* are probably the best budget option. Prices for these rooms average 200-300AS per night in the summer; slap on about 100AS more during winter. People traveling alone, in particular, should make reservations well before arriving; singles are few and far between. Wherever you stay, inquire about a **guest card** *(Kurkarte)* that discounts 10-20% off skiing, swimming, concerts, and local attractions. **Haus Felseneck,** Kirchwald 309 (tel. 25 40), is one of the least expensive guest houses. Walk straight out of the train station onto Bahnhofstr., which becomes Klosterstr. Take Klosterstr. past the sport center and all the way to the end. Turn left onto Mosererstr. At this intersection there is also a small narrow road with a guard rail on its left-hand side; this is Kirchwaldstr. The *Pension* is the third house on the right. Bask in luxurious bed chambers—balconies, TV, lace lamp shades and a view you'll wish you could write a quick message on the back of, stamp and send home. The owners yearn to practice their language skills with English-speaking visitors. (In summer, singles 260AS; in winter, singles 360AS. Breakfast and private shower included.) **Haus Carinthia,** Hocheggstr. 432 (tel. 29 55), sits all the way across town. Take a left after you exit the train station and cross over the train tracks to Reitherspitzstr., continue until you reach Milserstr. and take another left. Then take your second right onto Hocheggstr., off the road, on your left. Antlers hang on the wall in typical Tirolean style. (In summer, singles 180AS, doubles

340AS; in winter, singles 270AS, doubles 500AS. Toilet, shower, and breakfast included. Call ahead.)

Finding inexpensive food in Seefeld is less arduous than hunting down a cheap room; the entire *Fußgängerzone* which lies on parts of Bahnhofstr., Innsbruckerstr., Klosterstr., and Münsterstr. is stocked with rows of restaurants, outdoor cafés, and bars. **Luigi and Lois,** Innsbruckstr. 12 (Luigi, tel. 22 59 66; Lois, tel. 22 59 67), offers a double header—Italian fare on the Luigi side and Tirolean fare on Lois's. Move from an Adriatic villa to a rustic mountain farm by simply crossing the hall. Masterpieces in ice cream and chocolate (35-68AS). Equally expressive pasta and pizza (79-130AS) and Tirolean munchies (69-220AS). (Luigi open daily 11:30am-11pm; Lois open 6pm-1am.Visa, MC, AmEx accepted.) Locals recommend *Wiener Schnitzel al fresco* at the **Tiroler Weinstube,** Dorfpl. 130 (tel. 22 08), in front of the tourist office. Most dishes are 80-155AS, specials from the grill cost 135-250AS, and desserts run 45-90AS. Also has a kid's menu and limited vegetarian offerings (open daily 9am-midnight; Visa, MC accepted). The **Meinl supermarket** (tel. 31 62) is located on Klosterstr. (Open Mon.-Fri. 8:30am-noon and 3-6pm, Sat 8:30am-noon.)

Skiing and Entertainment Winter in Seefeld brings a blanket of snow and a multitude of skiers from around the globe. The town offers two ski passes; the **Seefelder Card** gives skiers access to slopes at Seefeld, Reith, Mösern, and Neuleut-asch, and is available for one or two days (1-day pass 330AS, children under 15 210AS). The other option is the **Happy Ski Pass,** which is valid for skiing at Seefeld, Reith, Neuleutasch, Mittenwald, Garmisch-Partenkirchen, Ehrwald, Lermoos, Biber-wier, Bichbach, Berwang, and Heiterwant. This pass is available for 3-20 days and a photograph is required. Three days of happy skiing cost 940AS, children under 15 620AS. This ski pass may include large, ecstatic facial expression which is often per-manent and rather annoying to all your friends back at home. There are ten different **sports equipment rental shops** in Seefeld willing to lease alpine and cross-country skis, snowboards, and toboggans, all at standardized prices. Downhill skis with poles and boots cost 140-250AS, children 80-130AS; snowboard 200-300AS. The tourist office can give you the *Seefeld A-Z* pamphlet to guide you to the nearest rental store and provide you with a schedule for the **ski bus,** free with the Seefeld guest card. The ski shuttle runs daily from 9:30am to 5pm (times are approx.), between the fire sta-tion, Rosshütte, and Gschwandtkopf systems. The *Seefeld Sport-Winter* and *Sport-Summer* packets describe the town's other outdoor pastimes, including ice skating, hockey, cycling, paragliding, and cross-country skiing. Those battered by a tough, knee-twisting day on the slopes can visit the massive **sauna** complex at the **Olympia Sport Center** (tel. 32 20; fax 32 28 83; indoor swimming pool open daily 9:30am-10pm, late fall and spring open daily 1-10pm; Sauna World open daily 2-10pm). **Mov-ies** are screened in the Sports Center nightly (80AS).

The tourist office and the **Tirol Alpine School** run an excellent summer **hiking** pro-gram that will satiate even the most accomplished veteran's *Wanderlust.* The four- to six-hour hikes wind among local towering peaks, including the **Pleisenspitze** (2569m) and the **Gehrenspitze** (2367m) among others. Hiking excursions are sched-uled by the tourist office to run every Tues. and Fri. from June 17 to mid-Sept. You must register by 5pm the day before at the tourist office. (Tues. hikes leave at 9am from the tourist office, Fri. hikes leave at 8am. All hikes 150AS. Transportation fees additional, and hiking equipment is available.) The **Kneipp Hiking Society** invites vis-itors to join its weekly five-hour outings (departures from the train station Thurs. 12:30pm; free). The **Bergbahn Rosshütte** (tel. (05242) 241 60) offers "four hours of mountain adventure" with its five-point program. Participants ride a street car, a cable car, and the Jochbahn railway to Alpine heights of over 2000m. For 205AS, hikers wander several short trails and then indulge in an immense "Austrian coffee break" at the Rosshütte restaurant. Summer glacier skiing, albeit slushy, is also available.

If not overwhelmed by Seefeld's immense sporting machinery, the renaissance jock may wish to take part in the full program of cultural events designed to intro-duce the visitor to the true Tirolean way (the ultimate harmonic quest). The tourist

---

Knee-Deep in Church

In 1384, a bratty Knight, Oswald Milser, put Seefeld on the map. Though dutifully attending Easter Mass, like a good little knight, Oswald felt a little bigger than his britches. Believing himself better than the masses, he rejected the small host usually given to lay-people and demanded the consecrated wafer reserved only for the clergy. The timid priest of the church complied, but when Oswald took the host in his mouth, he suddenly began to sink into the ground, lower and lower, until the priest pulled the now blood-red wafer from his mouth. This miracle and acute example of the Proverb "pride goeth before fall" turned Seefeld into a pilgrimage site. The devout still come to see the 1½-foot hole in the ground (now covered by a protective grate) and the deep hand-print on the altar on which the sinking Oswald attempted to support himself.

---

office prints a schedule of summer events from May to Oct. in its pamphlet *Sports Activities and Events Summer*. Listings include the annual **Village Festival** (third Sat. in July), choir concerts, and chamber music. **Tirol Evenings** take place three times a week from July through Sept. (Tues. at Café Corso and Ferienhotel, Thurs. and Fri. at Hotel Tirol). The tourist office lists the featured group for the twice-weekly **City Classics Concerts** in the Seefeld **Kurpark** (June-Sept. Thurs. and Sun. 8:15pm). Chamber music concerts are held at 8:30pm on summer Fridays in the Parish Church. The tourist office also prints a summer program for children which includes nature adventure days, horse-back riding, and puppet theater.

THE LECHTALER ALPS

The Lechtaler Alps, a region of 3000m peaks and lake-speckled valleys, hugs the German border in northwestern Tirol. Friendly to mountain beasts and mythical dwarves but not rear-wheel-drive cars, less than one-fifth of the alpine terrain is habitable by humankind. As a result, the supply of guest beds is heavily concentrated in large resort areas. Cheap lodgings are few and far between, though portions of the Lechtal do offer alternative accommodations—the Innsbruck branch of the Tirol Information Service, Adamgasse 3-7, A-6020 Innsbruck (tel. 56 18 82), prints *Urlaub am Bauernhof* (Vacation on the Farm).

The best time to visit the Lechtal is when the mountains are your only companions; consider a trip in the off-season, April to June or October to November. In these border lands, it is a good idea to carry your passport at all times, in case you encounter an urge to go international. The **Inn River,** the primary waterway of the valley, runs southwest to northeast from the Swiss frontier at Finstermünz to the German border by Kufstein. It cuts a swath of land through Innsbruck, Imst, and Landeck and then heads south to Switzerland; for the past two millennia it has served as a pivotal transport route. Parallel to and north of the Inn, the **Lech River** has eroded its own wide valley. Between the lowlands of the Inn and Lech, the mountains are virtually people-free.

The Lechtaler Alps offer some of the best skiing in Austria and the world. For a 24-hr. **weather report,** call (0512) 15 66. Swimming. Skiing. Hiking. All of this hearty cardiovascular activity is going to make you hungry. When your food gauge is running low, sit down for some local specialties—try the *Tiroler Speckknödel* (bacon fat balls), served either *zu Wasser* (in broth) or *zu Lande* (dry, with salad or sauerkraut); or *Gröstel* (a combination of potatoes, meat, bacon, and eggs).

■ Ehrwald

Of his beloved hometown Ehrwald, poet Ludwig Ganghofer once importuned God, "If You love me, please let me live here forever." Though at last report his request went unheeded (he died in 1920 and was buried near Munich), some divine power has certainly smiled on the city. Other than a few damaged buildings, the World Wars spared the hamlet, and to date nothing has blemished Ehrwald's *Wunderkind,* the majestic **Zugspitze.** This mountain, rising stark and monumental, straddles the German-Austrian border (at 2962m, it's Germany's highest), and brings 400,000 tourists a year to Ehrwald (pop. 2500). In return the town has set up a TV station that provides nothing but live footage of the mountain: hour after hour of trees, rocks, and dirt, designed to bring you by constant subliminal suggestion to the top.

The plan does not seem to be as successful as hoped, however. For some reason, visitors flock like lemmings to the more congested German resort **Garmisch-Partenkirchen,** perhaps because it was a former Olympic host. Ehrwald's motto is "Ehrwald—on the *sunny* side of the Zugspitze;" while no scientist has confirmed this meteorological oddity, Ehrwald *is* more pleasant than its German counterpart in many ways. It's quieter, it boasts a faster cable car (the **Tiroler Zugspitzbahn**), and it's cheaper (rooms average 50-100AS less in Ehrwald). Whatever the reason, there are plenty of opportunities to sample life on both sides of the border; trains cross from Austria to Germany and back ten times daily (don't forget your passport).

Orientation and Practical Information Autobahn A12 follows the Inn from Innsbruck to Imst, the old market town. Bundesstr. 314 runs north from Imst to Ehrwald, close to Germany and the popular resort, Garmisch-Partenkirchen. Bundesstr. 198 runs along the River Lech. To reach Ehrwald by **train,** disembark at Garmisch-Partenkirchen and switch onto the two-car train, which curves around to Ehrwald. The diminutive Ehrwald **train station** (tel. 22 01) offers a telephone and **luggage storage** (20AS), and cheery shutters with cut-out hearts. To reach the town center from the train station, turn left out of the station and cross over the tracks. Walk straight ahead on Bahnhofstr., and continue left when it feeds into Hauptstr. The town center will appear after approximately 20 minutes, when Hauptstr. forks off to the left. The **tourist office** (tel. 23 95; fax 33 14) is located in the town center just behind the church at Kirchpl. 1. The helpful staff is more than willing to answer questions and direct you to the best the town has to offer in sporting opportunities and entertainment. Various brochures are available (open Mon-Fri 8:30am-noon and 1:30-6pm; mid-June to mid-Sept. and Christmas-Feb., Mon.-Sat. 8:30am-noon and 1:30-6pm). **Currency exchange** is available at local banks (open Mon.-Fri. 8am-noon and 2-4:30pm). Unfortunately, there are no **ATMs** in town that accept Plus or Cirrus cards. **Telephones** are available at the post office, train station, and next to the town green about 100m before the church on the left side of the road. **Mountain bikes** can be rented at **Intersport Leitner** (tel. 23 71; 80AS per hour, 250AS per day, helmet included; also rents skis 210-350AS), or try **Sport Scheiber** (tel. 31 04), located in the town center (mountain bikes 200AS per day, road bikes 90AS). Closer to the train station, rent bikes at the tongue-twisting Zweirad Zirknitzer (tel. 32 19), appropriately located at Zugspitzstr. 16 (mountain bikes 50AS per hour, 200AS per day; road bikes 90AS per day). To reach the **post office** (tel. 33 66; fax 31 40), from the tourist office, head out of the town center and down Hauptstr. to #5. (Open Mon.-Fri. 8am-noon and 2-6pm, Sat. 8-10am. On weekdays money exchange open until 5pm.) **Postal code:** A-6632. **Telephone code:** 05673.

Accommodations and Food Ehrwald is filled with guest houses that offer the comforts of home while also sparing your wallet. **Pension Buchenhain,** Wettersteinstr. 33 (tel. 22 47), sits stunningly at the bottom of the surrounding mountains, only meters away from a forest filled with hiking trails. From the tourist office, walk down Kirchpl., which becomes Hauptstr. Take your first right onto Wettersteinstr., and the pension is at the end of a small dirt road on your left. Definitely make a reservation. (in summer 220-240AS, in winter 280-310AS. Toilet, shower, breakfast, and balcony included.) **Haus Edith,** Im Tal 22a (tel. 35 04), sits on a riverbank in a friendly residential neighborhood, full of kids on bikes and grandparents on porches. From the tourist office head down Wehnerwegstr, directly opposite the church spire. Im Tal is after the short but steep hill on Wehnerweg; turn right after the hill and Edith's is on your left, one house from the road. (in summer 220AS person, in winter 240AS. Breakfast, shower, toilet, and balcony included.) If you are planning a picnic on the summit of the Zugspitze, the local **SPAR Markt,** Hauptstr. 1, next to the post office, will help (open Mon.-Thurs. 8am-6:30pm, Fri. 8am-7:30pm, Sat. 7:30am-noon).

Sights and Entertainment The **Tiroler Zugspitzbahn** (tel. 23 09) is Ehrwald's leading tourist attraction and greatest engineering feat to date. This cable car climbs the 1750m to the summit of the Zugspitze in a hold-your-breath seven minutes and 12 seconds (and that's without the top secret turbo boost). The outdoor platforms of the crowded restaurant at the ride's end have what some call the most breath-taking view on the entire continent; on a clear day, visibility extends from Salzburg to Stuttgart (restaurant open mid-May to mid-Oct.). Be sure to bring a sweater, as there may still be snow on the ground (round-trip 410AS, children 240AS, age 16-17 290AS. Lift runs daily late May to late October and late November to mid-April 8:40am-4:40pm.) To reach the cable car, take a Summerrund bus from the town green or across the tracks from the train station to "Tiroler Zugspitzbahn" (20AS one-way, 34AS day ticket). Ehrwald offers the **Happy Ski Card,** so named because of the strange, ear-to-ear grin noticed on those who masochistically believe they can "ski it all." The card gives access to 128 lifts, 244km of alpine skiing runs, 100km of cross-country trails, and several other winter time sports arenas (for more information and prices see **Seefeld** listing above). The mountains also draw thrill-seeking visitors in summer. The Ehrwald tourist office organizes free **mountain bike tours** every Fri., leaving from the office at 8:30am, as well as daily guided mountain tours; registration for both is open until Thurs. at 5pm at the tourist office. The tourist office also provides information on walks and hikes in the area, as well as fishing, swimming, billiards, boats, skating, climbing, paragliding, horse-back riding, tobogganing, squash, tennis, kayaking, and rafting (whew), both in Ehrwald and the neighboring area. Ehrwald's annual triathlon is held at the end of July, with mountain climbing replacing biking (swim, run, then climb). Winter brings the Synchro Ski World Cup; two skiers tackle the mountain simultaneously and are judged not only on speed but on how closely they mirror each other's form. Anyone with a partner and a penchant for playing "Simon Says" may enter.

THE ARLBERG

Rising stark and massive, halfway between the Bodensee and Innsbruck, the jagged peaks of the Arlberg mountains make for an extreme Alpine experience. Since the first descent to the valley by Lech's parish priest in 1895, incomparable conditions have catapulted the area to powder glory. Where once only knickerbockered spitfires dared tread, Spandex-clad pedal pushers and stooped aristocrats now flock like lemmings. Though most lifts operate in summer for high-altitude hikes, **skiing** remains the area's main draw. With hundreds of miles of groomed ski runs ranging in altitude from 1000 to 3000m, the Arlberg offers unparalleled terrain from December through April. All resorts have ski schools in German and English for children and beginners as well as proficient skiers. In fact, the world's first-ever ski instructor still makes his home in the tiny village of Oberlech. Immensely long cross-country trails (up to 42km) traverse the valleys, linking the various villages. The comprehensive **Arlberg Ski Pass** allows you access to some of Austria's most coveted slopes, including the famed **Valluga** summit. The pass is valid for over 88 mountain railways and ski lifts in St. Anton, St. Jakob, St. Christoph, Lech, Zürs, and the tiny villages of Klösterle and Stuben, amounting to more than 192km of prime snow-draped terrain. Rumor has it that the Galzigbahn endures the longest morning lines, while the Rendl ski area remains largely pristine. Passes should be purchased at the Galzig, Vallugagrat, Vallugipfel, Gampen, and Kapall cable car stations from 8am to 4:30pm on the day prior to use. (455AS per day, 2 days 860AS, 1 week 2470AS, 2 weeks 4010AS; off-season

410AS, 770AS, 2220AS, and 3610AS. Seniors receive a 100AS discount per day; children under 15 pay approximately 60% of the adult price; before Dec. 1 and after April 20, prices are reduced more than 50%.)

Those looking to jump start their ski career should enroll in ski lessons at the **Arlberg Ski Club**—members have won an amazing 11 Olympic and 40 world championship medals. (Group classes for half day 350AS, 5 days 1300AS; private lessons for 1 day 1900AS.) **Equipment rental** is standardly priced throughout the Arlberg at 1800AS per week. For **weather reports,** call (05583) 18 in Lech or (05446) 226 90 in St. Anton; **to report accidents** call (05583) 28 55 in Lech, (05446) 235 20 in St. Anton. In summer, the equivalent of the Arlberg Ski Pass is available for access to cable car lifts for **hiking;** the pass can be obtained from any of the five stations mentioned in the Ski Pass description above (1-week pass 390AS, children 220AS).

On the eastern side of the Arlberg tunnel, in the province of Tirol, you'll find the hub of the region, **St. Anton,** and its distinctly less cosmopolitan cousin, **St. Jakob.** The western Arlberg is home to the classy resorts **Lech, Zürs,** and **St. Christoph,** which become, in order, increasingly more expensive. **Buses** bind the Arlberg towns together, and trains connect St. Anton to the rest of Austria. Bus #4235 runs from Landeck to St. Anton every hour; #4248 runs from St. Anton to St. Christoph, Zürs, and Lech five times per day and returns four times per day. In high season, book rooms six to eight weeks in advance; in off-season, two weeks is sufficient.

■ St. Anton am Arlberg

France has St. Tropez, Switzerland has St. Moritz, and Austria has St. Anton. Don't be fooled by the pious name, the hillside farms, or the cherubic schoolchildren. As soon as the first snowflake arrives, St. Anton (non-tourist pop. 2300) awakens with a vengeance; in winter, the town is an international playground brimming with playboys, partygoers, and plenty of physical activity (skiing, skating, and snow-shoeing, of course). Downhill skiing was born here at the turn of the century when a bevy of Austrian chaps barreled down the mountain with boards on their feet; the town has definitely retained its daredevil panache. To escape the tabloid reporters in St. Moritz, many members of the Euro jet-set (including Prince Edward of England) winter here. St. Anton *loves* its flock of traveling socialites. All major credit cards are accepted at almost every establishment; after all, dah-ling, it's awfully *gauche* to carry a wad of cash around. Language shouldn't be a problem either; salesmen have learned that a healthy knowledge of English tends to grease the wheels of commerce. Whether calculated for tourists or just standard practice, the many traditional touches—lederhosen-clad marching bands, colorful festivals and early evening cattle drives through the *Fußgängerzone*—round out the Tirolean experience. Be warned that the ski season drives this town—it doesn't emerge from spring hibernation until mid-July. The sleep is so deep that restaurants and museums often close during May and June for a late spring cleaning.

Orientation and Practical Information St. Anton is conveniently located along major rail and bus routes, at the administrative center of the Arlberg. More than 40 **trains** (tel. 22 42) come and go daily, with destinations including **Innsbruck** (1hr.20min., 13 daily, 128AS one-way), **Munich** (3hr.45min., two daily, 900AS round-trip, under 26 630AS), and **Zürich** (3hr.30min., 5 daily, 764AS round-trip, under 26 535AS); the St. Anton train station has **currency exchange, luggage storage** (30AS), and a restaurant for when you have to eat and run. **Buses** run every hour in winter, every 2hr. in summer among the neighboring Arlberg villages **Lech** (24AS), **Zürs,** and **St. Christoph** (10AS); buses run almost hourly to **Landeck** (6am-7pm; 46AS). You can purchase a day pass (80AS) which allows unlimited travel between the towns. The bus station is right across the street from the tourist office, under Sport Pangratz.

Many St. Anton streets lack names, which wreaks havoc on directions. Use the *Fußgängerzone* as a reference; head right from the train station, follow the street down the hill, and bear left at the fork to reach the pedestrian area. The **tourist office,** in the Arlberghaus (tel. 226 90; fax 25 32), sits just beyond the high end of the pedestrian zone. To find it, exit the train station, proceed down the hill, and turn right. You will see a souvenir shop just ahead of you. The tourist office is just to the left of the shop. The office is as chic as the town—luxurious leather chairs, mahogany reception stands, an invaluable 24-hr. electronic room finder outside, and no fewer than six full-size English brochures. (Open Dec.-April Mon.-Fri. 8:30am-noon and 2:30-6:30pm, Sat. 9am-noon and 1-7pm, Sun. 10am-noon and 3-6pm; May-early July Mon.-Fri. 8am-noon and 2-6pm; early July-mid-Sept. Mon.-Fri. 8am-noon and 2-6pm, Sat. 10am-noon, Sun. 10am-noon; mid-Sept.-Dec. Mon.-Fri. 8am-noon and 2-6pm.) The **Tiroler Landesreisebüro,** opposite the railway crossing (tel. 22 22; fax 22 21), is a well equipped regional **travel agency** offering **money exchange,** airplane and rail reservations, and **car rental** services through Hertz (in summer open Mon.-Fri. 8:30am-noon and 2:45-6pm, Sat. 8:30am-noon; in winter open Mon.-Sat. 9am-noon and 2:30-6pm). The smallest car available costs 732AS per day with unlimited mileage. You can also **exchange currency** at the ATM machines around town (though the commission may be exorbitant), or at any of the three local banks, all found in the *Fußgängerzone* (banking hours are Mon.-Fri. 8am-noon and 2-4:30pm). **Telephones** are available inside and outside the post office, and by the tourist office and train station. **Biking** in the Arlberg is arduous but extraordinarily rewarding—the folks at **Sporthaus Schneider,** in the pedestrian zone (tel. 22 09), will be glad to rent you a bike and dispense maps and trail advice. (Full day rental 280AS, morning rental 150AS, afternoon rental 180AS. Tennis racket rental 50AS per hour, hiking boot rental 80AS per day. Open end of June-Sept. Mon.-Sun. 8am-6:30pm, Dec.-April 8am-7pm.) A 24-hr. recording has updated **ski conditions** (tel. 25 65). **Police station:** tel. 23 62 13. **Emergency:** tel. 22 37. To find the **post office** (tel. 36 50), walk to the low end of the *Fußgängerzone,* and turn right; then take the second right, and the office will be on the left side of the street (also look for yellow Post P.S.K. signs; open Mon.-Fri. 8:30am-noon and 2-6pm; in winter Mon.-Fri. 8:30am-7pm, Sat. 9-11am). **Postal code:** A-6580. **Telephone code:** 05446.

Accommodations and Food The general rule in St. Anton is that prices double during the ski season. Book far enough in advance (about two months), and you *may* find relatively cheap housing. Since street anonymity makes directions unclear, the best bet is to ask for precise directions at the tourist office, or consult the electronic accommodation board outside. **Pension Pepi Eiter** (tel. 25 50; fax 36 57), is across the tracks from the railway station and up the hill to the left of the tourist office. Take the small, narrow road on your left as you head downhill. The owner will buzz you in the entrance at the back of the garage. Pepi Eiter provides luscious beds, hearty repasts, light pine rooms, and chocolate for weary guests. (In summer, singles 180-220AS, doubles 360AS; in winter, singles 420-480AS, doubles 800AS; breakfast and private shower included). **Pension Elisabeth** (tel. 24 96; fax 292 54) is one of the town's least expensive, three-star bed-and-breakfasts. From the tourist office, head straight across the train tracks and up the hill to the left and in front of you, which is lined with various eateries and guest houses. Pension Elizabeth is house #315 on the right hand side of the road, up the road from Pepi Eiter and across from the cable car. (In summer, 230AS per person, in winter, 520-530AS. Bath, TV, radio, breakfast, and parking included. English spoken.) To find **Pension Klöpfer** (tel. 28 00), turn left at the end of the *Fußgängerzone* by Club Amadeus, and follow the street as it forks to the right over the rail tracks; go up the hill, winding with the curves and turn on the first gravel road to your right. Look for the sign at #419. (In summer, singles 250AS, doubles 800-880AS; in winter, singles 500-600AS, doubles 800-1200AS. Breakfast and parking included.)

The *Fußgängerzone* is riddled with restaurants such as the **Amalien Stüberl** (tel. 22 18 12), which serves up the biggest pizzas around (94-119AS) and a stellar mixed salad with chicken breast (open mid-June to mid-Oct. and mid-Dec. to March daily 10am-midnight). To combat St. Anton's generally high prices, the local supermarkets may be your best bet for a meal. The **Nah und Frisch Supermarket** beckons from the left of the Stüberl (open Mon.-Fri. 7am-noon and 2-6pm, Sat. 7am-noon). The local **Spar Markt** lies just past the *Fußgängerzone* (open Mon.-Fri. 7am-noon and 2-6pm, Sat. 7am-noon).

Sights and Entertainment In the winter, the world famous Alpine slopes of St. Anton await, but you must pay for the fame and glamour. St. Anton's resorts boast a list of clientele that reads like the December special issue of *People* magazine. European royalty, public figures, and Hollywood stars roll incognito (they like the fact that no one can recognize them in their bulky ski wear and extra-terrestrial goggles). Prince Edward, John Kennedy Jr., Clint Eastwood, Charles Schulz, and Paul Anka have all graced the slopes at St. Anton. To follow in their ski tracks may be costly. If you stay in St. Anton and ski for more than six days, you become eligible for a minor reduction in price (about 100AS off your Arlberg Ski Pass).

If Demi Moore has crowded you out of the lift line, you might want to turn to St. Anton's smaller assortment of other pursuits. In summer, you can tack on 10AS to the weekly hiking pass (see Arlberg Ski Pass p. 429) to utilize all the facilities at the St. Anton **recreation park**—table tennis, miniature golf, and fishing, among others. 45AS more will get you into the St. Anton **swimming pool** and down its 36-m twisty red slide. The recreation park is good for beautiful summer hikes along a fast-flowing stream as well. St. Anton's 60km of marked mountain bike paths (bikers rave about Ferwall Valley and Moostal), as well as 90km of hiking paths complement the 220km of groomed ski slopes.Wednesdays in July, a local Alpine flower expert leads free day-long flower hikes from the tourist office that are very popular.

Avid sports fans can not only participate in St. Anton's numerous sporting events—they can watch as well. The town offers a professional **tennis tournament** and **World Cup skiing** for your viewing pleasure. The Isospeed Trophy, an indoor tennis tournament which comes to town in December, features some moderately famous European players, such as Goran Ivanisevic, Henri Leconte, and Javier Sanchez. Also in December, the **Kandahar Ski Race** (men's or women's, depending on the year) on the World Cup circuit, attracts the sport's best. Call the tourist office for information on specific dates and ticket availability. The **Arlberg Mountainbike Trophy** is bestowed every August upon the winner of a treacherous 20.5km race, composed of steep climbs and dangerously rapid downhill sections. Any psychotic velocipedist eager to undertake the journey may enter for a mere 200AS registration fee—it's a great way to pace yourself against Olympic and professional cyclists. In 2001, St. Anton will host the Alpine Skiing World Championships.

■ Near St. Anton: Lech

In 1300 the call went out: "There's gold in them thar hills," and the settlers came, leading their cattle from the Valais region of western Switzerland to Lech. As others found, however, the real gold here is really powdery and white. The converting process between snow and a large Swiss bank account was not discovered until the 20th century, when some lost Tirolean daredevil skiers happened upon the Swiss dairy men in their little valley between the Rüflikopf (2362m), Karhorn (2416m), and Braunarspitze (2648m) peaks. Gasping in awe at the mountains, they took a quick swig of schnapps, checked their bindings, and immediately shooshed to the nearest bank, mortgaging all they had to bring the sport of skiing (and its wealthy practitioners) to the valley. The skiing was so good that the Lech chaps couldn't head up the hill quickly enough; in 1939 the first T-bar lift was built. From these humble beginnings sprung a giant among resorts; no fewer than four Olympic gold medalist skiers call Lech home. However, if you think the mountains are steep, you should check out the prices. Advice—spend more time on the mountain and less at the bar. In the summer, the shiny peaks looming above the town beckon those ready to lace up their boots and exercise as God intended—before Stairmaster took over. In Lech it is just the peaks and the town, making for amazing **hiking** prospects.

In typical gold mining town fashion, Lech has no street names ("Well, past Louie's saloon and before the old horse hitch"), but one main road pretty much does it all. The **bus** from St.Anton, Zürs, or Bludenz (44AS) pulls in at the start of the main drag. The **tourist office** (tel. 21 61, fax 31 55) is close by, down the hill on the right, and provides a model of efficiency; check the board in the hall for vacant rooms. (Open Dec.-April Mon.-Fri. 9am-noon and 2-6pm, Sat. 9am-6pm, Sun. 10am-noon and 3-5pm; late June-mid-Sept. Mon.-Sat. 8am-noon and 2-6pm, Sun. 10am-noon and 3-5pm; other months, Mon. and Wed.-Fri. 8am-noon and 2-5pm, Tues. 9am-noon and 2-5pm). The banks are also but a few steps removed and are generally open 8:30am-noon and 2-4pm. **Raiffeisenbank** (opposite the church) has an **ATM** and **24-hr. money exchange**. Swim laps in the shadow of the mountains at the 1200 square meter outdoor, heated swimming pool, the **Waldbad**, down the road to Stubenbach. Keep walking down the hill to find the **post office** on your left (open Mon.-Fri. 8am-noon and 2-6pm; **postal code:** A-6764), which has **telephones** (**city code:** 05583).

Guest beds outnumber permanent Lech residents five to one, but when the snow-flakes fall the beds fill up and the prices rise. Luckily, there is a **youth hostel** in Lech kept discreetly at a distance. From the bus stop, head down the main road into town, cross over the river when the road cuts left, and continue along this road. Don't panic when you reach the *auf wiedersehen* sign, but turn right when the road splits, down the hill and back over the river. Continue for about 15 minutes, and when the road curves back toward Lech, bear right at the tiny white chapel, head up hill to the left of *Haus Tristeller*, and climb one more hill. **Jugendheim Stubenbach(HI)** is at the top of that hill, decorated by a large mural depicting a prophet right in the middle of a revelation (tel. 24 19; fax 24 194; in summer, 130-150AS per person; in winter, 260-280AS; breakfast included; open July-late April). **Pension Würfl** (tel. 26 27) also serves up a tasty deal on a night's sleep. Located on the slopes. Facing the post office, go to your right across the river and to your second left, winding up the road toward Oberlecht to the green shutters of #45 (summer 200AS, winter 300AS). The daredevil skiers, who brought hordes of people to the valley, were quick to learn that in order to ski, you have to eat. **Pizza Charly** (tel. 23 39) will do fine, thank you. Underneath the cables of the Schloßkopfbahn (where they hang their tablecloths in the summer), the place serves up pizza (68-110AS) and pasta (68-115AS) and gives free yodeling lessons with coffee. (Open July-late April daily 11am-2pm and 5-11pm. Take-out available.)

VORARLBERG

On Austria's panhandle, Vorarlberg (2600 sq. km, pop. 340,000) is the westernmost province (and the smallest, barring Vienna). Most residents speak an Allemannian, dialect of German more akin to the tongues of neighboring Switzerland and German Swabia than the language of the rest of Austria. Here, at the crossroads of four nations, make sure you carry your passport at all times; foreign borders are never more than two hours away, and thereby an easy daytrip may take on an international flavor. **Bludenz**, at the intersection of the Ill and Alfenz Rivers, lies about 15km north of Switzerland and 20km east of *petit* Liechtenstein. **Bregenz**, on the banks of the Bodensee (Lake Constance), would be German but for half a dozen kilometers. It is the capital of Vorarlberg and the seat of the provincial government.

The area between the Bodensee and the Arlberg massif contains a variety of sumptuous scenery—from the soft-edged contours of the lake's shoreline to the plains of the upper Rhine Valley, it is a landscape molded by Ice Age glaciers. Vorarlberg's culinary specialty is *Kässpätzle*, a cheese and noodle combination. Cheese is big here (the edible and not the ABBA type); a visit to a Vorarlberg cheese dairy is an *après*-ski option worth milking.

Snow conditions are dependably *wunderbar* from December to April, with trails as high as 2600m. Further, over 1610km of marked hiking paths, ranging in altitude from 400 to 3350m, crosscut Vorarlberg, with mountain railways carrying hikers to the summit quickly and conveniently. Alpine associations maintain dozens of huts that provide accommodations and refreshments for hikers between May and October; opening times depend on the altitude, so contact the local tourist offices. Vorarlberg's 161km network of cycling paths ranges from leisurely routes that meander through the Bodensee and Rhine plain to challenging mountain-bike routes in the Alps. The 125km Bodensee circuit circumnavigates the lake. Cycling maps are available at bookstores and tourist offices.

▓ Schruns

First immortalized by Ernest Hemingway's autobiography *A Moveable Feast,* Schruns has since become a vacation get-away for world leaders, opera singers, and various European actors and actresses. Hemingway arrived in the winter of 1925, and the small town still has his signature from the original Hotel Taube guest book.

Orientation and Practical Information Schruns is located 13km southeast of Bludenz, the closest city accessible by major highway. Besides secondary roads, the *Montafonerbahn* (Montafon Valley train) and local buses offer frequent transportation between Schruns and Bludenz (about 25 trains per day). All train passages to the major Austrian cities of Innsbruck, Salzburg, and Vienna must first travel from Schruns to Bludenz. Local bus transportation is also offered to the smaller towns neighboring Schruns. The **tourist office** is located at Silvrettastr. 6 (tel. 721 66; fax 725 54). From the train station take a right and continue straight until you reach the Sparkasse building. With the Sparkasse building on your right, take a left onto Bahnhofstr. Go up Bahnhofstr. until you reach Kirchpl., with the easily distinguishable *Pfarrkirche* on your left, and Silvrettastr. is on the right; the tourist office is 20m down Silvrettastr. on the right. (Open mid-June to mid-Oct. Mon.-Fri. 8am-noon and 2-6pm, Sat. 9am-noon and 4-6pm, Sun. and holidays 10:30am-noon; weekdays only in the off-season.) A **public reading room** is located next to the tourist office. **Currency** can be exchanged during the week at the post office and at local banks. Most banks are open Mon.-Fri. 8am-noon and 2-5pm. Several banks in town offer **ATMs** with 24-hr. currency exchange. There is **public parking** next to the post office (1st hr. free). **Telephones** are in front of the post office.

The **train station**, Bahnhofstr. 17 (tel. 723 82), has 14 trains daily from Schruns to **Innsbruck** via Bludenz (2½hr., 204AS; first train leaves Schruns at 6:20am, last departure at 10:34pm). The *Montafonerbahn* travels the 13km between Bludenz and Schruns about 24 times per day (20min., 26AS, one-way; first train leaves Schruns at 5:26am, last at 10:03pm). **Luggage storage** 20AS per day per bag (open daily 7am-7pm). **Taxis** are available at the train station or by calling 17 12. Mangeng, Bahnhofstr. 6 (tel. 721 25), is a convenience store that sells **English magazines** such as *Time* and *Newsweek* (open Mon.-Sat. 7am-noon and 2-6pm, Sun. 9-11am). To **rent bikes,** try Intersport, Silvretta Center (tel. 71 03 38). Rental costs 220AS per day or 60AS per hour. Groups larger than five receive a 10% discount. Large groups must call a few days in advance to ensure that there are enough bikes available (open Mon.-Fri. 8:30am-noon and 2-6pm, Sat. 8:30am-noon). **Police:** Wagenweg 4 (tel. 721 33). **Police:** 133. **Fire:** 122. **Medical emergency:** 144. The **post office,** Wagenweg 1 (tel. 724 00), is about 150m to the right of the train station. Money exchange, telegrams, fax machine, and self-service photocopies available. (Open Mon.-Fri. 8am-6pm; July 16-Oct. 15 and Dec.16-April 15 Mon.-Fri. 8am-6pm, Sat. 8-11am.) **Postal code:** A-6780. **Telephone code:** 05556.

Accommodations Guest rooms are the most reasonably priced places to stay, and some of their out-of-the-way locales offer outstanding views of the natural surroundings. Reservations are *strongly* recommended, especially during the winter season when many hotels and pensions cater only to returning clientele.

Just up the street from the Hochjochbahn, on the edge of a cow pasture, stands **Haus Agnes**, Bergbahnstr. 21 (tel. 726 34). Coming out of the tourist office, head right on Silvrettastr., then take the first left onto Bergbahnstr. Walk up the hill past *Hochjochbahn* and the mini-golf place, and bear right when the road splits. Haus Agnes is the large, white house past the wooden fence. A friendly, English-speaking family will show you to a quiet, pink-walled room. (In summer 200-220AS, with shower 220-250AS; in winter 210-230AS, with shower 240-300AS.) **Gästehaus Hanni Loretz,** Prof.-Tschohl-weg 8 (tel. 739 22), at the edge of town, offers a flower garden, fish pond (in summer), and a mountainside show. From the train station take a right and continue straight to the post office. Take a right onto the street directly in front of the post office, and take the first left onto Vettlinerweg. Follow the street until it intersects Prof.-Tschohl-Weg, take a right, and follow the street to #8. Rustic shutters give the impeccably clean, brown-carpeted rooms an old-fashioned touch. (In summer singles 210AS, doubles 400AS. In winter singles 230AS, doubles 440AS. Shower, toilet, and breakfast included.) If you're in the mood to rough it, **Thöny's,** Flurstr. (tel. and fax 726 74), will make your camping experience as enjoyable as possible. From the train station, turn left and then take the first left over the train tracks onto Batloggstr. Walk straight ahead for about 300m and there will be a sign pointing to the campground. They have hook-ups for mobile home owners and for those who plan to pitch a tent; they even have washers and driers. (80AS per site, 60AS per person, 13AS tax per person.)

Food For a traditional Italian meal, eat at the **Don Camillo Pizzeria Ristorante,** Im Gässle 6 (tel. 769 01). Under white, gently vaulted ceilings, Don Camillo provides a relaxed, sit-down meal. Many vegetarian options are served. From the train station go straight up Bahnhofstr. Bear right at the fork in the road, immediately after which there is a small path on your right leading to the restaurant, marked by its red, white, and green sign. (Entrées 80-225AS. Open daily 11:30am-2pm and 5pm-midnight. Closed Thurs. in the summer.) **Museo Gusto,** next to the church, at the head of Dorfstr., is your place for ice cream (10AS) or *Apfel Strudel* (25AS) in the center of town (open Tues.-Sat. 9am-1am). For a do-it-yourself meal, shop at **Spar,** Silvretta Center, next to the bike rental shop (tel. 71 03). The small store has everything, from toothpaste to turnips (open Mon.-Fri. 7:30am-6pm, Sat. 7:30am-12:30pm).

Sights and Entertainment Schruns prides itself on offering many opportunities for the outdoorsperson, from winter skiing at the local **Hochjoch resort** to summer hiking over its vast mountain country. A one-day ticket for skiing at Hochjoch (tel. 721 26) costs 405AS. **Montafon-Abos tickets** entitle the purchaser to use one of the 69 cableways and lifts that operate in the Montafon Valley, shuttle bus, and passage on the *Montafonerbahn* (1055AS for three days, children 655AS, seniors 845AS). The **Hochjochbahn** transports daring skiers to the mountain's steepest descent (1700m) spread over 11km. From June 15 to the end of October, the Hochjochbahn is in operation, transporting nature lovers, hikers, and mountain view enthusiasts to three stations (Kropfen, 1335m; Kopell, 1855m; and Sennigrat, 2300m) high above the Montafon Valley. A round-trip ticket to Sennigrat costs 190AS, with guest card 174AS. The *Hochjochbahn* runs daily between 8:30am and 5pm, with rides on the hour.

From mid-June to mid-October, the tourist office offers the **Montafoner Sommerpass**. It is valid for seven days and entitles the holder to free rides on eight mountain lifts (including the *Hochjochbahn*) in the valley, as well as unlimited travel on the Montafonerbahn and buses and admission to all pools and museums (480AS, seniors 380AS, children 290AS). A large sign at the bottom of the *Hochjochbahn,* as well as a free brochure, details 13 hiking trails, all marked 1-3hr., with bright colors. The **Wormser Hütte** is an easy 20-minute walk from the Sennigrat station. If you want to experience the mountain but spare your legs, try the one-hour downhill trek from Kapell to Kropfen. To satisfy more exotic urges, check out rafting (from 990AS), spelunking (840AS), mountain climbing (from 590AS), tandem paragliding (from 1000AS), riding (780AS for three hours), archery (150AS), or **canyoning** (a bizarre sport where the brave don wetsuits, helmets, life jackets, and harnesses and pay for the privilege of inching down icy Alpine rivers and waterfalls; 890AS). All activities include instruction and require a minimum number of participants (usually 4-5); check with the office.

Back indoors, the **Montafoner Heimat Museum** (Local Museum of the Montafon Valley) details the comprehensive history of the Montafon Valley through four floors of exhibits and paintings. The displays range from one of the earliest pairs of wooden skis (complete with primitive metal and leather bindings) to a modern series of paintings depicting the Stations of the Cross. One can also find furniture, traditional costumes, weaponry, and craftsmen's tools in the era before Sears & Roebuck. (Museum open July-Sept. 15 Tues.-Sat. 3-6pm, Sun. 10am-noon; Sept. 16-Oct. 26 and Dec.26-June Tues., Fri. 3-6pm. 25AS, students 5AS.)

The **Pfarrkirche,** whose domed, yellow tower shadows the town's Kirchplatz, contains intricate ceiling paintings and altarpieces. The beautiful, embedded mosaic of St. George slaying the dragon that adorns the outside of the 19th-century church only hints at the ornamentation that awaits inside. The stained-glass windows and triad of altarpieces topped with three-dimensional figures and gold leaf are overwhelming. The simple pine pews create an elegant balance (open daily 8am-6pm).

■ Feldkirch

As early as the 13th century, travelers lauded Feldkirch for its ancient castles, fiercely protected feudal lands, and fascinating history. The **Ill River** winds its way through the city and, in seeming defiance of its foreboding moniker, has been a balm of health and rejuvenation for road-weary wanderers and the city's 27,000 residents. Feldkirch is an excellent base for international expeditions; the city is just minutes from the Swiss and Liechtensteinian borders and handles all trains to Bregenz and the German Bodensee. The narrow streets, with their carefully restored buildings, are functional and fashionable reminders of the Middle Ages.

Orientation and Practical Information The **tourist office,** Herrengasse 12 (tel. 734 67; fax 798 67), is a short walk from the train station. Exit the station door and walk straight ahead until the road intersects Bahnhofstr. Take a left onto this road and proceed 5 minutes to the descending stairs of an underpass. Underneath the street, follow the arrow marked *Zentrum*. Back on street level, walk through the *Bezirkhauptmannschaft* building directly ahead. Herrengasse is slightly to your right. The office helps with hotel and *privatzimmer* reservations and hands out a good map with a walking tour of historic sights. Cultural information and a detailed city map are available outside after hours. Be sure to pick up the *Gäste-Anzeiger,* or guest newspaper, for free (open Mon.-Fri. 9am-7pm, Sat. 9am-noon; mid-Sept. to mid-June, Mon.-Fri. 8am-noon and 2-6pm, Sat. 9am-noon). **City buses** *(Stadt Bus)* connect Feldkirch's various subdivisions (12AS, 24AS for a day pass). **BundesBuses** connect Feldkirch to other parts of Austria (main departures from the train station), and Swiss PTT buses connect Vaduz, Buchs, and Sargens to Feldkirch. **Bicycle rental** (50AS with train ticket, 100AS without), **currency exchange,** and **lockers** (20-30AS) are available at the **train station** (open daily 6:25am-11:30pm). Trains run frequently to **Vienna** (7hr.30min., 770AS), **Salzburg** (4hr., 500AS), **Innsbruck** (2hr., 228AS), and **Bregenz** (45min., one-way 56AS, round-trip 74AS). **Taxis:** call 1718 or 1712. Lesbian travelers can contact **Auton. Feministisches Netzwerk Feldkirch,** Büro im Jugendhaus Graf Hugo, A-6800 Feldkirch (tel. 792 95; open Tues. 9-11am for information and counseling). Feldkirch's **post office** is across from the train station, on Bahnhofstr. (open Mon.-Fri. 7am-7pm, Sat. 7am-noon). There are **telephones** inside and outside. **Postal code:** A-6800. **Telephone Code:** 05522.

Accommodations and Food While there are no inexpensive hotels anywhere near the *Altstadt,* a short bus ride or walk leads to several promising opportunities. To reach the town's youth hostel, **Jugendherberge "Altes Siechenhaus,"** Reichstr. 111 (tel. 731 81), catch city bus #1 ("Ringbus"), 2, or 60 to "Jugendherberge." By foot, walk straight out of the train station past the post office to Bahnhof-str., and turn right; Bahnhofstr. now becomes Reichstr. Walk 15-20 minutes; the hostel is an ancient white brick-and-wood building on the right of the street, next to a small stone church. This nearly 600-year-old *Fachwerk* structure served as an infirmary during the Black Plague and several other epidemics. In 1640 it was used to house sick people outside the city walls. Later it was a poor house and was even used as a grammar school after the great fire of 1697. Today, all the lepers, paupers, and displaced school children are gone, replaced by a friendly proprietor and a spotlessly clean, modern house with thick wooden beams, white stucco walls and a decidedly medieval feel. The garden in back lets you laze the day away or strike up a game of ping pong. (Reception open 7-10am and 5-11pm. 160AS, breakfast included. Handi-capped accessible. To reserve a room outside of these hours, use the envelopes out-side the door and return by 5pm.) If the hostel is full, a short ride on bus #2 or #3 to "Egelseestr." leads to **Gasthof Löwen,** in Tosters-Feldkirch (tel. 72 868). Get off at stop "Burgweg" and walk half a block toward the tall pink and white building on Egel-seestr.; the green shutters of the Gasthof are visible on this corner. The hotel offers simple rooms in a quiet neighborhood (220-350AS per person, breakfast and showers included).

Dining in Feldkirch is fortunately not as difficult as finding a place to stay. **Pizzeria-Trattoria La Taverna,** Vorstadtstr. 18 (tel. 792 93), offers a cool Mediterranean atmo-sphere and affordable pizza (65-100AS) and pasta (70-100AS) as well as a vegetarian's Valhalla (open daily 11:30am-2pm and 5pm-midnight). For a quick, inexpensive bite, head for *Döner Kebabs* or pizza at **König Kebap,** Kreuzgasse 9 (tel. 380 42), right down from the tourist office (open Mon.-Sat. 9am-11pm, Sun. 11am-11pm). The res-taurant inside the huge iron doors of the **Schattenburg Castle** serves up enormous portions of *Wiener Schnitzel* (135AS) and *Apfel Strudel* (35AS; open Tues.-Sun. 10am-midnight). A stroll in the *Fußgängerzone,* with its many restaurants and cafés, can usually satisfy any appetite. Be sure to try the Feldkirch Spezi, a mixture of coke and lemonade. It's always relatively cheap—at least cheaper than the beer (!). In the center of the *Altstadt,* find picnic supplies at **Interspar Markt,** at the top of Johan-nitergasse, off Marktgasse (open Mon.-Thurs. 9am-6:30pm, Fri. 9am-7pm, Sat. 8am-1pm). Its smaller cousin, **Spar Markt,** is across from the Jugendherberge, one minute toward the Altstadt (open Mon.-Fri. 7am-noon and 2:30-6pm, Sat. 7am-noon). There is also a **market** in the Markplatz (Tues. and Sat. mornings).

Sights and Entertainment Begin your voyage to the era of chivalry at the green steeple of the Gothic **St. Nikolaus Kirche** in the center of the *Altstadt.* The edi-fice was mentioned in a document in 1287 and received a facelift in 1478 after a series of devastating fires. The **Pieta,** crafted in 1521 by Wolf Huber (a master of the Danube School), graces the altar on the right. Frescoes of Feldkirch history and the coats of arms of local potentates adorn the 15th-century **Rathaus** on Schmiedgasse, originally a granary. On nearby Schloßgasse stands the **Palais Liechtenstein,** com-pleted in 1697. The palace, which once supported the royal seat of the Prince of Liechtenstein (yes, the ones that own that tiny country), now houses the city archives and the town library. For two weeks in the middle of June, the plays of Johann Nestroy are performed in the courtyard of the Palais. The **Schattenburg Castle** pre-sides over the *Neustadt* quarter; stroll up either Schloßsteig or Burggasse for a great view of the *Altstadt.* From the early 1200s until 1390, the castle was the seat of the Count of Montfort. The town purchased the castle in 1825 to save it from demolition and converted it into the **Feldkirch Heimatmuseum.** Locks, weapons, paintings, and medallions lie side by side with small cradles and 18th-century stoves in the historic apartments of the erstwhile castle (open Tues.-Sun. 9am-noon and 1-5pm. 25AS, youth 15AS, child 5AS). Just outside the *Altstadt* lies the **Capuchin monastery,** built in 1605. In 1817, when a great famine struck Feldkirch, the monks fed 2000 people daily here with a soup made from potatoes and bone gratings.

December brings the annual Christmas bazaar, complete with crafts, candy canes, and creches, all sold throughout Advent. In the second weekend of July, Feldkirch's annual **wine festival** intoxicates all those who venture to the Marktplatz. Voralbergers laud one of their own during the **Schubertiade,** throughout which Schubert's works and modern interpretations of them are played at the *Landeskonservatorium* (School of Music), concert halls, and manor houses in the Feldkirch area. 1996 performers included pianist Andràs Schiff and the Alban Berg quartet. The festival will run from June 18 to July 1 in 1997. Ticket bookings are accepted beginning in October 1996 by phone (tel. 720 91; fax 175 450), or mail. (Write to Schubertiade Feldkirch GmbH, Postfach 625, Schubertpl. 1, A-6803 Feldkirch. Prices run 100-1300AS, depending on the specific event, location, and seat; outdoor concert tickets cost 100-400AS.)

Monforthaus, just past the castle entrance on Neustadtstr. is a 1000 seat auditorium and plaza with frequent concerts, musicals, plays, and other cultural events. Ice skaters blade the day away in Voralberghalle (tel. 733 88). The circus comes to town on the first weekend of August; the annual **Festival of Traveling Entertainers** sweeps jugglers, mimes, clowns, and those anatomically questionable balloon animals into every cobblestone path.

■ Bregenz

A playground city on the banks of the **Bodensee** (Lake Constance), Vorarlberg's capital, Bregenz, approaches tourist nirvana. Thousands of Swiss, Germans, and Austrians come—speedo-clad—to bake on the banks of the lake, occasionally exerting themselves to sail or to hike in the nearby mountains. When the Romans conquered Brigantium two millennia ago, they set up a thriving bath and spa center and ever since those first ancient sun-worshippers, Bregenz has been a shrine to the principles of pleasure. Gallus and Columban, two Irish missionaries, were captured by Bregenz's magnetism. As they lifted their heads from their medieval beach blankets, they observed the vast shimmering lake ringed by mountains, and so dubbed the locale "Bregenz" (Golden Bowl). The town's international locale has made it a military focal point for centuries. Happily, the only remnant from the bloody past is the inimitable **White Fleet,** an armada of Bodensee ferries that have abandoned belligerence and today deliver wealthy vacationers from three different currencies—er, countries—to the city's open palms—er, ports.

ORIENTATION AND PRACTICAL INFORMATION

Bregenz is a city of piled-on layers of history and architecture, ranging from *belle-epoque* townhouses and modern hotels in the *Zentrum,* to the *Fachwerk* (timber) style of the *Oberstadt* on the slopes surrounding the lake. The *Zentrum* extends its grasp along the shore of the lake, and ends along the Bregenzer Str. The turquoise train station is right on the lake, near the *Stadtzentrum.* Bahnhofstr., in front of the station, divides into Seestr. and Kornmarktstr., both of which lead to the town center. The other side of Bahnhofstr. becomes Rheinstr., which leads away from the city. On the eastern edge of the Bodensee, Bregenz is generally the first major city one passes when coming from Switzerland or the southwestern corner of Germany. Hourly trains chauffeur passengers to **Bludenz** and **St. Gallen.** Bregenz also has daily connections to **Zürich, Innsbruck, Vienna,** and **Munich. BundesBus** connections to the rest of Austria leave from the train station.

Tourist Office: Anton-Schneider-Str. 4A (tel. 433 91-0), makes hotel reservations (30AS), dispenses *Privatzimmer* lists, hiking and city maps, and concert info. English spoken. From the train station, head left along Bahnhofstr., turn right on Rathausstr., and then left onto Anton-Schneider-Str, or just cross the street and walk straight along the shopping strip, which leads to the same area.

Consulate: U.K., Bundesstr. 110, in neighboring Lauterach (tel. 78 586).

City Buses: Buses connect the train station to most points of interest in the city. 13AS per ride, Tagesnetzkarte 26AS.

Car Rental: Hertz, Immler Schneeweiss, Am Brand 2 (tel. 44 995). **Avis-ARBÖ,** Rheinstr. 86 (tel. 78 100).

Parking: Garage GWL (tel. 437 37), in Leutbühel. **Hypobank** parking garage, and metered parking lots and spaces throughout the city.

Taxis: tel. 1718

AIDS Information: AIDS-Hilfe Voralberg, Neugasse 5, A-6900 Bregenz (tel. 465 26). Hotline open Tues. and Thurs. 4-7pm, Wed. and Fri. 10am-1pm. HIV test Tues. and Thurs. 5-7pm.

Post Office: Seestr. 5 (tel. 490 00). Open Mon.-Sat. 7am-7pm, though the cashier's desk closes at 5pm, Sun. 9am-noon. **Postal Code:** A-6900.

Telephone Code: 05574.

ACCOMMODATIONS AND CAMPING

Though Bregenz caters to a wealthy tourist clientele, it's not impossible for the budget traveler to get a good night's rest. Be warned, though; notes and accommodation prices soar during the Bregenzer Festspiele.

Jugendherberge (HI), Belrupstr. 16a (tel. 228 67), a quick stroll from the tourist office. Head right on Anton-Schneider-Str. and turn right on Bergmannstr., at the Österreichischer Nationalbank building; then turn left on Belrupstr. A few blocks later, bear right up the hill at the hostel sign to the wood-and-stucco hostel. An elongated barn house, the easy one-corridor layout makes it hard to get lost. The sunny lawn is good for a sun bath, ping-pong, or a game of Frisbee. Reception open 5-8pm. Curfew 10pm. 121AS. Sheets 30AS. Breakfast and shower included. Free lockers on request. Open April-Sept.

Pension Sonne, Kaiserstr. 8 (tel. 425 72), off the Bahnhofstr., minutes from the train station. Clean, quiet rooms, centrally located in the *Fußgängerzone*. Terrace, historic location, and an English-speaking staff are some of the comforts of this pension. Singles 330-470AS, doubles 600-900AS, depending on the season and whether or not you have a private bath. Breakfast and shower included.

Pension Paar, Am Steinbach 10 (tel. 423 05). Walk left from the train station, up Bahnhofstr. to Seestr. until it becomes Reichstr., and make a right off that onto Steinbach at the "Hotel Germania" sign. This family-run mauve house is on a quiet street near the edge of Bregenz. Singles 380AS, doubles 680AS. Hall showers and breakfast included. Open May-Oct.

Seecamping, (tel. 718 96 or 718 95) is a long but pleasant walk from the train station, bearing left along Strandweg on the lake, or take Bus #2 (dir: Achsiedlung Weidach) to stop "Viktoria" and follow the signs. It boasts a beautiful lakeside location and sparkling white tile bathrooms. 60AS per person, showers included. Tent, car, or caravan 60AS. Guest tax 16AS. Open May 15-Sept. 15.

FOOD

Pizza Charly, Dr.-Anton-Schneider-Str. 19 (tel. 459 59). Pizza (65-100AS), pasta (70-90AS), and vegetarian pasture land (10 different salad plates 32-88AS), just down the street from the tourist office. Another location at Quellenstr. 32. Open Mon.-Sat. 11:45am-1:30pm and 5:30-11:30pm, Sun. 11:45am-2pm and 5-11:30pm.

Ikaros, Deuringstr. 5. A little taste of the mediterranean on the Bodensee. In this little café, fish nets and wine bottles line the walls, and *baklava* (10AS) warms the heart. Gorgeous Greek salads (58AS) and a glass of wine (22AS). Open Mon.-Fri. 10am-midnight, Sat. 9am-4pm.

Zum Goldenen Hirschen, Kirchstr. 8 (tel. 428 15), one block up on your way to the Oberstadt. Look for the old wooden building with the small stained glass windows and a flying gold reindeer over the door. Dark wooden furniture and outside patio. *Schnitzel* 110AS. Visa, MC.

SIGHTS AND ENTERTAINMENT

St. Martinsplatz is the center of the **Oberstadt** (medieval part of the city); its anchor, the **Martinskirche,** is filled with frescoes dating back to the early 14th century. Partic-

WEST AUSTRIA

ularly noteworthy are the depictions of St. Christopher, the Holy Symbol of Grief, and the 18th-century Stations of the Cross. The **Martinturm,** to the right of the church, rules the *Oberstadt* with 2000-year-old authority. It boasts Europe's largest onion dome and was the first Baroque structure built on the Bodensee. Though the dome is closed to the public, the view from the third floor of the tower is a breathtaking look out over the blue Boden expanse and into Germany and Switzerland. The first and second floors of the tower house the **Voralberg Military Museum** (open May-Sept. Tues.-Sun. 9am-6pm; 10AS, children 7AS).

Just past Ehrequta Square, at the top of Kirchstr. and Thalbachgasse stands the **Parish Church of St. Gallus.** The white stucco sanctuary of the 11-century church now glows under the lavish gold ornamentation and a detailed ceiling painting which dates from 1738. The shepherdesses in the altar has the face of Empress Maria Theresa, who donated 1500 guilders to the church in 1740. Climb the steps set into the hill or walk up under the overpass for a sweeping view of the *Oberstadt.* Look for the old city walls containing the Baker's Tower, where 16th-century bakers were locked up for the heinous crime of producing loaves that were too small. The **Alte Rathaus,** on Graf-Wilhelm-Str., is a marvelous example of the intricate *Fachwerk* architecture characteristic of the region. A wander along the narrow cobblestone streets will lead you to the **Deuring Castle.** An expensive hotel with one of the world's most perfect restaurants. If Austria's gorgeous gilt churches are all starting to look alike, check out the imposing **Herz-Jesu Kirche,** one block from the youth hostel. Built in 1907 and recently renovated in neo-Gothic style, the brick wood and sea-green accents in the huge sanctuary complement the abstract geometric stained glass windows.

To see Bregenz as it was before tourists, head over to the **Voralberg Landesmuseum,** Kornmarktpl. 1. The museum's collection spans thousands of years, with carefully explained exhibits (alas, all in German) on the Stone and Bronze Age inhabitants of Bregenz. (Open Tues.-Sun. 9am-noon and 2-5pm. 20AS, students 10AS.)

The main attraction of Bregenz is the Bodensee itself. All along the waterfront, carefully groomed paths and strategically placed ice cream stands surround fantastic playgrounds, mini-golf, and paddle boat rental shops. Away from the city center and down past the train station lies the **Strand-und-Freibad** (tel. 442 42), a huge swimming pool, sauna, and sunbathing area. (Open mid-May to mid-Sept. Tues.-Fri. 9am-9pm, Sat. 9am-7pm, Sun. 10am-6pm in fair weather. 33AS, students and seniors 20AS.) The black monstrosity on the edge of the lake is not a ski ramp gone awry, but the world's largest floating stage and the centerpiece for the annual Bregenzer Festspiele. Every year from mid-July to mid-August the Vienna Symphony Orchestra and other opera, theatrical, and chamber music companies come to town, bringing some 180,000 tourists with them. The main attraction is the floating stage's performance which plays to sold-out crowds of 6000 (*Porgy and Bess,* done in English for 1997 and 1998). Ticket sales for all events commence in October. (100-1250AS. Standing room tickets can only be purchased 1hr. before performance; arrive as early as possible, but expect to still face a huge line and painful wait.) For more information, write to Postfach 311, A-6901 Bregenz, call 407 223, or check it out on the Web (http://www.vol.at/bregenzerfestspiele).

To acquaint yourself with the lake from a different angle, hop aboard a ferry to the **Blumeninsel Mainau** (Mainau Flower Isle) and participate in one of the year-round tours of the island's Baroque castle, indoor tropical palm house, or new butterfly house. Orchids, tulips, dahlias, and 1100 kinds of roses fill the outside gardens. (Ferries depart Bregenz May-Sept. daily at 11am and leave Mainau at 3:55pm, returning to Bregenz at 6:40pm. Round-trip 280AS, under 16 half-price, plus the 112AS entrance fee at Mainau.) There is also an international tour from Bregenz in Austria, stopping at the ports of Rorschach, Switzerland, and Lindau, Germany (July-Aug., Tues. and Thurs., leaving at 1:45pm returning at 6:45pm; round-trip 160AS). Or join the afternoon cruise along the Swiss, German, and Austrian waterfronts on the **Drei-Länder-Rundfahrt.** (The boat departs Bregenz July-Aug. at 2:30pm, docks again at 5pm. 140AS. 50% off of all cruises with a Eurail pass or Austrian Rail Pass, and various discounts for children. Bring your passport on board all boat rides.) All cruises leave from the harbor, across from the post office (tel. 428 68).

Catch the **cable car** near the hostel that sways up the Pfänder mountain (the tallest peak around the Bodensee) for a panorama spanning from the Black Forest to the Swiss Alps. (Up 84AS, down 60AS, round-trip 120AS, discounts for seniors and children under 19.) Runs daily on the hour 9am-6pm, Sept. 22-March 9am-6pm, closed the second and third weeks in November (tel. 42 160). Adjacent to the lift's apex is a **wild park** with trails where animals wander in their natural habitat (free). The many hikes down (45min.-2hr.) are worth every step.

Gateway Cities

Travel often introduces one to a culture fashioned long before the advent of 20th century political boundaries. Such is certainly manifest in Austria, whose imperial flourish once covered a much larger part of Europe than what is now circumscribed by its national borders. Though now no longer a part of the Austrian nation, cities like Prague, the erstwhile capitol of the Holy Roman Empire, and Budapest were extremely close to the Habsburgs' heart. Both make an excellent and highly recommended weekend destination from Vienna. Munich, only 120km from its Baroque Austrian sister, Salzburg is another key destination for border hoping. It is often cheaper to fly into the German city and take the train down to Salzburg than it is to fly to Salzburg itself.

■ Prague (Praha)

According to legend, Princess Libuše stood on Vyšehrad above the Vltava and declared, "I see a city whose glory will touch the stars; it shall be called Praha (threshold)." Medieval kings, benefactors, and architects easily fulfilled the princess's prophecy, as soaring cathedrals and lavish palaces gave notice of Prague's status as the capital of the Holy Roman Empire. Curiously, though, the city's character differed sharply from the holy splendor of Rome and Constantinople: legends of demons, occult forces, and mazes of shady alleys lent this "city of dreams" a dark side and provided frightening fodder for Franz Kafka's tales of paranoia. Only this century has the spell been broken, as the fall of the Berlin Wall brought hordes of euro-trotting foreigners to the once-isolated capital. Sadly, Prague has now lost much of the mystery and intrigue of Kafka's day; tourists and entrepreneurs have long since explored and exploited every nook and cranny of the city. Yet these same visitors also lend the city a festive air which few places in the world can match. Come for the great beer, or world-class concerts and shows, or simply immerse yourself in the humbling magnificence of this 1000-year-old metropolis.

ORIENTATION AND PRACTICAL INFORMATION

Straddling a bend in the Vltava, Prague is a gigantic mess of suburbs and winding streets. **Staré Město** (Old Town) lies along the southeast riverbank; across the Vltava sits the **Hradčany** castle with **Malá Strana** at its south base. Southeast of the Old Town spreads **Nové Město** (New Town), and farther east across **Wilsonova** lie the **Žižkov** and **Vinohrady** districts. **Holešovice** in the north has an international train terminal; **Smíchov,** the southwest end, is the student-dorm suburb. All train and bus terminals are on or near the Metro system. Metro B: nám. Republiky is closest to the principal tourist offices and accommodations agencies.

Don't just refer to your map: study it. *Tabak* stands and bookstores vend indexed *plán města* (maps). The **Praha** booklet (190kč) contains maps of the city by suburb including up-to-date transport links and a comprehensive street index. The English-language weekly *The Prague Post* provides tips for visitors and the usual news.

> Prague is in the process of carrying out a telephone-system overhaul; throughout 1997 many numbers will change, though the eight-digit ones should not.

Tourist Offices: Signs with "i"s signal tourist agencies that book rooms, arrange tours, and sell maps and guidebooks. Be wary: these private firms didn't pop up just to help tourists. Prague Information Service (Pražská Informační Služba), Staromwstske nám. 1 (tel. 54 44 44; fax 24 21 19 89), happily sells maps, arranges tours, and books musical extravaganzas (open Mon.-Fri. 9am-7pm, Sat.-Sun. 9am-6pm). **Čedok,** Na příkopě 18 (tel. 24 19 73 50; fax 232 16 56), a Communist relic, once controlled all of Czech tourism. The staff can answer the trickiest travel and

Central Prague

Betlémská kaple (Bethlehem Chapel), 38
Čedok Office, 23
Čedok Office, 27
Clam-Gallasův palác (Clam-Gallas Palace), 32
Divadlo na zábradlí (Theatre at the Balustrade), 36
Dům umělců (Rudolfinum), 1
Golz-Kinsky Palace, 16
Jan Hus monument, 15
Jubilejní synagóga (Jubilee Synagogue), 24

Kafka museum, 13
Karolinum (Charles University), 28
Klausova synagóga (Klaus Synagogue), 4
Klementinum and sv Kliment (St. Clement church), 33
Maislova synagóga (Maisl Synagogue), 12
Masarykovo nádraží (Railway Station), 22
Náprstek Museum, 37
Obecní dům (Municipal House), 18
Pánělská Synagóga (Spanish Synagogue), 10
Panna Marie před Týnem (Týn Church), 17

Pinkasova synagóga (Pinkas Synagogue), 3
PIS (Pražská Informační Služba), 26
Prašná brána (Powder Tower), 19
Smetana Museum, 35
Social Democratic Party HQ, 21
Staroměstská radnice (Old Town Hall), 31
Staronová synagóga (Old-New Synagogue), 6
Starý Židovský hřbitov (Old Jewish Cemetery), 5
Stavovské divadlo (Estates Theatre), 29
sv Duch, 9

sv František (St. Francis church), 34
sv Havel (St. Gall Church), 30
sv Jindřich (St. Henry Church), 25
sv Mikuláš, 14
sv Salvátor, 11
sv Jiljí (St. Giles Church), 39
Umělecko-průmyslové muzeum (Museum of Decorative Arts), 2
U hybernů, 20
Vysoká synagóga (High Synagogue), 7
Židovnická radnice (Jewish Town Hall), 8

GATEWAY CITIES

transportation questions, but for more banal requests the bureaucracy isn't worth it. Open Mon.-Fri. 8:30am-6pm, Sat. 9am-1pm.

Budget Travel: CKM, Jindřišská 28 (tel. 26 85 32; fax 26 86 23), sells ISICs (150kč) and HI cards (350kč) and arranges trips to Scandinavia. Open Mon.-Fri. 9am-6pm. The office at Žitná 12 (tel. 29 12 40; fax 24 22 18 13) handles bus, rail, and train tickets. Open Mon.-Fri. 9am-6pm. **KMC,** Karoliny Světlé 30 (tel. 24 23 06 33; fax 855 00 13), sells HI cards (300kč) and can book HI hostels in Prague and virtually everywhere in the world. Open Mon.-Fri. 9am-noon and 2-4pm.

Passport Office: Foreigner police headquarters at Olšanská 2 (tel. 683 17 39). Take Metro A to "Flora." Walk down Jičinská, and turn right onto Olšanska, or take tram 9. Come here for a visa extension. Open Mon.-Tues. and Thurs. 7:30-11:45am and 12:30-2:30pm, Wed. 7:30-11:30am and 12:30-5pm, Fri. 7:30-noon.

Embassies: U.S., Tržiště 15 (tel. 24 51 08 47, after hours tel. 53 12 00). Take Metro A to "Malostranská." From Malostranské nám., turn onto Karmelitská, then right on Tržiště. Open Mon.-Fri. 9am-noon and 2-3pm. **Canada,** Mickiewiczova 6 (tel. 24 31 11 08, after hours 06 01 20 35 20). Take Metro A to "Hradčanská." Open Mon.-Fri. 9am-noon and 2-4pm. **U.K.,** Thunovská 14 (tel. 24 51 04 39). Take Metro A to "Malostranská." Open Mon.-Fri. 9am-noon. Travelers from **Australia** and **New Zealand** should contact the British embassy. **South Africa,** Ruská 65 (tel. 67 31 11 14). Take Metro A to "Jiřího z Poděbrad." Open Mon.-Fri. 9am-noon.

Currency Exchange: Visitors with AmEx and Thomas Cook traveler's checks can get currency commission-free at their respective offices. On weekends and holidays, exchange counters in large hotels will convert money. **Komerční Banka,** Na příkopě 33 (tel. 24 02 11 11; fax 24 24 30 20), offers 2% commission on traveler's checks and cash. Open Mon.-Fri. 9am-5pm. **Živnostenská Banka,** Na příkopě 20 (tel. 24 12 11 11; fax 24 12 55 55), gives cash advances on MasterCard and Visa. Commission 1% on cash, 2% on traveler's checks. Open Mon.-Fri. 8:30am-5:30pm. **Chequepoint,** in all highly touristed areas and sometimes open 24hr., requires a 10% commission and a service charge. **ATMs** are popping up everywhere; the one in the wall of the Krone supermarket on Václavské nám. is connected to the Cirrus, Eurocard, Eurocheque, MC, Plus, and Visa networks.

American Express: Václavské nám. 56 (tel. 24 21 99 92; fax 24 22 77 08). Take Metro A or C to "Muzeum." Address mail: "American Express, Client Letter Service, Václavské nám. 56, 113 26 Praha 1, Czech Republic." MC and Visa cash advances at 3% commission. **ATM.** Exchange office open May-Sept. daily 9am-7pm; Oct.-April Mon.-Fri. 9am-6pm and Sat. 9am-3pm. Travel office open May-Sept. Mon.-Fri. 9am-6pm, Sat. 9am-2pm; Oct.-April Mon.-Fri. 9am-5pm, Sat. 9am-noon.

Thomas Cook: Václavské nám. 47 (tel. 24 22 86 58; fax 26 56 95). Cash Thomas Cook's Eurocheques here. Flexible hours for clients. MC cash advances and emergency card replacement. Open Mon.-Fri. 9am-6pm, Sat. 9am-5pm.

Telephones: Jindřišská 14, in the post office. Open daily 7am-11pm. Buy phone cards at kiosks, the post office, or from the Telecom man at *Hlavní pošta.* But beware: some kiosks, especially near Malá Strana and Staré Město, charge above the usual 100kč for 50 units.

Flights: Ruzyně Airport (tel. 334 33 14), 20km northwest of city center. Take bus #119 from "Dejvická" or #176 from Metro B to "Nové Butovice." Private companies run expensive buses from the airport to downtown Prague (90-400kč). Fifteen carriers fly into Prague. **ČSA** (Czech National Airlines) has a main office at Revoluční 1 (tel. 24 80 61 11 or 24 80 62 25). Take Metro B to "nám. Republiky."

Trains: 24-hr. info in Czech tel. 24 21 76 54. Prague has 4 train depots; always ask what your departure point is. If you're confused, Čedok books seats and couchettes. **Praha Hlavní Nádraží** (or Wilsonovo Nádraží) handles international and domestic routes. Take Metro C to "Hlavní Nádraží." **B.I.J. Wasteels** (tel. 24 61 50 54; fax 24 22 18 72), in the station, offers under-26 train tickets for 20-40% off. Open Mon.-Fri. 8:45-11:30am and 12:30-5:45pm. To: **Berlin** (6hr.; 1301kč, Wasteels 1123kč); **Budapest** (9hr.; 906kč, Wasteels 670kč); **Vienna** (5hr.; 638kč, Wasteels 460kč); **Warsaw** (10hr.; 625kč, Wasteels 413kč). **Praha-Holešovice** is the other large terminal. Metro C to "Nádraží Holešovice." Five daily departures to **Berlin,** 5 to **Budapest,** and 2 to **Vienna.** The international ticket office sells Wasteels tickets (open 24hr.). **Masarykovo Nádraží** (formerly Střední), at Hybernská and Havlikčova, covers domestic routes to Central and West Bohemia. Metro B to "nám. Republiky." **Praha Smíchov,** across the river, opposite Vyšehrad, serves nearby domestic routes. Metro B to "Smíchovské Nádraží."

Buses: ČSAD has three *autobusové nádraží* (bus terminals). **Praha-Florenc,** Křižíkova (tel. 24 21 49 90; info in Czech 24 21 10 60), behind the Masarykovo Nádraží train station, sells tickets to Berlin (6hr., 1 per day, 820kč), Budapest (8hr., 5 per week, 740kč), and Vienna (8hr., 1-2 per day, 810kč). Metro B or C to "Florenc." The staff speaks little English, but schedules are legible and extensive. Buy tickets at least a day in advance; they often sell out. The Tourbus office upstairs (tel. 24 21 02 21) sells **Eurolines** tickets. Tourbus open daily 8am-8pm.

Public Transportation: The **Metro, tram,** and **bus** systems serve the city well. Tickets, available at newsstands, "DP" kiosks, and machines in the metro stations, are valid on all forms of transportation. 6kč tickets are good for 15min. after punching, and only for 1 ride; if you're switching lines or expect a longer trip, get a 10kč ticket (valid for 1hr.). The municipal transit authority **DP** *(Dopravní Podnik),* at Jungmannovo nám (tel. 24 22 51 35; Metro A and B to "Můstek") and Palackého nám (tel. 29 46 82; Metro B: "Karlovo nám"), sells **tourist passes** valid for the entire network (1-day pass 50kč, 3 days 130kč, 1 week 190kč, 2 weeks 220kč). DP offices open daily 7am-9pm. Baggage on all lines costs 5kč per piece, but you're allowed one large bag if you have a ticket valid for one day or more. The Metro's 3 main lines run daily 5am-midnight. On city maps, line A is green, line B is yellow, and line C is red; "Můstek" (lines A and B), "Muzeum" (lines A and C), and "Florenc" (lines B and C) are the primary junctions. Night trams #51-58 and buses #500-510 run midnight-5am; look for the dark blue signs at transport stops.

Taxis: Taxi Praha (tel. 24 91 66 66) and **AAA** (tel. 312 21 12) operate 24hr. The official fare is 12kč per 1km atop the flat fee of 20kč. Before entering the cab make sure the meter has been reset. On shorter trips, check that the meter is running by saying *"Zapněte taxametr";* for longer trips set a price beforehand. As you can guess, locals strongly distrust cab drivers.

Hitchhiking: Hitchhiking in and around Prague has become increasingly dangerous.*Let's Go* does not recommend hitchhiking. Those hitching east take tram 1, 9, or 16 to the last stop. To points south, they take Metro C to "Pražskeho povstání," walk left 100m, and cross náměstí Hrdinů to 5 Květná (highway D1). To Munich, hitchers take tram 4 or 9 to the intersection of Plzeňská at Kukulova/Bucharova, then hitch south. Those going north take a tram or bus to "Kobyliské nám.," then bus 175 up Horňátecká.

Luggage Storage: Lockers in all train and bus stations charge 10kč. In the main train terminal they're often full—try the 24-hr. baggage storage in the basement instead. 25kč per day for first 15kg. Watch your bags as you set your locker code.

English Bookstore: The Globe Bookstore, Janovského 14 (tel. 66 71 26 10). Take Metro C to "Vltavská." From the Metro, walk under the overpass on the right, then turn right onto Janovského. The store has many used books along with job, accommodation, and bungee-jumping listings. Open daily 9am-5pm.

Laundromat: If you're staying in a private flat, ask to include your laundry with the family's. Otherwise, go to **Laundry Kings,** Dejvická 16 (tel. 312 37 43), 1 block from Metro A: "Hradčanská." Cross the tram and railroad tracks, then turn left onto Dejvická. Wash 50kč. Dry 15kč per 8min. Soap 10-20kč. Beer 11kč (ah, Prague). The note-board aids apartment seekers and English teachers. Use the spinner to save on drying. Open Mon.-Fri. 6am-10pm, Sat.-Sun. 8am-10pm.

Pharmacies: Prague has many pharmacies which offer a variety of foreign products. Don't hesitate to ask for *kontrcepční prostředky* (contraceptives), *náplast* (bandages), or *dámské vložky* (tampons). The pharmacies at Koněvova 210 (tel. 644 18 95) and Štefánikova 6 (tel. 24 51 11 12) are open 24hr.

Emergencies: Medical Emergency Aid in English: tel. 29 93 81. **Na Homolce** (for foreigners), Roentgenova 2 (tel. 52 92 21 46, after hours 52 92 21 91).

Post Office: The main office is at Jindřišská 14. Take Metro A or B to "Můstek." **Poste Restante** at window 28. Open Mon.-Fri. 7am-8pm, Sat. 7am-1pm. Address mail: "Christopher BRECK, POSTE RESTANTE, Jindřišská 14, 110 00 Praha 1, Czech Republic." For stamps go to windows 20-23, for letters and parcels under 2kg win-

HOSTELS

1 Hostel Sokol
2 CKM
3 Junior Hotel Praha
4 Hotel Juventus

N ↑

LETENSKÉ
GARDENS

Milady Horákové

Badeniho

Navalech

Chotkova

pod Bruskou

Na Opyši

HRADČANY

U Prašného mostu

Mariánské hradby

náb. Edvarda Beneše

Kosářkovo nábřeží

M

Mánesův most

NÁMĚ
JANA
PALAC

Valdštejnská

Letenská

**VOJANOVY
GARDENS**

Karlův most

Thunovská

8

9

Úvoz Nerudova

MALOSTRANSKÉ
NÁMĚSTÍ

10

Vltava River

Křížovnická

**MALÁ
STRANA**

Tržiště

11

Mostecká

13

Karmelitská

12

MALTÉZSKÉ
NÁMĚSTÍ

Prague

1 Canadian Embassy
2 Palace Belvedere
3 National Gallery
4 St. Vitus Cathedral
5 Royal Palace
6 Basilica of St. George
7 Lobkovic Palace
8 U.K. Embassy
9 Wallenstein Palace
10 St. Nicholas Church
11 U.S. Embassy
12 Church of Our
Lady Victorious
13 Charles Bridge
14 National Theater
15 New Town Hall
16 National Museum
17 Smetana Theater
18 Praha hlavní nádraží
19 Church of Our Lady
of the Snows
20 Bethlehem Chapel
21 Kafka's Birthplace
22 Maislova Synagóga
23 Vysoká Synagóga
24 Staronová Synagóga
25 Old Town Hall
26 Týn Church
27 Church of St James
28 Powder Tower
29 Masarykovo nádraží
30 Florenc Bus Station
31 Pražská Informační
Sluzba (PIS)
32 Čedak Office
33 Main Post Office
34 Anežský klášter
(St. Agnes Convent)
35 American Express
Office
36 Kafka's Grave

Hellichova

1

KAMPA

Újezd

Malostranské náb.

Střelecký
ostrov

Betlémsk

Konv

Smetanovo náb.

Divadelní

**PETŘINSKÉ
GARDENS**

Říční

Šeříkova

Vítězná

most Legií

14

Plaská

Zborovská

Janáčkovo náb.

Petřínská

Masarykovo náb.

Slovanský
ostrov

Vodní

Dětský
ostrov

Malátova

Preslova

Kořenského

V. botanice

Jiráskův most

Resslo

Matoušova

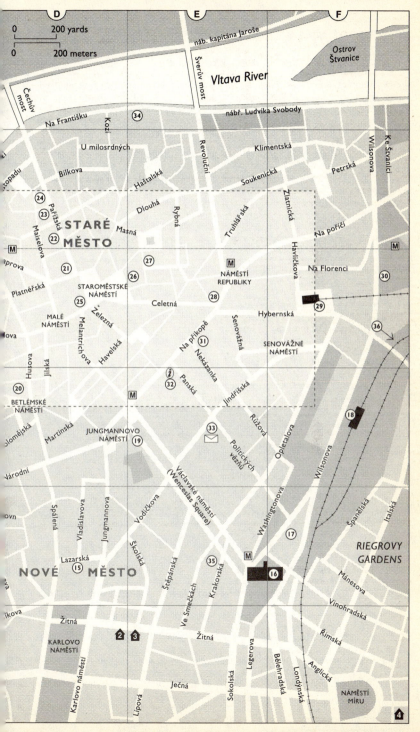

dows 10-12. Office open 24hr. Parcels over 2kg can be mailed only at **Pošta-Celnice,** Plzeňská 139. Take tram 9 west. **Postal Code:** 110 00.
Telephone Code: 02.

ACCOMMODATIONS AND CAMPING

While hotel prices have skyrocketed, the hostel market in Prague is glutted, and prices hover between 200-300kč per night. If you can't find a room, keep in mind that a growing number of Prague residents are taking advantage of the tourist influx by renting rooms. You may also find a few bare-bones hotels in your price range.

Accommodations Agencies

Hawkers and agents besiege visitors at the train station with offers of rooms for around US$15-30 (500-1000kč). Arrangements made in this way are generally safe, but if you're wary of bargaining on the street, call around or try one of the agencies listed below. Make sure any room you accept is close to public transportation and that you understand what you're paying for; if you're at all confused, have the staff write it down. Payment is usually accepted in Czech, German, or U.S. currency.

Hello Travel Ltd., Senovážné nám. 3 (tel. 24 21 26 47), between Na příkopě and Hlavní Nádraží. Arranges every sort of housing imaginable. Rooms in apartments start at US$14, hotels at US$35, and hostels at US$8. Payment in kč, DM, or by credit card (AmEx, Diners, MC, Visa). Open daily 10am-9pm.

Konvex 91, Ve Smekčách 29 (tel. 26 49 01; fax 24 21 49 37). The professional staff books hostels from 295kč and central apartments with kitchen and bathroom from 540kč per person. Open Mon.-Fri. 9am-12:30pm and 1:30-6pm.

Ave., Hlavní Nádraží (tel. 24 22 32 26; fax 24 23 07 83), left from the main hall of the train station. The burgeoning firm offers hundreds of rooms (shared and private) starting at 440kč per person and hostels from 170kč. Open daily 6am-11pm.

Hostels

Many dorms and hostels free up in July and August west of the river in the Strahov neighborhood, next to the Olympic stadium. These rooms may be the best bet for travelers who arrive in the middle of the night *sans* clue. Most hostels listed below are open year-round.

Hostel Sokol, Hellichova 1 (tel. 57 00 73 97; fax 54 74 47), at the end of Karmelitská. Take Metro B to "Malostranská," then tram 12 or 22 to Hellichova, and walk straight another 100m. The hostel is on the left in the passage 5min. from the Charles Bridge. Mega-hip receptionists will fill you in on "the scene" when asked. The hostel itself isn't sparkling, but the staff and guests are very friendly and energetic. Kitchen facilities. 80 beds in summer, 40 off season. Lockout 10am-3pm. 10-bed rooms 179kč per person. Pillow, sheets, and blanket 54kč.

Slavoj Wesico (a.k.a. **Hostel Boathouse**), V náklích 1a (tel. 402 10 76). Take Metro A to "Staroměstská," then tram #17 to Černý Kůň. Descend by the balustrade on the river side and walk all the way to the Vltava; be sure to look for it in the daytime. Clean 3-bed rooms and bathrooms scrubbed sparkling clean. No curfew or lockout. 190kč per person, 120kč for a bed in the hallway. 50kč deposit. Breakfast 30kč, hearty meals 50kč. Call ahead.

Domov Mládeže, Dykova 20 (tel. 25 06 88; fax 25 14 29). From Metro A: "nám. Jiřího z Poděbrad." Follow Nitranská, and turn left on Dykova. Possibly the most enjoyable hostel trek in the city. 60 beds in the tree-lined Vinohrady district. So peaceful you might forget you're in Prague. The 2- to 7-bed rooms are clean but not sterile. 300kč per person, breakfast included.

Hostel Hostel, Malá Veleslavínova (tel. 232 89 37). Ride Metro A to "Staroměstská," and walk south (left as you face the river) on Křížovnická. It's marked, in an alleyway to the right behind Křížovnická 7. The nameless hostel is quiet and in a central location. Four rooms with 11 beds each, plus one double. Lockout noon-5pm. 200kč per person, deckchairs 150kč. Open June 28-Sept. 2.

Traveller's Hostels, in 6 dorms throughout the city. The one at Husova 3 (tel. 24 21 53 26) is the classiest, with singles at 390kč and doubles at 490kč. Take Metro A to "Národní Třida," take a right onto Spálená (which turns into Na Perštýně after Národní), and turn onto Husova. Střelecký ostrov (tel. 24 91 01 88), on the island off most Legii, is the newest dorm. Take Metro B to "Národní třida." 270kč. Other dorms are located at Mikulandská 5 (tel. 24 91 07 39; Metro B to "Národní třída;" 240kč); Křížovnická 7 (tel. 232 09 87; Metro A to "Staroměstská;" 240kč); Růžova 5 (Metro C to "Hlavní nádraží"; 200-240kč); and U lanové drahy 3 (tel. 53 31 60; tram #6, 9, 12, or 22 to "Újezd" and up the stairs; 180kč).

ESTEC Hostel, Vaníkčova 5, blok (building) 5 (tel. 52 73 44). Take bus 217 or 143 from Metro A: Dejvická to "Koleje Stranov," or bus #176 from Metro B: "Karlovo nám." to the end "Stadión Strahov." 500 beds and a beer garden downstairs make for lively nights. Clean rooms, hall toilets, and showers. Check-in 4pm, check-out 9:30am. Singles 360kč. Doubles 240kč. Breakfast 50kč. Laundry service 150kč.

Hotels and Pensions

With so many tourists infiltrating Prague, hotels are upgrading both service and appearance. A few may try to bill you for a more expensive room than the one in which you stayed; come armed with pen, paper, and receipts. The hotels listed below require reservations up to a month in advance. Call, and confirm by fax.

Hotel Unitour, Senovážné nám. 21 (tel. 24 10 25 36; fax 24 22 15 79). Unbelievable find near the Old Town. Singles 470kč, with bathroom 820kč. Doubles 770kč, with bathroom 1200kč. Triples 1100kč, with bathroom 1420kč.

Penzion Unitas, Bartolomějská 9 (tel. 232 77 00; fax 232 77 09), in the Old Town. Take Metro B to "Národní." A Jesuit monastery where Beethoven once performed, transformed by the Communists into a state prison where Václav Havel was jailed; the iron prison doors remain. The dungeon rooms are understandably a bit damp. No alcohol. Check-in 2pm, check-out 10am. Lockout 1-6am. Singles 920kč. Doubles 1100kč. Triples 1500kč. Quads 1750kč. Breakfast included.

Hotel Standart, Přístavní 2 (tel. 87 52 58; fax 80 67 52). From Metro C: "Vltavská," take tram 1, 3, 14, or 25 to "Dělnická," continue along the street, and make a left onto Přístavní. Very quiet neighborhood gets very dark at night. Spotless hall showers and bathrooms. 740kč, HI members 345kč.

Junior Hotel Praha, Žitná 12 (tel. 29 29 84; fax 24 22 39 11), right next to CKM. Decor on the cutting edge of 1970s revival. Private showers and baths. Singles 1200kč. Doubles 1900kč. Huge buffet breakfast included. The hostel in the same building charges 400kč per person in 4-bed rooms.

Camping

Tourist offices sell a guide of campsites near the city (15kč). For a tranquil setting, try **Císařská Louka,** a peninsula on the Vltava. Take Metro B to "Smíchovské nádraží," then tram #12 to "Lihovar." Walk toward the river and onto the shaded path. **Caravan Park** (tel. 54 50 64 or 54 09 25; fax 54 33 05) and **Caravan Camping** (tel. 54 01 29 or tel./fax 54 56 82) charge 85kč per person and 80-120kč per tent. Caravan Park rents 2-person bungalows at 400kč, 4-person ones at 600kč. Caravan Camping offers rooms at 265kč per person. Reserve bungalows and rooms by fax.

FOOD

Restaurants in Prague eat careless travelers alive. *Anything* offered with your meal (even ketchup) costs extra, as will everything placed on your table, so check the bill scrupulously. You'll save money if you avoid the places that attract Old Town tourist mobs. For a quick bite, the window stands selling tasty *párek v rohlíku* (sausage in a roll) for 7-15kč are a bargain. Outlying Metro stops become impromptu marketplaces in summer; look for the daily **vegetable market** at the intersection of Havelská and Melantrichova in the Old Town. Supermarkets include the **K-mart/Maj department store,** on the corner of Národní and Spálena (open Mon.-Wed. 7am-7pm, Thurs.-Fri. 7am-8pm, Sat. 8am-6pm, Sun. 10am-6pm), and the **Krone department store,** on

Wenceslas Square at the intersection with Jindřišská (open Mon.-Fri. 8am-7pm, Sat. 8am-6pm, Sun. 10am-6pm).

Restaurants

U Rozvařlů, Na poříčí (tel. 24 21 93 57). The last of a Communist breed evolving to survive. Nowadays you can sit down with *guláš* (33kč) and soda or beer (12kč). Open Mon.-Fri. 8am-7:30pm, Sat. 8am-7pm, Sun. 10am-5pm.

Klub Architektů, Betlémské nám. 59 (tel. 24 40 12 14); walk through the gates and descend to the right. A 12th-century cellar thrust into the 20th century with sleek table-settings and fun copper pulley lamps. The menu features traditional dumpling plates (55-60kč) and new-fangled vegetarian burritos (32kč). Pilsner on tap for 20kč per 0.5liter. Open Mon.-Sat. 11:30am-midnight.

Bar bar, Všehrdova 17, a left off Karmelitská walking down from Malostranské nám. A jungle jungle of salads salads, meat meat, and fish fish. Most meals 49-69kč. Pancakes 12-89kč. Smoke-filled. *Velkopopovický kozel* is on tap at 15kč per 0.5L. Open Mon.-Fri. 11am-midnight, Sat.-Sun. noon-midnight.

Velryba (The Whale), Opatovická 24 (tel. 24 91 23 91). Trendy ex-pats without the cash enjoy inexpensive Czech dishes (50-80kč) and gallons of java (11-31kč). Open daily 11am-1am. Kitchen closes at 10pm. Last guests leave around 2am.

U Medvídků, Na Perštýně 7 (tel. 24 22 09 30), bordering on the Old Town. Upscale pub fare amid dark-wood furniture and yellow surroundings. *Guláš* 77kč, finger-food 20-30kč. Vegetarian choices (79-89kč) include spaghetti with Rocquefort cheese, veggie plate with cheese, and fried cheese *extraordinaire*. Draft *Budvars* 18kč per 0.5L. Open Mon.-Sat. 11:30am-11pm, Sun. 11:30am-10pm.

Malostranská Hospoda, Karmelitská 25 (tel. 53 20 76), 2 blocks south of Malostranské nám. Chairs spill out onto the square from the pub's vaulted interior. Good *guláš* 50kč. Draft *Staropramen* 13kč per 0.5L. English menu. Open Mon.-Sat. 10am-midnight, Sun. 11am-midnight.

Góvinda, Soukenická 27. Rama and Krishna gaze upon diners and their delicious vegetarian stews. Cafeteria-style, serving a plate with the works for a 50kč. Menu changes daily so you won't get bored. Open Mon.-Sat. 11am-5pm.

Jo's Bar, Malostranské nám. 7. You can bet the ranch that everyone here speaks English (and after they grow out of their hippie hair or baseball caps will carry a camera, have 2.6 kids, and an Oldsmobile). Burritos, quesadillas, and nachos 75-105kč. *Staropramen* 25kč.

Pizzeria Kmotra, V jirchářích 12 (tel. 24 91 58 09). Some argue it's the best pizza on both sides of Italy. Watch your crust cook in the brick oven of a vaulted underground eatery. Huge pizzas 54-93kč. Moravian wine runs 19kč a glass. Beer 16kč per 0.5L. Open daily 11am-1pm.

Cafés

Dozens of dimestore *kavárnas* have opened up in the Old Town, but for more than an expensive one-bite stand, try the outskirts where the real sippers hang out.

U malého Glena, Karmelitská 23 (tel. 535 81 15 or 90 00 39 67), just south off Malostranské nám. Light entrees 95-115kč, stuffed pita 55-60kč. Mixed crowd of dread-locked and multi-pierced Czechs and visitors. Frequent live music at night—consult the schedule on the tables. Open daily 7:30am-2am.

U Knihomola, Mánesova 79 (tel. 627 77 70). Metro A to "Jiřího z Poděbrad." Comfy couches and smooth jazz. Tea 30kč, coffee 20kč. Carrot cake 65kč. Open Mon.-Thurs. 10am-11pm, Fri.-Sat. 10am-midnight, Sun. 11am-8pm.

The Globe Coffeehouse, Janovského 14 (tel./fax 66 71 26 10), inside Prague's largest English bookstore. People come for the 0.4L teas, a cigarette, and expat gossip. Open daily 10am-midnight.

SIGHTS

Orient yourself before tackling the city's many scattered sights. Central Prague is structured by three streets that form a leaning *"T."* The long stem of the *T*, separating Old and New Towns, is the boulevard **Václavské nám.** (Wenceslas Sq.). The **National**

Museum sits at the bottom of the this street. Busy and pedestrian **Na příkopě** forms the right arm of the *T* and leads to **nám. Republiky;** on the left, **28. října** becomes **Národní** after a block, leading to the **National Theater** on the river. A maze of small streets leads to Staroměstské nám. two blocks above this area.

The festive heart of Prague, **Wenceslas Square** was actually designed as a quiet promenade in the late 19th century. The **statue** of the king and saint Václav (Wenceslas) has stood here since 1912 as an encouragement to Czech independence, and has witnessed no less than five revolutions from its pedestal in front of the National Museum. It was here that Czechoslovakia declared itself a nation in 1918, and here that in 1969 Jan Palach set himself ablaze to protest Soviet intervention in the Prague Spring. Stretching north from the monument, Art Nouveau buildings dominate the square. The premier example is the 1903 **Hotel Evropa;** since its construction, the hotel has been a socialite center with a side-street café of the same name. The post-revolution clientele is more kitschy than cultured, but people-watching possibilities still abound. Wenceslas Square, however, is one of the seediest areas in Prague, so be cautious. Under the arcades halfway down Národní stands a **memorial** honoring the hundreds of Prague's citizens beaten by the police during a government-sanctioned protest on November 17, 1989—the event which marked the start of the Velvet Revolution.

A labyrinth of narrow roads and Old World alleys leads to the thriving heart of the Old Town—**Staroměstské náměstí,** northwest of Wenceslas Square toward the river. **Jan Hus,** the Czech Republic's most famous martyred theologian, sweeps across the scene in bronze, and eight magnificent towers surround the square. The somewhat destroyed edifice of the **Staroměstská radnice** (Old Town Hall) has a tourist office inside that offers tours of the Hall. (Open in summer daily 9am-5pm; off season only when there are tourists. Tours 20kč, students 10kč.) Onlookers gather on the hour to see the Hall's fabulous **Astronomical Clock** *(orloj),* with 12 peering apostles and a bell-ringing skeleton representing death. The clockmaker's eyes were reputedly put out by his patron so he could not craft another.

Across from the town hall, the spires of **Panna Marie před Týnem** (Týn Church) rise above a huddled mass of medieval homes. To the left of the church, the austere **Dům U kamenného zvonu** (House at Stone Bell) shows the Gothic core that lurks beneath many of Prague's Baroque façades. **Sv. Mikuláš** (St. Nicholas Church) sits just across Staroměstské nám. (open Tues.-Sun. 10am-5pm). Between Maiselova and Sv. Mikuláš is **Franz Kafka's** former home, marked with a plaque.

Head out of the Old Town square on Jilská and take Karlova at the fork to reach **Kalův most** (Charles Bridge), one of the most active and festive bridges in Europe. The area is packed day and night with artisans and street performers. Continue along Jilská to reach the restored **Bethlehem Chapel,** where Jan Hus preached to his loyal congregation from 1402 until he was burned at the stake (20kč, students 10kč). At the center of the bridge is the statue of legendary hero **Jan Nepomucký** (John of Nepomuk), confessor to Queen Zofie. Brave Jan was tossed over the side of the Charles for faithfully guarding his queen's confidences from a suspicious King Václav IV. Climb the Gothic **defense tower** on the Malá Strana side of the bridge or the tower on the Old Town side for a superb view of the city (both towers open daily 10am-5:30pm; 20kč, students 10kč). The stairs on the left side of the bridge (as you face the castle district) lead to **Hroznová,** where a mural honors John Lennon and the peace movement of the 60s.

Prague's historic Jewish neighborhood, **Josefov,** is located north of Staromětstské nám. along Maiselova and several side streets. Its cultural wealth lies in five well-preserved synagogues. **Staronová synagóga** (Old-New Synagogue), now 700 years old, is Europe's oldest synagogue still in use. Next door, the 16th-century **Vysoká synagóga** (High Synagogue) holds exhibits of ceremonial items and religious tapestries. The neighboring **Židovská radnice** (Jewish Town Hall) features a clock that runs backwards. Walk down Maiselova and turn right on Široka until you reach the **Pinkasova synagóga** (Pinkas Synagogue); the synagogue's walls list victims from four centuries of persecution. Back on Maiselova to the right is **Maiselova synagóga** (Maisel Syna-

GATEWAY CITIES

gogue), the only temple-museum here with exhibitions describing the Jews' way of living and praying throughout the centuries. At the 90-degree bend in U Starého hřbitova, **Starý židovský hřbitov** (Old Jewish Cemetery) remains one of the most popular attractions in the area. (Admission to the entire quarter 340kč, students 230kč.)

Once the seedy hangout of criminals and counter-revolutionaries, the cobblestone streets of the **Malá Strana** (Lesser Side) have become the most prized real estate on either side of the Vltava. **Sv. Mikuláš** (St. Nicholas' Church) rises impressively above the square's mess of Baroque decorations. Mozart's works are performed here almost nightly (open daily 9am-5pm; 20kč, students 10kč; concert tickets 300kč, students 200kč). Nearby on Karmelitská rises the more modest **Panna Maria Vítězna** (Church of Our Lady Victorious), where the famous and reputedly miracle-bestowing polished-wax statue of the **Infant Jesus of Prague** resides (open daily 10am-7:30pm).

A simple wooden gate just down the street at Letenská 10 opens onto **Valdštejnská zahrada** (Wallenstein Garden), one of Prague's best-kept secrets. This tranquil 17th-century Baroque garden, adorned with statues and frescoes depicting scenes from the Trojan War, is enclosed by old buildings that glow golden on sunny afternoons (open May-Sept. daily 9am-7pm).

You could easily spend a day exploring **Pražský hrad** (Prague Castle) and the surrounding town, but come early, and not on Monday. The castle is crowned by the soaring **Chrám Sv. Víta** (St. Vitus's Cathedral), completed in 1930 after 600 years of construction. To the right of the high altar stands the **tomb of St. Jan Nepomucký,** three meters of solid, glistening silver, weighing two tons. Stroll across the third interior courtyard to enter **Starý královský palác** (Old Royal Palace), where gloomy halls exhibit gloomier art. Inside, the vast **Vladislav Hall** provides ample room for the jousting competitions that once took place here. Climb the 287 steps of the **Cathedral Tower** for a breathtaking view of the castle and the city (open daily 10am-4pm). In the nearby **Chancellery of Bohemia,** two Catholic Habsburg officials were lobbed out the window by fed-up Protestant noblemen in 1618 in the notorious **Defenestration of Prague** (see "the Habsburgs" p. 231). Though a dungheap broke their fall, the die was cast, and war ravaged Europe for the next 30 years. The Romanesque **Bazilika Sv. Jiří** (Basilica of St. George) was erected in 921 just behind the Old Royal Palace. On the right as you enter, note the wood-and-glass tomb enclosing St. Ludmila's skeleton—her missing thigh bone cursed the basilica's construction. (Castle complex open daily 9am-5pm; some parts close up to 45min. early. 80kč, students 40kč.) Exiting the castle through the main gate and walking straight for 200m brings you to the lovely **Loreto** (tel. 24 51 07 89). A garden of agonized statues guards the entrance to a popular pilgrimage site here (open Tues.-Sun. 9am-4:30pm; 30kč, students 20kč).

The **Petřínské sady,** the largest gardens in central Prague, are topped by a model of the Eiffel Tower and the wacky castle **Bludiště.** (Castle open April-Oct. daily 10am-4pm. Gardens open April-Oct. daily 9:30am-9pm; Nov.-March 9:30am-6pm. 20kč, students 10kč.) Take a cable car from just above the intersection of Vítézná and Újezd (6kč; look for *lanová dráha* signs) for spectacular views.

The former haunt of Prague's 19th-century romantics, **Vyšehrad** is clothed in nationalistic myths and the legends of a once-powerful Czech empire. It is here that Princess Libuše adumbrated Prague and embarked on her search for the first king of Bohemia. The 20th century has passed the castle by, and Vyšehrad's elevated pathways now escape the flood of tourists in the city center. Quiet walkways lead between crumbling stone walls to a magnificent **church,** a black Romanesque rotunda, and one of the Czech Republic's most celebrated sites, **Vyšehrad Cemetery,** where Dvořák and other national heros are laid to rest. To reach the complex, take Metro C to Vyšehrad (complex open 24hr.).

Museums

National Museum, Václavské nám. 68 (tel. 24 23 04 85). Take Metro A or C to "Muzeum." Soviet soldiers mistook this landmark for a government building and fired on it; traces of the damage are still visible. Open daily 9am-6pm; closed the first Tues. of each month. 40kč, students 15kč.

National Gallery: Collections are housed in 9 different historical buildings. The **National Gallery of European Art** is in the **Šternberský Palác,** Hradčanské nám. 15 (tel. 24 51 05 94), just outside the front gate of the Prague Castle. It includes works by Rubens, Bruegel, Dürer, Picasso, and your favorite Impressionists. The **National Gallery of Bohemian Art,** ranging from Gothic to Baroque, is housed in **Basilika Sv. Jíří,** nám. U Sv. Jíří 33 (tel. 24 51 06 95), inside the castle. It showcases works by Czech artists including Master Theodorik, court painter for Charles IV. More Bohemian creations are exhibited at **Anežský areal.,** at the corner of Anežská and Řásnovka, for centuries the Cloister of St. Agnes. All collections open Tues.-Sun. 10am-6pm. Admission to each gallery 50kč, students 15kč.

Bertramka Mozart Museum, Mozartova 169 (tel. 54 38 93). Ride Metro B to "Anděl," take a left on Plzeňská, and turn left onto Mozartova. Housed in Villa Bertramka, where Mozart lived (and reputedly wrote *Don Giovanni*) in 1787. Open daily 9:30am-6pm. 50kč, students 30kč. Garden concerts July-Aug. Fri. 7:30pm; call ahead for tickets. 220kč, students 120kč. The vast garden outside is free.

Muzeum Hlavního Města Prahy (Prague Municipal Museum), Na poříčí 52 (tel. 24 81 67 72). Take Metro B or C to "Florenc." Holds the original calendar board from the town hall's Astronomical Clock and a 1:480 scale model of old Prague. Other exhibits from the collection reside in the **House at Stone Bell,** Staroměstské nám., left of Týn Church. Both open Tues.-Sun. 10am-6pm. 20kč, students 15kč.

ENTERTAINMENT

For a list of current concerts and performances, consult *The Prague Post* or *Do města-Downtown* (the latter is free and distributed at most cafés and restaurants). Most shows begin at 7pm; unsold tickets are sometimes available a half-hour before showtime (this is rare in summer). **Národní Divadlo** (National Theater), Národní třída 2/4 (tel. 24 91 34 37), is perhaps Prague's most famous theater (box office open Mon.-Fri. 10am-6pm, Sat.-Sun. 10am-12:30pm and 3-6pm). Equally impressive is **Stavorské Divadlo** (Estates Theater), Ovocný trh 6 (tel. 24 21 50 01), where Mozart's *Don Giovanni* premiered in 1787. (Box office open same hours as National Theater. Earphones available for English translation.) Most of Prague's theaters shut down in July and return in August with attractions for tourists. In early June, the **Prague Spring Festival** draws musicians from around the world. Tickets (300-2000kč) may sell out a year in advance; try **Bohemia Ticket International,** Salvátorská 6, next to Čedok (tel. 24 22 78 32; open Mon.-Fri. 9am-6pm).

Prague nightlife is fluid—sometimes dark, quiet brews, sometimes shots of "screaming orgasm"—but always intoxicating and as fleeting as yesterday's hangover. Of the clubs listed below, a few will have become glossy tourist traps by 1997, so ask your hostel or hotel manager about the latest local favorites.

Slovanská Hospoda, Na příkopě 22; duck beneath the passage. A red-cheeked crowd of professionals enjoys 15kč brews on the terrace, while grunge thrives around benches under the tall trees. Open daily 11am-11pm.

Rock Club Bunkr, Lodecká 2 (tel. 231 07 35). From Metro B: "nám. Republiky," walk down Na poříčí, turn left on Zlatnická, then cross the parking lot diagonally. Hot Czech and foreign rock bands in an erstwhile Communist-regime nuclear bunker. Absorb the graffiti, and add your own. Cover 50kč, less on weekdays, women free. 0.3L of *Gambrinus* 12kč. Open daily 8pm-6am. Concerts start at 9pm. Café upstairs is a respite from the energy below. Open daily 9am-3am.

Café Gulu Gulu, Betlémské nám. 8. A hangout for the Czech university crowd. Graffiti by Salvador Miro and frequent impromptu musical jams. Live music Fridays. *Eggenberg* 20kč. Open daily 10am-1am.

Café Marquis de Sade, a.k.a. **Café Babylon,** Templová 8 (tel. 232 34 06), between nám. Republiky and Staroměstské nám. Take Metro B to "nám. Republiky." The band on the central podium strikes up old pops or jazz for a packed house. Beers 25kč. Open daily until 1am, often much later.

Reduta, Národní 20 (tel. 24 91 22 46). Like everything"original" in Prague, the city's oldest jazz club has fallen to the tourists. But if you can get a seat in the tiny red velvet audience hall, the "jazz and not jazz" might blow your mind. Open nightly 9pm-late. Cover 90kč, but the cashier is not 100% resistant to sweet eyes pleading for a student reduction (50kč).

U Hynků, Štupartská 6 (tel./fax 23 23 406), just off the west corner of Staroměstské nám. The cigarette smoke has permanently inscribed itself into the brown-gray walls of this bar-*cum*-café. The young, male, t-shirt-clad staff befriends only the cool clients and on request will play the tape you just bought. Light *Lobkowicz* beer 18kč per 0.5L, dark beer and *Fezané* 22kč. Open daily 11am-3am.

Molly Malone's, U obecního dvora 4. Irish and fun. A draft of *Staropramen* is 20 kč; *Guinness* is cheaper than in Ireland at 60kč per pint. Open daily 11am-7am.

Agharta, Krakovská 5 (tel. 24 21 29 14), just down Krakovská from Wenceslas Square. The "Jazz Centrum" also operates a CD shop. Cramped space featuring nightly live jazz ensembles (starting at 9pm). Open nightly 7pm-1am.

Roxy, Dlouhá 33 (tel. 24 81 09 51). This former theater rocks on the ground floor and chills in the peanut gallery (don't fall over the edge). Variety of reggae, ska, rock, and tribal rhythms. Cover 20-40kč. Beer 15kč. Open Tues.-Sun. 9pm-4am.

NEAR PRAGUE

A train ride southwest from Praha-Smíchov (45min., 12kč) brings you to **Karlštejn** (tel. (0311) 846 17), a walled and turreted fortress built by Charles IV to house his crown jewels and holy relics. The **Chapel of the Holy Cross** is decorated with more than 2000 inlaid precious stones and 128 apocalyptic paintings by medieval artist Master Theodorik. (Open Tues.-Sun. 9am-4pm. Admission with English guide 95kč, students 50kč; in Czech 25kč, students 10kč.)

An hour and a half east of Prague is the former mining town of **Kutná Hora** (Silver Hill). The 13th-century silver boom and subsequent bust in the 16th century left snapshots of a thriving medieval town here, replete with burghers' houses, cobblestone alleys, church spires, and a vaulted cathedral on a hill southwest of town. From Palackého nám., follow 28. října to Havlíčkovo nám. Originally a storehouse for Kutná Hora's stash, the imposing **Vlašský Dvůr** (Italian Court) served a stint as the royal mint. (Open daily 9am-5pm; guided tours every 15min. 40kč, students 20kč; written handout in English.) Near the Italian Court, Rutnardská leads to the Gothic **St. Barbara's Cathedral,** one of Europe's finest (open Tues.-Sun. 8am-5:30pm; 20kč, students 10kč). Two kilometers out of town, a *kostnice* (ossuary church) displays the bones of thousands killed during medieval wars and plagues.(open daily 8am-noon and 1-5pm; 20kč, students 10kč). **Buses** travel to Silver Hill from Prague's Florenc station (1¼hr., 5 per day, 1 on weekends; 41kč) and from station 2 at Metro A: "Želivského" (1¾hr., 9 per day, 2 on weekends; 41kč).

At the end of the 18th century, Austrian Empress Maria Theresa had a fortress built at the Labe's confluence with the Ohře known as **Terezín.** The Nazis established a concentration camp here in 1940, and nearby constructed **Terezín ghetto,** a sham model village to satisfy the International Red Cross (all Terezín residents were killed after the Red Cross visit). Following the Red Army's capture of the camp in May 1945, the Czech regime used Terezín as an internment camp. (Open May-Sept. daily 8am-6pm; April and Oct. 8am-5pm; Nov.-March 8am-4:30pm. 70kč, students 35kč. English guide 200kč. Combined ticket for fortress and museum 90kč, students 45kč.) **Buses** arrive from Prague-Florenc (1hr., every 1-2hr., 44kč).

■ Budapest

At once a cosmopolitan European capital and the stronghold of Magyar nationalism, Budapest has awakened from its Communist-era coma with the same vigor that rebuilt the city from the rubble of WWII. Endowed with an architectural majesty befitting the Habsburg Empire's number-two city, the Hungarian capital also possesses an intellectual and cultural scene often compared to that of Paris. Today, the city maintains its charm and a vibrant spirit—refusing to buckle under the relentless siege of glitzification—while pursuing a difficult course of modernization.

ORIENTATION AND PRACTICAL INFORMATION

Budapest straddles the **Duna** (Danube) in north-central Hungary 250km downstream from **Vienna.** On the west bank, **Buda** inspires countless artists with its hilltop citadel, trees, and cobblestone **Castle District,** while on the east side **Pest** pulses as the heart of the modern city. Three bridges bind the two halves together: **Széchenyi lánchíd,** slender, white **Erzsébet híd,** and green **Szabadság híd.**

Moszkva tér (Moscow Square), just down the north slope of the Castle District, is where virtually all trams and buses start or end their routes. One Metro stop away in the direction of Örs vezér tere, **Batthyány tér** lies opposite the Parliament building on the west bank; this is the starting node of the **HÉV commuter railway.** Budapest's three Metro lines converge at **Deák tér,** at the core of Pest's loosely concentric ring boulevards, beside the main international bus terminal at **Erzsébet tér.**

Many street names occur more than once in town; always check the district as well as the street. Moreover, streets arbitrarily change names from one block to the next. Because many have shed their Communist labels, an up-to-date **map** is essential. To check if your map of Budapest is useful, look at the avenue leading from Pest toward the City Park (Városliget) in the east: the modern name should be **Andrássy út.** The **American Express** and **Tourinform** offices have reliable and free tourist maps, or pick up *Belváros Idegenforgalmi Térképe* at any Metro stop (100Ft). Anyone planning an exhaustive visit should look into purchasing András Török's *Budapest: A Critical Guide.*

Tourist Offices: Tourinform, V, Sütő u. 2 (tel. 117 98 00; fax 117 95 78), off Deák tér just behind McDonald's. Take M1, 2, or 3 to "Deák tér." Busy, multilingual tourist office provides information ranging from sightseeing tours to opera performances. Open daily 8am-8pm. Sightseeing, accommodation bookings, and travel services available at **IBUSZ** and **Budapest Tourist** (offices in train stations and tourist centers). Ask for their free and helpful quarterly *For Youth.* The 24-hr. IBUSZ central office is at V, Apácsai Csere J. u. 1 (tel. 118 57 76; fax 117 90 00).

Budget Travel: Express, V, Zoltán u. 10 (tel. 111 64 18), 2 blocks south of the Parliament. Take M2 to "Kossuth tér." ISIC 500Ft. Some reduced international air and rail fares for the under-26 crowd (similar train ticket reductions available at train station). Open Mon.-Thurs. 8:30am-12:30pm and 1:30-3pm. Cashier closes ½hr. early. **Main office,** V, Szbadság tér 16 (tel. 131 77 77). Open Mon. and Wed.-Thurs. 8am-4:30pm, Tues. 8am-6pm, Fri. 8am-2:30pm.

Embassies: U.S., V, Szabadság tér 12 (tel. 267 44 00). Take M2 to "Kossuth Lajos," then walk 2 blocks down Akademia and turn left on Zoltán. Open Mon.-Tues. and Thurs.-Fri. 8:30am-noon. **Canada,** XII, Budakeszi út 32 (tel. 275 12 00). Take bus 22 5 stops from Moszkva tér. Open Mon.-Fri. 9-11am. **U.K.,** V, Harmincad u. 6 (tel. 266 28 88), off the corner of Vörösmarty tér. Take M1 to "Vörösmarty tér." Open Mon.-Fri. 9am-noon and 2-4:30pm. **Australia,** XII, Kriályhágó tér 8/9 (tel.201 88 99). Open Mon.-Fri. 9am-noon. **New Zealanders** contact the British embassy.

Currency Exchange: The bureaus with longer hours generally have less favorable rates. **General Banking and Trust Co. Ltd.,** Váci u. 19/21 (tel. 118 96 88; fax 118 82 30), has excellent rates. Open Mon.-Fri. 9am-4:30pm. **IBUSZ,** V, Petőfi tér 3, just north of Erzsébet híd, offers cash advances on Visa and ATM machine for Cirrus. Open 24hr. **GWK Tours** (tel. 322 90 11), in the Keleti Station. Good rates and convenient for rail travelers. Open daily 6am-9pm. **Citibank,** Vörösmarty tér 4 (tel. 138 26 66; fax 266 98 45). Efficient and pleasant. Open Mon.-Fri. 9am-4pm.

American Express: V, Deák Ferenc u. 10 (tel. 266 86 80; fax 267 20 28). Take M1 to "Vörösmarty tér," next to Hotel Kempinski. Sells AmEx Traveler's Cheques and cashes them in US$ for a 6% commission. Cash advances. Mail held free for cardholders or cheque carriers, 555Ft otherwise. AmEx **ATM.** Open July-Sept. Mon.-Fri. 9am-7:30pm, Sat. 9am-2pm; Oct.-June Mon.-Fri. 9am-5:30pm, Sat. 9am-1pm.

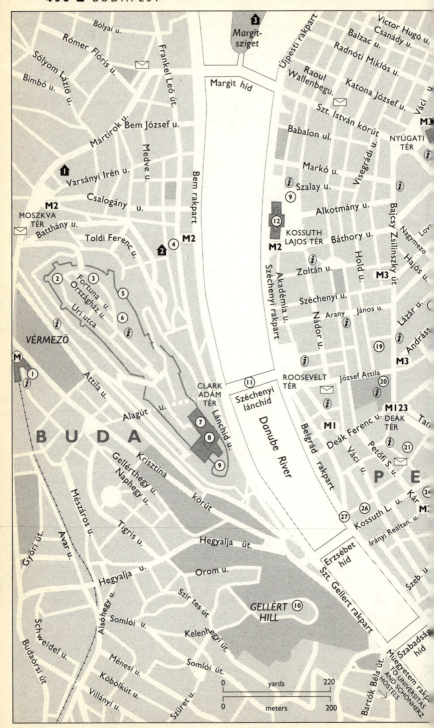

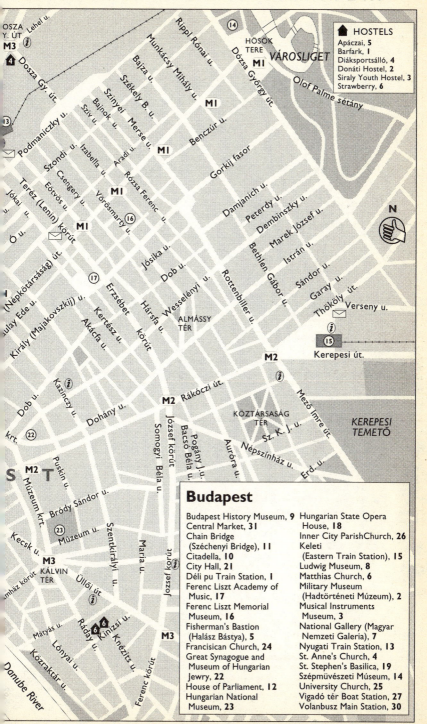

HOSTELS

Apáczai, 5
Barfark, 1
Diáksportsálló, 4
Donáti Hostel, 2
Siraly Youth Hostel, 3
Strawberry, 6

Budapest

Budapest History Museum, 9
Central Market, 31
Chain Bridge (Széchenyi Bridge), 11
Citadella, 10
City Hall, 21
Déli pu Train Station, 1
Ferenc Liszt Academy of Music, 17
Ferenc Liszt Memorial Museum, 16
Fisherman's Bastion (Halász Bástya), 5
Franciscian Church, 24
Great Synagogue and Museum of Hungarian Jewry, 22
House of Parliament, 12
Hungarian National Museum, 23

Hungarian State Opera House, 18
Inner City ParishChurch, 26
Keleti (Eastern Train Station), 15
Ludwig Museum, 8
Matthias Church, 6
Military Museum (Hadtörténeti Múzeum), 2
Musical Instruments Museum, 3
National Gallery (Magyar Nemzeti Galeria), 7
Nyugati Train Station, 13
St. Anne's Church, 4
St. Stephen's Basilica, 19
Szépmüvészeti Múseum, 14
University Church, 25
Vigadó tér Boat Station, 27
Volanbusz Main Station, 30

Telephones: V, Petőfi Sándor u. 17. English-speaking staff. Fax service. Open Mon.-Fri. 8am-8pm, Sat.-Sun. 8am-2pm. At other times, try the post office. Many public phones use **phone cards,** available at newsstands, post offices, and metro stations. 50-unit card 700Ft, 120-unit card 1500Ft. Use **card phones** for **international calls.**

Flights: Ferihegy Airport (tel. 267 43 33, info 157 71 55, reservations 157 91 23). Volánbusz takes 30min. to terminal 1 and 40min. to terminal 2 (300Ft) from Erzsébet tér. The **airport shuttle bus** (tel. 157 89 93) will pick you up anywhere in the city, or take you anywhere from the airport (800Ft). Call for pick-up a few hours in advance. Amazing youth and standby discounts available at the **Malév office,** V, Dorottya u. 2 (tel. 266 56 16; fax 266 27 84). Open Mon.-Fri. 7:30am-5pm.

Trains: For domestic info call 322 78 60; for international 142 91 50. The word for train station is *pályaudvar,* often abbreviated "pu." Those under 26 get a 33% discount on international tickets. Show your ISIC and tell the clerk *"diák"* (student). The three main stations—**Keleti pu., Nyugati pu.,** and **Déli pu.**—are also Metro stops. Each station has schedules for the others. To: Belgrade (6½hr., 6003Ft), Berlin (12½hr., 14,779Ft), Prague (7½hr., 7501Ft), Vienna (3½hr., 4819Ft), Warsaw (10hr., 8078Ft), and other cities. The daily **Orient Express** arrives from Berlin and continues on to Bucharest. **Luggage storage** at Keleti pu. costs 60Ft.

Buses: Volánbusz main station, V, Erzsébet tér (tel. 117 25 62). Take M1, 2, 3 to "Deák tér." To: Berlin (14½hr., 12,500Ft), Bratislava (3½hr., 1370Ft), Prague (8½hr., 2940Ft), Vienna (3hr., 2990Ft). Buses to the Czech Republic, Slovakia, Poland, Romania, Turkey, and Ukraine depart from the **Népstadion** terminal on Hungária körút 48/52, as do most domestic buses to East Hungary. Take M2 to "Népstadion." Buses to the Danube Bend leave from the **Árpád híd** station.

Public Transportation: The **Metro (M)** is rapid and punctual. There are 3 lines—M1 is yellow, M2 is red, and M3 is blue. "M" indicates a stop, but you won't always find the sign on the street; look for stairs leading down. Most public transportation stops about 11:30pm. The subway, buses, and trams all use the same yellow **tickets** which are sold in Metro stations and *Trafik* shops and by some sidewalk vendors. A single-trip ticket costs 50Ft; punch it in the orange boxes at the gate of the Metro or on board buses and trams (10-trip *tíz jegy* 450Ft, 1-day pass 400Ft, 3-day pass 800Ft). The **HÉV commuter rail** runs between Batthyány tér in Buda and Szentendre, 40min. north on the Danube Bend, every 15min.

Hydrofoils: MAHART International Boat Station, V, Belgrád rakpart (tel. 118 17 04; fax 118 77 40), on the Duna near Erzsébet híd, has information and tickets. Open Mon.-Fri. 8am-4pm. Or try **IBUSZ,** Károly krt. 3 (tel. 322 24 73). M2: Astoria. Open Mon.-Fri. 8am-4pm. Arrive at the docks 1hr. before departure for customs and passport control. Eurailpass holders receive a 50% discount. To: Vienna (6hr., one-way 10,990Ft, students 8,000Ft).

Taxis: Főtaxi, tel. 222 22 22. **Volántaxi,** tel. 166 66 66. 80Ft. base fare plus 80Ft per km. The Mercedes-Benz taxis charge double the jalopy fee. Taxis are more expensive at night.

English Bookstore: Bestsellers KFT, V, Október 6 u. 11, near Arany János u. M1 to "Vörösmarty tér." Open Mon.-Fri. 9am-6:30pm, Sat. 10am-6pm.

Gay Hotline: tel. 166 92 83. Line staffed daily 8am-4pm. Try **Dohotourist,** VI, Jókai tér 7 (tel. 111 04 06; fax 269 36 45), for a free brochure with gay spot listings and a gay map of Budapest. Open Mon.-Fri. 8:30am-4:30pm.

Laundromats: Irisz Szalon, VII, Rákóczi út 8b. M2: Astoria. Wash 300Ft per 5kg. Dry 100Ft per 15min. Pay the cashier before you start. Open Mon.-Fri. 7am-7pm, Sat. 7am-1pm. Many youth hostels have washing machines for a fee.

24-Hr. Pharmacies: I, Széna tér 1 (tel. 202 18 16); VI, Teréz krt. 41 (tel. 111 44 39); IX, Boráros tér 3 (tel. 117 07 43); and IX, Üllői út. 121 (tel. 133 89 47). At night, call the number on the door or ring the bell; there is a small fee for the service.

Medical Assistance: tel. 118 82 88 or 118 80 12. English spoken. Open 24hr.

Emergencies: Ambulance: tel. 04. **Fire:** tel. 05.

Police: tel. 07. For tourist police, call 112 15 37.

Post Office: Poste Restante at V, Városház u. 18 (tel. 118 48 11). Open Mon.-Fri. 8am-8pm, Sat. 8am-3pm. 24-hr. **branches** at Nyugati station, VI, Teréz krt. 105-107, and Keleti station, VIII, Baross tér 11c. After-hours staff does not speak English. Sending mail via American Express may be better. **Postal code:** 1052.

Telephone Code: 1

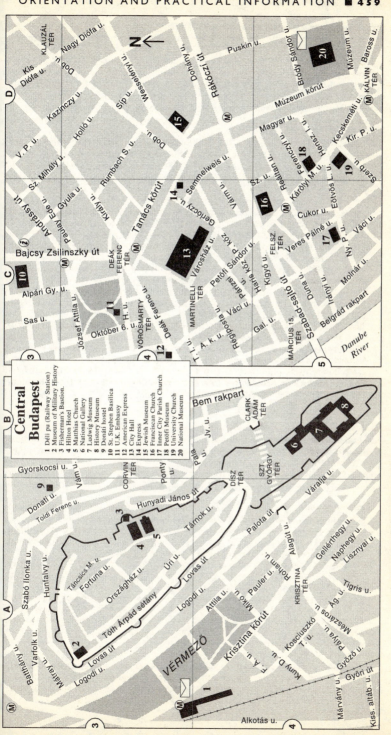

Central Budapest

1 Déli pu (Railway Station)
2 Museum of Military History
3 Fisherman's Bastion.
4 Hilton Hotel
5 Matthias Church
6 National Gallery
7 Ludwig Museum
8 History Museum
9 Donáti hostel
10 St. Stephen Basilica
11 U.K. Embassy
12 American Express
13 City Hall
14 Express
15 Jewish Museum
16 Franciscan Church
17 Inner City Parish Church
18 Petőfi Museum
19 University Church
20 National Museum

GATEWAY CITIES

ACCOMMODATIONS AND CAMPING

Travelers arriving in Keleti station enter a frenzy of hostel hucksters. Always ask that a solicitor show you on a map where the lodging is located, and inspect your room before you pay. It may be wiser to head directly to an accommodation agency, hostel, or guesthouse. Whatever approach you choose, make sure that the room is easily accessible by public transportation, preferably by Metro, which arrives more frequently than buses. The area around Keleti station can be dangerous at night.

Accommodations Agencies

Accommodation services are overrunning Budapest. The rates (800-3000Ft per person) depend on location and bathroom quality. Haggle stubbornly. Arrive around 8am and you may get a single for 1000Ft or a double for 1600Ft. Travelers who stay for more than four nights can obtain a somewhat better rate.

Pension Centrum, XII, Szarvas Gábor út 24 (tel. 201 93 86 or 176 00 57). A nonprofit group that makes reservations in private rooms. Open daily 10am-7pm.

IBUSZ, at all train stations and tourist centers. **24-hr. accommodation office,** V, Apáczai Csere J. u. 1 (tel. 118 39 25; fax 117 90 99). An established service offering the most rooms in Budapest. Private rooms for 1600-3000Ft per person. Swarms of people outside IBUSZ offices push "bargains"; quality varies, but they're legal. Old women asking *"Privatzimmer?"* are vending private rooms.

Budapest Tourist, V, Roosevelt tér 5 (tel. 117 35 55; fax 118 16 58), near Hotel Forum, 10min. from Deák tér on the Pest end of Széchenyi lánchíd. A well-established enterprise offering 1800-2400Ft singles and 4500Ft doubles. Open Mon.-Thurs. 9am-5pm, Fri. 9am-3pm. Same hours at branches throughout the city.

Duna Tours, Bajcsy-Zsilinszky út 17 (tel. 131 45 33 or 111 56 30; fax 111 68 27), next to Cooptourist, allows travelers to see rooms before accepting them. The English-speaking staff maintains that their rooms are located only in districts V and VI. Doubles from 2000Ft. Open Mon.-Fri. 9:30am-noon and 12:30-5pm.

To-Ma Tour, V, Oktober 6. u. 22 (tel. 153 08 19; fax 269 57 15), promises to find you a central room, even if only for one night. Doubles 1800-3000Ft, with private bathroom 2800Ft. 20% off if you stay more than a month. Open Mon.-Fri. 9am-noon and 1-8pm, Sat.-Sun. 9am-5pm.

Hostels

Most hostel-type accommodations, including university dorms, are under the aegis of **Express.** Try their office at V, Semmelweis u. 4 (tel. 117 66 34 or 117 86 00); leave Deák tér on Tanács krt., head right on Gerlóczy u., then take the first left. Or try the branch at V, Szabadság tér 16 (tel. 131 77 77), between M3: "Arany János" and M2: "Kossuth tér." Again, be cautious when accepting a room at the station.

Open year-round

Nicholas's Budget Hostel, XI, Takács Menyhért u. 12 (tel. 185 48 70). Follow the directions to the Back Pack Guesthouse (see below), then continue a half block down the road. A spacious and clean hostel with TV, garden, and kitchen. 800Ft, bedding 400Ft. Laundry 400Ft per 5kg. Reservations accepted.

Back Pack Guesthouse, XI, Takács Menyhért u. 33 (tel. 185 50 89). From Keleti pu. or the city center, take bus 1, 7, or 7A (black numbers) heading toward Buda and disembark at "Tétenyi u.," after the rail bridge. Go back under the bridge, turn left, and follow the street parallel to the train tracks for 3 blocks. Look for the small green signs. Carpeted rooms, clean bathrooms, and humor in every niche. 5- and 8-bed rooms 800-900Ft per person. Hot showers, breakfast, private locker, and use of kitchen, TV, and VCR included. Lends bikes; tennis courts nearby.

Summer Hostels

Almost all dorms of the **Technical University** (M-egyetem) become youth hostels in July and Aug.; they are conveniently located in district XI, around Móricz Zsigmond Körtér. From M3: "Kálvin Ter," ride tram 47 or 49 across the river to "M. Zsigmond."

For more information, call the **International Student Center** (tel. 166 77 58 or 166 50 11, ext. 1469). In summer, the center also has an office in Schönherz.

Baross, XI, Bartók Béla út 17 (tel. 186 83 65; fax 275 70 46), 2 blocks from Géllert tér. Open late June-Aug. Lived-in college dorms in a very central location. Reception open 24hr. Check-out 9am. No curfew. Triples and quads 1470Ft. 10% discount with an HI card. Laundry 140Ft, detergent 50Ft.

Schönherz, XI, Irinyi József u. 42 (tel. 166 54 60 or 166 50 21), two stops after crossing the river on tram 4 or 6. The blue high-rise has some of the better summer dorms in town with well-kept quads with bathrooms and refrigerators. Disco and bar in the building, but the rooms are still quiet. No curfew. 1550Ft per person. 10% off with HI card. Laundry 140Ft, dry 70Ft.

Martos, XI, Stoczek u. 5/7 (tel. 463 37 76; tel./fax 463 36 51; email reception@hotel.martos.bme.hu), opposite the hostel Vásárhely. This student-run summer hostel offers some of the cheapest rooms in town without sacrificing quality. No English spoken on weekends. No curfew. Check-out 9am. Free use of washing and drying machines. Internet access. Dorms and doubles 700-900Ft per person.

Guest Houses

Guest houses and rooms for rent in private homes include a personal touch for about the same as an anonymous hostel bed. Proprietors carry cellular telephones so they can always be reached for reservations. In stations, bypass the pushier hostel representatives and look for their more docile competitors.

Caterina, V, Andrássy út 47, III. 48 (tel. 291 95 38, cellular tel. 06 20 34 63 98). Take M1 or tram 4 or 6 to "Oktogon." A century-old building only a few min. from downtown Pest. One guest bathroom. 1000Ft. Owners speak only some English.

"Townhouser's" International Guesthouse, XVI, Attila u. 123 (cellular tel. 06 30 44 23 31; fax 342 07 95). Take M2 to "Örs Vezér tere," then 5 stops on bus #31 to "Diófa u." A quiet residential area ½hr. from downtown. Five spacious guest rooms, with 2 or 3 beds each, and 2 clean bathrooms. Kitchen available. Owners transport guests to and from the train station. 1000Ft per person.

Mrs. Ena Bottka, V, Garibaldi u. 5, 5th fl. (tel. 112 41 22), a block south of M2: "Kossuth tér." Live the Bohemian life in the tiny rooms overlooking gabled rooftops and the Parliament building. Small kitchen. Doubles 2900Ft. Call ahead.

Ms. Vali Németh, VIII, Osztály u. 20/24 A11 (tel. 113 88 46, cellular tel. 06 30 47 53 48), 400m east of M2: "Népstadion." Two doubles, a triple, and a bathroom close to the bus station, grocery stores, and a restaurant. 1300Ft per person.

Hotels

Budapest's few affordable hotels are frequently clogged with groups, so call ahead. Proprietors often speak English. All hotels should be registered with Tourinform.

Hotel Goliat, XIII, Kerekes út 12-20 (tel. 270 14 56). Take M1 to "Árpád híd.," then take the tram away from the river, and get off before the overpass. Walk down Reitler Ferere ut. until you see the 10-story yellow building on the left. Clean, spacious rooms. Singles 1800Ft. Doubles 2300Ft.

Hotel Citadella, Citadella Sétany (tel. 166 57 94; fax 186 03 05), atop Gellért Hill. Take tram #47 or 49 three stops into Buda to "Móricz Zsigmond Körter," then catch bus #27 to "Citadella." Perfect location and spacious rooms. Doubles, triples, and quads US$40-58. Usually packed, so write or fax to reserve.

Camping

Camping Hungary, available at tourist offices, has detailed information on Budapest's campgrounds.

Római Camping, III, Szentendrei út 189 (tel. 168 62 60; fax 250 04 26). Take M2 to "Batthyány tér," then take the HÉV commuter rail to "Római fürdő," and walk 100m towards the river. Tip-top security with grocery, swimming pool, and huge park on the site. Common showers. Reception open 24hr. 650Ft per person, students 500Ft. Tent 650Ft, students 500Ft. Bungalows 1600-5000Ft.

Hárs-hegyi, II, Hárs-hegyi út 5/7 (tel. 115 14 82; fax 176 19 21). Seven stops on bus 22 from "Moszkva tér" to "Dénes u." Currency exchange and a restaurant. 650Ft per person, students 500Ft. Tent 510Ft, students 460Ft. Bungalows 1600-5000Ft.

Riviera Camping, III, Királyok u. 257/259 (tel. 160 82 18). Take the HÉV commuter rail from Batthyány tér to "Romai fürdö," then bus #34 10min. until you see the campground. Tent 420Ft. Bungalows 2000Ft.

FOOD

Most restaurants in Budapest will fit your budget, though the food at family eateries may be cheaper and better tasting. An average meal runs 600-800Ft, and a 10% tip is usual. The listings below are just a nibble of what Budapest has to offer; seek out the *kifőzde* or *kisvendéglő* in your neighborhood for a taste of Hungarian life. Cafeterias lurk under **Önkiszolgáló Étterem** signs (vegetarian entrees 80Ft, meat entrees 160-200Ft). Fast food joints, though hardly Hungarian, are at least always there when you need them. Travelers may also rely on grocery stores and markets. The king of them all is the **Central Market**, V K¤zraktár tér u. 1 (M3: "Kelvin tér;" open Mon. 6am-4pm, Tues.-Fri. 6am-6pm, Sat. 6am-2pm). You can also shop at the **produce market,** IX, Vámház krt. 1/3, at Fővám tér (open Mon. 6am-3pm); the **ABC Food Hall,** I, Batthyány tér 5/7 (open Sun. 7am-1pm); or the **Non-Stops** at V, Október 6. u. 5 and V, Régi Posta u., off Váci u. past McDonald's.

Bohémtanya, V, Paulay Ede u. 6 (tel. 322 14 53). Take M to "Deák tér" or M1 to "Bajcsy-Zsilinsky." This place is packed due to its large portions of delicious Hungarian food. Full meals 290-780Ft. *Ropogös malacsüt* (roast suckling pig) 390Ft. English menu. Open daily noon-11pm.

Vegetárium, V, Cukor u. 3 (tel. 267 03 22). 1½ blocks from M3: "Ferenciek tere" (on map "Felszahadulás tér"). Walk up Ferenciek tere (formerly Károlyi M. u.) to Irány u. on the right, and take a quick left. Elaborate and imaginative vegetarian dishes 500-800Ft. 15% student discount with ISIC. Open daily noon-10pm.

Picasso Point Kávéhaz, VI, Hajós u. 31 (tel. 169 55 44). Make a right onto Hajos u., 2 blocks north of M3: "Arany János." A Bohemian hang-out with Hungarian, French, and Tex-Mex offerings. Dance club downstairs. Open daily noon-4am.

Alföldi Kisvendéglő, V, Kecskeméti u. 4 (tel. 267 02 24). M3: Kálvin tér, 50m past the Best Western. Traditional Hungarian folk cuisine—even the booths are paprika-red. The spicy, sumptuous homemade rolls (40Ft) are reason enough to come. Entrees 320-680Ft. Open daily 11am-midnight.

New York Bagels (The Sequel), VI, Bajesy-Zsilinszky út 21 (tel. 111 84 41). Take M3 to "Arany János utca." Assorted bagels baked hourly, freshly made spreads, sandwiches, salads, and cookies. Bagel sandwiches 250Ft, or design your own. Counter service. Open daily 7am-10pm.

Marquis de Salade, VI, Hajós u. 43 (tel. 153 49 31) corner of Bajzy-Zilinsky út, 2 blocks north of M3: "Arany János." A self-service mix of salads, Middle Eastern, and Bengali food in a cozy storefront the size of a large closet. English-speaking owner has been known to try new dishes on the spot at her patrons' urging. Most dishes are 420-500Ft. Open daily noon-midnight.

Remiz, II, Budakeszi út 5 (tel. 176 18 96). Take bus 158 from Moszkva tér to "Szépilona" (about 10min.), and walk past 3 stores. Traditional and tasty Hungarian cuisine in a fancy setting. Entrees 600-1200Ft. Outdoor seating in warm weather. Live music. Open daily 9am-1am. Call for reservations.

Marxim, II, Kis Rókus u. 23 (tel. 212 41 83). Take M2 to "Moszkva tér." With your back to the Lego-like castle, walk 200m along Margit krt., and turn left. KGB pizza (200-520Ft) and Lenin salad (100-170Ft) are just a few of the meals prepared by the staff according to their abilities, consumed by the patrons according to their needs. Open Mon.-Thurs. noon-1am, Fri.-Sat. noon-2am, Sun. 6pm-1am.

Paprika, V, Varosáz u. 10. Cafeteria food from 210Ft, but come here for the bakery with window service on the street. Open Mon.-Fri. 11am-4pm, Sat. 11am-3pm.

Cafés

These amazing establishments were the grandiloquent haunts of Budapest's literary, intellectual, and cultural elite. A café repose is a must for every visitor; best of all, the absurdly ornate pastries are inexpensive, even in the most genteel establishments.

Café New York, VII, Erzsébet krt. 9/11 (tel. 122 38 49). M2 to "Blaha Lujza tér." One of the most beautiful cafés in Budapest, with plenty of velvet, gold, and marble. Cappuccino 200Ft. Ice cream and coffee delights 20-400Ft. Filling Hungarian entrees (from 850Ft) served downstairs noon-10pm. Open daily 9am-midnight.

M>vész Kávéház, VI, Andrássy út 29 (tel. 267 06 89), diagonally across the street from the National Opera House. Take M1 to "Opera." Golden period wood paneling and gilded ceilings make this café one of Budapest's most elegant. Open daily 10am-midnight.

Lukács Cukrászda, VI, Andrássy út 70. M1: Vörösmarty u., near Hősök tere. One of Budapest's most stunning cafés. Dieters will wish the heavenly cakes and tortes were more expensive. Seated service costs more. Open Mon.-Fri. 9am-8pm.

Litia Literatura & Tea, I, Hess András tér 4 (tel. 175 69 87), in the Fortuna Passage. Choose from an immense selection of teas in this airy gardenhouse café in a quiet courtyard. Adjoining artsy bookstore. Coffee 70Ft. Open daily 10am-6pm.

SIGHTS

Buda The **Castle District** rests 100m above the Duna, atop the 2-km mound called **Várhegy** (Castle Hill). Built in the 13th century, the hilltop castle was leveled in consecutive sieges by the Mongols and Ottoman Turks. Christian Habsburg forces razed the rebuilt castle while ousting the Turks after a 145-year occupation. A reconstruction was completed just in time to be destroyed by the Germans in 1945. Today, the **Budavári palota** (Royal Palace) on the site houses several notable museums. During recent reconstruction of the palace, excavations revealed artifacts from the earliest castle here; they are now displayed in Wing E in the **Budapest History Museum.** (Open March-Oct. daily 10am-6pm; Nov.-Dec. 10am-5pm; Jan.-Feb. Tues.-Sun. 10am-4pm. 100Ft, students 50Ft, Wed. free.) Wing A contains the **Museum of Contemporary History** and the **Ludwig Museum,** a collection of international modern art (open Tues.-Sun. 10am-6pm; 100Ft, students 50Ft, Tues. free). Wings B-D hold the **Hungarian National Gallery,** a vast hoard of the best Hungarian painting and sculpture. (Open Tues.-Sun. 10am-6pm. 100Ft, students 40Ft, for all 3 wings. English tour 120Ft.) To reach Várhegy, follow a path up the hill, or cross the **Széchenyi lánchíd** (Chain Bridge) from Pest and ride the *sikló* (cable car) to the top (operates daily 7:30am-10pm; closed 2nd and 4th Mon. of each month; 150Ft).

From the castle, stroll down Színház u. and Tárnok u. to **Trinity Square,** site of the Disney-esque **Fisherman's Bastion.** This arcaded stone wall supports a squat, fairytale tower, but you'll have to pay for the magnificent view across the Duna (50Ft). Behind the tower stands the delicate, neo-Gothic **Mátyás templom** (St. Matthew's Church); it served as a mosque for 145 years after the Turks seized Buda. These days, high mass is celebrated Sundays at 10am with orchestra and choir. On summer Fridays at 8pm, organ concerts reverberate in the resplendent interior (open daily 7am-7pm). Intricate door-knockers and balconies adorn the Castle District's other historic buildings; ramble through **Úri u.** (Gentlemen's Street) with its Baroque townhouses, or **Táncsics Mihály u.** in the old Jewish sector. Enjoy a tremendous view of Buda from the Castle District's west walls.

The **Liberation Monument** crowns neighboring **Gellért Hill,** just south of the castle. This 30m bronze statue honors Soviet soldiers who died while "liberating" Hungary from the Nazis. The hill itself is named for the 11th-century bishop sent by the Pope to help King Stephen convert the Magyars; unconvinced, the Magyars hurled poor St. Gellért to his death from atop the hill. His statue, with colonnaded backdrop and waterfall, overlooks the **Erzsébet híd** (Elizabeth Bridge). The **Citadella** was built as a symbol of Habsburg power after the 1848 revolution; to get there, climb the hill from Hotel Gellért or take bus 27 from Móricz Zsigmond Körtér two stops beyond the hotel.

East of the **Vadaskert** (Game Park), the **Pál-völgyi Caves** boast 15m-high caverns and remarkable stalactite formations. Take bus #86 from Batthyany tér to "Kolosyi tér," and then bus #65 to the caves. Inquire at a tourist office for irregular tour times and prices. Between the caves and the Castle, the **Margit híd** spans the Duna to the **Margitsziget** (Margaret Island). Off-limits to private cars, the island offers capacious thermal baths, luxurious garden pathways, and numerous shaded terraces. According to legend, the *sziget* is named after King Béla IV's daughter; he vowed to rear young Margit as a nun if the nation survived the Mongol invasion of 1241. The Mongols left Hungary decimated but not destroyed, and Margaret was confined to the island convent. Take bus #26 from "Szt. István krt." to the island.

Pest Cross the Duna to reach Pest, the throbbing commercial and administrative center of the capital. The old **Inner City**, rooted in the pedestrian zone of Váci u. and Vörösmarty tér, is a tourist haven. On the riverbank, a string of modern luxury hotels leads up to the magnificent neo-Gothic **Parliament** in Kossuth tér (arrange 1500Ft tours at IBUSZ and Budapest Tourist). Nearby, at Kossuth tér 12 in the former Hungarian Supreme Court, the **Néprajzi múzeum** (Museum of Ethnography) hosts an outstanding exhibit of Hungarian folk culture from the late 18th century to World War I, and an exceptional collection of cultural artifacts from Asian, African, and Aboriginal peoples (open Tues.-Sat. 10am-5:45pm, Sun. 10am-6pm; 60Ft, students 20Ft).

St. Stephen's Basilica, two blocks north of Deák tér, is by far the city's largest church, with room for 8500 worshippers. Climb 302 spiraling steps to the Panorama tower for a 360° view of the city (open April-Oct. daily 10am-6:30pm; 200Ft, students 125Ft). St. Stephen's holy **right hand,** one of Hungary's most revered religious relics, is displayed in the Basilica's museum. (Basilica open Mon.-Sat. 9am-5pm, Sun. 1-5pm. 70Ft, students 50Ft. Museum open April-Sept. Mon.-Sat. 9am-4:30pm, Sun. 1-4:30pm; Oct.-March Mon.-Sat. 10am-4pm, Sun. 1-4pm.) At the corner of Dohány u. and Wesselényi u., the **Great Synagogue** is the largest temple in use in Europe and the second largest in the world (open Mon.-Fri. 10am-6pm; in winter 10am-3:30pm; donation requested). Next door, the **Jewish Museum** juxtaposes magnificent exhibits dating back to the Middle Ages with haunting documentation of the Holocaust. (Open April-Oct. Mon.-Fri. 10am-3pm, Sun. 10am-1pm. The museum may open year-round in the near future. 150Ft.)

To the east of the basilica, **Andrássy út,** Hungary's grandest boulevard, extends from the edge of Belváros in downtown Pest to H¤sök tere (Heroes' Square), some 2km away. The **Magyar állami operaház** (Hungarian National Opera House), VI, Andrássy út 22 (M1: Opera), is laden with sculptures and paintings in the ornate Empire style of the 1880s. If you can't actually see an opera, at least take a tour (daily at 3 and 4pm; 400Ft, students 200Ft). The **Millennium Monument,** commemorating the nation's most prominent leaders and national heroes from 896 to 1896, dominates Hősök tere. The **Szépművészti múzeum** (Museum of Fine Arts) on the square maintains a splendid collection; highlights include an entire room devoted to El Greco and an exhaustive display of Renaissance works. (Open Tues.-Sun. 10am-5:30pm. 200Ft, students with ISIC 100Ft. Tours for up to 5 people 1500Ft.)

Behind the monument, the **Városliget** (City Park) is home to a circus, an amusement park, a zoo, a castle, and the impressive **Széchenyi Baths.** The **Vajdahunyad Castle,** created for the Millenary Exhibition of 1896, incorporates Romanesque, Gothic, Renaissance, and Baroque styles. Outside the castle broods the hooded statue of **Anonymous,** the secretive scribe to whom we owe much of our knowledge of medieval Hungary, and, after Ibid., the most-quoted figure in history. Rent a **rowboat** (June to mid-Sept. daily 9am-8pm) or **ice skates** (Nov.-March daily 9am-1pm and 4-8pm; 60Ft in morning) on the lake next to the castle.

The ruins of the north Budapest garrison town of **Aquincum** (tel. 168 82 41 or 180 46 50) crumble in the outer regions of the third district. To reach the area, take M2 to "Batthyány tér," then the HÉV to "Aquincum;" the site is about 100m south of the

---

Like a Troubled Bridge over Water...

The citizens of Budapest are justly proud of the bridges that bind Buda to Pest. The four great lions that have guarded the **Széchenyi lánchíd** ("The Chain Bridge") since 1849 make this bridge one of the most recognizable in the city. These exotic beasts were created by the master János Marschalkō in a naturalistic style, with the tongues resting far back in their gaping mouths. The anatomical correctness of their new city mascots did not impress the Budapestians—distraught by public laughter over this apparently missing feature in his creations, Marschalkō jumped from the bridge to his death. Another version of the story has the king reprimanding Marschalkō, with the same result. *Let's Go* does not recommend sculpting lions without visible tongues.

HÉV stop. Here are the most impressive vestiges of the Roman occupation, which spanned the first four centuries AD. The **museum** on the grounds contains a model of the ancient city as well as musical instruments and other household items. The remains of the **Roman Military Baths** are visible to the south of the Roman encampment, beside the overpass at Flórián tér near the "Árpád híd" HÉV station. From the stop, just follow the main road away from the river.

ENTERTAINMENT AND NIGHTLIFE

Budapest hosts cultural events year-round. Pick up a copy of the English-language monthly *Programme in Hungary* or *Budapest Panorama*, both available free at tourist offices; they contain daily listings of all concerts, operas, and theater performances in the city. The "Style" section of the weekly English-language *Budapest Sun* is another excellent source for schedules of entertainment happenings.

The **Central Theater Booking Office,** VI, Andrassy út 18 (tel. 112 00 00; open Mon.-Thurs. 10am-1pm and 2-6pm, Fri. 10am-5pm), next to the Opera House, and the branch at Moszkva tér 3 (tel. 212 56 78; open Mon.-Fri 10am-5pm), both sell commission-free tickets to almost every performance in the city. An extravaganza at the gilded, Neo-Renaissance **State Opera House,** VI, Andrássy út 22 (tel. 131 25 50; M1: Opera), costs only US$4-5; the box office (tel. 153 01 70), on the left side of the building, sells unclaimed tickets at even better prices 30min. before showtime (open Tues.-Sat. 11am-1:45pm and 2:30-7pm, Sun. 10am-1pm and 4-7pm). The **Philharmonic Orchestra** is also world renowned; concerts thunder through town almost every evening September to June. The ticket office (tel. 117 62 22) is located at Vörösmarty tér 1. (Open Mon.-Fri. 10am-6pm, Sat.-Sun. 10am-2pm. Tickets 800-1200Ft; on the day of performance 300Ft.)

In late summer, the Philharmonic and Opera take sabbaticals, but summer theaters and concert halls are ready to pick up the slack. In July, classical music and opera are performed at 8:30pm in the **Hilton Hotel Courtyard,** I, Hess András tér 1/3 (tel. 175 10 00), next to St. Matthew's in the Castle District. The **Margitsziget Theater,** XIII, Margitsziget (tel. 111 24 96), features opera and Hungarian-music concerts on its open-air stage. Take tram #4 or 6 to "Margitsziget." Try **Zichy Mansion Courtyard,** III, F¤ tér 1, for orchestral concerts, or the **Pest Concert Hall** (Vigadó), V, Vigadó tér 2 (tel. 118 99 03; fax 175 62 22), on the Duna bank near Vörösmarty tér, for operettas (cashier open Mon.-Sat. 10am-6pm; tickets 3000Ft). Folk-dancers stomp across the stage at the **Buda Park Theater,** XI, Kosztolányi Dezső tér (tel. 117 62 22); brochures and concert tickets flood from the ticket office at Vörösmarty tér 1 (open Mon.-Fri. 11am-6pm; tickets 70-250Ft). For a psychedelic evening, try the laser shows at the **Planetarium** (tel. 134 11 61; M3: Népliget). The multi-media sorcery even brings Floyd to life on occasion. (Wed.-Thurs. and Sat. 6:30, 8, and 9:30pm; Mon. and Fri. 8 and 9:30pm; Tues. 6:30 and 9:30pm.)

A virtually unenforced drinking age and cheap drinks draw old and young alike to Budapest's clubs and bars. As clubs become more and more technically sophisticated, the cover prices are rising—a night of techno may soon cost the same as a night at the opera.

GATEWAY CITIES

Old Man's Pub, VII, Akácfa u. 13 (tel. 122 76 45). Take M2 to "Blaha Lujza tér." Live blues and jazz in a classy and upscale environment. Kitchen serves pizza, spaghetti, and salads. Occasional free samples of beer. Open Mon.-Sat. 12pm-2am.

Morrison's Music Pub, VI, Révay u. 25 (tel. 269 40 60), left of the State Opera House. Take M1 to "Opera." Pub and dance club with a young, international crowd. Functional English red telephone booth inside. Fri.-Sat. cover 200Ft. Open Mon.-Thurs. 7pm-4am, Fri.-Sat. 6pm-4am, Sun. 8pm-4am.

Angel Bar, VII, Rákóczi ut 51 (tel. 113 12 73). Take M2 to "Blaha Lujza tér." Bar and popular disco for the city's gay community. Open nightly 10pm to dawn.

Véndiák (Former Student), V, Egyetem tér 5 (tel. 267 02 26). M2: Kálvin tér. Walk up Kecskeméti u. Late-night bar with a lively dance floor after midnight. Popular with local students during school year. Open Mon. 9pm-2am, Tues.-Sat. 9pm-5am.

Bahnhof, on the north side of Nugati train station. Take M3 to "Nyugati pu." One of the most popular dance clubs and with good reason; no technical wizardry but two superb dance floors. Well ventilated. Cover 300Ft. Open Mon.-Sat. 6pm-4am.

Made-Inn Music Club, VI, Andrassy út 112. Take M1 to "Bajza u." Crowds come for the frequent live bands in this cavernous club. Open Wed.-Sun. 8pm-4am.

■ Danube Bend (Dunakanyar)

North of Budapest, the Danube sweeps south in a dramatic arc known as the Danube Bend *(Dunakanyar),* as it flows east from Vienna along the Slovak border. Within 45km of Budapest, the region offers a variety of daytrips and overnights from the capital. Ruins of first-century Roman settlements cover the countryside, and medieval palaces and fortresses overlook the river in **Esztergom** and **Visegrád.** An artist colony thrives today amidst the museums and churches of **Szentendre.**

Szentendre Szentendre is by far the most tourist-thronged of the Danube bend cities, but its proximity to Budapest, narrow cobblestone streets, and the artistry of its shops and museums keep the visitors coming. On Szentendre's **Templomdomb** (Church Hill) above Fő tér sits the 13th-century Roman Catholic **parish church.** Facing it, the **Czóbel Museum** exhibits works of Hungary's foremost Impressionist, Béla Czóbel (open Tues.-Sun. 10am-4pm; 60Ft, students 30Ft). To the north across Alkotmány u., the Baroque **Serbian Orthodox Church** displays Serbian religious art (open Wed.-Sun. 10am-4pm; 60Ft). Szentendre's most impressive museum, **Kovács Margit Múzeum,** Vastagh György u. 1, exhibits brilliant ceramic sculptures and tiles by the 20th-century Hungarian artist Margit Kovács (open Mon. 10am-4pm, Tues.-Sun. 10am-6pm; 200Ft, students 100Ft). **Szabó Marcipán Múzeum,** Dumtsa Jenő u. 7 (tel. (26) 31 14 84), chronicles marzipan's history and production with clever and flavorful displays (open daily 10am-6pm; 100Ft, students and seniors 50Ft).

■ Munich (München)

Berlin and Munich represent two irreconcilable poles of the German character: northern Berlin is fragmented, wry, and cerebral, reflecting a spirit that hovers somewhere between East and West; while southern Munich is unified, merry, sensual, and decidedly Western in feel. As the capital and cultural center of Bavaria, liberal Munich boasts world-class museums, handsome parks and architecture, a rambunctious arts scene, and astonishing vitality. *Münchners* party particularly zealously during *Fasching* (Feb. 15-20 in 1997), Germany's equivalent of Mardi Gras, and during the legendary *Oktoberfest* (Sept. 20-Oct. 5 in 1997).

ORIENTATION AND PRACTICAL INFORMATION

A map of Munich's center looks like a somewhat skewed circle quartered by one horizontal and one vertical line. The circle is the main traffic **Ring**; within it lies the lion's share of Munich's sights. The east-west and north-south thoroughfares cross at

Munich's epicenter, the **Marienplatz** (home to the **Neues Rathaus**), and meet the traffic ring at **Karlsplatz** in the west, **Isartorplatz** in the east, **Odeonsplatz** in the north, and **Sendlinger Tor** in the south. The **Hauptbahnhof** (main train station) is just beyond Karlspl. outside the Ring in the west. To get to Marienpl. from the station, go straight on Schützenstr. to Karlspl., then continue through Karlstor to Neuhauser Str., which becomes Kaufingerstr. before it reaches Marienpl. (15min.). Or, from the *Hauptbahnhof,* take any of S-Bahn lines 1-8 to Marienpl.

At Odeonsplatz, the giant **Residenz** palace appears. Odeonsplatz is also the starting point for the long, straight **Ludwigstraße**, stretching north to the university district. **Leopoldstraße,** the continuation of Ludwigstraße, reaches farther toward **Schwabing.** This district, also known as "Schwabylon," is student country. Farther west sits posh **Nymphenburg,** built around **Nymphenburg Palace.** Southwest of Marienpl., **Sendlingerstraße** leads past shops and the Baroque **Asamkirche** to **Sendlinger Tor.** From here, Lindwurmstr. proceeds onward to Goethepl., from which Mozartstr. leads to **Theresienwiese,** site of the *Oktoberfest.*

Tourist Office: Fremdenverkehrsamt (tel. 23 33 02 56 or 23 33 02 57), in the train station. The office books rooms for a DM5 fee plus DM3-9 deposit, and sells accommodations lists for DM0.50. The English/German guide *München Infopool* is aimed at students (DM7). The office also has excellent free maps. Open Mon.-Sat. 9am-9pm, Sun. 11am-7pm. The **branch office** (tel. 97 59 28 15), at the Flughafen Munich airport in the *Zentralgebäude,* offers general info but no bookings. Open Mon.-Sat. 8:30am-10pm, Sun. 1-9pm. A new office is opening in the **Neu Rathaus** in Marienplatz. **EurAide in English** (tel. 59 38 89; fax 550 39 65), along track 11 of the *Hauptbahnhof* near the Bayerstr. exit, is fast and friendly. The office reserves rooms for DM6 and validates Eurailpasses. *Inside Track,* with tips on rail travel, is available here and at the station's *Reisezentrum* (free). Open May daily 7:30am-noon and 1-4:30pm; June-Oct. 7:30am-noon and 1-6pm.

Tours: Mike's Bike Tours, St. Bonifatiusstr. 2 (tel. 651 42 75; e-mail 101372.2014@compuserve.com). 3½-4hr. tours leave daily at 11:30am and 4pm from the *Altes Rathaus.* DM28, bike rental included.

Budget Travel: Council Travel, Adalbertstr. 32 (tel. 39 50 22; fax 39 70 04), near the university. Distributes ISIC cards. Open Mon.-Fri. 9:30am-1pm and 2-6pm.

Consulates: U.S., Königinstr. 5 (tel. 288 80). Open Mon.-Fri. 8-11:30am. **Canada,** Tal 29 (tel. 219 95 70). Open Mon.-Thurs. 9am-noon and 2-5pm, Fri. 9am-noon and 2-3:30pm. **U.K.,** Bürkleinstr. 10 (tel. 21 10 90). Open Mon.-Fri. 8:45-11:30am and 1-3:15pm. **Ireland,** Mauerkircherstr. 1a (tel. 985 72 35). Open Mon.-Thurs. 9am-noon and 2-4pm, Fri. 9am-noon. The **Australian** consulate is in Frankfurt (tel. (069) 273 90 90). **South Africa,** Sendlinger-Tor-Platz 5 (tel. 231 16 30). Open Mon.-Fri. 9am-noon.

Currency Exchange: American Express offers the best deal; otherwise, the **post office** across from the station cashes traveler's checks for DM6 per check. **Deutsche Verkehrs-Bank (DVB),** at the main station, cashes traveler's checks, offers Western Union services, and handles cash transactions (DM2). Those with *Inside Track* get a 50% commission reduction when cashing U.S. traveler's checks over US$50. Open daily 6am-11pm.

American Express: Promenadepl. 6 (tel. 29 09 00, 24hr. hotline 0130 853 100; fax 29 09 01 18), in the Hotel Bayerischer Hof. The staff holds mail and cashes all traveler's checks. Open Mon.-Fri. 9am-5:30pm, Sat. 9:30am-12:30pm.

Telephones: You can make credit card and collect calls from the post office, on the 2nd level of the train station, and across the street from the station.

Flights: For flight information, call 97 52 13 13. To reach the **Flughafen München** from the train station, take S-Bahn 8 (daily 3:22am-12:42am, DM13.20).

Trains: Munich connects to major cities throughout Europe several times daily. For information call 194 19; for reservations (German only) call 12 23 23 33. To: Frankfurt (4hr.), Berlin (8½hr.), Prague (7hr.), Vienna (4-5hr.); Zürich (4-5hr.), Paris (10hr.). Station open daily 4:30am-1:30am.

Public Transportation: The **MVV** public transportation system runs weekdays 5am-12:30am, weekends 5am-1:30am. Railpasses are valid on the S-Bahn (com-

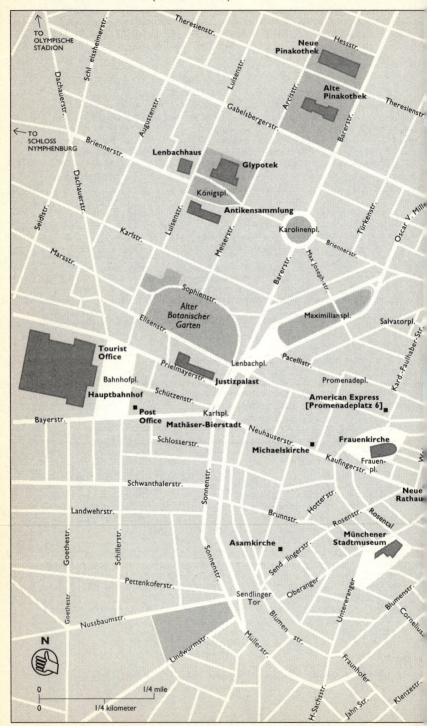

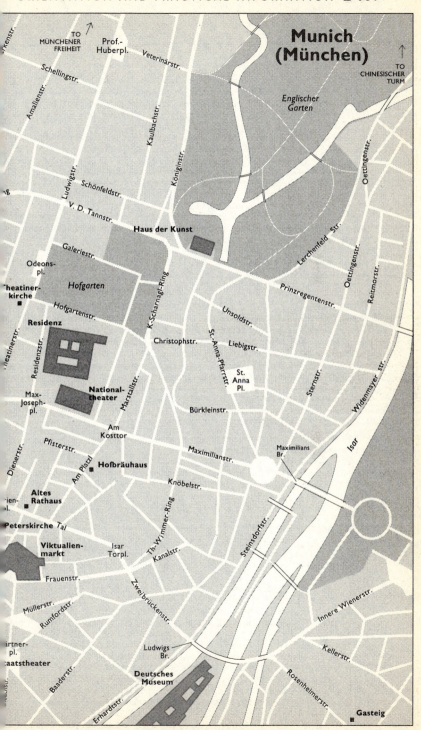

Munich (München)

TO MÜNCHENER FREIHEIT

Prof.-Huberpl.

TO CHINESISCHER TURM

Englischer Garten

kenstr.
Amalienstr.
Schellingstr.
Veterinärstr.
Kaulbachstr.
Königinstr.
Ludwigstr.
Schönfeldstr.
V. D. Tannstr.
Haus der Kunst
Galeriestr.
Odeons-pl.
Theatiner-kirche
Hofgarten
K.-Scharnagl-Ring
Lerchenfeld Str.
Oettingenstr.
Reitmorstr.
Prinzregentenstr.
Hofgartenstr.
Residenz
Unsoldstr.
St.-Anna-Pfarrstr.
Liebigstr.
Sternstr.
Widenmayer str.
Residenzstr.
Christophstr.
St. Anna Pl.
Theatinerstr.
Nationaltheater
Marsallstr.
Max-Joseph-pl.
Bürkleinstr.
Am Kosttor
Pfisterstr.
Maximilianstr.
Maximilians Br.
Isar
Dienerstr.
Am Platzl
Hofbräuhaus
Knöbelstr.
Altes Rathaus
ien-l.
Peterskirche Tal
Viktualien-markt
Isar Torpl.
Th.-Wimmer-Ring
Kanalstr.
Steinsdorfstr.
Frauenstr.
Müllerstr.
Rumfordstr.
Zweibrückenstr.
Innere Wienerstr.
ärtner-pl.
aatstheater
Baaderstr.
Ludwigs Br.
Deutsches Museum
Erhardtstr.
Kellerstr.
Rosenheimerstr.
Gasteig

muter rail), but *not* on the U-Bahn (subway), *Straßenbahn* (trams), or buses. Single rides within the *Innenraum* (inner city) cost DM3.30. Single-day tickets *(Single-Tages-Karte)* run DM8, one-week passes DM34. Cancel your ticket in the boxes marked with an "E" *before* you go to the platform. Pick up a transit maps at the tourist office, EurAide, or MVV counters.

Bike Rental: English-speaking **Radius Touristik** (tel. 59 61 13) is opposite tracks 30-31 at the station. DM10 for 2hr., DM25 for 24hr. DM100 deposit. Students and Eurailpass holders get 10% off. Open May-early Oct. daily 9am-6pm. **Aktiv-Rad,** Hans-Sachs-Str. 7 (tel. 266 506), rents 'em out for DM18 a day. U-Bahn 1 or 2: Frauenhoferstr. Open Mon.-Fri. 9am-1pm and 2-6:30pm, Sat. 9am-1pm.

Hitchhiking: Hitchers who want to reach *Autobahn* A8/E52 "Salzburg-Vienna-Italy" first ride U-Bahn 1 or 2 to Karl-Preis-Pl. To get to A8/E52 "Stuttgart/France," they take U-Bahn 1 to Rotkreuzpl., then tram 12 to Amalienburgstr.; or S-Bahn 2 to Obermenzing. Thumbers who want to reach the *Autobahn* A9/E45 interchange to Berlin take U-Bahn 6 to Studentenstadt and walk 500m to the Frankfurter Ring. A safer bet is **McShare Treffpunkt Zentrale,** Klenzestr. 57b and Lämmerstr. 4 (tel. 194 40), near the train station, which matches drivers and riders. Open Mon.-Sat. 8am-8pm. Also try **Känguruh,** Amalienstr. 87 (tel. 194 44), in the Amalienpassage near the university. Open Mon.-Fri. 8:30am-7pm, Sat. 9am-3pm, Sun. 10am-7pm. Scan bulletin boards in the *Mensa* at Leopoldstr. 13 for ride information.

Laundromat: Wäscherei, Paul-Heyse-Str. 21, near the station. Open daily 6am-10pm. **Münz Waschsalon,** Amalienstr. 61, near the university. Wash DM6, dry DM1. Soap DM1. Open Mon.-Fri. 8am-6:30pm, Sat. 8am-1pm.

Pharmacy: Bahnhof Apotheke (tel. 59 41 19 or 59 81 19), on the corner outside the station. Open Mon.-Fri. 8am-6:30pm, Sat. 8am-2pm. 24hr. service rotates; call 59 44 75 for info (in German) or get a schedule from the tourist office or EurAide.

Medical Assistance: University clinic, across the river on Ismaningerstr. U.S. and British consulates have lists of English-speaking doctors.

Emergencies: Ambulance: tel. 192 22. **Emergency medical service:** tel. 55 77 55. **Fire:** tel. 112.

Police: tel. 110.

Post Office: Post/Telegrafamt, Bahnhofpl. 1 (tel. 545 40), opposite the train station. **Poste Restante** and currency exchange available at windows 8-10. Open Mon.-Fri. 7am-10pm, Sat.-Sun. 8am-10pm. To send packages and insured letters, turn left out of the station onto Arnulfstr.; on the right is another post office. Open Mon.-Fri. 8am-7pm, Sat. 8am-2pm. **Postal Code:** 80335.

Telephone Code: 089.

ACCOMMODATIONS AND CAMPING

Munich accommodations fall into one of three categories: seedy, expensive, or booked. Reserve in advance in summer and during *Oktoberfest,* when all three often apply. Sleeping in the *Englischer Garten* or train station is unsafe and illegal. Augsburg's hostel (40min. by train) is an option, but mind the 1am curfew.

Hostels and Camping

Jugendlager Kapuzinerhölzl ("The Tent"), In den Kirchen 30 (tel. 141 43 00; fax 51 41 06 18). Take streetcar #17 from the *Hauptbahnhof* to "Botanischer Garten," Franz-Schrank-Str. (ticket inspections are rigorous along this route). Sleep with 400 other people in a big circus tent. 3-day max. stay. Under 24 only (flexible). Reception open daily 5pm-9am. DM13 for foam pad, blankets, bathrooms, and shower. Actual beds DM17. No reservations. Open late June to early Sept.

4 you münchen (ökologisches Jugendgästehaus), Hirtenstr. 18 (tel. 55 21 660; fax 55 21 66 66), 200m from the train station. This beautiful, ecological youth hostel has beech wood, large windows, and granola good cheer. Dorms DM20-25. Singles DM50. Doubles DM70. Sheets DM4. Wheelchair accessible. Adjoining hotel has singles for DM110 and doubles for DM130, shower included.

Jugendherberge (HI), Wendl-Dietrich-Str. 20 (tel. 13 11 56; fax 167 87 45). U-Bahn 1 to "Rotkreuzpl." Reception open daily 10am-1am. Check-in 10:30am, but lines form before 9am. Dorms for men only DM21.50. 4- to 6-bed rooms DM24 per person. DM20 key deposit. DM50 safe deposit. Breakfast and sheets included.

Jugendherberge Pullach Burg Schwaneck (HI), Burgweg 4-6 (tel. 793 06 43; fax 793 79 22). Ride S-Bahn 7 (dir: Wolfratshausen) to "Pullach." Romantic surroundings swarm with schoolkids. Reception open daily 5-11pm. Curfew 11:30pm. DM20, sheets DM5.50. Shower tokens DM1; buy them early. Breakfast included.

Jugendgästehaus München (HI), Miesingstr. 4 (tel. 723 65 50; fax 724 25 67). Hop on U-Bahn 1 or 2 to "Sendlinger Tor," then U-Bahn 3 (dir: Forstenrieder Allee) to "Thalkirchen." Crowded and distant, but the rooms are immaculate. Reception open daily 7am-1am. 8- to 15-bed rooms DM26. Singles DM34. Doubles DM60. Triples and quads DM28 per person. Sheets and breakfast included.

CVJM (YMCA) Jugendgästehaus, Landwehrstr. 13, 80336 München (tel. 552 14 10; fax 550 42 82; e-mail muenchen@cvjm.org). Take the Bayerstr. exit from the station, head down Goethestr., and take the second left. Clean, no-frills rooms. Reception open daily 8am-12:30am. Singles DM48. Doubles DM82. 15% surcharge for guests over 27. Breakfast included. Closed Easter and Dec. 20-Jan. 7.

Jugendhotel Marienberge, Goethestr. 9 (tel. 55 58 05), south of the train station. The hotel is in a rough area, but the building is secure and staffed by nuns. Open only to women under 26 years old. Reception open daily 8am-midnight. Curfew midnight. 6-bed rooms DM25 per person. Singles DM35. Doubles DM60. Triples DM90. Showers and breakfast included.

Haus International Youth Hotel, Elisabethstr. 87 (tel. 12 00 60; fax 12 00 62 51). Ride U-Bahn 2 (dir: Dülferstr.) to "Hohenzollernpl.," then streetcar 12 or bus 33 to "Barbarastr." Very clean, with an indoor pool and beer garden. Reception open 24hr. Singles DM53-83. Doubles DM100-140. Triples DM135. Quads DM164.

Campingplatz Thalkirchen, Zentrallandstr. 49 (tel. 723 17 07; fax 724 31 77). Take U-Bahn 1 or 2 to "Sendlinger Tor," then U-Bahn 3 to "Thalkirchen," then bus 57. Large and well-run but crowded. Curfew 11pm. DM7.80 per person. Small tents DM5.50, large tents DM7. Showers DM2. Open mid-March to Oct.

Hotels and Pensions

When the city is full, finding singles under DM55-65 and doubles under DM80-100 is nearly impossible. Also keep in mind that prices may rise DM5-20 during *Oktoberfest.* The tourist office and EurAide find rooms for a DM5-6 fee.

Hotel Kurpfalz, Schwanthalerstr. 121 (tel. 540 98 60; fax 54 09 88 11; email hotel-kurpfalz@munich-online.de). Walk 5-6 blocks on Bayerstr. to reach Schwanthalerstr. TV, showers, and hardwood furniture in spotless rooms. Reception open 24hr. Singles DM55-59. Doubles DM80-90. Laundry DM6. Breakfast included.

Hotel Haberstock, Schillerstr. 4 (tel. 55 78 55; fax 550 36 34), near the train station. Musky carpets and expansive pillows in a quiet and private hotel. Reception open 24hr. Singles DM66-105. Doubles DM116-176. Breakfast included.

Pension Locarno, Bahnhofplatz 5 (tel. 55 51 64; fax 59 50 45), under the AGFA sign outside the train station. Reception open daily 7am-midnight; key opens outside door. Singles DM 55-75. Doubles DM90. Tripes DM135. Quads DM140.

Pension Schillerhof, Schillerstr. 21 (tel. 59 42 70; fax 550 18 35). Bland rooms brightened by the hustle of neighborhood sex shops and kinos. Singles DM55-75. Doubles DM80-110. Shower and breakfast included.

Pension Hungaria, Briennerstr. 42 (tel. 52 15 58). Ride U-Bahn 1 to "Stiglmaierplatz," and take the Briennerstr./Volkstheater exit. Oriental rugs, comfortable furnishings, and a small travel library. Reception open daily 8am-10pm. Singles DM50-55. Doubles DM80-85. Triples DM105. Showers DM3. Breakfast included.

Pension Frank, Schellingstr. 24 (tel. 28 14 51; fax 280 09 10). From the Hauptbahnhof, take U-Bahn 4 or 5 to "Odeonsplatz," then U-Bahn 3 or 6 to "Universität." Campy, casual atmosphere. Reception open daily 7:30am-10pm. Dorms DM35. Singles DM55-65. Doubles DM78-85. Shower and breakfast included.

Pension am Kaiserplatz, Kaiserpl. 12 (tel. 34 91 90). Take U-Bahn 3 or 6 to "Münchner Freiheit," ride the escalator to Herzogstr., and turn left on Viktoriastr. Elegantly decorated. Reception open daily 7am-8pm. Singles DM49-59. Doubles DM75-89. Triples DM105. Quads DM120-130. Shower and breakfast included.

Hotel-Pension am Markt, Heiliggeiststr. 6 (tel. 22 50 14; fax 22 40 17). Hop on S-Bahn 1-8 to Marienpl., then walk through the *Altes Rathaus,* and turn right behind the *Heiliggeist* church. Sparsely furnished but thoroughly clean rooms. Singles DM60-100. Doubles DM112-155. Breakfast included.

FOOD

Munich's gastronomic center is the vibrant **Viktualienmarkt,** two minutes south of Marienpl., with a rainbow of bread, fruit, meat, pastry, cheese, wine, vegetable, and sandwich shops (open Mon.-Fri. 9am-6:30pm, Sat. 9am-2pm). Otherwise, look for cheap meals in the **university district** off Ludwigstr. **Tengelmann,** Schützenstr. 7, near the train station, satisfies grocery needs quickly and conveniently (open Mon.-Wed. and Fri. 8:30am-6:30pm, Thurs. 8:30am-8:30pm, Sat. 9am-2pm).

Münch'ner Suppenküche, at the Viktualienmarkt and at Schellingstr. 24, near the university. A Munich institution. Warm, hearty soup meals DM5.80-8; *Krustis* (sandwiches) DM3.60-5. Open Mon.-Fri. 8am-6:30pm, Sat. 10am-5pm.

Türkenhof, Türkenstr. 78. Smoky, relaxed, and buzzing at night. *Schnitzel,* omelettes, soups, and other entrees DM8-17. Open Sun.-Thurs. 11am-1am.

Café Puck, Türkenstr. 33 (tel. 280 22 80). Handsome café that exudes a hip, energetic bustle. Breakfasts DM4.50-15, soups DM5-7. Open daily 9am-1am.

Schelling Salon, Schellingstr. 54. Bavarian *Knödel* and billiard balls. Founded in 1872, this pool joint has racked the balls of Lenin, Rilke, and Hitler; Franz Josef Strauss used to drop by for a snack. Open Thurs.-Mon. 6:30am-midnight.

Atzinger, Schellingstr. 9. Pleasing pastas (DM9-11) and vegetarian dishes (DM8-10); other meals DM8-27. Open Mon.-Tues. 10am-1am, Wed.-Thurs. 10am-2am, Fri.-Sat. 10am-3am, Sun. 5pm-1am. Hot meals served until 1am.

Shoya, Orlandostr. 5, across from Hofbräuhaus. Fill up on teriyakis (DM8-16), sushi (DM5-30), and other dishes (DM4-16). Open daily 10:30am-midnight.

Café Ruffini, Orffstr. 22; take U-Bahn 1 to Rotkreuzplatz. Veggie dishes (DM 6-15) with good wine. Open Tues.-Sat. 10am-midnight, Sun. 10am-6pm.

SIGHTS

The **Marienplatz** serves as an interchange for major S-Bahn and U-Bahn lines as well as the social nexus of the city. On the square, the onion-domed towers of the 15th-century **Frauenkirche** have long been one of Munich's most notable landmarks (towers open April-Oct. Mon.-Sat. 10am-5pm; DM4, students DM2). At the neo-Gothic **Neues Rathaus,** the **Glockenspiel** marks the hour at 11am, noon, 5, and 9pm with jousting knights and dancing coopers. At 9pm, a mechanical watchman marches out and an angel escorts the *Münchner Kindl,* the city's symbol, to bed (tower open Mon.-Fri. 9am-7pm; DM3).

Munich's ritual past is represented by the 11th-century **Peterskirche,** at Rinder-markt and Peterspl.; 294 steps scale the saintly tower, christened *Alter Peter* (Old Peter) by locals (tower open Mon.-Sat. 9am-6pm, Sun. 10am-6pm; DM2.50, students DM1.50). Nearby, Ludwig II of Bavaria rests in peace in a crypt of the 16th-century Jesuit **Michaelskirche,** on Neuhauserstr. (crypt DM0.50). A Bavarian Rococo master-piece, the **Asamkirche,** Sendlingerstr. 32, is named after the brothers, Cosmas and Egid, who created it. The magnificent **Residenz,** Max-Joseph-Pl. 3, boasts richly deco-rated rooms built from the 14th to 19th centuries. The grounds now house several museums, and the **treasury** *(Schatzkammer)* contains jeweled baubles, crowns, swords, china, and ivorywork from as early as the 10th century (treasury open Tues.-Sun. 10am-4:30pm; DM5, students DM2.50). To reach the *Residenz,* take U-Bahn 3, 4, 5, or 6 to Odeonspl.

The royal summer residence of **Schloß Nymphenburg** is worth the trip northwest of town; take U-Bahn 1 to Rotkreuzpl., then streetcar 12 "Amalienburgstr." A Baroque wonder set in a winsome park, the palace hides a number of treasures, including a two-story granite marble hall seasoned with stucco, frescoes, and a Chinese lacquer cabinet. Check out King Ludwig's "Gallery of Beauties"—whenever a woman caught his fancy, he would have her portrait painted. (*Schloß* open April-Sept. Tues.-Sun. 9am-noon and 1-5pm; Oct.-March 10am-12:30pm and 1:30-4pm. Main palace DM4, students DM3; entire complex DM6, students DM5. Grounds free.) Next door is the immense **Botanischer Garten,** where greenhouses shelter rare and wonderful flora from around the world. (Garden open daily 9am-7pm. Greenhouses open 9am-11:45am and 1-6:30pm. DM3, students DM1.50.) Abutting the city center is the **Englischer Garten,** one of Europe's oldest landscaped parks.

Museums Munich is a supreme museum city. Take a break from Monet et al. at the **Deutsches Museum,** on the *Museumsinsel* (Museum Island) in the Isar River (S-Bahn 1-8: Isartor), one of the world's largest, most exciting museums of science and technology. Particularly interesting are the mining exhibit, which winds through a labyrinth of recreated subterranean tunnels, the planetarium (DM3), and the daily electrical show (museum open daily 9am-5pm; DM10, students DM4). The **Neue Pinakothek,** on Barerstr., boasts 18th- to 20th-century masterpieces. (Open Tues. and Thurs. 10am-8pm, Wed. and Fri.-Sun. 10am-5pm. DM7, students DM4, Sun. free.) **Lenbachhaus,** Luisenstr. 33, houses Munich cityscapes, along with works by Kandinsky, Klee, and the Blaue Reiter school, which helped to forge the modernist abstract aesthetic (open Tues.-Sun. 10am-6pm; DM8, students DM4, Sun. free.) Between them, **Glyptohek,** Königsplatz 3, and **Antikensammlung,** Königsplatz 1, hold Munich's finest collection of ancient art. (Glyptohek open Tues.-Wed. and Fri.-Sun. 10am-5pm, Thurs. 10am-8pm. Antikensammlung open Tues. and Thurs.-Sun. 10am-5pm, Wed. 10am-8pm. Joint admission DM10, students DM5.) **Staatsgalerie moderner Kunst,** Prinz-Regenten-Str. 1, in the Haus der Kunst, has a sterling 20th-century collection that includes works by Klee, Picasso, and Dalí. (Open Tues.-Wed. and Fri.-Sun. 10am-5pm, Thurs. 10am-8pm. DM6, students DM3.50, Sun. free.) The **ZAM: Zentrum für Außergewöhnliche Museen** (Center for Unusual Museums), Westenriederstr. 26, includes favorites like the Corkscrew Museum, Museum of Easter Rabbits, and the Chamberpot Museum (open daily 10am-6pm; DM8, students DM5).

ENTERTAINMENT

Munich's streets erupt with bawdy beer halls, rowdy discos, and cliquey cafés every night of the week. Pick up *Munich Found* (DM4), *In München* (free), or the hip and hefty *Prinz* (DM5) at any newsstand to find out what's up.

Beer To most visitors, Munich means beer. The six great city labels are *Augustiner, Hacker-Pschorr, Hofbräu, Löwenbräu, Paulaner-Thomasbräu,* and *Spaten-Franzinskaner;* each brand supplies its own beer halls. Beer is served by the *Maß* (about a liter, DM8-11). The biggest keg party in the world, Munich's **Oktoberfest** (Sept. 20-Oct. 5 in 1997) features speeches, a parade of horse-drawn beer wagons, and the mayor tapping the first ceremonial barrel. The world-famous **Hofbräuhaus,** Am Platzl 9, two blocks from Marienpl., has been tapping barrels for the commoners since 1897 and now seems reserved for drunken tourists; 15,000 to 30,000 liters of beer are sold per day (*Maß* DM9.90, most meals DM10-18; open daily 10am-midnight). Most *Müncheners* claim that **Augustiner,** Arnulfstr. 52 (S-Bahn 1-8 to "Hackerbrücke"), is the finest beer garden in town, with lush grounds and 100-year-old chestnut trees. (*Maß* DM9-10. Open daily 10am-1am; beer garden open 10:30am-midnight. Food served until 10pm.) The new **Augustiner Bräustuben,** Landsbergerstr. 19 (S-Bahn 1-8 to "Hackerbrücke"), in the Augustiner Brewery's former horse stalls, offers delicious Bavarian food at excellent prices (DM6-20; open daily until 11pm). The largest beer garden in Europe, **Hirschgarten,** Hirschgartenallee 1 (U-Bahn 1 to "Rotkreuzpl.," then streetcar #12 to "Romanpl."), is boisterous and verdant (*Maß* DM9; open daily 9am-midnight; restaurant open Nov.-Feb. Tues.-Sun.). **Waldwirtschaft Großhesselohe,** Georg-Kalb-Str. 3 (tel. 79 50 88; S-Bahn to "Großhesselohe"), has live music daily and was the site of Munich's recent "Beer Garden Revolution" (*Maß* DM9.80; open daily 11am-1am; beer garden open until 10pm).

Theater, Music, and Nightlife Stages sprinkled throughout the city span styles and tastes from dramatic classics at the **Residenztheater** and **Volkstheater,** to comic opera at the **Staatstheater am Gärtnerplatz,** to experimental works at the **Theater im Marstall** in Nymphenburg. The tourist office's *Monatsprogramm* (DM2.50) lists schedules for all of Munich's stages. Leftovers tickets sell for around DM10. Munich's **Opera Festival** (in July) is held in the **Bayerische Staatsoper** (tel. 55 59 33), accompanied by a concert series in the Nymphenburg and Schleissheim palaces. (Regular season standing-room and student tickets DM15-20. Box office open Mon.-Fri. 10am-6pm, Sat. 10am-1pm.) **Gasteig,** Rosenheimerstr. 5 (tel. 48 09 80, box office 54 89 89 89), hosts diverse musical performances on the former site of the *Bürgerbräukeller* where Adolf Hitler launched his abortive "Beer Hall *Putsch."* (Box office open Mon.-Fri. 10:30am-2pm and 3-6pm, Sat. 10:30am-2pm, and 1hr. before the beginning of a program.) The **Muffathalle,** Zellerstr. 4, in Haidhausen, is a former power plant that still generates energy with ethno, hip-hop, jazz, and dance performances (DM30).

Munich's nightlife is a curious mix of Bavarian *Gemütlichkeit* and trendy cliquishness. The hip bars, cafés, cabarets, discos, and galleries plugged into Leopoldstr. in the **Schwabing** district attract tourists from all over Europe. The blocks between **Viktualienmarkt** and **Gärtnerplatz** are the center of the gay and lesbian scene. At **Master's Home,** Frauenstr. 11, navigate the homey geography of a *faux*-private house with a subterranean bar (open daily 6pm-3am). Singles flock to **Wunderbar,** Hochbrückenstr. 3, on Wednesday nights when there's a phone on every table. (Wed. cover DM10. Open Tues.-Thurs. and Sun. 8pm-3am, Mon. and Fri.-Sat. 8pm-4am. Disco Fri. and Sat.) **Nachtcafé,** Maximilianspl. 5, plays live jazz, funk, soul, and blues until the wee hours, and features karaoke on Sun. (no cover; beers DM7.50; open daily 9pm-6am). **Park Café,** Sophienstr. 7, is a pleasant beer garden by day (*Maß* DM9.50; open daily 10am-1am) and a bumping disco by night. (Cover DM5-15 on weekends, DM5-8 on weekdays. Open Tues.-Thurs. and Sun. 10:30pm-4am, Fri.-Sat. 10:30pm-5am.) Fashionable gay men dance at **New York** disco, Sonnenstr. 25; take U-Bahn 1, 2, 3, or 6 to "Sendlinger Tor" (DM10 cover on Fri. and Sat. includes drinks; open daily 11pm-4am). **Fortuna Musikbar,** Maximiliansplatz 5 (Reginahaus), is a popular disco for lesbians; to get there, ride U-Bahn 4 or 5, or S-Bahn 1-8 to "Karlsplatz" (open Thurs. 10pm-4am).

Appendices

▓ International calls

Making international calls is relatively painless. Follow these steps:

1. Dial the international access code for the country from which you are calling:

Switzerland: 00
Austria: 900 from Vienna, 00 from elsewhere
Czech Republic: 00
Hungary: 00
United States and Canada: 011
United Kingdom: 010
Republic of Ireland: 00
Australia: 001
New Zealand: 00
South Africa: 09

Wait briefly; in some countries, such as the Czech Republic and Hungary, there will be a second dial tone after you have dialed the international access code. Then:

2. Dial the country code for the country you are calling

Switzerland: 41
Austria: 43
Czech Republic: 42
Hungary: 36
United States and Canada: 1
United Kingdom: 44
Republic of Ireland: 353
Australia: 61
New Zealand: 64
South Africa: 27

3. Dial the **area code** or **city code** for the establishment you are calling. When calling Austria, Switzerland, the Czech Republic, and most other countries (but excluding the U.S., Canada, and Hungary) from outside the country, omit the first number of this code, usually 1, 0, or 9.

4. Dial the establishment's number

Note: Austria's telephone system is currently being comverted to a digital network. Some phone numbers may change in the near future, particularly in Innsbruck and Vienna.

▓ Weights and Measures

Like the rest of the civilized world, Switzerland, Austria, Prague, and Budapest use the metric system. So does *Let's Go*. The following are more precise metric equivalents of common English measurements. To convert from Fahrenheit degrees into Celsius, subtract 32 and multiply by 5/9; from Celsius to Fahrenheit, multiply by 9/5 and add 32.

1 Millimeter (mm) = 0.04 inch	1 inch = 25mm
1 Meter (m) = 1.09 yards	1 yard = 0.92m
1 Kilometer (km) = 0.62 mile	1 mile = 1.61km

1 Gram (g) = 0.04 ounce   1 ounce = 25g
1 Kilogramm (kg) = 2.2 pounds   1 pound = 0.45kg
1 Liter (L) = 1.06 quarts   1 quart = 0.94L

■ Climate

Like its terrain, **Switzerland's** weather varies drastically from area to area. As one might expect, the rain falls mainly on the temperate swath of plain that extends across from Lake Constance in the northeast through Zurich and Berne down to Geneva. In the Alps, snow is the norm. The Italian-speaking canton of Ticino lies in a lowish plateau, and boasts a pseudo-tropical clime.

| Temp in °C | January | | April | | July | | October | |
Rain in cm	Temp	Rain	Temp	Rain	Temp	Rain	Temp	Rain
Basel	4/-3	5.3	16/4	6.4	26/13	8.0	15/6	5.2
Bern	2/-4	19	14/4	12	22/13	11	13/5	6
Geneva	4/-2	6.3	15/5	5.1	25/15	6.4	14/7	7.2
Lugano	6/-2	6.3	17/7	14.8	27/16	18.5	16/8	17.3
Lucerne	2/-3	7.4	14/4	7.6	25/14	13.6	14/6	7.7
Zermatt	-7/-11	20.2	-2/-6	16.6	8/3	30.2	2/-3	18.3
Zurich	2/-3	7.4	15/4	7.6	25/14	13.6	14/6	7.7

Austria's climate throughout the year resembles chilly New York City weather. Temperatures depend largely on altitude; as a rule, they decrease an average of 1.7°C (3F) for each additional thousand feet of elevation. Unless you're on a mountain, Austria doesn't usually get brutally cold, even in the dead of winter. Warm sweaters are the rule September to May, with a parka, hat, and gloves added on in the winter months. Winter snowcover lasts from late December to March in the valleys, from November to May at about 6000 ft., and becomes permanent above about 8500 ft. Summer temperatures can reach 38°C for brief periods, although summer evenings are usually cool. Summertime brings very frequent rains—almost one day out of two in Salzburg—so suitable raingear is a must. Budapest, on the other hand, glistens under approximately 2015 annual hours of sunshine. Figures below are degrees Celcius.

| Temp in °C | January | | April | | July | | October | |
Rain in cm	Temp	Rain	Temp	Rain	Temp	Rain	Temp	Rain
Graz	1/-5	2.5	15/5	5.0	25/14	12.5	14/6	7.5
Innsbruck	1/-7	5.4	16/4	5.2	25/13	13.4	15/5	6.7
Linz	1/-4	3.9	12/5	4.5	24/14	8.4	14/5	5.6
Salzburg	2/-5	6.5	12/3	8.5	23/13	19.5	14/4	8.0
Vienna	1/-4	3.9	15/6	4.5	25/15	8.4	14/7	5.6
Budapest	1/-4	3.7	17/7	4.5	28/16	5.6	16/7	5.7
Prague	0/-5	1.8	12/3	2.7	23/13	6.8	12/5	3.3

■ Time

Switzerland, Austria, Prague, and Budapest all use Central European time (abbreviated MEZ in German). Add six hours to Eastern Standard Time and one hour to Greenwich Mean Time. Subtract nine hours from Eastern Australia Time and 11 hours from New Zealand Time. Austria and Switzerland use the 24-hour clock for all official purposes: 8pm equals 20.00.

■ Mileage (distances shown in km)

	Vienna	Salzburg	Innsbruck	Graz	Linz
Vienna	—	295	481	195	181
Salzburg	295	—	180	264	130
Innsbruck	481	180	—	432	316
Graz	195	264	432	—	227
Linz	181	130	316	227	—

	Bern	Geneva	Zurich	Lugano	Interlaken
Bern	—	171	125	279	57
Geneva	171	—	292	446	230
Zurich	125	292	—	221	177
Lugano	279	446	221	—	221
Interlaken	57	230	177	221	—

■ Festivals and Holidays

The *International Herald-Tribune* lists national holidays in each daily edition. If you plan your itinerary around them, you can encounter the holidays that entice you and circumvent the crowds visiting the ones that don't. Also, you should be sure to arrive in any country on a non-holiday, when most services are operating. Check the individual town listings for information on the festivals below. Note also that in Austria the first Saturday of every month is "Long Shopping Saturday"; most stores open until 5 or 6pm.

SWITZERLAND

Summer		
June	*Zürich*	International June Festival: classical music, theater, art
June 2	*Regional*	Corpus Christi
June 15-20	*Basel*	International 20th-century art festival
July 2-17	*Montreux*	International Jazz Festival
Aug. 1	*National*	Swiss National Day
Aug. 24-27	*Fribourg*	Folklore Festival
Sept. 12-13	*Zürich*	*Knabenschiessen*
Autumn		
Oct. 22-Nov. 6	*Basel*	Autumn Fair
Nov. 21	*Bern*	Traditional Onion Market
Dec. 11-12	*Geneva*	*Escalade* (Historic Festival)
Winter		
Jan. 19-25	*Lausanne*	European Figure Skating Championships
March 1-3	*Basel*	*Fasnacht* (Carnival)

April 22-29	*Basel*	European Watch, Clock, and Jewelry Fair
Spring		
May	*Bern*	International Jazz Festival
May 1	*Regional*	Labor Day
May 11	*National*	Ascension
May 22	*National*	Whit Monday

AUSTRIA

Summer		
June 2	*National Holiday*	Corpus Christi Day
End of July	*Salzburg*	Salzburg Festival
late July to mid-August	*Bregenz*	Music Festival
late July to late August	*Salzburg*	Salzburg Music Festival
around August First	*Villach*	Folklore fair
First Monday and Tuesday in August	*Graz*	*Fröhlichgasse*
August 14	*Wörther See*	Eve of the First Feast of the Assumption
August 15	*Public Holiday*	Feast of the Assumption
Autumn		
October 26	*National Holiday.*	Flag Day
November 1	*National Holiday.*	All Saints' Day
November 11	*Regional Holiday*	St. Martin's Day
Sunday following November 25	*Regional Holiday*	*Kathreinsonntag*
December 8	*Public Holiday.*	Feast of the Immaculate Conception
Winter		
January 6		Twelfth Night or Epiphany
January	*Kitzbühel.*	World Cup Ski Races
Spring		
April 17-24	*Salzburg.*	Easter Festival
May 1	*Public Holiday.*	Labor Day
mid-May to mid-June	*Vienna.*	Vienna Festival
May 11	*Public Holiday.*	Ascension Day
Saturday and Sunday after Corpus Christi	*Tamsweg.*	Procession of Samson
May 21-22	*Public Holiday.*	Whit Sunday and Monday

■ Language

As the Germanic peoples extend their commercial tentacles into more and more ventures, German stakes a firmer claim to the status of international language. Nevertheless, it is a difficult tongue for many English speakers to learn, with three genders, four cases, and five ways of saying "the." Fortunately, most Viennese speak at least a smattering of English, and quite a few speak it better than the typical American college student. (The situation is considerably different in isolated villages of the Alps, where proprietors are considered proficient if they can regurgitate "hello," "good-bye," and "dollars.") All schoolchildren in Austria are required to take English, and most are quite anxious to practice. Don't, however, assume that all Austrians or Swiss speak English, especially outside the major cities; always preface your questions with a polite "*Sprechen Sie Englisch?*" or "*Parlez-vous anglais?*" in the appropriate regions.

Don't ever be afraid to attempt a bit of German or French; a few phrases will go a long way. Locals will generally appreciate your effort to acknowledge their culture, and will usually be significantly more helpful once they've heard a bit of their native language. There are a few caveats, though; German is an extremely polite and formal tongue, and it's fairly easy to unintentionally offend. Keep these few simple rules in mind to maintain the good graces of your listener. Always address an acquaintance with *Herr* (Mr.) or *Frau* (Ms.) and his or her surname, and always use the formal pronoun *Sie* with the plural form of the verb. *Fräulein* is used to address a younger waitress or stewardess only. The transition from formal to informal (*dutzen*) is occasion for a major ceremony; never assume that you are on informal terms—you will be *told*. Those who have achieved post-collegiate degrees or civic positions should be addressed with "Herr" or "Frau." *and* their secondary title, e.g. Frau Doktor Puka or Herr Bürgermeister Zabusky. French also differentiates between the formal and informal; however, it is not as strict. As with German, use the polite *vous* form until you are asked to use the *tu* form.

RESERVATIONS BY PHONE

Mastery of the following phrases should help you reserve a room by telephone. Many proprietors, particularly in larger cities, are used to dealing with the minimal German or French of callers; with a little patience and politeness you should be able to secure a room.

GERMAN

Phone greeting	Servus!
Do you speak English? (Hopefully, the answer is "Ja," or better yet, "Yes." If not, struggle bravely on...)	Sprechen Sie Englisch?
Do you have a room (single, double) free...	Haben Sie ein Zimmer (Einzelzimmer, Doppelzimmer) frei...
for tonight?	für heute abend?
for tomorrow?	für morgen?
for a day / for two days?	für einen Tag / zwei Tage?
from the fourth of July...	vom vierten Juli...
until the sixth of July?	bis zum sechsten Juli?
with bathroom/ shower?	mit W.C./ Dusche?
How much does it cost?	Wieviel kostet es?
My name is...	Ich heiße... (ikh HIGH-suh)
I'm coming immediately.	Ich komme gleich
I'm coming at eight in the morning/evening.	Ich komme um acht Uhr am Morgen/ Abend.
Return phrases to watch out for:	
No, we're booked / full.	Nein, es ist alles besetzt / voll.
Sorry.	Es tut mir leid.
We don't make reservations by phone.	Wir machen keine Vorbestellungen / Reservierungen am Telephon.
You have to arrive before two o'clock.	Sie müssen vor zwei Uhr ankommen.

FRENCH

Hello	Bonjour
Do you speak English?	Parlez-vous anglais?
Yes/No	Oui/Non

Do you have a (single, double) room?	Avez-vous une chambre (simple, pour deux)?
for tonight?	pour ce soir?
for tomorrow?	pour demain?
for a day? for two days?	pour un jour? pour deux jours?
with bathroom? shower?	avec toilettes? avec une douche?
with breakfast?	avec le petit déjeuner?
How much?	Combien?
My name is . . .	Je m'appelle
I'm coming immediately.	Je viens tout de suite.
I'm coming at eight in the morning/evening.	Je viens à huit heures du matin/du soir.
No, we're full.	Non, c'est complet.
Sorry.	Je suis desolé.
You have to arrive before two o'clock.	Vous devez arriver avant que deux heures.
Please	S'il vous plait

■ Numbers

	German	French
0	null	zero
1	eins	un
2	zwei (zwoh)	deux
3	drei	trois
4	vier	quatre
5	fünf	cinq
6	sechs	six
7	sieben	sept
8	acht	huit
9	neun	neuf
10	zehn	dix
11	elf	onze
12	zwölf	douze
13	dreizehn	treize
14	vierzehn	quatorze
15	fünfzehn	quinze
16	sechzehn	seize
17	siebzehn	dix-sept
18	achtzehn	dix-huit
19	neunzehn	dix-neuf
20	zwanzig	vingt
21	einundzwanzig	vingt et un
30	dreißig	trente
40	vierzig	quarante
50	fünfzig	cinquante
60	sechzig	soixante
70	siebzig	soixante-dix
80	achtzig	quatre-vingt
90	neunzig	quatre-vingt-dix
100	(ein)hundert	cent
101	hunderteins	cent-et-un
200	zweihundert	deux-cent
1000	(ein)tausend	mille
2000	zweitausend	deux-mille

There are a couple of peculiarities in the way Europeans render numbers that can trip up the unwary American. A space or period rather than a comma is used to indicate thousands, e.g. "10,000" is written "10 000" or "10.000". Instead of a decimal point, most Europeans use a comma, e.g. "3.1415" is written "3,1415." Months and days are written in the reverse of the American manner, e.g. "10.11.92" is November 10, not October 11. The numeral 7 is written with a slash through the vertical line, and the numeral 1 is written with an upswing, resembling an inverted "V." Ordinal numbers are written with a period after the digit, e.g. "1st" is written "1."

Note that, in German, the number in the ones place is pronounced *before* the number in the tens place; thus "zweihundertfünfundsiebzig" is 275, not 257. This can be excrutiatingly difficult to remember if you're not used to the system.

PHRASES

	German	French
At what time...?	Um wieviel Uhr...?	À quelle heure...?
What time is it?	Wie spät ist es?	Quelle heure est-il?
What's the date?	Der wievielte ist heute?	Quelle est la date?
June 1st	ersten Juni	le premier Juin
quarter past seven	viertel acht	sept heures et quart
half past seven	halb acht	sept heures et demi
quarter to eight	dreiviertel acht	huit heures moins le quart
morning	Morgen	matin
noon	Mittag	midi
afternoon	Nachmittag	après-midi
evening	Abend	le soir
night	Nacht	la nuit
midnight	Mitternacht	minuit
day	Tag	jour
week	Woche	semaine
month	Monat	mois
year	Jahr	an
yesterday	Gestern	hier
today	Heute	aujourd'hui
tomorrow	Morgen	demain

GLOSSARY

BASIC PHRASES

	German	French
hospital	das Krankenhaus	l'hôpital
pharmacy	die Apotheke	la pharmacie
sick	krank	malade
doctor	der Arzt	un médecin
police	die Polizei	la police
Help!	Hilfe!	Au secours!
Caution!	Achtung!/Vorsicht!	Avertissement!
Danger!	Gefahr!	Danger!
Fire!	Feuer!	Feu!
Stop!	Halt!	Arrêt!
consulate	das Konsulat	le consulat

English (language)	Englisch	Anglais
German (language)	Deutsch	Allemand
French (language)	Französisch	Français
Hungarian (language)	Ungarisch	Hongrois
American (person)	der Amerikaner/in	un(e) Américain(e)
Australian (person)	der Australier/in	un(e) Australien(ne)
Briton (person)	der Engländer/in	un(e)Anglais(e)
Canadian (person)	der Kanadier/in	un(e) Canadien(ne)
Irish (person)	der Irländer/in	un(e) Irlandais(e)
New Zealander (person)	der Neuseeländer/in	un(e) Néo-Zealandais(e)
South African (person)	der Südafrikaner/in	un(e) Sud-Africain(e)
Good morning	Guten Morgen	Bonjour
Good day	Servus/Grüß Gott/Guten tag/Tag/Szervusz	Bonjour
Good evening	Guten Abend	Bonsoir
Good night	Gute Nacht	Bonne nuit
Goodbye	Tschüß/Auf Wiedersehen/ Auf Wiederschauen	Au revoir
Hello	Hallo	Bonjour
Please	Bitte	S'il vous plait
Thank you	Danke	Merci
You're welcome	Bitte	De rien
Excuse me	Entschuldigung	Pardon
Yes	Ja	Oui
No	Nein	Non
Sir	Herr	Monsieur
Madam	Frau	Madame
I'm sorry.	Es tut mir leid.	Je suis desolé(e)
I don't speak…	Ich spreche kein…	Je ne parle pas…
Do you speak English?	Sprechen Sie Englisch?	Parlez-vous anglais?
Can you help me?	Könnten Sie mir helfen?	Pouvez-vous m'aider?
I don't understand.	Ich verstehe nicht.	Je ne comprends pas.
Do you understand?	Verstehen Sie?	Comprennez-vous?
Please speak slowly.	Sprechen Sie langsam.	Parlez lentement.
How do you say…in…	Wie sagt man…auf…?	Comment dit-on… en…?
What did you say?	Wie, bitte?	Qu'avez-vous dit?
I would like…	Ich möchte…	Je voudrais...
How much does…cost?	Wieviel kostet…?	Combien coute...
I'd like to pay.	Zahlen, bitte.	Je voudrais payer.
Where is…?	Wo ist…?	Où est...?
When is…?	Wann ist…?	Quand est...?
Non-smoking	Nichtraucher	Non-fumeur
Smoking	Raucher	Fumeur

DIRECTIONS

direction	die Richtung	la direction
left	links	à gauche
right	rechts	à droite
straight ahead	geradeaus	tout droit

here	hier	ici
there	da	là-bas
far	fern	loin
near	nah	près

TRAVEL

travel ticket	die Fahrkarte	un billet
reservation	die Reservierung	une réservation
one-way	einfache Fahrt	billet simple
round-trip	Hin- und Rückfahrt	aller-retour
window seat	der Fensterplatz	un siège à côte de la fenêtre
arrival	die Ankunft	l'arrivée
departure	die Abfahrt	le départ
schedule	der Fahrplan	les horaires
baggage	das Gepäck	les bagages
airplane	das Flugzeug	un avion
airport	der Flughafen	un aéroport
customs	der Zoll	la douane
train	der Zug	le train
train station	der Bahnhof	la gare
main train station	der Hauptbahnhof	le gare centrale
(train) track	das Gleis	les rails
train platform	der Bahnsteig	le quai
express train	der Eilzug	un train express
railway	die Bahn	le chemin de fer
subway	die U-Bahn	le métro
subway stop	die Haltestelle	un arrêt de métro
tram, trolley	die Straßenbahn	le tramway
urban railway	die S-Bahn	
ferry	die Fähre	un passage
bus	der Bus	un autobus
bus station	der Busbahnhof	la gare routière
bus stop	die Bushaltestelle	un arrêt d'autobus
car	das Auto	une voiture
no stopping	Halten verboten	interdit d'arrêter
parking	parken	parking
no parking	parken verboten	interdit de stationner
parking spot	Parkplatz	place de stationnement
short-term parking	Kurzfristzone	
speed limit	Geschwindigkeitsbegrenzung	limite de vitesse
do not enter	Eintritt verbotten	passage interdit
expressway	die Autobahn	autoroute
federal highway	die Bundesstraße	autoroute
highway	die Autobahn	autoroute
one-way street	die Einbahnstraße	rue à sens unique
dead-end street	die Sackgasse	une impasse/ cul de sac
bicycle	das Fahrrad	une bicyclette

| moped | das Moped | une mobylette |
| motorcycle | das Motorrad | une moto |

THE POST OFFICE

post office	die Post	la poste/ le bureau de poste
main post office	der Hauptpostamt	le bureau de poste principal
address	die Adresse	l'adresse
express	der Eilbote	express
air mail	die Luftpost	par avion
letter	der Brief	une lettre
parcel	das Paket	un paquet
postcard	die Postkarte	une carte postale
Poste restante	Postlagernde Briefe	Poste Restante
stamp	die Briefmarke	un timbre
telegram	das Telegramm	un télégramme
telephone	das Telefon	un téléphone
telephone number	die Telefonnummer	un numero de téléphone
to exchange	wechseln	échanger de l'argent
money	das Geld	l'argent

ACCOMMODATIONS

toilet	die Toilette/ das WC	les toilettes
shower	die Dusche	une douche
key	der Schlüssel	une clé
house	das Haus	une maison
youth hostel	die Jugendherberge	Auberge de jeunesse
campground	der Campingplatz	un terrain de camping
guest-house	die Pension	une maison d'hôtes
hotel	das Hotel	un hôtel
inn	das Gasthaus	une auberge
private apartment	das Privatzimmer	apartement privé
bed	das Bett	un lit
single	das Einzelzimmer	une chambre pour une personne
double	das Doppelzimmer	une chambre pour deux personnes

DINING

diabetic	der Diabetiker	un(e) diabétique
vegetarian	der Vegetarier	un(e) végétarien(ne)
hungry	hungrig	affamé
meal	das Essen	un repas
lounge, café	die Kneipe	un café
pastry shop	die Konditorei	la pâtisserie
restaurant	die Gaststätte	un restaurant
waiter	der Kellner	garçon
waitress	die Kellnerin	mademoiselle

bill, check	die Rechnung	l'addition
breakfast	das Frühstück	le petit-déjeuner
lunch	das Mittagessen	le déjeuner
dinner	das Mittagessen	le dîner
supper	das Abendessen	le souper
fork	die Gabel	la fourchette
knife	das Messer	le couteau
spoon	der Löffel	la cuillère

▓ Food and Drink

hors-d'oeuvres	gemischte Vorspeise	les hors-d'oeuvres
vegetables	*das Gemüse*	*les légumes*
beans	die Bohnen	les haricots
mushrooms	die Champignons	les champignons
potato	die Kartoffeln/Erdäpfel	les pommes de terre
cabbage	das Kraut/ der Kohl	le chou
french fries	die pommes frites	les pommes-frites
green salad	der grüne Salat	la salade verte
tomatoes	die Tomaten	les tomates
onions	die Zwiebeln	les oignons
pepper	der Paprika	le poivre
fruits	das Obst	les fruits
cheese	der Käse/Käsekrainer	le fromage
bread	das Brot	le pain
roll	das Brötchen/die Semmel	un petit pain
egg	das Ei	un oeuf
ham	*der Schinken*	*le jambon*
bacon	der Speck	le beicon/ le lard
sausage	die Wurst	le saucisse
poultry	*das Geflügel*	*la volaille*
duck	die Ente	le canard
goose	die Gans	l'oie
chicken	das Huhn/Hendl	le poulet
pasta	die Teigwaren	les nouilles
beer	das Bier	la bière
beer hall	die Bierstube	
wine	der Wein	le vin
wine hall	die Weinstube	
coffee	der Kaffee	le café
coffee and cream	Kaffee mit Sahne	le café au lait/ café crème
tea	der Tee	le thé
fruit juice	der Fruchtsaft	le jus de fruits
mineral water	das Mineralwasser	l'eau minéral
soda	das Soda	la soude
water	das Wasser	l'eau

Index

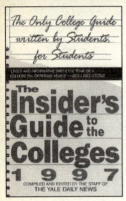

★Let's Go 1997 Reader Questionnaire ★

Please fill this out and return it to **Let's Go, St. Martin's Press,**
175 5th Ave. NY, NY 10010

Name: _____ **What book did you use?**_____

Address: _____

City: _____ **State:** _____ **Zip Code:** _____

How old are you? under 19   19-24   25-34   35-44   45-54   55 or over

Are you (circle one)   in high school   in college   in grad school
employed   retired   between jobs

Have you used Let's Go before? yes   no

Would you use Let's Go again? yes   no

How did you first hear about Let's Go? friend   store clerk   CNN
bookstore display   advertisement/promotion   review   other

Why did you choose Let's Go (circle up to two)? annual updating
reputation   budget focus   price   writing style
other: _____

Which other guides have you used, if any? Frommer's $-a-day   Fodor's
Rough Guides   Lonely Planet   Berkeley   Rick Steves
other: _____

Is Let's Go the best guidebook? yes   no

If not, which do you prefer? _____

**Which part of Let's Go do you feel needs most to be improved, if any
(circle up to two)?** packaging/cover   practical information
accommodations   food   cultural introduction   sights
practical introduction ("Essentials")   directions   entertainment
gay/lesbian information   maps   other: _____

How would you like to see these things improved?

_____

_____

How long was your trip? · one week   two weeks   three weeks
one month   two months or more

Have you traveled extensively before? yes   no

Do you buy a separate map when you visit a foreign city? yes   no

Have you seen the Let's Go Map Guides? yes   no

Have you used a Let's Go Map Guide? yes   no

If you have, would you recommend them to others? yes   no

Did you use the internet to plan your trip? yes   no

Would you buy a Let's Go phrasebook   adventure/trekking guide
gay/lesbian guide

**Which of the following destinations do you hope to visit in the next three
to five years (circle one)?** Australia   China   South America   Russia
other: _____

Where did you buy your guidebook? internet   chain bookstore
independent bookstore   college bookstore   travel store
other: _____